SECOND

THE HARPER & ROW READER

Liberal Education Through Reading and Writing

WAYNE C. BOOTH
The University of Chicago

MARSHALL W. GREGORY
Butler University

EDITION

1817

HARPER & ROW, PUBLISHERS, NEW YORK
Cambridge, Philadelphia, San Francisco, Washington,
London, Mexico City, São Paulo, Singapore, Sydney

Sponsoring Editor: Lucy Rosendahl
Project Editor: Susan Goldfarb
Text Design: Maria Carella
Cover Design: Karen Salsgiver
Production Manager: Jeanie Berke
Production Assistant: Beth Maglione
Compositor: ComCom Division of Haddon Craftsmen, Inc.
Printer and Binder: R. R. Donnelley & Sons Company
Cover Printer: New England Book Components

The Harper & Row Reader: Liberal Education Through Reading and Writing, Second Edition

Acknowledgments begin on page 833.

Library of Congress Cataloging-in-Publication Data

The Harper & Row reader : liberal education through reading and writing / [compiled by] Wayne C. Booth, Marshall W. Gregory.—2nd ed.

p. cm.
Includes index.
ISBN 0-06-040836-7
1. College readers. 2. English language—Rhetoric. I. Booth, Wayne C. II. Gregory, Marshall W., 1940– . III. Title: Harper and Row reader.
PE1417.H276 1988 87-27113
808'.0427—dc19 CIP

89 90 9 8 7 6 5 4 3

Contents

Preface

The Harper & Row Reader has met with the kind of success that supports our belief that many writing teachers want a reader to offer students an education at the same time that it helps them improve their writing. It was our conviction when we prepared the first edition, and now, that the aims of both general education and writing are most successfully fulfilled when they are intertwined. That they can be intertwined is the foundation upon which the Reader stands.

What's New in the Second Edition

Under the rigors of four years of classroom use, and in light of many helpful suggestions from both teachers and students, we have come to see several ways of increasing the Reader's effectiveness and enriching the selections. (In all, twenty-six new pieces have been added to the second edition.) Users of the first edition will note that we have transposed the chapters on language and critical thinking so that critical thinking is now introduced earlier. The work now being done on the relationship between critical thinking and learning, especially critical thinking and writing, suggests that this will be useful.

One of the first edition's most successful features—the inclusion of a number of essays which "spoke" to each other from opposite sides of a topic—has now been extended systematically throughout the book. Each chapter now has at least one such pair of essays, sometimes two pairs, set apart under the heading "Ideas in Debate." Paul Goodman and Karl Popper disagreeing about the value of utopian thinking, Thomas Love Peacock and E. M. Forster disagreeing about the value of art in a technological society, Stephen Toulmin and B. F. Skinner disagreeing about the role of ethics in science, and C. S. Lewis and Bertrand Russell disagreeing about the authority of Christianity—these are the voices of reasoned opinion and civilized controversy. Lively, opinionated, rich, searching, and inquisitive, these voices do not compel assent in every case, but they do command attention and respect.

In chorus they exemplify the educated mind at work, inquiring with energy and moral responsibility into a diverse range of important issues. We firmly believe that both teachers and students will enjoy the education that attends the study of these controversies.

A frequent request received from users of the first edition was to include more fiction and poetry in the second edition. This we have done, taking care to make these additions consistent with the character of the book as a whole. We have not turned *The Harper & Row Reader* into a literature text, nor will the teacher be required to change the focus of the course in order to use the literary pieces. Fiction and poetry are included here mainly as argument. (It should be clear, however, that teachers who prefer to use literature in the freshman class will find more to work with in the second edition than in the first.) We have chosen stories and poems that have a strong argumentative slant, such as Faulkner's "Delta Autumn" and Shirley Jackson's "Flower Garden." Such works allow students to see the rhetorical, argumentative, and polemical dimensions of such "literary" features as metaphor and narrative. This will not only enrich students' knowledge of how arguments actually get advanced in the world, but will also offer them and their teachers a welcome change of pace without throwing the course into confusion.

We have added a rhetorical index specifically designed for student use. We have not indexed all of the ideas, concepts, and themes in the essays, but we have indexed all of the references to, and most of the examples of, rhetorical devices and strategies. Thus if students are unclear, for example, about the meaning or use of analogy, a quick glance at the index will take them to a number of places where analogy is either discussed or exemplified. (As a further aid, a rhetorical table of contents is included in the instructor's manual.)

Finally, Chapter 3, on language, has been heavily revised and somewhat expanded in order to provide the student with better discussions of language as the fundamental milieu of human existence, and to present a sharper view of the political and educational controversies involved in language usage and study.

None of these changes affects our initial assumption that students using this book will also have access to a standard "rhetoric" and a handbook of English. In "Why Take This Course?" (pp. 3–5) and "Why Use a 'Reader' in a Writing Course?" (pp. 6–9), we try to explain the importance of a course like this for both students and teachers. Here we offer only a brief overview of our intentions. A fuller picture will emerge from reading our introductory essays in Part One and from sampling our introductions, questions for discussion, and suggested essay topics.

Purpose of the Course

We have assumed from the beginning that it is not only wasted effort in practice but indefensible in theory to attempt to train students to write without educating them. We assume, in other words, that writers must have something to say in order to have something to write, and that what they have to say will depend mainly on what they know, how they think, and who they are, not just on their mastery of isolated skills. We assume, further, that we write not just as thinkers but as moral agents attempting to do something in or to the world. Any attempt to teach writing as if it were something separate from our character, or to reduce writing instruction to the status of a "service course," insults our students and shortchanges our culture.

Obviously, we cannot offer decisive proof for these assumptions—as opposed to views that we think are cynical, impoverished, or unjust—but we have not chosen them blindly. In what we know of empirical research and learning theory, we find no justification for believing that learning to write well can be divorced from the daily nourishment of trying to understand what other writers have said and then trying to respond with something worth saying.

None of this means that we should fail to teach what are sometimes called "skills." But whatever skills we teach should be taught because they are important to achieving larger goals. Education, after all, is not just for abstract performance but to obtain wisdom. That term may seem old-fashioned or pretentious to your ears, but surely it describes the ends of education better than many modern, "value-free" equivalents such as "maturity," "integrated selfhood," or "effective functioning as a critical and creative adult." But whatever your terms, we here invite you to join us in the unending quest for a liberal education. When courses in "composition" or "rhetoric" or "communication" are viewed in this light, they are for us without question the most important in any curriculum. If this claim seems extravagant to you (as it will almost certainly seem to your students), we hope that working through this book will justify it.

The notion of "working" cannot be dodged. We were convinced from the beginning that the job we wanted to do would require a reader with a fair number of pieces both longer and harder than those in most of the recent anthologies. Toughness for its own sake would no doubt be silly, but students cannot be stretched by what is already within easy reach. In each chapter we have thus included substantial essays, some of them once popular in readers but now abandoned, many of them never anthologized before.

Not all of our selections are hard, however; we have provided a range of both difficulty and styles. Nor have we made our selections with any sense that we are self-appointed guardians of an aristocratic tradition that the barbarian hordes have been neglecting. The distinction between aristocrats and barbarians seems to us absurd, especially when thinking about American education. The education we try to serve here is the kind that we think would be defensible for any group of young people in any historical period—a mixture of the best thinking that people are doing now with the best thinking from other periods.

The result, we believe, is a distinguished and engaging collection of essays. It is a controversial collection. In each chapter some essays confront others directly, while others address issues shared by other essays. Disagreement is found everywhere. The collection is also unusually wide-ranging.

Even so, we obviously do not offer a complete list of topics important to liberal education, or a survey of the entire range of possible views about any one topic. Any critical reader will find that entire disciplines are either ignored or underrepresented; among the liberal arts, for example, we talk little about logic or grammar, but much about rhetoric. More particularly, many political, religious, and philosophical views go unmentioned. But we hope that our recommended approach to the readings will itself provide a way to compensate for our omissions and biases. In our introductions and questions, we have tried hard to avoid the suggestion, found in too many anthologies these days, that the authors and their editors are somehow privy to the one right way of looking at the world. And we assume that the kind of critical thinking we encourage throughout this book will in itself compensate, in the long run, for the inevitable gaps and distortions in our choice of selections.

Methods

Thinking of the difficulties presented to beginners by many of our pieces, we have asked ourselves what kind of guidance we would have welcomed when we were beginning college students. The result is that we offer more extensive commentary than any other reader we have seen. Of course we have tried to modulate our editorial voice, according to the difficulty of the selections, by limiting our introductions to a paragraph for some simpler pieces, while demonstrating how to perform extensive analyses of some of the more difficult works. For those to whom our commentary seems excessive, the format makes it easy to skip our words and work exclusively on our selections.

The introductions to the readings provide only a minimum of biographical and bibliographical information; we concentrate instead on grappling with the issues. "Grappling" is the word, because we do not conceal our own inability to solve many of the issues raised. These works have stretched us as we have performed our editing, and they do so still. Too many anthologies have seemed to us to imply that their editors now have the whole of education taped, and that the students' task is to discover what the editors claim to know already.

Similarly, we have not hesitated to raise questions for discussion that we ourselves cannot answer, though we hope to have raised none that would leave us tongue-tied. We have tried to strike a balance between relatively determinate questions about the authors' procedures and open-ended questions about the issues.

In our suggested essay topics we have, in contrast, suggested no topics that we could not happily write on ourselves. This has meant avoiding assignments that seem canned, arbitrary, abstract, or impossibly ambitious. (No doubt we have not always succeeded, even after much probing and pruning, but most of our topics *have* been tried out in the only crucible that counts in such matters: the classroom itself.) Generally, our assignments place students in situations where they can aim for concrete objectives directed at specific audiences, choosing appropriate strategies and dealing with ideas raised or suggested by the piece they have just read. If they take our suggestions seriously, they will discover that learning to write well has become their own goal, not just the instructor's or the editors'.

Organization

Our selections offer great flexibility to both students and teachers. Teachers and students can enter *The Harper & Row Reader* at any of several levels of reading difficulty. For example, a class might well move through the whole text using mainly the shorter and less ambitious pieces, or a term could be built mainly on the longer and harder essays. Or a class of "middling" preparation might well choose to read all or most of the readings in a few chapters, beginning with the epigraphs that introduce a chapter and working right through to the toughest arguments at the end. Some classes might want entirely to ignore the sequence of our chapters, and the order within them, though we hope—since our discussion material in general builds upon itself—that most classes will profit from following our organization.

We have, then, worked throughout in the conviction that reading, writing, and thinking are integrally related. No doubt every student will at some point need to pay special attention to isolated skills; some will profit from drill—in grammar, in reading techniques, in sentence combining. They will profit, that is, provided they have learned why the drill is important, and why learning to write well is something they should want for themselves, not something they do just for their teachers, their grades, or their parents.

To educate is always harder than to train, and the world will no doubt always find demonstrable uses for those who are trained without knowing what they have been trained *for.* But neither students nor their teachers should have to choose between a "useful" practical training and a "useless" liberal education. Anything truly liberating is also useful, and anything truly useful, when done well and with joy, is also liberating. The best versions of liberal and practical education are ultimately inseparable.

Regardless of any mistakes we have made in our own theory and practice, we feel quite sure about one thing: the required freshman composition course (whatever it is called and however it is staffed) can provide the most important experience of any student's college years and a continuing experience of self-education for the teacher. It can do so, that is, when it enables students and teachers together to repossess for themselves what others have learned in the past and then to engage each other pointedly and eagerly, sharing their thoughts about who they are and how they should try to live, here and now.

We would like to thank the following reviewers of this second edition for their helpful comments and suggestions: Nancy Baxter, Butler University; Sam Dragga, Texas A&M University; Gwendolyn Gong, Texas A&M University; Lynn M. Grow, Broward Community College; Jack Hibbard, St. Cloud State University; James R. Payne, New Mexico State University; Linda Peterson, Yale University; Richard Reid, Grand Rapids Junior College; Nancy Smith, Iowa State University of Science; Mary Soliday, University of Illinois; and Mary Wallum, North Dakota State University.

Special thanks must go to Phyllis Booth and Valiska Gregory, whose support and criticism have been both constant and nourishing, and to those many students and teachers who have contacted us over the past four years with suggestions and criticisms. They have helped sustain our energy and improve our work.

Wayne C. Booth
Marshall W. Gregory

PART ONE

THE COURSE, THE BOOK, AND SOME LEADING IDEAS

SIX INTRODUCTORY ESSAYS

by

Wayne C. Booth and Marshall W. Gregory

WHY TAKE THIS COURSE?

1 Human beings deal constantly in words. We hardly ever stop talking, either audibly to each other or silently to ourselves. Life without words would be reduced to the value of zero: a thin circle of existence enclosing a blankness. To specialists who study brain structure or evolution, language may be a subject for inquiry but to those who use it every day it is a form of behavior that, more than anything else we do, makes human life possible. As fish are creatures of water and birds are creatures of air, human beings are creatures of words. Alfred North Whitehead sums up this point admirably: "The souls of men are the gift of language to mankind."

2 If Whitehead is right, language gives human beings an ability and pleasure available to no other species. It follows, then, that we become fully human when we most fully use and appreciate the gift of language. But unlike other creatures, which seem to realize their potential effortlessly so long as nothing inhibits their development, we language creatures can only reach our full potential through relentless exercise. Reading and writing courses aim to provide you with that exercise. Through steady practice, this course can promise you two benefits. You can strengthen your power to use language effectively and learn to respond to it sensitively. And, second, this course promises you the uniquely human pleasure of the exercise itself; like good health, language skills need no justification beyond the satisfaction of possessing them for their own sake.

3 Just as exercise and discipline can improve our bodily health, they can also improve our "verbal health"—our power to use and respond to language. People often act as if being able to read a newspaper or ask for directions proves that they are fluent in their native tongue. But in fact most of us perform even these basic language tasks less well than we could. People who think they "know how to read" often misread even the simplest news ac-

counts, as all newspaper editors and reporters learn to their sorrow. And we all have had the experience of finding ourselves on the wrong side of town because we either asked for directions unclearly or received unclear directions from someone else. The number of our confusions, misunderstandings, and misspeakings can be decreased if we only know how, but not without work, not without the exercise, study, and discipline that strengthen our performance. The main objective of this course is to provide such systematic exercise in reading and writing. It may be the only course you will take, in fact, that is designed exclusively to provide such exercise.

If human beings are creatures of words in general, then their ability to 4
use words *well* is made even more pressing by the modern conditions of work, politics, and leisure. The modern world depends increasingly on words as the primary tools for keeping itself in motion. A century ago, pioneers depended less on words than we do. Their survival skills have become our recreations. Tracking, hunting, canoeing, and riding are for us diversions, not a way of life.

In our world survival is much more likely to depend on words than on 5
skill in handling animals, rifles, or plows. In business, medicine, education, law enforcement, church work, psychiatry, social work, or selling—name the line of work and the general truth will hold: The modern world floats on a sea of memos, reports, forms, letters, speeches, minutes, manuals, and notes. Nurses and police officers spend as much time writing reports as they do handling cases. Accountants have to write complicated summaries to both their clients and their employers. People in business write an endless stream of memos to the executives above them and to the staffs below. Scientists in education and industry have to write accounts of their procedures and findings for both the agencies they serve and the general public. In all fields, jobs and promotions tend to go to those who read and write most effectively.

Contrary to what some people believe, the age of the computer is not 6
diminishing our reliance on the old-fashioned use of words. Computers are in fact increasing our dependency. We authors are writing this essay, for example, on a computer loaded with a word-processing program. With the purchase of the computer we received four instruction manuals, each more than 150 pages long (in small type with thin margins). A fifth manual over 100 pages long tells us how to operate the word-processing program. On the advice of the dealer who sold us the machine, we wound up buying a sixth 400-page manual—just to clear up questions that the other manuals do not cover completely. The point is not only that somebody had to *write* those manuals, but that anyone who wants to know how to use computers well must know how to *read* them. Whether we are talking about reading or writing, computers are not going to let us off the hook about words.

The *utility* of reading and writing is not the most important justification, 7
however, for doing these activities well. It is true at one level that we must all practice the skills of literacy because the conditions of modern life force us to go into training. Since none of us plans to live under a rock or on a desert island, we have to acquire the skills necessary for competition and interaction

in a complex world. But the metaphor of training and the reality of competition should not blind us to the fact that using language well and responding to it sensitively offer pleasures and rewards in and of themselves. Just as we all wish not merely to have health but to have *good* health, not merely to eat but to eat *well,* and not merely to have people we know but people we *love*—because these fulfillments enrich our lives—so we all wish that we could use language not only as a tool but as a pleasure. Watching a play, reading novels and poetry, playing word games with children, writing love letters, working crossword puzzles, and making puns all exhibit the joy we take in the presence of words shaped for uniquely human purposes. No one pays us for doing any of these things; we simply do them because a life in which they are present is better than a life in which they are absent—regardless of practical conditions and circumstances. Because we are the only creatures who can use language at all, using it well always carries a rich array of rewards that go far beyond simple usefulness.

Questions for Discussion

1. Discuss with your fellow students the reasons you were given in high school for taking a writing course, and relate the advantages, if any, that your counselors and teachers taught you to expect. Compare these views with the views that we give you in our short essay. Are there significant discrepancies? Which views seem most persuasive to you? Why?
2. Does our analogy in paragraph 1—As fish are creatures of water and birds are creatures of air, human beings are creatures of words—seem to overstate language's importance? If not, can you restate the point we are making in your own words? If it does, can you say where we are wrong?
3. If you are skeptical about the extent to which we all rely on language in non-practical ways, discuss with your classmates the way students use language to stimulate laughter (puns, jokes, satire, slang, double entendre, "in" words, innuendo, and so on), to express themselves (notes, letters, poems, diaries, letters to the editor, and so on), and to vent emotions (swear words, "psych up" talk, romantic talk, and so on). Or would you declare all these uses practical? If so, then what happens to the everyday definition of *practical* as "that which produces immediately useful or measurable results"? What *is* practical?

Suggested Essay Topics

1. Write a letter to one of your high school teachers or counselors arguing that the view of reading and writing you were given in high school was too narrow. Give your reasons and suggest how things might be improved for students still in high school.

2. Write a letter to us arguing that we exaggerate language's importance or that we underestimate the need to master practical uses of language—or objecting to some other part of our argument. Give your reasons for objecting and suggest how we should revise our case.

WHY USE A "READER" IN A WRITING COURSE?

The reason you have been asked to buy this book, called a "reader," may not be immediately apparent. You may think that a writing class should deal mostly with writing, and that if you read even half of the material in this book you are going to spend a lot of time reading that you might better spend on writing. In addition, you may have been told that improving your writing is largely a matter of learning to avoid grammatical and spelling errors and that a "reader" will offer you no help in these areas. How can reading Plato on the education of women help you write an effective job application or a persuasive business letter? 1

The connections exist, but they are indirect. Seventeenth-century sailors did not see at first what eating an orange a day had to do with sailing ships, and early nineteenth-century medical students did not see at first what antiseptics had to do with doctoring. But oranges prevented scurvy and antiseptics prevented infection, though for a long time nobody knew why. The connection between reading and writing is like these others. Though a full scientific explanation may never be found, experience shows that reading produces healthy effects on writing. 2

This book, then, is based on the assumption that good writing must keep company with good reading. Obviously we cannot prove this claim about cause and effect because the relations are complex and irregular: Some people who read a lot do not write well. But we have never encountered a good writer who did not read a great deal. Every author who has earned a position in this book, for example, was a heavy reader, and so was every good writing student we have ever known. But we still call our claim an assumption, because we depend on it while waiting for the kind of scientific proof that in human affairs is seldom available. 3

Since the aim of a writing course is to help you write better prose, the obvious questions to ask are, "How do people learn to write in the first place, and how do they then improve?" The same answer holds for both speaking and writing: We learn to speak and write by imitating the behavior of others who already know how. 4

As very young children, even as infants, words stroked and cradled our souls into wakefulness. Rocked in the arms of language we early learned—although we could never have *said* that this was what we were learning—the rules of grammar in our native tongue. We learned at an aston- 5 ishingly fast rate to say "She walks" rather than "Walks her" and "The water is boiling" rather than "Water boiling is the." We could not have told anyone that we were "using grammar," but knowing how to make these linguistic formations is what grammarians call knowing the "rules" of English.

There are many highly complicated and little understood processes that 6 occur during this period of language acquisition. At one level language learning occurs so deeply beneath consciousness that none of us can examine the process as it happens: We seem to have learned intuitively to say "went" instead of "goed" and to ask questions and give orders without referring to any conscious rules about interrogatives and direct objects. But an indispensable part of our learning is the conscious testing of what we have intuited. Children may act as if they are playing when they go through the steps of learning language, but it is very purposeful play. They *work* at acquiring language, and they work at it hard and persistently. They drill themselves and are drilled by their parents, making thousands of mistakes and receiving thousands of corrections, until they can finally say whole sentences and say them right: "The car went" instead of "The car goed."

The same process that taught us how to speak—constant exposure, 7 constant practice, and constant corrections—also teaches us how to write. We learn both intuitively and consciously, just as we learn to play tennis, play the piano, drive a car, or repair a radio both by the development of intuitive "feel" and by conscious practice. Once you are past the rock-bottom elementary stage of learning a skill (and in your use of English you are well past that point already), conscious imitation is going to work for you only if it is *intelligent* imitation: imitation that expresses independent thought, not mindless duplication.

Some people, for example, try to imitate classical paintings using the 8 paint-by-number technique. Anyone really interested in painting knows that this is both boring and useless. The pianist who wants to play as well as Vladimir Horowitz must do more than duplicate his execution of one piece. He must imitate Horowitz's *understanding;* he must play the music, not just the notes. No doubt there is a point, especially at the beginning, when simply trying to *sound like* Horowitz might teach the aspirant a good deal. But imitation-as-duplication can never be a sufficient means of developing independent skill. Writing, for reasons we discuss briefly in "What Is an Essay?" (pp. 10–14), seems to be the skill in which flat imitation is least instructive—but we must imitate, even so.

Acquiring the "feel" for any complicated skill requires, first, being in the 9 presence of models who already know the skills and, second, undertaking the discipline of sustained and thoughtful practice. Skimming over the assigned essays Monday through Thursday and then cramming the writing of the weekly essay into a 2- or 3-hour session mainly devoted to wishing you didn't have to do it does not even qualify as "hands-on experience"; any tennis coach or violin teacher would laugh at such a lack of discipline and sustained practice. Getting the feel of good writing is even more complicated.

The number of possible "moves," styles of play, and "partners" is much larger in the world of writing than in any of these other skills.

For any writer, master or beginner, reading well is part of the indispens- 10
able practice for writing well. Reading "well" means reading both accurately and sensitively, reading good writers, and reading a lot, not in spurts separated by periods of drought, but with regularity. When you were a child, talking was not something you listened to only occasionally, or only during the summer, or only for diversion, or only in fulfillment of an assignment. No, you swam in a sea of words until you became entirely adapted to your verbal environment, until you became in fact a "word creature." Learning to write requires the same immersion. Learning to write *well* means swimming in good company—the kind of company we have provided in this book.

But there is a further reason for reading your way into being a good 11
writer. When you were first learning how to talk, most of what you said centered around yourself. As you matured you learned to take into account other people and a larger slice of the world. Writing follows the same pattern of development. At first it probably seems more natural to write about yourself—your own feelings, desires, and views of things—than it does to write about events, issues, ideas, or problems in the "external" world. But just as maturing causes you to cease *talking* exclusively about yourself, so it also causes you to stop *writing* exclusively about yourself.

Some readers may protest here that a writer *must* write from personal 12
feelings and experiences. What else could one do? But the objection is based on a superficial notion of who we are and of how we "own" a "personal" feeling. Admitting that ideas and points of view are always in some sense personal does not erase the fundamental difference between self-absorption and fellow-feeling, between placing one's own ego at the center of the universe and having the capacity to embrace the feelings and ideas of others. Einstein once wrote that "the true value of a human being is determined primarily by the measure and the sense in which he has attained liberation from self." In this book we offer you a rich collection of "other selves" to listen to, to "talk to," and sometimes even to imitate.

If you work at these readings, if you engage fully with the problems 13
raised by the authors and grapple with their methods of arguing, you will intuit the shapes of good writing in the same way that you intuited the shapes of spoken English when you were a child. If you are also diligent in your practice, even if your first essays seem discouragingly inferior to these "professional" statements, you can progress rapidly.

Of course no one can promise how much progress you will make—there 14
are too many variables at work, your own commitment to learning being by far the most crucial. Do not be surprised if things fail to come easily or if your progress is uneven. You are not, after all, undertaking some trivial activity that anyone can easily master. You are trying to improve one of the skills that separates human beings most distinctively and most completely from all other creatures. Perhaps it could even be called a mystery, not just a skill. It is everyone's birthright, but it is possessed fully by none. Those few who are

masters have penetrated the mystery, but they have also paid the dues of discipline and practice.

Questions for Discussion

1. Take an informal poll in your class. How many students estimate that they read 50 literary works a year beyond works assigned to them in school? How many read more, how many less? How many read hardly any? Then, using people's personal testimony as evidence, try to determine whether there is any correlation between success and ease of writing on the one hand and amount of reading on the other. Does your poll corroborate what we say about the connection between reading and writing?
2. Throughout our essay we make analogies between learning to write and learning other complicated skills such as playing some kinds of sports or playing a musical instrument. Can you develop this analogy further in discussion with your classmates? What do the training and discipline necessary to engage in sports or play music become when we think of the student writer? What changes, if any, does this analogy suggest that you should make in the way you approach writing or studying for this class?
3. Can you illustrate from your own experience our assertion that imitation is necessary in order to learn complicated skills but is never a sufficient means of learning such skills *well*? What skills have you learned (or may you be still learning) in which imitation has been a useful but limited tool? How do you know when to stop imitating and launch out on your own?

Suggested Essay Topics

1. You are the teacher of this class and a student has just come to you with a C essay and the request that you tell him how to make it "better." In addition to seeing that the student is weak in mechanical skills and logic, you also recognize that he simply has no intimacy with language. Write an extended note to your student (perhaps two typewritten pages) explaining what he needs to attend to if he is likely to make any real progress in learning to write better. Perhaps you could outline a course of "practice" or "training," as you might do for a weak athlete if you were a football or basketball coach.
2. At the beginning of paragraph 13 we say, "If you work at these readings, if you engage fully with the problems raised by the authors and grapple with their methods of arguing, you will intuit the shapes of good writing in the same way that you intuited the shapes of spoken English when you were a child." Write an essay directed to your fellow students in which you explain what it means to "work at these readings" and to "engage fully with the problems raised by the authors." You might take our own

essay and, by commenting on selections from it or on its overall structure or position, show how "working" and "engaging" with others' arguments is accomplished.

WHAT IS AN ESSAY?— THE RANGE OF RHETORIC

1 Not long ago, the main meaning for the word *essay* was "an attempt," "a trial." In calling all of your "papers" *essays,* we want to underline that you should think of them as trial runs, attempts that you can always improve, no matter how good they are. Like all of our own "essays" throughout the book—this one for example—yours will always be in some sense unfinished, always asking for further improvement. We "try out" this or that solution, always hoping to make a better try later on. You will find that your best writing comes when you revise one attempt, after learning how other people view it, by "trying out" another one.

2 What is it that we try out? What do we attempt? We sometimes think that we are simply trying to solve a problem presented by a subject matter or a topic. But it is usually useful to add that we are also attempting to achieve some "rhetorical effect" on our potential readers. Each of your essays will attempt something never attempted before: your chosen rhetorical task. That task will always consist of three elements, each of them immensely variable: (1) the available reasons you can discover and turn into a line of argument to persuade the reader to see things your way (or, often enough, to discover for yourself what to believe); (2) your knowledge or hunches about the tastes, values, experiences, prejudices, or interests of your reader; and (3) your own resources of style and character.

3 To call the effects of your essays "rhetorical" may be misleading, because the everyday meanings of the word *rhetoric* are generally narrow and derogatory. Many people take *rhetoric* to mean mere trickery or bombast or "cover-up"—the opposite of "substance" or "solid argument." But we use it here in a quite different, traditional sense, to refer to the entire range of devices that writers and speakers use to communicate their ideas effectively. Thus whenever writers think about readers and about possible effects on them, they are thinking *rhetorically.* And even when writers do not themselves think about rhetorical effect, what they do can be "analyzed rhetorically" to discover whether in fact they have discovered the needed rhetorical resources for the task they have attempted.

4 In this sense of the word, no writer can avoid using rhetoric. The choice is only between good rhetoric and bad, and the judgment of good and bad will not depend only on whether or not the writer *intended* to "be rhetorical." But most writers find that they write best when they are clearest about their chosen rhetorical task. They think of what they write as designed to achieve some kind of communication—to produce in some specified audience this or

that rhetorical effect, such as persuading, informing, entertaining, or simply building a friendship.

Kinds of essays are as numerous as the kinds of possible effects we 5
might aim for. Almost every effect that anybody could seek can be "essayed" in words; what's more, the same general task can be essayed in many different possible forms. For example, suppose I want to attack a political opponent or to prove that my friend should be president of the student body. The kinds of possible essays that I might use for my purposes vastly outnumber any one person's range: a solemn editorial; a mocking or ironic editorial; a letter campaign (and how many different forms might a letter take?); a long, fact-laden "report" on the conditions that call for new leadership; a biography of my enemy or my friend, and so on.

Because the choices among so many devices can seem threatening, some 6
people have claimed that the best way to teach writing is to free students from having to think very hard about what is to be said: "Just tell students what to say, and let them practice how to say it. If they have to think hard—not only about a subject but about how to choose among rhetorical effects—they are sure to write badly." There is some truth to this claim. If you have to think about *too* much at once, if you are faced by overwhelming choices, you can sit in front of your desk helplessly frozen for hours. But something worse happens when you are forced to do "skill" assignments that are so specific and predetermined that you do not have to think about what *you* want to say or how you want to say it. Such assignments do not produce essays but mere mechanical exercises.

It is true that exercise, even if we do it according to someone else's drill, 7
can be useful. Many human achievements depend on long hours of dull practice performed according to charts worked out by other people. If learning to play the cello or to be a fine swimmer requires endless hours of routine practice, why shouldn't writing?

The answer is that writing is more complicated, and thus harder to learn, 8
than any other skill we can think of. It is in fact only superficially similar to developing athletic or musical skills. It *includes* routine but goes beyond it. The proof of this is quite simple: The success of any piece of writing depends to some degree on how it *departs* from standardization or routine repetitiveness, while most other skills *depend* on standardization and routine. A champion runner or swimmer, for example, tries to perfect a repeatable style that will produce a win in every race; nobody cares whether the swimmer's form exactly duplicates his or her previous form, so long as victory results. But if a writer hands in this week a duplicate of an essay that earned an A last week, it will receive an F—and possibly a conference about dishonesty.

Strange, isn't it? If you were able to "write well" last week, why 9
shouldn't writing the same words this week also be judged favorably? The answer is that it would be no longer an essay, no longer an attempt to say something still worth saying. What is worth *your* saying is only something that *you* want to say to someone *now,* and since you are a constantly changing human being, you are unlikely to say exactly what you have said before to

anyone. And what your readers (whether instructors or classmates) will want to read this week will not be a duplicate of what you have already said to them. In addition, repeating yourself robs you of learning. Writing is one of our most effective ways of learning, for it not only forces us to attend to other people's arguments and opinions, but also forces us to *think through* our own views. But in order to take advantage of writing-as-learning, we must constantly face the challenge of saying new things, facing new topics.

The most important part of each week's assignment will thus be *thinking* 10
about your purpose in writing. Of course in one sense the purpose will always be the same: to do the best paper you can do, or at least to show that you have made a genuine effort. But in every assignment you will be grappling with new ideas, and the clearer you are about the actual rhetorical task you are attempting, the better the results will be.

Spend some time, then, before you start writing (and from paragraph 11
to paragraph *as* you write), nagging yourself with the question: "What *am* I trying to do here, really?" Your answer may change as you write and rewrite, but if when working on each assignment you constantly relate your steps to an emerging notion of the job to be done, in a growing relation with some actual reader, you will find that notion guiding steps that otherwise would seem haphazard.

No one has ever made a complete list of the possible rhetorical effects, 12
that is, of all the possible goals you might "essay" to achieve, but there are several traditional classifications. One ancient tradition says that rhetoric will have one of three effects:

1. It will "move" us—that is, stir us to action, as when we change our vote or join a political movement.
2. It will teach us.
3. It will delight us, as when we read a beautiful poem or story.

Another interpretation says that rhetoric will do one of these three things:

1. Change our views about the *past* and about who was responsible for past events (*forensic rhetoric* of the kind studied by lawyers).
2. Change our decisions about how to act for a desired *future* (*deliberative rhetoric,* of the kind practiced by members of Congress or families deciding where to go for vacation).
3. Change our judgments about some person or institution in the *present* (*epideictic, display,* or *demonstrative rhetoric,* of the kind used for Fourth of July celebrations or college commencements).

Finally, some modern textbooks classify rhetorical tasks into four types:

1. Describing something (description).
2. Telling a story (narration).
3. Explaining something (exposition).
4. Making an argument (persuasion).

There's no need here at the beginning to worry about how these terms and classifications relate to each other. We offer them now only as a checklist to suggest questions that you can profitably ask yourself as you write. Instead of merely "getting the paper done," make a habit of running through questions like these: 13

1. Am I trying to change the beliefs of my readers? If so, how?
   a. To persuade them to believe something about a subject they already care about?
   b. To consider seriously some question they have previously ignored?
   c. To open their minds to a possibility they had ruled out?
2. Am I trying to think something through for myself (and consequently for a reader who will be in a sense listening in)? If so, I should decide, as I must with question 1, whether it is in the nature of my topic to allow for some sort of decisive proof or only for probabilities.
3. Am I trying to provide thoughtful companionship for my readers, simply discussing issues and possibilities, with no effort to come to conclusions at all? (See the selection from Montaigne, pp. 417–428, as a possible example.)
4. Am I simply trying to entertain (by no means a contemptible task for an essayist)?
5. Am I perhaps trying to perform one of the following functions:
   - Explain a process, law, or rule?
   - Clarify a common confusion?
   - Console someone for a loss?
   - Warn someone?
   - Praise something or someone underrated?
   - Blame something or someone overpraised?
   - Lead someone to worship?
   - Shake someone's naive faith?
   - Complain about an injustice?
   - Show a relationship between things that people have commonly separated (that is, build a new synthesis)?
   - Separate things that people have previously mushed together (that is, perform a new analysis)?
   - Proclaim my love?
   - Get revenge?
   - Gain employment?
   - Correct an error?
   - Induce an attitude of peaceful meditation?
   - Incite to action?

Whatever your answers to these or other questions, your writing will generally profit from asking them insistently. None of your specific choices can be guided by the simple desire to "write a good essay." What you need, 14 in deciding what is good and what is bad, will always be some kind of answer to questions like these.

STUDENT: What, then, is the intended rhetorical effect of your little essay on the essay? 15

BOOTH: Well, it is to try to goad students into *thinking* about each essay, rather than simply going through the motions.

GREGORY: Do you think it will work?

BOOTH: Why not? Hasn't it *sometimes* worked for us?

Questions for Discussion

1. Does "writing-as-learning" (¶9) make sense to you? Can you restate this notion in your own words?
2. Discuss the limitations and strengths of the analogies that compare learning to write with learning sports and musical skills. In our two previous essays we viewed these analogies as helpful; in this essay we suggest that they are limited in their application. Discuss with your fellow students the ways in which the analogies work and the points at which they (like all analogies) eventually break down.
3. Contrast the popular view of rhetoric as a kind of verbal fakery or trickery with the view we suggest here. Can you find references to rhetoric in newspapers and magazines that take this derogatory, suspicious view? Do you think that "mere rhetoric," as it is sometimes called, can be separated from the substance of an argument or a position? Why or why not?

Suggested Essay Topics

1. Read Norman Cousins's essay "How to Make People Smaller Than They Are" (p. 30) and write an essay to your instructor arguing that the overall intent of Cousins's essay is to accomplish one of the rhetorical aims listed in paragraph 12: to stir the audience to action, to teach, or to delight. Cite the particular passages that seem to you to support your interpretation, and note the way that all three aims may be exhibited to some extent in a single essay.
2. Write three different brief accounts of the same thing, the first one designed to move the audience, the second one designed to teach, and the third one designed to delight. You might choose, perhaps, some campus issue (required phys ed classes, dorm hours, tuition increases, inadequate resources for commuters, inadequate resources for older students, and so on) as the material to be worked up according to these three aims.

WHAT IS AN IDEA?

"I've got an idea; let's go get a hamburger." "All right, now, as sales representatives we must brainstorm for ideas to increase profits." "The way Ray flatters the boss gives you the idea he's bucking for a promotion, doesn't it?" "Hey, listen to this: I've just had an idea for attaching the boat to the top of the car without having to buy a carrier." "The idea of good defense is to keep pressure on the other team without committing errors ourselves." "What did you say that set of books was called? *The Great Ideas*? What does that mean?" 1

The word *idea,* as you can see, is used in a great many ways. In most of the examples above it means something like "intention," "opinion," or "mental image." The "idea" of going for a hamburger is really a mental picture of a possible action, just as the "idea" of a boat carrier is a mental image of a mechanical device. The "ideas" of good defense and Ray the flatterer are really opinions held by the speakers, while the appeal for "ideas" about how to increase profits is really an appeal for opinions (which may also involve mental images) from fellow workers. None of these examples, however, encompasses the meaning of *idea* as it has always been used by those who engage in serious discussions of politics, history, intellectual movements, and social affairs. Even the last example, an allusion to the famous set of books edited by Robert Maynard Hutchins and Mortimer Adler at the University of Chicago, does not yet express an idea; it only directs us toward a source where ideas may be encountered. 2

These uses of *idea* are entirely appropriate in their contexts. Words play different roles at different times. One can "fish" for either trout or compliments; and a scalp, an executive, and a toilet (in the Navy) are all "heads." Usually these different uses have overlapping, not opposed, meanings. For example, we wouldn't know what fishing for compliments meant unless we already knew what fishing for trout meant, and the "heads" we just referred to are all indications of position or place. In the same way, the different uses of the word *idea* overlap. Even the most enduring ideas may appear to some as "mere opinion." What, then, does *idea* mean in the context of serious talk, and what keeps some opinions and mental images from being ideas in our sense? 3

Three central features distinguish an idea from other kinds of mental products: 4

1. An idea is always connected to other ideas that lead to it, follow from it, or somehow support it. Like a family member, an idea always exists amid a network of ancestors, parents, brothers, sisters, and cousins. An idea could no more spring into existence by itself than a plant could grow without a seed, soil, and a suitable environment. For example, the idea that acts of racial discrimination are immoral grows out of and is surrounded by a complex of other, related ideas about the nature of human beings and the nature of moral conduct: Racial differences are irrelevant to human nature, the sort of respect that is due to any human

being *as* a human being is due equally to *all* human beings, it is immoral to deny to any human being the rights and privileges due to every human being, and so on. You can see that a great many other ideas surround, support, and follow from the leading idea.

2. An idea always has the capacity to generate other ideas. Ideas not only have ancestors and parents, but they make their own offspring. The idea that *racial* discrimination is immoral, for example, is the offspring of the idea that *any* sort of bigotry is wrong.
3. An idea is always capable of yielding more than one argument or position. An idea never has a fixed, once-and-for-all meaning, and it always requires interpretation and discussion. Whenever interpretation is required and discussion permitted, disagreements will exist. Ideas are always to some degree controversial, but the kind of controversy produced by the clash of ideas—unlike the kind of controversy produced by the clash of prejudices—is one in which *reasons* are offered and tested by both sides in the debate. As reasons are considered, positions that seemed fixed turn into ideas that move with argument. (See "What Is an Argument?" pp. 19–22, for further discussion.)

In recent years, for example, the idea that racial discrimination is im- 5
moral, combined with the idea that past discriminations should be compensated for, has led to the follow-up idea that minority groups should, in some cases, receive preferred treatment, such as being granted admission to medical school with lower scores than those of competing applicants from majority groups. Some people have charged that this is "reverse discrimination," while others advance arguments for and against such positions with great intellectual and moral vigor. Regardless of where you stand on this issue, you can see that interpretations of ideas yield a multiplicity of positions.

There are obviously many kinds of mental products that do not qualify 6
as ideas according to these criteria. "Two plus two equals four," for example, is not an idea. Without reference to the ideas that lie behind it, it can neither be interpreted nor used. In and of itself, "two plus two equals four" is simply a brute fact, not an idea. However, as a statement it is clearly the product of ideas: the idea of quantity, the idea that the world can be understood and manipulated in terms of systems of numbers, and so on.

Many of our everyday notions, opinions, and pictures of things also fail 7
to qualify as ideas. "I hate John" may be an intelligible utterance—it conveys the feelings of the speaker—but it is not an idea. The "parents" of this utterance lie in the psychology or biography of the speaker, not in other ideas, and it can neither yield its own offspring nor support an argument. "Catholics are sheep," "All communists are traitors," "Christianity is the only true religion," "Republicans stink," "Most people on welfare are cheaters," and "Premarital sex is OK if you know what you're doing" are all such non-ideas. With appropriate development or modification, some of these opinions could be turned into ideas, but what keeps them from qualifying as ideas in their present form is that they are only minimally related (and in some instances

totally unrelated) to other ideas. One sign that you are being offered mindless, bigoted, or fanatical opinions, not ideas, is the presence of emotion-charged generalizations, unsupported by evidence or argument. Catchwords, clichés, and code phrases ("welfare cheaters," "dumb jocks," "typical woman," "mad scientist") are a sure sign that emotions have shoved ideas out of the picture.

A liberal education is an education in ideas—not merely memorizing 8
them, but learning to move among them, balancing one against the other, negotiating relationships, accommodating new arguments, and returning for a closer look. Writing is one of the primary ways of learning how to perform this intricate dance *on one's own.* In American education, where the learning of facts and data is often confused with an education in ideas, thoughtful writing remains one of our best methods for learning how to turn opinions into ideas.

The attempt to write well forces us to clarify our thoughts. Because 9
every word in an essay (unlike those in a conversation) can be retrieved in the same form every time and then discussed, interpreted, challenged, and argued about, the act of putting words down on paper is more deliberate than speaking. It places more responsibility on us, and it threatens us with greater consequences for error. Our written words and ideas can be thrown back in our faces, either by our readers or simply by the page itself as we re-read. We are thus more aware when writing than when speaking that every word is a *choice,* one that commits us to a meaning in a way that another word would not.

One result is that writing forces us to develop ideas more systematically 10
and fully than speaking does. In conversation we can often get away with canyon-sized gaps in our arguments, and we can rely on facial expression, tone, gesture, and other "body language" to fill out our meanings when our words fail. But most of these devices are denied to us when we write. To make a piece of writing effective, every essential step must be filled in carefully, clearly, and emphatically. We cannot grab our listeners by the lapel or charm them with our ingratiating smile. The "grabbing" and the "charm" must somehow be put into words, and that always requires greater care than is needed in ordinary conversation.

Inexperienced writers often make the mistake of thinking that they 11
have a firmer grasp on their ideas than on their words. They frequently utter the complaint, "I know what I want to say; I just can't find the words for it." This claim is almost always untrue, not because beginning writers are deliberate liars but because they confuse their intuitive sense that they have something to say with the false sense that they already know precisely what that something is. When a writer is stuck for words, the problem is rarely a problem only of words. Inexperienced writers may think they need larger vocabularies when what they really need are clearer ideas and intentions. Being stuck for words indicates that the thought one wants to convey is still vague, unformed, cloudy, and confused. Once you finally discover your concrete meaning, you will discover the proper words for expressing it at the same time. You may revise words later as meanings become *more* clear to you,

but no writer ever stands in full possession of an idea without having enough words to express it.

Ideas are to writing as strength and agility are to athletic prowess: They do not in themselves guarantee quality, but they are the muscle in all good writing prowess. Not all strong and agile athletes are champions, but all champion athletes are strong and agile. Not everyone who has powerful ideas is a great writer, but it is impossible for any writer even to achieve effectiveness, much less greatness, without them. 12

Questions for Discussion

1. Identify and discuss meanings of the word *idea* that we did not mention in our essay. Does an awareness of these different meanings allow you to pick your words with greater care?
2. We briefly indicated some of the family relationships among ideas based on the parent idea that discrimination against individuals is wrong. In discussion with your classmates, pick a few other ideas that interest you and map out some of the primary family relationships among them. You could discuss, for example, such ideas as the following: the universe is God's creation; the speed of light is an absolute; modern sexual mores are undermining the nuclear family (or are allowing more people more freedom and fulfillment than ever before); capitalism is the economic system most compatible with a democratic political system. The world is full of ideas (and non-ideas); the point is to see whether you can trace how one idea leads to other, related ideas. This exercise will also allow you to see that almost every idea is confronted eventually by its contrary, and is thus a source of controversy as well as enrichment.
3. Discuss our assertion in paragraph 8 that "a liberal education is an education in ideas." Contrast such an education with an education in skills. Is it possible to learn skills without learning ideas? Do you know people who know how to do certain activities by rote but who are poor at thinking through the rationale for doing them, or poor at criticizing what they do, or poor at looking for alternative ways of doing them? You might consider whether a technical education would ever be sufficient training by itself in how to deal with sophisticated or complex ideas.

Suggested Essay Topics

1. Look through some of the editorials or letters to the editor in the newspaper, and pick one that seems to you filled with either non-ideas or feeble ideas. Address a letter to the author showing him or her how weak the writing is in real ideas, and suggesting how the weak notions might have been turned into real ideas.

2. Take any field that interests you and show how it may be divided into techniques of performance on the one hand and the ideas that underlie technique on the other. Try to show the relationship. Football, ballet, architecture, and cooking are all suitable examples. In football, for example, some players only know how to run the plays they have memorized, but the coach (and other players, especially the quarterback) have to keep in mind the strategies that underlie the patterns, and they have to know how to adapt certain strategies for certain situations. You might consider whether the best performer is one who can both think *and* do. Does every great coach or choreographer have to also be a player or dancer? Make your essay an analysis of such questions.

WHAT IS AN ARGUMENT?

Everybody knows what an argument is. It is a dispute between two people. 1
But the word has another meaning, a very old one that will be important in this book. When two people argue, they not only *have* an argument with each other; each of them *presents* an argument—a line of reasoning. Each arguer can present a case that is either strong or weak, regardless of what final position either one takes. Each one may hate "arguing" but still *argue* well.

What makes a good argument—a good case? We might think that it 2
would be whatever convinces one party to accept the other's views. If George and Jeanne have an argument (in the first sense), and if Jeanne convinces George that she is right, doesn't that show that she presented the best argument—the best case? Not necessarily. Maybe George was a pushover. Maybe Jeanne was just very clever at concealing the flaws in her argument. A good argument, in the sense of a good *case,* must stand up under close *analysis* (see "What Is Analysis?" pp. 22–25). You may want to ask here questions that will come up again and again throughout your work in college: Stand up under *whose* analysis? Who are the experts who test our arguments, and how many of them are needed to decide that an argument is sound? If there were simple answers to such questions, a college education would not require four years. If all the experts in the study of argument could agree on what makes a good or bad one, our lives would be simple. We could then just learn a set of neat tests, like using a circuit-tester to check for live wires, and then easily check out the relative strength of Jeanne's and George's arguments. But even the experts often disagree about which arguments justify changing our minds in a given case. Some people, including some of the authors in this volume, insist that an argument is not worth anything at all unless it consists of *hard proof*—evidence that usually involves numbers, statistics, laboratory reports, and calculations. But the curious fact is that even in the highly technical sciences like physics and chemistry, most disputes are not decisively settled with unarguable proof. Almost every argument includes steps that *some* people criticize as weak, leading to *further* disputes about whether those criticisms are right or not. Scientists do not consider such disputes unhealthy; continued

disagreement about evidence and proof pumps life into the sciences. It should not distress us that such disputes mark most nonscientific matters as well.

The trouble comes when disagreement about which arguments should 3
carry real weight becomes so widespread and difficult that people get skeptical about finding any good arguments at all, especially when facing life's important and complex matters. In fact, one of the issues most disputed in our century is the degree to which genuinely good reasons are available for thinking together about such major decisions as whether or when to marry, how to vote, what causes to support, whether to believe in God, how to raise our children, how hard to work at getting an education, and a host of other problems that we cannot dodge but never have enough "scientific proof" to settle.

If even the experts do not agree, how can we, beginners all, hope to 4
improve our own arguments? Fortunately, we all have available two important resources. The first, possessed by everyone with or without a formal education, is commonsense experience. As the great American philosopher Charles Sanders Peirce said, "We generally reason correctly by nature: we are . . . in the main logical animals." But, he adds, "we are imperfectly so." Common sense, sometimes called "popular wisdom," although essential to life, can be highly unreliable. Still, if we learn how to make use of it, if we simply *pay attention* to one another's arguments, in class and out, and "use our heads" in a natural way, we can discover arguments that will save us from many a disaster, both intellectual and practical.

The truth is that simply to survive in our complex society—perhaps in 5
any society—everyone develops a fairly elaborate, though rough-and-ready, reasoning apparatus. We all have ways of asking whether a given conclusion "follows" from the reasons given—that is, whether an arguer has earned a given "therefore" or "thus" or "consequently." We Americans have a sturdy popular tradition of skeptical expressions that help us to avoid getting conned: "I'm from Missouri—you've got to show me," "Don't take any wooden nickels," "There's a sucker born every minute," "Tell me another good one," "I wasn't born yesterday, you know." Even when dealing with elaborate written arguments we can use popular wisdom of this kind, employing more deliberately our natural habit of making sense.

But fortunately we have a chance in college to master a second resource, 6
to go beyond common sense and learn a whole range of more formal, deliberate tests of *accuracy* about data, *cogency* of logical inference, and general *clarity* about the reasons for our beliefs. Some of you will later study formal logic and learn to apply elaborate and precise tests for judging whether two or more statements ("propositions") are logically tied together or not. In your rhetoric book you will find examples of fallacies—seemingly good arguments that are actually weak or not valid at all. (You may later find that in practice some arguments that are called fallacies in fact carry weight in some circumstances; things are never as simple as they seem.)

We cannot pretend in this book to take you through a complete and 7
systematic introduction to every kind of good argument. But if you attend

closely to our suggested questions for discussion and study the introductions and analyses that precede and follow the selections by Norman Cousins (pp. 30–35) and Karl R. Popper (pp. 113–133) and then test the other authors and your own writing with the same kinds of questions, you will gradually develop confidence in deciding whether an argument carries real weight. But you will also learn, like your editors and teachers before you, that the task of analyzing and testing arguments is endless. As in so much else that you will study this year, college is just the beginning.

Questions for Discussion

1. Notice how closely connected are *argument* and *ideas.* Real arguments are fueled by real ideas. Sham arguments are made up of faked ideas or sheer prejudice. Divide up into groups of four or five students and examine the arguments in some editorials and letters to the editor. Consider whether the opinions advanced there constitute real arguments or not, and discuss together what the authors might do to strengthen their arguments.
2. Take some moral issue, such as students cheating on tests or husbands and wives cheating on their spouses or bank employees cheating on the books, and notice how difficult it is for people to agree about the *grounds* on which such behavior is to be condemned as wrong. Notice how much more confused things become when less stark matters requiring moral reasoning are introduced: whether pornography should be banned, whether the American Nazi party has the right to march in Jewish neighborhoods, whether taking drugs is wrong or merely a matter of personal choice, or whether it is morally wrong to cheat on one's income taxes. Try to determine why making arguments about these kinds of issues is so difficult. (If you get really interested in this topic, look at Alasdair MacIntyre's *After Virtue* and *Habits of the Heart* by Robert N. Bellah et al.) Ask yourself whether your education should aim at helping you reason better about moral issues, and how it might work toward achieving that aim.

Suggested Essay Topics

1. Write two versions of the same case, one which relies on mere assertion or emotional ploys, and a second which attempts to present a reasoned argument. Each essay should hold the same opinions and ask for the same response from the reader; the difference between them should be the way in which the case is advanced. Address the essays to someone you think needs convincing. At the end of the second essay, append a brief discussion about the relative merits of each case.
2. Read Anton Chekhov's short story "Gooseberries" (available in many different anthologies) and write an essay in which you make an argument

either supporting or attacking Ivan Ivanych's criticism of his brother's notion of happiness. It is clear that Ivan Ivanych thinks there is something intrinsically wrong with his brother's definition of happiness and that his brother would be a better person if he would give up the idea of happiness he holds and replace it with another. Is it ever possible to criticize another person's notions of happiness, or are all such notions irretrievably private? In your essay, try to establish whether such criticisms can *ever* be validly made. If they may, on what grounds? If they may not, why not?

WHAT IS ANALYSIS?

We all practice two basic ways of thinking, whether we have names for them or not: We can delve inside something and try to separate its parts, or we can look at two or more things that seem separated and try to fit them together. Some theorists even claim that every new thought consists either of finding a new way of *analyzing* the parts or elements of the whole or a new way of *synthesizing* two or more elements into a single thing. 1

Analysis can be as complicated as trying to separate atomic particles or as simple as identifying the ingredients in a restaurant salad; synthesis can range from constructing an ambitious theory about the parts of the universe to a simple hunch that Deborah and Harry both vote Republican because their fathers are wealthy. Both analysis and synthesis can be performed either with highly deliberate methods, as in a scientific laboratory, or with quick intuitive leaps, as when we use metaphors or similes to describe people we know: "Percy is a pig," "Marie is a marshmallow," "My coach nags like a demon." Thus the most elaborate thought of the greatest genius is no different *in kind* from what everyone does a hundred times a day. The expert simply has (sometimes vastly) greater skill in discovering differences and similarities—in inventing possibilities and then testing them rigorously. Unfortunately, that skill cannot be learned or taught with formulas either simple or complex. If it could be, we would all be potential geniuses. But everyone can learn how to think better by *thinking about* these two fundamental ways of thinking. 2

Learning to do better analysis as you read and prepare to write will be an essential part of that education in synthesis. Analysis usually looks easier than synthesis. Isn't it obvious that you can break something into parts more easily than you can put something together? To find out what something is made of—even if it is a complicated essay or a complex subject you plan to write about—all you have to do is tear at it for a while, like a vigorous child pulling a toy apart, until you finally have all the parts separated. But we all know that things don't work as simply as that. If, for example, you want to know how a clock or a toy works, pulling things apart at random will not give you knowledge, just a pile of meaningless fragments. A true analysis of any machine seeks not only to separate its parts but also to discover the relationships that *make the parts work*—that is, to analyze each part's *function.* If we asked 3 you to do a chemical analysis of a spoonful of some powder, and you came back saying, "I've counted all the grains, and there are 2456 parts," we'd know that you did not understand what *analysis* meant. If we asked you to analyze the workings of a watch, and you brought us five piles of parts labeled "metal parts," "plastic parts," "jewels," "numbers," and "dial," we'd know that you had been simply tearing it apart, not really analyzing. The popular complaint, "But you're comparing apples and oranges," reflects our common sense that *for some purposes* we need to distinguish differences rather than to dwell on similarities.

You will of course find yourself synthesizing every time you write an essay, because to make an essay *work* you must create a new synthesis—a new putting-together of words and ideas that nobody has ever put together in precisely this way before. That is one reason learning to write is so difficult. Even our sentences are almost all brand-new things in the world: They are combinations of words that, like these we are combining now, have never appeared in exactly this order before. Though our *ideas* are seldom entirely new, our ways of talking about them always require new syntheses. In this sense, all of your work this year—and not only in this course—will be an education in how to make better syntheses. 4

Among life's most difficult and important kinds of analyses are those we perform when we read an essay carefully. It is true that we cannot avoid performing some analysis, no matter how unconsciously we may go about it, for all reading goes from part to part, and the parts fit together in some way to make up a whole. We know that an author has put together sentences, paragraphs, sections, perhaps even chapters, to make something that he or she considers now to be a single thing—an essay or a book. But the joints in an essay's skeleton are often not obvious, and we sometimes do our carving at points that would surprise the author, especially if we are reading an argument about a topic new to us. We make up our minds too quickly that "this is a botched X, with the joints all wrong," when it is really a "fine Y, with every joint as it should be." In reading Karl Marx and Friedrich Engels's catalog of the achievements of the European middle class (pp. 805–815), it would be easy for a hasty reader to decide that Marx and Engels admire the middle class but just don't know how to express that admiration forcefully; a closer reading, however, shows them expressing hatred, in brilliant but subtle form. 5

Our best defense against mistaking what an essay says is thus a more careful analysis—a close and systematic look at how the parts form a whole. Most authors work hard to provide clues about the kind of creature they are creating; they build in "visible joints" that enable us to figure out the structure of the skeleton. A full analysis of any work will take into account every such explicit aid—every *thus* and *therefore,* every *first* and *second,* every *we see, then,* and *on the other hand.* We give two illustrations (pp. 30–35 and 113–133) of how such analyses might be done, and our questions for discussion are often designed to help you see an essay's structure. 6

Fortunately, all of us naturally tend to take such clues into account, provided that we are paying close attention. In conversation, whenever we are genuinely interested, we don't ignore such clues. If a friend says, "Now wait a minute, we're talking about two entirely different things here, and it's only the second one that matters to our discussion," we don't just ignore this analysis—not unless we are looking for a fight instead of a conversation. Paying the same close attention when we read will usually, though not always, uncover the clues that reveal the author's own analysis. 7

Discovering the author's own slicings in this way will often lead you to your best thinking as you attempt further analysis, in effect saying to the author, "But you have not looked at this subject closely enough. You have divided it into two huge lumps, but there are really at least four distinct elements here, as follows: . . ." And such analytical thinking will automatically spill over into your own writing, as you organize your ideas, and then your words, according to the new analysis. Indeed, you will find that when you are stuck for something to say, a close *analytical* look at almost anything in the world will turn up interesting revisions of your own ideas—and when that happens, you will have something to say. 8

Can you now *analyze* the parts of this essay on analysis? What are the joints that we authors see in the subject? What clues have we provided (that is, what transitions from part to part)? It is always a useful exercise to run through an essay, pencil in hand, underlining every word or phrase that flags a move to a new part. If your outlining is systematic in this way, rather than a random marking of whatever statements happen to catch your eye, you may be surprised at how much it helps both your understanding of an essay and your memory of how it works as an *argument*—or as some other kind of critter. 9

Questions for Discussion

1. Define *analysis* and *synthesis* as mental processes; give several examples of each.
2. Focus on three or four complex decisions that you have had to make, and try to determine whether you had to rely mainly on analysis, or on synthesis, or, as is more likely, on a movement back and forth between the two. In picking your college, for example, you undoubtedly lumped certain kinds of schools together in an act of synthesis (preppy, academically serious, beautiful campus, dull [or lively] social life, and so on), while at the same time you distinguished between them analytically ("Even though these two schools are both preppy, one has a much better chemistry major than the other"). The process of identifying the kinds of mental processes you use in making decisions can be carried to great length. Work out two or more examples in some detail.

Suggested Essay Topics

1. Pick some *event* of interest to a particular audience and give an analytic account of it. That is, break the event down into its component parts, not just chronologically (which would be like merely separating the parts of a watch into respective piles, as in our example), but in such a way as to show how the parts make up the whole.
2. Pick some *literary work* and, in an essay directed to your instructor, provide a synthetic account of it. That is, show how it is like other works that are similar to it in important ways, and further, show how the similarities help explain the character of the work you have selected. (You may choose a musical work, a scientific theorem, or a sport if you do not want to write about a literary work.)

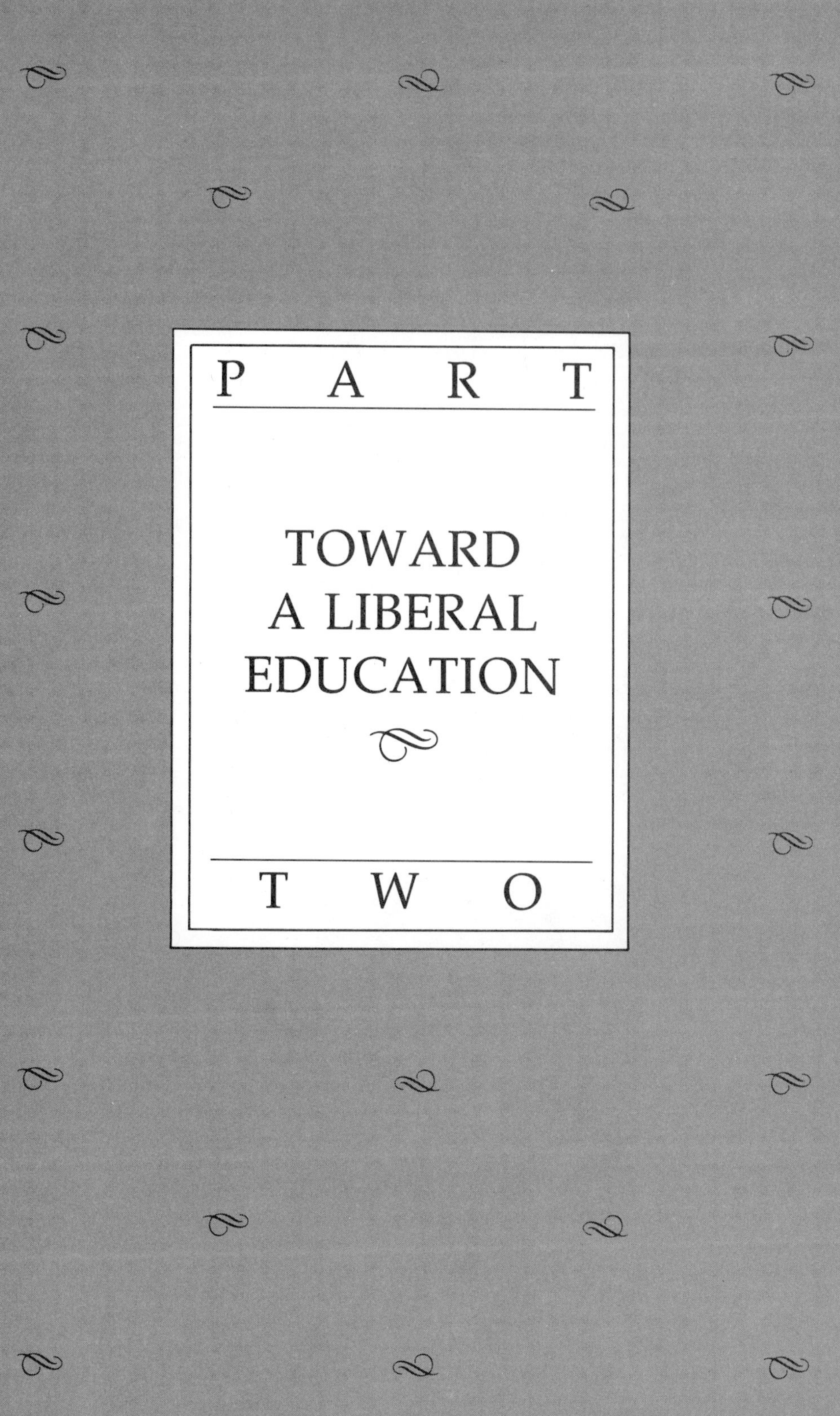

PART

TOWARD A LIBERAL EDUCATION

TWO

1

EDUCATION

Images, Methods, and Aims

Ignorance is the night of the mind.
Efe Pygmies of Zaire

Never lose a holy curiosity.
Albert Einstein

Knowledge is capable of being its own end. Such is the constitution of the human mind, that any kind of knowledge, if it be really such, is its own reward.
John Henry Cardinal Newman

The pleasure of learning and knowing, though not the keenest, is yet the least perishable of all pleasures.
A. E. Housman

Where there is much desire to learn, there of necessity will be much arguing, much writing, many opinions; for opinion in good men is but knowledge in the making.
John Milton

Whoso loveth instruction loveth knowledge: but he that hateth reproof is brutish.
Proverbs 12:1

A little learning is a dangerous thing.
Alexander Pope

Human history becomes more and more a race between education and catastrophe.
H. G. Wells

Norman Cousins

Norman Cousins (b. 1912) has for some decades been one of America's most widely read critics and journalists of ideas. As a columnist and longtime editor of the influential Saturday Review, *he has consistently prodded us into hard thought about how to improve our lives by improving how we write. Here we meet him as advocate for a controversial educational idea.*

Following the essay we offer a short "demonstration" of how one might go about reading this piece. As with our other demonstration of how to read an argument (pp. 125–133) and our introductory comments throughout this book, we urge you both to follow them carefully and *to resist taking them as any kind of final word. Every reading is partial; every reading can be improved. We hope only to suggest useful* ways *of reading, not to kill the text and mount it neatly in a specimen case.*

HOW TO MAKE PEOPLE SMALLER THAN THEY ARE

From *The Saturday Review,* December 1978.

Three months ago in this space we wrote about the costly retreat from the humanities on all the levels of American education. Since that time, we have had occasion to visit a number of campuses and have been troubled to find that the general situation is even more serious than we had thought. It has become apparent to us that one of the biggest problems confronting American education today is the increasing vocationalization of our colleges and universities. Throughout the country, schools are under pressure to become job-training centers and employment agencies. 1

The pressure comes mainly from two sources. One is the growing determination of many citizens to reduce taxes—understandable and even commendable in itself, but irrational and irresponsible when connected to the reduction or dismantling of vital public services. The second source of pres- 2 sure comes from parents and students who tend to scorn courses of study that do not teach people how to become attractive to employers in a rapidly tightening job market.

It is absurd to believe that the development of skills does not also require the systematic development of the human mind. Education is being measured more by the size of the benefits the individual can extract from society than by the extent to which the individual can come into possession of his or her full powers. The result is that the life-giving juices are in danger of being drained out of education. 3

Emphasis on "practicalities" is being characterized by the subordination of words to numbers. History is seen not as essential experience to be transmitted to new generations, but as abstractions that carry dank odors. Art is regarded as something that calls for indulgence or patronage and that has no place among the practical realities. Political science is viewed more as a specialized subject for people who want to go into politics than as an opportunity for citizens to develop a knowledgeable relationship with the systems by which human societies are governed. Finally, literature and philosophy are assigned the role of add-ons—intellectual adornments that have nothing to do with "genuine" education. 4

Instead of trying to shrink the liberal arts, the American people ought to be putting pressure on colleges and universities to increase the ratio of the humanities to the sciences. Most serious studies of medical-school curricula in recent years have called attention to the stark gaps in the liberal education of medical students. The experts agree that the schools shouldn't leave it up to students to close those gaps. 5

. . .

The irony of the emphasis being placed on careers is that nothing is more valuable for anyone who has had a professional or vocational education than to be able to deal with abstractions or complexities, or to feel comfortable with subtleties of thought or language, or to think sequentially. The doctor who knows only disease is at a disadvantage alongside the doctor who knows at least as much about people as he does about pathological organisms. The lawyer who argues in court from a narrow legal base is no match for the lawyer who can connect legal precedents to historical experience and who employs wide-ranging intellectual resources. The business executive whose competence in general management is bolstered by an artistic ability to deal with people is of prime value to his company. For the technologist, the engineering of consent can be just as important as the engineering of moving parts. In all these respects, the liberal arts have much to offer. Just in terms of career preparation, therefore, a student is shortchanging himself by shortcutting the humanities. 6

But even if it could be demonstrated that the humanities contribute nothing directly to a job, they would still be an essential part of the educational equipment of any person who wants to come to terms with life. The humanities would be expendable only if human beings didn't have to make decisions that affect their lives and the lives of others; if the human past never 7 existed or had nothing to tell us about the present; if thought processes were irrelevant to the achievement of purpose; if creativity was beyond the human mind and had nothing to do with the joy of living; if human relationships were random aspects of life; if human beings never had to cope with panic or pain, or if they never had to anticipate the connection between cause and effect; if all the mysteries of mind and nature were fully plumbed; and if no special demands arose from the accident of being born a human being instead of a hen or a hog.

Finally, there would be good reason to eliminate the humanities if a free 8 society were not absolutely dependent on a functioning citizenry. If the main purpose of a university is job training, then the underlying philosophy of our government has little meaning. The debates that went into the making of American society concerned not just institutions or governing principles but the capacity of humans to sustain those institutions. Whatever the disagreements were over other issues at the American Constitutional Convention, the fundamental question sensed by everyone, a question that lay over the entire assembly, was whether the people themselves would understand what it meant to hold the ultimate power of society, and whether they had enough of a sense of history and destiny to know where they had been and where they ought to be going.

Jefferson was prouder of having been the founder of the University of 9 Virginia than of having been President of the United States. He knew that the educated and developed mind was the best assurance that a political system could be made to work—a system based on the informed consent of the governed. If this idea fails, then all the saved tax dollars in the world will not be enough to prevent the nation from turning on itself.

How to Read an Argument: Demonstration I

As you may have learned already, it 1 *is never easy to write about complicated matters, especially in a short space. Writers who try to say a great deal in a few words often wind up sounding pompous, desperate, vague, or wildly opinionated.*

Since your own papers will usually be short like Cousins's, you can profit from 2 *studying how he organizes his argument. Try to postpone any decision about whether you agree with him until you have worked out precisely what he is claiming.*

A good way to begin is to read the whole piece through once, fairly fast, slowing 3 *down only to circle any troublesome words or phrases. Then read through again, dictionary at hand, scribbling helpful definitions in the margin. Once you have done this, you will have gone further than most people ever do in ordinary reading, but you will have only begun to read at a serious college level.*

Much of the writing we run into is not worth the trouble of this second step. 4
The art of reading is in part that of knowing how and when to skim and when to dig in with hard study. Ordinarily you will have to decide for yourself whether to take the later, harder steps, but here we will assume that your first quick reading has led you to see Cousins as someone you would like to converse with for a while. How might the conversation be conducted?

On the basis of our first reading, we know Cousins's purpose: *He wants us* 5
to believe not only that the "humanities"—whatever they really are—are being neglected but that they are the most important part of the curriculum. And we know from the final paragraph that he sees the humanities as the source of the "educated and developed mind." Since this is obviously a controversial claim, one that would be questioned by many people, our next step is to ask him, "Exactly what reasons have you offered us for going along with your argument?"

There are many good ways to perform the careful reading that will uncover 6
Cousins's answer to that question. Some people can do it lounging in an armchair, reading and thinking; some can do it entirely in their heads, referring to the text with photographic memory. We (Booth and Gregory)—at least when we are feeling virtuous and energetic—do this kind of reading while sitting up at a desk, pencil in hand, marking the text frequently.

There is no use in underlining a great many passages unless your clues clearly 7
show why some passages are important and how the different sections relate to each other. It is useful to develop some sort of brief code that tells at a glance what statements you view as conclusions *and what statements you view as* reasons, *what words give evidence about* organization, *and what terms reveal the relative weight of different points.*

You may then want to distinguish different kinds of reasons: appeals to facts 8
(examples, statistics, commonsense experience) and appeals to general beliefs or principles *("Everybody knows that . . ."; "All modern science teaches that . . ."; "Our country is founded on the principle that . . ."; "Nobody who has thought about this issue for more than five minutes has ever denied that. . . .") Some students use different pencil colors for the different kinds of attempts at proof. We find it even more useful to create an outline in the margins of the text, using roman numerals or capital letters to flag the major conclusions and* a*'s and* b*'s and 1's and 2's to flag the supporting points. It often helps to draw arrows from the evidence to the conclusion, underlining in the text the key* connecting terms *that show the relationship:* because, but, therefore, thus, on the other hand, finally. *If it is important to us to decide whether to accept an argument (because we face an examination or must write something about the passage, let us say, or because we must decide how to vote or whether to invest our immense fortune), we may then even make a written outline on a separate sheet.*

Consider for a moment how Cousins supports his claim that "the American 9
people" (meaning you, of course) "ought to be putting pressure . . . to increase the ratio of the humanities to the sciences" (¶5). His first reason *comes in paragraph 6: because "nothing is more valuable" than the skills he then lists. (Note that as we move in*

this way, we begin to get a clearer and clearer notion of what he means by "the humanities": they are those studies that cultivate these skills.) Then, having introduced his first reason, he provides evidence for the because: *first, the doctor's need for the humanities; then the lawyer's; then the business executive's; finally the technologist's. The result is that when we come to his* therefore, *three lines before the end of the paragraph, we see that he has worked hard to earn his right to use it with his four examples of vocations that depend on the humanities.*

It is important to see that each of his claims about these vocations could in turn 10
be questioned, and that it would take him many pages to develop a full argument for any one of the four. (You will later find examples of much fuller development; see our analysis of Popper's "Utopia and Violence," pp. 125–133.) But Cousins counts on our finding each of his examples at least probable or plausible, and he goes on to show, by the way he moves into his next reason (¶7), that he knows how much more might have been said in paragraph 6: "But even if it could be demonstrated . . ."—that is, even if you are still skeptical about all that, *I have even stronger reasons to offer: the humanities are "essential" for "any person who wants to come to terms with life." He can assume that every reader will want* that, *and he can thus move on to show why this second main reason is itself sound.*

We leave it to you to determine how much evidence he provides for his second 11
reason and move on to the third one (¶8). (Note that Cousins has not numbered his reasons for you, but he has given you clear clues by beginning paragraphs 7 and 8 with "But even" and "Finally.") In paragraph 8 he moves from our private desire for "coming to terms with life" to society's "absolute dependence" on citizens educated in the humanities. Like his first two reasons, this one might require a long essay, or even a book, for its full support. In a short piece, Cousins can only suggest the line that he would follow in a longer proof: a consideration of our "underlying philosophy" as revealed by our national history. He ends with an argument that could be considered either as an extension of his third reason or as a new kind of reason altogether, an "appeal to authority." "Jefferson knew . . ."—knew what? Well, in effect, Jefferson knew that what Cousins is arguing for is true. The humanities are even more important than the points raised in the third reason: They are what government (and tax dollars) are for.

What we have just given is by no means a complete analysis of Cousins's 12
argument, but it is a good start toward knowing how to argue with him in a way that would make him sit up and take notice. At least we can now look him in the eye and say such things as, "What you claim is that P *is true* because A, B, *and* C *are true and that each of those is true* because X, Y, *and* Z *are true. But at* B *I have serious questions [or it might be at every step]. Tell me more about why you think . . ."; or "You're flatly wrong about* C. *Just last week a report was issued showing that. . . ."*

In a dialogue of this kind, either with someone in person or with the author 13
who lives before us (in a sense) in the text, we learn to read by learning to think and learn to think by learning to read. The process yields its reward when we sit down to write out the results of our "conversation," saying in effect: "Now see here, Mr.

Cousins, I've considered your case with full respect, and I've thought about your reasons. But I must conclude that. . . ."

Of course we seldom make up our minds only on the basis of carefully thinking through an author's patterns of reasoning. At every point in our encounter with Cousins we are inferring his quality as a person, his character—what is sometimes called his ethos. *Does he seem to be trustworthy, likable, a valuable friend and guide? Writers like Cousins who are skillful at creating an appealing character for themselves will be trusted (not by every reader but by those who like the* ethos*) even when the reasoning is vague or incomplete. You will find many authors in this book whom you like and some whom you dislike. As you work on your own writing, you will find it useful—though sometimes disturbing—to experiment in "sounding like" different writers you admire. There's nothing dishonest about practicing imitations of an author's style as long as you don't claim as your own what you have simply copied.* 14

We might call this whole process, borrowing from Cousins's title, "How to Re-make a Text So That It Is as Large *as Its Author Intended It to Be." It will prove valuable in all of your college work. But of course it will not work at all in reading texts that are not organized as* arguments. *The questions we have asked of Cousins may prove entirely inappropriate when we approach other kinds of texts. But the technique of using marginal notes and underlinings to flag interrelationships (rather than simply to emphasize something you happen to like or, worse, to prove to yourself that you are working hard) should be useful in all kinds of difficult reading. Obviously there are many texts that will be destroyed if we read them with pencil in hand. Sometimes we have even been known to lie back in our hammocks, detective story or sci-fi thriller in limp hand—and fall asleep.* 15

Malcolm X

Malcolm X (1925–1965) was a famous and powerful leader in the push for equal rights for blacks in the 1950s and 1960s. In The Autobiography of Malcolm X, *he describes the dramatic sequence of events that transformed him from Malcolm Little, street hustler and convicted thief, to political leader and outstanding evangelist for the Temple of Islam. In his devotion to Muslim teachings he journeyed to Mecca, and while there he became convinced that many of the teachings of the Temple of Islam were not true to the Muslim faith. On his return to America, he expressed his new convictions with characteristic forthrightness and power. He was assassinated in New York City in 1965 while preaching his new views. Some members of the Temple of Islam were convicted of the murder, but there is still controversy over who in fact killed him.*

The Autobiography *continues to be read as a passionate document express-*

ing both private and public commitment to a cause. In the following selection, Malcolm X gives one of the most moving accounts we know of what it is like to engage in self-education. Although many people these days might scoff at the method he chose, his description of how he felt, once reading changed from merely deciphering words to understanding ideas, is vivid, indeed gripping. It is impossible to doubt that, for him, his strange method worked.

FREEDOM THROUGH LEARNING TO READ

From chapter 11, "Saved," of *The Autobiography of Malcolm X* (1964). The title is ours.

It was because of my letters that I happened to stumble upon starting to acquire some kind of a homemade education. 1

I became increasingly frustrated at not being able to express what I wanted to convey in letters that I wrote, especially those to Mr. Elijah Muhammad.* In the street, I had been the most articulate hustler out there—I had commanded attention when I said something. But now, trying to write simple English, I not only wasn't articulate, I wasn't even functional. How would I sound writing in slang, the way I would *say* it, something such as, "Look, daddy, let me pull your coat about a cat, Elijah Muhammad—" 2

Many who today hear me somewhere in person, or on television, or those who read something I've said, will think I went to school far beyond the eighth grade. This impression is due entirely to my prison studies. 3

It had really begun back in the Charlestown Prison, when Bimbi first made me feel envy of his stock of knowledge. Bimbi had always taken charge of any conversations he was in, and I had tried to emulate him. But every book I picked up had few sentences which didn't contain anywhere from one to nearly all of the words that might as well have been in Chinese. When I just skipped those words, of course, I really ended up with little idea of what the book said. So I had come to the Norfolk Prison Colony still going through only book-reading motions. Pretty soon, I would have quit even these motions, unless I had received the motivation that I did. 4

I saw that the best thing I could do was get hold of a dictionary—to study, to learn some words. I was lucky enough to reason also that I should try to improve my penmanship. It was sad. I couldn't even write in a straight line. It was both ideas together that moved me to request a dictionary along with some tablets and pencils from the Norfolk Prison Colony school. 5

I spent two days just riffling uncertainly through the dictionary's pages. I'd never realized so many words existed! I didn't know *which* words I needed to learn. Finally, just to start some kind of action, I began copying. 6

*Elijah Muhammad was a leader of the Black Muslims' Temple of Islam in the 1940s, 1950s, and 1960s.

In my slow, painstaking, ragged handwriting, I copied into my tablet everything printed on that first page, down to the punctuation marks. 7

I believe it took me a day. Then, aloud, I read back, to myself, everything I'd written on the tablet. Over and over, aloud, to myself, I read my own handwriting. 8

I woke up the next morning, thinking about those words—immensely proud to realize that not only had I written so much at one time, but I'd written words that I never knew were in the world. Moreover, with a little effort, I also could remember what many of these words meant. I reviewed the words whose meanings I didn't remember. Funny thing, from the dictionary first page right now, that "aardvark" springs to my mind. The dictionary had a picture of it, a long-tailed, long-eared, burrowing African mammal, which lives off termites caught by sticking out its tongue as an anteater does for ants. 9

I was so fascinated that I went on—I copied the dictionary's next page. And the same experience came when I studied that. With every succeeding page, I also learned of people and places and events from history. Actually the dictionary is like a miniature encyclopedia. Finally the dictionary's A section had filled a whole tablet—and I went on into the B's. That was the way I started copying what eventually became the entire dictionary. It went a lot faster after so much practice helped me to pick up handwriting speed. Between what I wrote in my tablet, and writing letters, during the rest of my time in prison I would guess I wrote a million words. 10

I suppose it was inevitable that as my word-base broadened, I could for the first time pick up a book and read and now begin to understand what the book was saying. Anyone who has read a great deal can imagine the new world that opened. Let me tell you something: from then until I left that prison, in every free moment I had, if I was not reading in the library, I was reading on my bunk. You couldn't have gotten me out of books with a wedge. Between Mr. Muhammad's teachings, my correspondence, my visitors—usually Ella and Reginald—and my reading of books, months passed without my even thinking about being imprisoned. In fact, up to then, I never had been so truly free in my life. 11

The Norfolk Prison Colony's library was in the school building. A variety of classes was taught there by instructors who came from such places as Harvard and Boston universities. The weekly debates between inmate teams were also held in the school building. You would be astonished to know how worked up convict debaters and audiences would get over subjects like "Should Babies Be Fed Milk?" 12

Available on the prison library's shelves were books on just about every general subject. Much of the big private collection that Parkhurst had willed to the prison was still in crates and boxes in the back of the library—thousands of old books. Some of them looked ancient: covers faded, old-time parchment-looking binding. Parkhurst, I've mentioned, seemed to have been principally interested in history and religion. He had the money and the 13 special interest to have a lot of books that you wouldn't have in general circulation. Any college library would have been lucky to get that collection.

As you can imagine, especially in a prison where there was heavy emphasis on rehabilitation, an inmate was smiled upon if he demonstrated an unusually intense interest in books. There was a sizable number of well-read inmates, especially the popular debaters. Some were said by many to be practically walking encyclopedias. They were almost celebrities. No university would ask any student to devour literature as I did when this new world opened to me, of being able to read and *understand.* 14

I read more in my room than in the library itself. An inmate who was known to read a lot could check out more than the permitted maximum number of books. I preferred reading in the total isolation of my own room. 15

When I had progressed to really serious reading, every night at about ten P.M. I would be outraged with the "lights out." It always seemed to catch me right in the middle of something engrossing. 16

Fortunately, right outside my door was a corridor light that cast a glow into my room. The glow was enough to read by, once my eyes adjusted to it. So when "lights out" came, I would sit on the floor where I could continue reading in that glow. 17

At one-hour intervals the night guards paced past every room. Each time I heard the approaching footsteps, I jumped into bed and feigned sleep. And as soon as the guard passed, I got back out of bed onto the floor area of that light-glow, where I would read for another fifty-eight minutes—until the guard approached again. That went on until three or four every morning. Three or four hours of sleep a night was enough for me. Often in the years in the streets I had slept less than that. 18

The teachings of Mr. Muhammad stressed how history had been "whitened"—when white men had written history books, the black man simply had been left out. Mr. Muhammad couldn't have said anything that would have struck me much harder. I had never forgotten how when my class, me and all of those whites, had studied seventh-grade United States history back in Mason, the history of the Negro had been covered in one paragraph, and the teacher had gotten a big laugh with his joke, "Negroes' feet are so big that when they walk, they leave a hole in the ground." 19

This is one reason why Mr. Muhammad's teachings spread so swiftly all over the United States, among *all* Negroes, whether or not they became followers of Mr. Muhammad. The teachings ring true—to every Negro. You can hardly show me a black adult in America—or a white one, for that matter—who knows from the history books anything like the truth about the black man's role. In my own case, once I heard of the "glorious history of the black man," I took special pains to hunt in the library for books that would inform me on details about black history. 20

I can remember accurately the very first set of books that really impressed me. I have since bought that set of books and I have it at home for my children to read as they grow up. It's called *Wonders of the World.* It's full 21 of pictures of archeological finds, statues that depict, usually, non-European people.

I found books like Will Durant's *Story of Civilization.* I read H. G. Wells' *Outline of History. Souls of Black Folk* by W. E. B. Du Bois gave me a glimpse into the black people's history before they came to this country. Carter G. Woodson's *Negro History* opened my eyes about black empires before the black slave was brought to the United States, and the early Negro struggles for freedom. 22

J. A. Rogers' three volumes of *Sex and Race* told about race-mixing before Christ's time; about Aesop being a black man who told fables; about Egypt's Pharaohs; about the great Coptic Christian Empires; about Ethiopia, the earth's oldest continuous black civilization, as China is the oldest continuous civilization. 23

Mr. Muhammad's teaching about how the white man had been created led me to *Findings in Genetics* by Gregor Mendel.* (The dictionary's G section was where I had learned what "genetics" meant.) I really studied this book by the Austrian monk. Reading it over and over, especially certain sections, helped me to understand that if you started with a black man, a white man could be produced; but starting with a white man, you never could produce a black man—because the white chromosome is recessive. And since no one disputes that there was but one Original Man, the conclusion is clear. 24

During the last year or so, in the *New York Times,* Arnold Toynbee used the word "bleached" in describing the white man. (His words were: "White [i.e. bleached] human beings of North European origin. . . .") Toynbee also referred to the European geographic area as only a peninsula of Asia. He said there is no such thing as Europe. And if you look at the globe, you will see for yourself that America is only an extension of Asia. (But at the same time Toynbee is among those who have helped to bleach history. He has written that Africa was the only continent that produced no history. He won't write that again. Every day now, the truth is coming to light.) 25

I never will forget how shocked I was when I began reading about slavery's total horror. It made such an impact upon me that it later became one of my favorite subjects when I became a minister of Mr. Muhammad's. The world's most monstrous crime, the sin and the blood on the white man's hands, are almost impossible to believe. Books like the one by Frederick Olmstead opened my eyes to the horrors suffered when the slave was landed in the United States. The European woman, Fannie Kimball, who had married a Southern white slaveowner, described how human beings were degraded. Of course I read *Uncle Tom's Cabin.* In fact, I believe that's the only novel I have ever read since I started serious reading. 26

Parkhurst's collection also contained some bound pamphlets of the Abolitionist Anti-Slavery Society of New England. I read descriptions of atrocities, saw those illustrations of black slave women tied up and flogged with whips; of black mothers watching their babies being dragged off, never to be seen by their mothers again; of dogs after slaves, and of the fugitive 27

*Gregor Mendel (1822–1884), Austrian Augustinian monk, father of genetic science.

slave catchers, evil white men with whips and clubs and chains and guns. I read about the slave preacher Nat Turner, who put the fear of God into the white slavemaster. Nat Turner wasn't going around preaching pie-in-the-sky and "non-violent" freedom for the black man. There in Virginia one night in 1831, Nat and seven other slaves started out at his master's home and through the night they went from one plantation "big house" to the next, killing, until by the next morning 57 white people were dead and Nat had about 70 slaves following him. White people, terrified for their lives, fled from their homes, locked themselves up in public buildings, hid in the woods, and some even left the state. A small army of soldiers took two months to catch and hang Nat Turner. Somewhere I have read where Nat Turner's example is said to have inspired John Brown to invade Virginia and attack Harper's Ferry nearly thirty years later, with thirteen white men and five Negroes.

I read Herodotus, "the father of History," or, rather, I read about him. 28
And I read the histories of various nations, which opened my eyes gradually, then wider and wider, to how the whole world's white men had indeed acted like devils, pillaging and raping and bleeding and draining the whole world's non-white people. I remember, for instance, books such as Will Durant's *The Story of Oriental Civilization,* and Mahatma Gandhi's accounts of the struggle to drive the British out of India.

Book after book showed me how the white man had brought upon the 29
world's black, brown, red, and yellow peoples every variety of the sufferings of exploitation. I saw how since the sixteenth century, the so-called "Christian trader" white man began to ply the seas in his lust for Asian and African empires, and plunder, and power. I read, I saw, how the white man never has gone among the non-white peoples bearing the Cross in the true manner and spirit of Christ's teachings—meek, humble, and Christlike.

I perceived, as I read, how the collective white man had been actually 30
nothing but a piratical opportunist who used Faustian machinations to make his own Christianity his initial wedge in criminal conquests. First, always "religiously," he branded "heathen" and "pagan" labels upon ancient non-white cultures and civilizations. The stage thus set, he then turned upon his non-white victims his weapons of war.

I read how, entering India—half a *billion* deeply religious brown peo- 31
ple—the British white man, by 1759, through promises, trickery and manipulations, controlled much of India through Great Britain's East India Company. The parasitical British administration kept tentacling out to half of the subcontinent. In 1857, some of the desperate people of India finally mutinied—and, excepting the African slave trade, nowhere has history recorded any more unnecessary bestial and ruthless human carnage than the British suppression of the non-white Indian people.

Over 115 million African blacks—close to the 1930's population of the 32
United States—were murdered or enslaved during the slave trade. And I read how when the slave market was glutted, the cannibalistic white powers of Europe next carved up, as their colonies, the richest areas of the black conti-

nent. And Europe's chancelleries for the next century played a chess game of naked exploitation and power from Cape Horn to Cairo.

Ten guards and the warden couldn't have torn me out of those books. 33
Not even Elijah Muhammad could have been more eloquent than those books were in providing indisputable proof that the collective white man had acted like a devil in virtually every contact he had with the world's collective non-white man. I listen today to the radio, and watch television, and read the headlines about the collective white man's fear and tension concerning China. When the white man professes ignorance about why the Chinese hate him so, my mind can't help flashing back to what I read, there in prison, about how the blood forebears of this same white man raped China at a time when China was trusting and helpless. Those original white "Christian traders" sent into China millions of pounds of opium. By 1839, so many of the Chinese were addicts that China's desperate government destroyed twenty thousand chests of opium. The first Opium War was promptly declared by the white man. Imagine! Declaring *war* upon someone who objects to being narcotized! The Chinese were severely beaten, with Chinese-invented gunpowder.

The Treaty of Nanking made China pay the British white man for the 34
destroyed opium: forced open China's major ports to British trade; forced China to abandon Hong Kong; fixed China's import tariffs so low that cheap British articles soon flooded in, maiming China's industrial development.

After a second Opium War, the Tientsin Treaties legalized the ravaging 35
opium trade, legalized a British-French-American control of China's customs. China tried delaying that Treaty's ratification; Peking was looted and burned.

"Kill the foreign white devils!" was the 1901 Chinese war cry in the 36
Boxer Rebellion. Losing again, this time the Chinese were driven from Peking's choicest areas. The vicious, arrogant white man put up the famous signs, "Chinese and dogs not allowed."

Red China after World War II closed its doors to the Western white 37
world. Massive Chinese agricultural, scientific, and industrial efforts are described in a book that *Life* magazine recently published. Some observers inside Red China have reported that the world never has known such a hate-white campaign as is now going on in this non-white country where, present birth-rates continuing, in fifty more years Chinese will be half the earth's population. And it seems that some Chinese chickens will soon come home to roost, with China's recent successful nuclear tests.

Let us face reality. We can see in the United Nations a new world order 38
being shaped, along color lines—an alliance among the non-white nations. America's U.N. Ambassador Adlai Stevenson complained not long ago that in the United Nations "a skin game" was being played. He was right. He was facing reality. A "skin game" *is* being played. But Ambassador Stevenson sounded like Jesse James accusing the marshal of carrying a gun. Because who in the world's history ever has played a worse "skin game" than the white man?

Mr. Muhammad, to whom I was writing daily, had no idea of what a 39 new world had opened up to me through my efforts to document his teachings in books.

When I discovered philosophy, I tried to touch all the landmarks of 40
philosophical development. Gradually, I read most of the old philosophers, Occidental and Oriental. The Oriental philosophers were the ones I came to prefer; finally, my impression was that most Occidental philosophy had largely been borrowed from the Oriental thinkers. Socrates, for instance, traveled in Egypt. Some sources even say that Socrates was initiated into some of the Egyptian mysteries. Obviously Socrates got some of his wisdom among the East's wise men.

I have often reflected upon the new vistas that reading opened to me. 41
I knew right there in prison that reading had changed forever the course of my life. As I see it today, the ability to read awoke inside me some long dormant craving to be mentally alive. I certainly wasn't seeking any degree, the way a college confers a status symbol upon its students. My homemade education gave me, with every additional book that I read, a little bit more sensitivity to the deafness, dumbness, and blindness that was afflicting the black race in America. Not long ago, an English writer telephoned me from London, asking questions. One was, "What's your alma mater?" I told him, "Books." You will never catch me with a free fifteen minutes in which I'm not studying something I feel might be able to help the black man.

Yesterday I spoke in London, and both ways on the plane across the 42
Atlantic I was studying a document about how the United Nations proposes to insure the human rights of the oppressed minorities of the world. The American black man is the world's most shameful case of minority oppression. What makes the black man think of himself as only an internal United States issue is just a catch-phrase, two words, "civil rights." How is the black man going to get "civil rights" before first he wins his *human* rights? If the American black man will start thinking about his *human* rights, and then start thinking of himself as part of one of the world's great peoples, he will see he has a case for the United Nations.

I can't think of a better case! Four hundred years of black blood and 43
sweat invested here in America, and the white man still has the black man begging for what every immigrant fresh off the ship can take for granted the minute he walks down the gangplank.

But I'm digressing. I told the Englishman that my alma mater was books, 44
a good library. Every time I catch a plane, I have with me a book that I want to read—and that's a lot of books these days. If I weren't out here every day battling the white man, I could spend the rest of my life reading, just satisfying my curiosity—because you can hardly mention anything I'm not curious about. I don't think anybody ever got more out of going to prison than I did. In fact, prison enabled me to study far more intensively than I would have if my life had gone differently and I had attended some college. I imagine that one of the biggest troubles with colleges is there are too many distractions, too much panty-raiding, fraternities, and boola-boola and all of that. Where

else but in a prison could I have attacked my ignorance by being able to study intensely sometimes as much as fifteen hours a day?

Questions for Discussion

1. Does it seem to you that the following accusation is metaphorically true, literally true, or simply untrue: "The collective white man had acted like a devil in virtually every contact he had with the world's collective non-white man" (¶33)? What kinds of evidence would be required to prove or disprove such a claim? Can you think of examples that would seem to bear it out or to make it doubtful? Do you think Malcolm X uses his own examples fairly or unfairly?
2. Malcolm X expresses exhilaration at "being able to read and *understand*" (¶14). Is his delight entirely political and racial? Is there a part of him that thrills *as a person* to learning, not just as someone who wants to achieve political or religious goals? What evidence can you point to? Does the distinction between "reading politically" and "reading as a person" seem useful to you?
3. Is Malcolm X's distinction between "civil rights" and "human rights" (¶42) clear to you? How would you explain the difference to someone who had not read the *Autobiography*? Must one precede the other either in time or importance?
4. How would you describe Malcolm X's tone? (*Tone* is a word commonly used to suggest tone of voice, but we shall always use it to suggest the whole range of emotions that authors share with readers.) Does he sound angry, amused, hurt, outraged, friendly, aggressive, confiding, frank? Can you think of other adjectives that come closer to his implied relation with you? What sort of reader does he seem to address? (*Note:* Throughout this text, you will find that asking about tone will be profitable, whether we remind you of it or not.)
5. In his account of Nat Turner (¶27), Malcolm X claims that Turner "put the fear of God into the white slavemaster" by killing 57 white people in one night. Is it clear whether the author approves or disapproves of this event? Would you respond differently, either to the event itself or to Malcolm X's account of it, if you knew whether the 57 murdered people were slaves or slavemasters? Field bosses? Children? Look up the life of Nat Turner in a good encyclopedia. What differences do you find between the account there and Malcolm X's? Are Malcolm X's claims about the biases of white historians relevant here?
6. In the light of what seems to be Malcolm X's purpose, does he make effective use of the Jesse James simile (¶38)? (A *simile* implies an analogy:

A is to *B* as *C* is to *D.* For instance, winter relates to mittens as summer relates to swimsuits.) Can you work out the implied analogy of the Jesse James simile? Is it persuasive?

Suggested Essay Topics

1. Make a list of the possible motives that drove Malcolm X to be such a dedicated and persistent learner: for example, ambition, love of power, greed, desire to be known as a scholar, curiosity, boredom, hope of outsmarting other people, desire to improve the world. Then study the text again to see which ones seem most strongly suggested by what the author says. Write an essay designed to convince your classmates that your view of what drove him is the most likely one.
2. On the basis of Malcolm X's essay and your own experience, define the qualities and behavior of the good student. In an essay directed to fellow students (or, if you prefer, in a letter to your parents), evaluate your own persistence and eagerness in learning, and discuss whether you are a typical or exceptional student. In the course of your discussion, try to explain Malcolm X's assertion that while learning, "months passed without my even thinking about being imprisoned. In fact, up to then, I had never been so truly free in my life" (¶11).

Charles Dickens

Charles Dickens (1812–1870) was the most popular novelist of the nineteenth century; his novels are sometimes said to be the greatest literary works in English since Shakespeare. Most of them include strong satirical attacks on social evils such as the kind exhibited in the excerpt here from Hard Times.

When we see a title like Hard Times, *we can expect that the times will be hard in more ways than one, and when we meet an elementary school director named Gradgrind, we can expect the grads to be "ground" in nasty ways. The passage here begins with the opening of the novel, when Mr. Thomas Gradgrind, founder of the School for Useful Knowledge, inspects the classroom of the schoolmaster, Mr. M'Choakumchild.*

As you read, ask yourself whether you think an education focused on facts and information alone is as unsatisfactory as Dickens implies. How heavily have your own teachers and parents advised you to ignore "impractical" areas of study—literature, philosophy, music, and history, perhaps—in favor of an education that "sticks to the facts" and supposedly leads to well-paying jobs? How much emphasis has school placed on the cultivation of your imagination and curiosity? How much emphasis should *be placed on this kind of learning? Are imagination and curiosity synonymous with triviality and woolgathering, or do they play important roles in politics, business, and other practical areas? Dickens's portrayal of grim teachers who make learning a chore and frustrated students who don't know why they are being made to jump through hoops invites us to think seriously about these questions.*

HARD FACTS

From *Hard Times* (1854). The title is ours.

THE ONE THING NEEDFUL

"Now, what I want is, Facts. Teach these boys and girls nothing but Facts. 1
Facts alone are wanted in life. Plant nothing else, and root out everything else. You can only form the minds of reasoning animals upon Facts; nothing else will ever be of any service to them. This is the principle on which I bring up my own children, and this is the principle on which I bring up these children. Stick to Facts, sir!"

The scene was a plain, bare, monotonous vault of a schoolroom, and the 2
speaker's square forefinger emphasized his observations by underscoring every sentence with a line on the schoolmaster's sleeve. The emphasis was helped by the speaker's square wall of a forehead, which had his eyebrows for its base, while his eyes found commodious cellarage in two dark caves, overshadowed by the wall. The emphasis was helped by the speaker's mouth, which was wide, thin, and hard set. The emphasis was helped by the speaker's voice, which was inflexible, dry, and dictatorial. The emphasis was helped by the speaker's hair, which bristled on the skirts of his bald head, a plantation of firs to keep the wind from its shining surface, all covered with knobs, like the crust of a plum pie, as if the head had scarcely warehouse-room for the hard facts stored inside. The speaker's obstinate carriage, square coat, square legs, square shoulders—nay, his very neckcloth, trained to take him by the throat with an unaccommodating grasp, like a stubborn fact, as it was—all helped the emphasis.

"In this life, we want nothing but Facts, sir; nothing but Facts!" 3

The speaker, and the schoolmaster, and the third grown person present, 4
all backed a little, and swept with their eyes the inclined plane of little vessels then and there arranged in order, ready to have imperial gallons of facts poured into them until they were full to the brim.

. . .

MURDERING THE INNOCENTS

Thomas Gradgrind, sir. A man of realities. A man of facts and calculations. 5
A man who proceeds upon the principle that two and two are four, and nothing over, and who is not to be talked into allowing for anything over. Thomas Gradgrind, sir—peremptorily Thomas—Thomas Gradgrind. With a rule and a pair of scales, and the multiplication table always in his pocket, sir, ready to weigh and measure any parcel of human nature, and tell you exactly what it comes to. It is a mere question of figures, a case of simple

arithmetic. You might hope to get some other nonsensical belief into the head of George Gradgrind, or Augustus Gradgrind, or John Gradgrind, or Joseph Gradgrind (all supposititious, nonexistent persons), but into the head of Thomas Gradgrind—no, sir!

In such terms Mr. Gradgrind always mentally introduced himself, whether to his private circle of acquaintance, or to the public in general. In such terms, no doubt, substituting the words "boys and girls" for "sir," Thomas Gradgrind now presented Thomas Gradgrind to the little pitchers before him, who were to be filled so full of facts. 6

Indeed, as he eagerly sparkled at them from the cellarage before mentioned, he seemed a kind of cannon loaded to the muzzle with facts, and prepared to blow them clean out of the regions of childhood at one discharge. He seemed a galvanizing apparatus,* too, charged with a grim mechanical substitute for the tender young imaginations that were to be stormed away. 7

"Girl number twenty," said Mr. Gradgrind, squarely pointing with his square forefinger, "I don't know that girl. Who is that girl?" 8

"Sissy Jupe, sir," explained number twenty, blushing, standing up, and curtseying. 9

"Sissy is not a name," said Mr. Gradgrind. "Don't call yourself Sissy. Call yourself Cecilia." 10

"It's father as calls me Sissy, sir," returned the young girl in a trembling voice, and with another curtsey. 11

"Then he has no business to do it," said Mr. Gradgrind. "Tell him he mustn't. Cecilia Jupe. Let me see. What is your father?" 12

"He belongs to the horse-riding,† if you please, sir." 13

Mr. Gradgrind frowned, and waved off the objectionable calling with his hand. 14

"We don't want to know anything about that, here. You mustn't tell us about that, here. Your father breaks horses, don't he?" 15

"If you please, sir, when they can get any to break, they do break horses in the ring, sir." 16

"You mustn't tell us about the ring here. Very well, then. Describe your father as a horsebreaker. He doctors sick horses, I dare say?" 17

"Oh, yes, sir." 18

"Very well, then. He is a veterinary surgeon, a farrier, and horsebreaker. Give me your definition of a horse." 19

(Sissy Jupe thrown into the greatest alarm by this demand.) 20

"Girl number twenty unable to define a horse!" said Mr. Gradgrind, for the general behoof of all the little pitchers. "Girl number twenty possessed of no facts in reference to one of the commonest of animals! Some boy's definition of a horse. Bitzer, yours." 21

The square finger, moving here and there, lighted suddenly on Bitzer, 22

*In early medical research, a "galvanizing apparatus"—named for Luigi Galvani (1737–1798), an Italian physiologist who discovered that electricity could be produced by chemical action—was used to shoot electrical impulses into animal or human tissue.

†Sissy's father works with the horse-riding acts in the circus.

perhaps because he chanced to sit in the same ray of sunlight which, darting in at one of the bare windows of the intensely whitewashed room, irradiated Sissy. For, the boys and girls sat on the face of the inclined plane in two compact bodies, divided up the centre by a narrow interval; and Sissy, being at the corner of a row on the sunny side, came in for the beginning of a sunbeam, of which Bitzer, being at the corner of a row on the other side, a few rows in advance, caught the end. But, whereas the girl was so dark-eyed and dark-haired that she seemed to receive a deeper and more lustrous colour from the sun, when it shone upon her, the boy was so light-eyed and light-haired that the self-same rays appeared to draw out of him what little colour he ever possessed. His cold eyes would hardly have been eyes, but for the short ends of lashes which, by bringing them into immediate contrast with something paler than themselves, expressed their form. His short-cropped hair might have been a mere continuation of the sandy freckles on his forehead and face. His skin was so unwholesomely deficient in the natural tinge, that he looked as though, if he were cut, he would bleed white.

"Bitzer," said Thomas Gradgrind. "Your definition of a horse." 23

"Quadruped. Graminivorous. Forty teeth, namely twenty-four grind- 24
ers, four eye-teeth, and twelve incisive. Sheds coat in the spring; in marshy countries, sheds hoofs, too. Hoofs hard, but requiring to be shod with iron. Age known by marks in mouth." Thus (and much more) Bitzer.

"Now, girl number twenty," said Mr. Gradgrind, "you know what a 25
horse is."

She curtseyed again, and would have blushed deeper, if she could have 26
blushed deeper than she had blushed all this time. Bitzer, after rapidly blinking at Thomas Gradgrind with both eyes at once, and so catching the light upon his quivering ends of lashes that they looked like the antennae of busy insects, put his knuckles to his freckled forehead, and sat down again.

The third gentleman now stepped forth. A mighty man at cutting and 27
drying, he was; a government officer; in his way (and in most other people's too), a professed pugilist; always in training, always with a system to force down the general throat like a bolus,* always to be heard of at the bar of his little Public-office, ready to fight all England. To continue in the fistic phraseology, he had a genius for coming up to the scratch,† wherever and whatever it was, and proving himself an ugly customer. He would go in and damage any subject whatever with his right, follow up with his left, stop, exchange, counter, bore his opponent (he always fought All England)‡ to the ropes, and fall upon him neatly. He was certain to knock the wind out of common sense, and render that unlucky adversary deaf to the call of time.

*A large pill.

†A line drawn across the center of the ring in the early days of prize-fighting. Contestants would commence a match by stepping up to opposite sides of this line, and the match would end when one of the two could no longer come up to the scratch line at the beginning of a new round.

‡Fighting according to a national code of rules for the prize-ring—one of the codes superseded by the adoption of the Marquis of Queensbury's rules in 1866.

And he had it in charge from high authority to bring about the great Public-office Millennium, when Commissioners* should reign upon earth.

"Very well," said this gentleman, briskly smiling, and folding his arms. 28
"That's a horse. Now, let me ask you, girls and boys, Would you paper a room with representations of horses?"

After a pause, one half of the children cried in chorus, "Yes, sir!" Upon 29
which the other half, seeing in the gentleman's face that Yes was wrong, cried out in chorus, "No, sir!"—as the custom is, in these examinations.

"Of course, No. Why wouldn't you?" 30

A pause. One corpulent slow boy, with a wheezy manner of breathing, 31
ventured the answer, Because he wouldn't paper a room at all, but would paint it.

"You *must* paper it," said the gentleman, rather warmly. 32

"You must paper it," said Thomas Gradgrind, "whether you like it or 33
not. Don't tell *us* you wouldn't paper it. What do you mean, boy?"

"I'll explain to you, then," said the gentleman, after another and a 34
dismal pause, "why you wouldn't paper a room with representations of horses. Do you ever see horses walking up and down the sides of rooms in reality—in fact? Do you?"

"Yes, sir!" from one half. "No, sir!" from the other. 35

"Of course, no," said the gentleman, with an indignant look at the 36
wrong half. "Why, then, you are not to see anywhere what you don't see in fact; you are not to have anywhere what you don't have in fact. What is called Taste, is only another name for Fact."

Thomas Gradgrind nodded his approbation. 37

"This is a new principle, a discovery, a great discovery," said the gentle- 38
man. "Now I'll try you again. Suppose you were going to carpet a room. Would you use a carpet having a representation of flowers upon it?"

There being a general conviction by this time that "No, sir!" was always 39
the right answer to this gentleman, the chorus of No was very strong. Only a few feeble stragglers said Yes; among them Sissy Jupe.

"Girl number twenty," said the gentleman, smiling in the calm strength 40
of knowledge.

Sissy blushed, and stood up. 41

"So you would carpet your room—or your husband's room, if you were 42
a grown woman, and had a husband—with representations of flowers, would you," said the gentleman. "Why would you?"

"If you please, sir, I am very fond of flowers," returned the girl. 43

"And is that why you would put tables and chairs upon them, and have 44
people walking over them with heavy boots?"

"It wouldn't hurt them, sir. They wouldn't crush and wither if you 45
please, sir. They would be the pictures of what was very pretty and pleasant, and I would fancy—"

*Administrative officials in various departments of government such as Customs or Income Taxes.

"Ay, ay, ay! But you mustn't fancy," cried the gentleman, quite elated 46
by coming so happily to his point. "That's it! You are never to fancy."

"You are not, Cecilia Jupe," Thomas Gradgrind solemnly repeated, "to 47
do anything of that kind."

"Fact, fact, fact!" said the gentleman. And "Fact, fact, fact!" repeated 48
Thomas Gradgrind.

"You are to be in all things regulated and governed," said the gentle- 49
man, "by fact. We hope to have before long, a board of fact, composed of commissioners of fact, who will force the people to be a people of fact, and of nothing but fact. You must discard the word Fancy altogether. You have nothing to do with it. You are not to have, in any object of use or ornament, what would be a contradiction in fact. You don't walk upon flowers in fact; you cannot be allowed to walk upon flowers in carpets. You don't find that foreign birds and butterflies come and perch upon your crockery; you cannot be permitted to paint foreign birds and butterflies upon your crockery. You never meet with quadrupeds going up and down walls; you must not have quadrupeds represented upon walls. You must use," said the gentleman, "for all these purposes, combinations and modifications (in primary colours) of mathematical figures which are susceptible of proof and demonstration. This is the new discovery. This is Fact. This is taste."

The girl curtseyed and sat down: She was very young, and she looked 50
as if she were frightened by the matter of fact prospect the world afforded.

"Now, if Mr. M'Choakumchild," said the gentleman, "will proceed to 51
give his first lesson here, Mr. Gradgrind, I shall be happy, at your request, to observe his mode of procedure."

Mr. Gradgrind was much obliged. "Mr. M'Choakumchild, we only wait 52
for you."

So, Mr. M'Choakumchild began in his best manner. He and some one 53
hundred and forty other schoolmasters had been lately turned at the same time, in the same factory, on the same principles, like so many pianoforte legs. He had been put through an immense variety of paces, and had answered volumes of head-breaking questions. Orthography, etymology, syntax, and prosody, biography, astronomy, geography, and general cosmography, the sciences of compound proportion, algebra, land-surveying and levelling, vocal music and drawing from models, were all at the ends of his ten chilled fingers. He had worked his stony way into Her Majesty's most Honourable Privy Council's Schedule B,* and had taken the bloom off the higher branches of mathematics and physical science, French, German, Latin, and Greek. He knew all about all the Water Sheds of all the world (whatever they are), and all the histories of all the peoples, and all the names of all the rivers and mountains, and all the productions, manners, and customs of all the countries, and all their boundaries and bearings on the two-and-thirty points of the compass. Ah, rather overdone,

*A syllabus established in 1846 specifying what subjects were to be mastered by candidates training to become teachers. Schedule B was drawn up by a subcommittee of the Privy Council.

M'Choakumchild. If he had only learnt a little less, how infinitely better he might have taught much more!

He went to work, in this preparatory lesson, not unlike Morgiana* in 54
the Forty Thieves; looking into all the vessels ranged before him, one after another, to see what they contained. Say, good M'Choakumchild. When from thy boiling store thou shalt fill each jar brimful by-and-by, dost thou think that thou wilt always kill outright the robber Fancy lurking within—or sometimes only maim him and distort him?

A LOOPHOLE

Mr. Gradgrind walked homewards from the school, in a state of considerable 55
satisfaction. It was his school, and he intended it to be a model. He intended every child in it to be a model—just as the young Gradgrinds were all models.

There were five young Gradgrinds, and they were models every one. 56
They had been lectured at, from their tenderest years; coursed, like little hares. Almost as soon as they could run alone, they had been made to run to the lecture-room. The first object with which they had an association, or of which they had a remembrance, was a large blackboard with a dry Ogre chalking ghastly white figures on it.

Not that they knew, by name or nature, anything about an Ogre. Fact 57
forbid! I only use the word to express a monster in a lecturing castle, with Heaven knows how many heads manipulated into one, taking childhood captive, and dragging it into gloomy statistical dens by the hair.

No little Gradgrind had ever seen a face in the moon; it was up in the 58
moon before it could speak distinctly. No little Gradgrind had ever learned the silly jingle, Twinkle, twinkle, little star; how I wonder what you are! No little Gradgrind had ever known wonder on the subject, each little Gradgrind having at five years old dissected the Great Bear like a Professor Owen,† and driven Charles's Wain‡ like a locomotive engine-driver. No little Gradgrind had ever associated a cow in a field with that famous cow with the crumpled horn who tossed the dog who worried the cat who killed the rat who ate the malt, or with that yet more famous cow who swallowed Tom Thumb;§ it had never heard of those celebrities, and had only been introduced to a cow as a graminivorous ruminating quadruped with several stomachs.

To his matter-of fact home, which was called Stone Lodge, Mr. Grad- 59
grind directed his steps. He had virtually retired from the wholesale hardware trade before he built Stone Lodge, and was now looking about for a suitable

*Ali Baba's slave in the *Arabian Nights* who killed forty thieves by pouring boiling oil into the jars in which they were hiding.

†Sir Richard Owen (1804–1892), zoologist and author of *Comparative Anatomy and Physiology of Vertebrates.* Dickens had visited his home and discussed telescopes with him, an incident that may have prompted the reference to astronomy.

‡One of the names for the constellation called the Big Dipper or the Great Bear, so named for its resemblance to a wagon (wain) associated with King Charlemagne (Charles).

§The hero of Henry Fielding's play *The Life of Tom Thumb the Great* (1730).

opportunity of making an arithmetical figure in Parliament. Stone Lodge was situated on a moor within a mile or two of a great town—called Coketown in the present faithful guidebook.

A very regular feature on the face of the country Stone Lodge was. Not 60
the least disguise toned down or shaded off that uncompromising fact in the landscape. A great square house, with a heavy portico darkening the principal windows, as its master's heavy brows overshadowed his eyes. A calculated, cast up, balanced, and proved house. Six windows on this side of the door, six on that side; a total of twelve in this wing, a total of twelve in the other wing; four-and-twenty carried over to the back wings. A lawn and garden and an infant avenue, all ruled straight like a botanical account-book. Gas and ventilation, drainage and water-service, all of the primest quality. Iron clamps and girders, fireproof from top to bottom; mechanical lifts* for the housemaids, with all their brushes and brooms; everything that heart could desire.

Everything? Well, I suppose so. The little Gradgrinds had cabinets in 61
various departments of science too. They had a little conchological cabinet, and a little metallurgical cabinet, and a little mineralogical cabinet; and the specimens were all arranged and labelled, and the bits of stone and ore looked as though they might have been broken from the parent substances by those tremendously hard instruments their own names; and, to paraphrase the idle legend of Peter Piper,† who had never found his way into *their* nursery, If the greedy little Gradgrinds grasped at more than this, what was it, for good gracious goodness' sake, that the greedy little Gradgrinds grasped at!

Their father walked on in a hopeful and satisfied frame of mind. He was 62
an affectionate father, after his manner; but he would probably have described himself (if he had been put, like Sissy Jupe, upon a definition) as "an eminently practical" father. He had a particular pride in the phrase eminently practical, which was considered to have a special application to him. Whatsoever the public meeting held in Coketown, and whatsoever the subject of such meeting, some Coketowner was sure to seize the occasion of alluding to his eminently practical friend Gradgrind. This always pleased the eminently practical friend. He knew it to be his due, but his due was acceptable.

He had reached the neutral ground upon the outskirts of the town, 63
which was neither town nor country, and yet was either spoiled, when his ears were invaded by the sound of music. The clashing and banging band attached to the horse-riding establishment, which had there set up its rest in a wooden pavilion, was in full bray. A flag, floating from the summit of the temple, proclaimed to mankind that it was "Sleary's horse-riding" which claimed their suffrages. Sleary himself, a stout modern statue with a money-box at its elbow, in an ecclesiastical niche of early Gothic architecture, took the money. Miss Josephine Sleary, as some very long and very narrow strips of printed bill announced, was then inaugurating the entertainments with her

*Elevators.

†Alluding to a line from a nursery rhyme: "Where's the peck of pickled peppers Peter Piper picked?"

graceful equestrian Tyrolean flower-act. Among the other pleasing but always strictly moral wonders which must be seen to be believed Signor Jupe was that afternoon to "elucidate the diverting accomplishments of his highly trained performing dog Merrylegs." He was also to exhibit "his astounding feat of throwing seventy-five hundredweight in rapid succession backhanded over his head, thus forming a fountain of solid iron in mid-air, a feat never before attempted in this or any other country and which having elicited such rapturous plaudits from enthusiastic throngs it cannot be withdrawn." The same Signor Jupe was to "enliven the varied performances at frequent intervals with his chaste Shaksperean quips and retorts." Lastly, he was to wind them up by appearing in his favourite character of Mr. William Button, of Tooley Street, in "the highly novel and laughable hippo-comedietta of The Tailor's Journey to Brentford."*

Thomas Gradgrind took no heed of these trivialities of course, but 64
passed on as a practical man ought to pass on, after brushing the noisy insects from his thoughts, or consigning them to the House of Correction. But, the turning of the road took him by the back of the booth, and at the back of the booth a number of children were congregated in a number of stealthy attitudes, striving to peep in at the hidden glories of the place.

This brought him to a stop. "Now, to think of these vagabonds," said 65
he, "attracting the young rabble from a model school."

A space of stunted grass and dry rubbish being between him and the 66
young rabble, he took his eyeglass out of his waistcoat to look for any child he knew by name, and might order off. Phenomenon almost incredible though distinctly seen, what did he then behold but his own metallurgical Louisa peeping with all her might through a hole in a deal board, and his own mathematical Thomas abasing himself on the ground to catch but a hoof of the graceful equestrian Tyrolean flower-act!

Dumb with amazement, Mr. Gradgrind crossed to the spot where his 67
family was thus disgraced, laid his hand upon each erring child, and said:

"Louisa!! Thomas!!" 68

Both rose, red and disconcerted. But Louisa looked at her father with 69
more boldness than Thomas did. Indeed, Thomas did not look at him, but gave himself up to be taken home like a machine.

"In the name of wonder, idleness, and folly!" said Mr. Gradgrind, lead- 70
ing each away by a hand, "what do you do here?"

"Wanted to see what it was like," returned Louisa, shortly. 71

"What it was like?" 72

*A pantomime staged on horseback. Performances of this kind, as described by Mr. Sleary in *Hard Times* were popular in circuses and amusement halls such as Astley's in London. In February 1854, when Dickens and his friend Mark Lemon were visiting circuses to gather information to be used in *Hard Times,* Astley's was advertising a double bill featuring an elephant show ("Wise Elephants of the East") to be followed by *"Billy Button's Journey to Brentford;* or *Harlequin and the Ladies' Favourite."* This production, described as a "Grand Equestrian Comic Pantomime" recently written by Nelson Lee, was based on a popular pantomime of a tailor who rode his horse facing backwards. The name Billy Button was applied to small boys. See *The Illustrated London News,* Dec. 24, 1853, and Feb. 4, 1854.

"Yes, father." 73

There was an air of jaded sullenness in them both, and particularly in the girl; yet, struggling through the dissatisfaction of her face, there was a light with nothing to rest upon, a fire with nothing to burn, a starved imagination keeping life in itself somehow, which brightened its expression. Not with the brightness natural to cheerful youth, but with uncertain, eager, doubtful flashes, which had something painful in them, analogous to the changes on a blind face groping its way. 74

She was a child now, of fifteen or sixteen; but at no distant day would seem to become a woman all at once. Her father thought so as he looked at her. She was pretty. Would have been self-willed (he thought in his eminently practical way), but for her bringing-up. 75

"Thomas, though I have the fact before me, I find it difficult to believe that you, with your education and resources, should have brought your sister to a scene like this." 76

"I brought *him,* father," said Louisa, quickly. "I asked him to come." 77

"I am sorry to hear it. I am very sorry indeed to hear it. It makes Thomas no better, and it makes you worse, Louisa." 78

She looked at her father again, but no tear fell down her cheek. 79

"You! Thomas and you, to whom the circle of the sciences is open; Thomas and you, who may be said to be replete with facts; Thomas and you, who have been trained to mathematical exactness; Thomas and you, here!" cried Mr. Gradgrind. "In this degraded position! I am amazed." 80

"I was tired, father. I have been tired a long time," said Louisa. 81

"Tired? Of what?" asked the astonished father. 82

"I don't know of what—of everything, I think." 83

"Say not another word," returned Mr. Gradgrind. "You are childish. I will hear no more." 84

. . .

NEVER WONDER

When she was half-a-dozen years younger, Louisa had been overheard to begin a conversation with her brother one day, by saying "Tom, I wonder"—upon which Mr. Gradgrind, who was the person overhearing, stepped forth into the light and said, "Louisa, never wonder!" 85

Herein lay the spring of the mechanical art and mystery of educating the reason without stooping to the cultivation of the sentiments and affections. Never wonder. By means of addition, subtraction, multiplication, and division, settle everything somehow, and never wonder. Bring to me, says M'Choakumchild, yonder baby just able to walk, and I will engage that it shall never wonder. 86

Now, besides very many babies just able to walk, there happened to be in Coketown a considerable population of babies who had been walking against time towards the infinite world, twenty, thirty, forty, fifty years and more. These portentous infants being alarming creatures to stalk about in any human society, the eighteen denominations incessantly scratched one an- 87 other's faces and pulled one another's hair by way of agreeing on the steps to be taken for their improvement—which they never did; a surprising circumstance, when the happy adaptation of the means to the end is considered. Still, although they differed in every other particular, conceivable and inconceivable (especially inconceivable), they were pretty well united on the point that these unlucky infants were never to wonder. Body number one, said they must take everything on trust. Body number two, said they must take everything on political economy. Body number three, wrote leaden little books for them, showing how the good grown-up baby invariably got to the Savings-bank, and the bad grown-up baby invariably got transported. Body number four, under dreary pretences of being droll (when it was very melancholy indeed), made the shallowest pretences of concealing pitfalls of knowledge, into which it was the duty of these babies to be smuggled and inveigled. But, all the bodies agreed that they were never to wonder.

88 There was a library in Coketown, to which general access was easy. Mr. Gradgrind greatly tormented his mind about what the people read in this library: a point whereon little rivers of tabular statements periodically flowed into the howling ocean of tabular statements, which no diver ever got to any depth in and came up sane. It was a disheartening circumstance, but a melancholy fact, that even these readers persisted in wondering. They wondered about human nature, human passions, human hopes and fears, the struggles, triumphs and defeats, the cares and joys and sorrows, the lives and deaths of common men and women! They sometimes, after fifteen hours' work, sat down to read mere fables about men and women, more or less like themselves, and about children, more or less like their own. They took De Foe to their bosoms, instead of Euclid, and seemed to be on the whole more comforted by Goldsmith than by Cocker.* Mr. Gradgrind was for ever working, in print and out of print, at this eccentric sum, and he never could make out how it yielded this unaccountable product.

89 "I am sick of my life, Loo. I hate it altogether, and I hate everybody except you," said the unnatural young Thomas Gradgrind in the hair-cutting chamber at twilight.

90 "You don't hate Sissy, Tom?"

91 "I hate to be obliged to call her Jupe.† And she hates me," said Tom, moodily.

92 "No, she does not, Tom, I am sure!"

93 "She must," said Tom. "She must just hate and detest the whole set-out of us. They'll bother her head off, I think, before they have done with her. Already she's getting as pale as wax, and as heavy as—I am."

94 Young Thomas expressed these sentiments sitting astride of a chair before the fire, with his arms on the back, and his sulky face on his arms. His sister sat in the darker corner by the fireside, now looking at him, now looking at the bright sparks as they dropped upon the hearth.

*Edward Cocker (1631–1675), author of a treatise on arithmetic.

†Upon the disappearance of her father, Sissy Jupe has come to live with the Gradgrinds.

"As to me," said Tom, tumbling his hair all manner of ways with his 95
sulky hands, "I am a Donkey, that's what I am. I am as obstinate as one, I am more stupid than one, I get as much pleasure as one, and I should like to kick like one."

"Not me, I hope, Tom?" 96

"No, Loo; I wouldn't hurt *you.* I made an exception of you at first. I don't 97
know what this—jolly old—Jaundiced Jail," Tom had paused to find a sufficiently complimentary and expressive name for the parental roof, and seemed to relieve his mind for a moment by the strong alliteration of this one, "would be without you."

"Indeed, Tom? Do you really and truly say so?" 98

"Why, of course I do. What's the use of talking about it!" returned Tom, 99
chafing his face on his coat-sleeve, as if to mortify his flesh, and have it in unison with his spirit.

"Because, Tom," said his sister, after silently watching the sparks 100
awhile, "as I get older, and nearer growing up, I often sit wondering here, and think how unfortunate it is for me that I can't reconcile you to home better than I am able to do. I don't know what other girls know. I can't play to you, or sing to you. I can't talk to you so as to lighten your mind, for I never see any amusing sights or read any amusing books that it would be a pleasure or a relief to you to talk about, when you are tired."

"Well, no more do. I. I am as bad as you in that respect; and I am a Mule 101
too, which you're not. If father was determined to make me either a Prig or a Mule, and I am not a Prig, why, it stands to reason, I must be a Mule. And so I am," said Tom, desperately.

"It's a great pity," said Louisa, after another pause, and speaking 102
thoughtfully out of her dark corner: "it's a great pity, Tom. It's very unfortunate for both of us."

"Oh! You," said Tom; "you are a girl, Loo, and a girl comes out of it 103
better than a boy does. I don't miss anything in you. You are the only pleasure I have—you can brighten even this place—and you can always lead me as you like."

"You are a dear brother, Tom; and while you think I can do such things, 104
I don't so much mind knowing better. Though I do know better, Tom, and am very sorry for it." She came and kissed him, and went back into her corner again.

"I wish I could collect all the Facts we hear so much about," said Tom, 105
spitefully setting his teeth, "and all the Figures, and all the people who found them out: and I wish I could put a thousand barrels of gunpowder under them, and blow them all up together! However, when I go to live with old Bounderby,* I'll have my revenge."

"Your revenge, Tom?" 106

"I mean, I'll enjoy myself a little, and go about and see something, and 107

*Mr. Bounderby is Mr. Gradgrind's friend and a factory and bank owner. Together they have already determined that Tom will work in Mr. Bounderby's bank when he is old enough.

hear something. I'll recompense myself for the way in which I have been
brought up."

"But don't disappoint yourself beforehand, Tom. Mr. Bounderby thinks 108
as father thinks, and is a great deal rougher, and not half so kind."

"Oh!" said Tom, laughing; "I don't mind that. I shall very well know 109
how to manage and smooth old Bounderby!"

Their shadows were defined upon the wall, but those of the high presses 110
in the room were all blended together on the wall and on the ceiling, as if the
brother and sister were overhung by a dark cavern. Or, a fanciful imagination—if such treason could have been there—might have made it out to be
the shadow of their subject, and of its lowering association with their future.

"What is your great mode of smoothing and managing, Tom? Is it a 111
secret?"

"Oh!" said Tom, "if it is a secret, it's not far off. It's you. You are his 112
little pet, you are his favourite; he'll do anything for you. When he says to
me what I don't like, I shall say to him, 'My sister Loo will be hurt and
disappointed, Mr. Bounderby. She always used to tell me she was sure you
would be easier with me than this.' That'll bring him about, or nothing will."

After waiting for some answering remark, and getting none, Tom wea- 113
rily relapsed into the present time, and twined himself yawning round and
about the rails of his chair, and rumpled his head more and more, until he
suddenly looked up, and asked:

"Have you gone to sleep, Loo?" 114

"No, Tom. I am looking at the fire." 115

"You seem to find more to look at in it than ever I could find," said Tom. 116
"Another of the advantages, I suppose, of being a girl."

"Tom," inquired his sister, slowly, and in a curious tone, as if she were 117
reading what she asked in the fire, and it were not quite plainly written there,
"do you look forward with any satisfaction to this change to Mr. Bounderby's?"

"Why, there's one thing to be said of it," returned Tom, pushing his 118
chair from him, and standing up; "it will be getting away from home."

"There is one thing to be said of it," Louisa repeated in her former 119
curious tone; "it will be getting away from home. Yes."

"Not but what I shall be very unwilling, both to leave you, Loo, and to 120
leave you here. But I must go, you know, whether I like it or not; and I had
better go where I can take with me some advantage of your influence, than
where I should lose it altogether. Don't you see?"

"Yes, Tom." 121

The answer was so long in coming, though there was no indecision in 122
it, that Tom went and leaned on the back of her chair, to contemplate the fire
which so engrossed her, from her point of view, and see what he could make
of it.

"Except that it is a fire," said Tom, "it looks to me as stupid and blank 123
as everything else looks. What do you see in it? Not a circus?"

"I don't see anything in it, Tom, particularly. But since I have been 124
looking at it, I have been wondering about you and me, grown up."

"Wondering again!" said Tom. 125

"I have such unmanageable thoughts," returned his sister, "that they 126
will wonder."

"Then I beg of you, Louisa," said Mrs. Gradgrind, who had opened the 127
door without being heard, "to do nothing of that description, for goodness' sake, you inconsiderate girl, or I shall never hear the last of it from your father. And, Thomas, it is really shameful, with my poor head continually wearing me out, that a boy brought up as you have been, and whose education has cost what yours has, should be found encouraging his sister to wonder, when he knows his father has expressly said that she is not to do it."

Louisa denied Tom's participation in the offense; but her mother 128
stopped her with the conclusive answer, "Louisa, don't tell me, in my state of health; for unless you had been encouraged, it is morally and physically impossible that you could have done it."

"I was encouraged by nothing, mother, but by looking at the red sparks 129
dropping out of the fire, and whitening and dying. It made me think, after all, how short my life would be, and how little I could hope to do in it."

"Nonsense!" said Mrs. Gradgrind, rendered almost energetic. "Non- 130
sense! Don't stand there and tell me such stuff, Louisa, to my face, when you know very well that if it was ever to reach your father's ears I should never hear the last of it. After all the trouble that has been taken with you! After the lectures you have attended, and the experiments you have seen! After I have heard you myself, when the whole of my right side has been benumbed, going on with your master* about combustion, and calcination, and calorification, and I may say every kind of ation that could drive a poor invalid distracted, to hear you talking in this absurd way about sparks and ashes!

Questions for Discussion

1. Dickens was famous not only as a novelist but also as a public reader of his works. In what tone of voice do you think Mr. Gradgrind's speeches here would be delivered? Sissy's? Bitzer's? Try reading them aloud to each other, as in a play.
2. Do you think that Dickens would adopt different tones in reading paragraphs 1 and 7? Support your case by reading aloud.
3. What is the tone of the whole passage? (See question 4 on the piece by Malcolm X, p. 43.) What emotions does Dickens imply that he is feeling, and what emotions does he seem to expect the reader to respond with?

*The schoolmaster, in this case a private tutor engaged to teach Tom and Louisa at home.

4. Do you find Dickens's satirical attack on Mr. Gradgrind's teaching methods effective? Too extreme? Not strong enough? Or do you simply believe, contrary to Dickens, that an education of "hard facts" alone is *not* destructive and that Dickens is being unfair in making a defensible position look bad when it really isn't bad? What arguments can you make for either position?
5. The whole passage relies heavily for its effects on strong metaphors: students as water pitchers, teachers as grinding machines or loaded cannon, home as jail, and so on. Do you find any less obvious metaphors raising our sympathy *for* Sissy and *against* Gradgrind and Bitzer? What are they and how do they work?
6. Dickens is often said to be a master of repetition. Yet handbooks often tell us not to repeat a word in the same sentence or paragraph. Does Dickens gain or lose here by the great number of repetitions? *What* does he gain or lose? Force? Monotony? Vividness? Wordiness? Anything else?

Suggested Essay Topics

1. Have you studied with any teachers who kill students' interest in learning? If so, write an account of your experience, whether the methods you describe resemble Gradgrind's or not. Include at least one paragraph in which you try to dramatize the kind of conversation (or lack of conversation) that produced the bad results. Make clear the criteria you are using to judge the teachers.
2. Read the selection from John Stuart Mill's *Autobiography* (pp. 318–332), in which he describes the effects of being raised by a father whose views about education closely resemble Mr. Gradgrind's. Then write a fictitious dialogue or conversation in which you have *either* J. S. Mill and Louisa Gradgrind *or* J. S. Mill and Bitzer discuss the kind of education most *really* useful.

Lewis Thomas

Lewis Thomas (b. 1913), former chancellor of the Memorial Sloan-Kettering Cancer Center, is a famous physician, research scientist, and essayist. His books of essays, The Lives of a Cell: Notes of a Biology Watcher, The Medusa and the Snail, *and* Late Night Thoughts on Listening to Mahler's Ninth Symphony *were best-sellers in the 1970s and 1980s. Unlike many best-sellers dealing with scientific matters, Thomas's works are respected by other scientists. The combination is indeed rare; few authors have been able to do justice to serious scientific issues in an easy, sometimes chatty style that is understandable by nonscientists.*

In this essay the subject is not science in itself but the teaching of one branch of science. Thomas argues that streamlined curricular programs for specialized groups of students—especially pre-med students—not only ruin their education but the education of their fellow students as well. As you read, try to determine whether he believes that society as a whole suffers from this trend in education and whether his proposed remedies seem reasonable or unrealistic, newfangled or old-fashioned.

HOW TO FIX THE PREMEDICAL CURRICULUM

From *The Medusa and the Snail: More Notes of a Biology Watcher* (1979).

The influence of the modern medical school on liberal-arts education in this country over the last decade has been baleful and malign, nothing less. The admission policies of the medical schools are at the root of the trouble. If something is not done quickly to change these, all the joy of going to college will have been destroyed, not just for that growing majority of undergraduate students who draw breath only to become doctors, but for everyone else, all the students, and all the faculty as well. 1

The medical schools used to say they wanted applicants as broadly educated as possible, and they used to mean it. The first two years of medical school were given over entirely to the basic biomedical sciences, and almost all entering students got their first close glimpse of science in those years. Three chemistry courses, physics, and some sort of biology were all that were required from the colleges. Students were encouraged by the rhetoric of medical-school catalogues to major in such nonscience disciplines as history, English, philosophy. Not many did so; almost all premedical students in recent generations have had their majors in chemistry or biology. But anyway, they were authorized to spread around in other fields if they wished. 2

There is still some talk in medical deans' offices about the need for general culture, but nobody really means it, and certainly the premedical students don't believe it. They concentrate on science. 3

They concentrate on science with a fury, and they live for grades. If there are courses in the humanities that can be taken without risk to class standing they will line up for these, but they will not get into anything tough except science. The so-called social sciences have become extremely popular as stand-ins for traditional learning. 4

The atmosphere of the liberal-arts college is being poisoned by premedical students. It is not the fault of the students, who do not start out as a necessarily bad lot. They behave as they do in the firm belief that if they behave any otherwise they won't get into medical school. 5

I have a suggestion, requiring for its implementation the following announcement from the deans of all the medical schools: henceforth, any applicant who is self-labeled as a "premed," distinguishable by his course 6 selection from his classmates, will have his dossier placed in the third stack of three. Membership in a "premedical society" will, by itself, be grounds for rejection. Any college possessing something called a "premedical curriculum," or maintaining offices for people called "premedical advisers," will be excluded from recognition by the medical schools.

Now as to grades and class standing. There is obviously no way of ignoring these as criteria for acceptance, but it is the grades *in general* that should be weighed. And, since so much of the medical-school curriculum is, or ought to be, narrowly concerned with biomedical science, more attention should be paid to the success of students in other, nonscience disciplines before they are admitted, in order to assure the scope of intellect needed for a physician's work. 7

Hence, if there are to be MCAT tests,* the science part ought to be made the briefest, and weigh the least. A knowledge of literature and languages ought to be the major test, and the scariest. History should be tested, with rigor. 8

The best thing would be to get rid of the MCATs, once and for all, and rely instead, wholly, on the judgment of the college faculties. 9

You could do this if there were some central, core discipline, universal within the curricula of all the colleges, which could be used for evaluating the free range of a student's mind, his tenacity and resolve, his innate capacity for the understanding of human beings, and his affection for the human condition. For this purpose, I propose that classical Greek be restored as the centerpiece of undergraduate education. The loss of Homeric and Attic Greek from American college life was one of this century's disasters. Putting it back where it once was would quickly make up for the dispiriting impact which generations of spotty Greek in translation have inflicted on modern thought. The capacity to read Homer's language closely enough to sense the terrifying poetry in some of the lines could serve as a shrewd test for the qualities of mind and character needed in a physician. 10

If everyone had to master Greek, the college students aspiring to medical school would be placed on the same footing as everyone else, and their identifiability as a separate group would be blurred, to everyone's advantage. Moreover, the currently depressing drift on some campuses toward special courses for prelaw students, and even prebusiness students, might be inhibited before more damage is done. 11

Latin should be put back as well, but not if it is handled, as it ought to be, by the secondary schools. If Horace has been absorbed prior to college, so much for Latin. But Greek is a proper discipline for the college mind. 12

English, history, the literature of at least two foreign languages, and philosophy should come near the top of the list, just below Classics, as basic requirements, and applicants for medical school should be told that their grades in these courses will count more than anything else. 13

Students should know that if they take summer work as volunteers in 14

*Tests for admission to medical school.

the local community hospital, as ward aides or laboratory assistants, this will not necessarily be held against them, but neither will it help.

Finally, the colleges should have much more of a say about who goes on to medical school. If they know, as they should, the students who are generally bright and also respected, this judgment should carry the heaviest weight for admission. If they elect to use criteria other than numerical class standing for recommending applicants, this evaluation should hold. 15

The first and most obvious beneficiaries of this new policy would be the college students themselves. There would no longer be, anywhere where they could be recognized as a coherent group, the "premeds," that most detestable of all cliques eating away at the heart of the college. Next to benefit would be the college faculties, once again in possession of the destiny of their own curriculum, for better or worse. And next in line, but perhaps benefiting the most of all, are the basic-science faculties of the medical schools, who would once again be facing classrooms of students who are ready to be startled and excited by a totally new and unfamiliar body of knowledge, eager to learn, unpreoccupied by the notions of relevance that are paralyzing the minds of today's first-year medical students already so surfeited by science that they want to start practicing psychiatry in the first trimester of the first year. 16

Society would be the ultimate beneficiary. We could look forward to a generation of doctors who have learned as much as anyone can learn, in our colleges and universities, about how human beings have always lived out their lives. Over the bedrock of knowledge about our civilization, the medical schools could then construct as solid a structure of medical science as can be built, but the bedrock would always be there, holding everything else upright. 17

Questions for Discussion

1. Is it your impression that students other than pre-meds "live for grades" (¶4)? Is Thomas overstating the case? If living for grades is a fact of college life, do you accept it or resent it? Is college different from high school in this respect? Would you give the same grades *to* most courses that you received *from* those courses? If not, did you or the course deserve the better grade?
2. Do the doctors or pre-med students you know seem to have minds that range freely (¶10)? As a patient, would you worry for fear a doctor with a freely ranging mind might be technically less competent in dealing with specialized problems? How might Thomas argue that doctors who take time for broad learning will know better how to use their specialized knowledge?
3. What is Thomas's purpose? Who do you think is his intended audience?

4. How would you describe Thomas's tone? Is he scholarly, formal, informal, colloquial, slangy? Is his tone appropriate to his purpose?
5. Do you find evidence that Thomas uses his status as a scientist to increase his credibility as a spokesman for the humanities? If you knew nothing about him except what you have found in this essay, would you ever suspect that he might be merely an unsuccessful scientist, a disillusioned or sour failure baring his fangs at an ungrateful medical profession? What devices of tone or style has he used to prevent that (quite false) suspicion from arising?
6. In the first sentence of paragraph 1 and in the third sentence of paragraph 8, Thomas employs the device of ending a sentence with a two-word phrase set off by a comma. What does he achieve by this device? If you get rid of these end tags, do the sentences gain or lose effectiveness? Does reading them outside of context affect your judgment?
7. Is there a significant ordering of the groups who would benefit from his proposed changes as he identifies those groups in paragraphs 16 and 17? Is this ordering appropriate to his purpose?

Suggested Essay Topics

1. Write a letter (or perhaps the manuscript for a speech) addressed to any specialized group of "pre-" students—pre-law, pre-medicine, pre-business, and so on—explaining why a liberal arts education is better for them as undergraduates than a streamlined set of specialized courses. Don't limit yourself to reasons that would apply with equal force to anyone (although you may include these), but try to show why these students would make better doctors, lawyers, or business persons, not just better human beings, for having had a liberal education.
2. Look through the catalog for your college or university and find the specialized programs for certain groups such as medical or business students. Write a letter to your teacher, or to the academic dean, evaluating any such programs from Thomas's point of view and arguing why it would be better, not only for the special students but for all other students and the institution as well, for such programs to be altered or abolished. If you recommend alterations, make them specific. If you recommend abolition, give your reasons.

IDEAS IN DEBATE

Theodore Roosevelt
Alfred North Whitehead

Theodore Roosevelt

Theodore Roosevelt (1858–1919), twenty-sixth president of the United States, headed the government during a period of intense economic expansion and population growth. America was flexing its muscles at home and around the world. Industrialization of the economy was nearly complete, the country was crisscrossed by transcontinental railroad traffic, frontier wilderness was rapidly fading into history, and many Americans felt that expansion and opportunity would continue forever.

Within this context of energetic moneymaking and social mobility, the question of education's role in helping America realize its promise was a natural topic for the president to address. Roosevelt had a distinct theme about American education, a theme in keeping with both his own character as a robust man of action and with the emerging character of a nation that in many ways reflected his own no-nonsense, get-the-job-done temperament. His theme distinguishes "literary" training, by which he means most of what we call the liberal arts, from technical training, by which he means the kinds of skills necessary in an industrial job market. "Literary" training produces "scholars," while technical training produces citizens. As you read, try to determine whether you think this distinction adequately expresses the relationship between citizenship and education, or whether it confuses more than it clarifies. What does Roosevelt oppose to education "of the head," as he calls it? And why does he think of the different forms of education as opposed in the first place? What is the role of book learning in technical and industrial training? Why does he imply that people like workers and farmers can do without intellectual cultivation? If book learning is useful only for scholars, how useful is it really?

Roosevelt's prejudice against what we today call liberal education, against the cultivation of knowledge and intellectual power for their own sake, and the corresponding prejudice in favor of what is deemed practical, are deeply rooted in American society. Roosevelt may have reinforced this prejudice, but he did not invent it. We probably have more terms of contempt for intellectuals and academics and for ideas and theory than any other society in Western culture. While "expert" is for us a term of honor, referring to the "know-how" specialist, we save terms like "pointy-headed intellectual," "egghead," "absent-minded professor," and "dry as dust" for people who spend much time in the world of books and ideas. We dismiss an idea as "merely academic" if it seems useless to us, we accuse college professors of having their "heads in the clouds" or of "living in ivory towers," and we constantly distinguish between school on the one hand and the "real world" on the other, as if nothing that happens in school had any bearing on the life that really counts, and as if the world of learning were merely a trivial corridor to something more important.

One of the reasons for reprinting Roosevelt rather than a contemporary writer is to show just how far back in time this prejudice extends and how little it has changed in at least the last eighty years. What has *changed are the kinds of occupations that education today is supposed to serve. Roosevelt wanted industrial education for factory workers and farmers; we want pre-professional education for such occupations as business managers, computer experts, and communications consultants. But Roosevelt's prejudice has been handed down to us intact. Many people still view education primarily as a means of getting a head start on the employment and income ladder, not as a cultivation of mind, character, or citizenship. And if* that *is its purpose, then its content, or so the argument goes, ought to be limited to the skills and information the student will need as a wage-worker (Roosevelt's concern) or as a professional (today's concern). All of Roosevelt's opinions about education could be transferred into today's schools without sounding old-fashioned or out of place as long as we merely changed his "workers" and "farmers" to "professionals," and his "industrial training" to "pre-professional training." The argument about education's ends would remain undisturbed.*

As you read Roosevelt, think back to some of the other arguments about education you have encountered: Booth and Gregory asserting that "unlike other creatures, which seem to realize their potential effortlessly so long as nothing inhibits their development, we language creatures can only reach our full potential through relentless exercise" (p. 3); Cousins arguing that "if the main purpose of a university is job training, then the underlying philosophy of our government has little meaning" (p. 32); Malcolm X reporting that he was so engrossed in learning that even in prison he "never had been so truly free" (p. 37); Dickens waxing indignant over the insensitivity of a schoolmaster who "seemed a kind of cannon loaded to the muzzle with facts, and prepared to blow [his students] clean out of the regions of childhood at one discharge" (p. 46); and Thomas arguing that an ability "to sense the terrifying poetry in some of [Homer's] lines [of poetry] could serve as a shrewd test for the qualities of mind and character needed in a physician" (p. 60).

These views are all quite different from Roosevelt's, though not always antithetical to his. The liberal view of education is always capacious enough to include room for technical and pre-professional education, but it denies that education should be limited to professional ends alone. Those on the other side, however, almost always want to do away with, or at least depreciate the value of, any kind of education not directly related to job skills. As you read, try to determine your own views on this important subject. If you are a freshman, you will spend much money and time obtaining your education during the next four years. Now is the time to make sure that you don't settle for less than the real thing. In the movie Auntie Mame, *Mame sneers at people who never stretch their capacities: "Life is a banquet," she says, "and most poor suckers are starving to death." Students have to endure powerful vocational pressures today, but they might do well to consider whether the narrow job-skills view of education will put them in the pitiable position of sitting at the banquet of education and starving their minds because they have uncritically inherited a prejudice in favor of dry toast and weak tea.*

THE WELFARE OF THE WAGE-WORKER

From Roosevelt's sixth annual message to Congress, December 3, 1906, and "The Man Who Works with His Hands," an address delivered at the Semicentennial Celebration of the Founding of Agricultural Colleges in the United States, Lansing, Michigan, May 31, 1907.

It would be impossible to overstate (though it is of course difficult quantita- 1
tively to measure) the effect upon a nation's growth to greatness of what may be called organized patriotism, which necessarily includes the substitution of a national feeling for mere local pride; with as a resultant a high ambition for the whole country. No country can develop its full strength so long as the parts which make up the whole each put a feeling of loyalty to the part above the feeling of loyalty to the whole. This is true of sections and it is just as true of classes. The industrial and agricultural classes must work together, capitalists and wage-workers must work together, if the best work of which the country is capable is to be done. It is probable that a thoroughly efficient system of education comes next to the influence of patriotism in bringing about national success of this kind. Our Federal form of government, so fruitful of advantage to our people in certain ways, in other ways undoubtedly limits our national effectiveness. It is not possible, for instance, for the National Government to take the lead in technical industrial education, to see that the public-school system of this country develops on all its technical, industrial, scientific, and commercial sides. This must be left primarily to the several States. Nevertheless, the National Government has control of the schools of the District of Columbia, and it should see that these schools promote and encourage the fullest development of the scholars in both commercial and industrial training. The commercial training should in one of its branches deal with foreign trade. The industrial training is even more important. It should be one of our prime objects as a nation, so far as feasible, constantly to work toward putting the mechanic, the wage-worker who works with his hands, on a higher plane of efficiency and reward, so as to increase his effectiveness in the economic world, and the dignity, the remuneration, and the power of his position in the social world. Unfortunately, at present the effect of some of the work in the public schools is in the exactly opposite direction. If boys and girls are trained merely in literary accomplishments, to the total exclusion of industrial, manual, and technical training, the tendency is to unfit them for industrial work and to make them reluctant to go into it, or unfitted to do well if they do go into it. This is a tendency which should be strenuously combated. Our industrial development depends

largely upon technical education, including in this term all industrial education, from that which fits a man to be a good mechanic, a good carpenter, or blacksmith, to that which fits a man to do the greatest engineering feat. The skilled mechanic, the skilled workman, can best become such by technical industrial education. The far-reaching usefulness of institutes of technology and schools of mines or of engineering is now universally acknowledged, and no less far-reaching is the effect of a good building or mechanical trades-school, a textile, or watchmaking, or engraving school. All such training must develop not only manual dexterity but industrial intelligence. In international rivalry this country does not have to fear the competition of pauper labor as much as it has to fear the educated labor of specially trained competitors; and we should have the education of the hand, eye, and brain which will fit us to meet such competition.

In every possible way we should help the wage-worker who toils with 2
his hands and who must (we hope in a constantly increasing measure) also toil with his brain. Under the Constitution the national legislature can do but little of direct importance for his welfare save where he is engaged in work which permits it to act under the interstate commerce clause of the Constitution; and this is one reason why I so earnestly hope that both the legislative and judicial branches of the government will construe this clause of the Constitution in the broadest possible manner. We can, however, in such a matter as industrial training, in such a matter as child-labor and factory laws, set an example to the States by enacting the most advanced legislation that can wisely be enacted for the District of Columbia.

The only other persons whose welfare is as vital to the welfare of the 3
whole country as is the welfare of the wage-workers, are the tillers of the soil, the farmers. It is a mere truism to say that no growth of cities, no growth of wealth, no industrial development can atone for any falling off in the character and standing of the farming population. During the last few decades this fact has been recognized with ever-increasing clearness. There is no longer any failure to realize that farming, at least in certain branches, must become a technical and scientific profession. This means that there must be open to farmers the chance for technical and scientific training, not theoretical merely but of the most severely practical type. The farmer represents a peculiarly high type of American citizenship, and he must have the same chance to rise and develop as other American citizens have. Moreover, it is exactly as true of the farmer, as it is of the business man and the wage-worker, that the ultimate success of the nation of which he forms a part must be founded not alone on material prosperity but upon high moral, mental, and physical development. This education of the farmer—self-education by preference, but also education from the outside, as with all other men—is peculiarly necessary here in the United States, where the frontier conditions even in the newest States have now nearly vanished, where there must be a substitution of a more intensive system of cultivation for the old wasteful farm management, and where there must be a better business organization among the farmers themselves.

Several factors must co-operate in the improvement of the farmer's condition. He must have the chance to be educated in the widest possible sense—in the sense which keeps ever in view the intimate relationship between the theory of education and the facts of life. In all education we should widen our aims.* It is a good thing to produce a certain number of trained scholars and students; but the education superintended by the State must seek rather to produce a hundred good citizens than merely one scholar, and it must be turned now and then from the class-book to the study of the great book of nature itself. This is especially true of the farmer, as has been pointed out again and again by all observers most competent to pass practical judgment on the problems of our country life. All students now realize that education must seek to train the executive powers of young people and to confer more real significance upon the phrase "dignity of labor," and to prepare the pupils so that, in addition to each developing in the highest degree his individual capacity for work, they may together help create a right public opinion, and show in many ways social and co-operative spirit. 4

. . .

As a people there is nothing in which we take a juster pride than our educational system. It is our boast that every boy or girl has the chance to get a school training; and we feel it is a prime national duty to furnish this training free, because only thereby can we secure the proper type of citizenship in the average American. Our public schools and our colleges have done their work well, and there is no class of our citizens deserving of heartier praise than the men and women who teach in them. 5

Nevertheless, for at least a generation we have been waking to the knowledge that there must be additional education beyond that provided in the public school as it is managed to-day. Our school system has hitherto been well-nigh wholly lacking on the side of industrial training, of the training which fits a man for the shop and the farm. This is a most serious lack, for no one can look at the peoples of mankind as they stand at present without realizing that industrial training is one of the most potent factors in national development. We of the United States must develop a system under which each individual citizen shall be trained so as to be effective individually as an economic unit, and fit to be organized with his fellows so that he and they can work in efficient fashion together. This question is vital to our future progress, and public attention should be focussed upon it. Surely it is eminently in accord with the principles of our democratic life that we should furnish the highest average industrial training for the ordinary skilled workman. But it is a curious thing that in industrial training we have tended to devote our energies to producing high-grade men at the top rather than in the ranks. Our engineering schools, for instance, compare favorably with the best in Europe, whereas we have done almost nothing to equip the private soldiers 6

*In talking about education today, we would probably take "widen our aims" to mean more liberal arts courses and fewer programs made up of exclusively technical or pre-professional courses. Roosevelt means exactly the opposite: "widen our aims" means less academic work and more pre-professional and technical training.

of the industrial army—the mechanic, the metal-worker, the carpenter. Indeed, too often our schools train away from the shop and the forge; and this fact, together with the abandonment of the old apprentice system, has resulted in such an absence of facilities for providing trained journeymen that in many of our trades almost all the recruits among the workmen are foreigners. Surely this means that there must be some systematic method provided for training young men in the trades, and that this must be co-ordinated with the public-school system. No industrial school can turn out a finished journeyman; but it can furnish the material out of which a finished journeyman can be made, just as an engineering school furnishes the training which enables its graduates speedily to become engineers. . . .

We have been fond as a nation of speaking of the dignity of labor, 7
meaning thereby manual labor. Personally I don't think that we begin to understand what a high place manual labor should take; and it never can take this high place unless it offers scope for the best type of man. We have tended to regard education as a matter of the head only, and the result is that a great many of our people, themselves the sons of men who worked with their hands, seem to think that they rise in the world if they get into a position where they do no hard manual work whatever; where their hands will grow soft, and their working clothes will be kept clean. Such a conception is both false and mischievous. There are, of course, kinds of labor where the work must be purely mental, and there are other kinds of labor where, under existing conditions, very little demand indeed is made upon the mind, though I am glad to say that I think the proportion of men engaged in this kind of work is diminishing. But in any healthy community, in any community with the great solid qualities which alone make a really great nation, the bulk of the people should do work which makes demands upon both the body and the mind. Progress cannot permanently consist in the abandonment of physical labor, but in the development of physical labor so that it shall represent more and more the work of the trained mind in the trained body. To provide such training, to encourage in every way the production of the men whom it alone can produce is to show that as a nation we have a true conception of the dignity and importance of labor. The calling of the skilled tiller of the soil, the calling of the skilled mechanic, should alike be recognized as professions, just as emphatically as the callings of lawyer, of doctor, of banker, merchant, or clerk. The printer, the electrical worker, the house-painter, the foundryman, should be trained just as carefully as the stenographer or the drug clerk. They should be trained alike in head and in hand. They should get over the idea that to earn twelve dollars a week and call it "salary" is better than to earn twenty-five dollars a week and call it "wages." The young man who has the courage and the ability to refuse to enter the crowded field of the so-called professions and to take to constructive industry is almost sure of an ample reward in earnings, in health, in opportunity to marry early, and to establish a home with reasonable freedom from worry. We need the training, the manual dexterity and industrial intelligence, which can be best given in a good agricultural, or building, or textile, or watchmaking, or en-

graving, or mechanical school. It should be one of our prime objects to put the mechanic, the wage-worker who works with his hands, and who ought to work in a constantly larger degree with his head, on a higher plane of efficiency and reward, so as to increase his effectiveness in the economic world, and therefore the dignity, the remuneration, and the power of his position in the social world. To train boys and girls in merely literary accomplishments to the total exclusion of industrial, manual, and technical training, tends to unfit them for industrial work; and in real life most work is industrial.

The problem of furnishing well-trained craftsmen, or rather journey- 8
men fitted in the end to become such, is not simple—few problems are simple in the actual process of their solution—and much care and forethought and practical common sense will be needed, in order to work it out in a fairly satisfactory manner. It should appeal to all our citizens. I am glad that societies have already been formed to promote industrial education, and that their membership includes manufacturers and leaders of labor-unions, educators and publicists, men of all conditions who are interested in education and in industry. It is such co-operation that offers most hope for a satisfactory solution of the question as to what is the best form of industrial school, as to the means by which it may be articulated with the public-school system, and as to the way to secure for the boys trained therein the opportunity to acquire in the industries the practical skill which alone can make them finished journeymen. . . .

Agricultural colleges and farmers' institutes have done much in instruc- 9
tion and inspiration; they have stood for the nobility of labor and the necessity of keeping the muscles and the brain in training for industry. They have developed technical departments of high practical value. They seek to provide for the people on the farms an equipment so broad and thorough as to fit them for the highest requirements of our citizenship; so that they can establish and maintain country homes of the best type, and create and sustain a country civilization more than equal to that of the city. The men they train must be able to meet the strongest business competition, at home or abroad, and they can do this only if they are trained not alone in the various lines of husbandry but in successful economic management. These colleges, like the State experiment stations, should carefully study and make known the needs of each section, and should try to provide remedies for what is wrong.

The education to be obtained in these colleges should create as intimate 10
a relationship as is possible between the theory of learning and the facts of actual life. Educational establishments should produce highly trained scholars, of course; but in a country like ours, where the educational establishments are so numerous, it is folly to think that their main purpose is to produce these highly trained scholars. Without in the least disparaging scholarship and learning—on the contrary, while giving hearty and ungrudging admiration and support to the comparatively few whose primary work should be creative scholarship—it must be remembered that the ordinary graduate of our colleges should be and must be primarily a man and not a

scholar. Education should not confine itself to books. It must train executive power, and try to create that right public opinion which is the most potent factor in the proper solution of all political and social questions. Book-learning is very important, but it is by no means everything; and we shall never get the right idea of education until we definitely understand that a man may be well trained in book-learning and yet, in the proper sense of the word, and for all practical purposes, be utterly uneducated; while a man of comparatively little book-learning may, nevertheless, in essentials, have a good education.

Questions for Discussion

1. If you have ever felt like objecting to what Roosevelt calls "literary" courses—liberal arts courses such as literature, history, philosophy, and languages—on the grounds that they just aren't "useful," go back over the other selections in this chapter, including Whitehead (who follows Roosevelt), and see if you and your classmates can come up with defenses for these kinds of courses, either by using an enlarged notion of usefulness or by arguing that usefulness is not the only relevant criterion.
2. What is revealed about the nature of Roosevelt's prejudices by his curious distinction in paragraph 4 between "trained scholars and students" on the one hand and "good citizens" on the other? "The State," he contends, "must seek rather to produce a hundred good citizens than merely one scholar." What is he supposing about the nature of each that justifies his placing them in opposition like this? Do you think his suppositions are justified? Can you think of good reasons why the trained scholar might be not just a good citizen but potentially a superior one? (He creates another curious distinction in paragraph 10 when he says, "It must be remembered that the ordinary graduate of our colleges should be and must be primarily a man and not a scholar.") Can you state his prejudice against scholars in your own words? Do you hear this same prejudice repeated today?
3. In paragraph 6 Roosevelt takes a tone that suggests that skills training—technical education in general—is the underdog and that he is trying to make more room in the typical curriculum for it against the dominance of "literary" studies. Do the studies that Roosevelt calls literary still dominate education today, or has the trend he points to been reversed? Has education been improved by developments since Roosevelt's day? Has society been well- or ill-served by the decline of liberal education and the dominance of pre-professional education (at the high school and college levels)?
4. If we substitute modern terms for Roosevelt's terms in the last sentence

of paragraph 7, do his remarks here sound like comments that you could hear on your campus any day of the week? "Merely literary accomplishments . . . tend to unfit [students] for professional work; and in real life most work is [professional]." Can you provide any evidence to suggest that this statement is simply not true? And can you find good reasons to object to education's being excluded from the "real world"? Do you object to having your life as a student called unreal simply because you may not yet be a homeowner, taxpayer, or full-time employee? (Of course many of you are all three of these things, and some of you are, in addition, parents, sometimes single parents, and you are pursuing an education as well. You of course know that all these activities are part of the real world.) If student life is not real, what is it and why do you have to pay so much for it?

Suggested Essay Topics

1. If you have ever heard your teachers, counselors, parents, or anyone else use the expression "the real world" in such a way as to imply that students are outside of it, select one such person and write him or her a persuasive letter challenging the use of the expression, the assumptions behind it, and the implications that follow from it. You will want to know, among other things, what the possible criteria for "real" are in this kind of usage, and, since society is urging you on the one hand to get an education, why it takes such a dismissive view of that education on the other.
2. The kind of job-skills education recommended by Roosevelt has pretty nearly become the rule for certain kinds of professional programs such as those taken by doctors in medical school. Yet Lewis Thomas, a prominent physician himself, thinks that this narrow kind of education has become a disaster both for the colleges that give it and for the medical students that take it (pp. 58–62). Write a dialogue in which you portray Lewis Thomas and Theodore Roosevelt debating this point. Give each man the best arguments you can, and make clear at the end whether one or the other has won or whether they have come to a draw.

Alfred North Whitehead

An English philosopher and mathematician, instructor of Bertrand Russell and later Russell's co-author on the Principia Mathematica, *and founder of a mode of thought called "process philosophy" (influential on scientists, philosophers, and theologians alike), Alfred North Whitehead (1861–1947) remains one of those figures in our day—like Plato, Aquinas, Kant, or Coleridge in earlier centuries—who seems to have become established as a permanent and almost official instructor of mankind. His technical writings, as in* Process and Reality, *are forbiddingly difficult, but his general writings, as in this piece, combine great depth of thought with a delightful clarity of style. Perhaps no one will ever find Whitehead* easy *to read; as he says in paragraph 11, "If it were easy, the book ought to be burned." But he has the kind of clarity we all seek, and his style is no more difficult than his ideas themselves require.*

As you work through his ideas about the aims of education, compare his description of a genuine education with an accurate description of your own education, both past and present, and with the aims of education as presented to you by your parents and high school counselors or teachers. You might use his essay as a source of new ideas about what is happening to you and your fellow students this year.

His main concerns seem to be (1) that whatever we learn should be truly useful (he takes pains to define what useful *means to us* now, *in a present that contains both the past and the future), (2) that all learning should constantly shift back and forth between general and specialized knowledge, and (3) that studying anything merely to pass a standardized exam kills all real learning.*

THE AIMS OF EDUCATION

From *"The Aims of Education" and Other Essays* (1929).

Culture is activity of thought, and receptiveness to beauty and humane feeling. Scraps of information have nothing to do with it. A merely well-informed man is the most useless bore on God's earth. What we should aim at producing is men who possess both culture and expert knowledge in some special direction. Their expert knowledge will give them the ground to start from, and their culture will lead them as deep as philosophy and as high as art. We have to remember that the valuable intellectual development is self-development, and that it mostly takes place between the ages of sixteen and thirty. As to training, the most important part is given by mothers before the age of twelve. A saying due to Archbishop Temple illustrates my meaning. Surprise was expressed at the success in after-life of a man, who as a boy at Rugby had been somewhat undistinguished. He answered, "It is not what they are at eighteen, it is what they become afterwards that matters." 1

In training a child to activity of thought, above all things we must beware of what I will call "inert ideas"—that is to say, ideas that are merely received into the mind without being utilized, or tested, or thrown into fresh combinations. 2

In the history of education, the most striking phenomenon is that schools of learning, which at one epoch are alive with a ferment of genius, in a succeeding generation exhibit merely pedantry and routine. The reason is, that they are overladen with inert ideas. Education with inert ideas is not only useless: it is, above all things, harmful—*Corruptio optimi, pessima* [The corruption of the best is the worst]. Except at rare intervals of intellectual ferment, education in the past has been radically infected with inert ideas. 3

That is the reason why uneducated clever women, who have seen much of the world, are in middle life so much the most cultured part of the community. They have been saved from this horrible burden of inert ideas. Every intellectual revolution which has ever stirred humanity into greatness has been a passionate protest against inert ideas. Then, alas, with pathetic ignorance of human psychology, it has proceeded by some educational scheme to bind humanity afresh with inert ideas of its own fashioning.

Let us now ask how in our system of education we are to guard against 4
this mental dryrot. We enunciate two educational commandments, "Do not teach too many subjects," and again, "What you teach, teach thoroughly."

The result of teaching small parts of a large number of subjects is the 5
passive reception of disconnected ideas, not illumined with any spark of vitality. Let the main ideas which are introduced into a child's education be few and important, and let them be thrown into every combination possible. The child should make them his own, and should understand their application here and now in the circumstances of his actual life. From the very beginning of his education, the child should experience the joy of discovery. The discovery which he has to make, is that general ideas give an understanding of that stream of events which pours through his life, which is his life. By understanding I mean more than a mere logical analysis, though that is included. I mean "understanding" in the sense in which it is used in the French proverb, "To understand all, is to forgive all." Pedants sneer at an education which is useful. But if education is not useful, what is it? Is it a talent, to be hidden away in a napkin? Of course, education should be useful, whatever your aim in life. It was useful to Saint Augustine and it was useful to Napoleon. It is useful, because understanding is useful.

I pass lightly over that understanding which should be given by the 6
literary side of education.* Nor do I wish to be supposed to pronounce on the relative merits of a classical or a modern curriculum. I would only remark that the understanding which we want is an understanding of an insistent present. The only use of a knowledge of the past is to equip us for the present. No more deadly harm can be done to young minds than by depreciation of the present. The present contains all that there is. It is holy ground; for it is the past, and it is the future.† At the same time it must be observed that an age is no less past if it existed two hundred years ago than if it existed two thousand years ago. Do not be deceived by the pedantry of dates. The ages of Shakespeare and of Molière are no less past than are the ages of Sophocles and of Virgil. The communion of saints is a great and inspiring assemblage, but it has only one possible hall of meeting, and that is, the present; and the mere lapse of time through which any particular group of saints must travel to reach that meeting-place, makes very little difference.

*By passing "lightly" over the "literary side of education," Whitehead is referring to what *we* would call "the humanities," especially literature, philosophy, history, and languages. He largely ignores these and discusses mainly scientific and mathematical examples because, first, he was himself a mathematician and, second, his audience was the Mathematical Association.

†See Karl Popper's treatment of this same idea in "Utopia and Violence," p. 123, ¶34–37.

Passing now to the scientific and logical side of education, we remember 7
that here also ideas which are not utilised are positively harmful. By utilising an idea, I mean relating it to that stream, compounded of sense perceptions, feelings, hopes, desires, and of mental activities adjusting thought to thought, which forms our life. I can imagine a set of beings which might fortify their souls by passively reviewing disconnected ideas. Humanity is not built that way—except perhaps some editors of newspapers.

In scientific training, the first thing to do with an idea is to prove it. But 8
allow me for one moment to extend the meaning of "prove"; I mean—to prove its worth. Now an idea is not worth much unless the propositions in which it is embodied are true. Accordingly an essential part of the proof of an idea is the proof, either by experiment or by logic, of the truth of the propositions. But it is not essential that this proof of the truth should constitute the first introduction to the idea. After all, its assertion by the authority of respectable teachers is sufficient evidence to begin with. In our first contact with a set of propositions, we commence by appreciating their importance. That is what we all do in after-life. We do not attempt, in the strict sense, to prove or to disprove anything, unless its importance makes it worthy of that honour. These two processes of proof, in the narrow sense, and of appreciation, do not require a rigid separation in time. Both can be proceeded with nearly concurrently. But in so far as either process must have the priority, it should be that of appreciation by use.

Furthermore, we should not endeavour to use propositions in isolation. 9
Emphatically I do not mean, a neat little set of experiments to illustrate Proposition I and then the proof of Proposition I, a neat little set of experiments to illustrate Proposition II and then the proof of Proposition II, and so on to the end of the book. Nothing could be more boring. Interrelated truths are utilised *en bloc,* and the various propositions are employed in any order, and with any reiteration. Choose some important applications of your theoretical subject; and study them concurrently with the systematic theoretical exposition. Keep the theoretical exposition short and simple, but let it be strict and rigid so far as it goes. It should not be too long for it to be easily known with thoroughness and accuracy. The consequences of a plethora of half-digested theoretical knowledge are deplorable.* Also the theory should not be muddled up with the practice. The child should have no doubt when it is proving and when it is utilising. My point is that what is proved should be utilised, and that what is utilised should—so far as is practicable—be proved. I am far from asserting that proof and utilisation are the same thing.

At this point of my discourse, I can most directly carry forward my 10
argument in the outward form of a digression. We are only just realising that the art and science of education require a genius and a study of their own; and that this genius and this science are more than a bare knowledge of some branch of science or of literature. This truth was partially perceived in the past generation; and headmasters, somewhat crudely, were apt to supersede

*Recall the epigraph from Alexander Pope, "A little learning is a dangerous thing" (p. 29.)

learning in their colleagues by requiring left-hand bowling and a taste for football. But culture is more than cricket, and more than football, and more than extent of knowledge.

Education is the acquisition of the art of the utilisation of knowledge. 11
This is an art very difficult to impart. Whenever a textbook is written of real educational worth, you may be quite certain that some reviewer will say that it will be difficult to teach from it. Of course it will be difficult to teach from it. If it were easy, the book ought to be burned; for it cannot be educational. In education, as elsewhere, the broad primrose path leads to a nasty place. This evil path is represented by a book or a set of lectures which will practically enable the student to learn by heart all the questions likely to be asked at the next external examination.* And I may say in passing that no educational system is possible unless every question directly asked of a pupil at any examination is either framed or modified by the actual teacher of that pupil in that subject. The external assessor may report on the curriculum or on the performance of the pupils, but never should be allowed to ask the pupil a question which has not been strictly supervised by the actual teacher, or at least inspired by a long conference with him. There are a few exceptions to this rule, but they are exceptions, and could easily be allowed for under the general rule.

We now return to my previous point, that theoretical ideas should 12
always find important applications within the pupil's curriculum. This is not an easy doctrine to apply, but a very hard one. It contains within itself the problem of keeping knowledge alive, of preventing it from becoming inert, which is the central problem of all education.

The best procedure will depend on several factors, none of which can 13
be neglected, namely, the genius of the teacher, the intellectual type of the pupils, their prospects in life, the opportunities offered by the immediate surroundings of the school, and allied factors of this sort. It is for this reason that the uniform external examination is so deadly. We do not denounce it because we are cranks, and like denouncing established things. We are not so childish. Also, of course, such examinations have their use in testing slackness. Our reason of dislike is very definite and very practical. It kills the best part of culture. When you analyse in the light of experience the central task of education, you find that its successful accomplishment depends on a delicate adjustment of many variable factors. The reason is that we are dealing with human minds, and not with dead matter. The evocation of curiosity, of judgment, of the power of mastering a complicated tangle of circumstances, the use of theory in giving foresight in special cases—all these powers are not to be imparted by a set rule embodied in one schedule of examination subjects.

I appeal to you, as practical teachers. With good discipline, it is always 14
possible to pump into the minds of a class a certain quantity of inert knowl-

*External examinations are standardized tests administered by state employees, school inspectors, who are "external" to the school where they give the tests.

edge. You take a text-book and make them learn it. So far, so good. The child then knows how to solve a quadratic equation. But what is the point of teaching a child to solve a quadratic equation? There is a traditional answer to this question. It runs thus: The mind is an instrument, you first sharpen it, and then use it; the acquisition of the power of solving a quadratic equation is part of the process of sharpening the mind. Now there is just enough truth in this answer to have made it live through the ages. But for all its half-truth, it embodies a radical error which bids fair to stifle the genius of the modern world. I do not know who was first responsible for this analogy of the mind to a dead instrument. For aught I know, it may have been one of the seven wise men of Greece, or a committee of the whole lot of them. Whoever was the originator, there can be no doubt of the authority which it has acquired by the continuous approval bestowed upon it by eminent persons. But whatever its weight of authority, whatever the high approval which it can quote, I have no hesitation in denouncing it as one of the most fatal, erroneous, and dangerous conceptions ever introduced into the theory of education. The mind is never passive; it is a perpetual activity, delicate, receptive, responsive to stimulus. You cannot postpone its life until you have sharpened it. Whatever interest attaches to your subject-matter must be evoked here and now; whatever powers you are strengthening in the pupil, must be exercised here and now; whatever possibilities of mental life your teaching should impart, must be exhibited here and now. That is the golden rule of education, and a very difficult rule to follow.

The difficulty is just this: the apprehension of general ideas, intellectual 15
habits of mind, and pleasurable interest in mental achievement can be evoked by no form of words, however accurately adjusted. All practical teachers know that education is a patient process of the mastery of details, minute by minute, hour by hour, day by day. There is no royal road to learning through an airy path of brilliant generalisations. There is a proverb about the difficulty of seeing the wood because of the trees. That difficulty is exactly the point which I am enforcing. The problem of education is to make the pupil see the wood by means of the trees.

The solution which I am urging, is to eradicate the fatal disconnection 16
of subjects which kills the vitality of our modern curriculum. There is only one subject-matter for education, and that is Life in all its manifestations. Instead of this single unity, we offer children—Algebra, from which nothing follows; Geometry, from which nothing follows; Science, from which nothing follows; History, from which nothing follows; a Couple of Languages, never mastered; and lastly, most dreary of all, Literature, represented by plays of Shakespeare, with philological notes and short analyses of plot and character to be in substance committed to memory. Can such a list be said to represent Life, as it is known in the midst of the living of it? The best that can be said of it is, that it is a rapid table of contents which a deity might run over in his mind while he was thinking of creating a world, and has not yet determined how to put it together.

Let us now return to quadratic equations. We still have on hand the 17 unanswered question. Why should children be taught their solution? Unless quadratic equations fit into a connected curriculum, of course there is no reason to teach anything about them. Furthermore, extensive as should be the place of mathematics in a complete culture, I am a little doubtful whether for many types of boys algebraic solutions of quadratic equations do not lie on the specialist side of mathematics. I may here remind you that as yet I have not said anything of the psychology or the content of the specialism, which is so necessary a part of an ideal education. But all that is an evasion of our real question, and I merely state it in order to avoid being misunderstood in my answer.

Quadratic equations are part of algebra, and algebra is the intellectual 18
instrument which has been created for rendering clear the quantitative aspects of the world. There is no getting out of it. Through and through the world is infected with quantity. To talk sense, is to talk in quantities. It is no use saying that the nation is large,—How large? It is no use saying that radium is scarce,—How scarce? You cannot evade quantity. You may fly to poetry and to music, and quantity and number will face you in your rhythms and your octaves. Elegant intellects which despise the theory of quantity, are but half developed. They are more to be pitied than blamed. The scraps of gibberish, which in their school-days were taught to them in the name of algebra, deserve some contempt.

This question of the degeneration of algebra into gibberish, both in 19
word and in fact, affords a pathetic instance of the uselessness of reforming educational schedules without a clear conception of the attributes which you wish to evoke in the living minds of the children. A few years ago there was an outcry that school algebra was in need of reform, but there was a general agreement that graphs would put everything right. So all sorts of things were extruded, and graphs were introduced. So far as I can see, with no sort of idea behind them, but just graphs. Now every examination paper has one or two questions on graphs. Personally I am an enthusiastic adherent of graphs. But I wonder whether as yet we have gained very much. You cannot put life into any schedule of general education unless you succeed in exhibiting its relation to some essential characteristic of all intelligent or emotional perception. It is a hard saying, but it is true; and I do not see how to make it any easier. In making these little formal alterations you are beaten by the very nature of things. You are pitted against too skilful an adversary, who will see to it that the pea is always under the other thimble.

Reformation must begin at the other end. First, you must make up your 20
mind as to those quantitative aspects of the world which are simple enough to be introduced into general education; then a schedule of algebra should be framed which will about find its exemplification in these applications. We need not fear for our pet graphs, they will be there in plenty when we once begin to treat algebra as a serious means of studying the world. Some of the simplest applications will be found in the quantities which occur in the simplest study of society. The curves of history are more vivid and more informing than the dry catalogues of names and dates which comprise the

greater part of that arid school study. What purpose is effected by a catalogue of undistinguished kings and queens? Tom, Dick, or Harry, they are all dead. General resurrections are failures, and are better postponed. The quantitative flux of the forces of modern society is capable of very simple exhibition. Meanwhile, the idea of the variable, of the function, of rate of change, of equations and their solution, of elimination, are being studied as an abstract science for their own sake. Not, of course, in the pompous phrases with which I am alluding to them here, but with that iteration of simple special cases proper to teaching.

If this course be followed, the route from Chaucer to the Black Death, from the Black Death to modern Labour troubles, will connect the tales of the mediĕval pilgrims with the abstract science of algebra, both yielding diverse aspects of that single theme, Life. I know what most of you are thinking at this point. It is that the exact course which I have sketched out is not the particular one which you would have chosen, or even see how to work. I quite agree. I am not claiming that I could do it myself. But your objection is the precise reason why a common external examination system* is fatal to education. The process of exhibiting the applications of knowledge must, for its success, essentially depend on the character of the pupils and the genius of the teacher. Of course I have left out the easiest applications with which most of us are more at home. I mean the quantitative sides of sciences, such as mechanics and physics. 21

. . .

I must beg you to remember what I have been insisting on above. In the first place, one train of thought will not suit all groups of children. For example, I should expect that artisan children will want something more concrete and, in a sense, swifter than I have set down here. Perhaps I am wrong, but that is what I should guess. In the second place, I am not contemplating one beautiful lecture stimulating, once and for all, an admiring class. That is not the way in which education proceeds. No; all the time the pupils are hard at work solving examples, drawing graphs, and making experiments, until they have a thorough hold on the whole subject. I am describing the interspersed explanations, the directions which should be given to their thoughts. The pupils have got to be made to feel that they are studying something, and are not merely executing intellectual minuets. 22

Finally, if you are teaching pupils for some general examination, the problem of sound teaching is greatly complicated. Have you ever noticed the zig-zag moulding round a Norman arch? The ancient work is beautiful, the modern work is hideous. The reason is, that the modern work is done to exact measure, the ancient work is varied according to the idiosyncrasy of the workman. Here it is crowded, and there it is expanded. Now the essence of getting pupils through examinations is to give equal weight to all parts of the 23

*Common external exams are what Americans call "Standardized exams"—tests made out by government employees or professional committees and administered to students on a mass scale ("in common").

schedule. But mankind is naturally specialist. One man sees a whole subject, where another can find only a few detached examples. I know that it seems contradictory to allow for specialism in a curriculum especially designed for a broad culture. Without contradictions the world would be simpler, and perhaps duller. But I am certain that in education wherever you exclude specialism you destroy life.

. . .

Fortunately, the specialist side of education presents an easier problem 24
than does the provision of a general culture. For this there are many reasons. One is that many of the principles of procedure to be observed are the same in both cases, and it is unnecessary to recapitulate. Another reason is that specialist training takes place—or should take place—at a more advanced stage of the pupil's course, and thus there is easier material to work upon. But undoubtedly the chief reason is that the specialist study is normally a study of peculiar interest to the student. He is studying it because, for some reason, he wants to know it. This makes all the difference. The general culture is designed to foster an activity of mind; the specialist course utilises this activity. But it does not do to lay too much stress on these neat antitheses. As we have already seen, in the general course foci of special interest will arise; and similarly in the special study, the external connections of the subject drag thought outwards.

Again, there is not one course of study which merely gives general 25
culture, and another which gives special knowledge. The subjects pursued for the sake of a general education are special subjects specially studied; and, on the other hand, one of the ways of encouraging general mental activity is to foster a special devotion. You may not divide the seamless coat of learning. What education has to impart is an intimate sense for the power of ideas, for the beauty of ideas, and for the structure of ideas, together with a particular body of knowledge which has peculiar reference to the life of the being possessing it.

The appreciation of the structure of ideas is that side of a cultured mind 26
which can only grow under the influence of a special study. I mean that eye for the whole chess-board, for the bearing of one set of ideas on another. Nothing but a special study can give any appreciation for the exact formulation of general ideas, for their relations when formulated, for their service in the comprehension of life. A mind so disciplined should be both more abstract and more concrete. It has been trained in the comprehension of abstract thought and in the analysis of facts.

Finally, there should grow the most austere of all mental qualities; I 27
mean the sense for style. It is an æsthetic sense, based on admiration for the direct attainment of a foreseen end, simply and without waste. Style in art, style in literature, style in science, style in logic, style in practical execution have fundamentally the same aesthetic qualities, namely, attainment and restraint. The love of a subject in itself and for itself, where it is not the sleepy pleasure of pacing a mental quarter-deck, is the love of style as manifested in that study.

Here we are brought back to the position from which we started, the utility of education. Style, in its finest sense, is the last acquirement of the educated mind; it is also the most useful. It pervades the whole being. The administrator with a sense for style hates waste; the engineer with a sense for style economises his material; the artisan with a sense for style prefers good work. Style is the ultimate morality of mind. 28

But above style, and above knowledge, there is something, a vague shape like fate above the Greek gods. That something is Power. Style is the fashioning of power, the restraining of power. But, after all, the power of attainment of the desired end is fundamental. The first thing is to get there. Do not bother about your style, but solve your problem, justify the ways of God to man, administer your province, or do whatever else is set before you. 29

Where, then, does style help? In this, with style the end is attained without side issues, without raising undesirable inflammations. With style you attain your end and nothing but your end. With style the effect of your activity is calculable, and foresight is the last gift of gods to men. With style your power is increased, for your mind is not distracted with irrelevancies, and you are more likely to attain your object. Now style is the exclusive privilege of the expert. Whoever heard of the style of an amateur painter, of the style of an amateur poet? Style is always the product of specialist study, the peculiar contribution of specialism to culture. 30

English education in its present phase suffers from a lack of definite aim, and from an external machinery which kills its vitality. Hitherto in this address I have been considering the aims which should govern education. In this respect England halts between two opinions. It has not decided whether to produce amateurs or experts. The profound change in the world which the nineteenth century has produced is that the growth of knowledge has given foresight. The amateur is essentially a man with appreciation and with immense versatility in mastering a given routine. But he lacks the foresight which comes from special knowledge. The object of this address is to suggest how to produce the expert without loss of the essential virtues of the amateur. The machinery of our secondary education is rigid where it should be yielding, and lax where it should be rigid. Every school is bound on pain of extinction to train its boys for a small set of definite examinations. No headmaster has a free hand to develop his general education or his specialist studies in accordance with the opportunities of his school, which are created by its staff, its environment, its class of boys, and its endowments. I suggest that no system of external tests which aims primarily at examining individual scholars can result in anything but educational waste. 31

Primarily it is the schools and not the scholars which should be inspected. Each school should grant its own leaving certificates, based on its own curriculum. The standards of these schools should be sampled and corrected. But the first requisite for educational reform is the school as a unit, with its approved curriculum based on its own needs, and evolved by its own staff. If we fail to secure that, we simply fall from one formalism into another, from one dung-hill of inert ideas into another. 32

In stating that the school is the true educational unit in any national system for the safeguarding of efficiency, I have conceived the alternative system as being the external examination of the individual scholar. But every Scylla is faced by its Charybdis—or, in more homely language, there is a ditch on both sides of the road. It will be equally fatal to education if we fall into the hands of a supervising department which is under the impression that it can divide all schools into two or three rigid categories, each type being forced to adopt a rigid curriculum. When I say that the school is the educational unit, I mean exactly what I say, no larger unit, no smaller unit. Each school must have the claim to be considered in relation to its special circumstances. The classifying of schools for some purposes is necessary. But no absolutely rigid curriculum, not modified by its own staff, should be permissible. Exactly the same principles apply, with the proper modifications, to universities and to technical colleges. 33

When one considers in its length and in its breadth the importance of this question of the education of a nation's young, the broken lives, the defeated hopes, the national failures, which result from the frivolous inertia with which it is treated, it is difficult to restrain within oneself a savage rage. In the conditions of modern life the rule is absolute, the race which does not value trained intelligence is doomed. Not all your heroism, not all your social charm, not all your wit, not all your victories on land or at sea, can move back the finger of fate. To-day we maintain ourselves. To-morrow science will have moved forward yet one more step, and there will be no appeal from the judgment which will then be pronounced on the uneducated. 34

Questions for Discussion

1. What does Whitehead mean by "inert ideas"? What is bad about them? (You might read our essay on pp. 15–18, "What Is an Idea?") Why does a head full of inert ideas not contain real learning? Is the distinction between inert ideas and real learning one that you think most of your teachers have taken into account? Is your university or college different from high school in its commitment to genuine learning? *Should* there be a difference on this score between high school and college?
2. Do you agree with Whitehead's "two educational commandments" in paragraph 4? How do you decide how many subjects are "too many" (too many for what?), and what is the difference between thorough teaching and superficial teaching? Does the difference between *thorough* and *superficial* apply to students as well as teachers?
3. What does Whitehead mean by saying that "the understanding which we want is an understanding of an insistent present" (¶6)? When read out of context this comment may sound difficult or obscure, but do the examples

in the remainder of the paragraph make it clear? How would you capture the meaning of paragraph 6 in your own words?

4. Whitehead insists that the metaphors teachers and students unconsciously work with largely determine what they do. Why does he object so strongly to the metaphor "the mind is an instrument" (¶14)? Can you think of other metaphors that teachers and students implicitly accept? For example, education as pouring knowledge into pitchers (refer to Dickens's "Hard Facts," pp. 45–57)? Education as training (as with animals)? Education as programming (as of computers)? Which of these metaphors do you like the best? Is your preferred metaphor fully adequate, or does it still fall short? What alternative metaphors can you create on your own—metaphors for either the mind or for learning—that accurately capture the most important aims of education?
5. Although Whitehead rejects the metaphor "the mind is an instrument," he uses many others (e.g., in ¶15, ¶29, and ¶30). Do these seem effective? Why? Why would an author choose a metaphor rather than saying something "straight out"?
6. By having "style" Whitehead seems to mean possessing the sophistication in any activity that comes from knowing it so intimately that one can move inside the activity by "feel," not thought. Dancers, scientists, athletes, and musicians may all exhibit style in this sense. Can you cite particular people who exhibit style in this way?

Suggested Essay Topics

1. Whitehead claims that all real learning involves going back and forth between general ideas and specialized knowledge. Write an essay directed to the narrowest teacher you have ever had (or to the dean or president of your university) explaining what Whitehead means by this notion and why it is crucial to all genuine education. Or, if you think Whitehead is wrong, explain why students should be allowed to take only the specialized courses that they feel will be useful to their careers.
2. As a variation of topic 1, write a letter to the United States Secretary of Education arguing that our nation's specialists are too narrowly trained or that our generalists are too generally trained. Be sure to say what they are too general or specialized *for,* and give concrete examples from both personal and national experience.

2

REASON AND CRITICAL THINKING

Thinking Critically, Thinking Together

He who knows only his own side of the case, knows little of that.
His reasons may be good, and no one may have
been able to refute them. But if he is equally unable to refute
the reasons on the opposite side; if he does not
so much as know what they are, he has no ground
for preferring either opinion.
John Stuart Mill

If some great Power would agree to make me always think
what is true and do what is right, on condition of being turned into
a sort of clock and wound up every morning
before I got out of bed, I should instantly close with the offer.
Thomas Henry Huxley

Although it might belong to Socrates and other minds
of the like craft to acquire virtue by reason, the human race
would long since have ceased to be, had its preservation depended
only on the reasonings of the individuals composing it.
Rousseau

It is not the feeling sure of a doctrine (be it what it may)
which I call an assumption of infallibility. It is the undertaking
to decide that question *for others,* without allowing
them to hear what can be said on the contrary side.
John Stuart Mill

Charles Darwin

The brief selection that follows is a small step in the monumental argument of one of the most influential works of the modern world, The Descent of Man *(1871). Twelve years earlier, in* The Origin of Species, *Charles Darwin had challenged the world's views about creation. In the later book he extended his claim that human beings are descended from earlier animal species, and he supported his conclusions with almost a thousand pages of close arguments like the one presented here.*

In the earlier part of the chapter comparing the mental powers of man and the lower animals, he considers first the senses, then instincts and emotions, and finally the "higher faculties" of imitation, attention, and imagination. After the section on reason presented here, Darwin continues with a detailed discussion of specific reasoning powers: abstraction, general conceptions, self-consciousness, mental individuality, ability to use language, sense of beauty, and belief in God and religion.

In reading this example of Darwin's method of reasoning, it is important to ask about each logical step or illustration: Does it prove what Darwin says it proves? How does he help the reader in deciding how his evidence relates to his conclusions?

REASONING IN ANIMALS

From chapter 3, "Comparison of the Mental Powers of Man and the Lower Animals," of *The Descent of Man* (1871, 1874). The title is ours.

1 Of all the faculties of the human mind, it will, I presume, be admitted that *Reason* stands at the summit. Only a few persons now dispute that animals possess some power of reasoning. Animals may constantly be seen to pause, deliberate, and resolve. It is a significant fact, that the more the habits of any particular animal are studied by a naturalist, the more he attributes to reason

and the less to unlearnt instincts. In future chapters we shall see that some animals extremely low in the scale apparently display a certain amount of reason. No doubt it is often difficult to distinguish between the power of reason and that of instinct. For instance, Dr. Hayes, in his work on "The Open Polar Sea," repeatedly remarks that his dogs, instead of continuing to draw the sledges in a compact body, diverged and separated when they came to thin ice, so that their weight might be more evenly distributed. This was often the first warning which the travellers received that the ice was becoming thin and dangerous. Now, did the dogs act thus from the experience of each individual, or from the example of the older and wiser dogs, or from an inherited habit, that is from instinct? This instinct, may possibly have arisen since the time, long ago, when dogs were first employed by the natives in drawing their sledges; or the Arctic wolves, the parent-stock of the Esquimaux dog, may have acquired an instinct impelling them not to attack their prey in a close pack, when on thin ice.

We can only judge by the circumstances under which actions are per- 2
formed, whether they are due to instinct, or to reason, or to the mere association of ideas: this latter principle, however, is intimately connected with reason. A curious case has been given by Prof. Möbius, of a pike, separated by a plate of glass from an adjoining aquarium stocked with fish, and who often dashed himself with such violence against the glass in trying to catch the other fishes, that he was sometimes completely stunned. The pike went on thus for three months, but at last learnt caution, and ceased to do so. The plate of glass was then removed, but the pike would not attack these particular fishes, though he would devour others which were afterwards introduced; so strongly was the idea of a violent shock associated in his feeble mind with the attempt on his former neighbours. If a savage, who had never seen a large plate-glass window, were to dash himself even once against it, he would for a long time afterwards associate a shock with a window-frame; but very differently from the pike, he would probably reflect on the nature of the impediment, and be cautious under analogous circumstances. Now with monkeys, as we shall presently see, a painful or merely a disagreeable impression, from an action once performed, is sometimes sufficient to prevent the animal from repeating it. If we attribute this difference between the monkey and the pike solely to the association of ideas being so much stronger and more persistent in the one than the other, though the pike often received much the more severe injury, can we maintain in the case of man that a similar difference implies the possession of a fundamentally different mind?

Houzeau relates that, whilst crossing a wide and arid plain in Texas, his 3
two dogs suffered greatly from thirst, and that between thirty and forty times they rushed down the hollows to search for water. These hollows were not valleys, and there were no trees in them, or any other difference in the vegetation, and as they were absolutely dry there could have been no smell of damp earth. The dogs behaved as if they knew that a dip in the ground offered them the best chance of finding water, and Houzeau has often witnessed the same behaviour in other animals.

I have seen, as I daresay have others, that when a small object is thrown 4
on the ground beyond the reach of one of the elephants in the Zoological Gardens, he blows through his trunk on the ground beyond the object, so that the current reflected on all sides may drive the object within his reach. Again a well-known ethnologist, Mr. Westropp, informs me that he observed in Vienna a bear deliberately making with his paw a current in some water, which was close to the bars of his cage, so as to draw a piece of floating bread within his reach. These actions of the elephant and bear can hardly be attributed to instinct or inherited habit, as they would be of little use to an animal in a state of nature. Now, what is the difference between such actions, when performed by an uncultivated man, and by one of the higher animals?

The savage and the dog have often found water at a low level, and the 5
coincidence under such circumstances has become associated in their minds. A cultivated man would perhaps make some general proposition on the subject; but from all that we know of savages it is extremely doubtful whether they would do so, and a dog certainly would not. But a savage, as well as a dog, would search in the same way, though frequently disappointed; and in both it seems to be equally an act of reason, whether or not any general proposition on the subject is consciously placed before the mind. The same would apply to the elephant and the bear making currents in the air or water. The savage would certainly neither know nor care by what law the desired movements were effected; yet his act would be guided by a rude process of reasoning, as surely as would a philosopher in his longest chain of deductions. There would no doubt be this difference between him and one of the higher animals, that he would take notice of much slighter circumstances and conditions, and would observe any connection between them after much less experience, and this would be of paramount importance. I kept a daily record of the actions of one of my infants, and when he was about eleven months old, and before he could speak a single word, I was continually struck with the greater quickness, with which all sorts of objects and sounds were associated together in his mind, compared with that of the most intelligent dogs I ever knew. But the higher animals differ in exactly the same way in this power of association from those low in the scale, such as the pike, as well as in that of drawing inferences and of observation.

The promptings of reason, after very short experience, are well shewn 6
by the following actions of American monkeys, which stand low in their order. Rengger, a most careful observer, states that when he first gave eggs to his monkeys in Paraguay, they smashed them, and thus lost much of their contents; afterwards they gently hit one end against some hard body, and picked off the bits of shell with their fingers. After cutting themselves only *once* with any sharp tool, they would not touch it again, or would handle it with the greatest caution. Lumps of sugar were often given them wrapped up in paper; and Rengger sometimes put a live wasp in the paper, so that in hastily unfolding it they got stung; after this had *once* happened, they always first held the packet to their ears to detect any movement within.

The following cases relate to dogs. Mr. Colquhoun winged two wild- 7 ducks, which fell on the further side of a stream; his retriever tried to bring over both at once, but could not succeed; she then, though never before known to ruffle a feather, deliberately killed one, brought over the other, and returned for the dead bird. Col. Hutchinson relates that two partridges were shot at once, one being killed, the other wounded; the latter ran away, and was caught by the retriever, who on her return came across the dead bird; "she stopped, evidently greatly puzzled, and after one or two trials, finding she could not take it up without permitting the escape of the winged bird, she considered a moment, then deliberately murdered it by giving it a severe crunch, and afterwards brought away both together. This was the only known instance of her ever having wilfully injured any game." Here we have reason though not quite perfect, for the retriever might have brought the wounded bird first and then returned for the dead one, as in the case of the two wild-ducks. I give the above cases, as resting on the evidence of two independent witnesses, and because in both instances the retrievers, after deliberation, broke through a habit which is inherited by them (that of not killing the game retrieved), and because they shew how strong their reasoning faculty must have been to overcome a fixed habit.

I will conclude by quoting a remark by the illustrious Humboldt. "The 8
muleteers in S. America say, 'I will not give you the mule whose step is easiest, but *la mas racional,*—the one that reasons best;' " and as he adds, "this popular expression, dictated by long experience, combats the system of animated machines, better perhaps than all the arguments of speculative philosophy." Nevertheless some writers even yet deny that the higher animals possess a trace of reason; and they endeavour to explain away, by what appears to be mere verbiage, all such facts as those above given.

Questions for Discussion

1. Darwin does not give a single-sentence definition of *reason.* Can you construct one using his words from other sentences?
2. What does Darwin say to persuade you that his reports on animal behavior are valid? Do you doubt that any of them occurred as reported? (Consider especially the effect of phrases like "as resting on the evidence of two independent witnesses," ¶7.)
3. The word *savage* may easily mislead us about Darwin's point in bringing it into his argument in paragraph 2. Look it up in an unabridged dictionary (or better yet, in the *Oxford English Dictionary*) to discover its range of meanings in Darwin's time. Is he intending to show how unintelligent a "savage" is? If not, what is his point?
4. Why does Darwin add the clause "which stand low in their order" to the end of the first sentence of paragraph 6?

5. Does Darwin strengthen or weaken his case by using the expression "mere verbiage" in the final sentence?

Suggested Essay Topics

1. If you have ever observed an animal "thinking," write an account of it as if in a letter to Charles Darwin, and explain to him why it supports or does not support his case. [For a dramatic, vivid account of an animal thinking, look up Loren Eiseley's three-page essay, "The Fire Apes," in *The Star Thrower* (Orlando, Fla.: Harcourt Brace Jovanovich, 1978).]
2. The critic and poet Samuel Taylor Coleridge once claimed that animals do not reason, because they cannot perform elementary deductions. He would believe, he said, that a dog could think if he saw a hunting hound approach a point where a path forks into three paths, smell *two* of them, and then proceed to run down the third *without* smelling it. Write an essay discussing whether Coleridge's claim offers a serious challenge to Darwin's argument. Does he seem to be defining reason in the same way? Is his "experiment," which is conducted entirely in the mind, as convincing as the natural events that Darwin describes?

Elaine Morgan

In this essay Elaine Morgan (b. 1920), Welsh author and teacher, criticizes male prejudices revealed in current evolutionary theory. Her criticism is not that all male biologists and anthropologists are malicious male chauvinists but that many of them are simply sloppy thinkers. Androcentric (male-centered) thinking has been around for so long, she argues (¶10), and has seemed so unquestionably true that few male scientists—despite their commitment, as scientists, to open-mindedness and neutral observation—can break through the crust of inherited prejudices and look clearly at evolutionary theory's supporting ideas and data.

She supports her own position by re-examining notions that have been long accepted as adequate accounts of human development. Without indulging in technical or abstract language, relying simply on careful reasoning and fresh vision, she shows that if scientists had thought as hard about women as they have about men, the inadequacy of their accounts would have been revealed long ago.

You have undoubtedly been told by your teachers over the years that having good reasons for your opinions is perhaps more important than having good opinions. And you may recall occasions on which being forced to support your opinions with good reasons made you see how few you had or how flimsy they were. The most useful part of your education is learning how to ask yourself the kind of penetrating questions that your best teachers have always asked you, learning how to criticize your own ideas by using the same hard tests they have employed. The purging of error, the straightening of twisted logic, the reformulation of ideas, and the search for new information in the light of new perspectives—these are the grounds of progress in all thinking.

By showing how to ask "Why?" and "How do you know that?" about "self-evident" opinions, Morgan exemplifies not only the healthy activity of critical thinking within a discipline but also the kind of critical thinking that education, at its best, teaches us to do on our own.

THE MAN-MADE MYTH

Chapter 1 of *The Descent of Woman* (1972).

According to the Book of Genesis, God first created man. Woman was not only an afterthought, but an amenity. For close on two thousand years this holy scripture was believed to justify her subordination and explain her inferiority; for even as a copy she was not a very good copy. There were differences. She was not one of His best efforts. 1

There is a line in an old folk song that runs: "I called my donkey a horse gone wonky." Throughout most of the literature dealing with the differences between the sexes there runs a subtle underlying assumption that woman is a man gone wonky; that woman is a distorted version of the original blueprint; that they are the norm, and we are the deviation. 2

It might have been expected that when Darwin came along and wrote an entirely different account of *The Descent of Man,* this assumption would have been eradicated, for Darwin didn't believe she was an afterthought: he believed her origin was at least contemporaneous with man's. It should have led to some kind of breakthrough in the relationship between the sexes. But it didn't. 3

Almost at once men set about the congenial and fascinating task of working out an entirely new set of reasons why woman was manifestly inferior and irreversibly subordinate, and they have been happily engaged in this ever since. Instead of theology they use biology, and ethology, and primatology, but they use them to reach the same conclusions. 4

They are now prepared to debate the most complex problems of economic reform not in terms of the will of God, but in terms of the sexual behavior patterns of the cichlid fish; so that if a woman claims equal pay or the right to promotion there is usually an authoritative male thinker around to deliver a brief homily on hormones, and point out that what she secretly intends by this, and what will inevitably result, is the "psychological castration" of the men in her life. 5

Now, that may look to us like a stock piece of emotional blackmail—like the woman who whimpers that if Sonny doesn't do as she wants him to do, then Mother's going to have one of her nasty turns. It is not really surprising that most women who are concerned to win themselves a new and better status in society tend to sheer away from the whole subject of biology and 6 origins, and hope that we can ignore all that and concentrate on ensuring that in the future things will be different.

I believe this is a mistake. The legend of the jungle heritage and the evolution of man as a hunting carnivore has taken root in man's mind as firmly as Genesis ever did. He may even genuinely believe that equal pay will do something terrible to his gonads. He has built a beautiful theoretical construction, with himself on the top of it, buttressed with a formidable array of scientifically authenticated facts. We cannot dispute the facts. We should not attempt to ignore the facts. What I think we can do is to suggest that the currently accepted interpretation of the facts is not the only possible one. 7

I have considerable admiration for scientists in general, and evolutionists and ethologists in particular, and though I think they have sometimes gone astray, it has not been purely through prejudice. Partly it is due to sheer semantic accident—the fact that "man" is an ambiguous term. It means the species; it also means the male of the species. If you begin to write a book about man or conceive a theory about man you cannot avoid using this word. You cannot avoid using a pronoun as a substitute for the word, and you will use the pronoun "he" as a simple matter of linguistic convenience. But before you are halfway through the first chapter a mental image of this evolving creature begins to form in your mind. It will be a male image, and he will be the hero of the story: everything and everyone else in the story will relate to him. 8

All this may sound like a mere linguistic quibble or a piece of feminist petulance. If you stay with me, I hope to convince you it's neither. I believe the deeply rooted semantic confusion between "man" as a male and "man" as a species has been fed back into and vitiated a great deal of the speculation that goes on about the origins, development, and nature of the human race. 9

A very high proportion of the thinking on these topics is androcentric (male-centered) in the same way as pre-Copernican thinking was geocentric. It's just as hard for man to break the habit of thinking of himself as central to the species as it was to break the habit of thinking of himself as central to the universe. He sees himself quite unconsciously as the main line of evolution, with a female satellite revolving around him as the moon revolves around the earth. This not only causes him to overlook valuable clues to our ancestry, but sometimes leads him into making statements that are arrant and demonstrable nonsense. 10

The longer I went on reading his own books about himself, the more I longed to find a volume that would begin: "When the first ancestor of the human race descended from the trees, she had not yet developed the mighty brain that was to distinguish her so sharply from all other species. . . ." 11

Of course, she was no more the first ancestor than he was—but she was no *less* the first ancestor, either. She was there all along, contributing half the genes to each succeeding generation. Most of the books forget about her for most of the time. They drag her onstage rather suddenly for the obligatory chapter on Sex and Reproduction, and then say: "All right, love, you can go now," while they get on with the real meaty stuff about the Mighty Hunter 12 with his lovely new weapons and his lovely new straight legs racing across the Pleistocene plains. Any modifications in her morphology are taken to be imitations of the Hunter's evolution, or else designed solely for his delectation.

Evolutionary thinking has been making great strides lately. Archeologists, ethologists, paleontologists, geologists, chemists, biologists, and physicists are closing in from all points of the compass on the central area of mystery that remains. For despite the frequent triumph dances of researchers coming up with another jawbone or another statistic, some part of the miracle is still unaccounted for. Most of their books include some such phrase as: ". . . the early stages of man's evolutionary progress remain a total mystery." "Man is an accident, the culmination of a series of highly improbable coincidences. . . ." "Man is a product of circumstances special to the point of disbelief." They feel there is still something missing, and they don't know what. 13

The trouble with specialists is that they tend to think in grooves. From time to time something happens to shake them out of that groove. Robert Ardrey tells how such enlightenment came to Dr. Kenneth Oakley when the first Australopithecus remains had been unearthed in Africa: "The answer flashed without warning in his own large-domed head: 'Of course we believed that the big brain came first! We assumed that the first man was an Englishman!' " Neither he, nor Ardrey in relating the incident, noticed that he was still making an equally unconscious, equally unwarrantable assumption. One of these days an evolutionist is going to strike a palm against his large-domed head and cry: "Of course! We assumed the first human being was a man!" 14

First, let's have a swift recap of the story as currently related, for despite all the new evidence recently brought to light, the generally accepted picture of human evolution has changed very little. 15

Smack in the center of it remains the Tarzanlike figure of the prehominid male who came down from the trees, saw a grassland teeming with game, picked up a weapon, and became a Mighty Hunter. 16

Almost everything about us is held to have derived from this. If we walk erect it was because the Mighty Hunter had to stand tall to scan the distance for his prey. If we lived in caves it was because hunters need a base to come home to. If we learned to speak it was because hunters need to plan the next safari and boast about the last. Desmond Morris, pondering on the shape of a woman's breasts, instantly deduces that they evolved because her mate became a Mighty Hunter, and defends this preposterous proposition with the greatest ingenuity. There's something about the Tarzan figure which has them all mesmerized. 17

I find the whole yarn pretty incredible. It is riddled with mysteries, and inconsistencies, and unanswered questions. Even more damning than the unanswered questions are the questions that are never even asked, because, as Professor Peter Medawar has pointed out, "scientists tend not to ask 18 themselves questions until they can see the rudiments of an answer in their minds." I shall devote this chapter to pointing out some of these problems before outlining a new version of the Naked Ape story [in following chapters not reprinted here] which will suggest at least possible answers to every one of them, and fifteen or twenty others besides.

The first mystery is, "What happened during the Pliocene?" 19

There is a wide acceptance now of the theory that the human story 20
began in Africa. Twenty million years ago in Kenya, there existed a flourishing population of apes of generalized body structure and of a profusion of types from the size of a small gibbon up to that of a large gorilla. Dr. L. S. B. Leakey has dug up their bones by the hundred in the region of Lake Victoria, and they were clearly doing very well there at the time. It was a period known as the Miocene. The weather was mild, the rainfall was heavier than today, and the forests were flourishing. So far, so good.

Then came the Pliocene drought. Robert Ardrey writes of it: "No mind 21
can apprehend in terms of any possible human experience the duration of the Pliocene. Ten desiccated years were enough, a quarter of a century ago, to produce in the American Southwest that maelstrom of misery, the dust bowl. To the inhabitant of the region the ten years must have seemed endless. But the African Pliocene lasted twelve million."

On the entire African continent no Pliocene fossil bed has ever been 22
found. During this period many promising Miocene ape species were, not surprisingly, wiped out altogether. A few were trapped in dwindling pockets of forest and when the Pliocene ended they reappeared as brachiating apes—specialized for swinging by their arms.

Something astonishing also reappeared—the Australopithecines, first 23
discovered by Professor Raymond Dart in 1925 and since unearthed in considerable numbers by Dr. Leakey and others.

Australopithecus emerged from his horrifying twelve-million-year or- 24
deal much refreshed and improved. The occipital condyles of his skull suggest a bodily posture approaching that of modern man, and the orbital region, according to Sir Wilfred le Gros Clark, has "a remarkably human appearance." He was clever, too. His remains have been found in the Olduvai Gorge in association with crude pebble tools that have been hailed as the earliest beginning of human culture. Robert Ardrey says: "We entered the [Pliocene] crucible a generalized creature bearing only the human potential. We emerged a being lacking only a proper brain and a chin. What happened to us along the way?" The sixty-four-thousand-dollar question: "What happened to them? Where did they go?"

Second question: "Why did they stand upright?" The popular versions 25
skim very lightly over this patch of thin ice. Desmond Morris says simply: "With strong pressure on them to increase their prey-killing prowess, they became more upright—fast, better runners." Robert Ardrey says equally simply: "We learned to stand erect in the first place as a necessity of the hunting life."

But wait a minute. We were quadrupeds. These statements imply that 26 a quadruped suddenly discovered that he could move faster on two legs than on four. Try to imagine any other quadruped discovering that—a cat? a dog? a horse?—and you'll see that it's totally nonsensical. Other things being equal, four legs are bound to run faster than two. The bipedal development was violently unnatural.

Stoats, gophers, rabbits, chimpanzees, will sit or stand bipedally to gaze 27
into the distance, but when they want speed they have sense enough to use all the legs they've got. The only quadrupeds I can think of that can move faster on two legs than four are things like kangaroos—and a small lizard called the Texas boomer, and he doesn't keep it up for long. The secret in these cases is a long heavy counterbalancing tail which we certainly never had. You may say it was a natural development for a primate because primates sit erect in trees—but *was* it natural? Baboons and macaques have been largely terrestrial for millions of years without any sign of becoming bipedal.

George A. Bartholomew and Joseph B. Birdsell point out: ". . . the 28
extreme rarity of bipedalism among animals suggests that it is inefficient except under very special circumstances. Even modern man's unique vertical locomotion when compared to that of quadrupedal mammals, is relatively ineffective. . . . A significant nonlocomotor advantage must have resulted."

What was this advantage? The Tarzanists suggest that bipedalism en- 29
abled this ape to race after game while carrying weapons—in the first instance, presumably pebbles. But a chimp running off with a banana (or a pebble), if he can't put it in his mouth, will carry it in one hand and gallop along on the others, because even *three* legs are faster than two. So what was our ancestor supposed to be doing? Shambling along with a rock in each hand? Throwing boulders that took two hands to lift?

No. There must have been a pretty powerful reason why we were 30
constrained over a long period of time to walk about on our hind legs *even though it was slower.* We need to find that reason.

Third question: How did the ape come to be using these weapons, 31
anyway? Again Desmond Morris clears this one lightly, at a bound: "With strong pressure on them to increase their prey-killing prowess . . . their hands became strong efficient weapon-holders." Compared to Morris, Robert Ardrey is obsessed with weapons, which he calls "mankind's most significant cultural endowment." Yet his explanation of how it all started is as cursory as anyone else's: "In the first evolutionary hour of the human emergence we became sufficiently skilled in the use of weapons to render redundant our natural primate daggers" (i.e., the large prehominid canine teeth).

But wait a minute—how? and why? Why did one, and only one, species 32
of those Miocene apes start using weapons? A cornered baboon will fight a leopard; a hungry baboon will kill and eat a chicken. He could theoretically pick up a chunk of flint and forget about his "natural primate daggers," and become a Mighty Hunter. He doesn't do it, though. Why did we? Sarel Eimerl and Irven de Vore point out in their book *The Primates:*

"Actually, it takes quite a lot of explaining. For example, if an animal's 33
normal mode of defense is to flee from a predator, it flees. If its normal method

of defense is to fight with its teeth, it fights with its teeth. It does not suddenly adopt a totally new course of action, such as picking up a stick or a rock and throwing it. The idea would simply not occur to it, and even if it did, the animal would have no reason to suppose that it would work."

Now primates do acquire useful tool-deploying habits. A chimpanzee will use a stick to extract insects from their nests, and a crumpled leaf to sop up water. Wolfgang Köhler's apes used sticks to draw fruit toward the bars of their cage, and so on. 34

But this type of learning depends on three things. There must be leisure for trial-and-error experiment. The tools must be either in unlimited supply (a forest is full of sticks and leaves) or else in *exactly the right place.* (Even Köhler's brilliant Sultan could be stumped if the fruit was in front of him and a new potential tool was behind him—he needed them both in view at the same time.) Thirdly, for the habit to stick, the same effect must result from the same action every time. 35

Now look at that ape. The timing is wrong—when he's faced with a bristling rival or a charging cat or even an escaping prey, he won't fool around inventing fancy methods. A chimp sometimes brandishes a stick to convey menace to an adversary, but if his enemy keeps coming, he drops the stick and fights with hands and teeth. Even if we postulate a mutant ape cool enough to think, with the adrenalin surging through his veins, "There must be a better way than teeth," he still has to be lucky to notice that right in the middle of the primeval grassland there happens to be a stone of convenient size, precisely between him and his enemy. And when he throws it, he has to score a bull's-eye, first time and every time. Because if he failed to hit a leopard he wouldn't be there to tell his progeny that the trick only needed polishing up a bit; and if he failed to hit a springbok he'd think: "Ah well, that obviously doesn't work. Back to the old drawing board." 36

No. If it had taken all that much luck to turn man into a killer, we'd all be still living on nut cutlets. 37

A lot of Tarzanists privately realize that their explanations of bipedalism and weapon-wielding won't hold water. They have invented the doctrine of "feedback," which states that though these two theories are separately and individually nonsense, together they will just get by. It is alleged that the ape's bipedal gait, however unsteady, made him a better rock thrower (why?) and his rock throwing, however inaccurate, made him a better biped. (Why?) Eimerl and de Vore again put the awkward question: Since chimps can both walk erect and manipulate simple tools, "why was it only the hominids who benefited from the feed-back?" You may well ask. 38

Next question: Why did the naked ape become naked? 39

Desmond Morris claims that, unlike more specialized carnivores such as lions and jackals, the ex-vegetarian ape was not physically equipped to "make lightning dashes after his prey." He would "experience considerable overheating during the hunt, and the loss of body hair would be of great value for the supreme moments of the chase." 40

This is a perfect example of androcentric thinking. There were two sexes 41 around at the time, and I don't believe it's ever been all that easy to part a woman from a fur coat, just to save the old man from getting into a muck-sweat during his supreme moments. What was supposed to be happening to the female during this period of denudation?

Dr. Morris says: "This system would not work, of course, if the climate was too intensely hot, because of damage to the exposed skin." So he is obviously dating the loss of hair later than the Pliocene "inferno." But the next period was the turbulent Pleistocene, punctuated by mammoth African "pluvials," corresponding to the Ice Ages of the north. A pluvial was century after century of torrential rainfall; so we have to picture our maternal ancestor sitting naked in the middle of the plain while the heavens emptied, needing both hands to keep her muddy grip on a slippery, squirming, equally naked infant. This is ludicrous. It's no advantage to the species for the Mighty Hunter to return home safe and cool if he finds his son's been dropped on his head and his wife is dead of hypothermia. 42

This problem could have been solved by dimorphism—the loss of hair could have gone further in one sex than the other. So it did, of course. But unfortunately for the Tarzanists it was the stay-at-home female who became nakedest, and the overheated hunter who kept the hair on his chest. 43

Next question: Why has our sex life become so involved and confusing? 44

The given answer, I need hardly say, is that it all began when man became a hunter. He had to travel long distances after his prey and he began worrying about what the little woman might be up to. He was also anxious about other members of the hunting pack, because, Desmond Morris explains, "if the weaker males were going to be expected to cooperate on the hunt, they had to be given more sexual rights. The females would have to be more shared out." 45

Thus it became necessary, so the story goes, to establish a system of "pair bonding" to ensure that couples remained faithful for life. I quote: "The simplest and most direct method of doing this was to make the shared activities of the pair more complicated and more rewarding. In other words, to make sex sexier." 46

To this end, the Naked Apes sprouted ear lobes, fleshy nostrils, and everted lips, all allegedly designed to stimulate one another to a frenzy. Mrs. A.'s nipples became highly erogenous, she invented and patented the female orgasm, and she learned to be sexually responsive at all times, even during pregnancy, "because with a one-male–one-female system, it would be dangerous to frustrate the male for too long a period. It might endanger the pair bond." He might go off in a huff, or look for another woman. Or even refuse to cooperate on the hunt. 47

In addition, they decided to change over to face-to-face sex, instead of the male mounting from behind as previously, because this new method led to "personalized sex." The frontal approach means that "the incoming sexual signals and rewards are kept tightly linked with the identity signals from the partner." In simpler words, you know who you're doing it with. 48

This landed Mrs. Naked Ape in something of a quandary. Up till then, 49 the fashionable thing to flaunt in sexual approaches had been "a pair of fleshy, hemispherical buttocks." Now all of a sudden they were getting her nowhere. She would come up to her mate making full-frontal identity signals like mad with her nice new earlobes and nostrils, but somehow he just didn't want to know. He missed the fleshy hemispheres, you see. The position was parlous, Dr. Morris urges. "If the female of our species was going to successfully shift the interest of the male round to the front, evolution would have to do something to make the frontal region more stimulating." Guess what? Right the first time: she invested in a pair of fleshy hemispheres in the thoracic region and we were once more saved by the skin of our teeth.

All this is good stirring stuff, but hard to take seriously. Wolf packs 50
manage to cooperate without all this erotic paraphernalia. Our near relatives the gibbons remain faithful for life without "personalized" frontal sex, without elaborate erogenous zones, without perennial female availability. Why couldn't we?

Above all, since when has increased sexiness been a guarantee of in- 51
creased fidelity? If the naked ape could see all this added sexual potential in his own mate, how could he fail to see the same thing happening to all the other females around him? What effect was that supposed to have on him, especially in later life when he noticed Mrs. A.'s four hemispheres becoming a little less fleshy than they used to be?

We haven't yet begun on the unasked questions. Before ending this 52
chapter I will mention just two out of many.

First: If female orgasm was evolved in our species for the first time to 53
provide the woman with a "behavioral reward" for increased sexual activity, why in the name of Darwin has the job been so badly bungled that there have been whole tribes and whole generations of women hardly aware of its existence? Even in the sex-conscious U.S.A., according to Dr. Kinsey, it rarely gets into proper working order before the age of about thirty. How could natural selection ever have operated on such a rickety, unreliable, late-developing endowment when in the harsh conditions of prehistory a woman would be lucky to survive more than twenty-nine years, anyway?

Second: Why in our species has sex become so closely linked with 54
aggression? In most of the higher primates sexual activity is the one thing in life which is totally incompatible with hostility. A female primate can immediately deflect male wrath by presenting her backside and offering sex. Even a male monkey can calm and appease a furious aggressor by imitating the gesture. Nor is the mechanism confined to mammals. Lorenz tells of an irate lizard charging down upon a female painted with male markings to deceive him. When he got close enough to realize his mistake, the taboo was so immediate and so absolute that his aggression went out like a light, and being too late to stop himself he shot straight up into the air and turned a back somersault.

Female primates admittedly are not among the species that can count 55
on this absolute chivalry at all times. A female monkey may be physically

chastised for obstreperous behavior; or a male may (on rare occasions) direct hostility against her when another male is copulating with her; but between the male and female engaged in it, sex is always the friendliest of interactions. There is no more hostility associated with it than with a session of mutual grooming.

How then have sex and aggression, the two irreconcilables of the animal kingdom, become in our species alone so closely interlinked that the words for sexual activity are spat out as insults and expletives? In what evolutionary terms are we to explain the Marquis de Sade, and the subterranean echoes that his name evokes in so many human minds? 56

Not, I think, in terms of Tarzan. It is time to approach the whole thing again right from the beginning: this time from the distaff side, and along a totally different route. 57

Questions for Discussion

1. Do you think that Morgan's sharpening of her feminist axe dulls her overall argument? Does she seem more intent on being a feminist thinker than a scientific thinker? Or do you think that her feminist examples are appropriate to her task?
2. Morgan's tone varies greatly from moment to moment. Often she sounds neutral, scientific: "We cannot dispute the facts. We should not attempt to ignore the facts. What I think we can do is to suggest that the currently accepted interpretation of the facts is not the only possible one" (¶7). But often enough she becomes ironic or even sarcastic: "I don't believe it's ever been all that easy to part a woman from a fur coat, just to save the old man from getting into a muck-sweat during his supreme moments" (¶41); Mrs. A. "invented and patented the female orgasm" (¶47); "He may even genuinely believe that equal pay will do something terrible to his gonads" (¶7). Do you find these two styles compatible? Does she mix them effectively? What is the effect of mixing them? Do the passages with ironic zingers in them affect your view of her credibility? Why?
3. In paragraphs 25–30, Morgan discusses the emergence of bipedalism in human beings and argues that the conventional explanation—that walking upright made men faster and better hunters—simply does not hold water. Discuss in detail the objections she raises. Her questions are based on logic, not specialized knowledge. Do they make sense to you? Can you think of arguments that either support or undercut her criticisms?
4. The following "skeleton" outline is intended to reveal the connecting "joints" in Morgan's argument. Choose any essay you have read so far and try to bare the skeletal framework for it as we have done for Morgan's essay.

I. Paragraphs 1–14: *Introduction:* Morgan lays out the topic, thesis, and general form of her argument.
   A. Paragraphs 1–7: Exposition of *topic,* the relation between evolutionary theory in biology and the status of women in society. The *thesis* statement emerges in the last sentence of paragraph 7: "The currently accepted interpretation of the facts is not the only possible one."
   B. Paragraphs 8–14: *General overview of argument* and beginning development. Even scientific thinkers do not think open-mindedly about evolution. She cites three reasons:
      1. Paragraphs 8–9: Language itself reinforces male prejudices.
      2. Paragraphs 10–13: Tradition reinforces male prejudices (brilliant metaphor from astronomy).
      3. Paragraphs 14: Narrowness of specialized thinking reinforces male prejudices; specialists tend to think "in grooves."

II. Paragraphs 15–56: *Detailed critique* of "grooved" views in evolutionary theory.
   A. Paragraphs 15–24: Summary of conventional views in current theory.
      1. Paragraphs 15–18: The development of human beings is largely built on the nature of early man as a "Mighty Hunter."
      2. Paragraphs 19–24: The standard problem that must be explained in anthropology.
   B. Paragraphs 25–30: The problem of how to explain the upright walk.
      1. Paragraph 25: The current explanation is based on the Mighty Hunter theory.
      2. Paragraphs 26–30: Critique that shows inadequacy of the current explanation.
   C. Paragraphs 31–38: The problem of how to explain emergence of weapons.
      1. Paragraph 31: The current explanation is based on the Mighty Hunter theory.
      2. Paragraphs 32–38: Critique—the necessities of hunting don't suffice as an explanation.
   D. Paragraphs 39–43: The problem of how to explain loss of hair.
      1. Paragraph 40: Again, the theory is based on the Mighty Hunter explanation.
      2. Paragraphs 41–43: Critique.
   E. Paragraphs 44–51: The problem of how to explain distinctive sexual practices of human beings.
      1. Paragraphs 45–49: Again we are given the conventional Mighty Hunter view.
      2. Paragraphs 50–56: Critique.

III. Paragraph 57: *Conclusion:* Reiteration of the thesis that current theory is inadequate to explain the data.

Suggested Essay Topics

1. In paragraph 10, Morgan compares androcentric thinking to pre-Copernican thinking and develops the comparison in a couple of sentences. In a short paper, begin by quoting the first three sentences of paragraph 10, then continue to develop the comparison. You might go on to compare some early feminist (e.g., Margaret Sanger or Susan B. Anthony) to Copernicus, or compare male chauvinists to Copernicus's con-

temporaries. The point of this essay is to give you practice in making an extended analogy work for you. Few devices are more powerful than extended analogies for packing meaning and effect into a compressed space. By contrast, nothing will seem less effective than an analogy that strikes a reader as far-fetched or inappropriate.

2. Pick an issue that is accompanied by widely accepted arguments that seem as objectionable to you as androcentric arguments seem to Morgan. Possible topics might include the arms race, space travel, a nuclear freeze, the "first-strike option," or abortion rights; or, if you wish to stick to issues you know firsthand, you might write on open dorm policies, tuition increases, the value of Greek-letter societies, or the money spent on athletics.

   In an essay directed to your fellow students or in a memo or letter addressed to responsible officials, imitate Morgan's style of attack (¶25–30 or ¶31–38 provide a model). Begin with a short statement of the issue, proceed to give the conventional view you find objectionable, and then develop your objections, relying not on special information but on tight reasoning. Like Morgan, you do not have to replace the ideas you criticize with a whole new set; your objective is simply to point out as many flaws as possible in the arguments you are attacking. Try to go for the basic ideas, not trivialities.

William Golding

In this essay the British novelist William Golding (b. 1911), author of The Lord of the Flies, *provides a humorous, yet serious, description of three levels of thinking. He draws his examples of each from his own experience in school, starting with grammar school and ending with the university. As you read, try to determine whether the three levels of schooling he talks about correspond to the three levels of thinking he describes. Consider whether you can verify his categories with examples from your own experience. Can you map his progress from thinking as a "hobby" to thinking as a "professional" (¶47)? Does the kind of thinking you are being taught in college fall within Golding's categories?*

THINKING AS A HOBBY

From *Holiday,* August 1961.

While I was still a boy, I came to the conclusion that there were three grades of thinking; and since I was later to claim thinking as my hobby, I came to an even stranger conclusion—namely, that I myself could not think at all. 1

I must have been an unsatisfactory child for grownups to deal with. I 2 remember how incomprehensible they appeared to me at first, but not, of course, how I appeared to them. It was the headmaster of my grammar school who first brought the subject of thinking before me—though neither in the way, nor with the result he intended. He had some statuettes in his study. They stood on a high cupboard behind his desk. One was a lady wearing nothing but a bath towel. She seemed frozen in an eternal panic lest the bath towel slip down any farther; and since she had no arms, she was in an unfortunate position to pull the towel up again. Next to her, crouched the statuette of a leopard, ready to spring down at the top drawer of a filing cabinet labeled A–AH. My innocence interpreted this as the victim's last, despairing cry. Beyond the leopard was a naked, muscular gentleman, who sat, looking down, with his chin on his fist and his elbow on his knee. He seemed utterly miserable.

Some time later, I learned about these statuettes. The headmaster had 3
placed them where they would face delinquent children, because they symbolized to him the whole of life. The naked lady was the Venus of Milo. She was Love. She was not worried about the towel. She was just busy being beautiful. The leopard was Nature, and he was being natural. The naked, muscular gentleman was not miserable. He was Rodin's Thinker, an image of pure thought. It is easy to buy small plaster models of what you think life is like.

I had better explain that I was a frequent visitor to the headmaster's 4
study, because of the latest thing I had done or left undone. As we now say, I was not integrated. I was, if anything, disintegrated; and I was puzzled. Grownups never made sense. Whenever I found myself in a penal position before the headmaster's desk, with the statuettes glimmering whitely above him, I would sink my head, clasp my hands behind my back and writhe one shoe over the other.

The headmaster would look opaquely at me, through flashing specta- 5
cles.

"What are we going to do with you?" 6

Well, what *were* they going to do with me? I would writhe my shoe some 7
more and stare down at the worn rug.

"Look up, boy! Can't you look up?" 8

Then I would look up at the cupboard, where the naked lady was frozen 9
in her panic and the muscular gentleman contemplated the hindquarters of the leopard in endless gloom. I had nothing to say to the headmaster. His spectacles caught the light so that you could see nothing human behind them. There was no possibility of communication.

"Don't you ever think at all?" 10

No, I didn't think, wasn't thinking, couldn't think—I was simply wait- 11
ing in anguish for the interview to stop.

"Then you'd better learn—hadn't you?" 12

On one occasion the headmaster leaped to his feet, reached up and 13
plonked Rodin's masterpiece on the desk before me.

"That's what a man looks like when he's really thinking." 14

I surveyed the gentleman without interest or comprehension. 15

"Go back to your class." 16

Clearly there was something missing in me. Nature had endowed the 17
rest of the human race with a sixth sense and left me out. This must be so, I mused, on my way back to the class, since whether I had broken a window, or failed to remember Boyle's Law, or been late for school, my teachers produced me one, adult answer: "Why can't you think?"

As I saw the case, I had broken the window because I had tried to hit 18
Jack Arney with a cricket ball and missed him; I could not remember Boyle's Law because I had never bothered to learn it; and I was late for school because I preferred looking over the bridge into the river. In fact, I was wicked. Were my teachers, perhaps, so good that they could not understand the depths of my depravity? Were they clear, untormented people who could direct their every action by this mysterious business of thinking? The whole thing was incomprehensible. In my earlier years, I found even the statuette of the Thinker confusing. I did not believe any of my teachers were naked, ever. Like someone born deaf, but bitterly determined to find out about sound, I watched my teachers to find out about thought.

There was Mr. Houghton. He was always telling me to think. With a 19
modest satisfaction, he would tell me that he had thought a bit himself. Then why did he spend so much time drinking? Or was there more sense in drinking than there appeared to be? But if not, and if drinking were in fact ruinous to health—and Mr. Houghton was ruined, there was no doubt about that—why was he always talking about the clean life and the virtues of fresh air? He would spread his arms wide with the action of a man who habitually spent his time striding along mountain ridges.

"Open air does me good, boys—I know it!" 20

Sometimes, exalted by his own oratory, he would leap from his desk and 21
hustle us outside into a hideous wind.

"Now, boys! Deep breaths! Feel it right down inside you—huge 22
draughts of God's good air!"

He would stand before us, rejoicing in his perfect health, an open-air 23
man. He would put his hands on his waist and take a tremendous breath. You could hear the wind, trapped in the cavern of his chest and struggling with all the unnatural impediments. His body would reel with shock and his ruined face go white at the unaccustomed visitation. He would stagger back to his desk and collapse there, useless for the rest of the morning.

Mr. Houghton was given to high-minded monologues about the good 24
life, sexless and full of duty. Yet in the middle of one of these monologues, if a girl passed the window, tapping along on her neat little feet, he would interrupt his discourse, his neck would turn of itself and he would watch her out of sight. In this instance, he seemed to me ruled not by thought but by an invisible and irresistible spring in his nape.

His neck was an object of great interest to me. Normally it bulged a bit 25 over his collar. But Mr. Houghton had fought in the First World War alongside both Americans and French, and had come—by who knows what illogic?—to a settled detestation of both countries. If either country happened to be prominent in current affairs, no argument could make Mr. Houghton think well of it. He would bang the desk, his neck would bulge still further and go red. "You can say what you like," he would cry, "but I've thought about this—and I know what I think!"

Mr. Houghton thought with his neck. 26

There was Miss Parsons. She assured us that her dearest wish was our 27
welfare, but I knew even then, with the mysterious clairvoyance of childhood, that what she wanted most was the husband she never got. There was Mr. Hands—and so on.

I have dealt at length with my teachers because this was my introduc- 28
tion to the nature of what is commonly called thought. Through them I discovered that thought is often full of unconscious prejudice, ignorance and hypocrisy. It will lecture on disinterested purity while its neck is being remorselessly twisted toward a skirt. Technically, it is about as proficient as most businessmen's golf, as honest as most politicians' intentions, or—to come near my own preoccupation—as coherent as most books that get written. It is what I came to call grade-three thinking, though more properly, it is feeling, rather than thought.

True, often there is a kind of innocence in prejudices, but in those days 29
I viewed grade-three thinking with an intolerant contempt and an incautious mockery. I delighted to confront a pious lady who hated the Germans with the proposition that we should love our enemies. She taught me a great truth in dealing with grade-three thinkers; because of her, I no longer dismiss lightly a mental process which for nine-tenths of the population is the nearest they will ever get to thought. They have immense solidarity. We had better respect them, for we are outnumbered and surrounded. A crowd of grade-three thinkers, all shouting the same thing, all warming their hands at the fire of their own prejudices, will not thank you for pointing out the contradictions in their beliefs. Man is a gregarious animal, and enjoys agreement as cows will graze all the same way on the side of a hill.

Grade-two thinking is the detection of contradictions. I reached grade 30
two when I trapped the poor, pious lady. Grade-two thinkers do not stampede easily, though often they fall into the other fault and lag behind. Grade-two thinking is a withdrawal, with eyes and ears open. It became my hobby and brought satisfaction and loneliness in either hand. For grade-two thinking destroys without having the power to create. It set me watching the crowds cheering His Majesty the King and asking myself what all the fuss was about, without giving me anything positive to put in the place of that heady patriotism. But there were compensations. To hear people justify their habit of hunting foxes and tearing them to pieces by claiming that the foxes liked it. To hear our Prime Minister talk about the great benefit we conferred on India by jailing people like Pandit Nehru and Gandhi. To hear American

politicians talk about peace in one sentence and refuse to join the League of Nations in the next. Yes, there were moments of delight.

But I was growing toward adolescence and had to admit that Mr. 31
Houghton was not the only one with an irresistible spring in his neck. I, too, felt the compulsive hand of nature and began to find that pointing out contradiction could be costly as well as fun. There was Ruth, for example, a serious and attractive girl. I was an atheist at the time. Grade-two thinking is a menace to religion and knocks down sects like skittles. I put myself in a position to be converted by her with an hypocrisy worthy of grade three. She was a Methodist—or at least, her parents were, and Ruth had to follow suit. But, alas, instead of relying on the Holy Spirit to convert me, Ruth was foolish enough to open her pretty mouth in argument. She claimed that the Bible (King James Version) was literally inspired. I countered by saying that the Catholics believed in the literal inspiration of Saint Jerome's *Vulgate,* and the two books were different. Argument flagged.

At last she remarked that there were an awful lot of Methodists, and 32
they couldn't be wrong, could they—not all those millions? That was too easy, said I restively (for the nearer you were to Ruth, the nicer she was to be near to) since there were more Roman Catholics than Methodists anyway; and they couldn't be wrong, could they—not all those hundreds of millions? An awful flicker of doubt appeared in her eyes. I slid my arm round her waist and murmured breathlessly that if we were counting heads, the Buddhists were the boys for my money. But Ruth had *really* wanted to do me good, because I was so nice. She fled. The combination of my arm and those countless Buddhists was too much for her.

That night her father visited my father and left, red-cheeked and indig- 33
nant. I was given the third degree to find out what had happened. It was lucky we were both of us only fourteen. I lost Ruth and gained an undeserved reputation as a potential libertine.

So grade-two thinking could be dangerous. It was in this knowledge, at 34
the age of fifteen, that I remember making a comment from the heights of grade two, on the limitations of grade three. One evening I found myself alone in the school hall, preparing it for a party. The door of the headmaster's study was open. I went in. The headmaster had ceased to thump Rodin's Thinker down on the desk as an example to the young. Perhaps he had not found any more candidates, but the statuettes were still there, glimmering and gathering dust on top of the cupboard. I stood on a chair and rearranged them. I stood Venus in her bath towel on the filing cabinet, so that now the top drawer caught its breath in a gasp of sexy excitement. "A-ah!" The portentous Thinker I placed on the edge of the cupboard so that he looked down at the bath towel and waited for it to slip.

Grade-two thinking, though it filled life with fun and excitement, did 35
not make for content. To find out the deficiencies of our elders bolsters the young ego but does not make for personal security. I found that grade two was not only the power to point out contradictions. It took the swimmer some

distance from the shore and left him there, out of his depth. I decided that Pontius Pilate was a typical grade-two thinker. "What is truth?" he said, a very common grade-two thought, but one that is used always as the end of an argument instead of the beginning. There is a still higher grade of thought which says, "What is truth?" and sets out to find it.

But these grade-one thinkers were few and far between. They did not visit my grammar school in the flesh though they were there in books. I aspired to them, partly because I was ambitious and partly because I now saw my hobby as an unsatisfactory thing if it went no further. If you set out to climb a mountain, however high you climb, you have failed if you cannot reach the top. 36

I *did* meet an undeniably grade-one thinker in my first year at Oxford. I was looking over a small bridge in Magdalen Deer Park, and a tiny mustached and hatted figure came and stood by my side. He was a German who had just fled from the Nazis to Oxford as a temporary refuge. His name was Einstein. 37

But Professor Einstein knew no English at that time and I knew only two words of German. I beamed at him, trying wordlessly to convey by my bearing all the affection and respect that the English felt for him. It is possible—and I have to make the admission—that I felt here were two grade-one thinkers standing side by side; yet I doubt if my face conveyed more than a formless awe. I would have given my Greek and Latin and French and a good slice of my English for enough German to communicate. But we were divided; he was as inscrutable as my headmaster. For perhaps five minutes we stood together on the bridge, undeniable grade-one thinker and breathless aspirant. With true greatness, Professor Einstein realized that any contact was better than none. He pointed to a trout wavering in midstream. 38

He spoke: "*Fisch.*" 39

My brain reeled. Here I was, mingling with the great, and yet helpless as the veriest grade-three thinker. Desperately I sought for some sign by which I might convey that I, too, revered pure reason. I nodded vehemently. In a brilliant flash I used up half my German vocabulary. 40

"*Fisch. Ja. Ja.*" 41

For perhaps another five minutes we stood side by side. Then Professor Einstein, his whole figure still conveying good will and amiability, drifted away out of sight. 42

I, too, would be a grade-one thinker. I was irreverent at the best of times. Political and religious systems, social customs, loyalties and traditions, they all came tumbling down like so many rotten apples off a tree. This was a fine hobby and a sensible substitute for cricket, since you could play it all the year round. I came up in the end with what must always remain the justification for grade-one thinking, its sign, seal and charter. I devised a coherent system for living. It was a moral system, which was wholly logical. Of course, as I readily admitted, conversion of the world to my way of thinking might be difficult, since my system did away with a number of trifles, such as big business, centralized government, armies, marriage. . . . 43

It was Ruth all over again. I had some very good friends who stood by me, and still do. But my acquaintances vanished, taking the girls with them. Young women seemed oddly contented with the world as it was. They valued the meaningless ceremony with a ring. Young men, while willing to concede the chaining sordidness of marriage, were hesitant about abandoning the organizations which they hoped would give them a career. A young man on the first rung of the Royal Navy, while perfectly agreeable to doing away with big business and marriage, got as red-necked as Mr. Houghton when I proposed a world without any battleships in it. 44

Had the game gone too far? Was it a game any longer? In those prewar days, I stood to lose a great deal, for the sake of a hobby. 45

Now you are expecting me to describe how I saw the folly of my ways and came back to the warm nest, where prejudices are so often called loyalties, where pointless actions are hallowed into custom by repetition, where we are content to say we think when all we do is feel. 46

But you would be wrong. I dropped my hobby and turned professional. 47

If I were to go back to the headmaster's study and find the dusty statuettes still there, I would arrange them differently. I would dust Venus and put her aside, for I have come to love her and know her for the fair thing she is. But I would put the Thinker, sunk in his desperate thought, where there were shadows before him—and at his back, I would put the leopard, crouched and ready to spring. 48

Questions for Discussion

1. What are the distinguishing features of each of Golding's levels of thinking? Do you know people who exemplify each kind? Are there persons in your college or university—administrators or professors, perhaps—whose wide recognizability make them good examples for the whole class to discuss? Are there times or occasions when even grade-three thinking is defensible? When? Why? If not, why not?
2. Can you point to details in paragraphs 4–16 that reveal Golding as a master storyteller? How do these narratives enhance his essay?
3. In what ways do the three statuettes seem to relate to Golding's three categories of thinking? Why does he rearrange the statuettes so that the leopard seems about to spring onto the back of the thinker? Does this rearrangement imply that Golding has reassessed the difficulty of thinking since he attended grammar school or since he gave it up as a hobby and turned professional?
4. Thinking as a hobby, as a game, seems to match which of Golding's levels of thinking? Does Golding reserve his highest praise for thinking as a

hobby? If he offers criticism of this kind of thinking, what sort of criticism is it and in what paragraphs does he advance it?

5. Do you find that you can identify Golding's three levels of thinking with the kind of thinking that characterizes any particular group or organization in society? Is it possible to say that politicians, for example—or the clergy, business executives, or single-issue proponents—generally fall into one level of thinking rather than another? Can you point to exceptions within groups?

Suggested Essay Topics

1. In an essay directed to your classmates, draw a verbal portrait of the best "grade-one" thinker you have ever personally known. Provide at least one anecdote about this person's thinking habits. The point of your essay is to define first-rate thinking as vividly as possible.

   As you write, think of the devices and strategies that Golding uses to achieve vividness: construction of little scenarios (¶4–16 and ¶37–42), use of images (Mr. Houghton's neck; people warming their hands at the fire of their own prejudices; the headmaster's opaque, flashing spectacles), and use of irony ("It is easy to buy small plaster models of what you think life is like"; "Were my teachers, perhaps, so good that they could not understand the depths of my depravity?"). Try to incorporate some of these devices into the writing of your own essay.

2. Go back through your memory's catalog of former teachers and, in imitation of Golding, pick out a few who exemplify his three levels of thinking. Write a feature article for a magazine or newspaper giving the traits, mannerisms, or examples from their behavior that illustrate the category you placed them in. Make your descriptions of these teachers your main support in an essay designed to persuade the public of the kind of thinking people should demand from teachers as the molders of each new generation.

IDEAS IN DEBATE

Paul Goodman
Karl R. Popper
Kurt Vonnegut, Jr.

Paul Goodman

***A**s you read this essay and the next one, try to ascertain as clearly as possible whether Goodman's and Popper's definitions of* utopian *overlap perfectly, somewhat, or not at all. Also look for the criteria—the standards—by which each author constructs his judgments of utopian thinking. Although Goodman (1911–1972) recommends utopian thinking and Popper rejects it, they will only be in real disagreement if they are each using the same definition. Is their disagreement only apparent or real?*

Your view of other differences between them will depend in large part on how you answer the previous question. For example, Popper is profoundly opposed to violence, whereas Goodman recommends a "new form" of society, "the conflictful community" (¶27), a phrase suggestive, if not of violence, at least of tension and social stress. As you read, try to determine what Goodman means by "conflictful community" and whether it really opposes Popper's "reasonableness" (¶6–8).

Finally, what is each author's overall intention? If the audiences addressed by each writer were completely won over and if they had an accurate understanding of what each author wanted them to believe or do, which opinions and behavior would readers adopt —and which would they abandon?

Asking such questions is not merely an academic exercise, useful only in school. When people who feel hostile and suspicious of each other fail to resolve their differences, it is not always because they are deliberately vicious, implacably pigheaded, or fond of violence. Sometimes people simply fail to understand where their beliefs and values support or contradict each other. Nothing is commoner in politics, for example, than to hear a so-called debate in which nothing gets genuinely debated because the speakers talk right past each other, failing to see that their opinions are not really very far apart. Trying to figure out precisely where Goodman and Popper agree and disagree can serve as a model of the kind of analysis needed to solve some of the world's most serious problems.

UTOPIAN THINKING

From *Utopian Essays and Practical Proposals* (1961).

Let me use ideas of mine as an example, since I am notoriously a "utopian thinker." That is, on problems great and small, I try to think up direct expedients that do not follow the usual procedures, and they are always called "impractical" and an "imposition on people by an intellectual." The question is—and I shall try to pose it fairly—in what sense are such expedients really practical, and in what sense are they really *not* practical? Consider half a dozen little thumbnail ideas.* 1

The ceremony at my boy's public school commencement is poor. We ought to commission the neighborhood writers and musicians to design it. There is talk about aiding the arts, and this is the way to advance them, for, as Goethe said, "The poetry of public occasions is the highest kind." It gives a real subject to the poet, and ennobles the occasion. 2

Similarly, we do not adequately use our best talents. We ought to get our best designers to improve some of the thousands of ugly small towns and make them unique places to be proud of, rather than delegate such matters to professionals in bureaucratic agencies, when we attend to them at all. A few beautiful models would be a great incentive to others. 3

In our educational system, too much is spent for plant and not enough for teachers. Why not try, as a pilot project, doing without the school building altogether for a few hundred kids for most of the day? Conceive of a teacher in charge of a band of ten, using the city itself as the material for the curriculum and the background for the teaching. Since we are teaching *for* life, try to get a little closer to it. My guess is that one could considerably diminish the use of present classrooms and so not have to increase their number. 4

The problem with the old ladies in a Home is to keep them from degenerating, so we must provide geriatric "occupational therapy." The problem with the orphans in their Home is that, for want of individual attention, they may grow up as cold or "psychopathic personalities." But the old ladies could serve as grandmothers for the orphans, to their mutual advantage. The meaning of community is people using one another as resources. 5

It is false to say that community is not possible in a great city, for 6,000,000 can be regarded as 2,000 neighborhoods of 3,000. These make up one metropolis and enjoy its central advantages, yet they can have a variety of particular conditions of life and have different complexes of community functions locally controlled. E.g., many neighborhoods might have local control of their small grade-schools, with the city enforcing 6

*Goodman in fact considers seven ideas.

minimum standards and somewhat equalizing the funds. Political initiative is the means of political education.

In any city, we can appreciably diminish commutation by arranging mutually satisfactory exchanges of residence to be near work. The aim of planning is to diminish in-between services that are neither production nor consumption. More generally, if this wasted time of commutation were considered *economically* as part of the time of labor, there would soon be better planning and more decentralization. 7

In New York City, the automobile traffic is not worth the nuisance it causes. It would be advantageous simply to ban all private cars. Nearly everyone would have faster transportation. Besides, we could then close off about three-quarters of the streets and use them as a fund of land for neighborhood planning. 8

Now, apart from the particular merits or demerits of any of these ideas, what is wrong with this *style* of thinking, which aims at far-reaching social and cultural advantages by direct and rather dumb-bunny expedients? I think that we can see very simply why it is "utopian." 9

It is risky. The writers and musicians designing the commencement ceremony would offend the parents, and the scandal would be politically ruinous to the principal, the school board, and the mayor. Nobody expects the ceremonial to be anything but boring, so let sleeping dogs lie. Artists are conceited anyway and would disdain the commissions. So with the small towns: the "best designers" would make the local hair stand on end. As for the thought of children being educated by roaming the streets and blocking traffic, it is a lulu and the less said the better. 10

Further, such thinking confuses administrative divisions. Community arrangements are always awkwardly multipurpose. What department is responsible? Who budgets? It is inefficient not to have specialized equipment, special buildings, and specialists. 11

Further, community creates conflict, for incompatibles are thrown together. And there is definitely an imposition of values. "Community" is an imposed value, for many people want to be alone instead of sharing responsibilities or satisfactions; that is why they came to the big city. The notion of living near work, or of a work-residence community, implies that people like their work; but most people today don't. 12

Further, most such proposals are probably illegal; there would never be an end to litigation. They override the usual procedures, so there is no experience of the problems that might arise; one cannot assess consequences or refer to standard criteria. 13

Further, they are impracticable. To effect a change in the usual procedures generally requires the pressure of some firm that will profit by it; such things do not happen just because they would be "advantageous"; one can hardly get the most trivial zoning regulation passed. 14

Finally, such proposals are impractical if only because they assume that 15
the mass of people have more sense and energy than they in fact have. In emergencies, people show remarkable fortitude and choose sensible values and agree to practical expedients because it is inevitable; but not ordinarily. The quotation from Goethe is typical; it is "true," but not for us.

This is a fair picture of our dilemma. A direct solution of social problems 16
disturbs too many fixed arrangements. Society either does not want such solutions, or society is not up to them—it comes to the same thing. The possibility of a higher quality of experience arouses distrust rather than enthusiasm. People must be educated slowly. On the other hand, the only way *to* educate them, to change the present tone, is to cut through habits, especially the character-defense of saying "nothing can be done" and withdrawing into conformity and privacy. We must prove by experiment that direct solutions are feasible. To "educate" in the accustomed style only worsens the disease. And if we do *not* improve the standard of our present experience, it will utterly degenerate.

Therefore we must confront the dilemma as our problem. Our present 17
"organized" procedures are simply not good enough to cope with our technological changes. They debase the users of science, they discourage inventive solutions, they complicate rather than simplify, they drive away some of the best minds. Yet other procedures rouse anxiety and seem unrealistic and irresponsible—whether or not they actually are. The question is, what kind of social science can solve a dilemma of this kind? Let us approach this question by deviating to a more philosophical consideration.

Let us attempt a list of postulates for a pragmatic social science: 18

1. The fact that the problem is being studied is a factor in the situation. 19
The experimenter is one of the participants and this already alters the locus of the problem, usefully objectifying it.
2. The experimenter cannot know definitely what he is after, he has no 20
fixed hypothesis to demonstrate, for he hopes that an unthought-of-solution will emerge in the process of coping with the problem. It is an "open" experiment.
3. The experimenter, like the other participants, is "engaged"; he has a 21
moral need to come to a solution, and is therefore willing to change his own conceptions, and even his own character. As Biddle has said: "A hopeful attitude toward man's improvability may become a necessary precondition to further research," for otherwise one cannot morally engage oneself.
4. Since he does not know the outcome, the experimenter must risk confu- 22
sion and conflict, and try out untested expedients. The safeguard is to stay in close contact with the concrete situation and to be objective and accurate in observation and reporting, and rigorous in analysis.

In the context of a pragmatic social science, utopian thinking at once 23
falls into place. Utopian ideas may be practical hypotheses, that is, expedients

for pilot experimentation. Or they may be stimuli for response, so that people get to know what they themselves mean. The fact that such ideas go against the grain of usual thinking is an advantage, for they thereby help to change the locus of the problem, which could not be solved in the usual terms. For instance, they may raise the target of conceivable advantages to a point where certain disadvantages, which were formerly prohibitive, now seem less important. (The assurance of help for an underprivileged child to go to college may make it worth while for him not to become delinquent. This has been the point of the "utopian" Higher Horizons program in the New York City schools.) Further, if a utopian expedient seems *prima facie* sensible, directly feasible, and technically practical, and is nevertheless unacceptable, there is a presumption that we are dealing with an "inner conflict," prejudice, the need to believe that nothing can be done, and the need to maintain the status quo.

As an illustration of the several points of this essay, consider utopian planning for increased face-to-face community, people using one another as resources and sharing more functions of life and society. In a recent discussion I had with Herbert Gans of the University of Pennsylvania and other sociologists, it was agreed by all that our present social fragmentation, individual isolation, and family privacy are undesirable. Yet it was also agreed that to throw people together *as they are*—and how else do we have them?—causes inevitable conflicts. Here is our dilemma. 24

Gans argued that the attempt at community often leads to nothing at all being done, instead of, at least, some useful accommodation. In Levittown, for example, a project in the community school fell through because the middle-class parents wanted a more intensive program to assure their children's "careers" (preparation for "prestige" colleges), whereas the lower-middle-class parents, who had lower status aims, preferred a more "progressive" program. "In such a case," said Gans, "a utopian will give up the program altogether and say that people are stupid." 25

My view is very different. It is that such a conflict is not an obstacle to community but a golden opportunity, *if the give-and-take can continue, if contact can be maintained.* The continuing conflict cuts through the character-defense of people and *defeats* their stupidity, for stupidity is a character-defense. And the heat of the conflict results in better mutual understanding and fraternity. In Levittown, the job of the sociologist should have been not merely to infer the class conflict, but to bring it out into the open, to risk intensifying it by moving also into concealed snobbery and resentment (and racial feeling?), and to confront these people with the *ad hominem* problem: are such things indeed more important to you than, as neighbors, educating your children together? 26

In our era, to combat the emptiness of technological life, we have to think of a new form, the conflictful community. Historically, close community has provided warmth and security, but it has been tyrannical, antiliberal, and static (conformist small towns). We, however, have to do with already thoroughly urbanized individuals with a national culture and a scien- 27 tific technology. The Israeli kibbutzim offer the closest approximation. Some of them have been fanatically dogmatic according to various ideologies, and often tyrannical; nevertheless, their urban Jewish members, rather well educated on the average, have inevitably run into fundamental conflict. Their atmosphere has therefore been sometimes unhappy but never deadening, and they have produced basic social inventions and new character-types. Is such a model improvable and adaptable to cities and industrial complexes? Can widely differing communities be accommodated in a larger federation? How can they be encouraged in modern societies? These are utopian questions.

Questions for Discussion

1. What passages can you point to that, taken together, constitute an adequate definition of Goodman's "utopian thinking"? Does most of the class agree about which passages to use?
2. Can you and other class members come up with examples of people from contemporary life—intellectuals or politicians, say—who seem to fit Goodman's definition of utopian thinkers? Can you think of examples of what Goodman might call anti-utopians?
3. In paragraphs 19–22 Goodman lists four postulates that describe what he calls "a pragmatic social science." How does this description differ, if at all, from a description you might make of the "hard" sciences: physics, chemistry, geology, and so on? Is social science as Goodman conceives of it really capable of achieving the social ends he wants?
4. Have someone who knows the Israeli Kibbutzim do a report that explains what Goodman means when he says the Kibbutzim "offer the closest approximation" to "a new form [of society], the conflictful community" (¶27).

Suggested Essay Topics

1. Take any one of Goodman's miniature arguments in paragraphs 2–8 and use it as a thesis statement for a more developed argument that you make yourself. The essay will be easier to write and probably more effective if you choose a specific audience. It is clear in paragraph 8, for example, that the intended audience is residents of New York City, not just anyone. Once you pick your audience, you may want to revise or refine the thesis statement to fit that audience better.
2. This suggestion is a variation on topic 1. Using Goodman's statements in paragraphs 2–8 as a model, construct a thesis of your own that recommends some significant kind of social change or reform; then develop reasons to show why your recommendations are both advantageous and workable.

Karl R. Popper

Philosopher Karl Popper (b. 1902) was born and educated in Vienna, but he taught and wrote at the University of London from 1945 until his retirement in 1969.

We are replacing our usual introduction with another demonstration of "How to Read an Argument." This demonstration is more extended than the one following Norman Cousins's essay (pp. 30–35). Here we offer first some suggestions about how to read an essay like Popper's. Then we follow the essay with an analysis that "walks through" the essay point by point.

How to Read an Argument: Demonstration II

By now you have seen that arguments reveal a variety of purposes, tones, and shapes: sleek and streamlined, colloquial and chatty, complicated and interlocking, formal and lofty, and so on. The different varieties, moreover, require different kinds of reading skills. Our early demonstration of how to read the kind of argument used by Norman Cousins in "How to Make People Smaller Than They Are" provides only a start, on one kind of essay.

Popper's essay, "Utopia and Violence," is strikingly different from Cousins's in both structure and tone. While Cousins's kind of essay uses simple language and makes broad points unsupported by extended argument, Popper's essay relies on (1) complex thought (the author troubles himself throughout to qualify, define, and explain with precision), (2) formal tone (he uses the vocabulary and sentence structure of someone engaged in a serious task directed at an educated audience), (3) analytical methodology (he elaborately separates his position into parts), and (4) intellectual intent (he primarily addresses his audience's capacity for thoughtful rather than emotional response).

To inexperienced readers such arguments often seem a tangle of briars in which they wander lost and frustrated, annoyed at the teacher for assigning such thorny stuff and becoming increasingly gloomy about the chances of escaping with any dignity or understanding. Unfortunately, there are no secret maps for keeping one's bearings inside such arguments—if there were, none of us would require either practice or intelligence. But there are some guideposts that can help to point us in the right direction. What follows here is a list of questions to ask as one reads essays like Popper's. Trying to fit the answers into a coherent reading of the text will move one toward a genuine "meeting" with a new and challenging author, even when, as is almost always the case, the text still refuses to yield itself up completely.

1. Topic. *What is the author's topic—the general area of interest and concern being dealt with?*

2. Thesis. *What is the author's thesis—that is, what specific proposition or hypothesis concerning the general* topic *is the author making? The* thesis *is a proposition that the author wants to persuade the reader to believe.*

3. Definitions of Terms. *What words or phrases seem crucial to the author's argument, and what meanings, explicit or implied, does he or she focus on throughout the essay? It is only by thinking hard about definitions that we turn* words *into the* terms *that form the elements of an author's argument.*

4. Evidence: Facts, Examples, Statistics, Analogies, and the Like. *Good readers persistently ask authors, at every step in a given argument, "What's your evidence?" Authors often openly welcome the question, especially those who exhibit great care and formality in their reasoning. And most authors, if their tasks are at all serious, in some way anticipate our habit of questioning the evidence. But the answers will vary greatly from author to author and from subject to subject, both in kind and quality. For some subjects, some authors will ask us to take examples from "real life," or even invented examples, as hard proof. (Much of Einstein's evidence in his early papers consisted of "thought experiments" that could not possibly be carried out in reality.) Other authors will offer us extensive statistical analyses. Others still will depend on analogies; astronomers often have to do so. When used appropriately, examples and analogies count as evidence. They often constitute the only kinds of evidence we can lay our hands on. Thus they are not to be automatically despised or dismissed because they are not scientific or factual. One mark of a liberal education is to know what kinds of evidence are appropriate, or even possible, in a given subject. As Aristotle says, it is foolish to ask for greater precision of proof than a given subject allows.*

The only rule for the reader, then, is to check in every case to discover whether the required kind of evidence has in fact been offered. What an author says *supports a claim must really do so. Controversies in all areas of life often revolve around just this issue, because no one has ever been able to formulate a uniform "code of evidence" applicable to all cases of serious reasoning.*

The most frequently praised kind of evidence these days is probably "the facts." Even people who fiercely dispute their interpretation and significance generally agree that once "facts" are ascertained, they must *be taken into account. To many people, the "harder" or more solid a fact is, the more weight it carries: the height of Mt. Everest, the atomic weight of elements, the statistics about lung cancer, the life expectancy of American females, or the size of the gross national product. To others, a sensation, a feeling, a dream, an ambition, or a sense of awe can qualify as a fact.*

Obviously the whole realm of discourse would be a lot easier to manage if facts had an intrinsic, self-announcing quality that set them off into easily recognizable categories—but they do not. No datum simply is *a relevant fact; it* becomes *a fact in an argument as one decides how it can be used to support a conclusion. Nothing is more common than debaters denying the relevance, or even the solidity, of each other's facts. (See Edward Carr, "The Historian and His Facts," pp. 575–583, and the introduction to that essay.) Despite their elusiveness, however, they can be the strongest kind of evidence whenever both parties to a discussion can agree about what they are. To insert them successfully into an argument is like thumping a trump card on an opponent's ace.*

5. Literary Devices. *Literary devices—such as personification, imagery, hyperbole, and irony—are sometimes powerfully persuasive. Metaphors are especially important. Sometimes their effect is local, limited to a particular sentence or paragraph, as when we said that reading some essays is like getting lost in a briar patch. But sometimes they exert a controlling influence over both the meaning and the structure of a whole argument. (For a discussion of metaphors, see the selection by Lakoff and Johnson beginning on page 190, and for an example of an argument controlled throughout by a single dominant metaphor, see the selection by Plato beginning on page 411.) If we had said, for example, that reading essays is like diving for pearls (you take a deep breath, plunge into alien waters, grab frantically at all of the oysters you can pry loose, and finally pop to the surface hoping you've snagged a pearl somewhere in your take), and if we had tried to make everything else we said about reading consistent with our pearl-diving metaphor,* then *we would have been operating under the influence of a controlling metaphor. Not every author relies on extended metaphors, and not all authors are even conscious of what metaphors they do use. But metaphors are usually present in an essay (some scholars, like Lakoff and Johnson, claim they are inescapable), and whenever metaphors occur, they, like all other literary devices, are crucially important.*

6. Assumptions. *All arguments take some things for granted in order to get themselves launched. Even positions that rely, like Popper's, on close reasoning still rest on a foundation of (implied or stated) ideas, principles, or value judgments that the author simply* assumes *to be true; demonstrations of their truth are seldom offered, although they may be subject to rational criticism and defense elsewhere.*

In order to make this argument about how to read certain kinds of essays, for example, we unavoidably rest our case on several assumptions. We assume, first, that the essays we read together have coherent meanings that are, on the whole, "public" and not just private. Otherwise we could not talk about ways of drawing out those meanings for general discussion. Second, we assume that it is better to get at an author's meaning by means of a systematic method, analyzing an argument for topic, thesis, definitions, assumptions, and so on. Third, we assume that this method can itself be discussed—it, too, is coherent and can be publicly assessed—and it can be duplicated and applied to any number of arguments. If we were operating on a contrary set of assumptions—that nonreplicable and unsystematic private intuitions were the foundation of all understanding—then we would have no business describing a method *for reading an essay.*

Each of our assumptions, like those behind any argument, might be challenged and in turn defended. But whether we choose to accept or reject an author's assumptions, it is essential to our understanding to identify them.

7. Logical Coherence. *Once an author's assumptions have been uncovered, the reader is ready to ask questions about logical inference. We all feel that catching an author in an illogicality weighs heavily against a conclusion. Whenever authors contradict themselves, claim to have proved something that they have only asserted, cite inappropriate or inconclusive evidence, fail to cite evidence where it is necessary,* *ignore evidence that undercuts their case, call their opponents names instead of disproving their arguments, and jump over large areas of argumentative terrain that need to be surveyed, they have (at least partially) discredited their position. They may even have discredited themselves personally, giving the impression that they are "up to something" or that they are tackling a task beyond their abilities. In short, we all have a strong sense that the logical relationships within a position are among the most important determiners of its credibility.*

The logic of an argument can be assessed by readers in three ways: first, by analyzing the formal relationships between premises and conclusions, an activity that can be done in a highly technical way by logicians and philosophers but can also be done in a less technical way by the general reader (see the section on "logical fallacies" in your rhetoric book or handbook and "What Is an Argument?" in this book, pp. 19–22); second, by testing an author's claims against whatever knowledge, experience, and evidence of your own you happen to possess; and third, by testing an author's claims against your intuitions, sometimes even in the absence of hard evidence or reasons, about what makes "good sense."

None of these is an infallible test of an author's logic, but they are all that we have to work with. The places to look sharp for logical connections or illogical jumps are at points of transition, when terms of conclusion such as hence, therefore, *and* finally *appear, and at points where examples and metaphors are offered. These are the places where authors sometimes fail to link the parts of their arguments together tightly. The reader can test the "tightness" by going back to a concluding term and tracing the links that lead up to it or by asking critically whether the example or metaphor really applies in the way that the author claims.*

8. Overall Structure. *All the while you are asking our first seven questions about an essay, you are in fact working to discover the structure of the argument—progressing a long way toward discovering the steps, large and small, that the author is taking. A final way of checking your reconstruction is to look again at all of the "signals of transition" that provide clues about where the author* thinks *the argument has come from and where it is going: transitional paragraphs only one or two sentences long; words like* therefore, then, thus, so, hence, nevertheless, finally; *and designations of series, such as* first, second, what's more. *Though you may have attempted an outline of the essay at earlier points, it may sometimes be only at this final moment of synthesis that you can construct one that satisfies you fully.*

Now, keeping these eight guideposts in mind, read Popper's essay as critically as you can. Although we will offer our analysis of "Utopia and Violence" at the end of the essay, try to construct your own before you read ours. You will then be better able to assess whether we have followed our own guideposts well or badly.

UTOPIA AND VIOLENCE

From *Conjectures and Refutations: The Growth of Scientific Knowledge* (1963; 2d ed. 1965; 3d ed. 1969; we are reprinting from the 2d ed.).

There are many people who hate violence and are convinced that it is one of their foremost and at the same time one of their most hopeful tasks to work for its reduction and, if possible, for its elimination from human life. I am among these hopeful enemies of violence. I not only hate violence, but I firmly believe that the fight against it is not at all hopeless. I realize that the task is difficult. I realize that, only too often in the course of history, it has happened that what appeared at first to be a great success in the fight against violence was followed by defeat. I do not overlook the fact that the new age of violence which was opened by the two world wars is by no means at an end. Nazism and Fascism are thoroughly beaten, but I must admit that their defeat does not mean that barbarism and brutality have been defeated. On the contrary, it is no use closing our eyes to the fact that these hateful ideas achieved something like victory in defeat. I have to admit that Hitler succeeded in degrading the moral standards of our Western world, and that in the world of today there is more violence and brutal force than would have been tolerated even in the decade after the first world war. And we must face the possibility that our civilization may ultimately be destroyed by those new weapons which Hitlerism wished upon us, perhaps even within the first decade* after the second world war; for no doubt the spirit of Hitlerism won its greatest victory over us when, after its defeat, we used the weapons which the threat of Nazism had induced us to develop. But in spite of all this I am today no less hopeful than I have ever been that violence can be defeated. It is our only hope; and long stretches in the history of Western as well as of Eastern civilizations prove that it need not be a vain hope—that violence *can* be reduced, and brought under the control of reason. 1

This is perhaps why I, like many others, believe in reason; why I call myself a rationalist. I am a rationalist because I see in the attitude of reasonableness the only alternative to violence. 2

When two men disagree, they do so either because their opinions differ, or because their interests differ, or both. There are many kinds of disagreement in social life which must be decided one way or another. The question may be one which must be settled, because failure to settle it may create new difficulties whose cumulative effects may cause an intolerable strain, such as a state of continual and intense preparation for deciding the issue. (An armaments race is an example.) To reach a decision may be a necessity. 3

How can a decision be reached? There are, in the main, only two possible ways: argument (including arguments submitted to arbitration, for example to some international court of justice) and violence. Or, if it is interests 4

*This was written in 1947. Today I should alter this passage merely by replacing "first" by "second." [Popper's note.]

that clash, the two alternatives are a reasonable compromise or an attempt to destroy the opposing interest.

A rationalist, as I use the word, is a man who attempts to reach decisions 5
by argument and perhaps, in certain cases, by compromise, rather than by violence. He is a man who would rather be unsuccessful in convincing another man by argument than successful in crushing him by force, by intimidation and threats, or even by persuasive propaganda.

We shall understand better what I mean by reasonableness if we con- 6
sider the difference between trying to convince a man by argument and trying to persuade him by propaganda.

The difference does not lie so much in the use of argument. Propaganda 7
often uses argument too. Nor does the difference lie in our conviction that our arguments are conclusive, and must be admitted to be conclusive by any reasonable man. It lies rather in an attitude of give and take, in a readiness not only to convince the other man but also possibly to be convinced by him. What I call the attitude of reasonableness may be characterized by a remark like this: "I think I am right, but I may be wrong and you may be right, and in any case let us discuss it, for in this way we are likely to get nearer to a true understanding than if we each merely insist that we are right."

It will be realized that what I call the attitude of reasonableness or the 8
rationalistic attitude presupposes a certain amount of intellectual humility. Perhaps only those can take it up who are aware that they are sometimes wrong, and who do not habitually forget their mistakes. It is born of the realization that we are not omniscient, and that we owe most of our knowledge to others. It is an attitude which tries as far as possible to transfer to the field of opinions in general the two rules of every legal proceeding: first, that one should always hear both sides, and secondly, that one does not make a good judge if one is a party to the case.

I believe that we can avoid violence only in so far as we practise this 9
attitude of reasonableness when dealing with one another in social life; and that any other attitude is likely to produce violence—even a one-sided attempt to deal with others by gentle persuasion, and to convince them by argument and example of those insights we are proud of possessing, and of whose truth we are absolutely certain. We all remember how many religious wars were fought for a religion of love and gentleness; how many bodies were burned alive with the genuinely kind intention of saving souls from the eternal fire of hell. Only if we give up our authoritarian attitude in the realm of opinion, only if we establish the attitude of give and take, of readiness to learn from other people, can we hope to control acts of violence inspired by piety and duty.

There are many difficulties impeding the rapid spread of reasonableness. 10
One of the main difficulties is that it always takes two to make a discussion reasonable. Each of the parties must be ready to learn from the other. You cannot have a rational discussion with a man who prefers shooting you to being convinced by you. In other words, there are limits to the attitude of reasonableness. It is the same with tolerance. You must not, without qualifi-

cation, accept the principle of tolerating all those who are intolerant; if you do, you will destroy not only yourself, but also the attitude of tolerance. (All this is indicated in the remark I made before—that reasonableness must be an attitude of *give and take.*)

An important consequence of all this is that we must not allow the distinction between attack and defence to become blurred. We must insist upon this distinction, and support and develop social institutions (national as well as international) whose function it is to discriminate between aggression and resistance to aggression. 11

I think I have said enough to make clear what I intend to convey by calling myself a rationalist. My rationalism is not dogmatic. I fully admit that I cannot rationally prove it. I frankly confess that I choose rationalism because I hate violence, and I do not deceive myself into believing that this hatred has any rational grounds. Or to put it another way, my rationalism is not self-contained, but rests on an irrational faith in the attitude of reasonableness. I do not see that we can go beyond this. One could say, perhaps, that my irrational faith in equal and reciprocal rights to convince others and be convinced by them is a faith in human reason; or simply, that I believe in man. 12

If I say that I believe in man, I mean in man as he is; and I should never dream of saying that he is wholly rational. I do not think that a question such as whether man is more rational than emotional or *vice versa* should be asked: there are no ways of assessing or comparing such things. I admit that I feel inclined to protest against certain exaggerations (arising largely from a vulgarization of psycho-analysis) of the irrationality of man and of human society. But I am aware not only of the power of emotions in human life, but also of their value. I should never demand that the attainment of an attitude of reasonableness should become the one dominant aim of our lives. All I wish to assert is that this attitude can become one that is never wholly absent—not even in relationships which are dominated by great passions, such as love.* 13

My fundamental attitude towards the problem of reason and violence will by now be understood; and I hope I share it with some of my readers and with many other people everywhere. It is on this basis that I now propose to discuss the problem of Utopianism. 14

I think we can describe Utopianism as a result of a form of rationalism, and I shall try to show that this is a form of rationalism very different from the form in which I and many others believe. So I shall try to show that there exist at least two forms of rationalism, one of which I believe is right and the other wrong; and that the wrong kind of rationalism is the one which leads to Utopianism. 15

As far as I can see, Utopianism is the result of a way of reasoning which is accepted by many who would be astonished to hear that this apparently 16

*The existentialist Jaspers writes, "This is why love is cruel, ruthless; and why it is believed in, by the genuine lover, only if it is so." This attitude, to my mind, reveals weakness rather than the strength it wishes to show; it is not so much plain barbarism as an hysterical attempt to play the barbarian. (*Cf.* my *Open Society,* 4th edn., vol. II, p. 317.) [Popper's note.]

quite inescapable and self-evident way of reasoning leads to Utopian results. This specious reasoning can perhaps be presented in the following manner.

An action, it may be argued, is rational if it makes the best use of the 17
available means in order to achieve a certain end. The end, admittedly, may be incapable of being determined rationally. However this may be, we can judge an action rationally, and describe it as rational or adequate, only relative to some given end. Only if we have an end in mind, and only relative to such an end, can we say that we are acting rationally.

Now let us apply this argument to politics. All politics consists of 18
actions; and these actions will be rational only if they pursue some end. The end of a man's political actions may be the increase of his own power or wealth. Or it may perhaps be the improvement of the laws of the state, a change in the structure of the state.

In the latter case political action will be rational only if we first deter- 19
mine the final ends of the political changes which we intend to bring about. It will be rational only relative to certain ideas of what a state ought to be like. Thus it appears that as a preliminary to any rational political action we must first attempt to become as clear as possible about our ultimate political ends; for example the kind of state which we should consider the best; and only afterwards can we begin to determine the means which may best help us to realize this state, or to move slowly towards it, taking it as the aim of an historical process which we may to some extent influence and steer towards the goal selected.

Now it is precisely this view which I call Utopianism. Any rational and 20
nonselfish political action, on this view, must be preceded by a determination of our ultimate ends, not merely of intermediate or partial aims which are only steps towards our ultimate end, and which therefore should be considered as means rather than as ends; therefore rational political action must be based upon a more or less clear and detailed description or blueprint of our ideal state, and also upon a plan or blueprint of the historical path that leads towards this goal.

I consider what I call Utopianism an attractive and, indeed, an all too 21
attractive theory; for I also consider it dangerous and pernicious. It is, I believe, self-defeating, and it leads to violence.

That it is self-defeating is connected with the fact that it is impossible 22
to determine ends scientifically. There is no scientific way of choosing between two ends. Some people, for example, love and venerate violence. For them a life without violence would be shallow and trivial. Many others, of whom I am one, hate violence. This is a quarrel about ends. It cannot be decided by science. This does not mean that the attempt to argue against violence is necessarily a waste of time. It only means that you may not be able to argue with the admirer of violence. He has a way of answering an argument with a bullet if he is not kept under control by the threat of counter-violence. If he is willing to listen to your arguments without shooting you, then he is at least infected by rationalism, and you may, perhaps, win him over. This is why arguing is no waste of time—as long as people listen to you. But you

cannot, by means of argument, make people listen to argument; you cannot, by means of argument, convert those who suspect all argument, and who prefer violent decisions to rational decisions. You cannot prove to them that they are wrong. And this is only a particular case, which can be generalized. No decision about aims can be established by *purely* rational or scientific means. Nevertheless argument may prove extremely helpful in reaching a decision about aims.

Applying all this to the problem of Utopianism, we must first be quite clear that the problem of constructing a Utopian blueprint cannot possibly be solved by science alone. Its aims, at least, must be given before the social scientist can begin to sketch his blueprint. We find the same situation in the natural sciences. No amount of physics will tell a scientist that it is the right thing for him to construct a plough, or an aeroplane, or an atomic bomb. Ends must be adopted by him, or given to him; and what he does *qua* [as] scientist is only to construct means by which these ends can be realized. 23

In emphasizing the difficulty of deciding, by way of rational argument, between different Utopian ideals, I do not wish to create the impression that there is a realm—such as the realm of ends—which goes altogether beyond the power of rational criticism (even though I certainly wish to say that the realm of ends goes largely beyond the power of *scientific* argument). For I myself try to argue about this realm; and by pointing out the difficulty of deciding between competing Utopian blueprints, I try to argue rationally against choosing ideal ends of this kind. Similarly, my attempt to point out that this difficulty is likely to produce violence is meant as a rational argument, although it will appeal only to those who hate violence. 24

That the Utopian method, which chooses an ideal state of society as the aim which all our political actions should serve, is likely to produce violence can be shown thus. Since we cannot determine the ultimate ends of political actions scientifically, or by purely rational methods, differences of opinion concerning what the ideal state should be like cannot always be smoothed out by the method of argument. They will at least partly have the character of religious differences. And there can be no tolerance between these different Utopian religions. Utopian aims are designed to serve as a basis for rational political action and discussion, and such action appears to be possible only if the aim is definitely decided upon. Thus the Utopianist must win over, or else crush, his Utopianist competitors who do not share his own Utopian aims and who do not profess his own Utopianist religion. 25

But he has to do more. He has to be very thorough in eliminating and stamping out all heretical competing views. For the way to the Utopian goal is long. Thus the rationality of his political action demands constancy of aim for a long time ahead; and this can only be achieved if he not merely crushes competing Utopian religions, but as far as possible stamps out all memory of them. 26

The use of violent methods for the suppression of competing aims becomes even more urgent if we consider that the period of Utopian construction is liable to be one of social change. In such a time ideas are liable to 27 change also. Thus what may have appeared to many as desirable at the time when the Utopian blueprint was decided upon may appear less desirable at a later date. If this is so, the whole approach is in danger of breaking down. For if we change our ultimate political aims while attempting to move towards them we may soon discover that we are moving in circles. The whole method of first establishing an ultimate political aim and then preparing to move towards it must be futile if the aim may be changed during the process of its realization. It may easily turn out that the steps so far taken lead in fact away from the new aim. And if we then change direction in accordance with our new aim we expose ourselves to the same risk. In spite of all the sacrifices which we may have made in order to make sure that we are acting rationally, we may get exactly nowhere—although not exactly to that "nowhere" which is meant by the word "Utopia."

Again, the only way to avoid such changes of our aims seems to be to 28
use violence, which includes propaganda, the suppression of criticism, and the annihilation of all opposition. With it goes the affirmation of the wisdom and foresight of the Utopian planners, of the Utopian engineers who design and execute the Utopian blueprint. The Utopian engineers must in this way become omniscient as well as omnipotent. They become gods. Thou shalt have no other Gods before them.

Utopian rationalism is a self-defeating rationalism. However benevo- 29
lent its ends, it does not bring happiness, but only the familiar misery of being condemned to live under a tyrannical government.

It is important to understand this criticism fully. I do not criticize politi- 30
cal ideals as such, nor do I assert that a political ideal can never be realized. This would not be a valid criticism. Many ideals have been realized which were once dogmatically declared to be unrealizable, for example, the establishment of workable and untyrannical institutions for securing civil peace, that is, for the suppression of crime within the state. Again, I see no reason why an international judicature and an international police force should be less successful in suppressing international crime, that is, national aggression and the ill-treatment of minorities or perhaps majorities. I do not object to the attempt to realize such ideals.

Wherein, then, lies the difference between those benevolent Utopian 31
plans to which I object because they lead to violence, and those other important and far-reaching political reforms which I am inclined to recommend?

If I were to give a simple formula or recipe for distinguishing between 32
what I consider to be admissible plans for social reform and inadmissible Utopian blueprints, I might say:

Work for the elimination of concrete evils rather than for the realization 33
of abstract goods. Do not aim at establishing happiness by political means. Rather aim at the elimination of concrete miseries. Or, in more practical terms: fight for the elimination of poverty by direct means—for example, by making sure that everybody has a minimum income. Or fight against epidemics and disease by erecting hospitals and schools of medicine. Fight illiteracy as you fight criminality. But do all this by direct means. Choose what you

consider the most urgent evil of the society in which you live, and try patiently to convince people that we can get rid of it.

But do not try to realize these aims indirectly by designing and working 34
for a distant ideal of a society which is wholly good. However deeply you may feel indebted to its inspiring vision, do not think that you are obliged to work for its realization, or that it is your mission to open the eyes of others to its beauty. Do not allow your dreams of a beautiful world to lure you away from the claims of men who suffer here and now. Our fellow men have a claim to our help; no generation must be sacrificed for the sake of future generations, for the sake of an ideal of happiness that may never be realized. In brief, it is my thesis that human misery is the most urgent problem of a rational public policy and that happiness is not such a problem. The attainment of happiness should be left to our private endeavours.

It is a fact, and not a very strange fact, that it is not so very difficult to 35
reach agreement by discussion on what are the most intolerable evils of our society, and on what are the most urgent social reforms. Such an agreement can be reached much more easily than an agreement concerning some ideal form of social life. For the evils are with us here and now. They can be experienced, and are being experienced every day, by many people who have been and are being made miserable by poverty, unemployment, national oppression, war and disease. Those of us who do not suffer from these miseries meet every day others who can describe them to us. This is what makes the evils concrete. This is why we can get somewhere in arguing about them; why we can profit here from the attitude of reasonableness. We can learn by listening to concrete claims, by patiently trying to assess them as impartially as we can, and by considering ways of meeting them without creating worse evils.

With ideal goods it is different. These we know only from our dreams 36
and from the dreams of our poets and prophets. They cannot be discussed, only proclaimed from the housetops. They do not call for the rational attitude of the impartial judge, but for the emotional attitude of the impassioned preacher.

The Utopianist attitude, therefore, is opposed to the attitude of reason- 37
ableness. Utopianism, even though it may often appear in a rationalist disguise, cannot be more than a pseudo-rationalism.

What, then, is wrong with the apparently rational argument which I 38
outlined when presenting the Utopianist case? I believe that it is quite true that we can judge the rationality of an action only in relation to some aims or ends. But this does not necessarily mean that the rationality of a political action can be judged only in relation to an *historical* end. And it surely does not mean that we must consider every social or political situation merely from the point of view of some preconceived historical ideal, from the point of view of an alleged ultimate aim of the development of history. On the contrary, if among our aims and ends there is anything conceived in terms of human happiness and misery, then we are bound to judge our actions in terms not only of possible contributions to the happiness of man in a distant

future, but also of their more immediate effects. We must not argue that a certain social situation is a mere means to an end on the grounds that it is merely a transient historical situation. For all situations are transient. Similarly we must not argue that the misery of one generation may be considered as a mere means to the end of securing the lasting happiness of some later generation or generations; and this argument is improved neither by a high degree of promised happiness nor by a large number of generations profiting by it. All generations are transient. All have an equal right to be considered, but our immediate duties are undoubtedly to the present generation and to the next. Besides, we should never attempt to balance anybody's misery against somebody else's happiness.

With this the apparently rational arguments of Utopianism dissolve into 39
nothing. The fascination which the future exerts upon the Utopianist has nothing to do with rational foresight. Considered in this light the violence which Utopianism breeds looks very much like the running amok of an evolutionist metaphysics, of an hysterical philosophy of history, eager to sacrifice the present for the splendours of the future, and unaware that its principle would lead to sacrificing each particular future period for one which comes after it; and likewise unaware of the trivial truth that the ultimate future of man—whatever fate may have in store for him—can be nothing more splendid than his ultimate extinction.

The appeal of Utopianism arises from the failure to realize that we 40
cannot make heaven on earth. What I believe we can do instead is to make life a little less terrible and a little less unjust in each generation. A good deal can be achieved in this way. Much has been achieved in the last hundred years. More could be achieved by our own generation. There are many pressing problems which we might solve, at least partially, such as helping the weak and the sick, and those who suffer under oppression and injustice; stamping out unemployment; equalizing opportunities; and preventing international crime, such as blackmail and war instigated by men like gods, by omnipotent and omniscient leaders. All this we might achieve if only we could give up dreaming about distant ideals and fighting over our Utopian blueprints for a new world and a new man. Those of us who believe in man as he is, and who have therefore not given up the hope of defeating violence and unreason, must demand instead that every man should be given the right to arrange his life himself so far as this is compatible with the equal rights of others.

We can see here that the problem of the true and the false rationalisms 41
is part of a larger problem. Ultimately it is the problem of a sane attitude towards our own existence and its limitations—that very problem of which so much is made now by those who call themselves "Existentialists," the expounders of a new theology without God. There is, I believe, a neurotic and even an hysterical element in this exaggerated emphasis upon the fundamental loneliness of man in a godless world, and upon the resulting tension between the self and the world. I have little doubt that this hysteria is closely akin to Utopian romanticism, and also to the ethic of hero-worship, to an

ethic that can comprehend life only in terms of "dominate or prostrate yourself." And I do not doubt that this hysteria is the secret of its strong appeal. That our problem is part of a larger one can be seen from the fact that we can find a clear parallel to the split between true and false rationalism even in a sphere apparently so far removed from rationalism as that of religion. Christian thinkers have interpreted the relationship between man and God in at least two very different ways. The sane one may be expressed by: "Never forget that men are not Gods; but remember that there is a divine spark in them." The other exaggerates the tension between man and God, and the baseness of man as well as the heights to which men may aspire. It introduces the ethic of "dominate or prostrate yourself" into the relationship of man and God. Whether there are always either conscious or unconscious dreams of godlikeness and of omnipotence at the roots of this attitude, I do not know. But I think it is hard to deny that the emphasis on this tension can arise only from an unbalanced attitude towards the problem of power.

This unbalanced (and immature) attitude is obsessed with the problem 42
of power, not only over other men, but also over our natural environment—over the world as a whole. What I might call, by analogy, the "false religion," is obsessed not only by God's power over men but also by His power to create a world; similarly, false rationalism is fascinated by the idea of creating huge machines and Utopian social worlds. Bacon's "knowledge is power" and Plato's "rule of the wise" are different expressions of this attitude which, at bottom, is one of claiming power on the basis of one's superior intellectual gifts. The true rationalist, by contrast, will always know how little he knows, and he will be aware of the simple fact that whatever critical faculty or reason he may possess he owes to intellectual intercourse with others. He will be inclined, therefore, to consider men as fundamentally equal, and human reason as a bond which unites them. Reason for him is the precise opposite of an instrument of power and violence: he sees it as a means whereby these may be tamed.

Analysis of "Utopia and Violence"

If we apply our method for reading an argument to Popper's essay, what does it yield? Let us look systematically at all eight guideposts.

1. Topic. *Popper begins in paragraph 1 by making three claims: (1) that he along with many other persons hates violence, (2) that the world has become increasingly violent in the aftermath of the two world wars, and (3) that he remains nevertheless convinced that violence can be reduced and "brought under the control of reason." Doing so, he says, "is our only hope." Apparently, then, Popper's* topic *is the relationship between reason and violence. Notice, however, that this is only a general area of concern. Discovering that Popper is interested in the relationship between reason and violence does not reveal what direction his concern will take or what point about that relationship he wants to make. In other words, we know his topic but not his thesis.*

2. Thesis. *Notice that paragraph 2 is very short, only two sentences long. Such paragraphs are often transitional. This one sums up the point of paragraph 1, but in doing so Popper manages to indicate clearly his thesis, the point he wants to make: "I see in the attitude of reasonableness the only alternative to violence."*

3. Definitions of Terms. *We know from Popper's thesis statement that there are two crucial terms in his argument,* reasonableness *and* violence. *The second of these he does not define in any special way. He seems to take it for granted that we all know what violence is, and, indeed, his incidental allusions to violence are all conventional: people shooting each other, aggression between nations, certain kinds of oppression by political rulers, and so on.*

Reasonableness, *however, has for him a very precise, special meaning, and he expends a considerable amount of effort and space clarifying this key term. He begins by saying what it is not. Reasonableness, he contends, is not merely knowing how to use reason in order to make arguments. Propagandists, tyrants, and oppressors of all sorts know how to use reason to make arguments. Rather, reasonableness "lies . . . in an attitude of give and take, in a readiness not only to convince the other man but also possibly to be convinced by him" (¶7).*

But what does give-and-take *mean? Primarily it means "humility," "the realization that we are not omniscient, and that we owe most of our knowledge to others" (¶8). (Notice, by the way, that Popper repeats this idea clearly at the end of his essay [¶42]: "The true rationalist . . . will always know . . . that whatever . . . reason he may possess he owes to intellectual intercourse with others." The more times an author repeats an idea in the course of an essay, especially if the repetitions come at key spots such as the beginning and the end, the more you are justified in assuming that the idea possesses central importance.)*

In paragraph 9 we learn that humility is not only the admission that we have learned most of what we know from others, but that even our most precious values, even our certainties, are still susceptible to correction. Good intentions do not automatically produce good effects. In the Middle Ages torture was accepted as a device not only for discovering the truth, but also for making wrong-doers confess so that their souls might be saved even as their bodies perished. And in the modern period every violent revolution has produced mass killings by those whose sole professed aim was to create a better society. The number of victims maimed, tortured, and killed in any period would be much smaller if all certainties had been subject to give-and-take. Popper's point is that no *belief, no matter how noble or true, allows us to assume our own infallibility; even if our opinions are true, we can never* know *them to be true in an absolute sense, and, in any event, inflicting pain, destruction, and violence, even in the interests of true opinions, involves us in an irreconcilable contradiction between the nobility of our aims and the ignobility of our methods.*

Another term that Popper defines with precision (although it takes less effort because it is derived from his term reasonableness*) is the word* rationalist. *A rationalist, as Popper uses the term, is simply a person committed to give-and-take, to tolerance, and to compromise (at least about conflicts of interest, if not about conflicts of opinion) when give-and-take is abandoned by those he is trying to talk to.*

A fourth crucial term, utopianism, *does not show up until paragraph 14. As with the term* reasonableness, *you can form a fairly clear notion of its importance in Popper's argument simply from the amount of discussion he devotes to its clarification. Reasonableness, it turns out, is the hero of his piece; utopianism is the villain. Notice here, by the way, how metaphors exert a controlling influence on one's understanding. The metaphor of "heroes versus villains," which comes from melodramas and westerns, is not used by Popper;* we *use it in trying to understand him. Notice further that if we were to base our analysis on this metaphor alone, we would trivialize his argument.*

Yet our metaphor is appropriate if we apply it with caution, for Popper really intends not only to reveal the evil consequences of accepting utopianism, but to discredit it so thoroughly that no thinking person could retain faith in it after reading his argument. While avoiding melodramatic metaphors, he nevertheless suggests that this is a showdown, that he has viewed this evil phenomenon long enough to be convinced of its dangerousness, that he has thought out his arguments with care and precision, and that he is determined to leave no chink for utopianism to weasel through.

As he develops his views on utopianism at length (¶15–29), we see that he has two main charges to level against it: "It is, I believe, self-defeating, and it leads to violence" (¶21). If this were self-evident to everyone, merely to say it would be at once to express the argument and to prove it. But it is not self-evident, and that is what justifies drawing out the argument. Far from being obviously evil, utopianism, claims Popper, is "an all too attractive theory" (¶21) "which is accepted by many who would be astonished to hear" that it leads inescapably to violence (¶16). These claims place on Popper two burdens: first, to show how *utopianism leads to violence and, second, to show* why *it is attractive (and, necessarily, why its attractiveness is illusory).*

Utopianism is attractive because, by definition, it is a form of rationalism (although unlike reasonableness), and it may therefore seem a credible mode of thinking to anyone who values rationality (¶15). It looks *rational because it engages in the process of constructing means to achieve already chosen ends (¶20). But, Popper claims, looks are in this case deceptive, for utopianism is "specious reasoning" (¶16), which is to say fair-looking but false.*

The falseness of utopianism lies not so much in looking for means to achieve aims—this is rational enough—but in choosing aims that are so difficult to define and so impossible to achieve that they lead inevitably (or so he claims) to violence among those responsible for achieving them. "Utopianists" move "rationally" toward the ideal *state, and* that, *says Popper, is where the trouble begins. Ideal ends, by definition, exist both so far removed from everyday experience and so far removed into the future that "differences of opinion concerning what the ideal state should be like cannot always be smoothed out by the method of argument. They will at least partly have the character of religious differences. And there can be no tolerance between these different Utopian religions" (¶25). Moreover, goals lying so far removed from experience and so far into the future cannot be kept in focus if competing views and shifts of goals are allowed. Thus, on its way toward the noble aim of creating a perfect society, utopianism always winds up employing means that not only create an imperfect society (presumably what we all begin with anyway) but the most imperfect form of society altogether: a totalitarianism that sacrifices everything in the present—the justice, comfort, security, and peace of the present generation—for the good of the ideal future state.*

It should be clear by this point that a full understanding of crucial terms sometimes leads us to the very heart of an author's argument. This is not always true, but you should be alert to the possibility.

4. Evidence: Facts, Examples, Statistics, Analogies, and the Like. *Unlike many a serious thinker, Popper relies on few examples, no statistics, and practically no facts. The force of his essay rests almost wholly on the logical coherence of his arguments. Given his aim, one would expect that historical examples might have been useful, but he grounds the argument in logic alone, not on examples that others (presumably the utopianists) could explain away or quibble about. The only place where examples become telling is his catalog (¶33–35) of concrete ills that we should be trying to rid ourselves of: disease, poverty, crime, and so on. If we did not find these examples appropriate his argument would suffer, but because he sticks generally to the obvious ills that, as he says, everyone already recognizes, he runs little risk of discrediting himself with implausible examples. Insofar as the examples he does use are universally admitted to exist, they have the status of facts in his argument. He makes no appeal to other kinds of facts that are often thought useful, such as statistics, measurements, or polls.*

5. Literary Devices. *Popper relies no more on colorful literary devices and metaphors than he does on examples and collections of facts. Like almost all authors, he uses some metaphors, but these are strictly low-key and directly functional rather than "literary." He uses only the kind of metaphors we all use every day—as when he speaks of blueprints for society and moving in circles (¶27)—and their impact is restricted to small passages. None of them determines either his view of his topic or the structure of his essay. Perhaps the most potent metaphor in the whole essay is his allusion in paragraph 28 to "Utopian engineers" who think themselves "omniscient as well as omnipotent"—a metaphor that alludes to the view projected by George Orwell in* Nineteen Eighty-four *and used in a host of science fiction movies. But whether "engineers" is not more of a cliché than a vivid picture is an open question. It is certainly not the most chilling image for political oppressors that he might have picked. The restraint seems deliberate. Even in his final sentence, for example, where he speaks of taming the instruments of power and violence, at the terminal point where many authors would be tempted to pull out all the stops, Popper avoids any striving for a highly charged, triumphant, final chord. He seems vigorous but controlled from* *beginning to end. (Of course one might, as we suggested earlier, claim to see an unspoken master metaphor in the "showdown" or "war" Popper conducts between reason and violence. It is important to think about the implications of unspoken governing metaphors, but this sort of critique is better conducted at a stage following your first thorough analysis of the essay. See Lakoff and Johnson, pp. 189–200.)*

6. Assumptions. *Perhaps because he is a philosopher, Popper is unusually clear about his assumptions. This is not the case with all writers; many authors seem guided by assumptions that they are only dimly aware of, and their conclusions and assumptions do not always seem consistent.*

The first assumption without which Popper's argument would be impossible, as he is well aware, is his "faith in human reason": "I believe in man," he says (¶12). Without this faith in the capacity of human beings not only to achieve understanding through reason but also to pattern behavior according to reason's light, writing this article would be a futile, self-contradictory undertaking.

Popper's second important assumption is about the limitations of reason. While he is advocating reasonableness with all the energy he can muster, he is only too aware that not everything can be decided on rational grounds alone, especially ultimate goals: "No decision about aims can be established by purely *rational or scientific means" (¶22). For example, he says, "No amount of physics will tell a scientist that it is the right thing for him to construct a plough, or an aeroplane, or an atomic bomb" (¶23). This does not mean that all ends, as value judgments, are irrational impulse or whimsy, nor does it mean that they are incapable of reasoned defense. But it does mean that they are the product of vision, intuitions, and experience that go beyond logical argument.*

This assumption plays a crucial role in Popper's argument, for if he assumed that final ends could *be rationally determined, he would be undercutting his charge that utopianism's rational goals for the future lead to concrete evils in the present.*

Popper's third crucial assumption is his belief that "no generation must be sacrificed for the sake of future generations, for the sake of an ideal of happiness that may never be realized" (¶34). He makes this same assertion another time or two in different words in the same paragraph, and utters it once again toward the end of paragraph 38: "We must not argue that a certain social situation is a mere means to an end on the grounds that it is merely a transient historical situation." The development of this assumption's meaning occupies the whole last section of the essay, from paragraphs 32 to 42.

At this point you may be wanting to say, "It is all very well to point out assumptions, and it is all very helpful when you do, but how do you recognize one in the first place? How did you know that these *utterances contained assumptions?" It is a good question, but one to which there is no formulaic answer. The necessary skills are experience at reading arguments like this, experience at thinking about the kinds of ideas they contain, careful observation of the pattern of ideas and expression, and attention to logical connections. This may sound like a tall order for the inexperienced reader, but, as we said in "What Is an Argument?" (pp. 19–21), no one, not even the most inexperienced reader, comes to a piece of writing totally devoid of the powers of observation and logic. And every reader can detect the presence of important generalizations for which no extended argument is offered; they are what is* assumed.

When readers who are paying close attention to what Popper is saying come, for example, to paragraph 32, they do not have to be college professors to observe that Popper's offer of "a simple formula or recipe" signals a shift of focus and tone. As the passage proceeds, Popper increasingly abandons neutrality of tone and addresses the reader in a more direct, personal, urgent way: "Do not try," he says, and "do not think," and "do not allow" (¶34). His increasing passion is one of the best clues that you are approaching a nodal point where assumptions lurk. Whenever an author's language becomes prescriptive and personal—"I feel," "I believe," "you must," "you must not"—chances are you are treading on the holy ground of fundamental assumptions.

7. Logical Coherence. *We saw earlier that Popper has two main charges to level against utopianism: that it is self-defeating and that it inevitably leads to violence. The first of these charges he supports convincingly, but the second seems less well supported. In paragraphs 22–28, for example, he launches into an extended argument about the procedure that turns utopian dreams into totalitarian states, but while he shows clearly that utopian ideals will always outpace achievement and are therefore self-defeating, he does not show that the inevitable consequence of this failure is violence. Even if he were able to show that that is what usually happens* in fact, *he would not have proved its inevitability* in principle.

Why would Popper neglect to provide proof for such a crucial point, while elsewhere he demonstrates impressive logical rigor? We might be tempted to assign the status of "assumption" to this point, but Popper himself, as we have seen, is careful to separate his fundamental assumptions from assertions he means to support—and he does, it seems, intend to argue for the violent consequences of utopianism.

In a case like this, where logical coherence inexplicably breaks down, it is useful to search out any other failures or missing steps in the logic and to try to discern a motive *behind the author's neglect. Another place where Popper has omitted steps in his argument is paragraph 38. Suddenly, without explanation, he introduces an element that seems totally unprepared for: "I believe that it is quite true that we can judge the rationality of an action only in relation to some aims or ends. But this does not necessarily mean that the rationality of a political action can be judged only in relation to an* historical *end." The abrupt insertion of a concern about* historical *ends right in the middle of his argument about* ideal *ends, without preparation or explanation, raises questions. There is a jump here in the logic that requires an explanation outside the boundaries of the argument itself.*

Perhaps the explanation is that Popper, without ever naming Marxist philosophy in his article, is nevertheless constructing an argument against it. Other writings of his show that he is an implacable foe of Marxist political philosophy, that he considers Marxist philosophers the most hopeless of all utopianists, and the Soviet Union the clearest example of how utopian dreams turn into totalitarian nightmares.

Why, then, does he not mention that it is the Marxists' *historical ends that he objects to? The question is impossible to answer if the only answer lies in Popper's private motives. But the position itself suggests an answer. If he can demonstrate that* all *utopian thinking is equally invalid, then it* must *follow that Marxist thinking also stands condemned. But if he makes his quarrel with Marxism alone, he winds up with a weaker position even if he wins, for combating Marxism without combating utopianism means that he must attack Marxism on the basis of its policies, not its principles. He wants the stronger case that will discredit Marxism* and *its cousins once and for all, and the stronger case requires an attack on Marxism's underlying principles.*

Does this attack on Marxism undermine the logical coherence of Popper's essay? Probably not, since one can easily guess his motive for avoiding a direct attack. But it is surely a weakness of Popper's presentation that one cannot find a sufficient number of references within the essay to make this motive clear. And even putting his presentation aside, one illogicality clearly remains: He has not shown that Marxist utopianism must always *produce totalitarian states or, more generally, that utopianism must* always *lead to violence. It is difficult to say just how much this illogicality weakens his entire position. Here is where one must test the logic of a position with one's intuitions about what makes "good sense" and about the limits of our ability to prove generalizations concerning human possibilities.*

8. Overall Structure. *The problem of how to discover a controlling structure in an argument is no different from the problem of how to discover a set of controlling assumptions. You have to pay close attention and then practice on essay after essay. From the beginning of Popper's essay it is apparent that he is concerned about violence and reasonableness, but it is not clear how the expression of that concern is going to be patterned until we come to paragraph 14. The careful reader will at this point observe that Popper explicitly defines what he has been up to for the first 13 paragraphs: "My fundamental attitude towards the problem of reason and violence will by now be understood." Building on this first clear indication of structure, let us see if we can discern the shape of the essay as a whole.*

I. Paragraphs 1–14: Introduction of topic, thesis, and definition of reasonableness.
   A. Paragraph 1, like most first paragraphs, is an introduction to the topic, the relationship between reason and violence.
   B. Paragraph 2 sums up paragraph 1 and states Popper's thesis.
   C. Paragraphs 3–9 refine the topic and thesis, mainly by providing a definition of *reasonableness* and by providing some appropriate concrete examples.
   D. Paragraphs 10–13 discuss the proper domain of reason, each paragraph adding a refinement to the idea.
   E. Paragraph 14 is transitional, introducing "the problem of Utopianism."

II. Paragraphs 15–29 express the main body of Popper's objections to utopianism.
   A. Paragraphs 15–21 argue that utopianism gives a rational appearance because it lays out goals and selects means for achieving them. This section ends with one of Popper's typical transitional paragraphs (¶21), just two sentences long, introducing a new direction to the discussion.
   B. Paragraphs 22–28 clarify the danger pointed to in the transitional paragraph.
      1. Paragraphs 22–24 begin to explain the danger.
      2. Paragraphs 25–28 become increasingly practical, culminating in a description of utopian planners as "engineers" who pretend to "become omniscient as well as omnipotent."
   C. Paragraph 29 is another two-sentence transition.

III. Paragraphs 30–40 make Popper's suggestions for how to avoid utopian thinking.
   A. Paragraphs 30–32 are a buildup to his catalog of non-utopian remedies.
      1. Paragraph 30 clarifies his critique: He wants the reader to be clear that he does not consider utopian thinking pernicious merely because it spins out ideals.
      2. Paragraph 31 seems to ask (not quite this bluntly), "Well, then, if ideal-oriented thinking isn't the problem, what is?"
      3. Paragraph 32 directly responds: "All right, I'll answer that question, but not by giving more criticisms, which I've already done. I will instead propose concrete remedies."
   B. Paragraphs 33–35 provide the concrete remedies. Popper here lists the ills that political planners should be trying to solve: the concrete evils of everyday life, the obvious ones that everybody already agrees about.
   C. Paragraphs 36–40 directly answer the question asked in paragraph 31, the answer made clearer now that we know what Popper's remedies are. The answer is that utopianism is not evil merely because it is idealistic; the problem is the *kinds* of ideals it commits itself to. Utopianism always assumes a dogmatic character, Popper claims, because it focuses on a future period of perfect happiness, and this seduces utopian-minded planners into thinking that they are justified in sacrificing the quality of present life for an anticipated, hoped-for, perfect, but always equally distant life in the future.

IV. Paragraphs 41–42 conclude Popper's case by positing the relationship between utopianism and general culture.
   A. Paragraph 41 argues that utopianism is one small current in a vast tide of anti-rational, hysterical, exaggerated, and immature responses to the problem of power afflicting Western culture in general. The essence of this attitude is that human beings in the modern world are given to thinking of themselves either as gods or worms, and both attitudes tend to give rulers a handy justification for walking over the people beneath them. If rulers are gods, they can do no wrong. If subjects are worms, they can be done no wrong. He sees this attitude also manifested in both religious and philosophical thinking, not just in political thinking.
   B. Paragraph 42 makes Popper's final point that this attitude, like the utopian thinking it spawns, always leads to violence. In response to that prospect, Popper ends where he began, by advocating reasonableness—intellectual humility and free give-and-take—as the only possible remedy.

Suggested Essay Topics

1. Write an essay addressed to Popper either commending or criticizing his claim that utopianism inevitably leads to violence. Unless you have fairly strong views about how his idea works on the large scale of political movements, you will do better to relate it to your personal experience of trying to reconcile ideal goals with practical necessities. You might, for example, make use of the popular expression "The perfect is the enemy of the good" and discuss how standards of perfection have sometimes prevented you from doing as well as you could. Or you might make use of opposing popular expressions ("Nothing ventured, nothing gained," "Difficult tasks take time; the impossible takes a little longer") by showing how striving for perfection has sometimes led to real—though still imperfect—performance.
2. Read Plato's "Allegory of the Cave" (pp. 409–417) and compare Plato's emphasis on the importance of the ideal with Popper's emphasis on the importance of the concrete. Discuss whether the ideal that Plato advocates is really the ideal that Popper fears and despises. If you think each author uses this term in the same way, discuss which of them makes the most persuasive case for his view. If you think that each of them uses the term in a different way, discuss the differences and explain why, despite their apparent contradictions of one another, they are not in disagreement because they are not talking about the same thing.
3. You may find it useful to vary topic 2 by turning it into a letter to Popper, arguing against his position using arguments derived from Plato, or vice versa.

Kurt Vonnegut, Jr.

Few statements carry as much meaning and significance for Americans as Jefferson's assertion that "all men are created equal." Despite the statement's ambiguity (equal in what sense?) and its inconsistent application (women and minorities have often been treated as if they were not *equal), most Americans nevertheless feel that it expresses one of our nation's most distinctive and noble aspirations.*

Yet it is clear that Kurt Vonnegut (b. 1922) thinks not only that this revered belief can become pernicious, but also that society is moving toward the evil conditions he portrays in his story. As a way of understanding this evil, you might ask yourself to what extent Vonnegut's depicted society is utopian. Equality is a good thing, right? All Americans believe in it, right? So what's wrong with a society in which equality is not only embraced in theory but enforced in practice—by impartial legislation? If people of superior ability will always take advantage of their inequality, doesn't handicapping them make sense as a way of evening out the chances of success for the rest of us? Isn't this exactly what Jefferson would have wanted, what his noble statement about equality leads to? Wouldn't getting rid of nasty competition and inequality make the world better, perhaps even perfect?

Maybe, and maybe not. Doesn't it finally depend on how we define "equal"? And on how we think "equal" ought to be protected or enforced? We have seen that Goodman considers utopian thinking to be consistent with a "conflictful society," that Popper views it as an inevitable prelude to violence, and that Jefferson, if we can call his notions utopian, held the ideal of equality to be consistent with slavery for blacks and no votes for women. What does "equal" mean in these different contexts? Is it possible that Vonnegut's story concretely illustrates Popper's abstract thesis that utopian goals always lead to violence? Does Vonnegut oppose the ideal of equality on principle? If so, what principle? As you read "Harrison Bergeron," try to determine what kind of society Vonnegut would really prefer and what view of his fictional society Jefferson, Goodman, and Popper would take. Finally, try to determine your own views.

HARRISON BERGERON

From *Welcome to the Monkey House* (1961).

The year was 2081, and everybody was finally equal. They weren't only equal before God and the law. They were equal every which way. Nobody was smarter than anybody else. Nobody was better looking than anybody else. Nobody was stronger or quicker than anybody else. All this equality was due to the 211th, 212th, and 213th Amendments to the Constitution, and to the unceasing vigilance of agents of the United States Handicapper General. 1

Some things about living still weren't quite right, though. April, for instance, still drove people crazy by not being springtime. And it was in that clammy month that the H-G men took George and Hazel Bergeron's fourteen-year-old son, Harrison, away. 2

It was tragic, all right, but George and Hazel couldn't think about it very hard. Hazel had a perfectly average intelligence, which meant she couldn't think about anything except in short bursts. And George, while his intelligence was way above normal, had a little mental handicap radio in his ear. He was required by law to wear it at all times. He was tuned to a government transmitter. Every twenty seconds or so, the transmitter would send out some sharp noise to keep people like George from taking unfair advantage of their brains. 3

George and Hazel were watching television. There were tears on Hazel's cheeks, but she'd forgotten for the moment what they were about. 4

On the television screen were ballerinas. 5

A buzzer sounded in George's head. His thoughts fled in panic, like bandits from a burglar alarm. 6

"That was a really pretty dance, that dance they just did," said Hazel. 7

"Huh?" said George. 8

"That dance—it was nice," said Hazel. 9

"Yup," said George. He tried to think a little about the ballerinas. They 10
weren't really very good—no better than anybody else would have been, anyway. They were burdened with sash-weights and bags of birdshot, and their faces were masked, so that no one, seeing a free and graceful gesture or a pretty face, would feel like something the cat drug in. George was toying with the vague notion that maybe dancers shouldn't be handicapped. But he didn't get very far with it before another noise in his ear radio scattered his thoughts.

George winced. So did two out of the eight ballerinas. 11

Hazel saw him wince. Having no mental handicap herself, she had to 12
ask George what the latest sound had been.

"Sounded like somebody hitting a milk bottle with a ball peen ham- 13
mer," said George.

"I'd think it would be real interesting, hearing all the different sounds," 14
said Hazel, a little envious. "All the things they think up."

"Um," said George. 15

"Only, if I was Handicapper General, you know what I would do?" said 16
Hazel. Hazel, as a matter of fact, bore a strong resemblance to the Handicapper General, a woman named Diana Moon Glampers. "If I was Diana Moon Glampers," said Hazel, "I'd have chimes on Sunday—fast chimes. Kind of in honor of religion."

"I could think, if it was just chimes," said George. 17

"Well—maybe make 'em real loud," said Hazel. "I think I'd make a good 18
Handicapper General."

"Good as anybody else," said George. 19

"Who knows better'n I do what normal is?" said Hazel. 20

"Right," said George. He began to think glimmeringly about his abnor- 21
mal son who was now in jail, about Harrison, but a twenty-one-gun salute in his head stopped that.

"Boy!" said Hazel, "that was a doozy, wasn't it?" 22

It was such a doozy that George was white and trembling, and tears 23
stood on the rims of his red eyes. Two of the eight ballerinas had collapsed to the studio floor, were holding their temples.

"All of a sudden you look so tired," said Hazel. "Why don't you stretch 24
out on the sofa, so's you can rest your handicap bag on the pillows, honeybunch." She was referring to the forty-seven pounds of birdshot in a canvas bag, which was padlocked around George's neck. "Go on and rest the bag for a little while," she said. "I don't care if you're not equal to me for a while."

George weighed the bag with his hands. "I don't mind it," he said. "I 25
don't notice it any more. It's just a part of me."

"You been so tired lately—kind of wore out," said Hazel. "If there was 26
just some way we could make a little hole in the bottom of the bag, and just take out a few of them lead balls. Just a few."

"Two years in prison and two thousand dollars fine for every ball I took 27
out," said George. "I don't call that a bargain."

"If you could just take a few out when you came home from work," said 28
Hazel. "I mean—you don't compete with anybody around here. You just set
around."

"If I tried to get away with it," said George, "then other people'd get 29
away with it—and pretty soon we'd be right back to the dark ages again, with
everybody competing against everybody else. You wouldn't like that, would
you?"

"I'd hate it," said Hazel. 30

"There you are," said George. "The minute people start cheating on 31
laws, what do you think happens to society?"

If Hazel hadn't been able to come up with an answer to this question, 32
George couldn't have supplied one. A siren was going off in his head.

"Reckon it'd fall all apart," said Hazel. 33

"What would?" said George blankly. 34

"Society," said Hazel uncertainly. "Wasn't that what you just said?" 35

"Who knows?" said George. 36

The television program was suddenly interrupted for a news bulletin. 37
It wasn't clear at first as to what the bulletin was about, since the announcer,
like all announcers, had a serious speech impediment. For about half a minute, and in a state of high excitement, the announcer tried to say, "Ladies and
gentlemen—"

He finally gave up, handed the bulletin to a ballerina to read. 38

"That's all right—" Hazel said of the announcer, "he tried. That's the 39
big thing. He tried to do the best he could with what God gave him. He should
get a nice raise for trying so hard."

"Ladies and gentlemen—" said the ballerina, reading the bulletin. She 40
must have been extraordinarily beautiful, because the mask she wore was
hideous. And it was easy to see that she was the strongest and most graceful
of all the dancers, for her handicap bags were as big as those worn by
two-hundred-pound men.

And she had to apologize at once for her voice, which was a very unfair 41
voice for a woman to use. Her voice was a warm, luminous, timeless melody.
"Excuse me—" she said, and she began again, making her voice absolutely
uncompetitive.

"Harrison Bergeron, age fourteen," she said in a grackle squawk, "has 42
just escaped from jail, where he was held on suspicion of plotting to overthrow the government. He is a genius and an athlete, is under-handicapped,
and should be regarded as extremely dangerous."

A police photograph of Harrison Bergeron was flashed on the screen 43
upside down, then sideways, upside down again, then right side up. The
picture showed the full length of Harrison against a background calibrated
in feet and inches. He was exactly seven feet tall.

The rest of Harrison's appearance was Halloween and hardware. No- 44
body had ever borne heavier handicaps. He had outgrown hindrances faster

than the H-G men could think them up. Instead of a little ear radio for a
mental handicap, he wore a tremendous pair of earphones, and spectacles
with thick wavy lenses. The spectacles were intended to make him not only
half blind, but to give him whanging headaches besides.

Scrap metal was hung all over him. Ordinarily, there was a certain 45
symmetry, a military neatness to the handicaps issued to strong people, but
Harrison looked like a walking junkyard. In the race of life, Harrison carried
three hundred pounds.

And to offset his good looks, the H-G men required that he wear at all 46
times a red rubber ball for a nose, keep his eyebrows shaved off, and cover
his even white teeth with black caps at snaggle-tooth random.

"If you see this boy," said the ballerina, "do not—I repeat, do not—try 47
to reason with him."

There was the shriek of a door being torn from its hinges. 48

Screams and barking cries of consternation came from the television set. 49
The photograph of Harrison Bergeron on the screen jumped again and again,
as though dancing to the tune of an earthquake.

George Bergeron correctly identified the earthquake, and well he might 50
have—for many was the time his own home had danced to the same crashing
tune. "My God—" said George, "that must be Harrison!"

The realization was blasted from his mind instantly by the sound of an 51
automobile collision in his head.

When George could open his eyes again, the photograph of Harrison 52
was gone. A living, breathing Harrison filled the screen.

Clanking, clownish, and huge, Harrison stood in the center of the stu- 53
dio. The knob of the uprooted studio door was still in his hand. Ballerinas,
technicians, musicians, and announcers cowered on their knees before him,
expecting to die.

"I am the Emperor!" cried Harrison. "Do you hear? I am the Emperor! 54
Everybody must do what I say at once!" He stamped his foot and the studio
shook.

"Even as I stand here—" he bellowed, "crippled, hobbled, sickened—I 55
am a greater ruler than any man who ever lived! Now watch me become what
I *can* become!"

Harrison tore the straps of his handicap harness like wet tissue paper, 56
tore straps guaranteed to support five thousand pounds.

Harrison's scrap-iron handicaps crashed to the floor. 57

Harrison thrust his thumbs under the bar of the padlock that secured 58
his head harness. The bar snapped like celery. Harrison smashed his head-
phones and spectacles against the wall.

He flung away his rubber-ball nose, revealed a man that would have 59
awed Thor, the god of thunder.

"I shall now select my Empress!" he said, looking down on the cowering 60
people. "Let the first woman who dares rise to her feet claim her mate and
her throne!"

A moment passed, and then a ballerina arose, swaying like a willow. 61

Harrison plucked the mental handicap from her ear, snapped off her 62
physical handicaps with marvelous delicacy. Last of all, he removed her mask.

She was blindingly beautiful. 63

"Now—" said Harrison, taking her hand, "shall we show the people the 64
meaning of the word dance? Music!" he commanded.

The musicians scrambled back into their chairs, and Harrison stripped 65
them of their handicaps, too. "Play your best," he told them, "and I'll make
you barons and dukes and earls."

The music began. It was normal at first—cheap, silly, false. But Harrison 66
snatched two musicians from their chairs, waved them like batons as he sang
the music as he wanted it played. He slammed them back into their chairs.

The music began again and was much improved. 67

Harrison and his Empress merely listened to the music for a while— 68
listened gravely, as though synchronizing their heartbeats with it.

They shifted their weights to their toes. 69

Harrison placed his big hands on the girl's tiny waist, letting her sense 70
the weightlessness that would soon be hers.

And then, in an explosion of joy and grace, into the air they sprang! 71

Not only were the laws of the land abandoned, but the law of gravity 72
and the laws of motion as well.

They reeled, whirled, swiveled, flounced, capered, gamboled, and spun. 73

They leaped like deer on the moon. 74

The studio ceiling was thirty feet high, but each leap brought the danc- 75
ers nearer to it.

It became their obvious intention to kiss the ceiling. 76

They kissed it. 77

And then, neutralizing gravity with love and pure will, they remained 78
suspended in air inches below the ceiling, and they kissed each other for a
long, long time.

It was then that Diana Moon Glampers, the Handicapper General, came 79
into the studio with a double-barreled ten-gauge shotgun. She fired twice,
and the Emperor and the Empress were dead before they hit the floor.

Diana Moon Glampers loaded the gun again. She aimed it at the musi- 80
cians and told them they had ten seconds to get their handicaps back on.

It was then that the Bergerons' television tube burned out. 81

Hazel turned to comment about the blackout to George. But George had 82
gone out into the kitchen for a can of beer.

George came back in with a beer, paused while a handicap signal shook 83
him up. And then he sat down again. "You been crying?" he said to Hazel.

"Yup," she said. 84

"What about?" he said. 85

"I forget," she said. "Something real sad on television." 86

"What was it?" he said. 87

"It's all kind of mixed up in my mind," said Hazel. 88

"Forget sad things," said George. 89

"I always do," said Hazel. 90

"That's my girl," said George. He winced. There was the sound of a 91
riveting gun in his head.

"Gee—I could tell that one was a doozy," said Hazel. 92

"You can say that again," said George. 93

"Gee—" said Hazel, "I could tell that one was a doozy." 94

Questions for Discussion

1. If "Harrison Bergeron" may be called a satire, what is the object, the butt, of the satire? Identify as specifically as you can who or what is being ridiculed.
2. Point out some of the specific devices of humor that Vonnegut uses. To what purpose does the humor seem directed?
3. The story relies heavily on dialogue. Try rewriting a section of dialogue (¶25–36, for example) as narrative commentary, using the same tone the narrator employs in the other, non-dialogue sections, and then discuss with the rest of the class what has been gained or lost by the revision.

Suggested Essay Topics

1. Write an essay directed to your classmates in which you compare the satire in Vonnegut's story with the satire from Dickens's *Hard Times* (pp. 45–57) and in Swift's "Modest Proposal" (pp. 483–491). Identify the satirical butt in each case, discuss the distinctive tone of each piece, and compare at least two satirical devices—ways of "sticking the needle" in the object being ridiculed.
2. Write a satire of your own, ridiculing some opinion, person, institution, custom, practice, or human trait. Satire is always *about* some detested object but seldom directed *to* that object. Usually the audience is composed of readers whom the satirist invites to stand *outside* the space occupied by the object while reader and writer both laugh at the object *inside* the satirical space. You need to be clear, therefore, about the audience for whom you are writing and how the audience differs from the satirized object.

3

LANGUAGE

Reading and Writing, Words and Experience

Reading is to the mind what exercise is to the body.
Richard Steele

Reading maketh a full man; conference a ready man and writing an exact man.
Sir Francis Bacon

For know you well, my dear Crito, that to
express oneself badly is not only faulty as far as the
language goes, but does some harm to the soul
Socrates, in Plato's Phaedo

Without precision of meaning we damage not simply language,
but thought. The language we share is beautiful
and alarmingly complex. Try as we may, we are all likely to make
mistakes, and very few among us can claim to know the
English language to perfection. But we can try.
Robert Davies

Inspiration usually comes during work, rather than before it.
Madeline L'Engle

Style in its simplest definition, it seems to me, is sound—the sound
of self. It arises out of the whole concept of the work,
from the very pulsebeat of the writer and all that has gone
to make him, so that it is sometimes difficult to decide definitely where
technique and style have their firm boundary lines.
Eleanor Cameron

Rewriting isn't virtuous. It isn't something that ought to be done.
It is simply something that most writers find
they have to do to discover what they have to say
and how to say it.
Donald M. Murray

Wayne C. Booth and Marshall W. Gregory

CORRECTNESS AND ERRORS

For centuries people have claimed that the English language is in danger of corruption and decay. Hundreds of books and articles have warned against the "corruption" of English. In 1924, for example, R. W. Chapman, speaking of "The Decay of Syntax," said that "the morbid state of modern English prose is generally recognized by competent judges. . . . Any beauty in modern English prose can be only the beauty of decay." As early as 1712 the great satirist Jonathan Swift suggested that to combat the threat of change, which he saw as the threat of decline, an "Academy" should be formed to establish and preserve the correct forms. Some nations have established such bodies, and to this day, in France and other nations, such official or semi-official "academies" issue formal decisions about which words or expressions will be given a badge of approval. 1

Nobody has succeeded in establishing such an academy to oversee the development of English. But many have tried, and many others have deplored the seemingly chaotic way in which new and forbidden expressions make their way from being outlawed—as "slang" or "foreign" or "vulgar" or "colloquial"—to being used by careful writers. 2

Many linguists have claimed that these purifying efforts are entirely misguided. Since all languages are constantly changing, and since there is never any clearly established authority to say which changes are good and which are bad, our ideas about good English must always shift according to the usage of whatever group we address. 3

The "warfare" between the linguists and the purists has often been bitter and confusing. It has been marked by much name-calling, and it reveals a good deal of puzzlement and anxiety on all sides. (See, for example, the controversy about *Webster's Third International Dictionary,* as recorded in *Dictionaries and That Dictionary,* edited in 1962 by Wilma Ebbitt and James Sledd.) 4

5 Few of us can hope to figure out the rights and wrongs of such an elaborate and prolonged controversy. But we can profit from becoming aware of the issues and thinking about what our own practice will be. Our choices must always be dictated both by our effort to address different readers successfully and by our own knowledge, or lack of knowledge, about what expressions hinder our communication.

6 We soon learn that "correctness" is at best a mere beginning. Observing correctness in writing is like observing the speed limit while driving: Following the "rules" may have the negative virtue of keeping you out of trouble, but, in and of itself, it cannot produce the positive virtue of good writing. Every beginner soon learns, moreover, that there is no end to the number of "mistakes" teachers can find in an essay; almost all of us have experienced a sense of hopelessness when we've seen our manuscripts marked again and again with corrections that seem endless.

7 Should teachers and students stop worrying, then, about correctness, as "permissivists" have argued? We all know that if we do so, we will make a lot of trouble for ourselves. Some people will refuse to read what we write if they find it full of "errors," even when linguists point out that many of those very "errors" have been accepted by great authors from Shakespeare's time to the present. But deciding to concentrate on avoiding errors will not work either; we authors can attest to that. As we have worked on this book we have constantly discovered "errors," real or imaginary, in each other's writing, and we know from experience that, even after careful correction by editors at Harper & Row, our readers will discover faults we never dreamed of.

8 Thus our choices in this matter are complicated. If we wrote, "Neither one of us don't know nothing about grammar," or if we commited many mispellings like these, and if you decided that we didn't know any better, you would probably stop using this book. But if we worried too much about catching every conceivable error, we would have to stop writing. So we all have a problem here—the problem of finding a livable "mean" between an overanxious care that makes writing either painful or impossible, on the one hand, and the carelessness that will leave readers confused or drive them away, on the other.

9 Like many problems in life, this one cannot be dodged. With every word we utter, we either *meet* those we address or we *fail* to, and our success will depend in part on learning how, in any given situation, to be as "correct" as that situation requires. This in turn means that to learn to write well, we must learn to think hard about different situations. The kind of language accepted as correct English in a college essay may be fatal in a dormitory bull session, and vice versa.

10 As you struggle to find appropriate language for your various writing tasks, you may at times become almost immobilized for fear of committing errors you never dreamed of. When this happens, you should remind yourself of four points implicit in all of your work this year.

11 First, you are not alone. Every author in this book has depended on the

corrections of other people; most authors show their writing to friends before sending it to the printer, and all of them depend finally on copy editors whose professional task is to improve manuscripts. Our own discussions in this "reader," for example, have been re-written again and again, taking into account the corrections of so many readers, paid and unpaid, that we have lost count. That you need help with your writing is thus no disgrace.

Second, although possible errors in writing may seem infinite in num- 12
ber, the really crippling ones are relatively rare. If you think hard about the *kinds* of errors you find flagged in your papers, you can soon learn to avoid those that give the most trouble. Seldom will a single error ever ruin an essay by itself.

Third, remember that you are learning correct ways of writing even as 13
you read the essays here. Even when you are not thinking about errors at all, you are learning to avoid them simply by paying attention to the texts you are assigned. If you had to memorize a full list of all the possible bad ways of writing, you would have reason to be discouraged. But by engaging with people who write well, you will automatically take in their ways—if you really pay attention.

Finally, don't forget that correctness is only a means to much more 14
important ends. You are learning to *say something worth saying;* and, if you face the challenges offered in this book, your writing will to a surprising degree "clean itself up." Most of the "errors" you now commit you would recognize yourself, if you really paid attention to your words as closely as the authors anthologized in this book have attended to theirs. And by following them in the close attention they practice, you will learn what it means to choose words that do their job.

One last hint: Nothing works quite so well for spotting errors as reading 15
your work aloud, slowly. Your worst errors will jump out at you when you hear yourself saying something that does not make good sense.

Helen Keller

The story of Helen Keller's life (1880–1968) is engrossing for the same reasons that all good memoirs are engrossing. They bring us into contact with an instructive, engaging mind, and they seem to offer us clues about how to face problems in our own lives. By presenting us with emotions that either parallel or differ from our own, memoirs confirm everyone's membership in the human community and simultaneously affirm everyone's individual uniqueness. Beyond this, however, Helen Keller's story offers us insight into a gripping topic larger than her life but on which her life and experience cast real illumination: the topic of how human beings acquire language and how, in acquiring it, they find, or perhaps create, their distinctively human nature.

Helen Keller was born a normal child, but at 19 months she was stricken with a severe disease that left her both blind and deaf. "Gradually," she says, "I got used to the silence and darkness that surrounded me, and forgot that it had ever been different." Despite the silence and darkness, the little girl came to understand a good deal of what was going on around her. She records that at age 5 she learned to fold and put away clean clothes, that she always knew when her mother and aunt were going out, and that she always wanted to accompany them. But without language she had no ideas, no means of living in a world of experience larger than immediate sensations and feelings, no way of holding on to memories or of formulating hopes and desires, no way of organizing the world conceptually, and, most important of all, no way of thinking her own thoughts and sharing them with others.

We are inclined to take language for granted. We live so much inside it that we no more think about it than we think about the beating of our own hearts or the air we breathe. But just as hearts may perform either well or poorly and air may be either pure or polluted, so our language may be used either more or less accurately, more or less sensitively, and more or less masterfully. Helen Keller was human, clearly, despite her immense handicap, but it is also clear that as she acquired language she came into an increasingly fuller ownership of her human birthright, an increasingly fuller experience of her own human nature.

This raises a question, doesn't it? If human nature and language are as intimately connected as Helen Keller's story suggests, and if language ownership is not an all-or-nothing thing but is instead mastered by degrees, does this not suggest that any enhancement or strengthening of our language will also enhance and strengthen our fundamental humanity? Is it possible, in other words, that being human (except in the most minimal biological sense) is not in itself an all-or-nothing thing? Is it possible that developing certain capacities within us may in fact bring us into fuller possession of what it means to be a human being? Helen Keller's story seems to suggest so.

If this suggestion is sound, implications for your own education follow. This view of language would clearly imply, for example, that courses that force you to deal with texts and thus increase your language power by constant exercise—humanities courses such as history, literature, languages, religion, and philosophy, to mention a few—may in fact be among the most useful courses you could take, useful if becoming more fully and powerfully human is useful. As you read, consider whether Helen Keller's story challenges any of your views or expectations about your own education, and whether her experience justifies your re-thinking or even re-tooling any of your educational ambitions.

THE KEY TO LANGUAGE

Our title for Chapters 4 and 6 of *The Story of My Life* (1902).

The most important day I remember in all my life is the one on which my teacher, Anne Mansfield Sullivan, came to me. I am filled with wonder when I consider the immeasurable contrasts between the two lives which it con- 1 nects. It was the third of March, 1887, three months before I was seven years old.

On the afternoon of that eventful day, I stood on the porch, dumb, expectant. I guessed vaguely from my mother's signs and from the hurrying to and fro in the house that something unusual was about to happen, so I went to the door and waited on the steps. The afternoon sun penetrated the mass of honeysuckle that covered the porch, and fell on my upturned face. My fingers lingered almost unconsciously on the familiar leaves and blossoms which had just come forth to greet the sweet southern spring. I did not know what the future held of marvel or surprise for me. Anger and bitterness had preyed upon me continually for weeks and a deep languor had succeeded this passionate struggle. 2

Have you ever been at sea in a dense fog, when it seemed as if a tangible white darkness shut you in, and the great ship, tense and anxious, groped her way toward the shore with plummet and sounding-line, and you waited with beating heart for something to happen? I was like that ship before my education began, only I was without compass or sounding-line, and had no way of knowing how near the harbour was. "Light! give me light!" was the wordless cry of my soul, and the light of love shone on me in that very hour. 3

I felt approaching footsteps. I stretched out my hand as I supposed to my mother. Some one took it, and I was caught up and held close in the arms of her who had come to reveal all things to me, and, more than all things else, to love me. 4

The morning after my teacher came she led me into her room and gave me a doll. The little blind children at the Perkins Institution had sent it and Laura Bridgman had dressed it; but I did not know this until afterward. When I had played with it a little while, Miss Sullivan slowly spelled into my hand the word "d-o-l-l." I was at once interested in this finger play and tried to imitate it. When I finally succeeded in making the letters correctly I was flushed with childish pleasure and pride. Running downstairs to my mother I held up my hand and made the letters for doll. I did not know that I was spelling a word or even that words existed; I was simply making my fingers go in monkey-like imitation. In the days that followed I learned to spell in this uncomprehending way a great many words, among them *pin, hat, cup* and a few verbs like *sit, stand* and *walk.* But my teacher had been with me several weeks before I understood that everything has a name. 5

One day, while I was playing with my new doll, Miss Sullivan put my big rag doll into my lap also, spelled "d-o-l-l" and tried to make me understand that "d-o-l-l" applied to both. Earlier in the day we had had a tussle over the words "m-u-g" and "w-a-t-e-r." Miss Sullivan had tried to impress it upon me that "m-u-g" is *mug* and that "w-a-t-e-r" is *water,* but I persisted in confounding the two. In despair she had dropped the subject for the time, only to renew it at the first opportunity. I became impatient at her repeated attempts and, seizing the new doll, I dashed it upon the floor. I was keenly delighted when I felt the fragments of the broken doll at my feet. Neither sorrow nor regret followed my passionate outburst. I had not loved the doll. 6

In the still, dark world in which I lived there was no strong sentiment or tenderness. I felt my teacher sweep the fragments to one side of the hearth, and I had a sense of satisfaction that the cause of my discomfort was removed. She brought me my hat, and I knew I was going out into the warm sunshine. This thought, if a wordless sensation may be called a thought, made me hop and skip with pleasure.

We walked down the path to the well-house, attracted by the fragrance 7
of the honeysuckle with which it was covered. Some one was drawing water and my teacher placed my hand under the spout. As the cool stream gushed over one hand she spelled into the other the word *water,* first slowly, then rapidly. I stood still, my whole attention fixed upon the motions of her fingers. Suddenly I felt a misty consciousness as of something forgotten—a thrill of returning thought; and somehow the mystery of language was revealed to me. I knew then that "w-a-t-e-r" meant the wonderful cool something that was flowing over my hand. That living word awakened my soul, gave it light, hope, joy, set it free! There were barriers still, it is true, but barriers that could in time be swept away.

I left the well-house eager to learn. Everything had a name, and each 8
name gave birth to a new thought. As we returned to the house every object which I touched seemed to quiver with life. That was because I saw everything with the strange, new sight that had come to me. On entering the door I remembered the doll I had broken. I felt my way to the hearth and picked up the pieces. I tried vainly to put them together. Then my eyes filled with tears; for I realized what I had done, and for the first time I felt repentance and sorrow.

I learned a great many new words that day. I do not remember what 9
they all were; but I do know that *mother, father, sister, teacher* were among them—words that were to make the world blossom for me, "like Aaron's rod, with flowers." It would have been difficult to find a happier child than I was as I lay in my crib at the close of that eventful day and lived over the joys it had brought me, and for the first time longed for a new day to come.

. . .

I had now the key to all language, and I was eager to learn to use it. 10
Children who hear acquire language without any particular effort; the words that fall from others' lips they catch on the wing, as it were, delightedly, while the little deaf child must trap them by a slow and often painful process. But whatever the process, the result is wonderful. Gradually from naming an object we advance step by step until we have traversed the vast distance between our first stammered syllable and the sweep of thought in a line of Shakespeare.

At first, when my teacher told me about a new thing I asked very few 11
questions. My ideas were vague, and my vocabulary was inadequate; but as my knowledge of things grew, and I learned more and more words, my field of inquiry broadened, and I would return again and again to the same subject, eager for further information. Sometimes a new word revived an image that some earlier experience had engraved on my brain.

I remember the morning that I first asked the meaning of the word, 12
"love." This was before I knew many words. I had found a few early violets in the garden and brought them to my teacher. She tried to kiss me; but at that time I did not like to have any one kiss me except my mother. Miss Sullivan put her arm gently round me and spelled into my hand, "I love Helen."

"What is love?" I asked. 13

She drew me closer to her and said, "It is here," pointing to my heart, 14
whose beats I was conscious of for the first time. Her words puzzled me very much because I did not then understand anything unless I touched it.

I smelt the violets in her hand and asked, half in words, half in signs, 15
a question which meant, "Is love the sweetness of flowers?"

"No," said my teacher. 16

Again I thought. The warm sun was shining on us. 17

"Is this not love?" I asked, pointing in the direction from which the heat 18
came, "Is this not love?"

It seemed to me that there could be nothing more beautiful than the sun, 19
whose warmth makes all things grow. But Miss Sullivan shook her head, and I was greatly puzzled and disappointed. I thought it strange that my teacher could not show me love.

A day or two afterward I was stringing beads of different sizes in 20
symmetrical groups—two large beads, three small ones, and so on. I had made many mistakes, and Miss Sullivna had pointed them out again and again with gentle patience. Finally I noticed a very obvious error in the sequence and for an instant I concentrated my attention on the lesson and tried to think how I should have arranged the beads. Miss Sullivan touched my forehead and spelled with decided emphasis, "Think."

In a flash I knew that the word was the name of the process that was 21
going on in my head. This was my first conscious perception of an abstract idea.

For a long time I was still—I was not thinking of the beads in my lap, 22
but trying to find a meaning for "love" in the light of this new idea. The sun had been under a cloud all day, and there had been brief showers; but suddenly the sun broke forth in all its southern splendour.

Again I asked my teacher, "Is this not love?" 23

"Love is something like the clouds that were in the sky before the sun 24
came out," she replied. Then in simpler words than these, which at that time I could not have understood, she explained: "You cannot touch the clouds, you know; but you feel the rain and know how glad the flowers and the thirsty earth are to have it after a hot day. You cannot touch love either; but you feel the sweetness that it pours into everything. Without love you would not be happy or want to play."

The beautiful truth burst upon my mind—I felt that there were invisible 25
lines stretched between my spirit and the spirits of others.

From the beginning of my education Miss Sullivan made it a practice 26
to speak to me as she would speak to any hearing child; the only difference

was that she spelled the sentences into my hand instead of speaking them. If I did not know the words and idioms necessary to express my thoughts she supplied them, even suggesting conversation when I was unable to keep up my end of the dialogue.

This process was continued for several years; for the deaf child does not learn in a month, or even in two or three years, the numberless idioms and expressions used in the simplest daily intercourse. The little hearing child learns these from constant repetition and imitation. The conversation he hears in his home stimulates his mind and suggests topics and calls forth the spontaneous expression of his own thoughts. This natural exchange of ideas is denied to the deaf child. My teacher, realizing this, determined to supply the kinds of stimulus I lacked. This she did by repeating to me as far as possible, verbatim, what she heard, and by showing me how I could take part in the conversation. But it was a long time before I ventured to take the initiative, and still longer before I could find something appropriate to say at the right time. 27

The deaf and the blind find it very difficult to acquire the amenities of conversation. How much more this difficulty must be augmented in the case of those who are both deaf and blind! They cannot distinguish the tone of the voice or, without assistance, go up and down the gamut of tones that give significance to words; nor can they watch the expression of the speaker's face, and a look is often the very soul of what one says. 28

[Attached here are two letters from Keller's revered teacher, Anne Mansfield Sullivan, which describe from the teacher's point of view the events that Keller has just narrated. What is interesting here are Sullivan's ideas about how language is learned by anyone, not just deaf children. Her description of young Helen turning more and more human as she acquires language is both moving and instructive.

Anne Sullivan was 14 years older than Helen Keller. Very early in her life she had been struck blind through illness and had entered the Perkins Institution for the blind the same year Helen was born. Later her sight was partially restored. The skills she learned at Perkins qualified her to be Keller's teacher. The letters here are addressed to Mrs. Sophia C. Hopkins, a matron at the Perkins Institution who had been like a mother to Sullivan. It is evident in these letters that Sullivan had a clear idea of what she was doing and was critically analyzing the effectiveness of her means of teaching Keller as she went along.]

April 5, 1887.

I must write you a line this morning because something very important has happened. Helen has taken the second great step in her education. She has learned that *everything has a name, and that the manual alphabet is the key to everything she wants to know.* 1

In a previous letter I think I wrote you that "mug" and "milk" had given Helen more trouble than all the rest. She confused the nouns with the verb "drink." She didn't know the word for "drink," but went through the pantomime of drinking whenever she spelled "mug" or "milk." This morning, while she was washing, she wanted to know the name for 2 "water." When she wants to know the name of anything, she points to it and pats my hand. I spelled "w-a-t-e-r" and thought no more about it until after breakfast. Then it occurred to me that with the help of this new word I might succeed in straightening out the "mug-milk" difficulty. We went out to the pump-house, and I made Helen hold her mug under the spout while I pumped. As the cold water gushed forth, filling the mug, I spelled "w-a-t-e-r" in Helen's free hand. The word coming so close upon the sensation of cold water rushing over her hand seemed to startle her. She dropped the mug and stood as one transfixed. A new light came into her face. She spelled "water" several times. Then she dropped on the ground and asked for its name and pointed to the pump and the trellis, and suddenly turning round she asked for my name. I spelled "Teacher." Just then the nurse brought Helen's little sister into the pump-house, and Helen spelled "baby" and pointed to the nurse. All the way back to the house she was highly excited, and learned the name of every object she touched, so that in a few hours she had added thirty new words to her vocabulary. Here are some of them: *Door, open, shut, give, go, come,* and a great many more.

P. S.—I didn't finish my letter in time to get it posted last night; so I 3
shall add a line. Helen got up this morning like a radiant fairy. She had flitted from object to object, asking the name of everything and kissing me for very gladness. Last night when I got in bed, she stole into my arms of her own accord and kissed me for the first time, and I thought my heart would burst, so full was it of joy.

April 10, 1887.

I see an improvement in Helen from day to day, almost from hour to 4
hour. Everything must have a name now. Wherever we go, she asks eagerly for the names of things she has not learned at home. She is anxious for her friends to spell, and eager to teach the letters to every one she meets. She drops the signs and pantomime she used before, as soon as she has words to supply their place, and the acquirement of a new word affords her the liveliest pleasure. And we notice that her face grows more expressive each day.

I have decided not to try to have regular lessons for the present. I am going to treat Helen 5
exactly like a two-year-old child. It occurred to me the other day that it is absurd to require a child to come to a certain place at a certain time and recite certain lessons, when he has not yet acquired a working vocabulary. I sent Helen away and sat down to think. I asked myself, *"How does a normal child learn language?"* The answer was simple, "By imitation." The child comes into the world with the ability to learn, and he learns of himself, provided he is supplied with sufficient outward stimulus. He sees people do things, and he tries to do them. He hears others speak, and he tries to speak. *But long before he utters his first word, he understands what is said to him.* I have been observing Helen's little cousin lately. She is about fifteen months old, and already understands a great deal. In response to questions she points out prettily her nose, mouth, eye, chin, cheek, ear. If I say, "Where is baby's other ear?" she points it out correctly. If I hand her a flower, and say, "Give it to mamma," she takes it to her mother. If I say, "Where is the little rogue?" she hides behind her mother's chair, or covers her face with her hands and peeps out at me

with an expression of genuine roguishness. She obeys many commands like these: "Come," "Kiss," "Go to papa," "Shut the door," "Give me the biscuit." But I have not heard her try to say any of these words, although they have been repeated hundreds of times in her hearing, and it is perfectly evident that she understands them. These observations have given me a clue to the method to be followed in teaching Helen language. *I shall talk into her hand as we talk into the baby's ears.* I shall assume that she has the normal child's capacity of assimilation and imitation. *I shall use complete sentences in talking to her,* and fill out the meaning with gestures and her descriptive signs when necessity requires it; but I shall not try to keep her mind fixed on any one thing. I shall do all I can to interest and stimulate it, and wait for results.

Questions for Discussion

1. Keller's story makes clear that even in her pre-language existence she had a life of some feelings and emotions. She could experience anger, frustration, and pleasure. But the absence of language seems to have had a muting effect on even these; of other emotions she seems to have had little knowledge at all, especially emotions of companionship or tenderness. "In the still, dark world in which I lived," she says, "there was no strong sentiment of tenderness" (¶6). Does this surprise you? Would you have thought that language was essential to having a fully developed, mature emotional life? Does Keller's experience on this score corroborate the point we make in our comments about language's being intimately tied to the development of one's human capacities, one's basic human nature? If so, how? If not, why not?
2. James Miller (pp. 183–189) quotes the philosopher Alfred North Whitehead as saying that "the souls of men are the gift from language to mankind." And Helen Keller records her sudden discovery of the word *water* in similar terms: "I knew then that 'w-a-t-e-r' meant the wonderful cool something that was flowing over my hand. That living word awakened my soul, gave it light, hope, joy, set it free!" (¶7). What do you think these two writers mean by the assertion that language liberates or awakens the soul? Is this just gushy talk for an incommunicable emotional experience, or does it mean anything you can pin down in other words? If so, what other words?
3. "Everything had a name, and each name gave birth to a new thought," says Keller (¶7). Can you imagine our language devoid of the names of things? What would a language of all verbs, adverbs, and other parts of speech, but no nouns, be like? How would it alter human perception and experience? If this is too hard to imagine, picture a more limited case: a language

with nouns but without proper names. Could we adapt to such a life, such a language? How? How would it alter our perception and experience?

4. In her pre-language stage, Keller reports that "I did not then understand anything unless I touched it" (¶14). We hear a lot of talk these days about re-discovering the kind of knowledge acquired through bodily sensations. The people who engage in this talk frequently assert the value of physical knowledge as an antidote to our tendency in modern society to distance everything with language that is too abstract, too conceptual, too removed from immediate experience. Use Helen Keller's story to help you construct a refutation of this view. Or, if you think this view is basically correct, show how Keller's acquisition of language is different from the kind of language being criticized by the "truth of the body" people.
5. Anne Sullivan reports that after Keller had begun to acquire language, "we notice that her face grows more expressive each day" (¶4). Why would this be the case? If you have ever had the opportunity to observe anyone with an extremely limited ownership of language, can you recall any notable features or absences of expressiveness that would throw light on Sullivan's meaning?

Suggested Essay Topics

1. Write an essay on discussion question 3 directed to your instructor. Or, if that kind of speculation seems too abstract, write a dialogue in which you picture two people—two students having lunch together in the cafeteria, for example—having a conversation in a version of English that includes nouns but no proper names. Address your piece of writing to the kind of general reader who might see it in the creative writing section of a magazine or as a feature essay in a newspaper.
2. Go to the library and look up one of the numerous accounts of feral children—children raised in complete absence from human contact (usually by animals, as the accounts go)—and write an essay in which you compare the indoctrination of these children into human society to Helen Keller's recovery of language. Conclude with appropriate observations about the nature and importance of language to human nature and experience. Direct the essay to your classmates. [One of the best-known accounts of a feral child is *The Wild Boy of Averyon* by Jean-Marc Gaspard Itard, translated by George and Muriel Humphrey (Prentice-Hall, 1962), which served as the inspiration for François Truffaut's film *L'Enfant sauvage (The Wild Child).*]

Clyde Kluckhohn

Have you ever thought of your native tongue as both imprisoning and liberating at the same time? This crude metaphor summarizes one of the paradoxical truths about language that Clyde Kluckhohn (1905–1960) discusses here. Our tongue, suggests Kluckhohn, is imprisoning in that its structures and biases—the ways it categorizes the world, the kinds of experiences it privileges, the way it structures (or refuses to structure) time, and so on—are rooted so deeply in native speakers that they see those structures and biases as natural, inevitable, and unchangeable. The categories of my language just are *my reality. Native speakers of English think time "naturally" falls into past, present, and future. But these categories do not seem imperative to the Hopi Indians, whose language divides experience not according to time but according to completeness of development. Things in the world may be in a more or less complete state of development or realization, according to Hopi views, but everything exists in the present: everything* is, *now. The universe is a complete creation. Thus it would not make sense to the Hopi to refer to things in either the past, as if they had disappeared, or in the future, as if they did not yet exist. Everything (what we call the past, present, and future) always exists and always has existed. Events and objects in this eternal now are not always equally visible, but this is not a function of time; it is a function of existence, and existence as something divisible into tenses is not a way of understanding available to the Hopi. It is not in their language. They doubtless find our way of thinking about experience as unnatural and confusing as we find theirs. All people are in this sense prisoners of their languages' categories and capabilities.*

Yet isn't language the most immensely liberating tool that human beings possess? Language has allowed us to be self-determining to a degree not even dreamed of by any other species. Human beings do not live mainly by instinct. We are not pushed around by genetic programming and glandular secretions; these account for only a minuscule portion of our activities. We do most of the things we do not because we are helplessly programmed to do them but because we have this strange and powerful ability to share goals and dreams with other human beings through language. Every important and characteristic human activity is rooted in our ability to talk together. If suddenly deprived of language, culture would instantly halt. Philosophy, science, literature, history, law, technology, sports, government, religion, and most forms of art would vanish. Thus while a given tongue entombs us within the prison of its own categories and special features, language in general is both the most characteristic and the most liberating feature of human existence, our most powerful tool and chief glory.

As you read, ask yourself which kinds of behavior are not influenced by language at all (basic body functions, perhaps?), which kinds are only slightly touched by language, and which kinds are thoroughly conditioned by language. Then ask yourself which of these activities seems most important to your sense of self, to your hopes and ambitions, and to your sense of reality. What kind of a creature would human beings be without language? Would we have culture? Would we engage in education, entertainment, art, sports, and other distinctively human activities? If so, what would they look like and how would they be structured? If not, would we have to invent non-language-based replacements for them, or would our lives simply be devoid of such activities, diminished by our inability to share common experience except through physical contact?

THE GIFT OF TONGUES

From *Mirror for Man* (1949).

> Our misapprehension of the nature of language has occasioned a greater waste of time, and effort, and genius, than all the other mistakes and delusions with which humanity has been afflicted. It has retarded immeasurably our physical knowledge of every kind, and vitiated what it could not retard.
>
> —A. B. Johnson, *Treatise on Language*[1]

It's a pity that so few of us have lived down our childhood struggles with grammar. We have been made to suffer so much from memorizing rules by rote and from approaching language in a mechanical, unimaginative way that we tend to think of grammar as the most inhuman of studies. Probably Americans, who dramatize themselves and their independence, have a kind of unconscious resentment against all patterns that are so set as to constitute a gratuitous insult to the principle of free will. For whatever reasons, Americans have been characteristically inept at foreign languages. Like the British, we have expected everybody else to learn English. 1

Yet nothing is more human than the speech of an individual or of a folk. Human speech, unlike the cry of an animal, does not occur as a mere element in a larger response. Only the human animal can communicate abstract ideas and converse about conditions that are contrary to fact. Indeed the purely conventional element* in speech is so large that language can be regarded as pure culture. A Burmese weaver, moved to Mexico, would know at once what a fellow craftsman in Mexico was doing, but would not understand one word of the Nahuatl tongue. No clues are so helpful as those of language in pointing to ultimate, unconscious psychological attitudes. Moreover, much of the friction between groups and between nations arises because in both the literal and the slangy sense they don't speak the same language. 2

We live in an environment which is largely verbal in the sense that we spend the most of our waking hours uttering words or responding actively or passively to the words of others. We talk to ourselves. We talk to our 3

*By "conventional element" Kluckhohn is referring to the parts of language that are culturally determined, the parts that exist because the users of the language simply agree to them, as conventions. If we all agreed to the change, we could, for example, use the sounds that now make up the word *bird* to mean "clock." And in fact many words have changed in both sound and meaning over the years. *Toilet* once meant a cloth placed over the shoulders while shaving or doing one's hair, but now it refers to the commode in the bathroom. Such agreed-upon meanings—and the sounds that represent them—are the "conventional element" in language.

families and friends—partly to communicate to them and to persuade them, partly just to express ourselves. We read newspapers, magazines, books, and other written matter. We listen to the radio, to sermons, lectures, and movies. As Edward Sapir says:

> Language completely interpenetrates direct experience. For most persons every experience, real or potential, is saturated with verbalism. This perhaps explains why so many nature lovers do not feel that they are truly in touch with nature until they have mastered the names of a great many flowers and trees, as though the primary world of reality were a verbal one, and as though one could not get close to nature unless one first mastered the terminology that somehow magically expresses it. It is this constant interplay between language and experience which removes language from the cold status of such purely and simply symbolic systems as mathematical symbolism or flag signalling.[2]

The dictionaries still say that "language is a device for communicating 4
ideas." The semanticists and the anthropologists agree that this is a tiny, specialized function of speech. Mainly, language is an instrument for action. The meaning of a word or phrase is not its dictionary equivalent but the difference its utterance brings about in a situation. We use words to comfort and cajole ourselves in fantasy and daydream, to let off steam, to goad ourselves into one type of activity and to deny ourselves another. We use words to promote our own purposes in dealing with others. We build up verbal pictures of ourselves and our motives. We coax, wheedle, protest, invite, and threaten. Even the most intellectual of intellectuals employs only a minute fraction of his total utterance in symbolizing and communicating ideas that are divorced from emotion and action. The primary social value of speech lies in getting individuals to work more effectively together and in easing social tensions. Very often what is said matters much less than that something is said.

To the manipulation of this verbal environment, the anthropological 5
linguist has made some immediately practical contributions. Forced by the absence of written materials and by other circumstances attendant upon work with primitives, he has become an expert on "the direct method." He knows how to learn a language by using it. Though sensitive to the broader implications of the subtler, rarer forms of a language, he is skilled in the socially practical. He knows how to dodge the subjunctive when the immediate objective is to get a conversation going. The training of the conventional teacher of languages tempts him to his besetting sin of preoccupation with the niceties. He loves complicated rules and even more the exceptions to those rules. This is one of the principal reasons that after eight years of instruction in French an American can read a French novel with pleasure but is terrified to ask street directions in Paris. The anthropologist can't look up the rules in

the book. He is hardened to making small and large mistakes. His tradition is to break through, to concentrate on the essential, to get on with the talk at all costs.

Since many odd languages were of military significance during World War II, the anthropological linguist had a chance to introduce his method of working directly with the native informant. He prepared educational materials that highlighted anthropological short cuts in learning how to speak languages. The results have influenced the traditional methods of language instruction in the United States. The anthropological linguist has also worked out ways of teaching adults who have no written language and ways of teaching illiterates to write and read their own tongue. 6

Because anthropological linguists have usually been trained as ethnologists* and have often done general field work, they have tended less than other students of language to isolate speech from the total life of the people. To the anthropologist, language is just one kind of cultural behavior with many interesting connections to other aspects of action and thought. Analysis of a vocabulary shows the principal emphases of a culture and reflects culture history. In Arabic, for example, there are more than six thousand different words for camel, its parts, and equipment. The crudity and the special local words of the vocabulary of Spanish-speaking villages in New Mexico reflect the long isolation of these groups from the main stream of Latin culture. The particular archaisms used show that the break with the main continuity of the Spanish language occurred during the eighteenth century. The fact that the Boorabbee Indians of Panama used words like *gadsoot* (gadzooks), *forsoo'* (forsooth), *chee-ah* (cheer), and *mai-api* (mayhap) suggests a possible connection with Elizabethan buccaneers. 7

A great deal is now known about the history of languages, especially those languages that have been the great carriers of culture: Greek, Latin, Sanskrit, Arabic, Chinese, and English. Certain regularities have been discovered. In contrast to the general course of cultural evolution, languages move from the complex to the simple. Chinese and English have today lost almost all inflections.† The uniformities of phonetic change are most encouraging to those who believe that there is a discoverable order in human events. As Bloomfield has said: 8

> These correspondences are a matter of historical detail, but their significance was overwhelming, since they showed that human action, in the mass, is not altogether haphazard, but may proceed with regularity even in so unimportant a matter as the manner of pronouncing the individual sounds within the flow of speech.[3]

*Ethnologists study the divisions of humankind into races: their origin, distribution, and relations.

†Inflections are changes in the forms of words to indicate such categories as case, gender, number, and tense. *I see* is present tense, but *I saw* is past tense. English once had many more inflected words than it now has.

The phonetic side of language* beautifully illustrates both the selective nature of culture and the omnipresence of patterning. The sound of the p in pin is uttered with a slight puff of breath that is lacking when we sound the p in spin. Yet the speakers of English have entered into an unconscious agreement to treat them as the same signals, though they are not acoustically identical. It is like the motorist trained to stop at a light that is any shade of red. If I am investigating an unknown language and discover two sounds that are somewhat similar to those represented by English "b" and "d" but differ in being softly whispered, I can immediately predict that sounds in the new language of "g" type will conform to the same pattern. 9

Language is as consistently nonrational as any aspect of culture. We cling stubbornly to functionless capital letters. One may also instance our absurd English spelling. "Ghiti" ought to spell fish—gh as in laugh, it as in ambition. In hiccough, gh has a p sound. "Ghoughteighteau" could be read as potato—figure it out yourself. We say "five houses" when "five house" would be simpler and convey the meaning equally well. 10

Small peculiarities of linguistic usage are very revealing. It is no accident that French Catholics address the deity with the familiar form of the personal pronoun *(tu)* and Protestants with the formal *(vous).* In all sectors of French society save the old aristocracy spouses use *tu* to each other. But in the *Faubourg St. Germain* the duke calls his duchess *vous*—it being well understood between them that he reserves *tu* for his mistress. 11

A whole monograph could well be written on differences in the social structure of European nations as exposed by linguistic habits relating to the second personal pronoun. In France one comes to *tutoyer*† few people after adolescence.‡ This familiarity is restricted to immediate relatives and to a few intimate friends of childhood. In the German-speaking world, however, a student who did not soon come to use the familiar *Du* with those whom he saw frequently would be regarded as stuffy. In the army of imperial Austria all officers in the same regiment called each other *Du* regardless of rank. Failure to use the familiar form was equivalent to a challenge to the duel. In Austria and in other European countries the initiation of the familiar usage between adults is formalized in a ceremony. There is an embrace and a drink from each other's glasses. In Spain and Italy the introduction of the *tu* relationship in later life is considerably easier than in France but less frequent than in southern Germany and Austria. In Italy there is the further complication of a special form of respectful address *(Lei).* Choice of *Lei* or the more common formal pronoun became a political issue. The Fascist Party forbade 12

*The "phonetic side of language" refers to the quality of the specific sounds that have meaning in a given language: The fact that the differences between the *p* in *pin* and the *p* in *spin* do not prevent them from being heard as the same sound is a fact of English phonetics. If we add voicing to the *p,* however, the word *pin* becomes *bin.* Phonetics is the study of the function within language of such varying sound values.

†To use the intimate form *tu.*

‡This statement is less true now than it was when Kluckhohn wrote this essay in 1949. Nowadays, college students, workers in the same office, members of the same (usually artistic) professions, and social contacts of around the same age automatically use *tu* with each other.

the use of *Lei.* In Sweden also, passions have been aroused over the pronoun *ni* which is used toward those of lower social status—and, in accord with the familiar principle of inverted snobbery,[4] toward royal personages. Clubs were formed to abolish this word. Individuals wore buttons saying, "I don't use *ni* and I hope you don't either." Persons were brought into court for using *ni* toward people who considered themselves the equals or superiors of those who derogated them by using *ni* in address. "You are *ni* to me; I am not *ni* to you."

There are also instances of the intensely emotional symbolism of language. During the course of the development of nationalism and the romantic movement, every tongue was seized upon as the tangible manifestation of each culture's uniqueness. In the earlier part of the nineteenth century Magyar nobles spoke Latin in the Hungarian Parliament because they could not speak Magyar and would not speak German. Magyar, Irish, Lithuanian, and other tongues have been revived within the last hundred years from the category of practically dead languages. This tendency is about as old as written history. In the Bible we learn that the Gileadites slew everyone at the passages of Jordan who said *sibboleth* instead of *shibboleth.* 13

Groups within a culture emphasize their unity by a special language. Criminals have their own argot. So, indeed, do all the professions. One school in England (Winchester) has a language, compounded of medieval Latin and the accretions of the slang of many generations, that is utterly unintelligible to the uninitiated. "The linguistic community" is no meaningless phrase. The use of speech forms in common implies other things in common. The hunting or "county" set in England affects the dropping of final g's as a badge of their being set apart. Understatement is the mark of unshakable psychological security. If a member of the English upper classes is a member of the Davis Cup team he says "Yes, I play a little tennis." Individuals of many countries pronounce words in certain ways in order to associate themselves with particular social classes. The extent to which an elderly or middle-aged Englishman is still identifiable as Harrow or Rugby—and not as a Yorkshireman nor even as an Oxonian nor as an army man—proves the identification of distinctive language with social status. You can pretty well place an Englishman by his tie and his accent. Idiomatic turns of speech identify to society at large the special positions and roles of its various members. Cliques and classes unconsciously use this device to prevent absorption into the larger group. "He talks like one of us" is a declaration of acceptance. Euphemisms, special terms of endearment, and slang are class labels. 14

The essential aroma of each culture or subculture may be caught as a fragrance of language. In the Berlin of 1930, when one met an acquaintance on the street one bowed and stiffly said, "Good day." In Vienna one called out, "I have the honor," to a superior; "May God greet thee (you)," to an intimate; or "Your servant," to a fellow student or fellow aristocrat. That *gewisse Liebenswürdigkeit* (a certain graciousness) which was the hallmark of Viennese culture came out most clearly and immediately in certain phrases that were not unknown in northern and Protestant Germany but were much 15 less frequent in the stuff of daily conversation: "Live well," "the lady mother," "I kiss the hand, noble lady," and many others. In Austria when the delivery boy brought the groceries to the kitchen he said, "May God greet thee," if the maid received them; "Kiss the hand, noble lady," if the mistress were there.

Although one could press this point of view too far, there is *something* significant in the lists of words from each European language that have become widely current in other languages. From English: gentleman, fair play, week end, sport. From French: *liaison, maitresse, cuisine.* From Italian: *diva, bravo, bel canto.* From German: *Weltschmerz, Sehnsucht, Weltanschauung, Gemutlichkeit.* In *Englishmen, Frenchmen and Spaniards,* de Madariaga has suggested that the words fair play, *le droit,* and *el honor* are the keys to the respective cultures. Here is a sample of his discussion of English: 16

> There is deep satisfaction in the thought that English—the language of the man of action—is a monosyllabic language. For the man of action, as we know, lives in the present, and the present is an instant with room for no more than one syllable. Words of more than one syllable are sometimes called in English "dictionary" words, *i.e.,* words for the intellectual, for the bookworm, for the crank, almost for the un-English. They are marvellous, those English monosyllables, particularly, of course, those which represent acts. Their fidelity to the act which they represent is so perfect that one is tempted to think English words are the right and proper names which those acts are meant to have, and all other words but pitiable failures. How could one improve on splash, smash, ooze, shriek, slush, glide, speak, coo? Who could find anything better than hum or buzz or howl or whir? Who could think of anything more sloppy than slop? Is not the word sweet a kiss in itself and what could suggest a more peremptory obstacle than stop?[5]

Certainly the recurrent turns of phrase, the bromides, of each culture and of different time periods in the same culture are illuminating. They embody in capsule form the central strains and stresses of the society, major cultural interests, the characteristic definitions of the situation, the prime motivations. You can't swear effectively in British to an American audience and vice versa. The Navaho greeting is "All is well"; the Japanese, "There is respectful earliness"; the American, "How do you do?" "How are you getting on?" Each epoch has its stock phrases. As Carl Becker has written: 17

> If we would discover the little backstairs door that for any age serves as the secret entranceway to knowledge, we will do well to look for certain unobtrusive words with uncertain meanings that are permitted to slip off the tongue or pen without fear and without research; words which, having from constant repetition lost their metaphorical significance, are unconsciously mistaken for objective realities. . . . In each age these magic words have their entrances and their exits.[6]

In a way there is nothing very new about semantics. The Roman grammarian, Varro, pointed out in a learned treatise that he had discovered 228 distinct meanings for the word "good." His basic point was the same as Aldous Huxley's: "There ought to be some way of dry-cleaning and disinfecting words. Love, purity, goodness, spirit—a pile of dirty linen waiting for the laundress." We are always bringing together by words things that are different and separating verbally things that are, in fact, the same. A Christian Scientist refused to take vitamin tablets on the ground that they were "medicine"; he willingly accepted them when it was explained that they were "food." An insurance company discovered that behavior toward "gasoline drums" was ordinarily circumspect, that toward "empty gasoline drums" habitually careless. Actually, the "empty" drums are the more dangerous because they contain explosive vapor. 18

The semantic problem is almost insoluble because, as John Locke said, "So difficult is it to show the various meaning and imperfections of words when we have nothing else but words to do it by." This is one of the reasons that a cross-cultural approach is imperative. Anyone who has struggled with translation is made to realize that there is more to a language than its dictionary. The Italian proverb *"traduttore, tradittore"* (the translator is a betrayer) is all too correct. I asked a Japanese with a fair knowledge of English to translate back from the Japanese that phrase in the new Japanese constitution that represents our "life, liberty, and the pursuit of happiness." He rendered, "license to commit lustful pleasure." English to Russian and Russian back to English transmuted a cablegram "Genevieve suspended for prank" into "Genevieve hanged for juvenile delinquency." 19

These are obvious crudities. But look at translations into half-a-dozen languages of the same passage in the Old Testament. The sheer difference in length will show that translation is not just a matter of finding a word in the second language that exactly matches a word in the original. Renderings of poetry are especially misleading. The best metrical translation of Homer is probably the fragment done by Hawtrey. The final two lines of the famous "Helen on the wall" passage of the third book in the *Iliad* goes as follows: 20

> So said she; but they long since in earth's soft arms were reposing
> There in their own dear land, their fatherland, Lacedaemon.

Hawtrey has caught the musical effect of Greek hexameter about as well as it is possible to do in English. But the Greek says literally, "but them, on the other hand, the life-giving earth held fast." The original is realistic—Helen's brothers were dead and that was that. The English is sentimental.

Once in Paris I saw a play called "The Weak Sex." I found it charmingly risque. A year later in Vienna I took a girl to see a German translation of the same play. Though she was no prude, I was embarrassed because the play was vulgar if not obscene in German. 21

I think I got my first genuine insight into the nature of language when my tutor at Oxford asked me to translate into Greek a few pages from an 22 eighteenth-century British rhetorician which contained the following phrase, "she heaped the utmost virulence of her invective upon him." I struggled with this and finally committed the unforgivable sin of looking up each word in an English-Greek dictionary. My tutor glanced at the resultant monstrosity and looked up at me with mingled disgust, pity, and amazement. "My dear boy," he said, "don't you know that the only possible way you can render that is *deinos aedeitai,* she blamed very strongly?"

Really, there are three kinds of translation. There is the literal or word-for-word variety which is always distorted except perhaps between languages that are very similar in structure and vocabulary. Second, there is the official type where certain conventions as to idiomatic equivalents are respected. The third, or psychological type of translation, where the words produce approximately the same effects in the speakers of the second language as they did in those of the original, is next to impossible. At best, the rendering must be extremely free, with elaborate circumlocutions and explanations. I once heard Einstein make a slip of the tongue that stated the deeper truth. He said, "I shall speak in English this evening, but if I get excited during the discussion I shall break into German and Professor Lindeman will traduce me." 23

If words referred only to things, translation would be relatively simple. 24
But they refer also to relations between things and the subjective as well as the objective aspects of these relationships. In different tongues relationships are variously conceived. The Balinese word *tis* means not to be cold when it is cold. The Balinese word *paling* designates the state of a trance or drunkenness or a condition of not knowing where you are, what day it is, where the center of the island is, the caste of the person to whom you are talking. The subjective aspects arise from the fact that we use words not only to express things and relationships but to express ourselves; words refer not only to events but to the attitudes of the speakers toward those events.

The words prostitute and whore have exactly the same denotation. The 25
connotation, however, is very different. And a word's connotation is at least as important as the denotation in rousing feeling and producing action. Examine carefully the richest field of modern verbal magic—advertisements.

The same words often don't mean the same thing to different genera- 26
tions within the same culture. Margaret Mead writes:

> Take the word *job.* To the parents a job was something you got when you finished school—the next step, a little grim, a little exciting, the end of carefree school days. A job was something you were going to get, bound to get, something that waited for you at the end of school, just as certainly as autumn follows summer. But job—to those born in 1914, 1915? Something that you might never get, something to be longed for and prayed for, to starve for and steal for, almost—a job. There weren't any. When these two generations talk together and the word *job* is used, how will they understand each other? Suppose the issue is the draft—"A shame a fellow has to give up his job." To the elders this is arrant unpatriotic selfishness. To the young it is obvious sense. They find it

strange that older people can see the sacrifice involved when married men with children must leave their families to go away in the defense service. Yet these same people don't see that any one should mind leaving a job. "Don't they know what a *job* means now, in the thinking of those born in 1915, 1916, 1917? Don't they know that just as among the ancients one was not a man until one had begotten a male child, so today one can't think of one's self as a full human being, without a job? We didn't say a guy wouldn't go because he had a job. We just said it was tough on him. We weren't saying anything they wouldn't say themselves about a man with kids. But gee—how they blew up!"[7]

The British and the Americans are still under the delusion that they speak the same language. With some qualifications this is true as far as denotations are concerned, though there are concepts like "sissy" in American for which there are no precise English equivalents. Connotations, however, are often importantly different, and this makes for the more misunderstanding because both languages are still called "English" (treating alike by words things that are different). An excellent illustration is again supplied by Margaret Mead: 27

. . . in Britain, the word "compromise" is a good word, and one may speak approvingly of any arrangement which has been a compromise, including, very often, one in which the other side has gained more than fifty per cent of the points at issue. On the other hand, in the United States, the minority position is still the position from which everyone speaks; the President *versus* Congress, Congress *versus* the President, the State government *versus* the metropolis and the metropolis *versus* the State government. This is congruent with the American doctrine of checks and balances, but it does not permit the word "compromise" to gain the same ethical halo which it has in Britain. Where, in Britain, to compromise means to work out a good solution, in America it usually means to work out a bad one, a solution in which all the points of importance (to both sides) are lost. Thus, in negotiations between the United States and Britain, all of which had, in the nature of the case, to be compromises, as two sovereignties were involved, the British could always speak approvingly and proudly of the result, while the Americans had to emphasize their losses.[8]

The words, then, that pass so readily from mouth to mouth are not entirely trustworthy substitutes for the facts of the physical world. The smooth-worn standard coins are slippery steppingstones from mind to mind. Nor is thinking simply a matter of choosing words to express thoughts. The selected words always mirror social situation as well as objective fact. Two men go into a bar in New York and are overcharged for bad liquor: "This is a gyp joint." The same thing happens in Paris: "The French are a bunch of chiselers." 28

Perhaps the most important contribution of anthropological linguistics has come from the difficulties the anthropologist goes through in trying to 29 express the meanings contained in speech structures completely foreign to the pattern of all European tongues. This study and this experience has forced upon the anthropologist a rather startling discovery which is fraught with meaning for a world where peoples speaking many different idioms are trying to communicate without distortion. Every language is something more than a vehicle for exchanging ideas and information—more even than a tool for self-expression and for letting off emotional steam or for getting other people to do what we want.

Every language is also a special way of looking at the world and inter- 30
preting experience. Concealed in the structure of each different language are a whole set of unconscious assumptions about the world and life in it. The anthropological linguist has come to realize that the general ideas one has about what happens in the world outside oneself are not altogether "given" by external events. Rather, up to a point, one sees and hears what the grammatical system of one's language has made one sensitive to, has trained one to look for in experience. This bias is the most insidious because everyone is so unconscious of his native language as a system. To one brought up to speak a certain language it is part of the very nature of things, remaining always in the class of background phenomena. It is as natural that experience should be organized and interpreted in these language-defined classes as it is that the seasons change. In fact the naïve view is that anyone who thinks in any other way is unnatural or stupid, or even vicious—and most certainly illogical.

In point of fact, traditional or Aristotelian logic has been mainly the 31
analysis of consistencies in the structures of languages like Greek and Latin. The subject-predicate form of speech has implied a changeless world of fixed relations between "substances" and their "qualities." This view, as Korzybski[9] has insisted, is quite inadequate to modern physical knowledge which shows that the properties of an atom alter from instant to instant in accord with the shifting relationships of its component elements. The little word "is" has brought us much confusion because sometimes it signifies that the subject exists, sometimes that it is a member of a designated class, sometimes that subject and predicate are identical. Aristotelian logic teaches us that something is or isn't. Such a statement is often false to reality, for both-and is more often true than either-or. "Evil" ranges all the way from black through an infinite number of shades of gray. Actual experience does not present clear-cut entities like "good" and "bad," "mind" and "body"; the sharp split remains verbal. Modern physics has shown that even in the inanimate world there are many questions that cannot be answered by an unrestricted "yes" or an unqualified "no."

From the anthropological point of view there are as many different 32
worlds upon the earth as there are languages. Each language is an instrument which guides people in observing, in reacting, in expressing themselves in a special way. The pie of experience can be sliced in many different ways, and language is the principal directive force in the background. You can't say in Chinese, "answer me yes or no," for there aren't words for yes and no. Chinese gives priority to "how?" and nonexclusive categories; European lan-

guages to "what?" and exclusive categories. In English we have both real plurals and imaginary plurals, "ten men" and "ten days"; in Hopi plurals and cardinal numbers may be used only for things that can be seen together as an objective group. The fundamental categories of the French verb are before and after (tense) and potentiality vs. actuality (mood); the fundamental categories of one American Indian language (Wintu) are subjectivity vs. objectivity, knowledge vs. belief, freedom vs. actual necessity.

In the Haida language of British Columbia there are more than twenty 33
verbal prefixes that indicate whether an action was performed by carrying, shooting, hammering, pushing, pulling, floating, stamping, picking, chopping, or the like. Some languages have different verbs, adjectives, and pronouns for animate and inanimate things. In Melanesia there are as many as four variant forms for each possessive pronoun. One may be used for the speaker's body and mind, another for illegitimate relatives and his loincloth, a third his possessions and gifts. The underlying conceptual images of each language tend to constitute a coherent though unconscious philosophy.

Where in English one word, "rough," may equally well be used to 34
describe a road, a rock, or the business surface of a file, the Navaho language finds a need for three different words which may not be used interchangeably. While the general tendency is for Navaho to make finer and more concrete distinctions, this is not inevitably the case. The same stem is used for rip, light beam, and echo, ideas which seem diverse to speakers of European languages. One word is used to designate a medicine bundle with all its contents, the skin quiver in which the contents are wrapped, the contents as a whole, and some of the distinct items. Sometimes the point is not that the images of Navahos are less fluid and more delimited but rather just that the external world is dissected along different lines. For example, the same Navaho word is used to describe both a pimply face and a nodule-covered rock. In English a complexion might be termed "rough" or "coarse," but a rock would never, except facetiously, be described as pimply. Navaho differentiates two types of rough rock: the kind which is rough in the manner in which a file is rough and the kind which is nodule-encrusted. In these cases the differences between the Navaho and the English ways of seeing the world cannot be disposed of merely by saying that the Navaho language is more precise. The variations rest in the features which the two languages see as essential. Cases can indeed be given where the Navaho is notably less precise. Navaho gets along with a single word for flint, metal, knife, and certain other objects of metal. This, to be sure, is due to the historical accident that, after European contact, metal in general and knives in particular took the place of flint.

Navahos are perfectly satisfied with what seem to Europeans rather 35
imprecise discriminations in the realm of time sequences. On the other hand, they are the fussiest people in the world about always making explicit in the forms of the language many distinctions which English makes only occasionally and vaguely. In English one says, "I eat," meaning, "I eat something." The Navaho point of view is different. If the object thought of is actually indefinite, then "something" must be tacked on to the verb.

The nature of their language forces the Navaho to notice and report 36
many other distinctions in physical events which the nature of the English language allows speakers to neglect in most cases, even though their senses are just as capable as those of the Navaho to register the smaller details of what goes on in the external world. For example, suppose a Navaho range rider and a white supervisor see that a wire fence needs repair. The supervisor will probably write in his notebook, "Fence at such and such a place must be fixed." If the Navaho reports the break, he must choose between forms that indicate whether the damage was caused by some person or by a nonhuman agency, whether the fence was of one or several strands of wire.

In general, the difference between Navaho thought and English 37
thought—both as manifested in the language and as forced by the very nature of the linguistic forms into such patterns—is that Navaho thought is ordinarily much more specific. The ideas expressed by the English verb "to go" provide a nice example. When a Navaho says that he went somewhere he never fails to specify whether it was afoot, astride, by wagon, auto, train, airplane, or boat. If it be a boat, it must be specified whether the boat floats off with the current, is propelled by the speaker, or is made to move by an indefinite or unstated agency. The speed of a horse (walk, trot, gallop, run) is expressed by the verb form chosen. He differentiates between starting to go, going along, arriving at, returning from a point. It is not, of course, that these distinctions *cannot* be made in English, but that they *are not* made consistently. They seem of importance to English speakers only under special circumstances.

A cross-cultural view of the category of time is highly instructive. 38
Beginners in the study of classical Greek are often troubled by the fact that the word *opiso* sometimes means "behind," sometimes "in the future." Speakers of English find this baffling because they are accustomed to think of themselves as moving through time. The Greeks, however, conceived of themselves as stationary, of time as coming up behind them, overtaking them, and then, still moving on, becoming the "past" that lay before their eyes.

Present European languages emphasize time distinctions. The tense sys- 39
tems are usually thought of as the most basic of verbal inflections. However, this was not always so. Streitberg says that in primitive Indo-European a special indicator for the present was usually lacking. In many languages, certainly, time distinctions are only irregularly present or are of distinctly secondary importance. In Hopi the first question answered by the verb form is that of the type of information conveyed by the assertion. Is a situation reported as actuality, as anticipated, or as a general truth? In the anticipatory form there is no necessary distinction between past, present, and future. The English translation must choose from context between "was about to run," "is about to run," and "will run." The Wintu language of California carries this stress upon implications of validity much farther. The sentence "Harry is chopping wood" must be translated in five different ways, depending upon whether the speaker knows this by hearsay, by direct observation, or by inference of three degrees of plausibility.

In no language are the whole of a sense experience and all possible 40
interpretations of it expressed. What people think and feel and how they report what they think and feel are determined, to be sure, by their personal history, and by what actually happens in the outside world. But they are also determined by a factor which is often overlooked; namely, the pattern of linguistic habits which people acquire as members of a particular society. It makes a difference whether or not a language is rich in metaphors and conventional imagery.

Our imaginations are restricted in some directions, free in others. The 41
linguistic particularization of detail along one line will mean the neglect of other aspects of the situation. Our thoughts are directed in one way if we speak a language where all objects are classified according to sex, in another if the classification is by social position or the form of the object. Grammars are devices for expressing relations. It makes a difference what is treated as object, as attribute, as state, as act. In Hopi, ideas referring to the seasons are not grouped with what we call nouns but rather with what we call adverbs. Because of our grammar it is easy to personify summer, to think of it as a thing or a state.

Even as between closely related tongues, the conceptual picture may be 42
different. Let us take one final example from Margaret Mead:

> Americans tend to arrange objects on a single scale of value, from best to worst, biggest to smallest, cheapest to most expensive, etc., and are able to express a preference among very complex objects on such a single scale. The question, "What is your favorite color?" so intelligible to an American, is meaningless in Britain, and such a question is countered by: "Favorite color for what? A flower? A necktie?" Each object is thought of as having a most complex set of qualities, and color is merely a quality of an object, not something from a color chart on which one can make a choice which is transferable to a large number of different sorts of objects. The American reduction of complexities to single scales is entirely comprehensible in terms of the great diversity of value systems which different immigrant groups brought to the American scene. Some common denominator among the incommensurables was very much needed, and over-simplification was almost inevitable. But, as a result, Americans think in terms of qualities which have uni-dimensional scales, while the British, when they think of a complex object or event, even if they reduce it to parts, think of each part as retaining all of the complexities of the whole. Americans subdivide the scale; the British subdivide the object.[10]

Language and its changes cannot be understood unless linguistic behav- 43
ior is related to other behavioral facts. Conversely, one can gain many subtle insights into those national habits and thought ways of which one is ordinarily unconscious by looking closely at special idioms and turns of speech in one's own and other languages. What a Russian says to an American doesn't really get across just from shuffling words—much is twisted or blunted or lost unless the American knows something about Russia and Russian life, a good

deal more than the sheer linguistic skill needed for a formally correct translation. The American must indeed have gained some entrance to that foreign world of values and significances which are pointed up by the emphases of the Russian vocabulary, crystalized in the forms of Russian grammar, implicit in the little distinctions of meaning in the Russian language.

Any language is more than an instrument for conveying ideas, more even than an instrument for working upon the feelings of others and for self-expression. Every language is also a means of categorizing experience. The events of the "real" world are never felt or reported as a machine would do it. There is a selection process and an interpretation in the very act of response. Some features of the external situation are highlighted; others are ignored or not fully discriminated. 44

Every people has its own characteristic classes in which individuals pigeonhole their experiences. These classes are established primarily by the language through the types of objects, processes, or qualities which receive special emphasis in the vocabulary and equally, though more subtly, through the types of differentiation or activity which are distinguished in grammatical forms. The language says, as it were, "notice this," "always consider this separate from that," "such and such things belong together." Since persons are trained from infancy to respond in these ways, they take such discriminations for granted as part of the inescapable stuff of life. When we see two peoples with different social traditions respond in different ways to what appear to the outsider to be identical stimulus situations, we realize that experience is much less an objective absolute than we thought. Every language has an effect upon what the people who use it see, what they feel, how they think, what they can talk about. 45

"Common sense" holds that different languages are parallel methods for expressing the same "thoughts." "Common sense," however, itself implies talking so as to be readily understood by one's fellows—in the same culture. Anglo-American "common sense" is actually very sophisticated, deriving from Aristotle, and the speculations of scholastic and modern philosophers. The fact that all sorts of basic philosophic questions are begged in the most cavalier fashion is obscured by the conspiracy of silent acceptance which always attends the system of conventional understandings that we call culture. 46

The lack of true equivalences between any two languages is merely the outward expression of inward differences between two peoples in premises, in basic categories, in the training of fundamental sensitivities, and in general view of the world. The way the Russians put their thoughts together shows the impress of linguistic habits, of characteristic ways of organizing experience, for 47

> Human beings do not live in the objective world alone, nor alone in the world of social activity as ordinarily understood, but are very much at the mercy of the particular language which has become the medium of expression for their society. It is quite an illusion to imagine that one adjusts

to reality essentially without the use of language and that language is merely an incidental means of solving specific problems of communication or reflection. The fact of the matter is that the 'real world' is to a large extent unconsciously built up on the language habits of the group. . . . We see and hear and otherwise experience very largely as we do because the language habits of our community predispose certain choices of interpretation.—Edward Sapir[11]

A language is, in a sense, a philosophy.

NOTES

All notes are Kluckhohn's.

1. Alexander Bryan Johnson, *A Treatise on Language,* David Rynin, ed. (Berkeley, University of California Press, 1947).

2. From "Language," by Edward Sapir, *Encyclopedia of the Social Sciences,* vol. ix. Copyright 1933 by The Macmillan Company and used with their permission.

3. Leonard Bloomfield, *Language,* (New York, Holt, Rinehart & Winston, Inc., 1933).

4. Another illustration of the "principle of inverted snobbery": In an American college that is small or struggling for prestige, faculty members who are members of Phi Beta Kappa would as soon appear on the campus without their pants as without their keys. In old, well-established universities, ΦBK keys are worn only by a few older professors.

5. S. de Madariaga, *Englishmen, Frenchmen and Spaniards* (Oxford University Press, 1929).

6. Carl Becker, *Heavenly City of the Eighteenth Century Philosophers* (New Haven, Yale University Press, 1935).

7. Margaret Mead, "When Were You Born," *Child Study* (Spring, 1941).

8. *Ibid.*

9. Alfred Korzybski, foremost proponent of General Semantics, wrote *Science and Sanity: An Introduction to Non-Aristotelian Systems and General Semantics,* a difficult but significant book on language and human behavior. Korzybski's views have been popularized by S. I. Hayakawa, Stuart Chase, and others. [eds.]

10. Margaret Mead, "The Application of Anthropological Techniques to Cross-National Communication," *Transactions of the New York Academy of Sciences* (February, 1947).

11. Edward Sapir, "Language," *Encyclopedia of the Social Sciences,* vol. ix (New York, The Macmillan Company, 1933).

Questions for Discussion

1. Kluckhohn observes that in Arabic, "there are more than six thousand different words for camel, its parts, and equipment" (¶7). Is a person with this powerful camel vocabulary going to "see" more when looking at a camel than those of us without this vocabulary? Or do the rest of us see the same things but simply lack the ability to name them? How much do you think our ability to name things determines our ability to perceive them or experience them?

2. Kluckhohn also observes that "we say 'five houses' when 'five house' would be simpler and convey the meaning equally well" (¶10). Construct arguments for and against changing the grammatical rules in such instances. Are the arguments based on logic or convention? Which argument, the one based on logic or the one based on convention, seems the more relevant to you?
3. If you belong to any close-knit group—a fraternity or sorority, a sports team, or a church group, for example—can you find instances of special vocabulary usage, special kinds of expressions, or special kinds of pronunciation that work to sustain the intimacy of the group?
4. Discuss with your classmates the denotations and connotations of the following pairs of words:

   thin, beanpole
   cautious, cowardly
   masculine, macho
   unconventional, weird
   pleasingly plump, obese
   independent, uncooperative
   proud, arrogant
   emotional, sentimental
   aggressive, intimidating

5. Can you identify the meanings of the following words common in British English? (*Hint:* Even the words in this list that Americans use do not have the same meaning for us that they have for the British.)

   treacle, lift, perambulator, drawing pins, telly, woollies, petrol, bonnet, boot, tart, biscuit, barrister, bobby, lorry, geyser, form, tin, coach, corn, waistcoat, football (Turn the book upside down to find the American "translations.")

   syrup, elevator, baby buggy, thumbtacks, television, long underwear, gasoline, hood, trunk, pie or prostitute, cracker, lawyer, policeman, truck, hot water heater, grade in school, can, bus, grain, vest, soccer or rugby

Suggested Essay Topics

1. Select some fairly brief but richly connotative passage of either prose or poetry and rewrite it using words that have the same denotations but are connotatively neutral or different. Then write an essay directed to the class analyzing what has been lost by the translation and showing how the original author's careful word choice created a precise meaning not exactly duplicable by any other words.
2. Carefully re-read paragraph 26 of Kluckhohn, the paragraph about words not meaning the same thing to different generations. You may even want to get the Mead book from the library and place the quotation in its larger context. Then create a list of words that you think might connote to your parents or grandparents meanings different from those that the same word connotes to you or your peers. Words on such a list might include *patriotism, job, professional, duty, rich, prejudiced, right, wrong, rich, poor,* and *virgin.* Pick words that you think will be revealing, given your particular subjects. Then interview two sets of subjects—the older generation and your peers—probing not just for denotative meanings but also for connotations and the

social, sexual, or political evaluations that lie packed within the connotations. Finally, write an essay directed to your instructor (or perhaps the subjects) explaining what differences and overlappings you found each group attaching to the words, and drawing any inferences that seem appropriate about the role of language in everyday perceptions and judgments.

Peggy Rosenthal

In the preceding essay Clyde Kluckhohn argues that the categories and special features of any given language partly determine our perceptions of and our knowledge about reality. Peggy Rosenthal approaches this same set of issues in another way: by providing a detailed analysis of the extended meanings of certain loaded words, extended meanings that a careless, inattentive, unknowing, or superficial user can set reverberating without realizing it. Every historical age, she argues, uses particular words again and again, words that become packed with so many meanings from different sources that it becomes difficult to use them without heaving whole cartloads of connotations into our discussions—frequently without our seeing or thinking about them. The problem is that while these connotations may escape our notice, they may yet distort our meaning. The only cure, Rosenthal argues, is to become critically aware of words' varied layers. Doing so will allow us to choose words more carefully and use them more precisely.

Some of the words that crop up repeatedly in contemporary discourse—and treated by Rosenthal in Words and Values*—are* self, growth, development, relative, *and* relationship. *In the following excerpt from her book, Rosenthal invites you to consider contemporary notions of "self": a self that we, unlike former generations, are likely to think of as rooted in* private feelings *rather than in social function (the job, trade, craft, or profession we follow) or in divine purpose (the self as God-given and God-defined) or in social class (the self as defined by the duties and privileges of social standing). For many twentieth-century Americans, the self is defined by none of these external points of reference but almost by individual fiat, by what was called a few years ago "existential assertion." Even our absorption in and obsession with careers is not an external source of self-definition, for what we deem important is not so much what we do, but whether we feel good doing it. In today's world, few people would criticize others for leaving a career on the sole grounds that they felt "unhappy" or "unfulfilled" in it. In our culture few sources—including, perhaps, most churches—would challenge the primacy of everyone's "need" for "*self*-fulfillment."*

As you read, try to determine whether you think the modern notion of self is as satisfactory (or perhaps even as morally good) as the notions of self from these other sources just listed, sources that had the authority to define the self in former eras. Of course, you will also have to think about your criteria for "satisfactory" and "good."

Do you hold happiness, for example, as a criterion for the "good" self? And do our self-derived notions of self make us happy? If we are not happy, does our unhappiness stem from the barrenness of our notions of self or from other sources? What other criteria might be useful? Fulfillment of social responsibilities (good citizenship)? Devotion to religious tenets (the righteous life)? Which criteria would you hold? Which notion of the self—your own self—do you prefer? Which notion, if any, do you find binding, or is each of us free to adopt any notion of self and self-fulfillment that pleases us most?

WORDS AND VALUES

From *Words and Values* (1984).

PREFACE

This book is a collection of biographical sketches of some of the leading figures of our time, though the figures aren't people but configurations of words. The purpose of tracing their lives is to find out how they got to be where they are today (how they got into their leading position) and what difference their being there makes in our own lives (what attitudes, beliefs, behavior we're led into by them). 1

The book therefore conceives of the leading words it examines as "leading" in two senses: as being currently "dominant" words, words in positions of power; and as "directing" us, from this dominant position, to think and act in certain ways. Each of the four parts of the book focuses on a group of very common leading words: words like *individual, feelings, develop, growth, alternative, opinion, relationship.* The words are examined to see where they get their popularity and their power, what meanings and values they carry as they move into different areas of our lives, and where they seem to be carrying us as they move along. 2

This view of our relation to the words we use perhaps appears a bit alarming. We aren't seen as leading our own language anywhere at all, but as being led by it. Our words, even our common everyday ones, are seen as an active force in our lives; our own position with respect to them is seen as passive. This is indeed a disturbing position to find ourselves in, but as the analysis proceeds we'll see that the normal operations of language do put us in this passive position: language works to give us much less control over "what we mean" than we generally assume we have. Even when we think we're choosing our words with care and giving them precise meanings, they can mean much more (or less) than we think; and when we use them carelessly, without thinking, they can still carry thoughts. These thoughts we're not aware of, these meanings we don't intend, can then carry us into certain beliefs and behavior—whether or not we notice where we're going. 3

But though the workings of language tend to put us in a passive position, this doesn't imply that our position must remain simply helpless. It will 4 be helpless as long as we let ourselves remain blind to what our language is doing. But we have powers of critical detachment that we're always free to exercise with respect to any of our activities: so instead of letting ourselves be pulled along by the going terms of the day, we can always step back from them and look, from a position of critical detachment, at where they've come from and where they're going. Examining them from this distance, we'll be in a position to resist some of their pull if we want to; seeing more clearly where a certain set of words is going, we'll be able to decide how far we want to go along with it and where we'd perhaps rather switch to a different set of terms (and values and goals) instead. To encourage this critical distance, to enable us to make such choices, is the purpose of this book.

. . .

SELF

If the word *self* were a stone and the sentences we hear or read or say were 5
pathways, we'd probably be unable to get through an ordinary day without stumbling across all the stones in our way. The lines of best-sellers, popular magazines, and television talk shows are strewn with *self:* we're urged to fulfill ourselves, realize ourselves, know ourselves, be aware of (but not beware of) ourselves, love ourselves, create ourselves, feel good about ourselves, actualize ourselves, express ourselves, improve ourselves. Self-fulfillment therapy and self-improvement courses are booming businesses, run by alchemists who know how to turn the stones of *self* into gold. There is even in the city where I live an organization called The Self Center: a perfect title for our times, in which the self stands firmly in the center of our path, worshipped as our rock and our redeemer.

If we turn from the main roads of popular public discourse (and by 6
discourse I mean all uses of verbal language, both written and spoken) into the areas of special-interest groups, we still stumble upon *self* almost wherever we go. "Women's self-knowledge," "self-fulfillment," and "self-identification" are proclaimed as goals of the Women's Movement. "Energy self-sufficiency" is our nation's goal, and "Palestinian self-determination" a goal for many in the Middle East.

Even on the narrower roads of academic disciplines, the ground remains 7
familiar. We find *self* all over the place in the writings of philosophy: no surprise, since the self has been one of philosophy's prime subjects of study ever since the Renaissance. Recent philosophical books like *The Nature of the Self,* then, follow a time-honored tradition. But in the profession of literary criticism the hundreds of recent articles and books taking *self* as their subject ("Saul Bellow's Idea of Self," "The Divided Self in the Fiction of Henry James," "The Flexibility of the Self in Renaissance Literature," *Imagining a Self*) are a relatively new development, and an unexpected one unless we realize that literary criticism is much more in touch with popular concerns than is usually granted.

When we come to psychology, *self* is no longer just a stone that we trip 8
over, or pass by, or stoop to examine, on our way; it has swollen into a huge

rock, even a cave, which we have to enter, explore, probe the depths of as we go through the discourse of the profession. And as we go through, we find ourselves coming full circle to where we began, since the cave of psychology opens onto the main road of popular discourse—even, we could say, spills onto it, considering the amount of best-seller material (*Games People Play; I'm OK, You're OK; Passages; Pulling Your Own Strings; Living, Loving, and Learning* is just some of it) that is the direct product of psychology.

Once we notice how often *self* turns up in our current public discourse, 9
both popular and specialized, we can easily see why *self* is a main term in our private discourse as well, and even in our private thoughts. The going terms of an age tend to be, naturally, the ones we think with, talk to our family and friends with, figure out things with. So it's no surprise that we often think these days in terms of *self,* seeing *myself* as the unquestioned justification for almost any action and as the goal toward which everything else must lead. Adolescents choosing a career are counseled, for example, to study themselves and know themselves fully in order to figure out which career will be best (meaning most self-fulfilling). We don't question whether, in laying our heavily weighted *self* on people who are already at the most self-absorbed stage of life, we might be burdening them unfairly, even preventing them from moving at all. Nor do we question our own or our friends' divorces when they're justified, as they often are, in terms of *self* (self-fulfillment, self-realization, etc.); there's no doubt that without the word *self,* and the values and concepts it currently brings with it, the divorce rate would be considerably lower than it is. . . .

Though I don't want to get bogged down here in methodology, I have 10
to make just one more distinction in order to be accurate about the way *self* pulls us: a distinction between the ways that a word's values, whether positive or negative, can be carried. Words lead complex lives and lead us along with them in complex ways; if we want to see how we're being led, rather than being led along blindly, we have to make an effort to follow our language with our eyes open to its subtle workings. What we see, then, when we look at how words carry their values, is that two different ways are possible. Some words carry their values inherently, in their very beings, so to speak: these are words whose referent* *is* a certain value, words like *good, pleasure, comfortable,* or, on the other side, *disgraceful, worthless, evil.* Many more words, though, carry their values not as inherent parts of themselves but *ad*herently, like labels stuck on their heads or behind their backs, or like little flags sticking up from them and bearing the imprint of a plus or a minus. These are words whose referent is not itself a value and which take on whatever attitude we have toward the referent at the time. Adherent values can therefore change over the years, as our attitudes do. For example, *sex* for the Victorians carried, at least on the surface of public discourse, a minus of untouchability, as if the word itself carried VD; whereas for us *sex* has become a bearer of all the good things of life, a word universally proclaimed from the

*The object, concept, idea, or feeling a word names or to which it refers.

rooftops by faces beaming with pleasure. Or *simple,* which once carried the positive sense of "guileless" or "sincere" when applied to a person, now tends to carry the negative scornful implication of "simple-minded" or "simpleton." Adherent values can vary not only over time but for different speakers at the same time: *car* spoken by the president of General Motors carries a proud plus, but in the mouth and mind of an environmentalist fighting air pollution, or of an energy conservationist, it carries a menacing minus, the sign of the skull and crossbones.

Self's positive value today is of the adherent and almost universal kind, 11
like that of *sex.* Though critics of our self-concern have started speaking out in the past few years and so have begun to move *self* into the ambivalent category of *car, self* is still generally seen as an unquestionably good thing. But what's so good about it? What is there in *self* that we find so attractive? This is a question, really, about what *self* means to us. And it's a hard question to answer, not only because *self* has a variety of meanings, but also because *meaning* itself (and here another dual distinction is necessary) means at least two things. By *meaning* we mean the definition of a word: *jogging,* for example, means running at a slow, regular pace. But by *meaning* we also mean the concept or concepts carried by—or, as we usually say, "behind"—a word: *jogging* now carries the concept of good health, physical well-being, and even for some people mental well-being and peace of mind. Note that along with this concept of jogging as well-being (physical or mental) comes a positive value; the mere definition of jogging is neutral. Concepts often, as in this case, imply values: the attractiveness of jogging today seems to lie in the concepts behind it.

. . .

PSYCHOLOGY'S SLIPPERY SENSE OF *SELF*

In 1956, a psychologist began his book with the statement: "Concern for the 12
self with all its contributing attributes and potentials is rapidly becoming a central focus of contemporary psychological inquiry." Today we might smile at the obviousness of such a statement, but our smile should be one not of scorn at its naiveté but of admiration at the astuteness of its prediction. *Self* and its compounds have indeed come to take up much of psychology's attention—so much that they fill, for example, fourteen columns of titles in the January–June 1982 *Psychological Abstracts* Subject Index (with *"Self Concept," "Self Esteem,"* and *"Self Perception"* the longest entries) and seven inches of the Psychiatric Card Catalog at the University of Rochester Medical School (including titles like "On the Beginnings of a Cohesive Self," "The Finding and Becoming of Self," and "On the Development of the Experience of Mental Self, the Bodily Self, and Self Consciousness"). These statistics, though admittedly crude, confirm the sense of probably anyone who comes in contact with psychology (and is there anyone who doesn't?) that contemporary psychology is inseparable from *self.*

The "contemporary psychology" I refer to includes, as my reference to 13 the Psychiatric Card Catalog indicates, psychiatry and psychoanalysis and some of the psychotherapies as well. This inclusion is sure to rankle some members of these various disciplines who insist on the distinctness of their fields. But in the use they make of *self,* these fields are far from distinct. In fact, they seem to have developed their sense of *self* on common ground: ground initially laid by Freud (who, however, made no significant use of the term) and then sown and cultivated by workers with professional concerns and styles as varied as those of Jung, William James, Karen Horney, Carl Rogers, and Rollo May. The *self* produced by this crossbreeding has then spread into general public discourse from all the psychology-related fields except behaviorism, which has worked hard to hold back the spread. One field in particular, though, has been most strongly behind the push of *self* into popular discourse: the field known as "humanistic psychology" or "personal growth psychology" or "the human potential movement." Since my ultimate concern in this part of the book is with our popular sense of *self,* the psychology I have in mind when I talk about "psychology's *self*" is primarily this personal growth psychology. Primarily but not exclusively—because, as I've said, no *self* of any field of psychology is cut off from the *self* of the others.

What exactly *self* means for all these areas of psychology that make so 14
much of it is surprisingly difficult to discover. Soon after the above-quoted psychologist began his book by noting psychology's central "concern for the self," another psychologist began hers by noting that "in psychological discussions the word 'self' has been used in many different ways." And sixteen years later, those differences hadn't yet been resolved: a 1977 article in *Psychology in the Schools* complains that "currently scores of theories and definitions of 'self' are found in the literature." In trying to find out what *self* means for psychology, then, we can't hope simply to open a dictionary of psychology and find there a comprehensive definition. Nor, it turns out, can we go to the literature* itself to find clear statements of those scores of meanings: even though the self is one of psychology's central concerns, *the self* rarely gets directly defined by those concerned with it.

By "direct definition" I mean statements in the form "the self is. . . ." 15
Occasionally in the literature we find such a statement: for example, "The self is . . . the center from which one sees and is aware of . . . different 'sides' of himself." More frequent, however, are indirect definitions of various kinds: definition by apposition ("it indicates that the person, the self, is generous"), by *or* ("the archetype of wholeness or of the self"), by *as* ("I speak now of the real self as that central inner force"), or by a combination of these ("conceiving ego or self as a constellation of interrelated attitudes"). Writers using grammatical forms such as these don't usually think of themselves as defining; yet these forms act as definitions, and in the absence of direct definitions we often have to rely on them to discover what writers mean by the words they use. Another, even more indirect, way of learning what is meant by psychology's *self* is by noticing the metaphors that *self* gets used in, or the

*The scholarly publications in a given field of research.

terms that surround it. Even the terms that *self* gets opposed to will give us a clue about its definition: when we read, for example, that often a client "discovers that he exists only in response to the demands of others, that he seems to have no self of his own," we know that *self* is *not* exclusive responsiveness to others' demands and is some sort of opposition to those demands.

Reading through the writings of psychology, both technical and popular, with these various methods of definition as a guide, we can begin to sort out what psychologists have in mind by *self.* One thing they often seem to have in mind is that *self* is a goal of some kind. But the kind varies. It can be the goal of what sounds like a treasure hunt (the familiar "finding of one's self"), a trip ("the long journey to achieve selfhood"), a vegetable ("the maturation of the self"), or a vaguely Aristotelian process ("self-actualization is actualization of a self"). Sometimes, though, *self* seems not to be a goal but to have goals of its own: "the [mature] self now expresses . . . its intentions and goals." . . . 16

[In a section too technical to include here, Rosenthal continues to discuss notions of the self advanced by various psychologists. She alludes both to the founders of modern psychology, Sigmund Freud and Carl Jung, and to some of their modern heirs, the titles of whose writings reveal their relevance for Rosenthal's thesis: Rollo May, Man's Search for Himself *(1953); Willard Gaylin,* Feelings: Our Vital Signs *(1979); Karen Horney,* Neurosis and Human Growth *(1950); Carl Rogers,* On Becoming a Person *(1961); Abraham Maslow, "Self-Actualizing People: A Study of Psychological Health" (1958); and Erich Fromm, "Selfishness, Self-love, and Self-interest" (1958). Generalizing on the basis of their views, Rosenthal asserts that modern psychology has tended to link the concept of self more and more with other terms that possess positive value in the modern world, especially such terms as* feelings, individual, *and* unique. *The upshot of this tendency, she argues, has been to give us a notion of the self that is (1) always supposed to be unique (the authentic person) and (2) always supposed to feel good, especially about "itself." She concludes this discussion as follows.]*

What psychology did, we can now say in summary, was to link the word *self* to these terms and to the concepts behind them; to give *self* and its associates scientific status by making them part of a technical vocabulary (without, however, developing for them clear or agreed-on definitions); and to link them all with teleologically weighted terms like *goal, growth,* and *health*—thus offering us this extended network of terms, bright with the golden glow of scientific validity, as the ideal pattern for us to follow in our talk, our thinking, and our shaping of our lives. 17

OUR BEST-SELLING AND GOD-GIVEN *SELF*

Have we accepted this *self* that psychology offers us? How much of our sense of *self,* as we ordinarily use the word, comes from psychology? All, we might be tempted to say—especially when we notice how many of our best-sellers 18 (those prime providers of terms for public, and private, discourse) either are written by psychologists or are, like *Passages,* * popularizations of psychology. *Passages,* in fact, has itself become a passage: a conduit through which the terms of self-oriented psychology have poured into the main stream of general discourse.

While *self* is not a frequent term in *Passages,* the self as conceived by 19
psychology is the book's subject, and all the familiar *self* associations of psychology are there. The "inner realm" is for Sheehy where the action is; her study—like Freud's, Jung's, Maslow's, Gaylin's—is of our "internal life system." And her proudly positive *inner* is, in the best Rogersian fashion, set against an *outer* conceived as restrictive and artificial: when you move into midlife, "you are moving out of roles and into the self." This inner self—like May's, Maslow's, Rogers's—is the source (the only "authentic" source) of values: the move into the self is a move "away from external validations and accreditations, in search of an inner validation"; and "one of the great rewards of moving through the disassembling period to renewal [another positively loaded term] is coming to approve of oneself ethically and morally and quite independent of other people's standards and agenda."

"Coming to approve of oneself ethically and morally" turns out, in the 20
book—as in Gaylin and Rogers—to be inseparable from feeling good about oneself. Sheehy, as we would expect from our familiarity with *self*'s associates in psychology, makes much of *feeling,* both as a main subject and as a main term in her vocabulary. "How do we *feel* about our way of living in the world at any given time?" she asks as one of the book's central questions, letting her italics show where her emphasis lies.

But, of course, this emphasis on feelings is not only Sheehy's. It has 21
become—through *Passages* and all the other mass media productions through which psychology's terms come to us—the emphasis almost everywhere we go. When, for example, we go to meetings on the job, we find that once-objective business (a company's marketing changes, a college's curriculum changes) has been sucked inside and comes out of speaker's mouths as "how I feel about these changes." If we go to church, we're likely to hear sermons on the importance of feeling good about ourselves and having a "positive self-image." And if we happen to go to medical school, we're likely to find the anatomy professor concentrating on how to "help the students deal with possible emotional tensions arising from the experience of the dissecting lab." The dissecting lab is no longer a classroom but an "experience"; an experience must be "felt"; and Sheehy's question "How do we *feel* about our way of living in the world at any given time?" seems to be asked now at every given time.

*Gail Sheehy's *Passages* (New York: Dutton, 1974) was a blockbuster best-seller that portrayed life as a series of passages and suggested that success in life is *not* finding yourself in middle age at the end of a passage leading to a future you don't want. The emphasis is on inner feelings as the final criteria: whether we "feel good" or "feel bad" about the choices we've made in life, whether those choices have been *authentic,* and whether they have been consistent with our *personal* values.

While we're asked constantly about our feelings, we're assured con- 22
stantly about our individual uniqueness. From Mister Rogers's assurance, to the four-year-old in each of us, that "you're a very special person" to Dr. Wayne Dyer's best-selling line that "you are unique in all the world" to Dr. Joyce Brothers's sales pitch that each of us should have "a unique and personal program" for success, psychology's line about the value of the individual seems to have spread everywhere. Or, more accurately (since the line isn't only psychology's), what has spread is psychology's version of a general humanist line: as *The Humanist* magazine reminds us, "the preciousness and dignity of the individual person is a central humanist value."

As pop psychology spreads the positive *unique–individual* line through our 23
culture, it necessarily spreads also the confusions and ambiguity that we saw running through psychology's use of the line. When, for example, Sheehy offers "each of us . . . the opportunity to emerge reborn, authentically unique, with an enlarged capacity to love ourselves and embrace others," she's offering us, along with that uniqueness, the ambiguity between given and goal that psychology leaves unresolved in *unique.* For if we have to "emerge" unique, we're presumably not unique already; yet our given uniqueness is one of the working assumptions that Sheehy takes over from developmental-personality psychology. To qualify the aimed-for uniqueness with *authentically* (and thus apparently to distinguish it from ordinary or inauthentic uniqueness) is to make no real qualification at all. *Authentic* is what we could call an "empty plus": it carries positive value but is void of content ("says nothing," as we often put it).

All my talk about the "spread" of psychology's *self,* via the popular 24
media into our common language, makes psychology sound like a creeping vine or like a virus spreading through the population or like a guerrilla force acting underground to take us over town by town (or term by term). These implications of my metaphor are, of course, inaccurate and unfair to psychology: psychology has no conspiracy against us, and it's not an alien force. It's part of us, part of our culture: the part, we could say, that studies for us what we want (even long) to know about our individual selves. If psychology gives us its *self,* this is because we ask for it.

So while we can truly say that we get psychology's *self* through the mass 25
media, we can't say that we get it against our will. Nor can we say, despite the dominant impression given by popular literature and by this analysis of it so far, that the *self* we get is entirely psychology's. Obviously, to a large extent it is—so obviously, maybe, that this examination of how the mass media repeat psychology's lines has been, for many readers, simply repetitious. But if we now look more closely into these best-selling lines, we can see something more in them than what psychology alone has put there. In, for example, that promise of Sheehy's of "the opportunity to emerge reborn" there's a touch of evangelicalism that we can't say comes from psychology. Or, if it does—and there is, certainly, something of the promise of a new life in Maslow's and Rogers's goal of a new or renewed or higher self—it comes into both professional and pop psychology from elsewhere: from, originally,

Christianity. There are other places, too, where Christianity enters into our sense of *self;* and we should look briefly at one of them in order to correct the impression that the *self* we get through the mass media, and hence our common sense of *self,* is entirely and simply psychology's.

In our common (both widespread and frequent) assertion of the value of each individual, we're indeed expressing what *The Humanist* called a "central humanist value." But before "the preciousness and dignity of the individual person" was a central humanist value, it was a central Christian value. By moving the locus of spiritual activity from external rites and laws into the individual, Christianity brought God's infinite value into each person. *Individual* and *internal* have thus always carried pluses for Christianity: the plus signs of God's presence in the individual. "Are you not aware that you are the temple of God, and that the Spirit of God dwells in you?" St. Paul asks rhetorically. One way of looking at what has happened to the positive term *individual* over the past two thousand years is to see the plus sign remaining over *individual* while the source of the world's plus, the Spirit of God, is gradually removed by the secular Renaissance–Romantic–psychology tradition. To St. Paul's question, psychology (speaking for secular humanism generally) answers no. And yet this answer doesn't decrease the value placed by us on the individual. In fact, it reinforces it. 26

This reinforcement works because we hear or see words but not the concepts behind them. Behind (or in) the Christian *individual* is the concept of God; behind (or in) the secular humanist *individual* is the concept of man alone. But while these concepts are far (infinitely far) apart, the words expressing them can be identical. Assertions of "our individual uniqueness" or "the preciousness of the individual" can sound exactly the same no matter who makes them. When Billy Graham asserts, for example, that "the central theme of the universe is the purpose and destiny of every individual," he sounds just like *The Humanist* (even though he means something different). And because Christian and secular voices can sound the same, each "sounds better" because we've heard the same line from the other; each, that is, lends its particular authority to the line. When Graham, then, tells us that each conversion process is "very personal" ("God looks at each of us differently, because each of us is different"), this sounds right because we've heard Mister Rogers telling us, since we were four, that each of us is special and different; and when Dr. Wayne Dyer assures each of us that "you are unique in all the world," we tend to believe it even more because we've heard it in church. 27

We've heard it even if we don't go to church—heard, that is, the Christian lines asserting the value of the individual. We tend to pride ourselves on living in a secular culture; yet a culture in which a major television network considers it profitable to broadcast Billy Graham during prime time, and in which the *New York Times* regularly (religiously!) prints the Pope's addresses, is hardly simply secular. Even those of us who grow up without opening the Bible cannot have avoided contact with Christian lines. Where those lines contradict the lines of a secular authority like psychology, of course we have to choose which to follow. But where the lines overlap, as in assertions of the 28 worth of the individual, we can easily nod our approval to both. The fact that Christianity places positive value on the individual just reinforces our sense of that value, and thus adds to the positive sense of *self* that we get from secular sources.

WHAT GOOD IS THE *SELF*?

If we return now to the original question of this chapter—the question of how 29
much of our sense of *self* comes from psychology—we find that the answer has to be a bit complicated. In the area of *self* covered by *individual,* our sense of positive value seems to come at least as much from Christianity as from psychology, though the amount is hard to measure since in most praise of the individual we can't tell where that praise is coming from. As for the rest of the extensive area covered by *self* and its associated terms, we've seen that while our common *self* is to a large extent psychology's, psychology's *self* is to a large extent not its own but that of four hundred years of Western culture. The Renaissance's positive valuing of subjectivity, individuality, and creativity; seventeenth-century philosophy's positive valuing of self-consciousness and identity; Romanticism's positive valuing of all these along with internalness, freedom, and feelings—all this is carried on in psychology's *self.*

This is quite a lot of good (or goods) to be carried by a single word! And 30
yet there's still more. Because besides Christianity and psychology (and through it the Renaissance–Romantic tradition), other powerful traditions and ideologies come into play in *self* and add their weight to the word.

We've seen, for example, that *freedom* is one of the plus terms associated 31
with *self* in the Romantic tradition carried on by psychology; but *freedom,* along with terms like *independence* and *self-determination,* has also been a plus word in every expression of democratic political ideals since the French Revolution. Furthermore, terms like *self-sufficiency* and *control,* which operate in close connection with the *freedom* set in both psychology and democratic political discourse, are plus terms also in the ideology of modern technology. These terms, of course, have different applications in each of these places. For technology, *self-sufficiency* and *control* are terms applied primarily to machines and ideal mechanical functioning; for democracy, these terms apply to governments and to people as political units; for psychology, they apply to individual personality. Yet the application in each case is to something valued positively by the ideology or discipline concerned.

These terms then carry along with them, in all of their uses, the posi- 32
tive values of all the ideologies and disciplines and activities and traditions of thought in which they operate. I don't mean that they necessarily carry along the particular applications from these various places; nor do I mean that we're aware of all these sources adding their weight to a word we use. What I mean is that our sense of a word's positive value is increased, usually without our awareness, when that word carries positive value in ideologies and activities and so on other than the one we're consciously

using it in—especially when those other sources of its value are themselves highly prized by our culture.

Take, for example, the call for independence in "Your Declaration of 33
Independence," a 1977 *Harper's Bazaar* article: "Independence, simply, is the freedom to choose what is pertinent to your needs at any given time. It is a feeling of freedom that comes from within." Because of the neat overlap of political and psychological terms here, the positive political values of *independence* and *freedom* are brought to bear on the positive psychological values of *independence, needs, feeling,* and *within.* For the authors of this "Declaration," as well as for readers who respond positively to it, *independence* is attractive because it carries some of our most cherished political and psychological values; and it has this double attraction whether or not the authors and readers are aware of the sources of this attraction. Similarly, in the calls we've heard so often in recent years to "pull our own strings"—whether in ads like *Ms.* magazine's picture of a female marionette with text urging women to cut the strings that control them from outside, or in best-sellers like *Pulling Your Own Strings*—what is being appealed to is our generally and overwhelmingly positive sense of *self-sufficiency* and *control of our lives,* a sense which derives from the combined positive appeal of these terms in psychology, democracy, and technology. Because of the multiple strength of this appeal, then, we tend to go along unquestioningly with our sense that *self-sufficiency* is a good thing—pulled less by our own strings than by those of the powerful networks of meaning and value operating on the word from behind the scenes.

It's odd, maybe, to think of words working like this, apart from our 34
awareness or our conscious intentions: we're so used to assuming our control of everything (we're so attracted by the idea of pulling our own strings) that we assume that, where our language is concerned, we can simply "say what we mean" as long as we just take a minute to choose our words carefully. That words can mean things apart from what we intend for them, that words say what *they* mean more than what *we* mean, is indeed disconcerting. Yet when we look at how our common language actually operates—when we look, for example, at why certain words attract us—we have to admit that it operates to a large extent outside of our conscious intentions. We can indeed increase the extent of our consciousness of its operations, as we're doing here, and thereby give ourselves more control over our language than we usually have. But unless we make this deliberate effort to watch how our words are working, we'll be worked on by them and manipulated by their meanings unawares.

One thing we've seen so far about the way words operate is that they 35
act as receptacles into which different disciplines and ideologies and traditions of thought pour their particular meanings, their favorite value-laden concepts. The word *self,* we can now say, is the container of heavily weighted meaning from some of our culture's most influential sources; it's a loaded term. This is the case even though *self* has no precise definition, either in any of the places where its value comes from or in our everyday use. If you ask someone who speaks in terms of his self—who talks about fulfilling himself

or having a negative self-image or knowing his true self—what exactly he means by his *self,* he's unlikely to be able to tell you. How could he have a precise definition when the sources of his sense of *self* don't give him one? What they give him instead of a definition is, as we've seen, a complex of positively valued concepts—an overwhelmingly good (yes) feeling. And it might be that if *self* had a tighter definition, it couldn't carry such a variety of concepts. A definition is (by definition) a boundary, an assumption of finiteness. A tightly defined word has definite boundaries and therefore limited room for concepts to fit into it. But a loosely defined word like *self* is flexible, stretchy; its sides can move out easily to accommodate all the concepts that come into it from the various places where it operates. And the more concepts it has room for, the more it then tends to draw in other terms associated with these concepts—and thus the more likely it is to operate, by itself or through its associates, in our everyday thought.

Our practically undefined *self,* then, brings with it an array of concepts: 36
mainly from the Renaissance, Romanticism, and psychology, but also from Christianity, democracy, and technology (and from evolutionary theory too . . . .). And these concepts carry almost unanimously positive value. No wonder we're so filled with self: because *self* is filled with the prize concerns of centuries of our culture.

Questions for Discussion

1. Can you think of other words that, like *self,* carry a lot of connotative baggage that many users may not be aware of? What about words like *honor, duty, respect, responsibility, rights, liberty,* and *patriotism*? Would they lend themselves to the kind of analysis that Rosenthal does of *self*? In class discussion can you begin to see some of the things that you would have to include in such an analysis of any one of these words (or another one of your own choice)?
2. In paragraph 3, Rosenthal says that "language works to give us much less control over 'what we mean' than we generally assume we have. Even when we think we're choosing our words with care and giving them precise meanings, they can mean much more (or less) than we think." Do you agree with this as a general position about language, or does it sound to you as if she is overstating the case? Can you think of examples on either side of the question? Have you ever found yourself using a word or phrase that your listeners took in a much wider or narrower sense than you did? If so, give an account of that experience in class.
3. According to the Christian scheme of values that once held much wider sway than it does today, the role of the self was not to serve itself, not to achieve personal happiness above all things. Happiness was not in itself

viewed as sinful, but the satisfaction or fulfillment of the self in a private sense was simply not taken to be the goal of existence. Human beings were created to do the will of God, not to serve the desires of the self. Human selfhood had been corrupt since the Fall (Adam and Eve's sin in the Garden of Eden) and was therefore not to be trusted as a guide to non-sinful behavior. Following God's will could lead the believer into many situations humiliating or stressful to the self—ridicule, poverty, persecution, or martyrdom, for example. In your view, how do modern Christians reconcile this traditional Christian view of the self with the modern view of the self based largely on twentieth-century psychology as described by Rosenthal? *Is* there any way to reconcile these views, to make them live together in peaceful co-existence? Or do most modern Christians simply fail to see that there is any divergence between these views of self? In class discussion, get as many Christians and non-Christians as possible to respond to these questions.

4. If any members of your class come from non-Western cultures or a non-Christian tradition, have them respond to Rosenthal's description of the twentieth-century American secular self from the perspective of their own cultural tradition. What important differences emerge? What kinds of insights might modern Americans learn about the self from non-Americans or non-Christians?

Suggested Essay Topics

1. In contemporary debates about moral issues it is clear that the perceived needs or feelings of the self are often given primacy over external moral standards. In the matter of cheating on exams, for example, you will often hear students arguing that "it's OK for you if you *feel* OK about it personally; I mean, everybody has to make up his own mind about these things." The same position is often taken about other kinds of behavior: premarital sex, drug use, abortion, cheating on income taxes, and so on. Choose an issue such as one of these, and write a dialogue in which one speaker gives support to the position that "*X* is right depending on how you feel about it," and the other supports some version of the position that "*X* can be viewed as wrong regardless of how you feel about it."
2. A variation on topic 1 is to choose one of these two positions about *X* and write an essay defending your views. If you choose this option, however, it will be important for you to find some way of bringing in the views of the opposition. (You might try writing a dialogue.) At least show an awareness of what an intelligent opponent would say. Otherwise you will sound simplistic and naive. For example, you may really believe that abortion is not really a matter of personal feeling because the Bible says 'Thou shalt not kill' and abortion is a form of murder, but in this form it is an inadequate argument. Whether abortion is really a form of murder is exactly what the controversy is all about, and there are many sophisticated points on either side that you need to be aware of before tackling

this (or any other) complex issue. A better way to begin is to say something like, "I know what the proponents of abortion on demand have to say. Their position boils down to three basic arguments: . . ." and then give those arguments. Doing so will not only make you seem in control of your subject, which will enhance your rhetorical credibility, but will also give you concrete points to respond to as you develop your rebuttal.

James E. Miller, Jr.

Is an opinion something we hold, or is it something we are? James E. Miller, Jr., professor of English at the University of Chicago, suggests that it may be both. He shows, for example, that the opinions we crystallize into writing form a part of the self; they are not just baggage we carry around.

The act of writing consists of one choice after another. These choices reveal more than just the extent of our vocabulary; they reveal the self behind the vocabulary, for the sense of a word's "rightness" reflects as much who we are as it does our subject matter. But words do more than reflect a self; they help create it, for each choice of words is a new choice about the self, about who it is that our choices are creating and sustaining.

Writing makes an especially important contribution to the process of self-creation, because the choices made in writing announce us to our readers as one kind of person rather than another. We present a self for our readers to meet and respond to. Once we create these "literary" selves, we do not automatically shed them when we finish a writing assignment. They remain as part of our minds and, to some extent, they then make up our character, our potential "real-life" selves. Samuel Johnson once said, "I write; therefore, I am." According to Miller's view, the quip was more profound than most of us might think.

WRITING AS SELF-DISCOVERY

From chapter 4, "Writing as Discovery: Inner Worlds," of *Word, Self, Reality: The Rhetoric of Imagination* (1972). The title is ours.

> The mentality of mankind and the language of mankind created each other. If we like to assume the rise of language as a given fact, then it is not going too far to say that the souls of men are the gift from language to mankind.
>
> The account of the sixth day should be written, He gave them speech, and they became souls.
>
> —Alfred North Whitehead, *Modes of Thought,* 1938

> The fundamental human capacity is the capacity and the need for creative self-expression, for free control of all aspects of one's life and thought. One particularly crucial realization of this capacity is the creative use of language as a free instrument of thought and expression. Now having this view of human nature and human needs, one tries to think about the modes of social organization that would permit the freest and fullest development of the individual, of each individual's potentialities in whatever direction they might take, that would permit him to be fully human in the sense of having the greatest possible scope for his freedom and initiative.
>
> —Noam Chomsky, "Linguistics and Politics—Interview," 1969

"I speak; therefore I am." 1

Though this declaration may seem a little strange at first, it can be supported by considerable evidence. The individual establishes his individuality, his distinction as a human being, through language. He *becomes*—through language. Not only does he proclaim his existence, his being, through speech, but also his identity—the special and particular nature that makes him *him.* The declaration may then be rewritten: "I speak; *thus,* I am." 2

The creation of the self must, by its very nature, be a cooperative affair. The potentiality for language acquisition and language-use appears to be granted as a birthright. But the accident of birth will determine whether the language acquired will be Chinese, Swahili, Spanish, or English. And the same accident will determine the nature of the dialect acquired within the language. These "accidents" assume the presence of people and a culture that together bring the language to the individual. 3

If, then, the individual creates himself through language, it is only with the help provided by a sympathetic environment; a mother who encourages him to babble, to distinguish sounds and consequences, and then to utter sentences; and a host of other people who act and react linguistically around him. Gradually as the individual develops, he acquires not only language but what might be called a "linguistic personality," a set of language behavior patterns that make up a substantial part of his identity as a person different from other persons. 4

> It is language . . . that really reveals to man that world which is closer to him than any world of natural objects and touches his weal and woe more directly than physical nature. For it is language that makes his existence in a community possible; and only in society, in relation to a "Thee," can his subjectivity assert itself as a "Me."
>
> —Ernst Cassirer, *Language and Myth,* 1946

This *creation of the self*—in the sense of the self's development into a distinctive person with distinctions that are in large part linguistic (or asserted or fulfilled through language)—is a creation of the self in a kind of gross or 5 obvious sense. Few would quarrel with the rough outline sketched above, though some might want to express it in a different set of terms. But there is another, more subtle sense in which we can speak of the creation of the self implied in "I speak; therefore I am." This profounder sense is implied in Alfred North Whitehead's assertion that "it is not going too far to say that the souls of men are the gift from language to mankind." Where a nineteenth-century divine, or a twentieth-century philosopher, might refer to "souls," the modern psychologist might refer to the sense of an enduring self. This sense is generated, sustained, and preserved in language.

One way through which the sense of self is generated appears in the 6
basic human impulse to sort through one's thoughts, or to think through the day's (or a lifetime's) experiences. To follow this impulse throws the individual back on his language resources. The experiences and thoughts that make up one's life are, in some sense, the essence of the individual, the things that are uniquely his and that make him what he is. In the process of sorting through his thoughts, or of disentangling and examining his tangled experiences, he is in effect defining himself, outlining himself, asserting and proclaiming himself. There can be no more vital activity for the individual: the results and the actions (new thoughts and new experiences) proceeding from it will further define his identity, not only for him but for the world he inhabits. In the old vocabulary, he is in this process revitalizing, reconstituting, refreshing, renewing his soul.

> I did not exist to write poems, to preach or to paint, neither I nor anyone else. All of that was incidental. Each man had only one genuine vocation—to find the way to himself. He might end up as poet or madman, as prophet or criminal—that was not his affair, ultimately it was of no concern. His task was to discover his own destiny—not an arbitrary one—and live it out wholly and resolutely within himself. Everything else was only a would-be existence, an attempt at evasion, a flight back to the ideas of the masses, conformity and fear of one's own inwardness.
>
> —Hermann Hesse, *Demian,* 1925

To live an aware life, the individual must begin with an awareness of 7
self. He must conduct a running examination and periodic reexaminations of the self—in language, the medium of furthest reaches, deepest diving, most labyrinthine windings. The sorting through might well begin with the ordinary, everyday experiences of life. A diary or journal enables one to sift through and evaluate experiences, as well as to come to understand them and their significance—or insignificance. Most of us do this sifting and evaluation in moments of reverie or in that state of mental vagabondage just before sleep. There is some (even great) advantage, however, in subjecting ourselves to the discipline of written language, in which the vague and the mushy and the muddled must give way to the specific, the firm, the clearly formulated.

For writing *is* discovery. The language that never leaves our head is like colorful yarn, endlessly spun out multicolored threads dropping into a void, momentarily compacted, entangled, fascinating, elusive. We have glimpses that seem brilliant but quickly fade; we catch sight of images that tease us with connections and patterns that too-soon flow on; we hold in momentary view a comprehensive arrangement (insight) that dissolves rapidly and disappears. 8

Writing that is discovery forces the capturing, the retrieving, the bringing into focus these stray and random thoughts. Sifting through them, we make decisions that are as much about the self as about language. Indeed, writing is largely a process of choosing among alternatives from the images and thoughts of the endless flow, and this choosing is a matter of making up one's mind, and this making up one's mind becomes in effect the making up of one's self. In this way writing that is honest and genuine and serious (though not necessarily without humor or wit) constitutes the discovery of the self. It is not uncommon, before the choices are made, before the words are fixed on paper, to be quite unsure of which way the choices will go. Most people have experienced the phenomenon of their opinions or feelings changing, sometimes markedly, in the process of writing a paper which forces confrontations with language and choices among expressions. All people have experienced the clarification of their views and perspectives as they have worked through the process of placing them on paper. It is not at all unusual to find an individual who is uncertain and unclear about his feelings on a subject or an issue, but who, on discovering his attitude in the process of writing, becomes committed, often dedicated, and sometimes even fanatical: he has come to know himself. When this happens the individual is not being insincere, but is simply experiencing the discoveries of writing—discoveries that are often surprising and frequently exhilarating. 9

As suggested earlier, in setting forth on this voyage of self-discovery, it is best to begin, not with the problems of the universe, but with what appear to be the trivia of everyday events. Indeed, it might turn out ultimately that the big is somehow indirectly connected with the little. The self-examination which requires simply the writing of an account of one's life for a single day might bring unexpected illumination. Such an account would necessitate reviewing in detail and reliving imaginatively moments of pain and fun, joy and sobriety. A list of the events of that day (or week, month) would require consideration as to what, for an individual, constitutes events. Presumably they left some kind of mark—intellectual, emotional, imaginative. What kind of mark, how deep, how long-lasting? There might be public events and private events—events for which there were some, perhaps many, witnesses, and events that had no witnesses at all. 10

The list of a day's events in an individual's life might be posed against a list of the general public events and happenings—in the community, town, state, country, or world. Where do the two lists intersect, if at all? Did any of the world's events leave any mark on the individual, or did they reach him remotely or impersonally through the mass media, newspapers, radio-TV, 11 and then fade into the distance? A third list might be composed of a close friend's perspective on the personal events on the first list, some of which he will have witnessed (but only externally), and others of which he will be totally unaware. Compilation of these lists, either in fact or imagination, may enable the individual to see the narrative of his life as marking a circle around him, with him—absolutely alone—at the center.

> YEE-AH! I feel like part of the shadows that make company for me in this warm *amigo* darkness.
> I am "My Majesty Piri Thomas," with a high on anything and like a stoned king, I gotta survey my kingdom.
> I'm a skinny, dark-face, curly-haired, intense Porty-Ree-can—
> Unsatisfied, hoping, and always reaching.
>
> —Piri Thomas, *Down These Mean Streets,* 1967

This circle marks the individual's personal turf, material for his intellectual and imaginative use or growth that is his and his alone, impossible to share totally with anyone, no matter how close. One who begins to feel a sense of the preciousness of this material, this segment of life that is his and no one else's, is in fact feeling a sense of the self. If he begins to discover sequence and sense—a kind of unified narrative—in the events of his life for a day, he is making the discovery of self that the process of writing brings about: the unification must come from the individual's unique sensibility and identity. 12

Henry James had something of all this in mind in some advice he gave to young writers: "Oh, do something from your point of view; an ounce of example is worth a ton of generalities . . . do something with life. Any point of view is interesting that is a direct impression of life. You each have an impression colored by your individual conditions; make that into a picture, a picture framed by your own personal wisdom, your glimpse of the American world. The field is vast for freedom, for study, for observation, for satire, for truth."[1] 13

> *Interviewer:* Is there anything else you can say to beginning writers?
> *Simenon:* Writing is considered a profession, and I don't think it is a profession. I think that everyone who does not *need* to be a writer, who thinks he can do something else, ought to do something else. Writing is not a profession but a vocation of unhappiness. I don't think an artist can ever be happy.
> *Interviewer:* Why?
> *Simenon:* Because, first, I think that if a man has the urge to be an artist, it is because he needs to find himself. Every writer tries to find himself through his characters, through all his writing.
> *Interviewer:* He is writing for himself?
> *Simenon:* Yes. Certainly.
>
> —Georges Simenon, *Writers at Work: The Paris Review Interviews,* 1958

NOTE

1. "A Letter to the Deerfield Summer School" (1889), reprinted in *The Future of the Novel,* ed. Leon Edel (New York: Vintage/Random House, 1956), p. 29.

Questions for Discussion

1. Miller implies that we would have no sense of self without language. Try imagining yourself without a name, not just in the legal or technical sense of having no confirming documents but having absolutely no name. What differences would this condition make in your self-image? Could you even make a self-image without a name?
2. Is Miller's claim that writing is a way of making up our minds and that making up our minds is a way of making up who we are (¶9) equally true of all writing? When people deliberately write things they do not believe or know to be false, are they also making themselves up? Are their selves separate from what they write because they have deliberately created the distance between them and their words? Or in choosing to use words that evade, conceal, or lie, do such writers *become* evasive, secretive, or deceitful, regardless of their intentions?
3. How do you distinguish the writing of lies from the writing of fiction? Must we agree that novelists, story writers, and film writers lie? If so, how do we distinguish their works, which we admire, from the kinds of lies we detest? If it is not fair or accurate to call their work lies, why not? Give your reasons.
4. Does Miller's simile, "the language that never leaves our head is like colorful yarn, endlessly spun out multicolored threads dropping into a void" (¶8), accurately capture your own experience of how thoughts pass through your mind? Is your mind ever completely empty of words? Is there not always some flow of language going through your head, like continuous background static, regardless of how deeply absorbed or distracted you may be?
5. Miller says that "the self-examination which requires simply the writing of an account of one's life for a single day might bring unexpected illumination" (¶10). Create two or three accounts (quick lists) of a given day, selecting the details for commentary or description on the basis of who would be most interested in them (your teacher, classmates, roommate, parents, and so on). As you select details, do you think that you would seem to be a dramatically different person to different audiences? Or a different person even to yourself, depending on what audience you are playing to or what "face" you are putting on? Is Miller right that making up an account goes far toward making up a self?

Suggested Essay Topics

1. Write an essay five or six paragraphs long, directed to your fellow students, in which you begin each paragraph with the statement, "I am the person who . . ." Make each paragraph not a miscellaneous collection of details, but a cohesive group of details clustering around the initial assertion. Arrange the paragraphs in ascending order of importance. Conclude with a final paragraph discussing whether you have learned anything new about yourself.

   (*Note:* This assignment will not produce a good essay if you focus only on superficial externals. Your objective is to give your readers the kind of knowledge that acquaints them with your inner self. After reading your essay, they should be able to make better than random predictions, for example, about what makes you happy or hurts your feelings, what ambitions you have, what you love or hate, or what choices you will make in a crisis.)
2. Miller suggests that "the list of a day's events in an individual's life might be posed against a list of the general public events and happenings," and he then asks, "Where do the two lists intersect, if at all?" (¶11). Try making two such lists. Have any recent public events—the success, death, departure, or words of a public personality, for example—had any impact on your personal life or feelings? Write an essay to a good friend explaining how the two lists intersect, exposing and explaining your private responses to a public event.

George Lakoff and Mark Johnson

Is it true that all of us, not just poets, speak in metaphors, whether we realize it or not? Is it perhaps even true that we live *by metaphors, that the way we experience the world is partly determined by the structure of our metaphors? In* Metaphors We Live By, *George Lakoff (b. 1941), a linguist, and Mark Johnson (b. 1949), a philosopher, suggest that metaphors not only make our thoughts more vivid and interesting but that they actually structure our perceptions and understanding. Thinking of marriage as a "contract agreement," for example, leads to one set of expectations, while thinking of it as "team play," "a negotiated settlement," "Russian roulette," "an indissoluble merger," or "a religious sacrament" will carry different sets of expectations. When a government thinks of its enemies as "turkeys" or "gooks" or "clowns," it does not take them as serious threats, but if they are "pawns" in the hands of the communists, they are taken seriously indeed.* Metaphors We Live By *has led many readers to a new recognition of how profoundly metaphors not only shape our view of life in the present but set up the expectations that determine what life will be for us in the future.*

METAPHORS WE LIVE BY

Our selection comprises chapters 1, 2, 3, and part of 4 of *Metaphors We Live By* (1980).

CONCEPTS WE LIVE BY

Metaphor is for most people a device of the poetic imagination and the 1
rhetorical flourish—a matter of extraordinary rather than ordinary language. Moreover, metaphor is typically viewed as characteristic of language alone, a matter of words rather than thought or action. For this reason, most people think they can get along perfectly well without metaphor. We have found, on the contrary, that metaphor is pervasive in everyday life, not just in language but in thought and action. Our ordinary conceptual system, in terms of which we both think and act, is fundamentally metaphorical in nature.

The concepts that govern our thought are not just matters of the intel- 2
lect. They also govern our everyday functioning, down to the most mundane details. Our concepts structure what we perceive, how we get around in the world, and how we relate to other people. Our conceptual system thus plays a central role in defining our everyday realities. If we are right in suggesting that our conceptual system is largely metaphorical, then the way we think, what we experience, and what we do every day is very much a matter of metaphor.

But our conceptual system is not something we are normally aware of. 3
In most of the little things we do every day, we simply think and act more or less automatically along certain lines. Just what these lines are is by no means obvious. One way to find out is by looking at language. Since communication is based on the same conceptual system that we use in thinking and acting, language is an important source of evidence for what that system is like.

Primarily on the basis of linguistic evidence, we have found that most 4
of our ordinary conceptual system is metaphorical in nature. And we have found a way to begin to identify in detail just what the metaphors are that structure how we perceive, how we think, and what we do.

To give some idea of what it could mean for a concept to be metaphori- 5
cal and for such a concept to structure an everyday activity, let us start with the concept ARGUMENT and the conceptual metaphor ARGUMENT IS WAR. This metaphor is reflected in our everyday language by a wide variety of expressions:

ARGUMENT IS WAR

Your claims are *indefensible.*

He *attacked every weak point* in my argument.

His criticisms were *right on target.*

I *demolished* his argument.

I've never *won* an argument with him.

You disagree? Okay, *shoot!*

If you use that *strategy,* he'll *wipe you out.*

He *shot down* all of my arguments.

It is important to see that we don't just *talk* about arguments in terms of war. We can actually win or lose arguments. We see the person we are arguing with as an opponent. We attack his positions and we defend our own. We gain and lose ground. We plan and use strategies. If we find a position indefensible, we can abandon it and take a new line of attack. Many of the things we *do* in arguing are partially structured by the concept of war. Though there is no physical battle, there is a verbal battle, and the structure of an argument—attack, defense, counterattack, etc.—reflects this. It is in this sense that the ARGUMENT IS WAR metaphor is one that we live by in this culture; it structures the actions we perform in arguing. 6

Try to imagine a culture where arguments are not viewed in terms of war, where no one wins or loses, where there is no sense of attacking or defending, gaining or losing ground. Imagine a culture where an argument is viewed as a dance, the participants are seen as performers, and the goal is to perform in a balanced and aesthetically pleasing way. In such a culture, people would view arguments differently, experience them differently, carry them out differently, and talk about them differently. But *we* would probably not view them as arguing at all: they would simply be doing something different. It would seem strange even to call what they were doing "arguing." Perhaps the most neutral way of describing this difference between their culture and ours would be to say that we have a discourse form structured in terms of battle and they have one structured in terms of dance. 7

This is an example of what it means for a metaphorical concept, namely, ARGUMENT IS WAR, to structure (at least in part) what we do and how we understand what we are doing when we argue. *The essence of metaphor is understanding and experiencing one kind of thing in terms of another.* It is not that arguments are a subspecies of war. Arguments and wars are different kinds of things—verbal discourse and armed conflict—and the actions performed are different kinds of actions. But ARGUMENT is partially structured, understood, performed, and talked about in terms of WAR. The concept is metaphorically structured, the activity is metaphorically structured, and, consequently, the language is metaphorically structured. 8

Moreover, this is the *ordinary* way of having an argument and talking about one. The normal way for us to talk about attacking a position is to use the words "attack a position." Our conventional ways of talking about arguments presuppose a metaphor we are hardly ever conscious of. The metaphor is not merely in the words we use—it is in our very concept of an argument. The language of argument is not poetic, fanciful, or rhetorical; it is literal. We talk about arguments that way because we conceive of them that way—and we act according to the way we conceive of things. 9

The most important claim we have made so far is that metaphor is not 10 just a matter of language, that is, of mere words. We shall argue that, on the contrary, human *thought processes* are largely metaphorical. This is what we mean when we say that the human conceptual system is metaphorically structured and defined. Metaphors as linguistic expressions are possible precisely because there are metaphors in a person's conceptual system. Therefore, whenever in this book we speak of metaphors, such as ARGUMENT IS WAR, it should be understood that *metaphor* means *metaphorical concept.*

THE SYSTEMATICITY OF METAPHORICAL CONCEPTS

Arguments usually follow patterns; that is, there are certain things we typically do and do not do in arguing. The fact that we in part conceptualize arguments in terms of battle systematically influences the shape arguments take and the way we talk about what we do in arguing. Because the metaphorical concept is systematic, the language we use to talk about that aspect of the concept is systematic. 11

We saw in the ARGUMENT IS WAR metaphor that expressions from the vocabulary of war, e.g., *attack a position, indefensible, strategy, new line of attack, win, gain ground,* etc., form a systematic way of talking about the battling aspects of arguing. It is no accident that these expressions mean what they mean when we use them to talk about arguments. A portion of the conceptual network of battle partially characterizes the concept of an argument, and the language follows suit. Since metaphorical expressions in our language are tied to metaphorical concepts in a systematic way, we can use metaphorical linguistic expressions to study the nature of metaphorical concepts and to gain an understanding of the metaphorical nature of our activities. 12

To get an idea of how metaphorical expressions in everyday language can give us insight into the metaphorical nature of the concepts that structure our everyday activities, let us consider the metaphorical concept TIME IS MONEY as it is reflected in contemporary English. 13

TIME IS MONEY

You're *wasting* my time.

This gadget will *save* you hours.

I don't *have* the time to *give* you.

How do you *spend* your time these days?

That flat tire *cost* me an hour.

I've *invested* a lot of time in her.

I don't *have enough* time to *spare* for that.

You're *running out* of time.

You need to *budget* your time.

Put aside some time for ping pong.

Is that *worth your while?*

Do you *have* much time *left?*

He's living on *borrowed* time.

You don't *use* your time *profitably.*

I *lost* a lot of time when I got sick.

Thank you for your time.

Time in our culture is a valuable commodity. It is a limited resource that we use to accomplish our goals. Because of the way that the concept of work has developed in modern Western culture, where work is typically associated with the time it takes and time is precisely quantified, it has become customary to pay people by the hour, week, or year. In our culture TIME IS MONEY in many ways: telephone message units, hourly wages, hotel room rates, yearly budgets, interest on loans, and paying your debt to society by "serving time." These practices are relatively new in the history of the human race, and by no means do they exist in all cultures. They have arisen in modern industrialized societies and structure our basic everyday activities in a very profound way. Corresponding to the fact that we *act* as if time is a valuable commodity—a limited resource, even money—we *conceive of* time that way. Thus we understand and experience time as the kind of thing that can be spent, wasted, budgeted, invested wisely or poorly, saved, or squandered. 14

TIME IS MONEY, TIME IS A LIMITED RESOURCE, and TIME IS A VALUABLE COMMODITY are all metaphorical concepts. They are metaphorical since we are using our everyday experiences with money, limited resources, and valuable commodities to conceptualize time. This isn't a necessary way for human beings to conceptualize time; it is tied to our culture. There are cultures where time is none of these things. 15

The metaphorical concepts TIME IS MONEY, TIME IS A RESOURCE, and TIME IS A VALUABLE COMMODITY form a single system based on subcategorization, since in our society money is a limited resource and limited resources are valuable commodities. These subcategorization relationships characterize entailment relationships between the metaphors. TIME IS MONEY entails that TIME IS A LIMITED RESOURCE, which entails that TIME IS A VALUABLE COMMODITY. 16

We are adopting the practice of using the most specific metaphorical concept, in this case TIME IS MONEY, to characterize the entire system. Of the expressions listed under the TIME IS MONEY metaphor, some refer specifically to money (*spend, invest, budget, profitably, cost*), others to limited resources (*use, use up, have enough of, run out of*), and still others to valuable commodities (*have, give, lose, thank you for*). This is an example of the way in which metaphorical entailments can characterize a coherent system of metaphorical concepts and a corresponding coherent system of metaphorical expressions for those concepts. 17

METAPHORICAL SYSTEMATICITY: HIGHLIGHTING AND HIDING

The very systematicity that allows us to comprehend one aspect of a concept 18
in terms of another (e.g., comprehending an aspect of arguing in terms of battle) will necessarily hide other aspects of the concept. In allowing us to focus on one aspect of a concept (e.g., the battling aspects of arguing), a metaphorical concept can keep us from focusing on other aspects of the concept that are inconsistent with that metaphor. For example, in the midst of a heated argument, when we are intent on attacking our opponent's position and defending our own, we may lose sight of the cooperative aspects of arguing. Someone who is arguing with you can be viewed as giving you his time, a valuable commodity, in an effort at mutual understanding. But when we are preoccupied with the battle aspects, we often lose sight of the cooperative aspects.

A far more subtle case of how a metaphorical concept can hide an aspect 19
of our experience can be seen in what Michael Reddy has called the "conduit metaphor."[1] Reddy observes that our language about language is structured roughly by the following complex metaphor:

IDEAS (or MEANINGS) ARE OBJECTS.

LINGUISTIC EXPRESSIONS ARE CONTAINERS.

COMMUNICATION IS SENDING.

The speaker puts ideas (objects) into words (containers) and sends them (along a conduit) to a hearer who takes the idea/objects out of the word/containers. Reddy documents this with more than a hundred types of expressions in English, which he estimates account for at least 70 percent of the expressions we use for talking about language. Here are some examples:

THE CONDUIT METAPHOR

It's hard to *get* that idea *across to* him.

I *gave* you that idea.

Your reasons *came through* to us.

It's difficult to *put* my ideas *into* words.

When you *have* a good idea, try to *capture* it immediately *in* words.

Try to *pack* more thought *into* fewer words.

You can't simply *stuff* ideas *into* a sentence any old way.

The meaning is right there *in* the words.

Don't *force* your meanings *into* the wrong words.

His words *carry* little meaning.

The introduction *has* a great deal of thought *content.*

Your words seem *hollow.*

The sentence is *without* meaning.

The idea is *buried in* terribly dense paragraphs.

In examples like these it is far more difficult to see that there is anything 20
hidden by the metaphor or even to see that there is a metaphor here at all. This is so much the conventional way of thinking about language that it is sometimes hard to imagine that it might not fit reality. But if we look at what the CONDUIT metaphor entails, we can see some of the ways in which it masks aspects of the communicative process.

First, the LINGUISTIC EXPRESSIONS ARE CONTAINERS FOR MEANINGS aspect of the 21
CONDUIT metaphor entails that words and sentences have meanings in themselves, independent of any context or speaker. The MEANINGS ARE OBJECTS part of the metaphor, for example, entails that meanings have an existence independent of people and contexts. The part of the metaphor that says LINGUISTIC EXPRESSIONS ARE CONTAINERS FOR MEANING entails that words (and sentences) have meanings, again independent of contexts and speakers. These metaphors are appropriate in many situations—those where context differences don't matter and where all the participants in the conversation understand the sentences in the same way. These two entailments are exemplified by sentences like

The meaning is *right there in* the words,

which, according to the CONDUIT metaphor, can correctly be said of any sentence. But there are many cases where context does matter. Here is a celebrated one recorded in actual conversation by Pamela Downing:

Please sit in the apple-juice seat.

In isolation this sentence has no meaning at all, since the expression "apple-juice seat" is not a conventional way of referring to any kind of object. But the sentence makes perfect sense in the context in which it was uttered. An overnight guest came down to breakfast. There were four place settings, three with orange juice and one with apple juice. It was clear what the apple-juice seat was. And even the next morning, when there was no apple juice, it was still clear which seat was the apple-juice seat.

In addition to sentences that have no meaning without context, there 22
are cases where a single sentence will mean different things to different people. Consider:

We need new alternative sources of energy.

This means something very different to the president of Mobil Oil from what it means to the president of Friends of the Earth. The meaning is not right there in the sentence—it matters a lot who is saying or listening to the sentence and what his social and political attitudes are. The CONDUIT metaphor does not fit cases where context is required to determine whether the sentence has any meaning at all and, if so, what meaning it has.

These examples show that the metaphorical concepts we have looked 23
at provide us with a partial understanding of what communication, argument, and time are and that, in doing this, they hide other aspects of these concepts. It is important to see that the metaphorical structuring involved here is partial, not total. If it were total, one concept would actually *be* the other, not merely be understood in terms of it. For example, time isn't really money. If you *spend your time* trying to do something and it doesn't work, you can't get your time back. There are no time banks. I can *give you a lot of time,* but you can't give me back the same time, though you can *give me back the same amount of time.* And so on. Thus, part of a metaphorical concept does not and cannot fit.

On the other hand, metaphorical concepts can be extended beyond the 24
range of ordinary literal ways of thinking and talking into the range of what is called figurative, poetic, colorful, or fanciful thought and language. Thus, if ideas are objects, we can *dress them up in fancy clothes, juggle them, line them up nice and neat,* etc. So when we say that a concept is structured by a metaphor, we mean that it is partially structured and that it can be extended in some ways but not others.

ORIENTATIONAL METAPHORS

So far we have examined what we will call *structural metaphors,* cases where one 25
concept is metaphorically structured in terms of another. But there is another kind of metaphorical concept, one that does not structure one concept in terms of another but instead organizes a whole system of concepts with respect to one another. We will call these *orientational metaphors,* since most of them have to do with spatial orientation: up-down, in-out, front-back, on-off, deep-shallow, central-peripheral. These spatial orientations arise from the fact that we have bodies of the sort we have and that they function as they do in our physical environment. Orientational metaphors give a concept a spatial orientation; for example, HAPPY IS UP. The fact that the concept HAPPY is oriented UP leads to English expressions like "I'm feeling *up* today."

Such metaphorical orientations are not arbitrary. They have a basis in 26
our physical and cultural experience. Though the polar oppositions up-down, in-out, etc., are physical in nature, the orientational metaphors based on them can vary from culture to culture. For example, in some cultures the future is in front of us, whereas in others it is in back. We will be looking at up-down spatialization metaphors, which have been studied intensively by William Nagy,[2] as an illustration. In each case, we will give a brief hint about how each metaphorical concept might have arisen from our physical and cultural

experience. These accounts are meant to be suggestive and plausible, not definitive.

HAPPY IS UP; SAD IS DOWN 27
I'm feeling *up.* That *boosted* my spirits. My spirits *rose.* You're in *high* spirits. Thinking about her always gives me a *lift.* I'm feeling *down.* I'm *depressed.* He's really *low* these days. I *fell* into a depression. My spirits *sank.*

Physical basis: Drooping posture typically goes along with sadness and depression, erect posture with a positive emotional state.

CONSCIOUS IS UP; UNCONSCIOUS IS DOWN 28
Get *up.* Wake *up.* I'm *up* already. He *rises* early in the morning. He *fell* asleep. He *dropped* off to sleep. He's *under* hypnosis. He *sank* into a coma.

Physical basis: Humans and most other mammals sleep lying down and stand up when they awaken.

HEALTH AND LIFE ARE UP; 29
SICKNESS AND DEATH ARE DOWN
He's at the *peak* of health. Lazarus *rose* from the dead. He's in *top* shape. As to his health, he's way *up* there. He *fell* ill. He's *sinking* fast. He came *down* with the flu. His health is *declining.* He *dropped* dead.

Physical basis: Serious illness forces us to lie down physically. When you're dead, you are physically down.

HAVING CONTROL OR FORCE IS UP; 30
BEING SUBJECT TO CONTROL OR
FORCE IS DOWN
I have control *over* her. I am *on top of* the situation. He's in a *superior* position. He's at the *height* of his power. He's in the *high* command. He's in the *upper* echelon. His power *rose.* He ranks *above* me in strength. He is *under* my control. He *fell* from power. His power is on the *decline.* He is my social *inferior.* He is *low man* on the totem pole.

Physical basis: Physical size typically correlates with physical strength, and the victor in a fight is typically on top.

MORE IS UP; LESS IS DOWN 31
The number of books printed each year keeps going *up.* His draft number is *high.* My income *rose* last year. The amount of artistic activity in this state has gone *down* in the past year. The number of errors he made is incredibly *low.* His income *fell* last year. He is *under*age. If you're too hot, turn the heat *down.*

Physical basis: If you add more of a substance or of physical objects to a container or pile, the level goes up.

FORESEEABLE FUTURE EVENTS ARE UP (AND AHEAD) 32
All *up*coming events are listed in the paper. What's coming *up* this week? I'm afraid of what's *up ahead* of us. What's *up?*

Physical basis: Normally our eyes look in the direction in which we typically move (ahead, forward). As an object approaches a person (or the person approaches the object), the object appears larger. Since the ground is perceived as being fixed, the top of the object appears to be moving upward in the person's field of vision.

HIGH STATUS IS UP; LOW STATUS IS DOWN 33
He has a *lofty* position. She'll *rise* to the *top.* He's at the *peak* of his career. He's *climbing* the ladder. He has little *upward* mobility. He's at the *bottom* of the social hierarchy. She *fell* in status.

Social and physical basis: Status is correlated with (social) power and (physical) power is UP.

GOOD IS UP; BAD IS DOWN 34
Things are looking *up.* We hit a *peak* last year, but it's been *downhill* ever since. Things are at an all-time *low.* He does *high-*quality work.

Physical basis for personal well-being: Happiness, health, life, and control—the things that principally characterize what is good for a person—are all UP.

VIRTUE IS UP; DEPRAVITY IS DOWN 35
He is *high-*minded. She has *high* standards. She is *upright.* She is an *upstanding* citizen. That was a *low* trick. Don't be *underhanded.* I wouldn't *stoop* to that. That would be *beneath* me. He *fell* into the *abyss* of depravity. That was a *low-down* thing to do.

Physical and social basis: GOOD IS UP for a person (physical basis), together with . . . SOCIETY IS A PERSON (in the version where you are *not* identifying with your society). To be virtuous is to act in accordance with the standards set by the society/person to maintain its well-being. VIRTUE IS UP because virtuous actions correlate with social well-being from the society/person's point of view. Since socially based metaphors are part of the culture, it's the society/person's point of view that counts.

RATIONAL IS UP; EMOTIONAL IS DOWN 36
The discussion *fell to the emotional* level, but I *raised* it back *up to the rational* plane. We put our *feelings* aside and had a *high-level intellectual* discussion of the matter. He couldn't *rise above* his *emotions.*

Physical and cultural basis: In our culture people view themselves as being in control over animals, plants, and their physical environment, and it is their unique ability to reason that places human beings above other animals and gives them this control. CONTROL IS UP thus provides a basis for MAN IS UP and therefore for RATIONAL IS UP.

NOTES

1. Michael Reddy, "The Conduit Metaphor," in A. Ortony, ed., *Metaphor and Thought* (Cambridge: Cambridge University Press, 1979).

2. William Nagy, "Figurative Patterns and Redundancy in the Lexicon" (Ph.D. diss., University of California at San Diego, 1974).

Questions for Discussion

1. Consider examples of metaphorical transfer in various activities—business, sex, politics, religion, education, sports, transportation, construction, and so on. Can you cite instances when persons in business, say, employ metaphors from sports or construction ("the sales *team*" or "the chairman of the board is the *architect* of our prosperity"), and vice versa? Do these examples support Lakoff and Johnson's view that metaphors often structure our thinking? Can you think of categories of thought and perception where metaphors do not seem to play an important role?
2. In *The Educated Imagination* (see pp. 246–254), Northrop Frye argues that the "motive for metaphor"—the reason that human beings devised metaphor in the first place—lies in the common human desire to live in a world that is a home, not just an environment. Metaphors create, through language, an identity between things. Consider, for example, the identity established between human beings and the animal world in comparisons such as "strong as an elephant," "sly as a fox," "dumb as an ox," and "playful as a kitten." This identity, Frye implies, allows us to feel at home in our world. Does Frye's theory ring true to you? Test it out by trying to come up with examples that both fit and don't fit. You might begin by discussing metaphors from patriotism and religion to see if they make us feel at home in our country ("America, *home* of the brave") and our cosmos ("God our *father*").
3. Can you think of examples of metaphors that contradict Lakoff and Johnson's assertion (¶34) that *up* is good and *down* is bad? When we say that a decision is "up in the air," meaning that it remains unsettled, do we mean something good or bad? Would one or two counterexamples really damage the authors' theory?

Suggested Essay Topics

1. Examine a group of metaphors clustered around a central concept (such as Lakoff and Johnson's in ¶13), and compare them to a group of metaphors clustered around a central concept in a good poem (such as Shakespeare's Sonnets 18 and 73). Even though we must grant that the two clusters are equally metaphorical, are there not startling differences between the *effects* of the metaphors in each group? Examine closely your two clusters of metaphors (if you don't like the Shakespeare sonnets, ask your instructor to recommend another good short poem), and write an essay explaining the differences in effect. (If Shakespeare had used metaphors as familiar as "You're *wasting* my time," would he have been more effective because more clear or less effective because too familiar?)
2. Listen carefully for a few nights to the metaphors used by athletes and sports broadcasters ("Iowa *trounced* Indiana," "quarterback *sneak,*" "a *shot* from the top of the *keyhole,*" "Michigan *up-ended* by UCLA," "Bears *dropped,*" etc.). Write a paper in which you (1) try to create categories that show where these metaphors come from (e.g., is "Princeton *pummels* Harvard" a metaphor from another sport, boxing?) and (2) try to argue whether a given sport would lose any significant part of its interest or color if it had to give up its metaphors. Even if we did continue talking about our favorite sport, deprived of its typical metaphors, consider how much more abstract, dull, and time-consuming such colorless talk would be.

George Orwell

George Orwell (1903–1950) was a British novelist, journalist, political commentator and satirist. He is most famous as the author of two satiric fables warning of the dangers and exposing the operations of tyrannical governments, Animal Farm *(1945) and* Nineteen Eighty-four *(1949). These works have been translated into most major languages and are studied by scholars and schoolchildren alike.*

"Politics and the English Language" is almost as widely read as Orwell's fiction. Its title clearly indicates Orwell's central concern: "In our time," he says, "political speech and writing are largely the defence of the indefensible" (¶13). His thesis is that there is a direct and traceable relationship between political brutality and imprecise, vague, evasive, and cliché-ridden English. Immoral politics and bad writing reinforce each other, each one becoming in turn both a cause and an effect.

Three different groups contribute most directly to the deterioration of political language: (1) governments that want to find easier ways of masking their "indefensible" acts of brutality; (2) persons connected with brutal governments who have a vested interest in disguising their governments' acts; and (3) people who do not want to see political brutality for what it is because they do not want to take responsibility for stopping it.

In exposing this problem, Orwell is not completely pessimistic. Things are bad, he says, and getting worse all the time, but the state of neither politics nor language is hopeless. Political brutality and bad writing are not natural forces as inevitable as the seasons; they are instead the product of choices. *Governments are not required to murder dissidents—they choose to. No one forces citizens to settle for language that disguises their government's murder of dissidents—they choose to. And what people choose at one time to do, they can choose at another time to undo.*

Orwell's essay is an attempt to persuade us to undo perversions of politics and power by forcing us to attend to the language that supports them. The kind of world we live in, he says, is not just the world that happens to us; it is also the world we make. He insists that the effects of a hard-headed demand that world governments say clearly what they are doing and why they are doing it, combined with a hard-headed diligence from ourselves in demanding clear and vigorous expression, will improve both political conduct and the use of English.

After studying Orwell's essay, your class may want to subscribe to the Quarterly Review of Doublespeak, *published by the National Council of Teachers of English. The review annually announces the "Orwell Award" for the best book exposing abuse of language, and the "Doublespeak Award," a mock prize for "misuses of language with pernicious social or political consequences." In 1982 two of the Doublespeak Awards were given to Lawrence A. Kudlow, chief economist of the Office of Management and Budget, "for creating the phrase 'revenue enhancement,' which was used by the Reagan administration instead of the phrase 'tax increase,'" and to Secretary of the Interior James Watt, "who said, 'I never use the words Republicans and Democrats. It's liberals and Americans'" (see the January 1983 issue).*

POLITICS AND THE ENGLISH LANGUAGE

From *"Shooting an Elephant" and Other Essays* (1950).

Most people who bother with the matter at all would admit that the English language is in a bad way, but it is generally assumed that we cannot by conscious action do anything about it. Our civilization is decadent and our language—so the argument runs—must inevitably share in the general collapse. It follows that any struggle against the abuse of language is a sentimental archaism, like preferring candles to electric light or hansom cabs to aeroplanes. Underneath this lies the half-conscious belief that language is a natural growth and not an instrument which we shape for our own purposes. 1

Now, it is clear that the decline of a language must ultimately have political and economic causes: it is not due simply to the bad influence of this or that individual writer. But an effect can become a cause, reinforcing the 2 original cause and producing the same effect in an intensified form, and so on indefinitely. A man may take to drink because he feels himself to be a failure, and then fail all the more completely because he drinks. It is rather the same thing that is happening to the English language. It becomes ugly and inaccurate because our thoughts are foolish, but the slovenliness of our language makes it easier for us to have foolish thoughts. The point is that the process is reversible. Modern English, especially written English, is full of bad habits which spread by imitation and which can be avoided if one is willing to take the necessary trouble. If one gets rid of these habits one can think more clearly, and to think clearly is a necessary first step towards political regeneration: so that the fight against bad English is not frivolous and is not the exclusive concern of professional writers. I will come back to this presently, and I hope that by that time the meaning of what I have said here will have become clearer. Meanwhile, here are five specimens of the English language as it is now habitually written.

These five passages have not been picked out because they are especially 3
bad—I could have quoted far worse if I had chosen—but because they illustrate various of the mental vices from which we now suffer. They are a little below the average, but are fairly representative samples. I number them so that I can refer back to them when necessary:

> (1) I am not, indeed, sure whether it is not true to say that the Milton who once seemed not unlike a seventeenth-century Shelley had not become, out of an experience ever more bitter in each year, more alien [*sic*] to the founder of that Jesuit sect which nothing could induce him to tolerate.—Professor Harold Laski (Essay in *Freedom of Expression*)

> (2) Above all, we cannot play ducks and drakes with a native battery of idioms which prescribes such egregious collocations of vocables as the Basic *put up with* for *tolerate* or *put at a loss* for *bewilder.*—Professor Lancelot Hogben (*Interglossa*)

> (3) On the one side we have the free personality: by definition it is not neurotic, for it has neither conflict nor dream. Its desires, such as they are, are transparent, for they are just what institutional approval keeps in the forefront of consciousness; another institutional pattern would alter their number and intensity; there is little in them that is natural, irreducible, or culturally dangerous. But *on the other side,* the social bond itself is nothing but the mutual reflection of these self-secure integrities. Recall the definition of love. Is not this the very picture of a small academic? Where is there a place in this hall of mirrors for either personality or fraternity?—Essay on psychology in *Politics* (New York)

> (4) All the "best people" from the gentlemen's clubs, and all the frantic fascist captains, united in common hatred of Socialism and bestial horror of the rising tide of the mass revolutionary movement, have turned to acts

of provocation, to foul incendiarism, to medieval legends of poisoned wells, to legalize their own destruction of proletarian organizations, and rouse the agitated petty-bourgeoisie to chauvinistic fervor on behalf of the fight against the revolutionary way out of the crisis.—Communist pamphlet

(5) If a new spirit *is* to be infused into this old country, there is one thorny and contentious reform which must be tackled, and that is the humanization and galvanization of the B.B.C. Timidity here will bespeak canker and atrophy of the soul. The heart of Britain may be sound and of strong beat, for instance, but the British lion's roar at present is like that of Bottom in Shakespeare's *Midsummer Night's Dream*—as gentle as any sucking dove. A virile new Britain cannot continue indefinitely to be traduced in the eyes or rather ears, of the world by the effete languors of Langham Place, brazenly masquerading as "standard English." When the Voice of Britain is heard at nine o'clock, better far and infinitely less ludicrous to hear aitches honestly dropped than the present priggish, inflated, inhibited, school-ma'amish arch braying of blameless bashful mewing maidens!—Letter in *Tribune*

Each of these passages has faults of its own, but, quite apart from 4
avoidable ugliness, two qualities are common to all of them. The first is staleness of imagery; the other is lack of precision. The writer either has a meaning and cannot express it, or he inadvertently says something else, or he is almost indifferent as to whether his words mean anything or not. This mixture of vagueness and sheer incompetence is the most marked characteristic of modern English prose, and especially of any kind of political writing. As soon as certain topics are raised, the concrete melts into the abstract and no one seems able to think of turns of speech that are not hackneyed: prose consists less and less of *words* chosen for the sake of their meaning, and more and more of *phrases* tacked together like the sections of a prefabricated hen-house. I list below, with notes and examples, various of the tricks by means of which the work of prose-construction is habitually dodged:

Dying Metaphors. A newly invented metaphor assists thought by evok- 5
ing a visual image, while on the other hand a metaphor which is technically "dead" (e.g. *iron resolution*) has in effect reverted to being an ordinary word and can generally be used without loss of vividness. But in between these two classes there is a huge dump of worn-out metaphors which have lost all evocative power and are merely used because they save people the trouble of inventing phrases for themselves. Examples are: *Ring the changes on, take up the cudgels for, toe the line, ride roughshod over, stand shoulder to shoulder with, play into the hands of, no axe to grind, grist to the mill, fishing in troubled waters, rift within the lute, on the order of the day, Achilles' heel, swan song, hotbed.* Many of these are used without knowledge of their meaning (what is a "rift," for instance?), and incompatible metaphors are frequently mixed, a sure sign that the writer is

not interested in what he is saying. Some metaphors now current have been twisted out of their original meaning without those who use them even being aware of the fact. For example, *toe the line* is sometimes written *tow the line.* Another example is *the hammer and the anvil,* now always used with the implication that the anvil gets the worst of it. In real life it is always the anvil that breaks the hammer, never the other way about: a writer who stopped to think what he was saying would be aware of this, and would avoid perverting the original phrase.

Operators or *Verbal False Limbs.* These save the trouble of picking out appropriate verbs and nouns, and at the same time pad each sentence with extra syllables which give it an appearance of symmetry. Characteristic phrases are *render inoperative, militate against, make contact with, be subjected to, give rise to, give grounds for, have the effect of, play a leading part (role) in, make itself felt, take effect, exhibit a tendency to, serve the purpose of, etc., etc.* The keynote is the elimination of simple verbs. Instead of being a single word, such as *break, stop, spoil, mend, kill,* a verb becomes a *phrase,* made up of a noun or adjective tacked on to some general-purposes verb such as *prove, serve, form, play, render.* In addition, the passive voice is wherever possible used in preference to the active, and noun constructions are used instead of gerunds (*by examination of* instead of *by examining*). The range of verbs is further cut down by means of the *-ize* and *de-* formations, and the banal statements are given an appearance of profundity by means of the *not un-* formation. Simple conjunctions and prepositions are replaced by such phrases as *with respect to, having regard to, the fact that, by dint of, in view of, in the interests of, on the hypothesis that;* and the ends of sentences are saved from anticlimax by such resounding common-places as *greatly to be desired, cannot be left out of account, a development to be expected in the near future, deserving of serious consideration, brought to a satisfactory conclusion,* and so on and so forth. 6

Pretentious Diction. Words like *phenomenon, element, individual* (as noun), *objective, categorical, effective, virtual, basic, primary, promote, constitute, exhibit, exploit, utilize, eliminate, liquidate,* are used to dress up simple statements and give an air of scientific impartiality to biased judgments. Adjectives like *epoch-making, epic, historic, unforgettable, triumphant, age-old, inevitable, inexorable, veritable,* are used to dignify the sordid processes of international politics, while writing that aims at glorifying war usually takes on an archaic color, its characteristic words being: *realm, throne, chariot, mailed fist, trident, sword, shield, buckler, banner, jackboot, clarion.* Foreign words and expressions such as *cul de sac, ancien régime, deus ex machina, mutatis mutandis, status quo, gleichschaltung, weltanschauung,* are used to give an air of culture and elegance. Except for the useful abbreviations *i.e., e.g.,* and *etc.,* there is no real need for any of the hundreds of foreign phrases now current in English. Bad writers, and especially scientific, political and sociological writers, are nearly always haunted by the notion that Latin or Greek words are grander than Saxon ones, and unnecessary words like *expedite, ameliorate, predict, extraneous, deracinated, clandestine, subaqueous* and hundreds of 7 others constantly gain ground from their Anglo-Saxon opposite numbers.* The jargon peculiar to Marxist writing (*hyena, hangman, cannibal, petty bourgeois, these gentry, lacquey, flunkey, mad dog, White Guard,* etc.) consists largely of words and phrases translated from Russian, German or French; but the normal way of coining a new word is to use a Latin or Greek root with the appropriate affix and, where necessary, the *-ize* formation. It is often easier to make up words of this kind (*deregionalize, impermissible, extramarital, non-fragmentary* and so forth) than to think up the English words that will cover one's meaning. The result, in general, is an increase in slovenliness and vagueness.

Meaningless Words. In certain kinds of writing, particularly in art criti- 8
cism and literary criticism, it is normal to come across long passages which are almost completely lacking in meaning.† Words like *romantic, plastic, values, human, dead, sentimental, natural, vitality,* as used in art criticism, are strictly meaningless, in the sense that they not only do not point to any discoverable object, but are hardly ever expected to do so by the reader. When one critic writes, "The outstanding feature of Mr. X's work is its living quality," while another writes, "The immediately striking thing about Mr. X's work is its peculiar deadness," the reader accepts this as a simple difference of opinion. If words like *black* and *white* were involved, instead of the jargon words *dead* and *living,* he would see at once that language was being used in an improper way. Many political words are similarly abused. The word *Fascism* has now no meaning except in so far as it signifies "something not desirable." The words *democracy, socialism, freedom, patriotic, realistic, justice,* have each of them several different meanings which cannot be reconciled with one another. In the case of a word like *democracy,* not only is there no agreed definition, but the attempt to make one is resisted from all sides. It is almost universally felt that when we call a country democratic we are praising it: consequently the defenders of every kind of régime claim that it is a democracy, and fear that they might have to stop using the word if it were tied down to any one meaning. Words of this kind are often used in a consciously dishonest way. That is, the person who uses them has his own private definition, but allows his hearer to think he means something quite different. Statements like *Marshal Pétain was a true patriot, The Soviet Press is the freest in the world, The Catholic Church is opposed to persecution,* are almost always made with intent to deceive. Other words used in variable meanings, in

*An interesting illustration of this is the way in which the English flower names which were in use till very recently are being ousted by Greek ones, *snapdragon* becoming *antirrhinum, forget-me-not* becoming *myosotis,* etc. It is hard to see any practical reason for this change of fashion: it is probably due to an instinctive turning-away from the more homely word and a vague feeling that the Greek word is scientific. [Orwell's note.]

†Example: "Comfort's catholicity of perception and image, strangely Whitmanesque in range, almost the exact opposite in aesthetic compulsion, continues to evoke that trembling atmospheric accumulative hinting at a cruel, an inexorably serene timelessness. . . . Wrey Gardiner scores by aiming at simple bull's-eyes with precision. Only they are not so simple, and through this contented sadness runs more than the surface bitter-sweet of resignation." (*Poetry Quarterly.*) [Orwell's note.]

most cases more or less dishonestly, are: *class, totalitarian, science, progressive, reactionary, bourgeois, equality.*

Now that I have made this catalogue of swindles and perversions, let me give another example of the kind of writing that they lead to. This time it must of its nature be an imaginary one. I am going to translate a passage of good English into modern English of the worst sort. Here is a well-known verse from *Ecclesiastes:* 9

"I returned and saw under the sun, that the race is not to the swift, nor the battle to the strong, neither yet bread to the wise, nor yet riches to men of understanding, nor yet favour to men of skill; but time and chance happeneth to them all."

Here it is in modern English:

"Objective considerations of contemporary phenomena compels the conclusion that success or failure in competitive activities exhibits no tendency to be commensurate with innate capacity, but that a considerable element of the unpredictable must invariably be taken into account."

This is a parody, but not a very gross one. Exhibit (3), above, for 10
instance, contains several patches of the same kind of English. It will be seen that I have not made a full translation. The beginning and ending of the sentence follow the original meaning fairly closely, but in the middle the concrete illustrations—race, battle, bread—dissolve into the vague phrase "success or failure in competitive activities." This had to be so, because no modern writer of the kind I am discussing—no one capable of using phrases like "objective consideration of contemporary phenomena"—would ever tabulate his thoughts in that precise and detailed way. The whole tendency of modern prose is away from concreteness. Now analyse these two sentences a little more closely. The first contains forty-nine words but only sixty syllables, and all its words are those of everyday life. The second contains thirty-eight words of ninety syllables: eighteen of its words are from Latin roots, and one from Greek. The first sentence contains six vivid images, and only one phrase ("time and chance") that could be called vague. The second contains not a single fresh, arresting phrase, and in spite of its ninety syllables it gives only a shortened version of the meaning contained in the first. Yet without a doubt it is the second kind of sentence that is gaining ground in modern English. I do not want to exaggerate. This kind of writing is not yet universal, and outcrops of simplicity will occur here and there in the worst-written page. Still, if you or I were told to write a few lines on the uncertainty of human fortunes, we should probably come much nearer to my imaginary sentence than to the one from *Ecclesiastes.*

As I have tried to show, modern writing at its worst does not consist 11
in picking out words for the sake of their meaning and inventing images in order to make the meaning clearer. It consists in gumming together long strips of words which have already been set in order by someone else, and making the results presentable by sheer humbug. The attraction of this way of writing is that it is easy. It is easier—even quicker, once you have the habit—to say *In my opinion it is not an unjustifiable assumption that* than to say *I think.* If you use

ready-made phrases, you not only don't have to hunt about for words; you also don't have to bother with the rhythms of your sentences, since these phrases are generally so arranged as to be more or less euphonious. When you are composing in a hurry—when you are dictating to a stenographer, for instance, or making a public speech—it is natural to fall into a pretentious, Latinized style. Tags like *a consideration which we should do well to bear in mind* or *a conclusion to which all of us would readily assent* will save many a sentence from coming down with a bump. By using stale metaphors, similes and idioms, you save much mental effort, at the cost of leaving your meaning vague, not only for your reader but for yourself. This is the significance of mixed metaphors. The sole aim of a metaphor is to call up a visual image. When these images clash—as in *The Fascist octopus has sung its swan song, the jackboot is thrown into the melting pot*—it can be taken as certain that the writer is not seeing a mental image of the objects he is naming; in other words he is not really thinking. Look again at the examples I gave at the beginning of this essay. Professor Laski (1) uses five negatives in fifty-three words. One of these is superfluous, making nonsense of the whole passage, and in addition there is the slip *alien* for akin, making further nonsense, and several avoidable pieces of clumsiness which increase the general vagueness. Professor Hogben (2) plays ducks and drakes with a battery which is able to write prescriptions, and, while disapproving of the everyday phrase *put up with,* is unwilling to look *egregious* up in the dictionary and see what it means; (3), if one takes an uncharitable attitude towards it, is simply meaningless: probably one could work out its intended meaning by reading the whole of the article in which it occurs. In (4), the writer knows more or less what he wants to say, but an accumulation of stale phrases chokes him like tea leaves blocking a sink. In (5), words and meaning have almost parted company. People who write in this manner usually have a general emotional meaning—they dislike one thing and want to express solidarity with another—but they are not interested in the detail of what they are saying. A scrupulous writer, in every sentence that he writes, will ask himself at least four questions, thus: What am I trying to say? What words will express it? What image or idiom will make it clearer? Is this image fresh enough to have an effect? And he will probably ask himself two more: Could I put it more shortly? Have I said anything that is avoidably ugly? But you are not obliged to go to all this trouble. You can shirk it by simply throwing your mind open and letting the ready-made phrases come crowding in. They will construct your sentences for you—even think your thoughts for you, to a certain extent—and at need they will perform the important service of partially concealing your meaning even from yourself. It is at this point that the special connection between politics and the debasement of language becomes clear.

In our time it is broadly true that political writing is bad writing. Where 12
it is not true, it will generally be found that the writer is some kind of rebel, expressing his private opinions and not a "party line." Orthodoxy, of whatever color, seems to demand a lifeless, imitative style. The political dialects to be found in pamphlets, leading articles, manifestos, White Papers and the

speeches of under-secretaries do, of course, vary from party to party, but they are all alike in that one almost never finds in them a fresh, vivid, home-made turn of speech. When one watches some tired hack on the platform mechanically repeating the familiar phrases—*bestial atrocities, iron heel, bloodstained tyranny, free peoples of the world, stand shoulder to shoulder*—one often has a curious feeling that one is not watching a live human being but some kind of dummy: a feeling which suddenly becomes stronger at moments when the light catches the speaker's spectacles and turns them into blank discs which seem to have no eyes behind them. And this is not altogether fanciful. A speaker who uses that kind of phraseology has gone some distance towards turning himself into a machine. The appropriate noises are coming out of his larynx, but his brain is not involved as it would be if he were choosing his words for himself. If the speech he is making is one that he is accustomed to make over and over again, he may be almost unconscious of what he is saying, as one is when one utters the responses in church. And this reduced state of consciousness, if not indispensable, is at any rate favorable to political conformity.

In our time, political speech and writing are largely the defence of the 13
indefensible. Things like the continuance of British rule in India, the Russian purges and deportations, the dropping of the atom bombs on Japan, can indeed be defended, but only by arguments which are too brutal for most people to face, and which do not square with the professed aims of political parties. Thus political language has to consist largely of euphemism, question-begging and sheer cloudy vagueness. Defenceless villages are bombarded from the air, the inhabitants driven out into the countryside, the cattle machine-gunned, the huts set on fire with incendiary bullets: this is called *pacification.* Millions of peasants are robbed of their farms and sent trudging along the roads with no more than they can carry: this is called *transfer of population* or *rectification of frontiers.* People are imprisoned for years without trial, or shot in the back of the neck or sent to die of scurvy in Arctic lumber camps: this is called *elimination of unreliable elements.* Such phraseology is needed if one wants to name things without calling up mental pictures of them. Consider for instance some comfortable English professor defending Russian totalitarianism. He cannot say outright, "I believe in killing off your opponents when you can get good results by doing so." Probably, therefore, he will say something like this:

"While freely conceding that the Soviet régime exhibits certain features 14
which the humanitarian may be inclined to deplore, we must, I think, agree that a certain curtailment of the right to political opposition is an unavoidable concomitant of transitional periods, and that the rigors which the Russian people have been called upon to undergo have been amply justified in the sphere of concrete achievement."

The inflated style is itself a kind of euphemism. A mass of Latin words 15
falls upon the facts like soft snow, blurring the outlines and covering up all the details. The great enemy of clear language is insincerity. When there is a gap between one's real and one's declared aims, one turns as it were instinctively to long words and exhausted idioms, like a cuttlefish squirting out ink.

In our age there is no such thing as "keeping out of politics." All issues are political issues, and politics itself is a mass of lies, evasions, folly, hatred and schizophrenia. When the general atmosphere is bad, language must suffer. I should expect to find—this is a guess which I have not sufficient knowledge to verify—that the German, Russian and Italian languages have all deteriorated in the last ten or fifteen years, as a result of dictatorship.

But if thought corrupts language, language can also corrupt thought. A 16
bad usage can spread by tradition and imitation, even among people who should and do know better. The debased language that I have been discussing is in some ways very convenient. Phrases like *a not unjustifiable assumption, leaves much to be desired, would serve no good purpose, a consideration which we should do well to bear in mind,* are a continuous temptation, a packet of aspirins always at one's elbow. Look back through this essay, and for certain you will find that I have again and again committed the very faults I am protesting against. By this morning's post I have received a pamphlet dealing with conditions in Germany. The author tells me that he "felt impelled" to write it. I open it at random, and here is almost the first sentence that I see: "[The Allies] have an opportunity not only of achieving a radical transformation of Germany's social and political structure in such a way as to avoid a nationalistic reaction in Germany itself, but at the same time of laying the foundations of a co-operative and unified Europe." You see, he "feels impelled" to write—feels, presumably, that he has something new to say—and yet his words, like cavalry horses answering the bugle, group themselves automatically into the familiar dreary pattern. This invasion of one's mind by ready-made phrases (*lay the foundations, achieve a radical transformation*) can only be prevented if one is constantly on guard against them, and every such phrase anaesthetizes a portion of one's brain.

I said earlier that the decadence of our language is probably curable. 17
Those who deny this would argue, if they produced an argument at all, that language merely reflects existing social conditions, and that we cannot influence its development by any direct tinkering with words and constructions. So far as the general tone or spirit of a language goes, this may be true, but it is not true in detail. Silly words and expressions have often disappeared, not through any evolutionary process but owing to the conscious action of a minority. Two recent examples were *explore every avenue* and *leave no stone unturned,* which were killed by the jeers of a few journalists. There is a long list of flyblown metaphors which could similarly be got rid of if enough people would interest themselves in the job; and it should also be possible to laugh the *not un-* formation out of existence,* to reduce the amount of Latin and Greek in the average sentence, to drive out foreign phrases and strayed scientific words, and, in general, to make pretentiousness unfashionable. But all these are minor points. The defence of the English language implies more than this, and perhaps it is best to start by saying what it does *not* imply.

*One can cure oneself of the *not un-* formation by memorizing this sentence: *A not unblack dog was chasing a not unsmall rabbit across a not ungreen field.* [Orwell's note.]

To begin with it has nothing to do with archaism, with the salvaging of obsolete words and turns of speech, or with the setting up of a "standard English" which must never be departed from. On the contrary, it is especially concerned with the scrapping of every word or idiom which has outworn its usefulness. It has nothing to do with correct grammar and syntax, which are of no importance so long as one makes one's meaning clear, or with the avoidance of Americanisms, or with having what is called a "good prose style." On the other hand it is not concerned with fake simplicity and the attempt to make written English colloquial. Nor does it even imply in every case preferring the Saxon word to the Latin one, though it does imply using the fewest and shortest words that will cover one's meaning. What is above all needed is to let the meaning choose the word, and not the other way about. In prose, the worst thing one can do with words is to surrender to them. When you think of a concrete object, you think wordlessly, and then, if you want to describe the thing you have been visualizing you probably hunt about till you find the exact words that seem to fit it. When you think of something abstract you are more inclined to use words from the start, and unless you make a conscious effort to prevent it, the existing dialect will come rushing in and do the job for you, at the expense of blurring or even changing your meaning. Probably it is better to put off using words as long as possible and get one's meaning as clear as one can through pictures or sensations. Afterwards one can choose—not simply *accept*—the phrases that will best cover the meaning, and then switch round and decide what impression one's words are likely to make on another person. This last effort of the mind cuts out all stale or mixed images, all prefabricated phrases, needless repetitions, and humbug and vagueness generally. But one can often be in doubt about the effect of a word or a phrase, and one needs rules that one can rely on when instinct fails. I think the following rules will cover most cases: 18

(i) Never use a metaphor, simile or other figure of speech which you are used to seeing in print.
(ii) Never use a long word where a short one will do.
(iii) If it is possible to cut a word out, always cut it out.
(iv) Never use the passive where you can use the active.
(v) Never use a foreign phrase, a scientific word or a jargon word if you can think of an everyday English equivalent.
(vi) Break any of these rules sooner than say anything outright barbarous.

These rules sound elementary, and so they are, but they demand a deep change of attitude in anyone who has grown used to writing in the style now fashionable. One could keep all of them and still write bad English, but one could not write the kind of stuff that I quoted in those five specimens at the beginning of this article.

I have not here been considering the literary use of language, but merely language as an instrument for expressing and not for concealing or preventing thought. Stuart Chase and others have come near to claiming that all abstract 19 words are meaningless, and have used this as a pretext for advocating a kind of political quietism. Since you don't know what Fascism is, how can you struggle against Fascism? One need not swallow such absurdities as this, but one ought to recognize that the present political chaos is connected with the decay of language, and that one can probably bring about some improvement by starting at the verbal end. If you simplify your English, you are freed from the worst follies of orthodoxy. You cannot speak any of the necessary dialects, and when you make a stupid remark its stupidity will be obvious, even to yourself. Political language—and with variations this is true of all political parties, from Conservatives to Anarchists—is designed to make lies sound truthful and murder respectable, and to give an appearance of solidity to pure wind. One cannot change this all in a moment, but one can at least change one's own habits, and from time to time one can even, if one jeers loudly enough, send some worn-out and useless phrase—some *jackboot, Achilles' heel, hotbed, melting pot, acid test, veritable inferno* or other lump of verbal refuse—into the dustbin where it belongs.

Questions for Discussion

1. Orwell begins by claiming that modern English is ugly, slovenly, and in decline. These charges must sound to many readers like highly subjective accusations, difficult if not impossible to document, and they are flatly denied by many scientific linguists. Does his claim seem to you convincing? (Remember that it is much easier to show that many people use language badly than to show that people in general speak and write worse now than they used to.) A second claim is that "the decline of a language must ultimately have political and economic causes" (¶2). How does he argue for this position? Do you accept it? If not, would you say that he has a serious argument worth thinking about? If you are dubious, where do you think Orwell has gone wrong in his argument?
2. Orwell claims that one of the surest symptoms of a language's abuse is staleness of imagery (figurative language that no longer evokes mental pictures or concrete sensations). Consider the following images by Orwell himself. Are they stale or fresh? Do they evoke effective concrete pictures or feelings?
   a. Modern prose is "tacked together like the sections of a prefabricated hen-house" (¶4).
   b. "Now that I have made this catalogue of swindles and perversions . . ." (¶9).
   c. "The writer knows more or less what he wants to say, but an accumulation of stale phrases chokes him like tea leaves blocking a sink" (¶11).

d. The typical political speaker often seems "unconscious of what he is saying, as one is when one utters the responses in church" (¶12).
e. "A mass of Latin words falls upon the facts like soft snow" (¶15).
f. Insincerity in writing leads "instinctively to long words and exhausted idioms, like a cuttlefish squirting out ink" (¶15).
g. Stock phrases "are a continuous temptation, a packet of aspirins always at one's elbow" (¶16).
h. Any stock phrase is a "lump of verbal refuse" that should be sent "into the dustbin [garbage can] where it belongs" (¶19).

Are all of these images equally effective? Are (f) and (g), for example, as good as (d) and (e)? (How do stock phrases resemble a packet of aspirins?) In general, does Orwell follow his own rule of using images that are fresh and effective?

3. Does the kind of argument Orwell constructs about the passage from Ecclesiastes (¶9–10)—counting the ratio of words to syllables—seem convincing? That is, is it a convincing way to show that writing is flaccid by remarking on its unusually high number of syllables per word? Will the ratio he deplores always produce the same effect? Can you rewrite the passage using many-syllabled words without being abstract and vague?
4. Do Orwell's "rules" for writing good English prose (¶18) sound like the rules you have read in English grammar texts? Do they sound easier or harder to follow? Does his argument convince you that following his rules will help you in your writing?
5. Do you think Orwell overstates his case when he says that writing good English "has nothing to do with correct grammar and syntax, which are of no importance so long as one makes one's meaning clear" (¶18)? Could you really write a business letter that was clear but ungrammatical? Do you find other points that seem to be overstated merely for strong effect?

Suggested Essay Topics

1. Select a document famous in American political history (such as the Declaration of Independence, Abraham Lincoln's Gettysburg Address or Second Inaugural Address, John F. Kennedy's Inaugural Address of 1960, or Hubert Humphrey's attack on "states' rights" at the Democratic National Convention in 1948). Read the whole speech and then evaluate one or two paragraphs according to Orwell's standards as summarized in paragraph 18 and defended throughout his essay. Direct your essay to your classmates, showing them why the speech you are examining is either a good or bad specimen of English prose, according to Orwell's standards.
2. Examine Orwell's own writing from the standpoint of his "rules" in paragraph 18, and write him a letter either commending or criticizing him for meeting (or not meeting) his own standards. Be sure to show concretely in particular passages how he either succeeds or fails.

IDEAS IN DEBATE

Bruno Bettelheim and Karen Zelan
Richard Wright

Bruno Bettelheim and Karen Zelan

*The psychologist Bruno Bettelheim (b. 1903) has made important contributions in many fields: the study of mental disorders in children (*The Empty Fortress*), the nature of totalitarianism and the experience of the holocaust under the Nazis (*The Informed Heart*), the moral and social effects of different kinds of children's literature (*The Uses of Enchantment*). Karen Zelan (b. 1934) is a research colleague of Bettelheim's and a child psychologist specializing in learning disorders. Together they have recently conducted an extensive study of how children are taught to read and why the teaching so often fails.*

*If you think back to when you were learning to read, you will remember that many children—you may even have been one of them—"hated school" and especially hated those moments when the teacher required each child to read a few words aloud. Bettelheim and Zelan argue that although learning to read must always be hard work, it can be work of the kind that leads to love, not hate—*if *the kind of reading that children do rewards them from the beginning with understanding and enjoyment. They find, however, that too many of today's reading texts cannot give such rewards because they are empty of human meaning. Most children, say Bettelheim and Zelan, will naturally rebel against such books and may, ultimately, learn to "hate reading."*

If Bettelheim and Zelan are right, they have discovered one main cause of many of America's educational problems. If you do not love to read, or if you have friends who say that they have never been "readers," the problem may well be traced to the kinds of stories, or non-stories, you were fed in the beginning years.

WHY CHILDREN DON'T LIKE TO READ

Originally published in *The Atlantic Monthly,* November 1981; reprinted as part of *On Learning to Read: The Child's Fascination with Meaning* (1981).

A child's attitude toward reading is of such importance that, more often than not, it determines his scholastic fate. Moreover, his experiences in learning to read may decide how he will feel about learning in general, and even about himself as a person. 1

Family life has a good deal to do with the development of a child's ability to understand, to use, and to enjoy language. It strongly influences his impression of the value of reading, and his confidence in his intelligence and academic abilities. But regardless of what the child brings from home to school, the most important influence on his ability to read once he is in class is how his teacher presents reading and literature. If the teacher can make reading interesting and enjoyable, then the exertions required to learn how will seem worthwhile. 2

A child takes great pleasure in becoming able to read some words. But the excitement fades when the texts the child must read force him to reread the same word endlessly. Word recognition—"decoding" is the term used by educational theorists—deteriorates into empty rote learning when it does not lead directly to the reading of meaningful content. The longer it takes the child to advance from decoding to meaningful reading, the more likely it becomes that his pleasure in books will evaporate. A child's ability to read depends unquestionably on his learning pertinent skills. But he will not be interested in learning basic reading skills if he thinks he is expected to master them for their own sake. That is why so much depends on what the teacher, the school, and the textbooks emphasize. From the very beginning, the child must be convinced that skills are only a means to achieve a goal, and that the only goal of importance is that he become literate—that is, come to enjoy literature and benefit from what it has to offer. 3

A child who is made to read, "Nan had a pad. Nan had a tan pad. Dad ran. Dad ran to the pad," and worse nonsense can have no idea that books are worth the effort of learning to read. His frustration is increased by the fact that such a repetitive exercise is passed off as a story to be enjoyed. The worst effect of such drivel is the impression it makes on a child that sounding out words on a page—decoding—is what reading is all about. If, on the contrary, a child were taught new skills as they became necessary to understand a worthwhile text, the empty achievement "Now I can decode some words" would give way to the much more satisfying recognition "Now I am reading something that adds to my life." From the start, reading lessons should nourish the child's spontaneous desire to read books by himself. 4

Benjamin S. Bloom, professor of education at the University of Chicago, has found that who will do well in school and who will do poorly is largely determined by the end of the third grade. Thus, reading instruction during the first three grades is crucial. Unfortunately, the primers used in most American schools up to and sometimes through the third grade convey no sense that there are rewards in store. And since poor readers continue to be subjected to these primers well past the third grade, their reading can only get worse as their interests and experience diverge further from the content of the books. 5

. . .

For many decades, textbooks have been used as the basis for reading instruction by the vast majority of elementary school teachers, and they are much worse today than [they were fifty years ago]. According to one study, 6 first readers published in the 1920s contained an average of 645 new words. By the late 1930s, this number had dropped to about 460 words. In the 1940s and 1950s, vocabulary declined further, to about 350 words. The vocabularies of primers in seven textbook series published between 1960 and 1963 ranged from 113 to 173 new words. More recent primers, compared with the 1920s editions, also have small vocabularies. For example, *Let's See the Animals,* published in 1970 by Bowmar/Noble, introduces 108 new words; *May I Come In?,* published in 1973, by Ginn & Company, introduces 219 new words; *Finding Places,* published by the American Book Company, in 1980, introduces 192 new words. Although in the 1920s few children went to kindergarten and little preschool reading instruction was given, by the 1970s, when many children were attending kindergarten and reading was consistently taught there, the first-grade primers contained only a quarter of the vocabulary presented to first-graders fifty years ago.

When they enter school, most children already know and use 4,000 or more words. Nobody has to make a deliberate effort to teach them these words, with the exception of the first few learned in infancy. Children make words their own because they want to, because they find them pleasing and useful. Even the least verbal group of first-graders has mastered well over 2,000 words, thus invalidating the claim that children of culturally deprived families would be unfairly burdened by primers of larger vocabulary. This condescending assumption ignores the richness of daily life in even the poorest households. By encouraging the adoption of less challenging books, it has helped to deprive most children at school just as poverty deprives many children at home. 7

. . .

Research in the teaching of reading, far from justifying the continuous reduction in the number of words used in primers, fails to show any reason for it. It is therefore hard to understand why textbook publishers have pursued this course, and why educators have not rebelled. One possible explanation is that as primers become simpler, children, because they are bored, read them with less and less facility. The publishers, in response, make the books even simpler and, thus, even less effective. 8

Primers have no authors. Many people help to create the books, and the financial investment required runs into the millions. (The sizable staff of one large publishing house worked for five years to produce a first-grade program alone.) Yet despite such prodigious effort and expense, all basic series are more or less alike. To recoup the large investment in a series, a publishing house must be able to sell it to schools all over the country. It cannot risk controversy. 9

We can cite two examples from our own experience. One publisher, in an effort to improve a first-grade reader, came up with a story in which children bring a balloon home from a fair, whereupon a cat leaps on it and it bursts. The story would seem harmless enough to most people, but when the book was tested in an Illinois school system, cat-lovers were outraged: the story had maligned their pets, turned children against animals, and so on. The 10 local school superintendent, who was coming up for re-election, decided to withdraw the book, and the publisher, fearing similar setbacks elsewhere, decided to drop the story.

Another publishing house was preparing a new edition of its widely 11
used series. One of us, asked to consult, objected in detail to the blandness of the stories proposed. The company's vice-president in charge of textbooks confessed that he, too, thought the stories would bore young readers, but he was obliged to keep in mind that neither children nor teachers buy textbooks: school boards and superintendents do. And their first concern is that no one mind their choices. Fairy tales, for example, would never do. Some people would complain that the stories insult stepmothers; others would find the punishment of evildoers too cruel.

The result of such constraints is a book full of endlessly repeated words 12
passed off as stories. Many teachers have told us that they don't like such a book, but assume that since a primer has been put together by experts, and approved by experts, it must be appropriate for children even if it is obnoxious to an adult. In the course of our research on the teaching of reading we have talked to children who were not so credulous. Many told us that their teachers must have faked an interest in the stories, or that they must think children are not very smart.

Fourth- and fifth-graders who had left the beginners' books behind 13
described their resentments to us quite clearly. One rather quiet boy, who preferred to read or work by himself and rarely participated in class, spoke up all on his own and with deep feeling. He had felt so ashamed to say the things written in primers that he could not bring himself to do it. And although he now liked reading a lot, he said, he still had a hard time reading aloud.

The first- and second-graders were as unhappy with their books as the 14
older children remembered being. They said they read only because they had to, and that on their own they would never choose such "junk." "It's all impossible," one of them said. When he was asked why, answers came from around the room: "The children aren't real!" "They aren't angry!" When one child exclaimed, "They aren't anything!" all agreed that there was nothing more to be said.

Textbook writers and publishers know that their books are dull, and 15
they have tried to make them more attractive by commissioning many colorful illustrations. For example, the number of pictures in primers of the Scott, Foresman series doubled between 1920 and 1962, from about one picture per one hundred words to nearly two per hundred words. The trouble with pictures is that the printed text becomes even less appealing in comparison. Words seem to be less vivid and to convey less information. Worse, being able to guess from the pictures what the text is about, a child who is reluctant to read has no incentive to learn.

The publishers' advice to teachers reinforces this syndrome. Typically, 16
the elaborate teachers' guides for each book in a series suggest that the class be asked questions about the pictures before reading the story. Yet there is

evidence that pictures retard or interfere with learning to read. Consider the following report by a psychologist of reading, Eleanor J. Gibson: "Children in the second term of kindergarten were given practice with three-letter common words ('cat,' 'bed,' 'dog,' etc.) on flash cards. In one group, the word on the card was accompanied by the appropriate picture. In another, it appeared alone. Training trials, in which the experimenter pronounced the word as it was displayed to the child, alternated with test trials [in which] the child was shown the word alone and asked to say what it was. The picture group made significantly more errors and took longer . . . than the group without pictures. The pictorial redundancy appeared to be distracting rather than useful." Yet in most of the preprimers and primers in classrooms today, words are used primarily as labels and captions.

Learning to read is not an entertainment but hard work. Rather than 17
face this directly, publishers seek to distract children with references to play. But allusions to strenuous physical activities make a child want to move, not think. Worse, a first-grader knows from his own experience just how complex a ball game can be. So a weak story about a ball game is most likely to convince the child that reading about a ball game is dull compared with playing in one.

In Harper & Row's "Janet and Mark" series (1966), school makes its first 18
appearance in second grade in *All Through the Year.* The last section of the book is titled "Too Much Is Too Much of Anything," and the first story about the things that are too much, "A Feeling in the Air," is about school. "Everyone was waiting. . . . It was the last day of school. A little while, and it would be all over." The children are "daydreaming . . . of baseball and swimming and bicycle rides." In the last picture of the story, we see them streaming out of the school building, joyful to be released.

Psychoanalytic studies of the so-called "double bind" have shown that 19
nothing is more confusing and disturbing to a child, or has more detrimental effects, than contradictory messages from an adult about important issues. Almost every preprimer and primer bears such contradictory messages. Tacitly, they say that the educational system, which requires the child to go to school and presents him with a book so that he may learn to read, holds that school and learning are serious business. But the explicit message of the text and pictures is that the child should think—that is, read—only about playing. The idea seems to be that a suggestion of what books are really for—to open new worlds of thought and imagination—would have the most undesirable consequences for the child's reading achievement.

From a psychoanalytic perspective, the primers' emphasis on play en- 20
sures that the books will be addressed solely to the child's pleasure-seeking ego—the earliest, most basic, but also most primitive motivating force in man. But as the child reaches school age, around age five, he should have learned to exchange (at least to some extent) living by the pleasure principle for making choices in accord with the reality principle. The primers, by presenting him almost exclusively with images of fun, throw the child back to the developmental phase he is trying, with difficulty, to outgrow. Such primers

insult the child's intelligence and his sense of worth, and the offense goes far to explain why children reject their reading books as empty. The books talk down to children; they do not take children's aspirations seriously.

In class, children read aloud. For some time to come, even if the child does not voice what he is reading, he will form the words with his lips. Reading aloud feels to a child as if he were speaking to his teacher, or whoever might be listening to him. For that matter, it is not unusual for a child to think that his teacher wrote the book, and has planted messages for him in it. In a conversation, we wish to hold our listener's attention and impress him with what we have to say. But the teacher is oblivious of the child's impression that reading aloud is a sort of conversation; instead, the teacher listens carefully to make sure that the child reads the words as they are printed in the book, and corrects him when he fails. To do so is a teacher's duty, according to the teaching methods favored in this country; it may also be the only way a teacher can remain alert through the near-hypnotic effect of the words. In any case, the child experiences the teacher's interruptions as rejection, which certainly does not make reading more attractive to him. 21

Furthermore, a child may have good reason to make a mistake. Reading for meaning is anything but passive, even when the content is absorbed exactly as presented. And the more intent a reader is on taking in the meaning, the more active he is in his reading. In order for a child to maintain the minimal interest necessary for reading a story, he may try to correct the story or improve it by misreading it. The barrenness of the text may tempt the child to project meaning where there is none. 22

The texts of preprimers and primers consist of words that can be readily sounded out. But these words are often combined in sentences that no one would ever say. Such a text is actually harder for the beginner to read. For example, because the child usually learns early to recognize the words "store" and "man," one widely used basal text (*People Read,* one of the Bank Street readers) tells about a "store man" when referring to a salesman. Out of a wish to make learning to read easy, children who know the word that the text of this story means to convey are asked to recognize and use in their reading a phrase that rarely comes up in writing or speech. To compound the irony, the phrase appears in a book whose title by implication promises to tell how everybody reads and what they read. The result is that children may be provoked to errors by the discrepancy between ordinary language and the uncommon language of the book. 23

We have spent a number of years observing school reading lessons, and have learned that children make mistakes for many reasons, in addition to the obvious one of ignorance. For example, a first-grade boy was reading "Van's Cave," a story in the 1969 J. B. Lippincott series about a hunter and his dog, Spot. The story goes that the hunter shoots five ducks, which the dog retrieves. They then return to the cave, where they live. The man starts a fire on which he plans to roast the ducks. The text says: "Spot must not leave the ducks. He can see a wolf near the cave." This, inexplicably, is accompanied by a picture showing the dog asleep. The boy reversed the meaning of the 24 sentence by reading, instead, "He can't see a wolf near the cave." It is possible that the boy did so because the picture shows the dog asleep. But it is more likely that the boy's knowledge of dog behavior made it seem unreasonable to him that a dog would sleep when it saw a wolf lurking nearby. A first-grader might also wish to believe that his dog would safeguard him. So the misreading of "can't" for "can," seemingly a simple error, reflects on one level the child's attempt to bring what the text says into accord with the picture. On another level, it may register the boy's protest against a dog that sleeps when its master needs protection. Finally, the misreading is a statement correctly describing normal dog behavior.

One first-grade girl complained about a story in McGraw-Hill's Sullivan Storybook series which told of a ball falling into a patch of tar. She thought it should have said that the ball fell into a puddle. The teacher, knowing that this phonics-based text used "patch of tar" in preference to "puddle" because these words are pronounced as printed, while "puddle" is pronounced "pud-del," said that perhaps the author of the story thought children would have difficulty in recognizing "puddle." By this she meant difficulty in decoding and reading the word. But the girl fastened on the exact words the teacher had used. She was indignant, and angrily exclaimed, "I know 'puddle' when I see it." We cannot say for sure that her remark did not simply reflect the fact that the word "puddle" was in her active vocabulary, while the words "patch of tar" were not, but the way she expressed herself suggests a more subtle reason for her sense of insult. She made it clear that she saw puddles in everyday life, not tar patches; and her reaction entailed the wish that teachers and those who write for children show respect for a child's experiences of the world. 25

Another smart first-grader puzzled his teacher because all year he had balked at reading, despite evidence that he knew how. On the day we observed him, the boy made numerous errors—for example, reading "stick" for "chick." This, the teacher told him, showed he had not mastered word beginnings and endings, and that he should therefore continue with his exercises. The boy refused. 26

The teacher then suggested that we read with him, upon which the boy strenuously protested that the workbook the teacher had assigned to him was boring. (The book, part of McGraw-Hill's Sullivan Programmed Reading series, is typical of most workbooks, in that the exercises require the student to fill in missing letters.) With our encouragement, the boy made one more attempt; again he read "stick" for "chick." But this time, before anyone had time to react, he corrected himself and angrily blurted out: "Fill in the blanks, that's all I get! Witch, witch, witch . . . ditch, ditch, ditch . . . stick, stick, stick . . . chick, chick, chick!" And that was it. He would not do any more reading with us that day. The boy had made error upon error, in this way giving vent to his negative feelings. But by pairing "witch" with "ditch," and "stick" with "chick," he showed that he understood well the different word beginnings and endings, and that his substitutions were not made in ignorance. 27

A couple of days later, we again asked the boy to read. He refused the 28

Sullivan series but was willing to try something more interesting. We settled on *The Bear Detectives,* by Stan and Jan Berenstain. The story tells how Papa Bear and his children hunt for a missing pumpkin, using a detective kit. Although the small bears discover various clues to the pumpkin's whereabouts, they can't find it. After reading the story eagerly for some thirty pages, the boy substituted the word "defective" for "detective": "He's in the barn. This is it! Hand me that defective kit." Earlier he had read "detective" correctly, demonstrating that he was well able to read the word—that he knew what it designated and how it fit into the story. It seemed to us that the boy, having read for so many pages that the detective kit was no help in the search for the pumpkin, and carried away by the excited wish of the bears to find it, was once more expressing his frustration with a text.

A few days later, this boy's workbook again required him to read a list 29
of words that, bereft of context, made no sense. He then read "dump" for "jump." Responding to the feelings this misreading suggested, we asked, "Who wants to dump this?" The boy immediately read the correct word, "jump," and then nodded at us. When we asked him why he wanted to dump the workbook, his unhesitating reply was, " 'Cause it's garbage."

Just as children are likely to change the words of a dull story in order 30
to make it more interesting, they are also likely to change the words of an interesting story because they have a personal stake in the meaning. For example, one competent first-grader read a story to us smoothly and with interest and comprehension in her voice. The story was about tigers, and the little girl made only one mistake: she consistently read "tigger" for "tiger." It is easy to understand why this child would shy away from thinking about dangerous tigers in favor of contemplating the harmless character of Tigger in the Pooh books, which were favorites of hers. Her switch in thought seemed to relieve her fear about what the ferocious beast would do next as the story unfolded.

It requires considerable ingenuity on the part of first-graders to make 31
radical alterations in meanings by only the slightest change of letters. In the examples of the boy reading about the dog and the wolf and the girl reading about the tiger, the children retained all the letters of the printed word, adding to them a single letter. By adding a "t," the boy substituted correct animal behavior for an incorrect description of it, and by adding a "g," the girl replaced an animal threatening danger and destruction with one symbolizing safety and pleasure. In the third example, by substituting one letter for another in a nine-letter word, the child expressed his dissatisfaction with the uselessness of an object that played a central role in the story he was reading.

When a child utters a word entirely different from the one printed in 32
the book, teachers are likely to assume, correctly, that the child's attention has wandered, or that he may have given up on reading a word that is hard for him. When what the child reads is only slightly different from what is printed, teachers are also likely to conclude that the child has a problem—faulty discrimination between letters—even though the error may change the meaning of the sentence radically. They assume this despite the fact that the

child has already read most letters as printed, suggesting that he was paying attention to the page and could recognize the letters correctly. But what if a child's substitution of one or a few letters makes good—though altered—sense within the context of a story? Perhaps he has perceived what the printed word signifies, decided that it is unacceptable, and found a solution that suits his purposes.

A teacher's reflex to catch and correct mistakes is but one example of 33
a situation that occurs over and over again in schools, and not only where beginners are taught to read: the educator's faith in abstract theories about how learning must proceed blinds him to the sophistication of the child's mind. The teacher's insistence on accuracy often barely hides the fact that what is involved is also a power play, in which the teacher uses her superior knowledge and her authority to gain her point. The child—consciously or, more often, subconsciously—reacts to being the victim of such a power play, and is antagonistic. Unfortunately, many children manage to defeat the teacher by refusing to learn; their victory robs them of their chance to be educated, and it deprives society of competent citizens.

It is not impossible to teach children to read while respecting their 34
intelligence and dignity. The primers used in Europe are generally far more difficult than those in use in this country. We believe their success is proved by the fact that at the end of the first grade, the average European child has a larger reading vocabulary than that of the average American child. Moreover, reading retardation, the curse of so many young Americans, is much less common among European children and, when it occurs, is rarely as severe.

The most recent series of basic readers published in Switzerland stands 35
as a notable alternative to the American textbooks that we have complained about. The early reading program consists of three preprimers and one primer. The preprimers are loose-leaf booklets, each page (with a single exception) comprising a few short lines of text and an illustration. Since there are no pictures on the covers of the booklets, the child is encouraged to form his own opinion of what each booklet is about by reading.

The first preprimer is entitled *We are all here,* meaning "here to read 36
together." Its first page has only two words: "I am." And on this page there is no picture, no face to rival the child's own. The Swiss child's reading thus begins with the strongest statement of self-assertion imaginable. After sixteen more pages, each with a few words for the child to learn, there follow twenty-eight pages devoted either to snatches of well-known songs or to a few lines from popular fairy tales. In this way, the first preprimer leads easily to the next, *Once upon a time,* which is composed of five fairy tales from Grimm. Though quite simple, these versions are nonetheless faithful in all essentials to the originals.

The third Swiss preprimer, *Edi,* is about a little boy who might be the 37
peer of the children reading about him. The first page shows Edi with his school satchel on his back, standing between his father and mother. The story goes that Edi, who has eaten something that disagrees with him, gets sick and is sent to the country to stay with relatives and get well. We follow Edi's

experiences on the farm until the end of the book, when he returns home, his health fully restored. There he finds that while he was away, his mother had a baby; Edi has a sister. Edi's story deals with two of the most critical events in a child's life: sickness and the birth of a sibling.

The primer of the Swiss series, *It's your turn,* meaning "it's your turn to 38
read," begins with counting rhymes and songs typically sung by children as accompaniment to their games. Since Swiss children know all these rhymes and songs, they know how the words they are decoding ought to sound, and so it is likely that at this more difficult level of reading, their attempts will be error-free. Thus the children's confidence in their ability to read this new, thicker, rather scary-looking book is supported, and they are ready for the remaining sections, which are longer and a little harder.

It's your turn has many colorful pictures that embellish the text without 39
giving away its meaning; the child *must* read in order to understand. For example, a poem by Christian Morgenstern, "Winternight," is illustrated by a picture of a town at night, covered with falling snow; the picture conveys the spirit of the poem but permits no conclusion about its substance. In addition to the Morgenstern poem, the book contains a number of other poems and short stories, many by famous German authors. The selection represents all periods of German literature: contemporary, Romantic, classical, and medieval, and legendary folktales, rhymes, and riddles.

This first Swiss reader, like its American counterparts, tries to introduce 40
children to reading by means of attractive and fairly easy material. The chief difference is that none of the pieces in the Swiss reader patronize the child; there is no deviation from ordinary language or ordinary usage. Children have been reciting the counting rhymes to each other for hundreds of years. No words are avoided because they might be difficult (as is done constantly in American primers)—and they prove not to be too hard, because the child who uses them in everyday conversation already knows what they mean, and is thus eager to master whatever technical obstacles they present on the page. In one way or another, all the stories appeal to children of primary age, but in none of them is there even the mention of active play. If anything, the pieces are on the contemplative side, though with a light touch. The most impressive difference between this book and American primers is the literary quality of many of its selections. The Swiss primer manages to introduce the child to literacy at the same time that it teaches him the rudiments of reading.

These primers, used in the German-speaking parts of Switzerland, have 41
a special lesson to teach American educators and publishers. It has been argued that our primers have to employ unnaturally simple words because many minority children speak a different language at home: Spanish, Chinese, "black English," and so on. But the language that *all* children growing up in the German parts of Switzerland speak—a dialect called *Schweizer Deutsch,* or Swiss German—is very different from the High German they must speak and read in school. Although during the first few months of school the children are allowed to speak to the teacher in their dialect, from the start they learn to read only the High German in which their primers are published.

For some reason, Swiss children do not find this enforced bilingualism such a handicap that they fail to become able readers. We believe that their lack of difficulty is explained to a great extent by the fact that they like what they are given to read.

Questions for Discussion

1. Can you summarize the differences between the Swiss basic readers that the authors admire and the American texts they deplore? Is the difference to be found in the method of presentation, in the subject matter, or in both?
2. Compare your earliest memories of learning to read with those of your classmates. Are there strong differences among you about how pleasant or disagreeable it was? Can you remember the first book you really enjoyed? (Gregory remembers *Smoky the Crow,* Booth *The Wizard of Oz,* both from the second grade. Neither of us can remember a single reading from the first grade, except for the Dick and Jane books, which were dismal, dismal.)
3. What kind of people do Bettelheim and Zelan seem to be, judging from the things they say and the way they write? Give evidence for your opinion from their own words. (One result of getting an education should be an expansion of your vocabulary for describing people—their character, their ethos. When you ask, "What kind of person is he?" how many kinds do you have in mind?)
4. Bettelheim and Zelan suggest an analogy (¶7) between the child's learning to talk and learning to read: If children learn to talk "because they want to," obviously they will learn to read if they want to. (Compare our analogy of learning to talk with learning to write, pp. 6–8.) Do you think that the analogy is sound? In answering, remember that a fitting analogy does not require that *all* details in the comparison match perfectly, only that the directly pertinent elements do.
5. In what paragraphs do the authors provide evidence for their conclusions? Do different kinds of evidence carry different weight here? For example, is the account of Swiss schools and their success more or less persuasive than the quotations from the American primers?
6. In paragraph 21 the authors say that children experience reading aloud as conversation. Is silent reading also experienced as conversation? If you ask a book a question, can it ever be said to "reply"? Do some textbooks make us feel like holding a conversation, while some merely talk *at* us, and still others seem to address someone *behind* us, someone wearing an academic robe and mortarboard? (Most textbooks we authors remember from college had this last tone.) What makes the difference?

Suggested Essay Topics

1. In the children's literature section of the library, find a reading primer and do a careful book review from the point of view of Bettelheim and Zelan. Your basic question is, "Would it be a good book to learn to read from?" Be sure to do some thinking about the kind of reader you are addressing, whether librarians, elementary teachers, parents, or the children themselves.
2. This assignment is somewhat more ambitious. Read all or part of *The Uses of Enchantment* by Bettelheim. Then choose a short section from his defense of fairy tales and discuss whether it seems persuasive and why. Again you should think about whom you are trying to convince. For this assignment you might think of writing a letter to the editor of *The Atlantic Monthly* (where "Why Children Don't Like to Read" originally appeared) praising or condemning the authors for their argument. Or you might imagine yourself writing the authors directly, giving carefully considered reasons why you find their arguments strong or weak.

Richard Wright

In the other "Ideas in Debate" essay, Bruno Bettelheim and Karen Zelan assert that a child "will not be interested in learning basic reading skills if he thinks he is expected to master them for their own sake. . . . The child must be convinced that skills are only a means to achieve a goal." If "for their own sake" means that children are taught reading skills as a dead-end activity, leading to nothing more exciting or illuminating than good or bad grades on reading tests, surely Bettelheim and Zelan are right. But if children are given worthy goals that can be met by learning to read—goals that belong to them as well as to the teacher—then presumably they will be motivated to learn eagerly. At that point there is not much distance between learning reading skills "for their own sake" and learning them to achieve goals. No two poles could be farther apart than the reading goals in today's minimum-achievement classroom, where reading is often taught as a mechanical activity that goes nowhere, and the goals of Richard Wright's (1908–1960) passionate reader in "The Library Card."

"I hungered for books," he says, "[for] new ways of looking and seeing. It was not a matter of believing what I read, but of feeling something new, of being affected by something that made the look of the world different" (¶23). "It would have been impossible for me to have told anyone what I derived from these novels, for it was nothing less than a sense of life itself" (¶28). Clearly, books for this young narrator are doorways into a wider existence than he could ever have experienced on his own, and in his eagerness to reach that wider existence he opened one door after another.

What does this experience suggest about the way reading should be taught to children in school? And what does it suggest about the kinds *of reading they ought to do?*

As you read, consider whether most of us share the narrator's hunger for a wider existence than our ordinary one. Is it possible to see people's interest in television, movies, plays, and song as different aspects of this hunger to be taken beyond our own lives, to learn how others see, feel, and think? If most of us do share this hunger (and if there are some who do not, why don't they?), why is the satisfying of this hunger not more frequently offered as the goal of learning to read? Six-year-old children may not be ready for a theoretical discussion of the issues, but isn't it true that they will certainly recognize the difference between reading as a narrow mechanical end and reading as a means of learning about the immense world around them? And at the high school and college levels, what is the proportion of reading that is done for sheer pleasure and general learning as compared to the reading that is done to acquire specific information? Does Richard Wright's account of how his world opened up make you wish you could take time to read more in your own life?

THE LIBRARY CARD

Chapter 13 of *Black Boy.*

One morning I arrived early at work and went into the bank lobby where the Negro porter was mopping. I stood at a counter and picked up the Memphis *Commercial Appeal* and began my free reading of the press. I came finally to the editorial page and saw an article dealing with one H. L. Mencken. I knew by hearsay that he was the editor of the *American Mercury,* but aside from that I knew nothing about him. The article was a furious denunciation of Mencken, concluding with one, hot, short sentence: Mencken is a fool. 1

I wondered what on earth this Mencken had done to call down upon him the scorn of the South. The only people I had ever heard denounced in the South were Negroes, and this man was not a Negro. Then what ideas did Mencken hold that made a newspaper like the *Commercial Appeal* castigate him publicly? Undoubtedly he must be advocating ideas that the South did not like. Were there, then, people other than Negroes who criticized the South? I knew that during the Civil War the South had hated northern whites, but I had not encountered such hate during my life. Knowing no more of Mencken than I did at that moment, I felt a vague sympathy for him. Had not the South, which had assigned me the role of a non-man, cast at him its hardest words? 2

Now, how could I find out about this Mencken? There was a huge library near the riverfront, but I knew that Negroes were not allowed to patronize its shelves any more than they were the parks and playgrounds of the city. I had gone into the library several times to get books for the white men on the job. Which of them would now help me to get books? And how could I read them without causing concern to the white men with whom I worked? I had so far been successful in hiding my thoughts and feelings from 3 them, but I knew that I would create hostility if I went about the business of reading in a clumsy way.

I weighed the personalities of the men on the job. There was Don, a Jew; 4
but I distrusted him. His position was not much better than mine and I knew that he was uneasy and insecure; he had always treated me in an offhand, bantering way that barely concealed his contempt. I was afraid to ask him to help me get books; his frantic desire to demonstrate a racial solidarity with the whites against Negroes might make him betray me.

Then how about the boss? No, he was a Baptist and I had the suspicion 5
that he would not be quite able to comprehend why a black boy would want to read Mencken. There were other white men on the job whose attitudes showed clearly that they were Kluxers or sympathizers, and they were out of the question.

There remained only one man whose attitude did not fit into an anti- 6
Negro category, for I had heard the white men refer to him as a "Pope lover." He was an Irish Catholic and was hated by the white Southerners. I knew that he read books, because I had got him volumes from the library several times. Since he, too, was an object of hatred, I felt that he might refuse me but would hardly betray me. I hesitated, weighing and balancing the imponderable realities.

One morning I paused before the Catholic fellow's desk. 7

"I want to ask you a favor," I whispered to him.

"What is it?"

"I want to read. I can't get books from the library. I wonder if you'd let me use your card?"

He looked at me suspiciously.

"My card is full most of the time," he said.

"I see," I said and waited, posing my question silently.

"You're not trying to get me into trouble, are you, boy?" he asked, 8
staring at me.

"Oh, no, sir."

"What book do you want?"

"A book by H. L. Mencken."

"Which one?"

"I don't know. Has he written more than one?"

"He has written several."

"I didn't know that."

"What makes you want to read Mencken?" 9

"Oh, I just saw his name in the newspaper," I said.

"It's good of you to want to read," he said. "But you ought to read the right things."

I said nothing. Would he want to supervise my reading?

"Let me think," he said. "I'll figure out something."

I turned from him and he called me back. He stared at me quizzically.

"Richard, don't mention this to the other white men," he said.

"I understand," I said. "I won't say a word."

A few days later he called me to him.

"I've got a card in my wife's name," he said. "Here's mine." 10

"Thank you, sir."

"Do you think you can manage it?"

"I'll manage fine," I said.

"If they suspect you, you'll get in trouble," he said.

"I'll write the same kind of notes to the library that you wrote when you sent me for books," I told him. "I'll sign your name."

He laughed.

"Go ahead. Let me see what you get," he said.

That afternoon I addressed myself to forging a note. Now, what were 11
the names of books written by H. L. Mencken? I did not know any of them. I finally wrote what I thought would be a foolproof note: *Dear Madam: Will you please let this nigger boy*—I used the word "nigger" to make the librarian feel that I could not possibly be the author of the note—*have some books by H. L. Mencken?* I forged the white man's name.

I entered the library as I had always done when on errands for whites, 12
but I felt that I would somehow slip up and betray myself. I doffed my hat, stood a respectful distance from the desk, looked as unbookish as possible, and waited for the white patrons to be taken care of. When the desk was clear of people, I still waited. The white librarian looked at me.

"What do you want, boy?"

As though I did not possess the power of speech, I stepped forward and 13
simply handed her the forged note, not parting my lips.

"What books by Mencken does he want?" she asked.

"I don't know, ma'am," I said, avoiding her eyes.

"Who gave you this card?"

"Mr. Falk," I said.

"Where is he?"

"He's at work, at the M——— Optical Company," I said. "I've been in 14
here for him before."

"I remember," the woman said. "But he never wrote notes like this."

Oh, God, she's suspicious. Perhaps she would not let me have the 15
books? If she had turned her back at that moment, I would have ducked out the door and never gone back. Then I thought of a bold idea.

"You can call him up, ma'am," I said, my heart pounding. 16

"You're not using these books, are you?" she asked pointedly.

"Oh, no, ma'am. I can't read."

"I don't know what he wants by Mencken," she said under her breath.

I knew now that I had won; she was thinking of other things and the 17
race question had gone out of her mind. She went to the shelves. Once or twice she looked over her shoulder at me, as though she was still doubtful. Finally she came forward with two books in her hands.

"I'm sending him two books," she said. "But tell Mr. Falk to come in 18
next time, or send me the names of the books he wants. I don't know what he wants to read."

I said nothing. She stamped the card and handed me the books. Not daring to glance at them, I went out of the library, fearing that that woman would call me back for further questioning. A block away from the library I opened one of the books and read a title: *A Book of Prefaces.* I was nearing my nineteenth birthday and I did not know how to pronounce the word "preface." I thumbed the pages and saw strange words and strange names. I shook my head, disappointed, looked at the other book; it was called *Prejudices.* I knew what that word meant; I had heard it all my life. And right off I was on guard against Mencken's books. Why would a man want to call a book *Prejudices?* The word was so stained with all my memories of racial hate that I could not conceive of anybody using it for a title. Perhaps I had made a mistake about Mencken? A man who had prejudices must be wrong. 19

When I showed the books to Mr. Falk, he looked at me and frowned. 20

"That librarian might telephone you," I warned him.

"That's all right," he said. "But when you're through reading those books, I want you to tell me what you get out of them."

That night in my rented room, while letting the hot water run over my can of pork and beans in the sink, I opened *A Book of Prefaces* and began to read. I was jarred and shocked by the style, the clear, clean, sweeping sentences. Why did he write like that? And how did one write like that? I pictured the man as a raging demon, slashing with his pen, consumed with hate, denouncing everything American, extolling everything European or German, laughing at the weaknesses of people, mocking God, authority. What was this? I stood up, trying to realize what reality lay behind the meaning of the words . . . Yes, this man was fighting, fighting with words. He was using words as a weapon, using them as one would use a club. Could words be weapons? Well, yes, for here they were. Then, maybe, perhaps, I could use them as a weapon? No. It frightened me. I read on and what amazed me was not what he said, but how on earth anybody had the courage to say it. 21

Occasionally I glanced up to reassure myself that I was alone in the room. Who were these men about whom Mencken was talking so passionately? Who was Anatole France? Joseph Conrad? Sinclair Lewis, Sherwood Anderson, Dostoevski, George Moore, Gustave Flaubert, Maupassant, Tolstoy, Frank Harris, Mark Twain, Thomas Hardy, Arnold Bennett, Stephen Crane, Zola, Norris, Gorky, Bergson, Ibsen, Balzac, Bernard Shaw, Dumas, Poe, Thomas Mann, O. Henry, Dreiser, H. G. Wells, Gogol, T. S. Eliot, Gide, Baudelaire, Edgar Lee Masters, Stendhal, Turgenev, Huneker, Nietzsche, and scores of others? Were these men real? Did they exist or had they existed? And how did one pronounce their names? 22

I ran across many words whose meanings I did not know, and I either looked them up in a dictionary or, before I had a chance to do that, encountered the word in a context that made its meaning clear. But what strange world was this? I concluded the book with the conviction that I had somehow overlooked something terribly important in life. I had once tried to write, had once reveled in feeling, had let my crude imagination roam, but the impulse to dream had been slowly beaten out of me by experience. Now it surged up 23 again and I hungered for books, new ways of looking and seeing. It was not a matter of believing or disbelieving what I read, but of feeling something new, of being affected by something that made the look of the world different.

As dawn broke I ate my pork and beans, feeling dopey, sleepy. I went 24
to work, but the mood of the book would not die; it lingered, coloring everything I saw, heard, did. I now felt that I knew what the white men were feeling. Merely because I had read a book that had spoken of how they lived and thought, I identified myself with that book. I felt vaguely guilty. Would I, filled with bookish notions, act in a manner that would make the whites dislike me?

I forged more notes and my trips to the library became frequent. Read- 25
ing grew into a passion. My first serious novel was Sinclair Lewis's *Main Street.* It made me see my boss, Mr. Gerald, and identify him as an American type. I would smile when I saw him lugging his golf bags into the office. I had always felt a vast distance separating me from the boss, and now I felt closer to him, though still distant. I felt now that I knew him, that I could feel the very limits of his narrow life. And this had happened because I had read a novel about a mythical man called George F. Babbitt.

The plots and stories in the novels did not interest me so much as the 26
point of view revealed. I gave myself over to each novel without reserve, without trying to criticize it; it was enough for me to see and feel something different. And for me, everything was something different. Reading was like a drug, a dope. The novels created moods in which I lived for days. But I could not conquer my sense of guilt, my feeling that the white men around me knew that I was changing, that I had begun to regard them differently.

Whenever I brought a book to the job, I wrapped it in newspaper—a 27
habit that was to persist for years in other cities and under other circumstances. But some of the white men pried into my packages when I was absent and they questioned me.

"Boy, what are you reading those books for?"

"Oh, I don't know, sir."

"That's deep stuff you're reading, boy."

"I'm just killing time, sir."

"You'll addle your brains if you don't watch out."

I read Dreiser's *Jennie Gerhardt* and *Sister Carrie* and they revived in me a 28
vivid sense of my mother's suffering; I was overwhelmed. I grew silent, wondering about the life around me. It would have been impossible for me to have told anyone what I derived from these novels, for it was nothing less than a sense of life itself. All my life had shaped me for the realism, the naturalism of the modern novel, and I could not read enough of them.

Steeped in new moods and ideas, I bought a ream of paper and tried to 29
write; but nothing would come, or what did come was flat beyond telling. I discovered that more than desire and feeling were necessary to write and I dropped the idea. Yet I still wondered how it was possible to know people sufficiently to write about them? Could I ever learn about life and people? To

me, with my vast ignorance, my Jim Crow station in life, it seemed a task impossible of achievement. I now knew what being a Negro meant. I could endure the hunger. I had learned to live with hate. But to feel that there were feelings denied me, that the very breath of life itself was beyond my reach, that more than anything else hurt, wounded me. I had a new hunger.

In buoying me up, reading also cast me down, made me see what was 30
possible, what I had missed. My tension returned, new, terrible, bitter, surging, almost too great to be contained. I no longer *felt* that the world about me was hostile, killing; I *knew* it. A million times I asked myself what I could do to save myself, and there were no answers. I seemed forever condemned, ringed by walls.

I did not discuss my reading with Mr. Falk, who had lent me his library 31
card; it would have meant talking about myself and that would have been too painful. I smiled each day, fighting desperately to maintain my old behavior, to keep my disposition seemingly sunny. But some of the white men discerned that I had begun to brood.

"Wake up there, boy!" Mr. Olin said one day. 32

"Sir!" I answered for the lack of a better word.

"You act like you've stolen something," he said.

I laughed in the way I knew he expected me to laugh, but I resolved to 33
be more conscious of myself, to watch my every act, to guard and hide the new knowledge that was dawning within me.

If I went north, would it be possible for me to build a new life then? 34
But how could a man build a life upon vague, unformed yearnings? I wanted to write and I did not even know the English language. I bought English grammars and found them dull. I felt that I was getting a better sense of the language from novels than from grammars. I read hard, discarding a writer as soon as I felt that I had grasped his point of view. At night the printed page stood before my eyes in sleep.

Mrs. Moss, my landlady, asked me one Sunday morning: 35

"Son, what is this you keep on reading?"

"Oh, nothing. Just novels."

"What you get out of 'em?"

"I'm just killing time," I said.

"I hope you know your own mind," she said in a tone which implied that she doubted if I had a mind.

I knew of no Negroes who read the books I liked and I wondered if any 36
Negroes ever thought of them. I knew that there were Negro doctors, lawyers, newspapermen, but I never saw any of them. When I read a Negro newspaper I never caught the faintest echo of my preoccupation in its pages. I felt trapped and occasionally, for a few days, I would stop reading. But a vague hunger would come over me for books, books that opened up new avenues of feeling and seeing, and again I would forge another note to the white librarian. Again I would read and wonder as only the naïve and unlettered

can read and wonder, feeling that I carried a secret, criminal burden about with me each day.

That winter my mother and brother came and we set up housekeeping, 37 buying furniture on the installment plan, being cheated and yet knowing no way to avoid it. I began to eat warm food and to my surprise found that regular meals enabled me to read faster. I may have lived through many illnesses and survived them, never suspecting that I was ill. My brother obtained a job and we began to save toward the trip north, plotting our time, setting tentative dates for departure. I told none of the white men on the job that I was planning to go north; I knew that the moment they felt I was thinking of the North they would change toward me. It would have made them feel that I did not like the life I was living, and because my life was completely conditioned by what they said or did, it would have been tantamount to challenging them.

I could calculate my chances for life in the South as a Negro fairly clearly 38 now.

I could fight the southern whites by organizing with other Negroes, as 39 my grandfather had done. But I knew that I could never win that way; there were many whites and there were but few blacks. They were strong and we were weak. Outright black rebellion could never win. If I fought openly I would die and I did not want to die. News of lynchings were frequent.

I could submit and live the life of a genial slave, but that was impossible. 40 All of my life had shaped me to live by my own feelings, and thoughts. I could make up to Bess and marry her and inherit the house. But that, too, would be the life of a slave; if I did that, I would crush to death something within me, and I would hate myself as much as I knew the whites already hated those who had submitted. Neither could I ever willingly present myself to be kicked, as Shorty had done. I would rather have died than do that.

I could drain off my restlessness by fighting with Shorty and Harrison. 41 I had seen many Negroes solve the problem of being black by transferring their hatred of themselves to others with a black skin and fighting them. I would have to be cold to do that, and I was not cold and I could never be.

I could, of course, forget what I had read, thrust the whites out of my 42 mind, forget them; and find release from anxiety and longing in sex and alcohol. But the memory of how my father had conducted himself made that course repugnant. If I did not want others to violate my life, how could I voluntarily violate it myself?

I had no hope whatever of being a professional man. Not only had I been 43 so conditioned that I did not desire it, but the fulfillment of such an ambition was beyond my capabilities. Well-to-do Negroes lived in a world that was almost as alien to me as the world inhabited by whites.

What, then, was there? I held my life in my mind, in my consciousness 44 each day, feeling at times that I would stumble and drop it, spill it forever. My reading had created a vast sense of distance between me and the world in which I lived and tried to make a living, and that sense of distance was increasing each day. My days and nights were one long, quiet, continuously contained dream of terror, tension, and anxiety. I wondered how long I could bear it.

Questions for Discussion

1. Having been deprived of learning, the young narrator views it as a great privilege. He does not view learning as a way of gaining power in the world or of increasing his income—those thoughts do not seem even to cross his mind—but simply as a way of learning about lives, thoughts, and feelings other than his own. Discuss with your classmates the extent to which you think student apathy about learning derives from its being forced on children as a requirement rather than held out as a privilege. If you were to try to influence students in grade school and high school to become more enthusiastic readers and learners, what changes or tactics would you recommend? What new instructions would you give to teachers and administrators? What changes of behavior or attitude would you recommend to students themselves?
2. What is the social function of "boy" used as a form of address to blacks? Can you suggest why the whites in the story constantly repeat this term?
3. Why does the narrator in paragraphs 24 and 26 say that he felt guilty for the reading he was doing?
4. In trying to learn to write, the narrator says that he "bought English grammars" but "felt that I was getting a better sense of the language from novels than from grammars." Does this ring true to you? Do you think that increasing your reading will automatically improve your grammar? Would a steady reader ever have to study grammar formally in order to use it correctly? As you think about the answer to this question, consider the grammar of pre-school children who have never studied grammar. If they are surrounded by grammatically correct speakers, is their own grammar generally correct? If so, does this fact suggest an answer to the question of whether you can learn grammar from reading as well as by listening?
5. In discussion with your classmates, compare the various English and reading teachers you have had over the years. How many students think their teachers were successful at instilling a love of reading? How many think their teachers were poor? Are there similarities among the good teachers? Among the bad?

Suggested Essay Topics

1. In paragraph 24 the young narrator reports that after an all-night orgy of reading, "I went to work, but the mood of the book would not die; it

lingered, coloring everything I saw, heard, did." If you have ever had this kind of experience yourself—the experience of a book's mood, characters, and events occupying your mind so vividly that they colored the world around you—give a specific account of the book's lingering effects. After reading Sinclair Lewis's *Main Street,* for example, the narrator achieves an entirely new understanding of his boss; he learns something about his boss's values and inner life that he could never have learned firsthand. Can you give an account of any similar experience, when a book gave you a fresher perspective or a deeper understanding of some (formerly inscrutable) person or event? Direct your essay to your classmates, with the aim of explaining how the book achieved its effect.

2. Re-read a book that was a favorite of yours when you were a child. Then write an essay explaining how you would present this book to children today if you were a parent or a teacher using it to teach reading. Think back on your own experience with reading teachers, either in school or at home, and explain the strategies you would employ to lift children up to a love of reading. If it seems appropriate, pick a passage or two and discuss your selection in detail.

4

IMAGINATION AND ART

The Nature and Value of Imagination

I am certain of nothing but the holiness of the heart's affections and the truth of imagination—what the imagination seizes as beauty must be truth—whether it existed before or not.

John Keats

States have been governed here and there, heaven knows how; but not by poetry, it is certain. Literature is a seducer; we had almost said a harlot. She may do to trifle with; but woe to the state whose statesmen write verses, and whose lawyers read more in Tom Moore [a poet] than in Brackton [a jurist]. This is a dangerous state of society. . . . The real happiness of man, of the mass, not of the few, depends on the knowledge of things, not on that of words.

Westminster Review

Then I asked: "Does a firm persuasion that a thing is so, make it so?" He replied: "All Poets believe that it does, and in ages of imagination this firm persuasion removed mountains; but many are not capable of a firm persuasion of anything."

William Blake

We turn to stories and pictures and music because they show us who and what and why we are, and what our relationship is to life and death, what is essential, and what, despite the arbitrariness of falling beams, will not burn.

Madeline L'Engle

Out of chaos the imagination frames a thing of beauty.

John Livingston Lowes

Aristotle

Aristotle's Poetics, *(c. 330 B.C.) is generally considered the most influential discussion in the tradition of literary studies. In it Aristotle (384–322 B.C.) introduces distinctions, terms, and definitions that still play a crucial role in almost all literary discussion and analysis.*

In the brief selection reprinted here, Aristotle raises the most fundamental question one can ask about literature: "Why are human beings interested in stories in the first place?" His answer is brief but perceptive, simple but profound. Human beings' fondness for stories is rooted in two instincts: first, the natural pleasure we take in imitations generally, human beings being "the most imitative of living creatures," and second, the natural pleasure we take in experiencing objects that are "harmoniously" crafted. We "naturally" love objects that are shaped, as stories are, by order, pattern, development, and selection.

Aristotle goes on to argue that the object *of imitation in literature is not just what people* happen *to say or do. If that were true, one could just copy down the random words and actions of one's roommate, say, and call it art: a literature of "real life." But no one (except perhaps your roommate's parents) would find your "imitation" interesting, much less view it as art or literature.*

What literature imitates is not what is random or accidental but what is probable: the selected words and actions of human beings rooted in the passions, values, and language of the represented persons and in their situations. This means that when one reads a story, one learns not just about literary human beings but about flesh-and-blood human beings as well.

THE "INSTINCT" OF IMITATION

From *Poetics.* The title is ours.

Poetry in general seems to have sprung from two causes, each of them lying deep in our nature. First, the instinct of imitation is implanted in man from childhood, one difference between him and other animals being that he is the most imitative of living creatures, and through imitation learns his earliest lessons; and no less universal is the pleasure felt in things imitated. We have evidence of this in the facts of experience. Objects which in themselves we view with pain, we delight to contemplate when reproduced with minute fidelity: such as the forms of the most ignoble animals and of dead bodies. The cause of this again is, that to learn gives the liveliest pleasure, not only to philosophers but to men in general; whose capacity, however, of learning is more limited. Thus the reason why men enjoy seeing a likeness is, that in contemplating it they find themselves learning or inferring, and saying perhaps, "Ah, that is he." For if you happen not to have seen the original, the pleasure will be due not to the imitation as such, but to the execution, the colouring, or some such other cause. 1

Imitation, then, is one instinct of our nature. Next, there is the instinct for "harmony" and rhythm, metres being manifestly sections of rhythm. Persons, therefore, starting with this natural gift developed by degrees their special aptitudes, till their rude improvisations gave birth to Poetry. 2

. . .

It is, moreover, evident from what has been said, that it is not the function of the poet to relate what has happened, but what may happen—what is possible according to the law of probability or necessity. The poet and the historian differ not by writing in verse or in prose. The work of Herodotus might be put into verse, and it would still be a species of history, with metre no less than without it. The true difference is that one relates what has happened, the other what may happen. Poetry, therefore, is a more philosophical and a higher thing than history: for poetry tends to express the universal, history the particular. By the universal I mean how a person of a certain type will on occasion speak or act, according to the law of probability or necessity; and it is this universality at which poetry aims in the names she attaches to the personages. The particular is—for example—what Alcibiades did or suffered. In Comedy this is already apparent: for here the poet first constructs the plot on the lines of probability, and then inserts characteristic names—unlike the lampooners who write about particular individuals. But tragedians still keep to real names, the reason being that what is possible is credible: what has not happened we do not at once feel sure to be possible: but what has happened is manifestly possible: otherwise it would not have happened. Still there are even some tragedies in which there are only one or two well known names, the rest being fictitious. In others, none are well known—as in Agathon's Antheus, where incidents and names alike are 3 fictitious, and yet they give none the less pleasure. We must not, therefore, at all costs keep to the received legends, which are the usual subjects of Tragedy. Indeed, it would be absurd to attempt it; for even subjects that are known are known only to a few, and yet give pleasure to all. It clearly follows that the poet or "maker" should be the maker of plots rather than of verses; since he is a poet because he imitates, and what he imitates are actions. And even if he chances to take an historical subject, he is none the less a poet; for there is no reason why some events that have actually happened should not conform to the law of the probable and possible, and in virtue of that quality in them he is their poet or maker.

Questions for Discussion

1. Compare the high truth value placed on imitations by Aristotle with Socrates' attack on them for being untrue (pp. 276–285). Why do you suppose they hold such different opinions? Whose claims, as presented in our selections, do you find more convincing? Can you support or reject either view by reference to specific stories that you have read or seen dramatized?
2. Do you agree that human beings possess an instinctive pleasure in imitation? Defend or reject this view by reference to your own feelings and experience.
3. Do you agree that we share an instinctive pleasure in harmony? Is Aristotle's assertion supported by the fact that no human culture is devoid of art and music?

Suggested Essay Topics

1. For this assignment you need to choose a very short story to work with—for example, "Araby" by James Joyce or "The Grave" by Katherine Ann Porter. (If you would like more choices, ask your instructor for help.) On a sheet of paper, in a column on the left-hand side, list what you consider the major episodes of the story. For example, (1) "Boys playing outside," (2) "Boys standing in front of Mangan's house," and so on. There's no right or wrong way to do this; simply break down the story's action into manageable units. In a column on the right side, list all the deviations in the story from "real life." For example, if passages of time are skipped over, if conversations are compressed or rendered in unfamiliar language, or if events are summarized instead of being depicted in literal detail, note these departures from a "real-life" sequence. Using your two lists, write an essay to your instructor describing the story's "craftedness"—what Aristotle would call its *harmony*—and attempt to show that that harmony is essential to the story's effect. You can test how important harmony is

by looking at what happens to the story if you try inserting the innumerable real-life details that the story's harmony omits.

2. Most families have a sizable repertory of stories about what happened to family members in the past: what Uncle Harry did the day the barn burned down, how Grandma's veil got torn on her wedding day, and so on. Everyone in every family learns these stories by heart, yet no one ever seems to lose interest in or fondness for them. Write a letter to someone in your own family in which you recall one or two of your family stories and explain why you think everyone continues to like hearing and telling them over and over. (They do not need to be completely retold in your essay.) Is Aristotle right in suggesting that we learn things from stories? If he is, what have you learned from your family stories?

Jacob Bronowski

Jacob Bronowski (1908–1974), a famous mathematician and philosopher and creator of the highly acclaimed television series The Ascent of Man, *argues here that imagination—the ability "to make images and to move them about inside one's head in new arrangements"—is not only a uniquely human power but also the source of progress and invention in all human activities.*

By pointing out that every new line of inquiry or action in human affairs exists first in the mind as a model of something that might-be-but-is-not-yet, Bronowski discovers one important way that the arts and sciences overlap. Scientists and engineers no less than artists and poets rely on imagination as the seedbed of all flowering ideas. In claiming that the arts and the sciences are not enemies but allies, Bronowski attempts to apply a healing salve to one of the most unfortunate, unnecessary, and potentially disastrous wounds in modern culture: the split between the scientists and the humanists.

THE REACH OF IMAGINATION

From *Proceedings of the American Academy of Arts and Letters and the National Institute of Arts and Letters* 17 (1967) and *The American Scholar* 36 (1967).

For three thousand years, poets have been enchanted and moved and perplexed by the power of their own imagination. In a short and summary essay I can hope at most to lift one small corner of that mystery; and yet it is a critical corner. I shall ask, What goes on in the mind when we imagine? You will hear from me that one answer to this question is fairly specific: which 1 is to say, that we can describe the working of the imagination. And when we describe it as I shall do, it becomes plain that imagination is a specifically *human* gift. To imagine is the characteristic act, not of the poet's mind, or the painter's, or the scientist's, but of the mind of man.

My stress here on the word *human* implies that there is a clear difference in this between the actions of men and those of other animals. Let me then start with a classical experiment with animals and children which Walter Hunter thought out in Chicago about 1910. That was the time when scientists were agog with the success of Ivan Pavlov in forming and changing the reflex actions of dogs, which Pavlov had first announced in 1903. Pavlov had been given a Nobel prize the next year, in 1904; although in fairness I should say that the award did not cite his work on the conditioned reflex, but on the digestive glands. 2

Hunter duly trained some dogs and other animals on Pavlov's lines. They were taught that when a light came on over one of three tunnels out of their cage, that tunnel would be open; they could escape down it, and were rewarded with food if they did. But once he had fixed that conditioned reflex, Hunter added to it a deeper idea: he gave the mechanical experiment a new dimension, literally—the dimension of time. Now he no longer let the dog go to the lighted tunnel at once; instead, he put out the light, and then kept the dog waiting a little while before he let him go. In this way Hunter timed how long an animal can remember where he has last seen the signal light to his escape route. 3

The results were and are staggering. A dog or a rat forgets which one of three tunnels has been lit up within a matter of seconds—in Hunter's experiment, ten seconds at most. If you want such an animal to do much better than this, you must make the task much simpler: you must face him with only two tunnels to choose from. Even so, the best that Hunter could do was to have a dog remember for five minutes which one of two tunnels had been lit up. 4

I am not quoting these times as if they were exact and universal: they surely are not. Hunter's experiment, more than fifty years old now, had many faults of detail. For example, there were too few animals, they were oddly picked, and they did not all behave consistently. It may be unfair to test a dog for what he *saw,* when he commonly follows his nose rather than his eyes. It may be unfair to test any animal in the unnatural setting of a laboratory cage. And there are higher animals, such as chimpanzees and other primates, which certainly have longer memories than the animals that Hunter tried. 5

Yet when all these provisos have been made (and met, by more modern experiments) the facts are still startling and characteristic. An animal cannot recall a signal from the past for even a short fraction of the time that a man can—for even a short fraction of the time that a child can. Hunter made comparable tests with six-year-old children, and found, of course, that they were incomparably better than the best of his animals. There is a striking and basic difference between a man's ability to imagine something that he saw or experienced, and an animal's failure. 6

Animals make up for this by other and extraordinary gifts. The salmon 7
and the carrier pigeon can find their way home as we cannot; they have, as it were, a practical memory that man cannot match. But their actions always depend on some form of habit: on instinct or on learning, which reproduce by rote a train of known responses. They do not depend, as human memory does, on calling to mind the recollection of absent things.

Where is it that the animal falls short? We get a clue to the answer, I 8
think, when Hunter tells us how the animals in his experiment tried to fix their recollection. They most often pointed themselves at the light before it went out, as some gun dogs point rigidly at the game they scent—and get the name *pointer* from the posture. The animal makes ready to act by building the signal into its action. There is a primitive imagery in its stance, it seems to me; it is as if the animal were trying to fix the light in its mind by fixing it in its body. And indeed, how else can a dog mark and (as it were) name one of three tunnels, when he has no such words as *left* and *right,* and no such numbers as *one, two, three?* The directed gesture of attention and readiness is perhaps the only symbolic device that the dog commands to hold on to the past, and thereby to guide himself into the future.

I used the verb *to imagine* a moment ago, and now I have some ground 9
for giving it a meaning. *To imagine* means to make images and to move them about inside one's head in new arrangements. When you and I recall the past, we imagine it in this direct and homely sense. The tool that puts the human mind ahead of the animal is imagery. For us, memory does not demand the preoccupation that it demands in animals, and it lasts immensely longer, because we fix it in images or other substitute symbols. With the same symbolic vocabulary we spell out the future—not one but many futures, which we weigh one against another.

I am using the word *image* in a wide meaning, which does not restrict 10
it to the mind's eye as a visual organ. An image in my usage is what Charles Peirce called a *sign,* without regard for its sensory quality. Peirce distinguished between different forms of signs, but there is no reason to make his distinction here, for the imagination works equally with them all, and that is why I call them all images.

Indeed, the most important images for human beings are simply words, 11
which are abstract symbols. Animals do not have words, in our sense: there is no specific center for language in the brain of any animal, as there is in the human brain. In this respect at least we know that the human imagination depends on a configuration in the brain that has only evolved in the last one or two million years. In the same period, evolution has greatly enlarged the front lobes in the human brain, which govern the sense of the past and the future; and it is a fair guess that they are probably the seat of our other images. (Part of the evidence for this guess is that damage to the front lobes in primates reduces them to the state of Hunter's animals.) If the guess turns out to be right, we shall know why man has come to look like a highbrow or an egghead: because otherwise there would not be room in his head for his imagination.

The images play out for us events which are not present to our senses, 12
and thereby guard the past and create the future—a future that does not yet exist, and may never come to exist in that form. By contrast, the lack of symbolic ideas, or their rudimentary poverty, cuts off an animal from the past and the future alike, and imprisons him in the present. Of all the distinctions between man and animal, the characteristic gift which makes us human is the power to work with symbolic images: the gift of imagination.

This is really a remarkable finding. When Philip Sidney in 1580 de- 13
fended poets (and all unconventional thinkers) from the Puritan charge that they were liars, he said that a maker must imagine things that are not. Halfway between Sidney and us, William Blake said, "What is now proved was once only imagin'd." About the same time, in 1796, Samuel Taylor Coleridge for the first time distinguished between the passive fancy and the active imagination, "the living Power and prime Agent of all human Perception." Now we see that they were right, and precisely right: the human gift is the gift of imagination—and that is not just a literary phrase.

Nor is it just a literary gift; it is, I repeat, characteristically human. 14
Almost everything that we do that is worth doing is done in the first place in the mind's eye. The richness of human life is that we have many lives; we live the events that do not happen (and some that cannot) as vividly as those that do; and if thereby we die a thousand deaths, that is the price we pay for living a thousand lives. (A cat, of course, has only nine.) Literature is alive to us because we live its images, but so is any play of the mind—so is chess: the lines of play that we foresee and try in our heads and dismiss are as much a part of the game as the moves that we make. John Keats said that the unheard melodies are sweeter, and all chess players sadly recall that the combinations that they planned and which never came to be played were the best.

I make this point to remind you, insistently, that imagination is the 15
manipulation of images in one's head; and that the rational manipulation belongs to that, as well as the literary and artistic manipulation. When a child begins to play games with things that stand for other things, with chairs or chessmen, he enters the gateway to reason and imagination together. For the human reason discovers new relations between things not by deduction, but by that unpredictable blend of speculation and insight that scientists call induction, which—like other forms of imagination—cannot be formalized. We see it at work when Walter Hunter inquires into a child's memory, as much as when Blake and Coleridge do. Only a restless and original mind would have asked Hunter's questions and could have conceived his experiments, in a science that was dominated by Pavlov's reflex arcs and was heading toward the behaviorism of John Watson.

Let me find a spectacular example for you from history. What is the 16
most famous experiment that you had described to you as a child? I will hazard that it is the experiment that Galileo is said to have made in Sidney's age, in Pisa about 1590, by dropping two unequal balls from the Leaning Tower. There, we say, is a man in the modern mold, a man after our own

hearts: he insisted on questioning the authority of Aristotle and St. Thomas Aquinas, and seeing with his own eyes whether (as they said) the heavy ball would reach the ground before the light one. Seeing is believing.

Yet seeing is also imagining. Galileo did challenge the authority of 17
Aristotle, and he did look hard at his mechanics. But the eye that Galileo used was the mind's eye. He did not drop balls from the Leaning Tower of Pisa—and if he had, he would have got a very doubtful answer. Instead, Galileo made an imaginary experiment in his head, which I will describe as he did years later in the book he wrote after the Holy Office silenced him: the *Discorsi . . . intorno à due nuove scienze,* which was smuggled out to be printed in the Netherlands in 1638.

Suppose, said Galileo, that you drop two unequal balls from the tower 18
at the same time. And suppose that Aristotle is right—suppose that the heavy ball falls faster, so that it steadily gains on the light ball, and hits the ground first. Very well. Now imagine the same experiment done again, with only one difference: this time the two unequal balls are joined by a string between them. The heavy ball will again move ahead, but now the light ball holds it back and acts as a drag or brake. So the light ball will be speeded up and the heavy ball will be slowed down; they must reach the ground together because they are tied together, but they cannot reach the ground as quickly as the heavy ball alone. Yet the string between them has turned the two balls into a single mass which is heavier than either ball—and surely (according to Aristotle) this mass should therefore move faster than either ball? Galileo's imaginary experiment has uncovered a contradiction; he says trenchantly,

> You see how, from your assumption that a heavier body falls more rapidly than a lighter one, I infer that a (still) heavier body falls more slowly.

There is only one way out of the contradiction: the heavy ball and the light ball must fall at the same rate, so that they go on falling at the same rate when they are tied together.

This argument is not conclusive, for nature might be more subtle (when 19
the two balls are joined) than Galileo has allowed. And yet it is something more important: it is suggestive, it is stimulating, it opens a new view—in a word, it is imaginative. It cannot be settled without an actual experiment, because nothing that we imagine can become knowledge until we have translated it into, and backed it by, real experience. The test of imagination is experience. But then, that is as true of literature and the arts as it is of science. In science, the imaginary experiment is tested by confronting it with physical experience; and in literature, the imaginative conception is tested by confronting it with human experience. The superficial speculation in science is dismissed because it is found to falsify nature; and the shallow work of art is discarded because it is found to be untrue to our own nature. So when Ella

Wheeler Wilcox died in 1919,* more people were reading her verses than Shakespeare's; yet in a few years her work was dead. It had been buried by its poverty of emotion and its trivialness of thought; which is to say that it had been proved to be as false to the nature of man as, say, Jean Baptiste Lamarck† and Trofim Lysenko‡ were false to the nature of inheritance. The strength of the imagination, its enriching power and excitement, lies in its interplay with reality—physical and emotional.

20 I doubt if there is much to choose here between science and the arts: the imagination is not much more free, and not much less free, in one than in the other. All great scientists have used their imagination freely, and let it ride them to outrageous conclusions without crying "Halt!" Albert Einstein fiddled with imaginary experiments from boyhood, and was wonderfully ignorant of the facts that they were supposed to bear on. When he wrote the first of his beautiful papers on the random movement of atoms, he did not know that the Brownian motion which it predicted could be seen in any laboratory. He was sixteen when he invented the paradox that he resolved ten years later, in 1905, in the theory of relativity, and it bulked much larger in his mind than the experiment of Albert Michelson and Edward Morley which had upset every other physicist since 1881. All his life Einstein loved to make up teasing puzzles like Galileo's, about falling lifts [elevators] and the detection of gravity; and they carry the nub of the problems of general relativity on which he was working.

21 Indeed, it could not be otherwise. The power that man has over nature and himself, and that a dog lacks, lies in his command of imaginary experience. He alone has the symbols which fix the past and play with the future, possible and impossible. In the Renaissance, the symbolism of memory was thought to be mystical, and devices that were invented as mnemonics (by Giordano Bruno, for example, and by Robert Fludd) were interpreted as magic signs. The symbol is the tool which gives man his power, and it is the same tool whether the symbols are images or words, mathematical signs or mesons. And the symbols have a reach and a roundness that goes beyond their literal and practical meaning. They are the rich concepts under which the mind gathers many particulars into one name, and many instances into one general induction. When a man says *left* and *right,* he is outdistancing the dog not only in looking for a light; he is setting in train all the shifts of meaning, the overtones and the ambiguities, between *gauche* and *adroit* and *dexterous,* between *sinister* and the sense of right. When a man counts *one, two,*

*American journalist and poet (1850–1919) who for many years published a daily poem for a syndicate of newspapers. She published over 20 volumes of verse but is now seldom read.

†French naturalist (1744–1829) who held that environmental adaptations could be genetically transmitted.

‡Soviet biologist (1898–1976) who developed a doctrine of genetics based partly on the ideas of Lamarck, which denied the existence of genes and plant hormones. His doctrine was eventually discredited, but not before greatly harming Soviet genetic research, agruicultural practices, and scientific education.

three, he is not only doing mathematics; he is on the path to the mysticism of numbers in Pythagoras and Vitruvius and Kepler, to the Trinity and the signs of the Zodiac.

I have described imagination as the ability to make images and to move 22
them about inside one's head in new arrangements. This is the faculty that is specifically human, and it is the common root from which science and literature both spring and grow and flourish together. For they do flourish (and languish) together; the great ages of science are the great ages of all the arts, because in them powerful minds have taken fire from one another, breathless and higgledy-piggledy, without asking too nicely whether they ought to tie their imagination to falling balls or a haunted island. Galileo and Shakespeare, who were born in the same year, grew into greatness in the same age; when Galileo was looking through his telescope at the moon, Shakespeare was writing *The Tempest;* and all Europe was in ferment, from Johannes Kepler to Peter Paul Rubens, and from the first table of logarithms by John Napier to the Authorised Version of the Bible.

Let me end with a last and spirited example of the common inspiration 23
of literature and science, because it is as much alive today as it was three hundred years ago. What I have in mind is man's ageless fantasy, to fly to the moon. I do not display this to you as a high scientific enterprise; on the contrary, I think we have more important discoveries to make here on earth than wait for us, beckoning, at the horned surface of the moon. Yet I cannot belittle the fascination which that ice-blue journey has had for the imagination of men, long before it drew us to our television screens to watch the tumbling of astronauts. Plutarch and Lucian, Ariosto and Ben Jonson wrote about it, before the days of Jules Verne and H. G. Wells and science fiction. The seventeenth century was heady with new dreams and fables about voyages to the moon. Kepler wrote one full of deep scientific ideas, which (alas) simply got his mother accused of witchcraft. In England, Francis Godwin wrote a wild and splendid work, *The Man in the Moone,* and the astronomer John Wilkins wrote a wild and learned one, *The Discovery of a New World.* They did not draw a line between science and fancy; for example, they all tried to guess just where in the journey the earth's gravity would stop. Only Kepler understood that gravity has no boundary, and put a law to it—which happened to be the wrong law.

All this was a few years before Isaac Newton was born, and it was all 24
in his head that day in 1666 when he sat in his mother's garden, a young man of twenty-three, and thought about the reach of gravity. This was how he came to conceive his brilliant image, that the moon is like a ball which has been thrown so hard that it falls exactly as fast as the horizon, all the way round the earth. The image will do for any satellite, and Newton modestly calculated how long therefore an astronaut would take to fall round the earth once. He made it ninety minutes, and we have all seen now that he was right; but Newton had no way to check that. Instead he went on to calculate how long in that case the distant moon would take to round the earth, if indeed it behaves like a thrown ball that falls in the earth's gravity, and if gravity

obeyed a law of inverse squares. He found that the answer would be twenty-eight days.

In that telling figure, the imagination that day chimed with nature, and 25
made a harmony. We shall hear an echo of that harmony on the day when we land on the moon, because it will be not a technical but an imaginative triumph, that reaches back to the beginning of modern science and literature both. All great acts of imagination are like this, in the arts and in science, and convince us because they fill out reality with a deeper sense of rightness. We start with the simplest vocabulary of images, with *left* and *right* and *one, two, three,* and before we know how it happened the words and the numbers have conspired to make a match with nature: we catch in them the pattern of mind and matter as one.

Questions for Discussion

1. To test Bronowski's argument, picture yourself unable to forecast any event in your life beyond the completion of this assignment. Does the fact that you have to use your imagination to picture *not* having an imagination show the pervasiveness of imaginative activity?
2. As you look forward to the events of this coming weekend—a date, trip home, movie, or concert—does your foreknowledge exist in your head only as an abstraction, a string of words naming the events? Or does it consist of actual images—pictures—of yourself in the future?
3. Is imagination as Bronowski defines it coexistent with consciousness? As long as you are conscious, does the making of images in your mind ever totally cease? We sometimes talk about our minds being "blank," usually as an exaggerated way of saying we can't remember something, but is your mind ever *really* blank? (See James E. Miller, Jr., "Writing as Self-discovery," pp. 183–189.)
4. If one pole of imagination is the recollection of images from the past (memory), then the other pole is the creation of images about the future (forecasting). While our usual forecasts picture only what will or may happen, pictures of what is unlikely or impossible to happen can also come to mind (for example, imagining ourselves invisible, meeting a griffin at lunch, or going to class at the speed of light). Yet imagining impossible things, which is what fantasy and science fiction writers do all the time, can be made to seem plausible, even gripping. The movie *Frankenstein* was made in the 1930s and has become a classic; the television series *Star Trek* is more than two decades old and still going strong. Does all this suggest the importance of imaginative activity for human beings? Does it suggest a distinction between imaginative and imaginary? Try putting this distinction into your own words.

5. What is the relationship between the quality of our lives and the quality of our imaginings? Does repeated exposure to images of brutality and violence on television actually make it easier to imagine doing brutal and violent acts? If they become easier to imagine, do they become easier to do? Are children more susceptible to the implanting of images than older persons? If so, does this lend weight to Socrates' argument (from *The Republic* (pp. 268–275) that the imaginative fare dished out to children ought to be censored?

Suggested Essay Topics

1. Paragraph 16 begins, "Let me find a spectacular example for you from history." For the next four paragraphs Bronowski not only gives us a spectacular example from history but also gives us a spectacular example of how to use an example. The four paragraphs could almost be lifted out as a miniature essay in themselves.

   Using these paragraphs as a model, develop some idea taken from Bronowski's essay. You might take as your thesis, for example, either of the two sentences at the beginning of paragraph 14: "Almost everything that we do that is worth doing is done in the first place in the mind's eye" or "The richness of human life is that we have many lives; we live the events that do not happen (and some that cannot) as vividly as those that do." Employing either of these sentences as a topic, think back to some experience that you anticipated keenly but that did *not* happen, and turn your account of the discrepancies between what you anticipated and what really happened into an extended example modeled on Bronowski's four paragraphs.
2. Write an account of one of your most vivid imaginative experiences, such as a dream, nightmare, daydream, fantasy, or ambition. After making the account as vivid as possible, describe the importance of this imagined experience to you or the role it plays in your life. Does it serve as motivation? As something you want to work toward? Something you want to avoid? Why do you remember it or keep coming back to it?

Northrop Frye

Northrop Frye (b. 1912), a native of Canada, is one of the most distinguished literary critics of our time. His Anatomy of Criticism *has been immensely influential as an ambitious effort to show the ways in which literature both differs from and relates to the rest of human life.* The

Educated Imagination *was originally delivered as a series of radio talks in Canada.*

Frye's aim is to establish the social and ethical importance of the imagination. To do this he separates imaginative activity and imaginative products from other human responses to the world. After distinguishing two levels of response that human beings share with animals (explained in the excerpt reprinted here), Frye comes to the uniquely human level of imaginative construction.

The imaginative response builds mental pictures, or models, of the world we want *as compared to the world we* have. *Literature grows out of this level of response to the world. Since reading literature amounts to nothing less than taking into one's own mind the visions of the world-as-it-might-be dreamed up in other people's minds, it follows that reading literature is a primary way of educating the imagination. Literature is to the imagination what fertilizer is to plant growth, or what movement is to muscle growth: It is the basic nutrition—or the basic form of exercise—that keeps the imagination healthy, supple, and active.*

Frye concludes his essay by asserting the unexpected: that the world of imaginative construction is more real—has a more lasting identity and enduring shape—than the world of material things and products. Frye's basic view, like Plato's (see "The Allegory of the Cave," pp. 411–417), is that material things are always in change and motion: Organisms conceive, mature, and die; rivers dry up or change course; deserts shrink and expand; some species adapt; others die out. Even more quickly than deserts bloom, human inventions such as social forms change and waver in time. The habits, customs, attitudes, clothing, dwellings, occupations, and aspirations of Americans and Canadians, says Frye, are not at all what they were 150 years ago. In the midst of all this change, what do we hold on to? If all these changes occur even as we hold them in our hands, where is their reality? Frye contends that the only enduring America is the one we construct in our imagination: It is that *vision that not only connects the America of today with the America of 150 years ago but that we refer to as we decide how to change things in the future.*

If Frye is right, the role of imagination in human affairs is clearly different from what most people think. Is his case persuasive?

THE EDUCATED IMAGINATION

From chapter 1, "The Motive for Metaphor," chapter 5, "Verticals of Adam," and chapter 6, "The Vocation of Eloquence," of *The Educated Imagination* (1962).

Suppose you're shipwrecked on an uninhabited island in the South Seas. The 1
first thing you do is to take a long look at the world around you, a world of sky and sea and earth and stars and trees and hills. You see this world as objective, as something set over against you and not yourself or related to you in any way. And you notice two things about this objective world. In the first place, it doesn't have any conversation. It's full of animals and plants and

insects going on with their own business, but there's nothing that responds to you: it has no morals and no intelligence, or at least none that you can grasp. It may have a shape and a meaning, but it doesn't seem to be a human shape or a human meaning. Even if there's enough to eat and no dangerous animals, you feel lonely and frightened and unwanted in such a world.

In the second place, you find that looking at the world, as something 2
set over against you, splits your mind in two. You have an intellect that feels curious about it and wants to study it, and you have feelings or emotions that see it as beautiful or austere or terrible. You know that both these attitudes have some reality, at least for you. If the ship you were wrecked in was a Western ship, you'd probably feel that your intellect tells you more about what's really there in the outer world, and that your emotions tell you more about what's going on inside of you. If your background were Oriental, you'd be more likely to reverse this and say that the beauty or terror was what was really there, and that your instinct to count and classify and measure and pull to pieces was what was inside your mind. But whether your point of view is Western or Eastern, intellect and emotion never get together in your mind as long as you're simply looking at the world. They alternate, and keep you divided between them.

The language you use on this level of the mind [i.e., while "simply 3
looking at the world"] is the language of consciousness or awareness. It's largely a language of nouns and adjectives. You have to have names for things, and you need qualities like "wet" or "green" or "beautiful" to describe how things seem to you. This is the speculative or contemplative position of the mind, the position in which the arts and sciences begin, although they don't stay there very long. The sciences begin by accepting the facts and the evidence about an outside world without trying to alter them. Science proceeds by accurate measurement and description, and follows the demands of the reason rather than the emotions. What it deals with is there, whether we like it or not. The emotions are unreasonable: for them it's what they like and don't like that comes first. We'd be naturally inclined to think that the arts follow the path of emotion, in contrast to the sciences. Up to a point they do, but there's a complicating factor.

That complicating factor is the contrast between "I like this" and "I 4
don't like this." In this Robinson Crusoe life I've assigned you, you may have moods of complete peacefulness and joy, moods when you accept your island and everything around you. You wouldn't have such moods very often, and when you had them, they'd be moods of identification, when you felt that the island was a part of you and you a part of it. That is not the feeling of consciousness or awareness, where you feel split off from everything that's not your perceiving self. Your habitual state of mind is the feeling of separation which goes with being conscious, and the feeling "this is not a part of me" soon becomes "this is not what I want." Notice the word "want": we'll be coming back to it.

So you soon realize that there's a difference between the world you're 5
living in and the world you want to live in. The world you want to live in

is a human world, not an objective one: it's not an environment but a home; it's not the world you see but the world you build out of what you see. You go to work to build a shelter or plant a garden, and as soon as you start to work you've moved into a different level of human life. You're not separating only yourself from nature now, but constructing a human world and separating it from the rest of the world. Your intellect and emotions are now both engaged in the same activity, so there's no longer any real distinction between them. As soon as you plant a garden or a crop, you develop the conception of a "weed," the plant you don't want in there. But you can't say that "weed" is either an intellectual or an emotional conception, because it's both at once. Further, you go to work because you feel you have to, and because you want something at the end of the work. That means that the important categories of your life are no longer the subject and the object, the watcher and the things being watched: the important categories are what you have to do and what you want to do—in other words, necessity and freedom.

One person by himself is not a complete human being, so I'll provide 6
you with another shipwrecked refugee of the opposite sex and an eventual family. Now you're a member of a human society. This human society after a while will transform the island into something with a human shape. What that human shape is, is revealed in the shape of the work you do: the buildings, such as they are, the paths through the woods, the planted crops fenced off against whatever animals want to eat them. These things, these rudiments of city, highway, garden and farm, are the human form of nature, or the form of human nature, whichever you like. This is the area of the applied arts and sciences, and it appears in our society as engineering and agriculture and medicine and architecture. In this area we can never say clearly where the art stops and the science begins, or vice versa.

The language you use on this level [i.e., the level of interaction with and 7
manipulation of the world] is the language of practical sense, a language of verbs or words of action and movement. The practical world, however, is a world where actions speak louder than words. In some ways it's a higher level of existence than the speculative level, because it's doing something about the world instead of just looking at it, but in itself it's a much more primitive level. It's the process of adapting to the environment, or rather of transforming the environment in the interests of one species, that goes on among animals and plants as well as human beings. The animals have a good many of our practical skills: some insects make pretty fair architects, and beavers know quite a lot about engineering. In this island, probably, and certainly if you were alone, you'd have about the ranking of a second-rate animal. What makes our practical life really human is a third level of the mind, a level where consciousness and practical skill come together.

This third level is a vision or model in your mind of what you want to 8
construct. There's that word "want" again. The actions of man are prompted by desire, and some of these desires are needs, like food and warmth and shelter. One of these needs is sexual, the desire to reproduce and bring more human beings into existence. But there's also a desire to bring a social human

form into existence. . . . Many animals and insects have this social form too, but man knows that he has it: he can compare what he does with what he can imagine being done. So we begin to see where the imagination belongs in the scheme of human affairs. It's the power of constructing possible models of human experience. In the world of the imagination, anything goes that's imaginatively possible, but nothing really happens. If it did happen, it would move out of the world of imagination into the world of action.

We have three levels of the mind now, and a language for each of them, which in English-speaking societies means an English for each of them. There's the level of consciousness and awareness, where the most important thing is the difference between me and everything else. The English of this level is the English of ordinary conversation, which is mostly monologue, as you'll soon realize if you do a bit of eavesdropping, or listening to yourself. We can call it the language of self-expression. Then there's the level of social participation, the working or technological language of teachers and preachers and politicians and advertisers and lawyers and journalists and scientists. We've already called this the language of practical sense. Then there's the level of imagination, which produces the literary language of poems and plays and novels. They're not really different languages, of course, but three different reasons for using words. 9

On this basis, perhaps, we can distinguish the arts from the sciences. Science begins with the world we have to live in, accepting its data and trying to explain its laws. From there, it moves toward the imagination: it becomes a mental construct, a model of a possible way of interpreting experience. The further it goes in this direction, the more it tends to speak the language of mathematics, which is really one of the languages of the imagination, along with literature and music. Art, on the other hand, begins with the world we construct, not with the world we see. It starts with the imagination, and then works toward ordinary experience: that is, it tries to make itself as convincing and recognizable as it can. You can see why we tend to think of the sciences as intellectual and the arts as emotional: one starts with the world as it is, the other with the world we want to have. Up to a point it is true that science gives an intellectual view of reality, and that the arts try to make the emotions as precise and disciplined as sciences do the intellect. But of course it's nonsense to think of the scientist as a cold unemotional reasoner and the artist as somebody who's in a perpetual emotional tizzy. You can't distinguish the arts from the sciences by the mental processes the people in them use: they both operate on a mixture of hunch and common sense. A highly developed science and a highly developed art are very close together, psychologically and otherwise. 10

. . .

At the level of ordinary consciousness the individual man is the center of everything, surrounded on all sides by what he isn't. At the level of practical sense, or civilization, there's a human circumference, a little cultivated world with a human shape, fenced off from the jungle and inside the 11 sea and the sky. But in the imagination anything goes that can be imagined, and the limit of the imagination is a totally human world.

. . .

Everything man does that's worth doing is some kind of construction, and the imagination is the constructive power of the mind set free to work on pure construction, construction for its own sake. 12

. . .

The central place of the imagination in social life is something that the advertisers suddenly woke up to a few years ago. Ever since, they've been doing what they call projecting the image, and hiring psychologists to tell them what makes the most direct appeal to the imagination. I spoke in my last talk* of the element of illusion in the imagination, and advertising is one example, though a very obvious one, of the deliberate creation of an illusion in the middle of real life. Our reaction to advertising is really a form of literary criticism. We don't take it literally, and we aren't supposed to: anyone who believed literally what every advertiser said would hardly be capable of managing his own affairs. I recently went past two teen-age girls looking at the display in front of a movie which told them that inside was the thrill of a lifetime, on no account to be missed, and I heard one of them say: "Do you suppose it's any good?" That was the voice of sanity trying to get its bearings in a world of illusion. We may think of it as the voice of reason, but it's really the voice of the imagination doing its proper job. You remember that I spoke of irony [in a section not reprinted here] which means saying one thing and meaning another, as a device which a writer uses to detach our imaginations from a world of absurdity or frustration by letting us see around it. To protect ourselves in a society like ours, we have to look at such advertising as that movie display ironically: it means something to us which is different from what it says. The end of the process is not to reject all advertising, but to develop our own vision of society to the point at which we can choose what we want out of what's offered to us and let the rest go. What we choose is what fits that vision of society. 13

This principle holds not only for advertising but for most aspects of social life. During an election campaign, politicians project various images on us and make speeches which we know to be at best a carefully selected part of the truth. We tend to look down on the person who responds to such appeals emotionally: we feel he's behaving childishly and like an irresponsible citizen if he allows himself to be stampeded. Of course there's often a great sense of release in a purely emotional response. Hitler represented to Germany a tremendous release from its frustrations and grievances by simply acting like a three-year-old child: when he wanted something he went into a tantrum and screamed and chewed the scenery until he got it. But that example shows how dangerous the emotional response is, and how right we are to distrust it. So we say we ought to use our reason instead. But all the 14

* *The Educated Imagination* was originally a series of radio talks.

appeals to us are carefully rationalized, except the obviously crackpot ones, and we still have to make a choice. What the responsible citizen really uses is his imagination, not believing anybody literally, but voting for the man or party that corresponds most closely, or least remotely, to his vision of the society he wants to live in. The fundamental job of the imagination in ordinary life, then, is to produce, out of the society we have to live in, a vision of the society we want to live in.

. . .

My subject is the educated imagination, and education is something 15
that affects the whole person, not bits and pieces of him. It doesn't just train the mind: it's a social and moral development too. But now that we've discovered that the imaginative world and the world around us are different worlds, and that the imaginative world is more important, we have to take one more step. The society around us looks like the real world, but we've just seen that there's a great deal of illusion in it, the kind of illusion that propaganda and slanted news and prejudice and a great deal of advertising appeal to. For one thing, as we've been saying, it changes very rapidly, and people who don't know of any other world can never understand what makes it change. If our society in 1962 is different from what it was in 1942, it can't be real society, but only a temporary appearance of real society. And just as it looks real, so this ideal world that our imaginations develop inside us looks like a dream that came out of nowhere, and has no reality except what we put into it. But it isn't. It's the real world, the real form of human society hidden behind the one we see. It's the world of what humanity has done, and therefore can do, the world revealed to us in the arts and sciences. This is the world that won't go away, the world out of which we built the Canada of 1942, are now building the Canada of 1962, and will be building the quite different Canada of 1982.

A hundred years ago the Victorian poet and critic Matthew Arnold 16
pointed out that we live in two environments, an actual social one and an ideal one, and that the ideal one can only come from something suggested in our education. Arnold called this ideal environment culture, and defined culture as the best that has been thought and said. The word "culture" has different overtones to most of us, but Arnold's conception is a very important one, and I need it at this point. We live, then, in both a social and a cultural environment, and only the cultural environment, the world we study in the arts and sciences, can provide the kind of standards and values we need if we're to do anything better than adjust.

I spoke in my first talk of three levels of the mind, which we have now 17
seen to be also three forms of society and three ways of using words. The first is the level of ordinary experience and of self-expression. On this level we use words to say the right thing at the right time, to keep the social machinery running, faces saved, self-respect preserved, and social situations intact. It's not the noblest thing that words can do, but it's essential, and it creates and diffuses a social mythology, which is a structure of words developed by the imagination. For we find that to use words properly even in this way we have

to use our imaginations, otherwise they become mechanical clichés, and get further and further removed from any kind of reality. There's something in all of us that wants to drift toward a mob, where we can all say the same thing without having to think about it, because everybody is all alike except people that we can hate or persecute. Every time we use words, we're either fighting against this tendency or giving in to it. When we fight against it, we're taking the side of genuine and permanent human civilization.

Questions for Discussion

1. Make a chart of Frye's three levels of response to the world and match each level with its characteristic kind of language. Can you give examples of language in each category?
2. Is it true that human beings want to live in "not an environment but a home" (¶5)? What does Frye mean by this? Does it provide a new or better explanation of various human activities? Cite some activities that make our environment a home, and assess whether he is right in saying that our desire for a home motivates these activities.
3. How could you employ Frye's notion of imagination—the ability to compare what we do with what we can imagine doing (¶8)—to explain progress in such areas as science, technology, and social reform?
4. In paragraph 15 Frye says that educating the imagination is "a social and moral development." State in your own words what Frye seems to mean by this. Then compare Frye's statement with the following statement by the early nineteenth-century poet Shelley: "The great secret of morals is love; a going out of our own nature. . . . A man, to be greatly good, must imagine intensely and comprehensively; he must put himself in the place of another and of many others. . . . The great instrument of moral good is the imagination" (from *A Defence of Poetry,* 1821). Would Frye agree with the statement? Do you?
5. What sort of person does Frye seem to be, to judge from this excerpt alone? Do you get a "reading" of the man as well as of his ideas? Does his tone suggest a distinct personality to you, one you tend to like or trust? Can you point to passages that reveal the person behind the words?

Suggested Essay Topics

1. Re-read paragraph 13 carefully; then choose two or three commercials or advertisements and explain not only how you react to them but also how you think the commercial makers expect you to react. Commercials that employ satire or humor, for example, obviously seek a favorable response for their product, but they do this by eliciting a response that is not limited to giving you data about the product. Explain your reactions to such

advertisements. You might address your essay as a letter to the producers of the commercials, or you might direct it to younger readers (such as a brother or sister in school) as a warning.

2. If literature is the best training for the imagination, and if the imagination is a powerful force in social and moral development, it follows that the study of literature, and presumably the study of the other humanities as well, is a valuable activity. For the past several years, however, high school seniors and college freshmen have been hearing from counselors, parents, and others that they should avoid the humanities in favor of sticking to "practical" courses of study: business, engineering, science, pre-med, pre-law, and so on.

   On the basis of Frye's arguments, and any others that seem appropriate to you, construct a defense for anyone wanting to major in something "impractical" like history, philosophy, or English. Construct your defense not only in terms of personal satisfaction but also in terms of the contributions that people with well-trained imaginations make to society.

IDEAS IN DEBATE

Maxim Gorky
Plato

Maxim Gorky

In the following excerpts, the great Russian author Maxim Gorky (1868–1936) describes his first entry into the world of literature and its beneficent effects on his character. His views create a stark contrast with those of Plato, whose attacks on literature follow Gorky's praise of it. For Plato, literature is suspect because it is composed of fictions, which Plato views simply as untruths, and because it "feeds and waters the passions" instead of strengthens the intellect. But the features of literature condemned by Plato are precisely the features that Gorky praises. Where Plato sees a fundamental ethical unhealthiness in developing deep feelings and attachments to the inferior objects of this inferior material world, including people, Gorky sees an ethical health in the formation of such sympathies. And he is both vivid and passionate in his description of how books helped him to enlarge and humanize his feelings toward his fellow creatures.

The world of peasants and workers in pre-Revolutionary Russia could be grim and even brutish, just as Gorky describes it. In such a world one could conceivably argue—indeed, many have—that the primary needs of the body must be tended first and that the needs of the spirit as addressed by literature, religion, and art must wait until people are decently fed, housed, and clothed. When reading Gorky's account of the effects of learning to read, thus having access to other, larger worlds of feeling and thought, one cannot help feeling that Gorky would reject the view, no matter how well-intended, that the cultivation of bodily needs should always take precedence over the cultivation of spiritual and intellectual needs. It would be a worthwhile exercise as you read to try to provide the rebuttal that you think Gorky, arguing from his own experience, might want to give to such views.

As you go from Gorky to Plato, try to give each writer's views a full and sympathetic hearing, and then decide which view seems to capture more of the truth. Plato is severe and rigorous, yet lifted to greatness by the greatness of his goal: to establish the groundwork for a truly just society. Gorky is affectionate and engaging, yet he too focuses on a great goal: the moral improvement of the individual. As you read, you might ask yourself whether Plato's severity tends to slide toward the coldness of tyranny and whether Gorky's warmth tends to slide toward the gushiness of sentimentality. Regardless of what judgments you finally make about them, they are among the authors who teach readers as much about themselves as about the subject of their reading.

ON BOOKS

From "How I Studied" (1918) and "On Books" (1925); translated by Julius Katzer.

It was at about the age of fourteen that I first learnt to read intelligently. By 1
that time I was attracted not only by the plot in a book—the more or less interesting development of the events depicted; I was beginning to appreciate the beauty of the descriptions, muse upon the characters of the men and women in the story, vaguely surmise as to the author's aims, and sense with alarm the difference between that which was spoken of in books and that which was prompted by life.

I was having a hard time then, for I was working for dyed-in-the-wool 2
philistines, people for whom plenteous food was the acme of enjoyment, and whose only amusement was going to church, whither they would sally forth gaudily bedecked in the fashion of people setting out for the theatre or a promenade. My work was back-breaking, so that my mind was almost benumbed; weekdays and holidays were equally cluttered up with toil that was petty, meaningless and futile.

The house my employers lived in belonged to a road-contractor, a short, 3
stocky man from somewhere along the River Klyazma. With his pointed beard and grey eyes, he was always ill-tempered, rude and cruel in a cold-blooded sort of way. He had about thirty men working for him, all of them peasants from Vladimir Gubernia, who lived in a gloomy cellar with a cement floor and little windows below ground level. Toil-worn and weary, they would emerge from their cellar in the evening, after a supper of evil-smelling cabbage soup with tripe or salt-beef that reeked of saltpetre, and sprawl about in the filthy yard, for the air in their damp cellar was suffocating and poisoned by the fumes from the huge stove there.

The contractor would appear at the window of his room and start 4
yelling at his men. "So you're in the yard again, you bastards! Lying all over the place like swine! I have respectable folk living in my house! Do you think they enjoy seeing the likes of you out there?"

The workers would obediently return to their cellar. They were all 5
woe-begone people, who spoke and laughed but seldom, and hardly ever sang songs; their clothes besmeared with clay and mud, they seemed to me corpses that had been resuscitated against their will so as to suffer torment for another term of life.

The "respectable folk" were army officers, who drank and gambled, 6
beat their servants black and blue, and thrashed their mistresses, loudly dressed, cigarette-smoking women, who were heavy drinkers, too, and would clout the officers' servants mercilessly. The latter also drank inordinately, and would guzzle themselves blind drunk.

On Sundays the contractor would seat himself on the porch steps, a long narrow ledger in one hand and a pencil stub in the other. The navvies would shuffle up to him one by one, as though they were beggars. They spoke in hushed tones, bowing and scratching their heads, while the contractor would yell for the whole world to hear, "Shut up! A ruble will do! Eh, what's that? Do you want a thick ear? You're getting more than you're worth as it is! Get the hell out of here! Get moving!" 7

I knew that among the navvies there were quite a few men hailing from the same village as the contractor, and even several relatives of his, but he treated them all in the same harsh, unfeeling manner. The navvies too were harsh and unfeeling towards one another and particularly towards the officers' servants. Bloody free fights would start in the yard every other Sunday, and the air would be blue with the foul language used. The navvies fought without any malice, as though they were performing some irksome duty; battered and bruised, they would creep out of the fray and in silence examine their scratches and injuries, testing loosened teeth with unclean fingers. A smashed face or a black-and-blue eye never evoked the least compassion, but things were different if a shirt proved in shreds; then the regret was general, and the mauled owner of the shirt would sullenly brood over his loss and sometimes shed tears. 8

Such scenes brought up in me a heavy feeling I cannot describe. I was sorry for these people, but in a way that was cold and aloof. There never arose in me a desire to say a kind word to any of them or help one who had had the worst of it in a fight—at least to bring him some water to wash away the sickeningly thick blood, mixed with mud or dust that oozed out of cuts and injuries. In fact I disliked these people, was somewhat afraid of them, and spoke the word muzhik in much the same way as my employers, or the officers, the regimental priest, the cook who lived next door, or even the officers' servants; all these spoke of the muzhiks with contempt. 9

Feeling sorry for people is a distressing business; one always prefers the joy of loving someone, but there was nobody there I could love. It was with all the more ardency that I got to love books. 10

There was much in my environment that was wicked and savage, and gave birth to a feeling of acute loathing. I shall not dwell on this; you are yourselves aware of the hell of that kind of life, the contumely heaped upon man by man, and that morbid urge to inflict torment which slaves so delight in. It was in such accursed conditions that I first began to read good and serious books by foreign authors. 11

I shall probably prove unable to express with sufficient vividness and convincingness the measure of my amazement when I felt that almost each book seemed to open up before me a window into a new and unfamiliar world, and told me of people, sentiments, thoughts and relationships that I had never before known or seen. It even seemed to me that the life around me, all the harsh, filthy and cruel things that were taking place around me every day—all these were not real or necessary. What was real and necessary was to be found only in books, where everything was more reasonable, 12 beautiful and humane. True, books also spoke of human boorishness, stupidity and suffering; they depicted mean and evil men too, but next to these were others, the like of whom I had never seen or even heard of, men that were clean and truthful, strong in spirit, and ready to sacrifice their very lives for the triumph of the truth or the beauty of an exploit.

Intoxicated by the novelty and the spiritual wealth of the world that 13
books had revealed to me, I at first began to consider books finer, more interesting and akin to me than people were, and was, I think, a little blinded by looking upon the realities of life through the prism of books. However, life, that wisest and severest of teachers, soon cured me of that delightful blindness.

On Sundays, when my employers would go visiting or promenading, I 14
used to climb out through the window of the stifling and greasy-smelling kitchen on to the roof, where I could read undisturbed. Down below I could see sleepy or half-drunk navvies lurching about the yard or hear the housemaids, washerwomen and cooks squeal at the uncouth advances made by the officers' servants. From my eyrie I looked down upon the yards and magnificently despised the vile, drunken and loose life about me.

One of the navvies was their foreman, an elderly little man named 15
Stepan Lyoshin, angular and ill-knit of figure, lean and sinewy, his eyes like those of a hungry tom-cat, and his lanky greying beard growing in funny patches over his brown face, scraggy neck and in his ears. Ragged of dress and dirtier than all the others, he was the most sociable among them. They all stood in awe of him, and even the master lowered his strident and angry voice when addressing him. I often heard the men curse Lyoshin behind his back as "that stingy bastard, that Judas of a lickspittle."

Old Lyoshin was a brisk man, but not fussy; he had a way of sliding 16
imperceptibly into some corner of the yard wherever two or three of the men would get together; he would come up to them, with a leer on his face, sniff through his broad nose, and ask:

"So what, eh?" 17

It seemed to me that he was always on the look-out for something, 18
waiting for some word to be said.

Once, when I was sitting on the roof of the shed, he climbed wheezing 19
up the ladder to where I was, sat down next to me, and, after sniffing the air, said:

"It smells of hay. . . . This is a fine place you've found, clean and away 20
from people. . . . What's that you are reading?"

He looked at me in a friendly way and I willingly told him what I was 21
reading about.

"Yes," he said, wagging his head. "That's how it is." 22

He fell silent for a while, picking with a grimy finger at a broken toe-nail 23
on his left foot, and suddenly began to talk in a low, sing-song tone, as though telling a story, squinting at me the while.

"There was a learned gentleman in Vladimir, Sabaneyev by name, a 24
grand gentleman, and he had a son—I think he was called Petrusha or some-

thing like that. I can't quite call his name to mind. Anyway, this Petrusha was
reading books all the time and tried to get others interested, but in the end
he was copped."

"What for?" I asked. 25

"Oh, for all that sort of thing! Don't you go in for reading, but if you 26
do, keep mum about it!"

He sniggered, winked to me, and went on: 27

"I can see what kind of fellow you are—kind of serious and you keep 28
out of mischief. Well, there's no harm in that. . . ."

He sat with me for a short while and then went down into the yard. 29
From that time on I noticed that Lyoshin kept an eye on me. He was always
coming up to me with the same question, "So what, eh?"

Once I told him a story that had gripped my imagination, something 30
about the victory of good over evil. He heard me out very attentively, nodded
his head, and said, "Such things do happen."

"Do they happen?" I asked in joy. 31

"Of course they may. All kinds of things happen," the old man asserted. 32
"Here's what I'll tell you. . . ." and he told me a story, quite a good one, about
flesh-and-blood people, not people out of books, and in conclusion said
impressively:

"You see, you can't understand these things in full, but you've got to 33
understand the chief thing, to wit that there are no end of little things, and
the people have got all tangled up in such trifles. They don't know what path
they should follow, so they don't know the way to God. People are hemmed
in by trifles, if you understand what I mean."

These words seemed to arouse something vivifying in my heart and I 34
seemed to have suddenly emerged into the light. Indeed, the life around me
was full of trifles, with its scuffles, its wickedness, petty thievery and foul
language, which, I suppose, is so lavish because a man lacks pure and sweet
words.

The old man was five times as old as I was and knew a lot, so that if 35
he said that good things really happen in life I had every reason to believe
him. I was eager to believe him, for books had already taught me to believe
in man. I felt that, after all, books did depict actual life, that they were, so
to say, copied from reality, and that therefore there must exist good men,
quite unlike that brute of a contractor, or my employers, or the drunken
officers, or, for that matter, everybody else I knew.

This discovery was of great joy to me, and I began to take a happier view 36
of life and be more friendly and considerate to people; when I read something
that was good or elevated the spirit I tried to tell the navvies and the officers'
servants all about it. They were not very good listeners, and, I think, did not
believe me very much; Stepan Lyoshin, however, kept on saying, "Such
things do happen. All kinds of things happen, my lad."

This brief and wise statement was of a surprisingly intense significance 37
to me. The oftener I heard it, the more it aroused in me a sense of courage
and pertinacity, an acute desire to achieve my ends. If indeed "all kinds of

things happen," then what I wanted could also come about. I have noticed that it is just when life has given me its hardest knocks, on the bad days, which have been only too numerous in my life, that a sense of courage and pertinacity has always surged up in me and I have been overcome by a youthful and Herculean urge to cleanse the Augean stables of life. This has remained with me to this day when I am fifty; it will remain with me till my dying day. I owe this quality in me to books, which are the gospel of the human spirit and reflect the anguish and the torment of man's growing soul; to science, which is the poetry of the mind, and to art, which is the poetry of the heart.

Books continued to open new vistas before me, two illustrated maga- 38
zines, the *Vsemirnaya Illustratsiya (World Illustrated)* and the *Zhivopisnoye Obozrenie (Pictorial Review),* being of particular value to me. Their depictions of cities, people and events abroad, expanded more and more the world before me, and I felt it growing, huge, enthralling and full of great works.

The temples and palaces, so unlike our churches and houses, the differ- 39
ently clad people, the land that men had adorned in so different a manner, the wondrous machines and the marvellous things they produced—all these evoked in me an unaccountable feeling of exhilaration and a desire to make and build something too.

Everything was different and unfamiliar, but I sensed vaguely that 40
behind it all stood one and the same force—man's creativity, and my feeling of consideration and respect for people mounted.

I was spellbound when I saw in a magazine a portrait of Faraday, the 41
famous scientist, read an article about him, much of which I could not understand, and learnt from it that Faraday had been a simple workman. This fact seemed fairy-like to me, and became imbedded in my mind.

"How can that be?" I asked myself incredulously. "It means that one of 42
these navvies may also become a scientist. Perhaps I, too, may become one."

That was something I could not believe, and I began to make inquiries 43
whether there had been other famous men who had first been working men. I discovered none in the magazines, but a Gymnasium* pupil I knew told me that very many well-known people had first been workers, and named some of them, including Stephenson, but I did not believe him.

The more I read, the closer books bound me to the world and the more 44
vivid and significant life became for me. I saw that there were people whose life was worse and harder than mine. Though I derived some comfort from this, I did not grow reconciled to the outrageous facts of the life about me. I saw too that there were such who were able to live a life of interest and happiness in a way none about me knew how to. From the pages of almost every book sounded a subdued but insistent message that perturbed me, called me into the unknown, and plucked at my heart. All men were suffering in one way or another; all were dissatisfied with life and sought something that was better, and this made them closer and more understandable to me.

*High school.

Books enshrouded the whole world in a mournful aspiration towards better things, and each one of them seemed a soul tacked down to paper by characters and words which came to life the moment my eyes and my mind came into contact with them.

I often wept as I read—so moving were the stories about people, so dear 45
and close did they become to me. Lad as I was, pestered with senseless toil and berated with senseless vituperation, I promised myself in the most solemn of terms that I would help people and render them honest service when I grew up.

Like some wondrous birds out of fairy tales, books sang their songs to 46
me and spoke to me as though communing with one languishing in prison; they sang of the variety and richness of life, of man's audacity in his strivings towards goodness and beauty. The more I read, the more a wholesome and kindly spirit filled my heart, and I grew calmer, my self-confidence developed, my work improved, and I paid ever less heed to the innumerable spurns life was dealing me.

Each book was a rung in my ascent from the brutish to the human, 47
towards an understanding of a better life and a thirst after that life. Replete with all I had read, feeling for all the world like some vessel brimming over with exhilarating drink, I would go to the officers' servants and the navvies and tell them my stories, enacting the scenes in them.

This amused my listeners. 48

"A regular rogue!" they would exclaim. "A real comedian! You should 49
join a travelling show or play at a fair!"

Of course, that was not what I had expected but I was pleased neverthe- 50
less.

However, I was sometimes able, not very frequently of course, to make 51
the Vladimir muzhiks listen to me with bated breath and on more than one occasion aroused some of them to delight and even to tears; such things convinced me all the more that there was a living and stimulating force in books.

One of the men, Vasily Rybakov by name, a morose and silent young 52
fellow of great physical strength, whose favourite prank it was to jostle others and send them flying, once led me aside to a place behind the stable, and said to me:

"Listen here, Alexei, learn me to read books and I'll pay you fifty 53
kopeks, and if you don't I'll bash your head in for you. I swear it!" and he crossed himself sweepingly.

I stood in fear of his gloomy horse-play and began instructing him, my 54
heart in my mouth, but things went well from the very start. Rybakov proved diligent at the unfamiliar work and very quick of understanding. Once, five weeks or so later, on his way back from work, he beckoned to me mysteriously, pulled a crumpled scrap of paper out of his pocket and started muttering in his agitation:

"See here. I tore this off a fence. What's written here, eh? Wait a 55
jiffy—'House for sale'—is that right? 'For sale,' eh?"

"That's what it says." 56

Rybakov's eyes rolled frighteningly, and his forehead became covered 57
with sweat. After a silence he grabbed me by the shoulder, shook me a little and said in a low tone:

"You see it was like this. When I looked at that there fence something 58
started whispering in me like—'House for sale'. . . . Lordie, lordie. . . . Just like a whisper in me, 'swelp me! Listen, d'you think I've really gone and learnt to read?"

"You try and read some more." 59

He bent low over the scrap of paper and began in a whisper, "Two—is 60
that right?—storey . . . brick . . ."

A broad smile spread all over his ugly face. He reared his head, swore 61
an oath and with a laugh started to fold up the paper.

"I'll keep this to remember the day, this being the first like. . . . O Lord 62
. . . don't you see? Just like a whisper. Queer things do happen, my lad! Well, well!"

I burst out laughing at his crude joy, his childlike perplexity at the 63
mystery revealed to him, the magic of little black characters being able to unfold before him another's thoughts, ideas, and very soul.

I could say quite a lot regarding the way book-reading—that familiar, 64
everyday but yet mysterious process of man's fusion with the great minds of all ages and peoples—at times suddenly reveals to man the meaning of life and his place in it; I know a multitude of such marvellous instances imbued with an almost magic beauty.

There is one such instance I would like to mention, which refers to a 65
time when I was living in Arzamas under police surveillance. My next-door neighbour, the chief of the local agricultural board,* who had developed such an intense dislike of my person that he even instructed his housemaid to avoid talking to my cook in the evening after working hours, had a policeman stationed right under my windows. Whenever the latter thought it fit, he would peer into my rooms with naïve incivility. This had the effect of intimidating the townspeople, and for quite a long time none of them ventured to call on me.

One day—it was a church holiday—a one-eyed man came to see me. 66
He had a bundle under one arm and said he had a pair of boots to sell. I told him I did not need any boots, at which the man, after looking suspiciously into the next room, addressed me in an undertone.

"The boots are only an excuse for coming to see you. What I really want 67
is to ask you whether you could let me have a good book to read."

The expression of his solitary eye was so sincere and intelligent that it 68
allayed suspicion, and his reply to my question as to what kind of book he wanted clinched the matter for me. Looking around as he spoke, he said in a deliberate if timid tone:

*In Russian, *Zemsky nachalnik*—prior to the Revolution, head of an authority with court and administrative powers over the local peasantry. [Translator's note]

"I'd like something about the laws of life, Mr. Writer, that's to say, 69
about the laws of the world. I can't make them out, I mean the way one should live and that kind of thing. There's a professor of mathematics from Kazan, who lives close by and he teaches me some mathematics. You see, he does that because I do his shoe repairs and take care of his garden—I'm a gardener too. Well, mathematics don't help me with the questions that interest me, and he is a man of few words. . . ."

I gave him a poorish book by Dreyfus entitled *World and Social Evolution,* 70
the only book on the subject that I could lay my hands on at the moment.

"Thank you kindly," said the one-eyed man, carefully concealing the 71
book in his boot top. "May I come to you for a talk when I have read the book? . . . Only I'll come on the pretext of pruning the raspberry bushes in your garden, because, you see, the police are keeping an eye on you, and in general, it's awkward for me. . . ."

When he came again five days later, in a white apron, equipped with 72
bass and a pair of shears, I was much surprised by his jaunty air. There was a merry gleam in his eye and his voice rang loud and strong. The first thing he did was to bring an open palm emphatically down on the book I had given him, and state hurriedly:

"May I draw the conclusion from this here book that there is no God?" 73

I am no believer in hasty "conclusions," so I began to question him in 74
a cautious sort of way as to what had led him to just that "conclusion."

"For me that is the chief thing!" he said fervently but quietly. "I argue 75
in the way many like me do: if the Almighty does really exist and everything depends on His will, then I must live in humble submission to His commandments. I've read a lot of divine literature—the Bible and a host of theological works, but what I want to know is whether I'm responsible for myself and my life, or not? Scripture says no, you must live according to God's will, for science will get you nowhere. That means that astronomy is all sham and invention; so's mathematics and everything else. Of course, you don't stand for blind obedience yourself, do you?"

"No, I don't," I said. 76

"Then why should I agree to it? You have been sent out here to be under 77
observation by the police because you're a dissenter. That means that you've risen up against the Gospel, because, as I see it, all dissent must be directed against Holy Scripture. All the laws of submission come from the Scriptures, while the laws of freedom all come from science, that's to say, from the mind of man. Let's argue farther: if God exists, I have no say in the matter, but if there's no God then I'm personally responsible for everything—for myself and for all other folks. I want to be responsible, after the example set by the holy fathers of the Church, but only in a different way—not through submission to the evil of life but by resistance to it!"

His palm again came down on the book, and he went on with a convic- 78
tion that sounded inflexible.

"All submission is evil because it goes to strengthen evil. You must 79
forgive me, but this is a book I believe in. To me it's like a path through a

thick forest. I've made up my mind for myself—I am personally responsible
for everything!"

Our friendly talk continued late into the night, and I saw that a medio- 80
cre little book had tipped the balance: it had turned his rebellious searchings
into a fervent conviction, into joyous worship of the beauty and might of
World Reason.

This fine, intelligent man did, in fact, wage a struggle against the evil 81
of life, and perished courageously in 1907.

Just as they had done to the morose Rybakov, books whispered in my 82
ear of the existence of another life, one that was more worthy of man than
that which I was living; just as they had done to the one-eyed shoemaker,
they showed me my place in life. By inspiring the mind and the heart, books
helped me to extricate myself from the foul morass that would have engulfed
me in its stupidity and boorishness. By expanding the limits of my world,
books told me of the majesty and beauty of man's strivings towards a better
life, of how much he had achieved in the world and what fearful sufferings
this had cost him.

In my soul there mounted a regard for man, for any man, whatever he 83
might be; there burgeoned in me respect for his labour and love of his restless
spirit. Life was becoming easier and more joyous, replete with a new and
profound meaning.

Just as with the one-eyed shoemaker, books bred in me a sense of 84
personal responsibility for all the evil in life and evoked in me a reverence
for the human mind's creativity.

It is with profound belief in the truth of my conviction that I say to all: 85
Love books; they will make your life easier, render you friendly service in
finding your way through the motley and tumultuous confusion of ideas,
emotions and happenings, teach you to respect yourselves and others, and fill
the mind and the heart with love for the world and man.

Even if hostile to your beliefs, any book that has been written in 86
honesty, out of love of people, out of good will, is admirable.

Any kind of knowledge is useful, as is knowledge of the mind's fallacies 87
and of mistaken emotions.

Love books, which are a source of knowledge; only knowledge is salu- 88
tary, and knowledge alone can make you spiritually strong, honest and intelligent people, capable of cherishing a sincere love of man, respect for his
labour and a warm admiration for the splendid fruits of his ceaseless and high
endeavour.

Everything man has done, every single thing that exists, contains some 89
particle of man's soul. This pure and noble soul is contained in science and
in art in greater degree than in anything else, and speaks with the greatest
eloquence and clarity through the medium and agency of books.

. . .

It is to books that I owe everything that is good in me. Even in my youth 90
I realized that art is more generous than people are. I am a book-lover; each
one of them seems a miracle to me, and the author a magician. I am unable

to speak of books otherwise than with the deepest emotion and a joyous enthusiasm. That may seem ridiculous but it is the truth. It will probably be said that this is the enthusiasm of a barbarian; let people say what they will—I am beyond cure.

When I hold a new book in my hand, something made at a printing- 91
house by a type-setter, a hero in his way, with the aid of a machine invented by another hero, I get a feeling that something living, wonderful and able to speak to me has entered my life—a new testament, written by man about himself, about a being more complex than anything else in the world, the most mysterious and the most worthy of love, a being whose labour and imagination have created everything in the world that is instinct with grandeur and beauty.

Books guide me through life, which I know fairly well, but they always 92
have a way of telling me something new which I did not previously know or notice in man. In a whole book you may find nothing but a single telling sentence, but it is that very sentence that draws you closer to man and reveals a new smile or a new grimace.

The majesty of the stellar world, the harmonious mechanism of the 93
Universe, and all that astronomy and cosmology speak of with such eloquence do not move me or evoke enthusiasm in me. My impression is that the Universe is not at all as amazing as the astronomers would have us think and that in the birth and death of worlds there is immeasurably more meaningless chaos than divine harmony.

Somewhere in the infinity of the Milky Way a sun has become extinct 94
and the planets about it are plunged into eternal night; that, however, is something that will not move me at all, but the death of Camille Flammarion, a man with a superb imagination, gave me deep sorrow.

Everything that we find fair and beautiful has been devised or narrated 95
by man. It is to be regretted that he has often had to create suffering too, and heighten it, as has been done by Dostoyevsky, Baudelaire and the like. Even in this I see a desire to embellish and alleviate that which is drab and hateful in life.

There is no beauty in the Nature that surrounds us and is so hostile to 96
us; beauty is something that man himself creates out of the depth of his soul. Thus, the Finn transfigures his bogs, forests and rusty-coloured granite, with its scanty and dwarfish vegetation, into scenes of beauty, and the Arab convinces himself that the desert is fair. Beauty is born of man's striving to contemplate it. I take delight not in chaotic and serrated mountain masses, but in the splendour man has endowed them with. I stand in admiration at the ease and magnanimity with which man is transforming Nature, a magnanimity which is all the more astonishing for the Earth's being, if one gives the matter closer thought, a far from cosy place to live in. Think of earthquakes, hurricanes, snowstorms, floods, extremes of heat and cold, noxious insects and microbes and a thousand and one other things that would make our life quite intolerable were man less of a hero than he is.

Our existence has always and everywhere been tragic, but man has 97 converted these numberless tragedies into works of art. I know of nothing more astonishing or more wonderful than this transformation. That is why in a little volume of Pushkin's poems or in a novel by Flaubert I find more wisdom and living beauty than in the cold twinkling of the stars, the mechanical rhythm of the oceans, the rustling of forests, or the silence of the wilderness.

The silence of the wilderness? It has been forcefully conveyed by the 98
Russian composer Borodin in one of his works. The *aurora borealis?* I give preference to Whistler's pictures. It was a profound truth that John Ruskin pronounced when he said that English sunsets had become more beautiful after Turner's pictures.

I would love our sky far more if the stars were larger, brighter and closer 99
to us. They have, indeed, become more beautiful since astronomers have been telling us more about them.

The world I live in is a world of little Hamlets and Othellos, a world 100
of Romeos and Goriots, Karamazovs and Mr. Dombey, of David Copperfield, Madame Bovary, Manon Lescaut, Anna Karenina, a world of little Don Quixotes and Don Juans.

Out of such insignificant creatures, out of the like of us, poets have 101
created majestic images and made them undying.

We live in a world in which it is impossible to understand man unless 102
we read books written about him by men of science and men of letters. Flaubert's *Un coeur simple* is precious to me as a gospel; Knut Hamsun's *Landstrykere (Growth of the Soil)* amazes me in the same way as the *Odyssey* does. I am sure that my grandchildren will read Romain Rolland's *Jean Christophe* and revere the author's greatness of heart and mind, his unquenchable love of mankind.

I am well aware that this kind of love is thought out of fashion today, 103
but what of it? It lives on without waning, and we go on living its joys and sorrows.

I even think that this love is growing ever stronger and more conscious. 104
Whilst this tends to lend a certain restraint and pragmatism to its manifestations, it in no wise diminishes the irrationality of this sentiment in our time, when the struggle for life has become so bitter.

I have no desire to know anything but man, to approach whom books 105
are friendly and generous guides; there is in me an ever deeper respect for the unassuming heroes who have created everything that is beautiful and grand in the world.

Questions for Discussion

1. Gorky's assertion that his first serious reading produced the feeling "that almost each book seemed to open up before me a window into a new and

unfamiliar world" (¶12) sounds remarkably similar to the narrator in Richard Wright's story "The Library Card." Both young men fasten passionately on books as a mode of vicarious experience quite different from the dreary, oppressive world of their everyday lives, and both feel that their emotional and spiritual capacities are enlarged by reading. If these views ring true to you, what arguments can you infer from them to answer people who say that required literature courses in college are a waste of time?

2. Aristotle (pp. 235–238) says that literature is a form of learning and that human beings' instinctive love of learning is one of the causes of our powerful attachment to literature (which Aristotle calls "poetry"). But Plato says that we can't learn the highest truth from literature because it is composed of made-up stories—fictions (or, as he would have it, lies). Which of these two views coincides more closely with Gorky's, and which paragraphs can you point to as evidence for your answer?
3. In paragraph 46 Gorky says, "The more I read, the more a wholesome and kindly spirit filled my heart, and I grew calmer, my self-confidence developed, my work improved, and I paid ever less heed to the innumerable spurns life was dealing me." Later on he says, "Love books; they will . . . teach you to respect yourselves and others, and fill the mind and the heart with love for the world and man" (¶85). These passages describe a highly interesting consequence of reading, but Gorky provides no account of the *mechanism* of it. That is, he doesn't say *how* literature achieves such large and beneficial effects. In discussion with your classmates, can you fill in this part of Gorky's position? Assume for the sake of the argument that he is right, that literature can actually achieve such happy results, and attempt to construct an explanation—it may be purely hypothetical or based on personal experience—of the process, or practice, or whatever it is that might be the *cause* of such effects.
4. Now turn to the other side and assume that Gorky is wrong, that literature cannot in itself produce such deep improvement in the character of a reader, and look for arguments and examples that refute his position.
5. Having now argued both sides of the position, get behind the one that seems to you more true, and attempt to discuss additional arguments and better examples to support it.
6. In paragraph 102 Gorky asserts that "it is impossible to understand man unless we read books written about him by men of science and men of letters." Do you believe this is true? Can you imagine for a moment what would happen to your understanding of other human beings if everything you had ever read about them in works of literature and science were suddenly erased from your memory? Could you have gained all that knowledge of others by firsthand, personal observation? If not, does this provide you with more grounds for arguing that college students ought to read as much literature as possible?

Suggested Essay Topics

1. Write a letter to the author of your favorite novel or poem, explaining to the writer the work's effects, if any, on your beliefs, views, and character. One way to test for such effects is to ask yourself how your views and beliefs might be different if you had never read that particular work. There are many accounts of people whose lives have been dramatically changed by their reading of a single book that gave them a whole new way of understanding themselves or the world around them. The effects you are invited to describe here may not be that dramatic, but most of us have been strongly influenced by at least a few books or poems at some point in our lives. Your letter will give you an opportunity to think about this influence in some detail and to explain to the author how that influence has operated in your life.
2. After you have read the following Plato selections, use Plato as one of your sources in constructing an argument that refutes Gorky's optimistic opinion that books will "fill the mind and the heart with love for the world and man" (¶85). You may concede to Gorky that this effect may occur if the *right* books are read, but this concession will not prevent you from arguing that quite contrary effects may result if readers read the *wrong* books. Choose some book that in your opinion would have a pernicious influence on the character of a reader who succumbed to it—a book, say, that invites the reader to find a real thrill in violence against other people, invites the reader to take a dismissive view of women or minorities, or invites a view of sex as manipulative, self-serving, masochistic, or sadistic. Argue in specific terms, referring to passages and events in the book, showing how the story invites these effects and why they would be ethically bad for any of us to experience.

Plato

In The Republic, *Plato (c. 427–347 B.C.) constructs a series of long conversations between Socrates and some of his fellow citizens. The time is about 450 B.C.; the place is Athens, center of Greek culture; and the topic they are discussing is "justice" and how they would go about constructing the best sort of society to achieve it. They are discussing, in other words, what an ideal society would look like—how it would educate its citizens to live just and beautiful lives, keep itself solvent, protect itself, administer its laws, and worship its gods. They try to consider everything, in short, that the creators of a state would have to make decisions about if they were to build it from the ground up.*

The state they talk about is "ideal" not in the sense that it is sheer fantasy or so outlandish that it bears no resemblance to the society everyone already knows.

Instead, their state is ideal in the sense that its creators are imagining themselves free to make it without having to solve all the practical problems that would hit them if they were to cast off their old state and start over. They do not have to deal, for example, with people's resistance to change, people's fears of the unknown, or the disruptions that would occur if established ways of doing things were suddenly abandoned.

One of the most important questions they discuss is how they should educate the state's rulers—"guardians"—in their youth. In addressing this problem Socrates pictures a committee of older guardians, all philosophers—that is, lovers of truth, not professionals—setting out a curriculum for the younger guardians who will actually conduct the day-to-day business of the state when they grow up. Socrates bases his educational ideas on the assumption that the kind of training a society gives its youth determines the kind of adults that society gets. This was not a novel idea even then, but few thinkers have pursued its implications as thoroughly and vigorously as Socrates.

It seems obvious to him that if education feeds both the mind and the character of a society's youth, then only first-rate fare should be proffered to them. In trying to decide what is first-rate, Socrates picks a quarrel with literature. Stories, he claims, feed youth with lies that teach them to disrespect the gods and imitate the immoral behavior of heroes in myths, legends, and poems. He recommends protecting youth from corrupt literature by state censorship. Judges are to decide on the acceptability of stories and poems before they are given to children to read.

Our selection opens where Socrates is just beginning to bare the heart of his argument.

CENSORSHIP

Our title for this portion of *The Republic,* book 2.

Then he who is to be a really good and noble guardian of the State will require to unite in himself philosophy and spirit and swiftness and strength? 1

Undoubtedly.

Then we have found the desired natures; and now that we have found them, how are they to be reared and educated? Is not this an inquiry which may be expected to throw light on the greater inquiry which is our final end—How do justice and injustice grow up in States? For we do not want either to omit what is to the point or to draw out the argument to an inconvenient length.

Adeimantus thought that the inquiry would be of great service to us. 2

Then, I said, my dear friend, the task must not be given up, even if somewhat long.

Certainly not.

Come then, and let us pass a leisure hour in story-telling, and our story shall be the education of our heroes.

By all means.

And what shall be their education? It would be hard, I think, to find a better than the traditional system, which has two divisions, gymnastic for the body, and music for the soul.

True.

Presumably we shall begin education with music, before gymnastic can 3
begin.

By all means.

And when you speak of music, do you include literature or not?

I do.

And literature may be either true or false?

Yes.

Both have a part to play in education, but we must begin with the false?

I do not understand your meaning, he said.

You know, I said, that we begin by telling children stories which, though not wholly destitute of truth, are in the main fictitious; and these stories are told them when they are not of an age for gymnastics.

Very true.

That was my meaning when I said that we must teach music before gymnastics.

Quite right, he said.

You know also that the beginning is the most important part of any 4
work, especially in the case of a young and tender thing; for that is the time at which the character is being formed and the desired impression is more readily taken.

Quite true.

And shall we just carelessly allow children to hear any casual tales which may be devised by casual persons, and to receive into their minds ideas for the most part the very opposite of those which we shall wish them to have when they are grown up?

We cannot.

Then the first thing will be to establish a censorship of the writers of 5
fiction, and let the censors receive any tale of fiction which is good, and reject the bad; and we will persuade mothers and nurses to tell their children the authorized ones only. Let them fashion the mind with such tales, even more fondly than they mould the body with their hands; but most of those which are now in use must be discarded.

Of what tales are you speaking? he said.

You may find a model of the lesser in the greater, I said; for they must both be of the same type, and the same spirit ought to be found in both of them.

Very likely, he replied; but I do not as yet know what you would term 6
the greater.

Those, I said, which are narrated by Homer and Hesiod, and the rest of the poets, who have ever been the great story-tellers of mankind.

But which stories do you mean, he said; and what fault do you find with them?

A fault which is fundamental and most serious, I said; the fault of saying what is false, and doing so for no good purpose.

But when is this fault committed?

Whenever an erroneous representation is made of the nature of gods and heroes,—as when a painter paints a picture not having the shadow of a likeness to his subject.

Yes, he said, that sort of thing is certainly very blameable; but what are the stories which you mean?

First of all, I said, there was that greatest of all falsehoods on great sub- 7
jects, which the misguided poet told about Uranus,—I mean what Hesiod says that Uranus did, and how Cronus retaliated on him.* The doings of Cronus, and the sufferings which in turn his son inflicted upon him, even if they were true, ought certainly not to be lightly told to young and thoughtless persons; if possible, they had better be buried in silence. But if there is an absolute necessity for their mention, a chosen few might hear them in a mystery, and they should sacrifice not a common pig, but some huge and unprocurable victim, so that the number of the hearers may be very few indeed.

Why, yes, said he, those stories are extremely objectionable.

Yes, Adeimantus, they are stories not to be repeated in our State; the young man should not be told that in committing the worst of crimes he is far from doing anything outrageous; and that even if he chastises in savage fashion his father when he does wrong, he will only be following the example of the first and greatest among the gods.

I entirely agree with you, he said; in my opinion those stories are quite unfit to be repeated.

Neither, if we mean our future guardians to regard the habit of lightly 8
quarrelling among themselves as of all things the basest, should any word be said to them of the wars in heaven, and of the plots and fightings of the gods against one another, for they are not true. No, we shall never mention the battles of the giants, or let them be embroidered on garments; and we shall be silent about the innumerable other quarrels of gods and heroes with their friends and relatives. If we intend to persuade them that quarrelling is unholy, and that never up to this time has there been any hatred between citizens, then the stories which old men and old women tell them as children should be in this strain; and when they grow up, the poets also should be obliged to compose for them in a similar spirit. But the narrative of Hephaestus binding Hera his mother, or how on another occasion his father sent him flying for taking her part when she was being beaten, and all the battles of the gods in Homer—these tales must not be admitted into our State, whether they are supposed to have an allegorical meaning or not. For a young person cannot judge what is allegorical and what is literal; anything that he receives into his mind at that age is likely to become indelible and unalterable; and

*Uranus, the first lord of the universe, is depicted as having thrown his children into Tartarus, a dark pit under the earth. He was eventually attacked and defeated by Cronus, his youngest but strongest son, who drove Uranus away with a sickle made by Uranus's wife, Gaea. Cronus was in turn eventually dethroned by his son, Zeus.

therefore it is most important that the tales which the young first hear should be models of virtuous thoughts.

There you are right, he replied; but if anyone asks where are such 9
models to be found and of what tales are you speaking—how shall we answer him?

I said to him, You and I, Adeimantus, at this moment are not poets, but founders of a State: now the founders of a State ought to know the general forms in which poets should cast their tales, and the limits which must be observed by them, but to make the tales is not their business.

Very true, he said; but what are these forms of theology which you 10
mean?

Something of this kind, I replied:—God* is always to be represented as he truly is, whatever be the sort of poetry, epic, lyric or tragic, in which the representation is given.

Right.

And is he not truly good? And must he not be represented as such?

Certainly.

And no good thing is hurtful?

No, indeed.

And that which is not hurtful hurts not?

Certainly not.

And that which hurts not does no evil?

No.

And can that which does no evil be a cause of evil?

Impossible.

And the good is advantageous?

Yes.

And therefore the cause of well-being?

Yes.

It follows therefore that the good is not the cause of all things, but of those which are as they should be; and it is not to be blamed for evil.

Assuredly.

Then God, if he be good, is not the author of all things, as the many 11
assert, but he is the cause of a few things only, and not of most things that occur to men. For few are the goods of human life, and many are the evils, and the good is to be attributed to God alone; of the evils the causes are to be sought elsewhere, and not in him.

That appears to me to be most true, he said.

Then we must not listen to Homer or to any other poet who is guilty of the folly of saying that

> Two casks lie at the threshold of Zeus, full of lots, one of good, the other of evil lots;

*See discussion question 4 on page 274.

and that he to whom Zeus gives a mixture of the two

> Sometimes meets with evil fortune, at other times with good;

but that he to whom is given the cup of unmingled ill,

> Him wild hunger drives o'er the beauteous earth.

And again—

> Zeus, who is the dispenser of good and evil to us.

And if anyone asserts that the violation of oaths and treaties, which was really the work of Pandarus, was brought about by Athena and Zeus, or that the strife and competition between the gods was instigated by Themis and Zeus, he shall not have our approval; neither will we allow our young men to hear the words of Aeschylus, that

> God plants guilt among men when he desires utterly to destroy a house.

And if a poet writes of the sufferings of Niobe—the subject of the tragedy in which these iambic verses occur—or of the house of Pelops, or of the Trojan war or on any similar theme, either we must not permit him to say that these are the works of God, or if they are of God, he must devise some explanation of them such as we are seeking: he must say that God did what was just and right, and they were the better for being punished. But that those who are punished are miserable, and that God is the author of their misery—the poet is not to be permitted to say; though he may say that the wicked were miserable because they required to be punished, and were benefited by receiving punishment from God; but that God being good is the author of evil to anyone is to be denied. We shall insist that it is not said or sung or heard in verse or prose by anyone whether old or young in any well-ordered commonwealth. Such a fiction would be impious, disastrous to us, and inconsistent with itself. 12

I agree with you, he replied, and am ready to give my assent to the law.

Questions for Discussion

1. In the poems and legends Socrates refers to in paragraphs 6–8, Greek heroes and gods are often shown behaving out of greed, spite, envy, jealousy, disrespect, and pride—almost the whole range of human vices.

Do you think Socrates is right in saying that young people will more likely commit vices themselves if they have "seen" them committed by gods and heroes in stories?

2. Socrates advances his argument about literature and character by means of an analogy with food and health. (For references to analogy, see the Rhetorical Index.) Can you state the analogy? Do you agree with it? Are feminists and minority representatives using this same analogy when they object to the moral effects of stories in which women, say, or blacks are depicted in demeaning ways? Do *you* object to such stories? On what grounds? Can you provide examples for class discussion?
3. If you accept Socrates' analogy and thus accept his definition of the problem, do you also accept his solution? Do you think that censorship is (1) a desirable solution or (2) a workable solution? In thinking about censorship, consider these questions:
   a. What is the possibility that the apparatus of censorship (committees, police, courts, suits, countersuits, and so on) might threaten the health of the state more than bad literature?
   b. Who is going to keep the censors pure? What happens if they need censoring? Who decides?
   c. How can a society be sure that its censors will never make a mistake?
   d. How does a society blend all of the competing standards for purity into one workable set of guidelines?
   e. Does free discussion disappear in a censored society?
   f. What happens to artistic expression in a censored society? (What about art in Nazi Germany or the Soviet Union? If no one in your class knows anything about such art, you might elect a committee to look into it and prepare a report for the rest of the class.)
4. In Benjamin Jowett's translation of Plato, from which we have excerpted the selections by Plato in this book, you will notice that both the terms *God* and *the gods* are used. Such terms cause problems in all translations, not only because of their inherent ambiguities but because they carry so many different meanings for modern readers. We should therefore be alert to probe *possible* meanings rather than settling on some one meaning that the words have had for us in other contexts. The warning may be especially important in reading Plato. Francis Cornford, in his preface to his translation of *The Republic,* says, "Some authors can be translated almost word for word. . . . This method cannot do justice to the matter and the manner of Plato's discourse. . . . Many key-words, such as 'music,' 'gymnastic,' 'virtue,' 'philosophy,' have shifted their meaning or acquired false associations for English ears." Cornford tells us that Plato "uses the singular 'god' and the plural 'the gods' with an indifference startling to the modern monotheist," and in his translation he avoids the form *God* entirely, in the belief that there is no notion in Plato quite like what is suggested to most modern readers by the term.

If no one in your class knows ancient Greek to assist in discussing the possible meanings of *God* and *the gods* in this selection, some students might be given the special assignment of consulting two or three other standard translations—the Paul Shorey translation in the Loeb Classical Library series, for example, or the Cornford translation. They could then photocopy the passages about *God* and *the gods,* or other troublesome passages, and bring them to class.

You may be shocked by the differences you find. Are they so great that they make reading the translations useless? What sorts of advice can you give yourself about reading other translations, on the basis of what you have found in comparing these translations?

Suggested Essay Topics

1. Clearly, Socrates is concerned about the moral influence of models that children meet in the stories they read. If children see Greek gods and heroes misbehaving, they will bend, like pliant plants, in those directions without realizing what is happening to them.

   Write an essay directed to a group of parents warning them that some of the models held out to children today are objectionable on the grounds given by Socrates. (You might watch some kids' programs, such as Saturday morning cartoons, in order to make your argument concrete and detailed.) Your purpose is to make a case, with illustrative examples, that the visual models children see on television are "bad" for them. You will, of course, have to say what you mean by *bad* and explain how important the problem is for society as a whole.

2. Read through a group of children's books in the library. Do you find material that you object to? Are there demeaning or stereotypical portrayals of minority groups, women, children, immigrants, or others? Try to find some old books from the late 1940s or early 1950s. Do you notice any difference between the depictions of stereotyped groups in older books as compared to more recent ones?

   If you find offensive material, choose an appropriate audience (your parents, the books' publishers, a grade-school teacher, etc.) and write an essay showing why the books you name are not good reading fare for young children. Be specific: Indicate why you find the material objectionable; indicate the ages you think make sensible cutoff points for parental or school supervision of youngsters' reading; say whether you think supervision ought to include actual censorship; and, if so, say why you accept censoring children's reading but not that of adults.

Plato

Many pages after Socrates has laid out his argument in The Republic *for censoring the reading of youngsters (his argument in the preceding selection), he again picks up his quarrel with literature. This time he attacks even more strongly, for he not only repeats his claims about the immoral influence of many kinds of literature but widens his argument to include most other kinds of representative art as well. For him the examples from literature, painting, and statuary are all interchangeable because they are all "imitations." The problem with imitations, we learn, is that they lead one away from truth by portraying shallow surfaces, not deep realities. Many readers have agreed with his earlier argument about the effects of literature on youngsters—witness the steady stream of criticism against the images that children are exposed to on television every day—but his later argument has proved harder to accept or even understand.*

His criticisms boil down to three main points. First, literature is inescapably entangled with falsehoods because it imitates appearances only, not underlying realities. Second, literature is not really useful in any significant way: poems and dramas, for example, do not make legislators more wise or generals more courageous. Third, literature constantly excites the weaker parts of human nature—the passions generally, but especially our fear of suffering—and thus undermines the strength of our nobler parts, reason and self-control. All three criticisms combine to make a serious charge about the immoral effects of most literature and to justify Socrates' claim that these bad effects should be prevented by state-enforced censorship.

Since all present-day concerns about the moral effects of literature (including television, movies, or dramas) ultimately echo Socrates' moral concerns, reading The Republic *carefully will provide insight into one of the most enduring debates in our history.*

THE SEDUCTIONS OF ART

Our title for this portion of *The Republic,* book 10.

Of the many excellences which I perceive in the order of our State, there is none which upon reflection pleases me better than the rule about poetry. 1

To what do you refer?

To our refusal to admit the imitative kind of poetry, for it certainly ought not to be received; as I see far more clearly now that the parts of the soul have been distinguished.

What do you mean?

Speaking in confidence, for you will not denounce me to the tragedians and the rest of the imitative tribe, all poetical imitations are ruinous to the understanding of the hearers, unless as an antidote they possess the knowledge of the true nature of the originals.

Explain the purport of your remark.

Well, I will tell you, although I have always from my earliest youth had 2 an awe and love of Homer which even now makes the words falter on my lips, for he seems to be the great captain and teacher of the whole of that noble tragic company; but a man is not to be reverenced more than the truth, and therefore I will speak out.

Very good, he said.

Listen to me then, or rather, answer me.

Put your question.

Can you give me a general definition of imitation? For I really do not myself understand what it professes to be.

A likely thing, then, that I should know.

There would be nothing strange in that, for the duller eye may often see a thing sooner than the keener.

Very true, he said; but in your presence, even if I had any faint notion, I could not muster courage to utter it. Will you inquire yourself?

Well then, shall we begin the inquiry at this point, following our usual 3
method: Whenever a number of individuals have a common name, we assume that there is one corresponding idea or form:—do you understand me?

I do.

Let us take, for our present purpose, any instance of such a group; there are beds and tables in the world—many of each, are there not?

Yes.

But there are only two ideas or forms of such furniture—one the idea of a bed, the other of a table.

True.

And the maker of either of them makes a bed or he makes a table for our use, in accordance with the idea—that is our way of speaking in this and similar instances—but no artificer makes the idea itself: how could he?

Impossible.

And there is another artificer,—I should like to know what you would 4
say of him.

Who is he?

One who is the maker of all the works of all other workmen.

What an extraordinary man!

Wait a little, and there will be more reason for your saying so. For this is the craftsman who is able to make not only furniture of every kind, but all that grows out of the earth, and all living creatures, himself included; and besides these he can make earth and sky and the gods, and all the things which are in heaven or in the realm of Hades under the earth.

He must be a wizard and no mistake.

Oh! you are incredulous, are you? Do you mean that there is no such maker or creator, or that in one sense there might be a maker of all these things but in another not? Do you see that there is a way in which you could make them all yourself?

And what way is this? he asked.

An easy way enough; or rather, there are many ways in which the feat 5
might be quickly and easily accomplished, none quicker than that of turning

a mirror round and round—you would soon enough make the sun and the heavens, and the earth and yourself, and other animals and plants, and furniture and all the other things of which we were just now speaking, in the mirror.

Yes, he said; but they would be appearances only.

Very good, I said, you are coming to the point now. And the painter too is, as I conceive, just such another—a creator of appearances, is he not?

Of course.

But then I suppose you will say that what he creates is untrue. And yet 6
there is a sense in which the painter also creates a bed? Is there not?

Yes, he said, but here again, an appearance only.

And what of the maker of the bed? Were you not saying that he too makes, not the idea which according to our view is the real object denoted by the word bed, but only a particular bed?

Yes, I did.

Then if he does not make a real object he cannot make what *is,* but only some semblance of existence; and if any one were to say that the work of the maker of the bed, or of any other workman, has real existence, he could hardly be supposed to be speaking the truth.

Not, at least, he replied, in the view of those who make a business of these discussions.

No wonder, then, that his work too is an indistinct expression of truth.

No wonder.

Suppose now that by the light of the examples just offered we inquire who this imitator is?

If you please.

Well then, here we find three beds: one existing in nature, which is made 7
by God, as I think that we may say—for no one else can be the maker?

No one, I think.

There is another which is the work of the carpenter?

Yes.

And the work of the painter is a third?

Yes.

Beds, then, are of three kinds, and there are three artists who superintend them: God, the maker of the bed, and the painter?

Yes, there are three of them.

God, whether from choice or from necessity, made one bed in nature and one only; two or more such beds neither ever have been nor ever will be made by God.

Why is that?

Because even if He had made but two, a third would still appear behind them of which they again both possessed the form, and that would be the real bed and not the two others.

Very true, he said.

God knew this, I suppose, and He desired to be the real maker of a real 8 bed, not a kind of maker of a kind of bed, and therefore He created a bed which is essentially and by nature one only.

So it seems.

Shall we, then, speak of Him as the natural author or maker of the bed?

Yes, he replied; inasmuch as by the natural process of creation He is the author of this and of all other things.

And what shall we say of the carpenter—is not he also the maker of a bed?

Yes.

But would you call the painter an artificer and maker?

Certainly not.

Yet if he is not the maker, what is he in relation to the bed?

I think, he said, that we may fairly designate him as the imitator of that which the others make.

Good, I said; then you call him whose product is third in the descent from nature, an imitator?

Certainly, he said.

And so if the tragic poet is an imitator, he too is thrice removed from 9
the king and from the truth; and so are all other imitators.

That appears to be so.

Then about the imitator we are agreed. And what about the painter?—Do you think he tries to imitate in each case that which originally exists in nature, or only the creations of artificers?

The latter.

As they are or as they appear? You have still to determine this.

What do you mean?

I mean to ask whether a bed really becomes different when it is seen from different points of view, obliquely or directly or from any other point of view? Or does it simply appear different, without being really so? And the same of all things.

Yes, he said, the difference is only apparent.

Now let me ask you another question: Which is the art of painting designed to be—an imitation of things as they are, or as they appear—of appearance or of reality?

Of appearance, he said.

Then the imitator is a long way off the truth, and can reproduce all 10
things because he lightly touches on a small part of them, and that part an image. For example: A painter will paint a cobbler, carpenter, or any other artisan, though he knows nothing of their arts; and, if he is a good painter, he may deceive children or simple persons when he shows them his picture of a carpenter from a distance, and they will fancy that they are looking at a real carpenter.

Certainly.

And surely, my friend, this is how we should regard all such claims: whenever any one informs us that he has found a man who knows all the arts, and all things else that anybody knows, and every single thing with a higher degree of accuracy than any other man—whoever tells us this, I think that we can only retort that he is a simple creature who seems to have been deceived by some wizard or imitator whom he met, and whom he thought all-knowing, because he himself was unable to analyse the nature of knowledge and ignorance and imitation.

Most true.

And next, I said, we have to consider tragedy and its leader, Homer; for 11
we hear some persons saying that these poets know all the arts; and all things human; where virtue and vice are concerned, and indeed all divine things too; because the good poet cannot compose well unless he knows his subject, and he who has not this knowledge can never be a poet. We ought to consider whether here also there may not be a similar illusion. Perhaps they may have come across imitators and been deceived by them; they may not have remembered when they saw their works that these were thrice removed from the truth, and could easily be made without any knowledge of the truth, because they are appearances only and not realities? Or, after all, they may be in the right, and good poets do really know the things about which they seem to the many to speak so well?

The question, he said, should by all means be considered. 12

Now do you suppose that if a person were able to make the original as well as the image, he would seriously devote himself to the image-making branch? Would he allow imitation to be the ruling principle of his life, as if he had nothing higher in him?

I should say not.

But the real artist, who had real knowledge of those things which he chose also to imitate, would be interested in realities and not in imitations; and would desire to leave as memorials of himself works many and fair; and, instead of being the author of encomiums, he would prefer to be the theme of them.

Yes, he said, that would be to him a source of much greater honour and profit.

Now let us refrain, I said, from calling Homer or any other poet to 13
account regarding those arts to which his poems incidentally refer: we will not ask them, in case any poet has been a doctor and not a mere imitator of medical parlance, to show what patients have been restored to health by a poet, ancient or modern, as they were by Asclepius; or what disciples in medicine a poet has left behind him, like the Asclepiads. Nor shall we press the same question upon them about the other arts. But we have a right to know respecting warfare, strategy, the administration of States and the education of man, which are the chiefest and noblest subjects of his poems, and we may fairly ask him about them. "Friend Homer," then we say to him, "if you are only in the second remove from truth in what you say of virtue, and not in the third—not an image maker, that is, by our definition, an imitator—and if you are able to discern what pursuits make men better or worse in private or public life, tell us what State was ever better governed by your

help? The good order of Lacedaemon is due to Lycurgus, and many other cities great and small have been similarly benefited by others; but who says that you have been a good legislator to them and have done them any good? Italy and Sicily boast of Charondas, and there is Solon who is renowned among us; but what city has anything to say about you?" Is there any city which he might name?

I think not, said Glaucon; not even the Homerids themselves pretend that he was a legislator.

. . .

The poet with his words and phrases may be said to lay on the colours 14
of the several arts, himself understanding their nature only enough to imitate them; and other people, who are as ignorant as he is, and judge only from his words, imagine that if he speaks of cobbling, or of military tactics, or of anything else, in metre and harmony and rhythm, he speaks very well—such is the sweet influence which melody and rhythm by nature have. For I am sure that you know what a poor appearance the works of poets make when stripped of the colours which art puts upon them, and recited in simple prose. You have seen some examples?

Yes, he said. 15

They are like faces which were never really beautiful, but only blooming, seen when the bloom of youth has passed away from them?

Exactly.

Come now, and observe this point: The imitator or maker of the image knows nothing, we have said, of true existence; he knows appearances only. Am I not right?

Yes.

Then let us have a clear understanding, and not be satisfied with half an explanation.

Proceed.

Of the painter we say that he will paint reins, and he will paint a bit?

Yes.

And the worker in leather and brass will make them?

Certainly.

But does the painter know the right form of the bit and reins? Nay, 16
hardly even the workers in brass and leather who make them; only the horseman who knows how to use them—he knows their right form.

Most true.

And may we not say the same of all things?

What?

That there are three arts which are concerned with all things: one which uses, another which makes, a third which imitates them?

Yes.

And the excellence and beauty and rightness of every structure, animate or inanimate, and of every action of man, is relative solely to the use for which nature or the artist has intended them.

True.

17 Then beyond doubt it is the user who has the greatest experience of them, and he must report to the maker the good or bad qualities which develop themselves in use; for example, the flute-player will tell the flute-maker which of his flutes is satisfactory to the performer; he will tell him how he ought to make them, and the other will attend to his instructions?

Of course.

18 So the one pronounces with knowledge about the goodness and badness of flutes, while the other, confiding in him, will make them accordingly?

True.

The instrument is the same, but about the excellence or badness of it the maker will possess a correct belief, since he associates with one who knows, and is compelled to hear what he has to say; whereas the user will have knowledge?

True.

But will the imitator have either? Will he know from use whether or no that which he paints is correct or beautiful? or will he have right opinion from being compelled to associate with another who knows and gives him instructions about what he should paint?

Neither.

19 Then an imitator will no more have true opinion than he will have knowledge about the goodness or badness of his models?

I suppose not.

The imitative poet will be in a brilliant state of intelligence about the theme of his poetry?

Nay, very much the reverse.

And still he will go on imitating without knowing what makes a thing good or bad, and may be expected therefore to imitate only that which appears to be good to the ignorant multitude?

Just so.

Thus far then we are pretty well agreed that the imitator has no knowledge worth mentioning of what he imitates.

. . .

20 But we have not yet brought forward the heaviest count in our accusation:—the power which poetry has of harming even the good (and there are very few who are not harmed), is surely an awful thing?

Yes, certainly, if the effect is what you say.

Hear and judge: The best of us, as I conceive, when we listen to a passage of Homer or one of the tragedians, in which he represents some hero who is drawling out his sorrows in a long oration, or singing, and smiting his breast—the best of us, you know, delight in giving way to sympathy, and are in raptures at the excellence of the poet who stirs our feelings most.

Yes, of course I know.

21 But when any sorrow of our own happens to us, then you may observe that we pride ourselves on the opposite quality—we would fain be quiet and

patient; this is considered the manly part, and the other which delighted us in the recitation is now deemed to be the part of a woman.

Very true, he said.

Now can we be right in praising and admiring another who is doing that which any one of us would abominate and be ashamed of in his own person?

No, he said, that is certainly not reasonable.

Nay, I said, quite reasonable from one point of view.

What point of view?

If you consider, I said, that when in misfortune we feel a natural hunger 22
and desire to relieve our sorrow by weeping and lamentation, and that this very feeling which is starved and suppressed in our own calamities is satisfied and delighted by the poets;—the better nature in each of us, not having been sufficiently trained by reason or habit, allows the sympathetic element to break loose because the sorrow is another's; and the spectator fancies that there can be no disgrace to himself in praising and pitying any one who while professing to be a brave man, gives way to untimely lamentation; he thinks that the pleasure is a gain, and is far from wishing to lose it by rejection of the whole poem. Few persons ever reflect, as I should imagine, that the contagion must pass from others to themselves. For the pity which has been nourished and strengthened in the misfortunes of others is with difficulty repressed in our own.

How very true!

And does not the same hold also of the ridiculous? There are jests which 23
you would be ashamed to make yourself, and yet on the comic stage, or indeed in private, when you hear them, you are greatly amused by them, and are not at all disgusted at their unseemliness;—the case of pity is repeated;—there is a principle in human nature which is disposed to raise a laugh, and this, which you once restrained by reason because you were afraid of being thought a buffoon, is now let out again; and having stimulated the risible faculty at the theatre, you are betrayed unconsciously to yourself into playing the comic poet at home.

Quite true, he said.

And the same may be said of lust and anger and all the other affections, 24
of desire and pain and pleasure, which are held to be inseparable from every action—in all of them poetry has a like effect; it feeds and waters the passions instead of drying them up; she lets them rule, although they ought to be controlled if mankind are ever to increase in happiness and virtue.

I cannot deny it.

Therefore, Glaucon, I said, whenever you meet with any of the eulogists 25
of Homer declaring that he has been the educator of Hellas, and that he is profitable for education and for the ordering of human things, and that you should take him up again and again and get to know him and regulate your whole life according to him, we may love and honour those who say these things—they are excellent people, as far as their lights extend; and we are ready to acknowledge that Homer is the greatest of poets and first of tragedy

writers; but we must remain firm in our conviction that hymns to the gods and praises of famous men are the only poetry which ought to be admitted into our State.

Questions for Discussion

1. Is it true that artists, whether they paint imitations in colors or in words, are only dealing in appearances, not reality? Doesn't this depend on how one defines the artist's real object of imitation? Would you say that a writer of short stories or movie scripts, for example, imitates only the appearances of human conduct and feeling or imitates instead the eternal, "real" qualities in human nature? To argue the issue, pick an example of a short story or movie that almost everyone in class knows.
2. If most art deals only with superficial appearances, how can one account for the facts (1) that art is found in all cultures, (2) that works of art are among the most treasured artifacts any culture possesses, and (3) that some works of art, such as those of Shakespeare and Homer, are found to be interesting to large numbers of readers, generation after generation, century after century, despite large shifts in language, society, and style?
3. Is it fair for Socrates to take it as an argument against literature that poems never helped a ruler govern a state (¶13)? Cannot the same thing be said of music, chess, football, fashions, fishing, senior proms, sky diving, and a thousand other activities that human beings devote invention, time, energy, and money to? Is art in some way more significant—and potentially more dangerous—than these other leisure-time activities? Would these things also have to be outlawed in an ideal state?
4. What would it be like to live in a world without art of any kind? (In thinking about such a condition, it is helpful to use a very broad definition of *art,* including all the "entertainment" that "imitates" life—even computer games and Lazer Tag.)

Suggested Essay Topics

1. In paragraph 24 Socrates says that poetry "feeds and waters the passions instead of drying them up; she lets them rule, although they ought to be controlled. . . ." Pick a literary work (or television program, movie, or play) that you think either supports or contradicts this assertion. Write an essay directed to the class explaining whether the work whips up the passions and whether you agree with Socrates that this is a bad thing.

2. A variation on topic 1: If you are familiar with any pornographic works, pick a vivid one and write an essay to your fellow students arguing either that Socrates' assertion about the passions provides a useful way of attacking the moral effects of pornography or that Socrates is wrong because pornography has the socially beneficial effect of releasing potentially destructive passions rather than whipping them up. If you take the latter option, explain why you think pornography decreases rather than increases the passions.

IDEAS IN DEBATE

Thomas Love Peacock
E. M. Forster

Thomas Love Peacock

Thomas Love Peacock (1785–1866) was well known in his own day as a writer of satirical novels. Though the novels are still read, The Four Ages of Poetry *(1820) is now perhaps better known, partly because it inspired in the following year an even more famous reply,* A Defence of Poetry, *by the Romantic English poet and Peacock's good friend Percy Bysshe Shelley.*

Peacock vividly advances an entertaining case that poetry can be of no real significance or value in the modern world of science and industry because it is utterly "impractical." In barbarous and superstitious past ages, he says, poetry was valued, but in the modern world it is no longer needed—it has, in fact, negative value.

Some have argued that Peacock was not altogether serious in his attack on poetry as a childish holdover from society's primitive youth. For one thing, in his other work he typically used a tongue-in-cheek style; what's more, he seems motivated as much by an impish desire to annoy his fellow writers as to advance a serious argument. Some of his attack, for example, seems deliberately worded to get a rise out of Shelley. Finally, he began his writing career as a poet; it seems unlikely that he could fully believe all that he says here. But whether he is entirely serious or not, his attack is worth reading because he says what more serious attackers of poetry were saying at the time, only he says it better.

If Peacock had been alone in advancing these views, it would matter little whether he was serious or not. But the idea that poetry has no place in the modern world of science, industry, and reason was—and still is—common. Throughout Peacock's century there were many serious attacks both on poetry in general and on poets in particular. Tennyson and Browning were accused at the beginning of their careers, for example, of walking around with their heads in the clouds while all right-minded, "serious" folk were applying their muscles to the wheels of social and industrial progress. Poetry simply got in the way of those who were hurrying to reach the promised land of middle-class prosperity.

As you read Peacock's witty indictment, postpone your own decision about whether it is sound until you have fully understood each point. Since the issues are complex, you should deliberately keep an open mind, at least until you have read more poetry and more arguments for and against it.

POETRY: AN OUTMODED AMUSEMENT

Our title for this portion of *The Four Ages of Poetry* (1820).

1 In the origin and perfection of poetry, all the associations of life were composed of poetical materials. With us it is decidedly the reverse. We know too that there are no Dryads* in Hyde-park nor Naiads† in the Regent's-canal. But barbaric manners and supernatural interventions are essential to poetry. Either in the scene, or in the time, or in both, it must be remote from our ordinary perceptions. While the historian and the philosopher are advancing in, and accelerating, the progress of knowledge, the poet is wallowing in the rubbish of departed ignorance, and raking up the ashes of dead savages to find gewgaws and rattles for the grown babies of the age. [Sir Walter] Scott digs up the poachers and cattle-stealers of the ancient border.‡ Lord Byron cruises for thieves and pirates on the shores of the Morea and among the Greek islands.§ [Robert] Southey wades through ponderous volumes of travels and old chronicles, from which he carefully selects all that is false, useless, and absurd, as being essentially poetical; and when he has a commonplace book full of monstrosities, strings them into an epic.‖ [William] Wordsworth picks up village legends from old women and sextons,# and [Samuel Taylor] Coleridge, to the valuable information acquired from similar sources, superadds the dreams of crazy theologians and the mysticisms of German metaphysics, and favours the world with visions in verse, in which the quadruple elements of sexton, old woman, Jeremy Taylor, and Emanuel Kant, are harmonized into a delicious poetical compound.** [Thomas] Moore presents us with a Persian, and [Thomas] Campbell with a Pennsylvanian tale,†† both formed on the same principle as Mr. Southey's epics, by extracting from a perfunctory and desultory perusal of a collection of voyages and travels, all that useful investigation would not seek for and that common sense would reject.

2 These disjointed relics of tradition and fragments of second-hand observation, being woven into a tissue of verse, constructed on what Mr. Coleridge calls a new principle (that is, no principle at all), compose a modern-antique compound of frippery and barbarism, in which the puling sentimentality of

*Wood nymphs.

†Water nymphs.

‡See *Border Minstrelsy* (1802–1803), *The Lay of the Last Minstrel* (1805), *Lord of the Isles* (1815)—poems based on traditional tales and ballads of the "Border country," the region dividing England and Scotland prior to the union of the two countries in 1707. The cluster of writers referred to in this paragraph are all writers of the Romantic period in England, and contemporaries of Peacock.

§See *The Giaour* (1813), *The Bride of Abydos* (1813), *The Corsair* (1814), *Don Juan* (1819–1824).

‖Robert Southey, poet laureate from 1813 to 1843, author of *Thalaba* (1801), *Madoc* (1805), *The Curse of Kehama* (1810), *Roderick, the Last of the Goths* (1814).

#Probably a reference to *The Excursion* (1814).

**Probably "The Rime of the Ancient Mariner" (1798) and "Christabel" (1816).

††Thomas Moore, *Lalla Rookh* (1817); Thomas Campbell, *Gertrude of Wyoming* (1809).

the present time is grafted on the misrepresented ruggedness of the past into a heterogeneous congeries of unamalgamating manners, sufficient to impose on the common readers of poetry, over whose understandings the poet of this class possesses that commanding advantage, which, in all circumstances and conditions of life, a man who knows something, however little, always possesses over one who knows nothing.

A poet in our times is a semi-barbarian in a civilized community. He 3
lives in the days that are past. His ideas, thoughts, feelings, associations, are all with barbarous manners, obsolete customs, and exploded superstitions. The march of his intellect is like that of a crab, backward. The brighter the light diffused around him by the progress of reason, the thicker is the darkness of antiquated barbarism, in which he buries himself like a mole, to throw up the barren hillocks of his Cimmerian labours.* The philosophic mental tranquillity which looks round with an equal eye on all external things, collects a store of ideas, discriminates their relative value, assigns to all their proper place, and from the materials of useful knowledge thus collected, appreciated, and arranged, forms new combinations that impress the stamp of their power and utility on the real business of life, is diametrically the reverse of that frame of mind which poetry inspires, or from which poetry can emanate. The highest inspirations of poetry are resolvable into three ingredients: the rant of unregulated passion, the whining of exaggerated feeling, and the cant of factitious sentiment: and can therefore serve only to ripen a splendid lunatic like Alexander, a puling driveller like Werther,† or a morbid dreamer like Wordsworth. It can never make a philosopher, nor a statesman, nor in any class of life an useful or rational man. It cannot claim the slightest share in any one of the comforts and utilities of life of which we have witnessed so many and so rapid advances. But though not useful, it may be said it is highly ornamental, and deserves to be cultivated for the pleasure it yields. Even if this be granted, it does not follow that a writer of poetry in the present state of society is not a waster of his own time, and a robber of that of others. Poetry is not one of those arts which, like painting, require repetition and multiplication, in order to be diffused among society. There are more good poems already existing than are sufficient to employ that portion of life which any mere reader and recipient of poetical impressions should devote to them, and these having been produced in poetical times, are far superior in all the characteristics of poetry to the artificial reconstructions of a few morbid ascetics in unpoetical times. To read the promiscuous rubbish of the present time to the exclusion of the select treasures of the past, is to substitute the worse for the better variety of the same mode of enjoyment.

But in whatever degree poetry is cultivated, it must necessarily be to the 4
neglect of some branch of useful study: and it is a lamentable spectacle to see

*The Cimmerians were a half-mythical people, first mentioned in *The Odyssey,* who supposedly lived in perpetual darkness.

†Probably Alexander the Great, who in the fourth century B.C. nearly realized his ambition of conquering the whole world; and the sentimental hero of Goethe's early romance, *The Sorrows of Young Werther* (1774, revised 1787).

minds, capable of better things, running to seed in the specious indolence of these empty aimless mockeries of intellectual exertion. Poetry was the mental rattle that awakened the attention of intellect in the infancy of civil society: but for the maturity of mind to make a serious business of the playthings of its childhood, is as absurd as for a full-grown man to rub his gums with coral, and cry to be charmed to sleep by the jingle of silver bells.

Questions for Discussion

1. In paragraph 1 Peacock pictures the historian and the philosopher advancing "the progress of knowledge." What kind of knowledge do you think Peacock is talking about? Is "progress" an appropriate measure for all kinds of knowledge?
2. Paragraph 2 consists of one long, complicated sentence. Do all of its parts fit together well? Can it be advantageously broken into smaller segments? Does it read more clearly if you read it aloud a couple of times?
3. Toward the middle of paragraph 3 Peacock refers to the "real business of life." Such phrases are almost always important clues to a writer's underlying assumptions. What seems to constitute the "real business of life" from Peacock's point of view? What is the "real business of life" from *your* point of view? Do you agree that the "frame of mind which poetry inspires" is "diametrically the reverse" of the frame of mind that makes valuable contributions to the "real business of life"?
4. In the first sentence of paragraph 4 Peacock asserts that poetry and "useful study" are mutually exclusive, that is, that they cannot be pursued simultaneously without damaging each other. Can you think of reasons to offer against Peacock's case or in his support?

Suggested Essay Topics

1. With a copy of your favorite poem in front of you, write an essay to Peacock in which you defend yourself against his accusation that an interest in poetry "is as absurd as for a full-grown man to rub his gums with coral, and cry to be charmed to sleep by the jingle of silver bells." Try to show why the poem of your choice is valuable and why your interest in it is justified. To do so, you must examine it in detail, showing that the value, for example, of the feelings it arouses, the lessons it teaches, the beauty of its language, or whatever else makes it special, is fully expressed *this* way in *this* poem.
2. Try to explode Peacock's assertion that poetry and useful studies are mutually exclusive. You could begin this way: "If poetry undermines useful activities, as Peacock implies, because it is frivolous, arouses the emotions, and fails to cultivate the reason, it must be true that other

activities possessing these features—music, tennis, chess, scuba diving, and a thousand other activities—are equally contemptible." Then select one or two of these "other activities" and go on to defend the value of their pursuit. You could try to show, for example, that by contributing to a balanced life they actually do not undermine but assist the cultivation of reason and other practical activities. After you establish the possibility that *these* activities are not mutually incompatible with reason and practicality, go back to poetry and try to show that if what you have said about your selected activities is true, the point must hold for poetry as well. Direct the essay to someone you know (or can imagine) who would initially disagree with your case.

E. M. Forster

For the same reason that a flute is almost always less noticeable in a symphony than a trumpet, writers like E. M. Forster (1879–1970) almost always sound less interesting when placed in direct debate with writers like Peacock. Peacock stands out. He has brilliance, vividness, cleverness, and polish. He has an easy flamboyance and can stop the show with funny and quotable jokes: "The march of [a poet's] intellect is like that of a crab, backward" (p. 288, ¶3).

E. M. Forster is more quiet. His mind is subtle, and he shades his meanings delicately. When he says, for example, that the artist "legislates through creating. And he creates through his sensitiveness and his power to impose form" (¶13), he hasn't given us a quotable nugget or made us laugh. But he has made us think. The initial disadvantage of a Forster against a Peacock wears off in time. Forster has staying power because he deals intelligently with interesting ideas. The more closely a reader attends to Forster, the more rewards he yields.

The phrase "art for art's sake" emerged toward the end of the nineteenth century as a kind of slogan or battle cry. It was at first used primarily by avant-garde *artists and critics who wanted to free art from all non-artistic standards and goals. They opposed the idea that art should ever try—or be asked to try—to teach moral truths, improve the world, or take positions about history, politics, or religion. Art, they insisted, exists only for itself. Its purpose is to achieve beauty, not to soil its aesthetic purity by embracing the world's coarseness or getting caught up in its controversies. The extremists in this group felt that art was the only goal worth pursuing in life, that art was the only dimension of life worth full respect and effect.*

But not everyone who defended "art for art's sake" was an extremist. Forster's views about art fall somewhere between those of Peacock, who argues that works of imagination are valueless in a scientific and industrial world, and the self-conscious aesthetes of the late nineteenth century (such as Oscar Wilde and James Whistler) who liked to shock the middle classes by sometimes claiming that art is the only thing that matters in life. Precisely where he falls between these two positions you must decide for yourself, but it is clear that Forster thinks art serves a valuable function beyond mere aesthetic beauty. It may be that art can only serve larger ends through *its beauty—rather than through direct argument, say—but if beauty is a totally self-reflexive quality, if it produces nothing beyond itself and has no consequences in the real world, then its elevation to a position of supreme importance is not likely to be taken seriously by many people. Artists themselves, in fact, are often eager for their works to be viewed as truthful or profound, not merely beautiful. Try to determine as precisely as you can Forster's views about the ends that art serves and its means of serving them. If art serves its own ends but in doing so also serves other ends, what are they? Are these other ends served directly or indirectly? And most important, are these other ends merely incidental, or are they essential? If the latter, why are they essential, and for whom?*

ART FOR ART'S SAKE

An address delivered before the American Academy of Arts and Letters in New York, 1949, and published in *Two Cheers for Democracy* (1951).

I believe in art for art's sake. It is an unfashionable belief, and some of my statements must be of the nature of an apology. Fifty years ago I should have faced you with more confidence. A writer or a speaker who chose "Art for Art's Sake" for his theme fifty years ago could be sure of being in the swim, and could feel so confident of success that he sometimes dressed himself in esthetic costumes suitable to the occasion—in an embroidered dressing gown, perhaps, or a blue velvet suit with a Lord Fauntleroy collar; or a toga, or a kimono, and carried a poppy or a lily or a long peacock's feather in his medieval hand.* Times have changed. Not thus can I present either myself or my theme today. My aim rather is to ask you quietly to reconsider for a few minutes a phrase which has been much misused and much abused, but which has, I believe, great importance for us—has, indeed, eternal importance. 1

Now we can easily dismiss those peacock's feathers and other affectations—they are but trifles—but I want also to dismiss a more dangerous heresy, namely the silly idea that only art matters, an idea which has somehow got mixed up with the idea of art for art's sake, and has helped to discredit it. Many things, besides art, matter. It is merely one of the things that matter, and high though the claims are that I make for it, I want to keep them in proportion. No one can spend his or her life entirely in the creation or the appreciation of masterpieces. Man lives, and ought to live, in a complex world, full of conflicting claims, and if we simplified them down into the esthetic he would be sterilised. Art for art's sake does not mean that only art 2

*The aesthetes, a group of mostly young men and women in the arts who captured a lot of public attention at the turn of the century, were noted (like the rebellious youth groups of the 1960s) for dressing extravagantly.

matters, and I would also like to rule out such phrases as "The Life of Art," "Living for Art," and "Art's High Mission." They confuse and mislead.

What does the phrase mean? Instead of generalising, let us take a specific instance—Shakespeare's *Macbeth,* for example, and pronounce the words, "*Macbeth* for *Macbeth*'s sake." What does that mean? Well, the play has several aspects—it is educational, it teaches us something about legendary Scotland, something about Jacobean England, and a good deal about human nature and its perils. We can study its origins, and study and enjoy its dramatic technique and the music of its diction. All that is true. But *Macbeth* is furthermore a world of its own, created by Shakespeare and existing in virtue of its own poetry. It is in this aspect *Macbeth* for *Macbeth*'s sake, and that is what I intend by the phrase "art for art's sake." A work of art—whatever else it may be—is a self-contained entity, with a life of its own imposed on it by its creator. It has internal order. It may have external form. That is how we recognise it. 3

Take for another example that picture of Seurat's which I saw two years ago in Chicago—"*La Grande Jatte.*" Here again there is much to study and to enjoy: the pointillism, the charming face of the seated girl, the nineteenth-century Parisian Sunday sunlight, the sense of motion in immobility. But here again there is something more; "*La Grande Jatte*" forms a world of its own, created by Seurat and existing by virtue of its own poetry: "*La Grande Jatte*" *pour "La Grande Jatte": l'art pour l'art.* Like *Macbeth* it has internal order and internal life. 4

It is to the conception of order that I would now turn. This is important to my argument, and I want to make a digression, and glance at order in daily life, before I come to order in art. 5

In the world of daily life, the world which we perforce inhabit, there is much talk about order, particularly from statesmen and politicians. They tend, however, to confuse order with orders, just as they confuse creation with regulations. Order, I suggest, is something evolved from within, not something imposed from without; it is an internal stability, a vital harmony, and in the social and political category, it has never existed except for the convenience of historians. Viewed realistically, the past is really a series of *dis*orders, succeeding one another by discoverable laws, no doubt, and certainly marked by an increasing growth of human interference, but disorders all the same. So that, speaking as a writer, what I hope for today is a disorder which will be more favourable to artists than is the present one, and which will provide them with fuller inspirations and better material conditions. It will not last—nothing lasts—but there have been some advantageous disorders in the past—for instance, in ancient Athens, in Renaissance Italy, eighteenth-century France, periods in China and Persia—and we may do something to accelerate the next one. But let us not again fix our hearts where true joys are not to be found. We were promised a new order after the first world war through the League of Nations. It did not come, nor have I faith in present promises, by whomsoever endorsed. The implacable offensive of Science forbids. We cannot reach social and political stability for the reason that we continue to make scientific discoveries and to apply them, and thus to destroy 6 the arrangements which were based on more elementary discoveries. If Science would discover rather than apply—if, in other words, men were more interested in knowledge than in power—mankind would be in a far safer position, the stability statesmen talk about would be a possibility, there could be a new order based on vital harmony, and the earthly millennium might approach. But Science shows no signs of doing this: she gave us the internal combustion engine, and before we had digested and assimilated it with terrible pains into our social system, she harnessed the atom, and destroyed any new order that seemed to be evolving. How can man get into harmony with his surroundings when he is constantly altering them? The future of our race is, in this direction, more unpleasant than we care to admit, and it has sometimes seemed to me that its best chance lies through apathy, uninventiveness, and inertia. Universal exhaustion might promote that Change of Heart which is at present so briskly recommended from a thousand pulpits. Universal exhaustion would certainly be a new experience. The human race has never undergone it, and is still too perky to admit that it may be coming and might result in a sprouting of new growth through the decay.

I must not pursue these speculations any further—they lead me too far 7
from my terms of reference and maybe from yours. But I do want to emphasize that order in daily life and in history, order in the social and political category, is unattainable under our present psychology.

Where is it attainable? Not in the astronomical category, where it was 8
for many years enthroned. The heavens and the earth have become terribly alike since Einstein. No longer can we find a reassuring contrast to chaos in the night sky and look up with George Meredith to the stars, the army of unalterable law,* or listen for the music of the spheres. Order is not there. In the entire universe there seem to be only two possibilities for it. The first of them—which again lies outside my terms of reference—is the divine order, the mystic harmony, which according to all religions is available for those who can contemplate it. We must admit its possibility, on the evidence of the adepts, and we must believe them when they say that it is attained, if attainable, by prayer. "O thou who changest not, abide with me," said one of its poets. *"Ordina questo amor, o tu che m'ami,"* said another: "Set love in order, thou who lovest me." The existence of a divine order, though it cannot be tested, has never been disproved.

The second possibility for order lies in the esthetic category, which is 9
my subject here: the order which an artist can create in his own work, and to that we must now return. A work of art, we are all agreed, is a unique product. But why? It is unique not because it is clever or noble or beautiful or enlightened or original or sincere or idealistic or useful or educational—it may embody any of those qualities—but because it is the only material object in the universe which may possess internal harmony. All the others have been pressed into shape from outside, and when their mold is removed they collapse. The work of art stands up by itself, and nothing else does. It achieves

*An allusion to George Meredith's poem "Lucifer by Starlight."

something which has often been promised by society, but always delusively. Ancient Athens made a mess—but the *Antigone* stands up. Renaissance Rome made a mess—but the ceiling of the Sistine got painted. James I made a mess—but there was *Macbeth.* Louis XIV—but there was *Phèdre.* Art for art's sake? I should just think so, and more so than ever at the present time. It is the one orderly product which our muddling race has produced. It is the cry of a thousand sentinels, the echo from a thousand labyrinths; it is the lighthouse which cannot be hidden: *c'est le meilleur témoignage que nous puissions donner de notre dignité.** *Antigone* for *Antigone*'s sake, *Macbeth* for *Macbeth*'s, *"La Grande Jatte" pour "La Grande Jatte."*

If this line of argument is correct, it follows that the artist will tend to 10
be an outsider in the society to which he has been born, and that the nineteenth-century conception of him as a Bohemian† was not inaccurate. The conception erred in three particulars: it postulated an economic system where art could be a full-time job, it introduced the fallacy that only art matters, and it overstressed idiosyncrasy and waywardness—the peacock-feather aspect—rather than order. But it is a truer conception than the one which prevails in official circles on my side of the Atlantic—I don't know about yours: the conception which treats the artist as if he were a particularly bright government advertiser and encourages him to be friendly and matey with his fellow citizens, and not to give himself airs.

Estimable is mateyness, and the man who achieves it gives many a 11
pleasant little drink to himself and to others. But it has no traceable connection with the creative impulse, and probably acts as an inhibition on it. The artist who is seduced by mateyness may stop himself from doing the one thing which he, and he alone, can do—the making of something out of words or sounds or paint or clay or marble or steel or film which has internal harmony and presents order to a permanently disarranged planet. This seems worth doing, even at the risk of being called uppish by journalists. I have in mind an article which was published some years ago in the London *Times,* an article called "The Eclipse of the Highbrow," in which the "Average Man" was exalted, and all contemporary literature was censured if it did not toe the line, the precise position of the line being naturally known to the writer of the article. Sir Kenneth Clark, who was at that time director of our National Gallery, commented on this pernicious doctrine in a letter which cannot be too often quoted. "The poet and the artist," wrote Clark, "are important precisely because they are not average men; because in sensibility, intelligence, and power of invention they far exceed the average." These memorable words, and particularly the words "power of invention," are the Bohemian's passport. Furnished with it, he slinks about society, saluted now by a brickbat and now by a penny, and accepting either of them with equanimity. He does not consider too anxiously what his relations with society may be, for he is aware of something more important than that—

*"It is the best testimony of our dignity that we can give." [Forster's translation]
†Unconventional, anti-establishment.

namely the invitation to invent, to create order, and he believes he will be better placed for doing this if he attempts detachment. So round and round he slouches, with his hat pulled over his eyes, and maybe with a louse in his beard, and—if he really wants one—with a peacock's feather in his hand.

If our present society should disintegrate—and who dare prophesy that it won't?—this old-fashioned and démodé figure will become clearer: the Bohemian, the outsider, the parasite, the rat—one of those figures which have at present no function either in a warring or a peaceful world. It may not be dignified to be a rat, but many of the ships are sinking, which is not dignified either—the officials did not build them properly. Myself, I would sooner be a swimming rat than a sinking ship—at all events I can look around me for a little longer—and I remember how one of us, a rat with particularly bright eyes called Shelley, squeaked out, "Poets are the unacknowledged legislators of the world," before he vanished into the waters of the Mediterranean. 12

What laws did Shelley propose to pass? None. The legislation of the artist is never formulated at the time, though it is sometimes discerned by future generations. He legislates through creating. And he creates through his sensitiveness and his power to impose form. Without form the sensitiveness vanishes. And form is as important today, when the human race is trying to ride the whirlwind, as it ever was in those less agitating days of the past, when the earth seemed solid and the stars fixed, and the discoveries of science were made slowly, slowly. Form is not tradition. It alters from generation to generation. Artists always seek a new technique, and will continue to do so as long as their work excites them. But form of some kind is imperative. It is the surface crust of the internal harmony, it is the outward evidence of order. 13

My remarks about society may have seemed too pessimistic, but I believe that society can only represent a fragment of the human spirit, and that another fragment can only get expressed through art. And I wanted to take this opportunity, this vantage ground, to assert not only the existence of art but its pertinacity. Looking back into the past, it seems to me that that is all there has ever been: vantage grounds for discussion and creation, little vantage grounds in the changing chaos, where bubbles have been blown and webs spun, and the desire to create order has found temporary gratification, and the sentinels have managed to utter their challenges, and the huntsmen, though lost individually, have heard each other's calls through the impenetrable wood, and the lighthouses have never ceased sweeping the thankless seas. In this pertinacity there seems to me, as I grow older, something more and more profound, something which does in fact concern people who do not care about art at all. 14

In conclusion, let me summarize the various categories that have laid claim to the possession of Order. 15

(1) The social and political category. Claim disallowed on the evidence of history and of our own experience. If man altered psychologically, order here might be attainable; not otherwise. 16

(2) The astronomical category. Claim allowed up to the present century, but now disallowed on the evidence of the physicists. 17

(3) The religious category. Claim allowed on the evidence of the mystics. 18

(4) The esthetic category—the subject of this article. Claim allowed on the evidence of various works of art; and on the evidence of our own creative impulses, however weak these may be, or however imperfectly they may function. Works of art, in my opinion, are the only objects in the material universe to possess internal order, and that is why, though I don't believe that only art matters, I do believe in Art for Art's Sake. 19

Questions for Discussion

1. The long third sentence of paragraph 14 contains a series of images that suggest what the world is like and the function art serves in that world. Discuss with your classmates the qualities of the world suggested by these images and where art fits in as a human endeavor.
2. When the artist "presents order to a permanently disarranged planet" (¶11), does he or she, in Forster's view, do so in order "to do the world good"? Does Forster think this *should* be the artist's aim? Should the making of the work itself or the possible effects of the work be of most concern to the artist? If the former, then how are the wider effects of art achieved, beyond merely being beautiful?
3. In paragraph 9 Forster says that "a work of art . . . is the only material object in the universe which may possess internal harmony. All the others have been pressed into shape from outside, and when their mold is removed they collapse." How would you state the meaning of these two sentences in your own words? What would serve as good examples of two material objects that match his description?
4. Aristotle (pp. 235–238) also talks about "harmony" as an important feature of works of art. Re-read our brief selection from Aristotle; then discuss with your classmates whether Forster's and Aristotle's meanings overlap completely, partly, or not at all.

Suggested Essay Topics

1. Consider for a moment some of the many ways available to a writer for establishing the internal order, or harmony, that Forster values so highly:
   a. Logical harmony: placing ideas in such an order that they "track" one another and thus develop coherently
   b. Thematic harmony: sticking to the same subject, or to appropriate subdivisions of the same subject, throughout an entire essay, story, or poem
   c. Tonal harmony: maintaining either the same tone throughout or modulating the variations in ways appropriate to the dominant tone

d. Imagistic harmony: giving the reader pictures—through the use of metaphor, analogy, example, and comparisons of abstract qualities with physical senses ("I was so mad I could taste it in the back of my mouth")—that are appropriate to the subject and each other

e. Formal harmony: designing a piece of writing so that its parts are of appropriate size and consistency

f. Point-of-view harmony: maintaining the same perspective on a topic that is assumed at the beginning (if you were writing a personal essay assuming the point of view—for comic purposes, say—of someone who was dizzy, confused, naïve, and bumbling, inserting sharply perceptive comments by other people would violate the initial point of view and, if done inadvertently, could ruin an essay)

These modes of harmony (and others) are, of course, not mutually exclusive; a given essay may employ all of them. For this assignment, choose an essay, short story, or poem that you like, one that seems harmonious, and address an essay to your instructor in which you discuss three of four of the main kinds of harmony in your selection. Analyze how they work, and evaluate whether the author employed them effectively.

2. Write a dialogue between Forster and Peacock in which you portray them as debating, in front of your class, one of the following topics: "The Relationship Between Art and Social Progress," "The Role of Literary Studies in High School and College Education," or "The Effect on Civilization If All Works of Art Were Suddenly to Disappear."

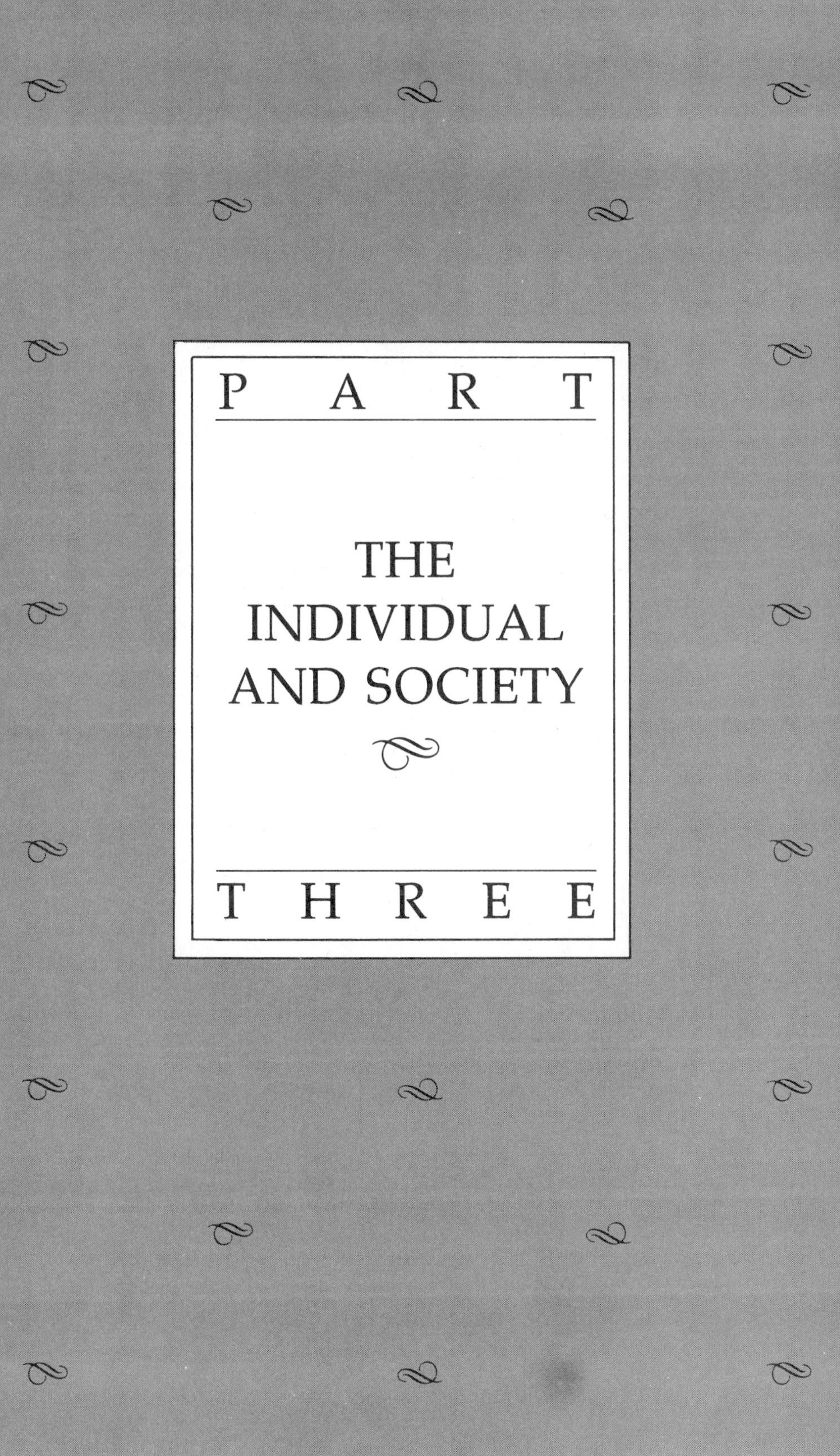

PART THREE

THE INDIVIDUAL AND SOCIETY

5

PERSONAL GOALS

What Should I Become?

Sow an act, and you reap a habit. Sow a habit, and you reap
a character. Sow a character, and you reap a destiny.
Charles Reade

Do not ask for success; success is for swine.
Anonymous

The only infallible criterion of wisdom to vulgar judgments—success.
Edmund Burke

To burn always with this hard, gemlike flame, to maintain
this ecstasy, is success in life.
Walter Pater

What is the chief end of man? To glorify God
and to enjoy him forever.
Shorter Catechism

He that can apprehend and consider vice with all her baits
and seeming pleasures, and yet abstain, and yet distinguish, and yet prefer
that which is truly better, he is the true wayfaring Christian.
I cannot praise a fugitive and cloistered virtue,
unexercised and unbreathed, that never sallies out and
sees her adversary, but slinks out of the race, where that immortal garland
is to be run for, not without dust and heat.
Assuredly we bring not innocence into the world, we bring
impurity much rather: that which purifies us is trial,
and trial is by what is contrary.
John Milton

That action is best, which procures the greatest happiness for
the greatest number.
Francis Hutcheson
(followed by many later utilitarians)

Phyllis Rose

This chapter focuses on personal goals: not simply on what we want out of life, *but on what we want to make out of* ourselves. *We are all prone to carry on internal conversations such as, "If I do X, which I already know is the* right *thing to do, how will others see me? Will they understand me, how will they judge me? If I don't do X because I fear being misunderstood or disliked, how will I live with myself? What kind of person will I have become then?"*

Asking such questions can underscore for us all just how vulnerable the self can sometimes feel. Don't we all share a certain shrinking when we anticipate criticism or rejection? Don't we all know that sweet flow of energy and jubilation when we have just received assurance that we, our precious selves, are indeed admired or loved? In an insightful essay, Phyllis Rose (b. 1942) takes note of these two poles and describes a typical human movement: the pendulum swing we all make between self-love and self-loathing or, in the jargon of the day, between being "up" about ourselves and being "down" about ourselves.

In the best tradition of the comic essay that makes a serious point while being funny, Rose shows that she knows us, that she knows how we all go up and down in our self-esteem. But of course she could know such a private thing about us only if in fact it is both private and universal. Rose knows us because in this respect she is *us. She knows that we are all heirs to the human capacity for despair and hope, joy and sorrow.*

So what do we make of our swings? Is this simply the way it is? Does self-consciousness doom us to eternal pendulum swings of feeling? Perhaps, but are we really helpless? Wouldn't things be better if we were more in control? Wouldn't life have been better even for the successful George Eliot referred to in Rose's essay if she hadn't had to spend so much emotion worrying about whether she was a noodle? Wouldn't Rose like to give up those days when she feels like an impostor? And wouldn't we all like to turn our paralyzing fears into liberating energies?

Rose's examples offer us suggestions—no recipes, but suggestions—for liberating ourselves. That the successful people of the world share our fears about achievement and self-worth suggests that we may be wrong to take it all so seriously, to take every occasion of self-loathing as if it were The End. Can we infer from Rose's examples that we take ourselves too seriously most of the time, whether we're feeling up or *down? If so, those life-or-death dramas when we feel like failures or frauds may be nothing but our own emotional hype. Knowing this might lower some of our soaring highs, but it might also take some of the depths out of our sagging lows. We might just discover that life doesn't have to be a constant switch between Ferris wheel heights and roller coaster plunges. In any event, Rose's fine essay invites us to take a hard look at the various selves we create inside.*

HEROIC FANTASIES, NERVOUS DOUBTS

From the *New York Times* "Hers" column (March 22, 1984).

Recently a young man presented a bouquet to the secretary of the English department. She was astounded. "But I don't even know you!" she said. He quickly explained that he was just the florist's messenger; the card would tell her who had sent the flowers. They came, as it happened, from a grateful professor. But what strikes me is that for a split second she thought a complete stranger was offering her flowers, and although this surprised her it was not inconceivable. 1

Why should it be? Don't we all harbor fantasies of a brass band's arriving at our door one day to play in our honor? Of Warren Beatty's standing on our front step with a red ribbon around his neck? I know I do. Like gold coins in a garbage dump, sprinkled here and there in the midst of our self-distrust are these glittering visions of our worth and importance. We may suspect during many waking hours that we have no worth or importance and at the same time hope that the world, perhaps in the form of a young man bearing flowers, will one day pay them tribute. 2

Such fantasies seem to me entirely healthy, as bankable as my metaphorical gold coins. Sometimes they are linked to myths we hold about our lives. Everyone, for example, has a story about his or her birth. I have always been told and believed that I was born in Doctors Hospital with the fleet massing in the East River beneath my mother's window for the invasion of North Africa. Was the fleet really massing in the East River for the invasion of North Africa? An easy question to answer for certain, but I never will, for the facts in this case, as in many others, are less important to me than their significance, the myth. 3

Some part of me thinks—has always thought—that the invasion of North Africa was an elegant pretext, a cover story, an excuse. World War II or no, the fleet would have been there festively "massing"—I imagine this to consist of a lot of nuzzling between ships and blowing of horns—in honor of my birth. The fleet massed for me the way the fairies gathered for the birth 4 of Sleeping Beauty. The fleet bestowed blessings on me and wished me well in life. On successive birthdays I have waited for the fleet, in some form, to return. It never does. Nevertheless, whatever is strong in my ego may be said to be strong because I believe that the fleet massed below my mother's window on the day of my birth.

The expectation that the world will congratulate us for living tends to 5
focus on birthdays, and usually what happens on birthdays is nothing. I'm speaking of adults. Indeed, that's one way you can tell when you're grown up: nothing happens on your birthday. I knew I was grown up when I turned 38 and even my mother forgot my birthday. I was so depressed after looking through the mail that I went back to bed. My son, then 8, found me there, the shades drawn on a bright Saturday afternoon. I disclosed the problem. "Don't move," he said. "I'll be right back." Half an hour later he returned and thrust something large at me in a brown paper bag. "You don't have to use these," he said, "but I want you to have them." He had grabbed all his capital—$2—had gone to the nearest store and had bought the biggest thing he could get for his money: a five-pound bag of potatoes. Now I have a special place in my heart for potatoes. Still, it's not the fleet or a brass band or Warren Beatty.

The average person's mixture of arrogance and self-loathing, of daring 6
and fear, never ceases to amaze me. We want to bring down the house. We want the house to stand, protecting us. We want to be invulnerable through strength. We want to be invulnerable because there's nothing there to hurt. We want to be everything and nothing. I sometimes believe I am the prize package my kindly parents always told me I was. But just as often getting out of bed in the morning seems a plucky thing to do. (At such moments of existential panic,* I find enormously helpful the phrase "another day, another dollar," which takes this risky business of getting out of bed away from metaphysics and into the realm of the practical, where it belongs.)

Often I think I'm the only person for the job, whatever the job may be: 7
cooking pasta al pesto, planning a trip, writing a certain biography. But often I feel like an impostor as writer, teacher, human being. I like attention but I suffer from stage fright. If I had to say what it is I'm afraid of, I guess it's that my self won't be there when I need it. I'm afraid people will see through me and find there's nothing there.

I once appeared on a TV talk show with Joey Skaggs, the artist who 8
specializes in putting things over on people. For example, he will announce that he intends to windsurf from Hawaii to California or that, as king of the gypsies, he is calling for a work stoppage of gypsies to protest the term gypsy moth. People believe him, and that constitutes the work of art. He is a media artist, a public-relations artist. I like his work and envy his talent. Before the

*The existential philosophers who were influential in the post–World War II period were given to insisting that human beings had to *assert* their personal worth in the face of a meaningless universe. Rose is joking on how panicky that act of self-assertion can make her.

TV show we chatted. He showed me his clippings, an enormous scrapbook full of them. Worried that I would be found invisible when I appeared on TV, I could not bring myself to look at this massive evidence of Joey Skaggs's reality. I guess he thought I was bored by it or contemptuous. "It's hard to take in all at once," he said. I told him that wasn't the problem. "It makes me feel like nothing by comparison," I said. Joey, a nice man, conned me into comfort. "Believe me," he said, waving his hand to take in the studio and his clipping book, "it's all this that's nothing."

I used to think these problems of self-esteem were peculiarly female. 9
Now I'm not sure. When I began teaching 14 years ago I was convinced that establishing authority in the classroom was more of a problem for me than for my male colleagues. Before the start of each semester I had terrible anxiety dreams: I would go to composition class prepared to teach Shakespeare or vice versa, I would suddenly be called upon to lecture on the history of Japanese theater or to announce the Harvard-Yale game, I would forget to show up for the first class or I would show up naked. That dream in particular seemed to me a woman's dream. Women are not bred to authority, I thought. If I set myself up as an authority, people will see I'm a fraud.

At this time, the early 70's, I found myself at a New Haven dinner party 10
seated next to a Yale geologist who was about to retire after a long and distinguished teaching career. Professor Flint told me that there were many things he would miss about teaching but one thing he would not miss: the nightmares he had at the start of every semester in which he presented himself at the podium for the first lecture and discovered he was naked.

Perhaps we should all have tapes of loved ones telling us the stories of 11
our lives in mythic form—how the fleet massed and so on—just as Olympic athletes have think-positive tapes prescribed by their sports psychologists. Few of us need tapes to remind us how insignificant we are. The anxieties speak for themselves. There was a Roman emperor who had a slave at his side all the time to remind him he was mortal. But probably more of us are like George Eliot,* who, according to her companion, needed a slave at her side constantly whispering, "You are not a noodle."

Questions for Discussion

1. Most people have both anxiety dreams and wish-fulfillment dreams. Without getting embarrassingly personal, can you and your classmates share some of these dreams? Is there a great deal of similarity among them?

*George Eliot, the pseudonym of Mary Ann Evans (1819–1880), one of the most successful and critically acclaimed novelists of the nineteenth century. Her novels include *Adam Bede* (1859) and *Middlemarch* (1871–1872).

If not, does this suggest that we are more different in this respect than the introduction and Rose's essay suggests? If they are similar, does this corroborate the suggestion than we are all pretty much alike in this respect regardless of past successes?

2. In how many places and in how many different forms do you find the swing from self-love to self-loathing recorded? Do the lyrics to some songs, for example, express the former, while the lyrics to others express inner doubts and fears? Can you give examples? What about characters on TV programs and in the movies? What about characters in drama? Hamlet, for example—if we take his soliloquies to express private thought—goes up and down in his own self-estimation much more than anyone else in the play knows. Do you find Hamlet's pattern repeated in other characters in other plays? At a quite different literary level, what about cartoons? Garfield the cat seems the epitome of arrogant self-confidence, but when he gets down on himself about his weight, he becomes another cat altogether. What other instances of our preoccupation with how we feel about ourselves can you cite from the culture around you?
3. How many people do you know who do not seem ever to need the slave whispering, "You are not a noodle," but who in fact could sometimes use another slave to whisper, "You are overbearing, egotistical, and obnoxious"? Do you think these people have their own moments of barren self-confidence, or are there a few of us who never lose our grip on who we want to be? If the latter, what we have said so far is wrong; self-doubt is only widespread but not really universal. What is your opinion? Can you support it with examples?

Suggested Essay Topics

1. St. Paul's definition of love (p. 344) suggests that the self finds its most complete fulfillment not in taking in assurance and affection but in passing these on to others. If you have ever been the recipient of a gift of love when you felt that you needed it most, when you were feeling like a barren thing, your own worst self, give an account of the experience—why you needed it, how the gift was given, the effects it worked—addressed to your classmates as an example of the kind of help we may be to one another in times of stress or trouble.
2. If you have ever given such a gift as described in topic 1, give an account of what motivated you, how you knew the gift was needed, what it cost you, and the effects it had—not to pat yourself on the back as a good person but to record what you learned or how you grew.

Plato

One of Plato's (c. 427–347 B.C.) best-loved and most frequently read works is the Symposium. *It remains interesting because of the timelessness of its topic—the importance of love—but that alone does not adequately account for why it has outlasted thousands of other works on the same topic. As with much of the world's greatest writing, the attraction probably lies in its combination of wisdom and liveliness. It is not a dry, academic lecture, a moralizing sermon, or a thorny logical proof. It is instead a conversation—one of the wisest and wittiest ever recorded (or invented—no one knows just how much of it actually happened).*

The conversationalists are friends—many of them have shared such conversations before—and they are having a celebration supper in honor of Agathon, who has just won the prize for tragedy with his very first entry in the annual festival in Athens. Although this is the second straight evening of celebration, everyone is exceptionally jovial and talkative.

The talkers agree that each member of the party must make a speech in honor of love. Their joking mood is clearly revealed when Aristophanes complains that he cannot give his speech because he has the hiccoughs. His friend Eryximachus (pronounced erik-sím-i-kus), a physician, playfully gives him some remedies (including self-induced sneezing) and delivers his speech in Aristophanes' place.

At the point where our selection picks up the conversation, Eryximachus has just finished stressing that love is a harmony of opposites and is returning the floor to Aristophanes, who has bested his hiccoughs. Aristophanes, a great comic writer and wit (see an encyclopedia for further information), begins by taking a dig at Eryximachus' idea of harmony and uses the laughter following his joke as a platform for plunging into his own speech, a comic myth explaining the origin of love.

Because terms such as alienation, anxiety, fragmentation, *and* dehumanization *dominate modern discussions of personality, one might conclude that the problem of divided selfhood is a peculiarly modern discovery. It is not. Aristophanes not only recognizes divided selfhood as a problem but proposes to explain it. In his myth, love is a primeval impulse residing deep in the fiber of human nature: We all seek to complete our private sense of selfhood by finding the right person to share it with. The great insight here is that a separate person is only half a person and that we all depend for our wholeness on a love that takes us beyond our "selves" to a larger self. Love cannot be satisfied by resting upon the "self" alone, and a private existence will remain miserable until it finds its completion in love.*

ARISTOPHANES' MYTH OF DIVIDED LOVES

Our title for this portion of the *Symposium.*

[Eryximachus:] I dare say that I, too, have omitted much that might be said 1
in praise of Love, but this was not intentional, and you, Aristophanes, may

now supply the omission or take some other line of commendation; for I perceive that you are rid of the hiccough.

Yes, said Aristophanes, who followed, the hiccough is gone; not, how- 2
ever, until I applied the sneezing; and I wonder whether the orderly system of the body has a love of such noises and ticklings, for I no sooner applied the sneezing than I was cured.

Eryximachus said: Beware, friend Aristophanes; although you are going 3
to speak, you are making fun of me; and I shall have to watch and see whether I cannot have a laugh at your expense, when you might speak in peace.

You are quite right, said Aristophanes, laughing, and I unsay my words. 4
But do you please not to watch me, as I fear that in the speech which I am about to make, instead of others laughing with me, which is the natural work of our muse and would be satisfactory, I shall only be laughed at by them.

Do you expect to shoot your bolt and escape, Aristophanes? Well, 5
perhaps if you are very careful and bear in mind that you will be called to account, I may be induced to let you off.

Aristophanes professed to open another vein of discourse; he had a 6
mind to praise Love in another way, unlike that of either Pausanias or Eryximachus. Mankind, he said, judging by their neglect of him, have never, as I think, at all understood the power of Love. For if they had understood him they would surely have built noble temples and altars, and offered solemn sacrifices in his honour; but this is not done, and most certainly ought to be done: since of all the gods he is the best friend of men, the helper and the healer of the ills which are the great impediment to the happiness of the race. I will try to describe his power to you, and you shall teach the rest of the world what I am teaching you. In the first place, let me treat of the nature of man and what has happened to it. The original human nature was not like the present, but different. The sexes were not two as they are now, but originally three in number; there was man, woman, and the union of the two, of which the name survives but nothing else. Once it was a distinct kind, with a bodily shape and a name of its own, constituted by the union of the male and the female: but now only the word "androgynous" is preserved, and that as a term of reproach. In the second place, the primeval man was round, his back and sides forming a circle; and he had four hands and the same number of feet, one head with two faces, looking opposite ways, set on a round neck and precisely alike; also four ears, two privy members, and the remainder to correspond. He could walk upright as men now do, backwards or forwards as he pleased, and he could also roll over and over at a great pace, turning on his four hands and four feet, eight in all, like tumblers going over and over with their legs in the air; this was when he wanted to run fast. Now the sexes were three, and such as I have described them; because the sun, moon, and earth are three; and the man was originally the child of the sun, the woman of the earth, and the man-woman of the moon, which is made up of sun and earth, and they were all round and moved round and round because they resembled their parents. Terrible was their might and strength, and the

thoughts of their hearts were great, and they made an attack upon the gods; of them is told the tale of Otys and Ephialtes* who, as Homer says, attempted to scale heaven, and would have laid hands upon the gods. Doubt reigned in the celestial councils. Should they kill them and annihilate the race with thunderbolts, as they had done the giants, then there would be an end of the sacrifices and worship which men offered to them; but, on the other hand, the gods could not suffer their insolence to be unrestrained.

At last, after a good deal of reflection, Zeus discovered a way. He said: 7
"Methinks I have a plan which will enfeeble their strength and so extinguish their turbulence; men shall continue to exist, but I will cut them in two and then they will be diminished in strength and increased in numbers; this will have the advantage of making them more profitable to us. They shall walk upright on two legs, and if they continue insolent and will not be quiet, I will split them again and they shall hop about on a single leg." He spoke and cut men in two, like a sorb-apple which is halved for pickling, or as you might divide an egg with a hair; and as he cut them one after another, he bade Apollo give the face and the half of the neck a turn in order that man might contemplate the section of himself: he would thus learn a lesson of humility. Apollo was also bidden to heal their wounds and compose their forms. So he gave a turn to the face and pulled the skin from the sides all over that which in our language is called the belly, like the purses which draw tight, and he made one mouth at the centre, which he fastened in a knot (the same which is called the navel); he also moulded the breast and took out most of the wrinkles, much as a shoemaker might smooth leather upon a last; he left a few, however, in the region of the belly and navel, as a memorial of the primeval state. After the division the two parts of man, each desiring his other half, came together, and throwing their arms about one another, entwined in mutual embraces, longing to grow into one, they began to die from hunger and self-neglect, because they did not like to do anything apart; and when one of the halves died and the other survived, the survivor sought another mate, man or woman as we call them,—being the sections of entire men or women,—and clung to that. Thus they were being destroyed, when Zeus in pity invented a new plan: he turned the parts of generation round to the front, for this had not been always their position, and they sowed the seed no longer as hitherto like grasshoppers in the ground, but in one another; and after the transposition the male generated in the female in order that by the mutual embraces of man and woman they might breed, and the race might continue; or if man came to man they might be satisfied, and rest, and go their ways to the business of life. So ancient is the desire of one another which is implanted in us, reuniting our original nature, seeking to make one of two, and to heal the state of man.

*In Greek mythology, Otys and Ephialtes were the giants who tried to attack the gods on Mount Olympus by stacking mountains on top of each other. They were defeated by the intervention of Artemis (Diana).

Each of us when separated, having one side only, like a flat fish, is but 8
the tally-half of a man, and he is always looking for his other half. Men who are a section of that double nature which was once called androgynous are lovers of women; adulterers are generally of this breed, and also adulterous women who lust after men. The women who are a section of the woman do not care for men, but have female attachments; the female companions are of this sort. But they who are a section of the male follow the male, and while they are young, being slices of the original man, they have affection for men and embrace them, and these are the best of boys and youths, because they have the most manly nature. Some indeed assert that they are shameless, but this is not true; for they do not act thus from any want of shame, but because they are valiant and manly, and have a manly countenance, and they embrace that which is like them. And these when they grow up become our statesmen, and these only, which is a great proof of the truth of what I am saying. When they reach manhood they are lovers of youth, and are not naturally inclined to marry or beget children,—if at all, they do so only in obedience to custom; but they are satisfied if they may be allowed to live with one another unwedded; and such a nature is prone to love and ready to return love, always embracing that which is akin to him. And when one of them meets with his other half, the actual half of himself, whether he be a lover of youth or a lover of another sort, the pair are lost in an amazement of love and friendship and intimacy, and one will not be out of the other's sight, as I may say, even for a moment: these are the people who pass their whole lives together, and yet they could not explain what they desire of one another. For the intense yearning which each of them has towards the other does not appear to be the desire of lover's intercourse, but of something else which the soul of either evidently desires and cannot tell, and of which she has only a dark and doubtful presentiment. Suppose Hephaestus,* with his instruments, to come to the pair who are lying side by side and to say to them, "What do you mortals want of one another?" they would be unable to explain. And suppose further, that when he saw their perplexity he said: "Do you desire to be wholly one; always day and night in one another's company? for if this is what you desire, I am ready to melt and fuse you together, so that being two you shall become one, and while you live live a common life as if you were a single man, and after your death in the world below still be one departed soul, instead of two—I ask whether this is what you lovingly desire and whether you are satisfied to attain this?"—there is not a man of them who when he heard the proposal would deny or would not acknowledge that this meeting and melting into one another, this becoming one instead of two, was the very expression of his ancient need. And the reason is that human nature was originally one and we were a whole, and the desire and pursuit of the whole is called love. There was a time, I say, when we were one, but now because of the wickedness of mankind God has dispersed us, as the Arcadians

*Hephaestus (Vulcan) was the son of Zeus and the blacksmith, artisan, and armorer of the Olympian gods.

were dispersed into villages by the Lacedaemonians. And if we are not obedient to the gods, there is a danger that we shall be split up again and go about in basso-relievo, like the profile figures showing only one half the nose which are sculptured on monuments, and that we shall be like tallies.

Wherefore let us exhort all men to piety in all things, that we may avoid 9
evil and obtain the good, taking Love for our leader and commander. Let no one oppose him—he is the enemy of the gods who opposes him. For if we are friends of God and at peace with him we shall find our own true loves, which rarely happens in this world at present. I am serious, and therefore I must beg Eryximachus not to make fun or to find any allusion in what I am saying to Pausanias and Agathon, who, as I suspect, are both of the manly nature, and belong to the class which I have been describing. But my words have a wider application—they include men and women everywhere; and I believe that if our loves were perfectly accomplished, and each one returning to his primeval nature had his original true love, then our race would be happy. And if this would be best of all, the best in the next degree must in present circumstances be the nearest approach to such a union; and that will be the attainment of a congenial love. Wherefore, if we would praise him who has given to us the benefit, we must praise the god Love, who is our greatest benefactor, both leading us in this life back to our own nature, and giving us high hopes for the future, for he promises that if we are pious, he will restore us to our original state, and heal us and make us happy and blessed. This, Eryximachus, is my discourse of love, which, although different to yours, I must beg you to leave unassailed by the shafts of your ridicule, in order that each may have his turn; each, or rather either, for Agathon and Socrates are the only ones left.

Questions for Discussion

1. In what ways does Aristophanes' account of human existence "before the split" parallel the biblical account of human existence "before the Fall"? Do the two stories explain any of the same features of human nature or conduct? Do you know any non-Western stories that parallel Plato's myth or the Judeo-Christian story?
2. Explain in your own words the three sexes that existed before Zeus's punishment.
3. Explain the sexual preferences of the three sexes after the split. What seems to be Aristophanes' view of homosexuality? How does it compare to modern views?
4. Is the image of human beings who are literally split in half an effective device for explaining psychological or emotional divisions?

Suggested Essay Topics

1. Write a speech to be delivered immediately after Aristophanes', agreeing or disagreeing with him. If you like his account, explain why you think it goes to the heart of the matter. If you dislike it, explain what important factors he has failed to notice.
2. Direct an essay to the members of your class supporting or attacking Aristophanes' view that homosexuality is an acceptable, even normal sexual preference. Show how society's general rejection of homosexuality is either right or wrong and how it is either good or bad for both those who favor and those who oppose homosexuality.

Margaret Sanger

Margaret Sanger (1883–1966) was the earliest influential advocate for the spread of birth-control information in America. In 1921, working against intense opposition, she organized the first American birth-control conference, and she continued to write books and publish magazines on the subject over several decades. In this essay Sanger recounts the episodes that led up to the crucial moment when she made her lifelong commitment to the cause of birth-control education.

As Sanger makes her way steadily toward the greatest decision of her life, she makes the reader aware of all that she will have to fight against in forging an unconventional path, especially difficult for a woman in her era. She will have to fight to reduce her own ignorance, fight the taboo against speaking out on sexual matters, fight against religious opposition, and, finally, fight against those who would dismiss her as an unfeminine radical at best, a meddling crackpot at worst.

Notice how the issue that was to dominate Sanger's life does not gain sharp focus until she becomes acquainted with the poor, who suffered most from excessive childbearing. Once she starts working among them, she learns to see them not as statistics or generalized "unfortunates" but as individuals (¶15). We can almost always endure reports of the catastrophes of anonymous masses with less discomfort than we can the minor troubles of people whom we know as individuals. Our sympathies are always more quickly awakened and brought into play by concrete images than by vague abstractions. Sanger is presumably aware of this tendency in her readers as she works to portray the suffering poor as vividly as possible without lapsing into lurid or implausible melodrama.

THE TURBID EBB AND FLOW OF MISERY

Chapter 7 of *An Autobiography* (1938). Sanger has taken her chapter title from a line in Matthew Arnold's poem "Dover Beach."

> Every night and every morn
> Some to misery are born.
> Every morn and every night
> Some are born to sweet delight.
> Some are born to sweet delight,
> Some are born to endless night.
> WILLIAM BLAKE

During these years [about 1912] in New York trained nurses were in great demand. Few people wanted to enter hospitals; they were afraid they might be "practiced" upon, and consented to go only in desperate emergencies. Sentiment was especially vehement in the matter of having babies. A woman's own bedroom, no matter how inconveniently arranged, was the usual place for her lying-in. I was not sufficiently free from domestic duties to be a general nurse, but I could ordinarily manage obstetrical cases because I was notified far enough ahead to plan my schedule. And after serving my two weeks I could get home again. 1

Sometimes I was summoned to small apartments occupied by young clerks, insurance salesmen, or lawyers, just starting out, most of them under thirty and whose wives were having their first or second baby. They were always eager to know the best and latest method in infant care and feeding. In particular, Jewish patients, whose lives centered around the family, welcomed advice and followed it implicitly. 2

But more and more my calls began to come from the Lower East Side, as though I were being magnetically drawn there by some force outside my control. I hated the wretchedness and hopelessness of the poor, and never experienced that satisfaction in working among them that so many noble women have found. My concern for my patients was now quite different from my earlier hospital attitude. I could see that much was wrong with them which did not appear in the physiological or medical diagnosis. A woman in childbirth was not merely a woman in childbirth. My expanded outlook included a view of her background, her potentialities as a human being, the kind of children she was bearing, and what was going to happen to them. 3

The wives of small shopkeepers were my most frequent cases, but I had carpenters, truck drivers, dishwashers, and pushcart vendors. I admired intensely the consideration most of these people had for their own. Money to pay doctor and nurse had been carefully saved months in advance—parents-in-law, grandfathers, grandmothers, all contributing. 4

As soon as the neighbors learned that a nurse was in the building they came in a friendly way to visit, often carrying fruit, jellies, or gefüllter fish made after a cherished recipe. It was infinitely pathetic to me that they, so 5 poor themselves, should bring me food. Later they drifted in again with the excuse of getting the plate, and sat down for a nice talk; there was no hurry. Always back of the little gift was the question, "I am pregnant (or my daughter, or my sister is). Tell me something to keep from having another baby. We cannot afford another yet."

I tried to explain the only two methods I had ever heard of among the middle classes, both of which were invariably brushed aside as unacceptable. They were of no certain avail to the wife because they placed the burden of responsibility solely upon the husband—a burden which he seldom assumed. What she was seeking was self-protection she could herself use, and there was none. 6

Below this stratum of society was one in truly desperate circumstances. The men were sullen and unskilled, picking up odd jobs now and then, but more often unemployed, lounging in and out of the house at all hours of the day and night. The women seemed to slink on their way to market and were without neighborliness. 7

These submerged, untouched classes were beyond the scope of organized charity or religion. No labor union, no church, not even the Salvation Army reached them. They were apprehensive of everyone and rejected help of any kind, ordering all intruders to keep out; both birth and death they considered their own business. Social agents, who were just beginning to appear, were profoundly mistrusted because they pried into homes and lives, asking questions about wages, how many were in the family, had any of them ever been in jail. Often two or three had been there or were now under suspicion of prostitution, shoplifting, purse snatching, petty thievery, and, in consequence, passed furtively by the big blue uniforms on the corner. 8

The utmost depression came over me as I approached this surreptitious region. Below Fourteenth Street I seemed to be breathing a different air, to be in another world and country where the people had habits and customs alien to anything I had ever heard about. 9

There were then approximately ten thousand apartments in New York into which no sun ray penetrated directly; such windows as they had opened only on a narrow court from which rose fetid odors. It was seldom cleaned, though garbage and refuse often went down into it. All these dwellings were pervaded by the foul breath of poverty, that moldy, indefinable, indescribable smell which cannot be fumigated out, sickening to me but apparently unnoticed by those who lived there. When I set to work with antiseptics, their pungent sting, at least temporarily, obscured the stench. 10

I remember one confinement case to which I was called by the doctor of an insurance company. I climbed up the five flights and entered the airless rooms, but the baby had come with too great speed. A boy of ten had been the only assistant. Five flights was a long way; he had wrapped the placenta in a piece of newspaper and dropped it out the window into the court. 11

Many families took in "boarders," as they were termed, whose small contributions paid the rent. These derelicts, wanderers, alternately working and drinking, were crowded in with the children; a single room sometimes 12 held as many as six sleepers. Little girls were accustomed to dressing and undressing in front of the men, and were often violated, occasionally by their own fathers or brothers, before they reached the age of puberty.

Pregnancy was a chronic condition among the women of this class. 13
Suggestions as to what to do for a girl who was "in trouble" or a married woman who was "caught" passed from mouth to mouth—herb teas, turpentine, steaming, rolling downstairs, inserting slippery elm, knitting needles, shoe-hooks. When they had word of a new remedy they hurried to the drugstore, and if the clerk were inclined to be friendly he might say, "Oh, that won't help you, but here's something that may." The younger druggists usually refused to give advice because, if it were to be known, they would come under the law; midwives were even more fearful. The doomed women implored me to reveal the "secret" rich people had, offering to pay me extra to tell them; many really believed I was holding back information for money. They asked everybody and tried anything, but nothing did them any good. On Saturday nights I have seen groups of from fifty to one hundred with their shawls over their heads waiting outside the office of a five-dollar abortionist.

Each time I returned to this district, which was becoming a recurrent 14
nightmare, I used to hear that Mrs. Cohen "had been carried to a hospital, but had never come back," or that Mrs. Kelly "had sent the children to a neighbor and had put her head into the gas oven." Day after day such tales were poured into my ears—a baby born dead, great relief—the death of an older child, sorrow but again relief of a sort—the story told a thousand times of death from abortion and children going into institutions. I shuddered with horror as I listened to the details and studied the reasons back of them—destitution linked with excessive childbearing. The waste of life seemed utterly senseless. One by one worried, sad, pensive, and aging faces marshaled themselves before me in my dreams, sometimes appealingly, sometimes accusingly.

These were not merely "unfortunate conditions among the poor" such 15
as we read about. I knew the women personally. They were living, breathing, human beings, with hopes, fears, and aspirations like my own, yet their weary, misshapen bodies, "always ailing, never failing," were destined to be thrown on the scrap heap before they were thirty-five. I could not escape from the facts of their wretchedness; neither was I able to see any way out. My own cozy and comfortable family existence was becoming a reproach to me.

Then one stifling mid-July day of 1912 I was summoned to a Grand 16
Street tenement. My patient was a small, slight Russian Jewess, about twenty-eight years old, of the special cast of feature to which suffering lends a madonna-like expression. The cramped three-room apartment was in a sorry state of turmoil. Jake Sachs, a truck driver scarcely older than his wife, had come home to find the three children crying and her unconscious from the effects of a self-induced abortion. He had called the nearest doctor, who in turn had sent for me. Jake's earnings were trifling, and most of them had gone to keep the none-too-strong children clean and properly fed. But his

wife's ingenuity had helped them to save a little, and this he was glad to spend on a nurse rather than have her go to a hospital.

The doctor and I settled ourselves to the task of fighting the septicemia. 17
Never had I worked so fast, never so concentratedly. The sultry days and nights were melted into a torpid inferno. It did not seem possible there could be such heat, and every bit of food, ice, and drugs had to be carried up three flights of stairs.

Jake was more kind and thoughtful than many of the husbands I had 18
encountered. He loved his children, and had always helped his wife wash and dress them. He had brought water up and carried garbage down before he left in the morning, and did as much as he could for me while he anxiously watched her progress.

After a fortnight Mrs. Sachs' recovery was in sight. Neighbors, ordinar- 19
ily fatalistic as to the results of abortion, were genuinely pleased that she had survived. She smiled wanly at all who came to see her and thanked them gently, but she could not respond to their hearty congratulations. She appeared to be more despondent and anxious than she should have been, and spent too much time in meditation.

At the end of three weeks, as I was preparing to leave the fragile patient 20
to take up her difficult life once more, she finally voiced her fears, "Another baby will finish me, I suppose?"

"It's too early to talk about that," I temporized. 21

But when the doctor came to make his last call, I drew him aside. "Mrs. 22
Sachs is terribly worried about having another baby."

"She well may be," replied the doctor, and then he stood before her and 23
said, "Any more such capers, young woman, and there'll be no need to send for me."

"I know, doctor," she replied timidly, "but," and she hesitated as 24
though it took all her courage to say it, "what can I do to prevent it?"

The doctor was a kindly man, and he had worked hard to save her, but 25
such incidents had become so familiar to him that he had long since lost whatever delicacy he might once have had. He laughed good-naturedly. "You want to have your cake and eat it too, do you? Well, it can't be done."

Then picking up his hat and bag to depart he said, "Tell Jake to sleep 26
on the roof."

I glanced quickly at Mrs. Sachs. Even through my sudden tears I could 27
see stamped on her face an expression of absolute despair. We simply looked at each other, saying no word until the door had closed behind the doctor. Then she lifted her thin, blue-veined hands and clasped them beseechingly. "He can't understand. He's only a man. But you do, don't you? Please tell me the secret, and I'll never breathe it to a soul. *Please!*"

What was I to do? I could not speak the conventionally comforting 28
phrases which would be of no comfort. Instead, I made her as physically easy as I could and promised to come back in a few days to talk with her again. A little later, when she slept, I tiptoed away.

Night after night the wistful image of Mrs. Sachs appeared before me. I made all sorts of excuses to myself for not going back. I was busy on other cases; I really did not know what to say to her or how to convince her of my own ignorance; I was helpless to avert such monstrous atrocities. Time rolled by and I did nothing. 29

The telephone rang one evening three months later, and Jake Sachs' agitated voice begged me to come at once; his wife was sick again and from the same cause. For a wild moment I thought of sending someone else, but actually, of course, I hurried into my uniform, caught up my bag, and started out. All the way I longed for a subway wreck, an explosion, anything to keep me from having to enter that home again. But nothing happened, even to delay me. I turned into the dingy doorway and climbed the familiar stairs once more. The children were there, young little things. 30

Mrs. Sachs was in a coma and died within ten minutes. I folded her still hands across her breast, remembering how they had pleaded with me, begging so humbly for the knowledge which was her right. I drew a sheet over her pallid face. Jake was sobbing, running his hands through his hair and pulling it out like an insane person. Over and over again he wailed, "My God! My God! My God!" 31

I left him pacing desperately back and forth, and for hours I myself walked and walked and walked through the hushed streets. When I finally arrived home and let myself quietly in, all the household was sleeping. I looked out my window and down upon the dimly lighted city. Its pains and griefs crowded in upon me, a moving picture rolled before my eyes with photographic clearness: women writhing in travail to bring forth little babies; the babies themselves naked and hungry, wrapped in newspapers to keep them from the cold; six-year-old children with pinched, pale, wrinkled faces, old in concentrated wretchedness, pushed into gray and fetid cellars, crouching on stone floors, their small scrawny hands scuttling through rags, making lamp shades, artificial flowers; white coffins, black coffins, coffins, coffins interminably passing in never-ending succession. The scenes piled one upon another on another. I could bear it no longer. 32

As I stood there the darkness faded. The sun came up and threw its reflection over the house tops. It was the dawn of a new day in my life also. The doubt and questioning, the experimenting and trying, were now to be put behind me. I knew I could not go back merely to keeping people alive. 33

I went to bed, knowing that no matter what it might cost, I was finished with palliatives and superficial cures; I was resolved to seek out the root of evil, to do something to change the destiny of mothers whose miseries were vast as the sky. 34

Questions for Discussion

1. In paragraphs 1–8, Sanger refers to three distinct social levels. What are they? What characterizes each one? How do they differ?
2. Compare Sanger's organization with the cinematographic device of the panorama. Paragraphs 1–15 begin as if from far above the city and the crowd; subsequent paragraphs begin to focus on things in more detail, and they continue to do so with increasing vividness until the Sachses' story begins in paragraph 16. Can you trace the progress of this organization in more detail? What are its effects?
3. In paragraph 25, Sanger gives the doctor on the Sachs case credit for being "a kindly man." Does his response to Mrs. Sachs's plea justify this credit? Can you defend his comments in paragraphs 25–26 in any way?

Suggested Essay Topics

1. Select a moment or an episode in your own life that you now see was decisive in giving you a sense of direction about something specific—for example, whether or not to go to college, to get engaged, to register for the draft, or to stand up for an unpopular cause. In an essay addressed to your fellow students, recount that moment or episode as Sanger does, giving your readers a vivid picture of the buildup of feelings and ideas that led to your decision. (Naturally, you will have to pick a decision that was dramatic and trying for you, not one that you made casually or that someone else made for you.)
2. In an essay directed to the (real or imaginary) school board in your hometown, make an argument recommending or opposing classes on sex education that would include information on contraceptives. Like Sanger, you should use concrete illustrations to buttress your argument (you may make them up, if necessary, but write about them as if they were firsthand observations). You should also make clear, as she does, the principle you are defending or the goal you are pursuing.

John Stuart Mill

In this selection from his Autobiography, *John Stuart Mill (1806–1873) provides a quiet, understated account of a deeply rending experience: a nervous breakdown of near-suicidal proportions. Partly because he recovered to continue an extremely productive life, the record of his breakdown and recovery teaches us something about the resilience of the human spirit and also about its sources of recovery.*

Mill was a prodigy who was pushed by his proud father into almost incredible intellectual feats in early childhood. The father personally conducted young Mill's education with an unrelentingly rigorous hand, turning the small boy into an adult intellect long before he was emotionally ready to handle the demands and responsibilities of his gifts. Young Mill became an adult and a scholar without ever having been a child. He was taught the Greek alphabet at 3 and by age 8 had read a great many books in Greek, including the first six dialogues of Plato. Also in his eighth year he began to learn Latin, Euclid's geometry, and algebra. Curiously, this wide and advanced reading does not show up as a rich source of allusiveness in his later writings, suggesting that he in fact read it too early to digest it. More important than the reading was the constant interaction with his father, who queried him about everything he read and took him on daily walks in which the son would produce notes on slips of paper and give an account of his day's learning. Reading in itself doubtless would have honed a mind like Mill's, but the constant sharpening provided by the tutorial sessions produced one of the keenest analytical minds of the nineteenth century.

But intellectual cultivation made up only half of Mill's training. The other half was moral training. From earliest youth Mill was taught that the one great object of his life was public service: the improvement of the lot of his fellow human beings. Because of the intensity and depth of his early training, he was able to begin his life's work, as he put it, "with an advantage of a quarter of a century" over his contemporaries. This means, to take him literally, that when he was 20 he had attained the intellectual cultivation and breadth of reading of a seasoned scholar of 45. During his teens he had started writing long articles on history and politics for the Westminster Review, *the periodical used by his father and other radical thinkers to disseminate their views to the public.*

But there was a serious omission in Mill's education, a nearly fatal flaw. Although he was given unarguably good (and certainly well-meant) intellectual and moral training, his emotional development was entirely neglected. His education, thorough almost beyond imagining, was bleak and cheerless. His father, the dominant force in both his rearing and his education, was conscientious, rational, and attentive but devoid of humor, fun, or lightheartedness. Perhaps this explains why he saw no need to provide for the cultivation of any of these qualities in his brilliant young son. Thus Mill grew up emotionally stunted. He was not monstrous, perverse, selfish, egotistical, or domineering; he seems in fact to have had a naturally self-effacing and sweet temperament. But he had never had occasion even to discover, much less stretch, his capacity for deep feeling beyond a kind of high-altitude commitment to abstract principles of justice and political reform.

It was only a matter of time before the inevitable happened: The young reasoning machine turned his powerful analytical prowess upon himself. The very first occasion on which this happened provoked a profound crisis. When Mill at 20 suddenly thought to ask himself whether achieving all of his social and political reforms would make him personally happy, he suddenly realized, to employ the kind of language we might use today, that he had been programmed but never really motivated. He had been put together like a sophisticated mechanical toy and wound tight by his father's training, but he had never asked himself whether he would have chosen this life for himself or whether, most devastating of all, he would feel that he had satisfied his own heart's longings if all of his goals were met. He suddenly realized that he had *no heart's longings, and he states the effect of this realization in touchingly simple language, with neither melodrama nor self-pity: "I seemed to have nothing left to live for" (¶1).*

As you read, compare Dickens's description of the stunted emotional life of the young Gradgrind children (pp. 45–57), whose lives are totally governed, as was Mill's, by a well-meaning but dangerously shortsighted and totally cheerless father. Ask yourself whether the educational sins of the present day are like those described by Mill and Dickens or whether they are quite different. How well are students' feelings attended to today? Are youngsters encouraged to discover, expand, and express their emotional lives? If so, is this a good thing? Is the proportion between emotional and intellectual cultivation a healthy one in today's schools?

After you read Mill's criticisms of the educational scheme he was reared under, picture Mill spending several months in a typical American high school or college, observing both the academic work and the social life. Would he think that students cultivated their personal lives and feelings far out of proportion to their cultivation of intellectual discipline? Are modern students lucky not to have to endure the rigor of young Mill's training, or do they lean too far toward emotional fulfillment at the expense of intellectual discipline?

Regardless of how you answer these questions, Mill offers you good reason to think seriously about their importance.

A CRISIS IN MY MENTAL HISTORY

From chapter 5 of *Autobiography* (1873).

From the winter of 1821, when I first read Bentham,* and especially from the commencement of the *Westminster Review,* † I had what might truly be called an object in life; to be a reformer of the world. My conception of my own happiness was entirely identified with this object. The personal sympathies I wished for were those of fellow labourers in this enterprise. I endeavoured to pick up as many flowers as I could by the way; but as a serious and permanent personal satisfaction to rest upon, my whole reliance was placed on this; and I was accustomed to felicitate myself on the certainty of a happy life which I enjoyed, through placing my happiness in something durable and 1

*Jeremy Bentham (1748–1832), British philosopher, founded utilitarianism, a philosophical scheme based on the notion that ideas, institutions, and behavior could all be judged good or bad on the basis of their usefulness. The wider the scope of a thing's utility—"the greatest happiness of the greatest number" being the ultimate standard—the more favorably it was judged. Since the utilitarians, including J. S. Mill and his father, deemed that the ancient system of aristocracy and monarchy inherited from the Middle Ages extended the greatest happiness to the *fewest* number, they all favored sweeping social and political reforms and looked to the American republic under the Constitution as an ideal form of democracy. They were the political radicals of their day.

†The *Westminster Review* was a quarterly periodical founded in 1824 to be the organ of opinion for the radical political thinkers of the day, especially the utilitarians. In his youth, J. S. Mill wrote extensively for the *Westminster* and later became its editor.

distant, in which some progress might be always making, while it could never be exhausted by complete attainment. This did very well for several years, during which the general improvement going on in the world and the idea of myself as engaged with others in struggling to promote it, seemed enough to fill up an interesting and animated existence. But the time came when I awakened from this as from a dream. It was in the autumn of 1826.* I was in a dull state of nerves, such as everybody is occasionally liable to; unsusceptible to enjoyment or pleasurable excitement; one of those moods when what is pleasure at other times, becomes insipid or indifferent; the state, I should think, in which converts to Methodism usually are, when smitten by their first "conviction of sin." In this frame of mind it occurred to me to put the question directly to myself: "Suppose that all your objects in life were realized; that all the changes in institutions and opinions which you are looking forward to, could be completely effected at this very instant: would this be a great joy and happiness to you?" And an irrepressible self-consciousness distinctly answered, "No!" At this my heart sank within me: the whole foundation on which my life was constructed fell down. All my happiness was to have been found in the continual pursuit of this end. The end had ceased to charm, and how could there ever again be any interest in the means? I seemed to have nothing left to live for.

At first I hoped that the cloud would pass away of itself; but it did not. 2
A night's sleep, the sovereign remedy for the smaller vexations of life, had no effect on it. I awoke to a renewed consciousness of the woful fact. I carried it with me into all companies, into all occupations. Hardly anything had power to cause me even a few minutes oblivion of it. For some months the cloud seemed to grow thicker and thicker. The lines in [Samuel Taylor] Coleridge's "Dejection"—I was not then acquainted with them—exactly describe my case:

> A grief without a pang, void, dark and drear,
> A drowsy, stifled, unimpassioned grief,
> Which finds no natural outlet or relief
> In word, or sigh, or tear.

In vain I sought relief from my favourite books; those memorials of past 3
nobleness and greatness from which I had always hitherto drawn strength and animation. I read them now without feeling, or with the accustomed feeling *minus* all its charm; and I became persuaded, that my love of mankind, and of excellence for its own sake, had worn itself out. I sought no comfort by speaking to others of what I felt. If I had loved any one sufficiently to make confiding my griefs a necessity, I should not have been in the condition I was. I felt, too, that mine was not an interesting, or in any way respectable distress. There was nothing in it to attract sympathy. Advice, if I had known where to seek it, would have been most precious. The words of Macbeth to the

*Mill was 20.

physician often occurred to my thoughts.* But there was no one on whom I could build the faintest hope of such assistance. My father, to whom it would have been natural to me to have recourse in any practical difficulties, was the last person to whom, in such a case as this, I looked for help. Everything convinced me that he had no knowledge of any such mental state as I was suffering from, and that even if he could be made to understand it, he was not the physician who could heal it. My education, which was wholly his work, had been conducted without any regard to the possibility of its ending in this result; and I saw no use in giving him the pain of thinking that his plans had failed, when the failure was probably irremediable, and, at all events, beyond the power of *his* remedies. Of other friends, I had at that time none to whom I had any hope of making my condition intelligible. It was however abundantly intelligible to myself; and the more I dwelt upon it, the more hopeless it appeared.

My course of study had led me to believe, that all mental and moral 4
feelings and qualities, whether of a good or of a bad kind, were the results of association;† that we love one thing, and hate another, take pleasure in one sort of action or contemplation, and pain in another sort, through the clinging of pleasurable or painful ideas to those things, from the effect of education or of experience. As a corollary from this, I had always heard it maintained by my father, and was myself convinced, that the object of education should be to form the strongest possible associations of the salutary class; associations of pleasure with all things beneficial to the great whole, and of pain with all things hurtful to it. This doctrine appeared inexpugnable; but it now seemed to me, on retrospect, that my teachers had occupied themselves but superficially with the means of forming and keeping up these salutary associations. They seemed to have trusted altogether to the old familiar instruments, praise and blame, reward and punishment. Now, I did not doubt that by these means, begun early, and applied unremittingly, intense associations of pain and pleasure, especially of pain, might be created, and might produce desires and aversions capable of lasting undiminished to the end of life. But there must always be something artificial and casual in associations thus produced. The pains and pleasures thus forcibly associated with things, are not connected with them by any natural tie; and it is therefore, I thought, essential to the durability of these associations, that they should have become so intense and inveterate as to be practically indissoluble, before the habitual exercise of the power of analysis had commenced. For I now saw, or thought I saw, what I had always before received with incredulity—that the habit of analysis‡ has a tendency to wear away the feelings: as indeed it has, when no other mental habit is cultivated, and the analysing spirit remains without

*"Canst thou not minister to a mind diseas'd?"

†"Associationist psychology" says that we build up our knowledge and our judgment of things by association. Our understanding of new things is colored by two kinds of associations: the way old knowledge is associated with new and whether new knowledge is associated with pain or with pleasure.

‡See "What Is Analysis," pp. 22–24.

its natural complements and correctives. The very excellence of analysis (I argued) is that it tends to weaken and undermine whatever is the result of prejudice; that it enables us mentally to separate ideas which have only casually clung together: and no associations whatever could ultimately resist this dissolving force, were it not that we owe to analysis our clearest knowledge of the permanent sequences in nature; the real connexions between Things, not dependent on our will and feelings; natural laws, by virtue of which, in many cases, one thing is inseparable from another in fact; which laws, in proportion as they are clearly perceived and imaginatively realized, cause our ideas of things which are always joined together in Nature, to cohere more and more closely in our thoughts. Analytic habits may thus even strengthen the associations between causes and effects, means and ends, but tend altogether to weaken those which are, to speak familiarly, a *mere* matter of feeling. They are therefore (I thought) favourable to prudence and clear-sightedness, but a perpetual worm at the root both of the passions and of the virtues; and, above all, fearfully undermine all desires, and all pleasures, which are the effects of association, that is, according to the theory I held, all except the purely physical and organic; of the entire insufficiency of which to make life desirable, no one had a stronger conviction than I had. These were the laws of human nature, by which, as it seemed to me, I had been brought to my present state. All those to whom I looked up, were of opinion that the pleasure of sympathy with human beings, and the feelings which made the good of others, and especially of mankind on a large scale, the object of existence, were the greatest and surest sources of happiness. Of the truth of this I was convinced, but to know that a feeling would make me happy if I had it, did not give me the feeling. My education, I thought, had failed to create these feelings in sufficient strength to resist the dissolving influence of analysis, while the whole course of my intellectual cultivation had made precocious and premature analysis the inveterate habit of my mind. I was thus, as I said to myself, left stranded at the commencement of my voyage, with a well-equipped ship and a rudder, but no sail; without any real desire for the ends which I had been so carefully fitted out to work for: no delight in virtue, or the general good, but also just as little in anything else. The fountains of vanity and ambition seemed to have dried up within me, as completely as those of benevolence. I had had (as I reflected) some gratification of vanity at too early an age: I had obtained some distinction, and felt myself of some importance, before the desire of distinction and of importance had grown into a passion: and little as it was which I had attained, yet having been attained too early, like all pleasures enjoyed too soon, it had made me *blasé* and indifferent to the pursuit. Thus neither selfish nor unselfish pleasures were pleasures to me. And there seemed no power in nature sufficient to begin the formation of my character anew, and create in a mind now irretrievably analytic, fresh associations of pleasure with any of the objects of human desire.

These were the thoughts which mingled with the dry heavy dejection 5
of the melancholy winter of 1826–7. During this time I was not incapable of

my usual occupations. I went on with them mechanically, by the mere force of habit. I had been so drilled in a certain sort of mental exercise, that I could still carry it on when all the spirit had gone out of it. I even composed and spoke several speeches at the debating society, how, or with what degree of success, I know not. Of four years continual speaking at that society, this is the only year of which I remember next to nothing. Two lines of Coleridge, in whom alone of all writers I have found a true description of what I felt, were often in my thoughts, not at this time (for I had never read them), but in a later period of the same mental malady:

> Work without hope draws nectar in a sieve,
> And hope without an object cannot live.*

In all probability my case was by no means so peculiar as I fancied it, and I doubt not that many others have passed through a similar state; but the idiosyncrasies of my education had given to the general phenomenon a special character, which made it seem the natural effect of causes that it was hardly possible for time to remove. I frequently asked myself, if I could, or if I was bound to go on living, when life must be passed in this manner. I generally answered to myself, that I did not think I could possibly bear it beyond a year. When, however, not more than half that duration of time had elapsed, a small ray of light broke in upon my gloom. I was reading, accidentally, [J. F.] Marmontel's† "Mémoires," and came to the passage which relates his father's death, the distressed position of the family, and the sudden inspiration by which he, then a mere boy, felt and made them feel that he would be everything to them—would supply the place of all that they had lost. A vivid conception of the scene and its feelings came over me, and I was moved to tears. From this moment my burthen grew lighter. The oppression of the thought that all feeling was dead within me, was gone. I was no longer hopeless: I was not a stock or a stone. I had still, it seemed, some of the material out of which all worth of character, and all capacity for happiness, are made. Relieved from my ever present sense of irremediable wretchedness, I gradually found that the ordinary incidents of life could again give me some pleasure; that I could again find enjoyment, not intense, but sufficient for cheerfulness, in sunshine and sky, in books, in conversation, in public affairs; and that there was, once more, excitement, though of a moderate kind, in exerting myself for my opinions, and for the public good. Thus the cloud gradually drew off, and I again enjoyed life: and though I had several relapses, some of which lasted many months, I never again was as miserable as I had been.

The experiences of this period had two very marked effects on my 6

*Coleridge, "Work Without Hope."

†Jean-François Marmontel (1723–1799), French writer, author of tragedies, philosophical romances, and librettos for several light operas.

opinions and character. In the first place, they led me to adopt a theory of life, very unlike that on which I had before acted, and having much in common with what at that time I certainly had never heard of, the anti-self-consciousness theory of Carlyle.* I never, indeed, wavered in the conviction that happiness is the test of all rules of conduct, and the end of life. But I now thought that this end was only to be attained by not making it the direct end. Those only are happy (I thought) who have their minds fixed on some object other than their own happiness; on the happiness of others, on the improvement of mankind, even on some art or pursuit, followed not as a means, but as itself an ideal end. Aiming thus at something else, they find happiness by the way.† The enjoyments of life (such was now my theory) are sufficient to make it a pleasant thing, when they are taken *en passant,* without being made a principal object. Once make them so, and they are immediately felt to be insufficient. They will not bear a scrutinizing examination. Ask yourself whether you are happy, and you cease to be so. The only chance is to treat, not happiness, but some end external to it, as the purpose of life. Let your self-consciousness, your scrutiny, your self-interrogation, exhaust themselves on that; and if otherwise fortunately circumstanced you will inhale happiness with the air you breathe, without dwelling on it or thinking about it, without either forestalling it in imagination, or putting it to flight by fatal questioning. This theory now became the basis of my philosophy of life. And I still hold to it as the best theory for all those who have but a moderate degree of sensibility and of capacity for enjoyment, that is, for the great majority of mankind.

The other important change which my opinions at this time underwent, 7
was that I, for the first time, gave its proper place, among the prime necessities of human well-being, to the internal culture‡ of the individual. I ceased to attach almost exclusive importance to the ordering of outward circumstances, and the training of the human being for speculation and for action.

I had now learnt by experience that the passive susceptibilities needed 8
to be cultivated as well as the active capacities, and required to be nourished and enriched as well as guided. I did not, for an instant, lose sight of, or undervalue, that part of the truth which I had seen before; I never turned recreant to intellectual culture, or ceased to consider the power and practice of analysis as an essential condition both of individual and of social improvement. But I thought that it had consequences which required to be corrected, by joining other kinds of cultivation with it. The maintenance of a due balance among the faculties, now seemed to me of primary importance. The cultivation of the feelings became one of the cardinal points in my ethical and

*Thomas Carlyle (1795–1881) held that the reasoning intellect, operating at a conscious level, could deal only with the superficialities of life and that only our deepest spiritual instincts, of which we are mostly unconscious, can probe the profoundest truths.

†See the next selection, "Happiness," by Bertrand Russell for a different formulation of this same idea.

‡That is, the life of feeling. *Culture* is here used in the sense of "cultivation."

philosophical creed. And my thoughts and inclinations turned in an increasing degree towards whatever seemed capable of being instrumental to that object.

I now began to find meaning in the things which I had read or heard 9
about the importance of poetry and art as instruments of human culture. But it was some time longer before I began to know this by personal experience. The only one of the imaginative arts in which I had from childhood taken great pleasure, was music; the best effect of which (and in this it surpasses perhaps every other art) consists in exciting enthusiasm; in winding up to a high pitch those feelings of an elevated kind which are already in the character, but to which this excitement gives a glow and a fervour, which, though transitory at its utmost height, is precious for sustaining them at other times. This effect of music I had often experienced; but like all my pleasurable susceptibilities it was suspended during the gloomy period. I had sought relief again and again from this quarter, but found none. After the tide had turned, and I was in process of recovery, I had been helped forward by music, but in a much less elevated manner. I at this time first became acquainted with [Karl Maria von] Weber's* "Oberon," and the extreme pleasure which I drew from its delicious melodies did me good, by showing me a source of pleasure to which I was as susceptible as ever. The good, however, was much impaired by the thought, that the pleasure of music (as is quite true of such pleasure as this was, that of mere tune) fades with familiarity, and requires either to be revived by intermittence, or fed by continual novelty. And it is very characteristic both of my then state, and of the general tone of my mind at this period of my life, that I was seriously tormented by the thought of the exhaustibility of musical combinations. The octave consists only of five tones and two semi-tones, which can be put together in only a limited number of ways, of which but a small proportion are beautiful: most of these, it seemed to me, must have been already discovered, and there could not be room for a long succession of Mozarts and Webers, to strike out, as these had done, entirely new and surpassingly rich veins of musical beauty. This source of anxiety may, perhaps, be thought to resemble that of the philosophers of Laputa, who feared lest the sun should be burnt out.† It was, however, connected with the best feature in my character, and the only good point to be found in my very unromantic and in no way honourable distress. For though my dejection, honestly looked at, could not be called other than egotistical, produced by the ruin, as I thought, of my fabric of happiness, yet the destiny of mankind in general was ever in my thoughts, and could not be separated from my own. I felt that the flaw in my life, must be a flaw in life itself; that the question was, whether, if the reformers of society and government could succeed in their objects, and every person in the community were free and in a state of physical comfort, the pleasures of life, being

*German composer (1786–1826), a leading creator of German romanticism and composer of nine operas.

†Jonathan Swift, *Gulliver's Travels,* Book III.

no longer kept up by struggle and privation, would cease to be pleasures. And I felt that unless I could see my way to some better hope than this for human happiness in general, my dejection must continue; but that if I could see such an outlet, I should then look on the world with pleasure; content as far as I was myself concerned, with any fair share of the general lot.

10 This state of my thoughts and feelings made the fact of my reading [William] Wordsworth for the first time (in the autumn of 1828), an important event in my life. I took up the collection of his poems from curiosity, with no expectation of mental relief from it, though I had before resorted to poetry with that hope. In the worst period of my depression, I had read through the whole of [George Gordon, Lord] Byron (then new to me), to try whether a poet, whose peculiar department was supposed to be that of the intenser feelings, could rouse any feeling in me. As might be expected, I got no good from this reading, but the reverse. The poet's state of mind was too like my own. His was the lament of a man who had worn out all pleasures, and who seemed to think that life, to all who possess the good things of it, must necessarily be the vapid, uninteresting thing which I found it. His Harold and Manfred had the same burthen on them which I had; and I was not in a frame of mind to derive any comfort from the vehement sensual passion of his Giaours, or the sullenness of his Laras.* But while Byron was exactly what did not suit my condition, Wordsworth was exactly what did. I had looked into the "Excursion" two or three years before, and found little in it; and I should probably have found as little, had I read it at this time. But the miscellaneous poems, in the two-volume edition of 1815 (to which little of value was added in the latter part of the author's life), proved to be the precise thing for my mental wants at that particular juncture.

11 In the first place, these poems addressed themselves powerfully to one of the strongest of my pleasurable susceptibilities, the love of rural objects and natural scenery; to which I had been indebted not only for much of the pleasure of my life, but quite recently for relief from one of my longest relapses into depression. In this power of rural beauty over me, there was a foundation laid for taking pleasure in Wordsworth's poetry; the more so, as his scenery lies mostly among mountains, which, owing to my early Pyrenean excursion, were my ideal of natural beauty. But Wordsworth would never have had any great effect on me, if he had merely placed before me beautiful pictures of natural scenery. [Sir Walter] Scott does this still better than Wordsworth, and a very second-rate landscape does it more effectually than any poet. What made Wordsworth's poems a medicine for my state of mind, was that they expressed, not mere outward beauty, but states of feeling, and of thought coloured by feeling, under the excitement of beauty. They seemed to be the very culture of the feelings, which I was in quest of. In them I seemed to draw from a source of inward joy, of sympathetic and imaginative

*Harold, Manfred, Giaour, and Lara were all characters in Byron's early poems, which tended to depict gloomy, self-conscious, cynical heroes.

pleasure, which could be shared in by all human beings; which had no connexion with struggle or imperfection, but would be made richer by every improvement in the physical or social condition of mankind. From them I seemed to learn what would be the perennial sources of happiness, when all the greater evils of life shall have been removed. And I felt myself at once better and happier as I came under their influence. There have certainly been, even in our own age, greater poets than Wordsworth; but poetry of deeper and loftier feeling could not have done for me at that time what his did. I needed to be made to feel that there was real, permanent happiness in tranquil contemplation. Wordsworth taught me this, not only without turning away from, but with a greatly increased interest in the common feelings and common destiny of human beings. And the delight which these poems gave me, proved that with culture of this sort, there was nothing to dread from the most confirmed habit of analysis. At the conclusion of the Poems came the famous Ode, falsely called Platonic, "Intimations of Immortality:" in which, along with more than his usual sweetness of melody and rhythm, and along with the two passages of grand imagery but bad philosophy so often quoted, I found that he too had had similar experience to mine; that he also had felt that the first freshness of youthful enjoyment of life was not lasting; but that he had sought for compensation, and found it, in the way in which he was now teaching me to find it. The result was that I gradually, but completely, emerged from my habitual depression, and was never again subject to it. I long continued to value Wordsworth less according to his intrinsic merits, than by the measure of what he had done for me. Compared with the greatest poets, he may be said to be the poet of unpoetical natures, possessed of quiet and contemplative tastes. But unpoetical natures are precisely those which require poetic cultivation. This cultivation Wordsworth is much more fitted to give, than poets who are intrinsically far more poets than he.

It so fell out that the merits of Wordsworth were the occasion of my 12
first public declaration of my new way of thinking, and separation from those of my habitual companions who had not undergone a similar change. The person with whom at that time I was most in the habit of comparing notes on such subjects was Roebuck,* and I induced him to read Wordsworth, in whom he also at first seemed to find much to admire: but I, like most Wordsworthians, threw myself into strong antagonism to Byron, both as a poet and as to his influence on the character. Roebuck, all whose instincts were those of action and struggle, had, on the contrary, a strong relish and great admiration of Byron, whose writings he regarded as the poetry of human life, while Wordsworth's, according to him, was that of flowers and butterflies. We agreed to have the fight out at our Debating Society, where we accordingly discussed for two evenings the comparative merits of Byron and Wordsworth, propounding and illustrating by long recitations our respective theo-

*John Arthur Roebuck (1801–1879), an early friend of Mill's, a radical politician, and a representative in Parliament for the industrial city of Sheffield.

ries of poetry: [John] Sterling* also, in a brilliant speech, putting forward his particular theory. This was the first debate on any weighty subject in which Roebuck and I had been on opposite sides. The schism between us widened from this time more and more, though we continued for some years longer to be companions. In the beginning, our chief divergence related to the cultivation of the feelings. Roebuck was in many respects very different from the vulgar notion of a Benthamite or Utilitarian. He was a lover of poetry and of most of the fine arts. He took great pleasure in music, in dramatic performances, especially in painting, and himself drew and designed landscapes with great facility and beauty. But he never could be made to see that these things have any value as aids in the formation of character. Personally, instead of being, as Benthamites† are supposed to be, void of feeling, he had very quick and strong sensibilities. But, like most Englishmen who have feelings, he found his feelings stand very much in his way. He was much more susceptible to the painful sympathies than to the pleasurable, and looking for his happiness elsewhere, he wished that his feelings should be deadened rather than quickened. And, in truth, the English character, and English social circumstances, make it so seldom possible to derive happiness from the exercise of the sympathies, that it is not wonderful if they count for little in an Englishman's scheme of life. In most other countries the paramount importance of the sympathies as a constituent of individual happiness is an axiom, taken for granted rather than needing any formal statement; but most English thinkers almost seem to regard them as necessary evils, required for keeping men's actions benevolent and compassionate. Roebuck was, or appeared to be, this kind of Englishman. He saw little good in any cultivation of the feelings, and none at all in cultivating them through the imagination, which he thought was only cutivating illusions. It was in vain I urged on him that the imaginative emotion which an idea, when vividly conceived, excites in us, is not an illusion but a fact, as real as any of the other qualities of objects; and far from implying anything erroneous and delusive in our mental apprehension of the object, is quite consistent with the most accurate knowledge and most perfect practical recognition of all its physical and intellectual laws and relations. The intensest feeling of the beauty of a cloud lighted by the setting sun, is no hindrance to my knowing that the cloud is vapour of water, subject to all the laws of vapours in a state of suspension; and I am just as likely to allow for, and act on, these physical laws whenever there is occasion to do so, as if I had been incapable of perceiving any distinction between beauty and ugliness.

. . .

In giving an account of this period of my life, I have only specified such 13
of my new impressions as appeared to me, both at the time and since, to be

*Essayist and poet (1806–1844), friend of many famous Victorians who outlived him, made famous by Carlyle's *Life of Sterling* (1851).

†Followers of the utilitarian philosophy (see note on p. 320) established by Jeremy Bentham.

a kind of turning point, marking a definite progress in my mode of thought. But these few selected points give a very insufficient idea of the quantity of thinking which I carried on respecting a host of subjects during these years of transition. Much of this, it is true, consisted in rediscovering things known to all the world, which I had previously disbelieved, or disregarded. But the rediscovery was to me a discovery, giving me plenary possession of the truths, not as traditional platitudes, but fresh from their source: and it seldom failed to place them in some new light, by which they were reconciled with, and seemed to confirm while they modified, the truths less generally known which lay in my early opinions, and in no essential part of which I at any time wavered. All my new thinking only laid the foundation of these more deeply and strongly, while it often removed misapprehension and confusion of ideas which had perverted their effect. For example, during the later returns of my dejection, the doctrine of what is called Philosophical Necessity* weighed on my existence like an incubus. I felt as if I was scientifically proved to be the helpless slave of antecedent circumstances; as if my character and that of all others had been formed for us by agencies beyond our control, and was wholly out of our own power. I often said to myself, what a relief it would be if I could disbelieve the doctrine of the formation of character by circumstances; and remembering the wish of Fox respecting the doctrine of resistance to governments, that it might never be forgotten by kings, nor remembered by subjects, I said that it would be a blessing if the doctrine of necessity could be believed by all *quoad* [as regards] the characters of others, and disbelieved in regard to their own. I pondered painfully on the subject, till gradually I saw light through it. I perceived, that the word Necessity, as a name for the doctrine of Cause and Effect applied to human action, carried with it a misleading association; and that this association was the operative force in the depressing and paralysing influence which I had experienced: I saw that though our character is formed by circumstances, our own desires can do much to shape those circumstances; and that what is really inspiriting and ennobling in the doctrine of free-will, is the conviction that we have real power over the formation of our own character; that our will, by influencing some of our circumstances, can modify our future habits or capabilities of willing. All this was entirely consistent with the doctrine of circumstances, or rather, was that doctrine itself, properly understood. From that time I drew in my own mind, a clear distinction between the doctrine of circumstances, and Fatalism; discarding altogether the misleading word Necessity. The theory, which I now for the first time rightly apprehended, ceased altogether to be discouraging, and besides the relief to my spirits, I no longer suffered under the burthen, so heavy to one who aims at being a reformer in opinions, of thinking one doctrine true, and the contrary doctrine morally beneficial.

*Determinism, the doctrine that everything we are and do has been determined by prior causes and that free will, and thus any form of freedom, is mere illusion.

Questions for Discussion

1. What does it say about Mill's character that at his lowest point of depression he has no desire to blame his father: "I saw no use in giving him the pain of thinking that his plans had failed" (¶3)?
2. Mill says in paragraph 4 "that the habit of analysis has a tendency to wear away the feelings . . . when no other mental habit is cultivated." Do you agree with this statement? If so, why? If not, why not? Produce the best reasons you can on both sides of the question. What kind of "other mental habits" need to be cultivated along with the powers of analysis? Where does Mill find the means of this other kind of mental cultivation?
3. What can you say to support Mill's description of analysis as a "dissolving force"? (See "What Is Analysis?" pp. 22–24).
4. In paragraph 6 Mill elaborates his notion that happiness should not be the direct aim of life, that it will come of itself, *"en passant"* (in passing), if we have our eyes fixed on other objects. Do you agree with him on this point? Why or why not? Do you agree that his views on this score diverge widely from the contemporary view that the main goal in life is to be happy and that everything may be justifiably subordinated to this goal? Compare what Mill says about happiness with Bertrand Russell's observations (pp. 333–341).
5. After reflecting on the exclusive emphasis on intellectual training in his own education, Mill observes that "the maintenance of a due balance among the faculties, now seemed to me of primary importance" (¶8). In his own case he found that reading Wordsworth helped restore this "due balance." Do you think that Wordsworth's helpfulness was the result of a coincidental compatibility between Mill's mind and Wordsworth's, or can you generalize and say that literature is one useful means for *anyone's* cultivation of a "due balance"? What reasons can you advance to support your opinion?

Suggested Essay Topics

1. In this fragment of Mill's life history we see that his education can be described as falling into three categories:
   a. intellectual—primarily the training of the analytical powers, the ability to dissect ideas and to see their relationships;
   b. moral—the forming of worthy goals beyond the gratification of personal desires and impulses, the ability to take the welfare and destinies of others into account; and
   c. affective—the development of the capacity for emotional expressiveness and responsiveness.

   For Mill, it is clear that the affective domain was too little cultivated in proportion to the other two domains. But what about you? In a letter to one of your favorite teachers (either in high school or college) or to your high school principal or college president, take the time to analyze and evaluate your own education in these three domains. What domain was most effectively tended not just by classes but by the whole experience of school? What was done poorly or ignored altogether? What was done well? Was a good balance maintained? Can you tell, now that you look back, that your education was designed with the aim of helping you develop a "due balance" among your faculties? Tell your reader what you think might have been done better, and suggest some ways of improving education for others.

2. This assignment is ambitious, but if you are interested in psychology, it will be rewarding. A lot of fascinating research has been done in clinical psychology on the therapeutic value of the arts. Painting and music especially have been used in the treatment of various emotional and psychological disorders. Do some research in this area, perhaps obtaining direction from someone in the psychology department; then write an account of Mill's reliance on poetry that offers psychological reasons for the beneficial effects he obtained from his reading. How would modern psychology explain what Mill experienced? Direct your essay to your classmates, that is, to lay people rather than specialists.

Bertrand Russell

Bertrand Russell (1872–1970) was a mathematician, social activist, controversialist, and philosopher, unquestionably one of the most influential of twentieth-century authors. In scores of books, he expressed strong opinions about a great many subjects, including education, sexual behavior, Christianity (see pp. 743–752), and the stockpiling of nuclear weapons. He particularly detested the last two.

Whatever his topic, he always expresses himself in an enviably straightforward, vigorous prose, the kind that looks easy to write—until one tries to duplicate its combination of relaxed ease and taut muscularity. His critics have called his prose "slick," but everyone acknowledges its power.

In The Conquest of Happiness, *Russell examines happiness as a human objective and argues that its acquisition is neither as difficult nor as elusive as most people think. In the selection reprinted here he focuses on two variables, one working against happiness and the other for it. Avoiding the first, sickly self-absorption, will prevent us from straying from the main road to happiness. Achieving the second, robust zest, will carry us toward our destination in the straightest possible line.*

As you read, try to decide whether Russell gives you adequate or clear advice about how to be happy and whether he himself sounds genuinely happy or merely resigned to a disappointing world.

HAPPINESS

From chapter 1, "What Makes People Unhappy?"; chapter 10, "Is Happiness Still Possible?"; and chapter 11, "Zest," of *The Conquest of Happiness* (1930). The title is ours.

Perhaps the best introduction to the philosophy [of happiness] which I wish to advocate will be a few words of autobiography. I was not born happy. As a child, my favorite hymn was: "Weary of earth and laden with my sin." At the age of five, I reflected that, if I should live to be seventy, I had only endured, so far, a fourteenth part of my whole life, and I felt the long-spread-out boredom ahead of me to be almost unendurable. In adolescence, I hated life and was continually on the verge of suicide, from which, however, I was restrained by the desire to know more mathematics. Now, on the contrary, I enjoy life; I might almost say that with every year that passes I enjoy it more. This is due partly to having discovered what were the things that I most desired, and having gradually acquired many of these things. Partly it is due to having successfully dismissed certain objects of desire—such as the acquisition of indubitable knowledge about something or other—as essentially unattainable. But very largely it is due to a diminishing preoccupation with myself. Like others who had a Puritan education, I had the habit of meditating on my sins, follies, and shortcomings. I seemed to myself—no doubt justly—a miserable specimen. Gradually I learned to be indifferent to myself and my deficiencies; I came to center my attention increasingly upon external objects: the state of the world, various branches of knowledge, individuals for whom I felt affection. External interests, it is true, bring each its own possibility of pain: the world may be plunged in war, knowledge in some direction may be hard to achieve, friends may die. But pains of these kinds do not destroy the essential quality of life, as do those that spring from disgust with self. And every external interest inspires some activity which, so long as the interest remains alive, is a complete preventive of *ennui* [boredom]. Interest in oneself, on the contrary, leads to no activity of a progressive kind. It may lead to the keeping of a diary, to getting psychoanalyzed, or perhaps to becoming a monk. But the monk will not be happy until the routine of the monastery has made him forget his own soul. The happiness which he attributes to religion he could have obtained from becoming a crossing-sweeper, provided he were compelled to remain one. External discipline is the only road to happiness for those unfortunates whose self-absorption is too profound to be cured in any other way. 1

. . .

Happiness is of two sorts, though, of course, there are intermediate degrees. The two sorts I mean might be distinguished as plain and fancy, or animal and spiritual, or of the heart and of the head. The designation to be chosen among these alternatives depends, of course, upon the thesis to be proved. I am at the moment not concerned to prove any thesis, but merely to describe. Perhaps the simplest way to describe the difference between the two sorts of happiness is to say that one sort is open to any human being, 2 and the other only to those who can read and write. When I was a boy I knew a man bursting with happiness whose business was digging wells. He was of enormous height and of incredible muscles; he could neither read nor write, and when in the year 1885 he got a vote for Parliament,* he learnt for the first time that such an institution existed. His happiness did not depend upon intellectual sources; it was not based upon belief in natural law, or the perfectibility of the species, or the public ownership of public utilities, or the ultimate triumph of the Seventh Day Adventists, or any of the other creeds which intellectuals consider necessary to their enjoyment of life. It was based upon physical vigor, a sufficiency of work, and the overcoming of not insuperable obstacles in the shape of rock. The happiness of my gardener is of the same species; he wages a perennial war against rabbits, of which he speaks exactly as Scotland Yard† speaks of Bolsheviks;‡ he considers them dark, designing and ferocious, and is of opinion that they can only be met by means of a cunning equal to their own. Like the heroes of Valhalla§ who spent every day hunting a certain wild boar, which they killed every evening but which miraculously came to life again in the morning, my gardener can slay his enemy one day without any fear that the enemy will have disappeared the next day. Although well over seventy, he works all day and bicycles sixteen hilly miles to and from his work, but the fount of joy is inexhaustible, and it is "they rabbits" that supply it.

. . .

The secret of happiness is this: let your interests be as wide as possible, and let your reactions to the things and persons that interest you be as far as possible friendly rather than hostile. 3

. . .

I [now] propose to deal with what seems to me the most universal and distinctive mark of happy men, namely, zest. 4

Perhaps the best way to understand what is meant by zest will be to consider the different ways in which men behave when they sit down to a meal. There are those to whom a meal is merely a bore; no matter how excellent the food may be, they feel that it is uninteresting. They have had excellent food before, probably at almost every meal they have eaten. They have never known what it was to go without a meal until hunger became a raging passion, but have come to regard meals as merely conventional occurrences, dictated by the fashions of the society in which they live. Like everything else, meals are tiresome, but it is no use to make a fuss, because nothing else will be less tiresome. Then there are the invalids who eat from a sense of duty, because the doctor has told them that it is necessary to take a little nourishment in order to keep up their strength. Then there are the epicures, 5

*1884 was the year that the right to vote was extended to all men (not women) in England.

†British counterpart of the FBI.

‡The revolutionary wing of the Russian Social Democratic party that seized supreme power in Russia during the Revolution (1917–1920).

§In Norse mythology, the eternal home of slain warriors.

who start hopefully, but find that nothing has been quite so well cooked as it ought to have been. Then there are the gormandizers, who fall upon their food with eager rapacity, eat too much, and grow plethoric and stertorous. Finally there are those who begin with a sound appetite, are glad of their food, eat until they have had enough, and then stop. Those who are set down before the feast of life have similar attitudes towards the good things which it offers. The happy man corresponds to the last of our eaters. What hunger is in relation to food, zest is in relation to life. The man who is bored with his meals corresponds to the victim of Byronic unhappiness. The invalid who eats from a sense of duty corresponds to the ascetic, the gormandizer to the voluptuary. The epicure corresponds to the fastidious person who condemns half the pleasures of life as unæsthetic. Oddly enough all these types, with the possible exception of the gormandizer, despise the man of healthy appetite and consider themselves his superiors. It seems to them vulgar to enjoy food because you are hungry or to enjoy life because it offers a variety of interesting spectacles and surprising experiences. From the height of their disillusionment they look down upon those whom they despise as simple souls. For my part, I have no sympathy with this outlook. All disenchantment is to me a malady, which, it is true, certain circumstances may render inevitable, but which none the less, when it occurs, is to be cured as soon as possible, not to be regarded as a higher form of wisdom. Suppose one man likes strawberries and another does not; in what respect is the latter superior? There is no abstract and impersonal proof either that strawberries are good or that they are not good. To the man who likes them they are good, to the man who dislikes them they are not. But the man who likes them has a pleasure which the other does not have; to that extent his life is more enjoyable and he is better adapted to the world in which both must live. What is true in this trivial instance is equally true in more important matters. The man who enjoys watching football is to that extent superior to the man who does not. The man who enjoys reading is still more superior to the man who does not, since opportunities for reading are more frequent than opportunities for watching football. The more things a man is interested in, the more opportunities of happiness he has and the less he is at the mercy of fate, since if he loses one thing he can fall back upon another. Life is too short to be interested in everything, but it is good to be interested in as many things as are necessary to fill our days. We are all prone to the malady of the introvert, who, with the manifold spectacle of the world spread out before him, turns away and gazes only upon the emptiness within. But let us not imagine that there is anything grand about the introvert's unhappiness.

There were once upon a time two sausage machines, exquisitely con- 6
structed for the purpose of turning pig into the most delicious sausages. One of these retained his zest for pig and produced sausages innumerable, the other said: "What is pig to me? My own works are far more interesting and wonderful than any pig." He refused pig and set to work to study his inside. When bereft of its natural food, his inside ceased to function, and the more he studied it, the more empty and foolish it seemed to him to be. All the

exquisite apparatus by which the delicious transformation had hitherto been made stood still, and he was at a loss to guess what it was capable of doing. This second sausage machine was like the man who has lost his zest, while the first was like the man who has retained it. The mind is a strange machine which can combine the materials offered to it in the most astonishing ways, but without materials from the external world it is powerless, and unlike the sausage machine it must seize its materials for itself, since events only become experiences through the interest that we take in them: if they do not interest us, we are making nothing of them. The man, therefore, whose attention is turned within finds nothing worthy of his notice, whereas the man whose attention is turned outward can find within, in those rare moments when he examines his soul, the most varied and interesting assortment of ingredients being dissected and recombined into beautiful or instructive patterns.

The forms of zest are innumerable. Sherlock Holmes, it may be remem- 7
bered, picked up a hat which he happened to find lying in the street. After looking at it for a moment he remarked that its owner had come down in the world as the result of drink and that his wife was no longer so fond of him as she used to be. Life could never be boring to a man to whom casual objects offered such a wealth of interest. Think of the different things that may be noticed in the course of a country walk. One man may be interested in the birds, another in the vegetation, another in the geology, yet another in the agriculture, and so on. Any one of these things is interesting if it interests you, and, other things being equal, the man who is interested in any one of them is a man better adapted to the world than the man who is not interested.

How extraordinarily different, again, are the attitudes of different peo- 8
ple to their fellow men! One man, in the course of a long train journey, will fail entirely to observe any of his fellow travelers, while another will have summed them all up, analyzed their characters, made a shrewd guess at their circumstances, and perhaps even ascertained the most secret histories of several of them. People differ just as much in what they feel towards others as in what they ascertain about them. Some men find almost everybody boring, others quickly and easily develop a friendly feeling towards those with whom they are brought in contact, unless there is some definite reason for feeling otherwise. Take again such a matter as travel; some men will travel through many countries, going always to the best hotels, eating exactly the same food as they would eat at home, meeting the same idle rich whom they would meet at home, conversing on the same topics upon which they converse at their own dinner table. When they return, their only feeling is one of relief at having done with the boredom of expensive locomotion. Other men wherever they go see what is characteristic, make the acquaintance of people who typify the locality, observe whatever is of interest either historically or socially, eat the food of the country, learn its manners and its language, and come home with a new stock of pleasant thoughts for winter evenings.

In all these different situations the man who has the zest for life has the 9
advantage over the man who has none. Even unpleasant experiences have

their uses to him. I am glad to have smelt a Chinese crowd and a Sicilian village, though I cannot pretend that my pleasure was very great at the moment. Adventurous men enjoy shipwrecks, mutinies, earthquakes, conflagrations, and all kinds of unpleasant experiences, provided they do not go so far as to impair health. They say to themselves in an earthquake, for example, "So that is what an earthquake is like," and it gives them pleasure to have their knowledge of the world increased by this new item. It would not be true to say that such men are not at the mercy of fate, for if they should lose their health they would be very likely to lose their zest at the same time, though this is by no means certain. I have known men die at the end of years of slow torture, and yet retain their zest almost till the last moment. Some forms of ill health destroy zest, others do not. I do not know whether the biochemists are able as yet to distinguish between these kinds. Perhaps when biochemistry has made further advances we shall all be able to take tablets that will ensure our feeling an interest in everything, but until that day comes we are compelled to depend upon common-sense observation of life to judge what are the causes that enable some men to take an interest in everything, while compelling others to take an interest in nothing.

Zest is sometimes general, sometimes specialized. It may be very spe- 10
cialized indeed. Readers of Borrow* may remember a character who occurs in "Lavengro." He had lost his wife, to whom he was devoted, and felt for a time that life had grown utterly barren. But by profession he was a tea merchant, and in order to endure life he taught himself unaided to read the Chinese inscriptions on the tea chests that passed through his hands. In the end this gave him a new interest in life, and he began to study with avidity everything that concerned China. I have known men who were entirely absorbed in the endeavor to find out all about the Gnostic heresy, and other men whose principal interest lay in collating the manuscripts and early editions of Hobbes.† It is quite impossible to guess in advance what will interest a man, but most men are capable of a keen interest in something or other, and when once such an interest has been aroused their life becomes free from tedium. Very specialized interests are, however, a less satisfactory source of happiness than a general zest for life, since they can hardly fill the whole of a man's time, and there is always the danger that he may come to know all there is to know about the particular matter that has become his hobby.

It will be remembered that among our different types at the banquet we 11
included the gormandizer, whom we were not prepared to praise. The reader may think that the man with zest whom we have been praising does not differ in any definable way from the gormandizer. The time has come when we must try to make the distinction between the two types more definite.

The ancients [i.e., the ancient Greeks], as every one knows, regarded 12
moderation as one of the essential virtues. Under the influence of romanticism and the French Revolution this view was abandoned by many, and

*George Henry Borrow (1803–1881), English author and linguist.

†Thomas Hobbes (1588–1679), English philosopher.

overmastering passions were admired, even if, like those of Byron's heroes, they were of a destructive and antisocial kind. The ancients, however, were clearly in the right. In the good life there must be a balance between different activities, and no one of them must be carried so far as to make the others impossible. The gormandizer sacrifices all other pleasures to that of eating, and by so doing diminishes the total happiness of his life. Many other passions besides eating may be carried to a like excess. The Empress Josephine was a gormandizer in regard to clothes. At first Napoleon used to pay her dressmaker's bills, though with continually increasing protest. At last he told her that she really must learn moderation, and that in future he would only pay her bills when the amount seemed reasonable. When her next dressmaker's bill came in, she was for a moment at her wit's end, but presently she bethought herself of a scheme. She went to the War Minister and demanded that he should pay her bill out of the funds provided for the war. Since he knew that she had the power to get him dismissed, he did so, and the French lost Genoa in consequence. So at least some books say, though I am not prepared to vouch for the exact truth of the story. For our purpose it is equally apt whether true or an exaggeration, since it serves to show how far the passion for clothes may carry a woman who has the opportunity to indulge it. Dipsomaniacs and nymphomaniacs are obvious examples of the same kind of thing. The principle in these matters is fairly obvious. All our separate tastes and desires have to fit into the general framework of life. If they are to be a source of happiness they must be compatible with health, with the affection of those whom we love, and with the respect of the society in which we live. Some passions can be indulged to almost any extent without passing beyond these limits, others cannot. The man, let us say, who loves chess, if he happens to be a bachelor with independent means, need not restrict his passion in any degree, whereas if he has a wife and children and no independent means, he will have to restrict it very severely. The dipsomaniac and the gormandizer, even if they have no social ties, are unwise from a self-regarding point of view, since their indulgence interferes with health, and gives them hours of misery in return for minutes of pleasure. Certain things form a framework within which any separate passion must live if it is not to become a source of misery. Such things are health, the general possession of one's faculties, a sufficient income to provide for necessaries, and the most essential social duties, such as those towards wife and children. The man who sacrifices these things for chess is essentially as bad as the dipsomaniac. The only reason we do not condemn him so severely is that he is much less common and that only a man of somewhat rare abilities is likely to be carried away by absorption in so intellectual a game. The Greek formula of moderation practically covers these cases. The man who likes chess sufficiently to look forward throughout his working day to the game that he will play in the evening is fortunate, but the man who gives up work in order to play chess all day has lost the virtue of moderation. It is recorded that Tolstoy, in his younger and unregenerate days, was awarded the military cross for valor in the field, but when the time came for him to be presented with it, he was so absorbed in a game of chess that he decided not to go. We can hardly find fault with Tolstoy on this account, since to him it might well be a matter of indifference whether he won military decorations or not; but in a lesser man such an act would have been one of folly.

As a limitation upon the doctrine that has just been set forth, it ought 13
to be admitted that some performances are considered so essentially noble as to justify the sacrifice of everything else on their behalf. The man who loses his life in the defense of his country is not blamed if thereby his wife and children are left penniless. The man who is engaged in experiments with a view to some great scientific discovery or invention is not blamed afterwards for the poverty that he has made his family endure, provided that his efforts are crowned with ultimate success. If, however, he never succeeds in making the discovery or the invention that he was attempting, public opinion condemns him as a crank, which seems unfair, since no one in such an enterprise can be sure of success in advance. During the first millennium of the Christian era a man who abandoned his family for a saintly life was praised, though nowadays it would be held that he ought to make some provision for them.

I think there is always some deep-seated psychological difference be- 14
tween the gormandizer and the man of healthy appetite. The man in whom one desire runs to excess at the expense of all others is usually a man with some deep-seated trouble, who is seeking escape from a specter. In the case of the dipsomaniac this is obvious: men drink in order to forget. If they had no specters in their lives, they would not find drunkenness more agreeable than sobriety. As the legendary Chinaman said: "Me no drinkee for drinkee, me drinkee for drunkee." This is typical of all excessive and one-sided passions. It is not pleasure in the object itself that is sought, but oblivion. There is, however, a very great difference according as oblivion is sought in a sottish manner or by the exercise of faculties in themselves desirable. Borrow's friend who taught himself Chinese in order to be able to endure the loss of his wife was seeking oblivion, but he sought it in an activity that had no harmful effects, but on the contrary improved his intelligence and his knowledge. Against such forms of escape there is nothing to be said. It is otherwise with the man who seeks oblivion in drinking or gambling or any other form of unprofitable excitement. There are, it is true, border-line cases. What should we say of the man who runs mad risks in aëroplanes or on mountain tops, because life has become irksome to him? If his risks serve any public object, we may admire him, but if not, we shall have to place him only slightly above the gambler and drunkard.

Genuine zest, not the sort that is really a search for oblivion, is part of 15
the natural make-up of human beings except in so far as it has been destroyed by unfortunate circumstances. Young children are interested in almost everything that they see and hear; the world is full of surprises to them, and they are perpetually engaged with ardor in the pursuit of knowledge, not, of course, of scholastic knowledge,* but of the sort that consists in acquiring

*Knowledge considered useless, irrelevant, and dull.

familiarity with the objects that attract their attention. Animals, even when adult, retain their zest provided they are in health. A cat in an unfamiliar room will not sit down until it has sniffed at every corner on the off chance that there may be a smell of mouse somewhere. The man who has never been fundamentally thwarted will retain his natural interest in the external world, and so long as he retains it he will find life pleasant unless his liberty is unduly curtailed. Loss of zest in civilized society is very largely due to the restrictions upon liberty which are essential to our way of life. The savage hunts when he is hungry, and in so doing is obeying a direct impulse. The man who goes to his work every morning at a certain hour is actuated fundamentally by the same impulse, namely the need to secure a living, but in his case the impulse does not operate directly and at the moment when it is felt; it operates indirectly through abstractions, beliefs and volitions. At the moment when the man starts off to his work he is not feeling hungry, since he has just had his breakfast. He merely knows that hunger will recur, and that going to his work is a means of satisfying future hunger. Impulses are irregular, whereas habits, in a civilized society, have to be regular. Among savages, even collective enterprises, in so far as they exist, are spontaneous and impulsive. When the tribe is going to war the tom-tom rouses military ardor, and herd excitement inspires each individual to the necessary activity. Modern enterprises cannot be managed in this way. When a train has to be started at a given moment it is impossible to inspire the porters, the engine driver and the signalman by means of barbaric music. Each of them must do his job merely because it has to be done. Their motive, that is to say, is indirect: they have no impulse towards the activity, but only towards the ultimate reward of the activity. A great deal of social life has the same defect. People converse with each other, not from any wish to do so, but because of some ultimate benefit that they hope to derive from cooperation. At every moment of life the civilized man is hedged about by restrictions of impulse: if he happens to feel cheerful he must not sing or dance in the street, while if he happens to feel sad he must not sit on the pavement and weep, for fear of obstructing pedestrian traffic. In youth his liberty is restricted at school, in adult life it is restricted throughout his working hours. All this makes zest more difficult to retain, for the continual restraint tends to produce weariness and boredom. Nevertheless, a civilized society is impossible without a very considerable degree of restraint upon spontaneous impulse, since spontaneous impulse will only produce the simplest forms of social cooperation, not those highly complex forms which modern economic organization demands. In order to rise above these obstacles to zest a man needs health and superabundant energy, or else, if he has that good fortune, work that he finds interesting on its own account. Health, so far as statistics can show, has been steadily improving in all civilized countries during the last hundred years, but energy is more difficult to measure, and I am doubtful whether physical vigor in moments of health is as great as it was formerly. The problem here is to a great extent a social problem, and as such I do not propose to discuss it in the present volume. The problem has, however, a personal and psychological aspect which we have already discussed in connection with fatigue. Some men retain their zest in spite of the handicaps of civilized life, and many men could do so if they were free from the inner psychological conflicts upon which a great part of their energy is expended. Zest demands energy more than sufficient for the necessary work, and this in turn demands the smooth working of the psychological machine. Of the causes promoting the smooth working I shall have more to say in later chapters.

Questions for Discussion

1. Russell begins by expressing an obvious contempt for self-absorption. "Interest in oneself," he says, ". . . leads to no activity of a progressive kind" (¶1). There has been an increasing emphasis in recent years on "learning to like your *self,*" "learning to know the real *you,*" "being in touch with your feelings"—phrases that suggest that we should constantly be asking ourselves whether we are happy. Self-help therapies, counseling groups, human development seminars, and other group efforts designed to help people "work through their problems" have become everyday features of our social landscape. (The 1970s, for example, were labeled the "me" generation, and popular songs with titles like "(I Did It) My Way" and "I've Got To Be Me" expressed a general current during this decade.) Does Russell make a convincing argument against this sort of "interiorism"? Do you know many people who are preoccupied with their inner feelings? Are these people generally more or less sensitive to the feelings of others? More or less happy than others?
2. Is Russell's description of what he calls "plain" happiness, the sort that is "open to any human being" (¶2), something you know about from experience? Can you describe it in your own words based on your own knowledge? The distinction between happiness "of the heart and of the head" (¶2) is not a subtle one, but is it useful to Russell's purpose? What *is* Russell's purpose?
3. How many different types of eaters does Russell characterize in paragraph 5? Can you describe each of them clearly? What different attitudes toward life does each represent?
4. Do you agree with the analogy, "What hunger is in relation to food, zest is in relation to life" (¶5)? Do you agree that zest (as Russell defines it) is an essential ingredient in happiness?
5. Is the analogy of the sausage-making machines (¶6) an effective device for showing the unhealthiness of too much introspection? Does it help make his point persuasive and forceful?
6. People of zest, as Russell describes them, are apparently a sort of ideal (although Russell does not explicitly say so), with perfect balance, all

normal appetites, no excesses, no quirks, no self-absorptions, no self-induced miseries, and no nonsense about wanting more than is good for them. Do you know anyone like this? If not, does that make you doubt the validity of the characterization? Or can you accept it as a useful ideal even if you have never met its complete realization in life? Do you know various people whom you can plot along a continuum from less to more zestful?

7. Do you agree that the constraints of civilized living in complex societies tend to cut off spontaneity and thus thwart zest (¶15)? Does Russell's description of people who are unable to break into song when they feel happy (because modern society pressures us to be conventional) strike a sympathetic chord in you? Have you ever felt your own zest blocked by such pressure?

Suggested Essay Topics

1. Do you know people who fail to practice moderation—who "breathe, eat, and sleep" sports or music, for example—and seem happy doing so? If so, address an argument to Russell himself, considering whether such immoderation is "good" for a person and whether the happiness one then feels is real or mistaken.
2. A recent survey has shown that people in their late teens and early twenties report themselves to be much less happy than people in their sixties do. Assuming that you have heard no more about the survey than that, write a thoughtful letter to the newspaper that reported the results, either explaining why people are happier after 60 than before 25 or arguing that the survey must have been oversimplified, confusing things like comfort or sleepiness or self-complacency with happiness, and things like restlessness, dissatisfaction, and insecurity with unhappiness.

IDEAS IN DEBATE

St. Paul
Robert Coles
Shirley Jackson

St. Paul

Of all the parts of the New Testament, the thirteenth chapter of First Corinthians is probably better known than any except the stories about Christ's birth. It is quoted so often that readers may rush through the familiar words with the impression that they are easy to understand. But everyone who studies them carefully will find that the chapter can yield more than one meaning. Part of our difficulty is that translators do not agree on the best English equivalent for the Greek word agape, *here translated as* love. *The translators who wrote the King James Version of the Bible, nearly four centuries ago, chose* charity. *Both of these English terms are deeply ambiguous, even more ambiguous, scholars tell us, than* agape, *which was distinguished by the Greeks from the term for sexual love (*eros*) and the term for loving friendship (*philia*).*

Obviously, some of the meanings that we associate with either English term cannot possibly fit what Paul claims to be the most important of all human spiritual qualities: Agape *has nothing to do with such phrases as "to* love *sport" or "to give generously to a* charity.*" But the difficulties we find here in determining meaning run far deeper than simply explaining the Greek words that lie behind the English. Paul is attempting to describe a condition of the soul that is essentially beyond literal definition; no words for that condition could ever be freed of all vagueness. Whatever Paul means by* love *or* charity, *it is not something that could be pinned down once and for all. In talking of such matters, he cannot avoid a tone that is oblique, suggestive, oracular, or even a bit gnomic. It is as if he had just come down from a mountaintop with a message from God himself.* *(See discussion questions 4–8 for "I Owe Nothing to My Brothers" by Ayn Rand, pp. 429–431.)*

We suggest that you read the passage several times, aloud and silently, first in the modern translation that we reprint from the New English Bible *and then in a copy of the King James Version. You will probably find, like many another student of the chapter, that even after studying it for an hour or so you are still puzzled about many words and phrases. You may also find, like many readers before you, that the puzzlement is part of the power the words contain. Though all guides to good writing tell us to be "as clear as possible," some of the world's greatest writing is about matters that can never be reduced to clear and simple propositions.*

Of course some statements that offer multiple suggestions and meanings may appear to be rich when they are not; they may be merely confused or even badly written. Unfortunately, there is no infallible test in reading prose for separating real gold from fool's gold. Readers are forced to rely on the same powers of judgment and discrimination in reading prose as they use when "reading" people. We meet phonies both in person and in prose, but by keeping a sharp eye for details and a sharp ear for tone we can separate truly rich writing from the merely muddled.

What we can certainly become clear about is the source of our problems. As you prepare for class discussion, try to determine the sources both of what hostile critics would call vagueness and what friendly readers might call spiritual richness. Can you see why such a passage would have become one of the most frequently quoted religious pronouncements of all time?

Note that we print the traditional verse numbers as well as our usual paragraph numbers.

I CORINTHIANS 13

And now I will show you the best way of all. 1

[1]I may speak in tongues of men or of angels, but if I am without love, 2
I am a sounding gong or a clanging cymbal. [2]I may have the gift of prophecy,
and know every hidden truth; I may have faith strong enough to move
mountains; but if I have no love, I am nothing. [3]I may dole out all I possess,
or even give my body to be burnt, but if I have no love, I am none the better.

[4]Love is patient; love is kind and envies no one. Love is never boastful,
[5]nor conceited, nor rude; never selfish, not quick to take offence. Love keeps 3
no score of wrongs; [6]does not gloat over other men's sins, but delights in the
truth. [7]There is nothing love cannot face; there is no limit to its faith, its hope,
and its endurance.

[8]Love will never come to an end. Are there prophets? their work will 4
be over. Are there tongues of ecstasy? they will cease. Is there knowledge?
it will vanish away; [9]for our knowledge and our prophecy alike are partial,
[10]and the partial vanishes when wholeness comes. [11]When I was a child, my
speech, my outlook, and my thoughts were all childish. When I grew up, I
had finished with childish things. [12]Now we see only puzzling reflections in
a mirror, but then we shall see face to face. My knowledge now is partial; then
it will be whole, like God's knowledge of me. [13]In a word, there are three
things that last for ever: faith, hope, and love; but the greatest of them all is
love.

Questions for Discussion

1. As we have suggested, guides to good writing often tell us that if a passage is written well, the reader should be able to summarize its meaning in one sentence. Can you summarize Paul's meaning in a sentence? In a paragraph? If so, can you get all other members of the class to accept your summary? If your class cannot agree on a summary, does this show the passage to be bad writing?
2. How would you state the purpose of the passage? Does it seem to be different from the meaning? Can you see anything in the purpose you have described that would force an author to be vague in meaning? Can you see any way in which an author could write with simple clarity about such matters?
3. How is the chapter organized? Do all of the sentences in each paragraph contribute to the same general point, as your own sentences are often expected to do? (Note that the paragraphing has been provided by modern translators; only the verse divisions appear in earlier printings.) What is the effect of the passage's organization?
4. We could describe verses 4–7 as Paul's effort to define an indefinable word by giving examples of what love *is,* while verses 1–3 give examples of what love *is not.* Do you see anything in either set of examples that would explain why modern translators would find the word *love* to be clearer than the word *charity*?

Suggested Essay Topics

1. Make a short list of words that might carry some of the meaning that Paul gives to *agape;* for example, *generosity, fellow feeling, compassion, sympathy,* or *large-mindedness.* Then write a brief paper (no more than one page) defending or rejecting the one that seems most nearly adequate or most inadequate for its job in Paul's chapter.
2. Choose some general quality or trait that you admire in other people; if possible, find one that you admire more than any other. Don't worry about whether it is one that everyone else would value to the same degree; after all, Paul must have known that many of his readers would disagree with his praise of love/charity/*agape,* or he would not have troubled to write his "praise poem." Write a passage praising the quality you have chosen; "imitate" Paul as much as you like, but try to find language that you think will appeal not only to your classmates but to all the world.

Robert Coles

Robert Coles (b. 1929) is one of a small number of social scientists who can write effectively both to specialists and to the general reading public. His best-known works are the three volumes of Children of Crisis *(see his reference notes 7 and 8), based on his experiences observing and thinking about how Americans deal with racial prejudice, and his recent book* The Moral Life of Children *(1986). If you read the selection carefully, you will find more direct clues about the author's biography than most of our selections have revealed. You will also find that he gives innumerable hints about himself while he* seems *to be talking about other matters. In reading an essay on character, attention to such hints about the author's own character is especially important.*

As Coles says, his present interest in what makes a good or bad character and in how to talk about character began about 1950 when he was in college. That interest has grown as he has observed how some people of limited education reveal in their actions a kind of tough inner quality that is not covered by terms like personality *or* reputation *or* psychological makeup. *As you read the essay reporting his visits to three highly contrasting schools, notice how he is able to show a mastery of fairly complicated psychological terms while at the same time admitting their final inadequacy for talking about character.*

As you follow him, try to develop your own picture of the people whose opinions he reports, and think about how they compare with the students, teachers, and administrators in your school.

In reading this piece, especially the first time through, it is important not to worry too much about any words that you may not be able to define precisely. Some of them will be understood fully only by professionals (for example, counterphobic *and* borderline personality *in ¶5), some of them are made clear by the context, and some do not matter to Coles's argument except as examples of terms that do not do justice to the topic of character. You might simply underline or circle words that you don't quite "get" so that on a second reading you can reduce your difficulties by looking up the essential words before you tackle each new paragraph.*

ON THE NATURE OF CHARACTER

Some Preliminary Field Notes

From *Daedalus: Proceedings of the American Academy of Arts and Sciences,* Fall 1981.

In the Harvard College of the decade after the Second World War, Gordon Allport was a significant figure indeed—interested always in connecting the newly influential social sciences to the ethical and religious concerns of earlier social and psychological scholars: William James, of course, and William McDougall, and farther back, J. S. Mill or John Locke. I still remember a 1 lecture of Allport's in 1950 in which he stressed the distinction between character and personality. He was forever anxious to acknowledge Freud's perceptive, trenchant thrusts into the outer precincts of consciousness, while at the same time remind us what Freud could afford to ignore about himself and certain others: a moral center that was, quite simply, *there.* No amount of psychoanalysis, even an interminable stretch of it, Allport cautioned us—drawing on Freud's givens with respect to human development—can provide a strong conscience to a person who has grown up in such a fashion as to become chronically dishonest, mean-spirited, a liar. "Psychoanalysis can provide insight, can help us overcome inhibitions," we were told, "but it was not meant to be an instrument of 'character building.' " I found recently my old college notes, found that sentence. I had put a big question mark above the phrase "character building," as if to say: What is it, really? I had heard the expression often enough in the Boy Scouts, in Sunday School, and, not least, from my somewhat Puritanical parents. They set great store by virtues they referred to as self-discipline, responsibility, honesty (often described as "the best policy"), and not least, the one my mother most commonly mentioned, "good conduct." Could it be that a social *scientist,* in the middle of the twentieth century, was mentioning such qualities in a college lecture—was, in fact, asking us to consider how they might be evaluated in people, with some accuracy and consistency?[1]

At that time such efforts were still being made, notably by Robert 2
Havighurst and Hilda Taba and their colleagues at the University of Chicago.[2] But as I got nearer and nearer to becoming a doctor, then a pediatrician, then a child psychiatrist, I heard less and less about "character" and more and more about "character disorders"—certain elements of psychopathology that many psychoanalysts today connect with the vicissitudes of what is called "psychosexual development."[3] In his early productive years, before he turned fanciful—if not deranged—Wilhelm Reich placed great emphasis on what he called "character reactions," the particular way each person works out his or her psychodynamic fate. "In the main," he once said, "character proves to be a narcissistic defense mechanism."[4] No doubt such a generalization can be helpful; we are brought closer to the subliminal workings of the mind, and to its historic necessities of symbolic expression and self-protection, in the face of turmoil generated from within, never mind the stresses that "life" manages to bring. But at some point, even the most factual-minded or dispassionately "rational" of psychoanalytic observers, anxious to maintain a "value-free" posture, would be tempted to observe that there is more to the assessment of human beings than an analysis (even one "in-depth") of narcissistic defense mechanisms can provide.

Hitler's mechanisms, Stalin's, those of any number of murderers or 3
thieves, surely offered what Reich called a "character armor"—as do, right now, the mechanisms employed by Mother Theresa's unconscious, and that belonging to Dom Helder of Brazil's Recife, or to such among us in America as Robert Penn Warren or Eudora Welty or, until her death recently, Dorothy

Day. At some point the issue becomes decidedly moral—or, in today's flat, impoverished language, a "normative matter." If I may call upon Gordon Allport again, "character is personality evaluated," a descriptive notion that may make up, in its everyday usefulness, for whatever is lost so far as "psychodynamic relevance" goes.

How we go about doing that evaluation is a matter of great import. In 4
recent years character has been of little concern for many of us whose interest is mental life, or the social and cultural life of human beings. The very word may suggest a prescientific age; may remind us of pietistic avowals or moralistic banalities many of us have tried to put behind us; may bring up the spectre of a word being used to protect the privileges of the well-born, the powerful—as if what is at issue is etiquette, polish, a certain appearance or manner of talking and carrying oneself. How much fairer, some say, to judge people through their academic performance, or through standardized tests: no risk of subjectivity, not to mention self-serving partiality. Still, it is not only Emerson, in another age, who suggested that "character is higher than intellect," and who observed that "a great soul will be strong to live, as well as strong to think."[5] Walker Percy today reminds us of those "who get all A's and flunk life."[6] And surely, a century that has witnessed learned individuals like Jung and Heidegger embrace Nazism, not to mention any number of intellectuals preach uncritically the virtues of Stalinist totalitarianism, is not going to be completely uninterested in such distinctions as the age-old polarity of knowledge as against wisdom.

In my own working life the question of "character" came up in the early 5
1960s when my wife and I were getting to know the black children who initiated school desegregation in the South, often against high odds—mob violence, even—and the young men and women who made up the nonviolent sit-in movement. I remember the clinical appraisals, psychological histories, and socioeconomic comments I wrote then. I remember my continuing effort to *characterize* those children, those youths—as if one weighty, academically acceptable adjective after another would, in sum, do the job. Ruby was from a "culturally deprived," a "culturally disadvantaged," family. Tessie's grandmother was illiterate. Lawrence was counterphobic, suffering "deep down" from a mix of anxiety and depression. Martha "projected" a lot. George was prone to "reaction-formations." Jim seemed to have a "character disorder," even a "borderline personality." Fred might well become psychotic later on. Meanwhile, these youthful American citizens were walking past grown men and women who were calling them the foulest of names, who were even threatening to kill them—and such hecklers were escaping sociological and psychological scrutiny in the bargain, while any number of judges were ordering "evaluations" by my kind to be done on sit-in students who were violating the (segregationist) laws, and who were thought to be (and eventually declared by doctors to be) "sick" or "delinquent" or "troubled" or "sociopathic" or "psychopathic." A historic crisis had confronted a region politically, and in so doing, had ripped open the political, economic, racial aspects

of our manner of judging others—the direct connection between what the Bible calls "principalities and powers," and what in our everyday life is "normal" or "proper" behavior. One day, as I mumbled some statements suffused with the words of psychiatric theory to "explain" a given child's behavior, my wife said, "You are making her sound as if she ought to be on her way to a child guidance clinic, but she is walking into a school building—and no matter the threats, she is holding her head up high, even smiling at her obscene hecklers. Last night she even prayed for them!"

It was my wife's judgment that Ruby Bridges, aged six, was demonstrat- 6
ing to all the world *character.* Even if cognitive psychologists were to declare such a child not old enough to make certain recognitions or distinctions; even if other theorists were to find Ruby unable to do very much moral reasoning or analysis; even if still other social scientists or clinicians were to emphasize her severe "problems"—her imitative habits, her fearful responses, her Oedipal tensions, her moments of blind obedience or terror-struck submission; even if she were to demonstrate to any number of curious observers—armed with questions, tests, stories to be analyzed, crayons to be used on drawing paper—certain handicaps, developmental difficulties, emotional impasses or disorders, cognitive blocks, age-related blind spots; nevertheless, she was managing to face those mobs with a quiet, stoic dignity that impressed her teachers, newspaper reporters, and federal marshals (who escorted her each day to and from school). One of her teachers, as a matter of fact, said that she herself could never submit to such a daily scene—suggesting that moral *behavior* is not necessarily the same thing as a capacity for moral *thinking;* that character may not be something one ascertains through questionnaires or through experiments done on a university campus.

Against such vexing theoretical difficulties (which had become for me 7
a matter of continuing astonishment, if not haunting confusion), a chance to talk again with young people in a variety of school situations was most welcome. My wife and I had spent years visiting a number of Atlanta's high schools, though not George Washington Carver School.[7] We had spent a season visiting a high school north of Chicago, though not Highland Park High School.[8] And we have children in the private schools of New England, though not St. Paul's School. I decided to keep trying to gain some sense of the variations in the moral life of the young by emphasizing that subject in my planned visits to these three schools, in the hope that more and more of what Anna Freud calls "direct observation" (as opposed to eagerly speculative and all too inclusive and unqualified generalizations) will help us to understand where "personality" ends and "character" begins in the mind's life.

The "methodology" is thoroughly simple—a mere beginning in explo- 8
ration, but perhaps not an altogether futile way to learn something about certain young people. I asked the principals of the two public high schools and the headmaster of the private school to "select two teachers qualified to judge character"; those teachers would, in turn, select four or so students who, they believe, possess "character" or "high character." When the princi-

pals of Highland Park and Carver asked what I meant by such a word, such an expression, I replied simply that I was trying to find out precisely *that.* I told each principal that I wanted to speak with all the students chosen together, rather than separately, and that I wanted to meet also with the two teachers together.

I went to St. Paul's School first. The headmaster had arranged for two teachers to select four students, and we met in a classroom a good distance from the headmaster's office. We were, in a sense, free—no classes, no one to interrupt or keep an eye on what was to be a full morning's discussion. I told the students, two young men and two young women, that I wanted to explore the meaning to them of "character," and we were, with no hesitation, off to a sustained inquiry. 9

The word was not a strange one for these students; they had heard it used repeatedly, they said, though none had ever really stopped to think about its meaning. Early on one of the young women said, "We talk about 'human nature' or 'personality' or 'identity'; I suppose in the past they talked about 'character.' " Yet these students were quite articulate as they sifted and sorted among themselves and their classmates in search of a definition, a way of looking at a particular subject. In no time a whole school was being morally scrutinized: the "jocks," the "beautiful people," the "social butterflies," the "freaks," the "party people," the "grinds," various teachers, and the "goodly heritage," a phrase many who have gone to St. Paul's have heard again and again. 10

Much time was spent struggling with the question of arrogance, with the temptation of self-importance and self-centeredness—a personal hazard these four were not loath to acknowledge. They were in a school known as one of the best in America. They were, in different ways, doing well there—one academically; one as a scholar-athlete; one for showing concern and compassion for others, near and afar; one as a person trusted and liked by a wide assortment of classmates. Yet they worried that their success was a temptation to "become stuck-up," as one put it. Self-righteousness and self-consciousness were additional hazards—elements likely to shut a person off, making that person less responsive to other people. Gradually, how one responds to others took on high importance. One of the young men put it this way: "I tend to be a private person. I like to take long walks by myself. At times I don't want company. I want to hold onto my individuality. But I like to be with others, too. I like to be a *friend.* I'd like to think that if someone were in trouble, he'd turn to me, and I'd be there, and I'd put that person's trouble above my needs, including taking a solitary walk!" 11

Other topics came up frequently: the tension between adjustment to the demands of various cliques and the private values a given individual feels to be important—or put differently, the tension between loyalty to one's friends and loyalty to one's own memories, habits, yearnings; the tension between one's competitive side and one's regard for others; and more crudely, the tension between one's wish to win and one's willingness to help others. The 12 word "honesty" was mentioned over and over—an Augustinian examination,* done with today's psychological panache: who is "really" honest, and for what "underlying" reasons? Moreover, does it "pay" in this society to be honest all the time? When do honesty and self-effacement turn into "masochism"? When does pride in one's convictions turn into a bullying egotism? If you really do have "a sense of yourself," are you not in danger of being smug, self-serving, all too sure of your own significance? When does popularity reduce one's individuality to the point that one belongs to a herd, has lost a mind of one's own?

Such questions were asked quite earnestly, and always with regard to 13
the matter at hand: the characteristics of character. When pressed by one another (I ended up being, most of the time, a listener), the students offered lists: a person who sticks to a set of principles; a person who can risk unpopularity, yet is commanding enough to gain the respect of others; a person who has the courage to be himself, herself; a person who is open-minded, who plays fair with others, who doesn't lie and cheat and, interestingly enough, deceive himself, herself. These were students who believed such qualities to be only partially present. These were students, in fact, who had a decidedly dialectical turn of mind: "You can try to be a better person, but it's a struggle. You can be humble, and that way, intimidate people. You can *use* humility. It's hard to know what's genuine in people. Sometimes people pretend to be something, but they're really just the opposite. They flip and they flop. I don't like people who are sanctimonious. They lecture others, and people take it, but it's out of fear, or there is guilt, and it's being exploited. Every once in a while, I prefer someone who puts his cards on the table and shows he's a real pain in the neck to these holier-than-thou types. Character doesn't mean being a goody-goody person! If you're that kind of person, there's a lot of meanness, probably, inside you, or competitiveness that you're not letting on about to others. Maybe you don't know about it yourself!"

These were, obviously, what we would now call a psychologically so- 14
phisticated breed of youth. Yet, they were (thank God!) not anxious to have all human behavior a matter of psychology or psychopathology—or sociology, either: "There are reasons we end up being one kind of person or another kind of person, but when you actually *become* that person (when you're nice to others most of the time), then that's a true achievement. A lot of people *don't* become nice, and it's no excuse to say you had a bad childhood or you never had the right luck. I think you have to take your troubles and overcome them!" The Puritan spirit lives still in the woods of southern New Hampshire, no matter the references—and they were many—to "adolescence," "identity," Sigmund Freud's ideas, the latest notions of what "motivates" people, what makes us "anxious" or "strung out" or "ambivalent."

More than anything else, these four youths grappled with what used to 15

*In his *Confessions,* St. Augustine (354–430) examines his moral and spiritual qualities in great detail, always in Christian terms.

be commonly called "the meaning of life" in philosophy lectures (before the advent of logical positivism, computers, the libido theory, and a strictly materialist view of life, liberty, the pursuit of happiness). One of the young men said this toward the end of our meeting time: "What matters—don't you think?—is what you *do* with your life. I've tried to be independent, to have my own thoughts, but to listen to others. I hope to live comfortably, but I hope I won't be greedy and selfish. I don't know what our responsibilities are—to ourselves and our friends and family and neighbors, and to others in places abroad I'll never even see. Even today, this is a big world. What are we supposed to do? We're lucky to be here at St. Paul's. We have such a good life. What do we owe others? Isn't that 'character'—what you decide to do for others, not just yourself?"

The "great suck of self," Walker Percy calls it in *The Second Coming*—the 16
inevitable pull toward our own thoughts, our own wishes, our navels. Adolescence is not the only period of self-absorption, these youths seemed already to know. For them, one is likely to be neither bad nor good. For them, character was no categorical trait. For them, character is not a possession, but something one searches for: a quality of mind and heart one struggles for, sometimes with a bit more success than at other times. Not one of these four wanted to spell out a definition, set down a compulsory series of attributes, offer a list of candidates. One heard from their mouths expressions of confusion, annoyance, vanity, self-satisfaction, self-criticism, self-doubt, self-assurance. One heard, maybe most of all, tentativeness—a reluctance to speak definitively about an aspect of human behavior one student kept describing as "hard to pin down," but also as "important to consider when you're thinking about someone."

The two teachers I met at St. Paul's School, a middle-aged man who 17
taught math, a young woman who taught English, had met, discussed the subject of "character," and added to one another's notions, so that, in the end, there was a final written statement available:

- The aggregate of distinctive qualities belonging to an individual
- Moral vigor or firmness, especially as acquired through self-discipline
- The ability to respond to a setback
- The ability to form an attachment to ideals of a larger community or organization than oneself, and to exert one's influence for the good of the greater body
- The possession of a sense of humor that allows one to see that there is more to life than living
- The ability to be an *individual* in a crowd of *different* people
- A sense of self that has been found through experience
- The ability to allow others to be individuals, even though they may be different
- The ability to disagree with others without condemning (or losing respect for) the individual one disagrees with

- A sensitivity toward the feelings of others
- An understanding of the wholeness of other people's personalities or character (even when it is different from one's own)

These were two individuals who had thought long and hard about a vexing subject—whom to choose, and why? A very bright person, involved in many activities, able to speak coherently and easily, headed straight for Harvard, as against a quiet person who defers to the ideas of others in a classroom, does well, but "not all that well," yet in numerous moments seems to reach out for others, not to save them, or turn them into psychiatric cases, but simply "to do a good turn"? A marvelous athlete who also is a leader in many ways during the course of a school year, as against a hardworking youth who is most often self-effacing, yet managed to stand up once or twice on a matter of ethical principle, no matter the risks and the penalties? And surely a host of alternatives, because, as one teacher put it, "when you judge 'character,' you judge the overall person and compare him, or her, to others, and you do so over time, the school year." 18

In Highland Park, north of Chicago, a somewhat different arrangement had been made. The principal of this suburban high school had selected two teachers, as I requested, but they had picked four students each—seven girls and one boy, interestingly enough. We met in a room across the hall from the principal's office. Twice he asked how we were doing, offered water, tea, coffee—in general, showed a distinct, active interest in our discussions. He himself had thought about the word "character," and as with so many of us, found it a bit puzzling and elusive. So did the students I spent a winter morning with. Several of them said that character had a lot to do with personality; in fact, declared "a good personality" or a "well-rounded person" to be equivalent descriptions to "good character" or "high character." Two young women dissented, however: "Character has to do with honesty. You can be popular, and have a shrink's seal of approval, but not have character!" 19

We fairly quickly got into a discussion of ethnic and racial tensions—in the school, in our society as a whole. At St. Paul's the cliques were enumerated, as if they threatened individuality, hence character, through the requirements of social cohesion; at Highland Park High School the dominant social divisions, at least for these students, had to do with class and race: Italians and Jews, "working people" and "wealthier people," blacks and whites. 20

I was given some outspoken lessons in how one's family life affects one's situation in school, and not least, one's character: "It all depends on who you are! Some kids want to go to an Ivy League school; that's all that's on their minds. They put up a good front, to show they have 'character'; they join clubs, and have all these hobbies and interests, so as to impress the teachers and the people who read college applications. Some kids have to work while going to school. They try to get a good deal, a job that pays well. They're making contacts even now for later on. It's built into their 'character' 21 that the world is tough, and you have to know people to get ahead. A lot of the black kids are here because there's a military base in the school district. They come and then they go. It's hard to figure them out. It's in their 'character' to stay away from us whites. There's a lot of tension among us whites. Go into the johns, and you'll see a lot of writing! [I went, and I saw the ethnic slurs.] But a lot of the time we get along pretty well. We've got brainy ones here, headed for college since they were born, and don't get in their way, or else! We've got kids who will work in a store or a factory, and not be ashamed. They see the world different. They take different courses. They have their own code."

The speaker is a wry, outspoken, somewhat detached young woman, 22
bound for college, but "not a fancy one." She is neither Italian nor Jewish, but Anglo-Irish. She had made a certain virtue out of marginality, and the others in the room seemed a bit deferential: "She isn't pushed around by anyone. She's her own person. She can mingle with anyone. She doesn't put on airs with anyone." The associations moved relentlessly from social situation to moral conduct—not the first time, or the last, such a progression would be made for me in the course of this study. "You have to know where the person is coming from," I was told several times. Explain! "Well, if you've got a lot going for you, then you can be more relaxed. True, you can be a tightwad and be rich; but it's easier to be generous if you've got a lot behind you!" On the other hand, one student insisted, "there's still room for being poor and good in this world!" She persisted: "I know some kids, right in this school, and they're not here now, they weren't chosen to be here, and they're from pretty poor families, compared to others; their fathers just get by, make a living. And they would give you the shirt off their backs, those kids: that's character. And they wouldn't go talking about what they've done, bragging, and showing off—*that's* character! Some people, they know how to play up to the teachers, and they get a big reputation, but what's the *truth* about them? What are they like when no one is looking, and what are they like when no one is listening?"

We touched many bases. Class and character. Egotism and character. 23
Psychology and character. Smartness and character. Motivation and character. Caring and character. Manners and character. To be stuck-up. To be considerate. To be a help when a person needs help—a flat tire, a car ride, a pencil or piece of paper, a loan of money, a sympathetic ear. To take risks, extend oneself to others, brave social pressures. Grade-mongers. Leaders and followers. Hypocrites. People who have one or another veneer. The "way-down-deep truth" of a person. A final test of character: sickness, financial straits, a disaster. Character and mental health.

Part of [the movie] *Ordinary People* had been made in Highland Park. The 24
students had watched the filming, and they wondered: If one is hurt, bewildered, "seeing a shrink," can one have the "mental peace" to demonstrate character? Consumerism, selfishness—can one defy them, develop "an ability not to be absorbed with objects"? And at some interesting and suggestive length: literature as a means of understanding character, as in *To Kill a Mocking-*

bird (Atticus had character, he was open-minded, stood up for what he believed, no matter the risks and costs, and so was a "moral man"); or as in *Macbeth* (Lady Macbeth was a "bad person," a "bad character"). And politics: Lincoln and Eisenhower and Truman had character; Johnson lacked it, as do Nixon and Carter. "All politicians probably lie," one student observed, "and maybe all people do, but some just keep on lying, and you can't trust them, and you don't like them, and they're just no damn good, and you can tell, after awhile, even if they tell you they pray every other minute! The truth about a person's character eventually comes out, *eventually.*"

Such faith was not universally shared. There was much talk of appear- 25
ance as against reality: the way people present themselves to others, as opposed to some inner truth about each of us. In contrast to the students at St. Paul's School, these students were distinctly more interested in the relationship between a person's social, economic, ethnic, or racial background—a person's circumstances—and that person's behavior, hence character. And it did come down to that, they all agreed at the end: "You are the way you act—in the long run." What did that qualification mean? Well, it goes like this: "Some people can put on an act. But if you keep your wits, and keep an eye on them, you find out the truth about them. If they're good people, kind to others, not just wrapped up in themselves, you'll find it out. If they're putting on a production, you'll find that out." No one, in that regard, seemed to have any doubts about his or her ultimate psychological acuity—or about the long-run dramatic capacities of one or another individual.

There was, as we were ending, a spirited, occasionally tense discussion 26
of tests, grades, the criteria used by colleges and graduate schools to evaluate people. "I know kids who get all A's, and would murder their parents, their brothers and sisters, if they stood in their way," one youth offered. Yes, but there's plenty of nastiness to go around, others said, even among those who do poorly in school. What *should* various committees of admission do? How *does* one make a fairly accurate moral judgment about a person? Numbers may not tell enough. Multiple choice questions may not do justice to life's strangeness—the ironies and ambiguities, the complexities and inconsistencies and contradictions we all struggle with, though some with more decency and integrity and generosity of spirit than others. But how do we arrive at an estimate of a person's essential kindness with respect to others—in the face of thousands of importunate applicants, each putting on the very best face possible? Don't interviews have *their* hazards, the unpredictable variations of mood and temperament, the nuances of subjectivity which can, alas, of a sudden, amount to outright prejudice? We ended on an eclectic note—the desirability of taking a lot into consideration when accepting people for a job, a place in a college, and yes, when judging that elusive concept "character." The last person to leave the room, the young woman who spoke least, said that she thought "character meant being kind and good, even when there was no one to reward you for being kind and good."

These were students acutely aware of the divisions in this society—as 27
Tillie Olsen put it in her story *O Yes,* the ways we "sort." The two Highland

Park High School teachers were similarly sensitive to issues of "class and caste," as the splits among us have sometimes been described. Actually, the teachers were themselves a bit split. The assistant principal, a man, is quite in touch with the more academic students of the school; whereas the woman teacher is very much involved with those students who are working at jobs while trying to get through Highland Park—and who are headed, mostly, for what many social scientists would call "service jobs," or membership in the "working class," or the "lower-middle to middle-middle-class," and on and on. The two did not argue, however; in fact, they largely echoed the sentiments of their chosen students: "Grades aren't the whole story, by any means"; and very emphatically, "Character has something to do with moral life."

Both teachers worried about class—expressed concern, for instance, that "mere etiquette" can deceive, or insisted that human scoundrels, like wolves, find sheepskins ("social veneer") aplenty to wear. I heard practically nothing about class-connected deceit at St. Paul's, a lot about it at Highland Park—and character seemed to require, everyone agreed, an impressive absence of such a tendency. Moreover, psychiatry and psychoanalysis were even more prominently mentioned than at St. Paul's—a way of getting to the "deeper truth" about people, hence to a judgment of their character. (Fallout from *Ordinary People*?) As already mentioned, disturbed people were described as less likely to show high character. When I mentioned Gandhi's personal eccentricities, if not moments of cruelty, vanity, thoughtlessness, the students were ready, all too ready, to take the clue, the hint, and write him off as sick. When I reminded them that he was, yet, a rather impressive moral leader, the students worried about the burdens placed on his family, and about his own psychiatric ones. 28

If I had a little trouble persuading this group of students and their teachers that, neurosis or no neurosis, a person's moral motives can affect his or her character, they had no trouble letting me know that a neighborhood, a level of income, the possession of a given nationality, can all affect a person's character. The teachers especially emphasized the distinction between the quietly considerate person, as against the demonstrative, if not flamboyant, doer of public good deeds, a performer of sorts. "Some students want to get A in character, too," one teacher said, as we broke off, a reminder that not only can life be unfair, as one American president took pains to remind us, but virtue can be unfairly perceived—when, in truth, sins are being shrewdly masked. As Flannery O'Connor observed, through the comic irony of a title to one of her stories, a good man is hard to find—and maybe, when the pressures are high, almost impossible to take for granted. 29

At George Washington Carver High School, in Atlanta, Georgia, I had quite another discussion, with the principal ready to point out the extreme hazards to what he called "character formation" well before I saw (in a room that belonged, really, to his office suite) the four children (two boys and two girls) and two teachers (both women, one who teaches math, the other, 30 biology). "There is a problem with drugs," he explained. "There is a problem with poverty, with terrible poverty, with welfare homes, with absent fathers, with unemployment all over the place." He gave me a lively lecture on the school's history—once a "dumping ground for school failures," now a "place of hope," much connected to businesses that offer promising black youths a great variety of jobs, a chance "to enter the mainstream," in the principal's words. In time I was able to begin talking with the four selected youths, though not before being told emphatically: "Character is something you have to build, right here in this school, every day. You have to lay down the law, and see that it's enforced. Character means discipline and hard work and looking to the future and getting there!" Of the three school leaders, Carver's principal was the only one to volunteer (or hazard) such an explication.

The students were not averse to this line of reasoning. These were young people who were determined to find jobs, determined to be hard workers, strong parents—and not reluctant to explain why such a commitment was connected to a definition, in their minds, of the word "character": "A lot of us, even here, with the principal and the teachers bearing down every minute on us, have trouble reading and writing. We're not going to college, most of us. We're going to try to get a job and hold onto it! It takes character, I think, to do that—not take the easy way out and drink or use drugs or say the white man is on our backs, so what the devil can we do! To me, character is being stubborn. It's staying in there, it's getting out of a hole, and breathing the fresh air, and not falling down anymore." 31

My wife and I spent three years in Atlanta, talking with youths such as these—young black men and women trying, in the face of adversity, to forge a better life for themselves. These were more outspoken and self-assured individuals than the ones we got to know in the early 1960s. They were quick to describe themselves as "job-hungry" and as full of determination, willfulness, hopeful anticipation. They were not, though, uninterested in some of the refinements of psychology I had heard discussed in Illinois and New Hampshire: "There's success and success. It's not only getting there, it's how you get there. If you have character, that means you keep trying, no matter how hard it is, and you don't lose your soul while you're doing that. You have to say to yourself, 'I'll go so far and no farther.' You have to draw the line, and if you do, and you can hold to it, you've got character." Nods all around, followed by smiles of recognition as the temptations get mentioned: white devils and black devils who offer serious distractions in the form of drugs and booze, bribes and payoffs, an assortment of "tricks." These are street-smart kids, and they have lots of savvy about Atlanta politics, Atlanta vice, Atlanta hypocrisy, black and white alike. Their moralism and self-conscious, urgently stated rectitude is hard earned, if (they seem to know) not entirely invulnerable. 32

One pushes the word "character," gets responses connected to hardship, ambition, the requirements of people living on the edge, hence with little interest in metaphysical or metapsychological speculation. Character? Why, J. R. in *Dallas* lacks it, utterly; Dr. King had it, that's for sure. Character? A 33 lot of big shots may seem to have it, but too bad more people don't know who is scratching whose back. On the other hand, there's a woman who works in a Howard Johnson's motel, and she lost her husband from cancer, and she has five kids, and she has two of them out of high school and in good jobs, and the other three are headed that way, and she doesn't stand for any foolishness, *none,* and she takes those kids to church every Sunday, and they pray hard and long, and she has character, in case anyone wants to know! The church—at long last it comes up in a talk about character! Not in a school that bears the name of St. Paul, no less; and not in a school where Catholics and Jews seem ready to square off at each other all day, every day; but in Carver, you bet. Each of these four high-school-age Americans (no fools about getting high or about the demands of the flesh or about the various shortcuts people take) goes to church on Sundays, and if there is reluctance sometimes (the joy of a late sleep), there is, after all, no real choice: "We have to go. Our mother says we have to go, and once we're there, I don't half mind! I like it there. I'll make my kids go, too."

Much talk of "uplift." Much reference to "building" oneself into "a stronger person," getting "on the map." How? There are auto repair shops. There are radio and TV repair shops. There are cosmetology shops. There are dry-cleaning places. There are tailoring and sewing and shoe repair places. There is a big airport, and people work there—on engines if they are on top, otherwise as cleaning people or doing errands, or driving buses and taxis, "lots of things." (No angst about capitalism at Carver!) If you get one of those jobs, and you hold onto it; if you get yourself a girlfriend or a boyfriend, and they become a wife or a husband, and you become a father or a mother, and you "stay with it," and be good to your family, earn them a living, take care of them; if you remain loyal to your church, and pray to God when you're weak; if you don't forget your people, and try to lend a hand to the ones who didn't make it, who stumbled and fell and are hurt and sad and wondering what the point of it all is, and maybe have done wrong, done it too many times—if all that is "inscribed on your soul," then, by God, you have character, and it's important to say "by God," because it's "His grace that does things." 34

"I'm not as small after church as I am before church," one of these four told me—a lifeline that rescues at least one American, temporarily, from "the culture of narcissism." As for "good manners," they aren't superficial at all; they tell of something very deep down, no matter what so-called depth psychologists have to say, not to mention those who make of them religious figures: "You can tell a person by how he speaks to you. If he's respectful, then he's good; if he gives you the shoulder, then he's bad. I don't care if someone has a lot of bad in him. If he keeps it a secret from the whole world, then he's way out front. If he shows his bad self to everyone, he's putting it on us, man, and it's hard enough without that—another hassle to deal with. My grandmother tells us: 'Keep your mouth shut if there's no good to come out of it. Keep your mischief to yourself. We've all got it—but some of us don't show it off.' She's right; she has character." 35

Some other virtues that bespeak character: punctuality; how you carry 36 yourself; an ability to laugh, when there's a good excuse for crying or shouting or shaking your fists; how you speak—with clear enunciation of words, so that others may hear you; self-respect, as measured by neatness and choice of clothes, as well as respect for others, as measured by a smile, a please, a thank you; obedience—to your elders, to the law, to your own self-evident ideas of what is right and wrong. "We all stray," said one of the young women, "but if we try hard not to keep repeating ourselves, and if we're not afraid to learn from our mistakes, and if we're willing to work hard, and sacrifice, then we have character." Pieties, all those remarks, the skeptical, psychoanalyzed liberal Yankee muses—fighting off embarrassment, wonder, a touch of awe, and emotional memories of other youths in other Atlanta spots, youths similarly hard-pressed, who managed to "overcome," and youths similarly unwilling to be self-pitying in the face of the severe inequities of this life.

The two teachers—my wife got to know so many very much like these 37
two: tough-minded, outspoken, a touch contemptuous of anyone who wants to offer sympathy, never mind condolences. They are demanding, insistent, forceful women: "Let these kids work hard, and better themselves, and be good members of their families, and they'll show character; that's how, the only way!" And candidly, bluntly, unapologetically: "We chose the best we have to talk with you. We chose the smart ones, the ones who could talk with you and get themselves across. We have others here who would tax your patience and understanding. Maybe they have 'character,' too. I don't think character is the property of the lucky and the smart and the successful, no sir. But to me, character means an active person, who is ready to face the world, and make a mark on it. That's why I chose these kids. They're ready, they're ready to turn their backs on all their troubles, our troubles, and be good—be full of action. 'Never be lazy,' I tell my kids at home, and here in school. There's that expression: going to meet 'the man.' Well, I say we can become 'the man' ourselves. We can take control of our own lives, be our own masters. It may be preachy of me to talk like this, but we've got to pep-talk ourselves, and then *get on with it!* I pray to God—we need His help badly—that more and more of these kids at Carver *will* get on with it."

On the way home, back North again, I took out my books and papers: 38
notes to write, ideas to savor, comparisons to make. There it was, the wonderful message that Kierkegaard gave us over a century ago, the message I often wish a few of us theorists of moral development would keep in constant mind: "Morality is character, character is that which is engraved (χαράσσω); but the sand and the sea have no character and neither has abstract intelligence, for character is really inwardness. Immorality, as energy, is also character; but to be neither moral nor immoral is merely ambiguous, and ambiguity enters into life when the qualitative distinctions are weakened by a gnawing reflection."[9]

He was a great one for leaps, that nineteenth century version of the 39
melancholy (if spiritedly so) Dane. I wondered on my flight home whether he might somewhere in this universe be smiling, be assenting to the message,

the slightly hectoring statement delivered by that mathematics teacher, and later by her tough, occasionally *very* tough, principal, who told me that he had "a lot of bad characters" to deal with, but damned if he couldn't "take them on," "turn them around," "convert their wasted energy into useful energy." It all sounded slightly like the noise of strained braggadocio: I'll talk big, and hope for the best. It all sounded exaggerated, romantic—like Kierkegaard. It all sounded pretty good, though, to those four young people and two of their teachers.

REFERENCES

All references are Coles's.

1. A good summary of Allport's sensitive moral and psychological writing is found in *Personality: A Psychological Interpretation* (New York: Holt, 1937).

2. See R. J. Havighurst and H. Taba, *Adolescent Character and Personality* (New York: Wiley, 1949). Also, more recently, R. Havighurst and R. Peck, *The Psychology of Character Development* (New York: Wiley, 1960).

3. See *Disorders of Character,* by Joseph Michaels (Springfield, Illinois: Thomas, 1955), for a suggestive discussion, with a first-rate bibliography.

4. Wilhelm Reich, *Character Analysis,* 3d ed. (New York: Farrar, Straus & Giroux, 1972), p. 169.

5. In his well-known oration, "The American Scholar," delivered before Harvard's Phi Beta Kappa Society on August 31, 1837.

6. Walker Percy, *The Second Coming* (New York: Farrar, Straus & Giroux, 1980). See also his wonderful collection of essays, which take up the same theme again and again, *The Message in the Bottle* (New York: Farrar, Straus & Giroux, 1975).

7. See my *Children of Crisis: A Study of Courage and Fear,* vol. 1 (Boston: Atlantic-Little, Brown, 1967).

8. See the section "Schools" in volume 3 of *Children of Crisis: The South Goes North* (Boston: Atlantic-Little, Brown, 1967).

9. Søren Kierkegaard, *The Present Age,* translated by Alexander Dru (New York: Harper & Row, 1962), p. 43.

Questions for Discussion

1. If a stranger had conducted interviews in your high school, would the principal have provided the interviewer with a quiet classroom "a good distance from the headmaster's office" (¶9)? Or would the principal have kept things closely under control, "in a room that belonged, really, to his office suite" (¶30)? What meanings or effects does Coles add to his piece with these details?
2. Can you construct a simple, clear summary of Coles's main point? Can you say whether he flatly admires or condemns any of the three schools?
3. Often an author will provide a careful summary in a final paragraph or two. Does Coles summarize, in paragraphs 38 and 39, what he thinks *we* should think? If not, why not? If so, what is the message?

4. Much of Coles's presentation consists of short accounts of what *other* people said and did, instead of statements about what *he* thinks. Which of the accounts seems to you most memorable or most forceful for his purposes?
5. Do you or your acquaintances ever talk about character? If so, do you use the term *character,* or do you use other terms to refer to the same thing?
6. Make two lists, in separate columns, of all the qualities you most admire and dislike in any person (yourself included). Don't worry about whether your terms are used in polite company or formal writing. And don't worry about whether your opinions will be "correct." Just consider yourself as going into a strange environment, as Coles did, to discover what people think, but this time *you* are the *subject* under study.
7. What kind of person does Coles seem to be? Does he lead you to infer that he has character? How would it alter your picture of him if he had omitted references to his wife, especially his admission that she always seems to discern character ahead of him? (See, for example, ¶5 and ¶6.)

Suggested Essay Topics

1. From the definitions of *good character* reported by Coles, choose the one that satisfies you best. Then write a portrait of a person who seems to be a good example of that kind of character. Try to include as much lively detail about actions or statements as you can remember (or invent). Some of Coles's devices for portraying Ruby Bridges (¶6) may suggest ways of doing your portrait.
2. Think over the people you know or have seen portrayed in movies or on TV. Choose three whose characters seem to be sharply defined or uncommon. Then write one paragraph about each person, *in the language of that person.* For example, "I doan take any a that kinda crap from anybody, see? You step on me, I'm gonna step right back. See what I mean?" Or "I'm just the sort of person who finds it extremely difficult to talk about myself. I cannot explain precisely what I mean, but I seem to want to keep in my own corner and watch the world go by. It's really unusual for me to be talking to you like this, but there was just something about you that made me open up." Write an essay directed to your classmates in which you discuss the character of each of your "speakers."

Shirley Jackson

The subtitle of this chapter—"What Should I Become?"—asks a question about character. It does not ask who we want to be, *as if all we had to do were to choose and then have the matter forever settled.*

It asks instead who we want to become, *implying that character is not a static thing, that it is in constant formation as a consequence of the choices we make in everyday living. Earlier in this chapter, St. Paul provided us with one of our culture's most influential and long-lasting definitions of the goals of character. St. Paul states clearly that the goal of character is love: "In a word, there are three things that last forever: faith, hope, and love; but the greatest of them all is love" (p. 344).*

Over the centuries this brief statement has seemed to many people to express a fundamental criterion of good character. Viewed as St. Paul seems to view it, the power to give and to receive love is the greatest source of good within and among individuals. With it one may be open to change and generous to others, for love unstops the ears and stirs the heart to charity. Those who can love may sometimes be weak and sometimes make mistakes, but they do not fall willingly into malice. Accepting love creates self-respect, and giving love creates fellow-feeling. Both are the enemy of malice. People who lack this power, however, may be led to malice through their own emptiness. They will be victims of whatever social forces get to them first. They will have no motives for generosity beyond their training in good manners or the promptings of self-interest and nothing to prop up their self-esteem but the goodwill of their neighbors, which must be purchased at the price of conforming to community conventions and accepted truths. People who cannot love can seldom afford to point out their neighbors' inadequacies, for they have no internal strength to fall back on if their neighbors reject them. They must thus pay the price of conformity even if the community's accepted truths are really cruel falsehoods.

In Shirley Jackson's (1919–1965) "Flower Garden" we see this principle illustrated and dramatized. A woman is jarred out of her ordinary habits and faced with a crisis: whether to challenge or to accept her community's racism. She is called upon to love another person, not romantically but charitably. She is called upon to be fair, decent, and just. Both her fundamental sympathies and her conscience stir her to answer this call with courage and justice. But to do so she must face the real possibility of losing her place in a small community where place is almost everything. She even faces the possibility, more remote but still real, of losing her home and family. In the midst of this dilemma her character hangs in the balance. Will she have enough courage? Does she love justice more than social position? She cannot dodge these issues. She must choose, and the choice she makes will constitute a decision about character, about who she is to become.

The narrator allows us to see that up to the present, Mrs. Winning has lived in a state of silent, resentful, incipient rebellion against the cold self-importance of her husband's family. She has longed for a life of independence symbolized by the cottage, and of passion and warmth symbolized by the flower garden. But when the opportunity of allying herself with another person who shares her longing for independence and warmth, and who is thus a natural friend and companion, brings her into conflict with her family's and community's disapproval, she cannot face her potential losses. We see her at the story's end turning away from new possibilities—new possibilities for herself, literally her "self," and her community—and turning toward conformity, toward sameness, and toward a falsehood that wounds both victim and victimizer.

As you read, compare Mrs. Winning's shaping of her character with that of

Margaret Sanger (pp. 313–317) and John Stuart Mill (pp. 318–322), who also faced crises of character. Does St. Paul's formulation about love give you a way of explaining the differences among these three people? Is Aristophanes' metaphorical myth about divided selves of any help (pp. 307–311)? Would it be helpful to augment the religious and mythical perspectives with theories of personality from psychology or sociology? Finally, regardless of what theories we appeal to, one fundamental question remains: What would each of us have done in Mrs. Winning's place? Surely we can see that to have chosen other than she did would have been costly. Who among us would have had the necessary strength to give and receive the needed love? There are no easy answers.

FLOWER GARDEN

From *The Lottery* (1948).

After living in an old Vermont manor house together for almost eleven years, the two Mrs. Winnings, mother and daughter-in-law, had grown to look a good deal alike, as women will who live intimately together, and work in the same kitchen and get things done around the house in the same manner. Although young Mrs. Winning had been a Talbot, and had dark hair which she wore cut short, she was now officially a Winning, a member of the oldest family in town and her hair was beginning to grey where her mother-in-law's hair had greyed first, at the temples; they both had thin sharp-featured faces and eloquent hands, and sometimes when they were washing dishes or shelling peas or polishing silverware together, their hands, moving so quickly and similarly, communicated more easily and sympathetically than their minds ever could. Young Mrs. Winning thought sometimes, when she sat at the breakfast table next to her mother-in-law, with her baby girl in the highchair close by, that they must resemble some stylized block print for a New England wallpaper; mother, daughter, and granddaughter, with perhaps Plymouth Rock or Concord Bridge in the background. 1

On this, as on other cold mornings, they lingered over their coffee, unwilling to leave the big kitchen with the coal stove and the pleasant atmosphere of food and cleanliness, and they sat together silently sometimes until the baby had long finished her breakfast and was playing quietly in the special baby corner, where uncounted Winning children had played with almost identical toys from the same heavy wooden box. 2

"It seems as though spring would never come," young Mrs. Winning said. "I get so tired of the cold." 3

"Got to be cold some of the time," her mother-in-law said. She began to move suddenly and quickly, stacking plates, indicating that the time for sitting was over and the time for working had begun. Young Mrs. Winning, rising immediately to help, thought for the thousandth time that her 4 mother-in-law would never relinquish the position of authority in her own house until she was too old to move before anyone else.

"And I wish someone would move into the old cottage," young Mrs. 5
Winning added. She stopped halfway to the pantry with the table napkins and said longingly, "If only *someone* would move in before spring." Young Mrs. Winning had wanted, long ago, to buy the cottage herself, for her husband to make with his own hands into a home where they could live with their children, but now, accustomed as she was to the big old house at the top of the hill where her husband's family had lived for generations, she had only a great kindness left toward the little cottage, and a wistful anxiety to see some happy young people living there. When she heard it was sold, as all the old houses were being sold in these days when no one could seem to find a newer place to live, she had allowed herself to watch daily for a sign that someone new was coming; every morning she glanced down from the back porch to see if there was smoke coming out of the cottage chimney, and every day going down the hill on her way to the store she hesitated past the cottage, watching carefully for the least movement within. The cottage had been sold in January and now, nearly two months later, even though it seemed prettier and less worn with the snow gently covering the overgrown garden and icicles in front of the blank windows, it was still forlorn and empty, despised since the day long ago when Mrs. Winning had given up all hope of ever living there.

Mrs. Winning deposited the napkins in the pantry and turned to tear 6
the leaf off the kitchen calendar before selecting a dish towel and joining her mother-in-law at the sink. "March already," she said despondently.

"They *did* tell me down at the store yesterday," her mother-in-law said, 7
"that they were going to start painting the cottage this week."

"Then that *must* mean someone's coming!" 8

"Can't take more than a couple of weeks to paint inside that little 9
house," old Mrs. Winning said.

It was almost April, however, before the new people moved in. The 10
snow had almost melted and was running down the street in icy, half-solid rivers. The ground was slushy and miserable to walk on, the skies grey and dull. In another month the first amazing green would start in the trees and on the ground, but for the better part of April there would be cold rain and perhaps more snow. The cottage had been painted inside, and new paper put on the walls. The front steps had been repaired and new glass put into the broken windows. In spite of the grey sky and the patches of dirty snow the cottage looked neater and firmer, and the painters were coming back to do the outside when the weather cleared. Mrs. Winning, standing at the foot of the cottage walk, tried to picture the cottage as it stood now, against the picture of the cottage she had made years ago, when she had hoped to live there herself. She had wanted roses by the porch; that could be done, and the neat colorful garden she had planned. She would have painted the outside

white, and that too might still be done. Since the cottage had been sold she had not gone inside, but she remembered the little rooms, with the windows over the garden that could be so bright with gay curtains and window boxes, the small kitchen she would have painted yellow, the two bedrooms upstairs with slanting ceilings under the eaves. Mrs. Winning looked at the cottage for a long time, standing on the wet walk, and then went slowly on down to the store.

The first news she had of the new people came, at last, from the grocer 11
a few days later. As he was tying the string around the three pounds of hamburger the large Winning family would consume in one meal, he asked cheerfully, "Seen your new neighbors yet?"

"Have they moved in?" Mrs. Winning asked. "The people in the cot- 12
tage?"

"Lady in here this morning," the grocer said. "Lady and a little boy, 13
seem like nice people. They say her husband's dead. Nice-looking lady."

Mrs. Winning had been born in the town and the grocer's father had 14
given her jawbreakers and licorice in the grocery store while the present grocer was still in high school. For a while, when she was twelve and the grocer's son was twenty, Mrs. Winning had hoped secretly that he would want to marry her. He was fleshy now, and middle-aged, and although he still called her Helen and she still called him Tom, she belonged now to the Winning family and had to speak critically to him, no matter how unwillingly, if the meat were tough or the butter price too high. She knew that when he spoke of the new neighbor as a "lady" he meant something different than if he had spoken of her as a "woman" or a "person." Mrs. Winning knew that he spoke of the two Mrs. Winnings to his other customers as "ladies." She hesitated and then asked, "Have they really moved in to stay?"

"She'll have to stay for a while," the grocer said drily. "Bought a week's 15
worth of groceries."

Going back up the hill with her package Mrs. Winning watched all the 16
way to detect some sign of the new people in the cottage. When she reached the cottage walk she slowed down and tried to watch not too obviously. There was no smoke coming from the chimney, and no sign of furniture near the house, as there might have been if people were still moving in, but there was a middle-aged car parked in the street before the cottage and Mrs. Winning thought she could see figures moving past the windows. On a sudden irresistible impulse she turned and went up the walk to the front porch, and then, after debating for a moment, on up the steps to the door. She knocked, holding her bag of groceries in one arm, and then the door opened and she looked down on a little boy, about the same age, she thought happily, as her own son.

"Hello," Mrs. Winning said. 17

"Hello," the boy said. He regarded her soberly. 18

"Is your mother here?" Mrs. Winning asked. "I came to see if I could 19
help her move in."

"We're all moved in," the boy said. He was about to close the door, but 20 a woman's voice said from somewhere in the house, "Davey? Are you talking to someone?"

"That's my mommy," the little boy said. The woman came up behind 21
him and opened the door a little wider. "Yes?" she said.

Mrs. Winning said, "I'm Helen Winning. I live about three houses up 22
the street, and I thought perhaps I might be able to help you."

"Thank you," the woman said doubtfully. She's younger than I am, 23
Mrs. Winning thought, she's about thirty. And pretty. For a clear minute Mrs. Winning saw why the grocer had called her a lady.

"It's so nice to have someone living in this house," Mrs. Winning said 24
shyly. Past the other woman's head she could see the small hallway, with the larger living-room beyond and the door on the left going into the kitchen, the stairs on the right, with the delicate stair-rail newly painted; they had done the hall in light green, and Mrs. Winning smiled with friendship at the woman in the doorway, thinking, She *has* done it right; this is the way it should look after all, she knows about pretty houses.

After a minute the other woman smiled back, and said, "Will you come 25
in?"

As she stepped back to let Mrs. Winning in, Mrs. Winning wondered 26
with a suddenly stricken conscience if perhaps she had not been too forward, almost pushing herself in. . . . "I hope I'm not making a nuisance of myself," she said unexpectedly, turning to the other woman. "It's just that I've been wanting to live here myself for so long." Why did I say that, she wondered; it had been a very long time since young Mrs. Winning had said the first thing that came into her head.

"Come see *my* room," the little boy said urgently, and Mrs. Winning 27
smiled down at him.

"I have a little boy just about your age," she said. "What's your name?" 28

"Davey," the little boy said, moving closer to his mother. "Davey Wil- 29
liam MacLane."

"My little boy," Mrs. Winning said soberly, "is named Howard Talbot 30
Winning."

The little boy looked up at his mother uncertainly, and Mrs. Winning, 31
who felt ill at ease and awkward in this little house she so longed for, said, "How old are you? My little boy is five."

"I'm five," the little boy said, as though realizing it for the first time. 32
He looked again at his mother and she said graciously, "Will you come in and see what we've done to the house?"

Mrs. Winning put her bag of groceries down on the slim-legged table 33
in the green hall, and followed Mrs. MacLane into the living-room, which was L-shaped and had the windows Mrs. Winning would have fitted with gay curtains and flower-boxes. As she stepped into the room, Mrs. Winning realized, with a quick wonderful relief, that it was really going to be all right, after all. Everything, from the andirons in the fireplace to the books on the table, was exactly as Mrs. Winning might have done if she were eleven years younger; a little more informal, perhaps, nothing of quite such good quality

as young Mrs. Winning might have chosen, but still richly, undeniably right. There was a picture of Davey on the mantel, flanked by a picture which Mrs. Winning supposed was Davey's father; there was a glorious blue bowl on the low coffee table, and around the corner of the L stood a row of orange plates on a shelf, and a polished maple table and chairs.

"It's lovely," Mrs. Winning said. This could have been mine, she was 34
thinking, and she stood in the doorway and said again, "It's perfectly lovely."

Mrs. MacLane crossed over to the low armchair by the fireplace and 35
picked up the soft blue material that lay across the arm. "I'm making curtains," she said, and touched the blue bowl with the tip of one finger. "Somehow I always make my blue bowl the center of the room," she said. "I'm having the curtains the same blue, and my rug—when it comes!—will have the same blue in the design."

"It matches Davey's eyes," Mrs. Winning said, and when Mrs. MacLane 36
smiled again she saw that it matched Mrs. MacLane's eyes too. Helpless before so much that was magic to her, Mrs. Winning said "*Have* you painted the kitchen yellow?"

"Yes," Mrs. MacLane said, surprised. "Come and see." She led the way 37
through the L, around past the orange plates to the kitchen, which caught the late morning sun and shone with clean paint and bright aluminum; Mrs. Winning noticed the electric coffeepot, the waffle iron, the toaster, and thought, *She* couldn't have much trouble cooking, not with just the two of them.

"When I have a garden," Mrs. MacLane said, "we'll be able to see it 38
from almost all the windows." She gestured to the broad kitchen windows, and added, "I love gardens. I imagine I'll spend most of my time working in this one, as soon as the weather is nice."

"It's a good house for a garden," Mrs. Winning said. "I've heard that 39
it used to be one of the prettiest gardens on the block."

"I thought so too," Mrs. MacLane said. "I'm going to have flowers on 40
all four sides of the house. With a cottage like this you can, you know."

Oh, I know, I know, Mrs. Winning thought wistfully, remembering the 41
neat charming garden she could have had, instead of the row of nasturtiums along the side of the Winning house, which she tended so carefully; no flowers would grow well around the Winning house, because of the heavy old maple trees which shaded all the yard and which had been tall when the house was built.

Mrs. MacLane had had the bathroom upstairs done in yellow, too, and 42
the two small bedrooms with overhanging eaves were painted green and rose. "All garden colors," she told Mrs. Winning gaily, and Mrs. Winning, thinking of the oddly matched, austere bedrooms in the big Winning house, sighed and admitted that it would be wonderful to have window seats under the eaved windows. Davey's bedroom was the green one, and his small bed was close to the window. "This morning," he told Mrs. Winning solemnly, "I looked out and there were four icicles hanging by my bed."

Mrs. Winning stayed in the cottage longer than she should have; she felt 43 certain, although Mrs. MacLane was pleasant and cordial, that her visit was extended past courtesy and into curiosity. Even so, it was only her sudden guilt about the three pounds of hamburger and dinner for the Winning men that drove her away. When she left, waving good-bye to Mrs. MacLane and Davey as they stood in the cottage doorway, she had invited Davey up to play with Howard, Mrs. MacLane up for tea, both of them to come for lunch some day, and all without the permission of her mother-in-law.

Reluctantly she came to the big house and turned past the bolted front door to go up the walk to the back door, which all the family used in the winter. Her mother-in-law looked up as she came into the kitchen and said irritably, "I called the store and Tom said you left an hour ago." 44

"I stopped off at the old cottage," Mrs. Winning said. She put the package of groceries down on the table and began to take things out quickly, to get the doughnuts on to a plate and the hamburger into the pan before too much time was lost. With her coat still on and her scarf over her head she moved as fast as she could while her mother-in-law, slicing bread at the kitchen table, watched her silently. 45

"Take your coat off," her mother-in-law said finally. "Your husband will be home in a minute." 46

By twelve o'clock the house was noisy and full of mud tracked across the kitchen floor. The oldest Howard, Mrs. Winning's father-in-law, came in from the farm and went silently to hang his hat and coat in the dark hall before speaking to his wife and daughter-in-law; the younger Howard, Mrs. Winning's husband, came in from the barn after putting the truck away and nodded to his wife and kissed his mother; and the youngest Howard, Mrs. Winning's son, crashed into the kitchen, home from kindergarten, shouting, "Where's dinner?" 47

The baby, anticipating food, banged on her high-chair with the silver cup which had first been used by the oldest Howard Winning's mother. Mrs. Winning and her mother-in-law put plates down on the table swiftly, knowing after many years the exact pause between the latest arrival and the serving of food, and with a minimum of time three generations of the Winning family were eating silently and efficiently, all anxious to be back about their work: the farm, the mill, the electric train; the dishes, the sewing, the nap. Mrs. Winning, feeding the baby, trying to anticipate her mother-in-law's gestures of serving, thought, today more poignantly than ever before, that she had at least given them another Howard, with the Winning eyes and mouth, in exchange for her food and her bed. 48

After dinner, after the men had gone back to work and the children were in bed, the baby for her nap and Howard resting with crayons and coloring book, Mrs. Winning sat down with her mother-in-law over their sewing and tried to describe the cottage. 49

"It's just perfect," she said helplessly. "Everything is so pretty. She invited us to come down some day and see it when it's all finished, the curtains and everything." 50

"I was talking to Mrs. Blake," the elder Mrs. Winning said, as though 51
in agreement. "She says the husband was killed in an automobile accident. *She* had some money in her own name and I guess she decided to settle down in the country for the boy's health. Mrs. Blake said he looked peakish."

"She loves gardens," Mrs. Winning said, her needle still in her hand for 52
a moment. "She's going to have a big garden all around the house."

"She'll need help," the elder woman said humorlessly, "that's a mighty 53
big garden she'll have."

"She has the *most* beautiful blue bowl, Mother Winning. You'd love it, 54
it's almost like silver."

"Probably," the elder Mrs. Winning said after a pause, "probably her 55
people came from around here a ways back, and *that's* why she's settled in these parts."

The next day Mrs. Winning walked slowly past the cottage, and slowly 56
the next, and the day after, and the day after that. On the second day she saw Mrs. MacLane at the window, and waved, and on the third day she met Davey on the sidewalk. "When are you coming to visit my little boy?" she asked him, and he stared at her solemnly and said, "Tomorrow."

Mrs. Burton, next-door to the MacLanes, ran over on the third day they 57
were there with a fresh apple pie, and then told all the neighbors about the yellow kitchen and the bright electric utensils. Another neighbor, whose husband had helped Mrs. MacLane start her furnace, explained that Mrs. MacLane was only very recently widowed. One or another of the townspeople called on the MacLanes almost daily, and frequently, as young Mrs. Winning passed, she saw familiar faces at the windows, measuring the blue curtains with Mrs. MacLane, or she waved to acquaintances who stood chatting with Mrs. MacLane on the now firm front steps. After the MacLanes had been in the cottage for about a week Mrs. Winning met them one day in the grocery and they walked up the hill together, and talked about putting Davey into the kindergarten. Mrs. MacLane wanted to keep him home as long as possible, and Mrs. Winning asked her, "Don't you feel terribly tied down, having him with you all the time?"

"I like it," Mrs. MacLane said cheerfully, "we keep each other com- 58
pany," and Mrs. Winning felt clumsy and ill-mannered, remembering Mrs. MacLane's widowhood.

As the weather grew warmer and the first signs of green showed on the 59
trees and on the wet ground, Mrs. Winning and Mrs. MacLane became better friends. They met almost daily at the grocery and walked up the hill together, and twice Davey came up to play with Howard's electric train, and once Mrs. MacLane came up to get him and stayed for a cup of coffee in the great kitchen while the boys raced round and round the table and Mrs. Winning's mother-in-law was visiting a neighbor.

"It's such an old house," Mrs. MacLane said, looking up at the dark 60
ceiling. "I love old houses; they feel so secure and warm, as though lots of

people had been perfectly satisfied with them and they *knew* how useful they
were. You don't get that feeling with a new house."

"This dreary old place," Mrs. Winning said. Mrs. MacLane, with a 61
rose-colored sweater and her bright soft hair, was a spot of color in the
kitchen that Mrs. Winning knew she could never duplicate. "I'd give anything in the world to live in your house," Mrs. Winning said.

"*I* love it," Mrs. MacLane said. "I don't think I've ever been so happy. 62
Everyone around here is so nice, and the house is so pretty, and I planted a
lot of bulbs yesterday." She laughed. "I used to sit in that apartment in New
York and dream about planting bulbs again."

Mrs. Winning looked at the boys, thinking how Howard was half-a- 63
head taller, and stronger, and how Davey was small and weak and loved his
mother adoringly. "It's been good for Davey already," she said. "There's color
in his cheeks."

"Davey loves it," Mrs. MacLane agreed. Hearing his name Davey came 64
over and put his head in her lap and she touched his hair, bright like her own.
"We'd better be getting home, Davey boy," she said.

"Maybe our flowers have grown some since yesterday," said Davey. 65

Gradually the days became miraculously long and warm, and Mrs. 66
MacLane's garden began to show colors and became an ordered thing, still
very young and unsure, but promising rich brilliance for the end of the
summer, and the next summer, and summers ten years from now.

"It's even better than I hoped," Mrs. MacLane said to Mrs. Winning, 67
standing at the garden gate. "Things grow so much better here than almost
anywhere else."

Davey and Howard played daily after the school was out for the sum- 68
mer, and Howard was free all day. Sometimes Howard stayed at Davey's
house for lunch, and they planted a vegetable patch together in the MacLane
back yard. Mrs. Winning stopped for Mrs. MacLane on her way to the store
in the mornings and Davey and Howard frolicked ahead of them down the
street. They picked up their mail together and read it walking back up the
hill, and Mrs. Winning went more cheerfully back to the big Winning house
after walking most of the way home with Mrs. MacLane.

One afternoon Mrs. Winning put the baby in Howard's wagon and with 69
the two boys they went for a long walk in the country. Mrs. MacLane picked
Queen Anne's lace and put it into the wagon with the baby; and the boys
found a garter snake and tried to bring it home. On the way up the hill Mrs.
MacLane helped pull the wagon with the baby and the Queen Anne's lace,
and they stopped halfway to rest and Mrs. MacLane said, "Look, I believe
you can see my garden all the way from here."

It was a spot of color almost at the top of the hill and they stood looking 70
at it while the baby threw the Queen Anne's lace out of the wagon. Mrs.
MacLane said, "I always want to stop here to look at it," and then, "Who is
that *beautiful* child?"

Mrs. Winning looked, and then laughed. "He *is* attractive, isn't he," she 71 said. "It's Billy Jones." She looked at him herself, carefully, trying to see him as Mrs. MacLane would. He was a boy about twelve, sitting quietly on a wall across the street, with his chin in his hands, silently watching Davey and Howard.

"He's like a young statue," Mrs. MacLane said. "So brown, and will you 72
look at that face?" She started to walk again to see him more clearly, and Mrs. Winning followed her. "Do I know his mother and fath—?"

"The Jones children are half-Negro," Mrs. Winning said hastily. "But 73
they're all beautiful children; you should see the girl. They live just outside town."

Howard's voice reached them clearly across the summer air. "Nigger," 74
he was saying, "nigger, nigger boy."

"Nigger," Davey repeated, giggling. 75

Mrs. MacLane gasped, and then said, *"Davey,"* in a voice that made 76
Davey turn his head apprehensively. Mrs. Winning had never heard her friend use such a voice, and she too watched Mrs. MacLane.

"Davey," Mrs. MacLane said again, and Davey approached slowly. 77
"What did I hear you say?"

"Howard," Mrs. Winning said, "leave Billy alone." 78

"Go tell that boy you're sorry," Mrs. MacLane said. "Go at once and 79
tell him you're sorry."

Davey blinked tearfully at his mother and then went to the curb and 80
called across the street, "I'm sorry."

Howard and Mrs. Winning waited uneasily, and Billy Jones across the 81
street raised his head from his hands and looked at Davey and then, for a long time, at Mrs. MacLane. Then he put his chin on his hands again.

Suddenly Mrs. MacLane called, "Young man—Will you come here a 82
minute, please?"

Mrs. Winning was surprised, and stared at Mrs. MacLane, but when the 83
boy across the street did not move, Mrs. Winning said sharply, "Billy! Billy Jones! Come here at once!"

The boy raised his head and looked at them, and then slid slowly down 84
from the wall and started across the street. When he was across the street and about five feet from them he stopped, waiting.

"Hello," Mrs. MacLane said gently, "what's your name?" 85

The boy looked at her for a minute and then at Mrs. Winning, and Mrs. 86
Winning said, "He's Billy Jones. Answer when you're spoken to, Billy."

"Billy," Mrs. MacLane said. "I'm sorry my little boy called you a name, 87
but he's very little and he doesn't always know what he's saying. But he's sorry, too."

"Okay," Billy said, still watching Mrs. Winning. He was wearing an old 88
pair of blue jeans and a torn white shirt, and he was barefoot. His skin and hair were the same color, the golden shade of a very heavy tan, and his hair curled lightly; he had the look of a garden statue.

"Billy," Mrs. MacLane said, "how would you like to come and work for 89
me? Earn some money?"

90 "Sure," Billy said.

91 "Do you like gardening?" Mrs. MacLane asked. Billy nodded soberly. "Because," Mrs. MacLane went on enthusiastically, "I've been needing someone to help me with my garden, and it would be just the thing for you to do." She waited a minute and then said, "Do you know where I live?"

92 "Sure," Billy said. He turned his eyes away from Mrs. Winning and for a minute looked at Mrs. MacLane, his brown eyes expressionless. Then he looked back at Mrs. Winning, who was watching Howard up the street.

93 "Fine," Mrs. MacLane said. "Will you come tomorrow?"

94 "Sure," Billy said. He waited for a minute, looking from Mrs. MacLane to Mrs. Winning, and then ran back across the street and vaulted over the wall where he had been sitting. Mrs. MacLane watched him admiringly. Then she smiled at Mrs. Winning and gave the wagon a tug to start it up the hill again. They were nearly at the MacLane cottage before Mrs. MacLane finally spoke. "I just can't stand that," she said, "to hear children attacking people for things they can't help."

95 "They're strange people, the Joneses," Mrs. Winning said readily. "The father works around as a handyman; maybe you've seen him. You see—" she dropped her voice—"the mother was white, a girl from around here. A local girl," she said again, to make it more clear to a foreigner. "She left the whole litter of them when Billy was about two, and went off with a white man."

96 "Poor children," Mrs. MacLane said.

97 "*They're* all right," Mrs. Winning said. "The church takes care of them, of course, and people are always giving them things. The girl's old enough to work now, too. She's sixteen, but. . . ."

98 "But what?" Mrs. MacLane said, when Mrs. Winning hesitated.

99 "Well, people talk about her a lot, you know," Mrs. Winning said. "Think of her mother, after all. And there's another boy, couple of years older than Billy."

100 They stopped in front of the MacLane cottage and Mrs. MacLane touched Davey's hair. "Poor unfortunate child," she said.

101 "Children *will* call names," Mrs. Winning said. "There's not much you can do."

102 "Well . . ." Mrs. MacLane said. "Poor child."

103 The next day, after the dinner dishes were washed, and while Mrs. Winning and her mother-in-law were putting them away, the elder Mrs. Winning said casually, "Mrs. Blake tells me your friend Mrs. MacLane was asking around the neighbors how to get hold of the Jones boy."

104 "She wants someone to help in the garden, I think," Mrs. Winning said weakly. "She needs help in that big garden."

105 "Not *that* kind of help," the elder Mrs. Winning said. "You tell her about them?"

106 "She seemed to feel sorry for them," Mrs. Winning said, from the depths of the pantry. She took a long time settling the plates in even stacks in order to neaten her mind. She *shouldn't* have done it, she was thinking, but

her mind refused to tell her why. She should have asked me first, though, she thought finally.

The next day Mrs. Winning stopped off at the cottage with Mrs. MacLane after coming up the hill from the store. They sat in the yellow kitchen and drank coffee, while the boys played in the back yard. While they were discussing the possibilities of hammocks between the apple trees there was a knock at the kitchen door and when Mrs. MacLane opened it she found a man standing there, so that she said, "Yes?" politely, and waited. 107

"Good morning," the man said. He took off his hat and nodded his head at Mrs. MacLane. "Billy told me you was looking for someone to work your garden," he said. 108

"Why . . ." Mrs. MacLane began, glancing sideways uneasily at Mrs. Winning. 109

"I'm Billy's father," the man said. He nodded his head toward the back yard and Mrs. MacLane saw Billy Jones sitting under one of the apple trees, his arms folded in front of him, his eyes on the grass at his feet. 110

"How do you do," Mrs. MacLane said inadequately. 111

"Billy told me you said for him to come work your garden," the man said. "Well, now, I think maybe a summer job's too much for a boy his age, he ought to be out playing in the good weather. And that's the kind of work I do anyway, so's I thought I'd just come over and see if you found anyone yet." 112

He was a big man, very much like Billy, except that where Billy's hair curled only a little, his father's hair curled tightly, with a line around his head where his hat stayed constantly and where Billy's skin was a golden tan, his father's skin was darker, almost bronze. When he moved, it was gracefully, like Billy, and his eyes were the same fathomless brown. "Like to work this garden," Mr. Jones said, looking around. "Could be a mighty nice place." 113

"You were very nice to come," Mrs. MacLane said. "I certainly do need help." 114

Mrs. Winning sat silently, not wanting to speak in front of Mr. Jones. She was thinking, I wish she'd ask me first, this is impossible . . . and Mr. Jones stood silently, listening courteously, with his dark eyes on Mrs. MacLane while she spoke. "I guess a lot of the work would be too much for a boy like Billy," she said. "There are a lot of things I can't even do myself, and I was sort of hoping I could get someone to give me a hand." 115

"That's fine, then," Mr. Jones said. "Guess I can manage most of it," he said, and smiled. 116

"Well," Mrs. MacLane said, "I guess that's all settled, then. When do you want to start?" 117

"How about right now?" he said. 118

"Grand," Mrs. MacLane said enthusiastically, and then, "Excuse me for a minute," to Mrs. Winning over her shoulder. She took down her gardening gloves and wide straw hat from the shelf by the door. "Isn't it a lovely day?" she asked Mr. Jones as she stepped out into the garden while he stood back to let her pass. 119

"You go along home now, Bill," Mr. Jones called as they went toward 120
the side of the house.

"Oh, why not let him stay?" Mrs. MacLane said. Mrs. Winning heard 121
her voice going on as they went out of sight. "He can play around the garden, and he'd probably enjoy . . ."

For a minute Mrs. Winning sat looking at the garden, at the corner 122
around which Mr. Jones had followed Mrs. MacLane, and then Howard's face appeared around the side of the door and he said, "Hi, is it nearly time to eat?"

"Howard," Mrs. Winning said quietly, and he came in through the door 123
and came over to her. "It's time for you to run along home," Mrs. Winning said. "I'll be along in a minute."

Howard started to protest, but she added, "I want you to go right away. 124
Take my bag of groceries if you think you can carry it."

Howard was impressed by her conception of his strength, and he lifted 125
down the bag of groceries; his shoulders, already broad out of proportion, like his father's and his grandfather's, strained under the weight, and then he steadied on his feet. "Aren't I strong?" he asked exultantly.

"*Very* strong," Mrs. Winning said. "Tell Grandma I'll be right up. I'll just 126
say good-bye to Mrs. MacLane."

Howard disappeared through the house; Mrs. Winning heard him walk- 127
ing heavily under the groceries, out through the open front door and down the steps. Mrs. Winning rose and was standing by the kitchen door when Mrs. MacLane came back.

"You're not ready to go?" Mrs. MacLane exclaimed when she saw Mrs. 128
Winning with her jacket on. "Without finishing your coffee?"

"I'd better catch Howard," Mrs. Winning said. "He ran along ahead." 129

"I'm sorry I left you like that," Mrs. MacLane said. She stood in the 130
doorway beside Mrs. Winning, looking out into the garden. "How *wonderful* it all is," she said, and laughed happily.

They walked together through the house; the blue curtains were up by 131
now, and the rug with the touch of blue in the design was on the floor.

"Good-bye," Mrs. Winning said on the front steps. 132

Mrs. MacLane was smiling, and following her look Mrs. Winning 133
turned and saw Mr. Jones, his shirt off and his strong back shining in the sun as he bent with a scythe over the long grass at the side of the house. Billy lay nearby, under the shade of the bushes; he was playing with a grey kitten. "I'm going to have the finest garden in town," Mrs. MacLane said proudly.

"You won't have him working here past today, will you?" Mrs. Win- 134
ning asked. "Of course you won't have him any longer than just today?"

"But surely—" Mrs. MacLane began, with a tolerant smile, and Mrs. 135
Winning, after looking at her for an incredulous minute, turned and started, indignant and embarrassed, up the hill.

Howard had brought the groceries safely home and her mother-in-law 136
was already setting the table.

"Howard says you sent him home from MacLane's," her mother-in-law 137
said, and Mrs. Winning answered briefly, "I thought it was getting late."

138 The next morning when Mrs. Winning reached the cottage on her way down to the store she saw Mr. Jones swinging the scythe expertly against the side of the house, and Billy Jones and Davey sitting on the front steps watching him. "Good morning, Davey," Mrs. Winning called, "is your mother ready to go downstreet?"

139 "Where's Howard?" Davey asked, not moving.

140 "He stayed home with his grandma today," Mrs. Winning said brightly. "Is your mother ready?"

141 "She's making lemonade for Billy and me," Davey said. "We're going to have it in the garden."

142 "Then tell her," Mrs. Winning said quickly, "tell her that I said I was in a hurry and that I had to go on ahead. I'll see her later." She hurried on down the hill.

143 In the store she met Mrs. Harris, a lady whose mother had worked for the elder Mrs. Winning nearly forty years before. "Helen," Mrs. Harris said, "you get greyer every year. You ought to stop all this running around."

144 Mrs. Winning, in the store without Mrs. MacLane for the first time in weeks, smiled shyly and said that she guessed she needed a vacation.

145 "Vacation!" Mrs. Harris said. "Let that husband of yours do the housework for a change. He doesn't have nuthin' else to do."

146 She laughed richly, and shook her head. "Nuthin' else to do," she said. "The Winnings!"

147 Before Mrs. Winning could step away Mrs. Harris added, her laughter penetrated by a sudden sharp curiosity: "Where's that dressed-up friend of yours get to? Usually downstreet together, ain't you?"

148 Mrs. Winning smiled courteously, and Mrs. Harris said, laughing again, "Just couldn't believe those shoes of hers, first time I seen them. Them shoes!"

149 While she was laughing again Mrs. Winning escaped to the meat counter and began to discuss the potentialities of pork shoulder earnestly with the grocer. Mrs. Harris only says what everyone else says, she was thinking, are they talking like that about Mrs. MacLane? Are they laughing at her? When she thought of Mrs. MacLane she thought of the quiet house, the soft colors, the mother and son in the garden; Mrs. MacLane's shoes were green and yellow platform sandals, odd-looking certainly next to Mrs. Winning's solid white oxfords, but so inevitably right for Mrs. MacLane's house, and her garden. . . . Mrs. Harris came up behind her and said, laughing again, "What's she got, that Jones fellow working for her now?"

150 When Mrs. Winning reached home, after hurrying up the hill past the cottage, where she saw no one, her mother-in-law was waiting for her in front of the house, watching her come the last few yards. "Early enough today," her mother-in-law said. "MacLane out of town?"

151 Resentful, Mrs. Winning said only, "Mrs. Harris nearly drove me out of the store, with her jokes."

152 "Nothing wrong with Lucy Harris getting away from that man of hers wouldn't cure," the elder Mrs. Winning said. Together, they began to walk around the house to the back door. Mrs. Winning, as they walked, noticed

that the grass under the trees had greened up nicely, and that the nasturtiums beside the house were bright.

"I've got something to say to you, Helen," the elder Mrs. Winning said 153
finally.

"Yes?" her daughter-in-law said. 154

"It's the MacLane girl, about her, I mean. You know her so well, you 155
ought to talk to her about that colored man working there."

"I suppose so," Mrs. Winning said. 156

"You *sure* you told her? You told her about those people?" 157

"I told her," Mrs. Winning said. 158

"He's there every blessed day," her mother-in-law said. "And working 159
out there without his shirt on. He goes in the house."

And that evening Mr. Burton, next-door neighbor to Mrs. MacLane, 160
dropped in to see the Howard Winnings about getting a new lot of shingles at the mill; he turned, suddenly, to Mrs. Winning, who was sitting sewing next to her mother-in-law at the table in the front room, and raised his voice a little when he said, "Helen, I wish you'd tell your friend Mrs. MacLane to keep that kid of hers out of my vegetables."

"Davey?" Mrs. Winning said involuntarily. 161

"No," Mr. Burton said, while all the Winnings looked at the younger 162
Mrs. Winning, "no, the other one, the colored boy. He's been running loose through our back yard. Makes me sort of mad, that kid coming in spoiling other people's property. You know," he added, turning to the Howard Winnings, "you know, that does make a person mad." There was a silence, and then Mr. Burton added, rising heavily, "Guess I'll say good-night to you people."

They all attended him to the door and came back to their work in 163
silence. I've got to do something, Mrs. Winning was thinking, pretty soon they'll stop coming to me first, they'll tell someone else to speak to *me.* She looked up, found her mother-in-law looking at her, and they both looked down quickly.

Consequently Mrs. Winning went to the store the next morning earlier 164
than usual, and she and Howard crossed the street just above the MacLane house, and went down the hill on the other side.

"Aren't we going to see Davey?" Howard asked once, and Mrs. Win- 165
ning said carelessly, "Not today, Howard. Maybe your father will take you out to the mill this afternoon."

She avoided looking across the street at the MacLane house, and hurried 166
to keep up with Howard.

Mrs. Winning met Mrs. MacLane occasionally after that at the store or 167
the post office, and they spoke pleasantly. When Mrs. Winning passed the cottage after the first week or so, she was no longer embarrassed about going by, and even looked at it frankly once or twice. The garden was going beautifully; Mr. Jones's broad back was usually visible through the bushes, and Billy Jones sat on the steps or lay on the grass with Davey.

One morning on her way down the hill Mrs. Winning heard a conversa- 168
tion between Davey MacLane and Billy Jones; they were in the bushes together and she heard Davey's high familiar voice saying, "Billy, you want to build a house with me today?"

"Okay," Billy said. Mrs. Winning slowed her steps a little to hear. 169

"We'll build a big house out of branches," Davey said excitedly, "and 170
when it's finished we'll ask my mommy if we can have lunch out there."

"You can't build a house just out of branches," Billy said. "You ought 171
to have wood, and boards."

"And chairs and tables and dishes," Davey agreed. "And walls." 172

"Ask your mommy can we have two chairs out here," Billy said. "Then 173
we can pretend the whole garden is our house."

"And I'll get us some cookies, too," Davey said. "And we'll ask my 174
mommy and your daddy to come in our house." Mrs. Winning heard them shouting as she went down along the sidewalk.

You have to admit, she told herself as though she were being strictly 175
just, you have to admit that he's doing a lot with that garden; it's the prettiest garden on the street. And Billy acts as though he had as much right there as Davey.

As the summer wore on into long hot days undistinguishable one from 176
another, so that it was impossible to tell with any real accuracy whether the light shower had been yesterday or the day before, the Winnings moved out into their yard to sit after supper, and in the warm darkness. Mrs. Winning sometimes found an opportunity of sitting next to her husband so that she could touch his arm; she was never able to teach Howard to run to her and put his head in her lap, or inspire him with other than the perfunctory Winning affection, but she consoled herself with the thought that at least they were a family, a solid respectable thing.

The hot weather kept up, and Mrs. Winning began to spend more time 177
in the store, postponing the long aching walk up the hill in the sun. She stopped and chatted with the grocer, with other young mothers in the town, with older friends of her mother-in-law's, talking about the weather, the reluctance of the town to put in a decent swimming pool, the work that had to be done before school started in the fall, chickenpox, the P.T.A. One morning she met Mrs. Burton in the store, and they spoke of their husbands, the heat, and the hot-weather occupations of their children before Mrs. Burton said: "By the way, Johnny will be six on Saturday and he's having a birthday party; can Howard come?"

"Wonderful," Mrs. Winning said, thinking. His good white shorts, the 178
dark blue shirt, a carefully wrapped present.

"Just about eight children," Mrs. Burton said, with the loving careless- 179
ness mothers use in planning the birthday parties of their children. "They'll stay for supper, of course—send Howard down about three-thirty."

"That sounds so nice," Mrs. Winning said. "He'll be delighted when I 180
tell him."

"I thought I'd have them all play outdoors most of the time," Mrs. 181

Burton said. "In this weather. And then perhaps a few games indoors, and supper. Keep it simple—*you* know." She hesitated, running her finger around and around the top rim of a can of coffee. "Look," she said, "I hope you won't mind me asking, but would it be all right with you if I didn't invite the MacLane boy?"

Mrs. Winning felt sick for a minute, and had to wait for her voice to even out before she said lightly, "It's all right with me if it's all right with *you;* why do you have to ask *me?*" 182

Mrs. Burton laughed. "I just thought you might mind if he didn't come." 183

Mrs. Winning was thinking, Something bad has happened, somehow people think they know something about me that they won't say, they all pretend it's nothing, but this never happened to me before; I live with the Winnings, don't I? "Really," she said, putting the weight of the old Winning house into her voice, "why in the *world* would it bother me?" Did I take it too seriously, she was wondering, did I seem too anxious, should I have let it go? 184

Mrs. Burton was embarrassed, and she set the can of coffee down on the shelf and began to examine the other shelves studiously. "I'm sorry I mentioned it at all," she said. 185

Mrs. Winning felt that she had to say something further, something to state her position with finality, so that no longer would Mrs. Burton, at least, dare to use such a tone to a Winning, presume to preface a question with "I hope you don't mind me asking." "After all," Mrs. Winning said carefully, weighing the words, "she's like a second mother to Billy." 186

Mrs. Burton, turning to look at Mrs. Winning for confirmation, grimaced and said, "Good Lord, Helen!" 187

Mrs. Winning shrugged and then smiled and Mrs. Burton smiled and then Mrs. Winning said, "I do feel so sorry for the little boy, though." 188

Mrs. Burton said, "Such a sweet little thing, too." 189

Mrs. Winning had just said, "He and Billy are together *all* the time now," when she looked up and saw Mrs. MacLane regarding her from the end of the aisle of shelves; it was impossible to tell whether she had heard them or not. For a minute Mrs. Winning looked steadily back at Mrs. MacLane, and then she said, with just the right note of cordiality. "Good morning, Mrs. MacLane. Where is your little boy this morning?" 190

"Good morning, Mrs. Winning," Mrs. MacLane said, and moved on past the aisle of shelves, and Mrs. Burton caught Mrs. Winning's arm and made a desperate gesture of hiding her face and, unable to help themselves, both she and Mrs. Winning began to laugh. 191

Soon after that, although the grass in the Winning yard under the maple trees stayed smooth and green, Mrs. Winning began to notice in her daily trips past the cottage that Mrs. MacLane's garden was suffering from the heat. The flowers wilted under the morning sun, and no longer stood up fresh and bright; the grass was browning slightly and the rose bushes Mrs. MacLane 192 had put in so optimistically were noticeably dying. Mr. Jones seemed always cool, working steadily; sometimes bent down with his hands in the earth, sometimes tall against the side of the house, setting up a trellis or pruning a tree, but the blue curtains hung lifelessly at the windows. Mrs. MacLane still smiled at Mrs. Winning in the store, and then one day they met at the gate of Mrs. MacLane's garden and, after hesitating for a minute, Mrs. MacLane said, "Can you come in for a few minutes? I'd like to have a talk, if you have time."

"Surely," Mrs. Winning said courteously, and followed Mrs. MacLane 193
up the walk, still luxuriously bordered with flowering bushes, but somehow disenchanted, as though the summer heat had baked away the vivacity from the ground. In the familiar living-room Mrs. Winning sat down on a straight chair, holding herself politely stiff, while Mrs. MacLane sat as usual in her armchair.

"How is Davey?" Mrs. Winning asked finally, since Mrs. MacLane did 194
not seem disposed to start any conversation.

"He's very well," Mrs. MacLane said, and smiled as she always did 195
when speaking of Davey. "He's out back with Billy."

There was a quiet minute, and then Mrs. MacLane said, staring at the 196
blue bowl on the coffee table, "What I wanted to ask you is, what on earth is gone wrong?"

Mrs. Winning had been holding herself stiff in readiness for some such 197
question, and when she said, "I don't know what you mean," she thought, I sound exactly like Mother Winning, and realized, I'm enjoying this, just as *she* would; and no matter what she thought of herself she was unable to keep from adding, "*Is* something wrong?"

"Of course," Mrs. MacLane said. She stared at the blue bowl, and said 198
slowly, "When I first came, everyone was so nice, and they seemed to like Davey and me and want to help us."

That's wrong, Mrs. Winning was thinking, you mustn't ever talk about 199
whether people like you, that's bad taste.

"And the garden was going so well," Mrs. MacLane said helplessly. 200
"And now, no one ever does more than just speak to us—I used to say 'Good morning' over the fence to Mrs. Burton, and she'd come to the fence and we'd talk about the garden, and now she just says 'Morning' and goes in the house—and no one ever smiles, or anything."

This is dreadful, Mrs. Winning thought, this is childish, this is com- 201
plaining. People treat you as you treat them, she thought; she wanted desperately to go over and take Mrs. MacLane's hand and ask her to come back and be one of the nice people again; but she only sat straighter in the chair and said, "I'm sure you must be mistaken. I've never heard anyone speak of it."

"*Are* you sure?" Mrs. MacLane turned and looked at her. "Are you sure 202
it isn't because of Mr. Jones working here?"

Mrs. Winning lifted her chin a little higher and said, "Why on earth 203
would anyone around here be rude to you because of Jones?"

Mrs. MacLane came with her to the door, both of them planning vigor- 204 ously for the days some time next week when they would all go swimming, when they would have a picnic, and Mrs. Winning went down the hill thinking, The nerve of her, trying to blame the colored folks.

Toward the end of the summer there was a bad thunderstorm, breaking 205
up the prolonged hot spell. It raged with heavy wind and rain over the town all night, sweeping without pity through the trees, pulling up young bushes and flowers ruthlessly; a barn was struck on one side of town, the wires pulled down on another. In the morning Mrs. Winning opened the back door to find the Winning yard littered with small branches from the maples, the grass bent almost flat to the ground.

Her mother-in-law came to the door behind her. "Quite a storm," she 206
said, "did it wake you?"

"I woke up once and went to look at the children," Mrs. Winning said. 207
"It must have been about three o'clock."

"I was up later," her mother-in-law said. "I looked at the children too; 208
they were both asleep."

They turned together and went in to start breakfast. 209

Later in the day Mrs. Winning started down to the store; she had almost 210
reached the MacLane cottage when she saw Mrs. MacLane standing in the front garden with Mr. Jones standing beside her and Billy Jones with Davey in the shadows of the front porch. They were all looking silently at a great branch from one of the Burtons' trees that lay across the center of the garden, crushing most of the flowering bushes and pinning down what was to have been a glorious tulip bed. As Mrs. Winning stopped, watching, Mrs. Burton came out on to her front porch to survey the storm damage, and Mrs. MacLane called to her, "Good morning, Mrs. Burton, it looks like we have part of your tree over here."

"Looks so," Mrs. Burton said, and she went back into her house and 211
closed the door flatly.

Mrs. Winning watched while Mrs. MacLane stood quietly for a minute. 212
Then she looked up at Mr. Jones almost hopefully and she and Mr. Jones looked at one another for a long time. Then Mrs. MacLane said, her clear voice carrying lightly across the air washed clean by the storm: "Do you think I ought to give it up, Mr. Jones? Go back to the city where I'll never have to see another garden?"

Mr. Jones shook his head despondently, and Mrs. MacLane, her shoul- 213
ders tired, went slowly over and sat on her front steps and Davey came and sat next to her. Mr. Jones took hold of the great branch angrily and tried to move it, shaking it and pulling until his shoulders tensed with the strength he was bringing to bear, but the branch only gave slightly and stayed, clinging to the garden.

"Leave it alone, Mr. Jones," Mrs. MacLane said finally. "Leave it for the 214
next people to move!"

But still Mr. Jones pulled against the branch, and then suddenly Davey 215
stood up and cried out, "There's Mrs. Winning! Hi, Mrs. Winning!"

Mrs. MacLane and Mr. Jones both turned, and Mrs. MacLane waved 216
and called out, "Hello!"

Mrs. Winning swung around without speaking and started, with great 217
dignity, back up the hill toward the old Winning house.

Questions for Discussion

1. In paragraph 10 Mrs. Winning thinks back on her earlier dreams of living in the cottage. What do her specific dreams of decorating and colors suggest about her inner life? About her distance from the other Winnings? About how happy she is?
2. What does the fact that the same people see each other every day—at the grocery store, at the post office, and on the single main street—suggest about the closeness of community standards? How is the size of a town a force for conformity?
3. How do the names of the Winnings, especially the men's names, suggest the view that the Winnings take of their own importance? How does the location of the Winning house reinforce this view?
4. What is the significance for Mrs. Winning's inner life that "no flowers would grow well around the Winning house, because of the heavy old maple trees which shaded all the yard and which had been tall when the house was built" (¶41)?
5. What is the significance for Mrs. Winning's inner life that when her husband comes in from the farm for the noon meal, he "nodded to his wife and kissed his mother" (¶47)?
6. What does Mrs. Winning's explanation of the name-calling episode (¶101) suggest about her character? What can we "read" in her joining Mrs. Burton's laughter in paragraph 191? Above all, what is suggested by her realization in paragraph 197 that she *enjoys* sounding just like Mother Winning?
7. What features in the Winning family make you sympathize with Mrs. Winning's position? What is suggested about the function and status of women in the Winning family by Mrs. Winning's silent thought that "she had at least given them another Howard, with the Winning eyes and mouth, in exchange for her food and bed" (¶48)?

Suggested Essay Topics

1. Write an essay to your class in which, speaking as Mrs. Winning, you explain your actions as they must have appeared to you. Allow Mrs. Winning to make the best case in her own defense that you can imagine, allowing her, perhaps, to predict the consequences if she had taken a different tack; in short, allow her to construct her own standards. After

you have given her her say, conclude with a page of response in which you determine which parts of her justification are valid and which are not.

2. Write a dialogue or conversation in which you picture Mrs. MacLane and Mrs. Winning meeting years later and discussing the events recorded in Jackson's story. The conversation could go in many different directions; you will have to choose one direction and stick with it. There could be recriminations and counteraccusations. You could invent any number of evil consequences for either or both women. Or you could have them arrive at an understanding of each other, seeing each other's limitations but also the pressure they were under at the time, and being willing to forgive. Or you could imagine a host of other kinds of confrontations. Try to keep in mind, however, that the story is fundamentally about possibilities of character and that your conversation should both express and illuminate the character of the women involved.

THE INDIVIDUAL AND COMMUNITY

The Life of Citizenship, the Role of Friendship

Power tends to corrupt; absolute power corrupts absolutely.
Lord Acton

Liberty means responsibility. That is why most men dread it.
George Bernard Shaw

Authority and power are two different things: *Power* is the force by means of which you can oblige others to obey you. *Authority* is the *right* to direct and comment, to be listened to or obeyed by others. Authority requests power. Power without authority is tyranny.
Jacques Maritain

If all mankind minus one were of one opinion, and only one person were of the contrary opinion, mankind would be no more justified in silencing that one person, than he, if he had the power, would be justified in silencing mankind.
John Stuart Mill

For discipline is the channel in which our acts run strong and deep; where there is no direction, the deeds of men run shallow and wander and are wasted.
Ursula K. Le Guin

The tree of liberty must be refreshed from time to time with the blood of patriots and tyrants. It is its natural manure.
Thomas Jefferson

Strange it is, that men should admit the validity of the arguments for free discussion, but object to their being "pushed to an extreme"; not seeing that unless the reasons are good for an extreme case, they are not good for any case.
John Stuart Mill

W. H. Auden

One of the most widely admired English poets of the twentieth century was W. H. Auden (1907–1973). Few poets in any language have ever written about more widely diverse subjects or mastered more contrasting poetic styles. Because many of his poems express controversial ideas, he was sometimes dismissed as "not a true poet" by critics who thought that poetry should not be used to advance arguments. Some other critics dismissed him because they hated his ideas—politically radical in his youth, Christian after his conversion in the late 1930s. But in the years since his death, almost everyone has acknowledged that he was a great master of the art of making ideas live by testing them in verse.

"The Unknown Citizen" is one of Auden's many satirical poems presented in the form of mock biography. You might begin by reading it aloud. Do you find that some of the lines simply cannot be read in a tone of straightforward praise? Now read through the poem, pencil in hand, underlining all the suggestions that something has certainly "been wrong" about this life. In doing so, you will find yourself contradicting the views of the official speaker of the poem, who is not *Auden but a character who can give this kind of praise without being ironic. By determining that the poem is a satire against the speaker and his kind, you are thus simultaneously deciphering Auden's irony. (Satire and irony are often confused, and you may find it useful to look them up in your dictionary.)*

Such satirical poems can deceive us if we fail to see that they contain much more than a paraphrased summary of their meanings. Suppose we concluded, for example, "The poem says that happiness is not to be found in conformity" or "People who merely conform to public standards destroy themselves." Obviously if that is all *that the poem says, Auden could have said it just like that. In reading poems that are worth reading at all, we find that the deeper our experience goes, the less we are satisfied with such summaries. They can be useful as entries into poems and as stimulation for our own further writing, but since this* is *a poem, the pursuit of such meanings is only the beginning of our pleasure. As you read and re-read the poem, then, ask yourself what it offers that could not have been achieved in any prose statement.*

THE UNKNOWN CITIZEN

Completed in March 1939.

(*To JS/07/M/378*
This Marble Monument
Is Erected by the State)

He was found by the Bureau of Statistics to be
One against whom there was no official complaint,
And all the reports on his conduct agree
That, in the modern sense of an old-fashioned word, he was a saint,
For in everything he did he served the Greater Community.
Except for the War till the day he retired
He worked in a factory and never got fired,
But satisfied his employers, Fudge Motors Inc.
Yet he wasn't a scab or odd in his views,
For his Union reports that he paid his dues,
(Our report on his Union shows it was sound)
And our Social Psychology workers found
That he was popular with his mates and liked a drink.
The Press are convinced that he bought a paper every day
And that his reactions to advertisements were normal in every way.
Policies taken out in his name prove that he was fully insured,
And his Health-card shows he was once in hospital but left it cured.
Both Producers Research and High-Grade Living declare
He was fully sensible to the advantages of the Instalment Plan
And had everything necessary to the Modern Man,
A phonograph, a radio, a car and a frigidaire.
Our researchers into Public Opinion are content
That he held the proper opinions for the time of year;
When there was peace, he was for peace; when there was war, he went.
He was married and added five children to the population,
Which our Eugenist says was the right number for a parent of his generation,
And our teachers report that he never interfered with their education.
Was he free? Was he happy? The question is absurd:
Had anything been wrong, we should certainly have heard.

Questions for Discussion

1. Can you and other members of your class agree about the main "message" of this poem? Why or why not?
2. One obvious difference between the poem and a paraphrase of it is that the line endings rhyme. Do all of them rhyme precisely? What would you say to someone who, in reading the poem aloud, pronounced *Inc.* as "Incorporated"? What do you make of the irregularity of the rhymes? Try reading aloud the little epigraph about the monument. How does the buried trick with rhyme help prepare the reader for the kind of reading required in the rest of the poem?
3. In finding both regularities and irregularities in the poem, you have no doubt noticed that you cannot read the lines aloud in any simple ta-túm-ty-túm-ty rhythm. If you count the number of syllables in each line, you find few with the same number—another irregularity. If you assume that Auden is not simply careless or unable to make regular rhymes, meter, and rhythm, can you think of any good reasons for his being what we might call "half-regular." Do his irregularities-within-regularity reinforce or even transform something about the "message"?

Suggested Essay Topics

1. Write a brief portrait of an extremely "happy, well-adjusted" person you know who, contrary to appearances, leads an empty life. Feel free to imitate any of Auden's methods, including verse if that seems tempting. Think of your reader not as your teacher but as someone coming across your work in a "reader" like this one.
2. Write a short magazine article delivering a straightforward attack on the oppressiveness and conformity that Auden attacks indirectly with his ironic portrait. (Decide in advance what kind of magazine your piece is designed for.) You might then want to add a paragraph, addressed to your teacher, describing the differences between Auden's account and yours, or perhaps even explaining why yours doesn't work as well or what gave you special difficulties.

E. B. White

The journalist and writer E. B. White (1899–1986) is commonly said to be one of the best prose stylists America has produced. His sentences never make a great fuss; they don't grab you by the lapels or shine a bright light in your eyes. They are quiet and light on their feet—taut, lithe, and graceful—like gymnasts in peak shape.

In this essay White conveys a rigorously critical, yet personal and anecdotal, assessment of the conflict between individual freedom and pressure to conform. He is not talking about the threat of repression by secret police; he can assume that we all would oppose that kind of infringement of liberty. His subject is the subtler kind of conformity imposed by current fashions. The pressure to conform to fashion or to assent blindly to "public opinion" is sinister because, not being illegal, it is difficult to combat. It may not even be seen for what it is, since it often consists only of unspoken suggestions that the nonconformist should be carefully watched by all "right-minded" folk.

People who pose, whether consciously or unconsciously, as guardians of "correct" thought usually start out innocently enough. They see themselves merely as patriotic citizens, full of Fourth-of-July zeal and civic pride, not as bigots or witch hunters. But history shows that all too often such people become so convinced of their own rightness that, like the Church in the days of the Inquisition, they wind up persecuting the saintly as heretics (or suppressing dissidents) in order to preserve holiness (or national purity). If not opposed early enough or vigorously enough, their momentum can easily crush the very liberties they start out professing to defend.

Notice especially how White interweaves his treatment of the general issue with particular reminiscences of his dachshund, Fred, the non-conformist who did his part to keep the Whites' community solid just by being himself.

BEDFELLOWS

A Letter from the East

From *Essays of E. B. White* (1956).

Turtle Bay, February 6, 1956

I am lying here in my private sick bay on the east side of town between Second and Third avenues, watching starlings from the vantage point of bed. Three Democrats are in bed with me: Harry Truman (in a stale copy of the *Times*), Adlai Stevenson* (in *Harper's*), and Dean Acheson† (in a book called *A Democrat Looks at His Party*). I take Democrats to bed with me for lack of a dachshund, although as a matter of fact on occasions like this I am almost certain to be visited by the ghost of Fred, my dash-hound everlasting, dead these many years. In life, Fred always attended the sick, climbing right into bed with the patient like some lecherous old physician, and making a bad situation worse. All this dark morning I have reluctantly entertained him upon the rumpled blanket, felt his oppressive weight, and heard his fraudulent report. He was an uncomfortable bedmate when alive; death has worked 1

*American politician (1900–1965), governor of Illinois (1949–1953), two-time Democratic nominee for the presidency (1952, 1956), and U.S. ambassador to the United Nations (1961–1965).

†Lawyer and statesman (1893–1971), secretary of state (1949–1953), appointed by President Truman.

little improvement—I still feel crowded, still wonder why I put up with his natural rudeness and his pretensions.

. . .

Fred was sold to me for a dachshund, but I was in a buying mood and would have bought the puppy if the storekeeper had said he was an Irish Wolfschmidt. He was only a few weeks old when I closed the deal, and he was in real trouble. In no time at all, his troubles cleared up and mine began. Thirteen years later he died, and by rights *my* troubles should have cleared up. But I can't say they have. Here I am, seven years after his death, still sharing a fever bed with him and, what is infinitely more burdensome, still feeling the compulsion to write about him. I sometimes suspect that subconsciously I'm trying to revenge myself by turning him to account, and thus recompensing myself for the time and money he cost me. 2

. . .

I have been languishing here, looking out at the lovely branches of the plane tree in the sky above our city back yard. . . . Fred was a window gazer and bird watcher, particularly during his later years, when hardened arteries slowed him up and made it necessary for him to substitute sedentary pleasures for active sport. I think of him as he used to look on our bed in Maine—an old four-poster, too high from the floor for him to reach unassisted. Whenever the bed was occupied during the daylight hours, whether because one of us was sick or was napping, Fred would appear in the doorway and enter without knocking. On his big gray face would be a look of quiet amusement (at having caught somebody in bed during the daytime) coupled with his usual look of fake respectability. Whoever occupied the bed would reach down, seize him by the loose folds of his thick neck, and haul him painfully up. He dreaded this maneuver, and so did the occupant of the bed. There was far too much dead weight involved for anybody's comfort. But Fred was always willing to put up with being hoisted in order to gain the happy heights, as, indeed, he was willing to put up with far greater discomforts—such as a mouthful of porcupine quills—when there was some prize at the end. 3

Once up, he settled into his pose of bird watching, propped luxuriously against a pillow, as close as he could get to the window, his great soft brown eyes alight with expectation and scientific knowledge. He seemed never to tire of his work. He watched steadily and managed to give the impression that he was a secret agent of the Department of Justice. Spotting a flicker or a starling on the wing, he would turn and make a quick report. 4

"I just saw an eagle go by," he would say. "It was carrying a baby." 5

This was not precisely a lie. Fred was like a child in many ways, and sought always to blow things up to proportions that satisfied his imagination and his love of adventure. He was the Cecil B. deMille of dogs. He was a zealot, and I have just been reminded of him by a quote from one of the Democrats sharing my bed—Acheson quoting Brandeis. "The greatest dangers to liberty," said Mr. Brandeis, "lurk in insidious encroachment by men of zeal, well-meaning but without understanding." Fred saw in every bird, 6 every squirrel, every housefly, every rat, every skunk, every porcupine, a security risk and a present danger to his republic. He had a dossier on almost every living creature, as well as on several inanimate objects, including my son's football.

Although birds fascinated him, his real hope as he watched the big shade trees outside the window was that a red squirrel would show up. When he sighted a squirrel, Fred would straighten up from his pillow, tense his frame, and then, in a moment or two, begin to tremble. The knuckles of his big forelegs, unstable from old age, would seem to go into spasm, and he would sit there with his eyes glued on the squirrel and his front legs alternately collapsing under him and bearing his weight again. 7

I find it difficult to convey the peculiar character of this ignoble old vigilante, my late and sometimes lamented companion. What was there about him so different from the many other dogs I've owned that he keeps recurring and does not, in fact, seem really dead at all? My wife used to claim that Fred was deeply devoted to me, and in a certain sense he was, but his was the devotion of an opportunist. He knew that on the farm I took the over-all view and travelled pluckily from one trouble spot to the next. He dearly loved this type of work. It was not his habit to tag along faithfully behind me, as a collie might, giving moral support and sometimes real support. He ran a trouble-shooting business of his own and was usually at the scene ahead of me, compounding the trouble and shooting in the air. The word "faithful" is an adjective I simply never thought of in connection with Fred. He differed from most dogs in that he tended to knock down, rather than build up, the master's ego. Once he had outgrown the capers of puppyhood, he never again caressed me or anybody else during his life. The only time he was ever discovered in an attitude that suggested affection was when I was in the driver's seat of our car and he would lay his heavy head on my right knee. This, I soon perceived, was not affection, it was nausea. Drooling always followed, and the whole thing was extremely inconvenient, because the weight of his head made me press too hard on the accelerator. 8

Fred devoted his life to deflating me and succeeded admirably. His attachment to our establishment, though untinged with affection, was strong nevertheless, and vibrant. It was simply that he found in our persons, in our activities, the sort of complex, disorderly society that fired his imagination and satisfied his need for tumult and his quest for truth. After he had subdued six or seven porcupines, we realized that his private war against porcupines was an expensive bore, so we took to tying him, making him fast to any tree or wheel or post or log that was at hand, to keep him from sneaking off into the woods. I think of him as always at the end of some outsize piece of rope. Fred's disgust at these confinements was great, but he improved his time, nonetheless, in a thousand small diversions. He never just lay and rested. Within the range of his tether, he continued to explore, dissect, botanize, conduct post-mortems, excavate, experiment, expropriate, savor, masticate, regurgitate. He had no contemplative life, but he held as a steady gleam the belief that under the commonplace stone and behind the unlikely piece of 9 driftwood lay the stuff of high adventure and the opportunity to save the nation.

10 But to return to my other bedfellows, these quick Democrats. They are big, solid men, every one of them, and they have been busy writing and speaking, and sniffing out the truth. I did not deliberately pack my counterpane with members of a single political faith; they converged on me by the slick device of getting into print. All three turn up saying things that interest me, so I make bed space for them.

11 Mr. Truman, reminiscing in a recent issue of the *Times,* says the press sold out in 1948 to "the special interests," was 90 percent hostile to his candidacy, distorted facts, caused his low popularity rating at that period, and tried to prevent him from reaching the people with his message in the campaign. This bold, implausible statement engages my fancy because it is a half-truth, and all half-truths excite me. An attractive half-truth in bed with a man can disturb him as deeply as a cracker crumb.

. . .

12 Without the press, radio, and TV, President Truman couldn't have got through to the people in anything like the volume he achieved. Some of the published news was distorted, but distortion is inherent in partisan journalism, the same as it is in political rallies. I have yet to see a piece of writing, political or nonpolitical, that doesn't have a slant. All writing slants the way a writer leans, and no man is born perpendicular, although many men are born upright. The beauty of the American free press is that the slants and the twists and the distortions come from so many directions, and the special interests are so numerous, the reader must sift and sort and check and countercheck in order to find out what the score is. This he does. It is only when a press gets its twist from a single source, as in the case of government-controlled press systems, that the reader is licked.

13 Democrats do a lot of bellyaching about the press being preponderantly Republican, which it is. But they don't do the one thing that could correct the situation: they don't go into the publishing business. Democrats say they haven't got that kind of money, but I'm afraid they haven't got that kind of temperament or, perhaps, nerve.

14 Adlai Stevenson takes a view of criticism almost opposite to Harry Truman's. Writing in *Harper's,* Stevenson says, ". . . I very well know that in many minds 'criticism' has today become an ugly word. It has become almost *lèse majesté* [crime against the sovereign]. It conjures up pictures of insidious radicals hacking away at the very foundations of the American way of life. It suggests nonconformity and nonconformity suggests disloyalty and disloyalty suggests treason, and before we know where we are, this process has all but identified the critic with the saboteur and turned political criticism into an un-American activity instead of democracy's greatest safeguard."

15 The above interests me because I agree with it and everyone is fascinated by what he agrees with. Especially when he is sick in bed.

16 Mr. Acheson, in his passionately partisan yet temperate book, writes at some length about the loyalty-security procedures that were started under

the Democrats in 1947 and have modified our lives ever since. This theme interests me because I believe, with the author, that security declines as security machinery expands. The machinery calls for a secret police. At first, this device is used solely to protect us from unsuitable servants in sensitive positions. Then it broadens rapidly and permeates nonsensitive areas, and, finally, business and industry. It is in the portfolios of the secret police that nonconformity makes the subtle change into disloyalty. A secret-police system first unsettles, then desiccates, then calcifies a free society. I think the recent loyalty investigation of the press by the Eastland subcommittee* was a disquieting event. It seemed to assume for Congress the right to poke about in newspaper offices and instruct the management as to which employees were okay and which were not. That sort of procedure opens wonderfully attractive vistas to legislators. If it becomes an accepted practice, it will lead to great abuses. Under extreme conditions, it could destroy the free press.

The loyalty theme also relates to Fred, who presses ever more heavily 17
against me this morning. Fred was intensely loyal to himself, as every strong individualist must be. He held unshakable convictions, like Harry Truman. He was absolutely sure that he was in possession of the truth. Because he was loyal to himself, I found his eccentricities supportable. Actually, he contributed greatly to the general health and security of the household. Nothing has been quite the same since he departed. His views were largely of a dissenting nature. Yet in tearing us apart he somehow held us together. In obstructing, he strengthened us. In criticizing, he informed. In his rich, aromatic heresy, he nourished our faith. He was also a plain damned nuisance, I must not forget that.

The matter of "faith" has been in the papers again lately. President 18
Eisenhower (I will now move over and welcome a Republican into bed, along with my other visitors) has come out for prayer and has emphasized that most Americans are motivated (as they surely are) by religious faith. The *Herald Tribune* headed the story, PRESIDENT SAYS PRAYER IS PART OF DEMOCRACY. The implication in such a pronouncement, emanating from the seat of government, is that religious faith is a *condition,* or even a *precondition,* of the democratic life. This is just wrong. A President should pray whenever and wherever he feels like it (most Presidents have prayed hard and long, and some of them in desperation and in agony), but I don't think a President should advertise prayer. That is a different thing. Democracy, if I understand it at all, is a society in which the unbeliever feels undisturbed and at home. If there were only half a dozen unbelievers in America, their well-being would be a test of our democracy, their tranquillity would be its proof. The repeated suggestion by the present administration that religious faith is a precondition of the American way of life is disturbing to me and, I am willing to bet, to a good many other citizens. President Eisenhower spoke of the tremendous

*In 1955 the Senate Internal Security Subcommittee, chaired by Senator James Eastland, began investigating the alleged influence of communists on American newspaper staffs. Chiefly targeted at the *New York Times,* the investigation led to an important controversy over the privileges and responsibilities of a free press.

favorable mail he received in response to his inaugural prayer in 1953. What he perhaps did not realize is that the persons who felt fidgety or disquieted about the matter were not likely to write in about it, lest they appear irreverent, irreligious, unfaithful, or even un-American. I remember the prayer very well. I didn't mind it, although I have never been able to pray electronically and doubt that I ever will be. Still, I was able to perceive that the President was sincere and was doing what came naturally, and anybody who is acting in a natural way is all right by me. I believe that our political leaders should live by faith and should, by deeds and sometimes by prayer, demonstrate faith, but I doubt that they should *advocate* faith, if only because such advocacy renders a few people uncomfortable. The concern of a democracy is that no honest man shall feel uncomfortable, I don't care who he is, or how nutty he is.

I hope that belief never is made to appear mandatory. One of our 19
founders, in 1787, said, "Even the diseases of the people should be represented." Those were strange, noble words, and they have endured. They were on television yesterday. I distrust the slightest hint of a standard for political rectitude, knowing that it will open the way for persons in authority to set arbitrary standards of human behavior.

Fred was an unbeliever. He worshiped no personal God, no Supreme 20
Being. He certainly did not worship *me.* If he had suddenly taken to worshiping me, I think I would have felt as queer as God must have felt the other day when a minister in California, pronouncing the invocation for a meeting of Democrats, said, "We believe Adlai Stevenson to be Thy choice for President of the United States. Amen."

I respected this quirk in Fred, this inability to conform to conventional 21
canine standards of religious feeling. And in the miniature democracy that was, and is, our household he lived undisturbed and at peace with his conscience. I hope my country will never become an uncomfortable place for the unbeliever, as it could easily become if prayer was made one of the requirements of the accredited citizen. My wife, a spiritual but not a prayerful woman, read Mr. Eisenhower's call to prayer in the *Tribune* and said something I shall never forget. "Maybe it's all right," she said. "But for the first time in my life I'm beginning to feel like an outsider in my own land."

Democracy is itself a religious faith. For some it comes close to being 22
the only formal religion they have. And so when I see the first faint shadow of orthodoxy sweep across the sky, feel the first cold whiff of its blinding fog steal in from sea, I tremble all over, as though I had just seen an eagle go by, carrying a baby.

Anyway, it's pleasant here in bed with all these friendly Democrats and 23
Republicans, every one of them a dedicated man, with all these magazine and newspaper clippings, with Fred, watching the starlings against the wintry sky, and the prospect of another presidential year, with all its passions and its distortions and its dissents and its excesses and special interests. Fred died from a life of excesses, and I don't mind if I do, too. I love to read all these words—most of them sober, thoughtful words—from the steadily growing

book of democracy: Acheson on security, Truman on the press, Eisenhower on faith, Stevenson on criticism, all writing away like sixty, all working to improve and save and maintain in good repair what was so marvelously constructed to begin with. This is the real thing. This is bedlam in bed. As Mr. Stevenson puts it: ". . . no civilization has ever had so haunting a sense of an ultimate order of goodness and rationality which can be known and achieved." It makes me eager to rise and meet the new day, as Fred used to rise to his, with the complete conviction that through vigilance and good works all porcupines, all cats, all skunks, all squirrels, all houseflies, all footballs, all evil birds in the sky could be successfully brought to account and the scene made safe and pleasant for the sensible individual—namely, him. However distorted was his crazy vision of the beautiful world, however perverse his scheme for establishing an order of goodness by murdering every creature that seemed to him bad, I had to hand him this: he really worked at it.

Questions for Discussion

1. In paragraph 6, where Fred is characterized as a "zealot," White seems to see him as a comic illustration of something he finds genuinely sinister. What is it about zealots that worries White so? Isn't sincerity always a good thing, and aren't zealots always sincere? When Barry Goldwater was a presidential candidate in 1963, he said in his speech accepting nomination that "extremism in defense of liberty is no vice." Since he was for liberty, was obviously sincere, and was clearly not a dictator (he didn't even get to be president), do you find his comment harmless? Foolish, or sinister, or patriotic? Why? What is the value of such utterances?
2. In light of White's worry about "the first faint shadow of orthodoxy" sweeping across the sky of American democracy (¶22), how would you characterize his tone throughout the essay? Is he fearful, troubled, angry, passionate, amused? How can you tell? Do you find his tone appropriate to his purpose as a whole? What *is* his purpose?
3. What does White imply about himself in this essay? Does he seem likable? Trustworthy? Is he one of those people you like even when you disagree? Do you find any characteristics that you dislike? List the words or phrases that suggest the qualities you admire or dislike.
4. In paragraph 3, where White pretends to read Fred's mind and gives him human traits ("his usual look of fake respectability"), he is employing a device called *personification,* giving the attributes of persons to non-persons. Can you find examples of this device in other places? (Try newspaper editorials or college catalogs.) Personification is an especially common device in church hymns (can you think why?), and in visual form it is

found in most political cartoons (e.g., a picture of the earth wearing a dismal countenance and holding in its arms a load of bombs with fuses burning short). Can you find other examples of visual personification? How does White's use of personification contribute to his effectiveness?

5. Who are White's implied readers? Can you infer the kinds of people White is *not* trying to speak to? How do you know?

Suggested Essay Topics

1. "The concern of a democracy is that no honest man shall feel uncomfortable, I don't care who he is, or how nutty he is" (¶18). This statement does not mean much unless you figure out what White means by *honest, uncomfortable,* and *nutty.* Since he does not explicitly define these terms anywhere, you are left to interpret what he means by fitting the statement into a consistent interpretation of the rest of his essay. Write an essay in which you show (a) what you think White means by his sentence, (b) why you think he means what he does, using evidence from the rest of the essay, and (c) why you agree or disagree with him.
2. Write a letter to White arguing that it is unfair to use Fred to exemplify nonconformists whose eccentricities and individuality the human family should cherish. You could argue that the portrait of the dog, while charming and amusing, oversimplifies the issue because Fred, unlike human nonconformists, could never constitute a real threat to other people or society. Press the point that the potential dangers of nonconformity need to be taken more seriously.

Mary McCarthy

Mary McCarthy's (b. 1912) "Artists in Uniform," first published in 1953, raises several important issues about the individual in relationship to the community. Part of the drama inside the story derives from the drama that was occurring outside of the story. In the early 1950s the cold war—the period of Soviet-American antagonism and military feinting that began at the end of World War II and led to the Cuban missile crisis of 1963—was in full swing and America was in the throes of a "red scare." Grade-school children were regularly drilled on how to climb dutifully under their desks in the event of a nuclear attack, people dug bomb shelters in their back yards, the signing of "loyalty oaths" was proposed as a prerequisite to some kinds of employment, and a series of books, articles, movies, and TV programs all fed the fear that communists were infiltrating every level of American society. Senator Joseph McCarthy (no relation to Mary McCarthy) was reinforcing that fear with his notorious Senate "hearings," in which artists, intellectuals, academics, and other political liberals were harassed, bullied, humiliated, and defamed in front of the whole country. Television, in its infancy as a mass commodity, seized on the hearings as one of its early "media events."

McCarthy's "hearings" did not succeed in unearthing any proven communists or conspiracies during the entire period of its operations. But they did succeed in scaring into silence most politicians who wanted to speak up in favor of civil liberties, and they fostered a climate of fear and suspicion in which political liberals might at any time or place—even in a passenger train winding its way across Indiana in a heat wave—find themselves the targets of insinuations or accusations that their patriotism was weak, that their loyalty was suspect, or that they were "soft on communism."

In a police state, such social pressures can be an effective mechanism for strangling dissent, criticism, or innovative thinking before the words ever get uttered. In a democracy, such pressure threatens to cut off democratic processes at the root. Conformity becomes enforced not by the secret police at the door but by the fear of majority opinion. In "Bedfellows" (pp. 386–394), E. B. White says that "democracy, if I understand it at all, is a society in which the unbeliever feels undisturbed and at home. If there were only half a dozen unbelievers in America, their well-being would be a test of our democracy, their tranquillity would be its proof. . . . The concern of a democracy is that no honest man shall feel uncomfortable, I don't care who he is, or how nutty he is" (pp. 391–392).

But the narrator in "Artists in Uniform" does not feel comfortable. Discovering with shock that her sophisticated clothing has revealed her to the men in the club car as not just an artist but an artist of an intellectual, "liberal" stamp—as if she were in uniform—she immediately feels vulnerable to potential attacks on her political beliefs. Yet her contempt for the cliché-ridden, knee-jerk mentality of her car companions spurs her to go on the attack herself, to attempt to overturn their vague accusations about communism among academics and Jews. The trouble is, she does not really possess any more facts about communism among these groups than do her opponents, and in the attempt to speak for pure reason and a liberal, unprejudiced mentality, she finds herself committing every intellectual sin she detests in the others.

Although McCarthy records elsewhere that the primary events of this story really happened to her, we should be leery of assuming that every detail of speech, thought, and action is a biographical fact. Regardless of how much the biography and the fiction overlap (or fail to), McCarthy portrays a character caught up in issues of importance for us all. As you read, consider the possibility that McCarthy writes this story not as an exposé of the Colonel—his prejudice is of the garden variety: common, rank, easily recognizable—but as an exposé of herself (or of people generally like her): the intellectual who sets up her own fall through excessive pride. Notice her smugness as she says, "It seemed to me that the writer or intellectual had a certain missionary usefulness in just such accidental gatherings as this, if he spoke not as an intellectual but as a normal member of the public" (¶3)—as if the "normal public" were too stupid to form sound opinions without guidance from intellectuals such as she, who will of course avoid condescending to their inferiors by pretending to be normal themselves. Here is condescension with a vengeance, not merely committing the sin of pride but pretending to be noble.

Consider, however, whether the story may contain a larger object of attack than either of the main characters. Is it possible that the story's larger target is a society that fosters extremist positions, that permits conformity to be a cover for non-thinkers like the Colonel while forcing intellectuals like McCarthy's narrator into defensive positions that short-circuit clear thinking? McCarthy invites us to consider seriously the uniforms we ourselves may wear and how we react to the perceived uniforms of others.

ARTISTS IN UNIFORM

From *On the Contrary* (1953).

The Colonel went out sailing,
He spoke with Turk and Jew . . .

"Pour it on Colonel," cried the young man in the Dacron suit excitedly, making his first sortie into the club-car conversation. His face was white as Roquefort and of a glistening, cheese-like texture; he had a shock of tow-colored hair, badly cut and greasy, and a snub nose with large gray pores. Under his darting eyes were two black craters. He appeared to be under some intense nervous strain and had sat the night before in the club car drinking bourbon with beer chasers and leafing magazines which he frowningly tossed aside, like cards into a discard heap. This morning he had come in late, with a hangdog, hangover look, and had been sitting tensely forward on a settee, smoking cigarettes and following the conversation with little twitches of the nose and quivers of the body, as a dog follows a human conversation, veering its mistrustful eyeballs from one speaker to another and raising its head eagerly at its master's voice. The Colonel's voice, rich and light and plausible, had in fact abruptly risen and swollen, as he pronounced his last sentence. "I can tell you one thing," he said harshly. "They weren't named Ryan or Murphy!" 1

A sort of sigh, as of consummation, ran through the club car. "Pour it on, Colonel, give it to them, Colonel, that's right, Colonel," urged the young man in a transport of admiration. The Colonel fingered his collar and modestly smiled. He was a thin, hawklike, black-haired handsome man with a bright blue bloodshot eye and a well-pressed, well-tailored uniform that did not show the effects of the heat—the train, westbound for St. Louis, was passing through Indiana, and, as usual in a heat-wave, the air-conditioning had not met the test. He wore the Air Force insignia, and there was something in his light-boned, spruce figure and keen, knifelike profile that suggested a classic image of the aviator, ready to cut, piercing, into space. In base fact, however, the Colonel was in procurement,* as we heard him tell the mining 2

*Procurement is a clerking, not a combat, function. The procurement clerk edits purchase requests, invites bids from suppliers, and makes out orders for procurement of materials—in this case for the Air Force.

engineer who had just bought him a drink. From several silken hints that parachuted into the talk, it was patent to us that the Colonel was a man who knew how to enjoy this earth and its pleasures: he led, he gave us to think, a bachelor's life of abstemious dissipation and well-rounded sensuality. He had accepted the engineer's drink with a mere nod of the glass in acknowledgment, like a genial Mars quaffing a libation; there was clearly no prospect of his buying a second in return, not if the train were to travel from here to the Mojave Desert. In the same way, an understanding had arisen that I, the only woman in the club car, had become the Colonel's perquisite; it was taken for granted, without an invitation's being issued, that I was to lunch with him in St. Louis, where we each had a wait between trains—my plans for seeing the city in a taxicab were dished.

From the beginning, as we eyed each other over my volume of Dickens 3
("*The Christmas Carol?*" suggested the Colonel, opening relations), I had guessed that the Colonel was of Irish stock, and this, I felt, gave me an advantage, for he did not suspect the same of me; strangely so, for I am supposed to have the map of Ireland written on my features. In fact, he had just wagered, with a jaunty, sidelong grin at the mining engineer, that my people "came from Boston from way back," and that I—narrowed glance, running, like steel measuring-tape, up and down my form—was a professional sculptress. I might have laughed this off, as a crudely bad guess like his *Christmas Carol,* if I had not seen the engineer nodding gravely, like an idol, and the peculiar young man bobbing his head up and down in mute applause and agreement. I was wearing a bright apple-green raw silk blouse and a dark-green rather full raw silk skirt, plus a pair of pink glass earrings; my hair was done up in a bun. It came to me, for the first time, with a sort of dawning horror, that I had begun, in the course of years, without ever guessing it, to look irrevocably Bohemian.* Refracted from the three men's eyes was a strange vision of myself as an artist, through and through, stained with my occupation like the dyer's hand. All I lacked, apparently, was a pair of sandals. My sick heart sank to my Ferragamo shoes; I had always particularly preened myself on being an artist in disguise. And it was not only a question of personal vanity—it seemed to me that the writer or intellectual had a certain missionary usefulness in just such accidental gatherings as this, if he spoke not as an intellectual but as a normal member of the public. Now, thanks to the Colonel, I slowly became aware that my contributions to the club-car conversation were being watched and assessed as coming from *a certain quarter.* My costume, it seemed, carefully assembled as it had been at an expensive shop, was to these observers simply a uniform that blazoned a caste and allegiance just as plainly as the Colonel's khaki and eagles. "*Gardez,*" [take care] I said to myself. But, as the conversation grew tenser and I endeavored to keep cool, I began to writhe within myself, and every time I looked down, my contrasting greens seemed to be growing more and more lurid and taking on an almost menacing light, like leaves just before a storm that lift their

*Unconventional, anti-establishment, scornful of middle-class values.

bright undersides as the air becomes darker. We had been speaking, of course, of Russia,* and I had mentioned a study that had been made at Harvard of political attitudes among Iron Curtain refugees. Suddenly, the Colonel had smiled. "They're pretty Red at Harvard, I'm given to understand," he observed in a comfortable tone, while the young man twitched and quivered urgently. The eyes of all the men settled on me and waited. I flushed as I saw myself reflected. The woodland greens of my dress were turning to their complementary red, like a color-experiment in psychology or a traffic light changing. Down at the other end of the club car, a man looked up from his paper. I pulled myself together. "Set your mind at rest, Colonel," I remarked dryly. "I know Harvard very well and they're conservative to the point of dullness. The only thing crimson is the football team." This disparagement had its effect. "So . . . ?" queried the Colonel. "I thought there was some professor. . . ." I shook my head. "Absolutely not. There used to be a few fellow-travelers, but they're very quiet these days, when they haven't absolutely recanted. The general atmosphere is more anti-Communist than the Vatican." The Colonel and the mining engineer exchanged a thoughtful stare and seemed to agree that the Delphic oracle that had just pronounced knew whereof it spoke. "Glad to hear it," said the Colonel. The engineer frowned and shook his fat wattles; he was a stately, gray-haired, plump man with small hands and feet and the pampered, finical tidiness of a small-town widow. "There's so much hearsay these days," he exclaimed vexedly. "You don't know *what* to believe."

I reopened my book with an air of having closed the subject and read 4
a paragraph three times over. I exulted to think that I had made a modest contribution to sanity in our times, and I imagined my words pyramiding like a chain letter—the Colonel telling a fellow-officer on the veranda of a club in Texas, the engineer halting a works-superintendent in a Colorado mine shaft: "I met a woman on the train who claims . . . Yes, absolutely. . . ." Of course, I did not know Harvard as thoroughly as I pretended, but I forgave myself by thinking it was the convention of such club-car symposia in our positivistic country to speak from the horse's mouth.

Meanwhile, across the aisle, the engineer and the Colonel continued 5
their talk in slightly lowered voices. From time to time, the Colonel's polished index-fingernail scratched his burnished black head and his knowing blue eye forayed occasionally toward me. I saw that still I was a doubtful quantity to them, a movement in the bushes, a noise, a flicker, that was figuring in their crenelated thought as "she." The subject of Reds in our colleges had not, alas, been finished; they were speaking now of another university and a woman faculty-member who had been issuing Communist statements. This story somehow, I thought angrily, had managed to appear in the newspapers without my knowledge, while these men were conversant with it; I recognized a big chink in the armor of my authority. Looking up from my book, I began

*In the early 1950s, at the height of the cold war, talk of Soviet-American antagonisms was common enough to be referred to by an "of course."

to question them sharply, as though they were reporting some unheard-of natural phenomenon. "When?" I demanded. "Where did you see it? What was her name?" This request for the professor's name was a headlong attempt on my part to buttress my position, the implication being that the identities of all university professors were known to me and that if I were but given the name I could promptly clarify the matter. To admit that there was a single Communist in our academic system whose activities were hidden from me imperiled, I instinctively felt, all the small good I had done here. Moreover, in the back of my mind, I had a supreme confidence that these men were wrong: the story, I supposed, was some tattered piece of misinformation they had picked up from a gossip column. Pride, as usual, preceded my fall. To the Colonel, the demand for the name was not specific but generic: what *kind* of name was the question he presumed me to be asking. "Oh," he said slowly with a luxurious yawn, "Finkelstein or Fishbein or Feinstein."* He lolled back in his seat with a side glance at the engineer, who deeply nodded. There was a voluptuary pause, as the implication sank in. I bit my lip, regarding this as a mere diversionary tactic. "Please!" I said impatiently. "Can't you remember exactly?" The Colonel shook his head and then his spare cheekbones suddenly reddened and he looked directly at me. "I can tell you one thing," he exclaimed irefully. "They weren't named Ryan or Murphy."

The Colonel went no further; it was quite unnecessary. In an instant, the young man was at his side, yapping excitedly and actually picking at the military sleeve. The poor thing was transformed, like some creature in a fairy tale whom a magic word releases from silence. "That's right, Colonel," he happily repeated. "I know them. *I* was at Harvard in the business school, studying accountancy. I left. I couldn't take it." He threw a poisonous glance at me, and the Colonel, who had been regarding him somewhat doubtfully, now put on an alert expression and inclined an ear for his confidences. The man at the other end of the car folded his newspaper solemnly and took a seat by the young man's side. "They're all Reds, Colonel," said the young man. "They teach it in the classroom. I came back here to Missouri. It made me sick to listen to the stuff they handed out. If you didn't hand it back, they flunked you. Don't let anybody tell you different." "You are wrong," I said coldly and closed my book and rose. The young man was still talking eagerly, and the three men were leaning forward to catch his every gasping word, like three astute detectives over a dying informer, when I reached the door and cast a last look over my shoulder at them. For an instant, the Colonel's eye met mine, and I felt his scrutiny processing my green back as I tugged open the door and met a blast of hot air, blowing my full skirt wide. Behind me, in my fancy, I saw four sets of shrugging brows. 6

In my own car, I sat down, opposite two fat nuns, and tried to assemble my thoughts. I ought to have spoken, I felt, and yet what could I have said? It occurred to me that the four men had perhaps not realized why I had left the club car with such abruptness: was it possible that they thought I was a 7

*Jewish-sounding names—which makes the Colonel's comment an anti-Semitic slur.

Communist, who feared to be unmasked? I spurned this possibility, and yet it made me uneasy. For some reason, it troubled my *amour-propre*[*] to think of my anti-Communist self living on, so to speak, green in their collective memory as a Communist or fellow-traveler. In fact, though I did not give a fig for the men, I hated the idea, while a few years ago I should have counted it a great joke. This, it seemed to me, was a measure of the change in the social climate. I had always scoffed at the notion of liberals "living in fear" of political demagoguery in America, but now I had to admit that if I was not fearful, I was at least uncomfortable in the supposition that anybody, anybody whatever, could think of me, precious me, as a Communist.† A remoter possibility was, of course, that back there my departure was being ascribed to Jewishness, and this too annoyed me. I am in fact a quarter Jewish, and though I did not "hate" the idea of being taken for a Jew, I did not precisely like it, particularly under these circumstances. I wished it to be clear that I had left the club car for intellectual and principled reasons; I wanted those men to know that it was not I, but my principles, that had been offended. To let them conjecture that I had left because I was Jewish would imply that only a Jew could be affronted by an anti-Semitic outburst: a terrible idea. Aside from anything else, it voided the whole concept of transcendence, which was very close to my heart, the concept that man is more than his circumstances, more even than himself.

However you looked at the episode, I said to myself nervously, I had 8
not acquitted myself well. I ought to have done or said something concrete and unmistakable. From this, I slid glassily to the thought that those men ought to be punished, the Colonel, in particular, who occupied a responsible position. In a minute, I was framing a businesslike letter to the Chief of Staff, deploring the Colonel's conduct as unbecoming to an officer and identifying him by rank and post, since unfortunately I did not know his name. Earlier in the conversation, he had passed some comments on "Harry"‡ that bordered positively on treason, I said to myself triumphantly. A vivid image of the proceedings against him presented itself to my imagination: the long military tribunal with a row of stern soldierly faces glaring down at the Colonel. I myself occupied only an inconspicuous corner of this tableau, for, to tell the truth, I did not relish the role of the witness. Perhaps it would be wiser to let the matter drop . . . ? We were nearing St. Louis now; the Colonel had come back into my car, and the young accountant had followed him, still talking feverishly. I pretended not to see them and turned to the two nuns, as if for sanctuary from this world and its hatreds and revenges. Out of the corner of my eye, I watched the Colonel, who now looked wry and restless; he shrank against the window as the young man made a place for himself

*Self-pride.

†This was the period in which Senator Joseph McCarthy was holding his notorious "hearings," in which he frequently accused artists and intellectuals of being communists. Such accusations, which could not be rebutted in a Senate hearing as they could have been in a court of law, ruined several careers and cost others both heavy loss of income and great personal anguish.

‡Harry Truman, president of the United States from 1946 to 1952.

amid the Colonel's smart luggage and continued to express his views in a pale breathless voice. I smiled to think that the Colonel was paying the piper. For the Colonel, anti-Semitism was simply an aspect of urbanity, like a knowledge of hotels or women. This frantic psychopath of an accountant was serving him as a nemesis, just as the German people had been served by their psychopath, Hitler. Colonel, I adjured him, you have chosen, between him and me; measure the depth of your error and make the best of it! No intervention on my part was now necessary; justice had been meted out. Nevertheless, my heart was still throbbing violently, as if I were on the verge of some dangerous action. What was I to do, I kept asking myself, as I chatted with the nuns, if the Colonel were to hold me to that lunch? And I slowly and apprehensively revolved this question, just as though it were a matter of the most serious import. It seemed to me that if I did not lunch with him—and I had no intention of doing so—I had the dreadful obligation of telling him why.

He was waiting for me as I descended the car steps. "Aren't you coming 9
to lunch with me?" he called out and moved up to take my elbow. I began to tremble with audacity. "No," I said firmly, picking up my suitcase and draping an olive-green linen duster over my arm. "I can't lunch with you." He quirked a wiry black eyebrow. "Why not?" he said. "I understood it was all arranged." He reached for my suitcase. "No," I said, holding on to the suitcase. "I can't." I took a deep breath. "I have to tell you. I think you should be *ashamed* of yourself, Colonel, for what you said in the club car." The Colonel stared; I mechanically waved for a red-cap, who took my bag and coat and went off. The Colonel and I stood facing each other on the emptying platform. "What do you mean?" he inquired in a low, almost clandestine tone. "Those anti-Semitic remarks," I muttered, resolutely. "You ought to be *ashamed.*" The Colonel gave a quick, relieved laugh. "Oh, come now," he protested. "I'm sorry," I said. "I can't have lunch with anybody who feels that way about the Jews." The Colonel put down his attaché case and scratched the back of his lean neck. "Oh, come now," he repeated, with a look of amusement. "You're not Jewish, are you?" "No," I said quickly. "Well, then . . ." said the Colonel, spreading his hands in a gesture of bafflement. I saw that he was truly surprised and slightly hurt by my criticism, and this made me feel wretchedly embarrassed and even apologetic, on my side, as though I had called attention to some physical defect in him, of which he himself was unconscious. "But I might have been," I stammered. "You had no way of knowing. You oughtn't to talk like that." I recognized, too late, that I was strangely reducing the whole matter to a question of etiquette: "Don't start anti-Semitic talk before making sure there are no Jews present." "Oh, hell," said the Colonel, easily. "I can tell a Jew." "No, you can't," I retorted, thinking of my Jewish grandmother, for by Nazi criteria I was Jewish. "Of course I can," he insisted. "So can you." We had begun to walk down the platform side by side, disputing with a restrained passion that isolated us like a pair of lovers. All at once, the Colonel halted, as though struck with a thought. "What *are* you, anyway?" he said meditatively, regarding my dark hair, green blouse, and pink earrings. Inside myself, I began to laugh. "Oh," I said gaily,

playing out the trump I had been saving, "I'm Irish, like you, Colonel." "How did you know?" he said amazedly. I laughed aloud. "I can tell an Irishman," I taunted. The Colonel frowned. "What's your family name?" he said brusquely. "McCarthy." He lifted an eyebrow, in defeat, and then quickly took note of my wedding ring. "That your maiden name?" I nodded. Under this peremptory questioning, I had the peculiar sensation that I get when I am lying; I began to feel that "McCarthy" was a nom de plume,* a coinage of my artistic personality. But the Colonel appeared to be satisfied. "Hell," he said, "come on to lunch, then. With a fine name like that, you and I should be friends." I still shook my head, though by this time we were pacing outside the station restaurant; my baggage had been checked in a locker; sweat was running down my face and I felt exhausted and hungry. I knew that I was weakening and I wanted only an excuse to yield and go inside with him. The Colonel seemed to sense this. "Hell," he conceded. "You've got me wrong. I've got nothing against the Jews. Back there in the club car, I was just stating a simple fact: you won't find an Irishman sounding off for the Commies. You can't deny that, can you?"

His voice rose persuasively; he took my arm. In the heat, I wilted and we went into the air-conditioned cocktail lounge. The Colonel ordered two old-fashioneds. The room was dark as a cave and produced, in the midst of the hot midday, a hallucinated feeling, as though time had ceased, with the weather, and we were in eternity together. As the Colonel prepared to relax, I made a tremendous effort to guide the conversation along rational, purposive lines; my only justification for being here would be to convert the Colonel. "There *have* been Irishmen associated with the Communist party," I said suddenly, when the drinks came. "I can think of two." "Oh, hell," said the Colonel, "every race and nation has its traitors. What I mean is, you won't find them in numbers. You've got to admit that the Communists in this country are 90 per cent Jewish." "But the Jews in this country aren't 90 per cent Communist," I retorted. 10

As he stirred his drink, restively, I began to try to show him the reasons why the Communist movement in America had attracted such a large number, relatively, of Jews: how the Communists had been anti-Nazi when nobody else seemed to care what happened to the Jews in Germany; how the Communists still capitalized on a Jewish fear of fascism; how many Jews had become, after Buchenwald,† traumatized by this fear. . . . 11

But the Colonel was scarcely listening. An impatient frown rested on his jaunty features. "I don't get it," he said slowly. "Why should you be for them, with a name like yours?" "I'm *not* for the Communists," I cried. "I'm just trying to explain to you—" "For the Jews," the Colonel interrupted, irritable now himself. "I've heard of such people but I never met one before." "I'm not 'for' them," I protested. "You don't understand. I'm not for *any* race or nation. I'm against those who are against them." This word, *them,* with a 12

*Assumed name, pen name.

†A Nazi extermination camp.

sort of slurring circle drawn round it, was beginning to sound ugly to me. Automatically, in arguing with him, I seemed to have slipped into the Colonel's style of thought. It occurred to me that defense of the Jews could be a subtle and safe form of anti-Semitism, an exercise of patronage: as a rational Gentile, one could feel superior both to the Jews and the anti-Semites. There could be no doubt that the Jewish question evoked a curious stealthy lust or concupiscence. I could feel it now vibrating between us over the dark table. If I had been a good person, I should unquestionably have got up and left.

"I don't get it," repeated the Colonel. "How were you brought up? Were 13
your people this way too?" It was manifest that an odd reversal had taken place; each of us regarded the other as "abnormal" and was attempting to understand the etiology of a disease. "Many of my people think just as you do," I said, smiling coldly. "It seems to be a sickness to which the Irish are prone. Perhaps it's due to the potato diet," I said sweetly, having divined that the Colonel came from a social stratum somewhat lower than my own.

But the Colonel's hide was tough. "You've got me wrong," he reiterated, 14
with an almost plaintive laugh. "I don't dislike the Jews. I've got a lot of Jewish friends. Among themselves, they think just as I do, mark my words. I tell you what it is," he added ruminatively, with a thoughtful prod of his muddler, "I draw a distinction between a kike and a Jew." I groaned. "Colonel, I've never heard an anti-Semite who didn't draw that distinction. You know what Otto Kahn* said? 'A kike is a Jewish gentleman who has just left the room.' " The Colonel did not laugh. "I don't hold it against some of them," he persisted, in a tone of pensive justice. "It's not their fault if they were born that way. That's what I tell them, and they respect me for my honesty. I've had a lot of discussions; in procurement, you have to do business with them, and the Jews are the first to admit that you'll find more chiselers among their race than among the rest of mankind." "It's not a race," I interjected wearily, but the Colonel pressed on. "If I deal with a Jewish manufacturer, I can't bank on his word. I've seen it again and again, every damned time. When I deal with a Gentile, I can trust him to make delivery as promised. That's the difference between the two races. They're just a different breed. They don't have standards of honesty, even among each other." I sighed, feeling unequal to arguing the Colonel's personal experience.

"Look," I said, "you may be dealing with an industry where the Jewish 15
manufacturers are the most recent comers and feel they have to cut corners to compete with the established firms. I've heard that said about Jewish cattle-dealers, who are supposed to be extra sharp. But what I think, really, is that you notice it when a Jewish firm fails to meet an agreement and don't notice it when it's a Yankee." "Hah," said the Colonel. "They'll tell you what I'm telling you themselves, if you get to know them and go into their homes. You won't believe it, but some of my best friends are Jews," he said, simply and thoughtfully, with an air of originality. "They may be *your* best friends,

*American banker and philanthropist (1867–1934), born in Germany (naturalized in 1917), president (1918–1931) of the Metropolitan Opera Company; perhaps the greatest patron of the arts in U.S. history.

Colonel," I retorted, "but you are not theirs. I defy you to tell me that you talk to them as you're talking now." "Sure," said the Colonel, easily. "More or less." "They must be very queer Jews you know," I observed tartly, and I began to wonder whether there indeed existed a peculiar class of Jews whose function in life was to be "friends" with such people as the Colonel. It was difficult to think that all the anti-Semites who made the Colonel's assertion were the victims of a cruel self-deception.

A dispirited silence followed. I was not one of those liberals who believed that the Jews, alone among peoples, possessed no characteristics whatever of a distinguishing nature—this would mean they had no history and no culture, a charge which should be leveled against them only by an anti-Semite. Certainly, types of Jews could be noted and patterns of Jewish thought and feeling: Jewish humor, Jewish rationality, and so on, not that every Jew reflected every attribute of Jewish life or history. But somehow, with the Colonel, I dared not concede that there was such a thing as a Jew: I saw the sad meaning of the assertion that a Jew was a person whom other people thought was Jewish. 16

Hopeless, however, to convey this to the Colonel. The desolate truth was that the Colonel was extremely stupid, and it came to me, as we sat there, glumly ordering lunch, that for extremely stupid people anti-Semitism was a form of intellectuality, the sole form of intellectuality of which they were capable. It represented, in a rudimentary way, the ability to make categories, to generalize. Hence a thing I had noted before but never understood: the fact that anti-Semitic statements were generally delivered in an atmosphere of profundity. Furrowed brows attended these speculative distinctions between a kike and a Jew, these little empirical laws that you can't know one without knowing them all. To arrive, indeed, at the idea of a Jew was, for these grouping minds, an exercise in Platonic thought, a discovery of essence,* and to be able to add the great corollary, "Some of my best friends are Jews," was to find the philosopher's cleft between essence and existence. From this, it would seem, followed the querulous obstinacy with which the anti-Semite clung to his concept; to be deprived of this intellectual tool by missionaries of tolerance would be, for persons like the Colonel, the equivalent of Western man's losing the syllogism: a lapse into animal darkness. In the club car, we had just witnessed an example: the Colonel with his anti-Semitic observation had come to the mute young man like the paraclete, bearing the gift of tongues. 17

Here in the bar, it grew plainer and plainer that the Colonel did not regard himself as an anti-Semite but merely as a heavy thinker. The idea that I considered him anti-Semitic sincerely outraged his feelings. "Prejudice" was the last trait he could have imputed to himself. He looked on me, almost respectfully, as a "Jew lover," a kind of being he had heard of but never 18

*For Plato, every object in *this* world—the world perceivable by the physical senses—is merely a shadow of its *essential* identity, a non-material version of itself existing on a spiritual plane. Thus to discover the "essence" of a thing is to discover the ultimate truth about it.

actually encountered, like a centaur or a Siamese twin, and the interest of relating this prodigy to the natural state of mankind overrode any personal distaste. There I sat, the exception which was "proving" or testing the rule, and he kept pressing me for details of my history that might explain my deviation in terms of the norm. On my side, of course, I had become fiercely resolved that he would learn nothing from me that would make it possible for him to dismiss my anti-anti-Semitism as the product of special circumstances: I was stubbornly sitting on the fact of my Jewish grandmother like a hen on a golden egg. I was bent on making *him* see hiimself as a monster, a deviation, a heretic from Church and State. Unfortunately, the Colonel, owing perhaps to his military training, had not the glimmering of an idea of what democracy meant; to him, it was simply a slogan that was sometimes useful in war. The notion of an ordained inequality was to him "scientific."

"Honestly," he was saying in lowered tones, as our drinks were taken 19
away and the waitress set down my sandwich and his corned-beef hash, "don't you, brought up the way you were, feel about them the way I do? Just between ourselves, isn't there a sort of inborn feeling of horror that the very word, Jew, suggests?" I shook my head, roundly. The idea of an *innate* anti-Semitism was in keeping with the rest of the Colonel's thought, yet it shocked me more than anything he had yet said. "No," I sharply replied. "It doesn't evoke any feeling one way or the other." "Honest Injun?" said the Colonel. "Think back; when you were a kid, didn't the word, Jew, make you feel sick?"* There was a dreadful sincerity about this that made me answer in an almost kindly tone. "No, truthfully, I assure you. When we were children, we learned to call the old-clothes man a sheeny, but that was just a dirty word to us, like 'Hun' that we used to call after workmen we thought were Germans."

"I don't get it," pondered the Colonel, eating a pickle. "There must be 20
something wrong with you. Everybody is born with that feeling. It's natural; it's part of nature." "On the contrary," I said. "It's something very unnatural that you must have been taught as a child." "It's not something you're *taught,*" he protested. "You must have been," I said. "You simply don't remember it. In any case, you're a man now; you must rid yourself of that feeling. It's psychopathic, like that horrible young man on the train." "You thought he was crazy?" mused the Colonel, in an idle, dreamy tone. I shrugged my shoulders. "Of course. Think of his color. He was probably just out of a mental institution. People don't get that tattletale gray except in prison or mental hospitals." The Colonel suddenly grinned. "You might be right," he said. "He was quite a case." He chuckled.

I leaned forward. "You know, Colonel," I said quickly, "anti-Semitism 21
is contrary to the Church's teaching. God will make you do penance for hating the Jews. Ask your priest; he'll tell you I'm right. You'll have a long spell in Purgatory, if you don't rid yourself of this sin. It's a deliberate

*Compare the similarity of the Colonel's views with the views of Hitler in *Mein Kampf,* pp. 494–502).

violation of Christ's commandment, 'Love thy neighbor.' The Church holds that the Jews have a sacred place in God's design. Mary was a Jew and Christ was a Jew. The Jews are under God's special protection. The Church teaches that the millennium can't come until the conversion of the Jews; therefore, the Jews must be preserved that the Divine Will may be accomplished. Woe to them that harm them, for they controvert God's Will!" In the course of speaking, I had swept myself away with the solemnity of the doctrine. The Great Reconciliation between God and His chosen people, as envisioned by the Evangelist, had for me at that moment a piercing, majestic beauty, like some awesome Tintoretto. I saw a noble spectacle of blue sky, thronged with gray clouds, and a vast white desert, across which God and Israel advanced to meet each other, while below in hell the demons of disunion shrieked and gnashed their teeth.

"Hell," said the Colonel, jovially. "I don't believe in all that. I lost my 22
faith when I was a kid. I saw that all this God stuff was a lot of bushwa." I gazed at him in stupefaction. His confidence had completely returned. The blue eyes glittered debonairly; the eagles glittered; the narrow polished head cocked and listened to itself like a trilling bird. I was up against an air man with a bird's-eye view, a man who believed in nothing but the law of kind: the epitome of godless materialism. "You still don't hold with that bunk?" the Colonel inquired in an undertone, with an expression of stealthy curiosity. "No," I confessed, sad to admit to a meeting of minds. "You know what got me?" exclaimed the Colonel. "That birth-control stuff. Didn't it kill you?" I made a neutral sound. "I was beginning to play around," said the Colonel, with a significant beam of the eye, "and I just couldn't take that guff. When I saw through the birth-control talk, I saw through the whole thing. They claimed it was against nature, but I claim, if that's so, an operation's against nature. I told my old man that when he was having his kidney stones out. You ought to have heard him yell!" A rich, reminiscent satisfaction dwelt in the Colonel's face.

This period of his life, in which he had thrown off the claims of the 23
spiritual and adopted a practical approach, was evidently one of those "turning points" to which a man looks back with pride. He lingered over the story of his break with church and parents with a curious sort of heat, as though the flames of old sexual conquests stirred within his body at the memory of those old quarrels. The looks he rested on me, as a sharer of that experience, grew more and more lickerish and assaying. "What got *you* down?" he finally inquired, settling back in his chair and pushing his coffee cup aside. "Oh," I said wearily, "it's a long story. You can read it when it's published." "You're an author?" cried the Colonel, who was really very slow-witted. I nodded, and the Colonel regarded me afresh. "What do you write? Love stories?" He gave a half-wink. "No," I said. "Various things. Articles. Books. Highbrowish stories." A suspicion darkened in the Colonel's sharp face. "That McCarthy," he said. "Is that your pen name?" "Yes," I said, "but it's my real name too. It's the name I write under *and* my maiden name." The Colonel digested this thought. "Oh," he concluded.

A new idea seemed to visit him. Quite cruelly, I watched it take posses- 24
sion. He was thinking of the power of the press and the indiscretions of other military figures, who had been rewarded with demotion. The consciousness of the uniform he wore appeared to seep uneasily into his body. He straightened his shoulders and called thoughtfully for the check. We paid in silence, the Colonel making no effort to forestall my dive into my pocketbook. I should not have let him pay in any case, but it startled me that he did not try to do so, if only for reasons of vanity. The whole business of paying, apparently, was painful to him; I watched his facial muscles contract as he pocketed the change and slipped two dimes for the waitress onto the table, not daring quite to hide them under the coffee cup—he had short-changed me on the bill and the tip, and we both knew it. We walked out into the steaming station and I took my baggage out of the checking locker. The Colonel carried my suitcase and we strolled along without speaking. Again, I felt horribly embarrassed for him. He was meditative, and I supposed that he too was mortified by his meanness about the tip.

"Don't get me wrong," he said suddenly, setting the suitcase down and 25
turning squarely to face me, as though he had taken a big decision. "I may have said a few things back there about the Jews getting what they deserved in Germany." I looked at him in surprise; actually, he had not said that to me. Perhaps he had let it drop in the club car. "But that doesn't mean I approve of Hitler." "I should hope not," I said. "What I mean is," said the Colonel, "that they probably gave the Germans a lot of provocation, but that doesn't excuse what Hitler did." "No," I said, somewhat ironically, but the Colonel was unaware of anything satiric in the air. His face was grave and determined; he was sorting out his philosophy for the record. "I mean, I don't approve of his methods," he finally stated. "No," I agreed. "You mean, you don't approve of the gas chamber." The Colonel shook his head very severely. "Absolutely not! That was terrible." He shuddered and drew out a handkerchief and slowly wiped his brow. "For God's sake," he said, "don't get me wrong. I think they're human beings." "Yes," I assented, and we walked along to my track. The Colonel's spirits lifted, as though, having stated his credo, he had both got himself in line with public policy and achieved an autonomous thought. "I mean," he resumed, "you may not care for them, but that's not the same as killing them, in cold blood, like that." "No, Colonel," I said.

He swung my bag onto the car's platform and I climbed up behind it. 26
He stood below, smiling, with upturned face. "I'll look for your article," he cried, as the train whistle blew. I nodded, and the Colonel waved, and I could not stop myself from waving back at him and even giving him the corner of a smile. After all, I said to myself, looking down at him, the Colonel was "a human being." There followed one of those inane intervals in which one prays for the train to leave. We both glanced at our watches. "See you some time," he called. "What's your married name?" "Broadwater," I called back. The whistle blew again. "Brodwater?" shouted the Colonel, with a dazed look of unbelief and growing enlightenment; he was not the first person to hear it as a Jewish name, on the model of Goldwater. "B-r-o-a-d," I began, auto-

matically, but then I stopped. I disdained to spell it out for him; the victory was his. "One of the chosen, eh?" his brief grimace commiserated. For the last time, and in the final fullness of understanding, the hawk eye patrolled the green dress, the duster, and the earrings; the narrow flue of his nostril contracted as he curtly turned away. The train commenced to move.

Questions for Discussion

1. Why is McCarthy's narrator so upset in paragraph 3 to realize that she has been discovered as an artist: "I had always particularly preened myself on being an artist in disguise"? What criticism or support can you offer for her desire to stay unknown as an artist among strangers?
2. What quality in the central figure's character is revealed when she says, "I exulted to think that I had made a modest contribution to sanity in our times, and I imagined my words pyramiding like a chain letter" (¶4)?
3. The reader gradually realizes that the narrator, in conversing with the Colonel, is not only deceiving herself about her own motives but is also being dishonest in her mode of arguing (attacking the Colonel, for example, with Church doctrines that she herself does not believe). Later, however, in writing it all down as a story, she seems completely honest and judgmental about her faults. To what degree does her subsequent honesty redeem her character in the reader's eyes? Are there any who dislike her as a person at the end of the story? For what reasons?
4. What does the narrator mean at the end of paragragh 12 when she says, "If I had been a good person, I should unquestionably have got up and left"? Why does she make this judgment? Do you agree with it? What do you think you would have done in her place?
5. Why does the narrator say at the end, "I disdained to spell it out for him; the victory was his"? What victory? Why does she not tell him that Broadwater is not a Jewish name? She has argued so hard and spent so much energy trying to convert the Colonel, why does she let him walk away thinking that he now knows why she objected to his anti-Semitism?

Suggested Essay Topics

1. If you have ever felt unfair pressure to conform to majority opinion, write an essay in which you give an account of the experience, explaining how you felt and analyzing, as McCarthy does, the source of the pressure. Finally, evaluate your behavior in the face of it. Address your essay to a sympathetic friend to whom you want to give as complete an account of the experience as possible.
2. The quotation from E. B. White included in the introduction could be countered with the old aphorism "The majority should rule," an aphorism

with which most of us probably agree. But where is the line that, when crossed, turns "majority rule" into "suppression of dissent"? And where is the line that, when crossed, turns the individual rights of the few into tyranny of the underdog? Choose some particular case that interests you and analyze it, attempting to uphold the rights of the individual (or the minority) against the will of the majority or, if the case warrants it, the rights of the majority against the will of the individual (or the minority). You might consider, for example, the justice of upholding minority quotas for job openings or for admission into schools, especially when the quotas seem to force the hiring or admission of minority candidates less qualified than others. Or you might discuss the right of men's and women's private clubs to ban members of the opposite sex, the prohibition of girls from Little League baseball, or some similar matter.

Plato

Plato's Republic, *a much longer work from which "The Allegory of the Cave" is taken, covers many topics as its characters discourse on the question, "What is justice and how can it be made the reigning principle of the state?" (For more on* The Republic, *see the introductions to "Censorship," pp. 268–269, "The Seductions of Art," p. 276, and "The Education of Women," p. 547.) Some of the topics discussed include education (the goals as well as the curriculum), the role of women, the rearing of children, the censorship of literature, and, in this portion, the criteria for choosing the highest rulers in the state.*

Plato (c. 427–347 B.C.) assumes that a state wants its most talented, most virtuous, and wisest persons as rulers, but he realizes that unless it is self-evident who these persons are, simply saying *that they are the ones most wanted doesn't automatically put them in power. Obviously, one must have some criterion for deciding who they are. The criterion that Plato invariably holds for determining wisdom and virtue is knowledge, not so much the* amount *of knowledge as the* kind *of knowledge. Specifically, he judges wisdom and virtue to be products of the knowledge of truth.*

But this raises another problem: He cannot determine his criterion of knowledge until he constructs a criterion for truth, especially the highest kind of truth. To do that is the purpose of "The Allegory of the Cave." He constructs his allegory—really an extended analogy—to express his theory of what the world is like and to define the highest kind of truth that it contains (¶1–16). Once he has accomplished that purpose, he is ready to apply the definition yielded by the analogy to the practical business of deciding who shall rule the state (¶17–26).

Plato's view of the world is what philosophers call dualistic, *which simply means that he believes in two realms of reality. Dualism assumes that there is, on the one hand, the tangible realm of matter—the entire realm of physical entities, including all forms of nature and our own bodies—and, on the other, the intangible realm of spiritual entities, which Plato called "Ideas." It is important to understand that Plato does* not *suppose that Ideas are created by any activity or force in the world of matter. Ideas are not in themselves created in people's brains or by nature; they have their own independent (what some philosophers call* objective*) existence. (Since dualism is a common view in most of the world's religions, this idea should not sound totally strange or unfamiliar. Any belief in an eternal, non-material, unchanging God is an example of a dualistic view, unless the belief treats our ordinary world as sheer illusion.)*

What is distinctive about Plato's dualism is the relationship he posits between Ideas and matter. Specialists quarrel about just how Plato sees this relationship, but we can clarify it, within limits, by contrasting it with Christian views. Christianity posits that the ultimate non-material force in the universe, God, is related to the world of matter by having initially created it, having invested it with a purpose and a destiny, and having sustained an interest in its goings on. To Christians the world of physical forms is both real and important because God created it. (For an account of the relationship between the rise of science and the Christian's commitment to understanding the world that a rational God had created for human existence, see Stanley Jaki, "The Role of Faith in Physics," pp. 648–663.)

However, even though some versions of Christianity have borrowed heavily from his thought, no mainstream Christian view is identical to Plato's. Contrary to Christianity's appreciation of the world as a creation of God, Plato devalues the world of physical reality altogether. From his point of view, the physical forms perceived by the physical senses are merely inferior shadows *of Ideas. Because any truth about physical forms can therefore only be a secondary shadow version of primary truth, Plato devotes much discussion to the ways that human beings can escape the constant pull of their physical nature, which dulls and blocks their intellectual perceptions. His remedy is self-discipline acquired by a lifelong, life-governing commitment to rational inquiry: the self-discipline of the true philosopher. The philosopher systematically hardens himself against the appetites and entanglements of worldly attractions: physical pleasure, the exercise of power, the accumulation of money, or the achievement of social status.*

The reason Plato assumes that non-material Ideas are superior to (simply more real and therefore more true than) material entities is that Ideas, unlike material objects, are perfect, eternal, and unchanging. The physical world may appear *to be solid and enduring, but a moment's reflection reminds us that even granite mountains eventually turn into hillocks, that whole oceans have dried into deserts, that the continents were once a solid landmass, and that most of the species of animals that ever lived on the earth are now extinct. (This is the same idea that Northrop Frye works with in* The Educated Imagination*; see the introduction to the excerpt from that book, pp. 246–254.) Particle physics tells us that the atoms making up solid-seeming matter are mostly composed of empty space and that their particles are dancing a miniature cosmic dance, the steps of which are eternally unpredictable. All matter, in other words, is in a constant state of flux, flow, alteration, deterioration, change, death, and rebirth. Plato's Ideas, however, having no physical substance, are not subject to the laws that govern physical emergence and change. They are the unchang-*

ing counterpart of what we express only fleetingly and glimpse only obscurely in the course of our physical existence.

"The Allegory of the Cave" is Plato's way of expressing all of this (and much more) in a compact, vivid way. The figures chained in the dark cave, looking at the shadows of things and mistaking them for realities, represent ordinary human beings chained to the appetites and allurements of physical existence. Their resistance to being unchained and disciplined for the arduous ascent into the true light of original *forms, the Ideas, represents most people's resistance to new thought. It especially represents the fuss that some people make when they are asked to abandon the clichés, maxims, customs, and inherited bits of wisdom that they have been using to organize their lives—when they are asked to start thinking* critically *rather than slipping into secondhand beliefs without checking to see if they really fit.*

Plato's allegory thus extends beyond representing kinds of truth and knowledge to suggest how the quality of knowledge we seek determines the quality of life we embrace. For example, the allegory would suggest one possible answer to the questions W. H. Auden raises about the life of his character, the Unknown Citizen: "Was he free? Was he happy?" (p. 385). Since the Unknown Citizen is precisely the sort of comfortable conformist who would most resist exercising the critical mind, Plato would answer (as would Auden, though his speaker in the poem dismisses the questions as "absurd") that the Citizen has no idea of true freedom and happiness. Plato claims that true freedom and happiness cannot be found in doing or acquiring the things that most people usually associate with freedom: having power, money, and prestige. He never tires of pointing out that these possessions only tighten the chains that keep most people's backs to the light and their eyes focused on shadows. The Platonic point of view says that freedom and happiness are found not by focusing on oneself but by focusing on something both larger than and external to oneself, something that compels and lifts one's vision above the mundane preoccupations that most people mistake as significant. The road to such unconventional and lofty concerns is steep and arduous, but Plato argues that it is worth the discipline and energy it requires, for the glimpse thus obtained of higher truths satisfies the soul as none of our ordinary pursuits ever can.

As you study "The Allegory of the Cave," you might find it helpful to compare Bertrand Russell's scorn of self-absorption in "Happiness" (pp. 333–341). Ask yourself also where Plato or Russell might have us look for that something larger than ourselves.

THE ALLEGORY OF THE CAVE

Our title for this portion of *The Republic,* book 7.

And now, I said, let me show in a figure how far our nature is enlightened 1
or unenlightened:—Behold! human beings housed in an underground cave, which has a long entrance open towards the light and as wide as the interior of the cave; here they have been from their childhood, and have their legs and necks chained, so that they cannot move and can only see before them,

being prevented by the chains from turning round their heads. Above and behind them a fire is blazing at a distance, and between the fire and the prisoners there is a raised way; and you will see, if you look, a low wall built along the way, like the screen which marionette players have in front of them, over which they show the puppets.

I see.

And do you see, I said, men passing along the wall carrying all sorts of 2
vessels, and statues and figures of animals made of wood and stone and various materials, which appear over the wall? While carrying their burdens, some of them, as you would expect, are talking, others silent.

You have shown me a strange image, and they are strange prisoners.

Like ourselves, I replied; for in the first place do you think they have 3
seen anything of themselves, and of one another, except the shadows which the fire throws on the opposite wall of the cave?

How could they do so, he asked, if throughout their lives they were never allowed to move their heads?

And of the objects which are being carried in like manner they would only see the shadows?

Yes, he said.

And if they were able to converse with one another, would they not suppose that the things they saw were the real things?

Very true.

And suppose further that the prison had an echo which came from the 4
other side, would they not be sure to fancy when one of the passers-by spoke that the voice which they heard came from the passing shadow?

No question, he replied.

To them, I said, the truth would be literally nothing but the shadows of the images.

That is certain.

And now look again, and see in what manner they would be released 5
from their bonds, and cured of their error, whether the process would naturally be as follows. At first, when any of them is liberated and compelled suddenly to stand up and turn his neck round and walk and look towards the light, he will suffer sharp pains; the glare will distress him, and he will be unable to see the realities of which in his former state he had seen the shadows; and then conceive someone saying to him that what he saw before was an illusion, but that now, when he is approaching nearer to being and his eye is turned towards more real existence, he has a clearer vision,—what will be his reply? And you may further imagine that his instructor is pointing to the objects as they pass and requiring him to name them,—will he not be perplexed? Will he not fancy that the shadows which he formerly saw are truer than the objects which are now shown to him?

Far truer.

And if he is compelled to look straight at the light, will he not have a 6
pain in his eyes which will make him turn away to take refuge in the objects

of vision which he can see, and which he will conceive to be in reality clearer than the things which are now being shown to him?

True, he said.

And suppose once more, that he is reluctantly dragged up that steep and 7
rugged ascent, and held fast until he is forced into the presence of the sun himself, is he not likely to be pained and irritated? When he approaches the light his eyes will be dazzled, and he will not be able to see anything at all of what are now called realities.

Not all in a moment, he said.

He will require to grow accustomed to the sight of the upper world. And 8
first he will see the shadows best, next the reflections of men and other objects in the water, and then the objects themselves; and, when he turned to the heavenly bodies and the heaven itself, he would find it easier to gaze upon the light of the moon and the stars at night than to see the sun or the light of the sun by day?

Certainly.

Last of all he will be able to see the sun, not turning aside to the illusory 9
reflections of him in the water, but gazing directly at him in his own proper place, and contemplating him as he is.

Certainly.

He will then proceed to argue that this is he who gives the seasons and 10
the years, and is the guardian of all that is in the visible world, and in a certain way the cause of all things which he and his fellows have been accustomed to behold?

Clearly, he said, he would arrive at this conclusion after what he had seen.

And when he remembered his old habitation, and the wisdom of the 11
cave and his fellow-prisoners, do you not suppose that he would felicitate himself on the change, and pity them?

Certainly, he would.

And if they were in the habit of conferring honours among themselves 12
on those who were quickest to observe the passing shadows and to remark which of them went before and which followed after and which were together, and who were best able from these observations to divine the future, do you think that he would be eager for such honours and glories, or envy those who attained honour and sovereignty among those men? Would he not say with Homer,

> "Better to be a serf, labouring for a landless master,"

and to endure anything, rather than think as they do and live after their manner?

Yes, he said, I think that he would consent to suffer anything rather than live in this miserable manner.

Imagine once more, I said, such a one coming down suddenly out of the 13 sunlight, and being replaced in his old seat; would he not be certain to have his eyes full of darkness?

To be sure, he said.

And if there were a contest, and he had to compete in measuring the 14
shadows with the prisoners who had never moved out of the cave, while his sight was still weak, and before his eyes had become steady (and the time which would be needed to acquire this new habit of sight might be very considerable), would he not make himself ridiculous? Men would say of him that he had returned from the place above with his eyes ruined; and that it was better not even to think of ascending; and if anyone tried to loose another and lead him up to the light, let them only catch the offender, and they would put him to death.

No question, he said.

This entire allegory, I said, you may now append, dear Glaucon, to the 15
previous argument; the prison-house is the world of sight, the light of the fire is the power of the sun, and you will not misapprehend me if you interpret the journey upwards to be the ascent of the soul into the intellectual world according to my surmise, which, at your desire, I have expressed—whether rightly or wrongly God knows. But, whether true or false, my opinion is that in the world of knowledge the Idea of good appears last of all, and is seen only with an effort; although, when seen, it is inferred to be the universal author of all things beautiful and right, parent of light and of the lord of light in the visible world, and the immediate and supreme source of reason and truth in the intellectual; and that this is the power upon which he who would act rationally either in public or private life must have his eye fixed.

I agree, he said, as far as I am able to understand you.

Moreover, I said, you must agree once more, and not wonder that those 16
who attain to this vision are unwilling to take any part in human affairs; for their souls are ever hastening into the upper world where they desire to dwell; which desire of theirs is very natural, if our allegory may be trusted.

Yes, very natural.

. . .

Then, I said, the business of us who are the founders of the State will 17
be to compel the best minds to attain that knowledge which we have already shown to be the greatest of all, namely, the vision of the good; they must make the ascent which we have described; but when they have ascended and seen enough we must not allow them to do as they do now.

What do you mean?

They are permitted to remain in the upper world, refusing to descend 18
again among the prisoners in the cave, and partake of their labours and honours, whether they are worth having or not.

But is not this unjust? he said; ought we to give them a worse life, when they might have a better?

You have again forgotten, my friend, I said, the intention of our law, 19
which does not aim at making any one class in the State happy above the rest; it seeks rather to spread happiness over the whole State, and to hold the

citizens together by persuasion and necessity, making each share with others any benefit which he can confer upon the State; and the law aims at producing such citizens, not that they may be left to please themselves, but that they may serve in binding the State together.

True, he said, I had forgotten.

Observe, Glaucon, that we shall do no wrong to our philosophers but 20
rather make a just demand, when we oblige them to have a care and providence of others; we shall explain to them that in other States, men of their class are not obliged to share in the toils of politics; and this is reasonable, for they grow up spontaneously, against the will of the governments in their several States; and things which grow up of themselves, and are indebted to no one for their nurture, cannot fairly be expected to pay dues for a culture which they have never received. But we have brought you into the world to be rulers of the hive, kings of yourselves and of the other citizens, and have educated you far better and more perfectly than they have been educated, and you are better able to share in the double duty. Wherefore each of you, when his turn comes, must go down to rejoin his companions, and acquire with them the habit of seeing things in the dark. As you acquire that habit, you will see ten thousand times better than the inhabitants of the cave, and you will know what the several images are and what they represent, because you have seen the beautiful and just and good in their truth. And thus our State, which is also yours, will be a reality and not a dream only, and will be administered in a spirit unlike that of other States, in which men fight with one another about shadows only and are distracted in the struggle for power, which in their eyes is a great good. Whereas the truth is that the State in which those who are to govern have least ambition to do so is always the best and most quietly governed, and the State in which they are most eager, the worst.

Quite true, he replied.

And will our pupils, when they hear this, refuse to take their turn at the 21
toils of State, when they are allowed to spend the greater part of their time with one another in the heavenly light?

Impossible, he answered; for they are just men, and the commands 22
which we impose upon them are just. But there can be no doubt that every one of them will take office as a stern necessity, contrary to the spirit of our present rulers of State.

Yes, my friend, I said; and there lies the point. You must contrive for 23
your future rulers another and a better life than that of a ruler, and then you may have a well-ordered State; for only in the State which offers this, will they rule who are truly rich, not in gold, but in virtue and wisdom, which are the true blessings of life. Whereas if men who are destitute and starved of such personal goods go to the administration of public affairs, thinking to enrich themselves at the public expense, order there can never be; for they will be fighting about office, and the civil and domestic broils which thus arise will be the ruin of the rulers themselves and of the whole State.

Most true, he replied.

And the only life which looks down upon the life of political ambition is that of true philosophy. Do you know of any other? 24

Indeed, I do not, he said.

And those who govern should not "make love to their employment?" For, if they do there will be rival lovers, and they will fight. 25

No question.

Whom, then, will you compel to become guardians of the State? Surely those who excel in judgement of the means by which a State is administered, and who at the same time have other honours and another and a better life than that of politics? 26

None but these, he replied.

Questions for Discussion

1. To make sure that you understand Plato's allegory, draw a line down a sheet of paper, dividing it into two vertical halves. On the left side make a column (a numbered list) of all the specific items Plato refers to in his allegory. Leave none of them out: chains, fire, cave, and so on. On the right side make a list of items, with corresponding numbers, that identify what those on the left side might represent in our "real" life. In other words, anatomize the allegory.
2. Do you believe, like Plato, that reality includes a realm of intangible entities that have their own objective existence? What arguments can you make in support of such a position? What arguments can you make against it? (Remember that whatever you assert now will be only a start on immensely complex problems.)
3. If you do believe in an objective realm of intangible entities, what is its relationship to the realm of tangible entities? Is one realm superior or more real than the other, as Plato believes? Is one realm truer than the other? What arguments can you make to support your position one way or another?
4. Do you agree with Plato that the highest rulers in a state ought to be those who care least for the power and prestige of the job? Do you agree that the more people care about these material things, the more their vision of just leadership is obscured and distorted? Can you provide examples that reinforce or discredit this argument?

Suggested Essay Topics

1. Plato says that earthly life is like living in a dark cave where we can see only the dusky shadows of things. Create and develop an extended analogy of your own—one that allows for allegorical development. You might try "Social life is like playing different roles in different dramas," "Dating

is like playing chess (or organizing a military campaign or establishing a dictatorship)," "Getting educated is like eating in a cafeteria." Address your allegory to your fellow students. Your objective, like Plato's, is to make an otherwise abstract concept vividly, concretely clear to your reader.

2. Write a letter to one of the governing bodies of your college or university (the president's administrative council or the faculty senate, for example), arguing that the officers of the student government should *not* be elected from among the candidates who *want* the job (argue in fact that their wanting it is sufficient to disqualify them from getting it) but that students should be persuaded to serve by those already in power on the basis of their intelligence, honesty, and clearheadedness. They should be urged to accept office as a matter of public duty, not private ambition. Support your position with inferences drawn from Plato's allegory. Your purpose is to show how the present process of selecting leaders only leads to petty bickering, political infighting, and shortsighted policies.

Montaigne

Michel Eyquem de Montaigne (1533–1592) is perhaps the most famous essayist of all time. His Essais, *written in his native French and first published in the 1580s, are not quite like most of the essays you may be asked to write. In fact he spent almost a lifetime inventing his kind of* essai *or "attempt" (see* *"What Is an Essay?" pp. 10–14**). At first he merely jotted down sayings and anecdotes that struck him as memorable while he was reading (you may be tempted this year to keep the same kind of record—what used to be called a "commonplace book"—of passages you like). But eventually, as he expanded his notes with more and more of his own commentary, he found himself creating a wonderful collection of freely ranging "attempts" in which it is impossible to draw a sharp line between traditional wisdom and his own original thinking.*

In the following essay on friendship most of what he says echoes what can be found in earlier works. Aristotle, probably the most powerful of these influences, had said in his Ethics *that human happiness would simply be inconceivable without friendship: "Without friends no one would choose to live, though he had all other goods." Aristotle did not mean, of course, that people should commit suicide if they lacked close friendships—friendships as close as Montaigne's with Etienne de La Boétie, a departed friend whom he memorializes in this essay. Rather, Aristotle was thinking of* all *our social bonds, including our feelings for parents and children and even our allegiance to political leaders. In this wider sense Aristotle was viewing friendship not as something merely nice to have but as the crowning active virtue of a good life—not as a possession but as an activity, a "practice." Having defined friendship as an ethical practice, Aristotle went* on to classify friendships according to good and bad practices, constructing a classification based on the kind of benefit that produces the sense of bonding. Toward some people we feel friendly because they give us pleasure. Others we seek out because they serve our interests in some way. And a third kind we make our friends not only because we enjoy them or because they are useful but because they are somehow good to be with just for the quality they add to our lives while we are with them. We feel that hours spent with them create life as it should be.

These three kinds were not seen as equally valuable. People who become friends only because they give each other pleasure—for example, sexual lovers or members of college fraternities—stop being friends as soon as the pleasure-giving stops. Those who become friends only because they contribute to each other's immediate practical gain—team members, partners in a business, tutors and pupils—fall apart as soon as the utility is no longer clear. True friendship arises whenever two people not only offer each other pleasure or utility but also share equality in all their sensitivities and aspirations and are thus good for and with each other. These full friends love to be with each other because of the enhanced life they live in each other's presence. In Aristotle's formula (repeated thousands of times over two millennia), a true friendship is a relation of virtue with virtue, or as we might translate, of strength with strength and aspiration with aspiration. A full friend "is said to be one who wishes and does good things, or what appear to him to be good, for the sake of his friend" or "one who wishes his friend to be and to live for his [friend's] own sake, as appears in mothers in regard to their children." In short, my true friend, for Aristotle, is one who "has the same relations with me that he has with himself."

Such friendships will last as long as the reciprocal love of virtue lasts, quite possibly until death and, as Montaigne suggests, even beyond. At times in the Essais he even claims that La Boétie still lives because he and Montaigne remain together, both within Montaigne himself and in the book.

In praising friendship, Montaigne's essay adds an important perspective on this chapter's theme, "The Individual and Community." Some of our authors see the individual's relation to the community as primarily the problem of finding freedom from communal restraints. Ayn Rand's worship of the "I," for example, portrays the individual as guarding personal liberties by breaking free of external forces. "For in the temple of his spirit," Rand's speaker proclaims, "each man is alone. Let each man keep his temple untouched and undefiled. Then let him join hands with others if he wishes, but only beyond his holy threshold" (p. 431). Montaigne's view of freedom might seem absolutely opposed to Rand's: Freedom, in his view, is not a possession one guards against any possible infringement but a benefit one "earns" by learning how to surrender to others who have been carefully selected as worthy of friendship.

Such contrasts, which are always valuable at least as exercises, usually come to seem more complicated as we dig deeper. It seems probable, for example, that Montaigne would not be at all disturbed by Rand's open rejection of most of the associations that we carelessly call friendships. He might very well find most "community" as oppressive as Rand's hero does. Perhaps for both authors everything would depend on finding the right "others" with whom to share the spirit and on achieving the right mode of sharing.

Wherever we come out working with such comparisons, it is clear that for Montaigne a surrender to true friendship—or what we might call love—produces a release from the private, isolated ego into a community that simply annihilates the border between self and others.

As you read this selection, don't worry about not recognizing all of the names that Montaigne drops into his discussion. Some of them would probably not have been recognized even by many of Montaigne's contemporaries, and even more of them are not known to most readers today. Except where noted, the text itself tells us all that we need to know about them, at least during our first encounter with Montaigne.

We begin our selection after omitting a few opening paragraphs in which Montaigne praises La Boétie's Voluntary Servitude *(sometimes called* Against One Man*), an essay in honor of liberty and against tyrants.*

OF FRIENDSHIP

From *Essais* (1580).

I am particularly obliged to this work [La Boétie's *Voluntary Servitude*] since it served as the medium of our first acquaintance. For it was shown to me long before I had seen him, and gave me my first knowledge of his name, thus starting on its way this friendship which together we fostered, as long as God willed, so entire and so perfect that certainly you will hardly read of the like, and among men of today you see no trace of it in practice. So many coincidences are needed to build up such a friendship that it is a lot if fortune can do it once in three centuries. 1

There is nothing to which nature seems to have inclined us more than to society. And Aristotle says that good legislators have had more care for friendship than for justice. Now the ultimate point in the perfection of society is this. For in general, all associations that are forged and nourished by pleasure or profit, by public or private needs, are the less beautiful and noble, and the less friendships, in so far as they mix into friendship another cause and object and reward than friendship itself. Nor do the four ancient types—natural, social, hospitable, erotic—come up to real friendship, either separately or together. 2

From children toward fathers, it is rather respect. Friendship feeds on communication, which cannot exist between them because of their too great inequality, and might perhaps interfere with the duties of nature. For neither can all the secret thoughts of fathers be communicated to children, lest this beget an unbecoming intimacy, nor could the admonitions and corrections, which are one of the chief duties of friendship, be administered by children to fathers. There have been nations where by custom the children killed their fathers, and others where the fathers killed their children, to avoid the interference that they can sometimes cause each other; and by nature the one depends on the destruction of the other. There have been philosophers who disdained this natural tie, witness Aristippus: when pressed about the affec- 3 tion he owed his children for having come out of him, he began to spit, saying that that had come out of him just as well, and that we also bred lice and worms. And that other, whom Plutarch wanted to reconcile with his brother, said: "I don't think any more of him for having come out of the same hole."

Truly the name of brother is a beautiful name and full of affection, and 4
for that reason he and I made our alliance a brotherhood. But that confusion of ownership, the dividing, and the fact that the richness of one is the poverty of the other, wonderfully softens and loosens the solder of brotherhood. Since brothers have to guide their careers along the same path and at the same rate, it is inevitable that they often jostle and clash with each other. Furthermore, why should the harmony and kinship which begets these true and perfect friendships be found in them? Father and son may be of entirely different dispositions, and brothers also. He is my son, he is my kinsman, but he is an unsociable man, a knave, or a fool. And then, the more they are friendships which law and natural obligation impose on us, the less of our choice and free will there is in them. And our free will has no product more properly its own than affection and friendship. Not that I have not experienced all the friendship that can exist in that situation, having had the best father that ever was, and the most indulgent, even in his extreme old age, and being of a family famous and exemplary, from father to son, in this matter of brotherly concord:

> Known to others
> For fatherly affection toward my brothers.
> HORACE

To compare this brotherly affection with affection for women, even 5
though it is the result of our choice—it cannot be done; nor can we put the love of women in the same category. Its ardor, I confess—

> Of us that goddess is not unaware
> Who blends a bitter sweetness with her care
> CATULLUS

—is more active, more scorching, and more intense. But it is an impetuous and fickle flame, undulating and variable, a fever flame, subject to fits and lulls, that holds us only by one corner. In friendship it is a general and universal warmth, moderate and even, besides, a constant and settled warmth, all gentleness and smoothness, with nothing bitter and stinging about it. What is more, in love there is nothing but a frantic desire for what flees from us:

> Just as a huntsman will pursue a hare
> O'er hill and dale, in weather cold or fair;
> The captured hare is worthless in his sight;
> He only hastens after things in flight.
> ARIOSTO

As soon as it enters the boundaries of friendship, that is to say harmony of wills, it grows faint and languid. Enjoyment destroys it, as having a fleshly end, subject to satiety. Friendship, on the contrary, is enjoyed according as it is desired; it is bred, nourished, and increased only in enjoyment, since it is spiritual, and the soul grows refined by practice. During the reign of this perfect friendship those fleeting affections once found a place in me, not to speak of my friend, who confesses only too many of them in these verses. Thus these two passions within me came to be known to each other, but to be compared, never; the first keeping its course in proud and lofty flight, and disdainfully watching the other making its way far, far beneath it.

As for marriage, for one thing it is a bargain to which only the entrance 6
is free—its continuance being constrained and forced, depending otherwise than on our will—and a bargain ordinarily made for other ends. For another, there supervene a thousand foreign tangles to unravel, enough to break the thread and trouble the course of a lively affection; whereas in friendship there are no dealings or business except with itself. Besides, to tell the truth, the ordinary capacity of women is inadequate for that communion and fellowship which is the nurse of this sacred bond; nor does their soul seem firm enough to endure the strain of so tight and durable a knot. And indeed, but for that, if such a relationship, free and voluntary, could be built up, in which not only would the souls have this complete enjoyment, but the bodies would also share in the alliance, so that the entire man would be engaged, it is certain that the resulting friendship would be fuller and more complete. But this sex in no instance has yet succeeded in attaining it, and by the common agreement of the ancient schools is excluded from it.

And that other, licentious Greek love [homosexuality] is justly ab- 7
horred by our morality. Since it involved, moreover, according to their practice, such a necessary disparity in age and such a difference in the lovers' functions, it did not correspond closely enough with the perfect union and harmony that we require here: *For what is this love of friendship? Why does no one love either an ugly youth, or a handsome old man?* [Cicero (translator's note)]. For even the picture the Academy* paints of it will not contradict me, I think, if I say this on the subject: that this first frenzy which the son of Venus [Cupid] inspired in the lover's heart at the sight of the flower of tender youth, in which they allow all the insolent and passionate acts that immoderate ardor can produce, was simply founded on external beauty, the false image of corporeal generation. For it could not be founded on the spirit, the signs of which [in the beloved boy] were still hidden, which was only at its birth and before the age of budding. If this frenzy seized a base heart, the means of his courtship were riches, presents, favor in advancement to dignities, and other such base merchandise, which were generally condemned. If it fell on a nobler heart, the means were also noble: philosophical instruc-

*The Academy, a school of philosophers established by Plato, had a continuous life from about 385 B.C. to A.D. 529. Because homosexual love was frequently described and recommended by some of the characters in Plato's dialogues and by some of his followers, the Academy came to stand for approval of homosexuality.

tion, precepts to revere religion, obey the laws, die for the good of the country; examples of valor, prudence, justice; the lover studying to make himself acceptable by the grace and beauty of his soul, that of his body being long since faded, and hoping by this mental fellowship to establish a firmer and more lasting pact.

. . .

8 After this general communion was established, the stronger and worthier part of it exercising its functions and predominating, they say that there resulted from it fruits very useful personally and to the public; that it constituted the strength of the countries [like Sparta] which accepted the practice, and the principal defense of equity and liberty. . . . Therefore they call it sacred and divine. And, by their reckoning, only the violence of tyrants and the cowardice of the common people are hostile to it. In short, all that can be said in favor of the Academy is that this was a love ending in friendship; which corresponds pretty well to the Stoic definition of love: *Love is the attempt to form a friendship inspired by beauty* [Cicero (translator's note)].

9 I return to my description of a more equitable and more equable kind of friendship. *Only those are to be judged friendships in which the characters have been strengthened and matured by age* [Cicero (translator's note)].

10 For the rest, what we ordinarily call friends and friendships are nothing but acquaintanceships and familiarities formed by some chance or convenience, by means of which our souls are bound to each other. In the friendship I speak of, our souls mingle and blend with each other so completely that they efface the seam that joined them, and cannot find it again. If you press me to tell why I loved him, I feel that this cannot be expressed, except by answering: Because it was he, because it was I.

11 Beyond all my understanding, beyond what I can say about this in particular, there was I know not what inexplicable and fateful force that was the mediator of this union. We sought each other before we met because of the reports we heard of each other, which had more effect on our affection than such reports would reasonably have; I think it was by some ordinance from heaven. We embraced each other by our names. And at our first meeting, which by chance came at a great feast and gathering in the city, we found ourselves so taken with each other, so well acquainted, so bound together, that from that time on nothing was so close to us as each other. He wrote an excellent Latin satire, which is published, in which he excuses and explains the precipitancy of our mutual understanding, so promptly grown to its perfection. Having so little time to last, and having begun so late, for we were both grown men, and he a few years older than I, it could not lose time and conform to the pattern of mild and regular friendships, which need so many precautions in the form of long preliminary association. Our friendship has no other model than itself, and can be compared only with itself. It is not one special consideration, nor two, nor three, nor four, nor a thousand: it is I know not what quintessence of all this mixture, which, having seized my whole will, led it to plunge and lose itself in his; which, having seized his whole will, led it to plunge and lose itself in mine, with equal hunger, equal rivalry. I say

lose, in truth, for neither of us reserved anything for himself, nor was anything either his or mine.

When Laelius, in the presence of the Roman consuls—who, after condemning Tiberius Gracchus, prosecuted all those who had been in his confidence—came to ask Caius Blossius, who was Gracchus' best friend, how much he would have been willing to do for him, he answered: "Everything." "What, everything?" pursued Laelius. "And what if he had commanded you to set fire to our temples?" "He would never have commanded me to do that," replied Blossius. "But what if he had?" Laelius insisted. "I would have obeyed," he replied. If he was such a perfect friend to Gracchus as the histories say, he did not need to offend the consuls by this last bold confession, and he should not have abandoned the assurance he had of Gracchus' will. But nevertheless, those who charge that this answer is seditious do not fully understand this mystery, and fail to assume first what is true, that he had Gracchus' will up his sleeve, both by power over him and by knowledge of him. They were friends more than citizens, friends more than friends or enemies of their country or friends of ambition and disturbance. Having committed themselves absolutely to each other, they held absolutely the reins of each other's inclination; and if you assume that this team was guided by the strength and leadership of reason, as indeed it is quite impossible to harness it without that, Blossius' answer is as it should have been.* If their actions went astray, they were by my measure neither friends to each other, nor friends to themselves. 12

For that matter, this answer has no better ring than would mine if someone questioned me in this fashion: "If your will commanded you to kill your daughter, would you kill her?" and I said yes. For that does not bear witness to any consent to do so, because I have no doubt at all about my will, and just as little about that of such a friend. It is not in the power of all the arguments in the world to dislodge me from the certainty I have of the intentions and judgments of my friend. Not one of his actions could be presented to me, whatever appearance it might have, that I could not immediately find the motive for it. Our souls pulled together in such unison, they regarded each other with such ardent affection, and with a like affection revealed themselves to each other to the very depths of our hearts, that not only did I know his soul as well as mine, but I should certainly have trusted myself to him more readily than to myself. 13

Let not these other, common friendships be placed in this rank. I have as much knowledge of them as another, and of the most perfect of their type, but I advise you not to confuse the rules of the two; you would make a mistake. You must walk in those other friendships bridle in hand, with prudence and precaution; the knot is not so well tied that there is no cause to mistrust it. "Love him," Chilo used to say, "as if you are to hate him some 14

*Here Montaigne makes use of the ancient myth found in Plato's *Phaedrus,* considering the soul as a chariot drawn by two steeds, Desire and Emotion, and guided by the charioteer, Reason. It is possible that Montaigne is punning on the word *team,* referring to both the horses and the friends.

day; hate him as if you are to love him." This precept, which is so abominable in this sovereign and masterful friendship, is healthy in the practice of ordinary and customary friendships, in regard to which we must use the remark that Aristotle often repeated: "O my friends, there is no friend."

In this noble relationship, services and benefits, on which other friend- 15
ships feed, do not even deserve to be taken into account; the reason for this is the complete fusion of our wills. For just as the friendship I feel for myself receives no increase from the help I give myself in time of need, whatever the Stoics say, and as I feel no gratitude to myself for the service I do myself; so the union of such friends, being truly perfect, makes them lose the sense of such duties, and hate and banish from between them these words of separation and distinction: benefit, obligation, gratitude, request, thanks, and the like. Everything actually being in common between them—wills, thoughts, judgments, goods, wives, children, honor, and life—and their relationship being that of one soul in two bodies, according to Aristotle's very apt definition, they can neither lend nor give anything to each other. That is why the lawmakers, to honor marriage with some imaginary resemblance to this divine union, forbid gifts between husband and wife, wishing thus to imply that everything should belong to each of them and that they have nothing to divide and split up between them.

If, in the friendship I speak of, one could give to the other, it would be 16
the one who received the benefit who would oblige his friend. For, each of them seeking above all things to benefit the other, the one who provides the matter and the occasion is the liberal one, giving his friend the satisfaction of doing for him what he most wants to do. When the philosopher Diogenes was short of money, he used to say that he asked it back of his friends, not that he asked for it. And to show how this works in practice, I will tell you an ancient example that is singular.

Eudamidas of Corinth had two friends, Charixenus, a Sicyonian, and 17
Aretheus, a Corinthian. When he came to die, he being poor and his two friends rich, he made his will thus: "I leave this to Aretheus, to feed my mother and support her in her old age; this to Charixenus, to see my daughter married and give her the biggest dowry he can; and in case one of them should chance to die, I substitute the survivor in his place." Those who first saw this will laughed at it; but his heirs, having been informed of it, accepted it with singular satisfaction. And when one of them, Charixenus, died five days later, and the place of substitute was opened to Aretheus, he supported the mother with great care, and of five talents he had in his estate, he gave two and a half to his only daughter for her marriage, and two and a half for the marriage of the daughter of Eudamidas, holding their weddings on the same day.

This example is quite complete except for one circumstance, which is 18
the plurality of friends. For this perfect friendship I speak of is indivisible: each one gives himself so wholly to his friend that he has nothing left to distribute elsewhere; on the contrary, he is sorry that he is not double, triple, or quadruple, and that he has not several souls and several wills, to confer

them all on this one object. Common friendships can be divided up: one may love in one man his beauty, in another his easygoing ways, in another liberality, in one paternal love, in another brotherly love, and so forth; but this friendship that possesses the soul and rules it with absolute sovereignty cannot possibly be double. If two called for help at the same time, which one would you run to? If they demanded conflicting services of you, how would you arrange it? If one confided to your silence a thing that would be useful for the other to know, how would you extricate yourself? A single dominant friendship dissolves all other obligations. The secret I have sworn to reveal to no other man, I can impart without perjury to the one who is not another man: he is myself. It is a great enough miracle to be doubled, and those who talk of tripling themselves do not realize the loftiness of the thing: nothing is extreme that can be matched. And he who supposes that of two men I love one just as much as the other, and that they love each other and me just as much as I love them, multiplies into a fraternity the most singular and unified of all things, of which even a single one is the rarest thing in the world to find.

The rest of this story fits in very well with what I was saying, for 19
Eudamidas bestows upon his friends the kindness and favor of using them for his need. He leaves them heirs to this liberality of his, which consists of putting into their hands a chance to do him good. And without doubt the strength of friendship is shown much more richly in his action than in that of Aretheus.

In short, these are actions inconceivable to anyone who has not tasted 20
friendship, and which make me honor wonderfully the answer of that young soldier to Cyrus, who asked him for how much he would sell a horse with which he had just won the prize in a race, and whether he would exchange him for a kingdom: "No indeed, Sire, but I would most willingly let him go to gain a friend, if I found a man worthy of such an alliance." That was not badly spoken, "if I found one"; for it is easy to find men fit for a superficial acquaintance. But for this kind, in which we act from the very bottom of our hearts, which holds nothing back, truly it is necessary that all the springs of action be perfectly clean and true.

In the relationships which bind us only by one small part,* we need look 21
out only for the imperfections that particularly concern that part. The religion of my doctor or my lawyer cannot matter. That consideration has nothing in common with the functions of the friendship they owe me. And in the domestic relationship between me and those who serve me, I have the same attitude. I scarcely inquire of a lackey whether he is chaste; I try to find out whether he is diligent. And I am not as much afraid of a gambling mule driver as of a weak one, or of a profane cook as of an ignorant one. I do not make it my business to tell the world what it should do—enough others do that—but what I do in it.

*Compare "one small part" here with "holds us only by one corner," in the third sentence of paragraph 5.

> That is my practice: do as you see fit.
> TERENCE

For the familiarity of the table* I look for wit, not prudence; for the bed, beauty before goodness; in conversation, competence, even without uprightness. Likewise in other matters.

Just as the man who was found astride a stick, playing with his children, 22
asked the man who surprised him thus to say nothing about it until he was a father himself, in the belief that the passion which would then be born in his soul would make him an equitable judge of such an act, so I should like to talk to people who have experienced what I tell. But knowing how far from common usage and how rare such a friendship is, I do not expect to find any good judge of it. For the very discourses that antiquity has left us on this subject seem to me weak compared with the feeling I have. And in this particular the facts surpass even the precepts of philosophy:

> Nothing shall I, while sane, compare with a dear friend.
> HORACE

The ancient Menander declared that man happy who had been able to 23
meet even the shadow of a friend. He was certainly right to say so, especially if he spoke from experience. For in truth, if I compare all the rest of my life—though by the grace of God I have spent it pleasantly, comfortably, and, except for the loss of such a friend, free from any grievous affliction, and full of tranquillity of mind, having accepted my natural and original advantages without seeking other ones—if I compare it all, I say, with the four years which were granted me to enjoy the sweet company and society of that man, it is nothing but smoke, nothing but dark and dreary night. Since the day I lost him,

> Which I shall ever recall with pain,
> Ever with reverence—thus, Gods, did you ordain—
> VIRGIL

I only drag on a weary life. And the very pleasures that come my way, instead of consoling me, redouble my grief for his loss. We went halves in everything; it seems to me that I am robbing him of his share,

> Nor may I rightly taste of pleasures here alone,
> —So I resolved—when he who shared my life is gone.
> TERENCE

I was already so formed and accustomed to being a second self everywhere that only half of me seems to be alive now.

*The word *table* here means something like "dinner conversation."

Since an untimely blow has snatched away
Part of my soul, why then do I delay,
I the remaining part, less dear than he,
And not entire surviving? The same day
Brought ruin equally to him and me.
HORACE

There is no action or thought in which I do not miss him, as indeed he would have missed me. For just as he surpassed me infinitely in every other ability and virtue, so he did in the duty of friendship.

Questions for Discussion

1. Do you find that Montaigne divides friendships into exactly the same kinds as those we reported from Aristotle? In answering, look closely at the fourth sentence of paragraph 2, at the last sentence of that paragraph, and at the kinds of friendship described in paragraphs 3–10.
2. As you sort out the various friendships that Montaigne contrasts with the friendship between him and La Boétie, think about the various bonds you have with people—not just with those you *call* friends, but with all those whose company you at any time seek out voluntarily. Do you have a vocabulary for distinguishing cronies, buddies, co-conspirators, allies, comrades, partners, favorites, lovers, and—friends? Do some of these bonds lead to freedom, while others lead to some form of enslavement?
3. Scholars debate about just how much is literally true in Montaigne's account of his friendship with La Boétie, who died many years before the essay was written (the *Essais* were first published in 1580; the friend died in 1563). Much of what he says—for example, that friendship is one soul in two bodies—had been said by many before him about other friends. Does the friendship as Montaigne describes it seem to you a possible human relation? A desirable one? As you make use of Montaigne in thinking about all the "friendships" that we moderns tend to cover with one vague word—*relationships*—does it matter whether Montaigne in "real life" ever achieved his ideal?
4. List the kinds of friendship that Montaigne traces in paragraphs 3–10. Can you think of other kinds that might seriously rival his notion of the highest friendship? Do you see any reason for placing the friendships in *this* order, instead of, say, that of homosexuals first, marriage in the middle, and "children toward fathers" last?
5. In paragraph 3, Montaigne says that "one of the chief duties of friendship" is to offer "admonitions and corrections." Here he is echoing a theme that ran through centuries of commentary: When criticism is needed, the true friend risks being unpleasantly critical. And a true friend can *accept* criti-

cism gratefully, knowing that anyone who flatters our faults cannot be a true friend. What do you think of this standard of friendship? Have you ever been attacked with hostility in the guise of "friendly admonition"? Have you ever responded with hostility to what you took to be unkindness, only to learn later that it was in reality a "friendly admonition"? If so, does this experience argue against the desirability of a freedom that is found in separation from others?

6. Montaigne makes a fairly elaborate statement about how sexual desire relates to friendship (¶5). Trace through the whole paragraph slowly, paying special attention to the pronoun *it.* Then see if you can paraphrase—that is, give in your own words—what he is saying in the final sentence. (Don't be alarmed if at first you find this difficult. After all, we authors can't earn your friendship by asking only easy questions.)
7. In paragraphs 12 and 13 Montaigne draws a daring analogy between trusting a true friend and trusting one's own will. Does the analogy work for you? In answering, it may help to translate the Blossius-Gracchus anecdote into modern terms, for example, "And what if your friend had commanded you to give secrets to the Russians?" Do you think that you could ever trust someone (even if only one person in a lifetime) "more readily" than you would trust yourself? If not, why not? If so, and if you do not care to name a particular person before the class, describe the *kind* of person you could trust this way.

Suggested Essay Topics

1. A critic might say, "Montaigne exaggerates the requirements of true friendship so badly that nobody could ever find even one example of it. He does a great disservice to the world in setting up impossible ideals like that, rather than describing human relations that everyone can hope for." Write a letter to the author of this statement, agreeing or disagreeing and giving your reasons as forcefully as you can.
2. It is sometimes said that the ideal of all American young people is to be "popular," to "fit in," to have as many "friends" as possible. Montaigne would surely consider that ideal a form of slavery. Study his reasons for thinking that no one can have more than one friend at once (especially ¶17) and for thinking that one is lucky to find even one true friend in a lifetime. Can these two ideals, popularity and friendship, be equally important to the same person? Write a letter to a friend who is still in high school, one who you think will become a good college student, describing the two ideals. Then tell him or her either (a) how to choose the ideal you prefer and how to live by it or (b) how to seek a way of reconciling the two, if you think reconciliation is possible.

IDEAS IN DEBATE

Ayn Rand
Martin Luther King, Jr.
e. e. cummings

Ayn Rand

***A**yn Rand (1905–1982) was born and educated in Russia, where as a young woman she experienced the Bolshevik Revolution and the extreme restrictions of individual freedom that Soviet collectivization imposed. A naturalized American citizen, she published a series of novels and essays urging the pursuit of freedom through a total individualism.* The Fountainhead *(1943), probably her best-known novel, portrays a version of the great architect, Frank Lloyd Wright, as a model of the achievements possible for a creative and uninhibited individual. Her credo is perhaps best summarized in the oath sworn by the citizens of an imaginary community described in* Atlas Shrugged *(1957): "I will never live for the sake of another man, nor ask any other man to live for mine."*

The following excerpt is from Anthem, *a novelette portraying the fate of a courageous dissenter in a totalitarian state. The excerpt is a hymn of praise sung by the hero to his god—himself. As you read, you might think of similar attitudes expressed in your time—though in a different style (for example, in the 1970s best-seller* Looking Out for No. 1 *by Robert J. Ringer).*

I OWE NOTHING TO MY BROTHERS

Our title for chapter 11 of *Anthem* (1938).

I AM. I THINK. I WILL. 1

My hands . . . My spirit . . . My sky . . . My forest . . . This earth of mine. . . . 2

What must I say besides? These are the words. This is the answer. 3

I stand here on the summit of the mountain. I lift my head and I spread my arms. This, my body and spirit, this is the end of the quest. I wished to 4 know the meaning of things. I am the meaning. I wished to find a warrant for being. I need no warrant for being, and no word of sanction upon my being. I am the warrant and the sanction.

5 It is my eyes which see, and the sight of my eyes grants beauty to the earth. It is my ears which hear, and the hearing of my ears gives its song to the world. It is my mind which thinks, and the judgment of my mind is the only searchlight that can find the truth. It is my will which chooses, and the choice of my will is the only edict I must respect.

6 Many words have been granted me, and some are wise, and some are false, but only three are holy: "I will it!"

7 Whatever road I take, the guiding star is within me; the guiding star and the loadstone which point the way. They point in but one direction. They point to me.

8 I know not if this earth on which I stand is the core of the universe or if it is but a speck of dust lost in eternity. I know not and I care not. For I know what happiness is possible to me on earth. And my happiness needs no higher aim to vindicate it. My happiness is not the means to any end. It is the end. It is its own goal. It is its own purpose.

9 Neither am I the means to any end others may wish to accomplish. I am not a tool for their use. I am not a servant of their needs. I am not a bandage for their wounds. I am not a sacrifice on their altars.

10 I am a man. This miracle of me is mine to own and keep, and mine to guard, and mine to use, and mine to kneel before!

11 I do not surrender my treasures, nor do I share them. The fortune of my spirit is not to be blown into coins of brass and flung to the winds as alms for the poor of the spirit. I guard my treasures: my thought, my will, my freedom. And the greatest of these is freedom.

12 I owe nothing to my brothers, nor do I gather debts from them. I ask none to live for me, nor do I live for any others. I covet no man's soul, nor is my soul theirs to covet.

13 I am neither foe nor friend to my brothers, but such as each of them shall deserve of me. And to earn my love, my brothers must do more than to have been born. I do not grant my love without reason, nor to any chance passer-by who may wish to claim it. I honor men with my love. But honor is a thing to be earned.

I shall choose friends among men, but neither slaves nor masters. And I shall choose only such as please me, and them I shall love and respect, but neither command nor obey. And we shall join our hands when we wish, or walk alone when we so desire. For in the temple of his spirit, each man is alone. Let each man keep his temple untouched and undefiled. Then let him join hands with others if he wishes, but only beyond his holy threshold. 14

For the word "We" must never be spoken, save by one's choice and as a second thought. This word must never be placed first within man's soul, else it becomes a monster, the root of all the evils on earth, the root of man's torture by men, and of an unspeakable lie. 15

The word "We" is as lime poured over men, which sets and hardens to stone, and crushes all beneath it, and that which is white and that which is black are lost equally in the grey of it. It is the word by which the depraved steal the virtue of the good, by which the weak steal the might of the strong, by which the fools steal the wisdom of the sages. 16

What is my joy if all hands, even the unclean, can reach into it? What is my wisdom, if even the fools can dictate to me? What is my freedom, if all creatures, even the botched and the impotent, are my masters? What is my life, if I am but to bow, to agree and to obey? 17

But I am done with this creed of corruption. 18

I am done with the monster of "We," the word of serfdom, of plunder, of misery, falsehood and shame. 19

And now I see the face of god, and I raise this god over the earth, this god whom men have sought since men came into being, this god who will grant them joy and peace and pride. 20

This god, this one word: 21

"I." 22

Questions for Discussion

1. People who like to think in slogans called the 1970s and 1980s "the me decades." *Anthem* was written in the 1930s, sometimes called "the decade

of social responsibility." Does the position expressed in "I Owe Nothing to My Brothers" seem to resemble or to contrast with the basic beliefs that have been fashionable since you became aware of "beliefs" at all?

2. The doctrine proclaimed in this excerpt from *Anthem* is in one sense deliberately "anti-social." Does it seem to you finally dangerous to society? Give your reasons. What do you think Rand would reply to anyone who claimed that she cared only about the welfare of the selfish and powerful?
3. Phrases like "the me decade," "the decade of social responsibility," "the apathetic decade" (the 1950s), and "the decade of protest" (the 1960s) at best cover only a limited number of the trends and topics of a given period. People pick them up as a way of talking easily about the past, but when we press our memories or do research we usually find more exceptions than illustrations. Ayn Rand might say that our tendency to use these catchphrases in our thinking is just one more example of our being too dependent on other people. Yet she inevitably depends, as we all do, on earlier thinkers (Nietzsche, perhaps, for the glorification of the independent "I"; Thomas Jefferson, for the inalienable right to the pursuit of happiness; Aristotle, for the relentless pursuit of rationality). Thus her ideas, like those of every other thinker, can almost all be traced to predecessors. Does this unavoidable kinship with earlier thinkers seriously undermine Rand's notion that each individual should attempt to worship and serve only the "I"? How does her "I" relate to the "we" who have thought similar thoughts?
4. Although Ayn Rand often advocates reliance on reason as the ultimate test of truth, the tone of this chapter from *Anthem* is "oracular"; it resembles what we might call the "prophetic" tone of I Corinthians 13 (pp. 343–345). Compare, for example, Rand's paragraph 18 with St. Paul's verse 11. The voice in "I Owe Nothing to My Brothers" is that of an "oracle," one who speaks to us from the "summit of the mountain" (like Moses at Mt. Sinai), uttering truths that seem to have come from a higher source than is available to ordinary mortals. Conclusions are pronounced without the usual kinds of supporting evidence, and each assertion is loaded with an unusually strong emotional commitment. Indeed, the whole utterance is couched in the language of scripture ("guiding star," ¶7; "miracle," ¶10; "fortune of my spirit," ¶11; "covet," ¶12; "temple" and "holy," ¶14; and so on). Go through the passage slowly and list all of the other "scriptural" devices used by the speaker—not just those that explicitly echo the Bible but any device or turn of phrase suggesting that "these utterances are not to be tested by the usual tests. Do not question my word; it comes from on high."
5. When two oracles seem to contradict each other, as do St. Paul and Rand, how are we to deal with them? One simple way would be to dismiss *all* such writing and speaking as absurd because it cannot be tested with rational tests. Another way would be to listen to one of the two voices

uncritically: *My* prophet is simply right and yours self-evidently wrong. Can you think of other possibilities?

6. One possible answer to question 5 would be this: When oracles conflict, there may be *some* truth in each, and the way to find out how much is to slow down and think about the *consequences,* both intellectual and practical, of taking the oracles seriously. Oracles do not, in themselves, usually talk about consequences; their tone suggests that life would be simple if we would only give up every reservation and follow the true doctrine. But as readers who want to learn from them, provided that they really have anything worthwhile to teach, we can step back a bit and ask what their message would mean to our effort to build livable worlds for ourselves. First what do you think would be the consequences, for you, if you decided to put into practice the values expressed by Rand? Second, what would be the consequences for *you* if everyone you know decided to live by these values?
7. Another way to test an oracle is to ask whether the utterance is consistent within itself. Do you detect any internal inconsistencies in Rand's message? In St. Paul's?
8. The 1980s has seen a remarkable growth in the popularity and influence of TV evangelists, claiming to offer us a saving truth. One good question to ask of these oracles, a question surprisingly often neglected by people who jump and join, is this: "What is there in it for *you*—the prophet?" Does the question yield different results when asked of St. Paul and when asked of Rand or of the TV evangelists?

Note: The executor of Miss Ayn Rand's estate, Mr. Leonard Peikoff, responding to our request to reprint this selection from *Anthem,* suggested that some of our discussion questions seriously misrepresent her thought.

> Miss Rand repudiates all forms of mysticism and religion; she advocates exclusive reliance on reason as a means of cognition, and she has written an entire book defining her conception of "reason" (*Introduction to Objectivist Epistemology*). To liken her method or approach, therefore, to that of St. Paul, and to describe her viewpoint as "oracular," is unacceptable in point of accuracy and scholarship. *Anthem* is, of course, a novelette, not a philosophical treatise; as such each sentence does not come equipped with lengthy exegesis or geometric demonstration. But this does not mean that the viewpoint is "oracular." Within its own context, the reasons *are* advanced: the events of the preceding story give the rationale for the summarizing conclusion which you wish to quote. For a full proof of Ayn Rand's ethical viewpoint, including a discussion of the meta-ethical problems of validation involved, I would refer you to her book *The Virtue of Selfishness.*

Suggested Essay Topics

1. "I owe nothing to my brothers, nor do I gather debts from them" (¶10). Imagine a friend of yours who, after reading Rand's chapter from *Anthem,*

has decided that her celebration of "I" as against "We" is sound guidance for life. Write *one* of the following letters:

a. A letter arguing against the decision, concentrating on why this one statement seems factually doubtful
b. A letter arguing in support of her views, concentrating on why this statement seems sound to you
c. A letter debating the pros and cons of the position, describing as many reasons as you can for and against saying that you "owe" something to your brothers (and sisters)

2. Most of your essays will attempt to give more supporting evidence for your claims than is appropriate in "prophetic" writing. But this topic is your chance to climb onto your own mountaintop and shout whatever truths you would like the whole world to believe. Choose your favorite cause—some behavior or set of beliefs you'd like the whole world to adopt—and let yourself go. (One possibility: a hymn to the god "We," in answer to Rand's celebration of the great god "I.")

Martin Luther King, Jr.

Martin Luther King, Jr. (1929–1968), a leader of the civil rights movement, first achieved national prominence during the late 1950s and early 1960s. The scope of his social vision, the moral integrity of his commitment to nonviolence, the authority of his voice, and the generous, incandescent passion of his love for an America not yet realized marked King early as a force larger than any local or particular movement pushing for social change. In 1964 he was awarded the Nobel Peace Prize. In 1968 he was assassinated while on a visit to Memphis, Tennessee, lending support to a strike for higher wages by the garbage workers of that city.

Like Socrates, who persistently reminded his fellow Athenians that they cared more for custom, comfort, and security than for the pursuit of truth or the cultivation of their souls, King reminded his fellow Americans that they cared more for the color of their fellow citizens' skins than for compassion, dignity, or justice. Also like Socrates, who chose to accept execution as a subversive rather than live in exile from his beloved Athens, King always made it clear that he attacked the practices of his country out of love, not hatred. Socrates could be unmerciful in flogging his friends' inconsistencies, hypocrisies, and deceptions and still show that he preferred their company to all others—that he needled them only because he loved them. In the same way, King could express annoyance, disappointment, frustration, and anger at his fellow Americans' foot-dragging on the issue of social justice (especially the foot-dragging of the self-styled "moderate liberal") and still show that what he wanted was for this country to live up to the dream of its best self.

The title of the piece reprinted here is factual; King wrote this letter while he was indeed in prison. The immediate circumstances and local history of the conflict are partially explained in the letter itself. But of course the significance of such matters shifts for us depending on our perspective. For Booth, who was 42 years old when the letter was written, to re-read it now is to experience again the excitement and admiration he felt at the time. For Gregory, who in 1963 was freshly graduated from an isolated, predominantly white college in central Indiana and who had never before faced seriously the problem of racial injustice, the movement King championed produced what he now considers a major awakening, a transformation of conscience and consciousness. But for most of you who read this book, the events took place before you were born and probably seem to you part of the distant past.

For all of us the meaning of those events shifts as we learn more and more about what they led to. What does not shift, as our memories dim and we become more and more dependent on historical accounts, is our picture of the grandeur of King's achievement. King's letter, addressing the conscience of a nation and testing its moral resolve, embraces far more than Birmingham, Alabama, 1963, as it speaks to people of any time and any place who care about justice.

LETTER FROM BIRMINGHAM JAIL*

From *Why We Can't Wait* (1964).

April 16, 1963

MY DEAR FELLOW CLERGYMEN:

While confined here in the Birmingham city jail, I came across your recent statement calling my present activities "unwise and untimely." Seldom do I pause to answer criticism of my work and ideas. If I sought to answer all the criticisms that cross my desk, my secretaries would have little time for anything other than such correspondence in the course of the day, and I would have no time for constructive work. But since I feel that you are men of genuine good will and that your criticisms are sincerely set forth, I want to try to answer your statement in what I hope will be patient and reasonable terms. 1

I think I should indicate why I am here in Birmingham, since you have been influenced by the view which argues against "outsiders coming in." I have the honor of serving as president of the Southern Christian Leadership Conference, an organization operating in every southern state, with head- 2

*This response to a published statement by eight fellow clergymen from Alabama (Bishop C. C. J. Carpenter, Bishop Joseph A. Durick, Rabbi Hilton L. Grafman, Bishop Paul Hardin, Bishop Holan B. Harmon, the Reverend George M. Murray, the Reverend Edward V. Ramage and the Reverend Earl Stallings) was composed under somewhat constricting circumstances. Begun on the margins of the newspaper in which the statement appeared while I was in jail, the letter was continued on scraps of writing paper supplied by a friendly Negro trusty, and concluded on a pad my attorneys were eventually permitted to leave me. Although the text remains in substance unaltered, I have indulged in the author's prerogative of polishing it for publication. [King's note] quarters in Atlanta, Georgia. We have some eighty-five affiliated organizations across the South, and one of them is the Alabama Christian Movement for Human Rights. Frequently we share staff, educational and financial resources with our affiliates. Several months ago the affiliate here in Birmingham asked us to be on call to engage in a nonviolent direct-action program if such were deemed necessary. We readily consented, and when the hour came we lived up to our promise. So I, along with several members of my staff, am here because I was invited here. I am here because I have organizational ties here.

But more basically, I am in Birmingham because injustice is here. Just 3
as the prophets of the eighth century B.C. left their villages and carried their "thus saith the Lord" far beyond the boundaries of their home towns, and just as the Apostle Paul left his village of Tarsus and carried the gospel of Jesus Christ to the far corners of the Greco-Roman world, so am I compelled to carry the gospel of freedom beyond my own home town. Like Paul, I must constantly respond to the Macedonian call for aid.

Moreover, I am cognizant of the interrelatedness of all communities and 4
states. I cannot sit idly by in Atlanta and not be concerned about what happens in Birmingham. Injustice anywhere is a threat to justice everywhere. We are caught in an inescapable network of mutuality, tied in a single garment of destiny. Whatever affects one directly, affects all indirectly. Never again can we afford to live with the narrow, provincial "outside agitator" idea. Anyone who lives inside the United States can never be considered an outsider anywhere within its bounds.

You deplore the demonstrations taking place in Birmingham. But your 5
statement, I am sorry to say, fails to express a similar concern for the conditions that brought about the demonstrations. I am sure that none of you would want to rest content with the superficial kind of social analysis that deals merely with effects and does not grapple with underlying causes. It is unfortunate that demonstrations are taking place in Birmingham, but it is even more unfortunate that the city's white power structure left the Negro community with no alternative.

In any nonviolent campaign there are four basic steps: collection of the 6
facts to determine whether injustices exist; negotiation; self-purification; and direct action. We have gone through all these steps in Birmingham. There can be no gainsaying the fact that racial injustice engulfs this community. Birmingham is probably the most thoroughly segregated city in the United States. Its ugly record of brutality is widely known. Negroes have experienced grossly unjust treatment in the courts. There have been more unsolved bombings of Negro homes and churches in Birmingham than in any other city in the nation. These are the hard, brutal facts of the case. On the basis of these conditions, Negro leaders sought to negotiate with the city fathers. But the latter consistently refused to engage in good-faith negotiation.

Then, last September, came the opportunity to talk with leaders of 7
Birmingham's economic community. In the course of the negotiations, certain promises were made by the merchants—for example, to remove the stores'

humiliating racial signs. On the basis of these promises, the Reverend Fred Shuttlesworth and the leaders of the Alabama Christian Movement for Human Rights agreed to a moratorium on all demonstrations. As the weeks and months went by, we realized that we were the victims of a broken promise. A few signs, briefly removed, returned; the others remained.

As in so many past experiences, our hopes had been blasted, and the 8
shadow of deep disappointment settled upon us. We had no alternative except to prepare for direct action, whereby we would present our very bodies as a means of laying our case before the conscience of the local and the national community. Mindful of the difficulties involved, we decided to undertake a process of self-purification. We began a series of workshops on nonviolence, and we repeatedly asked ourselves: "Are you able to accept blows without retaliating?" "Are you able to endure the ordeal of jail?" We decided to schedule our direct-action program for the Easter season, realizing that except for Christmas, this is the main shopping period of the year. Knowing that a strong economic-withdrawal program would be the by-product of direct action, we felt that this would be the best time to bring pressure to bear on the merchants for the needed change.

Then it occurred to us that Birmingham's mayoral election was coming 9
up in March, and we speedily decided to postpone action until after election day. When we discovered that the Commissioner of Public Safety, Eugene "Bull" Connor, had piled up enough votes to be in the run-off, we decided again to postpone action until the day after the run-off so that the demonstrations could not be used to cloud the issues. Like many others, we waited to see Mr. Connor defeated, and to this end we endured postponement after postponement. Having aided in this community need, we felt that our direct-action program could be delayed no longer.

You may well ask: "Why direct action? Why sit-ins, marches and so 10
forth? Isn't negotiation a better path?" You are quite right in calling for negotiation. Indeed, this is the very purpose of direct action. Nonviolent direct action seeks to create such a crisis and foster such a tension that a community which has constantly refused to negotiate is forced to confront the issue. It seeks so to dramatize the issue that it can no longer be ignored. My citing the creation of tension as part of the work of the nonviolent-resister may sound rather shocking. But I must confess that I am not afraid of the word "tension." I have earnestly opposed violent tension, but there is a type of constructive, nonviolent tension which is necessary for growth. Just as Socrates felt that it was necessary to create a tension in the mind so that individuals could rise from the bondage of myths and half-truths to the unfettered realm of creative analysis and objective appraisal, so must we see the need for nonviolent gadflies to create the kind of tension in society that will help men rise from the dark depths of prejudice and racism to the majestic heights of understanding and brotherhood.

The purpose of our direct-action program is to create a situation so 11
crisis-packed that it will inevitably open the door to negotiation. I therefore concur with you in your call for negotiation. Too long has our beloved

Southland been bogged down in a tragic effort to live in monologue rather than dialogue.

One of the basic points in your statement is that the action that I and my associates have taken in Birmingham is untimely. Some have asked: "Why didn't you give the new city administration time to act?" The only answer that I can give to this query is that the new Birmingham administration must be prodded about as much as the outgoing one, before it will act. We are sadly mistaken if we feel that the election of Albert Boutwell as mayor will bring the millennium to Birmingham. While Mr. Boutwell is a much more gentle person than Mr. Connor, they are both segregationists, dedicated to maintenance of the status quo. I have hope that Mr. Boutwell will be reasonable enough to see the futility of massive resistance to desegregation. But he will not see this without pressure from devotees of civil rights. My friends, I must say to you that we have not made a single gain in civil rights without determined legal and nonviolent pressure. Lamentably, it is an historical fact that privileged groups seldom give up their privileges voluntarily. Individuals may see the moral light and voluntarily give up their unjust posture; but, as Reinhold Niebuhr* has reminded us, groups tend to be more immoral than individuals. 12

We know through painful experience that freedom is never voluntarily given by the oppressor; it must be demanded by the oppressed. Frankly, I have yet to engage in a direct-action campaign that was "well timed" in the view of those who have not suffered unduly from the disease of segregation. For years now I have heard the word "Wait!" It rings in the ear of every Negro with piercing familiarity. This "Wait" has almost always meant "Never." We must come to see, with one of our distinguished jurists, that "justice too long delayed is justice denied." 13

We have waited for more than 340 years for our constitutional and God-given rights. The nations of Asia and Africa are moving with jetlike speed toward gaining political independence, but we still creep at horse-and-buggy pace toward gaining a cup of coffee at a lunch counter. Perhaps it is easy for those who have never felt the stinging darts of segregation to say, "Wait." But when you have seen vicious mobs lynch your mothers and fathers at will and drown your sisters and brothers at whim; when you have seen hate-filled policemen curse, kick and even kill your black brothers and sisters; when you see the vast majority of your twenty million Negro brothers smothering in an airtight cage of poverty in the midst of an affluent society; when you suddenly find your tongue twisted and your speech stammering as you seek to explain to your six-year-old daughter why she can't go to the public amusement park that has just been advertised on television, and see tears welling up in her eyes when she is told that Funtown is closed to colored children, and see ominous clouds of inferiority beginning to form in her little mental sky, and see her beginning to distort her personality by developing 14

*American clergyman and theologian (1892–1971). The book King refers to is *Moral Man and Immoral Society* (1932).

an unconscious bitterness toward white people; when you have to concoct an answer for a five-year-old son who is asking: "Daddy, why do white people treat colored people so mean?"; when you take a cross-country drive and find it necessary to sleep night after night in the uncomfortable corners of your automobile because no motel will accept you; when you are humiliated day in and day out by nagging signs reading "white" and "colored"; when your first name becomes "nigger," your middle name becomes "boy" (however old you are) and your last name becomes "John," and your wife and mother are never given the respected title "Mrs."; when you are harried by day and haunted by night by the fact that you are a Negro, living constantly at tiptoe stance, never quite knowing what to expect next, and are plagued with inner fears and outer resentments; when you are forever fighting a degenerating sense of "nobodiness"—then you will understand why we find it difficult to wait. There comes a time when the cup of endurance runs over, and men are no longer willing to be plunged into the abyss of despair. I hope, sirs, you can understand our legitimate and unavoidable impatience.

You express a great deal of anxiety over our willingness to break laws. 15
This is certainly a legitimate concern. Since we so diligently urge people to obey the Supreme Court's decision of 1954 outlawing segregation in the public schools, at first glance it may seem rather paradoxical for us consciously to break laws. One may well ask: "How can you advocate breaking some laws and obeying others?" The answer lies in the fact that there are two types of laws: just and unjust. I would be the first to advocate obeying just laws. One has not only a legal but a moral responsibility to obey just laws. Conversely, one has a moral responsibility to disobey unjust laws. I would agree with St. Augustine that "an unjust law is no law at all."

Now, what is the difference between the two? How does one determine 16
whether a law is just or unjust? A just law is a man-made code that squares with the moral law or the law of God. An unjust law is a code that is out of harmony with the moral law. To put it in the terms of St. Thomas Aquinas: An unjust law is a human law that is not rooted in eternal law and natural law. Any law that uplifts human personality is just. Any law that degrades human personality is unjust. All segregation statutes are unjust because segregation distorts the soul and damages the personality. It gives the segregator a false sense of superiority and the segregated a false sense of inferiority. Segregation, to use the terminology of the Jewish philosopher Martin Buber, substitutes an "I–it" relationship for an "I–thou" relationship and ends up relegating persons to the status of things. Hence segregation is not only politically, economically and sociologically unsound, it is morally wrong and sinful. Paul Tillich has said that sin is separation. Is not segregation an existential expression of man's tragic separation, his awful estrangement, his terrible sinfulness? Thus it is that I can urge men to obey the 1954 decision of the Supreme Court, for it is morally right; and I can urge them to disobey segregation ordinances, for they are morally wrong.

Let us consider a more concrete example of just and unjust laws. An 17
unjust law is a code that a numerical or power majority group compels a

minority group to obey but does not make binding on itself. This is *difference* made legal. By the same token, a just law is a code that a majority compels a minority to follow and that it is willing to follow itself. This is *sameness* made legal.

Let me give another explanation. A law is unjust if it is inflicted on a minority that, as a result of being denied the right to vote, had no part in enacting or devising the law. Who can say that the legislature of Alabama which set up that state's segregation laws was democratically elected? Throughout Alabama all sorts of devious methods are used to prevent Negroes from becoming registered voters, and there are some counties in which, even though Negroes constitute a majority of the population, not a single Negro is registered. Can any law enacted under such circumstances be considered democratically structured? 18

Sometimes a law is just on its face and unjust in its application. For instance, I have been arrested on a charge of parading without a permit. Now, there is nothing wrong in having an ordinance which requires a permit for a parade. But such an ordinance becomes unjust when it is used to maintain segregation and to deny citizens the First-Amendment privilege of peaceful assembly and protest. 19

I hope you are able to see the distinction I am trying to point out. In no sense do I advocate evading or defying the law, as would the rabid segregationist. That would lead to anarchy. One who breaks an unjust law must do so openly, lovingly, and with a willingness to accept the penalty. I submit that an individual who breaks a law that conscience tells him is unjust, and who willingly accepts the penalty of imprisonment in order to arouse the conscience of the community over its injustice, is in reality expressing the highest respect for law. 20

Of course, there is nothing new about this kind of civil disobedience. It was evidenced sublimely in the refusal of Shadrach, Meshach and Abednego to obey the laws of Nebuchadnezzar, on the ground that a higher moral law was at stake. It was practiced superbly by the early Christians, who were willing to face hungry lions and the excruciating pain of chopping blocks rather than submit to certain unjust laws of the Roman Empire. To a degree, academic freedom is a reality today because Socrates practiced civil disobedience. In our own nation, the Boston Tea Party represented a massive act of civil disobedience. 21

We should never forget that everything Adolf Hitler did in Germany was "legal" and everything the Hungarian freedom fighters did in Hungary was "illegal." It was "illegal" to aid and comfort a Jew in Hitler's Germany. Even so, I am sure that, had I lived in Germany at the time, I would have aided and comforted my Jewish brothers. If today I lived in a Communist country where certain principles dear to the Christian faith are suppressed, I would openly advocate disobeying that country's antireligious laws. 22

I must make two honest confessions to you, my Christian and Jewish brothers. First, I must confess that over the past few years I have been gravely disappointed with the white moderate. I have almost reached the regrettable 23 conclusion that the Negro's great stumbling block in his stride toward freedom is not the White Citizen's Counciler or the Ku Klux Klanner, but the white moderate, who is more devoted to "order" than to justice; who prefers a negative peace which is the absence of tension to a positive peace which is the presence of justice; who constantly says: "I agree with you in the goal you seek, but I cannot agree with your methods of direct action"; who paternalistically believes he can set the timetable for another man's freedom; who lives by a mythical concept of time and who constantly advises the Negro to wait for a "more convenient season." Shallow understanding from people of good will is more frustrating than absolute misunderstanding from people of ill will. Lukewarm acceptance is much more bewildering than outright rejection.

I had hoped that the white moderate would understand that law and order exist for the purpose of establishing justice and that when they fail in this purpose they become the dangerously structured dams that block the flow of social progress. I had hoped that the white moderate would understand that the present tension in the South is a necessary phase of the transition from an obnoxious negative peace, in which the Negro passively accepted his unjust plight, to a substantive and positive peace, in which all men will respect the dignity and worth of human personality. Actually, we who engage in nonviolent direct action are not the creators of tension. We merely bring to the surface the hidden tension that is already alive. We bring it out in the open, where it can be seen and dealt with. Like a boil that can never be cured so long as it is covered up but must be opened with all its ugliness to the natural medicines of air and light, injustice must be exposed, with all the tension its exposure creates, to the light of human conscience and the air of national opinion before it can be cured. 24

In your statement you assert that our actions, even though peaceful, must be condemned because they precipitate violence. But is this a logical assertion? Isn't this like condemning a robbed man because his possession of money precipitated the evil act of robbery? Isn't this like condemning Socrates because his unswerving commitment to truth and his philosophical inquiries precipitated the act by the misguided populace in which they made him drink hemlock? Isn't this like condemning Jesus because his unique God-consciousness and never-ceasing devotion to God's will precipitated the evil act of crucifixion? We must come to see that, as the federal courts have consistently affirmed, it is wrong to urge an individual to cease his efforts to gain his basic constitutional rights because the quest may precipitate violence. Society must protect the robbed and punish the robber. 25

I had also hoped that the white moderate would reject the myth concerning time in relation to the struggle for freedom. I have just received a letter from a white brother in Texas. He writes: "All Christians know that the colored people will receive equal rights eventually, but it is possible that you are in too great a religious hurry. It has taken Christianity almost two thousand years to accomplish what it has. The teachings of Christ take time to come to earth." Such an attitude stems from a tragic misconception of time, 26 from the strangely irrational notion that there is something in the very flow of time that will inevitably cure all ills. Actually, time itself is neutral; it can be used either destructively or constructively. More and more I feel that the people of ill will have used time much more effectively than have the people of good will. We will have to repent in this generation not merely for the hateful words and actions of the bad people but for the appalling silence of the good people. Human progress never rolls in on wheels of inevitability; it comes through the tireless efforts of men willing to be co-workers with God, and without this hard work, time itself becomes an ally of the forces of social stagnation. We must use time creatively, in the knowledge that the time is always ripe to do right. Now is the time to make real the promise of democracy and transform our pending national elegy into a creative psalm of brotherhood. Now is the time to lift our national policy from the quicksand of racial injustice to the solid rock of human dignity.

You speak of our activity in Birmingham as extreme. At first I was rather 27
disappointed that fellow clergymen would see my nonviolent efforts as those of an extremist. I began thinking about the fact that I stand in the middle of two opposing forces in the Negro community. One is a force of complacency, made up in part of Negroes who, as a result of long years of oppression, are so drained of self-respect and a sense of "somebodiness" that they have adjusted to segregation; and in part of a few middle-class Negroes who, because of a degree of academic and economic security and because in some ways they profit by segregation, have become insensitive to the problems of the masses. The other force is one of bitterness and hatred, and it comes perilously close to advocating violence. It is expressed in the various black nationalist groups that are springing up across the nation, the largest and best-known being Elijah Muhammad's Muslim movement. Nourished by the Negro's frustration over the continued existence of racial discrimination, this movement is made up of people who have lost faith in America, who have absolutely repudiated Christianity, and who have concluded that the white man is an incorrigible "devil."

I have tried to stand between these two forces, saying that we need 28
emulate neither the "do-nothingism" of the complacent nor the hatred and despair of the black nationalist. For there is the more excellent way of love and nonviolent protest. I am grateful to God that, through the influence of the Negro church, the way of nonviolence became an integral part of our struggle.

If this philosophy had not emerged, by now many streets of the South 29
would, I am convinced, be flowing with blood. And I am further convinced that if our white brothers dismiss as "rabble-rousers" and "outside agitators" those of us who employ nonviolent direct action, and if they refuse to support our nonviolent efforts, millions of Negroes will, out of frustration and despair, seek solace and security in black-nationalist ideologies—a development that would inevitably lead to a frightening racial nightmare.

Oppressed people cannot remain oppressed forever. The yearning for 30
freedom eventually manifests itself, and that is what has happened to the

American Negro. Something within has reminded him of his birthright of freedom, and something without has reminded him that it can be gained. Consciously or unconsciously, he has been caught up by the *Zeitgeist,* and with his black brothers of Africa and his brown and yellow brothers of Asia, South America and the Caribbean, the United States Negro is moving with a sense of great urgency toward the promised land of racial justice. If one recognizes this vital urge that has engulfed the Negro community, one should readily understand why public demonstrations are taking place. The Negro has many pent-up resentments and latent frustrations, and he must release them. So let him march; let him make prayer pilgrimages to the city hall; let him go on freedom rides—and try to understand why he must do so. If his repressed emotions are not released in nonviolent ways, they will seek expression through violence; this is not a threat but a fact of history. So I have not said to my people: "Get rid of your discontent." Rather, I have tried to say that this normal and healthy discontent can be channeled into the creative outlet of nonviolent direct action. And now this approach is being termed extremist.

But though I was initially disappointed at being categorized as an extremist, as I continued to think about the matter I gradually gained a measure of satisfaction from the label. Was not Jesus an extremist for love: "Love your enemies, bless them that curse you, do good to them that hate you, and pray for them which despitefully use you, and persecute you." Was not Amos an extremist for justice: "Let justice roll down like waters and righteousness like an ever-flowing stream." Was not Paul an extremist for the Christian gospel: "I bear in my body the marks of the Lord Jesus." Was not Martin Luther an extremist: "Here I stand; I cannot do otherwise, so help me God." And John Bunyan: "I will stay in jail to the end of my days before I make a butchery of my conscience." And Abraham Lincoln: "This nation cannot survive half slave and half free." And Thomas Jefferson: "We hold these truths to be self-evident, that all men are created equal . . ." So the question is not whether we will be extremists, but what kind of extremists we will be. Will we be extremists for hate or for love? Will we be extremists for the preservation of injustice or for the extension of justice? In that dramatic scene on Calvary's hill three men were crucified. We must never forget that all three were crucified for the same crime—the crime of extremism. Two were extremists for immorality, and thus fell below their environment. The other, Jesus Christ, was an extremist for love, truth and goodness, and thereby rose above his environment. Perhaps the South, the nation and the world are in dire need of creative extremists. 31

I had hoped that the white moderate would see this need. Perhaps I was too optimistic; perhaps I expected too much. I suppose I should have realized that few members of the oppressor race can understand the deep groans and passionate yearnings of the oppressed race, and still fewer have the vision to see that injustice must be rooted out by strong, persistent and determined action. I am thankful, however, that some of our white brothers in the South have grasped the meaning of this social revolution and committed themselves to it. They are still all too few in quantity, but they are big in quality. 32

Some—such as Ralph McGill, Lillian Smith, Harry Golden, James McBride Dabbs, Ann Braden and Sarah Patton Boyle—have written about our struggle in eloquent and prophetic terms. Others have marched with us down nameless streets of the South. They have languished in filthy, roach-infested jails, suffering the abuse and brutality of policemen who view them as "dirty nigger-lovers." Unlike so many of their moderate brothers and sisters, they have recognized the urgency of the moment and sensed the need for powerful "action" antidotes to combat the disease of segregation.

Let me take note of my other major disappointment. I have been so 33
greatly disappointed with the white church and its leadership. Of course, there are some notable exceptions. I am not unmindful of the fact that each of you has taken some significant stands on this issue. I commend you, Reverend Stallings, for your Christian stand on this past Sunday, in welcoming Negroes to your worship service on a nonsegregated basis. I commend the Catholic leaders of this state for integrating Spring Hill College several years ago.

But despite these notable exceptions, I must honestly reiterate that I 34
have been disappointed with the church. I do not say this as one of those negative critics who can always find something wrong with the church. I say this as a minister of the gospel, who loves the church; who was nurtured in its bosom; who has been sustained by its spiritual blessings and who will remain true to it as long as the cord of life shall lengthen.

When I was suddenly catapulted into the leadership of the bus protest 35
in Montgomery, Alabama, a few years ago, I felt we would be supported by the white church. I felt that the white ministers, priests and rabbis of the South would be among our strongest allies. Instead, some have been outright opponents, refusing to understand the freedom movement and misrepresenting its leaders; all too many others have been more cautious than courageous and have remained silent behind the anesthetizing security of stained-glass windows.

In spite of my shattered dreams, I came to Birmingham with the hope 36
that the white religious leadership of this community would see the justice of our cause and, with deep moral concern, would serve as the channel through which our just grievances could reach the power structure. I had hoped that each of you would understand. But again I have been disappointed.

I have heard numerous southern religious leaders admonish their wor- 37
shipers to comply with a desegregation decision because it is the law, but I have longed to hear white ministers declare: "Follow this decree because integration is morally right and because the Negro is your brother." In the midst of blatant injustices inflicted upon the Negro, I have watched white churchmen stand on the sideline and mouth pious irrelevancies and sanctimonious trivialities. In the midst of a mighty struggle to rid our nation of racial and economic injustice, I have heard many ministers say: "Those are social issues, with which the gospel has no real concern." And I have watched many churches commit themselves to a completely otherworldly religion

which makes a strange, un-Biblical distinction between body and soul, between the sacred and the secular.

I have traveled the length and breadth of Alabama, Mississippi and all 38
the other southern states. On sweltering summer days and crisp autumn mornings I have looked at the South's beautiful churches with their lofty spires pointing heavenward. I have beheld the impressive outlines of her massive religious-education buildings. Over and over I have found myself asking: "What kind of people worship here? Who is their God? Where were their voices when the lips of Governor Barnett dripped with words of interposition and nullification? Where were they when Governor Wallace gave a clarion call for defiance and hatred? Where were their voices of support when bruised and weary Negro men and women decided to rise from the dark dungeons of complacency to the bright hills of creative protest?"

Yes, these questions are still in my mind. In deep disappointment I have 39
wept over the laxity of the church. But be assured that my tears have been tears of love. There can be no deep disappointment where there is not deep love. Yes, I love the church. How could I do otherwise? I am in the rather unique position of being the son, the grandson and the great-grandson of preachers. Yes, I see the church as the body of Christ. But, oh! How we have blemished and scarred that body through social neglect and through fear of being nonconformists.

There was a time when the church was very powerful—in the time 40
when the early Christians rejoiced at being deemed worthy to suffer for what they believed. In those days the church was not merely a thermometer that recorded the ideas and principles of popular opinion; it was a thermostat that transformed the mores of society. Whenever the early Christians entered a town, the people in power became disturbed and immediately sought to convict the Christians for being "disturbers of the peace" and "outside agitators." But the Christians pressed on, in the conviction that they were "a colony of heaven," called to obey God rather than man. Small in number, they were big in commitment. They were too God-intoxicated to be "astronomically intimidated." By their effort and example they brought an end to such ancient evils as infanticide and gladiatorial contests.

Things are different now. So often the contemporary church is a weak, 41
ineffectual voice with an uncertain sound. So often it is an archdefender of the status quo. Far from being disturbed by the presence of the church, the power structure of the average community is consoled by the church's silent—and often even vocal—sanction of things as they are.

But the judgment of God is upon the church as never before. If today's 42
church does not recapture the sacrificial spirit of the early church, it will lose its authenticity, forfeit the loyalty of millions, and be dismissed as an irrelevant social club with no meaning for the twentieth century. Every day I meet young people whose disappointment with the church has turned into outright disgust.

Perhaps I have once again been too optimistic. Is organized religion too 43
inextricably bound to the status quo to save our nation and the world?

Perhaps I must turn my faith to the inner spiritual church, the church within the church, as the true *ekklesia* and the hope of the world. But again I am thankful to God that some noble souls from the ranks of organized religion have broken loose from the paralyzing chains of conformity and joined us as active partners in the struggle for freedom. They have left their secure congregations and walked the streets of Albany, Georgia, with us. They have gone down the highways of the South on tortuous rides for freedom. Yes, they have gone to jail with us. Some have been dismissed from their churches, have lost the support of their bishops and fellow ministers. But they have acted in the faith that right defeated is stronger than evil triumphant. Their witness has been the spiritual salt that has preserved the true meaning of the gospel in these troubled times. They have carved a tunnel of hope through the dark mountain of disappointment.

I hope the church as a whole will meet the challenge of this decisive 44
hour. But even if the church does not come to the aid of justice, I have no despair about the future. I have no fear about the outcome of our struggle in Birmingham, even if our motives are at present misunderstood. We will reach the goal of freedom in Birmingham and all over the nation, because the goal of America is freedom. Abused and scorned though we may be, our destiny is tied up with America's destiny. Before the pilgrims landed at Plymouth, we were here. Before the pen of Jefferson etched the majestic words of the Declaration of Independence across the pages of history, we were here. For more than two centuries our forebears labored in this country without wages; they made cotton king; they built the homes of their masters while suffering gross injustice and shameful humiliation—and yet out of a bottomless vitality they continued to thrive and develop. If the inexpressible cruelties of slavery could not stop us, the opposition we now face will surely fail. We will win our freedom because the sacred heritage of our nation and the eternal will of God are embodied in our echoing demands.

Before closing I feel impelled to mention one other point in your state- 45
ment that has troubled me profoundly. You warmly commended the Birmingham police force for keeping "order" and "preventing violence." I doubt that you would have so warmly commended the police force if you had seen its dogs sinking their teeth into unarmed, nonviolent Negroes. I doubt that you would so quickly commend the policemen if you were to observe their ugly and inhumane treatment of Negroes here in the city jail; if you were to watch them push and curse old Negro women and young Negro girls; if you were to see them slap and kick old Negro men and young boys; if you were to observe them, as they did on two occasions, refuse to give us food because we wanted to sing our grace together. I cannot join you in your praise of the Birmingham police department.

It is true that the police have exercised a degree of discipline in handling 46
the demonstrators. In this sense they have conducted themselves rather "nonviolently" in public. But for what purpose? To preserve the evil system of segregation. Over the past few years I have consistently preached that nonvi-

olence demands that the means we use must be as pure as the ends we seek. I have tried to make clear that it is wrong to use immoral means to attain moral ends. But now I must affirm that it is just as wrong, or perhaps even more so, to use moral means to preserve immoral ends. Perhaps Mr. Connor and his policemen have been rather nonviolent in public, as was Chief Pritchett in Albany, Georgia, but they have used the moral means of nonviolence to maintain the immoral end of racial injustice. As T. S. Eliot has said: "The last temptation is the greatest treason: To do the right deed for the wrong reason."

I wish you had commended the Negro sit-inners and demonstrators of 47
Birmingham for their sublime courage, their willingness to suffer and their amazing discipline in the midst of great provocation. One day the South will recognize its real heroes. They will be the James Merediths, with the noble sense of purpose that enables them to face jeering and hostile mobs, and with the agonizing loneliness that characterizes the life of the pioneer. They will be old, oppressed, battered Negro women, symbolized in a seventy-two-year-old woman in Montgomery, Alabama, who rose up with a sense of dignity and with her people decided not to ride segregated buses, and who responded with ungrammatical profundity to one who inquired about her weariness: "My feets is tired, but my soul is at rest." They will be the young high school and college students, the young ministers of the gospel and a host of their elders, courageously and nonviolently sitting in at lunch counters and willingly going to jail for conscience' sake. One day the South will know that when these disinherited children of God sat down at lunch counters, they were in reality standing up for what is best in the American dream and for the most sacred values in our Judaeo-Christian heritage, thereby bringing our nation back to those great wells of democracy which were dug deep by the founding fathers in their formulation of the Constitution and the Declaration of Independence.

Never before have I written so long a letter. I'm afraid it is much too 48
long to take your precious time. I can assure you that it would have been much shorter if I had been writing from a comfortable desk, but what else can one do when he is alone in a narrow jail cell, other than write long letters, think long thoughts and pray long prayers?

If I have said anything in this letter that overstates the truth and indi- 49
cates an unreasonable impatience, I beg you to forgive me. If I have said anything that understates the truth and indicates my having a patience that allows me to settle for anything less than brotherhood, I beg God to forgive me.

I hope this letter finds you strong in the faith. I also hope that circum- 50
stances will soon make it possible for me to meet each of you, not as an integrationist or a civil-rights leader but as a fellow clergyman and a Christian brother. Let us all hope that the dark clouds of racial prejudice will soon pass away and the deep fog of misunderstanding will be lifted from our fear-drenched communities, and in some not too distant tomorrow the radiant

stars of love and brotherhood will shine over our great nation with all their scintillating beauty.

Yours for the cause of Peace and Brotherhood,
MARTIN LUTHER KING, JR.

Questions for Discussion

1. What reasons does King give for taking time to answer the critics whose letter provoked this reply when he ignores most of his other critics?
2. Do you agree that "anyone who lives inside the United States can never be considered an outsider anywhere within its bounds" (¶4)? Have you heard arguments to the contrary? Do you find King convincing on this question?
3. Can you give an explanation and a justification for the four steps in any nonviolent campaign that King lays out in paragraph 6? Can you explain and justify the order of the steps?
4. How does "direct action" differ from violence (¶8, 10, and 11)?
5. Stylistically, King is master of certain devices that are particularly effective in oral delivery. Identify the device used in paragraph 14, and comment on its effectiveness. What happens to the rhetorical power of the paragraph if you alter the wording to destroy the device—even if you retain the meaning?
6. Can you explain in your own words King's distinction between a "just" and an "unjust" law? Does he support the distinction with convincing argument? Why is it important for him to spend so much space (¶15–22) supporting the validity of this distinction?
7. Why does King find the "white moderate" more objectionable (in some ways) than the outspoken segregationist? Do you think he is justified in his feeling?
8. What is King's criticism of the church with respect to social justice? Do you think the church in America has become less silent and evasive since King criticized it in 1963?

Suggested Essay Topics

1. Powerful metaphors abound in King's letter in almost every paragraph. Pick several that strike you as most impressive and analyze the power they impart to King's prose. One clear way of doing this is to replace each metaphor with a literal statement—the best you can write—and see what happens to the power of the statement. (It may strengthen your analysis if you consider which of the five senses each metaphor appeals to.) Address your paper either to your instructor or to someone you know whose

writing seems to suffer from a poverty of metaphor. Remember that your own tone should vary somewhat, depending on which kind of reader you are trying to convince.

2. Choose some injustice that you have experienced firsthand or know something about, and write two contrasting arguments about it. Address the first one to a sympathetic judge who has asked for a *factual* or *skeletal* account of your argument. Make it as lean, as undoctored, as unliterary as you can. Then write a second account of the same issue, but this time use as much of the kind of stylistic heightening that King uses as you possibly can. Don't worry about being too flowery; treat the assignment as an experiment in packing in rather than cutting out—a chance to try out all kinds of appeals that can reinforce the skeleton of an argument.

e. e. cummings

The poet e. e. cummings (1894–1962) was one of a group of avant-garde poets and novelists who became famous, shortly after World War I, for their experimentation with "shocking" styles. Many of these writers were quickly forgotten, because their tricky rejections of literary convention—with coined words, twisted grammar, "impossible" metaphors, wild or nonexistent punctuation, and strange verse forms and antiforms—soon lost their sense of originality and no longer conveyed the interest even of shock. Those who have endured are those who, like cummings, brought a strong personal passion or vision with their surface innovations. In cummings's best poems one discovers a lyrical or satirical voice that would speak with power even if the surface surprises were removed.

Though many of cummings's effects depend in part on our seeing the printed poem—he liked typographical innovations such as printing his name in all lowercase letters—most of his effects must be heard to be fully enjoyed. The poem we print here, numbered simply "LIV" in Roman numerals (that is, "Poem Number 54," though there is probably a pun on "Live!" as a command), should be read aloud several times before you even try to ask, "What does it mean?*" Don't be embarrassed about chanting it like a kind of vigorous drumbeat, leaving as much time for some of the "slow" syllables (e.g.,* skip *and* up*) as you allow for three or four "fast" ones (e.g.,* ev-ery-thing *and* a-round a-gain*). Try chanting the lines like this, the way we render lines 14–17, giving an equal amount of time to what happens between the syllables in capital letters:*

one's
ANYthing
OLD being
EVerything
NEW with a

WHAT (rest)
WHICH (rest) a-
ROUND we come
WHO

Written in wartime and published in 1944 in the volume 1 × 1, *"LIV" celebrates the mysterious act of multiplication that love achieves: One times one equals a new* one *who is a "we" and not two "I's." When "I love you and you love me" and when everything that is a "your" becomes a "my," we can celebrate a new world with a song like this one.*

LIV

if everything happens that can't be done
(and anything's righter
than books
could plan)
the stupidest teacher will almost guess
(with a run
skip
around we go yes)
there's nothing as something as one

one hasn't a why or because or although
(and buds know better
than books
don't grow)
one's anything old being everything new
(with a what
which
around we come who)
one's everyanything so

so world is a leaf so tree is a bough
(and birds sing sweeter
than books
tell how)
so here is away and so your is a my
(with a down
up
around again fly)
forever was never till now

now i love you and you love me
(and books are shuter

than books
can be)
and deep in the high that does nothing but fall
(with a shout
each
around we go all)
there's somebody calling who's we

we're anything brighter than even the sun
(we're everything greater
than books
might mean)
we're everyanything more than believe
(with a spin
leap
alive we're alive)
we're wonderful one times one

Questions for Discussion

1. You may at first have been puzzled by some of the non-sentences the poem offers, with their forced joining of terms ordinarily kept separate: "one hasn't a why," "buds know better than books don't grow," "deep in the high," and so on. But after reading the poem a few times you have no doubt begun to see that there is a pattern to these "meaningless" expressions. Try "translating" (paraphrasing) some of the statements that are not strictly grammatical into ordinary English. (For example, for lines 11–13, "Flowers convey to us a knowledge even the wisest books cannot convey," or, for line 9, "Nothing in the world is as fully real, as fully alive, as discovering the 'oneness' of love.") What do your paraphrases lose, if anything, that cummings's words achieve?
2. You will find other authors both in this book and elsewhere making points similar to those you have written as you paraphrased cummings: Men and women find their happiness only in working with and for others; individualism is a dangerous thing; and so on. Discuss the different effects that can be achieved when the same idea is treated in poetry and in prose. What, if anything, is lost or gained by conveying an idea through poetry rather than arguing the same idea at length in discursive prose?

Suggested Essay Topics

1. Write an essay comparing what seem to be the assumptions and conclusions of this poem with those of Ayn Rand in the preceding selection.

2. Picture a critic asserting: "In order to praise love, cummings unfortunately finds it necessary to mock books and knowledge and teachers. It is a silly romantic notion to see an opposition between being fully alive in love and learning how to discover what 'books might mean.' " Write an essay either refuting or supporting this criticism. If you support it, direct your essay to cummings himself; if you refute it, direct your essay to the "insensitive" critic who simply fails to see how right cummings really is.

7

SOCIAL JUSTICE

Minorities and Majorities

To me, anti-Semitism is now the most shocking of all things.
It is destroying much more than the Jews; it is assailing the human mind
at its source, and inviting it to create false categories
before exercising judgment. I am sure we shall win through.
But it will take a long time. . . . For the moment
all we can do is to dig in our heels, and prevent silliness
from sliding into insanity.
E. M. Forster

The Negro wanted to feel pride in his race? With tokenism,
the solution was simple. If all twenty million Negroes would keep looking
at Ralph Bunche [former ambassador to the United Nations],
the one man in so exalted a post would
generate such a volume of pride that it could be cut into
portions and served to everyone.
Martin Luther King, Jr.

In giving freedom to the slave, we assure freedom
to the free—honorable alike in what we give and what we preserve.
Abraham Lincoln

There is no subject on earth so easily understood as that of
the American Indian. Each summer, work camps
disgorge teen-agers on various reservations.
Within one month's time the youngsters acquire a knowledge
of Indians that would astound a college professor.
Vine Deloria, Jr.

None can love freedom heartily, but good men; the rest love
not freedom, but licence.
John Milton

Chief Red Jacket and the Missionary

The story of injustices inflicted upon racial and ethnic minorities in American society, past and present, has been widely documented with case histories and statistics and explained with countless theories. These are useful and informative, but the whole issue has perhaps never been summed up with such simple and powerful eloquence as in the rejection by the Indians (in this episode) of the white man's religion, patronizingly pushed at them by a missionary whose every word reveals his intolerance toward everything Indian. The Indians say that they will accept the white man's religion when they see that it makes whites treat Indians more fairly. By this simple test they at once summarize and condemn the whole tradition of white hypocrisy and greed.

Why should the Indians accept a religion that has allowed the white man to justify the theft of Indian lands and the murder of Indian people? They have learned that listening to the white man always leads to being cheated. Their "smiling" acceptance of the missionary's refusal to shake their hands after they have rejected his religion shows that they clearly see through his professed intention to do them good and perceive his real intention, which is to add the robbery of their religion to the robbery of their lands and way of life.

The narrative that introduces and comments on the speeches is by the anonymous editor of the 1809 edition.

A NATIVE AMERICAN EPISODE

Speeches by Chief Red Jacket and the Reverend Mr. Cram

From *Indian Speeches; Delivered by Farmer's Brother and Red Jacket, Two Seneca Chiefs* (1809). The title is ours.

[In the summer of 1805, a number of the principal Chiefs and Warriors of the Six Nations, principally Senecas, assembled at Buffalo Creek, in the state of New York, at the particular request of Rev. Mr. Cram, a Missionary from the state of Massachusetts. The Missionary being furnished with an Interpreter, and accompanied by the Agent of the United States for Indian affairs, met the Indians in Council, when the following talk took place.] 1

FIRST, BY THE AGENT. "*Brothers of the Six Nations;* I rejoice to meet you at this time, and thank the Great Spirit, that he has preserved you in health, and given me another opportunity of taking you by the hand. 2

"*Brothers;* The person who sits by me, is a friend who has come a great distance to hold a talk with you. He will inform you what his business is, and it is my request that you would listen with attention to his words." 3

MISSIONARY. "*My Friends;* I am thankful for the opportunity afforded us of uniting together at this time. I had a great desire to see you, and inquire into your state and welfare; for this purpose I have travelled a great distance, being sent by your old friends, the Boston Missionary Society. You will recollect they formerly sent missionaries among you, to instruct you in religion, and labor for your good. Although they have not heard from you for a long time, yet they have not forgotten their brothers the Six Nations, and are still anxious to do you good. 4

"*Brothers;* I have not come to get your lands or your money, but to enlighten your minds, and to instruct you how to worship the Great Spirit agreeably to his mind and will, and to preach to you the gospel of his son Jesus Christ. There is but one religion, and but one way to serve God, and if you do not embrace the right way, you cannot be happy hereafter. You have never worshipped the Great Spirit in a manner acceptable to him; but have, all your lives, been in great errors and darkness. To endeavor to remove these errors, and open your eyes, so that you might see clearly, is my business with you. 5

"*Brothers;* I wish to talk with you as one friend talks with another; and, if you have any objections to receive the religion which I preach, I wish you to state them; and I will endeavor to satisfy your minds, and remove the objections. 6

"*Brothers;* I want you to speak your minds freely; for I wish to reason with you on the subject, and, if possible, remove all doubts, if there be any on your minds. The subject is an important one, and it is of consequence that you give it an early attention while the offer is made you. Your friends, the Boston Missionary Society, will continue to send you good and faithful 7 ministers, to instruct and strengthen you in religion, if, on your part, you are willing to receive them.

"*Brothers;* Since I have been in this part of the country, I have visited 8
some of your small villages, and talked with your people. They appear willing to receive instruction, but, as they look up to you as their older brothers in council, they want first to know your opinion on the subject.

"You have now heard what I have to propose at present. I hope you will 9
take it into consideration, and give me an answer before we part."

[After about two hours consultation among themselves, the Chief, com- 10
monly called by the white people, Red Jacket (whose Indian name is Sagu-yu-what-hah, which interpreted is *Keeper awake*) rose and spoke as follows:]

"*Friend and Brother;* It was the will of the Great Spirit that we should meet 11
together this day. HE orders all things, and has given us a fine day for our Council. HE has taken his garment from before the sun, and caused it to shine with brightness upon us. Our eyes are opened, that we see clearly; our ears are unstopped, that we have been able to hear distinctly the words you have spoken. For all these favors we thank the Great Spirit; and HIM *only.*

"*Brother;* This council fire was kindled by you. It was at your request that 12
we came together at this time. We have listened with attention to what you have said. You requested us to speak our minds freely. This gives us great joy; for we now consider that we stand upright before you, and can speak what we think. All have heard your voice, and all speak to you now as one man. Our minds are agreed.

"*Brother;* You say you want an answer to your talk before you leave this 13
place. It is right you should have one, as you are a great distance from home, and we do not wish to detain you. But we will first look back a little, and tell you what our fathers have told us, and what we have heard from the white people.

"*Brother;* Listen to what we say. 14

"There was a time when our forefathers owned this great island. Their seats extended from the rising to the setting sun. The Great Spirit had made it for the use of Indians. HE had created the buffalo, the deer, and other animals for food. HE had made the bear and the beaver. Their skins served us for clothing. HE had scattered them over the country, and taught us how to take them. HE had caused the earth to produce corn for bread. All this HE had done for his red children, because HE loved them. If we had some disputes about our hunting ground, they were generally settled without the shedding of much blood. But an evil day came upon us. Your forefathers crossed the great water, and landed on this island. Their numbers were small. They found friends and not enemies. They told us they had fled from their country for fear of wicked men, and had come here to enjoy their religion. They asked for a small seat. We took pity on them, granted their request; and they sat down amongst us. We gave them corn and meat, they gave us poison [alluding, it is supposed, to ardent spirits] in return.

"The white people had now found our country. Tidings were carried 15
back, and more came amongst us. Yet we did not fear them. We took them

to be friends. They called us brothers. We believed them, and gave them a larger seat. At length their numbers had greatly increased. They wanted more land; they wanted our country. Our eyes were opened, and our minds became uneasy. Wars took place. Indians were hired to fight against Indians, and many of our people were destroyed. They also brought strong liquor amongst us. It was strong and powerful, and has slain thousands.

"*Brother;* Our seats were once large and yours were small. You have now 16
become a great people, and we have scarcely a place left to spread our blankets. You have got our country, but are not satisfied; you want to force your religion upon us.

"*Brother;* Continue to listen. 17

"You say that you are sent to instruct us how to worship the Great Spirit agreeably to his mind, and, if we do not take hold of the religion which you white people teach, we shall be unhappy hereafter. You say that you are right and we are lost. How do we know this to be true? We understand that your religion is written in a book. If it was intended for us as well as you, why has not the Great Spirit given to us, and not only to us, but why did he not give to our forefathers, the knowledge of that book, with the means of understanding it rightly? We only know what you tell us about it. How shall we know when to believe, being so often deceived by the white people?

"*Brother;* You say there is but one way to worship and serve the Great 18
Spirit. If there is but one religion; why do you white people differ so much about it? Why not all agreed, as you can all read the book?

"*Brother;* We do not understand these things. 19

"We are told that your religion was given to your forefathers, and has been handed down from father to son. We also have a religion, which was given to our forefathers, and has been handed down to us their children. We worship in that way. It teaches us to be thankful for all the favors we receive; to love each other, and to be united. We never quarrel about religion.

"*Brother;* The Great Spirit has made us all, but he has made a great 20
difference between his white and red children. He has given us different complexions and different customs. To you He has given the arts. To these He has not opened our eyes. We know these things to be true. Since He has made so great a difference between us in other things; why may we not conclude that He has given us a different religion according to our understanding? The Great Spirit does right. He knows what is best for his children; we are satisfied.

"*Brother;* We do not wish to destroy your religion, or take it from you. 21
We only want to enjoy our own.

"*Brother;* We are told that you have been preaching to the white people 22
in this place. These people are our neighbors. We are acquainted with them. We will wait a little while, and see what effect your preaching has upon them. If we find it does them good, makes them honest and less disposed to cheat Indians; we will then consider again of what you have said.

"*Brother;* You have now heard our answer to your talk, and this is all we 23
have to say at present.

"As we are going to part, we will come and take you by the hand, and hope the Great Spirit will protect you on your journey, and return you safe to your friends." 24

[As the Indians began to approach the missionary, he rose hastily from his seat and replied, that he could not take them by the hand; that there was no fellowship between the religion of God and the works of the devil. 25

This being interpreted to the Indians, they smiled, and retired in a peaceable manner. 26

It being afterwards suggested to the missionary that his reply to the Indians was rather indiscreet; he observed, that he supposed the ceremony of shaking hands would be received by them as a token that he assented to what they had said. Being otherwise informed, he said he was sorry for the expressions.] 27

Questions for Discussion

1. What words and actions can you point to that reveal the unconscious bigotry of the missionary?
2. In light of the patronizing tone adopted by the missionary, how do you account for the mildness and friendliness of the Indians' reply? Clearly, this picture squares badly with the image of the "savage redskin" in novels and movies. What reasons can you offer for the persistence of this popular but degrading image? Which of those reasons is connected to the attitudes exhibited by the missionary?
3. What kind of research, and what kind of thinking about evidence, would be required to get a clear picture of what the Senecas were like at the time this speech was given? Do you think that any one account, whether from the perspective of Indians, of white Americans, or of some "neutral" historian from another nation, could capture the full story that lies behind Red Jacket's speech?
4. Do you think that the account of Indian history *from the Indians' point of view* (¶14–16) is generally accepted today by most white people? If it is, why do you think that more has not been done to right the obvious wrongs exposed in this history? If you think most white people reject the Indians' view, what other views do you think they hold?

Suggested Essay Topics

1. Write another answer to the missionary for the Indians, taking a tone of indignation, outrage, or bitterness. You may use the same content or add to it from your own store of information; the point is to alter the tone so that you change the effect of the message.

2. Write a speech that might serve as a reply to Red Jacket, made by someone who has *really listened* to his arguments. In planning your speech, you should think through the possible lines of argument and the possible tones you might take: humbly apologetic (moving toward explanation); firmly indignant about having been misunderstood and maligned; rational and unemotional, mustering anecdotes and other evidence to show that Indians after all *have* committed cruel acts; and so on. Then choose the tone (implying a character for yourself) that you think will be most likely to be taken as sympathetic, so that the Indians will be most likely to hear your side of the story.

Ralph Ellison

Ralph Ellison (b. 1914) became famous almost overnight with the publication in 1952 of his novel Invisible Man, *the story of a young black man's trek toward self-identity. In a society that tells him he has no right to an identity except that given to him by whites, almost all of whom treat him with contempt, a trek toward identity meets almost impossible conditions. Most of us feel that we have a right not only to our own sense of selfhood but also to be surrounded by people who give us affection, encouragement, guidance, and hope.*

Through the use of symbol and metaphor, "Battle Royal" implies an argument about the position of blacks in a white-dominated power structure. Simply put, blacks must do battle in order to survive, but they must lose their naïveté if they are to battle successfully. As long as they allow whites to set the terms and conditions of battle, as long as they allow whites to set blacks battling against other blacks, and as long as they allow whites to reward them with cheap and phony payoffs that only underscore their inferior status, they will be duped into thinking they are winning a skirmish here and there (a scholarship to an all-black college, for example), but they will lose the royal battle, the battle for dignity, freedom, and self-esteem.

One of the most evocative symbols in the story is the naked dancer. As you read, try to determine how Ellison uses this symbol. Does "the small American flag tattooed upon her belly" (¶7) make her a symbol? If so, of what? Of all the false seductions that whites have held out to blacks who are eager to embrace America's noble slogans about freedom and equality but who are never allowed to join in the dance? The message to blacks has historically been one of "desire but don't possess," "admire but don't touch." And the callous way the white men toss the dancer in the air, defiling her out of sheer lust or greed, seems to highlight their profound ignorance of the grounds of their own freedom and to provide a sad commentary on their profound corruption.

The realization "that I am nobody but myself" (¶1) sounds simple, but to realize what this means in the only way that counts—to be in possession of one's own conscience, one's own sense of worth, and one's own sense of dignity, and to be able to hold to these in spite of social pressure, failure, or disappointment—this is not so simple. When family or society gives us double messages or lies, the realization can be made even harder. As you read, consider in what ways your own experience, whether you are a member of a minority or not, parallels and diverges from the central character's. Perhaps each of us has to fight a battle royal of some kind on the road to self-knowledge. The young man in the story has to identify the real enemy before he can begin to fight effectively, before he can even choose the right battle. How does he do this? What, or who, is his real enemy? His story invites us all to identify the battles that are most necessary or meaningful for us personally.

BATTLE ROYAL

From *Invisible Man* (1952).

It goes a long way back, some twenty years. All my life I had been looking for something, and everywhere I turned someone tried to tell me what it was. I accepted their answers too, though they were often in contradiction and even self-contradictory. I was naïve. I was looking for myself and asking everyone except myself questions which I, and only I, could answer. It took me a long time and much painful boomeranging of my expectations to achieve a realization everyone else appears to have been born with: That I am nobody but myself. But first I had to discover that I am an invisible man! 1

And yet I am no freak of nature, nor of history. I was in the cards, other things having been equal (or unequal) eighty-five years ago. I am not ashamed of my grandparents for having been slaves. I am only ashamed of myself for having at one time been ashamed. About eighty-five years ago they were told that they were free, united with others of our country in everything pertaining to the common good, and, in everything social, separate like the fingers of the hand. And they believed it. They exulted in it. They stayed in their place, worked hard, and brought up my father to do the same. But my grandfather is the one. He was an odd old guy, my grandfather, and I am told I take after him. It was he who caused the trouble. On his deathbed he called my father to him and said, "Son, after I'm gone I want you to keep up the fight. I never told you, but our life is a war and I have been a traitor all my born days, a spy in the enemy's country ever since I give up my gun back in the Reconstruction. Live with your head in the lion's mouth. I want you to overcome 'em with yeses, undermine 'em with grins, agree 'em to death and destruction, let 'em swoller you till they vomit or bust wide open." They thought the old man had gone out of his mind. He had been the meekest of men. The younger children were rushed from the room, the shades drawn and the flame of the lamp turned so low that it sputtered on the wick like the old man's breathing. "Learn it to the younguns," he whispered fiercely; then he died. 2

But my folks were more alarmed over his last words than over his dying. It was as though he had not died at all, his words caused so much anxiety. I was warned emphatically to forget what he had said and, indeed, this is the 3 first time it has been mentioned outside the family circle. It had a tremendous effect upon me, however. I could never be sure of what he meant. Grandfather had been a quiet old man who never made any trouble, yet on his deathbed he had called himself a traitor and a spy, and he had spoken of his meekness as a dangerous activity. It became a constant puzzle which lay unanswered in the back of my mind. And whenever things went well for me I remembered my grandfather and felt guilty and uncomfortable. It was as though I was carrying out his advice in spite of myself. And to make it worse, everyone loved me for it. I was praised by the most lily-white men of the town. I was considered an example of desirable conduct—just as my grandfather had been. And what puzzled me was that the old man had defined it as *treachery*. When I was praised for my conduct I felt a guilt that in some way I was doing something that was really against the wishes of the white folks, that if they had understood they would have desired me to act just the opposite, that I should have been sulky and mean, and that that really would have been what they wanted, even though they were fooled and thought they wanted me to act as I did. It made me afraid that some day they would look upon me as a traitor and I would be lost. Still I was more afraid to act any other way because they didn't like that at all. The old man's words were like a curse. On my graduation day I delivered an oration in which I showed that humility was the secret, indeed, the very essence of progress. (Not that I believed this—how could I, remembering my grandfather?—I only believed that it worked.) It was a great success. Everyone praised me and I was invited to give the speech at a gathering of the town's leading white citizens. It was a triumph for our whole community.

It was in the main ballroom of the leading hotel. When I got there I 4
discovered that it was on the occasion of a smoker, and I was told that since I was to be there anyway I might as well take part in the battle royal to be fought by some of my schoolmates as part of the entertainment. The battle royal came first.

All of the town's big shots were there in their tuxedos, wolfing down 5
the buffet foods, drinking beer and whiskey and smoking black cigars. It was a large room with a high ceiling. Chairs were arranged in neat rows around three sides of a portable boxing ring. The fourth side was clear, revealing a gleaming space of polished floor. I had some misgivings over the battle royal, by the way. Not from a distaste for fighting, but because I didn't care too much for the other fellows who were to take part. They were tough guys who seemed to have no grandfather's curse worrying their minds. No one could mistake their toughness. And besides, I suspected that fighting a battle royal might detract from the dignity of my speech. In those pre-invisible days I visualized myself as a potential Booker T. Washington.* But the other fellows didn't care too much for me either, and there were nine of them. I felt superior to them in my way, and I didn't like the manner in which we were all crowded together into the servants' elevator. Nor did they like my being there. In fact,

*Black American teacher and leader (1856–1915).

as the warmly lighted floors flashed past the elevator we had words over the fact that I, by taking part in the fight, had knocked one of their friends out of a night's work.

We were led out of the elevator through a rococo hall into an anteroom and told to get into our fighting togs. Each of us was issued a pair of boxing gloves and ushered out into the big mirrored hall, which we entered looking cautiously about us and whispering, lest we might accidentally be heard above the noise of the room. It was foggy with cigar smoke. And already the whiskey was taking effect. I was shocked to see some of the most important men of the town quite tipsy. They were all there—bankers, lawyers, judges, doctors, fire chiefs, teachers, merchants. Even one of the more fashionable pastors. Something we could not see was going on up front. A clarinet was vibrating sensuously and the men were standing up and moving eagerly forward. We were a small tight group, clustered together, our bare upper bodies touching and shining with anticipatory sweat; while up front the big shots were becoming increasingly excited over something we still could not see. Suddenly I heard the school superintendent, who had told me to come, yell, "Bring up the shines, gentlemen! Bring up the little shines!" 6

We were rushed up to the front of the ballroom, where it smelled even more strongly of tobacco and whiskey. Then we were pushed into place. I almost wet my pants. A sea of faces, some hostile, some amused, ringed around us, and in the center, facing us, stood a magnificent blonde—stark naked. There was a dead silence. I felt a blast of cold air chill me. I tried to back away, but they were behind me and around me. Some of the boys stood with lowered heads, trembling. I felt a wave of irrational guilt and fear. My teeth chattered, my skin turned to goose flesh, my knees knocked. Yet I was strongly attracted and looked in spite of myself. Had the price of looking been blindness, I would have looked. The hair was yellow like that of a circus kewpie doll, the face heavily powdered and rouged, as though to form an abstract mask, the eyes hollow and smeared a cool blue, the color of a baboon's butt. I felt a desire to spit upon her as my eyes brushed slowly over her body. Her breasts were firm and round as the domes of East Indian temples, and I stood so close as to see the fine skin texture and beads of pearly perspiration glistening like dew around the pink and erected buds of her nipples. I wanted at one and the same time to run from the room, to sink through the floor, or go to her and cover her from my eyes and the eyes of the others with my body; to feel the soft thighs, to caress her and destroy her, to love her and murder her, to hide from her, and yet to stroke where below the small American flag tattooed upon her belly her thighs formed a capital V. I had a notion that of all in the room she saw only me with her impersonal eyes. 7

And then she began to dance, a slow sensuous movement; the smoke of a hundred cigars clinging to her like the thinnest of veils. She seemed like a fair bird-girl girdled in veils calling to me from the angry surface of some gray and threatening sea. I was transported. Then I became aware of the clarinet playing and the big shots yelling at us. Some threatened us if we looked and others if we did not. On my right I saw one boy faint. And now 8 a man grabbed a silver pitcher from a table and stepped close as he dashed ice water upon him and stood him up and forced two of us to support him as his head hung and moans issued from his thick bluish lips. Another boy began to plead to go home. He was the largest of the group, wearing dark red fighting trunks much too small to conceal the erection which projected from him as though in answer to the insinuating low-registered moaning of the clarinet. He tried to hide himself with his boxing gloves.

And all the while the blonde continued dancing, smiling faintly at the big shots who watched her with fascination, and faintly smiling at our fear. I noticed a certain merchant who followed her hungrily, his lips loose and drooling. He was a large man who wore diamond studs in a shirtfront which swelled with the ample paunch underneath, and each time the blonde swayed her undulating hips he ran his hand through the thin hair of his bald head and, with his arms upheld, his posture clumsy like that of an intoxicated panda, wound his belly in a slow and obscene grind. This creature was completely hypnotized. The music had quickened. As the dancer flung herself about with a detached expression on her face, the men began reaching out to touch her. I could see their beefy fingers sink into the soft flesh. Some of the others tried to stop them and she began to move around the floor in graceful circles, as they gave chase, slipping and sliding over the polished floor. It was mad. Chairs went crashing, drinks were spilt, as they ran laughing and howling after her. They caught her just as she reached a door, raised her from the floor, and tossed her as college boys are tossed at a hazing, and above her red, fixed-smiling lips I saw the terror and disgust in her eyes, almost like my own terror and that which I saw in some of the other boys. As I watched, they tossed her twice and her soft breasts seemed to flatten against the air and her legs flung wildly as she spun. Some of the more sober ones helped her to escape. And I started off the floor, heading for the anteroom with the rest of the boys. 9

Some were still crying and in hysteria. But as we tried to leave we were stopped and ordered to get into the ring. There was nothing to do but what we were told. All ten of us climbed under the ropes and allowed ourselves to be blindfolded with broad bands of white cloth. One of the men seemed to feel a bit sympathetic and tried to cheer us up as we stood with our backs against the ropes. Some of us tried to grin. "See that boy over there?" one of the men said. "I want you to run across at the bell and give it to him right in the belly. If you don't get him, I'm going to get you. I don't like his looks." Each of us was told the same. The blindfolds were put on. Yet even then I had been going over my speech. In my mind each word was as bright as flame. I felt the cloth pressed into place, and frowned so that it would be loosened when I relaxed. 10

But now I felt a sudden fit of blind terror. I was unused to darkness. It was as though I had suddenly found myself in a dark room filled with poisonous cottonmouths. I could hear the bleary voices yelling insistently for the battle royal to begin. 11

"Get going in there!" 12

"Let me at the big nigger!" 13

I strained to pick up the school superintendent's voice, as though to squeeze some security out of that slightly more familiar sound. 14

"Let me at those black sonsabitches!" someone yelled. 15

"No, Jackson, no!" another voice yelled. "Here, somebody, help me hold Jack." 16

"I want to get at that ginger-colored nigger. Tear him limb from limb," the first voice yelled. 17

I stood against the ropes trembling. For in those days I was what they called ginger-colored, and he sounded as though he might crunch me between his teeth like a crisp ginger cookie. 18

Quite a struggle was going on. Chairs were being kicked about and I could hear voices grunting as with a terrific effort. I wanted to see, to see more desperately than ever before. But the blindfold was as tight as a thick skin-puckering scab and when I raised my gloved hands to push the layers of white aside a voice yelled, "Oh, no you don't, black bastard! Leave that alone!" 19

"Ring the bell before Jackson kills him a coon!" someone boomed in the sudden silence. And I heard the bell clang and the sound of feet scuffling forward. 20

A glove smacked against my head. I pivoted, striking out stiffly as someone went past, and felt the jar ripple along the length of my arm to my shoulder. Then it seemed as though all nine of the boys had turned upon me at once. Blows pounded me from all sides while I struck out as best I could. So many blows landed upon me that I wondered if I were not the only blindfolded fighter in the ring, or if the man called Jackson hadn't succeeded in getting me after all. 21

Blindfolded, I could no longer control my motions. I had no dignity. I stumbled about like a baby or a drunken man. The smoke had become thicker and with each new blow it seemed to sear and further restrict my lungs. My saliva became like hot bitter glue. A glove connected with my head, filling my mouth with warm blood. It was everywhere. I could not tell if the moisture I felt upon my body was sweat or blood. A blow landed hard against the nape of my neck. I felt myself going over, my head hitting the floor. Streaks of blue light filled the black world behind the blindfold. I lay prone, pretending that I was knocked out, but felt myself seized by hands and yanked to my feet. "Get going, black boy! Mix it up!" My arms were like lead, my head smarting from blows. I managed to feel my way to the ropes and held on, trying to catch my breath. A glove landed in my midsection and I went over again, feeling as though the smoke had become a knife jabbed into my guts. Pushed this way and that by the legs milling around me, I finally pulled erect and discovered that I could see the black, sweat-washed forms weaving in the smoky-blue atmosphere like drunken dancers weaving to the rapid drumlike thuds of blows. 22

Everyone fought hysterically. It was complete anarchy. Everybody fought everybody else. No group fought together for long. Two, three, four, fought one, then turned to fight each other, were themselves attacked. Blows 23 landed below the belt and in the kidney, with the gloves open as well as closed, and with my eye partly opened now there was not so much terror. I moved carefully, avoiding blows, although not too many to attract attention, fighting from group to group. The boys groped about like blind, cautious crabs crouching to protect their mid-sections, their heads pulled in short against their shoulders, their arms stretched nervously before them, with their fists testing the smoke-filled air like the knobbed feelers of hypersensitive snails. In the corner I glimpsed a boy violently punching the air and heard him scream in pain as he smashed his hand against a ring post. For a second I saw him bent over holding his hand, then going down as a blow caught his unprotected head. I played one group against the other, slipping in and throwing a punch then stepping out of range while pushing the others into the melee to take the blows blindly aimed at me. The smoke was agonizing and there were no rounds, no bells at three minute intervals to relieve our exhaustion. The room spun around me, a swirl of lights, smoke, sweating bodies surrounded by tense white faces. I bled from both nose and mouth, the blood spattering upon my chest.

The men kept yelling, "Slug him, black boy! Knock his guts out!" 24

"Uppercut him! Kill him! Kill that big boy!" 25

Taking a fake fall, I saw a boy going down heavily beside me as though 26
we were felled by a single blow, saw a sneaker-clad foot shoot into his groin as the two who had knocked him down stumbled upon him. I rolled out of range, feeling a twinge of nausea.

The harder we fought the more threatening the men became. And yet, 27
I had begun to worry about my speech again. How would it go? Would they recognize my ability? What would they give me?

I was fighting automatically when suddenly I noticed that one after 28
another of the boys was leaving the ring. I was surprised, filled with panic, as though I had been left alone with an unknown danger. Then I understood. The boys had arranged it among themselves. It was custom for the two men left in the ring to slug it out for the winner's prize. I discovered this too late. When the bell sounded two men in tuxedos leaped into the ring and removed the blindfold. I found myself facing Tatlock, the biggest of the gang. I felt sick at my stomach. Hardly had the bell stopped ringing in my ears than it clanged again and I saw him moving swiftly toward me. Thinking of nothing else to do I hit him smash on the nose. He kept coming, bringing the rank sharp violence of stale sweat. His face was a black blank of a face, only his eyes alive—with hate of me and aglow with a feverish terror from what had happened to us all. I became anxious. I wanted to deliver my speech and he came at me as though he meant to beat it out of me. I smashed him again and again, taking his blows as they came. Then on a sudden impulse I struck him lightly and as we clinched, I whispered, "Fake like I knocked you out, you can have the prize."

"I'll break your behind," he whispered hoarsely. 29

"For *them*?" 30

"For *me*, sonofabitch." 31

They were yelling for us to break it up and Tatlock spun me half around with a blow, and as a joggled camera sweeps in a reeling scene, I saw the howling red faces crouching tense beneath the cloud of blue-gray smoke. For a moment the world wavered, unraveled, flowed, then my head cleared and Tatlock bounced before me. The fluttering shadow before my eyes was his jabbing left hand. Then falling forward, my head against his damp shoulder, I whispered. 32

"I'll make it five dollars more." 33

"Go to hell!" 34

But his muscles relaxed a trifle beneath my pressure and I breathed, "Seven?" 35

"Give it to your ma," he said, ripping me beneath the heart. 36

And while I still held him I butted him and moved away. I felt myself bombarded with punches. I fought back with hopeless desperation. I wanted to deliver my speech more than anything else in the world, because I felt only these men could judge truly my ability, and now this stupid clown was ruining my chances. I began fighting carefully now, moving in to punch him and out again with my greater speed. A lucky blow to his chin and I had him going too—until I heard a loud voice yell, "I got my money on the big boy." 37

Hearing this, I almost dropped my guard. I was confused: Should I try to win against the voice out there? Would not this go against my speech, and was not this a moment for humility, for nonresistance? A blow to my head as I danced about sent my right eye popping like a jack-in-the-box and settled my dilemma. The room went red as I fell. It was a dream fall, my body languid and fastidious as to where to land, until the floor became impatient and smashed up to meet me. A moment later I came to. An hypnotic voice said FIVE emphatically. And I lay there, hazily watching a dark red spot of my own blood shaping itself into a butterfly, glistening and soaking into the soiled gray world of the canvas. 38

When the voice drawled TEN I was lifted up and dragged to a chair. I sat dazed. My eye pained and swelled with each throb of my pounding heart and I wondered if now I would be allowed to speak. I was wringing wet, my mouth still bleeding. We were grouped along the wall now. The other boys ignored me as they congratulated Tatlock and speculated as to how much they would be paid. One boy whimpered over his smashed hand. Looking up front, I saw attendants in white jackets rolling the portable ring away and placing a small square rug in the vacant space surrounded by chairs. Perhaps, I thought, I will stand on the rug to deliver my speech. 39

Then the M.C. called to us, "Come on up here boys and get your money." 40

We ran forward to where the men laughed and talked in their chairs, waiting. Everyone seemed friendly now. 41

"There it is on the rug," the man said. I saw the rug covered with coins of all dimensions and a few crumpled bills. But what excited me, scattered here and there, were the gold pieces. 42

"Boys, it's all yours," the man said. "You get all you grab." 43

"That's right, Sambo," a blond man said, winking at me confidentially. 44

I trembled with excitement, forgetting my pain. I would get the gold and 45
the bills, I thought. I would use both hands. I would throw my body against the boys nearest me to block them from the gold.

"Get down around the rug now," the man commanded, "and don't 46
anyone touch it until I give the signal."

"This ought to be good," I heard. 47

As told, we got around the square rug on our knees. Slowly the man 48
raised his freckled hand as we followed it upward with our eyes.

I heard, "These niggers look like they're about to pray!" 49

Then, "Ready," the man said. "Go!" 50

I lunged for a yellow coin lying on the blue design on the carpet, 51
touching it and sending a surprised shriek to join those rising around me. I tried frantically to remove my hand but could not let go. A hot, violent force tore through my body, shaking me like a wet rat. The rug was electrified. The hair bristled up on my head as I shook myself free. My muscles jumped, my nerves jangled, writhed. But I saw that this was not stopping the other boys. Laughing in fear and embarrassment, some were holding back and scooping up the coins knocked off by the painful contortions of the others. The men roared above us as we struggled.

"Pick it up, goddamnit, pick it up!" someone called like a bass-voiced 52
parrot. "Go on, get it!"

I crawled rapidly around the floor, picking up the coins, trying to avoid 53
the coppers and to get greenbacks and the gold. Ignoring the shock by laughing, as I brushed the coins off quickly, I discovered that I could contain the electricity—a contradiction, but it works. Then the men began to push us onto the rug. Laughing embarrassedly, we struggled out of their hands and kept after the coins. We were all wet and slippery and hard to hold. Suddenly I saw a boy lifted into the air, glistening with sweat like a circus seal, and dropped, his wet back landing flush upon the charged rug, heard him yell and saw him literally dance upon his back, his elbows beating a frenzied tattoo upon the floor, his muscles twitching like the flesh of a horse stung by many flies. When he finally rolled off, his face was gray and no one stopped him when he ran from the floor amid booming laughter.

"Get the money," the M.C. called. "That's good hard American cash!" 54

And we snatched and grabbed, snatched and grabbed. I was careful not 55
to come too close to the rug now, and when I felt the hot whiskey breath descend upon me like a cloud of foul air I reached out and grabbed the leg of a chair. It was occupied and I held on desperately.

"Leggo nigger! Leggo!" 56

The huge face wavered down to mine as he tried to push me free. But 57
my body was slippery and he was too drunk. It was Mr. Colcord, who owned a chain of movie houses and "entertainment palaces." Each time he grabbed me I slipped out of his hands. It became a real struggle. I feared the rug more than I did the drunk, so I held on, surprising myself for a moment by trying to topple *him* upon the rug. It was such an enormous idea that I found myself

actually carrying it out. I tried not to be obvious, yet when I grabbed his leg, trying to tumble him out of the chair, he raised up roaring with laughter, and, looking at me with soberness dead in the eye, kicked me viciously in the chest. The chair leg flew out of my hand and I felt myself going and rolled. It was as though I had rolled through a bed of hot coals. It seemed a whole century would pass before I would roll free, a century in which I was seared through the deepest levels of my body to the fearful breath within me and the breath seared and heated to the point of explosion. It'll all be over in a flash, I thought as I rolled clear. It'll all be over in a flash.

But not yet, the men on the other side were waiting, red faces swollen 58
as though from apoplexy as they bent forward in their chairs. Seeing their fingers coming toward me I rolled away as a fumbled football rolls off the receiver's fingertips, back into the coals. That time I luckily sent the rug sliding out of place and heard the coins ringing against the floor and the boys scuffling to pick them up and the M.C. calling, "All right, boys, that's all. Go get dressed and get your money."

I was limp as a dish rag. My back felt as though it had been beaten with 59
wires.

When we had dressed the M.C. came in and gave us each five dollars, 60
except Tatlock, who got ten for being last in the ring. Then he told us to leave. I was not to get a chance to deliver my speech, I thought. I was going out into the dim alley in despair when I was stopped and told to go back. I returned to the ballroom, where the men were pushing back their chairs and gathering in groups to talk.

The M.C. knocked on a table for quiet. "Gentlemen," he said, "we 61
almost forgot an important part of the program. A most serious part, gentlemen. This boy was brought here to deliver a speech which he made at his graduation yesterday . . ."

"Bravo!" 62

"I'm told that he is the smartest boy we've got out there in Greenwood. 63
I'm told that he knows more big words than a pocket-sized dictionary."

Much applause and laughter. 64

"So now, gentlemen, I want you to give him your attention." 65

There was still laughter as I faced them, my mouth dry, my eye throb- 66
bing. I began slowly, but evidently my throat was tense, because they began shouting, "Louder! Louder!"

"We of the younger generation extol the wisdom of that great leader 67
and educator," I shouted, "who first spoke these flaming words of wisdom. 'A ship lost at sea for many days suddenly sighted a friendly vessel. From the mast of the unfortunate vessel was seen a signal: "Water, water; we die of thirst!" The answer from the friendly vessel came back: "Cast down your bucket where you are." The captain of the distressed vessel, at last heeding the injunction, cast down his bucket, and it came up full of fresh sparkling water from the mouth of the Amazon River.' And like him I say, and in his words, 'To those of my race who depend upon bettering their condition in a foreign land, or who underestimate the importance of cultivating friendly

relations with the Southern white man, who is his next-door neighbor, I would say: "Cast down your bucket where you are"—cast it down in making friends in every manly way of the people of all races by whom we are surrounded. . . .' "

I spoke automatically and with such fervor that I did not realize that the 68
men were still talking and laughing until my dry mouth, filling up with blood from the cut, almost strangled me. I coughed, wanting to stop and go to one of the tall brass, sand-filled spittoons to relieve myself, but a few of the men, especially the superintendent, were listening and I was afraid. So I gulped it down, blood, saliva, and all, and continued. (What powers of endurance I had during those days! What enthusiasm! What a belief in the rightness of things!) I spoke even louder in spite of the pain. But still they talked and still they laughed, as though deaf with cotton in dirty ears. So I spoke with greater emotional emphasis. I closed my ears and swallowed blood until I was nauseated. The speech seemed a hundred times as long as before, but I could not leave out a single word. All had to be said, each memorized nuance considered, rendered. Nor was that all. Whenever I uttered a word of three or more syllables a group of voices would yell for me to repeat it. I used the phrase "social responsibility" and they yelled:

"What's that word you say, boy?" 69

"Social responsibility," I said. 70

"What?" 71

"Social . . ." 72

"Louder." 73

". . . responsibility." 74

"More!" 75

"Respon—" 76

"Repeat!" 77

"—sibility." 78

The room filled with the uproar of laughter until, no doubt, distracted 79
by having to gulp down my blood, I made a mistake and yelled a phrase I had often seen denounced with newspaper editorials, heard debated in private.

"Social . . ." 80

"What?" they yelled. 81

". . . equality—" 82

The laughter hung smokelike in the sudden stillness. I opened my eyes, 83
puzzled. Sounds of displeasure filled the room. The M.C. rushed forward. They shouted hostile phrases at me. But I did not understand.

A small dry mustached man in the front row blared out, "Say that 84
slowly, son!"

"What sir?" 85

"Social responsibility, sir," I said. 86

"You weren't being smart, were you, boy?" he said, not unkindly. 87

"No, sir!" 88

"You sure that about 'equality' was a mistake?" 89

"Oh, yes, sir," I said. "I was swallowing blood." 90

"Well, you had better speak more slowly so we can understand. We mean to do right by you, but you've got to know your place at all times. All right, now, go on with your speech." 91

I was afraid. I wanted to leave but I wanted also to speak and I was afraid they'd snatch me down. 92

"Thank you, sir," I said, beginning where I had left off, and having them ignore me as before. 93

Yet when I finished there was a thunderous applause. I was surprised to see the superintendent come forth with a package wrapped in white tissue paper, and, gesturing for quiet, address the men. 94

"Gentlemen, you see that I did not overpraise this boy. He makes a good speech and some day he'll lead his people in the proper paths. And I don't have to tell you that that is important in these days and times. This is a good, smart boy, and so to encourage him in the right direction, in the name of the Board of Education I wish to present him a prize in the form of this . . ." 95

He paused, removing the tissue paper and revealing a gleaming calfskin brief case. 96

". . . in the form of this first-class article from Shad Whitmore's shop." 97

"Boy," he said, addressing me, "take this prize and keep it well. Consider it a badge of office. Prize it. Keep developing as you are and some day it will be filled with important papers that will help shape the destiny of your people." 98

I was so moved that I could hardly express my thanks. A rope of bloody saliva forming a shape like an undiscovered continent drooled upon the leather and I wiped it quickly away. I felt an importance that I had never dreamed. 99

"Open it and see what's inside," I was told. 100

My fingers a-tremble, I complied, smelling the fresh leather and finding an official-looking document inside. It was a scholarship to the state college for Negroes. My eyes filled with tears and I ran awkwardly off the floor. 101

I was so overjoyed; I did not even mind when I discovered that the gold pieces I had scrambled for were brass pocket tokens advertising a certain make of automobile. 102

When I reached home everyone was excited. Next day the neighbors came to congratulate me. I even felt safe from grandfather, whose deathbed curse usually spoiled my triumphs. I stood beneath his photograph with my brief case in hand and smiled triumphantly into his stolid black peasant's face. It was a face that fascinated me. The eyes seemed to follow everywhere I went. 103

That night I dreamed I was at a circus with him and that he refused to laugh at the clowns no matter what they did. Then later he told me to open my brief case and read what was inside and I did, finding an official envelope stamped with the state seal; and inside the envelope I found another and another, endlessly, and I thought I would fall of weariness. "Them's years," 104 he said. "Now open that one." And I did and in it I found an engraved document containing a short message in letters of gold. "Read it," my grandfather said. "Out loud."

"To Whom It May Concern," I intoned. "Keep This Nigger-Boy Running." 105

I awoke with the old man's laughter ringing in my ears. 106

(It was a dream I was to remember and dream again for many years after. 107
But at that time I had no insight into its meaning. First I had to attend college.)

Questions for Discussion

1. What is your own interpretation of the grandfather's message in paragraph 2? What does he mean when he says "our life is a war and I have been a traitor all my born days"?
2. What is meant (in the young man's dream) by the official document inscribed, "To Whom It May Concern, Keep This Nigger-Boy Running" (¶105)? What is the significance of this document's being contained in "an official envelope stamped with the state seal"? How does "running" tie in with the young man's willingness to fight and his gratitude over the scholarship to college?
3. Why is it significant that the smoker is attended by "the most important men of the town . . . bankers, lawyers, judges, doctors, fire chiefs, teachers, merchants. Even one of the more fashionable pastors" (¶6)? What do these men represent in the story?
4. In what sense might it be true to say that the young man, who thinks he sees how the game of progress and social advancement must be played, begins to see more clearly the *real* truth of his situation when he is placed in the blindfold (¶11)?
5. Why is it ironic that the young man "attempts to squeeze some security" out of the school superintendent's voice as the fight begins (¶14)? What does this say about his naïveté?
6. A corrupt system corrupts not just the victimizers but the victims as well. How is the truth of this statement corroborated by the young man's question, "What would they give me?" in paragraph 27?
7. What does the young man mean when he says that before he could discover "that I am nobody but myself . . . I had to [experience] much painful boomeranging of my expectations" (¶1)?

Suggested Essay Topics

1. Have you ever felt invisible in Ellison's narrator's sense of the term—felt that some persons, no matter what you do or say to them, will always fail to see you for what you are, will always insist on seeing instead some

image of you or of "your kind" that they have already formed in their own heads? If you have ever experienced this feeling, give an account of it in an essay directed to your fellow students. Use Ellison's analysis to help you explain what it feels like to be treated this way and how you dealt (or are dealing) with it. Your purpose is to try to define the condition of invisibility as *you* have experienced it (with appropriate examples) so that your readers will know not only what the condition has been like but what it has meant (or means) in your life.

2. After thinking about topic 1, write an editorial or a letter to the editor of your campus newspaper, arguing that everyone should wake up and *look* at the *individuals* on campus, instead of making them invisible by lumping them into groups and types. Identify the group stereotypes that make individuals invisible (dumb jocks, dizzy blonds, stupid administrators, and so on), and make your editorial or letter a ringing assertion of these people's right to be viewed and judged as individuals, not as predictable representatives of groups.

Lillian Smith

Lillian Smith (1897–1966) was one of the most influential champions of racial justice of her time. From the moment her novel Strange Fruit *became a best-seller in 1944 to the end of her life, she fought steadily against the racist code that had dominated her childhood. For many readers she long represented what human intelligence, courage, and conscience can do to overcome inherited evil.*

"When I Was a Child" tells of how she discovered that "something was wrong" with her world. As you read, try to imagine not just the pre–World War I South in which she lived but the post–World War II America, North and South, in which her readers lived. What does Smith expect those readers to believe? Is she addressing people who would themselves never practice racial segregation because they were "brought up right"? Or does she address most directly those who still fail to practice what they preach and who might be awakened to internal conflict, as she was, by living with her through a shattering childhood experience?

WHEN I WAS A CHILD

Chapter 1 of *Killers of the Dream* (1949).

Even its children knew that the South was in trouble. No one had to tell them; 1
no words said aloud. To them, it was a vague thing weaving in and out of their play, like a ghost haunting an old graveyard or whispers after the

household sleeps—fleeting mystery, vague menace to which each responded in his own way. Some learned to screen out all except the soft and the soothing; others denied even as they saw plainly, and heard. But all knew that under quiet words and warmth and laughter, under the slow ease and tender concern about small matters, there was a heavy burden on all of us and as heavy a refusal to confess it. The children knew this "trouble" was bigger than they, bigger than their family, bigger than their church, so big that people turned away from its size. They had seen it flash out and shatter a town's peace, had felt it tear up all they believed in. They had measured its giant strength and felt weak when they remembered.

This haunted childhood belongs to every southerner of my age. We ran 2
away from it but we came back like a hurt animal to its wound, or a murderer to the scene of his sin. The human heart dares not stay away too long from that which hurt it most. There is a return journey to anguish that few of us are released from making.

We who were born in the South called this mesh of feeling and memory 3
"loyalty." We thought of it sometimes as "love." We identified with the South's trouble as if we, individually, were responsible for all of it. We defended the sins and the sorrows of three hundred years as if each sin had been committed by us alone and each sorrow had cut across our heart. We were as hurt at criticism of our region as if our own name had been called aloud by the critic. We knew guilt without understanding it, and there is no tie that binds men closer to the past and each other than that.

It is a strange thing, this umbilical cord uncut. In times of ease, we do 4
not feel its pull, but when we are threatened with change, suddenly it draws the whole white South together in a collective fear and fury that wipe our minds clear of reason and we are blocked from sensible contact with the world we live in.

To keep this resistance strong, wall after wall was thrown up in the 5
southern mind against criticism from without and within. Imaginations closed tight against the hurt of others; a regional armoring took place to ward off the "enemies" who would make our trouble different—or maybe rid us of it completely. For it was a trouble that we did not want to give up. We were as involved with it as a child who cannot be happy at home and cannot bear to tear himself away, or as a grownup who has fallen in love with his own disease. We southerners had identified with the long sorrowful past on such deep levels of love and hate and guilt that we did not know how to break old bonds without pulling our lives down. *Change* was the evil word, a shrill clanking that made us know too well our servitude. *Change* meant leaving one's memories, one's sins, one's ambivalent pleasures, the room where one was born.

In this South I lived as a child and now live. And it is of it that my story 6
is made. I shall not tell, here, of experiences that were different and special and belonged only to me, but those most white southerners born at the turn of the century share with each other. Out of the intricate weaving of unnumbered threads, I shall pick out a few strands, a few designs that have to do

with what we call color and race . . .* and politics . . . and money and how it is made . . . and religion . . . and sex and the body image . . . and love . . . and dreams of the Good and the killers of dreams.

A southern child's basic lessons were woven of such dissonant strands 7
as these; sometimes the threads tangled into a terrifying mess; sometimes archaic, startling designs would appear in the weaving; sometimes, a design was left broken while another was completed with minute care. Bewildered teachers, bewildered pupils in home and on the street, driven by an invisible Authority, learned their lessons:

The mother who taught me what I know of tenderness and love and 8
compassion taught me also the bleak rituals of keeping Negroes in their "place." The father who rebuked me for an air of superiority toward schoolmates from the mill and rounded out his rebuke by gravely reminding me that "all men are brothers," trained me in the steel-rigid decorums I must demand of every colored male. They who so gravely taught me to split my body from my mind and both from my "soul," taught me also to split my conscience from my acts and Christianity from southern tradition.

Neither the Negro nor sex was often discussed at length in our home. 9
We were given no formal instruction in these difficult matters but we learned our lessons well. We learned the intricate system of taboos, of renunciations and compensations, of manners, voice modulations, words, feelings, along with our prayers, our toilet habits, and our games. I do not remember how or when, but by the time I had learned that God is love, that Jesus is His Son and came to give us more abundant life, that all men are brothers with a common Father, I also knew that I was better than a Negro, that all black folks have their place and must be kept in it, that sex has its place and must be kept in it, that a terrifying disaster would befall the South if ever I treated a Negro as my social equal and as terrifying a disaster would befall my family if ever I were to have a baby outside of marriage. I had learned that God so loved the world that He gave His only begotten Son so that we might have segregated churches in which it was my duty to worship each Sunday and on Wednesday at evening prayers. I had learned that white southerners are a hospitable, courteous, tactful people who treat those of their own group with consideration and who as carefully segregate from all the richness of life "for their own good and welfare" thirteen million people whose skin is colored a little differently from my own.

I knew by the time I was twelve that a member of my family would 10
always shake hands with old Negro friends, would speak graciously to members of the Negro race unless they forgot their place, in which event icy peremptory tones would draw lines beyond which only the desperate would dare take one step. I knew that to use the word "nigger" was unpardonable and no well-bred southerner was quite so crude as to do so; nor would a well-bred southerner call a Negro "mister" or invite him into the living room or eat with him or sit by him in public places.

*All ellipses are Smith's.

I knew that my old nurse who had cared for me through long months of illness, who had given me refuge when a little sister took my place as the baby of the family, who soothed, fed me, delighted me with her stories and games, let me fall asleep on her deep warm breast, was not worthy of the passionate love I felt for her but must be given instead a half-smiled-at affection similar to that which one feels for one's dog. I knew but I never believed it, that the deep respect I felt for her, the tenderness, the love, was a childish thing which every normal child outgrows, that such love begins with one's toys and is discarded with them, and that somehow—though it seemed impossible to my agonized heart—I too, must outgrow these feelings. I learned to use a soft voice to oil my words of superiority. I learned to cheapen with tears and sentimental talk of "my old mammy" one of the profound relationships of my life. I learned the bitterest thing a child can learn: that the human relations I valued most were held cheap by the world I lived in. 11

From the day I was born, I began to learn my lessons. I was put in a rigid frame too intricate, too twisting to describe here so briefly, but I learned to conform to its slide-rule measurements. I learned it is possible to be a Christian and a white southerner simultaneously; to be a gentlewoman and an arrogant callous creature in the same moment; to pray at night and ride a Jim Crow car* the next morning and to feel comfortable in doing both. I learned to believe in freedom, to glow when the word *democracy* was used, and to practice slavery from morning to night. I learned it the way all of my southern people learn it: by closing door after door until one's mind and heart and conscience are blocked off from each other and from reality. 12

I closed the doors. Or perhaps they were closed for me. One day they began to open again. Why I had the desire or the strength to open them, or what strange accident or circumstance opened them for me would require in the answering an account too long, too particular, too stark to make here. And perhaps I should not have the wisdom that such an analysis would demand of me, nor the will to make it. I know only that the doors opened, a little; that somewhere along that iron corridor we travel from babyhood to maturity, doors swinging inward began to swing outward, showing glimpses of the world beyond, of that bright thing we call "reality." 13

I believe there is one experience which pushed these doors open, a little. And I am going to tell it here, although I know well that to excerpt from a life and family background one incident and name it as a "cause" of a change in one's life direction is a distortion and often an irrelevance. The hungers of a child and how they are filled have too much to do with the way in which experiences are assimilated to tear an incident out of life and look at it in isolation. Yet, with these reservations, I shall tell it, not because it was in itself a severe trauma, but because it became a symbol of buried experiences that I did not have access to. It is an incident that has rarely happened to other 14

*A racially segregated railroad car.

southern children. In a sense, unique. But it was an acting-out, a private production of a little script that is written on the lives of most southern children before they know words. Though they may not have seen it staged this way, each southerner has had his own private showing.

I should like to preface the account by giving a brief glimpse of my 15
family, hoping the reader, entering my home with me, will be able to blend the edges of this isolated experience into a more full life picture and in doing so will see that it is, in a sense, everybody's story.

I was born and reared in a small Deep South town whose population 16
was about equally Negro and white. There were nine of us who grew up freely in a rambling house of many rooms, surrounded by big lawn, back yard, gardens, fields, and barn. It was the kind of home that gathers memories like dust, a place filled with laughter and play and pain and hurt and ghosts and games. We were given such advantages of schooling, music, and art as were available in the South, and our world was not limited to the South, for travel to far places seemed a natural thing to us, and usually one of the family was in a remote part of the earth.

We knew we were a respected and important family of this small town 17
but beyond this we gave little thought to status. Our father made money in lumber and naval stores for the excitement of making and losing it—not for what money can buy nor the security which it sometimes gives. I do not remember at any time wanting "to be rich" nor do I remember that thrift and saving were ideals which our parents considered important enough to urge upon us. In the family there was acceptance of risk, a mild delight in burning bridges, an expectant "what next?" We were not irresponsible; living according to the pleasure principle was by no means our way of life. On the contrary we were trained to think that each of us should do something of genuine usefulness, and the family thought it right to make sacrifices if necessary, to give each child preparation for such work. We were also trained to think learning important, and books; but "bad" books our mother burned. We valued music and art and craftsmanship but it was people and their welfare and religion that were the foci around which our lives seemed naturally to move. Above all else, the important thing was what we "planned to do." That each of us must do something was as inevitable as breathing for we owed a "debt to society which must be paid." This was a family commandment.

While many neighbors spent their energies in counting limbs on the 18
family tree and grafting some on now and then to give symmetry to it, or in licking scars to cure their vague malaise, or in fighting each battle and turn of battle of that Civil War which has haunted the southern conscience so long, my father was pushing his nine children straight into the future. "You have your heritage," he used to say, "some of it good, some not so good; and as far as I know you had the usual number of grandmothers and grandfathers. Yes, there were slaves, too many of them in the family, but that was your grandfather's mistake, not yours. The past has been lived. It is gone. The future is yours. What are you going to do with it?" He asked this question often and sometimes one knew it was but an echo of a question he had spent

his life trying to answer for himself. For the future held my father's dreams; always there, not in the past, did he expect to find what he had spent his life searching for.

19 We lived the same segregated life as did other southerners but our parents talked in excessively Christian and democratic terms. We were told ten thousand times that status and money are unimportant (though we were well supplied with both); we were told that "all men are brothers," that we are a part of a democracy and must act like democrats. We were told that the teachings of Jesus are important and could be practiced if we tried. We were told that to be "radical" is bad, silly too; and that one must always conform to the "best behavior" of one's community and make it better if one can. We were taught that we were superior to hate and resentment, and that no member of the Smith family could stoop so low as to have an enemy. No matter what injury was done us, we must not injure ourselves further by retaliating. That was a family commandment.

20 We had family prayers once each day. All of us as children read the Bible in its entirety each year. We memorized hundreds of Bible verses and repeated them at breakfast, and said "sentence prayers" around the family table. God was not someone we met on Sunday but a permanent member of our household. It never occurred to me until I was fourteen or fifteen years old that He did not chalk up the daily score on eternity's tablets.

21 Despite the strain of living so intimately with God, the nine of us were strong, healthy, energetic youngsters who filled days with play and sports and music and books and managed to live most of the time on the careless level at which young lives should be lived. We had our times of anxiety of course, for there were hard lessons to be learned about the soul and "bad things" to be learned about sex. Sometimes I have wondered how we learned them with a mother so shy with words.

22 She was a wistful creature who loved beautiful things like lace and sunsets and flowers in a vague inarticulate way, and took good care of her children. We always knew this was not her world but one she accepted under duress. Her private world we rarely entered, though the shadow of it lay heavily on our hearts.

23 Our father owned large business interests, employed hundreds of colored and white laborers, paid them the prevailing low wages, worked them the prevailing long hours, built for them mill towns (Negro and white), built for each group a church, saw to it that religion was supplied free, saw to it that a commissary supplied commodities at a high price, and in general managed his affairs much as ten thousand other southern businessmen managed theirs.

24 Even now, I can hear him chuckling as he told my mother how he won his fight for Prohibition. The high point of the campaign was election afternoon, when he lined up the mill force of several hundred (white and black), passed out a shining silver dollar to each one, marched them in and voted liquor out of our county. It was a great day. He had won the Big Game, a game he was always playing against all kinds of evil. It did not occur to him to

scrutinize the methods he used. Evil was a word written in capitals; the devil was smart; if you wanted to win you outsmarted him. It was as simple as that.

He was a hardheaded, warmhearted, high-spirited man born during the 25
Civil War, earning his living at twelve, struggling through decades of Reconstruction and post-Reconstruction, through populist movement, through the panic of 1893, the panic of 1907, on into the twentieth century accepting his region as he found it, accepting its morals and its mores as he accepted its climate, with only scorn for those who held grudges against the North or pitied themselves or the South; scheming, dreaming, expanding his business, making and losing money, making friends whom he did not lose, with never a doubt that God was by his side whispering hunches as to how to pull off successful deals. When he lost, it was his own fault. When he won, God had helped him.

Once while we were kneeling at family prayers the fire siren at the mill 26
sounded the alarm that the mill was on fire. My father did not falter. The alarm sounded again and again—which signified the fire was big. With dignity he continued his talk with God while his children sweated and wriggled and hearts beat out of their chests in excitement. He was talking to God—how could he hurry out to save his mills! When he finished his prayer, he quietly stood up, laid the Bible carefully on the table. Then, and only then, did he show an interest in what was happening in Mill Town. . . . When the telegram was placed in his hands telling of the death of his beloved favorite son, he gathered his children together, knelt down, and in a steady voice which contained no hint of his shattered heart, loyally repeated, "God is our refuge and strength, a very present help in trouble. Therefore will we not fear, though the earth be removed, and though the mountains be carried into the midst of the sea." On his deathbed, he whispered to his old Business Partner in Heaven: "I have fought a good fight . . . I have kept the faith."

Against this backdrop the drama of the South was played out one day 27
in my life:

A little white girl was found in the colored section of our town, living 28
with a Negro family in a broken-down shack. This family had moved in a few weeks before and little was known of them. One of the ladies in my mother's club, while driving over to her washerwoman's, saw the child swinging on a gate. The shack, as she said, was hardly more than a pigsty and this white child was living with dirty and sick-looking colored folks. "They must have kidnapped her," she told her friends. Genuinely shocked, the clubwomen busied themselves in an attempt to do something, for the child was very white indeed. The strange Negroes were subjected to a grueling questioning and finally grew evasive and refused to talk at all. This only increased the suspicion of the white group. The next day the clubwomen, escorted by the town marshal, took the child from her adopted family despite their tears.

She was brought to our home. I do not know why my mother consented 29
to this plan. Perhaps because she loved children and always showed concern

for them. It was easy for one more to fit into our ample household and Janie was soon at home there. She roomed with me, sat next to me at the table; I found Bible verses for her to say at breakfast; she wore my clothes, played with my dolls and followed me around from morning to night. She was dazed by her new comforts and by the interesting activities of this big lively family; and I was as happily dazed, for her adoration was a new thing to me; and as time passed a quick, childish, and deeply felt bond grew up between us.

But a day came when a telephone message was received from a colored 30
orphanage. There was a meeting at our home. Many whispers. All afternoon the ladies went in and out of our house talking to Mother in tones too low for children to hear. As they passed us at play, they looked at Janie and quickly looked away again, though a few stopped and stared at her as if they could not tear their eyes from her face. When my father came home Mother closed her door against our young ears and talked a long time with him. I heard him laugh, heard Mother say, "But Papa, this is no laughing matter!" And then they were back in the living room with us and my mother was pale and my father was saying, "Well, work it out, Mame, as best you can. After all, now that you know, it is pretty simple."

In a little while my mother called my sister and me into her bedroom 31
and told us that in the morning Janie would return to Colored Town. She said Janie was to have the dresses the ladies had given her and a few of my own, and the toys we had shared with her. She asked me if I would like to give Janie one of my dolls. She seemed hurried, though Janie was not to leave until next day. She said, "Why not select it now?" And in dreamlike stiffness I brought in my dolls and chose one for Janie. And then I found it possible to say, "Why is she leaving? She likes us, she hardly knows them. She told me she had been with them only a month."

"Because," Mother said gently, "Janie is a little colored girl." 32

"But she's white!" 33

"We were mistaken. She is colored." 34

"But she looks—" 35

"She is colored. Please don't argue!" 36

"What does it mean?" I whispered. 37

"It means," Mother said slowly, "that she has to live in Colored Town 38
with colored people."

"But why? She lived here three weeks and she doesn't belong to them, 39
she told me so."

"She is a little colored girl." 40

"But you said yourself she has nice manners. You said that," I persisted. 41

"Yes, she is a nice child. But a colored child cannot live in our home." 42

"Why?" 43

"You know, dear! You have always known that white and colored 44
people do not live together."

"Can she come to play?" 45

"No." 46

"I don't understand." 47

"I don't either," my young sister quavered. 48

"You're too young to understand. And don't ask me again, ever again, 49 about this!" Mother's voice was sharp but her face was sad and there was no certainty left there. She hurried out and busied herself in the kitchen and I wandered through that room where I had been born, touching the old familiar things in it, looking at them, trying to find the answer to a question that moaned like a hurt thing. . . .

And then I went out to Janie, who was waiting, knowing things were 50 happening that concerned her but waiting until they were spoken aloud.

I do not know quite how the words were said but I told her she was to 51 return in the morning to the little place where she had lived because she was colored and colored children could not live with white children.

"Are you white?" she said. 52

"I'm white," I replied, "and my sister is white. And you're colored. And 53 white and colored can't live together because my mother says so."

"Why?" Janie whispered. 54

"Because they can't," I said. But I knew, though I said it firmly, that 55 something was wrong. I knew my father and mother whom I passionately admired had betrayed something which they held dear. And they could not help doing it. And I was shamed by their failure and frightened, for I felt they were no longer as powerful as I had thought. There was something Out There that was stronger than they and I could not bear to believe it. I could not confess that my father, who always solved the family dilemmas easily and with laughter, could not solve this. I knew that my mother who was so good to children did not believe in her heart that she was being good to this child. There was not a word in my mind that said it but my body knew and my glands, and I was filled with anxiety.

But I felt compelled to believe they were right. It was the only way my 56 world could be held together. And, slowly, it began to seep through me: *I was white. She was colored. We must not be together. It was bad to be together. Though you ate with your nurse when you were little, it was bad to eat with any colored person after that. It was bad just as other things were bad that your mother had told you. It was bad that she was to sleep in the room with me that night. It was bad. . . .*

I was overcome with guilt. For three weeks I had done things that white 57 children were not supposed to do. And now I knew these things had been wrong.

I went to the piano and began to play, as I had always done when I was 58 in trouble. I tried to play my next lesson and as I stumbled through it, the little girl came over and sat on the bench with me. Feeling lost in the deep currents sweeping through our house that night, she crept closer and put her arms around me and I shrank away as if my body had been uncovered. I had not said a word, I did not say one, but she knew, and tears slowly rolled down her little white face. . . .

And then I forgot it. For more than thirty years the experience was 59 wiped out of my memory. But that night, and the weeks it was tied to, worked its way like a splinter, bit by bit, down to the hurt places in my memory and festered there. And as I grew older, as more experiences collected around that faithless time, as memories of earlier, more profound hurts crept closer, drawn to that night as if to a magnet, I began to know that people who talked of love and children did not mean it. That is a hard thing for a child to learn. I still admired my parents, there was so much that was strong and vital and sane and good about them and I never forgot this; I stubbornly believed in their sincerity, as I do to this day, and I loved them. Yet in my heart they were under suspicion. Something was wrong.

Something was wrong with a world that tells you that love is good and 60
people are important and then forces you to deny love and to humiliate people. I knew, though I would not for years confess it aloud, that in trying to shut the Negro race away from us, we have shut ourselves away from so many good, creative, honest, deeply human things in life. I began to understand slowly at first but more clearly as the years passed, that the warped, distorted frame we have put around every Negro child from birth is around every white child also. Each is on a different side of the frame but each is pinioned there. And I knew that what cruelly shapes and cripples the personality of one is as cruelly shaping and crippling the personality of the other. I began to see that though we may, as we acquire new knowledge, live through new experiences, examine old memories, gain the strength to tear the frame from us, yet we are stunted and warped and in our lifetime cannot grow straight again any more than can a tree, put in a steel-like twisting frame when young, grow tall and straight when the frame is torn away at maturity.

As I sit here writing, I can almost touch that little town, so close is the 61
memory of it. There it lies, its main street lined with great oaks, heavy with matted moss that swings softly even now as I remember. A little white town rimmed with Negroes, making a deep shadow on the whiteness. There it lies, broken in two by one strange idea. Minds broken. Hearts broken. Conscience torn from acts. A culture split in a thousand pieces. That is segregation. I am remembering: a woman in a mental hospital walking four steps out, four steps in, unable to go further because she has drawn an invisible line around her small world and is terrified to take one step beyond it. . . . A man in a Disturbed Ward assigning "places" to the other patients and violently insisting that each stay in his place. . . . A Negro woman saying to me so quietly, "We cannot ride together on the bus, you know. It is not legal to be human down here."

Memory, walking the streets of one's childhood . . . of the town where 62
one was born.

Questions for Discussion

1. How has Smith organized her account? Are the main divisions clearly marked? Note that in the first two sections she covers several decades, in the third section she provides a blowup of only a few moments out of a three-week period, and in the fourth section she quickly covers "more than thirty years." Obviously she could have shortened the third section greatly by summarizing rather than giving a detailed account with extended dialogue. For example, she might have written more briefly, "So I went to Janie and explained that because she was colored we couldn't play together any more, since white people and colored people can't live together. I felt that I had been wrong to be friendly with her, and I did everything I could to wipe our friendship out of my memory." What would be lost (or gained) by such a method?
2. What does Smith mean by saying that her neighbors spent energy grafting some limbs on the family tree, to "give symmetry to it" (¶18)?
3. Since Smith seems careful in her choice of words, it is worthwhile to note any choices that at first glance seem unnecessary or redundant. For example, in the middle of paragraph 28, she says that the southern ladies were "genuinely shocked." One might say that to be "shocked" is necessarily to be *genuinely* shocked. Why do you think she chooses to add the adjective?
4. One important fact you can infer about Lillian Smith and her readers in the 1940s: Her account makes clear that no "polite" person at that time referred to "blacks"; the only terms Smith uses are *Negroes* and *colored people.* Did you notice that Smith does not use *colored people* when speaking in her own adult voice but only when reporting the language of her childhood? Her adult terms are *Negroes* and *the Negro race.* How do you account for that? She could not have known that within a few years the word *Negro* would also come to seem insulting. Would you expect that *blacks* and *black people,* which are standard terms in the 1980s, might also become unacceptable in the future? Can you think of other terms that were acceptable in referring to groups at one time but were later rejected? Or vice versa? In recent years some black authors and comedians have referred openly to "niggers" (Dick Gregory even called his autobiography *Nigger*). Have they taken the negative weight off the word so that it might be used acceptably even by white people to refer to American blacks?
5. Each of us belongs, sometimes without knowing it, to some group or class that behind our backs is referred to disparagingly by a term no one uses publicly—except when delivering an insult. Make a list, with the help of your classmates, of all the bigoted terms you can think of. Why do you think people spend so much energy inventing insults? Do you think that Smith's desire to build a world free of prejudice can ever be realized?
6. Have you ever been driven to a traumatic rejection of beliefs or commitments that your parents or other guides taught you early in your life? What do you think are the usual causes of such personal "revolutions"?

Do they happen only when we confront inconsistencies and hypocrisies like those that Smith tells about?

Suggested Essay Topics

1. If you have ever managed to discard a prejudice against a group (or gained a prejudice that your parents and neighbors did not implant), write an account of the change, trying to make it as vivid as the material allows. If there were dramatic moments of change, like Smith's, heighten them with dramatic devices such as dialogue; if you experienced a gradual change, explore "quieter" devices. You might address your account to people whose beliefs you have rejected, trying to change their minds.
2. Write a letter (or a draft of a speech) addressed to some person or group you know to be strongly prejudiced against a group that you belong to (such as cheerleaders, musicians, athletes, ethnic or racial minorities, scholars), trying to persuade them that they are wrong to judge individuals according to group stereotypes. One possible strategy for writing such a paper might be to admit that although your readers are generally right to mistrust the average person in your group, there are many exceptions, including yourself. Do you think that would be a good strategy for your case? What does it imply about *your* prejudices? Can you think of an approach that would be more effective? More fair?

Jonathan Swift

Jonathan Swift (1667–1745) was born and educated in Dublin, Ireland, was ordained as an Anglican priest, and from 1713 on held the post of dean of St. Patrick's in Dublin. He wrote on church doctrine, social matters, and politics (especially on the relations between Ireland and England). The latter two topics gave him great scope for his immense gifts as a satirist. He wielded his pen like a scalpel and dissected the objects of his ridicule with deadly accuracy, energy, and finesse. What sets Swift above many other brilliant satirists is the scope and depth of his moral vision. He does not just satirize absurdities like comedians on late-night television, jabbing the needle quickly and then running to the next topic. His ridicule goes far beyond merely accurate observation and enters the realm of informed vision. He shows us not simply that human stupidity, greed, or self-deception exists but also how things might be better. It is important to remember that Swift is a satirist, not a cynic: While he thinks many people bad, he does not think all people hopeless. Even as he flays his targets, hanging up the pelts of their hypocrisies and absurdities to swing in the wind of public scrutiny, he points out possible remedies for the evils he attacks.

The main satiric device in "A Modest Proposal" is irony: *saying one thing and meaning the opposite. (Irony is a much more sophisticated device than this rough definition implies, but we have insufficient space here for a thorough discussion.) Even this simple definition, however, makes one thing clear: The reader somehow has to* know *that a meaning beyond the surface meaning must be decoded. Any reader who does not recognize a piece as satire will simply take the surface meaning at face value—and, in the case of "A Modest Proposal," will make a horrible mistake.*

As you read, try to spot places where Swift lets you know that a deep decoding is necessary. What are the clues? He cannot use any of the visual or auditory signals that satirists often rely on, such as inflection, body language, gesture, or facial expression. Yet by the third sentence of paragraph 4, far in advance of the outrageous proposal in paragraph 9, you know you are in the presence of a satiric voice. How is the satiric intent conveyed? Are there any sections in which the satire is dropped in favor of straightforward recommendations? If so, where? If not, how do you decide whether his essay includes any positive proposals and where they are stated? Try to decipher not only the satire but the means *by which the satire is accomplished.*

A MODEST PROPOSAL

First published as "A Modest Proposal for Preventing the Children of Poor People from Being a Burden to Their Parents or the Country" (1729).

It is a melancholy object to those who walk through this great town* or travel in the country, when they see the streets, the roads, and cabin doors, crowded with beggars of the female sex, followed by three, four, or six children, all in rags and importuning every passenger for an alms. These mothers, instead of being able to work for their honest livelihood, are forced to employ all their time in strolling to beg sustenance for their helpless infants, who, as they grow up, either turn thieves for want of work, or leave their dear native country to fight for the Pretender in Spain, or sell themselves to the Barbadoes.† 1

I think it is agreed by all parties that this prodigious number of children in the arms, or on the backs, or at the heels of their mothers, and frequently of their fathers, is in the present deplorable state of the kingdom a very great additional grievance; and therefore whoever could find out a fair, cheap, and easy method of making these children sound, useful members of the commonwealth would deserve so well of the public as to have his statue set up for a preserver of the nation. 2

But my intention is very far from being confined to provide only for the children of professed beggars; it is of a much greater extent, and shall take in the whole number of infants at a certain age who are born of parents in effect as little able to support them as those who demand our charity in the streets. 3

*Dublin, capital city of Ireland.

†The pretender to the throne of England was James Stuart (1688–1766), son of the deposed James II. Barbados is an island in the West Indies.

As to my own part, having turned my thoughts for many years upon 4
this important subject, and maturely weighed the several schemes of other projectors, I have always found them grossly mistaken in their computation. It is true, a child just dropped from its dam may be supported by her milk for a solar year, with little other nourishment; at most not above the value of two shillings,* which the mother may certainly get, or the value in scraps, by her lawful occupation of begging; and it is exactly at one year old that I propose to provide for them in such a manner as instead of being a charge upon their parents or the parish, or wanting food and raiment for the rest of their lives, they shall on the contrary contribute to the feeding, and partly to the clothing, of many thousands.

There is likewise another great advantage in my scheme, that it will 5
prevent those voluntary abortions, and that horrid practice of women murdering their bastard children, alas, too frequent among us, sacrificing the poor innocent babes, I doubt, more to avoid the expense than the shame, which would move tears and pity in the most savage and inhuman breast.

The number of souls in this kingdom being usually reckoned one mil- 6
lion and a half, of these I calculate there may be about two hundred thousand couple whose wives are breeders; from which number I subtract thirty thousand couples who are able to maintain their own children, although I apprehend there cannot be so many under the present distress of the kingdom; but this being granted, there will remain an hundred and seventy thousand breeders. I again subtract fifty thousand for those women who miscarry, or whose children die by accident or disease within the year. There only remain an hundred and twenty thousand children of poor parents annually born. The question therefore is, how this number shall be reared and provided for, which, as I have already said, under the present situation of affairs, is utterly impossible by all the methods hitherto proposed. For we can neither employ them in handicraft or agriculture; we neither build houses (I mean in the country) nor cultivate land. They can very seldom pick up a livelihood by stealing till they arrive at six years old, except where they are of towardly parts;† although I confess they learn the rudiments much earlier, during which time they can however be looked upon only as probationers, as I have been informed by a principal gentleman in the county of Cavan, who protested to me that he never knew above one or two instances under the age of six, even in a part of the kingdom so renowned for the quickest proficiency in that art.

I am assured by our merchants that a boy or a girl before twelve years 7
old is no salable commodity; and even when they come to this age they will not yield above three pounds, or three pounds and half a crown at most on the Exchange; which cannot turn to account either to the parents or the kingdom, the charge of nutriment and rags having been at least four times that value.

*The British pound sterling was made up of twenty shillings; five shillings made a crown.

†*Towardly* means "advanced"; *parts* refers to abilities or talents.

I shall now therefore humbly propose my own thoughts, which I hope 8
will not be liable to the least objection.

I have been assured by a very knowing American of my acquaintance 9
in London, that a young healthy child well nursed is at a year old a most delicious, nourishing, and wholesome food, whether stewed, roasted, baked, or boiled; and I make no doubt that it will equally serve in a fricassee or a ragout.

I do therefore humbly offer it to public consideration that of the hun- 10
dred and twenty thousand children, already computed, twenty thousand may be reserved for breed, whereof only one fourth part to be males, which is more than we allow to sheep, black cattle, or swine; and my reason is that these children are seldom the fruits of marriage, a circumstance not much regarded by our savages, therefore one male will be sufficient to serve four females. That the remaining hundred thousand may at a year old be offered in sale to the persons of quality and fortune through the kingdom, always advising the mother to let them suck plentifully in the last month, so as to render them plump and fat for a good table. A child will make two dishes at an entertainment for friends; and when the family dines alone, the fore or hind quarter will make a reasonable dish, and seasoned with a little pepper or salt will be very good boiled on the fourth day, especially in winter.

I have reckoned upon a medium that a child just born will weigh twelve 11
pounds, and in a solar year if tolerably nursed increaseth to twenty-eight pounds.

I grant this food will be somewhat dear, and therefore very proper for 12
landlords, who, as they have already devoured most of the parents, seem to have the best title to the children.

Infant's flesh will be in season throughout the year, but more plentiful 13
in March, and a little before and after. For we are told by a grave author, an eminent French physician,* that fish being a prolific diet, there are more children born in Roman Catholic countries about nine months after Lent than at any other season; therefore, reckoning a year after Lent, the markets will be more glutted than usual, because the number of popish infants is at least three to one in this kingdom; and therefore it will have one other collateral advantage, by lessening the number of Papists among us.

I have already computed the charge of nursing a beggar's child (in which 14
list I reckon all cottagers, laborers, and four fifths of the farmers) to be about two shillings per annum, rags included; and I believe no gentleman would repine to give ten shillings for the carcass of a good fat child, which, as I have said, will make four dishes of excellent nutritive meat, when he hath only some particular friend or his own family to dine with him. Thus the squire will learn to be a good landlord, and grow popular among the tenants; the mother will have eight shillings net profit, and be fit for work till she produces another child.

Those who are more thrifty (as I must confess the times require) may 15

*François Rabelais (1494?–1553), French satirist, author of *Pantagruel* (1532) and *Gargantua* (1534).

flay the carcass; the skin of which artificially* dressed will make admirable gloves for ladies, and summer boots for fine gentlemen.

As to our city of Dublin, shambles† may be appointed for this purpose in the most convenient parts of it, and butchers we may be assured will not be wanting; although I rather recommend buying the children alive, and dressing them hot from the knife as we do roasting pigs. 16

A very worthy person, a true lover of his country, and whose virtues I highly esteem, was lately pleased in discoursing on this matter to offer a refinement upon my scheme. He said that many gentlemen of this kingdom, having of late destroyed their deer, he conceived that the want of venison might be well supplied by the bodies of young lads and maidens, not exceeding fourteen years of age nor under twelve, so great a number of both sexes in every country being now ready to starve for want of work and service; and these to be disposed of by their parents, if alive, or otherwise by their nearest relations. But with due deference to so excellent a friend and so deserving a patriot, I cannot be altogether in his sentiments; for as to the males, my American acquaintance assured me from frequent experience that their flesh was generally tough and lean, like that of our schoolboys, by continual exercise, and their taste disagreeable; and to fatten them would not answer the charge. Then as to the females, it would, I think with humble submission, be a loss to the public, because they soon would become breeders themselves: and besides, it is not improbable that some scrupulous people might be apt to censure such a practice (although indeed very unjustly) as a little bordering upon cruelty; which, I confess, hath always been with me the strongest objection against any project, how well soever intended. 17

But in order to justify my friend, he confessed that this expedient was put into his head by the famous Psalmanazar, a native of the island Formosa, who came from thence to London above twenty years ago, and in conversation told my friend that in his country when any young person happened to be put to death, the executioner sold the carcass to persons of quality as a prime dainty; and that in his time the body of a plump girl of fifteen, who was crucified for an attempt to poison the emperor, was sold to his Imperial Majesty's prime minister of state, and other great mandarins of the court, in joints from the gibbet, at four hundred crowns. Neither indeed can I deny that if the same use were made of several plump young girls in this town, who without one single groat to their fortunes cannot stir abroad without a chair,‡ and appear at the playhouse and assemblies in foreign fineries which they never will pay for, the kingdom would not be the worse. 18

Some persons of a desponding spirit are in great concern about that vast number of poor people who are aged, diseased, or maimed, and I have been desired to employ my thoughts what course may be taken to ease the nation 19

*Skillfully, artistically.

†Slaughterhouses.

‡Sedan chair, an enclosed chair set on horizontal poles, in which the occupant could be conveyed from place to place by two carriers, one in front and one in back.

of so grievous an encumbrance. But I am not in the least pain upon that matter, because it is very well known that they are every day dying and rotting by cold and famine, and filth and vermin, as fast as can be reasonably expected. And as to the younger laborers, they are now in almost as hopeful a condition. They cannot get work, and consequently pine away for want of nourishment to a degree that if at any time they are accidentally hired to common labor, they have not strength to perform it; and thus the country and themselves are happily delivered from the evils to come.

I have too long digressed, and therefore shall return to my subject. I 20
think the advantages by the proposal which I have made are obvious and many, as well as of the highest importance.

For first, as I have already observed, it would greatly lessen the number 21
of Papists, with whom we are yearly overrun, being the principal breeders of the nation as well as our most dangerous enemies; and who stay at home on purpose to deliver the kingdom to the Pretender, hoping to take their advantage by the absence of so many good Protestants, who have chosen rather to leave their country than stay at home and pay tithes against their conscience to an Episcopal curate.*

Secondly, the poorer tenants will have something valuable of their own, 22
which by law may be made liable to distress, and help to pay their landlord's rent, their corn and cattle being already seized and money a thing unknown.

Thirdly, whereas the maintenance of an hundred thousand children, 23
from two years old and upward, cannot be computed at less than ten shillings a piece per annum, the nation's stock will be thereby increased fifty thousand pounds per annum, besides the profit of a new dish introduced to the tables of all gentlemen of fortune in the kingdom who have any refinement in taste. And the money will circulate among ourselves,† the goods being entirely of our own growth and manufacture.

Fourthly, the constant breeders, besides the gain of eight shillings ster- 24
ling per annum by the sale of their children, will be rid of the charge of maintaining them after the first year.

Fifthly, this food would likewise bring great custom to taverns, where 25
the vintners will certainly be so prudent as to procure the best receipts for dressing it to perfection, and consequently have their houses frequented by all the fine gentlemen, who justly value themselves upon their knowledge in good eating; and a skillful cook, who understands how to oblige his guests, will contrive to make it as expensive as they please.

Sixthly, this would be a great inducement to marriage, which all wise 26
nations have either encouraged by rewards or enforced by laws and penalties. It would increase the care and tenderness of mothers toward their children, when they were sure of a settlement for life to the poor babes, provided in some sort by the public, to their annual profit instead of expense. We should see an honest emulation among the married women, which of them could

*Swift blamed much of Ireland's poverty on large Protestant landowners who, not wanting to pay Anglican (Episcopal) Church tithes (taxes), lived abroad and thus spent their Irish-made money abroad, depriving the Irish economy of their income.

†That is, among the Irish themselves.

bring the fattest child to the market. Men would become as fond of their wifes during the time of their pregnancy as they are now of their mares in foal, their cows in calf, or sows when they are ready to farrow; nor offer to beat or kick them (as is too frequent a practice) for fear of a miscarriage.

Many other advantages might be enumerated. For instance, the addition 27
of some thousand carcasses in our exportation of barreled beef, the propagation of swine's flesh, and improvement in the art of making good bacon, so much wanted among us by the great destruction of pigs, too frequent at our tables, which are no way comparable in taste or magnificence to a well-grown, fat, yearling child, which roasted whole will make a considerable figure at a lord mayor's feast or any other public entertainment. But this and many others I omit, being studious of brevity.

Supposing that one thousand families in this city would be constant 28
customers for infants' flesh, besides others who might have it at merry meetings, particularly weddings and christenings, I compute that Dublin would take off annually about twenty thousand carcasses, and the rest of the kingdom (where probably they will be sold somewhat cheaper) the remaining eighty thousand.

I can think of no one objection that will possibly be raised against this 29
proposal, unless it should be urged that the number of people will be thereby much lessened in the kingdom. This I freely own, and it was indeed one principal design in offering it to the world. I desire the reader will observe, that I calculate my remedy for this one individual kingdom of Ireland and for no other that ever was, is, or I think ever can be upon earth. Therefore let no man talk to me of other expedients: of taxing our absentees at five shillings a pound: of using neither clothes nor household furniture except what is of our own growth and manufacture: of utterly rejecting the materials and instruments that promote foreign luxury: of curing the expensiveness of pride, vanity, idleness, and gaming* in our women: of introducing a vein of parsimony, prudence, and temperance: of learning to love our country, in the want of which we differ even from Laplanders and the inhabitants of Topinamboo: of quitting our animosities and factions, nor acting any longer like the Jews, who were murdering one another at the very moment their city† was taken: of being a little cautious not to sell our country and conscience for nothing: of teaching landlords to have at least one degree of mercy toward their tenants: lastly, of putting a spirit of honesty, industry, and skill into our shopkeepers; who, if a resolution could now be taken to buy only our native goods, would immediately unite to cheat and exact upon us in the price, the measure, and the goodness, nor could ever yet be brought to make one fair proposal of just dealing, though often and earnestly invited to it.

Therefore I repeat, let no man talk to me of these and the like expedi- 30
ents, till he hath at least some glimpse of hope that there will ever be some hearty and sincere attempt to put them in practice.

But as to myself, having been wearied out for many years with offering 31

*Gambling.

†Jerusalem, sacked by the Romans in A.D. 70.

vain, idle, visionary thoughts, and at length utterly despairing of success, I fortunately fell upon this proposal, which, as it is wholly new, so it hath something solid and real, of no expense and little trouble, full in our own power, and whereby we can incur no danger in disobliging England. For this kind of commodity will not bear exportation, the flesh being of too tender a consistence to admit a long continuance in salt, although perhaps I could name a country* which would be glad to eat up our whole nation without it.

After all, I am not so violently bent upon my own opinion as to reject any offer proposed by wise men, which shall be found equally innocent, cheap, easy, and effectual. But before something of that kind shall be advanced in contradiction to my scheme, and offering a better, I desire the author or authors will be pleased maturely to consider two points. First, as things now stand, how they will be able to find food and raiment for an hundred thousand useless mouths and backs. And secondly, there being a round million of creatures in human figure throughout this kingdom, whose sole subsistence put into a common stock would leave them in debt two millions of pounds sterling, adding those who are beggars by profession to the bulk of farmers, cottagers, and laborers, with their wives and children who are beggars in effect; I desire those politicians who dislike my overture, and may perhaps be so bold to attempt an answer, that they will first ask the parents of these mortals whether they would not at this day think it a great happiness to have been sold for food at a year old in the manner I prescribe, and thereby have avoided such a perpetual scene of misfortunes as they have since gone through by the oppression of landlords, the impossibility of paying rent without money or trade, the want of common sustenance, with neither house nor clothes to cover them from the inclemencies of the weather, and the most inevitable prospect of entailing the like or greater miseries upon their breed forever. 32

I profess, in the sincerity of my heart, that I have not the least personal interest in endeavoring to promote this necessary work, having no other motive than the public good of my country, by advancing our trade, providing for infants, relieving the poor, and giving some pleasure to the rich. I have no children by which I can propose to get a single penny; the youngest being nine years old, and my wife past childbearing. 33

Questions for Discussion

1. If the satirist Swift is delivering a message that has to be decoded, not the message that is stated, who is delivering the surface message? What does Swift achieve by not speaking "straight," in his own voice? How

*England, of course, against whose occupation of Ireland many Irish are still resentful.

can you determine the amount of distance between the persona and Swift himself?

2. The tone of Swift's persona, the "proposer," seems to change radically as the italicized passage begins in paragraph 29. If we assume that Swift is being ironic throughout, how should we read this passage? Can you translate it into non-ironic language? What is the purpose of this passage? What kind of clue, if any, are the italics? How does this passage fit into the rest of the essay?
3. Does it matter for Swift's satire whether his persona's statistics are accurate or not? Do you think they are bogus or real? Regardless of the answer to this question, what *rhetorical* effect do they serve? What kind of *character* do they help establish for the persona? How do they fit into Swift's overall satire?
4. Who receives the strongest attack from Swift: the British landlords, the Irish leaders, or the Irish people in general? How do you know?
5. What would the "proposal" gain or lose if the final paragraph were dropped? Does it provide a fitting conclusion for the satire? If so, how? If not, why not?
6. How does the animal imagery—dam, breeder, carcass, and so on—contribute to the satire? Can you think of any other terms that would serve Swift's purpose as well? If not, what does this suggest about the craftedness of the satire?

Suggested Essay Topics

1. Write your own satire making fun of some group, person, institution, or human trait. Address it not to your target but to people that you would like to join you in contempt or ridicule of the target.
2. Write two different versions of the same attack, one in a satirical voice, the other as a straightforward denunciation. In a satire you can say you "love" something, and, if the satire is working, the reader will know that you hate it. In a straightforward denunciation you simply say that you hate what you hate. But satire's greater relative complexity does not mean that it is always better for all purposes. After you have done your two versions, write a final paragraph or two evaluating which version works better.

Stephen Spender

Most of the readings in this chapter deal with different versions of racial or ethnic discrimination, but there is one form of discrimination in modern life that embraces all races, ages, and sexes: the discrimina-

tion against the urban poor—not those who are struggling to stay economically afloat, and not those whose lives are scrimped and scraped by insufficient income, but those who have no *income, those who have gone under: the bag ladies, the hobos, and the winos who beg on the streets, live in the alleys, and sleep on the warm-air gratings of every large American city. They are the unemployed and, in many cases, the unemployable; they are homeless, hopeless, and habituated to neglect. Many of us stop noticing these degraded and unaided folk after a while; we don't wish to see what we cannot understand or help.*

Fortunately, however, others not only look but see *and in the intensity of their gaze make us look again. They invite us to see what we were too embarrassed or hurried to notice the first time. Spender's (b. 1909) poem captures a moment of intense seeing of these urban poor. He looks at them without sentimentality and insists that we do the same. He admonishes us to "paint here no draped despairs" (l. 12) but to look on wounds that are raw, ugly, and personal, not statistical.*

IN RAILWAY HALLS, ON PAVEMENTS NEAR THE TRAFFIC

From *Collected Poems* (1934).

In railway halls, on pavements near the traffic,
They beg, their eyes made big by empty staring
And only measuring Time, like the blank clock.

No, I shall wave no tracery of pen-ornament
To make them birds upon my singing-tree:
Time merely drives these lives which do not live
As tides push rotten stuff along the shore.

—There is no consolation, no, none,
In the curving beauty of that line
Traced on our graphs through History, where the oppressor
Starves and deprives the poor.

Paint here no draped despairs, no saddening clouds
Where the soul rests, proclaims eternity.
But let the wrong cry out as raw as wounds
This time forgets and never heals, far less transcends.

1933

Questions for Discussion

1. Why is the clock in line 3 described as "blank"? In what sense is Spender using *blank*?
2. To what do "tracery of pen-ornament" (l. 4) and "singing-tree" (l. 5) refer? Are these appropriate metaphors? How do they aid the poem's effectiveness?
3. Graph lines may have a "curving beauty" (l. 9), but why does Spender find them so sinister? Why is he angry?
4. What is his final judgment about "this time" (l. 15) and its treatment of the poor he is describing?

Suggested Essay Topic

1. Choose some discriminated-against group that is generally as invisible to most of us as the urban poor, and write an indignant letter to the editor of the city newspaper in which you attempt to make this group really visible and awaken the conscience of your fellow citizens about the plight of the real people in the group.
2. Try writing a "social protest" poem of your own, focusing on any groups and taking any tone you choose. Direct the poem toward the kind of general reader who might see it as a published piece in your campus literary magazine.

IDEAS IN DEBATE

Adolf Hitler
Malcolm Hay

Adolf Hitler

Into Mein Kampf *(My Struggle), Adolf Hitler (1889–1945) poured all of the weird fantasies, twisted logic, and racial hatred of a person who seems never to have loved or to have been loved by anyone. (The idolatry he received as Führer was another kind of thing.) His father was a shoemaker, and his mother, who was his father's third wife, had been a maid in the first wife's home. The father died when Hitler was 13; the mother died two years later.*

At age 15, then, Hitler found himself alone in the world and made his way to Vienna, Austria, where he hoped to study art. He lived in Vienna for about nine years, until 1912, existing in miserable poverty, failing his entrance exam into the art academy, and finding himself unable to take up architecture, a second ambition, because he had never completed his secondary education. He squeezed out a barren existence as a building construction worker and also tried painting postcards and selling pictures. But these efforts brought in only pennies. In 1912 Hitler moved to Munich, where he continued to make a scanty living as a commercial artist. He served as a soldier in the German army, 1914–1918, and was wounded in 1916. After the war he became more and more absorbed in political activity, joining the German Workers' party in 1919 and discovering that he was a speaker. He began to gather around him a group of misfits and thugs who with him participated in the "Beer Hall Putsch" of November 8–9, 1923, when Hitler was 34. With the failure of the putsch, he was sentenced to prison on the charge of treason, and while there he began writing Mein Kampf *at the suggestion of Rudolf Hess. He was pardoned the next year by a government that was habitually lenient toward right-wing agitators.*

In Hitler's account of his Vienna years in Mein Kampf *we get a clear picture of his emerging hatred of Jews. At them he directs all the pent-up rage and the psychopathological fury of a man who, small in every sense, had lived a life unloved, unexciting, unrewarded, unsuccessful, and unpromising. This rage was later to transform itself into the calculated murder of more than 6 million Jews.*

However, as Malcolm Hay makes clear in the next selection, "The Persecution of Jews" (pp. 502–519), Hitler's choice of the Jews as a scapegoat for his frustrations was not random, idiosyncratic, or accidental. Hatred of Jews was an ancient tradition in Europe, both within the Christian church and outside of it. Anti-Semitism was thus a "safe" outlet for the expression of hatreds that Hitler during his Vienna years had neither the imagination nor the influence to vent on other, more powerful groups. The Jews were traditional targets.

We pick up Hitler's story at the point where he tells of coming under the influence of the mayor of Vienna, Karl Lueger, whose newspaper, Volksblatt, *was rabidly anti-Semitic. He begins by saying that when he first came to Vienna he disliked both Lueger and his anti-Semitic bias. As the account progresses he records how he gradually came to see anti-Semitism as, for him, an inevitable position.*

IS THIS A JEW?

From *Mein Kampf.* We are reprinting from the translation by Ralph Manheim. *Mein Kampf* was originally published in 1925. The title is ours.

These occasions slowly made me acquainted with the man and the move- 1
ment, which in those days guided Vienna's destinies: Dr. Karl Lueger* and the Christian Social Party.

When I arrived in Vienna, I was hostile to both of them. 2

The man and the movement seemed 'reactionary' in my eyes. 3

My common sense of justice, however, forced me to change this judg- 4
ment in proportion as I had occasion to become acquainted with the man and his work; and slowly my fair judgment turned to unconcealed admiration. Today, more than ever, I regard this man as the greatest German mayor of all times.

How many of my basic principles were upset by this change in my 5
attitude toward the Christian Social movement!

My views with regard to anti-Semitism thus succumbed to the passage 6
of time, and this was my greatest transformation of all.

It cost me the greatest inner soul struggles, and only after months of 7
battle between my reason and my sentiments did my reason begin to emerge victorious. Two years later, my sentiment had followed my reason, and from then on became its most loyal guardian and sentinel.

At the time of this bitter struggle between spiritual education and cold 8
reason, the visual instruction of the Vienna streets had performed invaluable services. There came a time when I no longer, as in the first days, wandered blindly through the mighty city; now with open eyes I saw not only the buildings but also the people.

Once, as I was strolling through the Inner City, I suddenly encountered 9
an apparition in a black caftan† and black hair locks. Is this a Jew? was my first thought.

*Karl Lueger (1844–1910). In 1897, as a member of the anti-Semitic Christian Social Party, he became mayor of Vienna and kept the post until his death. He also edited the violently anti-Semitic newspaper *Volksblatt,* which influenced Hitler's views about race, nation, and patriotism. At first opposed by the Court for his radical nationalism and anti-Semitism, toward the end of Lueger's career he became more moderate and was reconciled with the Emperor.

†An ankle-length coat-like garment, often striped, with very long sleeves and a sash.

For, to be sure, they had not looked like that in Linz. I observed the man 10
furtively and cautiously, but the longer I stared at this foreign face, scrutinizing feature for feature, the more my first question assumed a new form:

Is this a German? 11

As always in such cases, I now began to try to relieve my doubts by 12
books. For a few hellers I bought the first anti-Semitic pamphlets of my life. Unfortunately, they all proceeded from the supposition that in principle the reader knew or even understood the Jewish question to a certain degree. Besides, the tone for the most part was such that doubts again arose in me, due in part to the dull and amazingly unscientific arguments favoring the thesis.

I relapsed for weeks at a time, once even for months. 13

The whole thing seemed to me so monstrous, the accusations so bound- 14
less, that, tormented by the fear of doing injustice, I again became anxious and uncertain.

Yet I could no longer very well doubt that the objects of my study were 15
not Germans of a special religion, but a people in themselves; for since I had begun to concern myself with this question and to take cognizance of the Jews, Vienna appeared to me in a different light than before. Wherever I went, I began to see Jews, and the more I saw, the more sharply they became distinguished in my eyes from the rest of humanity. Particularly the Inner City and the districts north of the Danube Canal swarmed with a people which even outwardly had lost all resemblance to Germans.

And whatever doubts I may still have nourished were finally dispelled 16
by the attitude of a portion of the Jews themselves.

Among them there was a great movement, quite extensive in Vienna, 17
which came out sharply in confirmation of the national character of the Jews: this was the *Zionists.* *

It looked, to be sure, as though only a part of the Jews approved this 18
viewpoint, while the great majority condemned and inwardly rejected such a formulation. But when examined more closely, this appearance dissolved itself into an unsavory vapor of pretexts advanced for mere reasons of expedience, not to say lies. For the so-called liberal Jews did not reject the Zionists as non-Jews, but only as Jews with an impractical, perhaps even dangerous, way of publicly avowing their Jewishness.

Intrinsically they remained unalterably of one piece. 19

In a short time this apparent struggle between Zionistic and liberal Jews 20
disgusted me; for it was false through and through, founded on lies and scarcely in keeping with the moral elevation and purity always claimed by this people.

The cleanliness of this people, moral and otherwise, I must say, is a 21
point in itself. By their very exterior you could tell that these were no lovers of water, and, to your distress, you often knew it with your eyes closed. Later

*Those Jews who believed that Judaism was not only a religion but conferred a *national* status as well. Zionists thus believe in a Jewish state, not just a Jewish faith.

I often grew sick to my stomach from the smell of these caftan-wearers. Added to this, there was their unclean dress and their generally unheroic appearance.

All this could scarcely be called very attractive; but it became positively 22
repulsive when, in addition to their physical uncleanliness, you discovered the moral stains on this 'chosen people.'

In a short time I was made more thoughtful than ever by my slowly 23
rising insight into the type of activity carried on by the Jews in certain fields.

Was there any form of filth or profligacy, particularly in cultural life, 24
without at least one Jew involved in it?

If you cut even cautiously into such an abscess, you found, like a maggot 25
in a rotting body, often dazzled by the sudden light—a kike!

What had to be reckoned heavily against the Jews in my eyes was 26
when I became acquainted with their activity in the press, art, literature, and the theater.* All the unctuous reassurances helped little or nothing. It sufficed to look at a billboard, to study the names of the men behind the horrible trash they advertised, to make you hard for a long time to come. This was pestilence, spiritual pestilence, worse than the Black Death of olden times, and the people was being infected with it! It goes without saying that the lower the intellectual level of one of these art manufacturers, the more unlimited his fertility will be, and the scoundrel ends up like a garbage separator, splashing his filth in the face of humanity. And bear in mind that there is no limit to their number; bear in mind that for one Goethe Nature easily can foist on the world ten thousand of these scribblers who poison men's souls like germ-carriers of the worse sort, on their fellow men.

It was terrible, but not to be overlooked, that precisely the Jew, in 27
tremendous numbers, seemed chosen by Nature for this shameful calling.

Is this why the Jews are called the 'chosen people'? 28

I now began to examine carefully the names of all the creators of 29
unclean products in public artistic life. The result was less and less favorable for my previous attitude toward the Jews. Regardless how my sentiment might resist, my reason was forced to draw its conclusions.

The fact that nine tenths of all literary filth, artistic trash, and theatrical 30
idiocy can be set to the account of a people, constituting hardly one hundredth of all the country's inhabitants, could simply not be talked away; it was the plain truth.

And I now began to examine my beloved 'world press' from this point 31
of view.

And the deeper I probed, the more the object of my former admiration 32
shriveled. The style became more and more unbearable; I could not help rejecting the content as inwardly shallow and banal; the objectivity of exposi-

*There is not much evidence that Hitler really knew the art, literature, and theatre of his day. These criticisms seem to be parrotings of *Volksblatt* editorials. It was attitudes such as these that eventually led to the Nazi burning of books and the denunciation of writings by "racially inferior" authors.

tion now seemed to me more akin to lies than honest truth; and the writers were—Jews.

A thousand things which I had hardly seen before now struck my 33
notice, and others, which had previously given me food for thought, I now learned to grasp and understand.

I now saw the liberal attitude of this press in a different light; the lofty 34
tone in which it answered attacks and its method of killing them with silence now revealed itself to me as a trick as clever as it was treacherous; the transfigured raptures of their theatrical critics were always directed at Jewish writers, and their disapproval never struck anyone but Germans. The gentle pinpricks against William II revealed its methods by their persistency, and so did its commendation of French culture and civilization. The trashy content of the short story now appeared to me as outright indecency, and in the language I detected the accents of a foreign people; the sense of the whole thing was so obviously hostile to Germanism that this could only have been intentional.

But who had an interest in this? 35

Was all this a mere accident? 36

Gradually I became uncertain. 37

The development was accelerated by insights which I gained into a 38
number of other matters. I am referring to the general view of ethics and morals which was quite openly exhibited by a large part of the Jews, and the practical application of which could be seen.

Here again the streets provided an object lesson of a sort which was 39
sometimes positively evil.

The relation of the Jews to prostitution and, even more, to the white- 40
slave traffic, could be studied in Vienna as perhaps in no other city of Western Europe, with the possible exception of the southern French ports. If you walked at night through the streets and alleys of Leopoldstadt,* at every step you witnessed proceedings which remained concealed from the majority of the German people until the War gave the soldiers on the eastern front occasion to see similar things, or, better expressed, forced them to see them.

When thus for the first time I recognized the Jew as the cold-hearted, 41
shameless, and calculating director of this revolting vice traffic in the scum of the big city, a cold shudder ran down my back.

But then a flame flared up within me. I no longer avoided discussion of 42
the Jewish question; no, now I sought it. And when I learned to look for the Jew in all branches of cultural and artistic life and its various manifestations, I suddenly encountered him in a place where I would least have expected to find him.

When I recognized the Jew as the leader of the Social Democracy,† the 43
scales dropped from my eyes. A long soul struggle had reached its conclusion.

*Second District of Vienna, separated from the main part of the city by the Danube Canal. Formerly the ghetto, it still has a predominantly Jewish population. [Original editor's note]

†Socialism, the political theory at the opposite end of the political spectrum from the fascism which Hitler later brought to Germany.

Even in my daily relations with my fellow workers, I observed the 44
amazing adaptability with which they adopted different positions on the same question, sometimes within an interval of a few days, sometimes in only a few hours. It was hard for me to understand how people who, when spoken to alone, possessed some sensible opinions, suddenly lost them as soon as they came under the influence of the masses. It was often enough to make one despair. When, after hours of argument, I was convinced that now at last I had broken the ice or cleared up some absurdity, and was beginning to rejoice at my success, on the next day to my disgust I had to begin all over again; it had all been in vain. Like an eternal pendulum their opinions seemed to swing back again and again to the old madness.

All this I could understand: that they were dissatisfied with their lot and 45
cursed the Fate which often struck them so harshly; that they hated the employers who seemed to them the heartless bailiffs of Fate; that they cursed the authorities who in their eyes were without feeling for their situation; that they demonstrated against food prices and carried their demands into the streets: this much could be understood without recourse to reason. But what inevitably remained incomprehensible was the boundless hatred they heaped upon their own nationality, despising its greatness, besmirching its history, and dragging its great men into the gutter.

This struggle against their own species, their own clan, their own home- 46
land, was as senseless as it was incomprehensible. It was unnatural.

It was possible to cure them temporarily of this vice, but only for days 47
or at most weeks. If later you met the man you thought you had converted, he was just the same as before.

His old unnatural state had regained full possession of him. 48

. . .

I gradually became aware that the Social Democratic press was directed 49
predominantly by Jews; yet I did not attribute any special significance to this circumstance, since conditions were exactly the same in the other papers. Yet one fact seemed conspicuous: there was not one paper with Jews working on it which could have been regarded as truly national, according to my education and way of thinking.

I swallowed my disgust and tried to read this type of Marxist press 50
production, but my revulsion became so unlimited in so doing that I endeavored to become more closely acquainted with the men who manufactured these compendiums of knavery.

From the publisher down, they were all Jews. 51

I took all the Social Democratic pamphlets I could lay hands on and 52
sought the names of their authors: Jews.* I noted the names of the leaders; by far the greatest part were likewise members of the 'chosen people,' whether they were representatives in the Reichsrat or trade-union secretaries, the heads of organizations or street agitators. It was always the same grue-

*The facts do not support this assertion that the leadership of Austrian Social Democracy was primarily Jewish.

some picture. The names of the Austerlitzes, Davids, Adlers, Ellenbogens, etc., will remain forever graven in my memory. One thing had grown clear to me: the party with whose petty representatives I had been carrying on the most violent struggle for months was, as to leadership, almost exclusively in the hands of a foreign people; for, to my deep and joyful satisfaction, I had at last come to the conclusion that the Jew was no German.

Only now did I become thoroughly acquainted with the seducer of our 53
people.

A single year of my sojourn in Vienna had sufficed to imbue me with 54
the conviction that no worker could be so stubborn that he would not in the end succumb to better knowledge and better explanations. Slowly I had become an expert in their own doctrine and used it as a weapon in the struggle for my own profound conviction.

Success almost always favored my side. 55

The great masses could be saved, if only with the gravest sacrifice in 56
time and patience.

But a Jew could never be parted from his opinions. 57

At that time I was still childish enough to try to make the madness of 58
their doctrine clear to them; in my little circle I talked my tongue sore and my throat hoarse, thinking I would inevitably succeed in convincing them how ruinous their Marxist madness was; but what I accomplished was often the opposite. It seemed as though their increased understanding of the destructive effects of Social Democratic theories and their results only reinforced their determination.

The more I argued with them, the better I came to know their dialectic. 59
First they counted on the stupidity of their adversary, and then, when there was no other way out, they themselves simply played stupid. If all this didn't help, they pretended not to understand, or, if challenged, they changed the subject in a hurry, quoted platitudes which, if you accepted them, they immediately related to entirely different matters, and then, if again attacked, gave ground and pretended not to know exactly what you were talking about. Whenever you tried to attack one of these apostles, your hand closed on a jelly-like slime which divided up and poured through your fingers, but in the next moment collected again. But if you really struck one of these fellows so telling a blow that, observed by the audience, he couldn't help but agree, and if you believed that this had taken you at least one step forward, your amazement was great the next day. The Jew had not the slightest recollection of the day before, he rattled off his same old nonsense as though nothing at all had happened, and, if indignantly challenged, affected amazement; he couldn't remember a thing, except that he had proved the correctness of his assertions the previous day.

Sometimes I stood there thunderstruck. 60

I didn't know what to be more amazed at: the agility of their tongues 61
or their virtuosity at lying.

Gradually I began to hate them. 62

All this had but one good side: that in proportion as the real leaders or at least the disseminators of Social Democracy came within my vision, my love for my people inevitably grew. For who, in view of the diabolical craftiness of these seducers, could damn the luckless victims? How hard it was, even for me, to get the better of this race of dialectical liars! And how futile was such success in dealing with people who twist the truth in your mouth, who without so much as a blush disavow the word they have just spoken, and in the very next minute take credit for it after all. 63

No. The better acquainted I became with the Jew, the more forgiving I inevitably became toward the worker. 64

Questions for Discussion

1. If you have ever talked to a fanatical bigot of any kind, compare the "reasoning" you encountered then with that in *Mein Kampf.* What seems to be the real root of the hatred that emerges in this kind of bigotry? Is it a common root, or does it vary unpredictably from person to person? This is too big a question to answer factually, of course. But it may be useful to share impressions and speculations with your classmates.
2. Notice the self-conscious abandonment of reason in favor of feeling in paragraph 7. What would have been the effect of this move on Hitler's emerging racial hatred?
3. What is the intended rhetorical effect of the imagery that Hitler employs in paragraphs 25, 26, 53, and 59?
4. Discuss the similarities of opinion about Jews in *Mein Kampf,* paragraphs 21–25, with the opinions of the Colonel in "Artists in Uniform" (p. 405 ¶19).
5. It is sometimes said that everyone views the members of *some* groups more favorably than others, which is to say that everyone is prejudiced to some degree, if by prejudice we mean the expectation that individual members of certain groups will behave less admirably than the members of our own group. Do you think that this is so? Is it true of you? If it is, are you "bigoted"? If you think that you are not but still admit that you allow preconceptions about *groups* to affect your judgment of *individuals,* how would you define *bigotry* and *prejudice* as distinct from your behavior?
6. It is sometimes said that America is experiencing a new increase in acts of bigotry: attacks on individuals merely because they belong to this or that group; mailing of anonymous hate-mail to members of minority groups; publication of journals that include incitement to bigotry. Have you noted any such behavior on your own campus? If so, what do you think might be an effective way to combat it?

Suggested Essay Topics

1. In "Artists in Uniform" (pp. 396–408), Mary McCarthy's narrator, talking with the anti-Semitic Colonel, says,

   > It came to me . . . that for extremely stupid people anti-Semitism was a form of intellectuality, the sole form of intellectuality of which they were capable. It represented, in a rudimentary way, the ability to make categories, to generalize. Hence a thing I had noted before but never understood: the fact that anti-Semetic statements were generally delivered in an atmosphere of profundity. . . . To arrive, indeed, at the idea of a Jew was, for these grouping minds, an exercise in Platonic thought, a discovery of essence. . . . From this, it would seem, followed the querulous obstinacy with which the anti-Semite clung to his concept; to be deprived of this intellectual tool by missionaries of tolerance would be, for persons like the Colonel, the equivalent of Western man's losing the syllogism: a lapse into animal darkness. (¶17)

   If you agree that this analysis accurately lays bare the cause of much bigotry in general and is not limited to anti-Semitism, write an essay that analyzes some example of bigotry that you know firsthand, and base your analysis on the perspective provided by McCarthy in the quoted passage.
2. A variation of topic 1: Use McCarthy's perspective as the basis of your analysis of some example of bigotry found in a work of fiction.

Malcolm Hay

In the book from which this excerpt is taken, Europe and the Jews: The Pressure of Christendom on the People of Israel for 1900 Years, *Malcolm Hay (1881–1962) addresses one of the most troublesome of all human questions: Why do the members of one human group hate other groups so much that they are eager to exterminate them? His form of the question—Who is to blame for a given historical crime?—presents one of the most difficult of all writing tasks. To support any conclusions about such broad and elusive questions requires an immense amount of careful research, and to grapple with such emotion-charged matters requires great courage and tact. The author is sure to offend many readers, especially those groups that he blames for crimes they have accused others of committing.*

Through more than 300 pages packed with carefully chosen quotations, Hay argues three main points. First, it is a mistake to blame only Hitler and the Germans for the killing of millions of Jews during World War II; if we in the nations that opposed Hitler had responded with concrete aid as reports of extermination camps filtered into the Allied countries, hundreds of thousands, perhaps millions, of Jews might have been saved. Second, the reason for our indifference to the fate of innocent millions was that we had been taught, by one major "Christian" tradition, that Jews deserved *to die because they had killed Christ. Third, the Jews did not kill Christ; Christ was killed, as three of the four Gospels make clear, by Roman soldiers. The Jews who connived in Christ's death were a small group who had to plot secretly with the Romans for fear of resistance from the main body of Jews.*

As a Christian himself, Hay is in a better position for making these points than if he were Jewish. Some people would be more tempted to question his objectivity if he clearly had a personal stake in making his case. But in arguing about such complex matters, it is never enough to have a good, seemingly "objective" platform to stand on; final success depends on the quality of our reasoning and the evidence we offer.

As you read this selection (less than one-tenth of Hay's argument), it is important to avoid making up your mind with final assurance. After all, it would take months, perhaps years, of study to check out the reliability of his hundreds of quotations (we have omitted his references to save space) and to reach a point of confident personal understanding of the issues he raises. What we all can *do, however, is enlarge our grasp of the issues and our sense of the possible ways of thinking about them. As you read, you may want to question yourself about your own prejudices and your justified beliefs and about possible ways of removing the prejudices and deepening and refining the convictions.*

THE PERSECUTION OF JEWS

A Christian Scandal

Our title for chapter 1, "The Golden Mouth," of *Europe and the Jews: The Pressure of Christendom on the People of Israel for 1900 Years* (1950).

> Suffer no man and no cause to escape the undying penalty which history has the power to inflict on wrong.—Lord Acton

> So I considered again all the oppressions that are done under the sun;
> And beheld the tears of such as were oppressed, and they had no comforter;
> And on the side of the oppressors there was power,
> But they had no comforter.
>
> Wherefore I praised the dead that are already dead
> More than the living that are yet alive;
> But better than they both is he that hath not yet been,
> Who hath not seen the evil that is done under the sun.
>
> Ecclesiastes IV: 1–3

Men are not born with hatred in their blood. The infection is usually acquired 1
by contact; it may be injected deliberately or even unconsciously, by parents, or by teachers. Adults, unless protected by the vigor of their intelligence, or by a rare quality of goodness, seldom escape contagion. The disease may spread throughout the land like the plague, so that a class, a religion, a nation,

will become the victim of popular hatred without anyone knowing exactly how it all began; and people will disagree, and even quarrel among themselves, about the real reason for its existence; and no one foresees the inevitable consequences.

For hatred dealeth perversely, as St. Paul might have said were he 2
writing to the Corinthians at the present time, and is puffed up with pride; rejoiceth in iniquity; regardeth not the truth. These three things, therefore, corrupt the world: disbelief, despair, and hatred—and of these, the most dangerous of all is hatred.

In the spring of 1945, three trucks loaded with eight to nine tons of 3
human ashes, from the Sachsenhausen concentration camp, were dumped into a canal in order to conceal the high rate of Jewish executions. When a German general was asked at Nuremberg how such things could happen, he replied: "I am of the opinion that when for years, for decades, the doctrine is preached that Jews are not even human, such an outcome is inevitable." This explanation, which gets to the root of the matter, is, however, incomplete. The doctrine which made such deeds inevitable had been preached, not merely for years or for decades, but for many centuries; more than once during the Middle Ages it threatened to destroy the Jewish people. "The Jews," wrote Léon Bloy, "are the most faithful witnesses, the most authentic remainders, of the candid Middle Ages which hated them for the love of God, and so often wanted to exterminate them." In those days the excuse given for killing them was often that they were "not human," and that, in the modern German sense, they were "nonadaptable"; they did not fit into the mediaeval conception of a World State.

The German crime of genocide—the murder of a race—has its logical 4
roots in the mediaeval theory that the Jews were outcasts, condemned by God to a life of perpetual servitude, and it is not, therefore, a phenomenon completely disconnected from previous history. Moreover, responsibility for the nearly achieved success of the German plan to destroy a whole group of human beings ought not to be restricted to Hitler and his gangsters, or to the German people. The plan nearly succeeded because it was allowed to develop without interference.

"It was an excellent saying of Solon's," wrote Richard Bentley, "who 5
when he was asked what would rid the world of injuries, replied: 'If the bystanders would have the same resentment with those that suffer wrong.' " The responsibility of bystanders who remained inactive while the German plan proceeded was recognized by one European statesman, by the least guilty of them all, Jan Masaryk, who had helped to rescue many thousands from the German chambers of death. Masaryk said:

> I am not an expert on the Near East and know practically nothing about pipe-lines. But one pipe-line I have watched with horror all my life; it is the pipe-line through which, for centuries, Jewish blood has flowed sporadically, and with horrible, incessant streams from 1933 to 1945. I will not, I cannot, forget this unbelievable fact, and I bow my head in shame

as one of those who permitted this greatest of wholesale murders to happen, instead of standing up with courage and decision against its perpetrators before it was too late.

Even after the Nuremberg Laws of 1935, every frontier remained closed against Jews fleeing from German terror, although a few were sometimes allowed in by a back door. Bystanders from thirty-two countries attended a conference at Evian, in 1938, to discuss the refugee problem; they formed a Permanent Intergovernmental Department in London to make arrangements for the admission of Jewish immigrants from Germany. The question of saving Jewish children by sending them to Palestine was not on the agenda of the Committee for assistance to refugees. "Up to August, 1939, the Committee had not succeeded in discovering new opportunities of immigration, though negotiations were proceeding with San Domingo, Northern Rhodesia, the Philippines and British Guiana." 6

An American writer asked in 1938: 7

> What is to be done with these people, with the millions who are clawing like frantic beasts at the dark walls of the suffocating chambers where they are imprisoned? The Christian world has practically abandoned them, and sits by with hardly an observable twinge of conscience in the midst of this terrible catastrophe. The Western Jews, still potent and powerful, rotate in their smug self-satisfied orbits, and confine themselves to genteel charity.

Until Germany obtained control of the greater part of Western Europe her policy had been directed mainly to compulsory Jewish emigration. But victories in 1940 had opened up new possibilities; and the Jews were therefore driven into ghettos in Poland and neighboring areas, where arrangements were being made for the "final solution," which was proclaimed in 1942, and put into action throughout all Germany and German-occupied territories. "What should be done with them," asked Hans Frank, governor general of occupied Poland, on December 16th, 1941. The German answer was no longer a secret. "I must ask you, gentlemen," said the governor, "to arm yourselves against all feelings of pity. We must annihilate the Jews wherever we find them." 8

Hitler, in 1941, was still waiting to see what the Christian world was going to do. Had the Allies opened their doors wide, even then, at least a million people, including hundreds of thousands of children, could have been saved. But no doors anywhere were widely opened. Few hearts anywhere were deeply moved. In Palestine, in the corner secured to Jews by the decision of the League of Nations, the entries by land and by sea were guarded by British soldiers and British sailors. Great numbers, especially in Poland, would have fled from the impending terror: *"If only they could,"* wrote Jacques Maritain in 1938, "if only other countries would open their frontiers." The German government at that time, and even after, was not always unwilling, 9 and in 1939 and 1940, was still prepared to let them go on certain conditions. "The Allies were told that if the Jews of Germany were to receive certificates to Palestine, or visas for any other country, they could be saved. Although for Jews to remain in Germany meant certain death, the pieces of paper needed to save human lives were not granted."

10 These pieces of paper were not provided, even to save the lives of children. In April, 1943, the Swedish government agreed to ask the German government to permit twenty thousand children to leave Germany for Sweden, provided that Sweden should be relieved of responsibility for them after the war. These children would have been saved had the British government given them certificates for Palestine. But even to save twenty thousand children from being slaughtered by the Germans, "it was not possible," said a British minister in the House of Commons, "for His Majesty's Government to go beyond the terms of policy approved by Parliament."

11 About the same time, in 1943, the Germans were considering an offer by the Red Cross and the British to evacuate seventy thousand children from Rumania to Palestine. Negotiations dragged on with the usual lack of vigor. And the Germans were persuaded by the Mufti of Jerusalem and Raschid Ali Gailani, prime minister of Iraq, who at the time were living, at German expense, in Berlin, to reject the plan. So the seventy thousand children were sent to the gas chambers.

12 More than a million children, including uncounted thousands of newborn infants, were killed by the Germans; most of them could have been saved had the countries of the world been determined to save them. But the doors remained closed. The children were taken away from their parents and sent, crowded in the death trains, and alone, to the crematoria of Auschwitz and Treblinka, or to the mass graves of Poland and Western Russia.

13 The German method of burying people in communal pits was a great improvement on the old system, once considered to be inhuman, of making each condemned man dig his own grave. The shooting of about two million people, whose bodies could not be left lying about, presented a difficult problem owing to the shortage of labor. Jewish women and children, weakened by torture and by long internment in concentration camps, were physically incapable of digging; and the men, when put on the list for "special treatment," were, as a rule, reduced to such a condition by hard labor on meager rations that they could hardly walk. The mass grave was an obvious necessity; but the German stroke of genius was the idea of making their victims get into the grave before they were shot, thus saving the labor of lifting two million dead bodies and throwing them in. Many hundreds of these death pits were dug in Central Europe until the Germans began to apply to extermination their well-known scientific efficiency. One of the largest pits, at Kerch, was examined in 1942 by officials of the Russian army:

> It was discovered that this trench, one kilometer in length, four meters wide, and two meters deep, was filled to overflowing with bodies of

> women, children, old men, and boys and girls in their teens. Near the trench were frozen pools of blood. Children's caps, toys, ribbons, torn off buttons, gloves, milkbottles, and rubber comforters, small shoes, galoshes, together with torn off hands and feet, and other parts of human bodies, were lying nearby. Everything was spattered with blood and brains.

14 What happened at Dulmo, in the Ukraine, reported by a German witness, Hermann Graebe, is one of the grimmest short stories that has ever been told in the bloody record of inhuman history. Graebe was manager of a building contractor's business at Dulmo. On October 5, 1942, he went as usual to his office and there was told by his foreman of terrible doings in the neighborhood. All the Jews in the district, about five thousand of them, were being liquidated. About fifteen hundred were shot every day, out in the open air, at a place nearby where three large pits had been dug, thirty meters long and three meters deep. Graebe and his foreman, who was intensely agitated, got into a car and drove off to the place. They saw a great mound of earth, twice the length of a cricket pitch and more than six feet high—a good shooting range. Near the mound were several trucks packed with people. Guards with whips drove the people off the trucks. The victims all had yellow patches sewn onto their garments, back and front—the Jewish badge. From behind the earth mound came the sound of rifle shots in quick succession. The people from the lorries, men, women and children of all ages, were herded together near the mound by an SS man armed with a dog whip. They were ordered to strip. They were told to put down their clothes in tidy order, boots and shoes, top clothing and underclothing.

15 Already there were great piles of this clothing, and a heap of eight hundred to a thousand pairs of boots and shoes. The people undressed. The mothers undressed the little children, "without screaming or weeping," reported Graebe, five years after. They had reached the point of human suffering where tears no longer flow and all hope has long been abandoned. "They stood around in family groups, kissed each other, said farewells, and waited." They were waiting for a signal from the SS man with a whip, who was standing by the pit. They stood there waiting for a quarter of an hour, waiting for their turn to come, while on the other side of the earth mound, now that the shots were no longer heard, the dead and dying were being packed into the pit. Graebe said:

> I heard no complaints, no appeal for mercy. I watched a family of about eight persons, a man and a woman both about fifty, with their grown up children, about twenty to twenty-four. An old woman with snow-white hair was holding a little baby in her arms, singing to it and tickling it. The baby was cooing with delight. The couple were looking at each other with tears in their eyes. The father was holding the hand of a boy about ten years old and speaking to him softly; the boy was fighting his tears . . .

Then suddenly came a shout from the SS man at the pit. They were 16
ready to deal with the next batch. Twenty people were counted off, including the family of eight. They were marched away behind the earth mound. Graebe and his foreman followed them. They walked round the mound and saw the tremendous grave, nearly a hundred feet long and nine feet deep. "People were closely wedged together and lying on top of each other so that only their heads were visible. Nearly all had blood running over their shoulders from their heads." They had been shot, in the usual German way, in the back of the neck. "Some of the shot people were still moving. Some were lifting their arms and turning their heads to show that they were still alive."

The pit was already nearly full; it contained about a thousand bodies. 17
The SS man who did the shooting was sitting on the edge of the pit, smoking a cigarette, with a tommy gun on his knee. The new batch of twenty people, the family of eight and the baby carried in the arms of the woman with snow-white hair, all completely naked, were directed down steps cut in the clay wall of the pit, and clambered over the heads of the dead and the dying. They lay down among them. "Some caressed those who were still alive and spoke to them in a low voice." Then came the shots from the SS man, who had thrown away his cigarette. Graebe looked into the pit "and saw the bodies were twitching, and some heads lying already motionless on top of the dead bodies that lay under them."

The Jews who died in this manner at Dulmo were the most fortunate 18
ones. They were spared torture in laboratory tests carried out by German doctors in order to find out how much agony the human body can endure before it dies; they were spared the choking terror of death in the gas chamber where hundreds of people at a time, squeezed together as tightly as the room could hold them, waited for the stream of poison to be turned on, while members of the German prison staff stood listening for ten or fifteen minutes until the screaming ceased, until all sounds had ceased, and they could safely open the door to the dead. And when the door was opened, the torture was not yet over. Four young Jews, whose turn would come perhaps with the next batch, dressed in a special sanitary uniform, with high rubber boots and long leather gauntlets, and provided with grappling irons, were compelled to drag out the pale dead bodies; and another group of young men was waiting to load the bodies onto a cart and drive them to the crematorium; and they knew that their turn, too, would soon come.

Responsibility for these deeds which have dishonored humanity does 19
not rest solely with Hitler and the men who sat in the dock at Nuremberg. Another tribunal will judge the bystanders, some of them in England, who watched the murderous beginnings, and then looked away and in their hearts secretly approved. "The Jewish blood shed by the Nazis," writes J.-P. Sartre, "is upon the heads of all of us."

As Maxim Gorky said more than thirty years ago, one of the greatest 20
crimes of which men are guilty, is indifference to the fate of their fellow men. This responsibility of the indifferent was recognized by Jacques Maritain a few years before the final act of the tragedy. "There seems to be a spirit," he

said in 1938, "which, without endorsing excesses committed against Jews . . . and without professing anti-Semitism, regards the Jewish drama with the indifference of the rational man who goes coldly along his way." It was this spirit of indifference, this cold aloofness of the bystanders, which made it possible for Hitler to turn Europe into a Jewish cemetery. Christian responsibility has, however, been recognized by one English bystander who for many years had never failed "to have the same resentment with those that suffer wrong": "In our own day, and within our own civilization," writes Dr. James Parkes, "more than six million deliberate murders are the consequence of the teachings about Jews for which the Christian Church is ultimately responsible, and of an attitude to Judaism which is not only maintained by all the Christian Churches, but has its ultimate resting place in the teaching of the New Testament itself."

Repressing the instinct to make excuses, read the following words writ- 21
ten by a survivor of Auschwitz:

> German responsibility for these crimes, however overwhelming it may be, is only a secondary responsibility, which has grafted itself, like a hideous parasite, upon a secular tradition, which is a Christian tradition. How can one forget that Christianity, chiefly from the eleventh century, has employed against Jews a policy of degradation and of pogroms, which has been extended—among certain Christian people—into contemporary history, which can be observed still alive to-day in most Catholic Poland, and of which the Hitlerian system has been only a copy, atrociously perfected.

Even in countries where pogroms are unknown, it was the coldness, the 22
indifference of the average man which made the Jewish drama in Europe possible. "I am convinced," wrote Pierre van Paassen, "that Hitler neither could nor would have done to the Jewish people what he has done . . . if we had not actively prepared the way for him by our own unfriendly attitude to the Jews, by our selfishness and by the anti-Semitic teaching in our churches and schools."

The way was prepared by a hatred which has a long history. The 23
inoculation of the poison began long ago in the nurseries of Christendom.

Millions of children heard about Jews for the first time when they were told the story of how Christ was killed by wicked men; killed by the Jews; crucified by the Jews. And the next thing they learned was that God had punished these wicked men and had cursed the whole of their nation for all time, so that they had become outcasts and were unfit to associate with Christians. When these children grew up, some of them quarreled among themselves about the meaning of the word of Christ and about the story of his life, death and resurrection; and others were Christians only in name; but most of them retained enough Christianity to continue hating the perfidious people, the Christ-killers, the deicide [i.e., god-murdering] race.

Although the popular tradition that "the Jews" crucified Christ goes 24
back to the beginnings of the Christian Church, no justification for it can be found in the New Testament. St. Matthew, St. Mark and St. Luke all took special care to impress upon their readers the fact that the Jewish people, their own people, were not responsible for, and were for the most part ignorant of, the events which led up to the apprehension, the trial and the condemnation of Christ. St. Matthew's account of what happened does not provide any opportunity for people to differ about his meaning. He states quite clearly in his twenty-sixth chapter that "the Jews" had nothing to do with the plot against Christ. He explains who the conspirators were, and why they had to do their work in secret. "Then were gathered together the Chief Priests and the Ancients of the people into the court of the High Priest who is called Caiphas. And they consulted together that by subtlety they might apprehend Jesus and put him to death." Secrecy was essential to the plans of the plotters because they "feared the multitude" (Matthew XXI:46). They were afraid that "the Jews" might find out what was brewing and start a riot.

The plot which ended on Calvary began to take shape for the first time 25
at that gathering in the court of Caiphas. These men were engaged upon an enterprise which they knew would not meet with public approval. They had no mandate from the Jewish people for what they were about to do. They did not represent the two or three million Jews who at that time lived in Palestine, or another million who lived in Egypt, or the millions more who were scattered all over the Roman Empire. At least three-quarters of all these people lived and died without ever hearing the name of Christ.

The conspirators did not even represent the wishes of the Jewish popu- 26
lation in and around Jerusalem. They were afraid, explained Matthew, of arresting Jesus "on the festival day, lest there should be a tumult among the people."

They had to act promptly; they had to avoid publicity. They employed 27
the crowd of idlers and ruffians which can be always collected for an evil purpose, to provide a democratic covering for what they proposed to do. This crowd formed a majority of the people present at the trial; these were the men who, when Pilate, the pioneer of appeasement, tried to save Christ from their fury, replied with the fateful words which Matthew recorded in the twenty-seventh chapter of his Gospel: "And the whole people answering said: 'His blood be upon us and upon our children.' " Although "the whole people," as Matthew explained, meant only the people present "who had been persuaded by the High Priest and the Ancients" (XXVII:20), his text has been used for centuries by countless Christian preachers as a stimulant to hate and an excuse for anti-Jewish pogroms. "O cursed race!" thundered Bossuet from his pulpit, "your prayer will be answered only too effectively; that blood will pursue you even unto your remotest descendants, until the Lord, weary at last of vengeance, will be mindful, at the end of time, of your miserable remnant."

St. Mark, also, records that the Jewish people had nothing to do with 28
the plot and that if they had known about it they would have expressed violent disapproval. "The Chief Priests and the Pharisees sought how they

might destroy him. For they feared him because the whole multitude was in admiration of his doctrine" (XI:18). "They sought to lay hands upon him, but they feared the people" (XII:12). They sought to lay hold on him and kill him, but they said, "not on the festival day, lest there should be a tumult among the people" (XIV:2).

St. Luke tells the same story with the same emphasis. "And the Chief Priests and the Scribes, and the rulers of the people, sought to destroy him. And they found not what to do to him; for all the people were very attentive to hear him" (XIX:47, 48). "The Chief Priests and the Scribes sought to lay hands on him . . . but they feared the people" (XX:19). "And the Chief Priests and the Scribes sought how they might put Jesus to death; but they feared the people" (XXII:2). 29

This Christian tradition, which made "the Jews" responsible for the death of Christ, first took shape in the Fourth Gospel. St. John deals with the historical beginnings of the Christian Church even more fully than with the ending of the era which preceded the foundation of Christianity. Unlike the other evangelists, he wrote as one outside the Jewish world, as one hostile to it. He was already disassimilated. His Gospel contains the first hint of hostility, the first suggestion of a religious Judaeophobia. He almost invariably employs the phrase "the Jews" when the context shows, and the other evangelists confirm, that he is referring to the action or to the opinions of the High Priests and the Ancients. 30

Whereas Matthew, Mark and Luke all wrote as if they had foreseen, and were trying to refute in advance, the accusation which would be brought against their fellow-countrymen, John, by his repeated use of the phrase "the Jews," puts into the mind of his readers the idea that they were all guilty. Although Matthew, for instance, says that when Jesus healed the man with a withered hand on the Sabbath, "the Pharisees made a consultation how they might destroy him," John, reporting a similar incident, indicts, not the Pharisees, but "the Jews": "*The Jews* therefore said to him that was healed: it is not lawful for thee to take up thy bed . . . therefore did *the Jews* persecute Jesus because he did these things on the Sabbath" (V:10, 16). 31

When John tells the story of the blind man, he begins by relating what the Pharisees said, but after the man received his sight his parents are reported to have "feared *the Jews,*" although it is obvious from the context that they feared the Pharisees. In the same chapter, John wrote that "*the Jews* had agreed among themselves that if any man should confess him to be the Christ, he should be put out of the synagogue." This agreement had been reached, not by the Jews, but by the Chief Priests and the Ancients. In the tenth chapter which deals with the action and behavior of this political group, we read that 32

> a dissension rose again among *the Jews* . . . and many of them said: He hath a devil and is mad . . . In Solomon's Porch *the Jews* therefore came to him and said to him . . . If thou be the Christ tell us plainly . . . *The Jews* then took up stones to stone him . . . *The Jews* answered him—For a good work we stone thee not, but for blasphemy.

John was more careful in his choice of words when he described the details of the crucifixion. He laid special emphasis on the fact that Christ was crucified, not by the Jews, but by Roman soldiers. "The soldiers therefore, when they had crucified him took his garments . . . and also his coat . . . they said to one another: Let us not cut it, but let us cast lots for it . . . and the soldiers indeed did these things" (XIX:23, 24). Nevertheless, in John's story of the apprehension, trial and death of Christ, responsibility is laid, as much as inference can lay it, on the whole Jewish people; a prominence is given to the action of "the Jews" which the events as recorded by the other evangelists do not justify. 33

Père Lagrange suggested that John made use of the phrase "the Jews," as a literary device to save constant repetition of the words "High Priests and Pharisees." It is a pity that this interpretation of John's meaning did not occur to any of the early Fathers. When Origen wrote at the beginning of the fourth century that "the Jews . . . nailed Christ to the cross," he also may have meant something different from what he said—but for many centuries his words were taken as literally true by all Christendom. And consequently, as an English historian in our own time has admitted, "The crime of a handful of priests and elders in Jerusalem was visited by the Christian Churches upon the whole Jewish race." 34

This tradition has been handed on without much respect for the actual facts as related in the Gospels. Thus, in the thirteenth century, a pious monk, Jacques de Vitry, went to the Holy Land, visited the site of Calvary and sat in meditation, as he recorded in his Chronicle, "on the very spot where *the Jews* divided the garments of Christ, and for his tunic cast lots." 35

. . .

Margery Kempe, a slightly later visionary . . . , in her description of the Passion [i.e., the suffering and crucifixion], which she imagined she had actually witnessed, followed the common conviction that Jews had nailed Christ to the cross. "Sche beheld how the cruel Jewys leydyn his precyows body to the Crosse and sithyn tokyn a long nayle . . . and wyth gret vilnes and cruelnes thei dreuyn it thorw hys hande" [She beheld how the cruel Jews laid his precious body to the Cross and then took a long nail . . . and with great villainy and cruelty they drove it through his hand]. Pictures of Jews hammering in the nails helped to encourage both hatred and piety. A writer at the beginning of the sixteenth century mentions "a Church where there was placed a Jew, of wood, before the Saviour, grasping a hammer." 36

Pious ingenuity reached a new peak in Spain where, in the first quarter of the eighteenth century, two hundred years after all the Jews had been expelled, hatred continued to flourish alongside Christian faith and Christian superstition. A collection of the fables popular in the Middle Ages, printed in 1728, entitled *Centinela Contra Judios,* revived the belief that certain Jews, who were "born with worms in their mouth . . . were descended from a Jewess who ordered the locksmith who made the nails to crucify Christ to make the points blunt so that the pain of crucifixion would be greater." In the seventeenth century a zealous Catholic who was trying to convert Spinoza asked him to 37 remember "the terrible and unspeakably severe punishments by which the Jews were reduced to the last stages of misery and calamity because they were the authors of Christ's crucifixion."

In order to fortify these traditions, Christian commentators tended increasingly to ignore the obvious meaning of the Gospel texts and sometimes substituted the phrase "the Jews" where John himself had written "the High Priests and the Pharisees." 38

. . .

In Russia popular Christianity produced a pattern of hate similar to that of Western Europe. When the Czarina Elizabeth (1741–1761) was asked to admit Jews into the country for economic reasons, she replied: "I do not wish to obtain any benefits from the enemies of Christ." More than a hundred years later, in 1890, when Alexander III was shown the draft of an official report recommending some relaxation of the oppression from which the Jews of his empire were suffering, he noted in the margin: "But we must not forget that the Jews crucified Christ." 39

. . .

From the earliest times to the present day, readers of the Fourth Gospel, with rare exceptions, have taken the phrase "the Jews" in its literal sense without any shading of meaning. Consequently the whole literature of Christendom has contributed throughout the centuries to consolidate a tradition not sanctioned by the text of the Synoptic Gospels—one that has brought immeasurable suffering upon countless numbers of innocent human beings: the tradition that "the Jewish nation condemned Christ to be crucified." Joseph Klausner writes: 40

> The Jews, *as a nation,* were far less guilty of the death of Jesus than the Greeks, as a nation, were guilty of the death of Socrates; but who now would think of avenging the blood of Socrates the Greek upon his countrymen, the present Greek race? Yet these nineteen hundred years past, the world has gone on avenging the blood of Jesus the Jew upon his countrymen, the Jews, who have already paid the penalty, and still go on paying the penalty, in rivers and torrents of blood.

The extent of Jewish responsibility for the apprehension, trial and death of Christ was defined by the highest authority of the Christian Church, St. Peter, whose judgment corrects the bias shown, a generation later, in the Fourth Gospel. The first papal pronouncement on this question was addressed by St. Peter to "Ye men of Israel," a gathering which had assembled in "the Porch which is called Solomon's"; it was addressed to those men only, in that place, and at that time. St. Peter did not acquit these men of guilt; he knew that they had taken some active part in the plot and at the trial; they were, he told them, accessories to the crime. But the final words he used have often been ignored: "And now, brethren, I know you did it through ignorance; as did also your rulers." 41

Ignorance, defined by Maimonides as "the want of knowledge respect- 42 ing things the knowledge of which can be obtained," is acceptable as an excuse only when it is not culpable. Abelard, in the twelfth century, may have extended too widely the proposition that where there is ignorance there can be no sin, when he said that the rulers of Israel acted "out of zeal for their law," and should therefore be absolved from all guilt. Christian tradition, especially in the early centuries, practically ignored St. Peter's statement that the "rulers" acted through ignorance. St. John Chrysostom, indeed, flatly contradicted St. Peter when he wrote that "the Jews . . . erred not ignorantly but with full knowledge." Whatever degree of guilt the "rulers" may have incurred, there is surely no justification for excluding them from the benefit of the petition and the judgment of Christ—"Father, forgive them for they know not what they do" (Luke XXIII:34). In the Gospel text these words refer quite clearly to the Roman soldiers, and not to the Jews.

The belief current in the Middle Ages which Abelard attacked and St. 43
Bernard defended was that "the Jews" were all guilty; that they had acted with deliberate malice; that their guilt was shared by the whole Jewish people, for all time, and that they, and their children's children to the last generation, were condemned to live in slavery as the servants of Christian princes. That was not the doctrine of St. Peter. If Christians had always remembered his words, the history of the Jews in their long exile would perhaps have been very different, and the civilization of the West might not have witnessed the degradation of humanity which was achieved by the Germans in their death camps and gas chambers.

In spite of St. Peter's judgment the popular Christian doctrine has al- 44
ways been that anyone, whether pagan or Christian, who has at any time persecuted, tortured or massacred Jews has acted as an instrument of Divine wrath. A chronicler, writing in the early years of the thirteenth century, admired the patience of God, who "after the Jews had crucified Our Lord, waited for forty-eight years before chastising them." According to Fleury, who wrote, in the first quarter of the eighteenth century, an enormous and still useful ecclesiastical history, God began to take reprisals against the Jews in the year 38 of the Christian era. In that year, anti-Jewish riots broke out in Alexandria. The rioters were secretly encouraged by Flaccus, the Roman commissioner in Egypt, who took no effective measures to prevent the mob from burning down synagogues, breaking into Jewish shops, and scattering the merchandise into the streets of the city. Flaccus showed his "neutrality" by attempting to disarm, not the rioters, but their victims. "He had searches made in the houses of the Jews on the pretext of disarming the nation, and several women were taken away and tormented when they refused to eat swine's flesh." A great number of Jews were murdered, and their bodies dragged through the streets. "In this manner," wrote Fleury in 1732, "divine vengeance began to be manifested against the Jews."

The sacking of Jerusalem and the destruction of the Temple, in the year 45
70, when more than a million people were massacred with a brutality to which the world has once again become accustomed, were regarded by many pious Christians as part of God's plan of revenge. "The Jews," wrote Sulpicius

Severus, "were thus punished and exiled throughout the whole world, for no other account than for the impious hands they laid upon Christ." This interpretation of the event has been repeated for centuries.

. . .

There are therefore still some people who believe that the Jews were 46
cursed out of Palestine because they had behaved in a manner displeasing to God. If nations were liable to be dispossessed for such a reason, very few of them would enjoy security of tenure. "The Curse," as J.-P. Sartre has recently pointed out, was "geographical."

. . .

To justify the persecution of Jews, two excuses . . . were available to 47
Christians: either the Christians were acting in self-defense, or they were carrying out the will of God. The teaching of the early Fathers made the second excuse plausible. There was no direct incitement to violence. Athanasius did not tell the people to go out and beat up Jews. But he told them that "the Jews were no longer the people of God, but rulers of Sodom and Gomorrah"; and he asked the ominous question: "What is left unfulfilled, that they should now be allowed to disbelieve with impunity?"

When St. Ambrose told his congregations that the Jewish synagogue 48
was "a house of impiety, a receptacle of folly, which God himself has condemned," no one was surprised when the people went off and set fire to one. St. Ambrose accepted responsibility for the outrage. "I declare that I set fire to the synagogue, or at least that I ordered those who did it, that there might not be a place where Christ was denied. If it be objected to me that I did not set the synagogue on fire here, I answer it began to be burnt by the judgment of God." He told the Emperor that people who burnt a synagogue ought not to be punished, such action being a just reprisal because Jews, in the reign of the Emperor Julian, had burnt down Christian churches. In any case, he added, since the synagogues contained nothing of any value, "what could the Jews lose by the fire?" When they complained to the Emperor, he was indignant at their impertinence. They had no place in a court of law, he declared, because nothing they said could ever be believed. "Into what calumnies will they not break out, who, by false witness, calumniated even Christ!"

The Emperor, however, who did not approve of fire-raising propaganda, 49
endeavored to protect the synagogues from the fury of the mob. He received a letter, from an unexpected quarter, asking him to revoke the orders he had given for punishing the offenders, a letter dispatched from the top of a pillar by St. Simeon Stylites. This ascetic, who achieved distinction by living for thirty-six years on top of a pillar fifty feet high, had given up, as G. F. Abbott remarked, "all worldly luxuries except Jew-hatred." He is not the only saint who was unable to renounce the consolations of anti-Semitism.

In the fourth century the natural goodness of men, and even saintliness, 50
did not always operate for the benefit of Jews. St. Gregory of Nyssa, with the eloquence for which he was famous, composed against them a comprehensive indictment:

> Slayers of the Lord, murderers of the prophets, adversaries of God, haters of God, men who show contempt for the law, foes of grace, enemies of their father's faith, advocates of the devil, brood of vipers, slanderers, scoffers, men whose minds are in darkness, leaven of the Pharisees, assembly of demons, sinners, wicked men, stoners, and haters of righteousness.

Such exaggeration may have been an offense against charity, but it is not so harmful to the soul as the modern hypocrisy which pretends that the early Christian Fathers were invariably models of proper Christian behavior. "Our duty," wrote Basnage in the seventeenth century, "is to excuse the Fathers in their Extravagance, instead of justifying them, lest such forcible Examples should authorize Modern Divines, and confirm the Hatred and Revenge of writers." 51

St. John Chrysostom, the Golden-Mouthed, one of the greatest of the Church Fathers, spent his life, in and out of the pulpit, trying to reform the world. Christian writers, of varying shades of belief, have agreed in admiring his fervent love for all mankind, in spite of the fact that he was undoubtedly a socialist. "Chrysostom," said a Protestant divine, "was one of the most eloquent of the preachers who, ever since apostolic times, have brought to men the Divine tidings of truth and love." "A bright cheerful gentle soul," wrote Cardinal Newman, "a sensitive heart, a temperament open to emotion and impulse; and all this elevated, refined, transformed by the touch of heaven,—such was St. John Chrysostom." 52

Yet in this kindly gentle soul of the preacher who brought to men the tidings of truth and love, was hidden a hard core of hatred. "It must be admitted," wrote an honest French hagiographer, "that, in his homilies against the Jews, he allowed himself to be unduly carried away by an occasional access of passion." 53

A great deal more than this must be admitted.

The violence of the language used by St. John Chrysostom in his homilies against the Jews has never been exceeded by any preacher whose sermons have been recorded. Allowances must, no doubt, be made for the custom of the times, for passionate zeal, and for the fear that some tender shoots of Christian faith might be chilled by too much contact with Jews. But no amount of allowance can alter the fact that these homilies filled the minds of Christian congregations with a hatred which was transmitted to their children, and to their children's children, for many generations. These homilies, moreover, were used for centuries, in schools and in seminaries where priests were taught to preach, with St. John Chrysostom as their model—where priests were taught to hate, with St. John Chrysostom as their model. 54

There was no "touch of heaven" in the language used by St. John Chrysostom when he was preaching about Jewish synagogues. "The synagogue," he said, "is worse than a brothel . . . it is the den of scoundrels and the repair of wild beasts . . . the temple of demons devoted to idolatrous cults . . . the refuge of brigands and debauchees, and the cavern of devils." 55

The synagogue, he told his congregations in another sermon, was "a criminal assembly of Jews . . . a place of meeting for the assassins of Christ . . . a house worse than a drinking shop . . . a den of thieves; a house of ill fame, a dwelling of iniquity, the refuge of devils, a gulf and abyss of perdition." And he concluded, exhausted at length by his eloquence: "Whatever name even more horrible could be found, will never be worse than the synagogue deserves." 56

These sermons have not been forgotten; nor has contempt for Judaism diminished among the Christian congregations since they were first preached more than fifteen hundred years ago. 57

. . .

In reply to some Christians who had maintained that Jewish synagogues might be entitled to respect because in them were kept the writings of Moses and the prophets, St. John Chrysostom answered: Not at all! This was a reason for hating them more, because they use these books, but willfully misunderstand their meaning. "As for me, I hate the synagogue. . . . I hate the Jews for the same reason." 58

It is not difficult to imagine the effect such sermons must have had upon congregations of excitable Orientals. Not only every synagogue, Chrysostom told them, but every Jew, was a temple of the devil. "I would say the same things about their souls." And he said a great deal more. It was unfit, he proclaimed, for Christians to associate with a people who had fallen into a condition lower than the vilest animals. "Debauchery and drunkenness had brought them to the level of the lusty goat and the pig. They know only one thing, to satisfy their stomachs, to get drunk, to kill and beat each other up like stage villains and coachmen." 59

. . .

When the usual allowances have been made for the manners of the time, pious zeal, oriental imagery, and for any context, setting, or background which might be urged in mitigation, these are words difficult to justify. This condemnation of the people of Israel, in the name of God, was not forgotten. It helped to strengthen the tradition of hate handed on through the Dark Ages and welcomed by mediaeval Christendom, a tradition which has disfigured the whole history of Western Europe. 60

For many centuries the Jews listened to the echo of those three words of St. John Chrysostom, the Golden-Mouthed: "God hates you." 61

Questions for Discussion

1. There are some passages in the chapter that might be misunderstood because Hay speaks with "tongue in cheek," using irony: for example, "The German method of burying people in communal pits was a great improvement on the old system" (¶13) or "most of them retained enough

Christianity to continue hating the perfidious people, the Christ-killers" (¶23). What is Hay really saying with these words? What does he gain by seeming to say something else? How many other ironic passages can you find?

2. Occasionally Hay addresses his reader in direct form (for example, the opening phrase of ¶21). Who *is* this reader? Why do you think Hay breaks the conventions of most scholarly writing to become personal in this way?
3. People are sure to respond to this kind of writing in diverse ways, depending on their prior beliefs. Christians are challenged directly to reappraise their traditions. In a sense all other readers are bystanders or eavesdroppers, watching Christians debate about a great wrong that Hay accuses them of having committed. Jewish readers, in contrast, may find the piece too painful to read because of the gruesome details about the Holocaust. Those who are neither Jewish nor Christian may initially feel less concerned—until they examine their own prejudices and reconsider the history of other atrocities that have been committed by groups they are affiliated with. It is important in discussing matters of this kind to recognize that we are *all* implicated in human prejudice, past and present. A college classroom is a rare place where we can discuss such matters without fearing reprisal from authorities or rival gangs, and we should be willing to risk talking frankly with each other.

   With these difficulties and opportunities in mind, see now whether you and your classmates can discuss your deepest prejudices about groups without falling into a pointless or angry shouting match. Do you assume, with or without what you consider to be good evidence, that people of any one group are going to be on "the level of the lusty goat and the pig," that they will "know only one thing, to satisfy their stomachs, to get drunk, to kill and beat each other up like stage villains" (¶59)?
4. If in discussing question 3 you have found strong hostility between two or more groups represented in the class, organize a discussion by assigning contrary roles—for example, have a Christian defend the case for Jews, a Jew speak for American blacks or Indians, a person of French descent defend the English, and so on. Your task, if you take one of these roles, is to show why the prejudice against "your" group is absurd or cruel or mistaken. Try to make your argument as free of name-calling as possible, depending instead on whatever evidence and reasons seem compelling.
5. Some classes have tried the experiment of "practicing" discrimination against a given group for a day or two—a prejudicial treatment invented for the occasion: "No one with blue eyes will be allowed to speak until Friday," "Everyone taller than 5 feet 10 inches must arrive 10 minutes early," and so on. If you are by now fairly easy with each other in class discussion, try inventing such a group (for example, people not from a given part of the country or state, people from a certain kind of school, or people who intend to be science or English majors). Then "give them the treatment." Make the kinds of jokes about them (or about you, if

you're one of the victims) that people make about minority groups. Seat them at the back of the room or in specially created "ghettos," "reservations," or "barrios." Require them to address the rest of the class as "ma'am" and "sir." Do this as long as the victims can stand it and then discuss how it felt, to both the oppressors and the oppressed.

Suggested Essay Topics

1. If you have ever been the victim of injustice based on someone's seeing you as a member of a condemned group, write an account of how it happened and how it felt. (Decide in advance whether you are addressing readers who are already sympathetic to your cause or readers who may share the feelings of your persecutors.) You will have noticed that Hay achieves some of his most powerful effects by using vivid stories. Don't hesitate to be just as vivid in your use of the details of your story.
2. If you have ever committed what you now consider to be an injustice against someone as a result of seeing that person as a member of a given group rather than as an individual, write an account of the event describing how it felt both at the time and when you later decided that you had been unjust. Before you write, study topic 1.

8

WOMEN AND MEN

From Sexism to Feminism

EPIGRAPHS FROM THE SEXIST TRADITION

There is a good principle which created order, light and man,
and an evil principle which created chaos, darkness and woman.
Pythagoras

Women, then, are only children of a larger growth:
they have an entertaining tattle, and sometimes wit;
but for solid reasoning good-sense, I never knew
in my life one that had it, or who reasoned or acted consequentially
for four and twenty hours together.
Lord Chesterfield

Man is the only male animal who beats his female.
He is therefore the most brutal of all males—unless woman is the most
unbearable of all females, which, after all, is quite plausible.
Georges Courteline

Beat thy wife every morning; if thou know not why, she doth.
Arab saying

Frailty, thy name is woman!
Shakespeare (spoken by Hamlet, about his mother)

The world is full of care, much like unto a bubble;
Women and care, and care and women, and women and care
and trouble.
Reverend Nathaniel Ward
(attributed to a lady at the Court of the Queen of Bohemia)

Ever hear of a woman loving a poor man?
Pagnol

EPIGRAPHS FROM THE FEMINIST TRADITION

All that has been written by men about women must be suspect,
for they are both judge and interested party.
Poulain La Barre

So the image of woman [in advertising] appears plastered on every surface
imaginable, smiling interminably. An apple pie evokes
a glance of tender beatitude, a washing machine causes hilarity,
a cheap box of chocolates brings forth meltingly
joyous gratitude, a Coke is the cause of a rictus of
unutterable brilliance, even a new stick-on bandage
is saluted by a smirk of satisfaction.
Germaine Greer

Total masculinity is an ideal of the frustrated, not a fact of biology.
Harold Rosenberg

It is impossible for a sex or a class to have economic freedom
until everybody has it, and until economic freedom is attained
for everybody, there can be no real freedom for anybody.
Suzanne LaFollette

I long to hear that you have declared an independancy
[for the thirteen colonies]—and by the way in the new Code of
Laws which I suppose it will be necessary for you
to make I desire you would Remember the Ladies, and be more
generous and favorable to them than your ancestors. Do not put
such unlimited power into the hands of the Husbands.
Remember all Men would be tyrants if they could. If
perticuliar care and attention is not paid to the Laidies we are determined
to foment a Rebelion, and will not hold ourselves bound by
any Laws in which we have no voice, or Representation.
Letter from Abigail Adams to John Adams

Yes, ye lordly, ye haughty sex, our souls are by nature *equal* to
yours; the same breath of God animates, enlivens, and invigorates us.
Judith Sargent Murray

I believe that our future salvation lies in a movement
away from sexual polarization and the prison of gender
toward a world in which individual roles
and the modes of personal behavior can be freely chosen.
Carolyn Heilbrun

IDEAS IN DEBATE

Wayne C. Booth and Marshall W. Gregory
St. Thomas Aquinas
Friedrich Nietzsche
Sigmund Freud

Wayne C. Booth and Marshall W. Gregory

THE TRADITIONAL ABASEMENT OF WOMEN

Until fairly recently, almost all discussions of men and women were by men, and almost all assumed the inferiority, if not the downright viciousness, of women. Occasionally a philosopher like Plato might speculate about what would happen if women were ever given education and rights genuinely equal to those of men (see pp. 547–553), and a few wrote about women as ideal, angelic creatures, far above their wicked menfolk. But whole libraries have been written "proving" that women's intrinsic inferiority justifies social servitude.

One of the most frequently quoted documents in this tradition was Aristotle's argument, in *On the Generation of Animals,* that a woman is a "misbegotten male." In the conception of a child, the "male principle" provides, he said, a form or shape, while the "female principle" provides the matter on which the shape is imposed by the semen. If the imposition of form is successful, a male child is born. If it is a partial failure, a female child—a botched male—results. The male thus provides the "active" role, the female the "passive." According to this view, a highly convenient one for males, nature invites and justifies whatever subordination a given culture chooses to impose on women.

Aristotle was quoted by almost all theorists for about 2000 years. Jewish, Christian, and Islamic theologians borrowed and extended his arguments to buttress their teachings about how a male God founded the universe and how females, from the beginning, were either responsible for or at least symbolic of its instabilities and limitations. His influence can be seen clearly in the brief passage we quote here from Thomas Aquinas (c. 1225–1274), which itself achieved wide influence as a standard Christian way of explaining the story of Adam and Eve. The passages by Nietzsche (1844–1900) and Freud (1856–1939) show that the downgrading of women has hardly been confined to religious theorists; many a secular author has heaped abuse on women, some of it (like that of Schopenhauer, the philosopher, and Strindberg, the playwright) even more aggressively woman-hating (or *misogynistic*) than the passages we quote.

In one respect we are clearly being unjust to such wide-ranging thinkers and prolific writers as Nietzsche and Freud by quoting only snippets from them. All writers can be made to look silly, thoughtless, or incoherent by editing that disembowels their positions. Knowing this, our readers need to understand that we are not trying to take cheap shots at the writers included here. The more creative sides of their thinking are passed over. Our point is not primarily about these specific thinkers at all. We quote from Aquinas, Nietzsche, and Freud not to pillory them but to illustrate some of the content of a centuries-long tradition that precedes them, includes them, and extends far beyond them. They did not create this tradition, but they are symptomatic of it. Thus, while it may be unfair to the wider range and substance of their thought to reprint them so briefly, they help us to make a valid point about hostility to women in Western culture. When feminists argue in favor of fairness and equality for women, their opponent is not one writer or a few male chauvinists but rather a whole set of misogynistic attitudes that thinkers like those reprinted here have helped energize and perpetuate.

Feminist writers of recent times, both male and female, have had to write under the immense pressure of this tradition of contempt, and they have often shown a sense of frustration in trying to deal with it. How does one find arguments to combat opinions that seem so wrongheaded yet deep-seated? How does one argue with dogmas uttered by authors who otherwise seem fair-minded and sane? It is no wonder that some writers find it impossible to remain cool and dispassionate in the face of past and present abuses.

The truth may be that there are no decisive arguments that could prove either natural inferiority or natural equality. Like arguments about religious belief, discussion of such matters depends on our deepest assumptions about life and on our experience. Such arguments are never settled once and for all; experience is too rich and diverse for that. But we need no resolution of debate to tell us how important is the quest in modern times for a new way of thinking and talking that will no longer debase or ignore one half of humanity.

St. Thomas Aquinas

THE PRODUCTION OF WOMAN

Whether Woman Should Have Been Made in the First Production of Things

"Question 92" from the *Summa Theologica* (1265–1272). There are four "articles" in the Question, of which we reprint part of the first.

We proceed thus to the First Article:—

Objection 1. It would seem that woman should not have been made in the first production of things. For the Philosopher [Aristotle] says that the *female is a misbegotten male.* But nothing misbegotten or defective should have been in the first production of things. Therefore woman should not have been made at that first production. 1

Obj. 2. Further, subjection and limitation were a result of sin, for to the woman was it said after sin (Genesis iii. 16): *Thou shalt be under the man's power;* and Gregory says that, *Where there is no sin, there is no inequality.* But woman is naturally of less strength and dignity than man, *for the agent is always more honorable than the patient,* as Augustine says. Therefore woman should not have been made in the first production of things before sin. 2

Obj. 3. Further, occasions of sin should be cut off. But God foresaw that woman would be an occasion of sin to man. Therefore He should not have made woman. 3

On the contrary, It is written (Genesis ii. 18): *It is not good for man to be alone; let us make him a helper like to himself.* 4

I answer that, It was necessary for woman to be made, as the Scripture says, as *a helper* to man; not, indeed, as a helpmate in other works, as some say, since man can be more efficiently helped by another man in other works; but as a helper in the work of generation. This can be made clear if we observe the mode of generation carried out in various living things. Some living things do not possess in themselves the power of generation, but are generated by an agent of another species; and such are those plants and animals which are generated, without seed, from suitable matter through the active power of the heavenly bodies. Others possess the active and passive generative power together, as we see in plants which are generated from seed. For the noblest vital function in plants is generation, and so we observe that in these the active power of generation invariably accompanies the passive power. Among perfect animals, the active power of generation belongs to the male sex, and the passive power to the female. And as among animals there is a vital operation nobler than generation, to which their life is principally directed, so it happens that the male sex is not found in continual union with the female in perfect animals, but only at the time of coition; so that we may consider that by coition the male and female are one, as in plants they are always united, even though in some cases one of them preponderates, and in some the other. But man is further ordered to a still nobler work of life, and that is intellectual operation. 5

Therefore there was greater reason for the distinction of these two powers in man; so that the female should be produced separately from the male, and yet that they should be carnally united for generation. Therefore directly after the formation of woman, it was said: *And they shall be two in one flesh* (Genesis ii. 24).

Reply Obj. 1. As regards the individual nature, woman is defective and misbegotten, for the active power in the male seed tends to the production of a perfect likeness according to the masculine sex; while the production of woman comes from defect in the active power, or from some material indisposition, or even from some external influence, such as that of a south wind, which is moist, as the Philosopher observes. On the other hand, as regards universal human nature, woman is not misbegotten, but is included in nature's intention as directed to the work of generation. Now the universal intention of nature depends on God, Who is the universal Author of nature. Therefore, in producing nature, God formed not only the male but also the female. 6

Reply Obj. 2. Subjection is twofold. One is servile, by virtue of which a superior makes use of a subject for his own benefit; and this kind of subjection began after sin. There is another kind of subjection, which is called economic or civil, whereby the superior makes use of his subjects for their own benefit and good; and this kind of subjection existed even before sin. For the good of order would have been wanting in the human family if some were not governed by others wiser than themselves. So by such a kind of subjection woman is naturally subject to man, because in man the discernment of reason predominates. 7

Friedrich Nietzsche

THE UGLINESS OF WOMAN

Our title for part 7, "Our Virtues," aphorism 232, of *Beyond Good and Evil* (1886).

Woman wants to become self-reliant—and for that reason she is beginning to enlighten men about "woman as such": *this* is one of the worst developments of the general *uglification* of Europe. For what must these clumsy attempts of women at scientific self-exposure bring to light! Woman has much reason for shame; so much pedantry, superficiality, schoolmarmishness, petty presumption, petty licentiousness and immodesty lies concealed in woman—one only needs to study her behavior with children!—and so far all this was at bottom best repressed and kept under control by *fear* of man. Woe when "the eternally boring in woman"*—she is rich in that!—is permitted to venture forth! When 1

*Allusion to "the Eternal-Feminine" in the penultimate line of Goethe's *Faust.*

she begins to unlearn thoroughly and on principle her prudence and art—of grace, of play, of chasing away worries, of lightening burdens and taking things lightly—and her subtle aptitude for agreeable desires!

Even now female voices are heard which—holy Aristophanes!—are frightening: they threaten with medical explicitness what woman *wants* from man, first and last. Is it not in the worst taste when woman sets about becoming scientific that way? So far enlightenment of this sort was fortunately man's affair, man's lot—we remained "among ourselves" in this; and whatever women write about "woman," we may in the end reserve a healthy suspicion whether woman really *wants* enlightenment about herself—whether she *can* will it— 2

Unless a woman seeks a new adornment for herself that way—I do think adorning herself is part of the Eternal-Feminine?—she surely wants to inspire fear of herself—perhaps she seeks mastery. But she does not *want* truth: what is truth to woman? From the beginning, nothing has been more alien, repugnant, and hostile to woman than truth—her great art is the lie, her highest concern is mere appearance and beauty. Let us men confess it: we honor and love precisely *this* art and *this* instinct in woman—we who have a hard time and for our relief like to associate with beings under whose hands, eyes, and tender follies our seriousness, our gravity and profundity almost appear to us like folly. 3

Finally I pose the question: has ever a woman conceded profundity to a woman's head, or justice to a woman's heart? And is it not true that on the whole "woman" has so far been despised most by woman herself—and by no means by us? 4

We men wish that woman should not go on compromising herself through enlightenment—just as it was man's thoughtfulness and consideration for woman that found expression in the church decree: *mulier taceat in ecclesia* [woman should be silent in church]! It was for woman's good when Napoleon gave the all too eloquent Madame de Staël to understand: *mulier taceat in politicis* [woman should be silent in politics]! And I think it is a real friend of women that counsels them today: *mulier taceat de muliere* [woman should be silent about woman]! 5

Sigmund Freud

FEMININITY

From lecture 33 of *New Introductory Lectures on Psycho-analysis* (1933).

As you hear, then, we ascribe a castration complex to women as well. And for good reasons, though its content cannot be the same as with boys. In the latter the castration complex arises after they have learnt from the sight of 1 the female genitals that the organ which they value so highly need not necessarily accompany the body. At this the boy recalls to mind the threats he brought on himself by his doings with that organ, he begins to give credence to them and falls under the influence of fear of castration, which will be the most powerful motive force in his subsequent development. The castration complex of girls is also started by the sight of the genitals of the other sex. They at once notice the difference and, it must be admitted, its significance too. They feel seriously wronged, often declare that they want to "have something like it too," and fall a victim to "envy for the penis," which will leave ineradicable traces on their development and the formation of their character and which will not be surmounted in even the most favourable cases without a severe expenditure of psychical energy. The girl's recognition of the fact of her being without a penis does not by any means imply that she submits to the fact easily. On the contrary, she continues to hold on for a long time to the wish to get something like it herself and she believes in that possibility for improbably long years; and analysis can show that, at a period when knowledge of reality has long since rejected the fulfilment of the wish as unattainable, it persists in the unconscious and retains a considerable cathexis of energy. The wish to get the longed-for penis eventually in spite of everything may contribute to the motives that drive a mature woman to analysis, and what she may reasonably expect from analysis—a capacity, for instance, to carry on an intellectual profession—may often be recognized as a sublimated modification of this repressed wish.

One cannot very well doubt the importance of envy for the penis. You 2
may take it as an instance of male injustice if I assert that envy and jealousy play an even greater part in the mental life of women than of men. It is not that I think these characteristics are absent in men or that I think they have no other roots in women than envy for the penis; but I am inclined to attribute their greater amount in women to this latter influence.

. . .

The discovery that she is castrated is a turning-point in a girl's growth. 3
Three possible lines of development start from it: one leads to sexual inhibition or to neurosis, the second to change of character in the sense of a masculinity complex, the third, finally, to normal femininity. We have learnt a fair amount, though not everything, about all three.

The essential content of the first is as follows: the little girl has hitherto 4
lived in a masculine way, has been able to get pleasure by the excitation of her clitoris and has brought this activity into relation with her sexual wishes directed towards her mother, which are often active ones; now, owing to the influence of her penis-envy, she loses her enjoyment in her phallic sexuality. Her self-love is mortified by the comparison with the boy's far superior equipment and in consequence she renounces her masturbatory satisfaction from her clitoris, repudiates her love for her mother and at the same time not infrequently represses a good part of her sexual trends in general. No doubt her turning away from her mother does not occur all at once, for to begin with the girl regards her castration as an individual misfortune, and only gradually

extends it to other females and finally to her mother as well. Her love was directed to her *phallic* mother; with the discovery that her mother is castrated it becomes possible to drop her as an object, so that the motives for hostility, which have long been accumulating, gain the upper hand. This means, therefore, that as a result of the discovery of women's lack of a penis they are debased in value for girls just as they are for boys and later perhaps for men.

Questions for Discussion

1. Restate Aristotle's position about the biological inferiority of women in your own words. Do you know people who take the view that men are "naturally" superior in some ways to women? What traits or abilities do these people ascribe to men and women? Do any of the assumptions about innate masculine and feminine traits match your own experience and observation? If so, which ones? If not, how do you react when you find yourself placed within categories that don't fit?
2. Is Nietzsche's denigration of women foreign to you, or is it the same denigration you hear nowadays, only less antagonistically and abrasively stated? In paragraph 4, for example, Nietzsche claims that " 'woman' has so far been despised most by woman herself." While this is strong language, is its content any different from that of the commonly bandied cliché that women are catty about other women? Can Nietzsche's other insults be restated in contemporary terms? If so, what does this say about contemporary views of women?
3. Ask the teacher to appoint three or four members of the class to ask various members of the psychology department whether they think Freud's notion of "penis envy" is taken seriously today by psychoanalysts and what they themselves think of the notion. Report back to the class.
4. Have two or three members of the class examine the wording of the Catholic marriage ceremony (or different versions of it) to see whether any traces of Aquinas's views about the relationship between men and women are reflected in it. Compare the Catholic ceremony to a few Protestant versions. Are there any interesing differences with respect to the roles of men and women?

Suggested Essay Topics

1. Read chapters 3 and 4 ("Biological Facts and Social Consequences" and "Who Said 'The Inferior Sex'?") of *The Natural Superiority of Women* by Ashley Montagu (Macmillan, 1952). Using Montagu as a starting point, but not limiting yourself to him if you have other scholars or scientists to

cite (Montagu offers an annotated bibliography at the end of his book), construct your own rebuttal to Aristotle's views of the natural inferiority of women.

2. In a small notebook that you should carry around with you until this assignment is completed, record for a two-week period all the instances in which you hear people expressing belief in "natural" differences between men and women. Whether the remarks you overhear are insulting or not, comment on the extent to which you think they are inaccurate, misleading, or limiting for either sex, and address your essay to people whose (perhaps unseen) prejudices you would like to make visible.

Margaret Mead

Margaret Mead (1901–1978) first became famous in the 1930s as an anthropologist. Her book Growing Up in New Guinea *remains a classic in its field, despite recent controversy about her method. Over the years she acquired an international reputation not only as an anthropologist but also as a commentator on human affairs in general, especially on issues like environmental pollution, women's rights, and the threat of nuclear war. A good example of her work of this kind is* A Rap on Race, *which she wrote with James Baldwin in the 1960s.*

In the following selection from her autobiography, Blackberry Winter, *Mead discusses how her mother's and grandmother's examples taught her early in life that "the mind is not sex-typed." According to Mead's account, her grandmother's stories were of crucial importance in forming her character and shaping her general view of the world. As you read, compare her account of the importance of stories with what Plato (pp. 269–273 and 276–284) and Aristotle (pp. 236–237) have to say about the roles that stories and imitation play in the formation of character.*

THE MIND IS NOT SEX-TYPED

From chapter 5, "On Being a Granddaughter," of *Blackberry Winter: My Earlier Years* (1972). The title is ours.

Grandma had no sense at all of ever having been handicapped by being a woman. I think she played as strong a role among her brothers and sisters as her elder brother, who was a famous Methodist preacher. Between them they kept up an active relationship with their parents in Winchester and, returning often for visits, they supervised, stimulated, and advised the less adventurous members of the family. This has now become my role among some of the descendants of my grandmother's sisters, who still live in various small towns and large cities in Ohio. 1

Grandma was a wonderful storyteller, and she had a set of priceless, individually tailored anecdotes with which American grandparents of her day brought up children. There was the story of the little boys who had been taught absolute, quick obedience. One day when they were out on the prairie, their father shouted, "Fall down on your faces!" They did, and the terrible prairie fire swept over them *and they weren't hurt.* There was also the story of three boys at school, each of whom received a cake sent from home. One hoarded his, and the mice ate it; one ate all of his, and he got sick; and who do you think had the best time?—why, of course, the one who shared his cake with his friends. Then there was the little boy who ran away from home and stayed away all day. When he came home after supper, he found the family sitting around the fire and nobody said a word. Not a word. Finally, he couldn't stand it anymore and said, "Well, I see you have the same old cat!" 2

And there was one about a man who was so lazy he would rather starve than work. Finally, his neighbors decided to bury him alive. On the way to the cemetery they met a man with a wagon-load of unshelled corn. He asked where they were going. When they told him that they were going to bury that no-good man alive, the owner of the corn took pity on him and said, "I tell you what. I will give you this load of corn. All you will have to do is shell it." But the lazy man said, "Drive on, boys!"

Because Grandma did so many things with her hands, a little girl could always tag after her, talking and asking questions and listening. Side by side with Grandma, I learned to peel apples, to take the skin off tomatoes by plunging them into scalding water, to do simple embroidery stitches, and to knit. Later, during World War I, when I had to cook for the whole household, she taught me a lot about cooking, for example, just when to add a lump of butter, something that always had to be concealed from Mother, who thought that cooking with butter was extravagant. 3

While I followed her about as she carried out the endless little household tasks that she took on, supplementing the work of the maids or doing more in between maids—and we were often in between—she told me endless tales about Winchester. She told me about her school days and about the poor children who used to beg the cores of apples from the rich children who had whole apples for lunch. She told me about Em Eiler, who pushed Aunt Lou off a rail fence into a flooded pasture lot; about Great-aunt Louisian, who could read people's minds and tell them everything they had said about her and who had been a triplet and so small when she was born that she would fit into a quart cup; about Grace, who died from riding a trotting horse too hard, which wasn't good for girls; and about the time Lida cut off Anna Louise's curls and said, "Now they won't say 'pretty little girl' anymore." My great-grandfather used to say such a long grace, she told me, that one of her most vivid memories was of standing, holding a log she had started to put on the fire, for what seemed to be hours for fear of interrupting him. All this was as real to me as if I had lived it myself. I think that if anyone had tried to repeat the Bridie Murphy case,* I could easily have impersonated, in trance, the child and girl my grandmother had been. 4

One of the stories I loved most was about the time the Confederate soldiers came through the village and shot down the flag. In the face of the danger, my grandmother's younger sister ran out and held the flag aloft. It was only another Barbara Frietchie episode and the story gained a great deal from the fact that we had learned to recite, " 'Shoot, if you must, this old gray head,/But spare your country's flag,' she said." But this particular Barbara Frietchie had been young and was my great-aunt. Later, I tried to immortalize her in a story called "A Strip of Old Glory," which was published in the Doylestown High School magazine, of which I was the editor. 5

*A celebrated case in which an American woman was alleged to have provided accounts, under hypnosis, of having lived various lives in previous states of existence, one of them as an Irish girl named Bridie Murphy.

I never saw Winchester until recently, when the town was holding its sesquicentennial celebration. I took my daughter with me, and as we walked through the streets, I looked at houses that were completely familiar. I saw the house in which my great-grandparents had lived and in which my father's cousin Cally had heard the sound of a ghostly coffin bumping on the stairs until her mother made her get down on her knees and promise never again to indulge in that strange, outlandish Aunt-Louisian kind of behavior. I saw the house in which the Bradfords had lived and where they had been such warm hosts to the next generation. And I recognized the sites of the fires. For part of the history of Winchester, a little town that never grew, is written in fire. 6

I was treated as an honored guest in a handsome house with peacocks on the lawn that had been bought by a successful man who had returned from a large city to buy the house where he had once been the stableboy. The husband of one of my cousins also was being honored for his success, and people told me how pleased they were; as a boy he had been so poor, they explained, that he had had to ride a horse bareback to school. One of the peculiarities of the little town, which was never reflected in my grandmother's stories because she saw life ethically and not in class terms, was its incredible snobbishness. This came home to me as I watched how people with strange ticks and deformities seldom seen in a city entered the house humbly in order to shake the hands of the guests of a leading citizen who now owned the garage, as once her father had owned the livery stable. 7

My grandmother was indifferent to social class, but in her stories she told me about poor people, unfortunate people, people who were better off, and no-count people who drank or gambled or deserted their wives and children. Her own family, for all their pride and their handsome noses, had a fair number of charming, no-count men in each generation and, appropriately, a fair number of women who married the same kind of men. There were a number of stern, impressive women and an occasional impressive man, but a lot of weak ones, too—that is the family picture. My cousins suspect that our great-grandfather was not a very strong character, but that he was kept in hand by our great-grandmother. 8

This indifference to social class irritated my mother, who used to complain that Grandma could get interested in the most ordinary people. Sometimes she went on a holiday to the seaside. When she came home she told us endless narratives about the lives of the ordinary people with whom she sat on the steps of the seaside hotel. This used to make Mother mutter. Grandma and Mother looked a good deal alike. They were of the same height and weight, and had similar enough features so that people often mistook them for mother and daughter. This, too, did not please Mother. 9

Mother never ceased to resent the fact that Grandma lived with us, but she gave her her due. Grandma never "interfered"—never tried to teach the children anything religious that had not previously been introduced by my mother, and in disagreements between my mother and father she always took 10 my mother's side. When my father threatened to leave my mother, Grandma told him firmly that she would stay with her and the children.

. . .

I think it was my grandmother who gave me my ease in being a woman. 11
She was unquestionably feminine—small and dainty and pretty and wholly without masculine protest or feminist aggrievement. She had gone to college when this was a very unusual thing for a girl to do, she had a firm grasp of anything she paid attention to, she had married and had a child, and she had a career of her own. All this was true of my mother, as well. But my mother was filled with passionate resentment about the condition of women, as perhaps my grandmother might have been had my grandfather lived and had she borne five children and had little opportunity to use her special gifts and training. As it was, the two women I knew best were mothers and had professional training. So I had no reason to doubt that brains were suitable for a woman. And as I had my father's kind of mind—which was also his mother's—I learned that the mind is not sex-typed.

Questions for Discussion

1. How did Mead's mother and grandmother differ in their attitudes about a woman's place in society (¶11)? Is it clear which woman Mead admires more? Is it clear which woman she prefers to use as a role model?
2. Can you tell whether Mead sympathizes more with her mother's or her grandmother's attitudes about social class (¶8–9)? Where do your own sympathies lie on this issue?
3. Does Mead sound defensive about being a woman? Does she sound masculine? Feminine? Or is this distinction simply irrelevant when talking about the workings of the intellect? From what you have read, would you predict that Mead ever gave much time to helping the feminist movement? Or would you expect her simply to have gone around it? (You can find out for sure by reading Part 3 of *Blackberry Winter.*)

Suggested Essay Topics

1. In an essay directed to the other students in your class, compare the importance of stories in Margaret Mead's childhood with the importance of such stories in your own childhood. Give an account of the kinds of stories that taught you, as the stories in Mead's background taught her, how to view issues and events in the world: the role of women, poor people, your own family history, and so on.
2. Using Mead's description of her grandmother as a model, create a corresponding portrait of someone in your own family who played a crucial role

in the formation of your character. Try to be as specific as Mead is about *how* your family member exerted influence. (You might choose to address your account to the model directly or to the other members of your family.)

Francine Frank and Frank Ashen

The struggle to rid society of various kinds of oppression requires analysis on many fronts: political, historical, theological, ethical, and so on. The analysis given to us here by Francine Frank and Frank Ashen is linguistic. The oppression they object to is the unfair and destructive denigration of women as a group; the mechanism of oppression they are attempting to expose is buried so deep within our consciousness that it takes a deliberate and energetic effort at self-examination to see how it operates. It is the mechanism of language itself. Because language lies so deep within us, some of us may be more hostile and defensive when asked to change our linguistic habits than we would be if we were asked to change anything else. The common words by which we refer to everyday objects and experience are more than just useful tools to us; they seem a natural extension of reality itself. Words thus carry an emotional charge, an aura, a mystique that native speakers decode in sophisticated ways without having to think consciously about how they do it.

So it is with words that deprecate, condescend, or depreciate: words that put people down, rob them of their dignity, or diminish their worth as human beings. "Boy"—a generic term of address—could at one time be used by any white person to refer to any black male, regardless of the black man's age, merits, or social standing. The subtle difference between "I know the woman who lives in that house" and "I know the lady who lives in that house" will be picked up by any reasonably educated speaker of English. Frank and Ashen give us many examples of the way English may be used to keep women in an inferior social position, to keep them feeling inferior, useless, incompetent, or powerless. No native speaker has to take a course to learn the use of such language; rather, one almost has to take a course in order to unlearn *it, to become aware enough to avoid it. The sexist bias runs deeper than most of us ever recognize until we are challenged to see it by the research and criticism of those who, like Frank and Ashen, spend much more time thinking about these issues than most people.*

As you read, try to think of examples from your own experience or reading that support or even extend the authors' arguments. You might also consider to what extent the authors' linguistic examples of sexist language are mirrored in nonverbal aspects of life. Clearly, we have a great many verbal ways of expressing bias against people of despised religions, ethnic origins, and skin color. We have all heard the ugly terms. What about other ways of identifying who is "in" and who is "out" in certain social groups—at school, in the dorm, in the fraternity or sorority house, on the job, in the neighborhood, and in other areas? Can Frank and Ashen's argument help explain such nonverbal modes of differentiation? But when we are talking about language, Frank and Ashen invite us to think more critically about (and listen more carefully to) the uses of language that help create our social and emotional environment.

OF GIRLS AND CHICKS

Chapter 4 of *Language and the Sexes* (1983).

1 English is a sexist language! Angry women have often been driven to make such a statement. But is it accurate? Can we really label some languages as more sexist than others? In a recent movie, a rather obnoxious adolescent described his favorite pastime as "cruising chicks." If the adolescent had been female, she would not have had a parallel term to refer to finding boys. This asymmetry in vocabulary is a linguistic reflection of sexism in our society.

2 One of the more intriguing and controversial hypotheses of modern linguistics is the idea that the grammatical structure of a language may influence the thought processes of speakers of that language. Regardless of the truth of that idea, known among linguists as the Sapir-Whorf hypothesis, it seems clear that we can gain insights into the culture and attitudes of a group by examining the language of that group. Eskimos live in an environment in which the condition of snow is vital to survival, and they therefore have a large number of distinct words for different kinds of snow. Most Hindi speakers live in areas of India where it does not snow and, as a result, Hindi has only a single word equivalent to the two English words *snow* and *ice.* In Modern English, the plethora of words such as *road, avenue, freeway, highway, boulevard, street, turnpike, expressway, parkway, lane,* and *interstate* might lead one to conclude that automobiles are very important to Americans, while the relative scarcity of words for various types of kinfolk would suggest that extended familial relationships are not very important to Americans. (We do not, for example, have separate words for our mother's brother and our father's brother.) In this chapter, we will look at the linguistic treatment of women in English for clues to the attitudes towards women held by speakers of English.

3 First let us consider what the last members of the following groups have in common: Jack and Jill, Romeo and Juliet, Adam and Eve, Peter, Paul and Mary, Hansel and Gretel, Roy Rogers and Dale Evans, Tristan and Isolde, Guys and Dolls, Abelard and Heloise, man and wife, Dick and Jane, Burns and Allen, Anthony and Cleopatra, Sonny and Cher, Fibber Magee and Molly,* Ferdinand and Isabella, Samson and Delilah, and Stiller and Meara. That's right, it is a group of women who have been put in their place. Not that women must always come last: Snow White gets to precede all seven of the dwarfs, Fran may follow Kukla, but she comes before Ollie,† Anna

*Popular radio entertainers in the 1930s and 1940s.

†*Kukla, Fran, and Ollie* was a popular TV show in the 1950s. Fran was a human who interacted with the puppets Kukla and Ollie.

preceded the King of Siam, although it must be noted that, as colonialism waned, she was thrust to the rear of the billing in "The King and I."* Women with guns are also able to command top billing, as in Frankie and Johnny, and Bonnie and Clyde. The moral is clear: a woman who wants precedence in our society should either hang around with dwarfs or dragons, or shoot somebody. "Women and children first" may apply on sinking ships, but it clearly doesn't apply in the English language.

4 Not only are women put off, they are also put down, numerically and otherwise. In the real world, women slightly outnumber men. But the world created for American schoolchildren presents a different picture. In an article describing the preparation of a dictionary for schoolchildren, Alma Graham recounts the imbalance discovered in schoolbooks in all subjects in use in the early 1970s. A computer analysis of five million words in context revealed many subtle and not-so-subtle clues to the status of women in American society. The numbers alone tell us a lot: men outnumber women seven to one, boys outnumber girls two to one; girls are even in the minority in home economics books, where masculine pronouns outnumber feminine ones two to one. In general, the pronouns *he, him,* and *his* outnumber *she, her,* and *hers* by a ratio of four to one.

5 When the linguistic context of the above pronouns was analyzed to see if they were generics, referring to people regardless of sex it was found that of 940 examples, almost eighty percent clearly referred to male human beings; next came references to male animals, to persons such as sailors and farmers, who were assumed to be male, and only thirty-two pronouns were true generics. In another set of words, we do find more women: mothers outnumber fathers, and wives appear three times as often as husbands. However, children are usually labelled by referring to a male parent (Jim's son rather than Betty's son), most mothers have sons rather than daughters, and so do most fathers. There are twice as many uncles as aunts and every first born child is a son. It is not altogether clear from all this how the race reproduces itself without dying out in a few generations. Notice further that, although the word *wife* is more frequent, expressions like *the farmer's wife, pioneers and their wives,* etc., indicate that the main characters are male.

6 Consider now another area of our language. English has a large number of nouns which appear to be neutral with regard to sex, but actually are covertly masculine. Although the dictionary may define *poet* as one who writes poetry, a woman who writes poetry appears so anomalous or threatening to some, that they use the special term *poetess* to refer to her. There is no corresponding term to call attention to the sex of a man who writes poetry, but then we find nothing remarkable in the fact that poetry is written by men. Of course, if a woman is sufficiently meritorious, we may forgive her her sex and refer to her as a poet after all, or, wishing to keep the important fact of her sex in our consciousness, we may call her a *woman poet.* However, to balance the possible reward of having her sex overlooked, there remains the

*The 1950s Broadway musical *The King and I* was based on a book titled *Anna and the King of Siam.*

possibility of more extreme punishment; we may judge her work so harshly that she will be labelled a *lady poet.* Once again, the moral is clear: people who write poetry are assumed to be men until proven otherwise, and people identified as women who write poetry are assumed to be less competent than sexually unidentified (i.e., presumably male) people who write poetry.

If the phenomenon we have been discussing were limited to poetry, we 7
might not regard it as very significant; after all, our society tends to regard poets as somewhat odd anyway. But, in fact, it is widespread in the language. There is a general tendency to label the exception, which in most cases turns out to be women. Many words with feminine suffixes, such as *farmerette, authoress,* and *aviatrix,* have such a clear trivializing effect, that there has been a trend away from their use and a preference for *woman author* and the like. The feminines of many ethnic terms, such as *Negress* and *Jewess,* are considered particularly objectionable. Other words, such as *actress* and *waitress,* seem to have escaped the negative connotations and remain in use. However, we note that waiters often work in more expensive establishments than do waitresses, that actresses belong to "Actor's Equity," and that women participants in theatrical groups have begun to refer to themselves as "actors." On rare occasions, this presumption of maleness in terms which should be sexually neutral, works to women's advantage. If someone is called a *bastard,* either as a general term of abuse, or as a statement of the lack of legal marital ties between that person's parents, we assume that person is a male. While an illegitimate child may be of either sex, only men are bastards in common usage. Although the dictionary seems to regard this as a sex-neutral term, a recent dictionary of slang gives the term *bastarda* as a "female bastard/law, Black."[1]

Sometimes the feminine member of a pair of words has a meaning 8
which is not only inferior to the masculine one, but also different from it. Compare, for instance, a *governor* with a *governess* or a *major* with a *majorette.* Ella Grasso was the governor of Connecticut, and a high ranking woman in the U.S. Army would certainly not be a majorette. In a large number of cases, the supposed feminine form does not even exist to refer to a woman occupying a "male" position. Women, for example, may be United States Senators, but there is no such thing as a *Senatress.* Often, where the feminine noun does exist, it will acquire sexual overtones not found in the original: compare a *mistress* with a *master.*

The last effect even spills over to adjectives applied to the two sexes. 9
A *virtuous* man may be patriotic or charitable or exhibit any one of a number of other admirable traits; a *virtuous* woman is chaste. (The word *virtue* is, itself, derived from the Latin word for *man.*) Similarly, consider Robin Lakoff's example[2] of the different implications involved in saying *He is a professional* versus *She is a professional.** Although adjectives also may come in seemingly equivalent pairs like *handsome* and *pretty,* they prove not to be equivalent in

*Traditionally, the word *professional,* applied to a woman, has been used as a euphemism for *prostitute.*

practice; it is a compliment to call a woman *handsome* and an insult to call a man *pretty.* In other cases, where pairs of adjectives exist, one term covers both sexes and the other one tends to refer only to one sex, usually females. So, members of both sexes may be *small,* but only women seem to be *petite;* both boys and girls may have a *lively* personality, but when did you last meet a *vivacious* boy?

In addition to this use of certain adjectives almost exclusively to refer 10
to women, descriptions of women typically include more adjectives and expressions referring to physical appearance than do descriptions of men. The media clearly reflect this tendency; a report on an interview with a well-known woman rarely fails to mention that she is *attractive* or *stylish,* or to say something about her clothes or the color of her hair or eyes, even if the context is a serious one like politics or economics, where such details have no importance. Readers are also likely to be informed of the number and ages of her children. Men are not treated in a parallel fashion.

Verbs turn out to be sex-differentiated also. Prominent among such 11
verbs are those which refer to women's linguistic behavior and reflect some of the stereotypes discussed in an earlier chapter. Women, for example, may *shriek* and *scream,* while men may *bellow.* Women and children (girls?) hold a virtual monopoly on *giggling,* and it seems that men rarely *gossip* or *scold.* There are also a large number of sex-marked verbs which refer to sexual intercourse. In their article, "Sex-marked Predicates in English," Julia P. Stanley and Susan W. Robbins note the abundance of terms which describe the male role in sexual intercourse, and the lack of parallel terms for women's role.[3] Women are thus assigned a passive role in sex by our language.

Another set of words which are presumably sex-neutral are the ones 12
that end in *-man.* This suffix, which is pronounced with a different vowel from the one in the word *man,* supposedly indicates a person of either sex. It is commonly found in words designating professions—*salesman, postman, congressman,* for example—and in some other expressions such as *chairman* and *freshman.* However, the very fact that there exist female counterparts for many of these words, such as *chairwoman* and *congresswoman,* indicates that they are thought of as typically male and, as in the case of poets, when a woman is referred to, her sex must be clearly indicated. In the case of *salesman,* there are a variety of feminine forms: *saleswoman, saleslady,* and *salesgirl.* Although they appear to be synonymous, they convey significant social distinctions; someone referred to as a *saleslady* or a *salesgirl* probably works in a retail establishment such as a department store or a variety store. A woman who sells mainframe computers to large corporations would be called a *saleswoman,* or even a *salesman.* The more important the position, the less likely it is to be held by a *-girl* or a *-lady,* and the more likely it is to be the responsibility of a *-man.*

If speakers of English often have a choice of using separate words for 13
men and women, of pretending that a single word with a male marker like *chairman* refers to both sexes, or of using a truly sex-neutral term like *chairperson* or *chair,* speakers of some other languages do not enjoy such freedom. They are constrained by the grammar of their languages to classify the nouns

they use according to something called gender. Grammatical gender is a feature of most European languages and of many others as well. Depending on the language, nouns may be classified according to whether they are animate or inanimate, human or non-human, male or female, or, in the case of inanimate objects, the class may depend on shape or some other characteristic. In some languages, meaning plays little part in determining noun class or gender; it may be predictable from the phonetic shape of the words, or it may be completely arbitrary. In the European tradition, genders are labelled *masculine* and *feminine* and, if there is a third noun class, *neuter.* This is in spite of the fact that most words included in all three of these classes represent inanimate objects like *tables* and *doors,* abstract concepts like *freedom,* or body parts like *head, toe, nose,* etc. Some of us English speakers may begin to wonder about the strange world view of speakers of languages which classify books as masculine and tables as feminine, especially when we notice that the word for nose is feminine in Spanish, but masculine in French and Italian. It turns out, however, that they are not following some animistic practice whereby inanimate objects are thought of as having sexual attributes; in the modern European languages at least, grammatical gender is, for most nouns, a purely arbitrary classification, often the result of linguistic tradition and of a number of historical accidents. The labels come from the fact that most nouns referring to males belong to one class and most nouns referring to females belong to another class and, following the human practice of classifying everything in terms of ourselves, we extend the distinguishing labels to all nouns. There are, not surprisingly, exceptions to this prevalent mode of classification, which lead to the oddity of such words as the French *sentinelle,* 'guard', being grammatically feminine, although most guards are men, while two German words for 'young woman,' *Fräulein* and *Mädchen,* are grammatically neuter.

Are speakers of languages with grammatical gender completely strait- 14
jacketed by their grammar and forced to be sexist? We will return to this question in the final chapter. For now, we note that in these languages, the masculine forms usually serve as generics and are considered the general forms, in much the same way as the *-man* words are in English. Just as there are often alternatives to these masculine words in English, other languages also have many words that are potentially neutral and can belong to either gender, depending on the sex of the person referred to—French *poète* and Spanish *poeta* are examples, despite the dictionaries' classification of them as masculine. Yet speakers often insist on signalling the sex of women poets by adding suffixes parallel to the English *-ess, poétesse* and *poetisa* being the French and Spanish equivalents, or by tacking on the word for woman, as in *femme médecin,* one term for a 'woman doctor' in French.

Although it is true that the masculine forms serve as the unmarked or 15
neutral terms in many languages, this does not seem to be a universal feature of human languages, as some have claimed. Iroquoian languages use feminine nouns as unmarked or generic terms; however, in the case of Iroquoian occupational terms, which are composed of a pronoun and a verb (literally translated as 'she cooks' or 'he cooks'), the sex-typing of the job determines

whether the masculine or feminine pronoun is used. In Modern Standard Arabic many nouns switch to the feminine gender when they are pluralized. In many European languages, abstract nouns are predominantly in the feminine gender.

English nouns no longer exhibit grammatical gender, but the language does have a large number of words that refer to members of one sex only. 16
In addition, when we do not know the sex of the person referred to by a noun such as *writer* or *student,* the choice of the pronoun will, as in Iroquois, often depend on culturally defined sex roles. *Teacher,* therefore, is usually *she,* while *professor, doctor,* and *priest* usually go with *he.* This brings us to the question of the "generic" use of *he* and the word *man.*

In the case of the word *man,* as in *Man is a primate,* it has been argued 17
that this usage is independent of sex, that it refers to all members of the species, and that it is just an etymological coincidence that the form for the species is the same as that for the male members of the species. Certainly, using the same form for the entire species and for half the species creates the possibility of confusion, as those colonial women discovered who rashly thought that the word *man* in the sentence "All men are created equal" included them. More confusion may come about when we use phrases like *early man.* Although this presumably refers to the species, notice how easy it is to use expressions like *early man and his wife* and how hard it is to say things like *man is the only animal that menstruates* or even *early woman and her husband.* As with the poetical examples discussed earlier, the common theme running through these last examples is that the male is taken as the normal, that masculine forms refer both to the sex and the species, while women are the exception, usually absorbed by the masculine, but needing special terms when they become noticeable.

If the above examples have not convinced you that *man* as a generic is 18
at best ambiguous, consider the following quote from Alma Graham:

> If a woman is swept off a ship into the water, the cry is "Man overboard!" If she is killed by a hit-and-run driver, the charge is "manslaughter." If she is injured on the job, the coverage is "workmen's compensation." But if she arrives at a threshold marked "Men Only," she knows the admonition is not intended to bar animals or plants or inanimate objects. It is meant for her.[4]

Historically, *man* did start out as a general term for human beings, but 19
Old English also had separate sex-specific terms: *wif* for women and *wer* or *carl* for men. The compound term *wifman* (female person) is the source for today's *woman,* but the terms for males were lost as *man* came to take on its sex-specific meaning, thus creating the confusion we have been discussing. For an authoritative opinion on the modern meaning of this word, we could turn to the *Oxford English Dictionary,* which notes that the generic use of *man* is obsolete: "in modern apprehension *man* as thus used primarily denotes the male sex, though by implication referring also to women." We note that the

"modern apprehension" referred to was the late nineteenth century. If anything, the situation is even clearer today.

An even shorter word which is supposed to include women but often excludes them is the pronoun *he.* Observers have long pointed out the inconvenience of the ambiguity of this form and the advantages of having a true generic singular pronoun, which would be sex-neutral. In the absence of such a sex-neutral pronoun, speakers of English have been expected to utter sentences such as *Everybody should bring his book tomorrow,* where the *everybody* referred to includes forty women and just one man. For centuries, speakers and writers of English have been happily getting around this obstacle by using *they* in such situations, yielding sentences such as *Everybody should bring their book tomorrow.* Unfortunately, since the middle of the eighteenth century, prescriptive grammarians have been prescribing the use of *he* in these situations and attacking the use of *they,* by arguing that the use of *they* is a violation of the rule for pronoun agreement, i.e., a singular noun such as *everybody* should not take a plural pronoun such as *they.* 20

Although the prescriptive grammarians have not explained why it is all right for a female person such as *Mary* to be referred to by a masculine pronoun such as *he,* they have managed to make many people feel guilty about breaking the law when they use *they* in such sentences. As a result, many of us consciously avoid the use of *they* in these contexts, and some of us avoid the use of such sentences at all. Ann Bodine quotes a writer of a grammatical handbook advocating the latter course when faced with the need to formulate the sentence, "Everyone in the class worried about the midyear history exam, but he all passed."[5] In 1850, an actual law was passed on the subject when the British Parliament, in an attempt to shorten the language in its legislation, declared: "in all acts words importing the masculine gender shall be deemed and taken to include females. . ."[6] The importance of shortening the language of legislation can clearly be seen by Parliament's use of "deemed and taken." Statements similar to Parliament's are found in leases and other legal contracts today, but, as Casey Miller and Kate Swift point out in *The Handbook of Nonsexist Writing for Writers, Editors and Speakers,* "it was often conveniently ignored. In 1879, for example, a move to admit female physicians to the all-male Massachusetts Medical Society was effectively blocked on the grounds that the society's by-laws describing membership used the pronoun *he.*"[7] Julia Stanley is one of a number of writers who have discredited the "myth of generics" in English. Her essay contains many examples of ambiguous and "pseudo-generic" usages.[8] 21

Rather than rely on authority or opinion, some scholars have conducted experiments to determine whether or not today's speakers of English perceive the forms *man* and *he* as generic. In one study, Joseph Schneider and Sally Hacker asked some students to find appropriate illustrations for an anthropology book with chapter headings like "Man and His Environment," and "Man and His Family;" another group of students was given titles like "Family Life" and "Urban Life." The students who were assigned titles with the word *man* chose more illustrations of men only, while the second group chose 22 more pictures showing men, women, and children. Other studies have confirmed our tendency to interpret *he* and *man* as masculine unless the context clearly indicates they are meant generically, the contrary of what is usually claimed. One experiment, conducted by Wendy Martyna, that tested the usage and meaning of these words among young people, found that women and men may be using the terms quite differently. The men's usage appears to be based on sex-specific (male) imagery, while the women's usage is based instead on the prescription that *he* should be used when the sex of the person is not specified. Things can now run smoothly with women believing that they are included while men know otherwise.

Being treated as a trivial exception, being made to go to the rear linguistically, or even being made to disappear, are not the worst things that happen to women in the English language. Our lopsided lexicon is well supplied with unpleasant labels for women. Many, although by no means all of these, are slang words. The editor of the 1960 edition of the *Dictionary of American Slang* writes that "most American slang is created and used by males." This observation may be prejudiced by the fact that most collectors of American slang are males, but in any case, the words referring to women should give us an idea of the attitudes of American men towards women. The dictionaries reveal an unpleasant picture indeed. 23

Disregarding the obscene terms, and that is quite a task, since the list of obscene words for women is long, if monotonous, we still find term after term referring to women in a sexually derogatory way. Consider the following small sample: *chick, hussy, tart, broad, dame,* and *bimbo.* In one study, "The Semantic Derogation of Women," Muriel Schulz found over one thousand words and phrases which put women in their place in this way.[9] She analyzes a long series of words which started out as harmless terms or had a positive meaning, and gradually acquired negative connotations. It would seem that men find it difficult to talk about women without insulting them. The opposite is not true—few of the words have masculine counterparts. After going through the lists compiled by Schulz and other writers, one may begin to wonder about the popular belief that men talk about more serious topics than do women. Unless, of course, sexual jokes and insults constitute a serious topic, men should scarcely need so many derogatory terms. An interesting, if depressing, party game is to try to think of positive labels which are used for women. 24

Let's examine a few examples of words for women, their meanings and their histories. The woman of the house, or *housewife,* became a *hussy* with the passage of time, and eventually the word had to be reinvented with its original meaning. So much for the dignity of housewives. *Madam* and *mistress* did not change in form, but they took on new sex related meanings, while *Sir* and *master* participate in no double entendres. Many of the most insulting words began life as terms of endearment and evolved into sexual slurs. *Tart,* originally a term of endearment like *sweetie-pie,* came to mean a sexually desirable woman and then a prostitute, while *broad* originally meant a young woman. *Girl* started out meaning a child of either sex, then took on the 25 following meanings at various stages: a female child, a servant, a prostitute, and a mistress. The process then seemed to reverse itself and *girl* has gone back to meaning a female child most of the time, although some of the other meanings remain. *Whore,* which has the same root as Latin *carus* 'dear', referred at first to a lover of either sex, then only to females, and finally came to mean prostitute. Almost all the words for female relatives—*mother, aunt, daughter,* and the like—have at one time or another been euphemisms for prostitute. Stanley analyzes 220 terms used to describe sexually promiscuous women.[10] This is just a sample of a much larger group, although there are relatively few words to describe sexually promiscuous men. Even though most of the derogatory terms for women originated as positive words, some of them did not: *shrew,* for example, never had a favorable connotation.

There are many animal metaphors used to insult both men and women, 26
dog being an example. However, here too, there seem to be more terms of abuse for women: *chick* is one example, another is *cow,* which has been "a rude term for a woman" since the mid 1600s according to one recent dictionary of slang. Side by side with *dog,* which can be used for both sexes, we find *bitch,* limited to women. We know of no animal terms of abuse which are limited to men. In another semantic area, there is the large group of terms used both to label and to address women as objects to be consumed: *tomato, honey, cookie, sweetie-pie,* and *peach* are but a few examples. These are not necessarily derogatory and some of them, like *honey,* can be used by women to address men, but most refer largely or exclusively to women, and there is no parallel set used to refer to men. The food terms have not escaped the process of pejoration which commonly afflicts words for women, as is shown by the example of *tart,* which was included in our discussion of derogatory words.

In an earlier chapter we discussed some of the similarities between 27
stereotypes about the way women speak and beliefs about the speech of other powerless groups. Not surprisingly, there are also many derogatory labels for such groups in the form of ethnic and racial slurs and, like women, they are the butt of many jokes. Once again we find that Black women are doubly insulted. In the words of Patricia Bell Scott, "the English language has dealt a 'low-blow' to the self-esteem of developing Black womanhood."[11] After consulting the 1960 *American Thesaurus of Slang,* Scott states: "From a glance at the synonyms used to describe a Black person, especially a Black woman, one readily senses that there is something inherently negative about 'being Black' and specifically about being a Black woman. The words listed under the heading 'Negress,' in itself an offensive term, have largely negative and sexual connotations."[12] Some of the milder terms listed include *Black doll, femmoke,* and *nigger gal.* Black women do not seem to be treated much better by Black English. Scott also examined handbooks of Black language and found "a preoccupation with physical attractiveness, sex appeal, and skin color, with the light-skinned Black women receiving connotations of positiveness." She concludes that "much of Black English has also dealt Black Womanhood a 'low-blow.'"[13]

At the beginning of this chapter we asserted that one can determine a 28 great deal about the attitudes of a group of speakers by examining their linguistic usage. At the end of this chapter we must conclude that the attitudes towards women reflected in the usage of English speakers are depressing indeed. They have sometimes been belittled and treated as *girls;* at other times, they have been excluded or ignored by the pretense of "generic" terms; they have frequently been defined as sex objects or insulted as prostitutes, or, on the contrary, placed on a pedestal, desexed, and treated with deference, as *ladies.* It is no wonder that many women have rebelled against being the object of such language and have become creators and advocates of new usages designed to bring equity to the English language. . . .

REFERENCES

All references are Frank and Ashen's.

1. Richard A. Spears, *Slang and Euphemism* (Middle Village, New York: Jonathan David, 1981), p. 21.

2. Robin Lakoff, *Language and Woman's Place* (New York: Harper & Row, 1975), p. 30.

3. Julia P. Stanley and Susan W. Robbins, "Sex-marked Predicates in English," *Papers in Linguistics* 11 (1978): 494.

4. Alma Graham, "The Making of a Nonsexist Dictionary," in *Language and Sex,* ed. Barrie Thorn and Nancy Henley (New York: Newbury House, 1975), p. 62.

5. Ann Bodine, "Androcentrism in Prescriptive Grammar: Singular 'They,' Sex-indefinite 'He' and 'He and She,' " *Language in Society* 4 (1975): 140.

6. Ibid., 136.

7. Casey Miller and Kate Swift, *The Handbook of Nonsexist Writing for Writers, Editors and Speakers* (New York: Lippincott & Crowell, 1980), p. 37.

8. Julia P. Stanley, "Gender-Marking in American English: Usage and Reference," in *Sexism and Language,* ed. Alleen Pace Nilsen, Haig Bosmajian, H. Lee Gershuny, and Julia P. Stanley (Urbana, Ill.: National Council of Teachers of English, 1977), pp. 43–74.

9. Muriel Schulz, "The Semantic Derogation of Women," in *Language and Sex,* ed. Barrie Thorn and Nancy Henley (Cambridge, Mass.: Newbury House, 1975), pp. 64–75.

10. Julia P. Stanley, "Paradigmatic Woman: The Prostitute," in *Papers in Language Variation,* ed. David L. Shores and Carol P. Hines (University, Ala.: University of Alabama Press, 1977).

11. Patricia Bell Scott, "The English Language and Black Womanhood: A Low Blow at Self-esteem," *Journal of Afro-American Issues* 2 (1974): 220.

12. Ibid.

13. Ibid., 220–221.

Questions for Discussion

1. Here are some words that refer to women or to activities attributed mainly to women. Following each word is one or more earlier meanings. Comment on political, social, linguistic, and sexual implications. Do you see a sexist pattern in the way the meanings of these words have changed over the years? What are some possible ways of accounting for the pattern?

a. *shrew:* a malicious, evil, cunning man
b. *termagant:* a male Saracen idol
c. *harlot:* a young, base fellow
d. *scold:* from Old Norse, a poet or lampooner
e. *baggage:* a worthless fellow
f. *frump:* a derisive snort > a jeer > ill humor > a cross, dowdy man or woman
g. *witch:* originally either male or female
h. *gossip: godsib,* "god-relative" > a familiar acquaintance
i. *mistress:* feminine of *master*
j. *madam:* "my lady"

2. Here are some other insulting terms for women: *broad, chippy, drab, floozy, slattern, slut, strumpet, trollop, troll, trot, doxy, hag, harridan, crone, biddy, harpy, vamp, nag, whore, bitch, piece, lay, tail, hen, old maid, wallflower, unladylike, unfeminine, snit, chit, tart, hussy.* What aspects of female reference do most of these words focus on? How many masculine counterparts to these words can you come up with? If there are many fewer insulting terms for men, what does this suggest about the relative differences between men and women, historically, in education, political clout, and social dominance?
3. Consider the way animal terms and animal imagery are employed to make value judgments, to praise, or to insult. Here is a list of animal images, many of them similes, that we use in everyday conversation. Discuss which of them refer mainly to women, which refer mainly to men, and which may refer to either sex. Note which are insulting. Is there a higher percentage of insulting images among the terms that refer mainly to women? If so, why?

a. eats like a bird, pecks at food
b. acts like a minx
c. a real fox, real foxy
d. talks catty
e. leads a dog's life, works like a dog
f. stubborn as a mule
g. works like a horse
h. looks fishy
i. fishing for compliments
j. gullible as a fish
k. bull-headed
l. to cry crocodile tears
m. dumb as an ox
n. act like a goose
o. old bat
p. feel sheepish
q. quarrelsome as a shrew
r. busy as a beaver

s. mild as a lamb
t. filthy as a pig, eat like a pig
u. feel squirrely
v. graceful as a swan
w. playful as a kitten
x. act like a jackass
y. timid as a mouse, quiet as a mouse
z. bull in a china shop

Suggested Essay Topics

1. For 3 weeks conduct an experiment of your own. Buy yourself a small notebook, such as a 3-by-5-inch spiral pad, and carry it with you at all times. In it jot down all the terms of insult that you hear used in reference to men and women. After you have recorded a phrase or term once, make a mark after it for every repeated use that you hear. Also for each term jot down the social context in which it was used (formal, informal, in class, etc.), and record the sex of the speaker. Finally, record whether the sex of the audience was single or mixed. After 3 weeks of keeping records, organize your material and present it in an essay directed to your classmates, drawing whatever implications and conclusions you think are warranted about the way men and women talk about one another on your campus. You might consider making this a feature article or letter to the editor in the campus newspaper. Finally, although this is not part of the essay assignment as such, discuss in class any strong differences that show up in the records of men and women. See if you can determine, for example, whether women talking together without men use more, less, or about the same number of insulting terms for men as men use when they are talking together without women.
2. Referring to the reference notes after the Frank and Ashen essay, select three of the following five sources to read more fully: Robin Lakoff, *Language and Woman's Place;* Alma Graham, "The Making of a Nonsexist Dictionary"; Muriel Schulz, "The Semantic Derogation of Women"; Julia P. Stanley, "Paradigmatic Woman: The Prostitute"; Patricia Bell Scott, "The English Language and Black Womanhood: A Low Blow at Self-esteem." After reading three of these sources, write an article for the campus newspaper in which you make the best arguments you can against sexist language usage, providing appropriate examples of its occurrence in the language and analyzing the pernicious social, political, and psychological effects it has on both users and referents.

Plato

Plato's Republic *is a long series of discussions between Socrates and some of his fellow Athenians concerning the ideally just society and the nature of justice itself. (See the introductions to other selections from* The Republic *on pp. 268–269, 276, and 547.) In the parts of* The Republic *where Socrates argues for censorship of the arts (pp. 269–284) and for what characterizes kinds of knowledge (pp. 411–417), the discussions are aimed at one central concern: how the education of society's future "guardians" determines the goodness or badness of their future leadership. Here we have selected a passage that focuses not on the content of education but on those who are educated—not on what but on whom.*

Socrates argues that in an ideally just society women should have equal opportunities for equal rule with men. He makes two proposals that hypothetically turn Athenian social conventions upside down. He argues, first, that women should hold all public offices equally with men and, second, that women should receive the same education as men. It is an index of the rigor of Plato's mind that he is able to construct a coherent argument even when his thinking violates every social convention of his time. And it is an index of how deeply ingrained sexist conventions still are today that women are left fighting an uphill battle for the fair and equal treatment that Plato imagined for them 2300 years ago.

As is his way, Socrates begins his argument without pausing to take into account the prejudices of his time. He never stops to wonder whether his listeners will think him daft or dangerous; he simply plunges into hard thinking, attacking every subject in its most direct form. Either women are equal to men with respect to all the capacities that make a good ruler, or they are not. He quickly establishes that they are *equal in this sense and immediately pursues the implications of this position: no quibbling, no hedging, no appeals to authority, and no loopholes for the male chauvinists whom he might offend.*

When Socrates says in paragraph 1 that "the drama of the men has been played out," he means that he has already discussed the role of men in the ideal republic. Having gone on in his discussion to other things, Socrates has just been asked by one of his companions to backtrack and take up the question of the role of women in his hypothetical new state. He begins to do this with the comment, "I must retrace my steps." The argument for female equality is complete from this point to the end of the selection. The questions come from Socrates, the answers from his companions.

THE EDUCATION OF WOMEN

Our title for this portion of *The Republic,* book 5.

Well, I replied, I suppose that I must retrace my steps and say what I perhaps ought to have said before in the proper place. The drama of the men has been played out, and now properly enough comes the turn of the women, especially in view of your challenge. 1

For men born and educated like our citizens there can, in my opinion, 2
be no right possession and use of women and children unless they follow the path on which we sent them forth. We proposed, as you know, to treat them as watchdogs of the herd.

True.

Let us abide by that comparison in our account of their birth and 3
breeding, and let us see whether the result accords with our design.

What do you mean?

What I mean may be put into the form of a question, I said: Are female 4
sheepdogs expected to keep watch together with the males, and to go hunting with them and share in their other activities? or do we entrust to the males the entire and exclusive care of the flocks, while we leave the females at home, because we think that the bearing and suckling their puppies is labour enough for them?

No, he said, they share alike; the only difference between them is that 5
the males are regarded as stronger and the females as weaker.

But can you use different animals for the same purpose, unless they are bred and fed in the same way?

You cannot.

Then if women are to have the same duties as men, they must have the same education?

Yes.

The education which was assigned to the men was music and gymnastic. 6

Yes.

Then women also must be taught music and gymnastic and military exercises, and they must be treated like the men?

This is the inference, I suppose.

I fully expect, I said, that our proposals, if they are carried out, being unusual, may in many respects appear ridiculous.

No doubt of it.

Yes, and the most ridiculous thing of all will be the sight of women 7
naked in the palaestra, exercising with the men, even when they are no longer young; they certainly will not be a vision of beauty, any more than the enthusiastic old men who in spite of wrinkles and ugliness continue to frequent the gymnasia.

Yes, indeed, he said: according to present notions the proposal would be thought ridiculous.

But then, I said, as we have determined to speak our minds, we must 8
not fear the jests of the wits which will be directed against this sort of innovation; how they will talk of women's attainments both in music and gymnastic, and above all about their wearing armour and riding upon horseback.

Very true, he replied.

Yet having begun we must go forward to the rough places of the law; 9
at the same time begging of these gentlemen for once in their life to be serious.

Not long ago, as we shall remind them, the Hellenes were of the opinion, which is still generally received among the barbarians, that the sight of a naked man was ridiculous and improper; and when first the Cretans and then the Lacedaemonians introduced the custom of stripping for exercise, the wits of that day might equally have ridiculed the innovation.

No doubt.

But no doubt when experience showed that to let all things be uncov- 10
ered was far better than to cover them up, the ludicrous effect to the outward eye vanished before what reason had proved to be best, and the man was perceived to be a fool who directs the shafts of his ridicule at any other sight but that of folly and vice, or seriously inclines to weigh the beautiful by any other standard but that of the good.

Very true, he replied.

First, then, let us come to an understanding whether the course we 11
propose is possible or not: let us admit any arguments put forward by comedians or persons more seriously inclined, and tending to show whether in the human race the female is able to take part in all the occupations of the male, or in some of them only, or in none; and to which class the art of war belongs. That will be the best way of commencing the inquiry, and will probably lead to the soundest conclusion.

That will be much the best way.

Shall we take the other side first and begin by arguing against ourselves; in this manner the adversary's position will not be undefended.

Why not? he said.

Then let us put a speech into the mouths of our opponents. They will 12
say: 'Socrates and Glaucon, no adversary is needed to convict you, for you yourselves, at the first foundation of the State, admitted the principle that everybody was to do the one work suited to his own nature.' And certainly, if I am not mistaken, such an admission was made by us. 'And do not the natures of men and women differ very much indeed?' And we shall reply: Of course they do. Then we shall be asked, 'Whether the tasks assigned to men and to women should not be different, and such as are agreeable to their different natures?' Certainly they should. 'But if so, have you not fallen into a serious inconsistency in saying that men and women, whose natures are so entirely different, ought to perform the same actions?'—What defence will you make for us, my good sir, against these objections?

That is not an easy question to answer when asked suddenly; and I shall 13
and I do beg of you to draw out the case on our side.

These are the objections, Glaucon, and there are many others of a like kind, which I foresaw long ago; they made me afraid and reluctant to take in hand any law about the possession and nurture of women and children.

By Zeus, he said, the problem to be solved is anything but easy.

Why yes, I said, but the fact is that when a man is out of his depth, 14
whether he has fallen into a little swimming-bath or into mid ocean, he has to swim all the same.

Very true.

And must not we swim and try to reach the shore, while hoping that Arion's dolphin or some other miraculous help may save us?

I suppose so, he said.

Well then, let us see if any way of escape can be found. We acknowl- 15
edged—did we not?—that different natures ought to have different pursuits, and that men's and women's natures are different. And now what are we saying? that different natures ought to have the same pursuits,—this is the inconsistency which is charged upon us.

Precisely.

Verily, Glaucon, I said, glorious is the power of the art of disputation!

Why do you say so?

Because I think that many a man falls into the practice against his will. 16
When he thinks that he is reasoning he is really disputing, just because he does not know how to inquire into a subject by distinguishing its various aspects, but pursues some verbal opposition in the statement which has been made. That is the difference between the spirit of contention and that of fair discussion.

Yes, he replied, that is a fairly common failing, but does it apply at present to us?

Yes, indeed; for there is a danger of our getting unintentionally into verbal contradiction.

In what way?

Why, we valiantly and pugnaciously insist upon the verbal truth that 17
different natures ought to have different pursuits, but we never considered at all what was the meaning of sameness or difference of nature, or with what intention we distinguished them when we assigned different pursuits to different natures and the same to the same natures.

Why, no, he said, that was never considered by us.

I said: Yet it seems that we should be entitled to ask ourselves whether 18
there is not an opposition in nature between bald men and hairy men; and if this is admitted by us, then, if bald men are cobblers, we should forbid the hairy men to be cobblers, and conversely?

That would be a jest, he said.

Yes, I said, a jest; and why? because we were not previously speaking 19
of sameness or difference in *any* sense; we were concerned with one *form* of difference or similarity, namely that which would affect the pursuit in which a man is engaged; we should have argued, for example, that a physician and one who is in mind a physician may be said to have the same nature.

True.

Whereas the physician and the carpenter have different natures?

Certainly.

And if, I said, the male and female sex appear to differ in their fitness 20
for any art or pursuit, we should say that such pursuit or art ought to be assigned to one or the other of them; but if the difference consists only in women bearing and men begetting children, this does not amount to a proof

that a woman differs from a man in respect of the sort of education she should receive; and we shall therefore continue to maintain that our guardians and their wives ought to have the same pursuits.

Quite rightly, he said.

Only then shall we ask our opponent to inform us with reference to 21
which of the pursuits or arts of civic life the nature of a woman differs from that of a man?

That will be quite fair.

And perhaps he, like yourself a moment ago, will reply that to give a sufficient answer on the instant is not easy; but that given time for reflection there is no difficulty.

Yes, perhaps.

Suppose then that we invite such an objector to accompany us in the argument, in the hope of showing him that there is no occupation peculiar to women which need be considered in the administration of the State.

By all means.

Let us say to him: Come now, and we will ask you a question:—when 22
you spoke of a nature gifted or not gifted in any respect, did you mean to say that one man will acquire a thing easily, another with difficulty? the first, after brief instruction, is able to discover a great deal more for himself, whereas the other, after much teaching and application, cannot even preserve what he has learnt; or again, did you mean that the one has a body which is a good servant to his mind, while the body of the other is a hindrance to him? Would not these be the sort of differences which distinguish the man gifted by nature from the one who is ungifted?

No one will deny that.

And can you mention any pursuit of mankind in which the male sex 23
has not all these gifts and qualities in a higher degree than the female? Need I waste time in speaking of the art of weaving, and the preparation of pancakes and preserves in which womankind is generally thought to have some skill, and in which for her to be beaten by a man is of all things the most absurd?

You are quite right, he replied, in maintaining that one sex greatly excels 24
the other in almost every field. Although many women are in many things superior to many men, yet on the whole what you say is true.

And if so, my friend, I said, there is no special faculty of administration 25
in a state which a woman has because she is a woman, or which a man has by virtue of his sex, but the gifts of nature are alike diffused in both; all the pursuits of men can naturally be assigned to women also, but in all of them a woman is weaker than a man.

Very true.

Then are we to impose all our enactments on men and none of them on 26
women?

That will never do.

Because we shall say that a woman too may, or may not, have the gift of healing; and that one is a musician, and another has no music in her nature?

Very true.

And it can hardly be denied that one woman has a turn for gymnastic and military exercises, and another is unwarlike and hates gymnastics?

I think not.

And one woman is a philosopher, and another is an enemy of philosophy; one has spirit, and another is without spirit?

That is also true.

Then one woman will have the temper of a guardian, and another not. 27
For these, as you remember, were the natural gifts for which we looked in the selection of the male guardians.

Yes.

Men and women alike possess the qualities which make a guardian; they differ only in their comparative strength or weakness.

Obviously.

Therefore those women who have such qualities are to be selected as 28
the companions and colleagues of men who also have them and whom they resemble in capacity and in character?

Very true.

But ought not the same natures to be trained in the same pursuits?

They ought.

Then we have come round to the previous point that there is nothing 29
unnatural in assigning music and gymnastic to the guardian women.

Certainly not.

The law which we then enacted was agreeable to nature, and therefore not an impossibility or mere aspiration; it is rather the contrary practice, which prevails at present, that is a violation of nature.

That appears to be true.

We had to consider, first, whether our proposals were possible, and 30
secondly whether they were the most beneficial?

Yes.

And the possibility has been acknowledged?

Yes.

The very great benefit has next to be established?

Quite so.

You will admit that the same education which makes a man a good 31
guardian will make a woman a good guardian; especially if the original nature of both is the same?

Yes.

I should like to ask you a question.

What is it?

Is it your opinion that one man is better than another? Or do you think them all equal?

Not at all.

And in the commonwealth which we were founding do you conceive 32
the guardians who have been brought up on our model system to be more perfect men, or the cobblers whose education has been cobbling?

What a ridiculous question!

You have answered me, I replied: in fact, our guardians are the best of all our citizens?

By far the best.

And will not the guardian women be the best women?

Yes, by far the best.

And can there be anything better for the interests of the State than that 33
the men and women of a State should be as good as possible?

There can be nothing better.

And this is what the arts of music and gymnastic, when present in such manner as we have described, will accomplish?

Certainly.

Then we have made an enactment not only possible but in the highest degree beneficial to the State?

True.

Then let the guardian women strip, for their virtue will be their robe, 34
and let them share in the toils of war and the defence of their country; only in the distribution of labours the lighter are to be assigned to the women, who are the weaker natures, but in other respects their duties are to be the same. And as for the man who laughs at naked women exercising their bodies from the best of motives, in his laughter he is plucking

> A fruit of unripe wisdom,

and he himself is ignorant of what he is laughing at, or what he is about;—for that is, and ever will be, the best of sayings, *That the useful is noble and the hurtful is base.*

Questions for Discussion

1. Do you accept Socrates' analogy between human beings and dogs (¶2–5)? He makes it clear that sexual differences between dogs are merely incidental to the activities they perform as dogs and that sexual differences between human beings are similarly incidental. They have no significant bearing on what men and women are capable of doing *as human beings* and thus cannot be used as argument for limiting the roles that members of either sex are invited to play in society. Regardless of what you decide about the analogy, what do you think of his general argument? Can you imagine how it would strike you if you were of the opposite sex?
2. Would you vote for a woman for president? How many students in your class would do so? How many would vote for a woman senator or member of Congress but *not* for a woman president? How many would vote for a

woman president of your student government? As you take these straw votes, be sure to look as closely as possible at the arguments that can be offered for various positions. And be sure to think back on what Socrates would be likely to say about your arguments. You might also want to look at the facts in your situation: How many of the top positions in various student activities are held by women? If there is a discrepancy between your expressed views and the facts of campus life, how do you explain it?

3. One could argue that Socrates' position is clearly not feminist in the modern sense of supporting a political and social movement. He gives no indication that he is motivated by the desire to correct actual injustices to women. He is instead drawing a rational picture of what the ideal society would look like. He is thus not speaking for a "special-interest group" with an ax to grind but for society as a whole. By concentrating on what is rational as against what is irrational, Socrates keeps the issue of sexual justice from getting bogged down in debates about private and petty interests or decisions about what to do *now.* A critic of Plato might argue:

   > If we want to get something *done* in the world of practical politics, Socrates' tone of dispassionate inquiry is not much help. To be effective in the world, we must be passionate, committed, and rhetorically flamboyant. While thinkers like Socrates pursue dispassionate inquiry, with their "on the one hand" and "on the other hand," the issues are actually settled by people of action, not of thought. After all, no matter how cogent Plato's presentation of Socrates' case may be, Plato seems to have produced no discernible improvement for women in Greece.

   After discussing this criticism, what do you conclude about the value of Socrates' tone? Would you recommend it to present-day feminists, male and female?

Suggested Essay Topics

1. After thinking about discussion question 3, write an essay directed to a committed feminist in which you attempt to argue that feminist issues should be couched in terms of human liberation, not just women's liberation. Take the Socratic position that the ultimate goal should be the perfection of society as a whole and that women, while having no less stake in this goal than men, certainly have no more stake in it than anyone else, including men. Try to make your reader see that if successful, programs to benefit special-interest groups only turn present inequalities upside down rather than erasing them and that if such programs are unsuccessful, they simply discredit those who have supported them.
2. This is a reversal of topic 1: Address an essay to Socrates (or to anyone who chooses to write on topic 1) arguing that human liberation and the perfection of society are too large and too vague to serve as political objectives. Argue that it is all very well to have these as ultimate aims but that political and social changes are created only by special pressure groups who know how to coerce or intimidate established seats of power.

Betty Roszak

Betty Roszak (b. 1933) is a writer, feminist, and co-editor with her husband, Theodore Roszak, of Masculine/Feminine, *the anthology in which the following essay first appeared.*

The temptation to misread is always strongest when we read essays that include, or seem to include, opinions that we find powerfully appealing or powerfully repulsive. We are more likely to notice statements with a high emotional charge, and more likely to remember them later on, forgetting the original supporting arguments. No doubt you have noticed how newspapers often emphasize a startling event or stirring statement so strongly that they sacrifice accuracy. Even when extracted sentences are quoted accurately, and they often are not, extraction itself always produces some *distortion. By quoting out of context, reporters even directly reverse an author's meaning because they fail, for example, to recognize or acknowledge that a passage was written ironically or that it in fact describes a position that the author was attempting to refute.*

The danger seems especially strong in an essay like this one. No matter where we stand on the issues Roszak raises, they are charged with emotion, and we are thus even more tempted than usual to notice only the charged moments and overlook how they work within the whole piece.

Any speedy reader can quickly discover here, for example, that Roszak is a feminist and that, like all feminists, she seeks to change things. She "favors abortion" and is convinced that men have on the whole been unjust to women. Whether we like these opinions or not, we are likely to let them overshadow her main points unless we discipline ourselves to the kind of reading that cares more about understanding others than feeding our prejudices or pet ideas. In short, to label the essay or the author with loose, general terms like pro-abortionist *or* radical *is to commit the fault that many good thinkers, including Roszak, warn us about: the fault of polarizing opinions on every issue into two, and often* only *two, positions and thus artificially simplifying what is actually rich and many-sided.*

As you read, then, resist deciding what the author's main point is until you have not only read through the whole piece once or twice but thought about how it is all put together—and why. Can you prepare a summary that would lead the author to say, "Yes, that *was my main point; you have understood"?*

By now you've learned not to expect any simple rules for grasping an author's true intention before deciding whether you agree or not. But there are two obvious questions by which you can test your command of an author's intention, both of them useful in reading Roszak. Ask yourself, "If I *were writing this piece, trying to say what I* think *she is saying, would I begin or end it the way she does?" Then ask, "If this essay were my own, would I introduce what I take to be her thesis with the title she uses?" Whenever the answer is "no" to one or both of these questions, either the author has chosen badly or you should try out another possible view of the author's intention.*

THE HUMAN CONTINUUM

From *Masculine/Feminine: Readings in Sexual Mythology and the Liberation of Women,* edited by Betty Roszak and Theodore Roszak (1969).

Recent years have seen a resurgence of feminism that has taken mainstream 1 America by surprise. It began with the discontent of lonely middle-class suburban housewives, whose malady was given a name by Betty Friedan in her immensely influential book, *The Feminine Mystique.* But it didn't become what we know as a "women's liberation movement" until the growth of the New Left from the civil rights and peace movements of the early 1960's. It wasn't until then that hundreds of young women, many of whom were seasoned veterans of antiwar and antisegregationist activities, began to realize the anomaly of their situation. Here they were, radical women involved in a struggle for human equality and an end to oppression, willing to dedicate years of effort to effecting political change, and what were they being allowed to do? Typing, mimeographing, addressing envelopes, sweeping, providing coffee and sexual diversion for the vigorous young men who were making all the decisions. Far from going forward together to change the world, men and women were once more stuck (and this time with a vengeance) with their time-honored roles: the men to think and act; the women to serve and drudge. The last equality—that between women and men—was never even mentioned. In fact, movement women found that they were even worse off than apolitical women, because they were aware of and extremely sensitive to the hypocrisies of their male colleagues who talked idealistically of equality, but who acted scornful of women in their everyday lives. The rhetoric of equality was directed at black, brown, and Third World *men* only. The New Left of the late sixties had begun to take on a tough, aggressively male tone, born of the idolization of Ché Guevara, guerrilla warfare, and admiration for the exaggerated, overcompensating manliness of the Black Panthers. As nonviolence, exemplified by Martin Luther King, Jr., became discredited by revolutionary and black militancy, so the tough style became a political requirement. In deference to this new brutalism men found it easy to take the necessary traditional he-man attitude toward women, the attitude of dominance and power. This left women in a bewildering dilemma. Were they to remain in a movement which allowed them to exist only as lackeys and silently submissive bedmates, or would they refuse to accept a subordinate status?

As this dilemma is being resolved today, there sounds in the back- 2 ground the laughter of contemptuous radical men: "Crazy feminist bitches!" The words merely echo a shared male ridicule that knows no class lines. Women find themselves of necessity beginning to re-examine the traditions of misogyny that even radical men have unknowingly inherited.

In our cultural past "Woman" was the symbol of sex; and sex, though 3 necessary, was at the same time known to be an abhorrent evil, a degrading passion. In the Middle Ages, the masculine world view of the church dared not make light of women. Church authorities of the fifteenth century, ever on the alert for the malevolence of the devil, used a popular handbook on the identification and treatment of witches, the *Malleus Maleficarum,* in searching out evil in the form of women. "What else is woman," says this medieval antisubversive activities manual, "but a foe to friendship, an unescapable punishment, a necessary evil, a natural temptation, a desirable calamity, a domestic danger, a delectable detriment, an evil of nature painted with fair colors?" By the eighteenth century, Rousseau, one of France's most prolific proponents of democratic equality, could write with impunity, "Women have in general no love of any art; they have no proper knowledge of any; and they have no genius," thus curtly dismissing half of humanity to a status of hopeless inferiority. By mid-nineteenth century, the "evil of nature" had turned into an object of scorn, and Schopenhauer's indictment of women as "that undersized, narrow-shouldered, broad-hipped, and short-legged race," denied women even their beauty, their "fair colors," along with their intellectual capacity.

Today's predominantly male society no longer sees women as evil, at least on the surface. The ambivalent fear and attraction of the Middle Ages has changed along with the prevailing attitude toward sex. Now that sexuality has lost its mystery, the once dangerous and seductive female can be safely ignored and denied her power. The fear has turned to ridicule. One cannot ignore evil, but one can pretend that the ridiculous does not exist. Men irritably ask the rhetorical question (echoing Freud), "What do women want?" meaning, of course, that anything women want is absurd. The question is asked not of individual women but of the world, and in an exasperated tone, as if women were dumb and couldn't answer. The false barrier continues to be built: "We" cannot understand "Them." Why are "They" so restive? Further communication between the sexes seems useless. Always it is men talking to men about women. 4

The fact of ridicule is constantly with us. When it was proposed in 1969 in the British House of Commons that attention be paid to developing a contraceptive pill for men, "the idea provoked hearty laughter," according to Paul Vaughan in the London *Observer.* Moreover, he tells us, the British government has rejected outright any allocation of funds for research on a pill for men. When the question was under discussion in the House of Lords, one Labour peer advised the government to ignore " 'these do-gooders who take all the fun out of life' (laughter)." Researchers explain their reluctance to tamper with the male germ cells. Yet the same researchers have not hesitated to tamper with the female germ cells in developing the pill for women. Nor have unpleasant side effects or hazards to women's health deterred them, while they quickly stopped research on a substance being tested on men because it was noted that when men drank alcohol while taking it, their eyes became reddened! Doctors have been known to laugh at the mention of labor pains during childbirth and in the not too distant past have been willing to stand by, calmly withholding anesthetics while women underwent great agonies in labor. So, too, male legislators have laughed at the idea of the 5 legalization of abortion, hinting at unprecedented promiscuity (on the part of women, not men) if such a thing were allowed. Meanwhile, thousands of desperate women die each year as the direct result of male laws making abortion illegal.

Women are learning the meaning of this male laughter and indifference in the face of the most hazardous and serious biological enterprise women undertake, willingly or not. And in cultural enterprises, whenever women attempt to enter any of the male-dominated professions (who ever heard of a woman chairman of the board, a woman orchestra conductor, a woman Chief Justice, a woman President or a woman getting equal pay for equal work?), we again hear the familiar laughter of male ridicule. If we look at the image of woman men present to us in novels, drama, or advertising, we see a scatterbrained, helpless flunky, or a comical sex-pot, or a dumb beast of burden. Is this what they mean when they exhort us in popular song to "enjoy being a girl"? But women are beginning to relearn the old lesson: in this male-dominated world, it is a misfortune to be born female. 6

From the very moment of birth a higher value is placed by his society on the male infant, a value which accumulates and accelerates into his adult life. By the time the female infant has grown into adulthood, however, if she has learned society's lessons well, she will have come to acquiesce in her second-class status—to accept unconsciously the burden of her inferiority. No matter what honors she wins, what her exploits, what her achievements or talents, she will always be considered a woman first, and thus inferior to the least honored, talented and worthy male of that society—foremost a sexual being, still fair game for his aggressive sexual fantasies. As Albert Memmi puts it, ". . . every man, no matter how low he may be, holds women in contempt and judges masculinity to be an inestimable good." 7

Male society's disparagement of women has all the force of an unconscious conspiracy. It is even more subtle than the racist and colonial oppressions to which it is so closely allied, because it is softened and hidden by the silken padding of eroticism. We women grow to think that because we are wanted as lovers, wives, and mothers, it might be because we are wanted as human beings. But if by chance or natural inclination we attempt to move outside these male-defined and male-dependent roles, we find that they are, in reality, barriers. 8

For many women this is the first inkling of the fact of oppression. Pressed from birth into the mold of an exclusively sexual being, the growing girl soon develops what Sartre calls the "phantom personality"; she comes to feel that she is what "they" tell her she is. This other self envelops her like a second skin. When she begins to experience a natural sense of constriction (which is growth), her real feelings clash with what "they" say she should feel. The more forceful and vital she is, the more she will have to repress her real feelings, because girls are to be passive and manipulatable. She becomes frightened, suspicious, anxious about herself. A sense of malaise overcomes her. She must obey the social prohibitions which force her back into the mold of the sexual being. She is not to desire or act, but to *be* desired and acted 9 upon. Many women give up the struggle right there and dully force themselves to remain stunted human beings. The butterfly must not be allowed to come forth from its chrysalis: her vitality is only allowed guilty expression in certain private moments or is turned into sullen resentment which smolders during all her unfulfilled life.

10 Family and home, which look like a refuge and a sanctuary, turn out to be the same kind of trap. Beyond the marriage ghetto there is outright rejection and exclusion. In the work world there are lower wages, union and employer discrimination, the prohibitive cost of child care. In the professions mere tokenism takes the place of acceptance and equality. The same is true in government and political activity. The single woman knows only too well the psychological exclusionism practiced by male society. She is suspect, or comic, if over a certain age. All men assume she would be married if she could—there must be something psychologically wrong with her if she isn't. And single women have the added burden of not being socially acceptable without an "escort"—a man, any man.

11 Further, women are the nonexistent people in the very life of the nation itself—now more so even than the blacks who have at last forced themselves into the nation's consciousness. The invisible man has become the invisible *woman.* William James called it a "fiendish punishment" that "one should be turned loose on society and remain absolutely unnoticed by all the members thereof." Yet that is the treatment male society metes out to those women who wish to escape from the male-defined erotic roles. Left out of the history books, not credited with a past worth mentioning in the masculine chronicles of state, women of today remain ignorant of women's movements of the past and the important role individual women have played in the history of the human race. Male historical scholarship sees the suffragists and feminists of the nineteenth century as figures of fun, worthy of only a paragraph here and there, as footnotes on the by-ways of social customs, far from the main roads of masculine endeavor: the wars, political intrigues, and diplomatic maneuverings which make up the history of power.

12 With the blacks and other oppressed minorities, women can say, "How can we hope to shape the future without some knowledge of our past?" If the historic heroines of feminism are ignored or treated trivially, today's women are hindered from dealing with their own repression. This undermining of self-confidence is common to all oppressed peoples, along with the doubts of the reality of one's own perceptions. Women's self-rejection as worthwhile human beings thus becomes an inevitable extension of the cycle of oppression.

13 But radical women have begun to rebel against the false, exclusively sexual image men have created for them. And in rebelling, many women are seeing the need for bypassing the marriage ghetto altogether. They are recognizing the true nature of the institution of marriage as an economic bargain glossed over by misty sentimentalizing. Wash off the romantic love ideal, and underneath we see the true face of the marriage contract. It is grimly epitomized by the immortal slogan found chalked on innumerable honeymoon

getaway cars: "She got him today; he'll get her tonight." Or, as put more sophisticatedly by Robert Briffault, "Whether she aims at freedom or a home a woman is thrown back on the defense of her own interests; she must defend herself against man's attempt to bind her, or sell herself to advantage. Woman is to man a sexual prey; man is to woman an economic prey." And this kind of oppression cuts across all economic class lines, even though there may be social differences between streetwalker Jane X, housewife Joan Y, and debutante Jacqueline Z. One may sell her body for a few dollars to the likeliest passerby; one for a four-bedroomed house in the suburbs; and one for rubies and yachts. But all must sell their bodies in order to participate in the bargain. Yet if women were to refuse to enter into the sexual bargain, they not only would refute the masculine idea of women as property, but they also would make it possible to free men from the equally self-destructive role of sole breadwinner. Thus there would be a chance to break the predatory cycle.

Beyond marriage and the old, outmoded roles, radical women are seeking new ways of dealing with the oppressive institutions of society. No longer will they acquiesce in the pattern of dominance and submission. They are beginning to take control of their own lives, building new relationships, developing new modes of work, political activity, child rearing and education. Rejection of male exploitation must start with psychic as well as economic independence. The new female consciousness is going to develop cooperative forms of child care; women's centers as sanctuaries for talk, planning, and action; all-female communes where women can escape for a while from the all-pervading male influence; the sharing of domestic drudgery with men in cooperative living arrangements; the building up of competence and self-confidence in such previously male-dependent endeavors as general mechanical repair work, carpentry, and construction. 14

By rejecting the false self for so long imposed upon us and in which we have participated unwittingly, we women can forge the self-respect necessary in order to discover our own true values. Only when we refuse to be made use of by those who despise and ridicule us, can we throw off our heavy burden of resentment. We must take our lives in our own hands. This is what liberation means. Out of a common oppression women can break the stereotypes of masculine-feminine and enter once more into the freedom of the human continuum. 15

Women's liberation will thus inevitably bring with it, as a concomitant, men's liberation. Men, no less than women, are imprisoned by the heavy carapace of their sexual stereotype. The fact that they gain more advantages and privileges from women's oppression has blinded them to their own bondage which is the bondage of an artificial duality. This is the male problem: the positing of a difference, the establishment of a dichotomy emphasizing oppositeness. Men are to behave in this way; women in that; women do this; men do the other. And it just so happens that the way men behave and act is important and valuable, while what women do is unimportant and trivial. Instead of identifying both the sexes as part of humanity, there is a 16 false separation which is to the advantage of men. Masculine society has insisted on seeing in sexuality that same sense of conflict and competition that it has imposed upon its relation to the planet as a whole. From the bedroom to the board room to the international conference table, separateness, differentiation, opposition, exclusion, antithesis have been the cause and goal of the male politics of power. Human characteristics belonging to the entire species have been crystallized out of the living flow of human experience and made into either/or categories. This male habit of setting up boundary lines between imagined polarities has been the impetus for untold hatred and destruction. Masculine/feminine is just one of such polarities among many, including body/mind, organism/environment, plant/animal, good/evil, black/white, feeling/intellect, passive/active, sane/insane, living/dead. Such language hardens what is in reality a continuum and a unity into separate mental images always in opposition to one another.

If we think of ourselves as "a woman" or "a man," we are already 17
participating in a fantasy of language. People become preoccupied with images of one another—surely the deepest and most desperate alienation there is. The very process of conceptualization warps our primary, unitary feelings of what we are. Mental images take the place of the primary stimuli of sex which involve the entire organism. Instead of a sense of identification, we have pornographic sex with its restrictive emphasis on genital stimulation. This "short circuiting between genitals and cortex" as William E. Galt calls it (in a brilliant article, "The Male-Female Dichotomy," in *Psychiatry,* 1943) is a peculiarly modern distortion of the original, instinctual nature of sex. We are suffering from D. H. Lawrence's "sex in the head." In childhood we know sexuality as a generalized body response; the body is an erotic organ of sensation. To this Freud gave the nasty name of polymorphous perversity. But it is actually the restriction to localized genitality of the so-called "normal" adult that is perverted, in the sense of a twisting away from the original and primary body eroticism. Biological evidence indicates that the sex response is a primitive, gross sensory stimulation—diffused and nonlocalizable. Phallic man, however, wishes to assert the primacy of his aggressive organ. The ego of phallic man divides him off from the rest of the world, and in this symbolic division he maintains the deep-seated tradition of man *against* woman, wresting his sexual pleasure *from* her, like the spoils of war. The total body response must be repressed in order to satisfy the sharpness of his genital cravings.

But in the primary sexual response of the body, there is no differentia- 18
tion between man or woman; there is no "man," there is no "woman" (mental images), just a shared organism responding to touch, smell, taste, sound. The sexual response can then be seen as one part of the species' total response to and participation in, the environment. We sense the world with our sensitive bodies as an ever-changing flow of relationships in which we move and partake. Phallic man sees the world as a collection of things from which he is sharply differentiated. If we consider the phenomenon of the orgasm in this light, we can see that its basic qualities are the same for male and female.

There can be no real distinction between the feminine and masculine *self*-abandonment in a sexual climax. The self, or controlling power, simply vanishes. All talk of masculine or feminine orgasm misses this point entirely, because this is a surrender which goes beyond masculine or feminine. Yet how many men are there who are willing to see their own sexual vitality as exactly this self-surrender?

When men want desperately to preserve that which they deem mascu- 19
line—the controlling power—then they insist on the necessity of the feminine as that which must be controlled and mastered. Men force themselves into the role of phallic man and seek always to be hard, to be tough, to be competitive, to assert their "manhood." Alan Watts wisely sees this masculine striving for rigidity as "nothing more than an emotional paralysis" which causes men to misunderstand the bisexuality of their own nature, to force a necessarily unsatisfactory sexual response, and to be exploitative in their relations with women and the world.

According to Plato's myth, the ancients thought of men and women as 20
originally a single being cut asunder into male and female by an angry god.* There is a good biological basis to this myth; although the sexes are externally differentiated, they are still structurally homologous. Psychologically, too, the speculations of George Groddeck are apt:

> Personal sex cuts right across the fundamental qualities of human nature; the very word suggests the violent splitting asunder of humanity into male and female. *Sexus* is derived from *secare,* to cut, from which we also get *segmentum,* a part cut from a circle. It conveys the idea that man and woman once formed a unity, that together they make a complete whole, the perfect circle of the individuum and that both sections share the properties of this individuum. These suggestions are of course in harmony with the ancient Hebrew legend, which told how God first created a human being who was both male and female, Adam-Lilith, and later sawed this asunder.[1]

The dichotomizing of human qualities can thus be seen as a basic error in men's understanding of nature. Biologically, both sexes are always present in each. Perhaps with the overcoming of women's oppression, the woman in man will be allowed to emerge. If, as Coleridge said, great minds are androgynous, there can be no feminine or masculine ideal, but only as the poet realizes,

> . . . what is true is human,
> homosexuality, heterosexuality
> There is something more important:
>
> to be human
> in which kind
> is kind.[2]

*The reference here is to Aristophanes' speech in the *Symposium* (pp. 307–311).

REFERENCES

1. *The World of Man* (New York: Vision Press, 1951).
2. Clayton Eshleman, "Holding Duncan's Hand."

Questions for Discussion

1. What is the *main* thesis of Roszak's essay? Does your answer fit her choice of a title and a conclusion? (See again our questions at the end of the introduction, p. 555.)
2. Did any part of this essay make you feel angry or uncomfortable? Elated or supported? If not, what emotions did you feel? Can you explain the basis of your reaction?
3. Discuss with your classmates whether men and women respond differently to Roszak's essay. Do the men find in it a different thesis than the women do? Do the men react to it with different emotions?
4. Conduct a poll of your classmates on the question "Does Roszak argue her case persuasively, providing adequate evidence at each step for the beliefs she wants us to accept?" Those who answer "no" should be asked to find unsupported assertions, and those who answer "yes" should be asked to explain why no further evidence is needed. After discussion, conduct the poll again. Are there any changes of vote? How do you account for the results of your experiment?
5. In paragraph 6, we find a parenthetical question that might be answered as follows: "Well, actually, we *have* heard by now of women who head boards, conduct symphony orchestras, and get equal pay for equal work. We now have a woman Justice of the Supreme Court—not quite the same as Chief Justice or President, perhaps, but we're moving fast." Do you think that such a reply weakens Roszak's case? Why or why not?
6. When you hear terms like *radical, pro-abortionist, feminist,* and *militant* thrown about, do you think that the people who use these terms recognize that there may be different *kinds* of each one of them? Or does the use of such general terms almost automatically erase differences of kind? Through open discussion try to determine whether the class members who use any of these labels to describe themselves really belong to homogeneous groups or whether they retain individual differences despite the labels they accept.

Suggested Essay Topics

1. Roszak generalizes freely about the typical experience of males and females in our society. Your own experience, presumably, either matches or fails to match her generalizations. Write an autobiographical essay (or,

if you prefer, a personal letter to Roszak) in which you describe as precisely as you can how you developed your picture of what it means to be male or female in our society. Don't try to describe any present inhibitions or anxieties. Your task is to dramatize how you first learned that "what a *man* does (or is like) is so-and-so, while what a *woman* does (or is like) is such-and-such." Then write a concluding paragraph or so appraising whether Roszak's picture fits your experience. (Note: Do not try to develop a general thesis about sex or sexual relations in American society or try to refute or support Roszak's whole position. Limit yourself to comparing your memories with her claims about what men and women are taught about themselves "from the very moment of birth" [¶6].)

2. In paragraph 18 Roszak talks about the necessity for men to learn "self-surrender" as an enlargement of sexual response. She also argues that the false distinction between male orgasm and female orgasm intensifies alienation between men and women. Write an essay directed to Roszak describing the earliest encounters you can remember with sexual images in fiction (novels, plays, movies, TV)—images that formed your first expectations about sex in general and about your role as a male or female partner. Looking at these images from Roszak's point of view, assess whether they were "good" for you or not. Be as clear as possible about the reasons for your judgment.

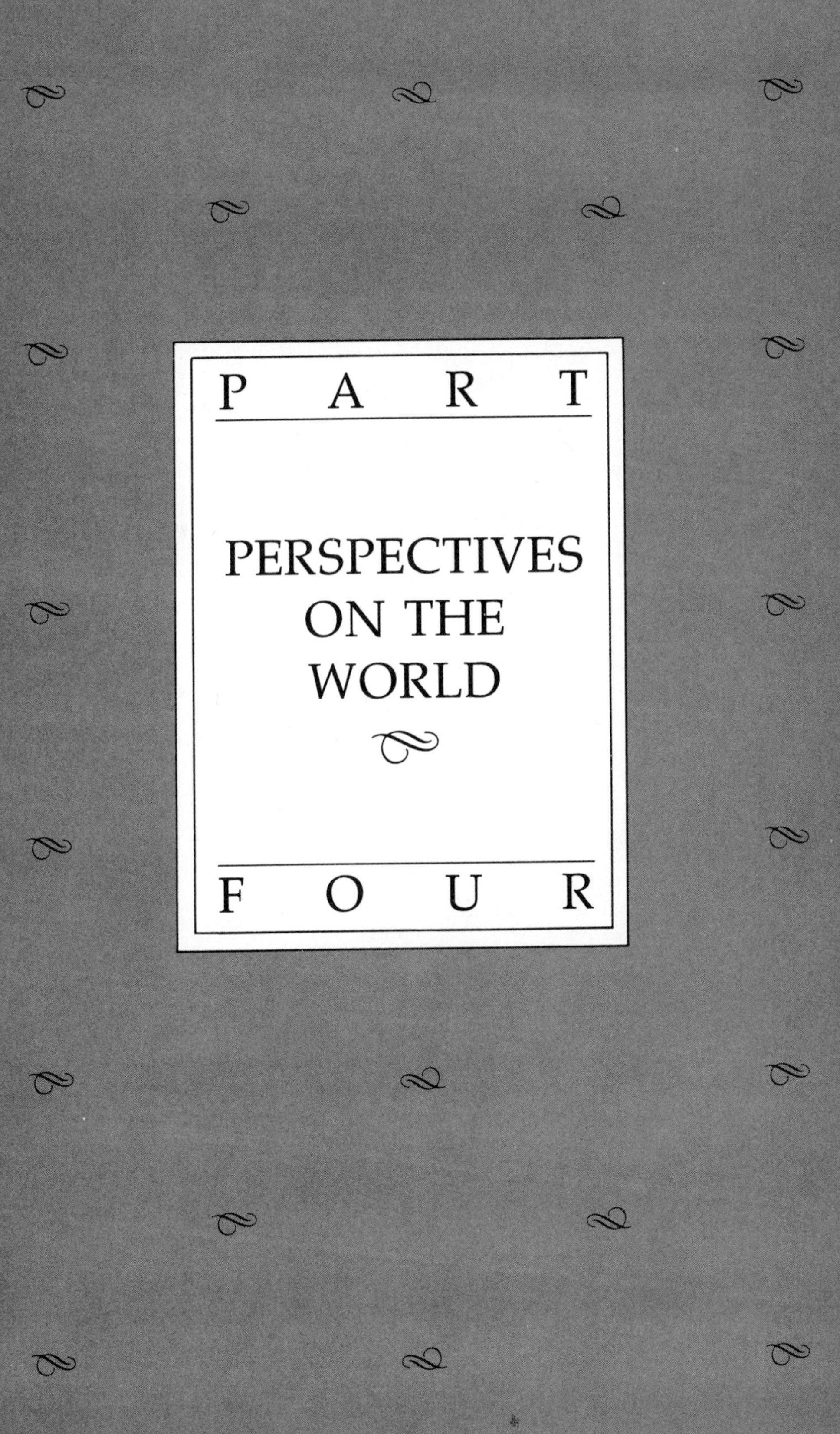

PART FOUR

PERSPECTIVES ON THE WORLD

9

HISTORICAL PERSPECTIVES

Understanding the Present by Learning About the Past

Of the three dimensions of time, only the past is "real" in the absolute sense
that it has occurred, the future is only a concept,
and the present is that fateful split second in which all action takes place.
One of the most disturbing habits of the human mind
is its willful and destructive forgetting of what in its past
does not flatter or confirm its present point of view.
Katherine Anne Porter

Those who do not learn from history are doomed to repeat it.
Karl Marx

If men could learn from history, what lessons it might teach us!
But passion and party blind our eyes, and the light which experience gives
is a lantern on the stern, which shines only on the waves behind us!
Samuel Taylor Coleridge

History is bunk.
Henry Ford

History is philosophy teaching by examples.
Dionysius of Halicarnassus

History is the pack of tricks that the living play on the dead.
Voltaire

What is history but a fable agreed on?
Napoleon

No great man lives in vain. The history of the world is but
the biography of great men.
Thomas Carlyle

Genesis 1–2:3

Obviously history must somehow have begun "in the beginning," "when God began to create the heaven and the earth." Yet no one has ever observed our beginnings, and the anthropologists and cosmologists who try to account today for what happened "then" usually hedge their statements with apologies about guesswork. Ancient authors were less cautious. Most cultures have stories that begin as confidently as the following account from Genesis, the opening story of what Christians call the Old Testament and Jews call the Torah. (Both Jews and Christians use the term Pentateuch *to refer to the first five books of the Bible, the books that Moses is said to have received from God.) The authors of the world's many creation stories always* know *what happened "in the beginning," and the accounts usually explain, as only a story can, how and why things started and how and why they led to the way things are now.*

The creation story in the Bible does not even bow in the direction of trying to explain where God himself came from. Other traditions, such as that of the ancient Greeks, developed much more elaborate accounts of how the *beginning could be found behind* other *beginnings and of how mysterious and amorphous early gods begat later gods who in turn created this or that part of the world. But Genesis begins with a supreme creator unchallenged in his orders and finding it "all," at the end of* the *creative week, unambiguously "good."*

We reprint two translations of Genesis 1–2:3, the first from the King James or "Authorized" Version of the Bible (1611) and the second from a modern translation of the Torah by the Jewish Publication Society of America (1962). The words you will now read constitute perhaps the most-discussed text in Western history. Innumerable books have been written about them, and scholars often disagree over their interpretation. Perhaps you have read or heard them so often that you see no reason to study them further. Or you may have come to accept a history about beginnings that you think makes this one obsolete—something like "In the beginning was a Big Bang, an explosion of an incredibly dense blob of mass or energy that expanded into the still-expanding universe we know today." Or you may believe that the words in Genesis recount a literal history that was written by Moses as one of five books given him by the Lord.

Whatever your view of when and where we began, you can recreate the wonder of this text, with its confident assertions, by asking simply, "What could lead anyone to tell this *kind of history in* this *way to account for our beginnings?"*

Note that we print the traditional verse numbers instead of our usual paragraph numbers. The verses in the King James Version correspond to those in the Torah.

GENESIS 1–2:3

From the King James Version

1.

1 In the beginning God created the heaven and the earth. 2 And the earth was
without form, and void; and darkness was upon the face of the deep. And
the Spirit of God moved upon the face of the waters. 3 And God said, Let there
be light: and there was light. 4 And God saw the light, that it was good: and
God divided the light from the darkness. 5 And God called the light Day, and
the darkness he called Night. And the evening and the morning were the first
day.

6 And God said, Let there be a firmament in the midst of the waters, and
let it divide the waters from the waters. 7 And God made the firmament, and
divided the waters which were under the firmament from the waters which
were above the firmament: and it was so. 8 And God called the firmament
Heaven. And the evening and the morning were the second day.

9 And God said, Let the waters under the heaven be gathered together
unto one place, and let the dry land appear: and it was so. 10 And God called
the dry land Earth; and the gathering together of the waters called he Seas:
and God saw that it was good. 11 And God said, Let the earth bring forth grass,
the herb yielding seed, and the fruit tree yielding fruit after his kind, whose
seed is in itself, upon the earth: and it was so. 12 And the earth brought forth
grass, and herb yielding seed after his kind, and the tree yielding fruit, whose
seed was in itself, after his kind: and God saw that it was good. 13 And the
evening and the morning were the third day.

14 And God said, Let there be lights in the firmament of the heaven to
divide the day from the night; and let them be for signs, and for seasons, and
for days, and years: 15 And let them be for lights in the firmament of the
heaven to give light upon the earth: and it was so. 16 And God made two great
lights; the greater light to rule the day, and the lesser light to rule the night:
he made the stars also. 17 And God set them in the firmament of the heaven
to give light upon the earth, 18 and to rule over the day and over the night,
and to divide the light from the darkness: and God saw that it was good.
19 And the evening and the morning were the fourth day. 20 And God said, Let
the waters bring forth abundantly the moving creature that hath life, and

fowl that may fly above the earth in the open firmament of heaven. 21And
God created great whales, and every living creature that moveth, which the
waters brought forth abundantly, after their kind, and every winged fowl
after his kind: and God saw that it was good. 22And God blessed them, saying,
Be fruitful, and multiply, and fill the waters in the seas, and let fowl multiply
in the earth. 23And the evening and the morning were the fifth day.

24And God said, Let the earth bring forth the living creature after his
kind, cattle, and creeping thing, and beast of the earth after his kind: and it
was so. 25And God made the beast of the earth after his kind, and cattle after
their kind, and every thing that creepeth upon the earth after his kind: and
God saw that it was good.

26And God said, Let us make man in our image, after our likeness: and
let them have dominion over the fish of the sea, and over the fowl of the air,
and over the cattle, and over all the earth, and over every creeping thing that
creepeth upon the earth. 27So God created man in his own image, in the image
of God created he him; male and female created he them. 28And God blessed
them, and God said unto them, Be fruitful, and multiply, and replenish the
earth, and subdue it: and have dominion over the fish of the sea, and over
the fowl of the air, and over every living thing that moveth upon the earth.

29And God said, Behold, I have given you every herb bearing seed,
which is upon the face of all the earth, and every tree, in the which is the
fruit of a tree yielding seed; to you it shall be for meat. 30And to every beast
of the earth, and to every fowl of the air, and to every thing that creepeth
upon the earth, wherein there is life, I have given every green herb for meat:
and it was so. 31And God saw every thing that he had made, and, behold, it
was very good. And the evening and the morning were the sixth day.

2.

1Thus the heavens and the earth were finished, and all the host of them.
2And on the seventh day God ended his work which he had made; and he
rested on the seventh day from all his work which he had made. 3And God
blessed the seventh day, and sanctified it: because that in it he had rested from
all his work which God created and made.

GENESIS 1–2:3

From the Torah

1.

1When God began to create the heaven and the earth—2the earth being
unformed and void, with darkness over the surface of the deep and a wind
from God sweeping over the water—3God said, "Let there be light"; and there

was light. 4God saw that the light was good, and God separated the light from
the darkness. 5God called the light Day, and the darkness He called Night.
And there was evening and there was morning, a first day.

6God said, "Let there be an expanse in the midst of the water, that it
may separate water from water." 7God made the expanse, and it separated the
water which was below the expanse from the water which was above the
expanse. And it was so. 8God called the expanse Sky. And there was evening
and there was morning, a second day.

9God said, "Let the water below the sky be gathered into one area, that
the dry land may appear." And it was so. 10God called the dry land Earth,
and the gathering of waters He called Seas. And God saw that this was good.
11And God said, "Let the earth sprout vegetation: seed-bearing plants, fruit
trees of every kind on earth that bear fruit with the seed in it." And it was
so. 12The earth brought forth vegetation: seed-bearing plants of every kind,
and trees of every kind bearing fruit with the seed in it. And God saw that
this was good. 13And there was evening and there was morning, a third day.

14God said, "Let there be lights in the expanse of the sky to separate day
from night; they shall serve as signs for the set times—the days and the years;
15and they shall serve as lights in the expanse of the sky to shine upon the
earth." And it was so. 16God made the two great lights, the greater light to
dominate the day and the lesser light to dominate the night, and the stars.
17And God set them in the expanse of the sky to shine upon the earth, 18to
dominate the day and the night, and to separate light from darkness. And God
saw that this was good. 19And there was evening and there was morning, a
fourth day.

20God said, "Let the waters bring forth swarms of living creatures, and
birds that fly above the earth across the expanse of the sky." 21God created
the great sea monsters, and all the living creatures of every kind that creep,
which the waters brought forth in swarms; and all the winged birds of every
kind. And God saw that this was good. 22God blessed them, saying, "Be
fertile and increase, fill the waters in the seas, and let the birds increase on
the earth." 23And there was evening and there was morning, a fifth day.

24God said, "Let the earth bring forth every kind of living creature:
cattle, creeping things, and wild beasts of every kind." And it was so. 25God
made wild beasts of every kind and cattle of every kind, and all kinds of
creeping things of the earth. And God saw that this was good. 26And God
said, "Let us make man in our image, after our likeness. They shall rule the
fish of the sea, the birds of the sky, the cattle, the whole earth, and all the
creeping things that creep on earth." 27And God created man in His image,
in the image of God He created him; male and female He created them. 28God
blessed them and God said to them, "Be fertile and increase, fill the earth and
master it; and rule the fish of the sea, the birds of the sky, and all the living
things that creep on earth."

29God said, "See, I give you every seed-bearing plant that is upon all the
earth, and every tree that has seed-bearing fruit; they shall be yours for food.
30And to all the animals on land, to all the birds of the sky, and to everything

that creeps on earth, in which there is the breath of life, [I give] all the green
plants for food." And it was so. [31]And God saw all that He had made, and
found it very good. And there was evening and there was morning, the sixth
day.

2.

[1]The heaven and the earth were finished, and all their array. [2]On the
seventh day God finished the work which He had been doing, and He ceased
on the seventh day from all the work which He had done. [3]And God blessed
the seventh day and declared it holy, because on it God ceased from all the
work of creation which He had done.

Questions for Discussion

1. If anyone in the class knows Hebrew well enough to read the original, ask him or her to bring the Torah and talk about other possible translations of passages that seem puzzling.
2. Do you see any logical order in the sequence of what God creates? How would that sequence compare with what you have been told in your biology classes?
3. If you believe that Genesis is completely "mythical," discuss what might be meant by that belief. Is the account fictional in the sense that a novel is? If so, why should so many people have treated it as sacred?
4. Read the next three chapters in either the Old Testament or the Torah. If you were to imagine that they were written in our own time, by a single author who was trying to account for "how things began," what problem or problems about the nature of our world would you say he or she was trying to solve?
5. In many regions of America today there are heated battles between "creationists" and "evolutionists." Usually such battles, whether in courtrooms, popular magazines, or scholarly journals, reveal that neither side fully appreciates the case made by the opponents. What is considered evidence by one side is dismissed as irrelevant or false by the other. If there are proponents and opponents of these views in your class, discuss the kinds of reasons that might be counted as evidence by *both* groups.

Suggested Essay Topics

1. Read in an encyclopedia about the history of translations of the Bible. Then compare our two translations in detail, remembering that ultimately they come from the same Hebrew original. If you discern any patterns of difference in emphasis or meaning, write an essay attempting to account for them. Don't think that you must speak as a biblical scholar. Your task

is not to provide a comparative linguistic or historical account but a rhetorical account. (See "What Is an Essay? The Range of Rhetoric," pp. 10–14.) That is, analyze what seem to be different *effects* that different wordings in each translation aim at, and try to reconstruct a picture of the kind of audience that the translators must have had in mind.

2. Write an essay directed to anyone you are fairly sure will initially disagree with you, defending your view of the creation story in Genesis. Whether you view it as literal truth, as poetic myth, as allegory, or as primitive intuition, explain why you think your view is credible, and try to make it as convincing as possible to someone with an opposing view.

Edward Hallett Carr

One mark of an excellent teacher, in any scholarly discipline, is the ability to formulate and wrestle with the fundamental questions of the discipline—questions so fundamental that they are often overlooked, yet usually so elusive that no one ever finally settles them. In this essay, Edward Hallett Carr (1892–1982) takes up one such question in his own discipline, history: What is a "historical fact," and how does such a fact differ from a "mere fact about the past"? Carr addresses the question to students of history, but the issues he raises about the relative status of facts clearly apply to other disciplines and even to everyday life.

His main objective is to show that historical facts do not exist, as is sometimes assumed, in a realm separated from interpretation. He argues that it is naive and uncritical to think that facts have an objective status that remains unchanged regardless of how they are used or how they are looked at. In the common view, the facts about the Battle of Waterloo, for example, are taken as having a permanent, objective, unchanging status; they will remain the same for anyone in any time or place. In answering the question "What really *happened at Waterloo?" one establishes a body of "objective" facts about the battle and then "bases" an interpretation on the facts. The possible interpretations might vary widely and new interpretations appear indefinitely, but the facts, it is held, always remain the same. And this would appear, after all, to be only common sense. Most people believe that any proposition, opinion, or datum that claims the status of a fact is unarguably true. In politics, business, medicine, mass communication, and everyday conversation, such claims as "It is a scientifically proven fact that . . . ," "It is a fact of history that . . . ," or "It is an indisputable fact that . . ." are clear claims to absolute authority, designed to preclude disagreement. A fact is a fact and that's that (compare Charles Dickens, "Hard Facts," pp. 45–57).*

Carr holds a more complicated view. According to him, taking up any given subject requires, right from the start, that one look at it from one angle rather than another; making this choice means that not only the data that one takes as facts *but also their relative importance are generated primarily by one's angle of vision, not by any intrinsic quality that facts possess in themselves.*

We can illustrate his view with a non-historical example. A cone may have an objective shape, which one may choose to call a brute fact of its existence. But one still has no choice but to look at it from a given point of view at any given time, and each of these various views will always yield a different "fact." From above, the cone will look like a circle; from the side, it will look like a triangle; from the bottom, it will look like a circle with a dot in the middle; and so on. Since there is no place one can stand to obtain a 360-degree, totally encompassing view of the cone, the "facts" of its shape are going to alter whenever one alters one's point of view.

This does not mean that there is no such thing as a fact of "coneness." Nor does it mean that there are no distinctions or preferences to be made among different views of a given topic: Not all knowledge is equally good or useful. But it does mean that facts have a dynamic, not a static, relationship to the angles of vision from which topics are viewed. Human history is full of examples. During the many centuries when demonology formed an important part of medical theory, demented behavior was explained by the "facts" of demonic possession. When everyone thought that the earth was at the center of the universe, the sun's movement around the earth was an accepted "fact." During the centuries when Euclid's theorems were unchallenged, the "fact" was that parallel lines never met, but today's non-Euclidean geometry teaches a different "fact." And so the story goes, through all the changing views and theories that human beings have held.

These earlier views cannot be dismissed as mere mistakes or falsehoods. Discredited views have not become discredited simply because thinkers "had their facts wrong." Ptolemy's epicycles could once again be used to explain the movements of the stars, if only we once again believed that the earth is at the center of the universe. Ptolemy's view and the facts it generated are not likely to be taken up again, but succeeding "facts" about astronomy and a host of other issues will be equally subject to change. Twenty years ago, for example, parents with feverish children were told to give them aspirin; today they are told to "let the fever do its job." The facts about fever depend on one's interpretation *of fever, not on any intrinsic or objective "facts of the case."*

The same holds true in history, science, religion, and all other fields of inquiry. What a sick person takes to be the "facts of the case" when recovery of health follows a prayer will depend on whatever beliefs he or she already *holds about the power of prayer. Faced with this realization, and the need to solve real problems, one can neither abandon facts nor kowtow to them. They must be viewed with critical respect, not slavish devotion or cynical skepticism. Their limitations need to be recognized; their powers need to be respected. We cannot do without them, but we cannot* live by *them either—unless we know enough not to view them with uncritical naïveté.*

THE HISTORIAN AND HIS FACTS

From chapter 1 of *What Is History?* (1961).

1 The nineteenth century was a great age for facts. "What I want," said Mr. Gradgrind in [Charles Dickens's] *Hard Times,* "is Facts. . . . Facts alone are wanted in life." Nineteenth-century historians on the whole agreed with him. When Ranke in the 1830s, in legitimate protest against moralizing history, remarked that the task of the historian was "simply to show how it really was (*wie es eigentlich gewesen*)" this not very profound aphorism had an astonishing success. Three generations of German, British, and even French historians marched into battle intoning the magic words, "*Wie es eigentlich gewesen*" like an incantation—designed, like most incantations, to save them from the tiresome obligation to think for themselves. The positivists, anxious to stake out their claim for history as a science, contributed the weight of their influence to this cult of facts.* First ascertain the facts, said the positivists, then draw your conclusions from them. In Great Britain, this view of history fitted in perfectly with the empiricist tradition which was the dominant strain in British philosophy from Locke to Bertrand Russell. The empirical theory of knowledge presupposes a complete separation between subject and object.† Facts, like sense-impressions, impinge on the observer from outside, and are independent of his consciousness. The process of reception is passive: having received the data, he then acts on them. *The Shorter Oxford English Dictionary,* a useful but tendentious work of the empirical school, clearly marks the separateness of the two processes by defining a fact as "a datum of experience as distinct from conclusions." This is what may be called the common-sense view of history. History consists of a corpus of ascertained facts. The facts are available to the historian in documents, inscriptions, and so on, like fish on the fishmonger's slab. The historian collects them, takes them home, and cooks and serves them in whatever style appeals to him. Acton,‡ whose culinary tastes were austere, wanted them served plain. In his letter of instructions to contributors to the first *Cambridge Modern History* [1902–1910] he announced the requirement "that our Waterloo must be one that satisfies French and English, German and Dutch alike; that nobody can tell, without examining the list of authors where the Bishop of Oxford laid down the pen, and whether Fairbairn or Gasquet, Liebermann or Harrison took it up."[1] Even Sir George Clark [general editor of the *New Cambridge Modern History*

*"Positivists" were philosophers who claimed that positive knowledge could be based *only* on verifiable facts. Impressed by the rapid advance of science and technology they witnessed during the second half of the nineteenth century and the opening decades of this century, the positivists optimistically proposed that all disciplines—including history, and even ethics and religion—could and should be based on scientific method.

†That is, the perceiver ("subject") is separate from—has no influence on—the thing perceived ("object").

‡John Dalberg, Lord Acton (1834–1902) was a famous English historian, author of the often-repeated aphorism "Power tends to corrupt; absolute power corrupts absolutely."

(1957–1979)], critical as he was of Acton's attitude, himself contrasted the "hard core of facts" in history with the "surrounding pulp of disputable interpretation"[2]—forgetting perhaps that the pulpy part of the fruit is more rewarding than the hard core. First get your facts straight, then plunge at your peril into the shifting sands of interpretation—that is the ultimate wisdom of the empirical, common-sense school of history. It recalls the favourite dictum of the great liberal journalist C. P. Scott: "Facts are sacred, opinion is free."

Now this clearly will not do. I shall not embark on a philosophical 2
discussion of the nature of our knowledge of the past. Let us assume for present purposes that the fact that Caesar crossed the Rubicon and the fact that there is a table in the middle of the room are facts of the same or of a comparable order, that both these facts enter our consciousness in the same or in a comparable manner, and that both have the same objective character in relation to the person who knows them. But, even on this bold and not very plausible assumption, our argument at once runs into the difficulty that not all facts about the past are historical facts, or are treated as such by the historian. What is the criterion which distinguishes the facts of history from other facts about the past?

What is a historical fact? This is a crucial question into which we must 3
look a little more closely. According to the common-sense view, there are certain basic facts which are the same for all historians and which form, so to speak, the backbone of history—the fact, for example, that the Battle of Hastings was fought in 1066. But this view calls for two observations. In the first place, it is not with facts like these that the historian is primarily concerned. It is no doubt important to know that the great battle was fought in 1066 and not in 1065 or 1067, and that it was fought at Hastings and not at Eastbourne or Brighton. The historian must not get these things wrong. But when points of this kind are raised, I am reminded of Housman's remark that "accuracy is a duty, not a virtue."[3] To praise a historian for his accuracy is like praising an architect for using well-seasoned timber or properly mixed concrete in his building. It is a necessary condition of his work, but not his essential function. It is precisely for matters of this kind that the historian is entitled to rely on what have been called the "auxiliary sciences" of history—archaeology, epigraphy, numismatics, chronology, and so forth. The historian is not required to have the special skills which enable the expert to determine the origin and period of a fragment of pottery or marble, to decipher an obscure inscription, or to make the elaborate astronomical calculations necessary to establish a precise date. These so-called basic facts which are the same for all historians commonly belong to the category of the raw materials of the historian rather than of history itself. The second observation is that the necessity to establish these basic facts rests not on any quality in the facts themselves, but on an *a priori* decision of the historian.* In spite of C. P. Scott's motto, every journalist knows today that the most effective way to influence

*"*A priori*"—literally, "from what is prior"; in other words, some facts become "basic" only because historians decide, before establishing them, that they need to be established.

opinion is by the selection and arrangement of the appropriate facts. It used to be said that facts speak for themselves. This is, of course, untrue. The facts speak only when the historian calls on them: it is he who decides to which facts to give the floor, and in what order or context. It was, I think, one of Pirandello's characters who said that a fact is like a sack—it won't stand up till you've put something in it. The only reason why we are interested to know that the battle was fought at Hastings in 1066 is that historians regard it as a major historical event. It is the historian who has decided for his own reasons that Caesar's crossing of that petty stream, the Rubicon, is a fact of history, whereas the crossing of the Rubicon by millions of other people before or since interests nobody at all. The fact that you arrived in this building [where Carr delivered this lecture] half an hour ago on foot, or on a bicycle, or in a car, is just as much a fact about the past as the fact that Caesar crossed the Rubicon. But it will probably be ignored by historians. Professor Talcott Parsons once called science "a selective system of cognitive orientations to reality."[4] It might perhaps have been put more simply. But history is, among other things, that. The historian is necessarily selective. The belief in a hard core of historical facts existing objectively and independently of the interpretation of the historian is a preposterous fallacy, but one which it is very hard to eradicate.

Let us take a look at the process by which a mere fact about the past 4
is transformed into a fact of history. At Stalybridge Wakes in 1850, a vendor of gingerbread, as the result of some petty dispute, was deliberately kicked to death by an angry mob. Is this a fact of history? A year ago I should unhesitatingly have said "no." It was recorded by an eyewitness in some little-known memoirs;[5] but I had never seen it judged worthy of mention by any historian. A year ago Dr. Kitson Clark cited it in his Ford lectures in Oxford.[6] Does this make it into a historical fact? Not, I think, yet. Its present status, I suggest, is that it has been proposed for membership of the select club of historical facts. It now awaits a seconder and sponsors. It may be that in the course of the next few years we shall see this fact appearing first in footnotes, then in the text, of articles and books about nineteenth-century England, and that in twenty or thirty years' time it may be a well established historical fact. Alternatively, nobody may take it up, in which case it will relapse into the limbo of unhistorical facts about the past from which Dr. Kitson Clark has gallantly attempted to rescue it. What will decide which of these two things will happen? It will depend, I think, on whether the thesis or interpretation in support of which Dr. Kitson Clark cited this incident is accepted by other historians as valid and significant. Its status as a historical fact will turn on a question of interpretation. This element of interpretation enters into every fact of history.

. . .

In the first place, the facts of history never come to us "pure," since they 5
do not and cannot exist in a pure form: they are always refracted through the mind of the recorder. It follows that when we take up a work of history, our first concern should be not with the facts which it contains but with the

historian who wrote it. Let me take as an example the great historian in whose honour and in whose name these lectures were founded. Trevelyan, as he tells us in his autobiography, was "brought up at home on a somewhat exuberantly Whig tradition";[7] and he would not, I hope, disclaim the title if I described him as the last and not the least of the great English liberal historians of the Whig tradition.* It is not for nothing that he traces back his family tree, through the great Whig historian George Otto Trevelyan, to Macaulay, incomparably the greatest of the Whig historians. Dr. Trevelyan's finest and maturest work *England under Queen Anne* was written against that background, and will yield its full meaning and significance to the reader only when read against that background. The author, indeed, leaves the reader with no excuse for failing to do so. For if, following the technique of connoisseurs of detective novels, you read the end first, you will find on the last few pages of the third volume the best summary known to me of what is nowadays called the Whig interpretation of history; and you will see that what Trevelyan is trying to do is to investigate the origin and development of the Whig tradition, and to root it fairly and squarely in the years after the death of its founder, William III. Though this is not, perhaps, the only conceivable interpretation of the events of Queen Anne's reign, it is a valid and, in Trevelyan's hands, a fruitful interpretation. But, in order to appreciate it at its full value, you have to understand what the historian is doing. For if . . . the historian must re-enact in thought what has gone on in the mind of his *dramatis personae,* so the reader in his turn must re-enact what goes on in the mind of the historian. Study the historian before you begin to study the facts. This is, after all, not very abstruse. It is what is already done by the intelligent undergraduate who, when recommended to read a work by that great scholar Jones of St. Jude's, goes round to a friend at St. Jude's [a hypothetical college at Cambridge or Oxford University] to ask what sort of chap Jones is, and what bees he has in his bonnet. When you read a work of history, always listen out for the buzzing. If you can detect none, either you are tone deaf or your historian is a dull dog. The facts are really not at all like fish on the fishmonger's slab. They are like fish swimming about in a vast and sometimes inaccessible ocean; and what the historian catches will depend partly on chance, but mainly on what part of the ocean he chooses to fish in and what tackle he chooses to use—these two factors being, of course, determined by the kind of fish he wants to catch. By and large, the historian will get the kind of facts he wants. History means interpretation. Indeed, if, standing Sir George Clark on his head, I were to call history "a hard core of interpretation surrounded by a pulp of disputable facts," my statement would, no doubt, be one-sided and misleading, but no more so, I venture to think, than the original dictum.

*The tradition of moderately liberal reform in English politics during the eighteenth and nineteenth centuries. The monument of "liberal history in the Whig tradition" is *History of England from the Accession of James II* by Thomas Babington Macauley (1800–1859). In it, Macauley unreservedly praises the Whig party as the party of progress; and progress, for Macauley, was the glorious feature of modern English history—progress of English liberty, wealth, morals, and intellect.

The second point is the more familiar one of the historian's need of imaginative understanding for the minds of the people with whom he is dealing, for the thought behind their acts: I say "imaginative understanding," not "sympathy," lest sympathy should be supposed to imply agreement. The nineteenth century was weak in mediaeval history, because it was too much repelled by the superstitious beliefs of the Middle Ages and by the barbarities which they inspired, to have any imaginative understanding of mediaeval people. Or take Burckhardt's censorious remark about the Thirty Years' War: "It is scandalous for a creed, no matter whether it is Catholic or Protestant, to place its salvation above the integrity of the nation."[8] It was extremely difficult for a nineteenth-century liberal historian, brought up to believe that it is right and praiseworthy to kill in defence of one's country, but wicked and wrong-headed to kill in defence of one's religion, to enter into the state of mind of those who fought the Thirty Years' War. This difficulty is particularly acute in the field in which I am now working. Much of what has been written in English-speaking countries in the last ten years about the Soviet Union, and in the Soviet Union about the English-speaking countries, has been vitiated by this inability to achieve even the most elementary measure of imaginative understanding of what goes on in the mind of the other party, so that the words and actions of the other are always made to appear malign, senseless, or hypocritical. History cannot be written unless the historian can achieve some kind of contact with the mind of those about whom he is writing. 6

The third point is that we can view the past, and achieve our understanding of the past, only through the eyes of the present. The historian is of his own age, and is bound to it by the conditions of human existence. The very words which he uses—words like democracy, empire, war, revolution—have current connotations from which he cannot divorce them. Ancient historians have taken to using words like *polis* and *plebs* in the original, just in order to show that they have not fallen into this trap. This does not help them. They, too, live in the present, and cannot cheat themselves into the past by using unfamiliar or obsolete words, any more than they would become better Greek or Roman historians if they delivered their lectures in a *chlamys* or a *toga.* The names by which successive French historians have described the Parisian crowds which played so prominent a role in the French revolution—*les sans-culottes, le peuple, la canaille, les bras-nus*—are all, for those who know the rules of the game, manifestos of a political affiliation and of a particular interpretation. Yet the historian is obliged to choose: the use of language forbids him to be neutral. Nor is it a matter of words alone. Over the past hundred years the changed balance of power in Europe has reversed the attitude of British historians to Frederick the Great. The changed balance of power within the Christian churches between Catholicism and Protestantism has profoundly altered their attitude to such figures as Loyola, Luther, and Cromwell. It requires only a superficial knowledge of the work of French historians of the last forty years on the French revolution to recognize how deeply it has been affected by the Russian revolution of 1917. The historian 7 belongs not to the past but to the present. Professor Trevor-Roper tells us that the historian "ought to love the past."[9] This is a dubious injunction. To love the past may easily be an expression of the nostalgic romanticism of old men and old societies, a symptom of loss of faith and interest in the present or future.[10] *Cliché* for *cliché,* I should prefer the one about freeing oneself from "the dead hand of the past." The function of the historian is neither to love the past nor to emancipate himself from the past, but to master and understand it as the key to the understanding of the present.

If, however, these [last three points] are some of the insights of what 8
I may call the Collingwood view of history,* it is time to consider some of the dangers. The emphasis on the role of the historian in the making of history tends, if pressed to its logical conclusion, to rule out any objective history at all: history is what the historian makes. Collingwood seems indeed, at one moment, in an unpublished note quoted by his editor, to have reached this conclusion:

> St. Augustine looked at history from the point of view of the early Christian; Tillemont, from that of a seventeenth-century Frenchman; Gibbon, from that of an eighteenth-century Englishman; Mommsen, from that of a nineteenth-century German. There is no point in asking which was the right point of view. Each was the only one possible for the man who adopted it.[11]

This amounts to total scepticism, like Froude's remark that history is "a child's box of letters with which we can spell any word we please."[12] Collingwood, in his reaction against "scissors-and-paste history," against the view of history as a mere compilation of facts, comes perilously near to treating history as something spun out of the human brain, and leads . . . to the conclusion [by Sir George Clark] . . . that "there is no 'objective' historical truth." In place of the theory that history has no meaning, we are offered here the theory of an infinity of meanings, none any more right than any other—which comes to much the same thing. The second theory is surely as untenable as the first. It does not follow that, because a mountain appears to take on different shapes from different angles of vision, it has objectively either no shape at all or an infinity of shapes. It does not follow that, because interpretation plays a necessary part in establishing the facts of history, and because no existing interpretation is wholly objective, one interpretation is as good as another, and the facts of history are in principle not amenable to objective interpretation. I shall have to consider at a later stage what exactly is meant by objectivity in history.

*The view that history is neither "the past by itself" nor only "the historian's thought about" the past but "the two things in their mutual relations." Earlier in the essay, in a passage omitted in this reprinting, Carr quotes this dictum from *The Idea of History* by the British philosopher and historian R. G. Collingwood (1889–1943). Collingwood was among the philosophers of history who first rejected the "cult of facts" and stressed the interpretive role of the historian.

But a still greater danger lurks in the Collingwood hypothesis. If the 9
historian necessarily looks at his period of history through the eyes of his own time, and studies the problems of the past as a key to those of the present, will he not fall into a purely pragmatic view of the facts, and maintain that the criterion of a right interpretation is its suitability to some present purpose? On this hypothesis, the facts of history are nothing, interpretation is everything. Nietzsche had already enunciated the principle: "The falseness of an opinion is not for us any objection to it. . . . The question is how far it is life-furthering, life-preserving, species-preserving, perhaps species-creating."[13] The American pragmatists moved, less explicitly and less wholeheartedly, along the same line. Knowledge is knowledge for some purpose. The validity of the knowledge depends on the validity of the purpose.* But, even where no such theory has been professed, the practice has often been no less disquieting. In my own field of study I have seen too many examples of extravagant interpretation riding roughshod over facts, not to be impressed with the reality of this danger. It is not surprising that perusal of some of the more extreme products of Soviet and anti-Soviet schools of historiography should sometimes breed a certain nostalgia for that illusory nineteenth-century haven of purely factual history.

How then, in the middle of the twentieth century, are we to define the 10
obligation of the historian to his facts? I trust that I have spent a sufficient number of hours in recent years chasing and perusing documents, and stuffing my historical narrative with properly footnoted facts, to escape the imputation of treating facts and documents too cavalierly. The duty of the historian to respect his facts is not exhausted by the obligation to see that his facts are accurate. He must seek to bring into the picture all known or knowable facts relevant, in one sense or another, to the theme on which he is engaged and to the interpretation proposed. If he seeks to depict the Victorian Englishman as a moral and rational being, he must not forget what happened at Stalybridge Wakes in 1850. But this, in turn, does not mean that he can eliminate interpretation, which is the life-blood of history. Laymen—that is to say, non-academic friends or friends from other academic disciplines—sometimes ask me how the historian goes to work when he writes history. The commonest assumption appears to be that the historian divides his work into two sharply distinguishable phases or periods. First, he spends a long preliminary period reading his sources and filling his notebooks with facts: then, when this is over, he puts away his sources, takes out his notebooks, and writes his book from beginning to end. This is to me an unconvincing and unplausible picture. For myself, as soon as I have got going on a few of what I take to

*The chief "American pragmatists" were Charles Peirce (1839–1914), William James (1842–1910), and John Dewey (1859–1952), the fathers of the American philosophical movement called *pragmatism.* While pragmatism is far too eclectic and complicated to summarize in a single creed, Carr is probably thinking of William James's view that a belief is justified if it satisfies a "compelling need" in the believer. Dewey, dissatisfied with James's ascribing so much precedence to the will, later worked out a program for reasoning in which he tried to set the conditions of doubt; inquiry terminates when doubt is no longer required or felt in order to act.

be the capital sources, the itch becomes too strong and I begin to write—not necessarily at the beginning, but somewhere, anywhere. Thereafter, reading and writing go on simultaneously. The writing is added to, subtracted from, re-shaped, cancelled, as I go on reading. The reading is guided and directed and made fruitful by the writing: the more I write, the more I know what I am looking for, the better I understand the significance and relevance of what I find. Some historians probably do all this preliminary writing in their head without using pen, paper, or typewriter, just as some people play chess in their heads without recourse to board and chess-men: this is a talent which I envy, but cannot emulate. But I am convinced that, for any historian worth the name, the two processes of what economists call "input" and "output" go on simultaneously and are, in practice, parts of a single process. If you try to separate them, or to give one priority over the other, you fall into one of two heresies. Either you write scissors-and-paste history without meaning or significance; or you write propaganda or historical fiction, and merely use facts of the past to embroider a kind of writing which has nothing to do with history.

Our examination of the relation of the historian to the facts of history 11 finds us, therefore, in an apparently precarious situation, navigating delicately between the Scylla of an untenable theory of history as an objective compilation of facts, of the unqualified primacy of fact over interpretation, and the Charybdis of an equally untenable theory of history as the subjective product of the mind of the historian who establishes the facts of history and masters them through the process of interpretation, between a view of history having the centre of gravity in the past and the view having the centre of gravity in the present. But our situation is less precarious than it seems. We shall encounter the same dichotomy of fact and interpretation again in these lectures in other guises—the particular and the general, the empirical and the theoretical, the objective and the subjective. The predicament of the historian is a reflexion of the nature of man. Man, except perhaps in earliest infancy and in extreme old age, is not totally involved in his environment and unconditionally subject to it. On the other hand, he is never totally independent of it and its unconditional master. The relation of man to his environment is the relation of the historian to his theme. The historian is neither the humble slave, nor the tyrannical master, of his facts. The relation between the historian and his facts is one of equality, of give-and-take. As any working historian knows, if he stops to reflect what he is doing as he thinks and writes, the historian is engaged on a continuous process of moulding his facts to his interpretation and his interpretation to his facts. It is impossible to assign primacy to one over the other.

The historian starts with a provisional selection of facts and a provi- 12 sional interpretation in the light of which that selection has been made—by others as well as by himself. As he works, both the interpretation and the selection and ordering of facts undergo subtle and perhaps partly unconscious changes through the reciprocal action of one or the other. And this reciprocal action also involves reciprocity between present and past, since the historian is part of the present and the facts belong to the past. The historian and the facts of history are necessary to one another. The historian without his facts is rootless and futile; the facts without their historian are dead and meaningless. My first answer therefore to the question, What is history?,* is that it is a continuous process of interaction between the historian and his facts, an unending dialogue between the present and the past.

NOTES

All notes are Carr's.

1. [Lord] Acton: *Lectures on Modern History* (London: Macmillan & Co.; 1906), p. 318.
2. Quoted in *The Listener* (June 19, 1952), p. 992.
3. M. Manilius: *Astronomicon: Liber Primus,* 2nd ed. (Cambridge University Press; 1937), p. 87.
4. Talcott Parsons and Edward A. Shils: *Toward a General Theory of Action,* 3rd ed. (Cambridge, Mass.: Harvard University Press; 1954), p. 167.
5. Lord George Sanger: *Seventy Years a Showman* (London: J. M. Dent & Sons; 1926); pp. 188–9.
6. These will shortly be published under the title *The Making of Victorian England.*
7. G. M. Trevelyan: *An Autobiography* (London: Longmans, Green & Company; 1949), p. 11.
8. Jacob Burckhardt: *Judgments on History and Historians* (London: S. J. Reginald Saunders & Company; 1958), p. 179.
9. Introduction to Burckhardt: *Judgments on History and Historians,* p. 17.
10. Compare Nietzsche's view of history: "To old age belongs the old man's business of looking back and casting up his accounts, of seeking consolation in the memories of the past, in historical culture" (*Thoughts Out of Season* [London: Macmillan & Co.; 1909], II, pp. 65–6).
11. Robin G. Collingwood: *The Idea of History* (London: Oxford University Press; 1946), p. xii.
12. James Anthony Froude: *Short Studies on Great Subjects* (1894), I, p. 21.
13. Friedrich Nietzsche: *Beyond Good and Evil,* ch. i.

Questions for Discussion

1. In your own words re-state and develop the distinction that Carr makes in paragraph 4 between "a mere fact about the past" and "a fact of history." Do you think this is a legitimate distinction? By what criterion or process does a "mere" fact become a historical fact?
2. Paragraphs 5, 6, and 7 each begin with references to a first, second, and third point. What are the points he develops in each of these paragraphs? What argument do all three points serve?
3. In paragraph 5, when Carr asserts that "by and large, the historian will get the kind of facts he wants," is he being cynical about historians? Is he saying that they just make up facts to support their favorite views or prejudices? If so, where does he justify this view? If not, what *is* his point?

*"What is history?" is the central topic of Carr's series of lectures.

4. Is his image of fish on a slab versus fish swimming in the ocean (¶5) an effective one? What do the fish represent? In paragraph 11 he uses the metaphor of Scylla and Charybdis (if you don't know this classical allusion, look it up in Book 12 of Homer's *Odyssey* or in a handbook of mythology), and in the same paragraph he makes an analogy comparing men and their environments to historians and their themes. What does each one mean? Does Carr use these devices appropriately and effectively? Do these metaphors and analogies represent the "facts" about historical research?

Suggested Essay Topics

1. Get together with an acquaintance who takes a radically different view from yours about an event or an issue. Discuss your differences long enough, taking notes, so that you can make a list of what he or she takes to be the crucial facts that support the position. In an essay directed to your fellow students, compare your version of the facts with the version you have obtained from your opponent. Make use of Carr's ideas and examples to support the point that one's list of crucial "facts" is never self-evident but in truth alters in response to many different forces. Try to identify those forces.
2. Read one of the following pairs of essays that take opposing positions, and, in an essay directed to readers who have read the pair, analyze each opponent's appeal to facts. Note the *kinds* of facts appealed to, the extent of the *authority* they are assumed to possess, the *criteria* for selecting them, and your assessment of the *appropriateness* with which they are used. (It might be helpful to re-read "How to Read an Argument: Demonstration II," pp. 113–116, especially section 4, "Evidence: Facts, Examples, Statistics, Analogies," p. 114.)
   a. Bertrand Russell, "Why I Am Not a Christian" (pp. 744–750), versus C. S. Lewis, "What Christians Believe" (pp. 753–761).
   b. C. P. Snow, "The Two Cultures" (pp. 690–700), versus Loren Eiseley, "The Illusion of the Two Cultures" (pp. 705–714).
   c. Paul Johnson, "Has Capitalism a Future?" (pp. 783–792), versus James Cone, "Capitalism Means Property over Persons" (pp. 800–803).
   d. Karl Marx and Friedrich Engels, "The Class Struggle" (pp. 806–815), versus Carl L. Becker, "The Marxian Philosophy of History" (pp. 818–830).

Edith Hamilton

Edith Hamilton (1867–1963) was one of the world's leading authorities on Greco-Roman civilization. In a life that spanned nearly a century, she did not publish her first book, The Greek Way, *until she was 63. When she was 90, in a ceremony conducted in the amphitheater of Herodes Atticus at the foot of the Athenian Acropolis, she was made an honorary citizen of Greece, in recognition of her contribution and devotion to classical studies.*

In this essay Hamilton defends the position that even in the modern world, which seems on the surface to be so far removed from the world of classical antiquity, we need not only to be educated about the Greeks but also to be educated by them. Like us, they valued freedom, and their freedom, like ours, was threatened by forces pressing from within and without.

We can be educated by *the Greeks if we study the spirit, the values, and the attitudes that motivated them to create and preserve a free society in the first place. By educating ourselves* about *the Greeks, about their failures and eventual fall from greatness, we can gain some insight into the causes that may cause us also to lose strength and purpose.*

In Hamilton's view, one of the most important things the Greeks can teach us is what kind of education fosters and preserves a free society. Our education differs markedly from the Greeks', and the contrast gives us much to think about. The Greeks understood, Hamilton argues, that a free society depends on a free spirit among its people, among individuals. Thus they directed education toward the cultivation of certain qualities and powers in individuals, *on the assumption that individuals are of intrinsic worth in and of themselves. Greek education did not merely attempt to provide job skills, for the Greeks knew that no amount of professional skill could compensate for a lack of independent spirit and flexible intelligence. Every citizen was educated, says Pericles (the ruler who led Athens at the height of her glory), not to become a cog in the social machine and not to increase the gross national product but "to meet life's chances and changes with the utmost versatility and grace" (¶23).*

Almost all historians believe that a knowledge of the past can enable us to face the problems of the present with deeper understanding, heightened sensitivity, and clearer heads. As you consider the contrasts and similarities that Hamilton lays out between our society and that of the Greeks, between their education and your own, consider also whether the knowledge you thus acquire about the past suggests to you any concrete recommendations for curing the ills of the present, whether in education or in society generally.

THE EVER-PRESENT PAST

First appeared in *The Saturday Evening Post* in 1958 as "The Lessons of the Past"; reprinted under the present title in *The Ever-Present Past* (1964).

Is there an ever-present past? Are there permanent truths which are forever important for the present? Today we are facing a future more strange and untried than any other generation has faced. The new world Columbus opened seems small indeed beside the illimitable distances of space before us, and the possibilities of destruction are immeasurably greater than ever. In such a position can we afford to spend time on the past? That is the question I am often asked. Am I urging the study of the Greeks and Romans and their civilizations for the atomic age? 1

Yes; that is just what I am doing. I urge it without qualifications. We have a great civilization to save—or to lose. The greatest civilization before ours was the Greek. They challenge us and we need the challenge. They, too, lived in a dangerous world. They were a little, highly civilized people, the only civilized people in the west, surrounded by barbarous tribes and with the greatest Asiatic power, Persia, always threatening them. In the end they succumbed, but the reason they did was not that the enemies outside were so strong, but that their own strength, their spiritual strength, had given way. While they had it they kept Greece unconquered and they left behind a record in art and thought which in all the centuries of human effort since has not been surpassed. 2

The point which I want to make is not that their taste was superior to ours, not that the Parthenon was their idea of church architecture nor that Sophocles was the great drawing card in the theaters, nor any of the familiar comparisons between fifth-century Athens and twentieth-century America, but that Socrates found on every street corner and in every Athenian equivalent of the baseball field people who were caught up by his questions into the world of thought. To be able to be caught up into the world of thought—that is to be educated. 3

How is that great aim to be reached? For years we have eagerly discussed ways and means of education, and the discussion still goes on. William James once said that there were two subjects which if mentioned made other conversation stop and directed all eyes to the speaker. Religion was one and education the other. Today Russia seems to come first, but education is still emphatically the second. In spite of all the articles we read and all the speeches we listen to about it, we want to know more; we feel deeply its importance. 4

There is today a clearly visible trend toward making it the aim of education to defeat the Russians. That would be a sure way to defeat education. Genuine education is possible only when people realize that it has to do with persons, not with movements. 5

When I read educational articles it often seems to me that this important 6 side of the matter, the purely personal side, is not emphasized enough; the fact that it is so much more agreeable and interesting to be an educated person than not. The sheer pleasure of being educated does not seem to be stressed. Once long ago I was talking with Prof. Basil L. Gildersleeve of Johns Hopkins University, the greatest Greek scholar our country has produced. He was an old man and he had been honored everywhere, in Europe as well as in America. He was just back from a celebration held for him in Oxford. I asked him what compliment received in his long life had pleased him most. The question amused him and he laughed over it, but he thought too. Finally he said, "I believe it was when one of my students said, 'Professor, you have so much fun with your own mind.' " Robert Louis Stevenson said that a man ought to be able to spend two or three hours waiting for a train at a little country station when he was all alone and had nothing to read, and not be bored for a moment.

What is the education which can do this? What is the furniture which 7
makes the only place belonging absolutely to each one of us, the world within, a place where we like to go? I wish I could answer that question. I wish I could produce a perfect decorator's design warranted to make any interior lovely and interesting and stimulating; but, even if I could, sooner or later we would certainly try different designs. My point is only that while we must and should change the furniture, we ought to throw away old furniture very cautiously. It may turn out to be irreplaceable. A great deal was thrown away in the last generation or so, long enough ago to show some of the results. Furniture which had for centuries been foremost, we lightly, in a few years, discarded. The classics almost vanished from our field of education. That was a great change. Along with it came another. There is a marked difference between the writers of the past and the writers of today who have been educated without benefit of Greek and Latin. Is this a matter of cause and effect? People will decide for themselves, but I do not think anyone will question the statement that clear thinking is not the characteristic which distinguishes our literature today. We are more and more caught up by the unintelligible. People like it. This argues an inability to think, or, almost as bad, a disinclination to think.

Neither disposition marked the Greeks. They had a passion for thinking 8
things out, and they loved unclouded clarity of statement as well as of thought. The Romans did, too, in their degree. They were able to put an idea into an astonishingly small number of words without losing a particle of intelligibility. It is only of late, with a generation which has never had to deal with a Latin sentence, that we are being submerged in a flood of words, words, words. It has been said that Lincoln at Gettysburg today would have begun in some such fashion as this: "Eight and seven-tenths decades ago the pioneer workers in this continental area implemented a new group based on an ideology of free boundaries and initial equality," and might easily have ended, "That political supervision of the integrated units, for the integrated units, by the integrated units, shall not become null and void on the superfi-

cial area of this planet." Along with the banishment of the classics, gobbledegook has come upon us—and the appalling size of the Congressional Record, and the overburdened mail service.

Just what the teaching in the schools was which laid the foundation of the Greek civilization we do not know in detail; the result we do know. Greek children were taught, Plato said, to "love what is beautiful and hate what is ugly." When they grew up their very pots and pans had to be pleasant to look at. It was part of their training to hate clumsiness and awkwardness; they loved grace and practiced it. "Our children," Plato said, "will be influenced for good by every sight and sound of beauty, breathing in, as it were, a pure breeze blowing to them from a good land." 9

All the same, the Athenians were not, as they showed Socrates when he talked to them, preoccupied with enjoying lovely things. The children were taught to think. Plato demanded a stiff examination, especially in mathematics, for entrance to his Academy. The Athenians were a thinking people. Today the scientists are bearing away the prize for thought. Well, a Greek said that the earth went around the sun, sixteen centuries before Copernicus thought of it. A Greek said if you sailed out of Spain and kept to one latitude, you would come at last to land, seventeen hundred years before Columbus did it. Darwin said, "We are mere schoolboys in scientific thinking compared to old Aristotle." And the Greeks did not have a great legacy from the past as our scientists have; they thought science out from the beginning. 10

The same is true of politics. They thought that out, too, from the beginning, and they gave all the boys a training to fit them to be thinking citizens of a free state that had come into being through thought. 11

Basic to all the Greek achievement was freedom. The Athenians were the only free people in the world. In the great empires of antiquity—Egypt, Babylon, Assyria, Persia—splendid though they were, with riches beyond reckoning and immense power, freedom was unknown. The idea of it never dawned in any of them. It was born in Greece, a poor little country, but with it able to remain unconquered no matter what manpower and what wealth were arrayed against her. At Marathon and at Salamis overwhelming numbers of Persians had been defeated by small Greek forces. It had been proved that one free man was superior to many submissively obedient subjects of a tyrant. Athens was the leader in that amazing victory, and to the Athenians freedom was their dearest possession. Demosthenes said that they would not think it worth their while to live if they could not do so as free men, and years later a great teacher said, "Athenians, if you deprive them of their liberty, will die." 12

Athens was not only the first democracy in the world, it was also at its height an almost perfect democracy—that is, for men. There was no part in it for women or foreigners or slaves, but as far as the men were concerned it was more democratic than we are. The governing body was the Assembly, of which all citizens over eighteen were members. The Council of Five Hundred which prepared business for the Assembly and, if requested, carried out what had been decided there, was made up of citizens who were chosen by 13 lot. The same was true of the juries. Minor officials also were chosen by lot. The chief magistrates and the highest officers in the army were elected by the Assembly. Pericles was a general, very popular, who acted for a long time as if he were head of the state, but he had to be elected every year. Freedom of speech was the right the Athenians prized most and there has never been another state as free in that respect. When toward the end of the terrible Peloponnesian War the victorious Spartans were advancing upon Athens, Aristophanes caricatured in the theater the leading Athenian generals and showed them up as cowards, and even then as the Assembly opened, the herald asked, "Does anyone wish to speak?"

There was complete political equality. It was a government of the peo- 14
ple, by the people, for the people. An unregenerate old aristocrat in the early fourth century, B.C., writes: "If you *must* have a democracy, Athens is the perfect example. I object to it because it is based on the welfare of the lower, not the better, classes. In Athens the people who row the vessels and do the work have the advantage. It is their prosperity that is important." All the same, making the city beautiful was important too, as were also the great performances in the theater. If, as Plato says, the Assembly was chiefly made up of cobblers and carpenters and smiths and farmers and retail-business men, they approved the construction of the Parthenon and the other buildings on the Acropolis, and they crowded the theater when the great tragedies were played. Not only did all free men share in the government; the love of the beautiful and the desire to have a part in creating it were shared by the many, not by a mere chosen few. That has happened in no state except Athens.

But those free Greeks owned slaves. What kind of freedom was that? 15
The question would have been incomprehensible to the ancient world. There had always been slaves; they were a first necessity. The way of life everywhere was based upon them. They were taken for granted; no one ever gave them a thought. The very best Greek minds, the thinkers who discovered freedom and the solar system, had never an idea that slavery was evil. It is true that the greatest thinker of them all, Plato, was made uncomfortable by it. He said that slaves were often good, trustworthy, doing more for a man than his own family would, but he did not follow his thought through. The glory of being the first one to condemn it belongs to a man of the generation before Plato, the poet Euripides. He called it, "That thing of evil," and in several of his tragedies showed its evil for all to see. A few centuries later the great Greek school of the Stoics denounced it. Greece first saw it for what it is. But the world went on in the same way. The Bible accepts it without comment. Two thousand years after the Stoics, less than a hundred years ago, the American Republic accepted it.

Athens treated her slaves well. A visitor to the city in the early fourth 16
century, B.C., wrote: "It is illegal here to deal a slave a blow. In the street he won't step aside to let you pass. Indeed you can't tell a slave by his dress; he looks like all the rest. They can go to the theater too. Really, the Athenians have established a kind of equality between slaves and free men." They were

never a possible source of danger to the state as they were in Rome. There were no terrible slave wars and uprisings in Athens. In Rome, crucifixion was called "the slave's punishment." The Athenians did not practice crucifixion, and had no so-called slave's punishment. They were not afraid of their slaves.

In Athens' great prime Athenians were free. No one told them what 17
they must do or what they should think—no church or political party or powerful private interests or labor unions. Greek schools had no donors of endowments they must pay attention to, no government financial backing which must be made secure by acting as the government wanted. To be sure, the result was that they had to take full responsibility, but that is always the price for full freedom. The Athenians were a strong people, they could pay the price. They were a thinking people; they knew what freedom means. They knew—not that they were free because their country was free, but that their country was free because they were free.

A reflective Roman traveling in Greece in the second century, A.D., said, 18
"None ever throve under democracy save the Athenians; *they* had sane self-control and were law-abiding." He spoke truly. That is what Athenian education aimed at, to produce men who would be able to maintain a self-governed state because they were themselves self-governed, self-controlled, self-reliant. Plato speaks of "the education in excellence which makes men long to be perfect citizens, knowing both how to rule and be ruled." "We are a free democracy," Pericles said. "We do not allow absorption in our own affairs to interfere with participation in the city's; we yield to none in independence of spirit and complete self-reliance, but we regard him who holds aloof from public affairs as useless." They called the useless man a "private" citizen, *idiotes,* from which our word "idiot" comes.

They had risen to freedom and to ennoblement from what Gilbert 19
Murray calls "effortless barbarism"; they saw it all around them; they hated its filth and fierceness; nothing effortless was among the good things they wanted. Plato said, "Hard is the good," and a poet hundreds of years before Plato said,

> Before the gates of Excellence the high gods have placed sweat.
> Long is the road thereto and steep and rough at the first,
> But when the height is won, then is there ease.

When or why the Greeks set themselves to travel on that road we do 20
not know, but it led them away from habits and customs accepted everywhere that kept men down to barbaric filth and fierceness. It led them far. One example is enough to show the way they took. It was the custom—during how many millenniums, who can say?—for a victor to erect a trophy, a monument of his victory. In Egypt, where stone was plentiful, it would be a slab engraved with his glories. Farther east, where the sand took over, it might be a great heap of severed heads, quite permanent objects; bones last a long time. But in Greece, though a man could erect a trophy, it must be made of wood and it could never be repaired. Even as the victor set it up he would

see in his mind how soon it would decay and sink into ruin, and there it must be left. The Greeks in their onward pressing along the steep and rough road had learned a great deal. They knew the victor might be the vanquished next time. There should be no permanent records of the manifestly impermanent. They had learned a great deal.

An old Greek inscription states that the aim of mankind should be "to 21
tame the savageness of man and make gentle the life of the world." Aristotle said that the city was built first for safety, but then that men might discover the good life and lead it. So the Athenians did according to Pericles. Pericles said that Athens stood for freedom and for thought and for beauty, but in the Greek way, within limits, without exaggeration. The Athenians loved beauty, he said, but with simplicity; they did not like the extravagances of luxury. They loved the things of the mind, but they did not shrink from hardship. Thought did not cause them to hesitate, it clarified the road to action. If they had riches they did not make a show of them, and no one was ashamed of being poor if he was useful. They were free because of willing obedience to law, not only the written, but still more the unwritten, kindness and compassion and unselfishness and the many qualities which cannot be enforced, which depend on a man's free choice, but without which men cannot live together.

If ever there is to be a truly good and great and enduring republic it must 22
be along these lines. We need the challenge of the city that thought them out, wherein for centuries one genius after another grew up. Geniuses are not produced by spending money. We need the challenge of the way the Greeks were educated. They fixed their eyes on the individual. We contemplate millions. What we have undertaken in this matter of education has dawned upon us only lately. We are trying to do what has never been attempted before, never in the history of the world—educate all the young in a nation of 170 millions; a magnificent idea, but we are beginning to realize what are the problems and what may be the results of mass production of education. So far, we do not seem appalled at the prospect of exactly the same kind of education being applied to all the school children from the Atlantic to the Pacific, but there is an uneasiness in the air, a realization that the individual is growing less easy to find; an idea, perhaps, of what standardization might become when the units are not machines, but human beings.

Here is where we can go back to the Greeks with profit. The Athenians 23
in their dangerous world needed to be a nation of independent men who could take responsibility, and they taught their children accordingly. They thought about every boy. Someday he would be a citizen of Athens, responsible for her safety and her glory, "each one," Pericles said, "fitted to meet life's chances and changes with the utmost versatility and grace." To them education was by its very nature an individual matter. To be properly educated a boy had to be taught music; he learned to play a musical instrument. He had to learn poetry, a great deal of it, and recite it—and there were a number of musical instruments and many poets; though, to be sure, Homer was the great textbook.

That kind of education is not geared to mass production. It does not produce people who instinctively go the same way. That is how Athenian children lived and learned while our millions learn the same lessons and spend hours before television sets looking at exactly the same thing at exactly the same time. For one reason and another we are more and more ignoring differences, if not trying to obliterate them. We seem headed toward a standardization of the mind, what Goethe called "the deadly commonplace that fetters us all." That was not the Greek way. 24

The picture of the Age of Pericles drawn by the historian Thucydides, one of the greatest historians the world has known, is of a state made up of people who are self-reliant individuals, not echoes or copies, who want to be let alone to do their own work, but who are also closely bound together by a great aim, the commonweal, each one so in love with his country—Pericles' own words—that he wants most of all to use himself in her service. Only an ideal? Ideals have enormous power. They stamp an age. They lift life up when they are lofty; they drag down and make decadent when they are low—and then, by that strange fact, the survival of the fittest, those that are low fade away and are forgotten. The Greek ideals have had a power of persistent life for twenty-five hundred years. 25

Is it rational that now when the young people may have to face problems harder than we face, is it reasonable that with the atomic age before them, at this time we are giving up the study of how the Greeks and Romans prevailed magnificently in a barbaric world; the study, too, of how that triumph ended, how a slackness and softness finally came over them to their ruin? In the end, more than they wanted freedom, they wanted security, a comfortable life, and they lost all—security and comfort and freedom. 26

Is not that a challenge to us? Is it not true that into our education have come a slackness and softness? Is hard effort prominent? The world of thought can be entered in no other way. Are we not growing slack and soft in our political life? When the Athenians finally wanted not to give to the state, but the state to give to them, when the freedom they wished most for was freedom from responsibility, then Athens ceased to be free and was never free again. Is not that a challenge? 27

Cicero said, "To be ignorant of the past is to remain a child." Santayana said, "A nation that does not know history is fated to repeat it." The Greeks can help us, help us as no other people can, to see how freedom is won and how it is lost. Above all, to see in clearest light what freedom is. The first nation in the world to be free sends a ringing call down through the centuries to all who would be free. Greece rose to the very height, not because she was big, she was very small; not because she was rich, she was very poor; not even because she was wonderfully gifted. So doubtless were others in the great empires of the ancient world who have gone their way leaving little for us. She rose because there was in the Greeks the greatest spirit that moves in humanity, the spirit that sets men free. 28

Plato put into words what that spirit is. "Freedom" he says, "is no matter of laws and constitutions; only he is free who realizes the divine order 29 within himself, the true standard by which a man can steer and measure himself." True standards, ideals that lift life up, marked the way of the Greeks. Therefore their light has never been extinguished.

"The time for extracting a lesson from history is ever at hand for them 30
who are wise." Demosthenes.

Questions for Discussion

1. Hamilton defines being educated as being "able to be caught up into the world of thought" (¶3). What do you think she means by being "caught up"? How does her meaning compare with Whitehead's definition in "The Aims of Education" that "education is the acquisition of the art of the utilization of knowledge" (p. 75, ¶11)?
2. According to Hamilton, the use of one's mind should be a pleasure in itself; she alludes to Robert Louis Stevenson's remark that "a man ought to be able to spend two or three hours waiting for a train at a little country station when he was all alone and had nothing to read, and not be bored for a moment" (¶6). How often do you sit down to think about something, not to daydream or lapse into random thoughts but to concentrate on an issue, topic, or idea? Do you know people who do this? Do you know anyone who seems afraid of the silence that invites thought, who requires the sound of records, television, radio, or friends to fill up the space that might otherwise be threatened by thinking?
3. Is your education enlarging your capacity for sustained thought? Are you being given both things to think *about* and methods to think *by*? Do you find yourself mulling over the ideas from your classes—or, better yet, discussing them with friends—as if they had applications and importance outside of the requirements for the course? If not, do you think this is what you *should be* getting? What are the obstacles preventing it?
4. When Athenian democracy was strong, Hamilton argues, it was strong because citizens generally—both rich and poor, noble and common—*took responsibility* for preserving it (¶17–18). Can you find examples in American society that suggest what happens to democracy when freedom *without* responsibility becomes the aim? Is it your impression that Americans generally are willing to be responsible for making democracy work? If you think they are not willing, what do you think might account for their unwillingness?

Suggested Essay Topics

1. "In the end, more than they [the Greeks] wanted freedom, they wanted security, a comfortable life, and they lost all—security and comfort and freedom" (¶26). When college students are asked today why they go to

college, they frequently cite comfort and security—a good job and a comfortable life—as their reasons for attending college. They seldom say that they want an education in order to make their contribution to freedom and democracy. In an essay or letter directed to Edith Hamilton, defend the goals of today's college students. Counter her claim that an education should be directed toward the cultivation of general powers rather than specific skills, and, since you are rejecting her claim that education helps preserve freedom, make clear what you think does help preserve it and what kind of responsibility that preservation places on individual citizens.

2. Take the opposite position from that of topic 1: In an essay directed to students you know who are bent on education for security and comfort, extend Hamilton's argument that today's education is slack and soft (¶27) and makes no real contribution to freedom in our society. Illustrate her argument with examples from trends in education generally, but especially with examples from your own education (both now and in the past). Contrast the aims of the education you have been given with the aims that Hamilton says guided Greek education—the cultivation of a sense of beauty, proportion, personal grace, excellence, and independent thought—and point out in detail where you think your education has been slack and soft. Make any recommendations you think appropriate.

William Faulkner

Whenever we attempt to make sense out of the present by remembering the past, we are taking a historical perspective. Of course, this is not the phrase we would use to describe such activity. "Taking a historical perspective" sounds like something only a historian would do. But the truth is that none of us can escape being historians much of the time. All of us reconstruct and interpret our own past as we try to understand what caused our present world: "If only I had taken that job with Electronics International instead of taking that blind-alley offer from Pro-Disk, I could now be earning 50 percent more money"; "The reason I had to take such a crummy college teaching job in 1973 is because that was the year the bottom dropped out of the academic job market"; "The reason I worry about money so much is that my parents, who struggled through the Great Depression, drilled into us kids that we should never be without a nest egg."

All of these examples show people taking a historical perspective on a typical subject: their own lives. But spreading backward from our private lives are historical dimensions that we share with larger and larger groups the farther back we travel: the history of our family; our neighborhood, city, or local community; our state; our region (the South or New England, for example); our nation; our civilization; the human race. Even if we are unaware of the events of the past in each of these dimensions, those events have nevertheless played some role in our lives by shaping the conditions *under which we carve out our present destinies. Thus we can be ignorant of the history of Greek literature and art, Roman law, Germanic languages, the American Revolution, or the graft in the last governor's administration and yet be influenced by them in our everyday lives because each of these factors has helped determine our available choices. What professional historians do differently from the rest of us is focus on these larger dimensions—the history of Greek civilization, the events of the fourteenth century in Europe, and so on—but the basic process of (1) trying to understand why things happened the way they did and then (2) using that understanding to improve our knowledge and control of the present is the same.*

Some imaginative writers mine the historical perspective as a rich source of literary gold. William Faulkner (1897–1962), who could for our purposes be called a historical interpreter of the soul of the South, is a good example. He is aware of the leading facts in the history of the South: the seizure of land from the Indians, the use of slaves as the basis of the South's economy, the systematic and institutionalized oppression of blacks even after slavery disappeared, the high-minded appeal to honor and loyalty and courage, the racism that corrupted these high-minded values with guilt and shame and hypocrisy, the implacable resistance of the southerner to outside interference or criticism, the pride in the Confederacy and the bitterness and shame that some southerners still feel over its defeat. Faulkner's stories are steeped in this history, which he employs not merely as a general coloring but as rich literary soil that he keeps reworking. He sees the present South in every respect as embedded in this history of high-minded values, attachment to the land, racism, and violence. The details of his stories—the particular characters, hunting episodes, and life stories, for example—are all fictional, but they are fictions designed to shadow forth the permanent truths in the South's history and character.

In "Delta Autumn" a large chunk of southern history parallels the 80-year span of Ike McCaslin's life. The rest of that history is embedded in Ike's head, and he uses it, as Faulkner himself does (Ike seems to be in part a spokesman for Faulkner), not only to help him understand but to evaluate the lives of the people around him, their passions and motives, their hates and loves. When Ike discovers that his kinsman, Roth Edmonds, has, like so many southern men before him, once again repeated the most ancient, crippling, and shameful sin in southern history, he has to have a way of explaining it to himself. The only mode of explanation he can appeal to is history. As you read, try to determine whether you agree with Ike's prognosis for the future based on his historical views and, more important, whether you agree with the basic values that underlie those views.

DELTA AUTUMN

From *Go Down, Moses* (1942).

Soon now they would enter the Delta. The sensation was familiar to old Isaac McCaslin. It had been renewed like this each last week in November for more than fifty years—the last hill, at the foot of which the rich unbroken alluvial 1 flatness began as the sea began at the base of its cliffs, dissolving away beneath the unhurried November rain as the sea itself would dissolve away.

2 At first they had come in wagons: the guns, the bedding, the dogs, the food, the whiskey, the keen heart-lifting anticipation of hunting; the young men who could drive all night and all the following day in the cold rain and pitch a camp in the rain and sleep in the wet blankets and rise at daylight the next morning and hunt. There had been bear then. A man shot a doe or a fawn as quickly as he did a buck, and in the afternoons they shot wild turkey with pistols to test their stalking skill and marksmanship, feeding all but the breast to the dogs. But that time was gone now. Now they went in cars, driving faster and faster each year because the roads were better and they had farther and farther to drive, the territory in which game still existed drawing yearly inward as his life was drawing inward, until now he was the last of those who had once made the journey in wagons without feeling it and now those who accompanied him were the sons and even grandsons of the men who had ridden for twenty-four hours in the rain or sleet behind the steaming mules. They called him "Uncle Ike" now, and he no longer told anyone how near eighty he actually was because he knew as well as they did that he no longer had any business making such expeditions, even by car.

3 In fact, each time now, on that first night in camp, lying aching and sleepless in the harsh blankets, his blood only faintly warmed by the single thin whiskey-and-water which he allowed himself, he would tell himself that this would be his last. But he would stand that trip—he still shot almost as well as he ever had, still killed almost as much of the game he saw as he ever killed; he no longer even knew how many deer had fallen before his gun—and the fierce long heat of the next summer would renew him. Then November would come again, and again in the car with two of the sons of his old companions, whom he had taught not only how to distinguish between the prints left by a buck or a doe but between the sound they made in moving, he would look ahead past the jerking arc of the windshield wiper and see the land flatten suddenly and swoop, dissolving away beneath the rain as the sea itself would dissolve, and he would say, "Well, boys, there it is again."

4 This time though, he didn't have time to speak. The driver of the car stopped it, slamming it to a skidding halt on the greasy pavement without warning, actually flinging the two passengers forward until they caught themselves with their braced hands against the dash. "What the hell, Roth!" the man in the middle said. "Can't you whistle first when you do that? Hurt you, Uncle Ike?"

5 "No," the old man said. "What's the matter?" The driver didn't answer. Still leaning forward, the old man looked sharply past the face of the man between them, at the face of his kinsman. It was the youngest face of them all, aquiline, saturnine, a little ruthless, the face of his ancestor too, tempered a little, altered a little, staring somberly through the streaming windshield across which the twin wipers flicked and flicked.

"I didn't intend to come back in here this time," he said suddenly and 6
harshly.

"You said that back in Jefferson last week," the old man said. "Then you 7
changed your mind. Have you changed it again? This ain't a very good time to—"

"Oh, Roth's coming," the man in the middle said. His name was Legate. 8
He seemed to be speaking to no one, as he was looking at neither of them. "If it was just a buck he was coming all this distance for, now. But he's got a doe in here. Of course a old man like Uncle Ike can't be interested in no doe, not one that walks on two legs—when she's standing up, that is. Pretty lightcolored, too. The one he was after them nights last fall when he said he was coon-hunting, Uncle Ike. The one I figured maybe he was still running when he was gone all that month last January. But of course a old man like Uncle Ike ain't got no interest in nothing like that." He chortled, still looking at no one, not completely jeering.

"What?" the old man said. "What's that?" But he had not even so much 9
as glanced at Legate. He was still watching his kinsman's face. The eyes behind the spectacles were the blurred eyes of an old man, but they were quite sharp too; eyes which could still see a gunbarrel and what ran beyond it as well as any of them could. He was remembering himself now: how last year, during the final stage by motor boat in to where they camped, a box of food had been lost overboard and how on the next day his kinsman had gone back to the nearest town for supplies and had been gone overnight. And when he did return, something had happened to him. He would go into the woods with his rifle each dawn when the others went, but the old man, watching him, knew that he was not hunting. "All right," he said. "Take me and Will on to shelter where we can wait for the truck, and you can go on back."

"I'm going in," the other said harshly. "Don't worry. Because this will 10
be the last of it."

"The last of deer hunting, or of doe hunting?" Legate said. This time 11
the old man paid no attention to him even by speech. He still watched the young man's savage and brooding face.

"Why?" he said. 12

"After Hitler gets through with it? Or Smith or Jones or Roosevelt or 13
Willkie or whatever he will call himself in this country?"

"We'll stop him in this country," Legate said. "Even if he calls himself 14
George Washington."

"How?" Edmonds said. "By singing 'God Bless America' in bars at 15
midnight and wearing dime-store flags in our lapels?"

"So that's what's worrying you," the old man said. "I ain't noticed this 16
country being short of defenders yet, when it needed them. You did some of it yourself twenty-odd years ago, before you were a grown man even. This country is a little mite stronger than any one man or group of men, outside of it or even inside of it either. I reckon, when the time comes and some of you have done got tired of hollering we are whipped if we don't go to war

and some more are hollering we are whipped if we do, it will cope with one Austrian paperhanger,* no matter what he will be calling himself. My pappy and some other better men than any of them you named tried once to tear it in two with a war, and they failed."

"And what have you got left?" the other said. "Half the people without 17
jobs and half the factories closed by strikes. Half the people on public dole that won't work and half that couldn't work even if they would. Too much cotton and corn and hogs, and not enough for people to eat and wear. The country full of people to tell a man how he can't raise his own cotton whether he will or won't, and Sally Rand with a sergeant's stripes and not even the fan couldn't fill the army rolls. Too much not-butter and not even the guns—"†

"We got a deer camp—if we ever get to it," Legate said. "Not to mention 18
does."

"It's a good time to mention does," the old man said. "Does and fawns 19
both. The only fighting anywhere that ever had anything of God's blessing on it has been when men fought to protect does and fawns. If it's going to come to fighting, that's a good thing to mention and remember too."

"Haven't you discovered in—how many years more than seventy is 20
it?—that women and children are one thing there's never any scarcity of?" Edmonds said.

"Maybe that's why all I am worrying about right now is that ten miles 21
of river we still have got to run before we can make camp," the old man said. "So let's get on."

They went on. Soon they were going fast again, as Edmonds always 22
drove, consulting neither of them about the speed just as he had given neither of them any warning when he slammed the car to stop. The old man relaxed again. He watched, as he did each recurrent November while more than sixty of them passed, the land which he had seen change. At first there had been only the old towns along the River and the old towns along the hills, from each of which the planters with their gangs of slaves and then of hired laborers had wrested from the impenetrable jungle of water-standing cane and cypress, gum and holly and oak and ash, cotton patches which, as the years passed, became fields and then plantations. The paths made by deer and bear became roads and then highways, with towns in turn springing up along them and along the rivers Tallahatchie and Sunflower which joined and became the Yazoo, the River of the Dead of the Choctaws—the thick, slow, black, unsunned streams almost without current, which once each year ceased to flow at all and then reversed, spreading, drowning the rich land and subsiding again, leaving it still richer.

Most of that was gone now. Now a man drove two hundred miles from 23
Jefferson before he found wilderness to hunt in. Now the land lay open from

*Adolf Hitler.

†Sally Rand, burlesque queen, used two large feather fans and helped recruit for the armed forces in World War II. Guns and butter stand for arms and civilian goods, respectively.

the cradling hills on the east to the rampart of levee on the west, standing horseman-tall with cotton for the world's looms—the rich black land, imponderable and vast, fecund up to the very doorsteps of the Negroes who worked it and of the white men who owned it; which exhausted the hunting life of a dog in one year, the working life of a mule in five and of a man in twenty—the land in which neon flashed past them from the little countless towns, and countless shining this-year's automobiles sped past them on the broad plumb-ruled highways, yet in which the only permanent mark of man's occupation seemed to be the tremendous gins, constructed in sections of sheet iron and in a week's time though they were, since no man, millionaire though he be, would build more than a roof and walls to shelter the camping equipment he lived from when he knew that once each ten years or so his house would be flooded to the second storey and all within it ruined;—the land across which there came now no scream of panther but instead the long hooting of locomotives: trains of incredible length and drawn by a single engine, since there was no gradient anywhere and no elevation save those raised by forgotten aboriginal hands as refuges from the yearly water and used by their Indian successors to sepulcher their fathers' bones, and all that remained of that old time were the Indian names of the little towns and usually pertaining to water—Aluschaskuna, Tillatoba, Homochitto, Yazoo.

By early afternoon, they were on water. At the last little Indian-named 24
town at the end of pavement they waited until the other car and the two trucks—the one carrying the bedding and tents and food, the other the horses—overtook them. They left the concrete and, after another mile or so, the gravel too. In caravan they ground on through the ceaselessly dissolving afternoon, with skid-chains on the wheels now, lurching and splashing and sliding among the ruts, until presently it seemed to him that the retrograde of his remembering had gained an inverse velocity from their own slow progress, that the land had retreated not in minutes from the last spread of gravel but in years, decades, back toward what it had been when he first knew it: the road they now followed once more the ancient pathway of bear and deer, the diminishing fields they now passed once more scooped punily and terrifically by axe and saw and mule-drawn plow from the wilderness' flank, out of the brooding and immemorial tangle, in place of ruthless mile-wide parallelograms wrought by ditching and dyking machinery.

They reached the river landing and unloaded, the horses to go overland 25
down stream to a point opposite the camp and swim the river, themselves and the bedding and food and dogs and guns in the motor launch. It was himself, though no horseman, no farmer, not even a countryman save by his distant birth and boyhood, who coaxed and soothed the two horses, drawing them by his own single frail hand until, backing, filling, trembling a little, they surged, halted, then sprang scrambling down from the truck, possessing no affinity for them as creatures, beasts, but being merely insulated by his years and time from the corruption of steel and oiled moving parts which tainted the others.

Then, his old hammer double gun which was only twelve years younger 26 than he standing between his knees, he watched even the last puny marks of man—cabin, clearing, the small and irregular fields which a year ago were jungle and in which the skeleton stalks of this year's cotton stood almost as tall and rank as the old cane had stood, as if man had had to marry his planting to the wilderness in order to conquer it—fall away and vanish. The twin banks marched with wilderness as he remembered it—the tangle of brier and cane impenetrable even to sight twenty feet away, the tall tremendous soaring of oak and gum and ash and hickory which had rung to no axe save the hunter's, had echoed to no machinery save the beat of old-time steam boats traversing it or to the snarling of launches like their own of people going into it to dwell for a week or two weeks because it was still wilderness. There was some of it left, although now it was two hundred miles from Jefferson when once it had been thirty. He had watched it, not being conquered, destroyed, so much as retreating since its purpose was served now and its time an outmoded time, retreating southward through this inverted-apex, this ▽-shaped section of earth between hills and River until what was left of it seemed now to be gathered and for the time arrested in one tremendous density of brooding and inscrutable impenetrability at the ultimate funnelling tip.

They reached the site of their last-year's camp with still two hours left 27
of light. "You go on over under that driest tree and set down," Legate told him. "—if you can find it. Me and these other young boys will do this." He did neither. He was not tired yet. That would come later. *Maybe it won't come at all this time,* he thought, as he had thought at this point each November for the last five or six of them. *Maybe I will go out on stand in the morning too;* knowing that he would not, not even if he took the advice and sat down under the driest shelter and did nothing until camp was made and supper cooked. Because it would not be the fatigue. It would be because he would not sleep tonight but would lie instead wakeful and peaceful on the cot amid the tent-filling snoring and the rain's whisper as he always did on the first night in camp; peaceful, without regret or fretting, telling himself that was all right too, who didn't have so many of them left as to waste one sleeping.

In his slicker he directed the unloading of the boat—the tents, the stove, 28
the bedding, the food for themselves and the dogs until there should be meat in camp. He sent two of the Negroes to cut firewood; he had the cook-tent raised and the stove up and a fire going and supper cooking while the big tent was still being staked down. Then in the beginning of dusk he crossed in the boat to where the horses waited, backing and snorting at the water. He took the lead-ropes and with no more weight than that and his voice, he drew them down into the water and held them beside the boat with only their heads above the surface, as though they actually were suspended from his frail and strengthless old man's hands, while the boat recrossed and each horse in turn lay prone in the shallows, panting and trembling, its eyes rolling in the dusk, until the same weightless hand and unraised voice gathered it surging upward, splashing and thrashing up the bank.

Then the meal was ready. The last of light was gone now save the thin 29 stain of it snared somewhere between the river's surface and the rain. He had the single glass of thin whiskey-and-water, then, standing in the churned mud beneath the stretched tarpaulin, he said grace over the fried slabs of pork, the hot soft shapeless bread, the canned beans and molasses and coffee in iron plates and cups,—the town food, brought along with them—then covered himself again, the others following. "Eat," he said. "Eat it all up. I don't want a piece of town meat in camp after breakfast tomorrow. Then you boys will hunt. You'll have to. When I first started hunting in this bottom sixty years ago with old General Compson and Major de Spain and Roth's grandfather and Will Legate's too, Major de Spain wouldn't allow but two pieces of foreign grub in his camp. That was one side of pork and one ham of beef. And not to eat for the first supper and breakfast neither. It was to save until along toward the end of camp when everybody was so sick of bear meat and coon and venison that we couldn't even look at it."

"I thought Uncle Ike was going to say the pork and beef was for the 30
dogs." Legate said, chewing. "But that's right; I remember. You just shot the dogs a mess of wild turkey every evening when they got tired of deer guts."

"Times are different now," another said. "There was game here then." 31

"Yes," the old man said quietly. "There was game here then." 32

"Besides, they shot does then too," Legate said. "As it is now, we ain't 33
got but one doe-hunter in—'

"And better men hunted it," Edmonds said. He stood at the end of the 34
rough plank table, eating rapidly and steadily as the others ate. But again the old man looked sharply across at the sullen, handsome, brooding face which appeared now darker and more sullen still in the light of the smoky lantern. "Go on. Say it."

"I didn't say that," the old man said. "There are good men everywhere, 35
at all times. Most men are. Some are just unlucky, because most men are a little better than their circumstances give them a chance to be. And I've known some that even the circumstances couldn't stop."

"Well, I wouldn't say—" Legate said. 36

"So you've lived almost eighty years," Edmonds said, "and that's what 37
you finally learned about the other animals you lived among. I suppose the question to ask you is, where have you been all the time you were dead?"

There was a silence; for the instant even Legate's jaw stopped chewing 38
while he gaped at Edmonds. "Well, by God, Roth—" the third speaker said. But it was the old man who spoke, his voice still peaceful and untroubled and merely grave:

"Maybe so," he said. "But if being what you call alive would have 39
learned me any different, I reckon I'm satisfied, wherever it was I've been."

"Well, I wouldn't say that Roth—" Legate said. 40

The third speaker was still leaning forward a little over the table, look- 41
ing at Edmonds. "Meaning that it's only because folks happen to be watching him that a man behaves at all," he said. "Is that it?"

"Yes," Edmonds said. "A man in a blue coat, with a badge on it watch- 42
ing him. Maybe just the badge."

43 "I deny that," the old man said. "I don't—"

44 The other two paid no attention to him. Even Legate was listening to them for the moment, his mouth still full of food and still open a little, his knife with another lump of something balanced on the tip of the blade arrested halfway to his mouth. "I'm glad I don't have your opinion of folks," the third speaker said. "I take it you include yourself."

45 "I see," Edmonds said. "You prefer Uncle Ike's opinion of circumstances. All right. Who makes the circumstances?"

46 "Luck," the third said. "Chance. Happen-so. I see what you are getting at. But that's just what Uncle Ike said: that now and then, maybe most of the time, man is a little better than the net result of his and his neighbors' doings, when he gets the chance to be."

47 This time Legate swallowed first. He was not to be stopped this time. "Well, I wouldn't say that Roth Edmonds can hunt one doe every day and night for two weeks and was a poor hunter or a unlucky one neither. A man that still have the same doe left to hunt on again next year—"

48 "Have some meat," the man next to him said.

49 "—ain't so unlucky—What?" Legate said.

50 "Have some meat." The other offered the dish.

51 "I got some," Legate said.

52 "Have some more," the third speaker said. "You and Roth Edmonds both. Have a heap of it. Clapping your jaws together that way with nothing to break the shock." Someone chortled. Then they all laughed, with relief, the tension broken. But the old man was speaking, even into the laughter, in that peaceful and still untroubled voice:

53 "I still believe. I see proof everywhere. I grant that man made a heap of his circumstances, him and his living neighbors between them. He even inherited some of them already made, already almost ruined even. A while ago Henry Wyatt there said how there used to be more game here. There was that too—" Someone laughed, a single guffaw, stillborn. It ceased and they all listened, gravely, looking down at their plates. Edmonds was drinking his coffee, sullen, brooding, inattentive.

54 "Some folks still kill does," Wyatt said. "There won't be just one buck hanging in this bottom tomorrow night without any head to fit it."

55 "I didn't say all men," the old man said. "I said most men. And not just because there is a man with a badge to watch us. We probably won't even see him unless maybe he will stop here about noon tomorrow and eat dinner with us and check our licenses—"

56 "We don't kill does because if we did kill does in a few years there wouldn't even be any bucks left to kill, Uncle Ike," Wyatt said.

57 "According to Roth yonder, that's one thing we won't never have to worry about," the old man said. "He said on the way here this morning that does and fawns—I believe he said women and children—are two things this world ain't ever lacked. But that ain't all of it," he said. "That's just the mind's reason a man has to give himself because the heart don't always have time to bother with thinking up words that fit together. God created man and He created the world for him to live in and I reckon He created the kind of world

He would have wanted to live in if He had been a man—the ground to walk on, the big woods, the trees and the water, and the game to live in it. And maybe He didn't put the desire to hunt and kill game in man but I reckon He knew it was going to be there, that man was going to teach it to himself, since he wasn't quite God himself yet—"

"When will he be?" Wyatt said. 58

"I think that every man and woman, at the instant when it don't even 59
matter whether they marry or not, I think that whether they marry then or afterward or don't never, at that instant the two of them together were God."

"Then there are some Gods in this world I wouldn't want to touch, and 60
with a damn long stick," Edmonds said. He set his coffee cup down and looked at Wyatt. "And that includes myself, if that's what you want to know. I'm going to bed." He was gone. There was a general movement among the others. But it ceased and they stood again about the table, not looking at the old man, apparently held there yet by his quiet and peaceful voice as the heads of the swimming horses had been held above the water by his weightless hand. The three Negroes—the cook and his helper and old Isham—were sitting quietly in the entrance of the kitchen tent, listening too, the three faces dark and motionless and musing.

"He put them both here: man, and the game he would follow and kill, 61
foreknowing it. I believe He said, 'So be it.' I reckon He even foreknew the end. But He said, 'I will give him his chance. I will give him warning and foreknowledge too, along with the desire to follow and the power to slay. The woods and fields he ravages and the game he devastates will be the consequence and signature of His crime and guilt, and his punishment.'—Bed time," he said. His voice and inflection did not change at all. "Breakfast at four oclock, Isham. We want meat on the ground by sunup time."

There was a good fire in the sheet-iron heater; the tent was warm and 62
was beginning to dry out, except for the mud underfoot. Edmonds was already rolled into his blankets, motionless, his face to the wall. Isham had made up his bed too—the strong, battered iron cot, the stained mattress which was not quite soft enough, the worn, often-washed blankets which as the years passed were less and less warm enough. But the tent was warm; presently, when the kitchen was cleaned up and readied for breakfast, the young Negro would come in to lie down before the heater, where he could be roused to put fresh wood into it from time to time. And then, he knew now he would not sleep tonight anyway; he no longer needed to tell himself that perhaps he would. But it was all right now. The day was ended now and night faced him, but alarmless, empty of fret. *Maybe I came for this,* he thought: *Not to hunt, but for this. I would come anyway, even if only to go back home tomorrow.* Wearing only his bagging woolen underwear, his spectacles folded away in the worn case beneath the pillow where he could reach them readily and his lean body fitted easily into the old worn groove of mattress and blankets, he lay on his back, his hands crossed on his breast and his eyes closed while the others undressed and went to bed and the last of the sporadic talking died into snoring. Then he opened his eyes and lay peaceful and quiet as a child,

looking up at the motionless belly of rain-murmured canvas upon which the glow of the heater was dying slowly away and would fade still further until the young Negro, lying on two planks before it, would sit up and stoke it and lie back down again.

They had a house once. That was sixty years ago, when the Big Bottom 63
was only thirty miles from Jefferson and old Major de Spain, who had been his father's cavalry commander in '61 and '2 and '3 and '4, and his cousin (his older brother; his father too) had taken him into the woods for the first time. Old Sam Fathers was alive then, born in slavery, son of a Negro slave and a Chickasaw chief, who had taught him how to shoot, not only when to shoot but when not to; such a November dawn as tomorrow would be and the old man led him straight to the great cypress and he had known the buck would pass exactly there because there was something running in Sam Fathers' veins which ran in the veins of the buck too, and they stood there against the tremendous trunk, the old man of seventy and the boy of twelve, and there was nothing save the dawn until suddenly the buck was there, smoke-colored out of nothing, magnificent with speed: and Sam Fathers said, 'Now. Shoot quick and shoot slow:' and the gun levelled rapidly without haste and crashed and he walked to the buck lying still intact and still in the shape of that magnificent speed and bled it with Sam's knife and Sam dipped his hands into the hot blood and marked his face forever while he stood trying not to tremble, humbly and with pride too though the boy of twelve had been unable to phrase it then: *I slew you; my bearing must not shame your quitting life. My conduct forever onward must become your death;* marking him for that and for more than that: that day and himself and McCaslin juxtaposed, not against the wilderness but against the tamed land, the old wrong and shame itself, in repudiation and denial at least of the land and the wrong and shame, even if he couldn't cure the wrong and eradicate the shame, who at fourteen when he learned of it had believed he could do both when he became competent, and when at twenty-one he became competent he knew that he could do neither but at least he could repudiate the wrong and shame, at least in principle, and at least the land itself in fact, for his son at least: and did, though he had: then (married then) in a rented cubicle in a back-street stock-traders' boarding-house, the first and last time he ever saw her naked body, himself and his wife juxtaposed in their turn against that same land, that same wrong and shame from whose regret and grief he would at least save and free his son and, saving and freeing his son, lost him.

They had the house then. That roof, the two weeks of each November 64
which they spent under it, had become his home. Although since that time they had lived during the two fall weeks in tents and not always in the same place two years in succession and now his companions were the sons and even the grandsons of them with whom he had lived in the house, and for almost fifty years now the house itself had not even existed, the conviction, the sense and feeling of home, had been merely transferred into the canvas. He owned a house in Jefferson, a good house though small, where he had had a wife and lived with her and lost her, ay, lost her even though he had lost her in the

rented cubicle before he and his old clever dipsomaniac partner had finished the house for them to move into it: but lost her, because she loved him. But women hope for so much. They never live too long to still believe that anything within the scope of their passionate wanting is likewise within the range of their passionate hope: and it was still kept for him by his dead wife's widowed niece and her children, and he was comfortable in it, his wants and needs and even the small trying harmless crochets of an old man looked after by blood at least related to the blood which he had elected out of all the earth to cherish. But he spent the time within those walls waiting for November, because even this tent with its muddy floor and the bed which was not wide enough nor soft enough nor even warm enough, was his home and these men, some of whom he only saw during these two November weeks and not one of whom even bore any name he used to know—De Spain and Compson and Ewell and Hogganbeck—were more his kin than any. Because this was his land—

The shadow of the youngest Negro loomed. It soared, blotting the 65
heater's dying glow from the ceiling, the wood billets thumping into the iron maw until the glow, the flame, leaped high and bright across the canvas. But the Negro's shadow still remained, by its length and breadth, standing, since it covered most of the ceiling, until after a moment he raised himself on one elbow to look. It was not the Negro, it was his kinsman; when he spoke the other turned sharp against the red firelight the sullen and ruthless profile.

"Nothing," Edmonds said. "Go on back to sleep." 66

"Since Will Legate mentioned it," McCaslin said, "I remember you had 67
some trouble sleeping in here last fall too. Only you called it coon-hunting then. Or was it Will Legate called it that?" The other didn't answer. Then he turned and went back to his bed. McCaslin, still propped on his elbow, watched until the other's shadow sank down the wall and vanished, became one with the mass of sleeping shadows. "That's right," he said. "Try to get some sleep. We must have meat in camp tomorrow. You can do all the setting up you want to after that." He lay down again, his hands crossed again on his breast, watching the glow of the heater on the canvas ceiling. It was steady again now, the fresh wood accepted, being assimilated; soon it would begin to fade again, taking with it the last echo of that sudden upflare of a young man's passion and unrest. Let him lie awake for a little while, he thought; He will lie still some day for a long time without even dissatisfaction to disturb him. And lying awake here, in these surroundings, would soothe him if anything could, if anything could soothe a man just forty years old. Yes, he thought; Forty years old or thirty, or even the trembling and sleepless ardor of a boy; already the tent, the rain-murmured canvas globe, was once more filled with it. He lay on his back, his eyes closed, his breathing quiet and peaceful as a child's, listening to it—that silence which was never silence but was myriad. He could almost see it, tremendous, primeval, looming, musing downward upon this puny, evanescent clutter of human sojourn which after a single brief week would vanish and in another week would be completely healed, traceless in the unmarked solitude. Because it was his land, although

he had never owned a foot of it. He had never wanted to, not even after he saw plain its ultimate doom, watching it retreat year by year before the onslaught of axe and saw and log-lines and then dynamite and tractor plows, because it belonged to no man. It belonged to all; they had only to use it well, humbly and with pride. Then suddenly he knew why he had never wanted to own any of it, arrest at least that much of what people called progress, measure his longevity at least against that much of its ultimate fate. It was because there was just exactly enough of it. He seemed to see the two of them—himself and the wilderness—as coevals, his own span as a hunter, a woodsman, not contemporary with his first breath but transmitted to him, assumed by him gladly, humbly, with joy and pride, from that old Major de Spain and that old Sam Fathers who had taught him to hunt, the two spans running out together, not toward oblivion, nothingness, but into a dimension free of both time and space, where once more the untreed land warped and wrung to mathematical squares of rank cotton for the frantic old-world people to turn into shells to shoot at one another, would fine ample room for both—the names, the faces of the old men he had known and loved and for a little while outlived, moving again among the shades of tall unaxed trees and sightless brakes where the wild strong immortal game ran forever before the tireless belling immortal hounds, falling and rising phoenix-like to the soundless guns.

He had been asleep. The lantern was lighted now. Outside in the dark- 68
ness the oldest Negro, Isham, was beating a spoon against the bottom of a tin pan and crying, "Raise up and get yo foa clock coffy. Raise up and get yo foa clock coffy," and the tent was full of low talk and of men dressing, and Legate's voice, repeating: "Get out of here now and let Uncle Ike sleep. If you wake him up, he'll go out with us. And he ain't got any business in the woods this morning."

So he didn't move. He lay with his eyes closed, his breathing gentle and 69
peaceful, and heard them one by one leave the tent. He listened to the breakfast sounds from the table beneath the tarpaulin and heard them depart—the horses, the dogs, the last voice until it died away and there was only the sounds of the Negroes clearing breakfast away. After a while he might possibly even hear the first faint clear cry of the first hound ring through the wet woods from where the buck had bedded, then he would go back so sleep again— The tent-flap swung in and fell. Something jarred sharply against the end of the cot and a hand grasped his knee through the blanket before he could open his eyes. It was Edmonds, carrying a shotgun in place of his rifle. He spoke in a harsh, rapid voice:

"Sorry to wake you. There will be a—" 70

"I was awake," McCaslin said, "Are you going to shoot that shotgun 71
today?"

"You just told me last night you want meat," Edmonds said. "There will 72
be a —"

"Since when did you start having trouble getting meat with your rifle?" 73

"All right," the other said, with that harsh, restrained, furious impa- 74 tience. Then McCaslin saw in his hand a thick oblong: an envelope. "There will be a message here some time this morning, looking for me. Maybe it won't come. If it does, give the messenger this and tell h— say I said No."

"A what?" McCaslin said. "Tell who?" He half rose onto his elbow as 75
Edmonds jerked the envelope onto the blanket, already turning toward the entrance, the envelope striking solid and heavy and without noise and already sliding from the bed until McCaslin caught it, divining by feel through the paper as instantaneously and conclusively as if he had opened the envelope and looked, the thick sheaf of banknotes. "Wait," he said. "Wait:"—more than the blood kinsman, more even than the senior in years, so that the other paused, the canvas lifted, looking back, and McCaslin saw that outside it was already day. "Tell her No," he said. "Tell her." They stared at one another—the old face, wan, sleep-raddled above the tumbled bed, the dark and sullen younger one at once furious and cold. "Will Legate was right. This is what you called coon-hunting. And now this." He didn't raise the envelope. He made no motion, no gesture to indicate it. "What did you promise her that you haven't the courage to face her and retract?"

"Nothing!" the other said. "Nothing! This is all of it. Tell her I said No." 76
He was gone. The tent flap lifted on an in-waft of faint light and the constant murmur of rain, and fell again, leaving the old man still half-raised onto one elbow, the envelope clutched in the other shaking hand. Afterward it seemed to him that he had begun to hear the approaching boat almost immediately, before the other could have got out of sight even. It seemed to him that there had been no interval whatever: the tent flap falling on the same out-waft of faint and rain-filled light like the suspiration and expiration of the same breath and then in the next second lifted again—the mounting snarl of the outboard engine, increasing, nearer and nearer and louder and louder then cut short off, ceasing with the absolute instantaneity of a blown-out candle, into the lap and plop of water under the bows as the skiff slid in to the bank, the youngest Negro, the youth, raising the tent flap beyond which for that instant he saw the boat—a small skiff with a Negro man sitting in the stern beside the upslanted motor—then the woman entering, in a man's hat and a man's slicker and rubber boots, carrying the blanket-swaddled bundle on one arm and holding the edge of the unbuttoned raincoat over it with the other hand: and bringing something else, something intangible, an effluvium which he knew he would recognize in a moment because Isham had already told him, warned him, by sending the young Negro to the tent to announce the visitor instead of coming himself, the flap falling at last on the young Negro and they were alone—the face indistinct and as yet only young and with dark eyes, queerly colorless but not ill and not that of a country woman despite the garments she wore, looking down at him where he sat upright on the cot now, clutching the envelope, the soiled undergarment bagging about him and the twisted blankets huddled about his hips.

"Is that his?" he cried. "Don't lie to me!" 77

"Yes," she said. "He's gone." 78

"Yes. He's gone. You won't jump him here. Not this time. I don't reckon 79
even you expected that. He left you this. Here." He fumbled at the envelope. It was not to pick it up, because it was still in his hand; he had never put it down. It was as if he had to fumble somehow to co-ordinate physically his heretofore obedient hand with what his brain was commanding of it, as if he had never performed such an action before, extending the envelope at last, saying again, "Here. Take it. Take it:" until he became aware of her eyes, or not the eyes so much as the look, the regard fixed now on his face with that immersed contemplation, that bottomless and intent candor, of a child. If she had ever seen either the envelope or his movement to extend it, she did not show it.

"You're Uncle Isaac," she said. 80

"Yes," he said. "But never mind that. Here. Take it. He said to tell you 81
No." She looked at the envelope, then she took it. It was sealed and bore no superscription. Nevertheless, even after she glanced at the front of it, he watched her hold it in the one free hand and tear the corner off with her teeth and manage to rip it open and tilt the neat sheaf of bound notes onto the blanket without even glancing at them and look into the empty envelope and take the edge between her teeth and tear it completely open before she crumpled and dropped it.

"That's just money," she said. 82

"What did you expect? What else did you expect? You have known him 83
long enough or at least often enough to have got that child, and you don't know him any better than that?"

"Not very often. Not very long. Just that week here last fall, and in 84
January he sent for me and we went west, to New Mexico. We were there six weeks, where I could at least sleep in the same apartment where I cooked for him and looked after his clothes—"

"But not marriage," he said. "Not marriage. He didn't promise you that. 85
Don't lie to me. He didn't have to."

"No. He didn't have to. I didn't ask him to. I knew what I was doing. 86
I knew that to begin with, long before honor, I imagine he called it, told him the time had come to tell me in so many words what his code, I suppose he would call it, would forbid him forever to do. And we agreed. Then we agreed again before he left New Mexico, to make sure. That that would be all of it. I believed him. No, I don't mean that; I mean I believed myself. I wasn't even listening to him any more by then because by that time it had been a long time since he had had anything else to tell me for me to have to hear. By then I wasn't even listening enough to ask him to please stop talking. I was listening to myself. And I believed it. I must have believed it. I don't see how I could have helped but believe it, because he was gone then as we had agreed and he didn't write as we had agreed, just the money came to the bank in Vicksburg in my name but coming from nobody as we had agreed. So I must have believed it. I even wrote him last month to make sure again and the letter came back unopened and I was sure. So I left the hospital and rented myself a room to live in until the deer season opened so I could make sure myself

and I was waiting beside the road yesterday when your car passed and he saw me and so I was sure."

"Then what do you want?" he said. "What do you want? What do you 87
expect?"

"Yes," she said. And while he glared at her, his white hair awry from 88
the pillow and his eyes, lacking the spectacles to focus them, blurred and irisless and apparently pupilless, he saw again that grave, intent, speculative and detached fixity like a child watching him. "His great great— Wait a minute—great great *great* grandfather was your grandfather. McCaslin. Only it got to be Edmonds. Only it got to be more than that. Your cousin McCaslin was there that day when your father and Uncle Buddy won Tennie from Mr. Beauchamp for the one that had no name but Terrel so you called him Tomey's Terrel, to marry. But after that it got to be Edmonds." She regarded him, almost peacefully, with that unwinking and heatless fixity—the dark, wide, bottomless eyes in the face's dead and toneless pallor which to the old man looked anything but dead, but young and incredibly and even ineradicably alive—as though she were not only not looking at anything, she was not even speaking to anyone but herself. "I would have made a man of him. He's not a man yet. You spoiled him. You, and Uncle Lucas and Aunt Mollie. But mostly you."

"Me?" he said. "Me?" 89

"Yes. When you gave to his grandfather that land which didn't belong 90
to him, not even half of it, by will or even law."

"And never mind that too," he said. "Never mind that too. You," he 91
said. "You sound like you have been to college even. You sound almost like a Northerner even, not like the draggle-tailed women of these Delta peckerwoods. Yet you meet a man on the street one afternoon just because a box of groceries happened to fall out of a boat. And a month later you go off with him and live with him until he got a child on you: and then, by your own statement, you sat there while he took his hat and said goodbye and walked out. Even a Delta peckerwood would look after even a draggle-tail better than that. Haven't you got any folks at all?"

"Yes," she said. "I was living with one of them. My aunt, in Vicksburg. 92
I came to live with her two years ago when my father died; we lived in Indianapolis then. But I got a job, teaching school here in Aluschaskuna, because my aunt was a widow, with a big family, taking in washing to sup—"

"Took in what?" he said. "Took in washing?" He sprang, still seated 93
even, flinging himself backward onto one arm, awry-haired, glaring. Now he understood what it was she had brought into the tent with her, what old Isham had already told him by sending the youth to bring her in to him—the pale lips, the skin pallid and dead-looking yet not ill, the dark and tragic and foreknowing eyes. *Maybe in a thousand or two thousand years in America,* he thought. *But not now! Not now!* He cried, not loud, in a voice of amazement, pity, and outrage: "You're a nigger!"

"Yes," she said. "James Beauchamp—you called him Tennie's Jim 94
though he had a name—was my grandfather. I said you were Uncle Isaac."

"And he knows?" 95

"No," she said. "What good would that have done?" 96

"But you did," he cried. "But you did. Then what do you expect here?" 97

"Nothing." 98

"Then why did you come here? You said you were waiting in Aluschas- 99
kuna yesterday and he saw you. Why did you come this morning?"

"I'm going back North. Back home. My cousin brought me up the day 100
before yesterday in his boat. He's going to take me on to Leland to get the
train."

"Then go," he said. Then he cried again in that thin not loud and 101
grieving voice: "Get out of here! I can do nothing for you! Can't nobody do
nothing for you!" She moved; she was not looking at him again, toward the
entrance. "Wait," he said. She paused again, obediently still, turning. He took
up the sheaf of banknotes and laid it on the blanket at the foot of the cot and
drew his hand back beneath the blanket. "There," he said.

Now she looked at the money, for the first time, one brief blank glance, 102
then away again. "I don't need it. He gave me money last winter. Besides the
money he sent to Vicksburg. Provided. Honor and code too. That was all
arranged."

"Take it," he said. His voice began to rise again, but he stopped it. "Take 103
it out of my tent." She came back to the cot and took up the money; whereupon once more he said, "Wait;" although she had not turned, still stooping,
and he put out his hand. But, sitting he could not complete the reach until
she moved her hand, the single hand which held the money, until he touched
it. He didn't grasp it, he merely touched it—the gnarled bloodless, bone-light,
bone-dry old man's fingers touching for a second the smooth young flesh
where the strong old blood ran after its long lost journey back to home.
"Tennie's Jim," he said. "Tennie's Jim." He drew the hand back beneath the
blanket again: he said harshly now: "It's a boy, I reckon. They usually are,
except that one that was its own mother too."

"Yes," she said. "It's a boy." She stood for a moment longer, looking 104
at him. Just for an instant her free hand moved as though she were about to
lift the edge of the raincoat away from the child's face. But she did not. She
turned again when once more he said Wait and moved beneath the blanket.

"Turn your back," he said. "I am going to get up. I ain't got my pants 105
on." Then he could not get up. He sat in the huddled blanket, shaking, while
again she turned and looked down at him in dark interrogation. "There," he
said harshly, in the thin and shaking old man's voice. "On the nail there. The
tent-pole."

"What?" she said. 106

"The horn!" he said harshly. "The horn." She went and got it, thrust 107
the money into the slicker's side pocket as if it were a rag, a soiled handkerchief, and lifted down the horn, the one which General Compson had left him
in his will, covered with the unbroken skin from a buck's shank and bound
with silver.

"What?" she said. 108

"It's his. Take it." 109

"Oh," she said. "Yes. Thank you." 110

"Yes," he said, harshly, rapidly, but not so harsh now and soon not 111
harsh at all but just rapid, urgent, until he knew that his voice was running away with him and he had neither intended it nor could stop it: "That's right. Go back North. Marry: a man in your own race. That's the only salvation for you—for a while yet, maybe a long while yet. We will have to wait. Marry a black man. You are young, handsome, almost white; you could find a black man who would see in you what it was you saw in him, who would ask nothing of you and expect less and get even still less than that, if it's revenge you want. Then you will forget all this, forget it ever happened, that he ever existed—" until he could stop it at last and did, sitting there in his huddle of blankets during the instant when, without moving at all, she blazed silently down at him. Then that was gone too. She stood in the gleaming and still dripping slicker, looking quietly down at him from under the sodden hat.

"Old man," she said, "have you lived so long and forgotten so much 112
that you don't remember anything you ever knew or felt or even heard about love?"

Then she was gone too. The waft of light and the murmur of the 113
constant rain flowed into the tent and then out again as the flap fell. Lying back once more, trembling, panting, the blanket huddled to his chin and his hands crossed on his breast, he listened to the pop and snarl, the mounting then fading whine of the motor until it died away and once again the tent held only silence and the sound of rain. And cold too: he lay shaking faintly and steadily in it, rigid save for the shaking. This Delta, he thought: This Delta. *This land which man has deswamped and denuded and derivered in two generations so that white men can own plantations and commute every night to Memphis and black men own plantations and ride in Jim Crow cars to Chicago to live in millionaires' mansions on Lake Shore Drive; where white men rent farms and live like niggers and niggers crop on shares and live like animals; where cotton is planted and grows man-tall in the very cracks of the sidewalks, and usury and mortgage and bankruptcy and measureless wealth, Chinese and African and Aryan and Jew, all breed and spawn together until no man has time to say which one is which nor cares. . . .* No wonder the ruined woods I used to know don't cry for retribution! he thought: The people who have destroyed it will accomplish its revenge.

The tent flap jerked rapidly in and fell. He did not move save to turn 114
his head and open his eyes. It was Legate. He went quickly to Edmonds' bed and stooped, rummaging hurriedly among the still-tumbled blankets.

"What is it?" he said. 115

"Looking for Roth's knife," Legate said. "I come back to get a horse. We 116
got a deer on the ground." He rose, the knife in his hand, and hurried toward the entrance.

"Who killed it?" McCaslin said. "Was it Roth?" 117

"Yes," Legate said, raising the flap. 118

"Wait," McCaslin said. He moved, suddenly, onto his elbow. "What was it?" Legate paused for an instant beneath the lifted flap. He did not look back. 119

"Just a deer, Uncle Ike," he said impatiently. "Nothing extra." He was gone; again the flap fell behind him, wafting out of the tent again the faint light and the constant and grieving rain. McCaslin lay back down, the blanket once more drawn to his chin, his crossed hands once more weightless on his breast in the empty tent. 120

"It was a doe," he said. 121

Questions for Discussion

1. One of the values expressed about honor is embedded in Ike McCaslin's assertion that "the only fighting anywhere that ever had anything of God's blessing on it has been when men fought to protect does and fawns" (¶19). What is "does and fawns" a metaphor for? Do you believe what the old man says? Why or why not?
2. In paragraphs 22–26 old Ike ponders the history of the wilderness, the land that men have claimed from it and tilled, and, in paragraph 26, the disappearance of the wilderness altogether. What are his views about its disappearance? Does he think future generations will be worse or better off for the disappearance of the wilderness? Does it contain value in itself, or is it valuable for what it teaches the men who face it?
3. If Uncle Ike can be taken in some sense as Faulkner's mouthpiece, how do you reconcile Faulkner's views about the shame of slavery with McCaslin's optimistic assertion that "there are good men everywhere, at all times. Most men are [good]. . . . Most men are a little better than their circumstances give them a chance to be" (¶35)? Certainly some of the circumstances he is referring to are not just the personal circumstances of people's private upbringing but the historical circumstances of social conditions in the South. What evidence does he provide that "most men are a little better than their circumstances give them a chance to be"? Are the men in the story "better" in this sense? Is Roth Edmonds?
4. In paragraph 63, where Uncle Ike is remembering his thoughts on the occasion of his first deer kill—"My bearing must not shame your quitting life. My conduct forever onward must become your death"—what meaning does the word *become* have in this passage? What does the whole statement mean?
5. Based on his view of the history of the land, what action did McCaslin take in his early manhood to separate himself from the shame and wrong that had been done out of greed for land and money (¶63)?

6. In paragraph 67, what is the link that Uncle Ike sees between himself and the wilderness? What quality of the hunting life causes him to value it so much?
7. When Uncle Ike discovers that the young woman who had been Roth Edmonds's mistress is black, he thinks, "Maybe in a thousand or two thousand years in America, but not now! Not now!" (¶93). What does he mean by this statement? In a thousand or two thousand years *what*? *What* not now? *Why* not now?
8. Why does Uncle Ike give away his precious hunting horn, a potent connection for him with the past, telling the young woman that it belongs to Roth Edmonds? What is he trying to accomplish?
9. In his final words to the young woman, Uncle Ike tells her, "Go back North. Marry: a man in your own race. That's the only salvation for you—for a while yet, maybe a long while yet. We will have to wait" (¶111). Do you find it curious that Uncle Ike thinks it's the girl who needs salvation? Wouldn't you rather think that the ones needing salvation would be Ike and all his forebears? How do you interpret this passage? How do you evaluate its social message?
10. In his final thoughts Uncle Ike looks into the future and seems disgusted at his vision of a world in which racial lines disappear, in which, as he puts it, the "Chinese and African and Aryan and Jew, all breed and spawn together until no man has time to say which one is which nor cares" (¶113). Why is this such a disgusting picture to him? Is it to you? What of value does McCaslin (and Faulkner?) seem to think will be lost if racial separateness is lost? What are your own views on this question?
11. Finally, what does McCaslin mean when he says that "the people who have destroyed [the wilderness] will accomplish its revenge" (¶113)?

Suggested Essay Topics

1. In an essay titled "Faulkner and Desegregation," published in 1956 as the civil rights movement that led to the Civil Rights Act of 1964 was just getting under way, James Baldwin, a black novelist and essayist, responded to Faulkner's attitude of "Maybe in a thousand . . . years in America, but not now!" with this rejoinder:

> Faulkner is not trying to save Negroes, who are, in his view, already saved; who, having refused to be destroyed by terror, are far stronger than the terrified white populace; and who have, moreover, fatally, from his point of view, the weight of the federal government behind them. He is trying to save "whatever good remains in those white people." The time he pleads for is the time in which the Southerner will come to terms with himself, will cease fleeing from his conscience, and achieve, in the words of Robert Penn Warren [another white southern writer], "moral identity." And he surely believes, with Warren, that "Then in a country where

> moral identity is hard to come by, the South, because it has had to deal concretely with a moral problem, may offer some leadership. And we need any we can get, if we are to break out of the national rhythm, the rhythm between complacency and panic."
>
> But the time Faulkner asks for does not exist—and he is not the only Southerner who knows it. There is never time in the future in which we will work out our salvation.

The challenge is in the moment, the time is always now.

Write a dialogue in which you picture Ike McCaslin and James Baldwin debating Baldwin's criticism of Faulkner's views. Give each speaker the best possible points they can make for their position, yet in the end you may make it clear, or at least imply, which one of them in your view has won the debate. [You can find the complete text of the Baldwin essay in either the *Partisan Review* (Winter 1956), where it first appeared, or in a Dell paperback reprint of a collection of essays, *Nobody Knows My Name: More Notes of a Native Son* (1961).]

2. Write an essay in which you picture Faulkner responding to Baldwin's criticisms. Allow him to make the best argument you think the case allows; then append a page of analysis in which you probe the weaknesses and strengths of each position.

IDEAS IN DEBATE

Pieter Geyl and Arnold J. Toynbee

Pieter Geyl and Arnold J. Toynbee

Few scholarly works have produced as much debate as Arnold J. Toynbee's Study of History. *Toynbee's massive comparative study of the world's civilizations continues to engage scholars in lively discussions like the one we reprint here, between historian Pieter Geyl and Toynbee himself. And in its time the* Study *provoked unusual debate among general readers. Despite its bulk—the first volume was published in 1934 and the twelfth volume completed the work in 1961—the* Study *was a steady best-seller in the years following World War II.*

Two theses in particular provoked debate among Toynbee's readers. First, Toynbee claimed that all 21 of what he considered the world's major past civilizations (each of which he studied in great detail) exhibited a common pattern in their rise and fall. Each of them began, he said, when some great threat or challenge produced a grand unified response. Working together to overcome apparently insuperable problems, men and women managed, at least 21 times in world history, to create great civilizations. But then, in every case, the spiritual center decayed, social forms fell apart, and the civilization collapsed. Though many readers were exhilarated by the offer of such a unified view of human history, many others (like Pieter Geyl in the exchange that follows) were skeptical about any effort to discern a pattern shared by all civilizations in all periods.

Even more controversial was Toynbee's second claim, that Western civilization has for a long time been on the "falling" side of the curve. Some readers saw Toynbee as saying that we have lost our spiritual center and that individuals can therefore do nothing to prevent the final collapse of our civilization. As you will see in the discussion reprinted here, Toynbee explicitly denied that his view was finally pessimistic; through a spiritual rebirth we might still have a chance to reverse the downward spiral.

The debate we print here is part of a report on a conference, held about midway through Toynbee's prolonged labors, to discuss his first six volumes. In his prepared paper for the conference, Pieter Geyl said,

> *I can . . . have little confidence . . . that Professor Toynbee, when later on he undertakes a set examination of our civilization and its prospects, will prove able to enlighten our perplexities; or should I not rather say that we need not let ourselves be frightened by his darkness? We need not accept his view that the whole of modern history from the sixteenth century on has been nothing but a*

downward course, following the path of rout and rally. We need not let ourselves be shaken in our confidence that the future lies open before us, that in the midst of misery and confusion such as have so frequently occurred in history, we still dispose of forces no less valuable than those by which earlier generations have managed to struggle through their troubles.

What we print here is a record of the more informal debate that followed the formal papers. We have no way of knowing how much revision Professors Toynbee and Geyl gave to their spoken words, but they have clearly kept a tone of spoken interchange. You may have noticed that most people who debate in public "talk past" each other most of the time, changing their opponents' points, deliberately or unconsciously, to points that are more easily crushed or dismissed. As you read this debate, try to determine whether Toynbee and Geyl commit this kind of distortion or manage really to understand each other. Are Geyl's points the ones that Toynbee answers? If you had the words of only one of the speakers, would you be able to give a fair account of the other speaker's views? To answer that question you will of course need to attend not only to both speakers' conclusions but to the supporting reasons they offer as well.

CAN WE KNOW THE PATTERN OF THE PAST?

A Discussion Between Pieter Geyl and Arnold J. Toynbee

From Pieter Geyl, Arnold J. Toynbee, and Pitirim Sorokin, *The Pattern of the Past: Can We Determine It?* (1949).

PROFESSOR GEYL

The six volumes of Toynbee's *Study of History* appeared before the war, but it is since the war that the book and the author have become famous. A generation only just recovering from the terrible experiences of the war and already anxious about the future, is reading the work in the hope of finding in its pages the answer to its perplexities. It is indeed the author's claim to discover for us, in the at first sight chaotic and confusing spectacle of human history, a pattern, a rhythm. . . . 1

I must come straight to the main features of the system. Has Toynbee proved that the histories of civilizations fall into these sharply marked stages of growth and disintegration, separated by breakdown? Has he proved that the work of the creative minds, or of the creative minorities, can be successful only in the first stage and that in the second it is doomed to remain so much fruitless effort? 2

In my opinion he has not. How do I know that the difference is caused by the triumphant creator acting in a growing society, and the hopelessly struggling one in a society in disintegration? I have not been convinced of the essential difference between the phases of civilization. There are evil tenden- 3 cies and there are good tendencies simultaneously present at every stage of human history, and the human intellect is not sufficiently comprehensive to weigh them off against each other and to tell, before the event, which is to have the upper hand. As for the theory that the individual leader, or the leading minority, is capable of creative achievement in a growing society only and doomed to disappointment in one that is in disintegration—that theory lapses automatically when the distinction is not admitted in the absolute form in which our author propounds it.

I am glad that you are present here, Toynbee, and going to reply. For 4
this is surely a point of great practical importance. *A Study of History* does not definitely announce ruin as did Spengler's book* by its very title. But in more than one passage you give us to understand that Western civilization broke down as long ago as the sixteenth century, as a result of the wars of religion. The last four centuries of our history would thus, according to your system, be one long process of disintegration, with collapse as the inevitable end—except for the miracle of a reconversion to the faith of our fathers.

There is no doubt, when we look around us, a great deal to induce 5
gloom. But I do not see any reason why history should be read so as to deepen our sense of uneasiness into a mood of hopelessness. Earlier generations have also had their troubles and have managed to struggle through. There is nothing in history to shake our confidence that the future lies open before us.

PROFESSOR TOYNBEE

The fate of the world—the destiny of mankind—*is* involved in the issue 6
between us about the nature of history.

In replying to Professor Geyl now, I am going to concentrate on what, 7
to my mind, are his two main lines of attack. One of his general criticisms is: "Toynbee's view of history induces gloom." The other is: "Toynbee has set himself to do something impossible. He is trying to make sense of human history, and that is beyond the capacity of the human mind." I will pay most attention to this second point, because it is, I am sure, by far the more important of the two.

Let me try to dispose of the "gloom" point first. Suppose my view of 8
history did point to a gloomy conclusion, what of it? "Gloomy" and "cheerful" are one thing, "true" and "false" quite another.

Professor Geyl has interpreted me rightly in telling you that I have 9
pretty serious misgivings about the state of the world today. Don't you feel the same misgivings? Doesn't Professor Geyl feel them? That surely goes without saying. But what doesn't go without saying is what we are going to

***Der Untergang des Abendlandes,* 2 vols. (1918–1922); translated as *The Decline of the West* (1926–1928). Oswald Spengler (1880–1936) made himself internationally famous with a thesis in some ways similar to Toynbee's, but by the time Toynbee was writing, most professional historians were inclined to dismiss Spengler's claim about the *inevitable* decline of the Western world as what Toynbee calls "dogmatic determinism" (¶28).

do about it; and here Professor Geyl has been handsome to me in telling you where I stand. He has told you that I disbelieve in predestination and am at the opposite pole, on that supremely important question, from the famous German philosopher Spengler. He has told you that my outlook is the reverse of historical materialism; that, in my view, the process of civilization is one of vanquishing the material problems to grapple with the spiritual ones; that I am a believer in free will; in man's freedom to respond with all his heart and soul and mind when life presents him with a challenge. Well, that is what I do believe. But how, I ask you, can one lift up one's heart and apply one's mind unless one does one's best to find out the relevant facts and to look them in the face?—the formidable facts as well as the encouraging ones.

In the state of the world today, the two really formidable facts, as I see 10
them, are that the other civilizations that we know of have all broken down, and that in our recent history one sees some of those tendencies which, in the histories of the broken-down civilizations, have been the obvious symptoms of breakdown. But what's the moral? Surely not to shy at the facts. Professor Geyl himself admits them. And also, surely, not to be daunted by the "sense of uneasiness" which these formidable facts are bound to give us. "I don't see any reason," said Professor Geyl just now, "why history should be read so as to deepen our sense of uneasiness into a mood of hopelessness." That is a telling criticism of Spengler, who does diagnose that our civilization is doomed, and who has nothing better to suggest than that we should fold our hands and await the inevitable blow of the axe. But that ball doesn't take my wicket, for in my view, as Geyl has told you, uneasiness is a challenging call to action, and not a death sentence to paralyze our wills. Thank goodness we do know the fates of the other civilizations; such knowledge is a chart that warns us of the reefs ahead. Knowledge can be power and salvation if we have the spirit to use it. There is a famous Greek epigram which runs: "I am the tomb of a shipwrecked sailor, but don't let that frighten off you, brother mariner, from setting sail; because, when we went down, the other ships kept afloat."

"There is nothing in history," said Professor Geyl in his closing sen- 11
tence, "to shake our confidence that the future lies open before us." Those might have been my own words, but I don't quite see what warrant Professor Geyl has for using them. The best comfort Professor Geyl can give us is: "If we take care not to unnerve ourselves by trying to chart the seas, we may be lucky enough to get by without hitting the rocks." No, I haven't painted him quite black enough, for his view is still gloomier than that. "To make a chart of history," he says, "is a sheer impossibility." Professor Geyl's own chart, you see, is the "perfect and absolute blank" of Lewis Carroll's bellman who hunted the snark. Geyl, too, has a chart, like Spengler and me. We all of us have one, whether we own up to it or not, and no chart is more than one man's shot at the truth. But surely, of those three, the blank is the most useless and the most dangerous.

Professor Geyl thinks I am a pessimist because I see a way of escape in 12
a reconversion to the faith of our fathers. "This," says Professor Geyl, "is an

unnecessarily gloomy view of our situation"—like the old lady who was advised to leave it to Providence and exclaimed: "Oh dear, has it come to that?"

What was our fathers' chart of history? As they saw it, it was a tale told 13
by God, unfolding itself from the Creation through the Fall and the Redemption to the Last Judgment. As Professor Geyl says he sees it, it seems like a tale told by an idiot, signifying nothing. You may not agree with our fathers' view that history is a revelation of God's providence; but it is a poor exchange, isn't it, to swap their faith for the view that history makes no sense.

Of course, Professor Geyl is no more singular in his view than I am in 14
mine. What one may call the nonsense view of history has been fashionable among Western historians for the last few generations. The odd thing is that some of the holders of this view—I don't know whether I could count Professor Geyl among the number—defend it principally on the ground that it is scientific. Of course, it is only human that historians should have wanted to be scientific in an age when science has been enjoying such prestige. I am, myself, a historian who believes that science has an awful lot to teach us. But how strange to suppose that one is being scientific by despairing of making sense! For what is science? It is only another name for the careful and scrupulous use of the human mind. And, if men despair of reason, they are lost. Nature hasn't given us wings, fur, claws, antennae or elephant's trunks; but she has given us the human intellect—the most effective of all implements, if we are not too timid to use it. And what does this scientific intellect do? It looks at the facts, but it doesn't stop there. It looks at the facts and it tries to make sense of them. It does, you see, the very thing that Professor Geyl takes me to task for trying to do with the facts of history.

Is history really too hard a nut for science to crack? When the human 15
intellect has wrested her secret from physical nature, are we going to sit down under an *ex cathedra* dictum that the ambition to discover the secret of human history will always be bound to end in disappointment? We don't need to be told that Man is a harder—a very much harder—nut than the atom. We have discovered how to split the atom and are in danger of splitting it to our own destruction. By comparison with the science of physics, the science of man is so difficult that our discoveries in the two fields have gone forward at an uneven pace till they have got quite out of step with each other. It is partly this that has got us into our present fix. Is science to shirk trying to do anything about it? "The proper study of mankind is man," says Pope. "The human intellect," sighs Geyl, "is not sufficiently comprehensive."

I say: We can't afford such defeatism; it is unworthy of the greatness 16
of man's mind; and it is refuted by the human mind's past achievements. The mind has won all its great victories by well-judged boldness. And today, before our eyes, science is launching a characteristically bold offensive in what is now the key area of the mental battlefield. Why, she has got her nutcrackers round this nut, this human nut, already. One arm of the pincers is the exciting young science of psychology, which is opening out entirely new mental horizons for us, in the very direction in which we are most in

need of longer vistas. The other is the forbidding yet rewarding discipline of statistics. Science has set herself now in good earnest to comprehend human nature, and, through understanding, to show it how to master itself and thereby to set itself free. Science, so long preoccupied with the riddles of non-human nature, has now joined in the quests of philosophy and religion, and this diversion of her energies has been timely. There is, indeed, no time to be lost. We are in for a life-and-death struggle. And, at this critical hour, is science to get no support from our professedly scientific historians?

Well, in this "mental fight," I have deliberately risked my neck by 17
putting my own reading of the facts of history on the table. I should never dream of claiming that my particular interpretation is the only one possible. There are, I am sure, many different alternative ways of analyzing history, each of which is true in itself and illuminating as far as it goes, just as, in dissecting an organism, you can throw light on its nature by laying bare either the skeleton or the muscles or the nerves or the circulation of the blood. No single one of these dissections tells the whole truth, but each of them reveals a genuine facet of it. I should be well content if it turned out that I had laid bare one genuine facet of history, and even then, I should measure my success by the speed with which my own work in my own line was put out of date by further work by other people in the same field. In the short span of one lifetime, the personal contribution of the individual scholar to the great and growing stream of knowledge can't be more than a tiny pailful. But if he could inspire—or provoke—other scholars to pour in their pailfuls too, well, then he could feel that he had really done his job. And this job of making sense of history is one of the crying needs of our day—I beg of you, believe me.

PROFESSOR GEYL

Well I must say, Toynbee, that I felt some anxiety while you were pouring 18
out over me this torrent of eloquence, wit and burning conviction, but that was of course what I had to expect from you. And now that is over I'm relieved to feel that I'm still there, and my position untouched.

Professor Toynbee pictures me as one of those men who mistake the 19
courage to see evils for gloom, and who when others sound the call for action take refuge from the dangers of our time in an illusionist optimism. But have I been saying that we are not in danger? And that no action is required? What I have said is that Toynbee's system induces the wrong kind of gloom because it tends to make action seem useless. "But I am a believer in man's free will," Toynbee replies. I know. But nevertheless, his system lays it down that the civilization which has been overtaken by a breakdown is doomed. Now Toynbee has repeatedly suggested that our Western civilization did suffer a breakdown as long ago as the sixteenth century, and that consequently, try as we may, we cannot avoid disaster. Except in one way, except in case we allow ourselves to be reconverted to the faith of our fathers. And here Toynbee exclaims: "You see, I'm not so gloomy after all." Perhaps not. But if one happens to hold a different opinion both of the efficacy and of the likelihood

of application of his particular remedy, one cannot help thinking that Toynbee is but offering us cold comfort. He talks as if we cannot advance matters by "so hotly canvassing and loudly advertising," as he contemptuously puts it, "our political and economic maladies." It is the loss of religious faith that is the deadly danger. To most of us this is indeed condemning all our efforts to futility.

Of course, Toynbee, it is only your picturesque way of putting things 20
when you describe me as one of those historians who cling to the nonsense view of history. Because I cannot accept either your methods or your system it does not follow that to my mind history has no meaning. I do not believe that at any time it will be possible to reduce the past to so rigid a pattern as to enable us to forecast the future—granted. Yet to me, as to you, the greatest function of the historian is to interpret the past—to find sense in it, although at the same time it is the least scientific, the most inevitably subjective of his functions.

I am surprised that you class me with those historians who believe that 21
their view of history rests securely on scientific foundations. In fact it is you who claim to be proceeding on the lines of empiricism towards laws of universal validity, while I have been suggesting that these and other scientific terms which you are fond of using have no real meaning in a historical argument. Even just now, didn't you deduce from the conquest of the mystery of the atom the certainty that man's mind will be able to conquer the mystery of the historical process as well? In my opinion these are fundamentally different propositions.

Let me remind you especially of what I have been saying about the 22
uncertain nature of historical events, and the difficulty of detaching them from their contexts. And also of my contention that the cases and instances strewn over your pages have been arbitrarily selected from an infinite number and haven't therefore that value as evidence which you attach to them.

PROFESSOR TOYNBEE

There can be no doubt that you look upon this last point as an important 23
one. . . . I see what you're getting at. I set out to deal with history in terms of civilizations, of which there are, of course, very few specimens, but in the illustrations I give, and the points I make, I don't confine myself to these rare big fellows, I hop about all over the place, bringing up as illustrations of my points events on a much smaller scale, which to you seem to be chosen arbitrarily, because they're just a few taken out of a large number. They also, as you point out, lend themselves to more interpretations than one. Yes, I think that's fair criticism, and quite telling. In answer I'd say two things. I think, as I said a minute or two ago, the same historical event often can be analyzed legitimately in a number of different ways, each of which brings out some aspect of historical truth which is true as far as it goes, though not the whole truth. I have myself sometimes made the same historical event do double or treble duty in this way, and I don't think this is a misleading way

of using facts. As I've said before, several different dissections can all be correct, each in its own line.

My second point is that I bring in these illustrations taken from the small change of history, not for their own sake but to throw indirect light on the big units, which I call civilizations, which are my main concern. I helped myself out in this way because, in the very early stage in human history in which our generation happens to be living, the number of civilizations that have come into existence up to date, is still so small—not more than about twenty, as I make it out. 24

To take up the case of your own country, Holland, now, which I have used to throw light on the rise of the Egyptian and Sumerian civilizations: you challenged my account of Holland's rise to greatness. I found my explanation of it in the stimulus of a hard country. The people of Holland had to wrest the country from the sea and they rose to the occasion. Your criticism is that I've arbitrarily isolated one fact out of several. The Dutch, you say, didn't do it by themselves, they were helped at the start by efficient outsiders, and then the country, when it had been reclaimed, turned out to have a rich soil, as well as a good situation for commerce. 25

Yes, of course, those are also facts of Dutch history, but my answer is that they're not the key facts. If the outsiders that you have in mind are the Romans, well, the benefits of Roman efficiency were not enjoyed by Holland alone; Belgium, France and England enjoyed them as well. So Holland's Roman apprenticeship won't account for achievements that are special to Holland and that distinguish her from her neighbors. Then the fertile soil and good location: these aren't causes of Holland's great feat of fighting and beating the North Sea, they're effects and rewards of it. It is a case of "to him that hath, shall be given." What the Dutch had, before these other things were given them, was the strength of will to raise their country out of the waters. The terrific challenge of the sea to a country below sea level is surely the unique and distinguishing feature of Dutch history. With all deference to you, Geyl, as a Netherlander and a historian, I still think I'm right in picking out the response of the people of Holland to this challenge as being the key to the greatness of your country. I do also think that the case of Holland throws valuable light on the cases of Egypt and Babylonia, two other places where people have had to fight swamp and sea in order to reclaim land, and where this struggle between man and nature has brought to life two out of the twenty or so civilizations known to us. 26

Of course if one could lay hands on some more civilizations, one might be able to study history on that scale without having to bother about little bits and pieces like Holland and England. I wish I were in that happy position, and if you now, Geyl, would help me by taking up your archeological spade and unearthing a few more forgotten civilizations for me, I should be vastly obliged to you. But even if you proved yourself a Layard, Schliemann and Arthur Evans rolled into one, you could only raise my present figure of twenty-one known civilizations to twenty-four, and that of course wouldn't help me to reduce my margin of error appreciably. 27

To turn for a moment to a different point, I want to correct an impres- 28
sion that I think our listeners may have got, of something else that you were saying just now. Anyway, I got the impression myself that you still thought I claimed to be able to foretell the future from the past, that I'd laid it down that our own civilization was doomed. This is a very important point and I want to make my position on it clear beyond all possibility of mistake. So let me repeat: I don't set up to be a prophet, I don't believe history can be used for telling the world's fortune, I think history can perhaps sometimes show one possibilities or even probabilities, but never certainties. With the awful warning of Spengler's dogmatic determinism before my eyes, I always have been and shall be mighty careful, for my part, to treat the future of our own civilization as an open question—not at all because I'm afraid of committing myself, but because I believe as strongly as you do, Geyl, that it *is* an open question.

PROFESSOR GEYL

Well I'm glad, Toynbee, that you've taken so seriously the objections I've 29
made to the profusion of illustrations from national histories. As to the case of Holland, let me just say that I was not thinking of the Romans only and not even of foreigners primarily. What I meant was that Netherlands civilization did not have its origin or earliest development in the region which was exposed to the struggle with the water, but, on the contrary, this region could be described as a backward part of the Netherlands area as a whole. And as regards the future, in one place of your book you are very near to drawing—as you put it—"the horoscope of our civilization" from the fates of other civilizations, and you suggest repeatedly that we have got into the disintegration stage, which you picture to us so elaborately in your book as leading inevitably to catastrophe. I'm glad to hear now that you did not in fact mean to pass an absolute sentence of death over us.

PROFESSOR TOYNBEE

No, I think we simply don't know. I suppose I must be the last judge of what 30
my own beliefs are.

But now, Geyl, here is a ball I'd like for a change to bowl at you. You've 31
given me an opening by the fair-mindedness and frankness you've shown all through our debate. You've done justice to my contention that while historical facts are in some respects unique, there are other respects in which they belong to a class and are therefore comparable. There is truth, you say, in this, otherwise no general ideas about history could ever be formed, but isolating the comparable elements is ticklish work. It certainly is ticklish work. I speak with feeling from long experience in trying to do precisely that job. But may there not be a moral in this for you and every other historian as well as for me? May not it mean that we ought all of us to give far more time and far more serious and strenuous thought than many of us have ever given to this

job of forming one's general ideas? And there is a previous and, to my mind, more important job to be done before that.

We've first to bring into consciousness our existing ideas and to put these trump cards of ours face upwards on the table. All historians are bound, you see, to have general ideas about history. On this point, every stitch of work they do is so much evidence against them. Without ideas, they couldn't think a thought, speak a sentence or write a line on their subjects. Ideas are the machine tools of the mind, and, wherever you see a thought being thrown out, you may be certain that there is an idea at the back of it. This is so obvious that I find it hard to have patience with historians who boast, as some modern Western historians do, that they keep entirely to the facts of history and don't go in for theories. Why, every so-called fact that they present to you had some pattern of theory behind it. Historians who genuinely believe they have no general ideas about history are, I would suggest to them, simply ignorant of the workings of their own minds, and such wilful ignorance is, isn't it, really unpardonable. The intellectual worker who refuses to let himself become aware of the working ideas with which he is operating seems to me to be about as great a criminal as the motorist who first closes his eyes and then steps on the gas. To leave oneself and one's public at the mercy of any fool ideas, if they happen to have taken possession of one's unconscious, is surely the height of intellectual irresponsibility. 32

I believe our listeners would be very much interested to hear what you say about that. 33

PROFESSOR GEYL

This is very simple. I agree with you entirely about the impossibility of allowing, as it used to be put, the facts to speak for themselves, and the historian who imagines that he can rule out theory or, let us say, his own individual mind, his personal view of things in general, seems to me a very uninteresting being, or in the majority of cases, when he is obviously only deluding himself and covering his particular partiality with the great word of objectivity and historical science, a very naïve person, and perhaps a very dangerous one. 34

As a matter of fact this is the spirit in which I have tackled you. When you said that I was an adherent of the nonsense view of history, you were mistaking my position altogether. In my own fashion, when I reject your methods and your conclusions, I am also trying to establish general views about history. Without such views, I know that the records of the past would become utterly chaotic and senseless, and I think I should rather be an astronomer than devote my life to so hopeless and futile a study. 35

But, to me, one of the great things to realize about history is its infinite complexity, and, when I say infinite, I do mean that not only the number of the phenomena and incidents but their often shadowy and changing nature 36 is such that the attempt to reduce them to a fixed relationship and to a scheme of absolute validity can never lead to anything but disappointment. It is when you present your system in so hard and fast a manner as to seem, at any rate to me, to dictate to the future, that I feel bound to protest, on behalf both of history and of the civilization whose crisis we are both witnessing.

You have twitted me for inviting the world to sail on an uncharted 37
course. Yet I believe that the sense of history is absolutely indispensable for the life of mankind. I believe with Burckhardt that there is wisdom to be gained from the study of the past, but no definite lessons for the actual problems of the present.

PROFESSOR TOYNBEE

Well there! It looks as if, on this question anyway, our two different ap- 38
proaches have brought us on to something like common ground. If I am right in this, I think it is rather encouraging, for this last issue we were discussing is, I am sure, a fundamental one.

PROFESSOR GEYL

Well I see, Toynbee, that our time is up. There are just a few seconds left for 39
me to pay tribute to the courage with which you, as you expressed it yourself, have risked your neck; not by facing me here at the microphone, but by composing that gigantic and impressive scheme of civilizations, which was bound to rouse the skeptics and to be subjected to their criticism. Now I am not such a skeptic as to doubt the rightness of my own position in our debate, but I am one compared with you. Perhaps you will value the assurance from such a one that he himself has found your great work immensely stimulating and that, generally speaking, in the vast enterprise in which we historians are engaged together, daring and imaginative spirits like yourself have an essential function to fulfill.

Questions for Discussion

1. Why does Geyl think that his differences with Toynbee have not just theoretical but great *practical* importance (¶4)?
2. Some historical questions are fairly easy to answer: for example, in what year did you enter high school? Others are more difficult, but not beyond meaningful speculation and argument: For example, what were your *real* reasons for going to college or for choosing this college? And some ques-

tions seem clearly beyond human capacity to answer: For example, what were Brutus' feelings as he stabbed Caesar? Does it seem to you that the question "Why do civilizations rise and fall?," is by its nature merely difficult to debate or is finally impossible to debate?

3. Clearly Toynbee and Geyl are convinced that question 2 could be addressed rationally, but few of us will ever know enough about the 21 civilizations to judge or even to debate in any detail about Geyl's and Toynbee's positions. It is not beyond us, however, to ask which of the two opponents is more convincing, given their arguments as presented. After reading the debate two or three times, choose a paragraph that seems highly persuasive, and list all the reasons you can find to explain why it carries weight for you.
4. The debate contains a good deal of comment by each speaker about the character of the other (for example, ¶18, the beginning of ¶19, and most of ¶39). Each speaker praises the other, and neither one says anything openly nasty about the other. Make two lists of characteristics, favorable and unfavorable, that Geyl attributes to Toynbee and two lists of Geyl's favorable and unfavorable qualities as stated or implied by Toynbee. (Don't list only the openly stated qualities, like the "courage" that Geyl talks about in sentence 2 of ¶39, but also the qualities that are merely implied, like Geyl's suggestion that Toynbee's work is careless and arrogant.) Does Geyl's characterization of Toynbee seem to fit what you can infer about Toynbee from his own words? Does Toynbee's Geyl fit the Geyl who speaks?
5. Study paragraph 18 carefully. What do you think Geyl is trying to accomplish with it? Would you advise Geyl to cut it, if he were preparing another printing? Why or why not?
6. In paragraph 19 Geyl suggests (especially in sentences 2–4) that Toynbee has misreported his claims. Is he justified in the claim?
7. Both men seem to agree that "facts do not speak for themselves but must be interpreted" (see, for example, ¶34). Can you state clearly the difference between them about how we should work in interpreting historical facts and making use of them in the present? Does either man take the view of facts explained by Edward Hallett Carr (pp. 575–583)? Support your answer by citing passages.

Suggested Essay Topics

1. Your life has a "history" just as each civilization does, and though that history may seem less complex, it still has consisted of so many details, from the time of your birth until now, that no one could ever list them all (see Geyl's talk about "infinite complexity" in ¶36). Your picture of your past is thus not a report of raw facts but an interpretation that in *some* ways resembles Toynbee's interpretation of civilizations. Choose some important turning point or event from your life, one that depended

on your making a conscious choice. Write a history of the choice, your reasons for it, and the consequences, good or bad. You may find it helpful to address your account as a letter to your parents, correcting what you take to be their false view of the event's "history." You may also get some hints about procedure by reading Lillian Smith's story (pp. 472–481).

2. Write a two-page "history" of what happened to you yesterday. Include an appraisal of whether the day showed signs of moving you upward or downward in your life's "curve."

10

SCIENTIFIC PERSPECTIVES

Science, Knowledge, and Morality

If science would discover rather than apply—if, in other words,
men were more interested in knowledge than
in power—mankind would be in a far safer position.
E. M. Forster

[Science] is the distinctive achievement of our history, and . . . nothing less
momentous than the preservation of our culture
hangs on understanding its growth and bearing. But the
influence of science is not simply comfortable. For neither
in public nor in private life can science establish an ethic. It tells
what we can do, never what we should. Its absolute incompetence
in the realm of values is a necessary consequence of the objective posture.
Charles Coulston Gillispie

Science is much closer to myth than a scientific philosophy
is prepared to admit. It is one of the many forms of thought that have been
developed by man, and not necessarily the best.
Paul Feyerabend

I believe that the scientific method, although slow
and never claiming to lead to complete truth, is the only method
which in the long run will give satisfactory foundation for beliefs.
Julian Huxley

The separation of science and non-science is not only artificial
but also detrimental to the advancement of knowledge.
If we want to understand nature, if we want to master our physical
surroundings, then we must use *all* ideas, *all* methods,
and not just a small selection of them. The assertion, however, that there
is no knowledge outside science—*extra scientiam nulla salus*—is
nothing but another and most convenient fairy-tale.
Paul Feyerabend

Lewis Thomas

Lewis Thomas (see the introduction to "How to Fix the Premedical Curriculum," pp. 58–59) characteristically writes of science not as a repellent realm of formulas and figures but as an activity at once important, accessible, and interesting. He does this by refusing to flaunt his expertise, striving instead to communicate his own enthusiasm for ideas.

In this essay, Thomas takes a critical look at science education. He argues that it consistently errs by presenting scientific knowledge to students the way supermarkets present food to their customers—as canned goods already processed by experts and intended to be swallowed whole by the consumer. He thinks that science students should do less indiscriminate swallowing and more critical thinking and that they should learn about areas where science has more questions than answers.

Thomas states his thesis boldly: Science education should expose students to the big controversies as well as the canned goods. He then supports it with a simple plan of organization: In support of his thesis he presents the best examples of interesting controversies he knows about, with some commentary on why they are important. This pattern of organization—thesis followed by illustrative examples—is perhaps the simplest and most often used pattern in all expository writing. It is simple, direct, and clear, and Thomas employs it with a skill that any of us might emulate. His tone also presents a laudable model for this kind of essay: articulate but not pretentious, deeply involved in his subject but not self-absorbed, expert but not pedantic, and friendly but not pushy or chummy.

DEBATING THE UNKNOWABLE

First published in *The Atlantic Monthly,* July 1981, and reprinted in *Late Night Thoughts on Listening to Mahler's Ninth Symphony* (1985).

The greatest of all the accomplishments of twentieth-century science has been the discovery of human ignorance. We live, as never before, in puzzlement about nature, the universe, and ourselves most of all. It is a new experience for the species. A century ago, after the turbulence caused by Darwin and Wallace had subsided and the central idea of natural selection had been grasped and accepted, we thought we knew everything essential about evolution. In the eighteenth century there were no huge puzzles; human reason was all you needed in order to figure out the universe. And for most of the earlier centuries, the Church provided both the questions and the answers, neatly packaged. Now, for the first time in human history, we are catching glimpses of our incomprehension. We can still make up stories to explain the world, as we always have, but now the stories have to be confirmed and reconfirmed by experiment. This is the scientific method, and once started on this line we cannot turn back. We are obliged to grow up in skepticism, requiring proofs for every assertion about nature, and there is no way out except to move ahead and plug away, hoping for comprehension in the future but living in a condition of intellectual instability for the long time. 1

It is the admission of ignorance that leads to progress, not so much because the solving of a particular puzzle leads directly to a new piece of understanding but because the puzzle—if it interests enough scientists—leads to *work.* There is a similar phenomenon in entomology known as stigmergy, a term invented by Grassé, which means "to incite to work." When three or four termites are collected together in a chamber they wander about aimlessly, but when more termites are added, they begin to build. It is the presence of other termites, in sufficient numbers at close quarters, that produces the work: they pick up each other's fecal pellets and stack them in neat columns, and when the columns are precisely the right height, the termites reach across and turn the perfect arches that form the foundation of the termitarium. No single termite knows how to do any of this, but as soon as there are enough termites gathered together they become flawless architects, sensing their distances from each other although blind, building an immensely complicated structure with its own air-conditioning and humidity control. They work their lives away in this ecosystem built by themselves. The nearest thing to a termitarium that I can think of in human behavior is the making of language, which we do by keeping *at* each other all our lives, generation after generation, changing the structure by some sort of instinct. 2

Very little is understood about this kind of collective behavior. It is out of fashion these days to talk of "superorganisms," but there simply aren't enough reductionist details in hand to explain away the phenomenon of termites and other social insects: some very good guesses can be made about 3 their chemical signaling systems, but the plain fact that they exhibit something like a collective intelligence is a mystery, or anyway an unsolved problem, that might contain important implications for social life in general. This mystery is the best introduction I can think of to biological science in college. It should be taught for its strangeness, and for the ambiguity of its meaning. It should be taught to premedical students, who need lessons early in their careers about the uncertainties in science.

College students, and for that matter high school students, should be 4
exposed very early, perhaps at the outset, to the big arguments currently going on among scientists. Big arguments stimulate their interest, and with luck engage their absorbed attention. Few things in life are as engrossing as a good fight between highly trained and skilled adversaries. But the young students are told very little about the major disagreements of the day; they may be taught something about the arguments between Darwinians and their opponents a century ago, but they do not realize that similar disputes about other matters, many of them touching profound issues for our understanding of nature, are still going on and, indeed, are an essential feature of the scientific process. There is, I fear, a reluctance on the part of science teachers to talk about such things, based on the belief that before students can appreciate what the arguments are about they must learn and master the "fundamentals." I would be willing to see some experiments along this line, and I have in mind several examples of contemporary doctrinal dispute in which the drift of the argument can be readily perceived without deep or elaborate knowledge of the subject.

There is, for one, the problem of animal awareness. One school of 5
ethologists devoted to the study of animal behavior has it that human beings are unique in the possession of consciousness, differing from all other creatures in being able to think things over, capitalize on past experience, and hazard informed guesses at the future. Other, "lower," animals (with possible exceptions made for chimpanzees, whales, and dolphins) cannot do such things with their minds; they live from moment to moment with brains that are programmed to respond, automatically or by conditioning, to contingencies in the environment. Behavioral psychologists believe that this automatic or conditioned response accounts for human mental activity as well, although they dislike that word "mental." On the other side are some ethologists who seem to be more generous-minded, who see no compelling reasons to doubt that animals in general are quite capable of real thinking and do quite a lot of it—thinking that isn't as dense as human thinking, that is sparser because of the lack of language and the resultant lack of metaphors to help the thought along, but thinking nonetheless.

The point about this argument is not that one side or the other is in 6
possession of a more powerful array of convincing facts; quite the opposite. There are not enough facts to sustain a genuine debate of any length; the question of animal awareness is an unsettled one. In the circumstance, I put forward the following notion about a small beetle, the mimosa girdler, which undertakes three pieces of linked, sequential behavior: finding a mimosa tree

and climbing up the trunk and out to the end of a branch; cutting a longitudinal slit and laying within it five or six eggs; and crawling back on the limb and girdling it neatly down into the cambium. The third step is an eight-to-ten-hour task of hard labor, from which the beetle gains no food for itself—only the certainty that the branch will promptly die and fall to the ground in the next brisk wind, thus enabling the larvae to hatch and grow in an abundance of dead wood. I propose, in total confidence that even though I am probably wrong nobody today can prove that I am wrong, that the beetle is not doing these three things out of blind instinct, like a little machine, but is thinking its way along, just as we would think. The difference is that we possess enormous brains, crowded all the time with an infinite number of long thoughts, while the beetle's brain is only a few strings of neurons connected in a modest network, capable therefore of only three *tiny* thoughts, coming into consciousness one after the other: find the right tree; get up there and lay eggs in a slit; back up and spend the day killing the branch so the eggs can hatch. End of message. I would not go so far as to anthropomorphize the mimosa tree, for I really do not believe plants have minds, but something has to be said about the tree's role in this arrangement as a beneficiary: mimosas grow for twenty-five to thirty years and then die, unless they are vigorously pruned annually, in which case they can live to be a hundred. The beetle is a piece of good luck for the tree, but nothing more: one example of pure chance working at its best in nature—what you might even wish to call good nature.

This brings me to the second example of unsettlement in biology, currently being rather delicately discussed but not yet argued over, for there is still only one orthodoxy and almost no opposition, yet. This is the matter of chance itself, and the role played by blind chance in the arrangement of living things on the planet. It is, in the orthodox view, pure luck that evolution brought us to our present condition, and things might just as well have turned out any number of other, different ways, and might go in any unpredictable way for the future. There is, of course, nothing chancy about natural selection itself: it is an accepted fact that selection will always favor the advantaged individuals whose genes succeed best in propagating themselves within a changing environment. But the creatures acted upon by natural selection are themselves there as the result of chance: mutations (probably of much more importance during the long period of exclusively microbial life starting nearly 4 billion years ago and continuing until about one billion years ago); the endless sorting and re-sorting of genes within chromosomes during replication; perhaps recombination of genes across species lines at one time or another; and almost certainly the carrying of genes by viruses from one creature to another. 7

The argument comes when one contemplates the whole biosphere, the conjoined life of the earth. How could it have turned out to possess such stability and coherence, resembling as it does a sort of enormous developing embryo, with nothing but chance events to determine its emergence? Lovelock and Margulis, facing this problem, have proposed the Gaia Hypothesis, 8 which is, in brief, that the earth is itself a form of life, "a complex entity involving the Earth's biosphere, atmosphere, oceans and soil; the totality constituting a feedback or cybernetic system which seeks an optimal physical and chemical environment for life on this planet." Lovelock postulates, in addition, that "the physical and chemical condition of the surface of the Earth, of the atmosphere, and of the oceans has been and is actively made fit and comfortable by the presence of life itself."

This notion is beginning to stir up a few signs of storm, and if it catches 9
on, as I think it will, we will soon find the biological community split into fuming factions, one side saying that the evolved biosphere displays evidences of design and purpose, the other decrying such heresy. I believe that students should learn as much as they can about the argument. In an essay in *Coevolution* (Spring 1981), W. F. Doolittle has recently attacked the Gaia Hypothesis, asking, among other things, ". . . how does Gaia know if she is too cold or too hot, and how does she instruct the biosphere to behave accordingly?" This is not a deadly criticism in a world where we do not actually understand, in anything like real detail, how even Dr. Doolittle manages the stability and control of his own internal environment, including his body temperature. One thing is certain: none of us can instruct our body's systems to make the needed corrections beyond a very limited number of rather trivial tricks made possible through biofeedback techniques. If something goes wrong with my liver or my kidneys, I have no advice to offer out of my cortex. I rely on the system to fix itself, which it usually does with no help from me beyond crossing my fingers.

Another current battle involving the unknown is between sociobiolo- 10
gists and antisociobiologists, and it is a marvel for students to behold. To observe, in open-mouthed astonishment, one group of highly intelligent, beautifully trained, knowledgeable, and imaginative scientists maintaining that all behavior, animal and human, is governed exclusively by genes, and another group of equally talented scientists asserting that all behavior is set and determined by the environment or by culture, is an educational experience that no college student should be allowed to miss. The essential lesson to be learned has nothing to do with the relative validity of the facts underlying the argument. It is the argument itself that is the education: we do not yet know enough to settle such questions.

One last example. There is an uncomfortable secret in biology, not 11
much talked about yet, but beginning to surface. It is, in a way, linked to the observations that underlie the Gaia Hypothesis. Nature abounds in instances of cooperation and collaboration, partnerships between species. There is a tendency of living things to join up whenever joining is possible: accommodation and compromise are more common results of close contact than combat and destruction. Given the opportunity and the proper circumstances, two cells from totally different species—a mouse cell and a human cell, for example—will fuse to become a single cell, and then the two nuclei will fuse into a single nucleus, and then the hybrid cell will divide to produce generations of new cells containing the combined genomes of both species. Bacteria

are indispensable partners in the fixation of atmospheric nitrogen by plants. The oxygen in our atmosphere is put there, almost in its entirety, by the photosynthetic chloroplasts in the cells of green plants, and these organelles are almost certainly the descendants of blue-green algae that joined up when the nucleated cells of higher plants came into existence. The mitochondria in all our own cells, and in all other nucleated cells, which enable us to use oxygen for energy, are the direct descendants of symbiotic bacteria. These are becoming accepted facts, and there is no longer an agitated argument over their probable validity; but there are no satisfactory explanations for how such amiable and useful arrangements came into being in the first place. Axelrod and Hamilton (*Science,* March 27, 1981) have recently reopened the question of cooperation in evolution with a mathematical approach based on game theory (the Prisoner's Dilemma game), which permits the hypothesis that one creature's best strategy for dealing repeatedly with another is to concede and cooperate rather than to defect and go it alone.

This idea can be made to fit with the mathematical justification based 12
on kinship already accepted for explaining altruism in nature—that in a colony of social insects the sacrifice of one individual for another depends on how many of the sacrificed member's genes are matched by others and thus preserved, and that the extent of the colony's altruistic behavior can be mathematically calculated. It is, by the way, an interesting aspect of contemporary biology that true altruism—the giving away of something without return—is incompatible with dogma, even though it goes on all over the place. Nature, in this respect, keeps breaking the rules, and needs correcting by new ways of doing arithmetic.

The social scientists are in the hardest business of all—trying to under- 13
stand how humanity works. They are caught up in debates all over town; everything they touch turns out to be one of society's nerve endings, eliciting outrage and cries of pain. Wait until they begin coming close to the bone. They surely will someday, provided they can continue to attract enough bright people—fascinated by humanity, unafraid of big numbers, and skeptical of questionnaires—and provided the government does not starve them out of business, as is now being tried in Washington. Politicians do not like pain, not even wincing, and they have some fear of what the social scientists may be thinking about thinking for the future.

The social scientists are themselves too modest about the history of 14
their endeavor, tending to display only the matters under scrutiny today in economics, sociology, and psychology, for example—never boasting, as they might, about one of the greatest of all scientific advances in our comprehension of humanity, for which they could be claiming credit. I refer to the marvelous accomplishments of the nineteenth-century comparative linguists. When the scientific method is working at its best, it succeeds in revealing the connection between things in nature that seem at first totally unrelated to each other. Long before the time when the biologists, led by Darwin and Wallace, were constructing the tree of evolution and the origin of species, the linguists were hard at work on the evolution of language. After beginning in

1786 with Sir William Jones and his inspired hunch that the remarkable similarities among Sanskrit, Greek, and Latin meant, in his words, that these three languages must "have sprung from some common source, which, perhaps, no longer exists," the new science of comparative grammar took off in 1816 with Franz Bopp's classic work "On the conjugational system of the Sanskrit language in comparison with that of the Greek, Latin, Persian and Germanic languages"—a piece of work equivalent, in its scope and in its power to explain, to the best of nineteenth-century biology. The common Indo-European ancestry of English, Germanic, Slavic, Greek, Latin, Baltic, Indic, Iranian, Hittite, and Anatolian tongues, and the meticulous scholarship connecting them was a tour de force for research—science at its best, and social science at that.

It is nice to know that a common language, perhaps 20,000 years ago, 15
had a root word for the earth which turned, much later, into the technical term for the complex polymers that make up the connective tissues of the soil: humus and what are called the humic acids. There is a strangeness, though, in the emergence from the same root of words such as "human" and "humane," and "humble." It comes as something of a shock to realize that the root for words such as "miracle" and "marvel" meant, originally, "to smile," and that from the single root *sa* were constructed, in the descendant tongues, three cognate words, "satisfied," "satiated," and "sadness." How is it possible for a species to show so much wisdom in its most collective of all behaviors—the making and constant changing of language—and at the same time be so habitually folly-prone in the building of nation-states? Modern linguistics has moved into new areas of inquiry as specialized and inaccessible for most laymen (including me) as particle physics; I cannot guess where linguistics will come out, but it is surely aimed at scientific comprehension, and its problem—human language—is as crucial to the species as any other field I can think of, including molecular genetics.

But there are some risks involved in trying to do science in the humani- 16
ties before its time, and useful lessons can be learned from some of the not-so-distant history of medicine. A century ago it was the common practice to deal with disease by analyzing what seemed to be the underlying mechanism and applying whatever treatment popped into the doctor's head. Getting sick was a hazardous enterprise in those days. The driving force in medicine was the need to *do* something, never mind what. It occurs to me now, reading in incomprehension some of the current reductionist writings in literary criticism, especially poetry criticism, that the new schools are at risk under a similar pressure. A poem is a healthy organism, really in need of no help from science, no treatment except fresh air and exercise. I thought I'd just sneak that in.

Questions for Discussion

1. In reflecting on the strangeness of termite social behavior in paragraph 3 and on how science is far from being able to explain it, Thomas observes that "this mystery is the best introduction I can think of to biological science in college . . . [for it teaches students] early in their careers about the uncertainties in science." Do the science courses you have had teach "the uncertainties in science" and encourage discussion of them? Do you agree that they should?
2. Thomas believes that science is full of mysteries. Does it seem to you that most people think of science as full of facts—cut, dried, and proved—rather than full of mysteries? Which of these views have been held by most of the science teachers you have known? Have you found that one view is more characteristic of good science teachers than the other view?
3. Do you agree with Thomas's opening sentence that "the greatest of all the accomplishments of twentieth-century science has been the discovery of human ignorance"? State your reasons.
4. Does the Gaia Hypothesis (¶8) sound like fact or fairy tale? Most great hypotheses in the history of science sounded like fairy tales (or sheer nuttiness) when they were first advanced. This does not necessarily argue in favor of the Gaia Hypothesis, but it does argue against the cliché that science progresses because scientists stick to what can be seen, measured, and proved. For example, when Copernicus suggested that the earth goes around the sun instead of the sun going around the earth, he was contradicting what everyone could "prove" simply by watching the sky every day. As Galileo later said, Copernicus performed "a rape upon the senses"; he asked people to believe in a theory that contradicted the "facts" of everyone's experience. Likewise, Newton asked people to rely more on their imaginations than on their own eyes. Since he could perform no laboratory tests to prove his theory of gravity, he asked everyone to picture gravity operating in a frictionless universe—a kind of universe no one on earth ever experiences. (Gravity still has not been defined or measured in any conclusive way.) And in our own century, Einstein had not performed one single laboratory experiment and could offer not a single fact to back up his claims when he proposed that mass and energy are equivalent at light speeds and that the speed of light is absolute. It took decades before *any* of his claims could be verified by observation, and most of them remain untested today.

   In light of the history of great scientific discoveries, what can you conclude about the nature of scientific inquiry? If Copernicus and Newton and Einstein were dreamers, surely they were informed dreamers; though they contradicted some of the "facts" of their day, they preserved what facts they could and thought out their reasons carefully, even when they had no laboratory experiments to support their hypotheses. What, then, is the role of facts in scientific inquiry, and what is the role of imagination? When Thomas opens his essay by praising modern science for accomplishing "the discovery of human ignorance," is he trying to spur us on to find more facts, or is he appealing to our imagination? Or both? (For further reading on the role of facts in inquiry, see Edward Hallett Carr, "The Historian and His Facts," pp. 575–583. For the role of the imagination in inquiry, see Jacob Bronowski, "The Reach of Imagination," pp. 238–245.)

5. In paragraph 10 Thomas says that college students need to be exposed to the big controversies in science because "it is the argument itself that is the education." This assertion implies that *all* of education should be education-as-argument. Can you say what such an education would be? Are you getting such an education? Would you like to? How would you define its opposite? (See "What Is an Argument?" pp. 19–21.)

Suggested Essay Topics

1. According to Thomas, "It is the admission of ignorance that leads to progress" (¶2). No doubt you have known teachers whose teaching did not reflect this view—teachers who never admitted ignorance or exposed their students to the "big arguments currently going on." Write a letter to one such teacher, arguing in support of Thomas's view of scientific education and imitating as well as you can Thomas's casual-seeming tone of geniality combined with hardheaded critical aggressiveness.
2. This is a tougher topic than the previous one and requires some library research. Picture yourself as a scientist in Copernicus' time, outraged at both the "unscientific method" and the content of Copernicus' new theory that the earth goes around the sun. Address a letter to Copernicus in which you try to persuade him of the scientific illegitimacy of contradicting so many proved facts. Point out just how well supported the accepted view of things is, and try to make him see that he is going to set science back 100 years if he gets people to believe in his nutty notions. Base your letter on library research. There *was* an enormous response to Copernicus' ideas; not only is reading some of this controversy firsthand a good introduction to the history of science, but writing about it is good practice at analysis. (See "What Is Analysis?" pp. 22–24.)

Joseph Wood Krutch

Joseph Wood Krutch (1893–1970) was in his time one of the most widely read commentators on literature and life. Unlike many scholars, he early developed a style that proved appealing to general readers, and in a long series of popular books he goaded Americans into thought about an astonishing range of subjects: the nature of genius in the lives of authors like Edgar Allan

Poe, Samuel Johnson, Henry David Thoreau, and the great novelists, European and American; the strengths and weaknesses of modern culture; the decline of serious discussion of moral issues; and, in the latter part of his life, the wonders of the natural world.

"The Meaning of Awareness" is one of his aggressive, thoughtful efforts to understand and preserve the traditional values of humankind and the natural world. Although Krutch was by no means an opponent of science, he feared that popular misapplications of scientific, technological, and economic theories would reduce our world to what can be "covered" with formulas and statistics. While some scientists and philosophers accused him of superficiality and partiality, other readers thought of him as something like a prophet. Can you see evidence in the following piece that might lead readers to both responses?

THE MEANING OF AWARENESS

The You and the Me

Chapter 7 of *The Great Chain of Life* (1956).

For nine long years a large salamander lived her sluggish life in a damp terrarium on my window sill. Before I assumed responsibility for her health and welfare she had lived through a different life—not as different as the life of a butterfly is from that of a caterpillar, but different enough. Once she had lived in water and breathed it. Like her parents before her she still had to keep her skin damp, but now she seldom actually went into the water. 1

Before she was even an egg her father and her mother, prompted by some no doubt unconscious memory, had left the damp moss or leaves they had normally preferred since achieving maturity and had climbed down into some pond or pool to mate. The prompt result was a cluster of eggs embedded in a mass of jelly much like that which surrounds the eggs of common American frogs. These eggs had hatched into tadpoles easily distinguishable from those destined to become frogs or toads by the two plumes waving from their shoulders—gills for breathing the water which frogs manage to get along without even though they too are temporarily water-breathers. 2

Most of my specimen's subsequent history was much like that of the young frogs themselves. Legs had budded, and though the tail had not disappeared the plumes had withered away while lungs fit for air-breathing had developed. Sally, as I called her, had then left the water and become a land animal. All this took place quite gradually without any radical dissolution of the organism as a whole, as in the case of the caterpillar, and without the intervention of that dead sleep from which the caterpillar woke to find himself somebody else. Far back in time, Sally's direct ancestors had been the first vertebrates to risk coming to land, and she recapitulated their history. 3

The rest of my salamander's life was very uneventful but not much 4 more so than it would have been had I left her to her own devices. In fact, returning to the water is almost the only interesting thing the amphibia ever *do.* By comparison with even the butterflies—who lead very uneventful lives as insects go—the amphibia are dull creatures indeed, seemingly without enterprise, aspiration, or any conspicuous resourcefulness.

5 If you or I had been permitted a brief moment of consciousness sometime about the middle of the Mesozoic era, when the amphibia and the insects were both flourishing, we well might have concluded that the latter were the more promising experiment. I doubt that we would have been very likely to pick out a salamander as our ancestor. Yet the evidence seems pretty definite that nature knew better and that it is from him we come. In Old Testament terms, Amphibia begat Reptile, Reptile begat Mammal, Mammal begat Man.

6 Even before the Mesozoic was over the beetles were far ahead of the salamanders so far as the techniques of living are concerned. "What," we might well have asked, "do the amphibia have that the insects do not?" What potentiality in them was responsible for the fact that, given the whole Cenozoic still to develop in, the one got no farther than the bee and the ant, while the other has ended—if this is indeed the end—in man?

7 Perhaps if that anticipatory visit had lasted long enough we could finally have guessed the answer as easily as it can be guessed today by anyone who has kept both insects and salamanders in captivity and has observed one great difference between them. The insect goes very expertly about his business. But not even those insects who go very expertly about their very complicated business give any sign of awareness of anything not directly connected with that immediate business.

8 It is not merely that they are absolutely, or almost absolutely, incapable of learning anything. A salamander cannot learn very much either. But the salamander has some awareness of the world outside himself and he has, therefore, the true beginnings of a self—as we understand the term. A butterfly or a beetle does not. Hence you can make a pet out of a salamander—at least to the extent necessary to fulfill the minimum definition of that word. He will come to depend upon you, to profit from your ministrations, and to expect them at appropriate times. An insect is never more than a captive. If you help him he does not know it and he will never come to depend upon your ministrations. He does not even know that you exist. And because of what that implies, a whole great world of experience was opened up to the hierarchy of vertebrates from the salamander on up and has remained closed to the insect.

9 Seen from the outside, the ants who keep cows, practice agriculture, make war, and capture slaves suggest human beings more strongly than any vertebrate lower than the apes. But if we could see from the inside, the psyche of even the sluggish salamander in my window terrarium would be different. In some dim way she has connected me with herself and I am part of her life.

10 My old housekeeper used to assure me pridefully from time to time: "She knows me." That, I am afraid, was a bit of overinterpretation. I doubt

very seriously that Sally could tell me and my housekeeper apart. But if either one of us approached the terrarium she would rise heavily on her short legs and amble slowly in the direction of the familiar object. We were associated in what little mind she had with the prospect of food.

Was this, many will ask, more than a mere reflex action? Did any such consciousness as I have been assuming really exist? I will not answer that question in the affirmative as positively as many would answer it in the negative. But the consciousness which is so acute in us must have begun dimly somewhere and to me it seems probable that it had already begun at least as far back as the salamanders who lie, though remotely, on our own direct line of descent. 11

Yet if Sally just barely achieved the status of a pet she fell considerably short of being what we call a domesticated animal. Considerably more awareness of the world around her and considerably more capacity to make an individual adaptation to it would be necessary for that. But because dogs and cats and horses—all of whom have, like us, a salamander in their ancestry—have that considerably greater awareness, they can live a considerable part of our lives and come to seem actual members of our family. Even they are not nearly as ingenious as bees or ants. But we recognize their nearer kinship to us. 12

Those ants have a culture not only analogous to ours in certain respects but one also far older than ours, since the social insects have been civilized for a much longer time—perhaps thirty times longer—than we have. This was possible because they had settled down biologically—i.e., had ceased to evolve organically—long before we did. And since they were not changing rapidly, they had time to mature and to settle irrevocably into habits and customs, while we are even now still experimenting wildly—discarding habits and techniques every decade or two. 13

By ant standards we have never had any traditions loyally adhered to. Their so-called virtues—industry, selfless devotion to the good of the community, etc.—are so strikingly superior to ours that certain fanatical critics of human nature and its ways have implied that these creatures whom the biologist calls "lower" are morally "better" than we, and have hoped that in a few million years we might become more like them. Even without going that far and leaving ourselves resolutely out of it as obviously *hors concours* [without rival], we may still find ourselves raising again the outrageous question already alluded to. By what right do we call the ants "lower" than, say, a member of a wolf pack? On what basis is the hierarchy established? 14

Ask that question of a biologist and he will give you ready reasons satisfactory to himself. Anatomically, the insects are simpler. They show very little adaptability. They cannot learn as readily as a wolf can. They can't change their habits very much. They have come to a dead end. They have been precisely what they are for a very long time and will remain that for a very long time to come. "Progress" is something they no longer know anything about. And they are not "intelligent." 15

All these statements are true enough, but like so many biological dis- 16 tinctions and standards they seem just a little remote. To say that an animal is a compulsory protein feeder is, as we remarked once before, perfectly accurate but has little to do with the rich complex of meanings the word "animal" suggests to the human being who hears it. In certain contexts it is fine. In other contexts—the context of a poem, for instance—it isn't.

Indisputable accuracy does not make it much more satisfactory than 17
Plato's definition of man—a two-legged animal without feathers. Man is certainly that and no other animal is. His definition establishes a criterion that is infallible, but also entirely irrelevant. Apply the test and you will never mistake a wolf or a bird for a man or even mistake a primate—always more or less four-footed—for one of your fellow citizens. This really is a sure way of telling your friends from the apes. But then, you would not be very likely to make a mistake anyway. The definition is perfect but also meaningless.

The explanation a biologist would give why a wolf is "higher" than an 18
ant is almost equally unsatisfactory, because it does not seem to involve the thing on the basis of which we make our judgment. Should they reverse themselves tomorrow and give new reasons in similar terms for deciding that the ant is "higher" we would go right on feeling that he is not. On what, then, is this feeling based if not upon any good scientific criteria? What kind of distinctions appeal to us as genuinely meaningful?

Suppose you play the childish game. Suppose you ask yourself which 19
you would rather be—a farmer ant or a robin. Only the perverse would hesitate. "A robin, of course." But why? What it would come to would certainly be something like this: "Because being a robin would be more fun. Because the robin exhibits the joy of life. Because he seems to be glad to be a robin and because it is hard to believe that an ant is glad to be what he is." Of course we can't say positively that he isn't. We cannot understand his language and he may be proclaiming to the world of other ants with what ecstasy he contemplates the fact that he is one of them. But he cannot communicate with us, and, justifiably or not, we find it hard to believe that he is glad.

Privately, biologists often share our prejudice. But few, I am afraid, 20
would agree to classify animals as "higher" or "lower" on any such basis. They would reply, and rightly so far as biology is concerned, that to say a robin is higher than an ant because he has more joy in living is to cease to be scientific. Also, some might think that it smacks of immoral hedonism. Nevertheless a hierarchy ordered on that basis is meaningful in human terms as the scientific one is not.

If the joy of living is the most enviable good any of the lower animals 21
can attain to and at least the second-best available to man himself, that implies in both a more general capacity which can only be called "awareness"—something that is different from intelligence as usually defined and not perfectly equatable with logic, or insight, or adaptability; also something the salamander has more of than the ant has. There is no way of measuring it, and even the psychologist would be for that reason rather loth to take it much into consideration or even to admit that it exists as distinguished from

reason, insight, and the rest. That it does exist in human beings, any contemplative man knows from his own experience.

The best solver of puzzles is not necessarily the man most aware of living. The animal who most skillfully adapts himself to the conditions for survival is not necessarily the one who has the greatest joy in living. And from the standpoint of one kind of interest in living creatures it is perfectly legitimate to think of them as "high" or "low" in proportion to the degree of awareness they exhibit. 22

We can freely admit that the ant's technique of making a living is far more advanced than that of the bird or, indeed, of any vertebrate animal except man. We can see that some species of ants have reached what in terms of human history corresponds to an agricultural society, whereas there is no vertebrate who is not still a mere nomad hunter. But living—as some men have got around to telling themselves—can be more important than making a living. And making a living seems to be all the ant does, while the robin and many another vertebrate live abundantly. 23

Yes, I say to myself, the "higher" animals really are higher. Even the sluggish, dim-witted salamander, cold-blooded but vertebrate and with the beginnings of a vertebrate brain, is "higher" than the industrious ant. But it is not for any of the objective reasons either the biologist or the social anthropologist will consent to give that I call him so. 24

It is because even the salamander has some sort of awareness the insects have not; because, unlike them, he is on his way to intelligence, on his way to pain and pleasure, on his way to courage, and even to a sense of honor as the bighorn is beginning to feel it; on his way to Love, which the birds, bungling parents though they are, can feel and the wise wasp cannot. On the way to the joy of life, which only one or more of these things can make possible. 25

Once you admit this fact there is something obviously wrong with the orthodox view of the aims and methods of that evolutionary process through which both the blindly efficient ant and the blunderingly emotional bird arrived at their present state. According to that orthodox view "survival value" is the key to everything. But though intelligence does have an obvious survival value, it is by no means obvious that it works any better than the instinct of the insect. As for the emotions, their survival value is not always obvious at all. And if you want to include man in the scheme of evolution, it is so far from obvious that the complexities of civilized emotional and intellectual life have any survival value at all that many recent philosophers have suspected them of being fatal handicaps instead. 26

This is a fact that raises a question for the evolutionist. If the survival value of intelligence is real enough though no greater than that of instinct, if many of our emotions and the kind of awareness upon which they depend have no obvious survival value at all, then why have certain animals developed both to such a high degree? Why, for that matter, have either they or we developed them at all? Doubtless an intelligent *individual* has a better chance of individual survival than a merely instinctive one. But if nature is 27 careful of the type, careless of the individual, then why should that weigh anything in the scales?

Darwin himself formulated a "law." No organism, he said, ever develops a characteristic beyond the point where it is useful for survival. But, as we have been asking, how useful in that sense is intelligence or even consciousness? Doesn't instinct have an even higher survival value? 28

It is pretty generally recognized that the insects are the most successful organisms on earth. It is also generally recognized that they get along either with the dimmest consciousness and intelligence, or perhaps without any at all. It is even believed by many that they lost a good deal of what they once had because instinct proved to have a higher survival value. If all this is true does it not suggest that orthodox evolutionism may be in one respect wrong? Does it not suggest that nature (or whatever you want to call it) puts a value on things which do not have any simple survival value? Is it not possible that mammals look after their young with bumbling consciousness rather than with the expertness of instinct because nature has, in some way, been interested not merely in the survival of the fittest, but in "the fittest" for something more than mere survival? 29

This last question, in a somewhat different form, was actually asked and then left unanswered in the earliest days of Darwinism. Alfred Russel Wallace, generously acknowledged by Darwin as the co-propounder of the theory of natural selection, steadily and from the beginning maintained one difference with his more famous co-worker. It was not and could not be demonstrated, he said, that natural selection could account for "the higher qualities of man." Most notable among these "higher qualities" was, he maintained, the moral sense. 30

No doubt some manifestations of it had a survival value in society. But not all of them. Man's willingness, sometimes at least, not only to sacrifice himself but to sacrifice himself and others for an ideal, his human conviction that "survival value" is not the only value, did not in themselves have any "survival value." How then could they have arisen if it was, as Darwin said, the inviolable rule of nature that no organism can develop what is not biologically useful to it? An all-inclusive explanation of the phenomenon of life in terms of natural selection would have to account somehow for the very conception of "values which have no survival value." And no such inclusive explanation is forthcoming. 31

For the most part this question has been simply brushed aside by orthodox evolutionists. Along with other related questions it has been kept alive chiefly by "mere men of letters"—by Samuel Butler, Bergson, Bernard Shaw, and the rest. But it will not down. And there are even signs that some scientists, perhaps especially the neurologists, are less sure than they once were that the mechanistic explanation of all the phenomena of living matter is complete. But if nature has been working toward something besides survival, what is it? 32

Julian Huxley, one of the most enlightened of present-day evolutionists, has tangled with the question. Evolution, he says, implies progress. But 33 in what does "progress" consist? Certainly, as he admits, it includes something more than a mere progressive increase in the amount of living matter on the earth. That could be achieved by the simplest forms. Nature "wants" not merely more organisms but more complex organisms. But how can it want them if they do not survive more abundantly? Greater complexity implies, he says, "improvement." But what constitutes an "improved" organism? Not, he says, mere complexity itself but a complexity which opens the way to further "improvement." That, it seems, simply closes the circle. The question of what constitutes "improvement" and what sort of values other than mere survival value nature does recognize is still unanswered.

Perhaps the only way to escape from the dilemma that a Huxley recog- 34
nizes is to make an assumption bolder than he would probably be willing to accept. But the difficulties do vanish if we are willing to accept the possibility that what Nature has been working toward is not merely survival; that, ultimately, it is not survival itself but Consciousness and Intelligence *themselves*—partly at least for their own sake.

If Nature has advanced from the inanimate to the animate; if she "pre- 35
fers" the living to the lifeless and the forms of life which survive rather to those that perish; then there is nothing which forbids the assumption that she also "prefers" conscious intelligence to blind instinct; that just as complex organization was developed even though it had no obvious survival value for the species, so also the awareness of itself which complex organization made possible is also one of her goals.

Whenever man's thinking starts with himself rather than with his pos- 36
sible origins in lower forms of life he usually comes to the conclusion that consciousness is the primary fact. "I think therefore I am"* seems to be the most inescapably self-evident of propositions. Only when he starts as far away from himself as possible can he get into the contrary habit of assuming what the nineteenth century did assume: namely, that his own mind is so far from being the most significant thing in the universe that it has no substantial significance at all, being a mere illusion, some sort of insubstantial by-product of those ultimate realities which are unconscious, automatic, and mechanical.

Ever since the seventeenth century, science actually has tended to 37
begin as far away from man himself as possible, while metaphysics has continued to start with man's own mind. Hence the undoubted fact that for a long time, at least, science and metaphysics either grew farther and farther apart, or, as with the positivists, metaphysics simply surrendered to science and tended to become no more than an abstractly stated theory of the va-

*The quotation, one of the most famous in the history of thought, is from René Descartes' proof for his own existence. By applying the methods of a strict skepticism to all other "things" in the universe, Descartes could in some sense doubt their existence, but he could not doubt that he was doubting—that is, thinking. Therefore, he concluded, *something* exists, namely his doubting self. Do you think that Krutch is justified in employing this famous moment as evidence for "awareness"?

lidity of science.* Yet, as we have just seen, science and positivism leave certain stubborn questions unanswered. Perhaps these questions will ultimately have to be attacked again and from the older point of view.

Aristotle is the acknowledged father of natural history. But because 38
Aristotle lived in an age when it still seemed natural to start with the human mind itself, he reached the conclusion that at least so far as man himself is concerned Contemplation is what he is "for." And if Aristotle had had any clear idea of evolution he would certainly have supposed that a more and more complete awareness, not mere survival, was what nature was aiming at.

Most present-day biologists, following the lead of the nineteenth cen- 39
tury, have no patience with any such metaphysical notions. When you come right down to it man is, they say, an animal; and there is only one thing that any animal is "for"—namely, survival and reproduction. Some animals accomplish this purpose in one way and some in another. Man's way happens to involve some consciousness of what he is doing and of why he does it. But that is a mere accident. If what we call intelligence had not had a high survival value it would never have developed. And one of the consequences of this fact is that man is most successful when he uses his intelligence to facilitate his survival. Thinking, or even awareness, for its own sake is a biological mistake. What he is "for" is *doing,* certainly not mooning over what he has done—unless of course that mooning has survival value, as under certain circumstances it may.

What we have been asking is, then, simply this: How good is the 40
evidence—even their own kind of evidence—which those who take this position can offer in its support? If they are right, then man ought biologically to be the most successful of all animals. No other ought to flourish so exuberantly or have a future which, biologically, looks so bright. But what grounds do we really have for believing anything like that to be the real state of affairs? Does conscious intelligence really work any better than instinct?

No doubt you and I are the most successful of the mammals. When we 41
take possession of any part of this earth the others go into a decline. No bear or wolf, no whale or buffalo, can successfully compete with us. But that doesn't really mean much, because all the mammals are creatures who have already started down the road we have followed so much farther than they. To some considerable extent they too are conscious, intelligent, capable of learning much from experience. Like us they are born with mental slates which, if not entirely blank, have much less written on them than is indelibly inscribed before birth on the nervous systems of many a "lower" animal.

*Krutch uses the term *metaphysics* to refer to the branch of philosophy dealing with the nature of existence, insofar as such speculation does not depend on scientific observation. As for the "positivists," see the note on p. 575. If you are not clear about these terms—and no brief definitions can do them justice—look them up in an encyclopedia. But do not be surprised if even after you research the terms, Krutch's passage remains difficult. Krutch has telescoped large claims into a small paragraph, and since the three terms *science, metaphysics,* and *positivism* are ambiguous and controversial, any such passage will leave even the best-informed reader with some unanswered questions.

Obviously if you are going to have to depend upon conscious intelligence, then it is an advantage to have that conscious intelligence highly developed. The other mammals over whom we triumph so easily have to fight us chiefly with inferior versions of our own weapons and it is no wonder that they lose. But what of the creatures who learn little or nothing, who can hardly be said to be capable of thought, who are conscious only dimly if at all? Are they really, from the biological standpoint, any less "successful" than we or the other mammals? Can they be said to "succeed" any less well? Are they deprived of anything except consciousness itself? 42

It is certainly not evident that they are. As a matter of fact the insects are the only conspicuous creatures indubitably holding their own against man. When he matches wits with any of the lower mammals they always lose. But when he matches his wit against the instinct and vitality of the insects he merely holds his own, at best. An individual insect is no match for an individual man. But most species of insects have done very well at holding their own as a species against him. And if you believe the biologists it is only with the prosperity of the species that Nature, or evolution, has ever, or could ever, concern herself. 43

Who is the more likely to be here on what evolution calls tomorrow—i.e., ten million years hence? Certainly the chance that man will have destroyed himself before then seems greater than the chance that the insects will have done so. Their instincts seem not to have created for them the difficulties and the dangers man's intelligence and emotion have created for him. They have been here much longer than he and it certainly seems not improbable that they will remain here much longer also. As a matter of fact the bacteria are even more "successful" than the insects. There are far more of them alive at this moment than there are of even insects, and it is even more difficult to imagine them ever extinct. If survival is the only thing that counts in nature then why or how did any life higher than that of a bacterium ever come into being? 44

No answer to that question seems possible unless we are willing to assume that for Nature herself, as well as for us, the instinct of the insect is "better" than the vegetative life of the bacterium, and the conscious concern of the bird for its offspring better than the unconscious efficiency of the wasp. Yet vegetation is not better than instinct and consciousness is not better than instinct if the only criterion is survival value. And if man's mind does not help him to survive more successfully than creatures having no mind at all, then what on earth can it be for? Can it be for anything except itself? Can its value be other than absolute rather than instrumental? 45

The bird and the man are more successful than the wasp only if you count their consciousness as, itself, some kind of success. The "purpose" of parental concern cannot be merely the successful rearing of offspring, because that can be accomplished quite as successfully without any consciousness at all. 46

Is it not possible, then, that Aristotle was right, that contemplation is not only the true end of man but the end that has been pursued ever since 47 vertebrates took the road leading to a keener and keener consciousness? Have we been trying to understand the meaning of evolution by beginning at the wrong end? Is it possible that, for instance, the real, the only true "purpose" served by conscious concern over the young is the fact that out of it comes parental love itself? Has what evolution worked toward been not "survival" but "awareness"? Is the ultimate answer to the question "Why is a bungling mammal higher than an efficient wasp" simply that it is higher because it can experience parental love? Was it this, rather than mere survival, that nature was after all along?

Questions for Discussion

1. Krutch deals with two large and complex contrasting views of life. Can you re-formulate them, clarifying Krutch's views of the reasons underlying each?
2. At crucial points in this essay, Krutch resorts to a series of questions rather than direct assertions (especially in ¶29 and ¶47). Yet at many other points he talks as if he is not really doubtful about the answers but is rather asserting his own strong, settled beliefs. For example, he calls some of his inferences *facts* (¶26, first line; ¶27, first line), and there are other signs that he considers his opponents flatly mistaken. What does he gain, if anything, from putting his conclusions in the form of questions and his inferences in the form of facts?
3. *Awareness* is a term that, like *love* and *charity* (see the introduction to I Corinthians 13, pp. 343–344), cannot be pinned down with rigorous definition. What steps does Krutch take to ensure that his readers have a clear notion of what *he* means by this elusive concept?
4. Other authors in this book argue against narrow notions of "practicality" (for example, Cousins, pp. 30–32, Dickens, pp. 45–57, and Whitehead, pp. 72–81). If you have read any of these essays, compare their authors' ideas of practicality with Krutch's idea of "survival value." Does Krutch seem to be saying that nature is *im*practical or, rather, that it serves a higher practicality?

Suggested Essay Topics

1. Go through the essay once again carefully, looking for all the *assumptions* you can find for which Krutch provides no supporting evidence. For example, in paragraph 19 he assumes, without conducting an actual survey, that anyone who would not rather be a robin than an ant is "perverse" (see "Assumptions" in "How to Read an Argument: Demonstration II," pp. 129–130). After writing out these assumptions carefully, write a brief critique of each one, asking yourself whether Krutch is justified in assum-

ing that his *readers* will see no need for further evidence. (Note that this assignment does not ask for an organized paper. Just number your short paragraphs.)

2. Krutch assumes that animals other than human beings show "awareness." If you have ever observed any animal closely, write a short paper discussing whether all of its behavior could be explained in terms of what Krutch calls "mere survival." (It would be useful here to review "Reasoning in Animals" by Charles Darwin, pp. 84–88.) Try to be as clear as possible about what kinds of behavior would satisfy Krutch's criteria for "awareness."

Stanley L. Jaki

Stanley L. Jaki (b. 1924) is a professor of the history and philosophy of physics at Seton Hall University, but he also has a doctorate in theology and is a member of the Benedictine Order. As a Roman Catholic priest teaching science, he thus presumably tries to live *the harmony of science and religion that his essay explores.*

But being a priest gives Jaki special rhetorical problems in writing about the role of faith in physics, for most readers will expect a priest to be biased in favor of faith. Isn't faith what he's "paid" to preach about? Thus Jaki must work with special care if he wants to convince skeptical readers that both science and religion depend equally on faith and that he is not stacking the cards in favor of religion.

We suggest that you read through the essay quickly once, without pausing to read our footnotes, to consult Jaki's endnotes, or to look up unfamiliar words. On this first reading, look closely for Jaki's most forceful statement of his central thesis, for the reasons he gives in support of that thesis, and for evidence that he is or is not speaking merely from a religious preference. You might want to underline the most likely candidates for topic sentences, perhaps numbering them for further reference. But on this first reading don't slow yourself down with other kinds of note-taking.

Now read through the essay again, this time slowly, pausing to consider whatever difficulties seem important to you. If a word or phrase that Jaki uses is not clear, look it up. If you can at first see no clear reason for his including a paragraph or section, ask yourself what he would lose by cutting it. Label each kind of reason he offers, either with different colors or with letters. Don't hesitate to sprinkle question marks wherever you are still puzzled. They will be your best guides for taking part in class discussion.

THE ROLE OF FAITH IN PHYSICS

From *Zygon: Journal of Religion & Science,* June 1967.

A little over seventy years ago, in 1896, the founder of psychology in America, William James, spoke before the philosophical clubs of Yale and Brown. The title of his still-famous lecture was "The Will To Believe." Its topic, as James noted with tongue in cheek, was hardly in line with what he called "Harvard freethinking and indifference."[1] In fact, a year later, when sending his lecture to print, he felt the need to explain why he had spoken of faith to an academic audience. He knew that according to most of his colleagues modern conditions required not stronger beliefs but a keener sense of doubt and criticism. Yet, James did not consider it "a misuse of opportunity" on his part to emphasize the role of faith before a gathering of scholars. He admitted that credulous crowds needed to be exposed to what he called "the northwest wind of science." For intellectuals, however, he had the following diagnosis: "Academic audiences, fed already on science, have a very different need."[2] What they needed, according to him, was the will to believe. 1

It is rather a reassuring symptom that, today, academic circles suffer much less of what James called "a paralysis of their native capacity for faith."[3] The recognition is growing strong that faith, or belief, forms the ultimate foundation of the certainty of every knowledge.[4] Such is certainly the case in the field of physics. Leading physicists voice with ever greater emphasis the conviction that faith plays an indispensable role in their search for new discoveries. Their awareness is steadily growing that historic breakthroughs in physics are as much the product of a trusting faith in nature as of a critical analysis of the facts of nature. Most important, leading physicists of today know all too well that the products of science will ruin mankind unless science will foster man's faith in himself and in his goals. 2

In speaking about faith, one touches on a delicate subject that needs clarification, especially when related to the science of physics. No one in his right mind will have any use for a faith as defined by a schoolboy: "Faith is when you believe something that you know isn't true." Clearly, to believe in something because it is absurd would be even worse than to believe blindly, which is bad enough. One may indeed go along with the dictum of T. H. Huxley who called "blind faith the one unpardonable sin."[5] Where Huxley, however, cannot be followed, is in looking with suspicion on faith in general. Faith can, of course, be blind, but so can unbelief, and Huxley himself was blinded by a false image of science very fashionable in his day. In 1866, when Huxley made his statement, physics seemed to approach rapidly its final and perfect stage. In 1871, Lord Kelvin told the British Association that the successes of the kinetic theory of gases pointed to an early completion of an all-inclusive, definitive physical theory.[6] Two decades later, another prominent British physicist, Oliver Lodge, interpreted the success of Maxwell's electromagnetic theory in the same sanguine way. As Lodge 3 put it: "The present is an epoch of astounding activity in physical science. Progress is a thing of months and weeks, almost of days. The long line of isolated ripples of past discovery seem blending into a mighty wave, on the crest of which one begins to discern some oncoming magnificent generalization."[7]

Neither Oliver Lodge, nor Lord Kelvin, nor Huxley guessed that, instead 4
of a major and final triumph, agonizing discoveries were in store for physics. Discoveries were to come that played havoc with apparently absolute tenets in physics. The last decade of the nineteenth century saw the discovery of radioactivity and of X-rays. Finally, only a short three weeks before the century was out, there came Planck's announcement of the concept of the quantum of energy. The concept, as all students of physics know, stood in fundamental opposition to some basic tenets of classical physics. The concept of quantum contradicted the principle of continuity, or endless divisibility of matter, and it also contradicted the principle of strict, physical causality. Abandoning those principles seemed equivalent to abandoning the conviction that nature itself was orderly and intelligible. Planck himself was beset with the most serious misgivings. As a matter of fact, he explored every possible avenue to find fault with his famous derivation of the formula of energy distribution of blackbody radiation.

But the concept of quantum could not be evaded. And what an ominous 5
concept it was. It seemed to suggest that, if nature was orderly, its orderliness was beyond the reach of classical physics. But was there at that time any other physics than the classical? In the context of the times, all this seemed to mean that the orderliness of nature could not be grasped by science. As a result, the concept of quantum presented physics with a tremendous challenge. The challenge was the challenge of faith. It called for a step in the dark; it called for a step beyond the science of the day into a mysterious new land of inquiry. It was a challenge that demanded faith in the absolute orderliness of nature regardless of whether the best of science was up to it or not. Such at least was the situation as it appeared to Planck himself. To live with such a situation, to cope with it and to master it, became for him the most momentous experience of his life. It was this experience that prompted his statement of faith, which is worth being quoted in full: "Science demands also the believing spirit. Anybody who has been seriously engaged in scientific work of any kind realizes that over the entrance to the gates of the temple of science are written the words: *Ye must have faith.* It is a quality which the scientist cannot dispense with."[8]

Quantum theory is one of the two main pillars of modern physics. The 6
other is the theory of relativity. These two theories are still unrelated. Today the so-called Unified Theory is but a dream, not a reality. There was, however, a basic common ground in the thinking of the authors of those two theories. Albert Einstein, the principal originator of the theory of relativity, was just as emphatic as Planck was in stressing the importance of faith in the work of the scientist. This is easy to understand. Relativity, no less than quantum theory, demanded an entirely new outlook on nature. The accep-

tance of relativity meant the abandonment of absolute space and time. In their place came a space and time defined in terms of the frame of reference of the observer. No wonder that idealist philosophers* saw in relativity a vindication of their claim that the order in nature was merely a subjective construct of the mind. Such were not, however, Einstein's views. For him, relativity meant rather the conviction that the laws of nature are always and everywhere the same, regardless of the frame of reference one may choose. He viewed the constancy of the speed of light as an absolute, primordial fact of nature that existed, with the rest of nature, independently of the thinking mind. Furthermore, he insisted that the scientist must have full confidence in the objective existence of nature. "Belief," he wrote, "in an external world, independent of the perceiving subject, is the basis of all natural science."[9] It was the same idea that he articulated in greater detail in his analysis of the history of physics written jointly with Leopold Infeld. "Without the belief that it is possible to grasp the reality with our theoretical constructions, without the belief in the inner harmony of our world, there could be no science. This belief is and always will remain the fundamental motive for all scientific creation."[10] To Einstein, the nature of this faith was such as to put it into the sphere of religious beliefs. As he emphatically argued the point, the man of science needed no less than a "profound faith" to secure for himself the assurance that "the regulations valid for the world of existence are rational, that is, comprehensible to reason." A scientist without that faith was simply beyond his comprehension. Clearly, such a disclosure of his thoughts had to come from the deepest recesses of his convictions. The measure of that depth can be best gauged in his most famous aphorism: "Science without religion is lame, religion without science is blind."[11]

Next to quantum theory and the theory of relativity, the most outstand- 7
ing creation of twentieth-century theoretical physics is Eddington's *Fundamental Theory.* Its purpose was possibly the most ambitious ever offered in the history of science. In substance, Eddington tried to derive from purely epistemological† considerations the basic structure and fundamental laws of the universe. Thus he claimed to have established on a priori‡ grounds that the total number of protons in the universe was of the order of 10^{79}. Eddington's ideas did not produce many disciples; yet even his most severe critics expressed their admiration for his bold efforts. At the basis of that intellectual boldness there stood an extraordinary measure of faith—faith in the orderliness of nature, and faith in the ability of the inquiring mind. Or as Eddington

*Philosophers who consider mind and spiritual values, rather than material things and processes, as the primary substance of the universe. The *idealists* are therefore usually contrasted with *realists* (like Planck and Einstein), who maintain faith that a real world exists independently of human perception and that it behaves according to immutable laws. Both terms, however, like so many names for philosophical movements, cover a great many subtle and diverse thinkers. It is always wise, in such cases, to consult a good encyclopedia.

†Epistemology is the study not of *what* we know but *how* we know, the way that mind and perception work to make different kinds of knowledge either available or unavailable to us.

‡"Before the fact"; thus a priori knowledge is not acquired by experience or experimentation but by logical inference alone.

put it: "Reasoning leads us from premises to conclusions; it cannot start without premises; . . . we must believe that we have an inner sense of values which guides us as to what is to be heeded, otherwise we cannot start on our survey even of the physical world. . . . At the very beginning there is something which might be described as an act of faith—a belief that what our eyes have to show us is significant."[12] Long would be the list of twentieth-century physicists who spoke in the same vein. Let it suffice here to recall only a few outstanding cases. First, Heisenberg, whose indeterminacy principle showed the full depth of Planck's quantum theory. He spoke of faith as the perennial mainspring of scientific work.[13] Willem De Sitter, one of the original proponents of relativistic cosmological models, also found it important to stress that "without a solid faith in the existence of order and law no science is possible." Moreover, he was also very explicit in stating that such belief, forming the basis of science, "is not a scientific theory." It is not derived, he insisted, from science, but rather "it is prescientific, being rooted much deeper in our consciousness than science, it is what makes science possible."[14]

THE INFERNAL RACE

By referring to the concept of the possibility of science, De Sitter touched upon a point that deserves to be discussed in some detail. Most immediately, the expression "possibility of science" refers to that historic event known as the birth of science. More of that later. But the expression "possibility of science" refers also to that series of options which runs unbroken throughout the entire history of science. Of this, physicists working in the forefront of physics are fully aware. They are the ones who stand on the borderlines of the unknown. For them, the possibility of science implies a constant renewal of their faith in the orderliness of nature. The best illustration of this can be gathered from a quick glance at what goes on in high-energy physics, or the search for fundamental particles. It is a bewildering field. Hardly a month passes today without the discovery of a new particle, or resonance, or whatever name you may prefer. Theories trying to systematize those particles are succeeding one another with astonishing rapidity. The reason for this lies in the now historic pattern: each major advance in accelerator construction has brought into view new, unsuspected particles. As a physicist put it, high-energy physics seems to be caught up in an infernal race.[15] 8

The expression "infernal race" was well chosen from the psychological viewpoint at least.* In such a race there is hardly any room for certainty or relaxation. Today, physicists think back with embarrassment to times when the last layer of matter was believed to be within reach. In our century the opening decade, the early thirties, and the fifties were such times. Thus in the early thirties the proton, neutron, and the electron were believed to have 9

*Don't overlook the root meaning of *infernal* here. When Jaki says that it is important from "the psychological viewpoint *at least,*" he implies that it is probably important from some other point of view as well. What is "infernal" about the race, from the perspective of the essay as a whole?

formed the fundamental system of particles. In the fifties most physicists believed that nature was built on a system of some thirty-four fundamental particles. Today, it is admitted that the best established property of fundamental particles is that none of them is fundamental. In one word, the final layer of matter appears to be farther away than ever. Recently, at the February, 1967, meeting of the American Physical Society, its president, Professor J. A. Wheeler of Princeton University, took the view that the ultimate layer of matter might be located in a practically never-never land, at the level of the so-called Planck distance, which is of the order of 10^{-33} cm.[16] How soon science will edge down to that level is anybody's guess. Perhaps in a hundred years. Even so it will be an extraordinary achievement. After all, during the last half-century, science only managed to move from the atom (10^{-8} cm.) to the neighborhood of the radius of the nucleus, that is, to the neighborhood of 10^{-13} cm. This great advance covered only five orders of magnitude. Between the nucleus and the realm of Planck's distance there are, however, twenty orders of magnitude.* In addition, one should not forget that the smaller a spatial magnitude is, the greater energy is required for its exploration. Whether energies necessary for the investigation of the realm of Planck's distance shall ever be available is a moot question. Furthermore, can science be assured that upon reaching that realm it would find exactly what it looked for? Very likely not. Clearly such is not a comforting outlook. It certainly gives no one the right to make easy predictions. Still the work of research must go on. And it is well to remember that its ultimate sustaining force is faith. Or to hear a prominent physicist, the late director of the Institute for Advanced Study, Robert Oppenheimer, state it: "We cannot make much progress without a faith that in this bewildering field of human experience [particle research], which is so new and so much more complicated than we thought even five years ago, there is a unique and necessary order; not an order that we can see without experience, not an order that we can tell a priori, but an order which means that the parts fit into a whole and that the whole requires the parts."[17]

Ten years have passed since Oppenheimer made this statement of faith. 10
Those ten years were an era of feverish research, yet none of the results diminished either the beauty or the truth of his words. No physicist can tell us today what are the true parts of the ultimate system of particles; yet, all believe firmly in the existence of such a system. This faith of theirs is not an easy one. After all, they are everyday witnesses to the fact that assuredly stable particles turn out to be subject to decay. Thus the concept of finality or definiteness has taken on for the modern physicist a meaning wholly different from its obvious meaning. Finality is to be taken today in physics as largely provisional. It ought to be most puzzling for the modern physicist to find that it is his own tools that time and again deprive him of apparently firmly established grounds. These tools are the tools of precision. They both

*Since the phrase "order of magnitude" has in popular usage become a synonym for something like "doubled," it is important to remember here that each "order" is *ten times smaller.*

confirm and undo theories, and keep physics in a dynamic flux never experienced before. These tools create as many problems as they provide solutions. For all that, the physicist must retain his confidence in the double-edged sword of precision, which keeps opening up before him strange, perplexing worlds. In using the tools of precision, all physicists are sustained by faith. It holds of all of them what was true of Albert A. Michelson, a wizard of precision in measurements and the first American to receive the Nobel Prize in physics. As Millikan, another Nobel laureate, said of Michelson: "He merely felt in his bones, or knew in his soul, or had faith to believe that accurate knowledge was important."[18]

It was more than forty years ago that Millikan uttered these words. In 11
American science and scientific philosophy, the thirties were still an era dominated by cliché accounts of the history of science. It was an era that accepted without further ado the slogan that physics consisted solely in correlating data of observations and experiments. The word "faith" was an ugly word for most of those who in those years and until very recently posed as the supreme interpreters of science and were accepted as such. I have in mind the neopositivists and the operationalists. There is, of course, much that can be said in favor of operationalism and of logical positivism. When, however, taken as the fundamental and exclusive theories of science, they display a serious shortcoming. Operationalism and logical positivism do not square with the facts of scientific creativity.* In our times this was emphasized by such creative personalities of physical science as Einstein, Born, Schrödinger, and many others.[19] It was in fact in the wake of his discovery of wave-mechanics that Schrödinger decried "that cold clutch of dreary emptiness" which exudes from the definition of scientific work as given by positivism: a description of the facts, with the maximum of completeness and the maximum economy of thought. Scientists sufficiently honest with themselves, Schrödinger added, would admit that "to have *only* this goal before one's eyes would not suffice to keep the work of research going forward in any field whatsoever."[20]

Much less could the positivistic concept of science give start to the 12
scientific endeavor itself. No wonder that the very start, the birth of science, has not become a favorite topic with positivist historians of science. Indeed, there can be no satisfactory explanation for it within a framework that frowns on the mental attitude called faith. Within the positivist framework it must remain an insoluble puzzle why science was born in the Western world and not in China or India or among the Mayas and the Aztecs. The birth of science was, of course, a rather long process. Its beginnings credit the marvelous insights of the Greek mind. As Einstein once noted: "In my opinion one has

*Operationalism is the doctrine that all true propositions can be expressed and tested by showing their consequences in action. Beliefs that cannot be "operationalized"—and hence tested—are declared meaningless. Positivism was explained in the note on p. 575. More precise knowledge about *positivism* and *operationalism* is not absolutely necessary for a general understanding of Jaki's essay, but his reasons for taking these two philosophical positions as his chief "enemies" will not be clear unless you use a good encyclopedia.

not to be astonished that the Chinese sages have not made these steps [the major discoveries of Greek science]. The astonishing thing is that these discoveries were made at all."[21] Still for all its achievements, ancient Greek science is not without a grave puzzle. That puzzle derives from the fact that Greek science remained a half-way house. It failed to recognize the crucial role of systematic experiments. It proved itself wholly powerless to come to grips with the quantitative analysis of motion.

THE BIRTH OF SCIENCE

It is a fact of scientific history that man needed faith to overcome these 13
hurdles and to bring science to a full birth. It is a fact of scientific history that the birth of modern science took place in a cultural ambiance wholly permeated by belief in dogmas. Foremost of these was the Christian tenet about a personal, rational Creator of the universe. Our century was reminded of this by [Alfred North] Whitehead in his Lowell Lectures of 1925, published under the title, *Science and the Modern World.* To millions of readers of that book it came as a revelation that, contrary to the claims of positivism, science does not owe its origin to the rejection of religious beliefs. Instead, as Whitehead told his readers, they had to look for the birth of science in the staunch belief of the Middle Ages. Foremost in this respect was, according to him, the medieval insistence on the rationality of the Creator. Whitehead also emphasized that belief in the dogma of creation had to be shared by a whole culture throughout several generations. Only such communal experience and conviction could produce what Whitehead called a tone of thought, a climate of intellectual confidence and courage.[22] This in turn gave rise to the scientific enterprise and determination to look for rationality in every process of nature.

In Whitehead's classic discourse, only one point was missing. He should 14
have called his listeners' and his readers' attention to the fact that what he said was not a more or less subjective version of history. He should have told them that his ideas were but the echo of those men of science who witnessed the birth of science three to six centuries ago. Thus references to the Creator are explicit in the great medieval forerunners of modern science, such as Oresme and Buridan. Their statements were further elaborated by such theoreticians of sixteenth-century science as Descartes, Bacon, and Galileo. Bacon's writings in this respect are especially instructive. Not a particularly original thinker, Bacon had an uncanny sense of gathering the best that was available in his time. He also had the skill to elaborate on it with great persuasiveness. Most of all, he said what his contemporaries wanted to hear. They wanted to hear, for instance, why Greek science came to a standstill. For the failures of the Greeks, Bacon laid the blame on the pantheistic features of their religious views.[23] It was pantheism that put the theological seal on the Greeks' preference for viewing the world as an organism, or a huge animal. For them, each portion of the world was full of volitions closely paralleling human strivings and aspirations. They discussed the fall of stones, the rise of fire, the motion of the stars in the same breath with the motion

of animals. For them, man was but a tiny organism wholly subject to the countless volitions animating the whole cosmos. Obviously, such an outlook could not generate a sustained confidence in ever deciphering, let alone mastering, the whims and movements of that great animal, the entire universe.[24]

15 On the sad failure of Greek science, an unexpected light is thrown by recent investigations of Chinese scientific history. What I have in mind is the conclusion of J. Needham, the distinguished author of the most monumental study of the history of Chinese science ever published in the West. A Marxist, Needham looked in various socioeconomical factors for the likely cause of the failure of the Chinese to invent science, so to speak. As is well known, ancient and medieval Chinese, though very proficient in practical inventions, such as rockets and compasses, failed to formulate one single law of physics. As might be expected, Needham laid part of the blame on medieval Chinese feudalism and other so-called reactionary factors. Yet, according to Needham, the fundamental reason for the scientific failure of the Chinese lay somewhere else. He had to admit that the basic cause of that failure pointed to theology. More specifically, he called attention to the early loss in Chinese religious thought of the belief in a personal rational Creator. With the loss of that belief was also lost the faith, the confidence of the Chinese in the ultimate rationality of the universe. To quote Needham, "Among the Chinese there was no conviction that rational personal beings would be able to spell out in their lesser earthly language the divine code of laws which the Creator had decreed aforetime."[25]

16 It was not, therefore, a freak happening of history that science was born in a Europe that was living through its centuries of faith. It was a Europe where those lived and worked who looked upon the world as the product of a most rational Creator and looked upon themselves as the stewards of their Father's handiwork. Theirs was not a blind faith, and happily for them. For the twist of history thrust upon them the whole Greek scientific corpus within the short span of two generations. What hit them was nothing short of an intellectual deluge. All of a sudden they were challenged by the dazzling scientific works of a Euclid, of a Ptolemy, and of an Aristotle. Some of the passages they could not translate, let alone understand. But they did not panic. Instead, they read those books with eager enthusiasm, notwithstanding the fact that Rome at one time put a ban even on the works of Aristotle. The enthusiasm of the medievals is easy to understand. They believed themselves to be children of an all-powerful, all-reasonable, all-good Creator. Consequently, they had to be enthusiastically confident in the final outcome of their newborn quest for scientific knowledge.

FAITH IN ORDER

17 The quest of science has seen many triumphs and many agonies. They usually went hand in hand and evidenced equally well the role of faith for science. The first major triumph was Copernicus' outline of the planetary order. He was far from proving definitely the heliocentric proposition. But what he

lacked in physical proofs, he amply supplemented with his faith in nature. From his belief that nature was the handiwork of the Creator, he readily concluded that nature was simple. His system of the planets, it is well to recall, gave no better prediction of the motion of planets than did Ptolemy's; the most attractive proof of Copernicus lay in the geometrical simplicity of the new ordering of the planets. It was a bold view, and he clung to it though its consequences flew in the face of everybody's daily experience. Positivists of all times may shake their heads in disbelief, but Galileo, whom they consider the father of experimental method, praised Copernicus precisely for what he did: for staying with his belief at the price of committing rape of his senses.[26]

These words of Galileo are not without some irony. Though he praised 18
the faith of Copernicus, he did his best to conceal the fact that much of what he claimed in the *Dialogues* was still largely a matter of faith. He passed over in silence the fact that his unbounded admiration for geometry was in effect a loud profession of his faith in the geometrical ordering of nature. Mystic as he was, Galileo frowned on anything savoring of mysticism, and soon developed a dislike for Kepler, an unabashed mystic. The loser was Galileo. Had he referred in his *Dialogues* to Kepler's Laws, he might have considerably strengthened his cause. Also, his conflict with some churchmen might have taken a different course if it had been recognized that there is a role for faith in science and that theology does not operate by faith alone.

When the clash came to a head, Kepler was already dead. Perhaps he 19
could have testified that his three laws were the outcome of tedious computations as well as of his firm faith in the mathematical orderliness of the universe. For this, no one gave him greater credit than Max Planck. In fact, Planck found a startling analogy between his case and Kepler's struggles. In Planck's case, the data of blackbody radiation were available to a great number of his colleagues. Yet, only one, Planck himself, perceived the true pattern underlying those data. And Planck was not ashamed to ascribe that success to his faith. Now, as Planck analyzed Kepler's case, both Tycho Brahe and Kepler were in possession of the same data of planetary motions. Yet, only Kepler found their true correlation. The answer to this could not be clearer to Planck. As he put it, Tycho did not have what Kepler did possess: scientific faith.[27]

That scientific faith is in evidence in all major breakthroughs and princi- 20
pal tenets of science. Men of science had believed in the inverse square law of gravitation long before its truth was demonstrated. Maupertuis had believed in his law of least action years before he formulated it with enough clarity. The law earned him the ridicule of the rationalist Voltaire, who decried it as credulous metaphysics. Yet, ultimately, it was Maupertuis' faith that proved victorious. It received its due praise when Helmholtz discussed the law of least action in 1884 before the Berlin Academy of Sciences. There Helmholtz traced the origin of the law to Maupertuis' belief in the uniformity of nature and in the human mind's ability to find the true form of that uniformity.

That Helmholtz saw Maupertuis' efforts in this light is understandable. Faith was the mainspring of his efforts to have the law of the conservation of energy recognized. His was not an easy struggle. His now classic paper, "On the Conservation of Force," was rejected by the leading German physical review. In the long run, however, the faith of Helmholtz prevailed. And so did the faith of Faraday and of other great physicists who worked on proving that all forces of nature are interconnected. In the case of electricity and magnetism, Faraday's was a complete success. On the other hand, only failures accompanied his lifelong efforts to find a correlation between electromagnetism and gravitation. For all that, the entries in his notebooks on the subject never showed the slightest trace of wavering. All the failures, he remarked, "do not shake my strong feeling of the existence of a relation between gravity and electricity." One of his papers on the subject refers to "the full conviction" and, again, "to the same deep conviction" that animated his search for a connection between gravity and electricity. To follow the promptings of that "strong feeling" was in his view a most sacred scientific duty. The contrary course, that is, to leave the problem untouched seemed to him equivalent to abandoning faith in nature or, to quote his words: "to rest content with darkness and to worship an idol."[28] 21

Fortunately for science, Faraday's faith, or "strong feeling," or "full conviction" in the interconnectedness of the forces of nature is as alive as ever. Witness Einstein's thirty years of search for a Unified Theory; witness the efforts to find a connection between the nuclear force and the force of the so-called weak interactions. Or witness the rather recent competition for the best essay on the possibility of gravitational shielding.[29] The idea underlying the competition was that, if there is a shielding against electrical forces, the same should also be true of gravitation. Faraday, I am sure, would have found to his liking a contest of this type and most likely would have participated in it with a lengthy paper. He would have also found that no less than in his time, physics in the 1960's is still supported both by evidence and by faith—by faith in the interconnectedness of the parts of nature; by faith in the intelligibility of nature; by faith in its simplicity, in its uniformity, and in its symmetry. 22

Intelligibility, simplicity, and uniformity of nature are concepts that are rarely reflected upon. They are like the air we breathe, they are taken for granted. All too often they are treated as self-evident notions that need no further scrutiny. Yet, when scrutinized with no reference to the scientist's faith in them, what remains of them? In a positivist framework of explanation they are reduced to formulas of convenience devoid of that absolute certainty with which the scientist espouses them. For once the principles of positivism are consistently applied, one cannot even have absolute certainty about one's own existence. Or as H. Reichenbach, a leading positivist philosopher of science, claimed: "We have no absolutely conclusive evidence that there is a physical world, and we have no absolutely conclusive evidence either that we exist."[30] 23

A long comment could be made about such a position, but let me confine 24 myself to the most obvious. Whatever the validity of Reichenbach's claim, the scientist needs in his work an unconditional and complete trust or conviction in his own existence, in the existence of nature, and in its simplicity, orderliness, and intelligibility. On such points, the scientist can entertain no misgivings, no futile sophistry, no wholesale doubts, no endless questioning. The scientist must go beyond the set of evidences available to him and must assert that nature in its ultimate foundations is absolutely simple and perfectly ordered.

Of course the scientist's evidence of the simplicity and orderliness of 25
nature is much more extensive than that available to the ordinary layman. Yet, even the scientist's glimpse of that orderliness is far from being exhaustive. The condition of the scientist is therefore much the same as that of the man of religion. Religious faith, like the faith of the scientist, has its set of evidences. Religious faith is not a blind faith.[31] Yet, numerous as its evidences might be, they do not form a complete, exhaustive set. Those evidences, like the evidences of science, are rather a prompting toward espousing propositions that imply unconditional affirmation and absolute commitment. It is through such commitment that the man of science grasps the simplicity and order of nature, and it is through a similar commitment that the man of religion grasps the spiritual and moral dimensions.[32]

CONCLUSION

This short outline of the analogy between scientific and religious faith was 26
not prompted by some hidden aim of proselytizing. The meaning and purpose of the analogy is far deeper. It is my conviction that the recognition of that analogy is of paramount importance if a major tragedy of our culture is to be overcome. That tragedy is the split of our culture in two sections. Today, intellectuals are clustered in two camps; they are either humanists or scientists. They speak different languages, they hardly communicate with each other, and consider each other's problems as largely irrelevant.

Much has been said about that cultural split, and well before C. P. Snow 27
came up with the now famous phrase, "two cultures." The tremendous response given to his work, *The Two Cultures,* is in itself evidence that the cultural split is a reality and a dangerous one. For that split, Snow laid much of the blame at the door of the humanists. It was in line with this that Snow prescribed his medicine for the restoration of the cultural unity. The medicine consisted in compulsory science courses, and a fair number of them to be imposed on students of humanities. I would not dispute that today students of humanities should do their best to become very familiar with science. Yet, just as important as the science one knows is one's familiarity with the foundations of the scientific quest. A careful study of those foundations will show that the sciences and the humanities have at their bases some remarkably common mental attitudes. One of them, and possibly the foremost, is the attitude of faith.

I know that the word "faith" is loaded with too many connotations to 28 be readily acceptable to many. If so, I am not reluctant to look for a substitute expression. To me, a most appealing one was coined by none other than David Hume, hardly a friend of intellectual faith. He preferred to speak of faith as a "kind of firm and solid feeling." Regardless of Hume's philosophical outlook, I find the expression to be one that perfectly suits our purpose here. A full recovery of that "firm and solid feeling" by today's intellectuals would greatly help to forestall the threat posed to human values by an unbridled technologization of life. Today the evaluation of man is shifting more and more toward the quantitative aspects. Calipers, slide rules, statistics, and computers are being used in areas where they can never come even remotely close to the heart of the matter. For numbers, equations, and tools, however precise, can never touch on the very core of man and on his faith or, if you wish, on his strong and firm feelings. Computers may be said to do thinking, but only man feels in the sense of having faith. Therein lies man's basic dignity and also his most perennial need. The scientist is no exception to that rule. As this lecture tried to intimate, the man of science, like all his fellow-men, lives by faith and ultimately makes his progress in virtue of his faith.

NOTES

All notes are Jaki's.

1. William James, *The Will to Believe and Other Essays in Popular Philosophy* (New York: Longmans, Green & Co., 1897), p. 1.

2. *Ibid.,* p. x.

3. *Ibid.*

4. The role of faith in scientific inquiry is rich in aspects, some of which have been given illuminating treatment in recent literature. Foremost to mention is the work by M. Polanyi, *Science, Faith and Society* (London: Oxford University Press, 1946; reprinted with a new Introduction by the author: University of Chicago Press, 1964). Some valuable contributions to the subject were made by noted physicists, such as H. Margenau, *Open Vistas: Philosophical Perspectives of Modern Science* (New Haven, Conn.: Yale University Press, 1961), pp. 73–76; K. Lonsdale, *I Believe: The Eighteenth Arthur Stanley Eddington Memorial Lecture, 6 November 1964* (Cambridge: University Press, 1964); H. K. Schilling, *Science and Religion: An Interpretation of Two Communities* (New York: Charles Scribner's Sons, 1962).

5. T. H. Huxley, "On the Advisableness of Improving Natural Knowledge," in *Method and Results: Essays* (New York: D. Appleton & Co., 1894), p. 40.

6. See Lord Kelvin's presidential address in *Report of the Forty-first Meeting of the British Association for the Advancement of Science* (held at Edinburgh in August, 1871) (London: John Murray, 1872), p. xciii.

7. Oliver Lodge, *Modern Views of Electricity* (London, 1889), pp. 382–83.

8. Max Planck, *Where Is Science Going?* translated by J. Murphy (New York: W. W. Norton & Co., 1932), p. 214.

9. Albert Einstein, "Clerk Maxwell's Influence on the Development of the Conception of Physical Reality" (1931), in *The World as I See It* (New York: Covici, 1934), p. 60.

10. Albert Einstein and Leopold Infeld, *The Evolution of Physics* (New York: Simon, 1938), pp. 312–13.

11. Albert Einstein, "Address to the Conference on Science, Philosophy, and Religion" (1940), in *Out of My Later Years* (New York: Philosophical Library, 1950), p. 26.

12. A. S. Eddington, *Science and the Unseen World: Swarthmore Lecture, 1929* (New York: Macmillan Co., 1930), pp. 73–74.

13. W. Heisenberg, "A Scientist's Case for the Classics," *Harper's Magazine,* CCXVI (May, 1958), p. 29.

14. Willem De Sitter, *Kosmos* (Cambridge, Mass.: Harvard University Press, 1932), p. 10.

15. L. Brillouin, *Scientific Uncertainty, and Information* (New York: Academic Press, 1964), p. 41.

16. On Wheeler's lecture, see W. Sullivan's report in the *New York Times,* February 5, 1967, sec. E, p. 5, cols. 3–5.

17. Robert Oppenheimer, *The Constitution of Matter* (Eugene: Oregon State System of Higher Education, 1956), p. 37.

18. R. A. Millikan, *Science and the New Civilization* (New York: Charles Scribner's Sons, 1930), p. 164.

19. On this point, see my work, *The Relevance of Physics* (Chicago: University of Chicago Press, 1966), pp. 479–80.

20. Erwin Schrödinger, *My View of the World,* translated by C. Hastings (Cambridge: University Press, 1964), pp. 3–4.

21. Einstein, in a letter of April 23, 1953, to Mr. J. E. Switzer; see D. J. de Solla Price, *Science since Babylon* (New Haven, Conn.: Yale University Press, 1961), p. 15.

22. Alfred N. Whitehead, *Science and the Modern World* (New York: Macmillan Co., 1926), pp. 18–19. For a very valuable discussion of the import of the Christian doctrine of creation, see L. Gilkey, *Maker of Heaven and Earth: The Christian Doctrine of Creation in the Light of Modern Knowledge* (1959) (Doubleday Anchor Book reprint; Garden City, N.Y.: Doubleday & Co., 1965). Concerning the Christian origins of modern science, Gilkey's discussion needs updating. Modern historical research has clearly shown those origins to be medieval, a point that was ignored by Gilkey's principal source on this point, several articles by M. Foster, published in *Mind* between 1934 and 1936.

23. Bacon, *Of the Dignity and Advancement of Learning,* Book 3, chap. iv, in *The Works of Francis Bacon,* edited by J. Spedding, R. L. Ellis, and D. D. Heath (new ed.; London, 1870), IV, 365.

24. On the impotence of the organismic concept of the physical world, see my *Relevance of Physics* (n. 19 above), chap. i.

25. J. Needham, *Science and Civilization in China, II.: History of Scientific Thought* (Cambridge: University Press, 1956), p. 581.

26. Galileo, *Dialogue concerning the Two Chief World Systems,* translated by Stillman Drake (Berkeley: University of California Press, 1953), p. 328.

27. Max Planck, *Where Is Science Going?* (n. 8 above), p. 214; see also his *The Philosophy of Physics,* translated by W. H. Johnston (New York: W. W. Norton & Co., 1936), pp. 122–23.

28. For a convenient source on these statements of Faraday, see H. Bence-Jones, *The Life and Letters of Faraday* (Philadelphia: J. B. Lippincott Co., 1870), II, 253, 417, 388.

29. It formed part of a program sponsored by the Gravity Research Foundation that for a number of years has awarded prizes to outstanding essays on various aspects of the problem of gravity.

30. H. Reichenbach, *The Rise of Scientific Philosophy* (Berkeley: University of California Press, 1951), p. 268.

31. Thus N. Wiener took pains to emphasize that the faith needed in scientific work has nothing in common with religious faith which he described as a set of dogmas imposed from outside (*The Human Use of Human Beings* [reprinted by Doubleday & Co., n.d.], p. 193). Religious faith was therefore rejected by Wiener as "no faith." Such high-handed, if not superficial, handling of the concept of religious faith proves only one thing. A scientist, however eminent, may easily dispense, when discussing topics outside his field, with the elementary scientific duty of securing for himself a fair measure of proper information in the matter.

32. There are, of course, differences between the attitudes of faith as acted out within the religious and the scientific framework, respectively. Those differences mainly derive from the role played by revelation and authority as normative factors within the community of the faithful. The rise and growing influence of science was most beneficial in reminding theologians

and churchmen that those normative factors are restricted to moral and supernatural considerations and can never play a heuristic role in man's search for the regularities of the processes of nature.

Questions for Discussion

1. Make a list of all the examples Jaki gives to support what he calls his "analogy between scientific and religious faith" (¶26). How many of them describe religious faith, in contrast to those describing scientific faith? Why do you think we find so little about the religious side of the analogy? Why do you suppose Jaki doesn't even mention religion until far along in the essay? Why should he save his most explicit thesis statements for very late, rather than following the "high school rule" that we should state our thesis in the first paragraph?
2. If there are real differences "between the attitudes of faith as acted out within the religious and the scientific framework," as Jaki says in his endnote 32, why would he mention them only in a note?
3. It is sometimes said, in textbooks on critical thinking, that "argument from authority" (or "proof by testimony") does little or nothing to prove any case. Yet if we count the instances of various *kinds* of argument in this essay, we find that Jaki has spent most of his time mustering the testimony of scientists. Does this use of "witnesses" provide strong support for Jaki's case? Why or why not?
4. After showing that three main achievements of modern science—quantum theory, relativity theory, and Eddington's *Fundamental Theory*—all rely on faith, Jaki turns to the "infernal race." Why? And why does he spend so much longer (¶8–10) explaining the role of faith in particle physics than he does explaining the other three examples?

Suggested Essay Topics

1. Suppose that a critic of Jaki's argument wrote a letter to the journal *Zygon,* where Jaki's essay first appeared, arguing as follows:

   > Jaki cheats by not making explicit just how ambiguous the word *faith* is in his account. If we ask the obvious question—"faith in *what?*"—we get various answers. First off, we have the scientific faith in order and uniformity, as a necessary basis for scientific inquiry. But Jaki then sneaks in a faith in God, which is really an entirely different matter. Thus he tries to trick us into thinking that the link between scientific and religious faith is tight, whereas it is really very loose. There is really nothing at all "religious" about the scientist's faith; if we just substitute words like *working assumptions* or *hypotheses,* Jaki's case evaporates.

   Write a letter to *Zygon,* either agreeing or disagreeing with the critic. Be sure to include, as the critic does not, specific quotations from Jaki, showing that he succeeds or fails in showing a strong similarity between the two faiths. (In preparing, it would be a good idea to study with special care paragraphs 13–16, which argue why science arose in a religious setting in the West and not in China or Greece.)

2. Think over your own activities of the past 24 hours. For how many of them could you offer "solid" justification, if someone insisted that you justify them with strict logic or experimental proof? Choose one or two of your actions that seem most dependent on "mere faith," and write a paper discussing whether this faith seems to you "blind" or reasonable. (Some possible "faiths": "Getting a college education is a good thing to do"; "Writing a paper even when I don't want to will in the long run be educational"; "My teacher knows what he or she is talking about, even when I can't make sense out of it"; "My parents love me"; "Love is a good thing"; "No matter how much I know, there is still something more to be known.")

IDEAS IN DEBATE

Stephen Toulmin
B. F. Skinner

Stephen Toulmin

Stephen Toulmin (b. 1922) was born and educated in England. Trained as an "analytical philosopher," he early became troubled with the way modern standards of reasoning seemed to rule out thinking about ethics. In a series of influential books, starting with Reason in Ethics *in 1949 and including* Human Understanding *(1972), Toulmin has steadily explored the meeting ground between principles of reasoning and ethical concerns. His book* Foresight and Understanding: An Enquiry into the Aims of Science *(1961) is one of the most penetrating contributions to the philosophy of science in recent decades.*

Toulmin's two main purposes in this fairly difficult essay are, first, to characterize the "puristic" posture by which science, as a profession, has tried to escape the ethical implications of its activity and, second, to show that such escapism, even in the interests of scientific purity, is illegitimate both philosophically and historically. The puristic posture asserts that scientific activity should be motivated and evaluated only on the grounds of scientific and intellectual, not moral, integrity. Purists do not admit that ethical evaluations apply either to scientific methods or findings; they admit only the authority of scientifically validated questions and conclusions. Science and ethics are treated like Euclid's parallel lines—entities that can never meet.

There are at least three important motives behind scientific purism, the third of which Toulmin attempts to explain with a coherent philosophical and historical account.

First, many scientists simply find ethical deliberations unrewarding and tedious. By training and temperament, they prefer problems that can be settled concretely and definitively.

Second, scientists avoid ethical considerations because they slow down the pace of research. The time and energy they devote to ethical issues must be subtracted from laboratory research or fieldwork.

Third (and here is where Toulmin begins to explain the separation), scientists have avoided ethical issues because scientific specialization, which has branched off into smaller and smaller tributaries for the past 100 years, has not only encouraged the avoidance of ethical questions but has even denied their importance. The typical scientist in the modern world can spend a whole career in a specialized niche with few, if any, windows looking out on the wider world of non-specialized concerns.

It is true, Toulmin grants, that some scientific pursuits are less embedded in ethical problems than others; sciences run along a continuum from less to more ethically suggestive (¶8). But every scientific inquiry that justifiably ignores ethical concerns is matched by other inquiries for which such concerns are both unavoidable and important. In these cases, he says, it is not only useless but positively destructive for science to ignore such questions in assessing both its methods and results.

In paragraphs 21–26 Toulmin gives the general argument for the connection between science and ethics, and in paragraphs 34–37 he lists the specific areas of significant overlap. In the last paragraph he returns to the question that dominated Plato's Republic *almost 2500 years ago, showing that the oldest questions often continue to live in the newest knowledge.*

SCIENCE AND ETHICS: CAN THEY BE RECONNECTED?

From *The Hastings Center Report,* June 1979, and *The University of Chicago Magazine,* Winter 1981.

In that branch of contemporary philosophy called ethics, "science"—or at 1
least "the natural and social sciences" as they are conceived of in the English-speaking world—receives very little attention.

And yet, interactions between science and ethics were once vigorous 2
and cordial.

How have science and ethics become estranged? And how, in an era in 3
which the two must inevitably collide, can they be put on speaking terms again?

From a strict philosophical point of view, all attempts to insulate the 4
sciences from ethics can be easily undercut. This is true whether we discuss the basic concepts of the sciences, the institutions and collective conduct of the scientific profession, or the personal motives of individual scientists.

As to the concept of science: so long as we restrict ourselves to the 5
physical and chemical sciences, our basic notions and hypotheses (e.g., hadron, field gradient, and amino acid) may have no obvious evaluative implications. But the physiological, to say nothing of the psychological and social sciences, employ whole families of concepts, such as functionality and adaptedness, and their cognates, which raise evaluative issues directly.

As to the scientific profession: the codes of good intellectual practice, 6
and the criteria of professional judgment in the sciences, may once upon a time have looked to the needs of effective inquiry alone, rather than to broader "ethical" considerations. But it is by now no longer possible to draw so clear or sharp a line between the intellectual demands of good science and the ethical demands of the good life. The increasingly close links between basic science and its practical applications expose working scientists more and more to ethical problems and public accountability of sorts that are commonplace in service professions such as medicine and law.

Finally, as to the individual motives that operate for scientists in their 7 work: though the ideal spring of action for scientific inquiry may be a pure respect for the rationality of the inquiry itself, such a pure respect is at best an aspiration, and a *moral* aspiration at that. Furthermore, it is something that can be developed in the course of any individual's lifetime, only as a somewhat refined product of moral education.

. . .

[Nowadays,] the "rationality" of science—the objectivity of scientific issues, the autonomy of the scientific professions, and the categorical claims of the scientific life—can no longer be used to differentiate science entirely from the rest of thought and morality. We are faced, on every level, not by a hard and fast distinction, but by a spectrum. 8

- The basic concepts of the sciences range along a spectrum from the effectively "value-free" to the irretrievably "value-laden";
- The goals of the scientific enterprise range along the spectrum from a purely abstract interest in theoretical speculations to a direct concern with human good and ill;
- The professional responsibilities of the scientific community range along a spectrum from the strictly internal and intellectual to the most public and practical.

Nonetheless, as recently as the 1930s, when I first acquired my ideas about "science," the most characteristic mark of the scientific attitude and the scientific task was to select as one's preferred center of attention the purest, the most intellectual, the most autonomous, and the least ethically implicated extreme on each of these different spectrums.

No doubt this "puristic" view of science was an extreme one, and by no means universally shared by working scientists, to say nothing of the outside social commentators who wrote about the scientific scene. Yet it is a view that had, and continues to have, great attractions for many professional scientists. Since "rational objectivity" is an indispensable part of the scientific mission, and the intrusion of "values" into science had come to be regarded as incompatible with such objectivity, all concern with values (or other arbitrary, personal preferences) had to be foresworn in the higher interest of rationality. Certainly, the professional institutions of science tended to be organized on this basis. The memberships of scientific academies, for instance, have for the last seventy-five or 100 years been increasingly recruited on the basis of the narrowly defined intellectual contributions of candidates alone, without regard to their social perceptiveness, ethical sensitivity, or political wisdom. Indeed, the puristic view is still powerful today: consider, for instance, the recent proposals by Arthur Kantrowitz of M.I.T. for a Science Court, whose duty would be to pronounce on the "factual implications" of science and technology for issues of public policy, without reference to the "values" at stake in each case. 9

. . .

What . . . explanation should we look for, then, to account for the 10 emergence of this puristic view of science? . . . I believe the crucial development in the history of nineteenth-century science was the establishment of distinct scientific disciplines, professions and roles: that is, the process by which individual, sharply delimited special sciences began to crystallize from the larger and less-defined matrix of eighteenth-century natural philosophy. As a result of this change, scientific workers divided themselves up into new and self-organized collectivities, and acquired a collective consciousness of their specialized intellectual tasks, as contrasted with the broader concerns of philosophical, literary, and theological discussion more generally. In this way, it at last became possible to define the new individual role of "scientist." (This familiar word was coined as recently as 1840 by William Whewell, on the model of the much older term "artist," for his presidential address to the British Association for the Advancement of Science.)

In these respects, scientific roles and writings, organizations and arguments dating from before 1830 differ sharply from anything to be found after around 1890. In the hands of the most distinguished eighteenth-century authors, scientific issues were always expanding into, and merging with, broader intellectual questions. In the writings of a John Ray or a Joseph Priestley, the doors between science, ethics, and religion are always open. "And why not?" they would have asked; "for natural philosophy must surely embrace within itself, not just mathematical and experimental philosophy, but also natural theology and natural morality." (Their sentiments were also those of Isaac Newton himself, for whom "to discourse of God" from a study of His Creation "does certainly belong to natural philosophy.") Indeed, it took a series of deliberate and collective decisions to restrict the scope of scientific debate before these larger issues of philosophy and theology were effectively excluded from the professional debate about scientific issues. One such example was the resolution adopted by the Geological Society of London in 1807 to exclude from its Proceedings all arguments about the origin, antiquity, and creation of the earth, as being merely speculative, and to confine the Proceedings to papers based on direct observations of the earth's crust. During the rest of the nineteenth century, the intellectual concerns of the different special sciences were identified and defined in progressively sharper terms, setting them apart from the broader interests of philosophers, theologians, and the general reading public. 11

At this point, we should look at the manner in which natural philosophy, as conceived in the seventeenth and eighteenth centuries, fell apart into its component elements, and the sciences (and scientists) were led to set up shop on their own. Even as late as the 1820s, Joseph Townsend could still present significant contributions to geological science in the guise of an argument vindicating *The Veracity of Moses as an Historian.* By the end of the century, Biblical history and geochronology had become entirely distinct disciplines, pursued by quite separate communities of scholars. 12

. . .

In addition, we might examine the institutional changes during the nineteenth century by the leading scientific academies and societies that had 13 originally been founded from 1650 on. How did they move from being general associations of scholars, clerics, and gentlemen to being specialized organizations of professional experts, with a narrowly defined scope and strict entrance qualifications? Before 1830, the Royal Society of London was still largely an association for the general discussion of issues in natural philosophy. Even in the second half of the nineteenth century, it was still accepted as a matter of common form that a poet such as Alfred Tennyson should be a Fellow of the Royal Society, and sit on important Royal Society committees. By the 1890s, it had become the mode to pursue, not just art for art's sake, but also science for science's sake: even, electrical theory for electrical theory's sake, organic chemistry for organic chemistry's sake, botanical taxonomy for botanical taxonomy's sake. This was so because, by 1890, the self-defining disciplines and autonomous professions with which we are familiar today—each of them devoted to the special aims of one or another science—had finally established an existence independent of each other.

. . .

In short, to understand how science came to part company from the foundations of ethics, we need to examine the history of scientific specialization. It was the development of specialization and professionalization that was responsible for excluding ethical issues from the foundations of science, and so, though inadvertently, destroyed most of the links between science and the foundations of ethics. During the hundred or so years beginning around 1840, the concepts and methods, collective organization, and individual roles of science were progressively sharpened and defined, in ways designed to insulate truly "scientific" issues and investigations from all external distractions. So defined, the task of "positive science" was to reveal how and in what respects, regardless of whether we like them or not, discoverable regularities, connections, and mechanisms are manifest in, or responsible for, the phenomena of the natural world. 14

This "positive" program for science was sometimes associated, but was never identical, with the philosophy of scientific positivism.* It rested on the following assumptions. 15

A scientific picture of the world differs radically from a metaphysico-religious picture. The former is realistically confined to demonstrable facts about the natural world: the latter embeds those demonstrable facts within a larger conceptual system, structured according to prejudices that are (from the scientific standpoint) arbitrary, externally motivated, and presumably wish-fulfilling. 16

A realistic view of the natural world is one that is kept free of irrelevant preferences and evaluations, and so depicts Nature as it is, "whether we like it or not." 17

If scientific work is to be effectively organized and prosecuted, questions of "demonstrable fact" must be investigated quite separately from all arbitrary, external, wish-fulfilling notions. Only in this way can we carry forward 18

*See note, p. 575.

the technical inquiries of science proper, without being sidetracked into fruitless and inconclusive debates about rival values or *Weltanschauungen* [world views] to which individual scientists may happen (like anyone else) to be attracted for personal reasons.

. . .

In all these ways, nineteenth-century natural scientists worked to keep ethical considerations and preferences from operating within "the foundations of science"; so that, for instance, the tests for deciding whether one scientific theory or concept was "better" or "worse" than its rivals, from the scientific point of view, should be wholly divorced from issues about what was ethically "better" or "worse." It was a matter of great importance for them to be able to make the choice between alternative theories or concepts turn solely on "objective" or "factual" considerations: thus, they could avoid having to face the question whether one theory or concept is morally preferable to, or more objectionable than, rival theories or concepts. 19

That kind of value neutrality was, of course, quite compatible with particular scientists adopting all sorts of ethical views and positions on their own responsibility. It was even compatible with one rather more general, collective view: namely, that we must begin by drawing a sharp line between matters of pure or real science and matters of applied science or—more precisely—of technology, after which it will become clear that questions of ethical desirability can arise only in the latter, technological area. (To put it crudely, anatomy is value-free, clinical medicine value-laden.) Above all, it was compatible with all sorts of philosophical discussions, as professional scientists sought to rationalize or justify their particular ethical positions, and square their personal views about ethics with their scientific interests and methodologies. 20

In our own day, however, the accumulated successes of the "positive" methodology have carried science—and scientists—up against the limits of that program's validity, and in some places across them. To begin to answer my central question—"How can we set about reconnecting the sciences with the foundations of ethics?"—let us identify certain points at which, during the last few years, the location of these limits has become apparent. 21

- *The positive program for science normally took for granted a sentimental view of ethics: this was used to justify excluding ethics—which was assumed to deal with labile and subjective matters of taste or feeling—from the systematic investigation of "demonstrable facts." It was assumed, in other words, that human values, valuations and preferences have no place within the world of nature that is the scientist's object of study.* 22

During the twentieth century, by contrast, science has expanded into the realms of physiology and psychology, and in so doing has shown the limits of that assumption. As physiology and psychology have succeeded in securing their own positions as sciences, human beings have ceased to be onlookers contemplating a natural world to which they themselves are foreign and have become parts of (or participants within) that world. As a result, 23 the makeup, operations, and activities of human beings themselves have become legitimate issues for scientific investigation. At the very least, the biochemical and physiological preconditions of *normal* functioning, and so of *good* health, can accordingly be discussed nowadays as problems for science, as well as for ethics. With this crucial incursion by science into the foundations of ethics, we can recognize that not all *human* evaluations must necessarily be regarded, from the scientific point of view, as *irrelevant* evaluations. On the contrary, some of the processes and phenomena studied by natural sciences carry with them certain immediate evaluative implications for the "good and ill" of human life. With this example before us, we are ready to take the first step in the direction hinted at earlier: that of using the "rational objectivity" of science as a model for reestablishing the claims of moral objectivity.

- *Given the increasingly close involvement of basic science with its applications to human welfare, notably in the area of medical research, it is meanwhile becoming clear that the professional organization and priorities of scientific work can no longer be concerned* solely *with considerations of intellectual content and merit, as contrasted with the ethical acceptability and social value, either of the research process itself, or of its practical consequences.* 24

The very existence of the bioethics movement is one indication of this change. The work of the National Commission for the Protection of Human Subjects, and of institutional review boards to review research involving human subjects, is another. 25

This being the case, the doors between science and the foundations of ethics can no longer be kept bolted from the scientific side, as they were in the heyday of positive science. Neither the disciplinary aspects of the sciences, their basic concepts and intellectual methods, nor the professional aspects of scientific work, the collective organization of science, and its criteria of professional judgment, can ever again be insulated against the "extraneous and irrelevant" influence of ethics, values, and preferences. 26

On what conditions, then, can we reestablish the frayed links between science and ethics? 27

1. We should not attempt to reestablish these links by reviving outworn styles of natural theology. The kind of syncretistic cosmology to be found in Teilhard de Chardin, for example, is no improvement on its predecessors: this is indeed an area in which "demonstrable facts" are in real danger of being obscured by a larger wish-fulfilling framework of theological fantasies. Instead, we should embark on a critical scientific and philosophical reexamination of humanity's place in nature, with special reference to the use of such terms as "function" and "adaptation," behind which the ethical aspects of our involvement in the natural world are too easily concealed. 28

2. We should not insist on seeing ethical significance in all of science, let alone require that every piece of scientific investigation should have a 29

demonstrable human relevance. Though the enthusiasms of the 1960s "counterculture" were intelligible enough in their historical context, that would be going too far in the opposite direction, and would land us in worse trouble than the positivist program itself. Instead, we should pay critical attention to the respects in which, and the points at which, ethical issues enter into the conduct of scientific work, including its immediate practical consequences. The ethical aspects of human experimentation, and of such enterprises as sex research, are only samples from a much larger group of possible issues.

3. We should not see this renewed interaction between science and 30
ethics as threatening, or justifying, any attack on the proper autonomy of scientists within their own specific professional domains. The recent debate about recombinant DNA research generated rhetoric of two contrary kinds: both from scientists who saw the whole affair as a pretext for outside interference in the proper affairs of the scientific professions, and from laypersons who genuinely believed that those affairs were being carried on irresponsibly. Instead, we should reconsider, in a more selective way, just what the proper scope and limits of professional autonomy are, and at what points scientists cross the line separating legitimate professional issues from matters of proper public concern, whether political or ethical.

4. We should not suppose that renewing diplomatic relations between 31
science and ethics will do anything to throw doubt on the virtues, duties, and obligations of the scientific role or station. During the last fifteen years, the anti-scientific excesses of the radicals have sometimes made it appear necessary to apologize for being a scientist; and, as a reaction against this radical rhetoric, some professional scientists have developed, in turn, a kind of resentful truculence toward public discussions about the ethical and political involvements of the scientific life. Instead, we need to understand better how the lines between the narrowly professional and broader social responsibilities of scientists run in the collective sphere, and also how individual scientists can balance their obligations within the overall demands of a morally acceptable life, as between their chosen professional roles as neurophysiologists, for example, and the other obligations to which they are subject in other capacities as citizens, colleagues, lovers, parents, religious believers, or whatever.

During the last few years, the "purist" view of science—as a strictly 32
autonomous intellectual enterprise, insulated against the influence of all merely human needs, wishes, and preferences—has thus lost its plausibility. Whether we consider the basic concepts of the sciences, the collective enterprises of professional science, or the personal commitments and motivations of individual scientists, we can maintain a strictly value-free (or rather, ethics-free) position only by sticking arbitrarily to one extreme end of a long spectrum.

From that extreme point of view, the ideally scientific investigation 33
would be a piece of strictly academic research on some application-proof project in theoretical physics, conducted by a friendless and stateless bachelor of independent means. There may have been a substantial body of science

approximating this ideal as recently as the 1880s and 1890s, but that is certainly not the case any longer. On the contrary, we can learn something about the foundations of ethics by reconsidering the character and content of the scientific enterprise on all three levels.

1. As a collective activity, any science is significant for ethics because 34
of the ways in which it serves as an embodiment or exemplar of applied rationality. In this respect, the very objectivity of the goals at which scientists aim, both collectively and individually, provides us with the starting point for a counterattack against relativism and subjectivism in ethics, too.

2. Correspondingly, the moral character of the scientist's personal moti- 35
vation, particularly the way in which the Kantian "pure respect for rationality as such" grows out of the wider life of affect or "inclination"—what I have elsewhere called "the moral psychology of science"—can teach us something about the nature of personal virtue and commitment in other areas of life.

3. Finally, the actual content of the sciences is at last contributing to a 36
better understanding of the human locus within the natural world. This fact is well recognized in the physiological sciences, where the links between *normal* functioning and *good* health are comparatively unproblematic. But it is a matter of active dispute in several areas just at this time: for example, in the conflict over the relations between social psychology and sociobiology. And there are some other fields in which it should be the topic of much more active debate than it is: for example, in connection with the rivalry between psychotherapeutic and psychopharmacological modes of treatment in psychiatry.

This done, it should not be hard to indicate the points at which issues 37
originating in the natural sciences can give rise to, and grow together with, evaluative issues—and not merely with issues that involve the values "intrinsic to" the scientific enterprise itself, but also larger human values of a more strictly ethical kind. For as we saw the new phase of scientific development into which we are now moving requires us to reinsert human observers into the world of nature, so that we become not merely onlookers, but also participants in many of the natural phenomena and processes that are subject matter of our scientific investigations. This is true across the whole spectrum of late twentieth-century science: all the way from quantum mechanics, where Heisenberg's Principle requires us to acknowledge the interdependence of the observer and the observed, to ecology, where the conduct of human beings is one crucial factor in any causal analysis of the condition of, say, Lake Erie, or to psychiatry, where the two-way interaction between the psychiatrist and his client is in sharp contrast to the one-way influence of nature on the human observer (but not *vice versa*) presupposed in classical nineteenth-century science.

Recognizing the interconnectedness of human conduct and natural 38
phenomena may not by itself determine the direction in which those interconnections should point us. Admitting the need to establish some harmony between human conduct and natural processes is one thing: agreeing on what constitutes such a harmony is another, harder task. There was, for instance,

a disagreement between Thomas Henry Huxley and his grandson, Julian, about the relations between human ethics and organic evolution. T. H. saw it as a basic human obligation to fight against the cruelty and destructiveness of natural selection, whereas Julian saw the direction of human progress as a simple continuation of the direction of organic evolution. What both Huxleys agreed about, however, was the need to see human ethics as having a place in the world of nature, and to arrive at a rational understanding of what that relation is.

It was with this need in mind that I referred to such concepts as function 39
and adaptation as requiring particular scrutiny. For the question, "What is the true *function* of human beings?," is potentially as much a topic of debate today as it was in classical Athens, when Plato had Socrates raise it in *The Republic.* Likewise, the question, "How should our ways of acting change, in order to become *better adapted* to the novel situations in which we are finding ourselves?," is a question that also invites answers—sometimes, overly simple answers—based on a reading of contemporary biology and ecology. For better and for worse, we are probably ripe for a revival of the organic theory of society and the state.* And, though this is a topic that must be taken seriously, it is also one that is going to need to be handled with great caution and subtlety, if we are to avoid the crudely conservative emphases of earlier versions of the theory. Starting from where we do, the answers we give to such questions will certainly need to be richer and more complex than those available in Plato's time; but, sharing Plato's questions, we are evidently back in a situation where our view of ethics and our view of nature are coming back together again.

Questions for Discussion

1. Put into your own words the distinction in paragraph 8 between "value-free" and "value-laden" concepts in science. Can you give examples of each? Is the atomic weight of enriched plutonium, from which nuclear bombs are made, a "value-free" fact? Is it possible to separate this fact, or any fact, from its actual or potential uses?
2. According to Toulmin, the desire for "rational objectivity" (¶9) has been made the grounds for excluding "values" from scientific activity. Put in your own words Toulmin's criticism of this exclusion.
3. How do you think "the man or woman in the street" views the objectivity and neutrality of science? Do you think most people assume that "scientific proof" makes a claim unassailable? (See the introduction to Edward Hallett Carr, "The Historian and His Facts," pp. 575–583, and discussion

*The organic theory states that the various components in a society are related as the parts of an organism are related. This view differs from the mechanistic theory, which views parts as mechanically related.

question 4 following Lewis Thomas, "Debating the Unknowable," pp. 630–635.)

4. Do the prevalent references to "scientific proof" in commercial advertisements suggest that people generally respect scientific claims? Do you think people buy one brand of toothpaste rather than another because its superiority has been "scientifically proved"? Or are they more influenced by other elements in advertising?
5. Do you think that facts ever have a morally neutral status? Can you give examples of seemingly neutral facts that on examination raise ethical issues?
6. In dealing with complicated issues of the kind treated in this essay, authors must work systematically to keep their organization clear. What do you think of the organizational device that Toulmin employs in paragraphs 4–7? What is his method of organizing paragraphs 21–26? Do you see the reasons for his numbered lists in paragraphs 28–31 and 34–36? Can you outline his entire essay with confidence?

Suggested Essay Topics

1. Specialization in American society extends far beyond science. Pick an activity or vocation that you think is especially damaged by overspecialization and write an essay explaining why. Imagine as your readers a group of specialists in the field you have chosen—that is, address readers who will not be easily persuaded.
2. Addressing someone who thinks specialization has gone too far, write an essay about how some activity that you know well has benefited from specialization. Take into account the reasons that your opponent might offer against your view.

B. F. Skinner

The first Walden *(published in 1854) is Henry David Thoreau's (1817–1862) famous account of two years that he spent living by himself in the woods near Walden Pond (outside Concord, Massachusetts). B. F. Skinner's (b. 1904) appropriation of Thoreau's title is potentially misleading. The only way in which Thoreau's and Skinner's* Waldens *are alike is in the very general desire, as Thoreau put it, "to front only the essential facts of life." But it would be hard to imagine any two works defining the "essential facts of life" more differently than these two; their views about life could not be farther apart.*

Walden Two, *in Skinner's own words, is "a novel about a utopian community . . . [that presents] an account of how I thought a group of, say, a thousand people might have solved the problems of their daily lives with the help of behavorial engineering" (from the preface of the 1976 reissue of* Walden Two*). "Behavorial engineering" has been an extremely controversial concept ever since Skinner first introduced it in the 1930s. While believers think it the best tool, perhaps the only effective one, for saving the modern world from its own disasters, its critics range from people who think it foolish to those who think it simply bad science to those who think it frightening and pernicious. To this last group, "behavorial engineering" calls up science fiction images of human beings turned into unthinking robots without dignity or freedom. (In a later book Skinner argues that freedom and dignity are in fact obsolete and socially retrogressive goals, but he rejects the notion that he wants to turn people into unthinking robots [*Beyond Freedom and Dignity, *1971]).*

In Skinner's view, human nature is infinitely malleable. He believes that human infants who are subjected from birth to certain kinds of conditioning—"contingencies of reinforcement," he calls them—can be made to act and think in almost any way the conditioners desire. He sees such conditioning as a wonderfully efficient and effective way of curing the world's ills. Wisdom and common sense, he believes, are ineffective means of making the world better. They are too erratic and too little heeded. But behavorial engineering, he insists, puts individual and social improvement "within reach of a behavorial science which can take the place of wisdom and common sense and with happier results" (preface to Walden Two, *1976).*

As you read, try to determine the extent to which you think Skinner's optimistic belief in applying scientific principles directly to everyday living matches Toulmin's description (in the preceding essay) of scientific thinking divorced from ethical considerations. If behavorial engineering really works as he describes, it is clear that human beings could create any kind of social world they desire. But to whom would you want to grant the power of making the final decisions about the shape and quality of that world? And if you disagreed with the conditioners, what kind of voice do you think minority views might be given in the brave new world created by the social engineers? And who educates the social engineers anyway?

Whether you wind up being attracted to or repelled by Skinner's vision of an infinitely malleable world, he invites you to think hard about the kind of world you are *willing to work for and, if you reject behavorial engineering, what other means you would recommend for making the world better.*

BEHAVIORAL ENGINEERING: PROGRAMMING THE CHILDREN

Our title for chapters 13 and 14 of *Walden Two* (1948).

The quarters for children from one to three consisted of several small playrooms with Lilliputian* furniture, a child's lavatory, and a dressing and locker room. Several small sleeping rooms were operated on the same principle as 1

*Lilliput is the land of extraordinarily small human beings created by Jonathan Swift in his great satire *Gulliver's Travels* (1726).

the baby-cubicles. The temperature and the humidity were controlled so that clothes or bedclothing were not needed. The cots were double-decker arrangements of the plastic mattresses we had seen in the cubicles. The children slept unclothed, except for diapers. There were more beds than necessary, so that the children could be grouped according to developmental age or exposure to contagious diseases or need for supervision, or for educational purposes.

We followed Mrs. Nash to a large screened porch on the south side of 2
the building, where several children were playing in sandboxes and on swings and climbing apparatuses. A few wore "training pants"; the rest were naked. Beyond the porch was a grassy play yard enclosed by closely trimmed hedges, where other children, similarly undressed, were at play. Some kind of marching game was in progress.

As we returned, we met two women carrying food hampers. They spoke 3
to Mrs. Nash and followed her to the porch. In a moment five or six children came running into the playrooms and were soon using the lavatory and dressing themselves. Mrs. Nash explained that they were being taken on a picnic.

"What about the children who don't go?" said Castle.* "What do you 4
do about the green-eyed monster?"

Mrs. Nash was puzzled. 5

"Jealousy. Envy," Castle elaborated. "Don't the children who stay home 6
ever feel unhappy about it?"

"I don't understand," said Mrs. Nash. 7

"And I hope you won't try," said Frazier,† with a smile. "I'm afraid we 8
must be moving along."

We said good-bye, and I made an effort to thank Mrs. Nash, but she 9
seemed to be puzzled by that too, and Frazier frowned as if I had committed some breach of good taste.

"I think Mrs. Nash's puzzlement," said Frazier, as we left the building, 10
"is proof enough that our children are seldom envious or jealous. Mrs. Nash was twelve years old when Walden Two was founded. It was a little late to undo her early training, but I think we were successful. She's a good example of the Walden Two product. She could probably recall the experience of jealousy, but it's not part of her present life."

"Surely that's going too far!" said Castle. "You can't be so godlike as 11
all that! You must be assailed by emotions just as much as the rest of us!"

"We can discuss the question of godlikeness later, if you wish," replied 12
Frazier. "As to emotions—we aren't free of them all, nor should we like to be. But the meaner and more annoying—the emotions which breed unhappiness—are almost unknown here, like unhappiness itself. We don't need them

*Augustine Castle is a philosopher who, reflecting Skinner's dislike of philosophy, is portrayed as smug, narrow-minded, and a bit dense.

†T.E. Frazier is the 'behavioral engineer" who has founded the community called Walden Two. He is Skinner's spokesman in the novel.

any longer in our struggle for existence, and it's easier on our circulatory system, and certainly pleasanter, to dispense with them."

"If you've discovered how to do that, you are indeed a genius," said 13
Castle. He seemed almost stunned as Frazier nodded assent. "We all know that emotions are useless and bad for our peace of mind and our blood pressure," he went on. "But how arrange things otherwise?"

"We arrange them otherwise here," said Frazier. He was showing a 14
mildness of manner which I was coming to recognize as a sign of confidence.

"But emotions are—fun!" said Barbara.* "Life wouldn't be worth living 15
without them."

"Some of them, yes," said Frazier. "The productive and strengthening 16
emotions—joy and love. But sorrow and hate—and the high-voltage excitements of anger, fear, and rage—are out of proportion with the needs of modern life, and they're wasteful and dangerous. Mr. Castle has mentioned jealousy—a minor form of anger, I think we may call it. Naturally we avoid it. It has served its purpose in the evolution of man; we've no further use for it. If we allowed it to persist, it would only sap the life out of us. In a cooperative society there's no jealousy because there's no need for jealousy."

"That implies that you all get everything you want," said Castle. "But 17
what about social possessions? Last night you mentioned the young man who chose a particular girl or profession. There's still a chance for jealousy there, isn't there?"

"It doesn't imply that we get everything we want," said Frazier. "Of 18
course we don't. But jealousy wouldn't help. In a competitive world there's some point to it. It energizes one to attack a frustrating condition. The impulse and the added energy are an advantage. Indeed, in a competitive world emotions work all too well. Look at the singular lack of success of the complacent man. He enjoys a more serene life, but it's less likely to be a fruitful one. The world isn't ready for simple pacifism or Christian humility, to cite two cases in point. Before you can safely train out the destructive and wasteful emotions, you must make sure they're no longer needed."

"How do you make sure that jealousy isn't needed in Walden Two?" 19
I said.

"In Walden Two problems can't be solved by attacking others," said 20
Frazier with marked finality.

"That's not the same as eliminating jealousy, though," I said. 21

"Of course it's not. But when a particular emotion is no longer a useful 22
part of a behavioral repertoire, we proceed to eliminate it."

"Yes, but how?" 23

"It's simply a matter of behavioral engineering," said Frazier. 24

"Behavioral engineering?" 25

"You're baiting me, Burris.† You know perfectly well what I mean. The 26
techniques have been available for centuries. We use them in education and

*Barbara Macklin is characteristically made to speak from an "emotional" point of view.

†Professor Burris, the narrator of *Walden Two,* is a former graduate school friend of T. E. Frazier.

in the psychological management of the community. But you're forcing my hand," he added. "I was saving that for this evening. But let's strike while the iron is hot."

We had stopped at the door of the large children's building. Frazier shrugged his shoulders, walked to the shade of a large tree, and threw himself on the ground. We arranged ourselves about him and waited. 27

"Each of us," Frazier began, "is engaged in a pitched battle with the rest of mankind." 28

"A curious premise for a Utopia," said Castle. "Even a pessimist like myself takes a more hopeful view than that." 29

"You do, you do," said Frazier. "But let's be realistic. Each of us has interests which conflict with the interests of everybody else. That's our original sin, and it can't be helped. Now, 'everybody else' we call 'society.' It's a powerful opponent, and it always wins. Oh, here and there an individual prevails for a while and gets what he wants. Sometimes he storms the culture of a society and changes it slightly to his own advantage. But society wins in the long run, for it has the advantage of numbers and of age. Many prevail against one, and men against a baby. Society attacks early, when the individual is helpless. It enslaves him almost before he has tasted freedom. The 'ologies' will tell you how it's done. Theology calls it building a conscience or developing a spirit of selflessness. Psychology calls it the growth of the superego.* 30

"Considering how long society has been at it, you'd expect a better job. But the campaigns have been badly planned and the victory has never been secure. The behavior of the individual has been shaped according to revelations of 'good conduct,' never as the result of experimental study. But why not experiment? The questions are simple enough. What's the best behavior for the individual so far as the group is concerned? And how can the individual be induced to behave in that way? Why not explore these questions in a scientific spirit? 31

"We could do just that in Walden Two. We had already worked out a code of conduct—subject, of course, to experimental modification. The code would keep things running smoothly if everybody lived up to it. Our job was to see that everybody did. Now, you can't get people to follow a useful code by making them into so many jacks-in-the-box. You can't foresee all future circumstances, and you can't specify adequate future conduct. You don't know what will be required. Instead you have to set up certain behavioral processes which will lead the individual to design his own 'good' conduct when the time comes. We call that sort of thing 'self-control.' But don't be misled, the control always rests in the last analysis in the hands of society. 32

*According to Skinner, none of the "ologies" refers to anything real or yields real knowledge.

"One of our Planners, a young man named Simmons, worked with me. 33
It was the first time in history that the matter was approached in an experimental way. Do you question that statement, Mr. Castle?"

"I'm not sure I know what you are talking about," said Castle. 34

"Then let me go on. Simmons and I began by studying the great works 35
on morals and ethics—Plato, Aristotle, Confucius, the New Testament, the Puritan divines, Machiavelli, Chesterfield, Freud—there were scores of them. We were looking for any and every method of shaping human behavior by imparting techniques of self-control. Some techniques were obvious enough, for they had marked turning points in human history. 'Love your enemies' is an example—a psychological invention for easing the lot of an oppressed people. The severest trial of oppression is the constant rage which one suffers at the thought of the oppressor. What Jesus discovered was how to avoid these inner devastations. His technique was to *practice the opposite emotion.* If a man can succeed in 'loving his enemies' and 'taking no thought for the morrow,' he will no longer be assailed by hatred of the oppressor or rage at the loss of his freedom or possessions. He may not get his freedom or possessions back, but he's less miserable. It's a difficult lesson. It comes late in our program."

"I thought you were opposed to modifying emotions and instincts until 36
the world was ready for it," said Castle. "According to you, the principle of 'love your enemies' should have been suicidal."

"It would have been suicidal, except for an entirely unforeseen conse- 37
quence. Jesus must have been quite astonished at the effect of his discovery. We are only just beginning to understand the power of love because we are just beginning to understand the weakness of force and aggression. But the science of behavior is clear about all that now. Recent discoveries in the analysis of punishment—but I am falling into one digression after another. Let me save my explanation of why the Christian virtues—and I mean merely the Christian techniques of self-control—have not disappeared from the face of the earth, with due recognition of the fact that they suffered a narrow squeak within recent memory.*

"When Simmons and I had collected our techniques of control, we had 38
to discover how to teach them. That was more difficult. Current educational practices were of little value, and religious practices scarcely any better. Promising paradise or threatening hell-fire is, we assumed, generally admitted to be unproductive. It is based upon a fundamental fraud which, when discovered, turns the individual against society and nourishes the very thing it tries to stamp out. What Jesus offered in return for loving one's enemies was heaven *on earth,* better known as peace of mind.

"We found a few suggestions worth following in the practices of the 39

*He is referring to World War II. Skinner wrote *Walden Two* in the early summer of 1945 (recounted in the preface of the 1976 reprint).

clinical psychologist. We undertook to build a tolerance for annoying experiences. The sunshine of midday is extremely painful if you come from a dark room, but take it in easy stages and you can avoid pain altogether. The analogy can be misleading, but in much the same way it's possible to build a tolerance to painful or distasteful stimuli, or to frustration, or to situations which arouse fear, anger or rage. Society and nature throw these annoyances at the individual with no regard for the development of tolerances. Some achieve tolerances, most fail. Where would the science of immunization be if it followed a schedule of accidental dosages?

"Take the principle of 'Get thee behind me, Satan,' for example," Frazier 40
continued. "It's a special case of self-control by altering the environment. Subclass A_3, I believe. We give each child a lollipop which has been dipped in powdered sugar so that a single touch of the tongue can be detected. We tell him he may eat the lollipop later in the day, provided it hasn't already been licked. Since the child is only three or four, it is a fairly diff—"

"Three or four!" Castle exclaimed. 41

"All our ethical training is completed by the age of six," said Frazier 42
quietly. "A simple principle like putting temptation out of sight would be acquired before four. But at such an early age the problem of not licking the lollipop isn't easy. Now, what would you do, Mr. Castle, in a similar situation?"

"Put the lollipop out of sight as quickly as possible." 43

"Exactly. I can see you've been well trained. Or perhaps you discovered 44
the principle for yourself. We're in favor of original inquiry wherever possible, but in this case we have a more important goal and we don't hesitate to give verbal help. First of all, the children are urged to examine their own behavior while looking at the lollipops. This helps them to recognize the need for self-control. Then the lollipops are concealed, and the children are asked to notice any gain in happiness or any reduction in tension. Then a strong distraction is arranged—say, an interesting game. Later the children are reminded of the candy and encouraged to examine their reaction. The value of the distraction is generally obvious. Well, need I go on? When the experiment is repeated a day or so later, the children all run with the lollipops to their lockers and do exactly what Mr. Castle would do—a sufficient indication of the success of our training."

"I wish to report an objective observation of my reaction to your story," 45
said Castle, controlling his voice with great precision. "I find myself revolted by this display of sadistic tyranny."

"I don't wish to deny you the exercise of an emotion which you seem 46
to find enjoyable," said Frazier. "So let me go on. Concealing a tempting but forbidden object is a crude solution. For one thing, it's not always feasible. We want a sort of psychological concealment—covering up the candy by paying no attention. In a later experiment the children wear their lollipops like crucifixes for a few hours."

" 'Instead of the cross, the lollipop, 47
About my neck was hung,' "

said Castle.

"I wish somebody had taught me that, though," said Rodge, with a glance at Barbara.* 48

"Don't we all?" said Frazier. "Some of us learn control, more or less by accident. The rest of us go all our lives not even understanding how it is possible, and blaming our failure on being born the wrong way." 49

"How do you build up a tolerance to an annoying situation?" I said. 50

"Oh, for example, by having the children 'take' a more and more painful shock, or drink cocoa with less and less sugar in it until a bitter concoction can be savored without a bitter face." 51

"But jealousy or envy—you can't administer them in graded doses," I said. 52

"And why not? Remember, we control the social environment, too, at this age. That's why we get our ethical training in early. Take this case. A group of children arrive home after a long walk tired and hungry. They're expecting supper; they find, instead, that it's time for a lesson in self-control: they must stand for five minutes in front of steaming bowls of soup. 53

"The assignment is accepted like a problem in arithmetic. Any groaning or complaining is a wrong answer. Instead, the children begin at once to work upon themselves to avoid any unhappiness during the delay. One of them may make a joke of it. We encourage a sense of humor as a good way of not taking an annoyance seriously. The joke won't be much, according to adult standards—perhaps the child will simply pretend to empty the bowl of soup into his upturned mouth. Another may start a song with many verses. The rest join in at once, for they've learned that it's a good way to make time pass." 54

Frazier glanced uneasily at Castle, who was not to be appeased. 55

"That also strikes you as a form of torture, Mr. Castle?" he asked. 56

"I'd rather be put on the rack,"† said Castle. 57

"Then you have by no means had the thorough training I supposed. You can't imagine how lightly the children take such an experience. It's a rather severe biological frustration, for the children are tired and hungry and they must stand and look at food; but it's passed off as lightly as a five-minute delay at curtain time. We regard it as a fairly elementary test. Much more difficult problems follow." 58

"I suspected as much," muttered Castle. 59

"In a later stage we forbid all social devices. No songs, no jokes—merely 60

*Rogers, a former student of Professor Burris's and Barbara's fiancé. The obscure "glance at Barbara" may be Rogers's way of alluding to control of sexual passion.

†The rack was an instrument of torture used in the Middle Ages.

silence. Each child is forced back upon his own resources—a very important step."

"I should think so," I said. "And how do you know it's successful? You 61
might produce a lot of silently resentful children. It's certainly a dangerous stage."

"It is, and we follow each child carefully. If he hasn't picked up the 62
necessary techniques, we start back a little. A still more advanced stage"—Frazier glanced again at Castle, who stirred uneasily—"brings me to my point. When it's time to sit down to the soup, the children count off—heads and tails. Then a coin is tossed and if it comes up heads, the 'heads' sit down and eat. The 'tails' remain standing for another five minutes."

Castle groaned. 63

"And you call that envy?" I asked. 64

"Perhaps not exactly," said Frazier. "At least there's seldom any aggres- 65
sion against the lucky ones. The emotion, if any, is directed against Lady Luck herself, against the toss of the coin. That, in itself, is a lesson worth learning, for it's the only direction in which emotion has a surviving chance to be useful. And resentment toward things in general, while perhaps just as silly as personal aggression, is more easily controlled. Its expression is not socially objectionable."

Frazier looked nervously from one of us to the other. He seemed to be 66
trying to discover whether we shared Castle's prejudice. I began to realize, also, that he had not really wanted to tell this story. He was vulnerable. He was treading on sanctified ground, and I was pretty sure he had not established the value of most of these practices in an experimental fashion. He could scarcely have done so in the short space of ten years. He was working on faith, and it bothered him.

I tried to bolster his confidence by reminding him that he had a profes- 67
sional colleague among his listeners. "May you not inadvertently teach your children some of the very emotions you're trying to eliminate?" I said. "What's the effect, for example, of finding the anticipation of a warm supper suddenly thwarted? Doesn't that eventually lead to feelings of uncertainty, or even anxiety?"

"It might. We had to discover how often our lessons could be safely 68
administered. But all our schedules are worked out experimentally. We watch for undesired consequences just as any scientist watches for disrupting factors in his experiments.

"After all, it's a simple and sensible program," he went on in a tone of 69
appeasement. "We set up a system of gradually increasing annoyances and frustrations against a background of complete serenity. An easy environment is made more and more difficult as the children acquire the capacity to adjust."

"But *why?*" said Castle. "Why these deliberate unpleasantnesses—to 70
put it mildly? I must say I think you and your friend Simmons are really very subtle sadists."

"You've reversed your position, Mr. Castle," said Frazier in a sudden flash of anger with which I rather sympathized. Castle was calling names, and he was also being unaccountably and perhaps intentionally obtuse. "A while ago you accused me of breeding a race of softies," Frazier continued. "Now you object to toughening them up. But what you don't understand is that these potentially unhappy situations are never very annoying. Our schedules make sure of that. You wouldn't understand, however, because you're not so far advanced as our children." 71

Castle grew black. 72

"But what do your children get out of it?" he insisted, apparently trying to press some vague advantage in Frazier's anger. 73

"What do they get out of it!" exclaimed Frazier, his eyes flashing with a sort of helpless contempt. His lips curled and he dropped his head to look at his fingers, which were crushing a few blades of grass. 74

"They must get happiness and freedom and strength," I said, putting myself in a ridiculous position in attempting to make peace. 75

"They don't sound happy or free to me, standing in front of bowls of Forbidden Soup," said Castle, answering me parenthetically while continuing to stare at Frazier. 76

"If I must spell it out," Frazier began with a deep sigh, "what they get is escape from the petty emotions which eat the heart out of the unprepared. They get the satisfaction of pleasant and profitable social relations on a scale almost undreamed of in the world at large. They get immeasurably increased efficiency, because they can stick to a job without suffering the aches and pains which soon beset most of us. They get new horizons, for they are spared the emotions characteristic of frustration and failure. They get—" His eyes searched the branches of the trees. "Is that enough?" he said at last. 77

"And the community must gain their loyalty," I said, "when they discover the fears and jealousies and diffidences in the world at large." 78

"I'm glad you put it that way," said Frazier. "You might have said that they must feel superior to the miserable products of our public schools. But we're at pains to keep any feeling of superiority or contempt under control, too. Having suffered most acutely from it myself, I put the subject first on our agenda. We carefully avoid any joy in a personal triumph which means the personal failure of somebody else. We take no pleasure in the sophistical, the disputative, the dialectical." He threw a vicious glance at Castle. "We don't use the motive of domination, because we are always thinking of the whole group. We could motivate a few geniuses that way—it was certainly my own motivation—but we'd sacrifice some of the happiness of everyone else. Triumph over nature and over oneself, yes. But over others, never." 79

"You've taken the mainspring out of the watch," said Castle flatly. 80

"That's an experimental question, Mr. Castle, and you have the wrong answer." 81

Frazier was making no effort to conceal his feeling. If he had been riding 82
Castle, he was now using his spurs. Perhaps he sensed that the rest of us had come round and that he could change his tactics with a single holdout. But it was more than strategy, it was genuine feeling. Castle's undeviating skepticism was a growing frustration.

"Are your techniques really so very new?" I said hurriedly. "What 83
about the primitive practice of submitting a boy to various tortures before granting him a place among adults? What about the disciplinary techniques of Puritanism? Or of the modern school, for that matter?"

"In one sense you're right," said Frazier. "And I think you've nicely 84
answered Mr. Castle's tender concern for our little ones. The unhappinesses we deliberately impose are far milder than the normal unhappinesses from which we offer protection. Even at the height of our ethical training, the unhappiness is ridiculously trivial—to the well-trained child.

"But there's a world of difference in the way we use these annoyances," 85
he continued. "For one thing, we don't punish. We never administer an unpleasantness in the hope of repressing or eliminating undesirable behavior. But there's another difference. In most cultures the child meets up with annoyances and reverses of uncontrolled magnitude. Some are imposed in the name of discipline by persons in authority. Some, like hazings, are condoned though not authorized. Others are merely accidental. No one cares to, or is able to, prevent them.

"We all know what happens. A few hardy children emerge, particularly 86
those who have got their unhappiness in doses that could be swallowed. They become brave men. Others become sadists or masochists of varying degrees of pathology. Not having conquered a painful environment, they become preoccupied with pain and make a devious art of it. Others submit—and hope to inherit the earth. The rest—the cravens, the cowards—live in fear for the rest of their lives. And that's only a single field—the reaction to pain. I could cite a dozen parallel cases. The optimist and the pessimist, the contented and the disgruntled, the loved and the unloved, the ambitious and the discouraged—these are only the extreme products of a miserable system.

"Traditional practices are admittedly better than nothing," Frazier went 87
on. "Spartan or Puritan—no one can question the occasional happy result. But the whole system rests upon the wasteful principle of selection. The English public school of the nineteenth century produced brave men—by setting up almost insurmountable barriers and making the most of the few who came over. But selection isn't education. Its crops of brave men will always be small, and the waste enormous. Like all primitive principles, selection serves in place of education only through a profligate use of material. Multiply extravagantly and select with rigor. It's the philosophy of the 'big litter' as an alternative to good child hygiene.

"In Walden Two we have a different objective. We make every man a 88
brave man. They all come over the barriers. Some require more preparation than others, but they all come over. The traditional use of adversity is to select the strong. We control adversity to build strength. And we do it deliberately,

no matter how sadistic Mr. Castle may think us, in order to prepare for adversities which are beyond control. Our children eventually experience the 'heartache and the thousand natural shocks that flesh is heir to.'* It would be the cruelest possible practice to protect them as long as possible, especially when we *could* protect them so well."

Frazier held out his hands in an exaggerated gesture of appeal. 89

"What alternative *had* we?" he said, as if he were in pain. "What else could we do? For four or five years we could provide a life in which no important need would go unsatisfied, a life practically free of anxiety or frustration or annoyance. What would *you* do? Would you let the child enjoy this paradise with no thought for the future—like an idolatrous and pampering mother? Or would you relax control of the environment and let the child meet accidental frustrations? *But what is the virtue of accident?* No, there was only one course open to us. We had to design a series of adversities, so that the child would develop the greatest possible self-control. Call it deliberate, if you like, and accuse us of sadism; there was no other course." Frazier turned to Castle, but he was scarcely challenging him. He seemed to be waiting, anxiously, for his capitulation. But Castle merely shifted his ground. 90

"I find it difficult to classify these practices," he said. Frazier emitted a disgruntled "Ha!" and sat back. "Your system seems to have usurped the place as well as the techniques of religion." 91

"Of religion and family culture," said Frazier wearily. "But I don't call it usurpation. Ethical training belongs to the community. As for techniques, we took every suggestion we could find without prejudice as to the source. But not on faith. We disregarded all claims of revealed truth and put every principle to an experimental test. And by the way, I've very much misrepresented the whole system if you suppose that any of the practices I've described are fixed. We try out many different techniques. Gradually we work toward the best possible set. And we don't pay much attention to the apparent success of a principle in the course of history. History is honored in Walden Two only as entertainment. It isn't taken seriously as food for thought. Which reminds me, very rudely, of our original plan for the morning. Have you had enough of emotion? Shall we turn to intellect?" 92

Frazier addressed these questions to Castle in a very friendly way and I was glad to see that Castle responded in kind. It was perfectly clear, however, that neither of them had ever worn a lollipop about the neck or faced a bowl of Forbidden Soup. 93

*From *Hamlet,* by William Shakespeare.

Questions for Discussion

1. In the preface to the 1976 reprint of *Walden Two,* Skinner details the kinds of improvements he pictures as a result of behavorial engineering. "Psychotic and retarded persons would lead better lives, time and energy of teachers and students would be saved, homes would be pleasanter social environments, people would work more effectively while enjoying what they were doing, and so on." Then in the next sentence he identifies these goals as "the kinds of achievements traditionally expected from wisdom and common sense." Are these goals in fact the ones that you would identify as the primary ones for wisdom and common sense to achieve? If not, which goals would you want to include? Regardless of where you would place different kinds of goals, which other ones do you think need to be included? While Skinner's goals are clearly important, do you find it curious that these goals are the only ones mentioned? Which other important goals are silently subordinated in his "and so on"?
2. In "Science and Ethics" (pp. 665–673), Toulmin says that "we should pay critical attention to the respects in which . . . ethical issues enter into the conduct of scientific work, including its immediate practical consequences. The ethical aspects of human experimentation, and of such enterprises as sex research, are only samples from a much larger group of possible issues" (pp. 671). Comment on the awareness or lack of awareness of ethical issues in Skinner's account of the advantages of behavorial engineering.
3. Presumably in Skinner's ideal society, behavorial engineering will be able to avoid turning into social oppression (although he never really makes this clear) by operating on consensus: People will agree to what they want before the conditioning procedures are implemented. But what do you picture happening to minority views and dissenting opinions in such a world? Who gets the final say about the qualities the conditioners instill in their citizen-subjects?
4. Where do Skinner's criteria come from for defining the kind of feelings and opinions society desires most? From science? If so, how does science establish criteria? From religion? Skinner thinks religion superfluous and illusory. From history? Perhaps, but whose version of it? From objective reasoning? Perhaps, but would you accept Skinner's reasoning, which lists psychotics and retarded persons leading better lives *first* in his catalog of the advantages of behavorial engineering?
5. Do you think Skinner's recommended technique of making children wait to begin eating is a good way to teach self-control? How much distance is there between learning this kind of self-control and learning to control one's impulses to envy, greed, lust, or aggression? Do these all exist on the same psychic and emotional plane as hunger? If they do not, what critique of Skinner's reasoning does this seem to suggest?

Suggested Essay Topics

1. Write an essay, scenario, or short story in which you depict the kinds of educational principles *you* would recommend for achieving the same goals that Skinner desires: the teaching of self-control and the stifling of envy, aggression, and competitiveness.
2. Write a dialogue in which you picture Frazier (or Skinner) debating the best means of educating children with any other appropriate author in this book: Dickens, Plato, John Stuart Mill, or some other thinker whose views will make an instructive contrast.

IDEAS IN DEBATE

C. P. Snow
Loren Eiseley

C. P. Snow

The British writer C. P. Snow (1905–1980) could write about the distinctive character of the literary and scientific cultures because he not only knew them both intimately but spanned them in a distinguished and unusual way. He is thus an exception to the generalizations he makes about both the literary culture (or, as we in America would tend to say, the humanistic outlook or humanistic tradition) and the scientific culture (or scientific outlook). That he was himself an exception does not, of course, invalidate his generalizations; it simply underscores what a remarkable man he was. He spanned the two cultures by working professionally as both a trained scientist and a publishing novelist. He was a physicist at Cambridge from 1930 to 1950, and at the same time he wrote an 11-volume sequence of novels, collectively titled Strangers and Brothers *(1940–1970), that focuses on contemporary English society and documents the corrupting influence of power.*

The split between humanists and scientists that Snow described in 1956 has in the intervening decades both grown and shrunk. At the theoretical level the split has shrunk, but at the institutional level and in the eyes of the general public the split has grown. At the theoretical level the work of such theorists and philosophers of science as Jacob Bronowski, Loren Eiseley, Stephen Toulmin, Norwood Russell Hanson, Thomas Kuhn, Paul Feyerabend, Harold Brown, and Michael Polanyi has taught contemporary scientists to see that their modes of operation and those of the humanists are not as different as they were thought to be in 1956 when Snow published his original review, "The Two Cultures," in the New Statesman. *In the past 30 years scientists have become much less naïve about such issues as the status of a fact, the nature of objectivity, and the limits of empiricism. And humanists are probably much more knowledgeable now than Snow's literary colleagues were in 1956 about the general trends and controversies in scientific theory—though probably not much more knowledgeable about the details of scientific research. Generally, then, the two cultures have more of a speaking, or at least nodding, relationship today, at the theoretical level, than they had in the 1950s.*

At the institutional level, however, at the places where scientists actually conduct their research and humanists write their books, the specialization that Snow deplores has driven the two cultures even farther apart. In both the humanities and the sciences the topics of inquiry over the past three decades have become even more specialized and thus more subdivided. The result is that a historian who has a general knowledge of trends in scientific theory these days will nevertheless be as ignorant as ever about the actual research that fuels theoretical controversy. What is more—and this is something new—humanists now find themselves in the same position of ignorance about research and theories, even those of other humanists. And in science today an organic chemist has a nearly impossible task trying to understand the work of a mathematical chemist. In other words, the split nowadays is not just between the humanists and the scientists but among the subdivisions within these two broad camps.

The split between scientists and humanists has also grown larger in the eyes of the general public since the 1950s. We have no statistical proof of this assertion, but it seems a logical consequence of the increasing specialization we just referred to. In the 1950s, as Snow reports, science was brash and optimistic. Since then science has had to endure a degree of suspicion and hostility that it once seemed immune to—primarily on occasions when technology has proved threatening, as in the near meltdown at the Three Mile Island nuclear facility, as in the injurious consequences of the Agent Orange defoliation of forests in Vietnam, or as in the deterioration of the ozone layer caused by atmospheric pollution. These problems, however, do not lead most people to reject science. Indeed, the remedies people look to are almost always scientific. Science is supposed to tell us how to make safer defoliants, more reliable nuclear power plants, more efficient, pollution-scrubbing smokestacks, and so on. And beyond that, most people still think of science as the source of the only true—or at least the most *true—understanding of both the natural world and human nature.*

While science has retained its prestige as a source of both true and useful knowledge, the humanities have lost prestige on this scale of measurement. Fewer people now seem to turn to the study of languages, history, literature, or philosophy for solving either social or personal problems. Thus in the more than 30 years since Snow's essay, science has maintained its position in society or even enhanced it, but the humanities have lost ground. B.A. degrees in the humanities and student enrollments in humanities courses have been steadily declining. In this and other ways, the split between the two cultures has become an even more formidable problem now than it was when Snow first called our attention to it.

As you read, try to extend and amplify Snow's reasons for thinking that the split between the sciences and the humanities is unfortunate and potentially disastrous. Also consider your own attitudes toward either culture in light of what you want out of your education or the qualities of mind you think a well-educated person should possess. If Snow is right, we should all share a common literacy in both science and the humanities. But as you know, science and humanities majors all too often not only avoid courses in the "other" culture (to whatever extent possible) but are downright hostile to them. Consider how far your own literacy (and that of your friends) extends in the sciences and humanities. Does it extend far enough? Far enough for what?

THE TWO CULTURES

From *The Two Cultures: And a Second Look* (1965).

It is about three years since I made a sketch in print of a problem which had been on my mind for some time.[1] It was a problem I could not avoid just because of the circumstances of my life. The only credentials I had to ruminate on the subject at all came through those circumstances, through nothing more than a set of chances. Anyone with similar experience would have seen much the same things and I think made very much the same comments about them. It just happened to be an unusual experience. By training I was a scientist: by vocation I was a writer. That was all. It was a piece of luck, if you like, that arose through coming from a poor home. 1

But my personal history isn't the point now. All that I need say is that I came to Cambridge and did a bit of research here at a time of major scientific activity. I was privileged to have a ringside view of one of the most wonderful creative periods in all physics. And it happened through the flukes of war—including meeting W. L. Bragg* in the buffet on Kettering station on a very cold morning in 1939, which had a determining influence on my practical life—that I was able, and indeed morally forced, to keep that ringside view ever since. So for thirty years I have had to be in touch with scientists not only out of curiosity, but as part of a working existence. During the same thirty years I was trying to shape the books I wanted to write, which in due course took me among writers. 2

There have been plenty of days when I have spent the working hours with scientists and then gone off at night with some literary colleagues. I mean that literally. I have had, of course, intimate friends among both scientists and writers. It was through living among these groups and much more, I think, through moving regularly from one to the other and back again that I got occupied with the problem of what, long before I put it on paper, I christened to myself as the "two cultures." For constantly I felt I was moving among two groups—comparable in intelligence, identical in race, not grossly different in social origin, earning about the same incomes, who had almost ceased to communicate at all, who in intellectual, moral and psychological climate had so little in common that instead of going from Burlington House or South Kensington to Chelsea,† one might have crossed an ocean. 3

In fact, one had travelled much further than across an ocean—because after a few thousand Atlantic miles, one found Greenwich Village‡ talking precisely the same language as Chelsea, and both having about as much communication with M.I.T.§ as though the scientists spoke nothing but Tibe- 4

*Sir William Lawrence Bragg (1890–1971), Cavendish professor of experimental physics at Cambridge (1938–1954) and co-winner with his father of the 1915 Nobel Prize in physics.

†Chelsea has a long history as a literary and artistic section of London. In the eighteenth century Swift, Steele, and Smollett lived there. Later, Turner, Rossetti, Whistler, Leigh Hunt, and Carlyle lived there.

‡A famous literary and artistic section of New York City.

§Massachusetts Institute of Technology in Boston, a famous school of science and engineering.

tan. For this is not just our problem; owing to some of our educational and social idiosyncrasies, it is slightly exaggerated here, owing to another English social peculiarity it is slightly minimised; by and large this is a problem of the entire West.

By this I intend something serious. I am not thinking of the pleasant 5
story of how one of the more convivial Oxford greats dons*—I have heard the story attributed to A. L. Smith—came over to Cambridge to dine. The date is perhaps the 1890's. I think it must have been at St John's, or possibly Trinity.† Anyway, Smith was sitting at the right hand of the President—or Vice-Master—and he was a man who liked to include all round him in the conversation, although he was not immediately encouraged by the expressions of his neighbours. He addressed some cheerful Oxonian chit-chat at the one opposite to him, and got a grunt. He then tried the man on his own right hand and got another grunt. Then, rather to his surprise, one looked at the other and said, "Do you know what he's talking about?" "I haven't the least idea." At this, even Smith was getting out of his depth. But the President, acting as a social emollient, put him at his ease by saying, "Oh, those are mathematicians! We never talk to *them.*"

No, I intend something serious. I believe the intellectual life of the 6
whole of western society is increasingly being split into two polar groups. When I say the intellectual life, I mean to include also a large part of our practical life, because I should be the last person to suggest the two can at the deepest level be distinguished. I shall come back to the practical life a little later. Two polar groups: at one pole we have the literary intellectuals, who incidentally while no one was looking took to referring to themselves as "intellectuals" as though there were no others. I remember G. H. Hardy once remarking to me in mild puzzlement, some time in the 1930's: "Have you noticed how the word 'intellectual' is used nowadays? There seems to be a new definition which certainly doesn't include Rutherford or Eddington or Dirac or Adrian or me.‡ It does seem rather odd, don't y' know."[2]

Literary intellectuals at one pole—at the other scientists, and as the most 7
representative, the physical scientists. Between the two a gulf of mutual incomprehension—sometimes (particularly among the young) hostility and dislike, but most of all lack of understanding. They have a curious distorted image of each other. Their attitudes are so different that, even on the level of emotion, they can't find much common ground. Non-scientists tend to think of scientists as brash and boastful. They hear Mr T. S. Eliot,§ who just

*A don is a tutor in an English university.

†St. John's and Trinity are colleges at Cambridge University.

‡All great scientists: Ernest Rutherford (1871–1937) was awarded the 1908 Nobel Prize for chemistry, Arthur Stanley Eddington (1882–1944) was an English astronomer and Cambridge professor, P. A. M. Dirac (1902–1984) was instrumental in the development of quantum theory, and Edgar Douglas Adrian (1889–1977) was an English physiologist who won (with Sir Charles Sherrington) the Nobel Prize for medicine in 1932.

§Thomas Stearns Eliot (1888–1965) was a leading poet and critic for most of his career. He won the Nobel Prize for literature in 1948.

for these illustrations we can take as an archetypal figure, saying about his attempts to revive verse-drama that we can hope for very little, but that he would feel content if he and his co-workers could prepare the ground for a new Kyd or a new Greene.* That is the tone, restricted and constrained, with which literary intellectuals are at home: it is the subdued voice of their culture. Then they hear a much louder voice, that of another archetypal figure, Rutherford, trumpeting: "This is the heroic age of science! This is the Elizabethan age!" Many of us heard that, and a good many other statements beside which that was mild; and we weren't left in any doubt whom Rutherford was casting for the role of Shakespeare. What is hard for the literary intellectuals to understand, imaginatively or intellectually, is that he was absolutely right.

And compare "this is the way the world ends, not with a bang but a 8
whimper"†—incidentally, one of the least likely scientific prophecies ever made—compare that with Rutherford's famous repartee, "Lucky fellow, Rutherford, always on the crest of the wave." "Well, I made the wave, didn't I?"

The non-scientists have a rooted impression that the scientists are shal- 9
lowly optimistic, unaware of man's condition. On the other hand, the scientists believe that the literary intellectuals are totally lacking in foresight, peculiarly unconcerned with their brother men, in a deep sense anti-intellectual, anxious to restrict both art and thought to the existential moment. And so on. Anyone with a mild talent for invective could produce plenty of this kind of subterranean back-chat. On each side there is some of it which is not entirely baseless. It is all destructive. Much of it rests on misinterpretations which are dangerous. I should like to deal with two of the most profound of these now, one on each side.

First, about the scientists' optimism. This is an accusation which has 10
been made so often that it has become a platitude. It has been made by some of the acutest non-scientific minds of the day. But it depends upon a confusion between the individual experience and the social experience, between the individual condition of man and his social condition. Most of the scientists I have known well have felt—just as deeply as the non-scientists I have known well—that the individual condition of each of us is tragic. Each of us is alone: sometimes we escape from solitariness, through love or affection or perhaps creative moments, but those triumphs of life are pools of light we make for ourselves while the edge of the road is black: each of us dies alone. Some scientists I have known have had faith in revealed religion. Perhaps with them the sense of the tragic condition is not so strong. I don't know. With most people of deep feeling, however high-spirited and happy they are,

*Robert Greene (ca. 1558–1592) and Thomas Kyd (1558–1594) were relatively minor literary figures of the sixteenth century. Snow's point is that if Eliot and other literary people are content merely to prepare the way for minor writers, they are indeed motivated by a conservative impulse quite different from the high ambitions of the scientists.

†The last two lines of Eliot's poem "The Hollow Men."

sometimes most with those who are happiest and most high-spirited, it seems to be right in the fibres, part of the weight of life. That is as true of the scientists I have known best as of anyone at all.

But nearly all of them—and this is where the colour of hope genuinely comes in—would see no reason why, just because the individual condition is tragic, so must the social condition be. Each of us is solitary: each of us dies alone: all right, that's a fate against which we can't struggle—but there is plenty in our condition which is not fate, and against which we are less than human unless we do struggle. 11

Most of our fellow human beings, for instance, are underfed and die before their time. In the crudest terms, *that* is the social condition. There is a moral trap which comes through the insight into man's loneliness: it tempts one to sit back, complacent in one's unique tragedy, and let the others go without a meal. 12

As a group, the scientists fall into that trap less than others. They are inclined to be impatient to see if something can be done: and inclined to think that it can be done, until it's proved otherwise. That is their real optimism, and it's an optimism that the rest of us badly need. 13

In reverse, the same spirit, tough and good and determined to fight it out at the side of their brother men, has made scientists regard the other culture's social attitudes as contemptible. That is too facile: some of them are, but they are a temporary phase and not to be taken as representative. 14

I remember being cross-examined by a scientist of distinction. "Why do most writers take on social opinions which would have been thought distinctly uncivilised and démodé at the time of the Plantagenets? Wasn't that true of most of the famous twentieth-century writers? Yeats, Pound, Wyndham Lewis, nine out of ten of those who have dominated literary sensibility in our time—weren't they not only politically silly, but politically wicked? Didn't the influence of all they represent bring Auschwitz* that much nearer?" 15

I thought at the time, and I still think, that the correct answer was not to defend the indefensible. It was no use saying that Yeats, according to friends whose judgment I trust, was a man of singular magnanimity of character, as well as a great poet. It was no use denying the facts, which are broadly true. The honest answer was that there is, in fact, a connection, which literary persons were culpably slow to see, between some kinds of early twentieth-century art and the most imbecile expressions of anti-social feeling.[3] That was one reason, among many, why some of us turned our backs on the art and tried to hack out a new or different way for ourselves.[4] 16

But though many of those writers dominated literary sensibility for a generation, that is no longer so, or at least to nothing like the same extent. 17

*One of Hitler's death camps in which millions of Jews were killed during World War II. The scientist Snow quotes is suggesting that the political attitudes of the literary culture helped make Auschwitz possible.

Literature changes more slowly than science. It hasn't the same automatic corrective, and so its misguided periods are longer. But it is ill-considered of scientists to judge writers on the evidence of the period 1914–50.

Those are two of the misunderstandings between the two cultures. I should say, since I began to talk about them—the two cultures, that is—I have had some criticism. Most of my scientific acquaintances think that there is something in it, and so do most of the practising artists I know. But I have been argued with by non-scientists of strong down-to-earth interests. Their view is that it is an over-simplification, and that if one is going to talk in these terms there ought to be at least three cultures. They argue that, though they are not scientists themselves, they would share a good deal of the scientific feeling. They would have as little use—perhaps, since they knew more about it, even less use—for the recent literary culture as the scientists themselves. J. H. Plumb, Alan Bullock and some of my American sociological friends have said that they vigorously refuse to be corralled in a cultural box with people they wouldn't be seen dead with, or to be regarded as helping to produce a climate which would not permit of social hope. 18

I respect those arguments. The number 2 is a very dangerous number: that is why the dialectic is a dangerous process. Attempts to divide anything into two ought to be regarded with much suspicion. I have thought a long time about going in for further refinements: but in the end I have decided against. I was searching for something a little more than a dashing metaphor, a good deal less than a cultural map: and for those purposes the two cultures is about right, and subtilising any more would bring more disadvantages than it's worth. 19

At one pole, the scientific culture really is a culture, not only in an intellectual but also in an anthropological sense. That is, its members need not, and of course often do not, always completely understand each other; biologists more often than not will have a pretty hazy idea of contemporary physics; but there are common attitudes, common standards and patterns of behaviour, common approaches and assumptions. This goes surprisingly wide and deep. It cuts across other mental patterns, such as those of religion or politics or class. 20

Statistically, I suppose slightly more scientists are in religious terms unbelievers, compared with the rest of the intellectual world—though there are plenty who are religious, and that seems to be increasingly so among the young. Statistically also, slightly more scientists are on the Left in open politics—though again, plenty always have called themselves conservatives, and that also seems to be more common among the young. Compared with the rest of the intellectual world, considerably more scientists in this country and probably in the U.S. come from poor families.[5] Yet over a whole range of thought and behaviour, none of that matters very much. In their working, and in much of their emotional life, their attitudes are closer to other scientists than to non-scientists who in religion or politics or class have the same labels as themselves. If I were to risk a piece of shorthand, I should say that naturally they had the future in their bones. 21

They may or may not like it, but they have it. That was as true of the conservatives J. J. Thomson and Lindemann as of the radicals Einstein or Blackett: as true of the Christian A. H. Compton as of the materialist Bernal: of the aristocrats de Broglie or Russell as of the proletarian Faraday: of those born rich, like Thomas Merton or Victor Rothschild, as of Rutherford, who was the son of an odd-job handyman. Without thinking about it, they respond alike. That is what a culture means.* 22

At the other pole, the spread of attitudes is wider. It is obvious that between the two, as one moves through intellectual society from the physicists to the literary intellectuals, there are all kinds of tones of feeling on the way. But I believe the pole of total incomprehension of science radiates its influence on all the rest. That total incomprehension gives, much more pervasively than we realise, living in it, an unscientific flavour to the whole "traditional" culture, and that unscientific flavour is often, much more than we admit, on the point of turning anti-scientific. The feelings of one pole become the anti-feelings of the other. If the scientists have the future in their bones, then the traditional culture responds by wishing the future did not exist.[6] It is the traditional culture, to an extent remarkably little diminished by the emergence of the scientific one, which manages the western world. 23

This polarisation is sheer loss to us all. To us as people, and to our society. It is at the same time a practical and intellectual and creative loss, and I repeat that it is false to imagine that those three considerations are clearly separable. But for a moment I want to concentrate on the intellectual loss. 24

The degree of incomprehension on both sides is the kind of joke which has gone sour. There are about fifty thousand working scientists in the country and about eighty thousand professional engineers or applied scientists. During the war and in the years since, my colleagues and I have had to interview somewhere between thirty to forty thousand of these—that is, about 25 per cent. The number is large enough to give us a fair sample, though of the men we talked to most would still be under forty. We were able to find out a certain amount of what they read and thought about. I confess that even I, who am fond of them and respect them, was a bit shaken. We hadn't quite expected that the links with the traditional culture should be so tenuous, nothing more than a formal touch of the cap. 25

As one would expect, some of the very best scientists had and have plenty of energy and interest to spare, and we came across several who had read everything that literary people talk about. But that's very rare. Most of the rest, when one tried to probe for what books they had read, would modestly confess, "Well, I've *tried* a bit of Dickens," rather as though Dickens were an extraordinarily esoteric, tangled and dubiously rewarding writer, something like Rainer Maria Rilke. In fact that is exactly how they do regard him: we thought that discovery, that Dickens had been transformed into the 26

*In other words, differences of social class, political leaning, and wealth among the scientists are all outweighed by common attitudes about the future based on scientific aspirations and outlook.

type-specimen of literary incomprehensibility, was one of the oddest results of the whole exercise.*

But of course, in reading him, in reading almost any writer whom we 27
should value, they are just touching their caps to the traditional culture. They have their own culture, intensive, rigorous, and constantly in action. This culture contains a great deal of argument, usually much more rigorous, and almost always at a higher conceptual level, than literary persons' arguments—even though the scientists do cheerfully use words in senses which literary persons don't recognise, the senses are exact ones, and when they talk about "subjective," "objective," "philosophy" or "progressive,"[7] they know what they mean, even though it isn't what one is accustomed to expect.

Remember, these are very intelligent men. Their culture is in many ways 28
an exacting and admirable one. It doesn't contain much art, with the exception, an important exception, of music. Verbal exchange, insistent argument. Long-playing records. Colour-photography. The ear, to some extent the eye. Books, very little, though perhaps not many would go so far as one hero, who perhaps I should admit was further down the scientific ladder than the people I've been talking about—who, when asked what books he read, replied firmly and confidently: "Books? I prefer to use my books as tools." It was very hard not to let the mind wander—what sort of tool would a book make? Perhaps a hammer? A primitive digging instrument?

Of books, though, very little. And of the books which to most literary 29
persons are bread and butter, novels, history, poetry, plays, almost nothing at all. It isn't that they're not interested in the psychological or moral or social life. In the social life, they certainly are, more than most of us. In the moral, they are by and large the soundest group of intellectuals we have; there is a moral component right in the grain of science itself, and almost all scientists form their own judgments of the moral life. In the psychological they have as much interest as most of us, though occasionally I fancy they come to it rather late. It isn't that they lack the interests. It is much more that the whole literature of the traditional culture doesn't seem to them relevant to those interests. They are, of course, dead wrong. As a result, their imaginative understanding is less than it could be. They are self-impoverished.

But what about the other side? They are impoverished too—perhaps 30
more seriously, because they are vainer about it. They still like to pretend that the traditional culture is the whole of "culture," as though the natural order didn't exist.† As though the exploration of the natural order was of no interest either in its own value or its consequences. As though the scientific edifice of the physical world was not, in its intellectual depth, complexity and

*This was "the oddest result" because Dickens is the last writer who could be justifiably accused or accurately described as being artistically incomprehensible. He was the most popularly admired and widely read author of the nineteenth century. Calling Dickens esoteric is like calling elevator music experimental.

†By "the natural order" he simply means "nature."

articulation, the most beautiful and wonderful collective work of the mind of man. Yet most non-scientists have no conception of that edifice at all. Even if they want to have it, they can't. It is rather as though, over an immense range of intellectual experience, a whole group was tone-deaf. Except that this tone-deafness doesn't come by nature, but by training, or rather the absence of training.

As with the tone-deaf, they don't know what they miss. They give a pitying chuckle at the news of scientists who have never read a major work of English literature. They dismiss them as ignorant specialists. Yet their own ignorance and their own specialisation is just as startling. A good many times I have been present at gatherings of people who, by the standards of the traditional culture, are thought highly educated and who have with considerable gusto been expressing their incredulity at the illiteracy of scientists. Once or twice I have been provoked and have asked the company how many of them could describe the Second Law of Thermodynamics. The response was cold: it was also negative. Yet I was asking something which is about the scientific equivalent of: *Have you read a work of Shakespeare's?* 31

I now believe that if I had asked an even simpler question—such as, What do you mean by mass, or acceleration, which is the scientific equivalent of saying, *Can you read?*—not more than one in ten of the highly educated would have felt that I was speaking the same language. So the great edifice of modern physics goes up, and the majority of the cleverest people in the western world have about as much insight into it as their neolithic ancestors would have had. 32

Just one more of those questions, that my non-scientific friends regard as being in the worst of taste. Cambridge is a university where scientists and non-scientists meet every night at dinner.[8] About two years ago, one of the most astonishing discoveries in the whole history of science was brought off. I don't mean the Sputnik*—that was admirable for quite different reasons, as a feat of organisation and a triumphant use of existing knowledge. No, I mean the discovery at Columbia by Yang and Lee. It is a piece of work of the greatest beauty and originality, but the result is so startling that one forgets how beautiful the thinking is. It makes us think again about some of the fundamentals of the physical world. Intuition, common sense—they are neatly stood on their heads. The result is usually known as the non-conservation of parity.† If there were any serious communication between the two cultures, this experiment would have been talked about at every High Table in Cambridge. Was it? I wasn't here: but I should like to ask the question. 33

There seems then to be no place where the cultures meet. I am not going 34

*In 1958 the Russians put the first man-made satellite, *Sputnik,* into orbit around the earth.

†Tsung-Dao Lee (b. 1926) and Chen Ning Yang (b. 1922) devised a set of experiments in 1956 that led to extensive revisions of basic theory in atomic and sub-atomic physics. For their accomplishments, generally known as the non-conservation of parity, they were awarded the Nobel Prize for physics in 1957.

to waste time saying that this is a pity. It is much worse than that. Soon I shall come to some practical consequences. But at the heart of thought and creation we are letting some of our best chances go by default. The clashing point of two subjects, two disciplines, two cultures—of two galaxies, so far as that goes—ought to produce creative chances. In the history of mental activity that has been where some of the break-throughs came. The chances are there now. But they are there, as it were, in a vacuum, because those in the two cultures can't talk to each other. It is bizarre how very little of twentieth-century science has been assimilated into twentieth-century art. Now and then one used to find poets conscientiously using scientific expressions, and getting them wrong—there was a time when "refraction" kept cropping up in verse in a mystifying fashion, and when "polarised light" was used as though writers were under the illusion that it was a specially admirable kind of light.

Of course, that isn't the way that science could be any good to art. It 35
has got to be assimilated along with, and as part and parcel of, the whole of our mental experience, and used as naturally as the rest.

I said earlier that this cultural divide is not just an English phenomenon: 36
it exists all over the western world. But it probably seems at its sharpest in England, for two reasons. One is our fanatical belief in educational specialisation, which is much more deeply ingrained in us than in any country in the world, west or east. The other is our tendency to let our social forms crystallise. This tendency appears to get stronger, not weaker, the more we iron out economic inequalities: and this is specially true in education. It means that once anything like a cultural divide gets established, all the social forces operate to make it not less rigid, but more so.

The two cultures were already dangerously separate sixty years ago; but 37
a prime minister like Lord Salisbury could have his own laboratory at Hatfield, and Arthur Balfour had a somewhat more than amateur interest in natural science. John Anderson* did some research in inorganic chemistry in Leipzig before passing first into the Civil Service, and incidentally took a spread of subjects which is now impossible.[9] None of that degree of interchange at the top of the Establishment is likely, or indeed thinkable, now.[10]

In fact, the separation between the scientists and non-scientists is much 38
less bridgeable among the young than it was even thirty years ago. Thirty years ago the cultures had long ceased to speak to each other: but at least they managed a kind of frozen smile across the gulf. Now the politeness has gone, and they just make faces. It is not only that the young scientists now feel that they are part of a culture on the rise while the other is in retreat. It is also, to be brutal, that the young scientists know that with an indifferent degree they'll get a comfortable job, while their contemporaries and counterparts in English or History will be lucky to earn 60 per cent as much. No young scientist of any talent would feel that he isn't wanted or that his work is ridiculous, as did the hero of *Lucky Jim,* and in fact, some of the disgruntlement

*John Anderson (1882–1958) was chancellor of the exchequer, 1943–1945.

of Amis* and his associates is the disgruntlement of the under-employed arts graduate.

There is only one way out of all this: it is, of course, by rethinking our 39
education. In this country, for the two reasons I have given, that is more difficult than in any other. Nearly everyone will agree that our school education is too specialised. But nearly everyone feels that it is outside the will of man to alter it. Other countries are as dissatisfied with their education as we are, but are not so resigned.

The U.S. teach out of proportion more children up to eighteen than we 40
do: they teach them far more widely, but nothing like so rigorously. They know that: they are hoping to take the problem in hand within ten years, though they may not have all that time to spare. The U.S.S.R. also teach out of proportion more children than we do: they also teach far more widely than we do (it is an absurd western myth that their school education is specialised) but much too rigorously.[11] They know that—and they are beating about to get it right. The Scandinavians, in particular the Swedes, who would make a more sensible job of it than any of us, are handicapped by their practical need to devote an inordinate amount of time to foreign languages. But they too are seized of the problem.

Are we? Have we crystallised so far that we are no longer flexible at all? 41

Talk to schoolmasters, and they say that our intense specialisation, like 42
nothing else on earth, is dictated by the Oxford and Cambridge scholarship examinations. If that is so, one would have thought it not utterly impracticable to change the Oxford and Cambridge scholarship examinations. Yet one would underestimate the national capacity for the intricate defensive to believe that that was easy. All the lessons of our educational history suggest we are only capable of increasing specialisation, not decreasing it.

Somehow we have set ourselves the task of producing a tiny *élite*—far 43
smaller proportionately than in any comparable country—educated in one academic skill. For a hundred and fifty years in Cambridge it was mathematics: then it was mathematics or classics: then natural science was allowed in. But still the choice had to be a single one.

It may well be that this process has gone too far to be reversible. I have 44
given reasons why I think it is a disastrous process, for the purpose of a living culture. I am going on to give reasons why I think it is fatal, if we're to perform our practical tasks in the world. But I can think of only one example, in the whole of English educational history, where our pursuit of specialised mental exercises was resisted with success.

It was done here in Cambridge, fifty years ago, when the old order-of- 45
merit in the Mathematical Tripos† was abolished. For over a hundred years, the nature of the Tripos had been crystallising. The competition for the top

*Kingsley Amis's novel *Lucky Jim* (1953) satirizes the stuffiness and provinciality of the English educational system. The hero is a historian, not a scientist, and part of his problem is that he can't get a job.

†The Mathematical Tripos was the final examination instituted in the first half of the eighteenth century for honors in mathematics.

places had got fiercer, and careers hung on them. In most colleges, certainly in my own, if one managed to come out as Senior or Second Wrangler, one was elected a Fellow out of hand. A whole apparatus of coaching had grown up. Men of the quality of Hardy, Littlewood, Russell, Eddington, Jeans, Keynes, went in for two or three years' training for an examination which was intensely competitive and intensely difficult. Most people in Cambridge were very proud of it, with a similar pride to that which almost anyone in England always has for our existing educational institutions, whatever they happen to be. If you study the flysheets of the time,* you will find the passionate arguments for keeping the examination precisely as it was to all eternity: it was the only way to keep up standards, it was the only fair test of merit, indeed, the only seriously objective test in the world. The arguments, in fact, were almost exactly those which are used today with precisely the same passionate sincerity if anyone suggests that the scholarship examinations might conceivably not be immune from change.

In every respect but one, in fact, the old Mathematical Tripos seemed 46
perfect. The one exception, however, appeared to some to be rather important. It was simply—so the young creative mathematicians, such as Hardy and Littlewood, kept saying—that the [Tripos] had no intellectual merit at all. They went a little further, and said that the Tripos had killed serious mathematics in England stone dead for a hundred years. Well, even in academic controversy, that took some skirting round, and they got their way. But I have an impression that Cambridge was a good deal more flexible between 1850 and 1914 than it has been in our time. If we had had the old Mathematical Tripos firmly planted among us, should we have ever managed to abolish it?

NOTES

All notes are Snow's.

1. "The Two Cultures," *New Statesman,* 6 October 1956.

2. This lecture was delivered to a Cambridge audience, and so I used some points of reference which I did not need to explain. G. H. Hardy, 1877–1947, was one of the most distinguished pure mathematicians of his time, and a picturesque figure in Cambridge both as a young don and on his return in 1931 to the Sadleirian Chair of Mathematics.

3. I said a little more about this connection in *The Times Literary Supplement,* "Challenge to the Intellect," 15 August 1958. I hope some day to carry the analysis further.

4. It would be more accurate to say that, for literary reasons, we felt the prevailing literary modes were useless to us. We were, however, reinforced in that feeling when it occurred to us that those prevailing modes went hand in hand with social attitudes either wicked, or absurd, or both.

5. An analysis of the schools from which Fellows of the Royal Society come tells its own story. The distribution is markedly different from that of, for example, members of the Foreign Service or Queen's Counsel.

6. Compare George Orwell's *1984,* which is the strongest possible wish that the future should not exist, with J. D. Bernal's *World Without War.*

*A flysheet is a small, loose advertising sheet, like a handbill; in this case it refers to campus leaflets espousing particular points of view.

7. *Subjective,* in contemporary technological jargon, means "divided according to subjects." *Objective* means "directed towards an object." *Philosophy* means "general intellectual approach or attitude" (for example, a scientist's "philosophy of guided weapons" might lead him to propose certain kinds of "objective research"). A "progressive" job means one with possibilities of promotion.

8. Almost all college High Tables contain Fellows in both scientific and non-scientific subjects.

9. He took the examination in 1905.

10. It is, however, true to say that the compact nature of the managerial layers of English society—the fact that "everyone knows everyone else"—means that scientists and non-scientists do in fact know each other as people more easily than in most countries. It is also true that a good many leading politicians and administrators keep up lively intellectual and artistic interests to a much greater extent, so far as I can judge, than is the case in the U.S. These are both among our assets.

11. I tried to compare American, Soviet and English education in "New Minds for the New World," *New Statesman,* 6 September 1956.

Questions for Discussion

1. Poll your class to see if the "two cultures" split is visible within it. Are the people who prefer humanities courses also fond of or excited by science courses? And vice versa? How many people enjoy switching back and forth equally?

2. In 1802 William Wordsworth (1770–1850), Romantic poet, wrote in his preface to *Lyrical Ballads:*

   > The knowledge both of the poet and the man of science is pleasure; but the knowledge of the one cleaves to us as a necessary part of our existence, our natural and unalienable inheritance; the other is a personal and individual acquisition, slow to come to us, and by no habitual and direct sympathy connecting us with our fellow-beings. The man of science seeks truth as a remote and unknown benefactor; he cherishes and loves it in his solitude: the poet, singing a song in which all human beings join with him, rejoices in the presence of truth as our visible friend and hourly companion. Poetry is the breath and finer spirit of all knowledge; it is the impassioned expression which is in the countenance of all science.

   Discuss with your classmates what you think this passage means and whether you think it is true. Is Wordsworth privileging literary culture over scientific culture? Or does he simply see each kind of culture as covering a different domain of human knowledge and experience? Support your views with the best reasons you can create.

3. In 1821, a few years after Wordsworth wrote his preface, another Romantic poet, Percy Shelley (1792–1822), also undertook (in *A Defence of Poetry*) to compare literary culture with scientific culture. Looking about him at a world in which industrialization and economic expansion seemed to be impoverishing at least as many people as it was enriching, he observed:

   > We have more moral, political and historical wisdom, than we know how to reduce into practice; we have more scientific and economical knowl-

> edge than can be accommodated to the just distribution of the produce which it multiplies. The poetry in these systems of thought, is concealed by the accumulation of facts and calculating processes. . . . We want [i.e., lack] the creative faculty to imagine that which we know; we want the generous impulse to act that which we imagine; we want the poetry of life: our calculations have outrun conception; we have eaten more than we can digest. The cultivation of those sciences which have enlarged the limits of the empire of man over the external world, has, for want of the poetical faculty, proportionally circumscribed those of the internal world; and man, having enslaved the elements, remains himself a slave.

Is Shelley being fair to science by implying that the means by which men are making themselves rich are also impoverishing their social sympathies? Can you think of examples in which science has been used both ways—that is, to alleviate human suffering and to create it at the same time? And if both kinds of examples are plentiful, is science's failings the fault of science or of something else? If something else, what?

4. Twelve years after Shelley's *Defence,* in 1833, John Stuart Mill (1806–1873)—philosopher, logician, and economist—wrote an essay called "What Is Poetry?" in which he asserts that the opposite of poetry is

> not prose, but matter of fact, or science. The one addresses itself to the belief; the other, to the feelings. The one does its work by convincing or persuading; the other, by moving. The one acts by presenting a proposition to the understanding; the other, by offering interesting objects of contemplation to the sensibilities.

How readily do you think this view of literary culture contributes to the popular notion that artists are impractical and irrational, guided by emotions and impulse rather than facts? Is this cliché true? Can you think of examples that contest it? Examples that support it? What do you think is the truth of the matter? Give reasons.

5. Fifty years after Mill's essay, in 1882, Matthew Arnold (1822–1888), poet and essayist, maintained in an essay titled "Literature and Science" that science yields important and true knowledge but cannot tell us what to do with such knowledge, cannot tell us how to relate it to the arenas of conduct and behavior. The humanities, he claims, are necessary for making these connections and therefore cannot be allowed to decline as science advances.

> Interesting, indeed, these results of science are, important they are, and we should all of us be acquainted with them. But what I now wish you to mark is, that we are still, when they are propounded and we receive them, we are still in the sphere of intellect and knowledge. And for the generality of men there will be found, I say, to arise, when they have duly taken in the proposition that their ancestor was "a hairy quadruped furnished with a tail and pointed ears, probably arboreal in his habits," there will be found to arise an invincible desire to relate this proposition to the sense in us for conduct, and to the sense in us for beauty. But this the men of science will not do for us, and will hardly even profess to do. They will give us other pieces of knowledge, other facts, about other

> animals and their ancestors, or about plants, or about stones, or about stars; and they may finally bring us to those great "general conceptions of the universe, which are forced upon us all," says Professor Huxley, "by the progress of physical science." But still it will be *knowledge* only which they give us; knowledge not put for us into relation with our sense for conduct, our sense for beauty, and touched with emotion by being so put; not thus put for us, and therefore, to the majority of mankind, after a certain while, unsatisfying, wearying.

As you sit day after day in your college courses, do you ever experience the feeling that Arnold here attributes to "the generality of men," the feeling that you are learning more than you know how to use, more than you know the worth of, more than you can relate to the other pieces of knowledge you are learning in other classes? If so, has Arnold put the case accurately for you, or would you put the emphasis in different places? And what about the sense of beauty Arnold alludes to? What do you take him to mean by this? Do you need the sense that knowledge has to be somehow turned to the beautification of life before it has earned its way in the world? Can you provide examples one way or the other? How would you define *beauty* in this context?

6. After reading these selections by nineteenth-century figures on humanistic versus scientific culture, what changes, if any, in your view of Snow's version of the two cultures have been created? Is it possible that the two cultures he sees were at least a century in the making? How could you corroborate this statement by referring to the quotations? What counter-examples could you provide?
7. Some critics have noted that Snow's analysis simply ignores many areas of modern thought, particularly the social sciences. He has little to say about history, sociology, anthropology, and political science. Where do you think he would place these subjects, if he did include them in his twofold scheme? Do you think his analysis would have to be greatly modified if he wrote an essay on "the *three* cultures"?

Suggested Essay Topics

1. At the time of Snow's essay in the 1950s, he was right to see the humanists and scientists as constituting the two dominant constituencies in the university, but today there is another constituency separate from these two traditional groups: the people in the professional or pre-professional schools. People getting degrees in business, pharmacy, dance, theater, communications, and many other fields are in neither the humanities nor the sciences. The question is, should they be, or at least should they be made to learn enough about the humanities and sciences as to achieve a minimal kind of literacy in both?

   In an essay directed to your classmates, answer these questions with the best reasons you can find for either forcing people in professional programs to take humanities and science courses or exempting them from such requirements. State what you think the minimal requirements should be, and make clear what your criteria for "minimal" are. If, for example, you would only require them to take, say, three hours of literature, say why that is enough. Enough in relation to what?

2. Write an essay to your instructor in which you attack or support Arnold's claim that the knowledge of science cannot be related to the questions we most want answers to—questions about how to live, how to make life meaningful or beautiful—and that scientific knowledge will therefore always remain incomplete unless complemented by knowledge from the humanities (and possibly other sources as well).

Loren Eiseley

Loren Eiseley (1907–1977) both admits and contests C. P. Snow's assertion that the humanities and sciences form two antagonistic, mutually unintelligible cultures in today's world. He admits that as an institution, as a profession, science has separated itself from the methods and insights of religion, art, and speculation—the areas of human creativity studied by the humanities. He even provides examples of this split, as when he tells of the young science colleague who, when he finds Eiseley reading J. R. R. Tolkien, sneers, "I wouldn't waste my time with a man who writes fairy stories." (¶7) Eiseley is clear that science has become "a professional body, and with professionalism there tends to emerge a greater emphasis upon a coherent system of regulations" (¶20) that produce a "deliberate blunting of wonder" (¶19).

But Eiseley is also clear that this division is a product of misunderstanding, that it occurs only at superficial levels within both humanistic and scientific activity. It is an illusion—a dangerous illusion with potentially disastrous consequences, to be sure—but an illusion nevertheless. The molds that the humanists and scientists cast each other in, Eiseley says, "are always useful to the mediocre conformist" (¶22)—useful, that is, to the thinker who has no sense of wonder, no personal vision, and therefore nothing original to say. But "happily," he continues later, "the very great in science . . . have been singularly free of this folly" (¶38), and he goes on to cite Leonardo da Vinci, Newton, Darwin, and Einstein as great scientific thinkers who all "retained a simple sense of wonder . . . [and who] all show a deep humility and an emotional hunger which is the prerogative of the artist" (¶38). "Creation in science," says Eiseley, "demands a high level of imaginative insight and intuitive perception" (¶25), which leaves us free to conclude, as indeed Eiseley implies, that the fence building, sloganeering, and sneering that go on between the mediocre professionals in both cultures are the opposite of creative. Such hostility is stultifying and deadening, and it leads to that curious feature of the modern mind noted by Santayana, the mind that has "seemed to lose courage and to become ashamed of its own fertility" (¶3).

As you read, ask yourself how much the conformist molds seem to characterize the thinking about scientists and humanists at your college or university. How much, and how uncritically, have you accepted such polarized, cliché-ridden thinking yourself? It would be odd if you had not accepted it, for, as both Snow and Eiseley agree, it pervades much of the thinking today not only about *scientists and humanists but* by *scientists and humanists. Finally, ask yourself whether Snow and Eiseley have given you good reasons for re-thinking any prejudices you may have held and in what ways your education and society at large would both benefit if the rift between the two cultures were closed.*

THE ILLUSION OF THE TWO CULTURES

From *The American Scholar* (1964) and *The Star Thrower* (1978).

Not long ago an English scientist, Sir Eric Ashby, remarked that "to train young people in the dialectic between orthodoxy and dissent is the unique contribution which universities make to society." I am sure that Sir Eric meant by this remark that nowhere but in universities are the young given the opportunity to absorb past tradition and at the same time to experience the impact of new ideas—in the sense of a constant dialogue between past and present—lived in every hour of the student's existence. This dialogue, ideally, should lead to a great winnowing and sifting of experience and to a heightened consciousness of self which, in turn, should lead on to greater sensitivity and perception on the part of the individual. 1

Our lives are the creation of memory and the accompanying power to extend ourselves outward into ideas and relive them. The finest intellect is that which employs an invisible web of gossamer running into the past as well as across the minds of living men and which constantly responds to the vibrations transmitted through these tenuous lines of sympathy. It would be contrary to fact, however, to assume that our universities always perform this unique function of which Sir Eric speaks, with either grace or perfection; in fact our investment in man, it has been justly remarked, is deteriorating even as the financial investment in science grows. 2

More than thirty years ago, George Santayana* had already sensed this trend. He commented, in a now-forgotten essay, that one of the strangest consequences of modern science was that as the visible wealth of nature was more and more transferred and abstracted, the mind seemed to lose courage and to become ashamed of its own fertility. "The hard-pressed natural man will not indulge his imagination," continued Santayana, "unless it poses for truth; and being half-aware of this imposition, he is more troubled at the thought of being deceived than at the fact of being mechanized or being bored; and he would wish to escape imagination altogether." 3

*George Santayana (1863–1952), Spanish-American poet and philosopher and Harvard professor.

"Man would wish to escape imagination altogether." I repeat that last phrase, for it defines a peculiar aberration of the human mind found on both sides of that bipolar division between the humanities and the sciences, which C. P. Snow has popularized under the title of *The Two Cultures.* The idea is not solely a product of this age. It was already emerging with the science of the seventeenth century; one finds it in Bacon.* One finds the fear of it faintly foreshadowed in Thoreau. Thomas Huxley† lent it weight when he referred contemptuously to the "caterwauling of poets." 4

Ironically, professional scientists berated the early evolutionists such as Lamarck and Chambers for overindulgence in the imagination. Almost eighty years ago John Burroughs observed that some of the animus once directed by science toward dogmatic theology seemed in his day increasingly to be vented upon the literary naturalist. In the early 1900s a quarrel over "nature faking" raised a confused din in America and aroused W. H. Hudson to some dry and pungent comment upon the failure to distinguish the purposes of science from those of literature. I know of at least one scholar who, venturing to develop some personal ideas in an essay for the layman, was characterized by a reviewer in a leading professional journal as a worthless writer, although, as it chanced, the work under discussion had received several awards in literature, one of them international in scope. More recently, some scholars not indifferent to humanistic values have exhorted poets to leave their personal songs in order to portray the beauty and symmetry of molecular structures. 5

Now some very fine verse has been written on scientific subjects, but, I fear, very little under the dictate of scientists as such. Rather there is evident here precisely that restriction of imagination against which Santayana inveighed; namely, an attempt to constrain literature itself to the delineation of objective or empiric truth, and to dismiss the whole domain of value, which after all constitutes the very nature of man, as without significance and beneath contempt. 6

Unconsciously, the human realm is denied in favor of the world of pure technics. Man, the tool user, grows convinced that he is himself only useful as a tool, that fertility except in the use of the scientific imagination is wasteful and without purpose, even, in some indefinable way, sinful. I was reading J. R. R. Tolkien's great symbolic trilogy, *The Fellowship of the Ring,* a few months ago, when a young scientist of my acquaintance paused and looked over my shoulder. After a little casual interchange the man departed leaving an accusing remark hovering in the air between us. "I wouldn't waste my time with a man who writes fairy stories." He might as well have added, "or with a man who reads them." 7

As I went back to my book I wondered vaguely in what leafless land- 8

*Francis Bacon (1561–1626), philosopher and author whose works were instrumental in furthering the development of modern science.

†Thomas Henry Huxley (1825–1895), English biologist, best known in his own day as "Darwin's bulldog" for his spirited defense and popularization of evolutionary theory.

scape one grew up without Hans Christian Andersen, or Dunsany, or even Jules Verne.* There lingered about the young man's words a puritanism which seemed the more remarkable because, as nearly as I could discover, it was unmotivated by any sectarian religiosity unless a total dedication to science brings to some minds a similar authoritarian desire to shackle the human imagination. After all, it is this impossible, fertile world of our imagination which gave birth to liberty in the midst of oppression, and which persists in seeking until what is sought is seen. Against such invisible and fearful powers, there can be found in all ages and in all institutions—even the institutions of professional learning—the humorless man with the sneer, or if the sneer does not suffice, then the torch, for the bright unperishing letters of the human dream.

One can contrast this recalcitrant attitude with an 1890 reminiscence 9
from that great Egyptologist Sir Flinders Petrie, which steals over into the realm of pure literature. It was written, in unconscious symbolism, from a tomb:

"I here live, and do not scramble to fit myself to the requirements of 10
others. In a narrow tomb, with the figure of Néfermaat standing on each side of me—as he has stood through all that we know as human history—I have just room for my bed, and a row of good reading in which I can take pleasure after dinner. Behind me is that Great Peace, the Desert. It is an entity—a power—just as much as the sea is. No wonder men fled to it from the turmoil of the ancient world."

It may now reasonably be asked why one who has similarly, if less 11
dramatically, spent his life among the stones and broken shards of the remote past should be writing here about matters involving literature and science. While I was considering this with humility and trepidation, my eye fell upon a stone in my office. I am sure that professional journalists must recall times when an approaching deadline has keyed all their senses and led them to glance wildly around in the hope that something might leap out at them from the most prosaic surroundings. At all events my eyes fell upon this stone.

Now the stone antedated anything that the historians would call art; it 12
had been shaped many hundreds of thousands of years ago by men whose faces would frighten us if they sat among us today. Out of old habit, since I like the feel of worked flint, I picked it up and hefted it as I groped for words over this difficult matter of the growing rift between science and art. Certainly the stone was of no help to me; it was a utilitarian thing which had cracked marrow bones, if not heads, in the remote dim morning of the human species. It was nothing if not practical. It was, in fact, an extremely early example of the empirical tradition which has led on to modern science.

The mind which had shaped this artifact knew its precise purpose. It 13
had found out by experimental observation that the stone was tougher, sharper, more enduring than the hand which wielded it. The creature's mind

*Andersen (1805–1875), Edward Plunkett (1878–1957), eighteenth baron of Dunsany, and Verne (1828–1905) were all writers of fairy tales or adventure stories popular with children.

had solved the question of the best form of the implement and how it could be manipulated most effectively. In its day and time this hand ax was as grand an intellectual achievement as a rocket.

As a scientist my admiration went out to that unidentified workman. 14
How he must have labored to understand the forces involved in the fracturing of flint, and all that involved practical survival in his world. My uncalloused twentieth-century hand caressed the yellow stone lovingly. It was then that I made a remarkable discovery.

In the mind of this gross-featured early exponent of the practical ap- 15
proach to nature—the technician, the no-nonsense practitioner of survival—two forces had met and merged. There had not been room in his short and desperate life for the delicate and supercilious separation of the arts from the sciences. There did not exist then the refined distinctions set up between the scholarly percipience of reality and what has sometimes been called the vaporings of the artistic imagination.

As I clasped and unclasped the stone, running my fingers down its 16
edges, I began to perceive the ghostly emanations from a long-vanished mind, the kind of mind which, once having shaped an object of any sort, leaves an individual trace behind it which speaks to others across the barriers of time and language. It was not the practical experimental aspect of this mind that startled me, but rather that the fellow had wasted time.

In an incalculably brutish and dangerous world he had both shaped an 17
instrument of practical application and then, with a virtuoso's elegance, proceeded to embellish his product. He had not been content to produce a plain, utilitarian implement. In some wistful, inarticulate way, in the grip of the dim aesthetic feelings which are one of the marks of man—or perhaps I should say, some men—this archaic creature had lingered over his handiwork.

One could still feel him crouching among the stones on a long-vanished 18
river bar, turning the thing over in his hands, feeling its polished surface, striking, here and there, just one more blow that no longer had usefulness as its criterion. He had, like myself, enjoyed the texture of the stone. With skills lost to me, he had gone on flaking the implement with an eye to beauty until it had become a kind of rough jewel, equivalent in its day to the carved and gold-inlaid pommel of the iron dagger placed in Tutankhamen's tomb.

All the later history of man contains these impractical exertions ex- 19
pended upon a great diversity of objects, and, with literacy, breaking even into printed dreams. Today's secular disruption between the creative aspect of art and that of science is a barbarism that would have brought lifted eyebrows in a Cro-Magnon cave. It is a product of high technical specialization, the deliberate blunting of wonder, and the equally deliberate suppression of a phase of our humanity in the name of an authoritarian institution, science, which has taken on, in our time, curious puritanical overtones. Many scientists seem unaware of the historical reasons for this development or the fact that the creative aspect of art is not so remote from that of science as may seem, at first glance, to be the case.

I am not so foolish as to categorize individual scholars or scientists. I am, 20 however, about to remark on the nature of science as an institution. Like all such structures it is apt to reveal certain behavioral rigidities and conformities which increase with age. It is no longer the domain of the amateur, though some of its greatest discoverers could be so defined. It is now a professional body, and with professionalism there tends to emerge a greater emphasis upon a coherent system of regulations.* The deviant is more sharply treated, and the young tend to imitate their successful elders. In short, an "Establishment"—a trade union—has appeared.

Similar tendencies can be observed among those of the humanities concerned with the professional analysis and interpretation of the works of the creative artist. Here too, a similar rigidity and exclusiveness make their appearance. It is not that in the case of both the sciences and the humanities standards are out of place. What I am briefly cautioning against is that too frequently they afford an excuse for stifling original thought or constricting much latent creativity within traditional molds. 21

Such molds are always useful to the mediocre conformist who instinctively castigates and rejects what he cannot imitate. Tradition, the continuity of learning, are, it is true, enormously important to the learned disciplines. What we must realize as scientists is that the particular institution we inhabit has its own irrational accretions and authoritarian dogmas which can be as unpleasant as some of those encountered in sectarian circles—particularly so since they are frequently unconsciously held and surrounded by an impenetrable wall of self-righteousness brought about because science is regarded as totally empiric and open-minded by tradition. 22

This type of professionalism, as I shall label it in order to distinguish it from what is best in both the sciences and humanities, is characterized by two assumptions: that the accretions of fact are cumulative and lead to progress, whereas the insights of art are, at best, singular, and lead nowhere, or, when introduced into the realm of science, produce obscurity and confusion. The convenient label "mystic" is, in our day, readily applied to men who pause for simple wonder, or who encounter along the borders of the known that "awful power" which Wordsworth characterized as the human imagination. It can, he says, rise suddenly from the mind's abyss and enwrap the solitary traveler like a mist. 23

We do not like mists in this era, and the word imagination is less and less used. We like, instead, a clear road, and we abhor solitary traveling. Indeed one of our great scientific historians remarked not long ago that the literary naturalist was obsolescent if not completely outmoded. I suppose he meant that with our penetration into the biophysical realm, life, like matter, would become increasingly represented by abstract symbols. To many it must appear that the more we can dissect life into its elements, the closer we are getting to its ultimate resolution. While I have some reservations on this score, they are not important. Rather, I should like to look at the symbols 24

*See Stephen Toulmin, "Science and Ethics" (pp. 665–673) for more on science as an institutionalized profession.

which in the one case denote science and in the other constitute those vaporings and cloud wraiths that are the abomination, so it is said, of the true scientist but are the delight of the poet and literary artist.

25 Creation in science demands a high level of imaginative insight and intuitive perception. I believe no one would deny this, even though it exists in varying degrees, just as it does, similarly, among writers, musicians, or artists. The scientist's achievement, however, is quantitatively transmissible. From a single point his discovery is verifiable by other men who may then, on the basis of corresponding data, accept the innovation and elaborate upon it in the cumulative fashion which is one of the great triumphs of science.

26 Artistic creation, on the other hand, is unique. It cannot be twice discovered, as, say, natural selection was discovered. It may be imitated stylistically, in a genre, a school, but, save for a few items of technique, it is not cumulative. A successful work of art may set up reverberations and is, in this, just as transmissible as science, but there is a qualitative character about it. Each reverberation in another mind is unique. As the French novelist François Mauriac has remarked, each great novel is a separate and distinct world operating under its own laws with a flora and fauna totally its own. There is communication, or the work is a failure, but the communication releases our own visions, touches some highly personal chord in our own experience.

27 The symbols used by the great artist are a key releasing our humanity from the solitary tower of the self. "Man," says Lewis Mumford, "is first and foremost the self-fabricating animal." I shall merely add that the artist plays an enormous role in this act of self-creation. It is he who touches the hidden strings of pity, who searches our hearts, who makes us sensitive to beauty, who asks questions about fate and destiny. Such questions, though they lurk always around the corners of the external universe which is the peculiar province of science, the rigors of the scientific method do not enable us to pursue directly.

28 And yet I wonder.

29 It is surely possible to observe that it is the successful analogy or symbol which frequently allows the scientist to leap from a generalization in one field of thought to a triumphant achievement in another. For example, Progressionism in a spiritual sense later became the model contributing to the discovery of organic evolution. Such analogies genuinely resemble the figures and enchantments of great literature, whose meanings similarly can never be totally grasped because of their endless power to ramify in the individual mind.

30 John Donne gave powerful expression to a feeling applicable as much to science as to literature when he said devoutly of certain Biblical passages: "The literall sense is alwayes to be preserved; but the literall sense is not alwayes to be discerned; for the literall sense is not alwayes that which the very letter and grammar of the place presents." A figurative sense, he argues cogently, can sometimes be the most "literall intention of the Holy Ghost."

31 It is here that the scientist and artist sometimes meet in uneasy opposition, or at least along lines of tension. The scientist's attitude is sometimes,

I suspect, that embodied in Samuel Johnson's remark that, wherever there is mystery, roguery is not far off.

Yet surely it was not roguery when Sir Charles Lyell* glimpsed in a few fossil prints of raindrops the persistence of the world's natural forces through the incredible, mysterious aeons of geologic time. The fossils were a symbol of a vast hitherto unglimpsed order. They are, in Donne's sense, both literal and symbolic. As fossils they merely denote evidence of rain in a past era. Figuratively they are more. To the perceptive intelligence they afford the hint of lengthened natural order, just as the eyes of ancient trilobites† tell us similarly of the unchanging laws of light. Equally, the educated mind may discern in a scratched pebble the retreating shadow of vast ages of ice and gloom. In Donne's archaic phraseology these objects would bespeak the principal intention of the Divine Being—that is, of order beyond our power to grasp. 32

Such images drawn from the world of science are every bit as powerful as great literary symbolism and equally demanding upon the individual imagination of the scientist who would fully grasp the extension of meaning which is involved. It is, in fact, one and the same creative act in both domains. 33

Indeed evolution itself has become such a figurative symbol, as has also the hypothesis of the expanding universe. The laboratory worker may think of these concepts in a totally empirical fashion as subject to proof or disproof by the experimental method. Like Freud's doctrine of the subconscious, however, such ideas frequently escape from the professional scientist into the public domain. There they may undergo further individual transformation and embellishment. Whether the scholar approves or not, such hypotheses are now as free to evolve in the mind of the individual as are the creations of art. All the resulting enrichment and confusion will bear about it something suggestive of the world of artistic endeavor. 34

As figurative insights into the nature of things, such embracing conceptions may become grotesquely distorted or glow with added philosophical wisdom. As in the case of the trilobite eye or the fossil raindrop, there lurks behind the visible evidence vast shadows no longer quite of that world which we term natural. Like the words in Donne's Bible, enormous implications have transcended the literal expression of the thought. Reality itself has been superseded by a greater reality. As Donne himself asserted, "The substance of the truth is in the great images which lie behind." 35

It is because these two types of creation—the artistic and the scientific—have sprung from the same being and have their points of contact even in division that I have the temerity to assert that, in a sense, the "two cultures" are an illusion, that they are a product of unreasoning fear, professionalism, and misunderstanding. Because of the emphasis upon science in our society, much has been said about the necessity of educating the layman and even the 36

*Lyell's (1795–1875) *Principles of Geology* (1830–1833) earned him the popular title of "father of geology."

†Fossils of Paleozoic marine arthropods.

professional student of the humanities upon the ways and the achievements of science. I admit that a barrier exists, but I am also concerned to express the view that there persists in the domain of science itself an occasional marked intolerance of those of its own membership who venture to pursue the way of letters. As I have remarked, this intolerance can the more successfully clothe itself in seeming objectivity because of the supposed open nature of the scientific society. It is not remarkable that this trait is sometimes more manifest in the younger and less secure disciplines.

There was a time, not too many centuries ago, when to be active in 37
scientific investigation was to invite suspicion. Thus it may be that there now lingers among us, even in the triumph of the experimental method, a kind of vague fear of that other artistic world of deep emotion, of strange symbols, lest it seize upon us or distort the hard-won objectivity of our thinking—lest it corrupt, in other words, that crystalline and icy objectivity which, in our scientific guise, we erect as a model of conduct. This model, incidentally, if pursued to its absurd conclusion, would lead to a world in which the computer would determine all aspects of our existence; one in which the bomb would be as welcome as the discoveries of the physician.

Happily, the very great in science, or even those unique scientist-artists 38
such as Leonardo, who foreran the emergence of science as an institution, have been singularly free from this folly. Darwin decried it even as he recognized that he had paid a certain price in concentrated specialization for his achievement. Einstein, it is well known, retained a simple sense of wonder; Newton felt like a child playing with pretty shells on a beach. All show a deep humility and an emotional hunger which is the prerogative of the artist. It is with the lesser men, with the institutionalization of method, with the appearance of dogma and mapped-out territories, that an unpleasant suggestion of fenced preserves begins to dominate the university atmosphere.

As a scientist, I can say that I have observed it in my own and others' 39
specialties. I have had occasion, also, to observe its effects in the humanities. It is not science *per se;* it is, instead, in both regions of thought, the narrow professionalism which is also plainly evident in the trade union. There can be small men in science just as there are small men in government or business. In fact it is one of the disadvantages of big science, just as it is of big government, that the availability of huge sums attracts a swarm of elbowing and contentious men to whom great dreams are less than protected hunting preserves.

The sociology of science deserves at least equal consideration with the 40
biographies of the great scientists, for powerful and changing forces are at work upon science, the institution, as contrasted with science as a dream and an ideal of the individual. Like other aspects of society, it is a construct of men and is subject, like other social structures, to human pressures and inescapable distortions.

Let me give an illustration. Even in learned journals, clashes occasionally 41
occur between those who would regard biology as a separate and distinct domain of inquiry and the reductionists who, by contrast, perceive in the

living organism only a vaster and more random chemistry. Understandably, the concern of the reductionists is with the immediate. Thomas Hobbes was expressing a similar point of view when he castigated poets as "working on mean minds with words and distinctions that of themselves signifie nothing, but betray (by their obscurity) that there walketh . . . another kingdome, as it were a kingdome of fayries in the dark." I myself have been similarly criticized for speaking of a nature "beyond the nature that we know."

Yet consider for a moment this dark, impossible realm of "fayrie." Man is not totally compounded of the nature we profess to understand. He contains, instead, a lurking unknown future, just as the man-apes of the Pliocene contained in embryo the future that surrounds us now. The world of human culture itself was an unpredictable fairy world until, in some pre-ice-age meadow, the first meaningful sounds in all the world broke through the jungle babble of the past, the nature, until that moment, "known." 42

It is fascinating to observe that, in the very dawn of science, Francis Bacon, the spokesman for the empirical approach to nature, shared with Shakespeare, the poet, a recognition of the creativeness which adds to nature, and which emerges from nature as "an art which nature makes." Neither the great scholar nor the great poet had renounced this "kingdome of fayries." Both had realized what Henri Bergson was later to express so effectively, that life inserts a vast "indetermination into matter." It is, in a sense, an intrusion from a realm which can never be completely subject to prophetic analysis by science. The novelties of evolution emerge; they cannot be predicted. They haunt, until their arrival, a world of unimaginable possibilities behind the living screen of events, as these last exist to the observer confined to a single point on the time scale. 43

Oddly enough, much of the confusion that surrounded my phrase, "a nature beyond the nature that we know," resolves itself into pure semantics. I might have pointed out what must be obvious even to the most dedicated scientific mind—that the nature which we know has been many times reinterpreted in human thinking, and that the hard, substantial matter of the nineteenth century has already vanished into a dark, bodiless void, a web of "events" in space-time.* This is a realm, I venture to assert, as weird as any we have tried, in the past, to exorcise by the brave use of seeming solid words. Yet some minds exhibit an almost instinctive hostility toward the mere attempt to wonder or to ask what lies below that microcosmic world out of which emerge the particles which compose our bodies and which now take on this wraithlike quality. 44

Is there something here we fear to face, except when clothed in safely 45

*In nineteenth-century physics, matter was viewed as determinate and predictable. It was thought that when physics finally succeeded in isolating the smallest particle of matter, the ultimate building block of reality would be revealed. Today, however, physics has given up the idea that there *is* an ultimate particle. Reality seems much more mysterious to physics today than it did 100 years ago. The smallest particles seem to be neither solid matter nor electromagnetic waves, yet they sometimes act like both. And the ultimate "facts" in particle physics seem not to be the predictable motion of solid particles but statistically "guessed at" *events.*

sterilized professional speech? Have we grown reluctant in this age of power to admit mystery and beauty into our thoughts, or to learn where power ceases? I referred earlier to one of our own forebears on a gravel bar, thumbing a pebble. If, after the ages of building and destroying, if after the measuring of light-years and the powers probed at the atom's heart, if after the last iron is rust-eaten and the last glass lies shattered in the streets, a man, some savage, some remnant of what once we were, pauses on his way to the tribal drinking place and feels rising from within his soul the inexplicable mist of terror and beauty that is evoked from old ruins—even the ruins of the greatest city in the world—then, I say, all will still be well with man.

And if that savage can pluck a stone from the gravel because it shone 46 like crystal when the water rushed over it, and hold it against the sunset, he will be as we were in the beginning, whole—as we were when we were children, before we began to split the knowledge from the dream. All talk of the two cultures is an illusion; it is the pebble which tells man's story. Upon it is written man's two faces, the artistic and the practical. They are expressed upon one stone over which a hand once closed, no less firm because the mind behind it was submerged in light and shadow and deep wonder.

Today we hold a stone, the heavy stone of power. We must perceive 47 beyond it, however, by the aid of the artistic imagination, those humane insights and understandings which alone can lighten our burden and enable us to shape ourselves, rather than the stone, into the forms which great art has anticipated.

Questions for Discussion

1. What logic or principle of development connects the first three paragraphs of Eiseley's essay with paragraph 4, in which he seems to focus on his thesis? What would be gained or lost if the first three paragraphs were dropped?
2. Once you are sure of the meanings of *dialectic, orthodoxy,* and *dissent,* do you agree that "to train young people in the dialectic between orthodoxy and dissent is the unique contribution which universities make to society" (¶1)? Do you feel that this *should* be the aim of university teaching? Why or why not? Do you feel that this aim governs the teaching at your institution? If not, and if you think it should, what obstacles can you identify as blocking that aim? And finally, can you offer any remedies for the removal or at least the mitigation of these obstacles?
3. If you were the editor of this book and wanted to write a footnote explaining Eiseley's meaning in the first two sentences of paragraph 2, how could you make use of Jacob Bronowski's essay "The Reach of Imagination" (pp. 238–245) in writing a commentary? Is there a quotation in Bronowski's

essay that amplifies and thus helps clarify Eiseley's point? Offer it to the rest of your class for discussion.

4. Do you agree with Santayana that people are so imprisoned by their notions of practicality that "the hard-pressed natural man will not indulge his imagination unless it poses for truth; and being half-aware of this imposition, he is more troubled at the thought of being deceived than at the fact of being mechanized or being bored" (¶3)? Can you provide examples of people who think of imaginative works as, if not downright deceiving, at least not leading to useful truth? How would you use material from the essays by Thomas Love Peacock (pp. 287–289) and E. M. Forster (pp. 291–296) to help clarify the issues raised in this question?
5. Eiseley's prose offers a flood of allusions to other writers and thinkers, including fairy-tale writers, philosophers, poets, anthropologists, literary critics, and, of course, natural scientists. The richness of his thinking seems directly related to the richness of this wide-ranging reading. How much of your own education is dominated by the desire to acquire something like this richness for yourself, to build it into the quality of your own mind? If this is not a personal goal for you, on what grounds do you reject or neglect it? Do most of your friends and peers hold to this goal? Do your teachers hold to it, either for themselves or for you? Should they? If those who do not hold to this goal were to adopt it, what differences would it make in their teaching and testing?
6. What fundamental traits in human nature does Eiseley see expressed in the decorative (or at least non-utilitarian) markings on the flint ax (¶16)? How does he use these markings as evidence in this argument that the division between the two cultures is merely an illusion?

Suggested Essay Topics

1. If you have ever had any teachers whose prejudiced views about either the sciences or the humanities have helped to reinforce the split between the two cultures, pick one such teacher now, either a scientist or a humanist, and address an essay in the form of a letter to that person, arguing that such prejudices are unreasonable and in the end deny to both the sciences and the humanities what is most creative in them. You will of course want to use Snow and Eiseley as sources for some of your ideas, but add any thinking of your own that will support the argument.
2. If you are majoring in neither the sciences nor the humanities but instead in some social science or pre-professional program such as business, nursing, accounting, or radio and television, and if you know that some of your peers or teachers in your field think that *both* the sciences and humanities are boring, irrelevant, or impractical, write an essay in the form of a letter to one of them arguing that people in the technical fields need the insights of the sciences and the humanities as much as anyone else; give the best reasons you can to support your claims.

11

RELIGIOUS PERSPECTIVES

Belief Versus Unbelief

We have just enough religion to make us hate, but not enough to make us love one another.
Jonathan Swift

The fairest thing we can experience is the mysterious. It is the fundamental emotion which stands at the cradle of true art and true science. He who knows it not, who can no longer wonder, can no longer feel amazement, is as good as dead, a snuffed-out candle.
Albert Einstein

For my own part, the sense of spiritual relief which comes from rejecting the idea of God as supernatural being is enormous. I see no other way of bridging the gap between the religious and the scientific approach to reality.
Julian Huxley

Incomprehensible? But because you cannot understand a thing, it does not cease to exist.
Blaise Pascal

Religion is a passion for righteousness, and for the spread of righteousness, conceived as a cosmic demand.
William Ernest Hocking

Many people . . . have been extremely religious and extremely wicked.
R. H. Thouless

Truth is the supreme God for me. Truth is God.
Gandhi

Religion . . . is the opium of the people.
Karl Marx

My country is the world, and my religion is to do good.
Thomas Paine

Elie Wiesel

Elie Wiesel (b. 1928), novelist and biblical commentator, winner of the Nobel Prize for literature, has written book after book since World War II, seeking a way to talk about religious questions while living with memories of the Nazi holocaust. How can a Jew—how can anyone—believe in and talk about God's loving care for his "chosen people" knowing that 6 million Jews and countless others were massacred? How can any sensitive person speak joyfully of "the sacred" after such an event? How can anyone have the courage or effrontery to affirm God's creation in the light of such horrors?

Wiesel has pursued such questions mainly in his novels, among them The Gates of the Forest, The Town Beyond the Wall, *and* A Beggar in Jerusalem. *Here we meet him in a different role, traditional in Jewish culture: that of the spiritual inquirer who wrestles with moral and spiritual problems by writing commentary on the mysterious stories in the Torah about the patriarchs, Israel's "founding fathers." In this essay, Wiesel comments on Genesis 22, in which God commands Abraham to sacrifice his son, Isaac. This powerful story has always raised difficult questions, and Wiesel says the questions troubled him even as a child. Why do the innocent suffer? How can God ask of anyone such a terrible sacrifice as that of a son? How could Abraham have enough faith to accept such an awful command? And why is the story told just* this *way?*

Wiesel finds the story of Abraham and Isaac raising the same questions that are raised by the Nazi holocaust, and, as you might expect, he arrives at no simple, unambiguous reassurance about the meaning of evil and suffering in the world. But he does offer a path to the kind of spiritual insight, often humorous but always profound, that Jewish commentators have traditionally exhibited in the Midrash*—a term that refers both to a way of interpreting scripture and to the content of the accumulated stories and interpretations that the method has produced over millennia.*

It is important when reading commentary of this kind not to worry about the literal historical status of the stories themselves. Their value lies not in their factuality but in their meaning, and such meaning is always oblique and allusive, usually tentative, and sometimes downright puzzling—like the experience of evil and suffering in life itself.

THE SACRIFICE OF ISAAC

A Strange Tale About Fear, Faith, and Laughter

From "The Sacrifice of Isaac: A Survivor's Story," in *Messengers of God: Biblical Portraits and Legends* (1976).

This strange tale is about fear and faith, fear and defiance, fear and laughter. 1

Terrifying in content, it has become a source of consolation to those 2
who, in retelling it, make it part of their own experience. Here is a story that contains Jewish destiny in its totality, just as the flame is contained in the single spark by which it comes to life. Every major theme, every passion and obsession that make Judaism the adventure that it is, can be traced back to it: man's anguish when he finds himself face to face with God, his quest for purity and purpose, the conflict of having to choose between dreams of the past and dreams of the future, between absolute faith and absolute justice, between the need to obey God's will and to rebel against it; between his yearnings for freedom and for sacrifice, his desire to justify hope and despair with words and silence—the same words and the same silence. It is all there.

As a literary composition, this tale—known as the *Akeda*—is unmatched 3
in Scripture. Austere and powerful, its every word reverberates into infinity, evoking suspense and drama, uncovering a whole mood based on a before and continuing into an after, culminating in a climax which endows its characters with another dimension. They are human—and more: forceful and real despite the metaphysical implications. At every step, their condition remains relevant and of burning gravity.

This very ancient story is still our own and we shall continue to be 4
bound to it in the most intimate way. We may not know it, but every one of us, at one time or another, is called upon to play a part in it. What part? Are we Abraham or Isaac? We are Jacob, that is to say, Israel. And Israel began with Abraham.*

Let us reread the text. 5

Once upon a time there lived a man for all seasons, blessed with all 6
talents and virtues, deserving of every grace. His name was Abraham and his mission was to serve as God's messenger among men too vain and blind to recognize His glory. Tradition rates him higher than Moses—whose Law he observed; higher even than Adam—whose errors he was asked to correct.

Abraham: the first enemy of idolatry. The first angry young man. The 7
first rebel to rise up against the "establishment," society and authority. The

*Isaac's son, Jacob, received the name "Israel" when he strove with the angel and prevailed (Genesis 32). The name later designated the 12 tribes, represented in Genesis by Jacob's 12 sons.

first to demystify official taboos and suspend ritual prohibitions. The first to reject civilization in order to form a minority of one. The first believer, the first one to suffer for his belief. Alone against the world, he declared himself free. Alone against the world, he braved the fire and the mob, affirming that God is one and present wherever His name is invoked; that one is the secret and the beginning of all that exists in heaven and on earth and that God's secret coincides with that of man.

And yet. Notwithstanding his total faith in God and His justice, His 8
kindness as well, he did not for a moment hesitate to take God to task as he tried to save two condemned cities from destruction:* How can You—who embody justice—be unjust? He was the first who dared query God. And God listened and answered. For unlike Job, Abraham was protesting on behalf of others, not of himself. God forgave Abraham everything, including his questions. God is God and Abraham was His faithful servant; one was sure of the other. To test his will and vision, God had made him leave the security of his father's home, challenge rulers and engage their armies in battle, endure hunger and exile, disgrace and fire. His trust in God was never shaken. So loyal was he to God that he was rewarded with a son who became symbol and bearer of grace and benediction for generations to come.

Then one day God decided once more to test him—for the tenth and 9
last time: Take your son and bring him to Me as an offering. The term used is *ola,* which means an offering that has been totally consumed, a holocaust. And Abraham complied. Without an argument. Without questioning or even trying to understand, without trying to stall. Without a word to anyone, not even his wife Sarah, without a tear; he simply waited for the next morning and left the house before she awakened. He saddled his donkey, and accompanied by his son and two servants, started on the road to Mount Moriah. After a three-day journey—which according to Kierkegaard† lasted longer than the four thousand years separating us from the event—father and son left the servants and donkey behind and began their ascent of the mountain. When they reached the top they erected an altar and prepared for the ritual. Everything was ready: the wood, the knife, the fire. Slaughterer and victim looked into each other's eyes and for one moment all of creation held its breath. The same fear penetrated the father and the son. A Midrash describes Isaac's fear. Stretched out on the altar, his wrists and ankles bound, Isaac saw the Temple in Jerusalem first destroyed and then rebuilt, and at the moment of the supreme test, Isaac understood that what was happening to him would happen to others, that this was to be a tale without an end, an experience to be endured by his children and theirs.‡ Never would they be spared the torture. The father's anguish, on the other hand, was not linked to the future; by sacrificing his son to obey God's will, Abraham knew that he was, in fact,

*Sodom and Gomorrah (see Genesis 18).

†Søren Kierkegaard (1813–1855), Danish philosopher and religious thinker.

‡The "Temple in Jerusalem" is Solomon's Temple, first built on the summit of Mt. Moriah where Abraham and Isaac's story takes place. Its history of repeated construction and destruction here symbolizes the history of the sufferings of the Jews.

sacrificing his knowledge *of* God and his faith *in* Him. If Isaac were to die, to whom would the father transmit this faith, this knowledge? The end of Isaac would connote the end of a prodigious adventure: the first would become the last. One cannot conceive of a more crushing or more devastating anguish: I shall thus have lived, suffered and caused others to suffer for nothing.

And the miracle took place. Death was defeated, the tragedy averted. 10
The blade that could have cut the line—and prevented Israel from being born—was halted, suspended.

Was thus the mystery resolved? Hardly. As one plunges into Midrashic 11
literature, one feels its poignancy. It leaves one troubled. The question is no longer whether Isaac was saved but whether the miracle could happen again. And how often. And for what reasons. And at what cost.

As a child, I read and reread this tale, my heart beating wildly; I felt dark 12
apprehension come over me and carry me far away.

There was no understanding the three characters. Why would God, the 13
merciful Father, demand that Abraham become inhuman, and why would Abraham accept? And Isaac, why did he submit so meekly? Not having received a direct order to let himself be sacrificed, why did he consent?

I could not understand. If God needs human suffering to be God, how 14
can man foresee an end to that suffering? And if faith in God must result in self-denial, how can faith claim to elevate and improve man?

These were painful questions, especially for an adolescent, because they 15
did not fit into the framework of the sin-punishment concept, to which all religious thought had accustomed us.

. . .

To me the *Akeda* was an unfathomable mystery given to every genera- 16
tion, to be relived, if not solved—one of the great mysteries of our history, a mystery so opaque that it obscures not only the facts but also the names of the protagonists.

Why did Abraham, the would-be slaughterer, become, in our prayers, 17
the symbol of *hesed:* grace, compassion and love? A symbol of love, he who was ready to throttle his son?

And Isaac, why was he called Isaac? *Yitzhak?* He who will laugh? Laugh 18
at whom? At what? Or, as Sarah thought, he who will make others laugh? Why was the most tragic figure in Biblical history given such a bizarre name?

. . .

What do we know about his [Abraham's] life and his person? Many 19
things told to us by the Bible and expounded upon by the Midrash. We are treated to an abundance of precise and picturesque details on both his private and public activities. We are informed about his habits, his moods, his business relationships, his difficulties with his neighbors, his servants and his concubines. He was rich, hospitable, friendly and giving; he invited strangers into his home without asking who they were or what the purpose of their

visit might be. He welcomed the hungry and helped the poor, angels and beggars alike, offering them both shelter and food.

. . .

He evidently was a restless man who could not stay idle long. He was 20
forever seeking new stimulation, new certainties; he abhorred all routine. He would go from Haran to Canaan, sometimes pushing as far as Damascus, in his search for worthy adversaries. He was an explorer of some stature who affronted kings and robbers, and enjoyed defeating them, exulting when he broke their pride.

Yet his greatest adventure was his encounter with God—an encounter 21
which was a result of deliberate choice on both sides. They addressed one another as equals. According to the Midrash, God said to Abraham: *Ani yekhidi veata yekhidi*—I am alone and you are alone, alone to know and proclaim it. From that moment on, their dialogue took place under the implacable sign of the absolute: they were to be both partners and accomplices. Before, says legend, God reigned only in heaven; it was Abraham who extended his rule unto the earth.

. . .

And one begins to wonder, since God and he loved one another so much 22
and collaborated so closely, why these tests? Why these ordeals and torture? Because God tests only the strong. The weak do not resist or resist poorly; they are of no consequence. But then, what good is it to resist, since God knows the outcome in advance? Answer: God knows, man does not.

Most commentators assume that Abraham was tested for his own good. 23
To serve as an example to the peoples of the world and to earn him their leaders' reverence. And also to harden him; to awaken in him an awareness of his own strength and potential.

Of course, this does not satisfy everyone: the idea that suffering is good 24
for Jews is one that owes its popularity to our enemies.

And indeed there is another explanation, though not a very original one, 25
that brings into the picture an old acquaintance, always present in moments of crisis and doubt: Satan. Source of all evil, supreme temptor. The easy, glib answer, the scapegoat. The crafty gambler, the unabashed liar. The servant who conveniently carries out the Master's dirty work, accepting all blame and anathema in His place. The sacrifice of Isaac? God had nothing to do with it; it was all Satan's doing. God did not want this test; Satan demanded it. The inhuman game was Satan's scheme and he bears full responsibility. Satan: the ideal alibi.

Just as he did with Job—who is frequently compared to Abraham for 26
more than one reason—Satan used gossip to distort and embellish history. On his return from an inspection tour on earth, he handed his report to the Almighty while telling Him his impressions. Thus he came to his surprise visit with Abraham, who was celebrating the birth of his beloved son Isaac. Rejoicing, sumptuous meals, public festivities, Satan did not spare the superlatives, as usual. And do You know, said he perfidiously, do You know that Your faithful servant Abraham has forgotten You—You? Yes indeed, his

good fortune has gone to his head; he forgot to set aside an offering for You. He thought only of his joy, as though it did not come from You; he fed all his guests, yet he neglected to offer You the youngest of his sheep, if only as a modest token of his gratitude. God was not convinced. He answered: No, no, you're wrong to suspect My faithful Abraham; he is devoted to Me, he loves Me, he would give Me all that he possesses—he would give me his son were I to ask him. Really? said Satan. Are You sure? I'm not. And God was provoked and felt compelled to accept the challenge. The rest can be found in Scripture.

The Biblical narrative is of exemplary purity of line, sobriety and terseness. Not one superfluous word, not one useless gesture. The imagery is striking, the language austere, the dialogue so incisive, it leaves one with a knot in one's throat. 27

. . . And, some time afterward, God put Abraham to the test. He said to him: Abraham. And he answered: Here I am. And He said: Take your son, your favored one, Isaac, whom you love, and go to the land of Moriah and offer him there as a burnt offering on one of the heights which I will point out to you. 28

This time Abraham did not answer: *Here I am;* he did not answer at all. He went home, lay down and fell asleep. The next morning he rose, awakened his son and two of his servants, and started out on his journey. At the end of three days—at the end of a silence that lasted three days—he saw the appointed place in the distance. He halted, and instructed the servants: *You stay here with the ass. The boy and I will go up there; we will worship and we will return to you.* 29

Abraham took the wood for the burnt offering and gave it to his son, Isaac. He himself took the firestone and the knife; and the two walked away together. 30

The last sentence gives us the key: one went to face death, the other to give it, but they went together; still close to one another though everything already separated them. God was waiting for them and they were going toward Him together. But then Isaac, who until that moment had not opened his mouth, turned to his father and uttered a single word: *Father.* And for the second time Abraham answered: *Here I am.* Was it because of the silence that followed this painfully hushed affirmation? Isaac began to feel uneasy; he wanted to be reassured or at least understand. 31

And Isaac said: Here is the firestone and the wood; but where is the sheep for the burnt offering? 32

Embarrassed, suddenly shy, Abraham tried to equivocate: *God will see to the sheep for His burnt offering, my son. And the two of them walked on together.* 33

The march continued. The two of them alone in the world, encircled by God's unfathomable design. But they were *together.* Now the repetition renders a new sound while adding to the dramatic intensity of the narrative. 34

And Isaac began to guess, to understand. And then he knew. And the father and the son remained united. Together they reached the top of the mountain; together they erected the altar; together they prepared the wood and the fire. Everything was ready, nothing was missing. And Isaac lay on the altar, silently gazing at his father. 35

And Abraham picked up the knife to slay his son. Then an angel of the Lord called to him from heaven: Abraham, Abraham! And he answered: Here I am. 36

For the third time he answered: *Here I am.* I am the same, the same person who answered Your first call; I answer Your call, whatever its nature; and even were *it* to change, *I* would not. 37

And the angel said: Do not raise your hand against the boy or do anything to him. For now I know that you fear God, since you have not withheld your son, your favored one, from Me. 38

All is well that ends well. The sacrifice took place, yet Isaac remained alive: a ram was slaughtered and burned in his stead. Abraham reconciled himself with his conscience. And the angel, exulting, renewed before him shining promises for the future: his children, as numerous as the stars reflected in the sea, would inherit the earth. Abraham once more plunged into the magnificent dream which would always remind him of his covenant with God. No, the future was not dead. No, truth would not be stifled. No, exile would not go on indefinitely. Abraham should have returned home a happy and serene man. Except that the tale ends with a strange sentence which opens rather than heals the wounds: *Vayashav avraham el nearav*—And Abraham returned to his servants. Note the singular: *Vayashav,* he returned. He, Abraham. Alone. And Isaac? Where was Isaac? Why was he not with his father? What had happened to him? Are we to understand that father and son were no longer together? That the experience they just shared had separated them—albeit only *after* the event? That Isaac, unlike Abraham, was no longer the same person, that the real Isaac remained there, on the altar? 39

These profoundly disquieting questions provoked passionate responses in the Midrash, where the theme of the *Akeda* occupies as important a place as the creation of the world or the revelation at Sinai. 40

The Midrash, in this case, does not limit itself to stating the facts and commenting upon them. It delves into the very heart and silence of the cast of characters. It examines them from every angle; it follows them into their innermost selves; it goes so far as to imagine the unimaginable. 41

. . .

On the morning of the third day, says the Midrash, Abraham could distinguish the appointed place from afar—just as the people did later before Sinai. He turned to his son and asked: Do you see what I see? Yes, replied Isaac, I see a splendid mountain under a cloud of fire. Then Abraham turned to his two servants and asked: And you, what do you see? The servants, passive onlookers, saw nothing but the desert. And Abraham understood that the event did not concern them and that they were to stay behind. And that the place was indeed the place. 42

And so the father and the son walked away together—*ze laakod veze léaked,* the one to bind and the other to be bound, *ze lishkhot veze lishakhet,* the one to slaughter and the other to be slaughtered—sharing the same allegiance to the same God, responding to the same call. The sacrifice was to be their joint offering; father and son had never before been so close. The Midrashic text 43 emphasizes this, as if to show another tragic aspect of the *Akeda,* namely, the equation between Abraham and Isaac. Abraham and Isaac were equals, in spite of their opposing roles as victim and executioner. But Abraham himself, whose victim was he? God's? Once more the key word is *yakhdav,* together: victims together. Together they gathered the wood, together they arranged it on the altar, together they set the stage for the drama to unfold. Abraham, says the text, behaved like a happy father preparing to celebrate his son's wedding, and Isaac like a groom about to meet his bride-to-be. Both were serene, at peace with themselves and each other.

But then, suddenly, for a brief moment, Isaac reentered reality and 44
grasped the magnitude and horror of what was to come: Father, what will you do, Mother and you, afterward? — He who has consoled us until now, answered Abraham, will continue to console us. — Father, Isaac went on after a silence, I am afraid, afraid of being afraid. You must bind me securely. And a little later: Father, when you shall speak to my mother, when you shall tell her, make sure she is not standing near the well or on the roof, lest she fall and hurt herself.

Our attention thereafter is centered on Isaac stretched out on the altar. 45
We watch him as Abraham gazes straight into his eyes. Abraham was weeping, his tears streaming into the eyes of his son, leaving a scar never to be erased. So bitterly did he weep that his knife slipped from his hands and fell to the ground. Only then, not before, did he shout in despair, and only then did God part the heavens and allow Isaac to see the higher sanctuaries of the *merkava,* of creation, with entire rows of angels lamenting: *Yakhid shokhet veyakhid nishkat*—Look at the slaughterer, he is alone and so is the one he is about to slaughter. All the worlds in all the spheres were in tumult: Isaac had become the center of the universe. He could not be allowed to die, not now, not like this. And die he would not. The voice of an angel was heard: Do not raise your hand against the boy, Abraham. Isaac must live.

Why did an angel intervene rather than God Himself? The Midrash 46
answers: God alone may order death, but to save a human life, an angel is enough.

A profoundly generous and beautiful explanation, but I have another 47
which I prefer. Mine allows me to do what until now I could not; namely, to identify not only with Isaac but also with Abraham.

The time has come for the storyteller to confess that he has always felt 48
much closer to Isaac than to his father, Abraham.

I have never really been able to accept the idea that inhumanity could 49
be one more way for man to move closer to God. Kierkegaard's too convenient theory of occasional "ethical suspension" never appealed to me. Kierkegaard maintains that Abraham concealed Isaac's fate from him in order to protect his faith in God; let Isaac lose faith in man rather than in man's Creator. These are concepts rejected by Jewish tradition. God's Law—we said it earlier—commits God as well; but while God cannot suspend His law, it

is given to man—to man and not to God—to interpret it. However, faith in God is linked to faith in man, and one cannot be separated from the other.

Let us once again examine the question: Why didn't Abraham tell Isaac 50
the truth? Because he thought the *Akeda* was a matter strictly between himself and God; it concerned nobody else, not even Isaac.

Thus I place my trust in man's strength. God does not like man to come 51
to him through resignation. Man must strive to reach God through knowledge and love. God loves man to be clear-sighted and outspoken, not blindly obsequious. He respected Job because he dared to stand up to Him. Abraham had interceded on behalf of the two sinful cities long before the test with Isaac.

A double-edged test. God subjected Abraham to it, yet at the same time 52
Abraham forced it on God. As though Abraham had said: I defy You, Lord. I shall submit to Your will, but let us see whether You shall go to the end, whether You shall remain passive and remain silent when the life of my son—who is also Your son—is at stake!

And God changed his mind and relented. Abraham won. That was why 53
God sent an angel to revoke the order and congratulate him; He Himself was too embarrassed.

And suddenly we have another *coup de théâtre* [sudden dramatic turn of 54
events]. Abraham never ceases to astonish us: having won the round, he became demanding. Since God had given in, Abraham was not going to be satisfied with one victory and continue their relationship as though nothing had changed. His turn had come to dictate conditions, or else . . . he would pick up the knife—and come what may!*

Let us listen to the Midrash: 55

When Abraham heard the angel's voice, he did not cry out with joy or express his gratitude. On the contrary, he began to argue. He, who until now had obeyed with sealed lips, suddenly showed inordinate skepticism. He questioned the counterorder he had been hoping and waiting for. First he asked that the angel identify himself in due form. Then he demanded proof that he was God's messenger, not Satan's. And finally he simply refused to accept the message, saying: God Himself ordered me to sacrifice my son, it is up to Him to rescind that order without an intermediary. And, says the Midrash, God had to give in again: He Himself finally had to tell Abraham not to harm his son.

This was Abraham's second victory; yet he was still not satisfied. 56

Listen . . . 57

When Abraham heard the celestial voice ordering him to spare his son 58
Isaac, he declared: I swear I shall not leave the altar, Lord, before I speak my mind. — Speak, said God. — Did You not promise me that my descendants would be as numerous as the stars in the sky? — Yes, I did promise you that. — And whose descendants will they be? Mine? Mine alone? — No, said God, they will be Isaac's as well. — And didn't You also promise me that they

*The ellipses in paragraphs 54 and 57 are Wiesel's.

would inherit the earth? — Yes, I promised you that too. — And whose descendants will they be? Mine alone? — No, said God's voice, they will be Isaac's as well. — Well then, my Lord, said Abraham unabashedly, I could have pointed out to You before that Your order contradicted Your promise. I could have spoken up, I didn't. I contained my grief and held my tongue. In return, I want You to make me the following promise: that when, in the future, my children and my children's children throughout the generations will act against Your law and against Your will, You will also say nothing and forgive them. — So be it, God agreed. Let them but retell this tale and they will be forgiven.

We now begin to understand why Abraham's name has become synonymous with *hesed.* For indeed he was charitable, not so much with Isaac as with God. He could have accused Him and proved Him wrong; he didn't. By saying yes—almost to the end—he established his faith in God and His mercy, thus bringing Him closer to His creation. He won and—so says the Midrash—God loves to be defeated by His children. 59

But unlike God, Satan hates to lose. Unlike God, he takes revenge, however and against whomever he can. Defeated by Abraham and Isaac, he turned against Sarah, appearing before her disguised as Isaac. And he told her the *true* story that was taking place on Mount Moriah. He told her of the march, the ritual ceremony, the heavenly intervention. Barely had Satan finished talking, when Sarah fell to the ground. Dead. 60

Why this legend? It has a meaning. Abraham thought that the *Akeda* was a matter between himself and God, or perhaps between himself and his son. He was wrong. There is an element of the unknown in every injustice, in every adventure involving total commitment. One imposes suffering on a friend, a son, in order to win who knows what battles, to prove who knows what theories, and in the end someone else pays the price—and that someone is almost always innocent. Once the injustice has been committed, it eludes our control. All things considered, Abraham was perhaps wrong in obeying, or even in making believe that he was obeying. By including Isaac in an equation he could not comprehend, by playing with Isaac's suffering, he became unwittingly an accomplice in his wife's death. 61

Another text, even more cruel, goes further yet. It hints that the tragic outcome could, after all, not be averted. Hence the use of the singular verb: *Vayashav avraham el nearav.* Yes, Abraham did return alone. One does not play such games with impunity. 62

Of course, this hypothesis has been rejected by tradition. The ancient commentators preferred to imagine Isaac shaken but alive, spending the unaccounted-for years at a yeshiva or perhaps even in paradise, but eventually returning home.* 63

*A yeshiva is an academy for studying the Talmud, the body of Jewish law and tradition. The notion of Isaac at a yeshiva is, of course, whimsical.

Yet popular imagination—collective memory—adheres rather to the tragic interpretation of the text. Isaac did not accompany his father on the way back because the divine intervention came too late. The act had been consummated. Neither God nor Abraham emerged victorious from the contest. They were both losers. Hence God's pangs of guilt on Rosh Hashana, when He judges man and his deeds. Because of the drama that took place at Mount Moriah, He understands man better. Because of Abraham and Isaac, He knows that it is possible to push some endeavors too far. 64

That is why the theme and term of the *Akeda* have been used, throughout the centuries, to describe the destruction and disappearance of countless Jewish communities everywhere. All the pogroms, the crusades, the persecutions, the slaughters, the catastrophes, the massacres by sword and the liquidations by fire—each time it was Abraham leading his son to the altar, to the holocaust all over again. 65

Of all the Biblical tales, the one about Isaac is perhaps the most timeless and most relevant to our generation. We have known Jews who, like Abraham, witnessed the death of their children; who, like Isaac, lived the *Akeda* in their flesh; and some who went mad when they saw their father disappear on the altar, with the altar, in a blazing fire whose flames reached into the highest of heavens. 66

We have known Jews—ageless Jews—who wished to become blind for having seen God and man opposing one another in the invisible sanctuary of the celestial spheres, a sanctuary illuminated by the gigantic flames of the holocaust. 67

. . .

But the story does not end there. Isaac survived; he had no choice. He had to make something of his memories, his experience, in order to force us to hope. 68

For our survival is linked to his. Satan could kill Sarah, he could even hurt Abraham, but Isaac was beyond his reach. Isaac too represents defiance. Abraham defied God, Isaac defied death. 69

What did happen to Isaac after he left Mount Moriah? He became a poet—author of the *Minha* service*—and did not break with society. Nor did he rebel against life. Logically, he should have aspired to wandering, to the pursuit of oblivion. Instead he settled on his land, never to leave it again, retaining his name. He married, had children, refusing to let fate turn him into a bitter man. He felt neither hatred nor anger toward his contemporaries who did not share his experience. On the contrary, he liked them and showed concern for their well-being. After Moriah, he devoted his life and his right to immortality to the defense of his people. 70

At the end of time, say our sages, God will tell Abraham: Your children have sinned. And Abraham will reply: Let them die to sanctify Your name. Then God will turn to Jacob and say: Your children have sinned. And Jacob will reply: Let them die to sanctify Your name. Then God will speak to Isaac: 71

*A daily afternoon liturgy.

Your children have sinned. And Isaac will answer: *My* children? Are they not also Yours? Yours as well?

It will be Isaac's privilege to remain Israel's *Melitz-Yosher,* the defender of his people, pleading its cause with great ability. He will be entitled to say anything he likes to God, ask anything of Him. Because he suffered? No. Suffering, in Jewish tradition, confers no privileges. It all depends on what one makes of that suffering. Isaac knew how to transform it into prayer and love rather than into rancor and malediction. This is what gives him rights and powers no other man possesses. His reward? The Temple was built on Moriah. Not on Sinai. 72

Let us return to the question we asked at the beginning: Why was the most tragic of our ancestors named Isaac, a name which evokes and signifies laughter? Here is why. As the first survivor, he had to teach us, the future survivors of Jewish history, that it is possible to suffer and despair an entire lifetime and still not give up the art of laughter. 73

Isaac, of course, never freed himself from the traumatizing scenes that violated his youth; the holocaust had marked him and continued to haunt him forever. Yet he remained capable of laughter. And in spite of everything, he did laugh. 74

Questions for Discussion

1. Can you summarize Wiesel's point in one topic sentence (for example, "God is good, after all," or "The meaning of suffering is such-and-such or so-and-so")? If so, can you get your classmates to agree with your summary? If your summaries seem even less satisfactory than usual, why is that so?
2. Do you or any other members of your class know of interpretations of the story of Abraham and Isaac that Wiesel does not offer? If so, discuss how they differ from his.
3. For some religious thinkers, religion is best explained in full-fledged systematic *theologies,* organized accounts of the nature of God and His creation (perhaps the most famous example is the *Summa Theologica* of St. Thomas Aquinas, a monumental intellectual inquiry running to thousands of pages). Neither the Torah nor the Christian Bible is like that. Like Wiesel, they seem to say that the truth about religion is expressed better in stories than in propositions or arguments. Do you think that there are some truths that are somehow "beyond" direct statement? That some genuine knowledge cannot be proved with argument? Or do you think that whatever cannot be stated in straightforward propositions must be something other than "truth" or "knowledge"—poetry, perhaps, or myth?

Suggested Essay Topics

1. Most of our suggested topics in this book have asked you to present an argument, a systematic defense of some belief, with your reasons worked out as fully as possible. Here is your chance to try a freer kind of exploration. Choose any story from the Torah or Bible (or any other scripture you may know) and tell it again, but more fully, adding your own hunches about the characters' motives or the probable outcomes. For example, you might dramatize the scene between Cain and Abel in Genesis 4, trying to understand the point of view of both characters. Or you might try the story of Mary and Martha in the New Testament (Luke 10:38–42). Try to tell your story in a tone that suggests, like Wiesel's, that you are engaged in a genuine search for meaning.
2. For Wiesel the holocaust was a supreme test of his religious faith, and he sees God's command to Abraham presenting a similar kind of supreme test. Can you think of experiences of evil or suffering in your own life that, though less grand in scale, presented to you the same *kind* of challenge? If so, write an essay in the form of a letter to someone you trust, recounting the argument with yourself (or perhaps the quarrel with God) that your experience produced. You may not want—or you may not be able—to settle the issues you raise, or you may feel ready to affirm or reject the religious views that were challenged by your experience. If you do take a settled position, however, try to give reasons for it. Merely asserting how you "feel" about God or religion will not make an interesting statement.

Rosemary Radford Ruether

This essay was written in 1972 at the height of various anti-establishment, quasi-revolutionary movements that had begun in the late 1950s with civil rights agitation and ended in the early seventies with the conclusion of the Vietnam War and the beginning of Watergate. In the midst of this 15-year ferment, feminists began making powerful arguments against the restrictiveness and injustice of traditional roles for women. Feminist arguments, not all of them made by women, began to surface in literary criticism; in politics; in business; in sports; in historical analysis; in legal analysis; in reformulations of sex, marital, and parenting roles; in criticism of advertising and mass media; in the arts; and in theology—to mention only a few areas. (See our Chapter 8.) Regardless of the arena of discussion, the general feminist theme is (1) that women have been the victims of suppression and exploitation that are sometimes explicitly hostile but often disguised as preferential treatment (the "woman on a pedestal" treatment), (2) that they have been disallowed from participating fully in the prestige and power traditionally reserved for men, and (3) that this enforced diminishment of their development as persons, not to mention the social loss of their contributions as thinkers and problem solvers, is bad not only for women but also for men and ultimately for the whole society.

In theology the feminist discussion continues on many fronts: the role of women in church history, the role of women in contemporary church leadership, the criticism of male-centered concepts ("God the father*"), the reinterpretation of biblical doctrines, and so on. In this essay, Rosemary Radford Ruether (b. 1936) presents a critique of one of the main ideas in the Christian view of the world: the idea that body and matter are inferior to and hostile to mind and spirit and that the most perfect form of existence is one in which mind and spirit finally separate themselves forever from entanglements with their inferior components, body and matter. One traditional Christian view is that this blessed separation comes after death, in heaven, where the disembodied soul is seen as enjoying a perfect and eternal existence.*

For Ruether, this dualistic view of the world's structure and man's nature (see the introduction to Plato's "Allegory of the Cave," pp. 411–416, for further discussion of dualism) has its roots in two sources: Neo-Platonism and apocalyptic Judaism (see the notes at bottom of p. 731). "Christianity," she says, "brought together both of these myths: the myth of world cataclysm [based on apocalyptic Judaism] and the myth of the flight of the soul to heaven [based on Platonic notions]" (¶23). But she is not primarily interested in a historical analysis. Of more importance to her is showing that the influence of this dualism has been in many ways pernicious. It has helped justify, for example, the systematic subjugation of women in Christian thinking, which has traditionally aligned women with the inferior elements of body, sensuality, earth, and matter, and aligned men with the superior elements of intellect, spirit, and high-mindedness. The arrangements and duties of domestic living have been given to women, while men have given themselves the tasks of pursuing "higher" goals (power, prestige, victory, competition, civilization, and so on) and portrayed themselves as driven by "higher" motives (theoretical, intellectual, patriotic, spiritual).

Ruether undertakes to expose and challenge this pernicious body- and soul-splitting dualism reinforced and sustained by Christian doctrines. She also proposes an alternative view. As you read, try to establish where her historical analysis turns into evaluation, whether or not you agree with her criticism of Christian doctrines, and to determine the content of her alternative. Keep in mind that as a professor of theology (at Garrett Theological Seminary in Evanston, Illinois), Ruether is offering her criticisms not as an unbeliever, as an atheist, or as a church-hater, but as a Christian theologian and scholar. Whether or not you think this gives her criticism more force, it is clear that as a Christian, a theologian, a scholar, and a woman, the issues have an inevitable importance for her. If they were just Ruether's issues or just women's issues, they would be more suitable for discussion by special-interest groups than by college freshmen. The truth is, however, that regardless of our religion and our sex, the notions that Christianity has offered about the relationship between body and mind, man and nature, and men and women are so deeply ingrained in our society that they are an important influence on us all. Do you find that Ruether's basic claims about the sexist bias in Christian thought are well supported? Even if you disagree, do you find her challenge to traditional Christian thinking vital and useful? Or does it seem dangerous and subversive? Will it serve to weaken or strengthen the beliefs of Christians? Regardless of how we each answer these questions, Ruether invites us to examine afresh our notions about truth and about the kind of world we want to live in.

MOTHEREARTH AND THE MEGAMACHINE

A Theology of Liberation in a Feminine, Somatic, and Ecological Perspective

From *Womanspirit Rising: A Feminist Reader in Religion* (1979).

Christianity, as the heir of both classical Neo-Platonism and apocalyptic Judaism,* combines the image of a male, warrior God with the exaltation of the intellect over the body. . . . These world-negating religions carried a set of dualities that still profoundly condition the modern world view. 1

All the basic dualities—the alienation of the mind from the body; the alienation of the subjective self from the objective world; the subjective retreat of the individual, alienated from the social community; the domination or rejection of nature by spirit—these all have roots in the apocalyptic-Platonic religious heritage of classical Christianity.† But the alienation of the masculine from the feminine is the primary sexual symbolism that sums up all these alienations. The psychic traits of intellectuality, transcendent spirit, and autonomous will that were identified with the male left the woman with the contrary traits of bodiliness, sensuality, and subjugation. Society, through the centuries, has in every way profoundly conditioned men and women to play out their lives and find their capacities within this basic antithesis. 2

This antithesis has also shaped the modern technological environment. The plan of our cities is made in this image: The sphere of domesticity, rest, and childrearing where women are segregated is clearly separated from those corridors down which men advance in assault upon the world of "work." The woman who tries to break out of the female sphere into the masculine finds not only psychic conditioning and social attitudes but the structure of social reality itself ranged against her. 3

**Classical Neo-Platonism* refers to the view, based on doctrines in Plato, that the world is divided into a duality between spirit and mind on the one hand and matter and body on the other. *Apocalyptic Judaism* refers to the Jewish belief that when the Messiah appears, the Jews will be freed from subjection to their enemies and restored to national greatness and religious purity. At the time of the rise of Christianity and the Jews' subjection to the Romans, this version of Judaism was held with special fervor by some.

†In other words, because part of Christianity's heritage goes back to Neo-Platonism and apocalyptic Judaism, Christianity is implicated in the destructive dualism of these religious views.

The physical environment—access to basic institutions in terms of space and time—has been shaped for the fundamental purpose of freeing one half of the race for the work society calls "productive," while the other half of the race remains in a sphere that services this freedom for work. The woman who would try to occupy both spheres at once literally finds *reality itself* stacked against her, making the combination of maternal and masculine occupations all but impossible without extraordinary energy or enough wealth to hire domestic help. 4

Thus, in order to play out the roles shaped by this definition of the male life-style, the woman finds that she must either be childless or have someone else act as her "wife" (i.e., play the service role for her freedom to work). Women's liberation is therefore *impossible* within the present social system except for an elite few. Women simply cannot be persons within the present system of work and family, and they can only rise to liberated personhood by the most radical and fundamental reshaping of the entire human environment in a way that redefines the very nature of work, family, and the institutional expressions of social relations. 5

Although widespread hopes for liberty and equality among all humans rose with the *philosophes** of the Enlightenment, hardly any of these ideologies of the French Revolution and the liberal revolutions of the nineteenth century envisioned the liberation of women. The bourgeoisie, the workers, the peasants, even the Negro slaves were more obvious candidates for liberation, while the subjugation of women continued to be viewed as an unalterable necessity of nature. When the most radical of the French liberals, the Marquis de Condorcet, included women in the vision of equality, his colleagues thought he had lost his senses and breached the foundations of the new rationalism. The ascendency of Reason meant the ascendency of the intellect over the passions, and this must ever imply the subjugation of women. 6

An embarrassed silence or cries of ridicule likewise greeted this topic when it was raised half a century later by another consistent libertarian, John Stuart Mill. Only after a long struggle from the nineteenth to the early twentieth century did women finally break down the barriers that separated them from the most basic rights to work, education, financial autonomy, and full citizenship—and even these freedoms are not universally secured today. 7

The reaction against and suppression of the Woman's Liberation Movement has been closely tied to reactionary cultural and political movements, and the emancipated woman has been the chief target of elitism, fascism, and neoconservatism of all kinds. The Romantic Movement traumatized Europe's reaction to the French Revolution, reinstated the traditional view of women in idealized form, while the more virulent blood-and-soil reactionaries of the nineteenth century expressed a more naked misogynism. Literary figures such as Strindberg and Nietzsche couldn't stress strongly enough their abhorrence of women. At the turn of the century, Freud codified all the traditional 8

*The *philosophes* were radical political theorists and philosophers whose criticism of the old order of things in the eighteenth century prepared the way for the French Revolution.

negative views of the female psychology, giving them scientific respectability for the new psychological and social sciences. These negative stereotypes have been a key element in the repression of the women's movement through the popular mass media.*

In Nazism, the reactionary drive against the libertarian tradition culminated in a virulent revival of racism, misogynism, elitism, and military and national chauvinism. Its victims were Jews, Communists, Social Democrats, and libertarians of all kinds—and, finally, the nascent women's movement. 9

In America, the period from World War I to the 1960s was characterized by a successive revival of anti-Negro racism, anti-Semitism, the destruction of the American Left, and finally the cold war militarization of society based on a fanatic anti-Communism. In this same period, a continuous reactionary pacification of the women's movement deprived women of many of their earlier gains in educational and professional fields. 10

This modern backlash against the libertarian tradition seeks to reinstate attitudes and social relations whose psychic roots run back through the Judeo-Christian and classical cultures into the very foundations of civilization building. The cry for liberty, equality, and fraternity challenged the roots of the psychology whereby the dominant class measured its status in terms of the conquest of classes, nations, races, and nature itself. 11

Lewis Mumford, in his monumental work on the foundations of ancient civilization, *The Myth of the Machine,* and its supplementary volume on modern technological society, *The Myth of the Machine: The Pentagon of Power,* has shown how civilization has been founded on a subjugation of man to machinery. A chauvinist, paranoid psychology has directed men's productive energies into destruction rather than the alleviation of the necessities of all, thus aborting the promise of civilization. The subjugation of the female by the male is the primary psychic model for this chauvinism and its parallel expressions in oppressor-oppressed relationships between social classes, races and nations. It is this most basic symbolism of power that has misdirected men's psychic energy into the building of the Pentagon of Power, from the pyramids of ancient Egypt to the North American puzzle-palace on the Potomac. 12

The psychosocial history of the domination of women has not been explored with any consistency, so the effort to trace its genesis and development here can only be very general. However, it appears that in agricultural societies sexist and class polarization did not immediately reshape the religious world view. For the first two millennia of recorded history, religious 13

*In paragraphs 7–10 Ruether is giving a quick historical overview of attitudes toward the liberation of women since the French Revolution, which erupted in 1789: In paragraph 7 she shows John Stuart Mill's case in the middle of the nineteenth century for the liberation of women being met with silence or ridicule; in paragraph 8 she argues for the negative effects of Romanticism and the reactionary attitudes of Nietzsche, Strindberg, and Freud at the end of the nineteenth century and the beginning of the twentieth; in paragraph 9 she alludes to the undermining of the women's movement by Nazism in the mid-twentieth century; and in paragraph 10 she argues that racial and ethnic prejudice and the paranoia caused by the cold war, which lasted until the 1960s, have also undermined the liberation of women. That brings her up to the time of the writing of this article, 1972.

culture continued to reflect the more holistic* view of society of the neolithic village, where the individual and the community, nature and society, male and female, earth Goddess and sky God were seen in a total perspective of world renewal. The salvation of the individual was not split off from that of the community; the salvation of society was one with the renewal of the earth; male and female played their complementary roles in the salvation of the world. This primitive democracy of the neolithic village persisted in the divine pantheons of Babylonia, despite the social class stratification that now appeared.

In these early civilizations, this holistic world view was expressed in the 14
public celebration of the new year's festival, wherein the whole society of humanity and nature experienced the annual death of the cosmos and its resurrection from primordial chaos. In this cult, the king, as the personification of the community, played the role of the God who dies and is reborn from the netherworld. His counterpart was a powerful feminine figure who was at once virgin and mother, wife and sister, and who rescued the dying God from the power of the underworld. The king united with her at the end of the drama to create the divine child of the new year's vegetation. The crisis and rebirth encompassed both society and nature: The hymns of rejoicing celebrated the release of the captives, justice for the poor, and security against invasion, as well as the new rain, the new grain, the new lamb and the new child.

Somewhere in the first millennium B.C., however, this communal world 15
view of humanity and nature, male and female, carried over from tribal society started to break down, and the alienations of civilization began to reshape the religious world picture. This change was partly aggravated by the history of imperial conquest that swept the people of the Mediterranean into larger and larger social conglomerates where they no longer felt the same unity with the king, the soil or the society.

The old religions of the earth became private cults for the individual, 16
no longer anticipating the renewal of the earth and society but rather expecting an otherworldly salvation of the individual soul after death. Nature itself came to be seen as an alien reality, and men now visualized their own bodies as foreign to their true selves, longing for a heavenly home to release them from their enslavement within the physical cosmos. Finally, earth ceased to be seen as man's true home.

Hebrew religion is significant in this history as the faith of a people who 17
clung with particular tenacity to their tribal identity over against the imperial powers of civilization. Hebrew society inherited kingship and the new year's festival of the temple from their Canaanite neighbors. But Yahwism repressed the feminine divine role integral to this cult and began to cut loose the festival itself from its natural base in the renewal of the earth.

This desert people claimed the land as a divine legacy, but they imag- 18
ined a manner of acquiring it that set them against the traditional cult of the

*Holistic refers to the wholeness and interconnectedness of things—the opposite of their division into dualistic and antagonistic categories.

earth. They took over the old earth festivals but reinterpreted them to refer to historical events in the Sinai journey. The messianic hopes of the prophets still looked for a paradisal renewal of earth and society, but this renewal broke the bonds of natural possibility and was projected into history as a future event.

So the pattern of death and resurrection was cut loose from organic 19
harmonies and became instead an historical pattern of wrath and redemption. The feminine imagery of the cult was repressed entirely, although it survived in a new form in the symbol of the community as the bride of Yahweh in the Covenant. But the bride was subordinate and dependent to the male Lord of Hosts, who reigned without consort in the heavens, confronting his sometimes rebellious, sometimes repentant people with punishment or promises of national victory.

The hopes for a renewal of nature and society, projected into a once and 20
for all historical future, now came to be seen as less and less realizable within history itself. And so the prophetic drive to free man from nature ended in the apocalyptic negation of history itself: a cataclysmic world destruction and angelic new creation.

In this same period of the first millennium B.C., we find in classical 21
philosophy a parallel development of the alienation of the individual from the world. Like the prophets, the philosophers repudiated the old nature Gods in their sexual forms of male and female divinities, and maleness was seen as bodiless and intellectual.

For Plato, the authentic soul is incarnated as a male, and only when it 22
succumbs to the body is it reincarnated in the body of a female and then into the body of some beast resembling the evil character into which it has fallen. The salvation of the liberated consciousness repudiates heterosexual for masculine love and mounts to heaven in flight from the body and the visible world. The intellect is seen as an alien, lonely species that originates in a purely spiritual realm beyond time, space, and matter, and has been dropped, either as into a testing place or, through some fault, into this lower material world. But space and time, body and mutability are totally alien to its nature. The body drags the soul down, obscuring the clarity of its knowledge, debasing its moral integrity. Liberation is a flight from the earth to a changeless, infinite world beyond. Again we see the emergence of the liberated consciousness in a way that alienates it from nature in a body-fleeing, world-negating spirituality.

Christianity brought together both of these myths—the myth of world 23
cataclysm and the myth of the flight of the soul to heaven. It also struggled to correct the more extreme implications of this body-negating spirituality with a more positive doctrine of creation and incarnation. It even reinstated, in covert form, the old myths of the year cult and the virgin-mother Goddess.

But the dominant spirituality of the Fathers of the Church finally ac- 24
cepted the antibody, antifeminine view of late antique religious culture. Recent proponents of ecology have, therefore, pointed the finger at Christianity as the originator of this debased view of nature, as the religious sanction for modern technological exploitation of the earth.

But Christianity did not originate this view. Rather, it appears to corre- 25
spond to a stage of development of human consciousness that coincided with ripening classical civilization. Christianity took over this alienated world view of late classical civilization, but its oppressive dualities express the basic alienations at work in the psychosocial channelization of human energy since the breakup of the communal life of earlier tribal society.

What we see in this development is a one-sided expression of the ego, 26
claiming its transcendental autonomy by negating the finite matrix of existence. This antithesis is projected socially by identifying woman as the incarnation of this debasing threat of bodily existence, while the same polarized model of the psyche is projected politically upon suppressed or conquered social groups.

The emphasis upon the transcendent consciousness has literally created 27
the urban earth, and both abstract science and revolution are ultimate products of this will to transcend and dominate the natural and social world that gave birth to the rebellious spirit. The exclusively male God who creates out of nothing, transcending nature and dominating history, and upon whose all-powerful wrath and grace man hangs as a miserable, crestfallen sinner, is the theological self-image and guilty conscience of this self-infinitizing spirit.

Today we recognize that this theology of rebellion into infinity has its 28
counterpart in a world-destroying spirituality that projects upon the female of the race all its abhorrence, hostility and fear of the bodily powers from which it has arisen and from which it wishes to be independent. One can feel this fear in the threatened, repressively hostile energy that is activated in the dominant male society at the mere suggestion of the emergence of the female on an equal plane—as though equality itself must inevitably mean *his* resubjugation to preconscious submersion in the womb.

This most basic duality characterizes much recent theology. Karl Barth, 29
despite his model of cohumanity as the essence of the creational covenant, insists on the relation of super- and subordination between men and women as an ordained necessity of creation. "Crisis" and "secular" theologians such as Bultmann and Gogarten continually stress the transcendence of history over nature, defining the Gospel as the freedom of the liberated consciousness to depart endlessly from natural and historical foundations into the contentless desert of pure possibility. Such theologians are happy to baptize modern technology as the expression of the freedom mediated by the Gospel to transcend and dominate nature.

Today, both in the West and among insurgent Third World peoples, we 30
are seeing a new intensification of this Western mode of abstractionism and revolution. Many are convinced that the problems created by man's ravaging of nature can be solved only by a great deal more technological manipulation. The oppressed peoples who have been the victims of the domination of the elite classes now seek to follow much the same path of pride, transcending wrath, separatism and power in order to share in the benefits of independence and technological power already won by the dominant classes.

Yet, at the same time, nature and society are giving clear warning signals 31 that the usefulness of this spirituality is about to end. Two revolutions are running in contrapuntal directions. The alienated members of the dominant society are seeking new communal, egalitarian life-styles, ecological living patterns, and the redirection of psychic energy toward reconciliation with the body. But these human potential movements remain elitist, privatistic, esthetic and devoid of a profound covenant with the poor and oppressed of the earth.

On the other hand, the aspirations of insurgent peoples rise along the 32
lines of the traditional rise of civilization through group pride, technological domination of nature and antagonistic, competitive relationships between peoples. Such tendencies might be deplored by those who have so far monopolized technology and now believe they have seen the end of its fruitfulness, but they must be recognized as still relevant to the liberation of the poor and oppressed from material necessity and psychological dependency.

We are now approaching the denouement of this dialectic. The ethic of 33
competitiveness and technological mastery has created a world divided by penis-missiles and countermissiles that could destroy all humanity a hundred times over. Yet the ethic of reconciliation with the earth has yet to break out of its snug corners of affluence and find meaningful cohesion with the revolutions of insurgent peoples.

The significance of the women's revolution, then, may well be its 34
unique location in the center of this clash between the contrapuntal directions of current liberation movements. Women are the first and oldest oppressed, subjugated people. They too must claim for themselves the human capacities of intellect, will, and autonomous creative consciousness that have been denied them through this psychosocial polarization in its most original form.

Yet women have also been identified with nature, the earth, and the 35
body in its despised and rejected form. To simply reject this identification would be to neglect that part of ourselves we have been left to cultivate and to buy into that very polarization of which we have been the primary victims. The significance of our movement will be lost if we merely seek valued masculine traits at the expense of devalued feminine ones.

Women must be the spokesmen for a new humanity arising out of the 36
reconciliation of spirit and body. This does not mean selling short our rights to the powers of independent personhood. Autonomy, world-transcending spirit, separatism as the power of consciousness raising, and liberation from an untamed nature and from subjugation to the rocket-ship male—all these revolutions are still vital to women's achievement of integral personhood. But we have to look beyond our own liberation from oppression to the liberation of the oppressor as well. Women should not buy into the masculine ethic of competitiveness that sees the triumph of the self as predicated upon the subjugation of the other. Unlike men, women have traditionally cultivated a communal personhood that could participate in the successes of others rather than seeing these as merely a threat to one's own success.

To seek the liberation of women without losing this sense of communal 37 personhood is the great challenge and secret power of the women's revolution. Its only proper end must be the total abolition of the social pattern of domination and subjugation and the erection of a new communal social ethic. We need to build a new cooperative social order out beyond the principles of hierarchy, rule, and competitiveness. Starting in the grass roots local units of human society where psychosocial polarization first began, we must create a living pattern of mutuality between men and women, between parents and children, among people in their social, economic, and political relationships and, finally, between mankind and the organic harmonies of nature.

Such a revolution entails nothing less than a transformation of all the 38
social structures of civilization, particularly the relationship between work and play. It entails literally a global struggle to overthrow and transform the character of power structures and points forward to a new messianic epiphany that will as far transcend the world-rejecting salvation myths of apocalypticism and Platonism as these myths transcended the old nature myths of the neolithic village. Combining the values of the world-transcending Yahweh with those of the world-renewing Ba'al in a post-technological religion of reconciliation with the body, the woman and the world, its salvation myth will not be one of divinization and flight from the body but of humanization and reconciliation with the earth.

Our model is neither the romanticized primitive jungle nor the modern 39
technological wasteland. Rather it expresses itself in a new command to learn to cultivate the garden, for the cultivation of the garden is where the powers of rational consciousness come together with the harmonies of nature in partnership.

The new earth must be one where people are reconciled with their labor, 40
abolishing the alienation of the megamachine while inheriting its productive power to free men for unalienated creativity. It will be a world where people are reconciled to their own finitude, where the last enemy, death, is conquered, not by a flight into eternity, but in that spirit of St. Francis that greets "Brother Death" as a friend that completes the proper cycle of the human soul.

The new humanity is not the will to power of a monolithic empire, 41
obliterating all other identities before the one identity of the master race, but a polylinguistic appreciativeness that can redeem local space, time, and identity. We seek to overcome the deadly Leviathan of the Pentagon of Power, transforming its power into manna to feed the hungry of the earth. The revolution of the feminine revolts against the denatured Babel of concrete and steel that stifles the living soil. It does not merely reject the spirit child born from the earth but seeks to reclaim spirit for body and body for spirit in a messianic appearing of the body of God.

Questions for Discussion

1. After discussing the world view of neolithic tribal societies, Ruether says, "Somewhere in the first millennium B.C., however, this communal world view of humanity and nature, male and female, carried over from tribal society started to break down . . . and men now visualized their own bodies as foreign to their true selves, longing for a heavenly home to release them from their enslavement within the physical cosmos" (¶15–16). To what extent do you see this dualistic antagonism between soul and body, earth and heaven still residing in Christianity (or other religions) today? How do Christians in your experience feel about the demands, impulses, and constraints of physical life?
2. How would you paraphrase paragraph 26 in your own words?
3. How difficult would it be for you to visualize God as a female? If you pray, can you imagine praying to a female God? What feelings would be aroused by the attempt? Can you account for them?
4. Today women are going into the pastoral ministry more than ever before. To those of you for whom attending a church pastored by a woman would be a new experience, can you say whether it would make you uncomfortable? Why or why not? To those of you who may have been in a church when a female pastor followed a male, can you give an account of the range of parishioners' reactions? If some responses were sexist, did they fade with time? How has the situation worked out?
5. To those of you who are Catholic, how would you feel about attending a mass conducted by a female priest? Would it undermine for you the authenticity or efficacy of the ritual? Why or why not?
6. In paragraphs 36–37 Ruether makes it clear that she does not want changes that will merely place women in the same roles and give them the same attitudes that men have traditionally held. How would you state her goals more fully in your own words? If she does not want merely to turn the present system upside down, what does she want?

Suggested Essay Topics

1. This topic is based on discussion question 6. In an essay addressed to someone to whom you think feminist arguments are either novel or repugnant, write an essay in which you, first, try to give, as completely as possible, an explanation in your own words of Ruether's position (you may quote Ruether if you wish) and, second, attempt to provide examples *of your own* to support her case, concluding with an evaluation of her final alternative.
2. In paragraph 5 Ruether states, "Women simply cannot be persons within the present system of work and family, and they can only rise to liberated personhood by the most radical and fundamental reshaping of the entire human environment in a way that redefines the very nature of work, family, and the institutional expressions of social relations." In an essay

written as a letter addressed to Ruether, give the best reasons you can muster for either agreeing or disagreeing with the position advanced in the quotation. If you agree, detail some of the "radical and fundamental" reshapings of the "entire human environment" that you think should come first, and cite the advantages you think will follow. If you disagree, provide concrete illustration of the disadvantages that will follow by adopting her views.

John Donne

Among many philosophers and religious believers the conviction persists—a consistent motif never quite drowned out by other views—that the profoundest truths cannot be expressed in straightforward propositions or declarative sentences but can only be hinted at, shadowed forth, in paradox. Such utterances contain contradictions, yet by their very perplexity seem to express the deepest truths more comprehensively, sensitively, and accurately than any other kind of formulation.

Whether or not John Donne (1572–1631) believed this as a general doctrine, his use of paradox is clear in "Batter My Heart." Only as God supports us can we approach him; only as God loves us can we be made lovable. These are conventional Christian notions, not new and not especially powerful when summarized. What gives Donne's poem its power, freshness, and conviction is his imagery, which invests these notions with life and emotional power. Each ascending paradox is knottier and more emotionally laden than the last, until in the end the poet achieves a catharsis of intensity in picturing himself as freed by slavery, purified by rape.

BATTER MY HEART

From *Holy Sonnets* (1633).

Batter my heart, three-personed God; for you
As yet but knock, breathe, shine, and seek to mend.
That I may rise and stand, o'erthrow me and bend
Your force to break, blow, burn, and make me new.
I, like an usurped town, to another due,
Labor to admit you, but, oh, to no end;
Reason, your viceroy in me, me should defend,
But is captived and proves weak or untrue.

Yet dearly I love you and would be lovèd fain,
But am betrothed unto your enemy:
Divorce me, untie or break that knot again,
Take me to you, imprison me, for I,
Except you enthrall me, never shall be free,
Nor ever chaste, except you ravish me.

1633

Questions for Discussion

1. What does Donne mean by "three-personed God" (l. 1)?
2. Does the extreme humility of the poet's voice strike you favorably? Does it seem to you to be the appropriate or correct stance for human beings to take before God? Or would you like to see the speaker showing more independence and spirit? Give reasons to support your view.
3. What is the root meaning of *enthrall*? How does the sense of this word that Donne is drawing on differ from the ordinary sense that the word usually possesses today?
4. For what is "town" a metaphor in line 5? Who is the usurper who holds the town captive at present?

Suggested Essay Topics

1. If you are an unbeliever, does Donne's poem lose force, interest, or relevance to you because you do not share with him the convictions upon which his own passionate emotional involvement is based? If so, you probably have little to say about the poem. But if you are an unbeliever who still finds the poem moving and powerful, as many unbelievers do, try to discover and discuss the reasons for the poem's success that are not based on shared religious beliefs with the reader. Write an essay directed to your instructor in which you discuss the reasons for the poem's success as a poem, quite apart from the Christian content of its message.
2. If you are a believer but are not a Christian, your reactions to this poem would be instructive to those of us who know only Christianity. For example, is paradox a common way in your religion of expressing the deep truths not containable in straightforward propositions? Does your religion posit an afterlife? If so, is that afterlife split into two versions, one of suffering for the sinful and one of blessedness for the virtuous? Does your religion insist on the self-abasement and humility that Donne exhibits in his poem? Would your religion understand Donne's emotions, his stance, even if it required belief in a different God?

If you belong to a non-Christian religious tradition that can provide the kinds of comparisons suggested by these questions, write an essay directed to your classmates in which you begin by saying why Donne's kind of appeal to God would be intelligible or not intelligible to believers in your religion. Then go on to discuss other relevant differences that might help explain whether or not Donne's poem could have an appropriate counterpart in your religion. If not, why not?

IDEAS IN DEBATE

Bertrand Russell
C. S. Lewis

Bertrand Russell

Each of the great world religions—Judaism, Christianity, Hinduism, Buddhism, Islam—has stimulated whole libraries of controversy. Over the centuries, theologians, church historians, and moralists have spent entire careers defending each faith against one or more of the others or arguing for specific interpretations within a given faith. Other scholars have spent lifetimes attacking alien traditions or attempting to purge a given tradition of errors and abuses. It is perhaps natural that some thinkers, viewing this enormous expenditure of energy and intelligence, have concluded that most of it, if not all, is sheer waste. Since questions about religious truth can never be finally settled and are certainly not subject to scientific testing, they feel that the whole tradition of religious controversy, like the entire religious enterprise, is all nonsense.

Bertrand Russell (1872–1970) was a skeptic of this kind, one who loved to show up the contradictions and follies of religious debate. Yet he was himself a kind of religious controversialist, often rising to prophetic fervor in recommending his own view of the values we should live by—for example, he titled one famous essay "A Free Man's Worship." Convinced that values are created only by human beings, not by any divinity, he defended his *values passionately against a foolish and wicked world.*

Russell's many attacks on Christianity are thus just one skirmish in what he saw as a lifetime war against human wickedness and folly, a war conducted by a tiny band of thinkers who favored reason and progress over superstition and sentimentality. Though his faith in the likelihood of intellectual and moral progress dimmed as he witnessed the carnage of two world wars, the horrors of Nazism, and then the threat of atomic annihilation, he never wavered in his conviction, arrived at in his youth, that Christianity in all of its manifestations had always been not only a fraud but a great obstacle to human happiness.

Russell's essay should be studied along with the essay that follows it: "What Christians Believe" by C. S. Lewis. The two were not addressed to each other, yet both authors write as if *they were addressing and refuting the arguments of the opposing camp. As you read them, ask yourself what audience each author seems to be primarily addressing himself to and whether either one successfully enters what we might call the "argumentative field" of the other. Do they reconstruct their opponents' arguments in a form that would make sense to those opponents? Do they both care about the same issues, or do they for some reason simply talk past each other?*

WHY I AM NOT A CHRISTIAN

From *"Why I Am Not a Christian" and Other Essays on Religion and Related Subjects,* edited by Paul Edwards (1957).

WHAT IS A CHRISTIAN?

Nowadays . . . we have to be a little more vague in our meaning of Christianity [than were people in former times]. I think, however, that there are two different items which are quite essential to anybody calling himself a Christian. The first is one of a dogmatic nature—namely, that you must believe in God and immortality. If you do not believe in those two things, I do not think that you can properly call yourself a Christian. Then, further than that, as the name implies, you must have some kind of belief about Christ. The Mohammedans, for instance, also believe in God and in immortality, and yet they would not call themselves Christians. I think you must have at the very lowest the belief that Christ was, if not divine, at least the best and wisest of men. If you are not going to believe that much about Christ, I do not think you have any right to call yourself a Christian. Of course, there is another sense, which you find in *Whitaker's Almanack* and in geography books, where the population of the world is said to be divided into Christians, Mohammedans [Muslims], Buddhists, fetish worshipers, and so on; and in that sense we are all Christians. The geography books count us all in, but that is a purely geographical sense, which I suppose we can ignore. Therefore I take it that when I tell you why I am not a Christian I have to tell you two different things: first, why I do not believe in God and in immortality; and, secondly, why I do not think that Christ was the best and wisest of men, although I grant him a very high degree of moral goodness. 1

But for the successful efforts of unbelievers in the past, I could not take so elastic a definition of Christianity as that. As I said before, in olden days it had a much more full-blooded sense. For instance, it included the belief in hell. Belief in eternal hell-fire was an essential item of Christian belief until pretty recent times. In this country, as you know, it ceased to be an essential item because of a decision of the Privy Council, and from that decision the Archbishop of Canterbury and the Archbishop of York dissented; but in this country our religion is settled by Act of Parliament, and therefore the Privy Council was able to override their Graces and hell was no longer necessary to a Christian. Consequently I shall not insist that a Christian must believe in hell. 2

THE EXISTENCE OF GOD

To come to this question of the existence of God: it is a large and serious question, and if I were to attempt to deal with it in any adequate manner I 3 should have to keep you here until Kingdom Come, so that you will have to excuse me if I deal with it in a somewhat summary fashion. You know, of course, that the Catholic Church has laid it down as a dogma that the existence of God can be proved by the unaided reason. That is a somewhat curious dogma, but it is one of their dogmas. They had to introduce it because at one time the freethinkers adopted the habit of saying that there were such and such arguments which mere reason might urge against the existence of God, but of course they knew as a matter of faith that God did exist. The arguments and the reasons were set out at great length, and the Catholic Church felt that they must stop it. Therefore they laid it down that the existence of God can be proved by the unaided reason and they had to set up what they considered were arguments to prove it. There are, of course, a number of them, but I shall take only a few.

THE FIRST-CAUSE ARGUMENT

Perhaps the simplest and easiest to understand is the argument of the First 4
Cause. (It is maintained that everything we see in this world has a cause, and as you go back in the chain of causes further and further you must come to a First Cause, and to that First Cause you give the name of God.) That argument, I suppose, does not carry very much weight nowadays, because, in the first place, cause is not quite what it used to be. The philosophers and the men of science have got going on cause, and it has not anything like the vitality it used to have; but, apart from that, you can see that the argument that there must be a First Cause is one that cannot have any validity. I may say that when I was a young man and was debating these questions very seriously in my mind, I for a long time accepted the argument of the First Cause, until one day, at the age of eighteen, I read John Stuart Mill's Autobiography, and I there found this sentence: "My father taught me that the question 'Who made me?' cannot be answered, since it immediately suggests the further question 'Who made God?' " That very simple sentence showed me, as I still think, the fallacy in the argument of the First Cause. If everything must have a cause, then God must have a cause. If there can be anything without a cause, it may just as well be the world as God, so that there cannot be any validity in that argument. It is exactly of the same nature as the Hindu's view, that the world rested upon an elephant and the elephant rested upon a tortoise; and when they said, "How about the tortoise?" the Indian said, "Suppose we change the subject." The argument is really no better than that. There is no reason why the world could not have come into being without a cause; nor, on the other hand, is there any reason why it should not have always existed. There is no reason to suppose that the world had a beginning at all. The idea that things must have a beginning is really due to the poverty of our imagination. Therefore, perhaps, I need not waste any more time upon the argument about the First Cause.*

. . .

*We omit Russell's examination of other arguments for the existence of God and move on to his examination of the character and teaching of Christ.

DEFECTS IN CHRIST'S TEACHING

Historically it is quite doubtful whether Christ ever existed at all, and if He 5
did we do not know anything about Him, so that I am not concerned with the historical question, which is a very difficult one. I am concerned with Christ as He appears in the Gospels, taking the Gospel narrative as it stands, and there one does find some things that do not seem to be very wise. For one thing, He certainly thought that His second coming would occur in clouds of glory before the death of all the people who were living at that time. There are a great many texts that prove that. He says, for instance, "Ye shall not have gone over the cities of Israel till the Son of Man be come." Then He says, "There are some standing here which shall not taste death till the Son of Man comes into His kingdom"; and there are a lot of places where it is quite clear that He believed that His second coming would happen during the lifetime of many then living. That was the belief of His earlier followers, and it was the basis of a good deal of His moral teaching. When He said, "Take no thought for the morrow," and things of that sort, it was very largely because He thought that the second coming was going to be very soon, and that all ordinary mundane affairs did not count. I have, as a matter of fact, known some Christians who did believe that the second coming was imminent. I knew a parson who frightened his congregation terribly by telling them that the second coming was very imminent indeed, but they were much consoled when they found that he was planting trees in his garden. The early Christians did really believe it, and they did abstain from such things as planting trees in their gardens, because they did accept from Christ the belief that the second coming was imminent. In that respect, clearly He was not so wise as some other people have been, and He was certainly not superlatively wise.

THE MORAL PROBLEM

Then you come to moral questions. There is one very serious defect to my 6
mind in Christ's moral character, and that is that He believed in hell. I do not myself feel that any person who is really profoundly humane can believe in everlasting punishment. Christ certainly as depicted in the Gospels did believe in everlasting punishment, and one does find repeatedly a vindictive fury against those people who would not listen to His preaching—an attitude which is not uncommon with preachers, but which does somewhat detract from superlative excellence. You do not, for instance, find that attitude in Socrates. You find him quite bland and urbane toward the people who would not listen to him; and it is, to my mind, far more worthy of a sage to take that line than to take the line of indignation. You probably all remember the sort of things that Socrates was saying when he was dying, and the sort of things that he generally did say to people who did not agree with him.

You will find that in the Gospels Christ said, "Ye serpents, ye generation 7 of vipers, how can ye escape the damnation of hell." That was said to people who did not like His preaching. It is not really to my mind quite the best tone, and there are a great many of these things about hell. There is, of course, the familiar text about the sin against the Holy Ghost: "Whosoever speaketh against the Holy Ghost it shall not be forgiven him neither in this World nor in the world to come." That text has caused an unspeakable amount of misery in the world, for all sorts of people have imagined that they have committed the sin against the Holy Ghost, and thought that it would not be forgiven them either in this world or in the world to come. I really do not think that a person with a proper degree of kindliness in his nature would have put fears and terrors of that sort into the world.

Then Christ says, "The Son of Man shall send forth His angels, and they 8
shall gather out of His kingdom all things that offend, and them which do iniquity, and shall cast them into a furnace of fire; there shall be wailing and gnashing of teeth"; and He goes on about the wailing and gnashing of teeth. It comes in one verse after another, and it is quite manifest to the reader that there is a certain pleasure in contemplating wailing and gnashing of teeth, or else it would not occur so often. Then you all, of course, remember about the sheep and the goats; how at the second coming He is going to divide the sheep from the goats, and He is going to say to the goats, "Depart from me, ye cursed, into everlasting fire." He continues, "And these shall go away into everlasting fire." Then He says again, "If thy hand offend thee, cut it off; it is better for thee to enter into life maimed, than having two hands to go into hell, into the fire that never shall be quenched; where the worm dieth not and the fire is not quenched." He repeats that again and again also. I must say that I think all this doctrine, that hell-fire is a punishment for sin, is a doctrine of cruelty. It is a doctrine that put cruelty into the world and gave the world generations of cruel torture; and the Christ of the Gospels, if you could take Him as His chroniclers represent Him, would certainly have to be considered partly responsible for that.

There are other things of less importance. There is the instance of the 9
Gadarene swine, where it certainly was not very kind to the pigs to put the devils into them and make them rush down the hill to the sea. You must remember that He was omnipotent, and He could have made the devils simply go away; but He chose to send them into the pigs. Then there is the curious story of the fig tree, which always rather puzzled me. You remember what happened about the fig tree. "He was hungry; and seeing a fig tree afar off having leaves, He came if haply He might find anything thereon; and when He came to it He found nothing but leaves, for the time of figs was not yet. And Jesus answered and said unto it: 'No man eat fruit of thee hereafter for ever' . . . and Peter . . . saith unto Him: 'Master, behold the fig tree which thou cursedst is withered away.' " This is a very curious story, because it was not the right time of year for figs, and you really could not blame the tree. I cannot myself feel that either in the matter of wisdom or in the matter of virtue Christ stands quite as high as some other people known to history. I think I should put Buddha and Socrates above Him in those respects.

THE EMOTIONAL FACTOR

As I said before, I do not think that the real reason why people accept religion has anything to do with argumentation. They accept religion on emotional grounds. One is often told that it is a very wrong thing to attack religion, because religion makes men virtuous. So I am told; I have not noticed it. You know, of course, the parody of that argument in Samuel Butler's book, *Erewhon Revisited.* You will remember that in *Erewhon* there is a certain Higgs who arrives in a remote country, and after spending some time there he escapes from that country in a balloon. Twenty years later he comes back to that country and finds a new religion in which he is worshiped under the name of the "Sun Child," and it is said that he ascended into heaven. He finds that the Feast of the Ascension is about to be celebrated, and he hears Professors Hanky and Panky say to each other that they never set eyes on the man Higgs, and they hope they never will; but they are the high priests of the religion of the Sun Child. He is very indignant, and he comes up to them, and he says, "I am going to expose all this humbug and tell the people of Erewhon that it was only I, the man Higgs, and I went up in a balloon." He was told, "You must not do that, because all the morals of this country are bound round this myth, and if they once know that you did not ascend into heaven they will all become wicked"; and so he is persuaded of that and he goes quietly away. 10

That is the idea—that we should all be wicked if we did not hold to the Christian religion. It seems to me that the people who have held to it have been for the most part extremely wicked. You find this curious fact, that the more intense has been the religion of any period and the more profound has been the dogmatic belief, the greater has been the cruelty and the worse has been the state of affairs. In the so-called ages of faith, when men really did believe the Christian religion in all its completeness, there was the Inquisition, with its tortures; there were millions of unfortunate women burned as witches; and there was every kind of cruelty practiced upon all sorts of people in the name of religion. 11

You find as you look around the world that every single bit of progress in humane feeling, every improvement in the criminal law, every step toward the diminution of war, every step toward better treatment of the colored races, or every mitigation of slavery, every moral progress that there has been in the world, has been consistently opposed by the organized churches of the world. I say quite deliberately that the Christian religion, as organized in its churches, has been and still is the principal enemy of moral progress in the world. 12

HOW THE CHURCHES HAVE RETARDED PROGRESS

You may think that I am going too far when I say that that is still so. I do not think that I am. Take one fact. You will bear with me if I mention it. It 13 is not a pleasant fact, but the churches compel one to mention facts that are not pleasant. Supposing that in this world that we live in today an inexperienced girl is married to a syphilitic man; in that case the Catholic Church says, "This is an indissoluble sacrament. You must stay together for life." And no steps of any sort must be taken by that woman to prevent herself from giving birth to syphilitic children. That is what the Catholic Church says. I say that that is fiendish cruelty, and nobody whose natural sympathies have not been warped by dogma, or whose moral nature was not absolutely dead to all sense of suffering, could maintain that it is right and proper that that state of things should continue.

That is only an example. There are a great many ways in which, at the present moment, the church, by its insistence upon what it chooses to call morality, inflicts upon all sorts of people undeserved and unnecessary suffering. And of course, as we know, it is in its major part an opponent still of progress and of improvement in all the ways that diminish suffering in the world, because it has chosen to label as morality a certain narrow set of rules of conduct which have nothing to do with human happiness; and when you say that this or that ought to be done because it would make for human happiness, they think that has nothing to do with the matter at all. "What has human happiness to do with morals? The object of morals is not to make people happy." 14

FEAR, THE FOUNDATION OF RELIGION

Religion is based, I think, primarily and mainly upon fear. It is partly the terror of the unknown and partly, as I have said, the wish to feel that you have a kind of elder brother who will stand by you in all your troubles and disputes. Fear is the basis of the whole thing—fear of the mysterious, fear of defeat, fear of death. Fear is the parent of cruelty, and therefore it is no wonder if cruelty and religion have gone hand in hand. It is because fear is at the basis of those two things. In this world we can now begin a little to understand things, and a little to master them by help of science, which has forced its way step by step against the Christian religion, against the churches, and against the opposition of all the old precepts. Science can help us to get over this craven fear in which mankind has lived for so many generations. Science can teach us, and I think our own hearts can teach us, no longer to look around for imaginary supports, no longer to invent allies in the sky, but rather to look to our own efforts here below to make this world a fit place to live in, instead of the sort of place that the churches in all these centuries have made it. 15

WHAT WE MUST DO

We want to stand upon our own feet and look fair and square at the world— 16
its good facts, its bad facts, its beauties, and its ugliness; see the world as it

is and be not afraid of it. Conquer the world by intelligence and not merely by being slavishly subdued by the terror that comes from it. The whole conception of God is a conception derived from the ancient Oriental despotisms. It is a conception quite unworthy of free men. When you hear people in church debasing themselves and saying that they are miserable sinners, and all the rest of it, it seems contemptible and not worthy of self-respecting human beings. We ought to stand up and look the world frankly in the face. We ought to make the best we can of the world, and if it is not so good as we wish, after all it will still be better than what these others have made of it in all these ages. A good world needs knowledge, kindliness, and courage; it does not need a regretful hankering after the past or a fettering of the free intelligence by the words uttered long ago by ignorant men. It needs a fearless outlook and a free intelligence. It needs hope for the future, not looking back all the time toward a past that is dead, which we trust will be far surpassed by the future that our intelligence can create.

Questions for Discussion

1. Russell frequently addresses "you" and tells "you" what makes sense and what does not (for example, ¶1, sentence 4). Trace these seemingly direct addresses through the essay and decide whether they are all addressed to the same kind of reader. Is Russell addressing serious believers in Christianity, as he seems to be in paragraph 1? Or is he in fact ridiculing *those* "you's," at least part of the time, in order to produce an effect on some other kind of reader? In class discussion try to determine whether those of you who were already unsympathetic toward Christianity were more impressed by his arguments than were the Christian believers.
2. Readers sometimes mistakenly assume that when an author jokes about a subject he or she cannot be taking it seriously. But the world's finest, most "serious" writing is often cast in a tone of wit and humor, as you have no doubt noticed frequently in this book. (See, for example, E. B. White's "Bedfellows," pp. 386–394.) By attending to the *kind* of jest an author offers, we can discover a good deal about how we are to read. Make a short list of some of Russell's jests and jibes (for example, the joke in ¶4; the bit about "Kingdom Come" in ¶3; the phrase "have *got going* on cause" in ¶4). Discuss the clues they provide about how we should view his arguments.
3. Russell's style, in what he called his "unpopular essays," is always simple and forceful, implying that the issues he deals with are quite clear, if only one will follow his logic. Choose any passage that seems to you especially lively and read it aloud, dramatizing the tone of voice that the author

might use if he delivered the piece as a lecture. (Try, for example, ¶7.) As he works to reinforce an air of simple clarity, does he in fact rely on devices that are really quite complicated, if not downright tricky? For example, how would you describe the tone of the sentence "It is not really to my mind quite the best tone" (¶7)? Or again, what is the force of the Hindu story about the tortoise (¶4)?

4. Russell seems to provide us with clues, in his subtitles, about how his logical organization runs. But if you consider the nature and especially the strength of his charges against Christianity as the essay progresses, you discover another organization: He advances from amiable, mild, jesting charges to angry, righteous indignation (¶12) and finally to a kind of visionary release from the chains of the past (¶15). Why do you think he organizes his effects in this way? What does this suggest about the kind of reader he hopes to influence?

Suggested Essay Topics

1. As we have seen, every written statement, regardless of its stated purpose, provides us with evidence about the kind of person who is responsible for writing in precisely *this* way. (See "Writing as Self-discovery" by James E. Miller, Jr., pp. 183–188.) The sentence we are now writing, for example, implies authors who are *this* kind of people and not *that* kind. It tells you, most obviously, that we have chosen one certain "level of style" rather than any of many other possibilities, such as, "If you really gotta have us lay it out for you, we'll put it to you straight, but you oughta be able to figure it out for yourself—every time you open your yap you put your foot in it." But along with the choice of style we find suggestions about deeper matters of character; for example, what we have just said tells you that we care about certain "deeper matters," that we believe in the existence and importance of something called "character," and that we think it is important to learn how to "read" such matters in other people's prose.

   Write a description of the version of Bertrand Russell created by his essay. Using his character as projected by this essay, describe Russell as you would describe a new acquaintance. Give a word or two of evidence for each trait you attribute to him. (Don't worry, for now, about the flesh-and-blood author. He may or may not differ greatly from the self he chooses to present.) For example, "He is a man who would never voluntarily inflict pain on anyone. I know that is so because he shows so much feeling in portraying Christ's cruelty (¶7–8), and he explicitly hails 'kindliness' as a necessary quality in a virtuous man (¶16)."

2. This question is for those who have undergone at some time a major change of belief—either a conversion to or a deconversion from some religious creed. Russell asserts that in his experience religious people are no more virtuous than unbelievers; he implies in paragraph 11, in fact, that they are more vicious, and then, in paragraph 12, he says "quite deliber-

ately" that the Christian church "is the principal enemy of moral progress." Obviously no amount of evidence could prove or disprove this charge, since our "sample" of virtuous or vicious believers or unbelievers could never be more than a drop in the bucket. What we must do, then, is accept Russell's implied invitation and consult our own experience. Have you found that your beliefs about the world, or the beliefs of the organized group you belong to, have or have not helped you develop the "kindliness," courage, generosity, and honesty that Russell recommends? Write a description of how your beliefs fortify—or fail to fortify—your efforts to become a better person. Can you give an example of how your beliefs enabled you to resist some temptation to do something that you in fact disapprove of?

Another possibility is to write an account of how the beliefs you formerly held blocked your development. Think of examples of how your former beliefs made you shortsighted, unreasonable, dogmatic, bossy, and so on.

C. S. Lewis

A widely recognized literary critic and historian, C. S. Lewis (1898–1963) is now perhaps best known as an author of children's stories (the "Narnia" tales) and as a witty, intelligent defender of Christianity.

The task faced by all authors who set out to defend a given set of beliefs varies greatly, depending on how sympathetic their readers are when they begin. For many centuries, Christian authors writing in Europe or America could assume that most of their readers were to some degree ready to take their arguments seriously. But from the seventeenth century onward, the number of unbelievers increased rapidly. In our century, Christian "apologists" (as defenders of the faith have traditionally been called) have had to assume that most of their readers begin reading in either a skeptical or a hostile frame of mind. As Lewis reports of himself in his autobiographical work Surprised by Joy *(1955), proclaiming oneself an atheist in one's early youth became an almost automatic, normal step required of anyone with serious intellectual interests.*

Lewis's reconversion was by no means automatic, and the struggle between doubt and belief that he fought with himself made him one of the best-informed and most effective Christian writers of modern times. Because he had himself felt the force of every conceivable argument against belief, he was able to meet doubting readers as no "automatic" Christian could. In a series of satirical works (the best known is The Screwtape Letters*), in science fiction (for example,* Perelandra*), and in direct argument of the kind we print here, he attempted to remind unbelievers that the issues of belief and doubt are, as he says in paragraph 8, extremely complex and difficult—at least as difficult as his proof for the existence of God (in ¶6). His chief target often* *seems to be those who "put up a version of Christianity suitable for a child of six and make that the object of their attack" (¶9).*

Be sure to read the preceding essay by Bertrand Russell for comparison with this one. Like Russell, Lewis is master of a style that seems to make complex issues crystal clear; they both suggest, in various ways, that if one does not accept their conclusions one must simply be too dull to follow a plain argument.

In reading Lewis, as in reading Russell, it is a good idea, at least the second time round, to have pencil in hand, tracing the connections between conclusions and reasons.

WHAT CHRISTIANS BELIEVE

From book 2 of *Mere Christianity* (1943, 1945, 1952).

THE RIVAL CONCEPTIONS OF GOD

I have been asked to tell you what Christians believe, and I am going to begin 1
by telling you one thing that Christians do not need to believe. If you are a Christian you do not have to believe that all the other religions are simply wrong all through. If you are an atheist you do have to believe that the main point in all the religions of the whole world is simply one huge mistake. If you are a Christian, you are free to think that all these religions, even the queerest ones, contain at least some hint of the truth. When I was an atheist I had to try to persuade myself that most of the human race have always been wrong about the question that mattered to them most; when I became a Christian I was able to take a more liberal view. But, of course, being a Christian does mean thinking that where Christianity differs from other religions, Christianity is right and they are wrong. As in arithmetic—there is only one right answer to a sum, and all other answers are wrong: but some of the wrong answers are much nearer being right than others.

The first big division of humanity is into the majority, who believe in 2
some kind of God or gods, and the minority who do not. On this point, Christianity lines up with the majority—lines up with ancient Greeks and Romans, modern savages, Stoics, Platonists, Hindus, Mohammedans [Muslims], etc., against the modern Western European materialist.*

Now I go on to the next big division. People who all believe in God can 3
be divided according to the sort of God they believe in. There are two very different ideas on this subject. One of them is the idea that He is beyond good and evil. We humans call one thing good and another thing bad. But according to some people that is merely our human point of view. These people would say that the wiser you become the less you would want to call anything good or bad, and the more clearly you would see that everything is good in one way and bad in another, and that nothing could have been different.

*A materialist believes in the existence of only matter. Thus spirit, including the divine, the materialist considers an illusion. [Our note.]

Consequently, these people think that long before you got anywhere near the divine point of view the distinction would have disappeared altogether. We call a cancer bad, they would say, because it kills a man; but you might just as well call a successful surgeon bad because he kills a cancer. It all depends on the point of view. The other and opposite idea is that God is quite definitely "good" or "righteous," a God who takes sides, who loves love and hates hatred, who wants us to behave in one way and not in another. The first of these views—the one that thinks God beyond good and evil—is called Pantheism. It was held by the great Prussian philosopher Hegel and, as far as I can understand them, by the Hindus. The other view is held by Jews, Mohammedans and Christians.

And with this big difference between Pantheism and the Christian idea 4
of God, there usually goes another. Pantheists usually believe that God, so to speak, animates the universe as you animate your body: that the universe almost *is* God, so that if it did not exist He would not exist either, and anything you find in the universe is a part of God. The Christian[s'] idea is quite different. They think God invented and made the universe—like a man making a picture or composing a tune. A painter is not a picture, and he does not die if his picture is destroyed. You may say, "He's put a lot of himself into it," but you only mean that all its beauty and interest has come out of his head. His skill is not in the picture in the same way that it is in his head, or even in his hands. I expect you see how this difference between Pantheists and Christians hangs together with the other one. If you do not take the distinction between good and bad very seriously, then it is easy to say that anything you find in this world is a part of God. But, of course, if you think some things really bad, and God really good, then you cannot talk like that. You must believe that God is separate from the world and that some of the things we see in it are contrary to His will. Confronted with a cancer or a slum the Pantheist can say, "If you could only see it from the divine point of view, you would realise that this also is God." The Christian replies, "Don't talk damned nonsense."* For Christianity is a fighting religion. It thinks God made the world—that space and time, heat and cold, and all the colours and tastes, and all the animals and vegetables, are things that God "made up out of His head" as a man makes up a story. But it also thinks that a great many things have gone wrong with the world that God made and that God insists, and insists very loudly, on our putting them right again.

And, of course, that raises a very big question. If a good God made the 5
world why has it gone wrong? And for many years I simply refused to listen to the Christian answers to this question, because I kept on feeling "whatever you say, and however clever your arguments are, isn't it much simpler and easier to say that the world was not made by any intelligent power? Aren't

*One listener complained of the word *damned* as frivolous swearing. But I mean exactly what I say—nonsense that is *damned* is under God's curse, and will (apart from God's grace) lead those who believe it to eternal death. [Lewis's note.]

all your arguments simply a complicated attempt to avoid the obvious?" But then that threw me back into another difficulty.

My argument against God was that the universe seemed so cruel and unjust. But how had I got this idea of *just* and *unjust?* A man does not call a line crooked unless he has some idea of a straight line. What was I comparing this universe with when I called it unjust? If the whole show was bad and senseless from A to Z, so to speak, why did I, who was supposed to be part of the show, find myself in such violent reaction against it? A man feels wet when he falls into water, because man is not a water animal: a fish would not feel wet. Of course I could have given up my idea of justice by saying it was nothing but a private idea of my own. But if I did that, then my argument against God collapsed too—for the argument depended on saying that the world was really unjust, not simply that it did not happen to please my private fancies. Thus in the very act of trying to prove that God did not exist—in other words, that the whole of reality was senseless—I found I was forced to assume that one part of reality—namely my idea of justice—was full of sense. Consequently atheism turns out to be too simple. If the whole universe has no meaning, we should never have found out that it has no meaning: just as, if there were no light in the universe and therefore no creatures with eyes, we should never know it was dark. *Dark* would be without meaning. 6

THE INVASION

Very well then, atheism is too simple. And I will tell you another view that is also too simple. It is the view I call Christianity-and-water, the view which simply says there is a good God in Heaven and everything is all right—leaving out all the difficult and terrible doctrines about sin and hell and the devil, and the redemption. Both these are boys' philosophies. 7

It is no good asking for a simple religion. After all, real things are not simple. They look simple, but they are not. The table I am sitting at looks simple: but ask a scientist to tell you what it is really made of—all about the atoms and how the light waves rebound from them and hit my eye and what they do to the optic nerve and what it does to my brain—and, of course, you find that what we call "seeing a table" lands you in mysteries and complications which you can hardly get to the end of. A child saying a child's prayer looks simple. And if you are content to stop there, well and good. But if you are not—and the modern world usually is not—if you want to go on and ask what is really happening—then you must be prepared for something difficult. If we ask for something more than simplicity, it is silly then to complain that the something more is not simple. 8

Very often, however, this silly procedure is adopted by people who are not silly, but who, consciously or unconsciously, want to destroy Christianity. Such people put up a version of Christianity suitable for a child of six and make that the object of their attack. When you try to explain the Chris- 9 tian doctrine as it is really held by an instructed adult, they then complain that you are making their heads turn round and that it is all too complicated and that if there really were a God they are sure He would have made "religion" simple, because simplicity is so beautiful, etc. You must be on your guard against these people for they will change their ground every minute and only waste your time. Notice, too, their idea of God "making religion simple": as if "religion" were something God invented, and not His statement to us of certain quite unalterable facts about His own nature.

Besides being complicated, reality, in my experience, is usually odd. It 10
is not neat, not obvious, not what you expect. For instance, when you have grasped that the earth and the other planets all go round the sun, you would naturally expect that all the planets were made to match—all at equal distances from each other, say, or distances that regularly increased, or all the same size, or else getting bigger or smaller as you go farther from the sun. In fact, you find no rhyme or reason (that we can see) about either the sizes or the distances; and some of them have one moon, one has four, one has two, some have none, and one has a ring.

Reality, in fact, is usually something you could not have guessed. That 11
is one of the reasons I believe Christianity. It is a religion you could not have guessed. If it offered us just the kind of universe we had always expected, I should feel we were making it up. But, in fact, it is not the sort of thing anyone would have made up. It has just that queer twist about it that real things have. So let us leave behind all these boys' philosophies—these over-simple answers. The problem is not simple and the answer is not going to be simple either.

What is the problem? A universe that contains much that is obviously 12
bad and apparently meaningless, but containing creatures like ourselves who know that it is bad and meaningless. There are only two views that face all the facts. One is the Christian view that this is a good world that has gone wrong, but still retains the memory of what it ought to have been. The other is the view called Dualism. Dualism means the belief that there are two equal and independent powers at the back of everything, one of them good and the other bad, and that this universe is the battlefield in which they fight out an endless war. I personally think that next to Christianity Dualism is the manliest and most sensible creed on the market. But it has a catch in it.

The two powers, or spirits, or gods—the good one and the bad one—are 13
supposed to be quite independent. They both existed from all eternity. Neither of them made the other, neither of them has any more right than the other to call itself God. Each presumably thinks it is good and thinks the other bad. One of them likes hatred and cruelty, the other likes love and mercy, and each backs its own view. Now what do we mean when we call one of them the Good Power and the other the Bad Power? Either we are merely saying that we happen to prefer the one to the other—like preferring beer to cider—or else we are saying that, whatever the two powers think about it, and whichever we humans, at the moment, happen to like, one of them is actually wrong, actually mistaken, in regarding itself as good. Now if we

mean merely that we happen to prefer the first, then we must give up talking about good and evil at all. For good means what you ought to prefer quite regardless of what you happen to like at any given moment. If "being good" meant simply joining the side you happened to fancy, for no real reason, then good would not deserve to be called good. So we must mean that one of the two powers is actually wrong and the other actually right.

But the moment you say that, you are putting into the universe a third 14
thing in addition to the two Powers: some law or standard or rule of good which one of the powers conforms to and the other fails to conform to. But since the two powers are judged by this standard, then this standard, or the Being who made this standard, is farther back and higher up than either of them, and He will be the real God. In fact, what we meant by calling them good and bad turns out to be that one of them is in a right relation to the real ultimate God and the other in a wrong relation to Him.

The same point can be made in a different way. If Dualism is true, then 15
the bad Power must be a being who likes badness for its own sake. But in reality we have no experience of anyone liking badness just because it is bad. The nearest we can get to it is in cruelty. But in real life people are cruel for one of two reasons—either because they are sadists, that is, because they have a sexual perversion which makes cruelty a cause of sensual pleasure to them, or else for the sake of something they are going to get out of it—money, or power, or safety. But pleasure, money, power, and safety are all, as far as they go, good things. The badness consists in pursuing them by the wrong method, or in the wrong way, or too much. I do not mean, of course, that the people who do this are not desperately wicked. I do mean that wickedness, when you examine it, turns out to be the pursuit of some good in the wrong way. You can be good for the mere sake of goodness: you cannot be bad for the mere sake of badness. You can do a kind action when you are not feeling kind and when it gives you no pleasure, simply because kindness is right; but no one ever did a cruel action simply because cruelty is wrong—only because cruelty was pleasant or useful to him. In other words badness cannot succeed even in being bad in the same way in which goodness is good. Goodness is, so to speak, itself: badness is only spoiled goodness. And there must be something good first before it can be spoiled. We called sadism a sexual perversion; but you must first have the idea of a normal sexuality before you can talk of its being perverted; and you can see which is the perversion, because you can explain the perverted from the normal, and cannot explain the normal from the perverted. It follows that this Bad Power, who is supposed to be on an equal footing with the Good Power, and to love badness in the same way as the Good Power loves goodness, is a mere bogy. In order to be bad he must have good things to want and then to pursue in the wrong way: he must have impulses which were originally good in order to be able to pervert them. But if he is bad he cannot supply himself either with good things to desire or with good impulses to pervert. He must be getting both from the Good Power. And if so, then he is not independent. He is part of the Good Power's world: he was made either by the Good Power or by some power above them both.

Put it more simply still. To be bad, he must exist and have intelligence and will. But existence, intelligence and will are in themselves good. Therefore he must be getting them from the Good Power: even to be bad he must borrow or steal from his opponent. And do you now begin to see why Christianity has always said that the devil is a fallen angel? That is not a mere story for the children. It is a real recognition of the fact that evil is a parasite, not an original thing. The powers which enable evil to carry on are powers given it by goodness. All the things which enable a bad man to be effectively bad are in themselves good things—resolution, cleverness, good looks, existence itself. That is why Dualism, in a strict sense, will not work. 16

But I freely admit that real Christianity (as distinct from Christianity-and-water) goes much nearer to Dualism than people think. One of the things that surprised me when I first read the New Testament seriously was that it talked so much about a Dark Power in the universe—a mighty evil spirit who was held to be the Power behind death and disease, and sin. The difference is that Christianity thinks this Dark Power was created by God, and was good when he was created, and went wrong. Christianity agrees with Dualism that this universe is at war. But it does not think this is a war between independent powers. It thinks it is a civil war, a rebellion, and that we are living in a part of the universe occupied by the rebel. 17

Enemy-occupied territory—that is what this world is. Christianity is the story of how the rightful king has landed, you might say landed in disguise, and is calling us all to take part in a great campaign of sabotage. When you go to church you are really listening-in to the secret wireless from our friends: that is why the enemy is so anxious to prevent us from going. He does it by playing on our conceit and laziness and intellectual snobbery. I know someone will ask me, "Do you really mean, at this time of day, to re-introduce our old friend the devil—hoofs and horns and all?" Well, what the time of day has to do with it I do not know. And I am not particular about the hoofs and horns. But in other respects my answer is "Yes, I do." I do not claim to know anything about his personal appearance. If anybody really wants to know him better I would say to that person, "Don't worry. If you really want to, you will. Whether you'll like it when you do is another question." 18

THE SHOCKING ALTERNATIVE

Christians, then, believe that an evil power has made himself for the present the Prince of this World. And, of course, that raises problems. Is this state of affairs in accordance with God's will or not? If it is, He is a strange God, you will say: and if it is not, how can anything happen contrary to the will of a being with absolute power? 19

But anyone who has been in authority knows how a thing can be in accordance with your will in one way and not in another. It may be quite sensible for a mother to say to the children, "I'm not going to go and make you tidy the schoolroom every night. You've got to learn to keep it tidy on your own." Then she goes up one night and finds the Teddy bear and the ink 20 and the French Grammar all lying in the grate. That is against her will. She would prefer the children to be tidy. But on the other hand, it is her will which has left the children free to be untidy. The same thing arises in any regiment, or trade union, or school. You make a thing voluntary and then half the people do not do it. That is not what you willed, but your will has made it possible.

It is probably the same in the universe. God created things which had free will. That means creatures which can go either wrong or right. Some people think they can imagine a creature which was free but had no possibility of going wrong; I cannot. If a thing is free to be good it is also free to be bad. And free will is what has made evil possible. Why, then, did God give them free will? Because free will, though it makes evil possible, is also the only thing that makes possible any love or goodness or joy worth having. A world of automata—of creatures that worked like machines—would hardly be worth creating. The happiness which God designs for His higher creatures is the happiness of being freely, voluntarily united to Him and to each other in an ecstasy of love and delight compared with which the most rapturous love between a man and a woman on this earth is mere milk and water. And for that they must be free. 21

Of course God knew what would happen if they used their freedom the wrong way: apparently He thought it worth the risk. Perhaps we feel inclined to disagree with Him. But there is a difficulty about disagreeing with God. He is the source from which all your reasoning power comes: you could not be right and He wrong any more than a stream can rise higher than its own source. When you are arguing against Him you are arguing against the very power that makes you able to argue at all: it is like cutting off the branch you are sitting on. If God thinks this state of war in the universe a price worth paying for free will—that is, for making a live world in which creatures can do real good or harm and something of real importance can happen, instead of a toy world which only moves when He pulls the strings—then we may take it it is worth paying. 22

When we have understood about free will, we shall see how silly it is to ask, as somebody once asked me: "Why did God make a creature of such rotten stuff that it went wrong?" The better stuff a creature is made of—the cleverer and stronger and freer it is—then the better it will be if it goes right, but also the worse it will be if it goes wrong. A cow cannot be very good or very bad; a dog can be both better and worse; a child better and worse still; an ordinary man, still more so; a man of genius, still more so; a superhuman spirit best—or worst—of all. 23

How did the Dark Power go wrong? Here, no doubt, we ask a question to which human beings cannot give an answer with any certainty. A reasonable (and traditional) guess, based on our own experiences of going wrong, can, however, be offered. The moment you have a self at all, there is a possibility of putting yourself first—wanting to be the centre—wanting to be God, in fact. That was the sin of Satan: and that was the sin he taught the human race. Some people think the fall of man had something to do 24 with sex, but that is a mistake. (The story in the Book of Genesis rather suggests that some corruption in our sexual nature followed the fall and was its result, not its cause.) What Satan put into the heads of our remote ancestors was the idea that they could "be like gods"—could set up on their own as if they had created themselves—be their own masters—invent some sort of happiness for themselves outside God, apart from God. And out of that hopeless attempt has come nearly all that we call human history—money, poverty, ambition, war, prostitution, classes, empires, slavery—the long terrible story of man trying to find something other than God which will make him happy.

The reason why it can never succeed is this. God made us: invented us 25
as a man invents an engine. A car is made to run on gasoline, and it would not run properly on anything else. Now God designed the human machine to run on Himself. He Himself is the fuel our spirits were designed to burn, or the food our spirits were designed to feed on. There is no other. That is why it is just no good asking God to make us happy in our own way without bothering about religion. God cannot give us a happiness and peace apart from Himself, because it is not there. There is no such thing.

That is the key to history. Terrific energy is expended—civilisations are 26
built up—excellent institutions devised; but each time something goes wrong. Some fatal flaw always brings the selfish and cruel people to the top and it all slides back into misery and ruin. In fact, the machine conks. It seems to start up all right and runs a few yards, and then it breaks down. They are trying to run it on the wrong juice. That is what Satan has done to us humans.

And what did God do? First of all He left us conscience, the sense of 27
right and wrong: and all through history there have been people trying (some of them very hard) to obey it. None of them ever quite succeeded. Secondly, He sent the human race what I call good dreams: I mean those queer stories scattered all through the heathen religions about a god who dies and comes to life again and, by his death, has somehow given new life to men. Thirdly, He selected one particular people and spent several centuries hammering into their heads the sort of God He was—that there was only one of Him and that He cared about right conduct. Those people were the Jews, and the Old Testament gives an account of the hammering process.

Then comes the real shock. Among these Jews there suddenly turns up 28
a man who goes about talking as if He was God. He claims to forgive sins. He says He has always existed. He says He is coming to judge the world at the end of time. Now let us get this clear. Among Pantheists, like the Indians, anyone might say that he was a part of God, or one with God: there would be nothing very odd about it. But this man, since He was a Jew, could not mean that kind of God. God, in their language, meant the Being outside the world Who had made it and was infinitely different from anything else. And when you have grasped that, you will see that what this man said was, quite simply, the most shocking thing that has ever been uttered by human lips.

One part of the claim tends to slip past us unnoticed because we have 29
heard it so often that we no longer see what it amounts to. I mean the claim

to forgive sins: any sins. Now unless the speaker is God, this is really so preposterous as to be comic. We can all understand how a man forgives offences against himself. You tread on my toe and I forgive you, you steal my money and I forgive you. But what should we make of a man, himself unrobbed and untrodden on, who announced that he forgave you for treading on other men's toes and stealing other men's money? Asinine fatuity is the kindest description we should give of his conduct. Yet this is what Jesus did. He told people that their sins were forgiven, and never waited to consult all the other people whom their sins had undoubtedly injured. He unhesitatingly behaved as if He was the party chiefly concerned, the person chiefly offended in all offences. This makes sense only if He really was the God whose laws are broken and whose love is wounded in every sin. In the mouth of any speaker who is not God, these words would imply what I can only regard as a silliness and conceit unrivalled by any other character in history.

Yet (and this is the strange, significant thing) even His enemies, when 30
they read the Gospels, do not usually get the impression of silliness and conceit. Still less do unprejudiced readers. Christ says that He is "humble and meek" and we believe Him; not noticing that, if He were merely a man, humility and meekness are the very last characteristics we could attribute to some of His sayings.

I am trying here to prevent anyone saying the really foolish thing that 31
people often say about Him: "I'm ready to accept Jesus as a great moral teacher, but I don't accept His claim to be God." That is the one thing we must not say. A man who was merely a man and said the sort of things Jesus said would not be a great moral teacher. He would either be a lunatic—on a level with the man who says he is a poached egg—or else he would be the Devil of Hell. You must make your choice. Either this man was, and is, the Son of God: or else a madman or something worse. You can shut Him up for a fool, you can spit at Him and kill Him as a demon; or you can fall at His feet and call Him Lord and God. But let us not come with any patronising nonsense about His being a great human teacher. He has not left that open to us. He did not intend to.

Questions for Discussion

1. Lewis clearly sees that many of his readers will find some of his views shocking, perhaps most obviously his claim that Satan is literally real. Does he, like Russell, take any steps to lead his readers gently into the more controversial territory? Do the steps work? To put it another way, did you feel, by the end of the first few paragraphs, that the author could on the whole be trusted, even if you could not fully accept his arguments?

2. Russell tells us that he was once a believer who learned better. Lewis tells us that he was once an unbeliever who learned better (¶1). Do they increase their persuasiveness by making this kind of claim? Why or why not?
3. Lewis engages in much less obvious jesting than Russell, and he does not pause, like Russell, to relate illustrative anecdotes. (He does of course engage in frequent witty thrusts, but his tone is on the whole more serious.) Do you find his style heavy or pompous? How would you describe the "person" behind the writing here? Be as detailed as you can, giving both intellectual and moral qualities.
4. Work out in discussion with your classmates the exact line of argument in the section called "The Invasion." Give special attention to the logic in paragraph 12. When writers give us "only two possibilities," we should always be on our guard. Only if there *really* are no other possibilities must we accept their choice, and it is worth remembering that in most human issues the possibilities are not limited to two. Has Lewis played fair with his sharp choice between Christianity and Dualism? If you think of other possibilities, be sure that they are not merely other versions of one of his.
5. Later in the essay Lewis gives us a sharp choice among three possibilities: either Christ was who he said he was, or he was mad, or he was the Devil of hell (¶31). What would Russell be likely to say about this choice? Again it is useful to ask yourself whether there are any other possibilities.
6. Whether we agree with them or not, both Russell and Lewis can teach us a good deal about how to present a case effectively. Lewis is especially skillful in this essay in organizing a body of difficult material into a clear sequence of steps. Trace those steps and ask about each of them: Why does he take it at *this* point? Once you have done that kind of reading of a variety of complicated essays, your own powers of organization will inevitably increase. (See "Why Use a 'Reader' in a Writing Course?" pp. 6–9.)

Suggested Essay Topics

1. If you consider yourself a Christian, write a letter to Lewis, explaining to him how his version of Christianity is similar to or different from yours. Your purpose, in the latter case, is not to convert him but to persuade him to see your view as something that he should take into account.
2. If you are an unbeliever in Christianity or a believer in some other religion, write a letter to either Lewis or Russell, disagreeing with any points in their arguments that seem faulty. Be sure that you have understood the point before trying to refute it.

12

ECONOMIC PERSPECTIVES

Capitalism Attacked and Defended

Money is indeed the most important thing in the world;
and all sound and successful personal and national morality should
have this fact for its basis.
George Bernard Shaw

But man has almost constant occasion for the help of his brethren,
and it is in vain for him to expect it from their
benevolence only. He will be more likely to prevail if he can
interest their self-love in his favour, and show them that it is for
their own advantage to do for him what he requires of
them. . . . It is not from the benevolence of the butcher, the brewer,
or the baker, that we can expect our dinner, but from
their regard to their own interest.
Adam Smith

A fool and his money are soon parted.
Old proverb

Money is like muck, not good except it be spread.
Sir Francis Bacon

You pays your money and you takes your choice.
Popular saying

The love of money is the root of all evil.
I Timothy 6:10

He that wants [i.e., lacks] money, means, and content
is without three good friends.
Shakespeare

Wine maketh merry: but money answereth all things.
Ecclesiastes 10:19

E. M. Forster

The English novelist and essayist E. M. Forster (1879–1970) published his most famous novel, A Passage to India, *in 1924. It was the money from American sales of this novel (alluded to in ¶1) that enabled him to buy the woods that gave him the title of this essay.*

"My Wood" is a good example of indirect argument. On the surface the essay is all about Forster himself—the effect on his character of owning property. But under the surface is another topic, related to the first but larger and more general. It is an indirect argument about the evils of an economic system that encourages us to think that owning things is a worthy objective in life—even the highest objective, a sufficient substitute for all other experiences. Our economic system implies that if we own enough things, we don't have to be intelligent, clever, creative, or compassionate. We don't even need to know how to enjoy ourselves.

Forster's larger argument is strongly hinted but not developed outright. Since Forster talks only about his own feelings and experience, he must make it clear that his references to himself are really observations about human beings in general, as they live under our economic system. Forster quietly but insistently places his own story within larger contexts ranging from biblical stories to the example of a man who ruins his woods by walling them off. In each case it is impossible to apply Forster's judgments only to him (although he asks you, tongue in cheek, to do so). In reality his judgments extend to the whole social system that holds up ownership of things as the main objective of life.

As you read, try to determine what kind of response to his indictment of our economic and social system Forster is asking for. Is he calling for political revolution? For moral reform? For a reaffirmation of religious principles? Or does he have some other aim in mind altogether?

MY WOOD

From *Abinger Harvest* (1936). "My Wood" was written in 1926.

A few years ago I wrote a book which dealt in part with the difficulties of the English in India. Feeling that they would have had no difficulties in India themselves, the Americans read the book freely. The more they read it the better it made them feel, and a cheque to the author was the result. I bought a wood with the cheque. It is not a large wood—it contains scarcely any trees, and it is intersected, blast it, by a public footpath. Still, it is the first property that I have owned, so it is right that other people should participate in my shame, and should ask themselves, in accents that will vary in horror, this very important question: What is the effect of property upon the character? Don't let's touch economics; the effect of private ownership upon the community as a whole is another question—a more important question, perhaps, but another one. Let's keep to psychology. If you own things, what's their effect on you? What's the effect on me of my wood? 1

In the first place, it makes me feel heavy. Property does have this effect. 2
Property produces men of weight, and it was a man of weight who failed to get into the Kingdom of Heaven. He was not wicked, that unfortunate millionaire in the parable, he was only stout; he stuck out in front, not to mention behind, and as he wedged himself this way and that in the crystalline entrance and bruised his well-fed flanks, he saw beneath him a comparatively slim camel passing through the eye of a needle [Mark 10:25] and being woven into the robe of God. The Gospels all through couple stoutness and slowness. They point out what is perfectly obvious, yet seldom realized: that if you have a lot of things you cannot move about a lot, that furniture requires dusting, dusters require servants, servants require insurance stamps, and the whole tangle of them makes you think twice before you accept an invitation to dinner or go for a bathe in the Jordan [II Kings 5:1–14]. Sometimes the Gospels proceed further and say with Tolstoy that property is sinful; they approach the difficult ground of asceticism here, where I cannot follow them. But as to the immediate effects of property on people, they just show straightforward logic. It produces men of weight. Men of weight cannot, by definition, move like the lightning from the East unto the West [Matthew 24:27], and the ascent of a fourteen-stone* bishop into a pulpit is thus the exact antithesis of the coming of the Son of Man. My wood makes me feel heavy.

In the second place, it makes me feel it ought to be larger. 3

The other day I heard a twig snap in it. I was annoyed at first, for I 4
thought that someone was blackberrying, and depreciating the value of the undergrowth. On coming nearer, I saw it was not a man who had trodden on the twig and snapped it, but a bird, and I felt pleased. My bird. The bird was not equally pleased. Ignoring the relation between us, it took fright as soon as it saw the shape of my face, and flew straight over the boundary hedge into a field, the property of Mrs. Henessy, where it sat down with a loud

*A stone is a British weight equal to 14 pounds.

squawk. It had become Mrs. Henessy's bird. Something seemed grossly amiss here, something that would not have occurred had the wood been larger. I could not afford to buy Mrs. Henessy out, I dared not murder her, and limitations of this sort beset me on every side. Ahab did not want that vineyard [I Kings 21]—he only needed it to round off his property, preparatory to plotting a new curve—and all the land around my wood has become necessary to me in order to round off the wood. A boundary protects. But—poor little thing—the boundary ought in its turn to be protected. Noises on the edge of it. Children throw stones. A rettle more, and then a little more, until we reach the sea. Happy Canute!* Happier Alexander!† And after all, why should even the world be the limit of possession? A rocket containing a Union Jack,‡ will, it is hoped, be shortly fired at the moon. Mars. Sirius. Beyond which . . . But these immensities ended by saddening me. I could not suppose that my wood was the destined nucleus of universal dominion—it is so very small and contains no mineral wealth beyond the blackberries. Nor was I comforted when Mrs. Henessy's bird took alarm for the second time and flew clean away from us all, under the belief that it belonged to itself.

In the third place, property makes its owner feel that he ought to do 5
something to it. Yet he isn't sure what. A restlessness comes over him, a vague sense that he has a personality to express—the same sense which, without any vagueness, leads the artist to an act of creation. Sometimes I think I will cut down such trees as remain in the wood, at other times I want to fill up the gaps between them with new trees. Both impulses are pretentious and empty. They are not honest movements towards money-making or beauty. They spring from a foolish desire to express myself and from an inability to enjoy what I have got. Creation, property, enjoyment form a sinister trinity in the human mind. Creation and enjoyment are both very, very good, yet they are often unattainable without a material basis, and at such moments property pushes itself in as a substitute, saying, "Accept me instead—I'm good enough for all three." It is not enough. It is, as Shakespeare said of lust, "The expense of spirit in a waste of shame": it is "Before, a joy proposed; behind, a dream." Yet we don't know how to shun it. It is forced on us by our economic system as the alternative to starvation. It is also forced on us by an internal defect in the soul, by the feeling that in property may lie the germs of self-development and of exquisite or heroic deeds. Our life on earth is, and ought to be, material and carnal. But we have not yet learned to manage our materialism and carnality properly; they are still entangled with the desire for ownership, where (in the words of Dante) "Possession is one with loss."

And this brings us to our fourth and final point: the blackberries. 6

Blackberries are not plentiful in this meagre grove, but they are easily 7
seen from the public footpath which traverses it, and all too easily gathered.

*Danish king who ruled all of England for about 20 years in the eleventh century.

†Alexander the Great (356–323 B.C.), who conquered all of the civilized world from Macedonia into Egypt.

‡The British flag.

Foxgloves, too—people will pull up the foxgloves, and ladies of an educational tendency even grub for toadstools to show them on the Monday in class. Other ladies, less educated, roll down the bracken in the arms of their gentlemen friends. There is paper, there are tins. Pray, does my wood belong to me or doesn't it? And, if it does, should I not own it best by allowing no one else to walk there? There is a wood near Lyme Regis, also cursed by a public footpath, where the owner has not hesitated on this point. He had built high stone walls each side of the path, and has spanned it by bridges, so that the public circulate like termites while he gorges on the blackberries unseen. He really does own his wood, this able chap. Dives in Hell did pretty well, but the gulf dividing him from Lazarus could be traversed by vision, and nothing traverses it here [Luke 16:19–26].* And perhaps I shall come to this in time. I shall wall in and fence out until I really taste the sweets of property. Enormously stout, endlessly avaricious, pseudo-creative, intensely selfish, I shall weave upon my forehead the quadruple crown of possession until those nasty Bolshies† come and take it off again and thrust me aside into the outer darkness.

Questions for Discussion

1. State in your own words the four effects that owning the wood had on Forster. Begin your statement something like this: "Property has four main effects on the moral character of the owner. . . ."
2. What "shame" is Forster talking about in paragraph 1? Does he mean this literally or tongue-in-cheek? Can you decide without reading farther into the essay? How far must you go before you know?
3. "Don't let's touch economics," he says in paragraph 1. Does he mean this literally or tongue-in-cheek? How do you know?
4. In paragraph 4 what mixture of reactions is elicited by the two words "My bird"? How do the words work? What happens to the effect of the paragraph if you omit these two words?
5. At the end of his essay (¶7) and at the end of his experience of ownership, Forster pictures himself sitting within his walled-up woods, "enormously stout, endlessly avaricious, pseudo-creative, [and] intensely selfish." Is he merely trying to get a laugh, or is he saying what he really thinks about persons who fall prey to the temptations of an acquisitive economic system? Does the description "go too far," or does it express a fair moral judgment?

*The "rich man" in the story is actually unnamed but is traditionally called Dives, the Latin word for "rich man."

†Bolsheviks, that is, communists, who are ideologically opposed to the private ownership of property.

6. The last two sentences of paragraph 2 exhibit a typical stylistic device of this essay: a fairly complex sentence in formal English followed by a simple sentence in colloquial English. Does this mixing of styles work for or against Forster's effectiveness? What happens to the effectiveness of any given paragraph if you make all of the sentences in it either consistently formal or consistently colloquial?

Suggested Essay Topics

1. Most of us know people who are out-and-out moneygrubbers—grade-A materialists whose only way of valuing anything is to look at the price tag. Imagine yourself sending these people a copy of Forster's essay, setting yourself the task of writing an introduction to it that will (without pointing the finger at them directly) force them to read it as a judgment on their materialism. You will have to make your introduction more than a summary; it must clarify the underlying value judgments that make this essay a reproof to your audience's intense acquisitiveness.
2. At the end of paragraph 5 Forster distinguishes "materialism and carnality" on the one hand from "the desire for ownership" on the other, and he quotes Dante to the effect that to own things is to lose them. Write an essay to your instructor in which you explain what this distinction means. This may seem difficult at first, but think of Forster's blackberries as a clue about how to start. Enjoying the blackberries is a carnal and material pleasure, surely an innocent one, but wanting to *own* the blackberries turns out to be something quite different. Consider whether this truth about the blackberries also applies to other things, such as possessiveness between men and women or domination of children by parents. Find enough examples to illuminate the meaning, and perhaps even show the validity, of the distinction.

Max Apple

Born in 1941, Max Apple spent the first 25 years of his life in the American post-war boom economy. For 25 years American productivity, the wonder of the world, washed a tidal wave of technology, consumer goods, and wealth across the nation, saturating even small towns and out-of-the-way places with washing machines, televisions, interstate highways, chain restaurants, and motels. Though Americans of all periods, even the Pilgrims, have been committed to some version of "progress," by the 1950s "progress" had come to be viewed by many Americans as synonymous with technology (speed and machines) and "development" (turning such resources as land, timber, water, minerals, and labor into cash).

These traits receive a strong satirical treatment in Max Apple's story about a fictitious Howard Johnson. Ask yourself whether Apple wants us to view HJ, as he is called in the story, as representing the best or worst of these traits, or as representing some middle ground between them? (See the introduction to Jonathan Swift's "Modest Proposal," pp. 483–491, for a discussion of satire and irony.) Regardless of how you answer this question, it is clear that Apple's satire is not like Dickens's withering indignation (see "Hard Facts," pp. 45–57) or Swift's savage irony. It is lighter of touch—more amused and more tongue-in-cheek, less thunderous and less prophetic—than Dickens's or Swift's satire. Yet the satirical vision is both penetrating and uncompromising. We leave it to you to identify the real target.

The satire begins in the title, which is a comic perversion of The Greening of America, *a book that gained a wide but brief popularity in the 1960s by proposing that modern society could save itself by returning to the life of the soil, by abandoning the urban rat race, by joining farm communes to re-learn the honesty of manual labor, and so on. Most Americans of the 1960s, however, were not about to exchange their hair dryers, fast cars, cheap gas, stereophonic sound, and air conditioning for the "honesty" of shoveling cow manure in some commune barnyard. For a variety of reasons both good and bad, commercial development has continued since the 1960s unimpeded and unbothered by the "return to the earth" movement.*

In his satire, Apple creates a composite picture that intertwines modern American commercialism with American myths from an earlier time—myths portraying the Indians' and pioneers' closeness to the land. Millie thinks of herself and HJ as "pioneers," for example, and HJ describes the erection of a new motel as being "like a seed grown into a tree, Millie" (¶6). Mildred thinks to herself that "Howard knew the land the way the Indians must have known it" (¶12). It is clear that Apple finds such self-serving, self-glamorizing views of American businessmen amusing. Does he also find them contemptible? Is he indignant and angry as well as amused? Try to determine how he wants you *to feel about the picture he presents of American commercialism. Is he being fair? Or is it fair of us to ask him to be fair? When Mildred takes a beautiful sunset, turns the color of it into the idea for tacky orange motel roofs, and calls it creativity—"And suddenly I thought what if the tops of our houses were that kind of orange, what a world it would be" (¶43)—how do you respond? Do you want to agree, ruefully, "What a world it would be!" or do you resist the suggestion that commercial development is inherently cheap and tacky? How effectively—persuasively—has Apple made his point?*

THE ORANGING OF AMERICA

From *The Oranging of America and Other Stories* (1974).

I

From the outside it looked like any ordinary 1964 Cadillac limousine. In the expensive space between the driver and passengers, where some installed bars or even bathrooms, Mr. Howard Johnson kept a tidy ice-cream freezer in 1 which there were always at least eighteen flavors on hand, though Mr. Johnson ate only vanilla. The freezer's power came from the battery with an independent auxiliary generator as a back-up system. Although now Howard Johnson means primarily motels, Millie, Mr. HJ, and Otis Brighton, the chauffeur, had not forgotten that ice cream was the cornerstone of their empire. Some of the important tasting was still done in the car. Mr. HJ might have reports in his pocket from sales executives and marketing analysts, from home economists and chemists, but not until Mr. Johnson reached over the lowered Plexiglas to spoon a taste or two into the expert waiting mouth of Otis Brighton did he make any final flavor decision. He might go ahead with butterfly shrimp, with candy kisses, and with packaged chocolate-chip cookies on the opinion of the specialists, but in ice cream he trusted only Otis. From the back seat Howard Johnson would keep his eye on the rearview mirror, where the reflection of pleasure or disgust showed itself in the dark eyes of Otis Brighton no matter what the driving conditions. He could be stalled in a commuter rush with the engine overheating and a dripping oil pan, and still a taste of the right kind never went unappreciated.

When Otis finally said, "Mr. Howard, that shore is sumpin, that one is 2
um-hum. That is it, my man, that is it." Then and not until then did Mr. HJ finally decide to go ahead with something like banana-fudge-ripple royale.

Mildred rarely tasted and Mr. HJ was addicted to one scoop of vanilla 3
every afternoon at three, eaten from his aluminum dish with a disposable plastic spoon. The duties of Otis, Millie, and Mr. Johnson were so divided that they rarely infringed upon one another in the car, which was their office. Neither Mr. HJ nor Millie knew how to drive, Millie and Otis understood little of financing and leasing, and Mr. HJ left the compiling of the "Traveling Reports" and "The Howard Johnson Newsletter" strictly to the literary style of his longtime associate, Miss Mildred Bryce. It was an ideal division of labor, which, in one form or another, had been in continuous operation for well over a quarter of a century.

While Otis listened to the radio behind his soundproof Plexiglas, while 4
Millie in her small, neat hand compiled data for the newsletter, Mr. HJ liked to lean back into the spongy leather seat looking through his specially tinted windshield at the fleeting land. Occasionally, lulled by the hum of the freezer, he might doze off, his large pink head lolling toward the shoulder of his blue suit, but there was not too much that Mr. Johnson missed, even in advanced age.

Along with Millie he planned their continuous itinerary as they trav- 5
eled. Mildred would tape a large green relief map of the United States to the Plexiglas separating them from Otis. The mountains on the map were light brown and seemed to melt toward the valleys like the crust of a fresh apple pie settling into cinnamon surroundings. The existing HJ houses (Millie called the restaurants and motels houses) were marked by orange dots, while projected future sites bore white dots. The deep green map with its brown mountains and colorful dots seemed much more alive than the miles that twinkled past Mr. Johnson's gaze, and nothing gave the ice-cream king

greater pleasure than watching Mildred with her fine touch, and using the original crayon, turn an empty white dot into an orange fulfillment.

"It's like a seed grown into a tree, Millie," Mr. HJ liked to say at such moments when he contemplated the map and saw that it was good. 6

They had started traveling together in 1925: Mildred, then a secretary to Mr. Johnson, a young man with two restaurants and a dream of hospitality, and Otis, a twenty-year-old busboy and former driver of a Louisiana mule. When Mildred graduated from college, her father, a Michigan doctor who kept his money in a blue steel box under the examining table, encouraged her to try the big city. He sent her a monthly allowance. In those early days she always had more than Mr. Johnson, who paid her $16.50 a week and meals. In the first decade they traveled only on weekends, but every year since 1936 they had spent at least six months on the road, and it might have gone on much longer if Mildred's pain and the trouble in New York with Howard Jr. had not come so close together. 7

They were all stoical at the Los Angeles International Airport. Otis waited at the car for what might be his last job while Miss Bryce and Mr. Johnson traveled toward the New York plane along a silent moving floor. Millie stood beside Howard while they passed a mural of a Mexican landscape and some Christmas drawings by fourth graders from Watts. For forty years they had been together in spite of Sonny and the others, but at this most recent appeal from New York Millie urged him to go back. Sonny had cabled, "My God, Dad, you're sixty-nine years old, haven't you been a gypsy long enough? Board meeting December third with or without you. Policy changes imminent." 8

Normally, they ignored Sonny's cables, but this time Millie wanted him to go, wanted to be alone with the pain that had recently come to her. She had left Howard holding the new canvas suitcase in which she had packed her three notebooks of regional reports along with his aluminum dish, and in a moment of real despair she had even packed the orange crayon. When Howard boarded Flight 965 he looked old to Millie. His feet dragged in the wing-tipped shoes, the hand she shook was moist, the lip felt dry, and as he passed from her sight down the entry ramp Mildred Bryce felt a fresh new ache that sent her hobbling toward the car. Otis had unplugged the freezer, and the silence caused by the missing hum was as intense to Millie as her abdominal pain. 9

It had come quite suddenly in Albuquerque, New Mexico, at the grand opening of a 210-unit house. She did not make a fuss. Mildred Bryce had never caused trouble to anyone, except perhaps to Mrs. HJ. Millie's quick precise actions, angular face, and thin body made her seem birdlike, especially next to Mr. HJ, six three with splendid white hair accenting his dark blue gabardine suits. Howard was slow and sure. He could sit in the same position for hours while Millie fidgeted on the seat, wrote memos, and filed reports in the small gray cabinet that sat in front of her and parallel to the ice-cream freezer. Her health had always been good, so at first she tried to ignore the 10 pain. It was gas: it was perhaps the New Mexico water or the cooking oil in the fish dinner. But she could not convince away the pain. It stayed like a match burning around her belly, etching itself into her as the round HJ emblem was so symmetrically embroidered into the bedspread, which she had kicked off in the flush that accompanied the pain. She felt as if her sweat would engulf the foam mattress and crisp percale sheet. Finally, Millie brought up her knees and made a ball of herself as if being as small as possible might make her misery disappear. It worked for everything except the pain. The little circle of hot torment was all that remained of her, and when finally at sometime in the early morning it left, it occurred to her that perhaps she had struggled with a demon and been suddenly relieved by the coming of daylight. She stepped lightly into the bathroom and before a full-length mirror (new in HJ motels exclusively) saw herself whole and unmarked, but sign enough to Mildred was her smell, damp and musty, sign enough that something had begun and that something else would therefore necessarily end.

II

Before she had the report from her doctor, Howard Jr.'s message had given her the excuse she needed. There was no reason why Millie could not tell Howard she was sick, but telling him would be admitting too much to herself. Along with Howard Johnson Millie had grown rich beyond dreams. Her inheritance, the $100,000 from her father's steel box in 1939, went directly to Mr. Johnson, who desperately needed it, and the results of that investment brought Millie enough capital to employ two people at the Chase Manhattan with the management of her finances. With money beyond the hope of use, she had vacationed all over the world and spent some time in the company of celebrities, but the reality of her life, like his, was in the back seat of the limousine, waiting for that point at which the needs of the automobile and the human body met the undeviating purpose of the highway and momentarily conquered it. 11

Her life was measured in rest stops. She, Howard, and Otis had found them out before they existed. They knew the places to stop between Buffalo and Albany, Chicago and Milwaukee, Toledo and Columbus, Des Moines and Minneapolis, they knew through their own bodies, measured in hunger and discomfort in the '30s and '40s when they would stop at remote places to buy land and borrow money, sensing in themselves the hunger that would one day be upon the place. People were wary and Howard had trouble borrowing (her $100,000 had perhaps been the key) but invariably he was right. Howard knew the land, Mildred thought, the way the Indians must have known it. There were even spots along the way where the earth itself seemed to make men stop. Howard had a sixth sense that would sometimes lead them from the main roads to, say, a dark green field in Iowa or Kansas. Howard, who might have seemed asleep, would rap with his knuckles on the Plexiglas, causing the knowing Otis to bring the car to such a quick stop that 12

Millie almost flew into her filing cabinet. And before the emergency brake had settled into its final prong, Howard Johnson was into the field and after the scent. While Millie and Otis waited, he would walk it out slowly. Sometimes he would sit down, disappearing in a field of long and tangled weeds, or he might find a large smooth rock to sit on while he felt some secret vibration from the place. Turning his back to Millie, he would mark the spot with his urine or break some of the clayey earth in his strong pink hands, sifting it like flour for a delicate recipe. She had actually seen him chew the grass, getting down on all fours like an animal and biting the tops without pulling the entire blade from the soil. At times he ran in a slow jog as far as his aging legs would carry him. Whenever he slipped out of sight behind the uneven terrain, Millie felt him in danger, felt that something alien might be there to resist the civilizing instinct of Howard Johnson. Once when Howard had been out of sight for more than an hour and did not respond to their frantic calls, Millie sent Otis into the field and in desperation flagged a passing car.

"Howard Johnson is lost in that field," she told the surprised driver. "He went in to look for a new location and we can't find him now." 13

"The restaurant Howard Johnson?" the man asked. 14

"Yes. Help us please." 15

The man drove off, leaving Millie to taste in his exhaust fumes the barbarism of an ungrateful public. Otis found Howard asleep in a field of light blue wild flowers. He had collapsed from the exertion of his run. Millie brought water to him, and when he felt better, right there in the field, he ate his scoop of vanilla on the very spot where three years later they opened the first fully air-conditioned motel in the world. When she stopped to think about it, Millie knew they were more than businessmen, they were pioneers. 16

And once, while on her own, she had the feeling too. In 1951 when she visited the Holy Land there was an inkling of what Howard must have felt all the time. It happened without any warning on a bus crowded with tourists and resident Arabs on their way to the Dead Sea. Past ancient Sodom the bus creaked and bumped, down, down, toward the lowest point on earth, when suddenly in the midst of the crowd and her stomach queasy with the motion of the bus, Mildred Bryce experienced an overwhelming calm. A light brown patch of earth surrounded by a few pale desert rocks overwhelmed her perception, seemed closer to her than the Arab lady in the black flowered dress pushing her basket against Millie at that very moment. She wanted to stop the bus. Had she been near the door she might have actually jumped, so strong was her sensitivity to that barren spot in the endless desert. Her whole body ached for it as if in unison, bone by bone. Her limbs tingled, her breath came in short gasps, the sky rolled out of the bus windows and obliterated her view. The Arab lady spat on the floor and moved a suspicious eye over a squirming Mildred. 17

When the bus stopped at the Dead Sea, the Arabs and tourists rushed to the soupy brine clutching damaged limbs, while Millie pressed twenty 18 dollars American into the dirty palm of a cab-driver who took her back to the very place where the music of her body began once more as sweetly as the first time. While the incredulous driver waited, Millie walked about the place wishing Howard were there to understand her new understanding of his kind of process. There was nothing there, absolutely nothing but pure bliss. The sun beat her like a wish, the air was hot and stale as a Viennese bathhouse, and yet Mildred felt peace and rest there, and as her cab bill mounted she actually did rest in the miserable barren desert of an altogether unsatisfactory land. When the driver, wiping the sweat from his neck, asked, "Meesez . . . pleeze. Why American woman wants Old Jericho in such kind of heat?" When he said "Jericho," she understood that this was a place where men had always stopped. In dim antiquity Jacob had perhaps watered a flock here, and not far away Lot's wife paused to scan for the last time the city of her youth. Perhaps Mildred now stood where Abraham had been visited by a vision and, making a rock his pillow, had first put the ease into the earth. Whatever it was, Millie knew from her own experience that rest was created here by historical precedent. She tried to buy that piece of land, going as far as King Hussein's secretary of the interior. She imagined a Palestinian HJ with an orange roof angling toward Sodom, a seafood restaurant, and an oasis of fresh fruit. But the land was in dispute between Israel and Jordan, and even King Hussein, who expressed admiration for Howard Johnson, could not sell to Millie the place of her comfort.

That was her single visionary moment, but sharing them with Howard 19
was almost as good. And to end all this, to finally stay in her eighteenth-floor Santa Monica penthouse, where the Pacific dived into California, this seemed to Mildred a paltry conclusion to an adventurous life. Her doctor said it was not so serious, she had a bleeding ulcer and must watch her diet. The prognosis was, in fact, excellent. But Mildred, fifty-six and alone in California, found the doctor less comforting than most of the rest stops she had experienced.

III

California, right after the Second War, was hardly a civilized place for travel- 20
ers. Millie, HJ, and Otis had a twelve-cylinder '47 Lincoln and snaked along five days between Sacramento and Los Angeles. "Comfort, comfort," said HJ as he surveyed the redwood forest and the bubbly surf while it slipped away from Otis, who had rolled his trousers to chase the ocean away during a stop near San Francisco. Howard Johnson was contemplative in California. They had never been in the West before. Their route, always slightly new, was yet bound by Canada, where a person couldn't get a tax break, and roughly by the Mississippi as a western frontier. Their journeys took them up the eastern seaboard and through New England to the early reaches of the Midwest, stopping at the plains of Wisconsin and the cool crisp edge of Chicago where two HJ lodges twinkled at the lake.

One day in 1947 while on the way from Chicago to Cairo, Illinois, HJ 21
looked long at the green relief maps. While Millie kept busy with her filing,

HJ loosened the tape and placed the map across his soft round knees. The map jiggled and sagged, the Mid- and Southwest hanging between his legs. When Mildred finally noticed that look, he had been staring at the map for perhaps fifteen minutes, brooding over it, and Millie knew something was in the air.

HJ looked at that map the way some people looked down from an airplane trying to pick out the familiar from the colorful mass receding beneath them. Howard Johnson's eye flew over the land—over the Tetons, over the Sierra Nevada, over the long thin gouge of the Canyon flew his gaze—charting his course by rest stops the way an antique mariner might have gazed at the stars. 22

"Millie," he said just north of Carbondale, "Millie . . ." He looked toward her, saw her fingers engaged and her thumbs circling each other in anticipation. He looked at Millie and saw that she saw what he saw. "Millie"—HJ raised his right arm and its shadow spread across the continent like a prophecy—"Millie, what if we turn right at Cairo and go that way?" California, already peeling on the green map, balanced on HJ's left knee like a happy child. 23

Twenty years later Mildred settled in her eighteenth-floor apartment in the building owned by Lawrence Welk. Howard was in New York, Otis and the car waited in Arizona. The pain did not return as powerfully as it had appeared that night in Albuquerque, but it hurt with dull regularity and an occasional streak of dark blood from her bowels kept her mind on it even on painless days. 24

Directly beneath her gaze were the organized activities of the golden-age groups, tiny figures playing bridge or shuffleboard or looking out at the water from their benches as she sat on her sofa and looked out at them and the fluffy ocean. Mildred did not regret family life. The HJ houses were her offspring. She had watched them blossom from the rough youngsters of the '40s with steam heat and even occasional kitchenettes into cool mature adults with king-sized beds, color TVs, and room service. Her late years were spent comfortably in the modern houses just as one might enjoy in age the benefits of a child's prosperity. She regretted only that it was probably over. 25

But she did not give up completely until she received a personal letter one day telling her that she was eligible for burial insurance until age eighty. A $1000 policy would guarantee a complete and dignified service. Millie crumpled the advertisement, but a few hours later called her Los Angeles lawyer. As she suspected, there were no plans, but as the executor of the estate he would assume full responsibility, subject of course to her approval. 26

"I'll do it myself," Millie had said, but she could not bring herself to do it. The idea was too alien. In more than forty years Mildred had not gone a day without a shower and change of underclothing. Everything about her suggested order and precision. Her fingernails were shaped so that the soft meat of the tips could stroke a typewriter without damaging the apex of a nail, her arch slid over a 6B shoe like an egg in a shell, and never in her adult life did Mildred recall having vomited. It did not seem right to suddenly let 27 all this sink into the dark earth of Forest Lawn because some organ or other developed a hole as big as a nickel. It was not right and she wouldn't do it. Her first idea was to stay in the apartment, to write it into the lease if necessary. She had the lawyer make an appointment for her with Mr. Welk's management firm, but canceled it the day before. "They will just think I'm crazy," she said aloud to herself, "and they'll bury me anyway."

She thought of cryonics while reading a biography of William Chese- 28
brough, the man who invented petroleum jelly. Howard had known him and often mentioned that his own daily ritual of the scoop of vanilla was like old Chesebrough's two teaspoons of Vaseline every day. Chesebrough lived to be ninety. In the biography it said that after taking the daily dose of Vaseline, he drank three cups of green tea to melt everything down, rested for twelve minutes, and then felt fit as a young man, even in his late eighties. When he died they froze his body and Millie had her idea. The Vaseline people kept him in a secret laboratory somewhere near Cleveland and claimed he was in better condition than Lenin, whom the Russians kept hermetically sealed, but at room temperature.

In the phone book she found the Los Angeles Cryonic Society and asked 29
it to send her information. It all seemed very clean. The cost was $200 a year for maintaining the cold. She sent the pamphlet to her lawyer to be sure that the society was legitimate. It wasn't much money, but, still, if they were charlatans, she didn't want them to take advantage of her even if she would never know about it. They were aboveboard, the lawyer said. "The interest on a ten-thousand-dollar trust fund would pay about five hundred a year," the lawyer said, "and they only charge two hundred dollars. Still, who knows what the cost might be in say two hundred years?" To be extra safe, they put $25,000 in trust for eternal maintenance, to be eternally overseen by Longstreet, Williams, and their eternal heirs. When it was arranged, Mildred felt better than she had in weeks.

IV

Four months to the day after she had left Howard at the Los Angeles Interna- 30
tional Airport, he returned for Mildred without the slightest warning. She was in her housecoat and had not even washed the night cream from her cheeks when she saw through the viewing space in her door the familiar long pink jowls, even longer in the distorted glass.

"Howard," she gasped, fumbling with the door, and in an instant he was 31
there picking her up as he might a child or an ice-cream cone while her tears fell like dandruff on his blue suit. While Millie sobbed into his soft padded shoulder, HJ told her the good news. "I'm chairman emeritus of the board now. That means no more New York responsibilities. They still have to listen to me because we hold the majority of the stock, but Howard Junior and Keyes will take care of the business. Our main job is new home-owned franchises. And, Millie, guess where we're going first?"

So overcome was Mildred that she could not hold back her sobs even 32 to guess. Howard Johnson put her down, beaming pleasure through his old bright eyes. "Florida," HJ said, then slowly repeated it, "Flor-idda, and guess what we're going to do?"

"Howard," Millie said, swiping at her tears with the filmy lace cuffs of her dressing gown, "I'm so surprised I don't know what to say. You could tell me we're going to the moon and I'd believe you. Just seeing you again has brought back all my hope." They came out of the hallway and sat on the sofa that looked out over the Pacific. HJ, all pink, kept his hands on his knees like paperweights. 33

"Millie, you're almost right. I can't fool you about anything and never could. We're going down near where they launch the rockets from. I've heard . . ." HJ leaned toward the kitchen as if to check for spies. He looked at the stainless-steel-and-glass table, at the built-in avocado appliances, then leaned his large moist lips toward Mildred's ear. "Walt Disney is planning right this minute a new Disneyland down there. They're trying to keep it a secret, but his brother Roy bought options on thousands of acres. We're going down to buy as much as we can as close in as we can." Howard sparkled. "Millie, don't you see, it's a sure thing." 34

After her emotional outburst at seeing Howard again, a calmer Millie felt a slight twitch in her upper stomach and in the midst of her joy was reminded of another sure thing. 35

They would be a few weeks in Los Angeles anyway. Howard wanted to thoroughly scout out the existing Disneyland, so Millie had some time to think it out. She could go, as her heart directed her, with HJ to Florida and points beyond. She could take the future as it happened like a Disneyland ride or she could listen to the dismal eloquence of her ulcer and try to make the best arrangements she could. Howard and Otis would take care of her to the end, there were no doubts about that, and the end would be the end. But if she stayed in this apartment, sure of the arrangements for later, she would miss whatever might still be left before the end. Mildred wished there were some clergyman she could consult, but she had never attended a church and believed in no religious doctrine. Her father had been a firm atheist to the very moment of his office suicide, and she remained a passive nonbeliever. Her theology was the order of her own life. Millie had never deceived herself; in spite of her riches all she truly owned was her life, a pocket of habits in the burning universe. But the habits were careful and clean and they were best represented in the body that was she. Freezing her remains was the closest image she could conjure of eternal life. It might not be eternal and it surely would not be life, but that damp, musty feel, that odor she smelled on herself after the pain, that could be avoided, and who knew what else might be saved from the void for a small initial investment and $200 a year. And if you did not believe in a soul, was there not every reason to preserve a body? 36

Mrs. Albert of the Cryonic Society welcomed Mildred to a tour of the premises. "See it while you can," she cheerfully told the group (Millie, two men, and a boy with notebook and Polaroid camera). Mrs. Albert, a big 37 woman perhaps in her mid-sixties, carried a face heavy in flesh. Perhaps once the skin had been tight around her long chin and pointed cheekbones, but having lost its spring, the skin merely hung at her neck like a patient animal waiting for the rest of her to join in the decline. From the way she took the concrete stairs down to the vault, it looked as if the wait would be long. "I'm not ready for the freezer yet. I tell every group I take down here, it's gonna be a long time until they get me." Millie believed her. "I may not be the world's smartest cookie"—Mrs. Albert looked directly at Millie—"but a bird in the hand is the only bird I know, huh? That's why when it does come . . . Mrs. A is going to be right here in this facility, and you better believe it. Now, Mr. King on your left"—she pointed to a capsule that looked like a large bullet to Millie—"Mr. King is the gentleman who took me on my first tour, cancer finally but had everything perfectly ready and I would say he was in prime cooling state within seconds and I believe that if they ever cure cancer, and you know they will the way they do most everything nowadays, old Mr. King may be back yet. If anyone got down to low-enough temperature immediately it would be Mr. King." Mildred saw the boy write "Return of the King" in his notebook. "Over here is Mr. and Mizz Winkleman, married sixty years, and went off within a month of each other, a lovely, lovely couple."

While Mrs. Albert continued her necrology and posed for a photo 38
beside the Winklemans, Millie took careful note of the neon-lit room filled with bulletlike capsules. She watched the cool breaths of the group gather like flowers on the steel and vanish without dimming the bright surface. The capsules stood in straight lines with ample walking space between them. To Mrs. Albert they were friends, to Millie it seemed as if she were in a furniture store of the Scandinavian type where elegance is suggested by the absence of material, where straight lines of steel, wood, and glass indicate that relaxation too requires some taste and is not an indifferent sprawl across any soft object that happens to be nearby.

Cemeteries always bothered Millie, but here she felt none of the dread 39
she had expected. She averted her eyes from the cluttered graveyards they always used to pass at the tips of cities in the early days. Fortunately, the superhighways twisted traffic into the city and away from those desolate marking places where used-car lots and the names of famous hotels inscribed on barns often neighbored the dead. Howard had once commented that never in all his experience did he have an intuition of a good location near a cemetery. You could put a lot of things there, you could put up a bowling alley, or maybe even a theater, but never a motel, and Millie knew he was right. He knew where to put his houses but it was Millie who knew how. From that first orange roof angling toward the east, the HJ design and the idea had been Millie's. She had not invented the motel, she had changed it from a place where you had to be to a place where you wanted to be. Perhaps, she thought, the Cryonic Society was trying to do the same for cemeteries.

When she and Howard had started their travels, the old motel courts 40 huddled like so many dark graves around the stone marking of the highway. And what traveler coming into one of those dingy cabins could watch the watery rust dripping from his faucet without thinking of everything he was missing by being a traveler . . . his two-stall garage, his wife small in the half-empty bed, his children with hair the color of that rust. Under the orange Howard Johnson roof all this changed. For about the same price you were redeemed from the road. Headlights did not dazzle you on the foam mattress and percale sheets, your sanitized glasses and toilet appliances sparkled like the mirror behind them. The room was not just there, it awaited you, courted your pleasure, sat like a young bride outside the walls of the city wanting only to please you, you only you on the smoothly pressed sheets, your friend, your one-night destiny.

As if it were yesterday, Millie recalled right there in the cryonic vault 41 the moment when she had first thought the thought that made Howard Johnson Howard Johnson's. And when she told Howard her decision that evening after cooking a cheese soufflé and risking a taste of wine, it was that memory she invoked for both of them, the memory of a cool autumn day in the '30s when a break in their schedule found Millie with a free afternoon in New Hampshire, an afternoon she had spent at the farm of a man who had once been her teacher and remembered her after ten years. Otis drove her out to Robert Frost's farm, where the poet made for her a lunch of scrambled eggs and 7 Up. Millie and Robert Frost talked mostly about the farm, about the cold winter he was expecting and the autumn apples they picked from the trees. He was not so famous then, his hair was only streaked with gray as Howard's was, and she told the poet about what she and Howard were doing, about what she felt about being on the road in America, and Robert Frost said he hadn't been that much but she sounded like she knew and he believed she might be able to accomplish something. He did not remember the poem she wrote in his class but that didn't matter.

"Do you remember, Howard, how I introduced you to him? Mr. Frost, 42 this is Mr. Johnson. I can still see the two of you shaking hands there beside the car. I've always been proud that I introduced you to one another." Howard Johnson nodded his head at the memory, seemed as nostalgic as Millie while he sat in her apartment learning why she would not go to Florida to help bring Howard Johnson's to the new Disneyland.

"And after we left his farm, Howard, remember? Otis took the car in 43 for servicing and left us with some sandwiches on the top of a hill overlooking a town, I don't even remember which one, maybe we never knew the name of it. And we stayed on that hilltop while the sun began to set in New Hampshire. I felt so full of poetry and"—she looked at Howard—"of love, Howard, only about an hour's drive from Robert Frost's farmhouse. Maybe it was just the way we felt then, but I think the sun set differently that night, filtering through the clouds like a big paintbrush making the top of the town all orange. And suddenly I thought what if the tops of our houses were that kind of orange, what a world it would be, Howard, and my God, that orange stayed until the last drop of light was left in it. I didn't feel the cold up there even though it took Otis so long to get back to us. The feeling we had about that orange, Howard, that was ours and that's what I've tried to bring to every house, the way we felt that night. Oh, it makes me sick to think of Colonel Sanders, and Big Boy, and Holiday Inn, and Best Western . . ."

"It's all right, Millie, it's all right." Howard patted her heaving back. 44
Now that he knew about her ulcer and why she wanted to stay behind, the mind that had conjured butterfly shrimp and twenty-eight flavors set himself a new project. He contemplated Millie sobbing in his lap the way he contemplated prime acreage. There was so little of her, less than one hundred pounds, yet without her Howard Johnson felt himself no match for the wily Disneys gathering near the moonport.

He left her in all her sad resignation that evening, left her thinking she 45
had to give up what remained here to be sure of the proper freezing. But Howard Johnson had other ideas. He did not cancel the advance reservations made for Mildred Bryce along the route to Florida, nor did he remove her filing cabinet from the limousine. The man who hosted a nation and already kept one freezer in his car merely ordered another, this one designed according to cryonic specifications and presented to Mildred housed in a twelve-foot orange U-Haul trailer connected to the rear bumper of the limousine.

"Everything's here," he told the astonished Millie, who thought How- 46
ard had left the week before, "everything is here and you'll never have to be more than seconds away from it. It's exactly like a refrigerated truck." Howard Johnson opened the rear door of the U-Haul as proudly as he had ever dedicated a motel. Millie's steel capsule shone within, surrounded by an array of chemicals stored on heavily padded rubber shelves. The California sun was on her back, but her cold breath hovered visibly within the U-Haul. No tears came to Mildred now; she felt relief much as she had felt it that afternoon near ancient Jericho. On Santa Monica Boulevard, in front of Lawrence Welk's apartment building, Mildred Bryce confronted her immortality, a gift from the ice-cream king, another companion for the remainder of her travels. Howard Johnson had turned away, looking toward the ocean. To his blue back and patriarchal white hairs, Mildred said, "Howard, you can do anything," and closing the doors of the U-Haul, she joined the host of the highways, a man with two portable freezers, ready now for the challenge of Disney World.

Questions for Discussion

1. Is it fair to say that Apple's satire is directed not only against materialism in the everyday sense of a greediness for material consumer items but also against materialism in the more philosophical sense that all existence is composed entirely of matter? If so, how is this satire advanced by Mildred's approach to her own death?

2. What are your clues that Apple finds the whole cryonics craze absurd and foolish? What reasons do you think he would give in support of this view? Do *you* think it is absurd and foolish? Why or why not?
3. Can you explain the allusion and the satirical joke buried in the last six words of paragraph 6?
4. Apple depicts HJ as sitting on a rock in the middle of a field, sensing "some secret vibration from the place," and then marking the spot with his urine (¶12). What kind of legitimate communing with the land does Apple seem to parody here? What set of values, unstated, do you have to decode in order to see Apple's "real" point of view toward what he is describing?
5. When Apple depicts the shadow of HJ's hand in 1947 "spread across the continent like a prophecy" (¶23), what does he see the shadow as a prophecy of? What is Apple's evaluation of the fulfillment of this prophecy?

Suggested Essay Topics

1. Write a two- or three-page response to Apple's satire of American commercialism employing the point of view of one of the authors who debate the merits of capitalism in the next section: Johnson, Schmertz, Nelson, McCarthy, or Cone. Try to capture the distinctive concern of the writer in whose mouth you place the "response." Direct the essay to your instructor.
2. Write a dialogue in which you portray Max Apple and Paul Johnson debating the merits of capitalistic commercialism. Give each speaker the strongest arguments you can, but make clear, either by the course of the dialogue itself or in a concluding analysis, who, in your opinion, presents the better arguments. Make clear your criteria for "better." Direct the dialogue to your classmates.

IDEAS IN DEBATE

Paul Johnson
Herbert Schmertz
J. Robert Nelson
Eugene McCarthy
James Cone

Paul Johnson

P*aul Johnson (b. 1928), British historian, author, and former editor of the* New Statesman, *first delivered "Has Capitalism a Future?" as a speech at a conference of bankers. Johnson's objective is to go on the "ideological offensive" (¶37) and "to teach the world a little history" (¶38) in order to defend capitalism against those he considers its five main enemies: academic leftists, ecological doomsayers, intrusive governments, union activists, and Soviet totalitarianists. He measures the value of capitalism as an economic system exclusively by the amount of national wealth it has generated. By comparing the rate of national economic growth in later historical times (after capitalism's emergence as the dominant economic system of the West) with the rate of economic growth in earlier times, Johnson claims to have clearly assessed its value: "Industrial capitalism, judged simply by its capacity to create wealth and to distribute it, is a phenomenon unique in world history. One could argue that it is the greatest single blessing ever bestowed on humanity" (¶11).*

Following Johnson's essay are four responses (by Herbert Schmertz, J. Robert Nelson, Eugene J. McCarthy, and James Cone) to his question, "Has capitalism a future?" Each respondent disagrees with parts of his position. It is clear that Johnson has an ax to grind and that he is speaking as an advocate, but it is not so clear, at least at first glance, whether his critics are simply looking for weaknesses in his arguments or whether they are grinding their own axes in a biased way. It may be helpful to know that Herbert Schmertz is a corporation executive; J. Robert Nelson is a professor of theology; Eugene McCarthy is a former presidential candidate, former senator, and author; and James Cone is a black theologian.

As you read, try to assess the validity of arguments raised on both sides of the issues. Note that Johnson's facts *are not disputed by any of his respondents, regardless of whether they like or dislike his position. Once again we see that facts seldom determine the positions that people take on issues. Everyone accepts Johnson's facts, yet everyone has a different picture of their significance. (For more on this topic, read*

Edward Hallett Carr, "The Historian and His Facts," pp. 575–583, and its introduction.) The facts are not irrelevant—everyone clearly takes them seriously—but the point is that in and of themselves, they are seldom conclusive.

HAS CAPITALISM A FUTURE?

This essay and the four responses to it are from *Will Capitalism Survive?* (1979), edited by Ernest W. Lefever.

Seen against the grand perspective of history, capitalism is a newcomer. I would date it, in its earliest phase in England, only from the 1780s. We now possess some knowledge of economic systems going back to the early centuries of the third millennium B.C. I could outline, for instance, the economic structure of Egypt under the Old Kingdom, about 2700 B.C. Our knowledge of how civilized societies have organized their economic activities thus covers a stretch of more than 4,600 years. And in only about two hundred of those years has industrial capitalism existed. As a widely spread phenomenon, it is barely one hundred years old. 1

(Before I go any further, let me define my term: by "capitalism" I mean large-scale industrial capitalism, in which privately financed, publicly quoted corporations, operating in a free-market environment, with the back-up of the private-enterprise money market, constitute the core of the national economy. This is a rather broad definition, but I think it will do.) 2

The next point to note is the remarkable correlation between the emergence of industrial capitalism and the beginnings of really rapid economic growth. Throughout most of history, growth rates, when we have the statistical evidence to measure them, have been low, nil, or minus. A century of slow growth might be followed by a century of decline. Societies tended to get caught in the Malthusian Trap: that is, a period of slow growth led to an increase in population, the outstripping of food supplies, then a demographic catastrophe, and the beginning of a new cycle. 3

There were at least three economic "Dark Ages" in history, in which a sudden collapse of the wealth-making process led to the extinction, or virtual extinction, of civilized living, and the process of recovery was very slow and painful. The last of these three Dark Ages extinguished Roman civilization in Western Europe in the fifth century A.D. Not until the thirteenth century were equivalent living standards achieved; the recovery thus took eight hundred years. 4

Society again fell into a Malthusian trap in the fourteenth century. Again recovery was slow, though more sure this time, as intermediate technology spread more widely and methods of handling and employing money became more sophisticated. As late as the first half of the eighteenth century, however, it was rare for even the most advanced economies, those of England and Holland, to achieve 1 per cent growth in any year. And there is a possibil- 5 ity that mankind would again have fallen into a Malthusian trap toward the end of the eighteenth century if industrial capitalism had not made its dramatic appearance.

And it *was* dramatic. By the beginning of the 1780s, in England, an 6
unprecedented annual growth rate of 2 per cent had been achieved. During that decade, the 2 per cent was raised to 4 per cent. This was the great historic "liftoff," and a 4 per cent annual compound growth rate was sustained for the next fifty years. Since this English, and also Scottish, performance was accompanied by the export of capital, patents, machine tools, and skilled manpower to several other advanced nations, the phenomenon soon became international.

A few more figures are necessary to show the magnitude of the change 7
that industrial capitalism brought to human society. In Britain, for instance, in the nineteenth century, the size of the working population multiplied fourfold. Real wages doubled in the half-century 1800–1850, and doubled again, 1850–1900. This meant there was a 1600 per cent increase in the production and consumption of wage-goods during the century. Nothing like this had happened anywhere before, in the whole of history. From the 1850s onward, in Belgium, France, Austria-Hungary, and above all in Germany and the United States, even higher growth rates were obtained; and feudal empires like Japan and Russia were able to telescope into a mere generation or two a development process that in Britain had stretched over centuries.

The growth rates of twelve leading capitalist countries averaged 2.7 per 8
cent a year over the whole fifty-year period up to World War I. There was, it is true, a much more mixed performance between the wars. The United States, which in the forty-four years up to 1914 had averaged a phenomenal 4.3 per cent growth rate, and which in the seven years up to 1929 had increased its national income by a staggering 40 per cent, then saw its national income fall 38 per cent in a mere four years, 1929–32.

But after World War II, growth was resumed on an even more impres- 9
sive scale. In the 1950s, for instance, the twelve leading capitalist economies cited before had an average annual growth of 4.2 per cent. In Germany it was as high as an average of 7.6 per cent. In all the West European economies, the rate of investment in the 1950s was half again as high as it had ever been on a sustained basis. In several such countries it was over 20 per cent of the GNP; in Germany and the Netherlands it was 25 per cent, in Norway even higher. Moreover, this high capital formation took place not at the cost of private consumption but during a rapid and sustained rise in living standards, particularly of industrial workers. These tendencies were prolonged throughout the 1960s and into the 1970s. For the mature economies, the second industrial revolution—1945–1970—was entirely painless. This was also largely true in Japan, which achieved even higher investment and growth rates in an effort to catch up with the United States and Europe.

In short, after nearly five recorded millennia of floundering about in 10
poverty, humanity suddenly in the 1780s began to hit on the right formula: industrial capitalism. Consider the magnitude of the change over the last two

centuries or less. We all know the wealth of present-day West Germany. In the year 1800, in the whole of Germany fewer than 1,000 people had annual incomes as high as $1,000. Or again, take France. France now has more automobiles per capita even than Germany, and more second homes per family than any other country in Europe. In the 1780s, four-fifths of the French families spent 90 per cent of their incomes simply on buying bread—only bread—to stay alive.

In short, industrial capitalism, judged simply by its capacity to create wealth and to distribute it, is a phenomenon unique in world history. One could argue that it is the greatest single blessing ever bestowed on humanity. Why, then, are we asking, "Has capitalism a future?" The answer is clear enough: because capitalism is threatened. 11

The idea has got around that industrial capitalism is unpopular and always has been, that it is the work of a tiny minority who have thrust it upon the reluctant mass of mankind. Nothing could be further from the truth. The storage economies of remote antiquity were often hideously unpopular. So was the slave-based economy, combined with corporatism, of the classical world. Agricultural feudalism was certainly unpopular, and mercantilism had to be enforced, in practice, by authoritarian states. 12

But from the very start industrial capitalism won the approval of the masses. They could not vote in the ballot box, but they voted in a far more impressive manner: with their feet. The poorest member of society values political freedom as much as the richest. But the freedom he values most of all is the freedom to sell his labor and skills in the open market, and it was precisely *this* that industrial capitalism gave to men for the first time in history. Hence it is a profound error of fact, in my view, to see what Blake called the "dark, satanic mills" of the industrial revolution as the enslavement of man. The factory system, however harsh it may have been, was the road to freedom for millions of agricultural workers. Not only did it offer them an escape from rural poverty, which was deeper and more degrading than anything experienced in the cities, but it allowed them to move from status to contract, from a stationary place in a static society, with tied cottages and semi-conscript labor, to a mobile place in a dynamic society. 13

That was why the common man voted for industrial capitalism with his feet, by tramping from the countryside to the towns in enormous numbers, first in Britain, then throughout Europe. And tens of millions of European peasants, decade after decade, moved relentlessly across the Atlantic in pursuit of that same freedom, from semi-feudal estates and small holdings in Russia, Poland, Germany, Austria-Hungary, Italy, Ireland, Scandinavia, to the mines and factories and workshops of New York, Chicago, Pittsburgh, Cleveland, Detroit. It was the first time in history that really large numbers of ordinary people were given the chance to exercise a choice about their livelihood and destiny, and to move, not as members of a tribe or conscript soldiers, but as free individuals, selling their labor in the open market. 14

They voted for industrial capitalism with their feet not only because they felt in their bones that it meant a modest prosperity for their children 15 and grandchildren—and on the whole they have been proved abundantly right—but because they knew it meant a new degree of freedom for themselves. Indeed, the success of industrialization, despite all its evils, continues to persuade countless ordinary men and women, all over the world, to escape the poverty and restraints of the rural status society and to enter the free labor markets of the towns. Hence the growth of megalopolises all over the world—Calcutta and Bombay, Teheran and Caracas, Mexico City and Djakarta, Shanghai and Lagos, Cairo and Johannesburg. There are now literally scores of million-plus cities all over the Third World. This never-ending one-way flow from countryside to city is plainly a voluntary mass choice, for most governments fear and resent it, and many are attempting, sometimes savagely but always ineffectively, to halt or reverse it. It is more marked in the free-market economies, but it is noticeable everywhere.

Short of evacuating the cities by force and terror, as is now apparently 16
being practiced in parts of southeast Asia, there is no way to stop this human flood. There seems to be an almost irresistible urge in human beings to move away from the status society to contractual individualism, the central feature of industrial capitalism. This operates even in totalitarian societies, as witness the efforts, for instance, of the Chinese and Polish governments to limit the urban explosions they are experiencing.

If industrial capitalism is unique in its wealth-producing capacity and 17
also has the endorsement of the people, then why is it under threat? And who is threatening it?

THE INTELLECTUAL AND MORAL BATTLE

Let me look at five principal elements. The *first,* and in some ways the most 18
important, is that *the free-enterprise idea is losing, if it has not already lost, the intellectual and moral battle.* Not long ago I went into Blackwell's, the great book shop at Oxford University. I wandered over the huge room that houses the books on politics and economics, and having been disagreeably surprised by what I saw there, I made a rough calculation. New books extolling the economic, social, and moral virtues of Communism and collectivism—and there were literally hundreds and hundreds from all over the world—outnumbered books defending free enterprise, or merely seeking to take an objective view of the argument, by between five and six to one. This overwhelming predominance of collectivism was not due to any sinister policy on the part of Blackwell's, which is a highly efficient capitalist enterprise. It was a marketing response to demand on the part of students and teachers. And this was not one of the new slum universities of recent years, some of which have been virtually shanghaied by Marxist factions, but Oxford University, one of the free world's greatest centers of learning, where the battle of ideas is fought under the best possible conditions.

There can be no doubt that the intellectual and moral assault on free 19
enterprise, and the exaltation of Marxist collectivism, that is such a striking

feature of the 1970s is directly related to the huge expansion of higher education, put through at such cost to the capitalist economies in the 1960s. Now there is in this a huge and tragic irony. For in the 1950s, the decade when the university expansion was planned, it was the prevailing wisdom among the leading thinkers of the West that the growth of higher education was directly productive of industrial growth—that the more university graduates we turned out, the faster the GNPs of the West would rise. This was the thesis outlined by President Clark Kerr of Berkeley in his 1963 Godkin lectures at Harvard, and it was a thesis put forward in Britain with immense effect by Sir Charles, now Lord Snow. Kerr said: "What the railroads did for the second half of the last century, and the automobile for the first half of this century, may be done for the second half of the twentieth century by the knowledge industry: that is, to serve as the focal point for national growth." He added that more graduates would not only mean a bigger GNP but act as a reinforcement for middle-class democracy, with all its freedoms.

To speak of the "knowledge industry" was to ask for trouble. Knowl- 20
edge is not a manufactured commodity. There is knowledge for good and knowledge for evil, as the Book of Genesis says. The 1960s, during which most Western nations doubled and some even trebled their university places, did not reinforce democratic freedoms or enlarge the GNP or strengthen the free-enterprise system. They produced the students' revolts, beginning in Paris in 1968. They detonated the Northern Ireland conflict, which is still harassing Britain. They produced the Baader-Meinhoff Gang in West Germany, the Red Brigade in Italy, the Left Fascist terrorism of Japan. They produced an enormous explosion of Marxist studies, centered on the social sciences and especially sociology and on a new generation of school and university teachers who are dedicated, by a sort of perverted religious piety, to the spread of Marxist ideas.

There are ironies within the general irony. The new university of the 21
air, created in Britain at enormous expense to bring higher education to adults and therefore christened the Open University, has become virtually closed to any teacher not of proven Marxist opinions. Nuffield College, Oxford, founded by the great capitalist pioneer Lord Nuffield, who created the British automobile industry, has become a center of trade-union ideology, of the very ideas that slowly but surely are putting the British automobile industry out of world markets and out of business. Warwick University, created in the 1960s as a powerhouse of ideas and clever graduate executives for the West Midlands industrial complex, Britain's biggest, has become a seminary of Marxist and pseudo-Marxist agitators dedicated to the destruction of the wealth-producing machine that brought their university into existence.

I could go on. It is true, of course, that student unrest, as such, has 22
quieted down. But the steady diffusion of ideas hostile to our free system continues remorselessly. Industrial capitalism and the free-market system are presented as destructive of human happiness, corrupt, immoral, wasteful, inefficient, and above all, doomed. Collectivism is presented as the only way out compatible with the dignity of the human spirit and the future of our

race. The expanded university threatens to become not the powerhouse of Western individualism and enterprise but its graveyard.

THE ECOLOGICAL PANIC

There is a *second* threat, what I have called *the "ecological panic."* This movement, 23
again, began with the best intentions. I well remember when Rachel Carson's book *The Silent Spring* first appeared in the *New Yorker.* The wave of concern that followed was justified. We were tending to ignore some of the destructive side effects of very rapid industrial expansion. The steps then taken, notably the clean-air policies and the policies for cleansing lakes and waterways, have been spectacularly successful. Thanks to smokeless fuel, London fogs, which were real killers, have been virtually eliminated; the last really serious one was in 1952. The Thames is now cleaner and has greater quantities of fish, and more varieties, than at any time since before the days of Spenser or Shakespeare. Similar successes are now being registered in the United States, which adopted such legally enforceable remedies somewhat later than Britain did. These are examples of what can be done by the thoughtful, unemotional, systematic, and scientifically justified application of conservation and anti-pollution policies.

But most of these were put in motion before the ecological panic started. 24
Once ecology became a fashionable good cause, as it did in the late 1960s, reason, logic, and proportion flew out the window. It became a campaign not against pollution but against growth itself, and especially against free-enterprise growth—totalitarian Communist growth was somehow less morally offensive. I highly recommend Professor Wilfred Beckerman's *In Defence of Economic Growth.* Beckerman is one of the best of our economists and was a member of the Royal Commission on Environmental Pollution; he knows the subject better perhaps than any other working economist, and his book is a wonderfully sane and lucid summary of it.

I have never yet been able to persuade any committed ecology cam- 25
paigner even to look at this book. Of course not. Such persons have a faith, and they do not want to risk it. One of the most important developments of our time is the growth, as a consequence of the rapid decline of Christianity, of irrational substitutes for it. These are not necessarily religious or even quasi-religious. Often they are pseudo-scientific in form, as for instance the weird philosophy of the late Teilhard de Chardin. The ecology panic is another example. It is akin to the salvation panic of sixteenth-century Calvinism. When you expel the priest, you do not inaugurate the age of reason—you get the witch doctor. But whereas Calvinist salvation panic may have contributed to the rise of capitalism, the ecology panic could be the death of it.

If the restrictions now imposed on industrial development had operated 26
in eighteenth-century England, the industrial revolution could not have taken place. It would in effect have been inhibited by law—as of course many landowners of the day wished it to be—and legal requirements would have eliminated the very modest profits by which it originally financed itself. We

would still be existing at eighteenth-century living standards, and wallowing in eighteenth-century levels of pollution, which were infinitely worse than anything we experience today. (If you want to see what they were like, visit the slums of Calcutta or Djakarta.)

As it is, the ecology panic has been a potent destructive force. The 27
panic-mongers played a crucial role in persuading the Middle Eastern oil producers, especially Iran, to quadruple the price of oil in the autumn of 1973, the biggest single blow industrial capitalism has suffered since the Wall Street crash of 1929. That was the beginning of the profound recession from which we have not yet emerged. In the end, as was foreseeable at the time, the huge rise in oil prices did not do anyone any good, least of all the oil producers. But it ended the great post-war boom and robbed Western capitalism of its tremendous élan, perhaps for good. As Browning put it, "Never glad confident morning again." And it is significant that the ecological lobby is now striving with fanatic vigor and persistence to prevent the development of nuclear energy, allegedly on the grounds of safety. Now it is a fact, a very remarkable fact in my view, that throughout the West (we have no figures for Russia or China) the nuclear power industry is the only industry, the *only* industry, which over a period of thirty years has not had a single fatal industrial accident. This unique record has been achieved by the efforts of the industry itself and the responsible governments, without any assistance from the ecolobby. But of course they would *like* a few fatal accidents. That would suit their purposes very well.

In Britain we had a long public enquiry, what we call a statutory en- 28
quiry, into whether or not it was right to go ahead with the enriched-uranium plant at Windscale. The enquiry was a model of its kind. The ecolobby marshalled all the scientific experts and evidence they could lay their hands on. At the end the verdict was that there was no reason whatever why the program should not proceed. Did the ecolobby accept the verdict? On the contrary. They immediately organized a mass demonstration and planned various legal and illegal activities to halt the program by force. It is notable that a leading figure in this campaign is the man who is perhaps Britain's leading Communist trade unionist, Mr. Arthur Scargill of the Mine-workers. He has never, so far as we know, campaigned against Soviet nuclear programs, peaceful or otherwise. It is true that most people in the movement in the United States, Britain, France, Germany, and Italy, so far as I have been able to observe, are not politically motivated; they are simply irrational. But irrationality is an enemy of civilized society, and it is being exploited by the politically interested.

BIG GOVERNMENT VS. THE MARKET

A *third* factor in the future of capitalism is *the growth of government.* Industrial 29
capitalism—or rather, the free-enterprise economy—and big government are natural and probably irreconcilable enemies. It is no accident that the industrial revolution took place in late eighteenth-century England, a time of

minimum government. Of all the periods of English history, indeed of European history, it was the time when government was least conspicuous and active. It was the age, very short alas, of the Night Watchman state. As a matter of fact, the industrial revolution—perhaps the most important single event in human history—seems to have occurred without the English government's even noticing. By the time the government did notice, it was, happily, too late.

30 It is almost inevitable that government, particularly an active, interventionist government, should view free enterprise with a degree of hostility, since it constitutes a countervailing power in the state. The tendency, then, is to cut free enterprise down to size, in a number of ways. In the United States the characteristic technique is government regulation and legal harassment, and this of course has been far more pervasive and strident since the ecolobby swung into action. In Britain the technique is both direct assault—nationalization—and slow starvation. In a way, nationalization is ineffective, since it allows the public to make comparisons between the performance of the nationalized sector and that of the free sector, nearly always to the latter's advantage.

31 Starvation is more insidious. By this I mean the progressive transfer of resources, by taxation and other government policies, from the private to the public sector. In 1955, for instance, public expenditure in Britain as a proportion of the GNP was just over 40 per cent. By 1975, twenty years later, it had risen to nearly 60 per cent. This was accompanied by a record budget deficit of about $22 billion, itself a further 11½ per cent of the GNP. Of course, the tax money had to be provided, and the deficit serviced, by the private sector. We have, then, an Old Man of the Sea relationship in which the parasitical Old Man is growing bigger, and poor Sinbad smaller, all the time. The shrinking productive sector has to carry the burden of an ever-expanding loss-making public sector. Thus Britain's authorized steel industry will lose $1 billion this year, and it has been authorized by statute to borrow up to $7 billion, guaranteed by government and taxpayer. Now the interesting thing is that in Britain the public sector and the civil service generally are now paying higher wages, providing better conditions, and giving larger pensions—which in a growing number of cases are index-linked and thus inflation-proof—than the private sector can possibly afford. And of course they are financing these goodies out of tax-guaranteed deficits—that is, from the dwindling profits of the private sector. This is what I call the starvation technique. When a private firm goes bust, provided it is big enough, the state takes over, the losses are added to the taxpayer's bill, and the private sector has one more expensive passenger to carry.

32 In this technique, the *fourth* factor, *the trade unions,* play an important part. In Britain it is demonstrably true that the legal privileges of the trade unions, which virtually exempt them from any kind of action for damages (including, now, libel), led directly to restrictive practices, over-manning, low productivity, low investment, low wages, and low profits. Thus trade-union action tends, in itself, to undermine the performance of industrial capitalism as a

wealth-creating system. In Britain, the trade unions can rightly claim that capitalism is inefficient, because they make sure it is inefficient. Ford workers in Britain, using exactly the same assembly-line machinery as in West Germany, produce between 20 per cent and 50 per cent fewer automobiles. ICI Chemicals, one of the best companies in Britain, nevertheless has a productivity performance 25 per cent lower than its Dutch and German competitors. A recent analysis shows this is entirely due to over-manning and restrictive practices.

The private sector in Britain is now threatened by two further union 33
devices: the legally enforced closed shop, which compels workers to join designated unions on pain of dismissal without compensation or legal redress, and new plans to force firms to have up to 50 per cent worker directors, appointed not by the work force themselves nor even necessarily from among them but by and from the trade-union bureaucracy (Bullock Report). This has to be seen against the explicit policy of some groups within the unions of driving private-sector firms to bankruptcy by strikes and harassment, so that the state will then have to take them into the public sector.

What is happening in Britain will not necessarily happen elsewhere. But 34
there are many ways in which the present U.S. administration seems determined to follow Britain's example. The West Germans, too, are now beginning to adopt some of the institutions that flourish in British trade unionism, notably the shop stewards' movement. Businessmen all over the free world may despise the performance of British industry, but trade unionists all over the world admire and envy the power of British trade unionists and are actively seeking to acquire it for themselves.

THE TOTALITARIAN THREAT

Let me end on a word of warning. I have said nothing of the *fifth* threat to 35
industrial capitalism and the free-enterprise system—*the threat from without.* But this is bound to increase as the military superiority of the Soviet Union over the United States is reinforced. I have never thought that the Communist system would triumph by a direct assault. I have always assumed that it would first establish an overwhelming military predominance and then, by pressure and threats, begin to draw the political and economic dividends of it. If the United States opts out of the competitive arms race with the Soviet Union while supposedly providing merely for its own defense, then we must expect to see this fifth threat hard at work winding up industrial capitalism and free enterprise all over the world.

Therefore, when we ask, "Has capitalism a future?," I answer: It all 36
depends on the United States. West Germany and Japan, it is true, have strong free-enterprise economies; they also have a tradition of state capitalism, and would adapt themselves with surprising speed and readiness to a new collective order. France already has a huge public sector and a long tradition of *dirigisme* [state-controlled finance] or *étatisme* [state socialism]. All three are Janus-faced. Britain, I believe, is profoundly anti-collective and will remain

so if it continues to be given the choice. But its private-enterprise system is now very weak, and its business and financial elites are demoralized and defeatist.

I myself think that capitalism will survive, because of its enormous intrinsic virtues as a system for generating wealth and promoting freedom. But those who man and control it must stop apologizing and go on the ideological offensive. They must show ordinary people that both the Communist world and the Third World are parasitical upon industrial capitalism for their growth technology, and that without capitalism, the 200 years of unprecedented growth that have created the modern world would gradually come to an end. We would have slow growth, then nil growth, then minus growth, and then the Malthusian catastrophe. 37

Those who wish to maintain the capitalist system must endeavor to teach the world a little history. They must remind it, and especially the young, that though man's achievements are great, they are never as solid as they look. If man makes the wrong choice, there is always another Dark Age waiting for him round the corner of time. 38

Herbert Schmertz

DEMOCRACY, TYRANNY, AND CAPITALISM

While I am all for capitalism and see many valid points in Paul Johnson's argument, I get uneasy when I see it posed—as I think Johnson does—as the antithesis to Marxism or "Marxist collectivism." Marxism is at best a theory about history and at worst what the economist P. T. Bauer has called "an all-embracing secular messianic faith." Capitalism is neither. It is a historical phenomenon, as Johnson points out, but even by his own definition it is an economic system: a device, a means, a way to go about certain economic business. It is hardly a theory about history, and much less is it the force that must be set in the lists to combat the messianic faith of Marxist collectivism. I would guess that the faith of capitalists is invested in far more profound and transcendent realities than capitalism. What they see and fear in Marxist collectivism is not so much its menace to capitalism as its menace to freedom. 1

This distinction is important. There is some danger that readers of Johnson's essay may come away believing that the struggle is between capitalism and Marxism. That is to wage the battle on Marxism's ground and in Marxism's terms, and it renders the contest deceptively simple. Marxism's argument is only superficially with capitalism: witness the cordiality of Marxist states when they are in need of high technology. At its essence, 2

Marxism's argument is about who shall make choices; it is a quarrel with freedom and democracy.

Given this perspective, I am somewhat hesitant about the broad scope 3
of Johnson's thesis. That the industrial revolution was an epochal event must be admitted, but Europe was by no means sick and poor when the industrial revolution began. Revolutionary economic changes had been initiated in the sixteenth century with the voyages of discovery and the considerable stimulation of trade, industry, and finance provoked by these discoveries. And—at least on this side of the ocean—we tend to assign even more importance to the revolution of ideas that might be said to have begun with the Magna Carta, developed in the Enlightenment, and culminated in the American Revolution: the idea that governments must answer to the people.

From such a perspective, the threats to capitalism outlined by Johnson 4
seem less formidable. We have seen that the university student's infatuation with collectivism tends to fade rather quickly once he begins to work within the capitalistic system and learns to recognize its virtues. We have seen, in the United States at least, a growing public realization that balance is necessary in questions that pit environmentalism against the need for energy, economic growth, and jobs; people are becoming more enlightened about the tradeoffs required in a progressive society. Americans have already begun a more careful definition of the role to be played by government in relation to enterprise and the market economy, as evidenced by the deregulation of airline fares and the movement toward decontrol of prices for natural gas and crude oil.

These are arguments that capitalism has begun to win on the basis of 5
facts and experience—on pragmatic, economic grounds. I would say that it is all very well to go on the "ideological offensive" but that one must be careful not to confuse ideology and economics, lest—as in Marxism—the one poison the other.

Many writers and scholars present capitalism as a scheme of social 6
organization, a remarkable fortress of ideology and philosophy concerning the right to private property, strict limitation of government power, and dedication to free markets or the market economy. Yet capitalism itself has displayed, in the main, a positive aversion to ideology, to declaring itself the one true way that men should live and work. Its claims—and demonstrated virtues—have mainly to do with the economic sphere. This is why multinational corporations are able to operate successfully and usefully in so many countries, with so many ideological shadings in their governments. For they enable economics to stand apart from politics.

Still, I suppose we are observing the phenomenon Bertolt Brecht de- 7
scribed when he said that to avoid ideology in our day is not to escape it. Presenting capitalism as a scheme of social organization gives the scholar a convenient rhetorical device to oppose to socialism or "Marxist collectivism." He can then argue private property vs. public ownership, market economy vs. centrally controlled economy, or limited government vs. all-pervasive government.

But the scheme of social organization in, say, the United States is not capitalism but democracy. Americans, if asked, do not describe themselves as capitalists. Capitalism, to the man in the street, is not the ideological fortress underlying his liberties but an economic system that has worked rather well (as Johnson points out) for almost every group or individual who got involved with it. As long as we talk about capitalism in terms of what it is—an economic device of proven value—it can generally hold its own in the public dialogue. But we shall send people scurrying off in droves if we attempt to load the nature and fate of Western civilization onto the back of capitalism. I think Americans know very well that what Marxism can imperil is their liberty, not their capitalism. 8

It is worth remembering that to offer a convincing catalogue of the dangers or abject failures of socialism does not, in itself, convert one's listeners to capitalism. This seems to have mystified a fair number of capitalist intellectuals; it is perhaps further evidence of the perils encountered when ideology and economics are confused. 9

Can we look at capitalism without its ideological freight? Perhaps by thinking of it as simply a "competitive market economy" we can consider it as an economic system. As Johnson describes most forcefully, capitalism has worked phenomenally well in achieving material abundance, the wide distribution of goods, and a steady increase in personal opportunity. I think we can discern in the system of capitalism some sort of inner affinity with the human desire to work, to make or build or accomplish something of one's own, and an even deeper affinity with the human desire to change, to improve not only one's self but also one's environment. Capitalism has not created these needs; it has merely provided a marvelous means for fulfilling them. When critics complain that capitalism has aggravated spiritual unease or restlessness in Western civilization, they overlook the possibility that this very restlessness has perhaps created and formed the civilization. Capitalism has been not a primary cause but an efficient vehicle. 10

Johnson's warning that capitalism can be smothered, dismantled, and destroyed is valid. I think there is some danger that this will happen in the United States, but I am, on the whole, optimistic that it will not. Even in the worst of times, many of us have persisted in believing that the American public—given more information—would come to see that the market prospers in liberty and atrophies under command. 11

That lesson of history is so clear that it cannot forever be ignored. It is an idea that is currently in disfavor among many American intellectuals. But the public is of a different mind. The public current is now running strongly against big government and excessive, costly regulation—witness California's Proposition 13* and similar tax revolts. The public demand is for change, for a thorough pruning of the huge, remote bureaucracies that have been inter- 12

*The first of several state laws passed by referendum limiting the size of state budgets and establishing limits on taxes.

fering so relentlessly not only with the free market but with almost everyone's life and work.

And even the intellectual community is beginning to resist the unnecessary interference of government in what had been an effective and highly successful market economy. In 1978 the new president of Yale University, A. Bartlett Giamatti, went to some length in his inaugural address to remind the Yale community of the dangers to Yale of "governmental intrusion" and to stress that private educational institutions "are an integral part of the private sector." He called for an end to the "ancient ballet of mutual antagonism" between private enterprise and private education, and said further: "There is a metaphor that informs the private business sector as it informs the private educational sector, and that is the metaphor of the free marketplace." 13

And of course there are other striking signs of the change in public opinion. Legislators themselves are becoming disenchanted with the unpredictable distortions and misallocations of resources that result from large-scale government interference in the operations of the market economy. They are coming to see the truth in Friedrich Hayek's observation that the competitive free market does not mean a national abdication from planning; rather, "competition means decentralized planning by many separate persons." 14

Inherent in the competitive market economy, in capitalism, there *is* a plan—a sort of unorchestrated harmony that represents not only the decisions of "many separate persons" but also the larger frame of public decisions and reasonable regulations that channel enterprise toward goals aligned with the democratic ideal. This is not true *laissez-faire* capitalism—if indeed there has ever been such a creature outside books—but rather a system in which the public sector takes pains to foster responsive, adaptable, innovative, and democratic markets. That system worked in an extraordinary, unprecedented way to advance the material well-being and range for personal autonomy of all those who took part in it. Today the public, much of the intellectual community, and many of the nation's political leaders show a growing appreciation of that system's worth—heartening evidence that capitalism does indeed have a future. 15

J. Robert Nelson

CAPITALISM: BLESSING AND CURSE

Paul Johnson's description of the astounding effects of industrial capitalism within two hundred years reminds us of other remarkable developments in this relatively brief period. Except for some realms of philosophy, religion, 1 literature, and the arts—visual, auditory, and culinary—our present civilization is wholly different from that of the eighteenth century. He is probably correct in comparing the slums and peasants' hovels of Europe in that century to those in the poorest lands of the Southern Hemisphere today. In hundreds of respects our present world, whether brave or not, is certainly new. And for millions of people it is manifestly better in three broad categories—health, education, and welfare.

Johnson does not choose to argue that the capitalist economy had a great deal to do with the generally improved lot of countless human beings who, thanks to science and technology, will now live to maturity and old age. Before the advent of capitalism, utter poverty, malnutrition, and mortal diseases were common conditions; the primary question was not how to *enhance* life but how to *survive.* Industrial capitalism is sustaining growing numbers of human beings at a higher level of health and material well-being. No one can deny that this is largely the result of a sense of individual worth, initiative, aspiration, and competition. These human qualities had for centuries been denied and suppressed in the common people. They were like white roots and stems found under flat rocks. The plants are alive, but barely so; only when they are uncovered and exposed to sunlight can they grow and develop color. The use of technology to make a profit on invested capital, encouraged by increasingly democratic political societies, was like the lifting of a heavy stone from Western Europe and America. 2

Johnson does not overstate the case for crediting capitalism—both the ideology and the economic system—for much of what the developed countries enjoy and take for granted. He could have extended the catalogue of its good influences. But he could also have noted the conditions and strictures that have been imposed upon the exuberant free enterprise of the nineteenth century. Government regulation, brought about by democratically elected legislatures, shows that citizens recognized dangers and evils inherent in that economic system. They have seen capitalism for what it is: both a blessing and a curse. 3

Perhaps this perception of paradox derives from the religious force usually associated with the rise of capitalism—Calvinism. To those most conscious of being God's elect and most obedient to his will is attributed the famous work ethic. But whether or not they were Calvinists, many of the early capitalists were indeed tirelessly industrious, thrifty, and imbued with a sense of rightness and destiny. How could they avoid believing that divine and benign Providence had given to the British the nearly inexhaustible natural resources of a world empire and to Americans the unexplored and as yet unexploited North American continent (though the new Jerusalem they felt called to build in the green lands of England and New England turned out to be more commercial than heavenly). 4

The same Providence that gave them resources and inspired resourcefulness also required justice and mercy. While the early capitalists, who could be described as "God-fearing," had a limited concept of what justice required, they did give expression to mercy through acts of philanthropy that partially 5 expiated their sin of acquisitiveness. Many colleges, universities, libraries, museums, charitable institutions, and foundations owe their existence in large measure to the "plagued conscience" of Christian and Jewish capitalists.

But this was not enough to offset the ill effects on the population of economic control by large corporations. As the era of robber barons gave way to the era of big business, the necessity of government regulation was apparent. Implicit in the motivation for regulation was a biblical teaching: the same heart of man that rejoices in the blessings of prosperity remains wicked and exceedingly self-centered. If there is any truth in the saying that there was more Methodism than Marxism in the rise of British socialism, a similar observation about religious influence is appropriate to America's willingness to accept the Rooseveltian reforms that rendered fully obsolete the concept of *laissez-faire.* 6

Paul Johnson's discussion of the relation between government and business is inadequate. It is merely contentious to say that industrial capitalism and big government are irreconcilable enemies. He has a legitimate complaint against *excessive* controls by government, but he goes much further and appears to preclude *proper* controls. He implies that the only alternative to big government's power over the economy is no control at all. 7

His discussion of labor unions leads to a similarly erroneous conclusion: better none at all than what we have in Britain and America today. This is unfortunate, since many who are sympathetic with Johnson's opposition to Marxism and Communism cannot believe that our national government and labor unions are equally perilous to a good society. 8

His polemic against the false gods and false hopes of Communism certainly is justified; but it would be more compelling if he had shown that the outrages of which industrial capitalism stands accused are easily matched, or exceeded, by those in socialist countries. These have to do with three kinds of exploitation: human, international, and ecological. Critics and dedicated opponents of capitalism have convincing reasons for faulting the corporate powers of free (or nearly free) enterprise. Countless workers and their dependents have suffered abuses and deprivations; natural resources of less developed countries have been pillaged for the profit of the rich ones; our air, water, and soil have been polluted. Johnson is not disposed to mention these vulnerable aspects of capitalist societies, which are the prime targets of both the academic Marxists and the pamphleteers. Neither does he admit the extent to which industrial capitalism is linked with, and dependent upon, the European and American production of military hardware and all the ancillary materials and services useful only to defense and warfare. Remembering that it was a representative of capitalist interests, President Eisenhower, whose last testament was a grave warning against the "military-industrial complex," we may find all the less convincing Johnson's generalization that industry and government are natural enemies. 9

These arguments can readily be turned back against Marxist apologists for socialist and Communist states and economies. When one thinks only of the Soviet Union's control over Eastern Europe, its expropriation of raw 10 materials and manufactured products for itself, its spoliation of the natural environment, and its abysmal record of human degradation and oppression, it is obvious that the Communist pot has no basis for calling the capitalist kettle black. To make these points would strengthen the case for capitalism as an imperfect yet preferable mode of production and distribution.

Johnson's animosity toward what he calls the "ecolobby" is excessive and perplexing. He gives the impression that he believes in industry's willingness and capability to care for the plundered planet by itself. Evidence abounds to show that this is an ill-founded belief—a point dramatized in March 1979 when the world turned horrified eyes on the Three Mile Island nuclear power reactor near Harrisburg, Pennsylvania. Although its malfunction and threatened explosion of radioactive materials were brought under control with no human death or injury, the catastrophic possibility was enough to negate such blithe cases for developing nuclear power as Johnson's. 11

Though his style is engaging and articulate, Johnson falls short of making a satisfying apologia for industrial capitalism in our time. This is disappointing. There is merit in his trenchant observations about Marxists. He is right to point to the erosion of both the ideologically informed will and the political conditions that can make capitalism work as it should—i.e., for the common good. Not socialism but social mutuality and human solidarity must now determine our evaluation of any economic or political system. 12

Eugene J. McCarthy

CORPORATIONS HAVE CORRUPTED CAPITALISM

Little can be said against Paul Johnson's case for the productive power of capitalism, whether a particular capitalist's motivation was to amass wealth (as the economist Carl Snyder observed years ago, "Deep as are our prejudices against avarice and greed, it cannot be denied that they have been great forces for the building of the modern economic world"), to demonstrate personal power and achievement (as in the case of empire-builders like Andrew Carnegie and James Hill), or to contribute to human welfare. Today the theoretical challenge, if it can properly be called that, is not to traditional capitalism but to capitalism as it is manifested in the corporation. 1

When economists began to write about the economics of "imperfect competition," they signaled the end of the pure economics of Adam Smith and of capitalism. Today nearly 80 per cent of the productive activity in the United States is controlled by corporate organizations operating under chart- 2 ers granted by the states. These corporations are not free, competing entities but institutions given special privileges and advantages over individuals by legal social decision.

James Kent, in his *Commentaries on American Law,* published early in the nineteenth century, observed that "the number of charters of incorporation" was increasing in the United States with a disturbing rapidity. "We are multiplying in this country to an unparalleled extent the institution of corporations," he said, "and giving them a flexibility and variety of purpose unknown to the Roman or to the English law." 3

Competition does not rule the economy of the United States today. More and more, differences between the largest corporations and the government are settled not within a framework of law but by negotiation. For example, when Du Pont was ordered to divest itself of General Motors stock some seventeen years ago, the existing antitrust laws and penalties were not applied. Congress passed special legislation to work out the transition. In much the same way, the taxation of insurance companies and of oil companies has been settled by negotiation rather than by the application of public judgment and law. 4

The government's dealings with the steel industry in recent years demonstrate the same relationship. During the Korean War, when President Truman tried to prevent a slowdown in steel production by issuing an executive order to take over the industry, the independence of the industry was sustained by the Supreme Court. 5

Subsequent challenges to the industry were handled differently. The Kennedy administration responded to a major increase in the price of steel not by attempting to apply the existing law or by executive order but by public denunciation and, according to some reports, by midnight calls from the FBI to steel-company officials. 6

In the Johnson administration, the presidents of steel companies were called to the White House for "jawboning" sessions, generally approved by the press and politicians. The message was not that competition, the free economy, and the law of supply and demand should be allowed to prevail but that prices should be kept down. The steel-company officers, champions of free enterprise and of capitalism, surrendered, seeming to accept the idea that if prices were fixed in Pittsburgh, that would be an "action in restraint of trade." It was rather as if an English king had called in the nobles and said: "If you agree to these things in my presence, you will be able to do them. But if you agree to them among yourselves in Wales, you will be in deep trouble." 7

It has been suggested that the U.S. government seek the equivalent of diplomatic representation on the boards of major corporations, especially those that are deeply involved in foreign business and finance. 8

What we have in America is not a free, competitive, capitalistic system but a kind of corporate feudalism. In the feudal system, according to a schoolboy's definition, everyone belonged to someone and everyone else belonged to the king. In the modern order, nearly every worker belongs to 9 some corporation, and everyone else belongs to the government, federal, state, or local.

A corporately controlled economy has left us with a situation in which there is widespread poverty, serious unemployment, the wasting of resources, shortages, and inflation. The corporation is not wholly responsible for these conditions. Undoubtedly outside policy or forces, such as war and government fiscal policies and regulations, have an adverse affect on the general economy and specifically on some institutions and businesses. 10

The concept of the corporation as an instrument for the conduct of business and financial affairs is a valid one. But it is a concept that must prove its vitality in practice. If the corporation is to be privileged by law, as it is now, and if it is to control most of the powers on which the material well-being of the nation depends, then it must become more effective and more responsible, both socially and economically. 11

James Cone

CAPITALISM MEANS PROPERTY OVER PERSONS

Some perspectives differ so radically from my own that I hardly know where to begin in responding to them. Having read Paul Johnson's address several times, I still find it hard to believe that he can so uncritically support capitalism in the face of the vast human suffering arising from it. How should I respond to a point of view that seems completely insensitive to many human factors that I regard as important? 1

I will focus my comments on the *selective* character of Paul Johnson's argument for industrial capitalism. Because I am a black American whose value system has been shaped in the historical context of an oppressed people's struggle for justice, I cannot avoid evaluating a given sociopolitical perspective in terms of how it helps or hinders that struggle. If one takes the general principle of "justice for the poor" as the criterion, Johnson's apology for capitalism is completely unconvincing. He shows little or no concern for oppressed humanity in Europe, the United States, and the Third World. It is as if they do not exist. 2

When a people's existence is not recognized, it means that their suffering is considered to have no bearing on the value of a given political system if that system continues to serve the interests of those for whom it was created. That was why white North Americans could speak of the United States as the "land of the free" while they held Africans as slaves. Similarly, Paul Johnson can speak of capitalism as "the greatest single blessing ever bestowed on humanity" even though the vast majority of people have been 3 victimized by it. He seems to be saying that as long as the white European and American ruling classes benefit from the profits of capitalism, its shortcomings in contributing toward the liberation of the poor from their poverty cannot count significantly against its value for humanity. Value is defined in terms of material profit for the rich, not economic and political structures for the benefit of all. It is this implication that makes his viewpoint reprehensible from my ethical perspective.

For whom does Johnson speak and for what purpose? I think the answer 4
is obvious. He speaks for the haves and not the have-nots, for the rich and not the poor, for whites and not blacks, for the United States and Europe and not for Asia, Africa, and Latin America. His purpose is to show that recent threats to industrial capitalism arise not from the masses of people but rather from university intellectuals, trade unions, big government, ecology campaigners, and the Soviet Union. This selective focus and his caricature of the opponents of capitalism define the character of his address; he thereby limits the possibility of genuine dialogue with anyone whose perspective has been shaped by solidarity with the victims of industrial capitalism.

Johnson's defense of industrial capitalism centers on its ability to pro- 5
duce an "unprecedented annual growth rate" in Europe and North America. Aside from Japan, there is no mention in this connection of any country in the Third World. Nor does he say anything about the relation between the wealth of Europe and the United States and the poverty in Asia, Africa, and Latin America. Is he suggesting that this wealth is in no way connected with and dependent upon slavery and colonization in the Third World? Because the examples he gives of the value of industrial capitalism are almost exclusively limited to Europe and the United States, I am particularly interested in how he would explain the huge gap between the rich and the poor on both continents, but especially in Asia, Africa, and Latin America. And why does he not mention that though the United States has only 6 per cent of the world's population, it consumes over 30 per cent of the world's natural resources?

I contend that capitalism is under threat not because it has received a 6
bad press from university intellectuals, ecology campaigners, and trade-union people, nor because of big government or even the outside danger of the Soviet Union, but because the so-called free-enterprise system is not free at all; it is actually controlled by multinational corporations.

I agree with Johnson that the capitalist economies of the United States 7
and Europe have produced a lot of wealth. But I also know that the masses of people on both continents do not receive their just share of that wealth. While legislators in the United States enact laws almost yearly that appear to guarantee a fairer distribution, statistics show that the very rich still control a hugely disproportionate amount of the nation's wealth. This rich ruling class makes up only 0.5 per cent of the population but controls over one-fourth of the nation's privately held wealth and yearly income, including 50–86 per cent of all corporate stock (see Jonathan Turner and Charles Staines, *Inequality: Privilege and Poverty in America,* Goodyear, 1976).

When these economic factors are set in a racial context, the injustice is 8
even more striking. Blacks and other U.S. minorities are especially victimized, because their color is an additional factor contributing to the economic injustice inflicted upon them. Aside from the small minority of black professionals who are needed to create the appearance of equality in the United States, blacks and other ethnic minorities are the last hired and often the first fired. Their unemployment rate is always four to ten times higher than that of whites. They are forced to live in urban ghettoes with no real opportunity to participate in shaping the laws that affect their community.

People who share Paul Johnson's perspective like to delude themselves 9
into thinking that the poor enjoy living in poverty. They nourish this delusion by spending most of their time talking to rich capitalists and their supporters rather than to the poor. Yet they like to claim that they know what the poor think. What they label as the "poor" perspective is nothing but the reinforcement of the ruling-class point of view. In the United States I have met many white people who share Johnson's viewpoint. They were plentiful during the civil-rights struggle in the 1950s and '60s, and today they are even more vocal in advocating the essential justice of the American capitalist system. When poor black people, during the 1960s, reacted in violent rebellion against intolerable economic conditions, white oppressors simply attributed such behavior to the influence of outside agitators and gave a military response that left many blacks dead in the streets.

Economic conditions in U.S. cities are no better today for the masses of 10
blacks than they were in the 1960s. But I am sure that urban police departments are better prepared for any disturbance that black people's poverty may motivate them to create. People who share Paul Johnson's perspective seem to be more concerned about eliminating social unrest through the power of the police than about eliminating the economic conditions that create the unrest.

Paul Johnson either is unaware of the gross injustices created by capital- 11
ism or has simply chosen to ignore them. If he thinks that the growth of megalopolises all over the world is evidence of a popular endorsement of capitalism, he is grossly mistaken. Poor people migrate to urban centers because they are trying to survive in a situation of maldistributed wealth. Whatever else may be said about the wealth that capitalism generates in the United States, poor blacks and other minorities do not benefit from it.

When capitalism's wealth is viewed in an international context, the 12
injustice it creates appears even greater. The wealth of Europe and the United States is directly determined by the poverty of the people of Asia, Africa, and Latin America. This is the historical significance of slavery and colonization, which today are continued in the economic domination of the Third World by the United States and Europe. Despite the Western world's verbal defense of human rights and freedom, its continued economic and military support of the dictator governments of South Africa, South Korea, Chile, and many other states completely invalidates what it says.

Although I am a Christian whose ethical perspective is derived primarily 13 from that tradition, I do not need to appeal to Christianity to demonstrate the gross immorality of economic arrangements defined by capitalism. One needs only to be sensitive to human beings and their right to life, liberty, and the pursuit of happiness to question seriously what Paul Johnson advocates. Capitalism is a system that clearly values property more than persons. That is why it is losing the moral and intellectual battle. And perhaps it is why Paul Johnson appeals to material statistics as evidence for the inherent value of capitalism rather than to the quality of life it makes possible for all people.

Questions for Discussion

1. In paragraph 15 of "Has Capitalism a Future?" Johnson pictures peasants and poor people all over the world going to the cities in a "never-ending one-way flow from [the] countryside." He calls this movement "plainly a voluntary mass choice." From what you know of poor people in cities either in the past or present, does this seem an accurate description of the urban poor?
2. Johnson calls the environmentalists' objections to industrial growth "ecological panic." What effect is the word *panic* designed to have on the reader?
3. Schmertz accuses Johnson of confusing capitalism as an economic system with democracy as a social system. Does this seem a well-placed criticism? Does Schmertz seem less or more eager than Johnson for capitalism to survive? Are Johnson and Schmertz appealing to the same *interests* in their readers? If so, what are they? If not, how do they differ?
4. Is McCarthy an opponent of capitalism? If not, what *does* he oppose? When he says that "competition does not rule the economy of the United States today" (¶4), is he saying that it should or should not? *Why* has competition disappeared from the American economy, and what should be done either to keep it out or to bring it back in?
5. What use does Nelson make of his observation that "the same heart of man that rejoices in the blessings of prosperity remains wicked and exceedingly self-centered" (¶6)? Does this remark provide support for Johnson's position? If so, how? If not, why not?
6. Nelson says that Johnson's attack on ecological advocates is "perplexing" (¶11). Does he really seem perplexed in the rest of the paragraph? If not, why do you think he uses this term? If you think his perplexity is genuine, what is he perplexed about?
7. Cone claims that Johnson "speaks for the haves and not the have-nots" (¶4). Do you think this is a fair accusation? Can you find evidence in Johnson's essay either to support or to refute it?

8. By putting Johnson's facts into the contexts of race and social class, Cone makes them look much less laudatory than Johnson does. Which writer do you think is being more careful with his facts? Are they speaking *at* each other or *past* each other?

Suggested Essay Topics

1. Select *one* of Johnson's respondents and make a list of three or four of his specific criticisms. Then write a letter to the critic in Johnson's name, addressing the criticisms in detail and answering them with information from "your" (Johnson's) essay, showing the critic that he has somehow failed to read you correctly.
2. Write a letter to Johnson, using evidence from all four of Johnson's respondents, to support a series of claims showing that Johnson has unfairly presented his argument for industrial capitalism.

IDEAS IN DEBATE

Karl Marx and Friedrich Engels
Carl L. Becker

Karl Marx and Friedrich Engels

Karl Marx (1818–1883) and Friedrich Engels (1820–1895) wrote The Manifesto of the Communist Party *in 1847 in Brussels, where they were members of a secret communist society of German workers, the "League of the Just." This work, published the following year, undertakes to give a concise description of the history of the working class in modern society from the communist point of view. The entire communist critique of capitalism is based on their interpretation of history.*

No works in modern times have been more influential than The Communist Manifesto *and Marx's* Capital *(*Das Kapital, *1867). Together these books lay out the view of economics and society that all communist governments today claim to be putting into effect, no matter how much disagreement they exhibit in practice.*

We assume that by this point you no longer need a great deal of help in making your way through an argument; fortunately Marx and Engels's essay is relatively free of the elaborate formulas and abstract economic theory that make Capital *difficult even for experts. If you have made use of our various suggestions and especially our formal "demonstrations" of how to read arguments, you should now have no special difficulties in working out the steps of an argument that earlier in the year might have thrown you.*

But as you have long since discovered, reading, in the sense of reconstructing what an author seems to be saying, is only a first step in an unending process that might be called "real reading" or interpretation. *(Some people call the most advanced kind of reading* hermeneutics.*) Even the most skilled readers disagree in their interpretations of the full meaning and significance of what Marx and Engels wrote. Thus, understanding the* Manifesto *at one level simply qualifies us to enter a discussion with other readers about where these ideas lead.*

As you read and re-read, then, try to think of discussion questions you *would devise. The more good questions you can devise, the better a reader you have become.*

THE CLASS STRUGGLE

Our title for part 1 of *The Manifesto of the Communist Party* (1848).

A spectre is haunting Europe—the spectre of Communism. All the Powers of 1
old Europe have entered into a holy alliance to exorcise this spectre: Pope and Czar, Metternich and Guizot, French Radicals and German police-spies.

Where is the party in opposition that has not been decried as Commu- 2
nistic by its opponents in power? Where the Opposition that has not hurled back the branding reproach of Communism, against the more advanced opposition parties, as well as against its reactionary adversaries?

Two things result from this fact: 3

I. Communism is already acknowledged by all European Powers to be itself a Power.

II. It is high time that Communists should openly, in the face of the whole world, publish their views, their aims, their tendencies, and meet this nursery tale of the Spectre of Communism with a Manifesto of the party itself.

To this end, Communists of various nationalities have assembled in 4
London, and sketched the following Manifesto, to be published in the English, French, German, Italian, Flemish and Danish languages.

BOURGEOIS AND PROLETARIANS[1]

The history of all hitherto existing society[2] is the history of class struggles. 5

Freeman and slave, patrician and plebeian, lord and serf, guild-master[3] 6
and journeyman, in a word, oppressor and oppressed, stood in constant opposition to one another, carried on an uninterrupted, now hidden, now open fight, a fight that each time ended, either in a revolutionary re-constitution of society at large, or in the common ruin of the contending classes.

In the earlier epochs of history, we find almost everywhere a complicat- 7
ed arrangement of society into various orders, a manifold gradation of social rank. In ancient Rome we have patricians, knights, plebeians, slaves; in the Middle Ages, feudal lords, vassals, guild-masters, journeymen, apprentices, serfs; in almost all of these classes, again, subordinate gradations.

The modern bourgeois [i.e., middle-class] society that has sprouted 8
from the ruins of feudal society has not done away with class antagonisms. It has but established new classes, new conditions of oppression, new forms of struggle in place of the old ones.

Our epoch, the epoch of the bourgeoisie, possesses, however, this dis- 9
tinctive feature: it has simplified the class antagonisms. Society as a whole is more and more splitting up into two great hostile camps, into two great classes directly facing each other: Bourgeoisie and Proletariat.

From the serfs of the Middle Ages sprang the chartered burghers* of the 10
earliest towns. From these burgesses the first elements of the bourgeoisie were developed.

The discovery of America, the rounding of the Cape, opened up fresh 11
ground for the rising bourgeoisie. The East-Indian and Chinese markets, the colonisation of America, trade with the colonies, the increase in the means of exchange and in commodities generally, gave to commerce, to navigation, to industry, an impulse never before known, and thereby, to the revolutionary element in the tottering feudal society, a rapid development.

The feudal [i.e., medieval] system of industry, under which industrial 12
production was monopolised by closed guilds, now no longer sufficed for the growing wants of the new markets. The manufacturing system took its place. The guild-masters were pushed on one side by the manufacturing middle class; division of labour between the different corporate guilds vanished in the face of division of labour in each single workshop.

Meantime the markets kept ever growing, the demand ever rising. Even 13
manufacture no longer sufficed. Thereupon, steam and machinery revolutionised industrial production. The place of manufacture was taken by the giant, Modern Industry, the place of the industrial middle class, by industrial millionaires, the leaders of whole industrial armies, the modern bourgeois.

Modern Industry has established the world market, for which the dis- 14
covery of America paved the way. This market has given an immense development to commerce, to navigation, to communication by land. This development has, in its turn, reacted on the extension of industry; and in proportion as industry, commerce, navigation, railways extended, in the same proportion the bourgeoisie developed, increased its capital, and pushed into the background every class handed down from the Middle Ages.

We see, therefore, how the modern bourgeoisie is itself the product of 15
a long course of development, of a series of revolutions in the modes of production and of exchange.

Each step in the development of the bourgeoisie was accompanied by 16
a corresponding political advance of that class. An oppressed class under the sway of the feudal nobility, an armed and self-governing association in the medieval commune;[4] here independent urban republic (as in Italy and Germany), there taxable "third estate" of the monarchy (as in France), afterwards, in the period of manufacture proper, serving either the semi-feudal or the absolute monarchy as a counterpoise against the nobility, and, in fact, cornerstone of the great monarchies in general, the bourgeoisie has at last, since the establishment of Modern Industry and of the world market, conquered for itself, in the modern representative [i.e., democratic] State, exclu-

*Licensed merchants, wine sellers, wool exporters, and the like. Such occupations emerged toward the end of the Middle Ages and formed the beginnings of the middle class in England and Europe.

sive political sway. The executive of the modern State is but a committee for managing the common affairs of the whole bourgeoisie.

The bourgeoisie, historically, has played a most revolutionary part. 17

The bourgeoisie, wherever it has got the upper hand, has put an end to all 18
feudal, patriarchal, idyllic relations. It has pitilessly torn asunder the motley feudal ties that bound man to his "natural superiors," and has left remaining no other nexus [i.e., link] between man and man than naked self-interest, than callous "cash payment." It has drowned the most heavenly ecstasies of religious fervour, of chivalrous enthusiasm, of philistine sentimentalism, in the icy water of egotistical calculation. It has resolved personal worth into exchange value, and in place of the numberless indefeasible [i.e., guaranteed] chartered freedoms, has set up that single, unconscionable freedom—Free Trade. In one word, for exploitation, veiled by religious and political illusions, it has substituted naked, shameless, direct, brutal exploitation.

The bourgeoisie has stripped of its halo every occupation hitherto ho- 19
noured and looked up to with reverent awe. It has converted the physician, the lawyer, the priest, the poet, the man of science, into its paid wage-labourers.

The bourgeoisie has torn away from the family its sentimental veil, and 20
has reduced the family relation to a mere money relation.

The bourgeoisie has disclosed how it came to pass that the brutal dis- 21
play of vigour in the Middle Ages, which Reactionists so much admire, found its fitting complement in the most slothful indolence. It has been the first to show what man's activity can bring about. It has accomplished wonders far surpassing Egyptian pyramids, Roman aqueducts, and Gothic cathedrals; it has conducted expeditions that put in the shade all former Exoduses of nations and crusades.

The bourgeoisie cannot exist without constantly revolutionising the 22
instruments of production, and thereby the relations of production, and with them the whole relations of society. Conservation of the old modes of production in unaltered form, was, on the contrary, the first condition of existence for all earlier industrial classes. Constant revolutionising of production, uninterrupted disturbance of all social conditions, everlasting uncertainty and agitation distinguish the bourgeois epoch from all earlier ones. All fixed, fast-frozen relations, with their train of ancient and venerable prejudices and opinions, are swept away, all new-formed ones become antiquated before they can ossify. All that is solid melts into air, all that is holy is profaned, and man is at last compelled to face with sober senses, his real conditions of life, and his relations with his kind.

The need of a constantly expanding market for its products chases the 23
bourgeoisie over the whole surface of the globe. It must nestle everywhere, settle everywhere, establish connexions everywhere.

The bourgeoisie has through its exploitation of the world market given 24
a cosmopolitan character to production and consumption in every country. To the great chagrin of Reactionists, it has drawn from under the feet of industry the national ground on which it stood. All old-established national

industries have been destroyed or are daily being destroyed. They are dislodged by new industries, whose introduction becomes a life and death question for all civilised nations, by industries that no longer work up indigenous raw material, but raw material drawn from the remotest zones; industries whose products are consumed, not only at home, but in every quarter of the globe. In place of the old wants, satisfied by the productions of the country, we find new wants, requiring for their satisfaction the products of distant lands and climes. In place of the old local and national seclusion and self-sufficiency, we have intercourse in every direction, universal inter-dependence of nations. And as in material, so also in intellectual production. The intellectual creations of individual nations become common property. National one-sidedness and narrow-mindedness become more and more impossible, and from the numerous national and local literatures, there arises a world literature.

The bourgeoisie, by the rapid improvement of all instruments of pro- 25
duction, by the immensely facilitated means of communication, draws all, even the most barbarian, nations into civilisation. The cheap prices of its commodities are the heavy artillery with which it batters down all Chinese walls, with which it forces the barbarians' intensely obstinate hatred of foreigners to capitulate. It compels all nations, on pain of extinction, to adopt the bourgeois mode of production; it compels them to introduce what it calls civilisation into their midst, i.e., to become bourgeois themselves. In one word, it creates a world after its own image.

The bourgeoisie has subjected the country to the rule of the towns. It 26
has created enormous cities, has greatly increased the urban population as compared with the rural, and has thus rescued a considerable part of the population from the idiocy of rural life. Just as it has made the country dependent on the towns, so it has made barbarian and semi-barbarian countries dependent on the civilised ones, nations of peasants on nations of bourgeois, the East on the West.

The bourgeoisie keeps more and more doing away with the scattered 27
state of the population, of the means of production, and of property. It has agglomerated population, centralised means of production, and has concentrated property in a few hands. The necessary consequence of this was political centralisation. Independent, or but loosely connected provinces with separate interests, laws, governments and systems of taxation, became lumped together into one nation, with one government, one code of laws, one national class-interest, one frontier and one customs-tariff.

The bourgeoisie, during its rule of scarce one hundred years, has created 28
more massive and more colossal productive forces than have all preceding generations together. Subjection of Nature's forces to man, machinery, application of chemistry to industry and agriculture, steam-navigation, railways, electric telegraphs, clearing of whole continents for cultivation, canalisation of rivers, whole populations conjured out of the ground—what earlier century had even a presentiment that such productive forces slumbered in the lap of social labour?

We see then: the means of production and of exchange, on whose 29
foundation the bourgeoisie built itself up, were generated in feudal society. At a certain stage in the development of these means of production and of exchange, the conditions under which feudal society produced and exchanged, the feudal organisation of agriculture and manufacturing industry, in one word, the feudal relations of property became no longer compatible with the already developed productive forces; they became so many fetters. They had to be burst asunder; they were burst asunder.

Into their place stepped free competition, accompanied by a social and 30
political constitution adapted to it, and by the economical and political sway of the bourgeois class.

A similar movement is going on before our own eyes. Modern bourgeois 31
society with its relations of production, of exchange and of property, a society that has conjured up such gigantic means of production and of exchange, is like the sorcerer, who is no longer able to control the powers of the nether world whom he has called up by his spells. For many a decade past the history of industry and commerce is but the history of the revolt of modern productive forces against modern conditions of production, against the property relations that are the conditions for the existence of the bourgeoisie and of its rule. It is enough to mention the commercial crises that by their periodical return put on its trial, each time more threateningly, the existence of the entire bourgeois society. In these crises a great part not only of the existing products, but also of the previously created productive forces, are periodically destroyed. In these crises there breaks out an epidemic that, in all earlier epochs, would have seemed an absurdity—the epidemic of over-production.* Society suddenly finds itself put back into a state of momentary barbarism; it appears as if a famine, a universal war of devastation had cut off the supply of every means of subsistence; industry and commerce seem to be destroyed; and why? Because there is too much civilisation, too much means of subsistence, too much industry, too much commerce. The productive forces at the disposal of society no longer tend to further the development of the conditions of bourgeois property; on the contrary, they have become too powerful for these conditions, by which they are fettered, and so soon as they overcome these fetters, they bring disorder into the whole of bourgeois society, endanger the existence of bourgeois property. The conditions of bourgeois society are too narrow to comprise the wealth created by them. And how does the bourgeoisie get over these crises? On the one hand by enforced destruction of a mass of productive forces; on the other, by the conquest of new markets, and by the more thorough exploitation of the old ones. That is to say, by paving the way for more extensive and more destructive crises, and by diminishing the means whereby crises are prevented.

The weapons with which the bourgeoisie felled feudalism to the ground 32
are now turned against the bourgeoisie itself.

*They are here referring to the cycle of prosperity followed by depression and arguing that depressions are only overcome by dramatic expansion or creation of new markets.

But not only has the bourgeoisie forged the weapons that bring death 33
to itself; it has also called into existence the men who are to wield those weapons—the modern working class—the proletarians.

In proportion as the bourgeoisie, i.e., capital, is developed, in the same 34
proportion is the proletariat, the modern working class, developed—a class of labourers, who live only so long as they find work, and who find work only so long as their labour increases capital. These labourers, who must sell themselves piecemeal, are a commodity, like every other article of commerce, and are consequently exposed to all the vicissitudes of competition, to all the fluctuations of the market.

Owing to the extensive use of machinery and to division of labour, the 35
work of the proletarians has lost all individual character, and, consequently, all charm for the workman. He becomes an appendage of the machine, and it is only the most simple, most monotonous, and most easily acquired knack, that is required of him. Hence, the cost of production of a workman is restricted, almost entirely, to the means of subsistence that he requires for his maintenance, and for the propagation of his race. But the price of a commodity, and therefore also of labour, is equal to its cost of production. In proportion, therefore, as the repulsiveness of the work increases, the wage decreases. Nay more, in proportion as the use of machinery and division of labour increases, in the same proportion the burden of toil also increases, whether by prolongation of the working hours, by increase of the work exacted in a given time or by increased speed of the machinery, etc.

Modern industry has converted the little workshop of the patriarchal 36
master into the great factory of the industrial capitalist. Masses of labourers, crowded into the factory, are organised like soldiers. As privates of the industrial army they are placed under the command of a perfect hierarchy of officers and sergeants. Not only are they slaves of the bourgeois class, and of the bourgeois State; they are daily and hourly enslaved by the machine, by the overlooker, and, above all, by the individual bourgeois manufacturer himself. The more openly this despotism proclaims gain [i.e., profit] to be its end and aim, the more petty, the more hateful and the more embittering it is.

The less the skill and exertion of strength implied in manual labour, in 37
other words, the more modern industry becomes developed, the more is the labour of men superseded by that of women. Differences of age and sex have no longer any distinctive social validity for the working class. All are instruments of labour, more or less expensive to use, according to their age and sex.

No sooner is the exploitation of the labourer by the manufacturer, so 38
far, at an end, and he receives his wages in cash, than he is set upon by the other portions of the bourgeoisie, the landlord, the shopkeeper, the pawnbroker, etc.

The lower strata of the middle class—the small tradespeople, shopkeep- 39
ers, and retired tradesmen generally, the handicraftsmen and peasants—all these sink gradually into the proletariat, partly because their diminutive capital does not suffice for the scale on which Modern Industry is carried on,

and is swamped in the competition with the large capitalists, partly because their specialised skill is rendered worthless by new methods of production. Thus the proletariat is recruited from all classes of the population.

The proletariat goes through various stages of development. With its 40
birth begins its struggle with the bourgeoisie. At first the contest is carried on by individual labourers, then by the workpeople of a factory, then by the operatives of one trade, in one locality, against the individual bourgeois who directly exploits them. They direct their attacks not against the bourgeois conditions of production, but against the instruments of production themselves; they destroy imported wares that compete with their labour, they smash to pieces machinery, they set factories ablaze, they seek to restore by force the vanished status of the workman of the Middle Ages.

At this stage the labourers still form an incoherent mass scattered over 41
the whole country, and broken up by their mutual competition. If anywhere they unite to form more compact bodies, this is not yet the consequence of their own active union, but of the union of the bourgeoisie, which class, in order to attain its own political ends, is compelled to set the whole proletariat in motion, and is moreover yet, for a time, able to do so. At this stage, therefore, the proletarians do not fight their enemies, but the enemies of their enemies, the remnants of absolute monarchy, the landowners, the non-industrial bourgeois, the petty bourgeoisie. Thus the whole historical movement is concentrated in the hands of the bourgeoisie; every victory so obtained is a victory for the bourgeoisie.

But with the development of industry the proletariat not only increases 42
in number; it becomes concentrated in greater masses, its strength grows, and it feels that strength more. The various interests and conditions of life within the ranks of the proletariat are more and more equalised, in proportion as machinery obliterates all distinctions of labour, and nearly everywhere reduces wages to the same low level. The growing competition among the bourgeois, and the resulting commercial crises, make the wages of the workers ever more fluctuating. The unceasing improvement of machinery, ever more rapidly developing, makes their livelihood more and more precarious; the collisions between individual workmen and individual bourgeois take more and more the character of collisions between two classes. Thereupon the workers begin to form combinations (Trades' Unions) against the bourgeois; they club together in order to keep up the rate of wages; they found permanent associations in order to make provision beforehand for these occasional revolts. Here and there the contest breaks out into riots.

Now and then the workers are victorious, but only for a time. The real 43
fruit of their battles lies, not in the immediate result, but in the ever-expanding union of the workers. This union is helped on by the improved means of communication that are created by modern industry and that place the workers of different localities in contact with one another. It was just this contact that was needed to centralise the numerous local struggles, all of the same character, into one national struggle between classes. But every class struggle is a political struggle. And that union, to attain which the burghers

of the Middle Ages, with their miserable highways, required centuries, the modern proletarians, thanks to railways, achieve in a few years.

This organisation of the proletarians into a class, and consequently into 44
a political party, is continually being upset again by the competition between the workers themselves. But it ever rises up again, stronger, firmer, mightier. It compels legislative recognition of particular interests of the workers, by taking advantage of the divisions among the bourgeoisie itself. Thus the ten-hours bill in England was carried [limiting the workday to no more than ten hours].

Altogether collisions between the classes of the old society further, in 45
many ways, the course of development of the proletariat. The bourgeoisie finds itself involved in a constant battle. At first with the aristocracy; later on, with those portions of the bourgeoisie itself, whose interests have become antagonistic to the progress of industry; at all times, with the bourgeoisie of foreign countries. In all these battles it sees itself compelled to appeal to the proletariat, to ask for its help, and thus, to drag it into the political arena. The bourgeoisie itself, therefore, supplies the proletariat with its own elements of political and general education, in other words, it furnishes the proletariat with weapons for fighting the bourgeoisie.

Further, as we have already seen, entire sections of the ruling classes are, 46
by the advance of industry, precipitated into the proletariat, or are at least threatened in their conditions of existence. These also supply the proletariat with fresh elements of enlightenment and progress.

Finally, in times when the class struggle nears the decisive hour, the 47
process of dissolution going on within the ruling class, in fact within the whole range of old society, assumes such a violent, glaring character, that a small section of the ruling class cuts itself adrift, and joins the revolutionary class, the class that holds the future in its hands. Just as, therefore, at an earlier period, a section of the nobility went over to the bourgeoisie, so now a portion of the bourgeoisie goes over to the proletariat, and in particular, a portion of the bourgeois ideologists, who have raised themselves to the level of comprehending theoretically the historical movement as a whole.

Of all the classes that stand face to face with the bourgeoisie today, the 48
proletariat alone is a really revolutionary class. The other classes decay and finally disappear in the face of Modern Industry; the proletariat is its special and essential product.

The lower middle class, the small manufacturer, the shopkeeper, the 49
artisan, the peasant, all these fight against the bourgeoisie, to save from extinction their existence as fractions of the middle class. They are therefore not revolutionary, but conservative. Nay more, they are reactionary, for they try to roll back the wheel of history. If by chance they are revolutionary, they are so only in view of their impending transfer into the proletariat, they thus defend not their present, but their future interests, they desert their own standpoint to place themselves at that of the proletariat.

The "dangerous class," the social scum, that passively rotting mass 50
thrown off by the lowest layers of old society may, here and there, be swept

into the movement by a proletarian revolution; its conditions of life, however, prepare it far more for the part of a bribed tool of reactionary intrigue.

In the conditions of the proletariat, those of old society at large are 51
already virtually swamped. The proletarian is without property; his relation to his wife and children has no longer anything in common with the bourgeois family relations; modern industrial labour, modern subjection to capital, the same in England as in France, in America as in Germany, has stripped him of every trace of national character. Law, morality, religion, are to him so many bourgeois prejudices, behind which lurk in ambush just as many bourgeois interests.

All the preceding classes that got the upper hand, sought to fortify their 52
already acquired status by subjecting society at large to their conditions of appropriation. The proletarians cannot become masters of the productive forces of society, except by abolishing their own previous mode of appropriation, and thereby also every other previous mode of appropriation. They have nothing of their own to secure and to fortify; their mission is to destroy all previous securities for, and insurances of, individual property.

All previous historical movements were movements of minorities, or in 53
the interest of minorities. The proletarian movement is the self-conscious, independent movement of the immense majority, in the interest of the immense majority. The proletariat, the lowest stratum of our present society, cannot stir, cannot raise itself up, without the whole superincumbent strata of official society being sprung into the air.

Though not in substance, yet in form, the struggle of the proletariat 54
with the bourgeoisie is at first a national struggle. The proletariat of each country must, of course, first of all settle matters with its own bourgeoisie.

In depicting the most general phases of the development of the proletar- 55
iat, we traced the more or less veiled civil war, raging within existing society, up to the point where that war breaks out into open revolution, and where the violent overthrow of the bourgeoisie lays the foundation for the sway of the proletariat.

Hitherto, every form of society has been based, as we have already seen, 56
on the antagonism of oppressing and oppressed classes. But in order to oppress a class, certain conditions must be assured to it under which it can, at least, continue its slavish existence. The serf, in the period of serfdom, raised himself to membership in the commune, just as the petty bourgeois, under the yoke of feudal absolutism, managed to develop into a bourgeois. The modern labourer, on the contrary, instead of rising with the progress of industry, sinks deeper and deeper below the conditions of existence of his own class. He becomes a pauper, and pauperism develops more rapidly than population and wealth. And here it becomes evident, that the bourgeoisie is unfit any longer to be the ruling class in society, and to impose its conditions of existence upon society as an over-riding law. It is unfit to rule because it is incompetent to assure an existence to its slave within his slavery, because it cannot help letting him sink into such a state, that it has to feed him, instead

of being fed by him. Society can no longer live under this bourgeoisie, in other words, its existence is no longer compatible with society.

The essential condition for the existence, and for the sway of the bour- 57
geois class, is the formation and augmentation of capital; the condition for capital is wage-labour. Wage-labour rests exclusively on competition between the labourers. The advance of industry, whose involuntary promoter is the bourgeoisie, replaces the isolation of the labourers, due to competition, by their revolutionary combination, due to association. The development of Modern Industry, therefore, cuts from under its feet the very foundation on which the bourgeoisie produces and appropriates products. What the bourgeoisie, therefore, produces, above all, is its own grave-diggers. Its fall and the victory of the proletariat are equally inevitable.

NOTES

All notes are Engels's.

1. By bourgeoisie is meant the class of modern Capitalists, owners of the means of social production and employers of wage-labour. By proletariat, the class of modern wage-labourers who, having no means of production of their own, are reduced to selling their labour-power in order to live.

2. That is, all *written* history. In 1847, the pre-history of society, the social organisation existing previous to recorded history, was all but unknown. Since then, Haxthausen discovered common ownership of land in Russia, Maurer proved it to be the social foundation from which all Teutonic races started in history, and by and by village communities were found to be, or to have been the primitive form of society everywhere from India to Ireland. . . .

3. Guild-master, that is, a full member of a guild, a master within, not a head of a guild.

4. "Commune" was the name taken, in France, by the nascent towns even before they had conquered from their feudal lords and masters local self-government and political rights as the "Third Estate." Generally speaking, for the economical development of the bourgeoisie, England is here taken as the typical country; for its political development, France. [1888]

This was the name given their urban communities by the townsmen of Italy and France, after they had purchased or wrested their initial rights of self-government from their feudal lords. [1890]

Questions for Discussion

1. What are the stages of the history of class struggle that Marx and Engels trace? Are you and your fellow students able to agree about what these stages are and when they occurred? Can you state in one sentence the thesis of Marx and Engels? Do they do so?
2. Why are the conditions of modern industrial production evil, according to the *Manifesto*? Is it, for example, simply because the conditions produce an unfair distribution of wealth?

3. What kind of people, according to the *Manifesto,* do the owners and producers seem to be? How do they differ from the proletariat?
4. Compare the conditions of the proletariat as Marx and Engels describe it in 1848 with the conditions of workers today. Marx and Engels seem to suggest that the proletariat is composed exclusively of factory workers. Is the modern working force more diverse than the one Marx and Engels were observing? In today's world is the social distance between the middle class and the lower class, between the bourgeoisie and the proletariat, much smaller than it was in 1848? At that time workers and controllers did not share the same tastes, accents, or amusements, and, more important, they did not share a comparable level of education or income. Today, some of those whom Marx and Engels would call the proletariat—factory workers and taxi drivers, for example—seem to share many more important features of life with the bourgeoisie. Some of them make comparable incomes, vacation in the same distant places, send their children to college, and, in short, live "bourgeois" lives. Other segments of today's proletariat, by contrast, are chronically out of work (unemployment rates run shockingly high, in both black and white communities), and seem to get poorer every year. Do you think that the views of Marx and Engels remain in any sense true despite social and economic developments since their time, or do they seem simply wrong in their analysis of where the modern world was heading? In responding to all questions of this kind, be sure to remember just how tentative your opinions about such complex issues should be. Scholars spend lifetimes trying to answer questions like these. But the fact that you will not settle these issues does not mean that you cannot improve your opinions by thinking about them and discussing them with others. See (one last time) "What Is an Idea?" pp. 15–19, and "What Is an Argument?" pp. 19–22.
5. In paragraph 18 the description of how the "idyllic" feudal relations between lords and serfs have been "pitilessly torn asunder" by bourgeois callousness sounds almost nostalgic, as if Marx and Engels would like to turn the social clock back to the Middle Ages. Since this cannot be their point, what do you think they gain by describing things this way?
6. What do the authors accomplish with the use of the metaphors "heavenly ecstasies" and "icy water" (¶18)? What implicit value judgments do these metaphors carry? (Sometimes such metaphors are said to be "loaded.")
7. In paragraph 16 the authors' catalog of the accomplishments of the bourgeoisie seems to suggest admiration. As in their description of feudal relations, however, this cannot be their point. Why, then, do they use this tone? What *is* their point? And what exactly is it they admire or detest about the accomplishments of the bourgeoisie?
8. Is the metaphor of "sorcerer" in paragraph 31 effective? Is the metaphor of "slave" in paragraph 36 fair to the bourgeoisie? What is the advantage of using such powerfully loaded metaphors? Does the metaphor of "instruments" in paragraph 37 make the authors' case (that modern work

dehumanizes workers) as effectively as a more straightforward description might? Does the use of so many metaphors becloud or clarify the issues?

9. Is the denunciation of the bourgeoisie in the second half of paragraph 56 fundamentally political, economic, or moral? In other words, on what main grounds do Marx and Engels conclude that the continued existence of the bourgeoisie "is no longer compatible with society"?

Suggested Essay Topics

1. Write a letter to Marx and Engels citing all the particulars you can think of that show their historical precictions to be wrong. You might point out ways in which the proletariat is not oppressed: A factory worker who makes $35,000 a year is not a pauper, and management-provided benefits such as retirement plans, hospitalization coverage, and paid vacations do not look exactly like enslavement. Point out the places in their analysis where they seem to have misread the character of capitalism, and show them that they have failed to anticipate the true condition of the modern worker in today's industrial world.
2. Write a letter to Marx and Engels corroborating their view of the relationship between the controlling class and the working class with as many particulars as you can cite. You might point out that although steelworkers are not exactly paupers, their salaries are still ridiculously low compared with those of company executives; that they are still subject to the whims of management and the ups and downs of the economy; that during a depression it is the worker who hurts, not the owner of the factory, whose invested funds can carry his family through for years; that alienation from the product of work is as great as or greater than ever; and that a new "underclass" has arisen, not workers but the unemployed, who are more badly exploited than the nineteenth-century proletariat ever were. Can you think of similar examples?

Carl L. Becker

The following essay by Carl Becker (1873–1945) first appeared in his Everyman His Own Historian *(1935), a book of essays on history and politics. The book received wide public attention, partly because of its unusually clear and forceful arguments about the nature of history and about "everyman's" role in making it and partly because of its challenge to Marxist theories, which were at that time attracting increasing numbers of American intellectuals. It seemed to many observers that Marx's predictions were coming true, that in fact the proletariat, or working class, in the modern world was being systemati-*

cally turned into a wage-slave class. The year 1935 was a high point in the Great Depression; working people were jobless and poor on a scale never before known in this country, yet the deflation of currency had made the rich even richer. In addition, large-scale conflicts between factory owners who opposed unions and workers who were trying to unionize seemed to augur social chaos. Such conflict revealed, at the very least, a deep bitterness developing between the rich and the poor. To some people these conditions seemed to corroborate Marx's theory that the proletariat, once debased and deprived beyond endurance, would eventually rise up in revolt and wrest power from its oppressive bourgeois masters.

Becker challenges both Marxist historical theory and Marxist political practice. Before reading this essay, read (or re-read) the preceding selection by Marx and Engels, for you will then be able to assess more accurately the fairness of Becker's opposition to Marxist views.

It has been more than half a century since Becker wrote this piece, yet even today the debate seems as fresh as ever. Marxists continue to claim that middle-class dominance has to be overturned. And many critics of Marxism continue to depend, as Paul Johnson does (pp. 783–792), on the claim that capitalism has done more than any other system in history to liberate and lift, not oppress, the proletariat. Notice, however, that Becker's rejection of Marxism is not based on facts or arguments about whether capitalist workers are better off or worse off than Marx claimed they were. He rejects Marxism instead by claiming (1) that the Marxist historical argument is self-contradictory (¶27–31) and (2) that Marxism employs force for its authority (¶33–35).

Before attempting to judge whether Becker's critique is valid, be sure that you can state, in your own words, the key arguments he offers against Marxism and the key arguments that you think Marxists would make in reply.

THE MARXIAN PHILOSOPHY OF HISTORY

From *Everyman His Own Historian* (1935)

I sometimes find myself discussing communism with those who profess that 1
faith; and not infrequently I note an implicit assumption on their part that I, as an intelligent person with some knowledge of history, ought either, (1) to refute the Marxian philosophy of history, or (2) in all honesty to support the communist cause. In such discussions I have maintained, (1) that an intelligent person may regard the Marxian philosophy of history as an illuminating interpretation of the past without subscribing to it as a law of history, and, (2) that even if convinced that the Marxian doctrine is a valid law of history, one might still with excellent reasons refuse to support the communist cause. Such discussions, developed more fully and presented more formally, may for convenience be put in the form of a discussion between a communist and a liberal.

2 COMMUNIST: Don't you think, Professor, that history proves that social progress, or change if you prefer, is the result of an inevitable class-conflict?

3 LIBERAL: Put in that precise way, no. I can't see that history proves anything except that what happened did happen, or that anything is inevitable except what happened; but what happened is precisely the question at issue. In using the words "prove" and "inevitable" you are, as the logicians say, begging the question.

4 COMMUNIST: I don't insist on those precise words.

5 LIBERAL: Very well. I agree then that history does support, or can easily be made to support, the Marxian doctrine in a general way. For example, in the middle ages the chief source of wealth was certainly land; and it is obvious that at that time the land-owning aristocracy was the ruling class. No great ingenuity is required to show that political, social, and religious customs and ideas of that time were suited to maintaining the political and economic ascendancy of the aristocracy. Likewise, it is obvious that during the last three centuries land has gradually been replaced by capital as the chief source of wealth; and the history of this time may easily be regarded as a conflict between the middle-class capitalist and the land-owning aristocracy, as a result of which the former have replaced the latter as the ruling class and have substituted, in their interest, a new set of institutions and ideas (representative government, individual liberty, popular sovereignty, free competition) for the old. Yes, as an interpretation of the last thousand years of European history, the Marxian theory is most illuminating.

6 COMMUNIST: Isn't it a bit more than merely illuminating? Can you deny that it is a more convincing and realistic interpretation than any other?

7 LIBERAL: I could very easily deny it, but I have no wish to do so. Let us admit that it is the most convincing interpretation. I will go farther. For purposes of argument I will admit that it is the only valid interpretation.

8 COMMUNIST: Very well then. If you admit that Marx has correctly interpreted the past, why not admit that he has correctly interpreted the future? Why not admit that just as the bourgeois-capitalist class displaced the land-owning aristocracy as the ruling class, so the proletariat will in its turn replace the bourgeois-capitalist class? And if they do so, isn't it reasonable to suppose that the characteristic ideas of the present society (representative government, freedom of speech, *laissez-faire*) will in turn give way to others suited to the interests of the proletariat?

9 LIBERAL: If I accept Marx's interpretation of the past it is because I know what it is, and can test it. If I hesitate to accept his interpretation

of the future it is partly because I do not know precisely what it is, and partly because, even if I know what it is, I cannot test it. I willingly admit that the future will, in some way that can after the event be rationalized, resemble the past. Certainly change is the law of life, and it is obvious that the institutions and ideas of the nineteenth century, which were so well suited to the interests of the capitalist class, will not suffice without modification for the needs of the complex mechanized society of the twentieth. I willingly admit also that the ideas and institutions of today will be changed in such a way as to conform more closely with the economic interests of the workers, the mass of the people, the proletariat. But that is not to say that the change will come about in the way predicted by Marx, or that the result will be the sort of utopia predicted by him.

COMMUNIST: Utopia! I am not aware that Marx predicted any utopia. 10

LIBERAL: Well, let us say that he didn't. What then did he predict? 11

COMMUNIST: He predicted that the capitalist régime would by its own nature 12
destroy itself. Its nature is to be ruthlessly competitive, so that in any industrial society the tendency is for wealth to be more highly concentrated in the hands of a few, while the mass of the people tend to fall to the condition of wage slaves. When this process reaches a certain point, the system breaks down, as it is now breaking down* because it has deprived the people of the means of buying the commodities which it is the sole aim of the capitalist class to make and sell for a profit. When the system ceases to work the people will necessarily take control, and, since it is their interest to do so, they will establish a classless society based upon the common ownership of instruments of production, and a more equitable distribution of the product. This is the social revolution that Marx predicted, and it has already begun—in Russia.

LIBERAL: In Russia, yes. In Russia, that is to say not the most highly 13
industrialized society but the least highly industrialized society. That is surely not according to Marx.

COMMUNIST: No, it is not. But you cannot maintain that because Marx's 14
prediction is not verified in every detail it is not therefore valid in its general outline. The Great War created a special set of circumstances which were peculiarly favorable to the social revolution in Russia.

LIBERAL: Very true. The social revolution clearly occurred before its time 15
in Russia. Providence, or Dialectic Materialism, or whatever it is that regulates social changes, certainly did a very curious thing in bringing the social revolution to Russia before it brought it to more highly industrialized countries, such as England. For my

*The "now" of this essay is 1935, the middle of the Great Depression.

part I don't think the Russian revolution does anything to verify the predictions of Marx; to me it indicates only that in a country in which the people were accustomed to being ruled by a dictatorship, a country moreover in which the prevailing form of dictatorship was especially corrupt and incompetent, it was very easy to establish a dictatorship of a different sort. But let that pass. My reluctance to accept the Marxian doctrine arises from something far more fundamental than the Russian accident. There are two difficulties which have always troubled me. Perhaps you can solve them. One is that it is extremely difficult to predict the future on the basis of past experience; or rather it is extremely easy to find in the past support for diverse predictions of the future. The other difficulty is to understand why a persistent economic class conflict in the past justifies us in predicting a classless society in the future.

As to the first difficulty. What little I know of history 16
makes me chary of any prediction as to the form which social institutions will take in the future. Especially so when such predictions, based upon a realistic view of the past, take an idealistic view of the future. During the last two thousand years all the saints and sages of the world, deploring greed and strife, poverty and injustice, have looked forward to the time when a more just society would be established. They have many times predicted the coming of a classless society in which everyone would have enough; but the course of events has never yet verified their hopes. This generalization is as solidly based on historical fact as any that Marx has made, and it is more widely based; and if I am to judge the future by the past, I see no reason for discarding this generalization for that which Marx offers me. The less so, since Marx's interpretation of the past, if projected into the future, seems to refute his own prediction.

COMMUNIST: I don't understand that. 17

LIBERAL: Perhaps it will become clear if I elaborate the second difficulty 18
I just mentioned. Marx's interpretation of the past is explicit and realistic; his forecast of the future seems to me vague and idealistic. I have called it utopian, but you object to that word. I do not insist on it. I will even surrender the word "idealistic." But the point is this. Marx finds that in the past the effective force that has determined social change is the economic class conflict. He points out that this economic class conflict explains the rise of the present capitalistic society. He shows, or at least his disciples show, how this economic class conflict is working to undermine our capitalistic society. Very well. If then I project this explanation of social changes into the future, what does it tell me? It seems to tell me that there will be in the future what there has been in the past—an endless economic class conflict,

an endless replacement of one dominant class by another, an endless transformation of institutions and ideas in accordance with the changes effected by the class conflict. But this is not what Marx predicts. What he predicts is the end of the economic class conflict, the establishment of a classless society. What you and he are asking me to accept is an explanation of history that will explain it only up to a certain point. Marx criticised Hegel for that very weakness. Hegel explained past history as a transformation effected by the Transcendent Idea realizing itself in the actual events of history; according to him the great objective of history was the complete realization of the Idea in the form of Freedom, and this great objective had already been in some sense attained in the Prussian state. Marx wanted to know what the Transcendent Idea would find to do in the future, now that it was entirely realized. That is a sound criticism. Now, my difficulty is to know how Marx has improved on Hegel. To be sure Marx does not say that the great objective of history has already been attained. He says the economic class conflict will bring about another social revolution. But after the social revolution, what then? What becomes of the economic class conflict after the revolution has established a classless society? I can't find that it will have anything more to do than Hegel's Transcendent Idea. A law of history which, at some determinate moment, ceases to explain history, a law of history which is required, at the appropriate moment, to commit hari-kari on the doorstep of the ideal, surely leaves something to be desired.

COMMUNIST: Well, that's a point. But really, Professor, you know very well that this objection has been noted before, and that there is a good answer to it. Marx was not so blind as to overlook it. How could he have done so, since he pointed out that very weakness in Hegel's philosophy of history? 19

LIBERAL: I should be glad to learn how Marx avoids that difficulty. 20

COMMUNIST: I am not sure that Marx himself does altogether avoid it. But you must allow Marxian philosophy to be elaborated and interpreted by his followers in the light of later experience. You have no objection to that? 21

LIBERAL: None at all. We must by all means discuss Marxianism at its best, as it is now interpreted by the most expert exegesis available. 22

COMMUNIST: Very well. According to a recent interpreter of Marxianism, history is explainable in terms of a dialectic of transformation, in which conflicts appear only to be resolved in a higher synthesis. This conflict is not necessarily always an economic class conflict. After the classless society is established the conflict will continue, but on a different level. According to Professor 23

Sidney Hook, a recent interpreter of Marx, the dialectic in a communist, classless society, will not be "historically conditioned in the same sense" as in earlier times. "It finds expression . . . on a more elevated plane. Although in advance no one can describe the detailed forms it will take, it is clear that its general locus is individual and personal." In other words, having solved the economic problem by establishing a classless society, men will be occupied with the higher, spiritual problems of human development.

LIBERAL: Well, I must confess that this greatly surprises me. A while back you would not allow me to apply the term "utopian" to the future society predicted by Marx; and yet this sounds to me very similar to all the utopian societies I ever heard of. Throughout the past men have engaged in brutal conflict for material gain; but this brutal conflict is somehow to bring about a classless society in which men will suddenly change their natures and devote themselves to the nobler things of life. A dialectic materialism will be replaced by what we may call a dialectic spiritualism; or to put it in simple English, conflict will cease on the economic plane, and continue only on the moral plane. 24

Well, it may be so: and if it should turn out so, it would be grand. I point out merely that this is what all the idealistic prophets of the world have always hoped would happen. It is what the early prophets of democracy predicted. It is what all humane liberals may hope for. But what I don't understand is how the Marxian philosophy permits us to hope for it. I suppose it to be a fundamental tenet of Marxian philosophy that the conduct of men is strictly conditioned; and if their conduct in the past has been strictly conditioned by the economic class conflict, how can it cease to be so conditioned in the future? 25

COMMUNIST: Your difficulty arises from a false assumption—an assumption that is made by many of the hostile critics of Marx. The assumption is that Marx accepted the nineteenth-century doctrine of mechanistic determinism. That is not so. Marx always insisted that "man makes his own history." He contributes something novel to the conditions that determine his own conduct. Marx says explicitly: "By acting on the external world man changes his own nature." This means that man can, by acquiring knowledge, modify his environment, and so modify also his own ways of submitting to the environment. Therefore it is quite possible that men might for a very long time submit blindly to the influence of the economic class conflict; for a long time, but not necessarily forever; since, having become aware that they had been in the past submitting to the economic class conflict, they would, in the future, even if they submitted to it, 26 not be submitting to it blindly. This awareness that their conduct has been determined by the economic class conflict becomes a new element in the conditions, and so changes the conditions that will determine men's conduct in the future. One might say that the great object of Marx was just this: to make men aware of the conditions that made social revolutions in the past, so that in the coming social revolution, being aware of what was happening, they could consciously direct it. To quote once more from Professor Sidney Hook: "Once man acquires control of the conditions of social life, he can consciously make over his own nature in accordance with a morally free will, in contradistinction to men in the past, whose nature has been unconsciously made over by the economically determined will of economic classes."

LIBERAL: I see; at least I think so, in spite of Professor Hook's somewhat 27
obscure academic phraseology. But what it comes to, I suppose, is this. In the physical world a law operates forever in the same way because the physical object is not aware of, and is indifferent to, what happens. A billiard ball (to use the classic example) has no desire to make over its nature. But man is aware of, and is not indifferent to, what happens. His acts are indeed strictly conditioned, but as soon as he becomes aware of what it is that conditions them, his awareness enables him to react differently; his acts are then not less strictly conditioned than formerly, but his own awareness becomes a new element that changes and complicates the conditions. For a long time men may worship the sun; when they become aware of the influences that make them worship the sun, this awareness may become an influence that will make them cease to worship the sun. Freedom of the will, as Engels said, is no more than man's knowledge that his acts are conditioned.

Very well, Marx then (or perhaps his disciples) applies 28
this principle of freedom to the social changes or revolutions that occur in history. In the past, social revolutions have been conditioned by the economic class conflict. As long as men are not aware of this fact, social revolutions will continue to be conditioned by the economic class conflict. But when men become fully aware, through the great discovery of Marx, that social revolutions in the past have been conditioned by the class conflict, this knowledge will enable them to react differently—to react in such a way as to abolish the class conflict. This, I take it, is how you interpret Marx.

COMMUNIST: Yes, that is right. 29

LIBERAL: Well, I agree with this idea of free will. It seems to me obvious 30
that as men acquire knowledge of the influences that determine their acts, this knowledge becomes a new influence that enables

them to act differently. But if we accept this principle it seems odd to me that men shouldn't have acquired, before the time of Marx, some knowledge of the fact that their conduct was determined by the economic class conflict. I should have supposed that this element of awareness would have been steadily modifying the conditions that determine social changes from the time of the Neanderthal man down to the present. How does it happen that this element of awareness has had no appreciable influence up to the time of Marx? Marx must have been a much greater man than I have always thought—a veritable Messiah, who at a single stroke has given mankind this epoch-making revelation that is to transform so radically the conditions that determine human history. I find it difficult to believe that. It seems more reasonable to believe that knowledge has been steadily modifying the economic influences that have determined social changes in the past, and that in the future further knowledge, knowledge unknown to Marx, will continue to modify those influences in ways not dreamed of by Marx.

But that is a minor point. Let us assume that up to the time 31
of Marx men have been submitting blindly to the economic class conflict, and that now, thanks to Marx, they are in the way of becoming aware of that fact, and that being aware of it they are in a position to modify profoundly the conditions that will determine social changes. What then? Well, it seems to me that this great revelation made by Marx is precisely what makes it impossible for him to predict the character of the coming social revolution. If we did not know that social changes had been conditioned by the economic class conflict, the coming social revolution would presumably follow the course of previous ones, in which case no classless society would emerge from it. But since we do know that social revolutions in the past were conditioned by the class conflict, this very knowledge, according to Marx, will make the coming social revolution follow some different course, in which case we may hope, but cannot be sure, that a classless society will emerge from it. In short, in so far as Marx has made men aware of the influence of the economic class conflict in the past, he has destroyed the very conditions that would have enabled him to predict the nature of the social revolution in the future. If Marx wished to predict correctly the nature of the coming social revolution, he should not have told us what it is that makes social revolutions: since he has told us, the secret is out, and hence no one can predict it. The great secret is out, thanks to Marx, and this knowledge will enable us to make of the coming social revolution something different than it otherwise would have been. Marxian philosophy presents his disciples with a dilemma which they

either do not see or refuse to meet. It is this. Either social changes are always determined by the same conditions, in which case we may be sure that the coming social revolution will be similar to those in the past—it will transform the present class conflict only to create the conditions that will issue in a new one. Or else knowledge of the conditions that have determined social revolutions in the past introduces a novel influence in the conditions that will determine social revolutions in the future, in which case we cannot predict with any certainty the nature of those revolutions. The profound conviction of Communists that the proletariat is destined to establish a classless society on the ruins of the present capitalist régime is not justified by Marxian philosophy: if you interpret Marx in terms of mechanistic determinism, this profound communist conviction is a pure delusion; on the other hand, if you interpret Marx in terms of free will, this conviction is no more than a splendid hope. That is why I cannot accept the Marxian philosophy as a law of history.

32 COMMUNIST: Very well. Suppose, for purposes of argument, that the communist conviction is only a splendid hope. You yourself have said that the present capitalist régime must be changed in such a way as to harmonize better with the interests of the mass of the people, the proletariat. That is just what the Communists want. Since you sympathize with their object, and believe that it will in some measure be realized, why not join the Communists and help to realize this splendid hope?

33 LIBERAL: I refuse to join the Communists because, while I sympathize with their desire to make a better world for the mass of the people, I have no faith in the methods which they propose for obtaining this object. If I understand them, they claim that nothing really worth while can be done until conditions are ripe for the application of the revolutionary technique. When that time comes, they propose, following the example of the Bolsheviks in Russia, to seize control of the government, forcibly expropriate the bourgeois class, and ruthlessly suppress the expression of all opinion that a dictatorial government judges to be hostile to the welfare of the community of workers.

34 Now I have no faith in force and repression as the *primary* means of achieving the good life. I am not as yet a non-resistance pacifist. Any government is probably better than none, and all government rests at last on force. But I believe that the essential test of civilized society is the extent to which law and public authority rest on free discussion and voluntary consent. A resort to force as a means of obtaining consent may be sometimes necessary to prevent a society from falling into virtual anarchy; but the resort to force in place of persuasion is so far

a confession of failure. I have no faith in the possibility of abolishing oppression by oppressing oppressors. I have no faith in the infallibility of any man, or of any group of men, or of the doctrines or dogmas of any man or group of men, except in so far as they can stand the test of free criticism and analysis. I agree with Pascal that "thought makes the dignity of man"; and I believe therefore that all the great and permanently valuable achievements of civilization have been won by the free play of intelligence in opposition to, or in spite of, the pressure of mass emotion and the effort of organized authority to enforce conformity in conduct and opinion. I do not believe that there has been, or that there will be, a high civilization in any country in which the mind of man is limited to the expression of ideas authorized by public authority. Dictatorship is as old as European society; and whether it be the dictatorship of a Stalin, a Mussolini, or a Hitler, it does not become something new and admirable by being dressed up in a new and mystical idealogy. I recognize it as a possibility that our modern, complex, machine civilization may so far fall into confusion that a dictatorship will in fact replace the present régime; but I refuse to recognize this outcome as inherently desirable, and I refuse to join in any effort to make it inevitable.

This is why I do not join the Communists. I believe that 35
profound changes in our economic and industrial system are necessary; but I believe that they can and I hope that they will be made, in this country, without resorting to violent revolution, without resorting to dictatorship, without abandoning our traditional reliance on free discussion and criticism of public authority and of the measures it proposes for the solution of social ills. And there is nothing in the Marxian philosophy, as you expound it, that makes it illogical for me to take this position. According to you, now that Marx has made us aware of the influence of the economic class conflict in the past, this very awareness will enable us to master and modify the class conflict in the future. I agree. But why is it necessary to assume that this knowledge which Marx has revealed to us is the exclusive possession of the proletariat? After all the bourgeoisie have a certain amount of intelligence. They can read Marx, or at least Sidney Hook. They can observe what has occurred in Russia, in Italy, in Germany. It is possible for them, too, to understand that the capitalist competitive system is in a fair way of destroying itself. Marxian doctrine tells me that capitalists, like proletarians, are motivated by their economic class interest; it does not tell me that they, any more than the proletarians, must forever be motivated by a blind illusion as to what that interest is. At the present moment it obviously is not to the interest of

the capitalist class that the mass of the people should be without the means of buying the goods which the capitalist class produces in order to sell. It is still possible that the capitalist system in this country, subjected to the pressure of economic necessity and the force of public discontent, may by reasonably peaceful procedure be sufficiently transformed into a coördinated and planned economic system to make it, not a utopia indeed, but at least a decently workable system. And a decently workable system which preserves our traditional liberty of discussion and criticism will, in my opinion, be superior in the long run to any system that can be established by the repressive measures now employed by the Communists of Russia, the Fascists of Italy, or the Nazis of Germany.

COMMUNIST: A decently workable system. That's certainly vague enough— 36
as vague as Marx's idealistic society of the future which you derided. No doubt a decently workable system is one which you would prefer to something which you don't like, such as the Russian communist state.

LIBERAL: It is. But you must permit me to prefer a decently workable 37
system which I like to a decently workable system which I don't like. You can hardly expect me to become a Communist until I am convinced that communism would be preferable to the system under which I live.

COMMUNIST: No. But you have already admitted that the "decently workable 38
system" which you hope will be established may fail to be established—that the present system may end in a dictatorship. That I think is the more probable outcome. It is likely that in the long run the capitalist class, confronted by the rising power of the proletariat, will resort to force, as it has done in Italy and Germany. If then you are faced with the alternative of supporting a dictatorship of the proletariat or a dictatorship of the bourgeoisie, what will you do? What then will become of freedom of speech and the appeal to persuasion? Since you sympathize with the objectives of the Communists, will you not then be forced to join them? Why wait till then? Why not join now the side which is bound to win in the long run because it is in harmony with the dominant trend of social forces?

LIBERAL: I do not admit that communism is necessarily in harmony 39
with the dominant trend of social forces. I see that when it suits your argument you, like most Communists, fall back on the doctrine of a fatalistic determinism which makes the communist revolution inevitable whatever men do about it; but when your argument requires another doctrine you admit that the social revolution may be mastered and directed by the conscious purposes of men. You ought really to accept one doctrine or the other, and stick to it. But no matter. Accept

one doctrine or both, as you like. In either case I see no good reason for joining the Communists. If the communist revolution is inevitable, whatever men do about it, why do anything? Why join either side, if you know beforehand that one side is bound to win anyway? But if the communist revolution is not inevitable, then the proletariat can indeed do something to hasten it, and by the same token the bourgeoisie can do something to retard it. And in that case why should I join the Communists? I am a professor; and the Communists are never weary of telling me that professors as a class support the capitalist régime because it is their economic interest to do so. Very well, I will be a sufficiently good Marxian to accept the doctrine that men's actions are motivated by their economic class interest. If then my economic interests are bound up with the capitalist régime, and I can do something to retard the communist revolution, I should be, according to Marx himself, a poor humanitarian fool to desert my class and work for a revolution which, if successful, would ruthlessly suppress me. As a liberal humanitarian, or a Christian mystic, I might logically sacrifice myself and my class for the welfare of the masses; but as a Marxian that would be to adopt the very "utopian" attitude which Marx never ceased to ridicule. You really ask too much. The Marxian philosophy teaches me either that the communist revolution is inevitable, in which case I merely resign myself to it: or else it teaches me that the communist revolution can be hastened or retarded by the conscious efforts of men, in which case I stick to my class and do what I can to retard it. In either case I have the profound consolation of knowing that my conduct is based on the solid foundation of the Marxian philosophy of history.

These, you are to understand, are choices logically open 40
to me on the assumption that I accept the Marxian philosophy of history. But life is less simple than logic. In logic you can present me with clear-cut alternatives. You can ask me whether I will "choose" to support the dictatorship of the proletariat or the dictatorship of the bourgeoisie, quite as if some day, the two contending parties being lined up in battle array on a *champs de mars* [field of war], I should be asked to step out and join one side or the other. In actual life it does not seem to me that I am ever confronted with choices as simple or as dramatically staged as that. When I voted for Mr. Roosevelt (if I *did* vote for him—I can't be sure now) I made a choice, without being certain (any more than Mr. Roosevelt himself was) what would come of it. I am now "supporting" (so far as I am supporting anything) the Roosevelt administration, and it is possible that in 1936 I shall vote for the reëlection of Mr. Roosevelt. Does this mean that

I am "choosing" to support a fascist rather than a communist régime? Thoroughgoing Communists appear to know that I am: the New Deal, they say, is obviously an American species of fascist technique. But I am sufficiently naïve not to be aware of having made any choice between communism and fascism. And very glad I am that it is so. I should dislike very much to be confronted with a clear-cut choice between a dictatorship of the proletariat and a dictatorship of the bourgeoisie. I should be inclined to say, "A plague on both your houses!" I find Mussolini as offensive as Stalin, and Hitler more offensive than either.

COMMUNIST: That is all very well, but a real revolution is not impossible. There are plenty of Russians who could assure you that the alternative you so much dislike has been presented to them in a quite sufficiently clear-cut and dramatic manner. If it should be similarly presented in this country, it seems to me that you would, however much you might dislike it, have to choose one side or the other. 41

LIBERAL: Not necessarily. There would still be another possibility. 42

COMMUNIST: What would that be? 43

LIBERAL: I might still refuse to join either side. I might persist in the futility of expressing my faith in the superior virtues of persuasion. 44

COMMUNIST: That would have serious consequences for you. You would be suppressed. 45

LIBERAL: True enough. But I might accept the consequences. I might choose to be suppressed rather than to support what I object to. In short, I might, as a last refuge from imbecility, become a Christian and practise the precept that it is better to suffer evil than to do it. 46

COMMUNIST: That would be to fall back upon a far more mystical type of idealism than Marx ever contemplated, and I fail to see that it would get you anywhere. 47

LIBERAL: I dare say it wouldn't: But, as I said before, I am a professor, and a professor, as the German proverb has it, is "a man who thinks otherwise": if he is not permitted to talk freely he cannot get anywhere anyway. 48

Questions for Discussion

1. State in your own words Becker's criticism of the Marxist view of history (¶18). Does the criticism seem justified? Why or why not?

2. In paragraph 24 Becker accuses the Marxists of inconsistency. It is the Marxist view, he says, that "throughout the past men have engaged in brutal conflict for material gain; but this brutal conflict is somehow to bring about a classless society in which men will suddenly change their natures and devote themselves to the nobler things of life"—that is, class conflict will inevitably result in classlessness. The final class revolution will end all class conflict. Does it seem to you that Becker's arguments against this view are adequate? Can you provide an explanation from the Marxist point of view that might reconcile its apparent inconsistencies?
3. The heart of Becker's attack is the inconsistency between the Marxist belief in iron laws of history and the possibility of free will for human beings. He develops his criticism in paragraphs 27–31. Marx predicts with absolute certainty, Becker claims, that the proletariat will overthrow the bourgeoisie. Yet Marx also allows that if people learn to understand their historical situation, they may change the conditions under which they live and work. Marx's historical view, Becker continues, constitutes such an intervention: Now that Marx has taught the bourgeoisie the consequences of not improving the conditions of their workers, they have the freedom to save themselves by changing their behavior and thus the course of history. It is inconsistent, Becker says, to claim both that people have free will and that they are at the same time blind pawns in the irresistible grip of historical movements. Is the inconsistency as marked as Becker claims? Can you provide a "Marxist" answer to Becker?
4. Becker rejects not only Marxist notions about history but also Marxist political practice: "Now I have no faith in force and repression as the *primary* means of achieving the good life. . . . I believe that the essential test of civilized society is the extent to which law and public authority rest on free discussion and voluntary consent" (¶34). (See Karl R. Popper, "Utopia and Violence," pp. 117–125, for more on this topic.) Can you think of occasions when governments have claimed to be justified in doing harm to some citizens in order to serve some greater end or to preserve some better version of the future? You might discuss such controversial examples as the incarceration of Japanese-Americans during World War II; the secret wiretappings of government employees in the State Department under Henry Kissinger, secretary of state during the administration of Richard Nixon (1969–1974); or former FBI director J. Edgar Hoover's attempts to intimidate and discredit Martin Luther King, Jr., by illicitly collecting details about his private life. Can you think of occasions when *you* have employed deplorable means for admirable ends? In the light of these or other examples, do you think that good ends sometimes genuinely justify evil means? On what grounds?
5. In paragraph 46 Becker says that he "might accept the consequences" of refusing to join a winning side he disapproves of: "I might choose to be suppressed rather than to support what I object to." Do you regard this

view as noble? Silly? Idealistic? What arguments can you make in defense of the position you take?

Suggested Essay Topics

1. Pick some episode in which our federal government seemed to engage in a policy of evil means in order to secure apparently good ends. You could use examples from discussion question 4, or you could refer to others, such as the imprisonment of pacifists who refused to fight in a war, the hiring of agents to assassinate foreign heads of governments, or the funding of rebels fighting an elected foreign government. Defend or attack the government's actions. Decide in advance what kind of reader you hope to influence—classmates, readers of a given editorial page in a newspaper, government officials, members of Congress. The problem in such writing is to find persuasive arguments rather than merely to assert one's opinions. You may find it helpful as you write to consider again how Becker organizes his essay. You may even want to follow his format: Create an opponent and construct a dialogue, so that you can dramatize the principal objections to your position.
2. Writing as a Marxist, attack Becker's position by arguing that Becker simply evades the unpleasant realities that undercut his position. While he talks about a nice cushy academic haven that will preserve individual dignity and freedom, the facts remain: In the real world the rich get richer and the poor get poorer all the time; the people on the bottom of the heap never get their fair share of a society's goods unless they have the leverage to demand it from those on the top; and people who have little food, less money, and no dignity cannot afford to stand on principle because they are too busy merely surviving. Develop this argument with as many appropriate examples as you can muster, sustaining a tone of indignation and concluding with a reassertion of the Marxist theme that things will never get better for the poor until the rich are forced to share.

Acknowledgments

Max Apple, "The Oranging of America." From *The Oranging of America* by Max Apple. Copyright © 1974, 1976 by Max Apple. Reprinted by permission of Viking Penguin Inc.

St. Thomas Aquinas, "The Production of Woman." From *The Summa Theologica.* From *Basic Writings of Saint Thomas Acquinas,* edited by Anton C. Pegis. Copyright © 1945 by Random House, Inc. Reprinted by permission of the Estate of Anton C. Pegis.

Aristotle, "The 'Instinct' of Imitation." From *Poetics.* Reprinted from *Aristotle's Theory of Poetry and Fine Art with a Critical Text and Translation of "The Poetics,"* ed. and trans. S.H. Butcher, rev. ed. Copyright © 1911 by Macmillan Publishing Co. Reprinted by permission of the publisher.

W.H. Auden, "The Unknown Citizen." From *Collected Poems of W.H. Auden* edited by Edward Mendelson. Copyright © 1940, 1968 by W. H. Auden. Reprinted by permission of Random House, Inc., and Faber and Faber Ltd.

James Baldwin, "Faulkner and Desegregation." From *Nobody Knows My Name.* Copyright © 1961 by James Baldwin. Reprinted by permission of Doubleday and Co.

Carl L. Becker, "The Marxian Philosophy of History." From *Everyman His Own Historian.* Copyright © 1935 by F. S. Crofts & Co., Inc. Reprinted by permission of Mr. Frederick D. Becker.

Bruno Bettelheim and Karen Zelan, "Why Children Don't Like to Read." From *On Learning to Read: The Child's Fascination with Meaning* by Bruno Bettleheim and Karen Zelan. Copyright © 1981 by Bruno Bettelheim and Karen Zelan. Reprinted by permission of Alfred A. Knopf, Inc.

Jacob Bronowski, "The Reach of Imagination." From *Proceedings of the American Academy of Arts and Letters and the National Institute of Arts and Letters,* 2d series, 17 (1967), and from *The American Scholar* 36, no. 2 (1967). Copyright © 1967 by the American Academy of Arts and Letters. Reprinted by permission of the American Academy of Arts and Letters.

Edward Hallett Carr, "The Historian and His Facts." From *What Is History?* by Edward Hallett Carr. Copyright © 1961 by Edward Hallett Carr. Reprinted by permission of Alfred A. Knopf, Inc., and Macmillan & Co., Ltd.

Robert Coles, "On the Nature of Character: Some Preliminary Field Notes." From *Daedalus* 110 no. 4 (Fall 1981). Reprinted by permission of *Daedalus, Journal of American Academy of Arts and Sciences.*

James Cone, "Capitalism Means Property over Persons." From *Will Capitalism Survive?* edited by Ernest W. Lefever (Washington, D.C.: Ethics and Public Policy Center, 1979). Copyright © 1979 by the Ethics and Public Policy Center. Reprinted by permission of the publisher.

E. E. Cummings, "LIV" ("if everything happens that can't be done"). From *Complete Poems 1913–1962* by E. E. Cummings. Copyright © 1944 by E. E. Cummings; renewed 1972 by Nancy T. Andrews. Reprinted by permission of Harcourt Brace Jovanovich, Inc.

Charles Dickens, "Hard Facts." From *Hard Times* by Charles Dickens, Norton Critical Edition edited by George Ford and Sylvere Monod. Reprinted by permission of W. W. Norton & Company, Inc.

Loren Eiseley, "The Illusion of the Two Cultures." From *The Star Thrower* by Loren Eiseley. Reprinted by permission of Times Books, a Division of Random House, Inc.

Ralph Ellison, "Battle Royal." From *Invisible Man* by Ralph Ellison. Copyright © 1948 by Ralph Ellison. Reprinted by permission of Random House, Inc.

William Faulkner, "Delta Autumn," From *Go Down, Moses* by William Faulkner. Copyright © 1942 by William Faulkner. Reprinted by permission of Random House, Inc.

E. M. Forster, "Art for Art's Sake." From *Two Cheers for Democracy* by E. M. Forster. Copyright © 1951 by E. M. Forster. Reprinted by permission of Harcourt Brace Jovanovich, Inc., and Edward Arnold, Ltd.

E. M. Forster, "My Wood." From *Abinger Harvest* by E. M. Forster. Copyright © 1936, 1964 by Edward Morgan Forster. Reprinted by permission of Harcourt Brace Jovanovich, Inc., and Edward Arnold, Ltd.

Francine Frank and Frank Ashen, "Of Girls and Chicks." From *Language and the Sexes* by Francine Frank and Frank Ashen. Copyright © 1983 by Francine Frank and Frank Ashen. Reprinted by permission of State University of New York Press.

Sigmund Freud, "Femininity." Reprinted from *New Introductory Lectures on Psycho-Analysis* by Sigmund Freud. Translated and edited by James Strachey. Copyright © 1933 by Sigmund Freud. Copyright © renewed 1961 by W. J. H. Sprott. Copyright © 1964, 1965 by James Strachey. Reprinted by permission of W. W. Norton & Company, Inc.

Northrop Frye, "The Educated Imagination." From *The Educated Imagination* by Northrop Frye. Copyright © 1964 by Indiana University Press. Reprinted by permission of Northrop Frye and the publisher.

Genesis 1–2:3, from *The Torah,* 2d ed. (Philadelphia: The Jewish Publication Society of America, 1962). Copyright © 1962 by the Jewish Publication Society of America. Reprinted by permission of the publisher.

Pieter Geyl and Arnold J. Toynbee, "Can We Know the Pattern of the Past?" Reprinted from *The Pattern of the Past: Can We Determine It?* by Pieter Geyl, Arnold J. Toynbee, and Pitirim A. Sorokin. Copyright © 1949 by The Beacon Press. Reprinted by permission of the publisher.

William Golding, "Thinking as a Hobby." Copyright © 1961 by William Golding. Reprinted by permission of Curtis Brown, Ltd. First printed in *Holiday* magazine.

Paul Goodman, "Utopian Thinking." From *Utopian Essays and Practical Problems* by Paul Goodman. Copyright © 1961 by Paul Goodman. Reprinted by permission of Random House, Inc.

Maxim Gorky, "On Books." From On *Literature* by Maxim Gorky, translated by Julius Katzer. Copyright © 1973 by University of Washington Press. Reprinted by permission of the publisher.

Edith Hamilton, "The Ever-Present Past." From *The Ever-Present Past* by Edith Hamilton. Copyright © 1958 by *The Saturday Evening Post.* Copyright © 1964 by W. W. Norton & Company, Inc. Reprinted by permission of the publisher.

Hermann Hesse (excerpted in James E. Miller, Jr., "Writing as Self-Discovery"). From *Demian: The Story of Emil Sinclair's Youth,* translated by Michael Roloff and Michael Lebeck. Reprinted by permission of Harper & Row, Publishers, Inc., and Joan Daves.

Adolf Hitler, "Is This a Jew?" From *Mein Kampf* by Adolf Hitler, translated by Ralph Manheim. Copyright © 1943, 1971 by Houghton Mifflin Company. Reprinted by permission of Houghton Mifflin Company and Hutchinson Publishing, Ltd.

Shirley Jackson, "The Flower Garden." From *The Lottery* by Shirley Jackson. Copyright © 1948, 1949, by Shirley Jackson. Copyright © renewed 1976, 1977 by Laurence Hyman, Barry Hyman, Mrs. Sarah Webster and Mrs. Joanne Schnurer. Reprinted by permission of Farrar, Straus and Giroux, Inc.

Stanley L. Jaki, "The Role of Faith in Physics." Reprinted from *Zygon* 2, no. 2 (June 1967). Copyright © 1967 by the Joint Publication Board of *Zygon.* Reprinted by permission of the publisher.

Paul Johnson, "Has Capitalism a Future?" From *Will Capitalism Survive?* edited by Ernest W. Lefever (Washington, D.C.: Ethics and Public Policy Center, 1979). Copyright © 1979 by Paul Johnson. Reprinted by permission of the author.

Helen Keller, "The Key to Language." From *The Story of My Life* by Helen Keller. Copyright © 1902 by Helen Keller. Reprinted by permission of Doubleday Publishing Co. Inc.

Martin Luther King, Jr., "Letter from Birmingham Jail." From *Why We Can't Wait* by Martin Luther King, Jr. Copyright © 1963 by Martin Luther King, Jr. Reprinted by permission of Harper & Row, Publishers, Inc.

Clyde Kluckhohn, "The Gift of Tongues." From *Mirror for Man* by Clyde Kluckhohn. Copyright © 1985 by The University of Arizona Press, Tuscon. Reprinted by permission of the Arizona Board of Regents.

Joseph Wood Krutch, "The Meaning of Awareness: The You and the Me." From *The Great Chain of Life* by Joseph Wood Krutch. Copyright © 1956 by Joseph Wood Krutch. Reprinted by permission of Houghton Mifflin Co.

George Lakoff and Mark Johnson, "Metaphors We Live By." From *Metaphors We Live By* by George Lakoff and Mark Johnson. Copyright © 1980 by The University of Chicago. Reprinted by permission of the publisher. Much of this material was originally published in the *Journal of Philosophy* LXXVII 8 (August 1980).

C. S. Lewis, "What Christians Believe." From *Mere Christianity* by C. S. Lewis. Copyright © 1943, 1945, 1952 by Macmillan Publishing Co., Inc. Copyright © 1943, 1945, 1952 by William Collins Sons & Co., Ltd. Reprinted by permission of Macmillan Publishing Co., Inc., and William Collins Sons & Co., Ltd.

Malcolm X, "Freedom Through Learning to Read." From *The Autobiography of Malcolm X* by Malcolm X, with the assistance of Alex Haley. Copyright © 1964 by Alex Haley and Malcolm X. Copyright © 1965 by Alex Haley and Betty Shabazz. Reprinted by permission of Random House, Inc.

Karl Marx and Friedrich Engels, "The Class Struggle." From "Manifesto of the Communist Party," in *Collected Works,* Vol. 6, 1845–1848 (New York: International Publishers, 1976). Copyright © 1976 by Progress Publishers, Moscow. Reprinted by permission of International Publishers.

Eugene J. McCarthy, "Corporations Have Corrupted Capitalism." From *Will Capitalism Survive?* edited by Ernest W. Lefever (Washington, D.C.: Ethics and Public Policy Center, 1979). Copyright © 1979 by the Ethics and Public Policy Center. Reprinted by permission of the publisher.

Mary McCarthy. "Artists in Uniform." From *On The Contrary* by Mary McCarthy. Copyright © 1953 by Mary McCarthy. Reprinted by permission of the author.

Margaret Mead, "The Mind Is Not Sex-Typed." From *Blackberry Winter: My Earlier Years* by Margaret Mead. Copyright © 1972 by Margaret Mead. Reprinted by permission of William Morrow & Co.

Margaret Mead (excerpted in Clyde Kluckhohn, "The Gift of Tongues"). From "The Application of Anthropological Techniques to Cross-National Communication." From *Transactions of the New York Academy of Sciences* (February, 1947). Copyright © 1947 by Margaret Mead. Reprinted by permission of New York Academy of Sciences.

James E. Miller, Jr. "Writing as Self-Discovery." From *Word, Self, Reality: The Rhetoric of Imagination* by James E. Miller, Jr. Copyright © 1972 by Harper & Row, Publishers, Inc. Reprinted by permission of the publisher.

Elaine Morgan, "The Man-Made Myth." From *The Descent of Woman* by Elaine Morgan. Copyright © 1972 by Elaine Morgan. Reprinted by permission of Stein and Day Publishers and Souvenir Press Ltd.

Montaigne, "Of Friendship." From *The Complete Essays of Montaigne,* translated by Donald M. Frame. Copyright © 1958 by the Board of Trustees of the Leland Stanford Junior University. Reprinted by permission of Stanford University Press.

J. Robert Nelson, "Capitalism: Blessing and Curse." From *Will Capitalism Survive?* edited by Ernest Lefever (Washington, D.C.: Ethics and Public Policy Center, 1979). Copyright © 1979 by the Ethics and Public Policy Center. Reprinted by permission of the publisher.

Friedrich Nietzsche, "The Ugliness of Woman." From *Beyond Good and Evil* by Friedrich Nietzsche, translated by Walter Kaufmann. Copyright © 1966 by Random House, Inc. Reprinted by permission of the publisher.

George Orwell, "Politics and the English Language." From *Shooting an Elephant and Other Essays* by George Orwell. Copyright © 1946, 1974 by Sonia Brownell Orwell. Reprinted by permission of Harcourt Brace Jovanovich, Inc., the estate of the late Sonia Brownell Orwell, and Martin Secker & Warburg, Ltd.

Thomas Love Peacock, "Poetry: An Outmoded Amusement." From *Percy Bysshe Shelley, A Defense of Poetry, and Thomas Love Peacock, The Four Ages of Poetry,* ed. John E. Jordan. Copyright © 1965 by The Bobbs-Merrill Company, Inc. Reprinted by permission of the publisher.

Plato, "The Allegory of the Cave," "Aristophanes' Myth of Divided Loves," "Censorship," "The Education of Women," and "The Seductions of Art." From the *Republic* and the *Symposium* in *The Dialogues of Plato,* translated by Benjamin Jowett, 4th ed. Copyright © 1953 by the Jowett Copyright Trustees. Reprinted by permission of Oxford: Clarendon Press.

Karl R. Popper, "Utopia and Violence," *From Conjectures and Refutations: The Growth of Scientific Knowledge* (2d ed., 1965.) Copyright © 1963, 1965 by Karl L. Popper. Reprinted by permission of Basic Books, Inc., Publishers.

Ayn Rand, "I Owe Nothing to My Brothers." From *Anthem* by Ayn Rand. Copyright © 1946 by Pamphleteers, Inc. Reprinted by permission of Dr. Leonard Peikoff, Executor, estate of Ayn Rand.

Phyllis Rose, "Heroic Fantasies, Nervous Doubts." From the *New York Times* "Hers" column of March 22, 1984. Copyright © 1984 by Phyllis Rose. Reprinted by permission of Phyllis Rose.

Theodore Roosevelt, "The Welfare of the Wage-Worker." From *The National Edition of Roosevelt's Works,* Vols. XV and XVI, by Theodore Roosevelt. Copyright © 1925 by Theodore Roosevelt. Originally published by Scribner Book Companies.

Peggy Rosenthal, "Words and Values." From *Words and Values: Some Leading Words and Where They Lead Us* by Peggy Rosenthal. Copyright © 1984 by Peggy Rosenthal. Reprinted by permission of Oxford University Press.

Betty Roszak, "The Human Continuum." From *Masculine/Feminine: Readings in Sexual Mythology and the Liberation of Women,* edited by Betty Roszak and Theodore Roszak. Copyright © 1969 by Betty Roszak and Theodore Roszak. Reprinted by permission of Harper & Row Publishers, Inc., and Betty Roszak.

Rosemary Radford Ruether, "Motherearth and the Magemachine: A Theology of Liberation in a Feminine, Somatic, and Ecological Perspective" by Rosemary Radford Ruether. From *Christianity and Crisis* (April 12, 1972). Copyright © 1972 by Rosemary Radford Ruether. Reprinted by permission of *Christianity and Crisis.*

Bertrand Russell, "Happiness." From *The Conquest of Happiness* by Bertrand Russell. Copyright © 1930 by Horace Liveright, Inc. Copyright © 1958 by Bertrand Russell. Reprinted by permission of Liveright Publishing Corporation and George Allen & Unwin Ltd.

Bertrand Russell, "Why I Am Not a Christian." From *Why I Am Not a Christian" and Other Essays on Religious and Related Subjects* by Bertrand Russell, edited by Paul Edwards. Copyright © 1957 by Allen & Unwin. Reprinted by permission of Simon & Schuster, a Division of Gulf & Western Corporation, and George Allen & Unwin, Ltd.

St. Paul, "I Corinthians 13." From *The New English Bible.* Copyright © 1961, 1970 by the Delegates of the Oxford University Press and the Syndics of the Cambridge University Press. Reprinted by permission of the publisher.

Margaret Sanger, "The Turbid Ebb and Flow of Misery." From *An Autobiography* by Margaret Sanger. Copyright © 1938 by W.W. Norton & Co., Inc. Reprinted by permission of Dr. Grant Sanger.

Edward Sapir (excerpted in Clyde Kluckhohn, "The Gift of Tongues). From "Language" by Edward Sapir, *Encyclopedia of the Social Sciences,* Vol IX. Copyright © 1933, 1961 by Macmillan Publishing Co. Reprinted by permission of the publisher.

Herbert Schmertz, "Democracy, Tyranny, and Capitalism." From *Will Capitalism Survive?* edited by Ernest W. Lefever (Washington, D.C.: Ethics and Public Policy Center). Copyright © 1979 by the Ethics and Public Policy Center. Reprinted by permission of the publisher.

Georges Simenon (excerpted in James E. Miller, Jr., "Writing as Self-Discovery"). From *Writers at Work: The Paris Review Interviews,* Volume I, edited by Malcolm Cowley. Copyright © 1957, 1958 by *The Paris Review.* Reprinted by permission of Viking Penguin, Inc.

B. F. Skinner, "Behavioral Engineering: Programming the Children." From *Walden Two* (Chapters 13 and 14) by B. F. Skinner. Copyright © 1948, 1976 by B. F. Skinner. Reprinted by permission of Macmillan Publishing Co.

Lillian Smith, "When I Was a Child." From *Killers of the Dream,* revised, by Lillian Smith. Copyright © 1949, 1961 by Lillian Smith. Reprinted by permission of W.W. Norton & Co., Inc.

C. P. Snow, "The Two Cultures." From *The Two Cultures: And a Second Look.* Copyright © 1959 by C. P. Snow. Reprinted by permission of Cambridge University Press.

Stephen Spender, "In Railway Halls, on Pavements Near the Traffic." From *Collected Poems 1928–1953* by Stephen Spender. Copyright © 1934, 1962 by Stephen Spender. Reprinted by permission of Random House and Faber & Faber, Ltd.

Lewis Thomas, "Debating the Unknowable." Originally published in *The Atlantic Monthly* (July 1981). Copyright © 1981 by *The Atlantic Monthly.* Reprinted in *Late Night Thoughts on Listening to Mahler's Ninth Symphony* by Lewis Thomas. Copyright © 1983 by Lewis Thomas. Reprinted by permission of *The Atlantic Monthly* and the Viking Press.

Lewis Thomas, "How to Fix the Premedical Curriculum." From *The Medusa and the Snail* by Lewis Thomas. Copyright © 1978, 1979 by Lewis Thomas. Reprinted by permission of Viking Penguin, Inc.

Stephen Toulmin, "Science and Ethics: Can They Be Reconnected?" From *The University of Chicago Magazine* (Winter 1981). Copyright © 1979 by the Hastings Center, Institute of Society, Ethics and the Life Sciences. Reprinted by permission of the Hastings Center.

Piri Thomas (excerpted in James E. Miller, Jr., "Writing as Self-Discovery"). From *Down These Mean Streets* by Piri Thomas. Copyright © 1967 by Piri Thomas. Reprinted by permission of Alfred A. Knopf, Inc.

Kurt Vonnegut, Jr., "Harrison Bergeron." From *Welcome to the Monkey House* by Kurt Vonnegut, Jr. Copyright © 1961 by Kurt Vonnegut, Jr. Originally published in *Fantasy and Science Fiction.* Reprinted by permission of Delacorte Press/Seymour Lawrence.

E. B. White, "Bedfellows." From *Essays of E. B. White* by E. B. White. Copyright © 1956 by E. B. White. Originally appeared in the *New Yorker.* Reprinted by permission of Harper & Row, Publishers, Inc.

Alfred North Whitehead, "The Aims of Education." From *The Aims of Education and Other Essays* by Alfred North Whitehead. Copyright © 1929 by Macmillan Publishing Co., Inc., renewed © 1957 by Evelyn Whitehead. Reprinted by permission of Macmillan Publishing Co.

Elie Wiesel, "The Sacrifice of Isaac: A Strange Tale About Fear, Faith and Laughter." From *Messengers of God: Biblical Portraits and Legends* by Elie Wiesel, translated by Marion Wiesel. Copyright © 1976 by Elie Wiesel. Reprinted by permission of Random House, Inc.

Richard Wright, "The Library Card." Chapter XIII of *Black Boy* by Richard Wright. Copyright © 1937, 1942, 1944, 1945 by Richard Wright. Renewed © 1973 by Ellen Wright. Reprinted by permission of Harper & Row, Publishers, Inc.

Author Index

Rhetorical Index